The Blackwell Encyclopedia of Sociology

Volume X

ST–Z

Edited by

George Ritzer

Blackwell
Publishing

© 2007 by Blackwell Publishing Ltd

BLACKWELL PUBLISHING
350 Main Street, Malden, MA 02148-5020, USA
9600 Garsington Road, Oxford OX4 2DQ, UK
550 Swanston Street, Carlton, Victoria 3053, Australia

The right of George Ritzer to be identified as the Author of the Editorial Material in this Work has been asserted in accordance with the UK Copyright, Designs, and Patents Act 1988.

First published 2007 by Blackwell Publishing Ltd

1   2007

Library of Congress Cataloging-in-Publication Data

Blackwell encyclopedia of sociology, the / edited by George Ritzer.
   p. cm.
Includes bibliographical references and index.
ISBN 1-4051-2433-4 (hardback : alk. paper) 1. Sociology—Encyclopedias. I. Ritzer, George.

HM425.B53 2007
301.03—dc22

2006004167

ISBN-13: 978-1-4051-2433-1 (hardback : alk. paper)

A catalogue record for this title is available from the British Library.

Set in 9.5/11pt Ehrhardt
by Spi Publisher Services, Pondicherry, India
Printed in Singapore
by COS Printers Pte Ltd

The publisher's policy is to use permanent paper from mills that operate a sustainable forestry policy, and which has been manufactured from pulp processed using acid-free and elementary chlorine-free practices. Furthermore, the publisher ensures that the text paper and cover board used have met acceptable environmental accreditation standards.

For further information on
Blackwell Publishing, visit our website:
www.blackwellpublishing.com

Contents

stereotyping and stereotypes

Michael Pickering

STEREOTYPING DEFINED

Stereotyping is a way of representing and judging other people in fixed, unyielding terms. These revolve around an alleged characteristic of the category to which they are assigned. They are reduced to the stereotype that results from this, rather than being viewed as individuals with their own personal features and qualities. Instead of being considered and treated as particular and distinctive, they are represented simply through their category assignment and the essentialized and naturalized attribute this is made to carry. The force of the stereotype is strongest when it is commonly held to be irrevocable.

In countering stereotypes, individuality can be exaggerated. The fallacy of individualism lies in its conception of personal uniqueness. For social, cultural, and historical reasons, all individuals share in the characteristics of certain groups, such as those of their social class or status, or their gender or ethnicity; people have group memberships and possess the insider knowledge required to operate efficiently within those groups and the milieux associated with them. The question is where to strike the line between group membership and individuality. Stereotypes involve refusing this distinction. Those who wield them see the people they represent entirely in terms of prescriptive assumptions about their biology, nationality, sexual orientation, disability, or whatever. Such assumptions fix on what is putatively most characteristic of broad, indiscriminate categories. Stereotypes make categories seem categorical. Since they are unconditional and not amenable to qualification, we could say that they are individualism in reverse. Anyone assigned to a stereotype is perceived primarily, if not solely, through the alleged characteristic that is considered to be definitive of who they are and what they do. Their identity and conduct is seen as the natural – and therefore necessary and unchangeable – consequence of this one key element. That is the fallacy of essentialism.

There are certainly cases where people adapt themselves to the alleged characteristic, at least in certain circumstances. They internalize the stereotype of them under the pressures of social conformity, censure, or fear of what will happen if they buck the stereotype. This may appear to confirm and validate it. All it does is conceal and possibly confuse or hedge in the subjectivity of the person stereotyped, along with the capacity of self-determination upon which subjectivity depends. Stereotyping denies this capacity in others. It is important here to distinguish stereotyping from the way we operate all the time with preconceptions and mental schemas as a means of cognitively mapping the world and negotiating different situations and circumstances, including those with which we are not necessarily familiar. These help us in our encounters and interactions in everyday life; they can be modified, updated, and flexibly used as our lives develop and move on. Stereotyping is by contrast a rigid form of cultural representation that creates barriers between people. It attempts to place and fix other people – who they are and what they represent – once and for all. The fact that this is not possible increases the effort to make it seem so, to make stereotypes seem absolute, not relative. That is why they are in the first place inflexibly based on homogenous, naturalized features regarded as integral to members of a specific group or category. Resisting stereotypes involves contesting the necessity of this in the name of self-determination. Three questions follow from this: who does the stereotyping; what purpose does stereotyping serve; and has stereotyping always existed?

PRACTICE, PURVEYORS, AND PURPOSES OF STEREOTYPING

Those who generate and perpetuate stereotypes of others are usually in positions of greater power and status than those who are stereotyped. Stereotypes not only define and place others as inferior, but also implicitly affirm and legitimate those who stereotype in their own position and identity. That has, for example, usually been the case with anti-Semitic stereotypes. For this reason stereotypes say far more about those who stereotype than about their stereotypical targets. This is usual, but not invariable. There are times when stereotypes may speak to a sense of deficiency in people's own identities or a sense of alienation from their own mainstream cultures. The stereotypes may involve selective idealizations of others, as for instance with the way some white men have regarded black jazz, blues, or rap musicians. They may then appear more positive as images, but they are still one-sided projections and may have negative consequences for the other, as for example in confining them to a set role or ability. Other stereotypes have figured as a juncture of both disavowal and desire on the part of dominant groups or nations; various Orientalist stereotypes have operated historically in this way. It is also the case that stereotypes are held by those with relatively little power and status in society. Those who are stereotyped may then serve as scapegoats for the feelings of frustration, disaffection, or anger connected with this lack of power and status. Travelers, foreign workers, and refugees (or so-called asylum seekers) are examples of people who have suffered from this displaced aggression, not least when it is given vent by a commercially driven press. The aggression is projected negatively onto whoever is targeted by the stereotype, and the stereotype then acts as a source of consolation for those who are relatively powerless or low in social status and esteem.

This is closely related to the various purposes which stereotyping can have. It may not only bolster the sense of superiority of those among whom the stereotype circulates, but also act as a means of validating elements of an existing social order or cultural hierarchy. Stereotyping creates symbolic boundaries between peoples and cultures, as for instance in the nineteenth century when Africans or people of African descent were considered socially and culturally backward, or when women were confined to certain functions (such as carers and housekeepers) and excluded from certain activities (such as participation in certain "higher art" genres like history painting and musical composition). The symbolic boundaries which stereotypes patrol strategically exclude those who are targeted by them. This is the political dimension of stereotypical representation. It is the focus of much of the struggle that goes into contesting stereotypes. We should remember and take heart from the successes of such struggle, for they tell us that stereotypes are not, of necessity, historically unchanging. Both women and black people have over time challenged the negative closure of their stereotypical representations; they have achieved, even if as yet incompletely, a greater inclusiveness within society, an expansion of opportunities and scope, and a more positive social identity. As the content of stereotypes diminishes and recedes, so the targets of stereotyping change historically, across different times and conjunctures. This brings us to the issue of whether stereotyping itself has always existed.

Prejudiced attitudes and hostility towards collectivities different to one's own are problems that stretch back a long way in time. They have occurred in many societies and cultures, and because of this it seems that stereotyping can be conceptually applied to various social contexts and circumstances, over both time and space. The difficulty here is that it has only been developed as a concept in modern times, with particular reference to modern societies or societies becoming modern. In various ways it is specific to such times, and may even be said to be characteristically modern in the problems it addresses. Its historical or anthropological application outside the context of these times is possible, but transposing a period-related formulation as a tool for interpreting phenomena beyond its usual social and cultural range requires care and caution. The concept is perhaps strongest when used with reference to specifically modern conditions, though of course these conditions have not been realized to the same extent, or in the same invariant combinations, across time and space.

MODERNITY AND LIPPMANN'S DILEMMA

That is why we need to remember that in the first place the concept arose specifically in western societies during the process of their becoming modern. Conceptual thought often develops through a metaphorical amplification in the semantics of an existing term. This was the case with the stereotype, which was initially used in printing to describe the process of type-setting: fixing characters and text in rigid form for the sake of their repeated use without subsequent modification or change. During the nineteenth century it was figuratively adapted as a synonym for commonplaces or over-conventionalized diction, but its conceptual power was only realized later when it became, metaphorically and then in its own right, a term of reference for reductionist forms of social and cultural representation – fixing and perpetuating such categories as "woman," "foreigner," "native," or the "undeserving poor" in their pejorative forms. The same applies to any of the stereotypical variants of these broad categories, such as "blonde bimbo," "wops," "chinks," or "welfare scroungers."

The American political columnist and social commentator Walter Lippmann is generally acknowledged as the first person to elaborate the term in this way, particularly in his book *Public Opinion* (1965). Lippmann not only offered the initial formulation of the concept – from which point it became a key term in the social and human sciences – but was also the first to link it to the problems of modernity. In this respect, he conceived of stereotyping as a dilemma attendant on living in the increasingly differentiated formations characteristic of modern urban societies, along with the expansion of encounters with cultural difference and of contact with multiple social groups which they have entailed.

The dilemma can be summarized in the following way. On the one hand, it can be argued that the difficulties of understanding and response that accompany our proliferating social and cultural relations under conditions of modern life create the need for informational short-cuts, readymade devices of discourse and representation that help us process the otherwise overwhelming data of daily social realities. We may turn to the modern media as sources of information and knowledge, and we may find that at their honest best they help us build mental bridges and enrich our experience of the complex world around us. On the other hand, this modern social need provides a fertile bed for the cultivation of stereotypes, as for instance in media such as film, advertising, and tabloid journalism. Once established and widely accepted, stereotypes diminish or block our appreciation and understanding of other social groups and categories because of the stunted, fixed manner of their representations. As already noted, stereotyping works by making these representations seem natural and absolute, and when it is successful the resulting view of others becomes entrenched and difficult to shift, even in the face of empirical evaluation or conflicting experience. The media are certainly not the only sites in which this process occurs, but media stereotyping attains influence and power beyond that of everyday conversation and interpersonal exchange because of the broad distribution and circulation of the products of modern communications, and the extent to which they are accredited as sources of authority or truth. Media accreditation increases the rhetorical force of stereotypes, whether this involves young people reading teen magazines or adults watching the news on television.

The dual sense of stereotypes as both necessary and undesirable modes of representation encapsulated for Lippmann an endemic contradiction of modernity, a simultaneous product of the imperatives of development, expansion, and change *and* the drive to order, control, and the enforcement of social norms. A key line of response to this contradictory combination involves a hardening and entrenchment of people's mental schemas or cognitive structures, converting aspects of them into stereotypes or making people more receptive to stereotypes already in circulation. Lippmann's resolution of the problems thrown up by these opposed imperatives was to side with the need for order, stability, and control in producing a consistent view of the world and securing public opinion on this basis. This was a diminution of conceptual vision. It undermines the need to critique stereotypes as ideological forms of representation which strive to repress both politics and history by injecting into social and cultural processes the fixity of their naturalized forms.

CONCEPTUAL REFINEMENTS AND CRITICAL ISSUES

There is a strong temptation to adopt some form of stereotyping when people are faced with ambivalence, uncertainty, loss, or bewildering change. They may also then be more vulnerable to influence from the media use of stereotypes. In these circumstances, the fast-frozen figures of stereotypes promote an intolerance of social and cultural difference on the basis of their categorical, unbending views of particular ethnic, gender, sexual, or other categories. In the face of these undesirable views and their various consequences, we should not lose sight – as Lippmann did himself – of the epistemological dilemma we face in modernity of embracing complexity and contingency without resorting to reductive simplification, either/or forms of thinking, and the absolute judgments of others that go with the territory of mediated and situated stereotyping.

All too often, this is what has happened in the subsequent application and development of the concept. It is as if those concerned with stereotyping in the social and human sciences see only one side of the dilemma, and not the other. For example, there is a strong tendency to see stereotyping as a problem associated only with other people, a critical distantiation that sets off "us" against "them" in a process which is akin to stereotyping itself. Stereotyping creates and maintains rigid boundaries between "us" and "them." Ironically, this is what happened after Lippmann's initial formulation of the concept, when stereotyping became widely conceived as a pathological process, an abnormal and irrational way of responding to others conveniently set apart from normal and rational forms of categorization. It could then be seen as entirely the product of deficient schooling, damaged personalities, or extreme beliefs – such as the anti-Semitic views of mid-twentieth century Fascists – and the propagandist dissemination of these in contemporary media. Partly because of the dominance of behaviorism in both mid-twentieth century psychology and communications research, this response to stereotyping was common to both from roughly the 1930s to the 1960s. The us/them dichotomy it set up between stereotyping and the rational coming to terms with difference may have appeared to resolve the dilemma identified by Lippmann, but it did this by all-too-cleanly separating the (rational) researcher from the (irrational) acceptance and use of stereotypes.

The model had no way of explaining the widespread social prevalence of stereotypical views – as for instance in the Nazi period of the Third Reich or the apartheid era in South Africa.

What followed from this unsatisfactory resolution was that the opposed senses of stereotyping in Lippmann's formulation became split off from each other. In late twentieth-century psychology, for instance, social cognition and social identity theory reacted to the pathologization of stereotypical prejudice by questioning the rigid divide between irrational ("false") and rational ("correct") thinking. However, in pointing up its wider social occurrence, they turned the pathological model on its head and began to conceive of stereotyping as a necessary component of ordinary human cognition, vital for the way we process and utilize information. The question of ideology was repressed, not because it is overburdened with all sorts of past intellectual baggage, but because stereotyping itself was normalized. This occurred around another binary opposition, that of ingroups and outgroups. The dichotomy distinguished between the assimilation of people into their own social groups and categories where their similarities are exaggerated, and the division between such social groups and categories and others where their differences are blown out of proportion and heavily biased. In this simplistic conception of culture, association, and belonging, stereotypes are vital to positive group identities, so being a member of any group inevitably leads to bias, distortion, and denigration of others. Stereotyping comes to appear as cognitively universal and natural whereas, from a critical sociological perspective, it is stereotyping which naturalizes its own universalized definitions of others.

More recently, the emphasis on just one side of Lippmann's epistemological problem has been redressed by other psychologists who have attended more fully to the social dimensions of stereotyping and other forms of representation or to the cultural models they involve, though these developments have occurred with cognition as their general informing background, and with the media being almost completely ignored. Social psychologists who pay explicit attention to the issues of power and ideology and their discursive accomplishments remain exceptional. For example, Augoustinos and Walker's (1995) definition of stereotypes as "ideological representations which are used to justify and legitimize existing social and power relations" is made against prevailing traditions within their discipline. Media and cultural studies, along with many areas of sociology, have moved mainly in the other direction to these traditions, opting to focus only on ideology and power at the expense of the psychological dimensions of experience, perception, knowledge, and belief. Much of the work that has resulted has been of enormous significance for sociology and other disciplines – the conceptual formulation and analysis of representations of the stereotypical Other in postcolonial and historical studies is just one example of this – but again there has been a tendency to lose sight of Lippmann's dual conception of stereotyping. The benefit of this is that it offsets the academic split between cognition and culture, or psychology and politics, and reminds us of the dilemma underlying stereotyping which stereotyping seeks to annul: the dilemma of how "we" are going to go about getting to know "you." Is this to be accomplished in terms of one-dimensional representations that help maintain existing structures of power, order, and control, or should we treat these representations critically for the way they help to produce and perpetuate inequality and oppression, and so try to develop a more complex vision characterized by its openness, flexibility, and tolerance?

Critical sociological commentary on stereotypes needs to focus not only on the pernicious images of public stereotyping and their discursive properties, but also on the broad relational dynamics of power and conflict that are always present in stereotyping as a social process. It has certainly proved fruitful to apply philosophical, feminist, and psychoanalytical theory to these dynamics, but we should remember that they are always definite and contingent, which means that methodologically the relations between identity, representation, and difference need to be historicized, understood within specific social and cultural contexts in time and space, across the different periods and formations of modernity and late modernity. These relations are fluid and changing, and

although the belief that they are not may itself be the result of stereotyping and its underlying self-assertions, it is important to see how stereotypes have been historically situated within such modern constellations of identity and discourse as sexual politics, nationalism, militarism and war, colonialism and postcolonialism, imperialism and neoimperialism, crime, normality and deviance, race and ethnicity, disability and disease. This may be something of a wish-list for further research, but such research is necessary wherever the relations of identity, representation, and difference generate the production or reproduction of those tight knots of symbolic figuration we refer to as stereotypes.

SEE ALSO: Anti-Semitism (Religion); Deviance, the Media and; Essentalism and Constructionism; Generalized Other; Ideology; Racist Movements; Representation; Social Cognition; Social Identity Theory; Stigma

REFERENCES AND SUGGESTED READINGS

Allport, G. W. (1954) *The Nature of Prejudice*. Addison Wesley, Cambridge, MA.

Augoustinos, M. & Walker, I. (1995) *Social Cognition*, Sage, Thousand Oaks, CA.

Bhabha, H. K. (1994) *The Location of Culture*. Routledge, New York.

Billig, M. (1991) *Ideology and Opinions*. Sage, Thousand Oaks, CA.

Dyer, R. (1993) *The Matter of Images*. Routledge, London.

Hall, S. (1997) The Spectacle of the "Other." In: Hall, S. (Ed.), *Representation: Cultural Representations and Signifying Practices*. Sage, Thousand Oaks, CA, pp. 223–90.

Hinton, P. R. (2000) *Stereotypes, Cognition and Culture*. Psychology Press, Hove.

Lippmann, W. (1965 [1922]) *Public Opinion*. Free Press/Collier Macmillan, London.

Perkins, T. E. (1979) Rethinking Stereotypes. In: Barrett, M., Corrigan, P., Kohn, A., & Wolff, J. (Eds.), *Ideology and Cultural Production*. Croom Helm, London.

Pickering, M. (2001) *Stereotyping: The Politics of Representation*. Palgrave Macmillan, New York.

Pickering, M. (2004) Bigotry. In Cashmore, E. (Ed.), *Encyclopedia of Race and Ethnic Studies*. Routledge, New York, pp. 53–7.

Pickering, M. (2004) Racial Stereotypes. In: Taylor, G. & Spencer, S. (Eds.), *Perspectives on Social Identity*. Routledge, New York.

Riggins, S. H. (Ed.) (1997) *The Language and Politics of Exclusion*. Sage, Thousand Oaks, CA.

Said, E. (1978) *Orientalism*. Harmondsworth, Penguin.

Shohat, E. & Stam, R. (1994) *Unthinking Eurocentrism*. Routledge, New York.

Tajfel, H. (1981) *Human Groups and Social Categories*. Cambridge University Press, Cambridge.

stigma

Abdi M. Kusow

The term stigma refers to a social or individual attribute that is devalued and discredited in a particular social context. As Goffman (1963) noted, however, this definition requires an important qualification, one that defines stigma in terms of "a language of relationship" that can link attributes to particular stereotypes, rather than a priori objectified attributes. The language of relationship between attributes and stereotypes is extremely important because an attribute, in and of itself, does not carry an inherent quality that makes it credible or discredible outside the nature of the stereotype that corresponds to it.

Link and Phelan (2001) defined stigma in terms of the presence and convergence of four interrelated components. First, people distinguish and label human differences. Second, members of the dominant cultural group link labeled persons with certain undesirable attributes. Third, negatively labeled groups or individuals are placed in distinct and separate categories from the non-stigmatized. Fourth, as a result of the first three components, labeled individuals experience status loss. Finally, the process of stigma placement, and therefore management, is dependent on the degree of one's access to social, economic, and political power.

Regardless of how stigma is defined, however, in order for an attribute to be designated as a mark of stigma, two conditions must be present. First, the designation of stigma must be informed by a collectively shared understanding by all participants of which attributes are stigmatizing in the available pool of socially meaningful categories in a particular social context. This statement is important because an attribute that is stigmatizing in one social context may not be stigmatizing in another. The second condition relates to the degree to which a mark of stigma is visible. The degree of visibility determines the stigmatized person's feelings about themselves and their interactions and relationship with non-stigmatized groups and individuals, particularly in situations perceived as potentially stigmatizing encounters.

There are two general categories of stigma attributes. The first category refers to attributes that are immediately or potentially visible upon social encounters. Three types of stigma attributes can be outlined within this category. The first relates to outward and clear physical deformations. The second relates to what Goffman described as "the tribal stigma of race, nation, and religion." The latter is transmitted through lineage, and affects all members of the stigmatized group. This type of stigma can be characterized as collective or group stigma, while the first, physical deformities, affects only individuals, and can therefore be referred to as individual stigma.

The second broad category relates to stigma attributes that are not clearly and outwardly visible, but may or may not become visible upon social interaction and where the stigmatized person believes that their stigma is not known to those with whom they interact. The distinction between whether or not a particular stigma attribute is visible is important because it determines the nature of social interaction between those who are perceived as stigmatized and the normals. More importantly, it situates the nature of the reactions and information management by stigmatized individuals that appear to reveal their stigma attributes. In the case where the stigma attribute is readily and clearly visible, the process of information management involves attempts to minimize tensions generated during social interactions.

If the stigma attribute is visible, the process of information management shifts from mere tension management to information management about one's feelings of having a spoiled identity. The concern of the stigmatized in this case becomes one of whether or not to display discrediting information, and ultimately leads to what Goffman described as information management techniques.

There are a number of information management techniques employed by stigmatized individuals. One common technique is "covering." Covering refers to attempts by stigmatized individuals to conceal signs commonly considered stigma symbols. Another strategy is "distancing," where stigmatized individuals or groups disassociate themselves from those roles, associations, and institutions that may be considered as stigmatizing. Still another strategy is "compartmentalization," where individuals divide their worlds into two social worlds: a small and intimate one to which the stigmatized reveals their identity, and a larger group from which the stigmatized individual conceals their identity. Finally, individuals may engage in "embracement" through the expressive confirmation of the social roles and statuses associated with stigma (Snow & Anderson 1987).

A recent criticism of the nature of stigma, however, pertains to the uncritical assumption of the existence of a normatively shared understanding of the distribution of stigma symbols (Kusow 2004). The conventional literature on the distribution of stigma divides a society into stigmatized and normals. This distinction is less tenable than before, however, because the current demographic, social, political, and economic context in which stigma symbols are distributed is radically different from those when Goffman's seminal essay *Stigma* first appeared. Due to changes in the political and social climate, particularly as a result of the impacts of multiculturalism and the embracement of wider social identities in the US, we are approaching a situation or an era in which who and what is normal, and therefore the question of who stigmatized whom, is under constant revision. Given this situation, future scholars must also consider how stigmatized individuals disavow dominant perspectives regarding the distribution of stigma, instead of merely concentrating on information management on the part of the stigmatized.

SEE ALSO: Deviance; Facework; Goffman, Erving; Interaction Order

REFERENCES AND SUGGESTED READINGS

Goffman, E. (1963) *Stigma: Notes on the Management of Spoiled Identities*. Prentice-Hall, Englewood Cliffs, NJ.
Killian, L. (1985) The Stigma of Race: Who Now Bears the Mark of Cain? *Symbolic Interaction* 8(2): 1–14.
Kusow, A. M. (2004) Contesting Stigma: On Goffman's Assumption of Normative Order. *Symbolic Interaction* 27(2): 179–97.
Link, B. & Phelan, J. (2001) Conceptualizing Stigma. *Annual Review of Sociology* 27(3): 363–85.
Riessman, C. (2000) Stigma and Everyday Resistance Practices: Childless Women in South India. *Gender and Society* 14(5): 111–35.
Snow, D. & Anderson, L. (1987) Identity Work among the Homeless: The Verbal Construction and Avowal of Personal Identities. *American Journal of Sociology* 92(6): 1336–71.

strain theories

Robert Agnew

Strain theories argue that strain or stress is a major cause of crime. Individuals engage in crime to reduce or escape from their strain (e.g., theft to reduce monetary strain, running away to escape abusive parents), seek revenge against the source of their strain or related targets, or cope with the negative emotions caused by strain (e.g., illicit drug use). There are several major versions of strain theory in sociology, distinguished in terms of the types of strain they examine and their description of the factors that influence or condition the effect of strain on crime. This entry describes the major versions of strain theory, beginning with Durkheim and ending with Agnew, whose general strain theory builds on previous strain theories.

DURKHEIM

Durkheim presented the first modern version of strain theory in his book *Suicide* (1951). Durkheim argues that healthy societies set limits on individual goals, such that individuals have a reasonable chance of achieving their goals. During periods of rapid social change or turmoil, however, societies may lose their ability to limit individual goals. Individuals, lacking the ability to limit their own goals, come to pursue unlimited or ever-escalating goals. The despair that inevitably results from the pursuit of unlimited goals was said to be a major cause of suicide and was also linked to other-directed violence. Durkheim's view of strain as the pursuit of unlimited goals, however, never had a significant effect on the study of crime, in part because it was overshadowed by Merton's version of strain theory (see Passas & Agnew 1997).

MERTON

Like Durkheim, Merton (1938) focuses on that type of strain involving the inability to achieve one's goals, particularly economic goals. Merton departs from Durkheim, however, in two important ways. While Durkheim focuses on the pursuit of unlimited goals, Merton focuses on the inability of lower-class individuals to achieve more limited economic goals. This difference may reflect the fact that Merton's theory was developed during the height of the Depression. Further, while for Durkheim the failure of society to regulate individual goals is the source of strain, the opposite is the case in Merton. Merton argues that society encourages individuals to pursue the goal of monetary success, but prevents large segments of the population from achieving this goal through legitimate channels. In particular, Merton argues that all individuals in the US – regardless of class – are encouraged to strive for monetary success. Many individuals, however, particularly those in the lower classes, are prevented from achieving such success through the legitimate routes of educational and occupational advancement. Such individuals experience much frustration and, according to Merton, they may respond in one of five ways.

Conformity is the most common response: individuals continue to strive for monetary success through legitimate channels, living with their frustration. Innovation involves the attempt to achieve monetary success through illegitimate channels, like theft, drug-selling, and prostitution. Ritualism involves lowering

the desire for monetary success to the point where it can be achieved through legitimate channels. Retreatism involves rejecting the goal of monetary success and the means to achieve it. Retreatists, according to Merton, include skid-row alcoholics, drug addicts, and in the most extreme case, those who commit suicide. Rebellion also involves rejecting the goal of monetary success and the means to achieve it, but individuals substitute new goals and means in their place. While rebellion may assume political forms, it can assume criminal forms, as illustrated in the discussion of Cohen, below.

It is of course critical to understand why some people adapt to strain in ways that involve crime while others do not. Merton provides some guidance here. He states, for example, that lower-class individuals are more likely to employ criminal adaptations because they are less committed to legitimate norms due to their inadequate socialization. The revisions in Merton's theory by Cohen and by Cloward and Ohlin shed additional light on the ways in which individuals, particularly lower-class juveniles, adapt to strain.

COHEN

Cohen (1955) drew on Merton's theory in an effort to explain lower-class gang delinquency. According to Cohen, lower-class boys do not simply desire money; rather, they desire middle-class status more generally – including respect from others. Such boys, however, have trouble achieving this status through legitimate channels. Most notably, they are often frustrated and humiliated when they compete with middle-class students in the school system and try to meet the expectations of middle-class teachers.

There are several ways to cope with this frustration, but the response of innovation is not a viable option. Middle-class status is not easily achieved through illegitimate channels. Many lower-class boys, however, cope through the response of rebellion. They reject the goal of middle-class status and set up an alternative status system in which they can successfully compete. Their hostility toward the middle class leads them to set up an oppositional status system which places high value on criminal acts like theft and fighting. Cohen's description of this oppositional subculture has been challenged as extreme, but Cohen's use of strain theory to explain the origin of delinquent groups is a fundamental contribution to criminology. Most contemporary researchers view delinquent groups as an adaptation to the strain experienced by group members.

CLOWARD AND OHLIN

Cloward and Ohlin (1960) also apply strain theory to the explanation of lower-class gang delinquency. Drawing on Merton, they argue that lower-class people want to achieve monetary success, but are often prevented from doing so through legitimate channels. Drawing on Cohen, they argue that if conditions are right, adolescents sometimes adapt to their strain by forming or joining delinquent groups like gangs. These delinquent groups facilitate law-violation; among other things, they provide rationalizations or justifications for delinquency. But Cloward and Ohlin go on to argue that there are different types of delinquent groups; some specializing in fighting, some in theft, and some in drug use. The type(s) of delinquent group available depends, in part, on the characteristics of the individual's community.

Cloward and Ohlin have been criticized because research suggests that most gang members do not specialize in particular types of delinquency. Their work is nevertheless important because it makes the point that explanations of crime must not only consider the factors that predispose individuals to crime, like strain, but also the opportunities that are available for crime – referred to as illegitimate opportunities.

CRITIQUES OF CLASSIC STRAIN THEORIES

The classic strain theories of Merton, Cohen, and Cloward and Ohlin were perhaps the dominant explanations of crime during the 1950s and 1960s. They were also part of the inspiration behind the War on Poverty, which was designed to make it easier for individuals to achieve economic success through legitimate channels. Certain of the programs that were part of the War on Poverty (like Head Start and Job Corps) are still in existence. Classic strain theories came

under heavy attack in the late 1960s and 1970s, however. Self-report surveys showed that delinquency was common in all social classes. This fact was taken as evidence against classic strain theories, although these theories can explain middle-class delinquency if one focuses on relative deprivation (Passas & Agnew 1997). Also, empirical tests provided little support for classic strain theory. Such tests typically examined the individual's educational or occupational aspirations and expectations, in an effort to determine if crime was highest among those who did not expect to achieve their aspirations. Crime, however, was found to be highest among those with both low aspirations and expectations, a finding usually interpreted in terms of control theories (Hirschi 1969).

These tests have been criticized; among other things, they do not focus on the key goal of monetary success. More recent data suggest that dissatisfaction with one's monetary situation is related to crime (Agnew 2001). Further, qualitative studies frequently report that criminals engage in income-generating crimes because they have a desperate need for money, but few legal prospects for obtaining it. Nevertheless, classic strain theories fell into decline. There were several attempts to revise strain theory in the 1970s and 1980s, most of which argued that people may pursue a ranges of goals and that goal achievement is a function of more than social class. In 1992 Agnew drew on classic strain theories, the revisions in these theories, and the broader stress literature to develop his general strain theory of crime, which led to a renewed interest in strain theory.

AGNEW'S GENERAL STRAIN THEORY (GST)

Agnew's (1992) general strain theory focuses on a broad range of strains or stressors. Certain of these strains involve the inability to achieve positively valued goals – the type of strain emphasized in previous versions of strain theory. Other strains involve the loss of positively valued stimuli (e.g., romantic partners) and the presentation of negatively valued stimuli (e.g., verbal and physical abuse) – the types of strain emphasized in the stress literature. Hundreds of specific types of strain fall under these broad categories, but GST argues that those strains most likely to lead to crime are (1) seen as unjust, (2) are high in magnitude, (3) are associated with low social control, and (4) create some pressure or incentive to engage in criminal coping. Specific strains that meet these criteria include the inability to achieve goals such as monetary success, thrills/excitement, autonomy, and masculine status; the experience of parental rejection; discipline that is very strict, erratic, excessive, and/or harsh; child abuse and neglect; negative secondary school experiences like low grades and negative relations with teachers; work in the secondary labor market; homelessness; criminal victimization; and experiences with prejudice or discrimination based on ascribed characteristics.

These types of strain lead to a range of negative emotions, including anger, frustration, and depression. These negative emotions in turn create pressure for corrective action. Crime is one possible response, since it may allow individuals to reduce or escape from their strain (e.g., running away from abusive parents), seek revenge, or alleviate negative emotions through illicit drug use. Whether strained individuals turn to crime is influenced by a range of factors which affect the individual's ability to engage in legal coping, the costs of crime, and the individual's disposition for crime. Such factors include coping skills and resources (e.g., intelligence, financial resources), level of conventional social support, parental supervision, personality traits like low constraint and negative emotionality, beliefs regarding crime, and association with delinquent peers.

GST has some empirical support, with studies suggesting that the above strains increase the likelihood of crime and that their effect on crime is partly mediated by negative emotions (Agnew 2001). Evidence on the extent to which the effect of strain on crime is influenced by the above factors is mixed, although some recent studies provide support for GST. Recent work has applied GST to the explanation of group differences in crime, including age, gender, community, and race/ethnic differences in offending rates. It is argued that some groups are more likely to experience those types of strain conducive to crime, react to strain with strong negative emotions, and respond to such strain and negative emotions with crime. Strain

theory, then, is once again playing an important role in the explanation of crime and deviance.

SEE ALSO: Anomie; Deviance, Crime and; Deviance, Explanatory Theories of; Durkheim, Émile; Merton, Robert K.

REFERENCES AND SUGGESTED READINGS

Agnew, R. (1992) Foundation for a General Strain Theory of Crime and Delinquency. *Criminology* 30: 47–87.
Agnew, R. (2001) An Overview of General Strain Theory. In: Paternoster, R. & Bachman, R. (Eds.), *Explaining Criminals and Crime*. Roxbury, Los Angeles, pp. 161–74.
Cloward, R. A. & Ohlin, L. E. (1960) *Delinquency and Opportunity*. Free Press, New York.
Cohen, A. (1955) *Delinquent Boys*. Free Press, New York.
Durkheim, E. (1951) *Suicide*. Free Press, New York.
Hirschi, T. (1969) *Causes of Delinquency*. University of California Press, Berkeley.
Merton, R. K. (1938) Social Structure and Anomie. *American Sociological Review* 3: 672–82.
Merton, R. K. (1968) *Social Theory and Social Structure*. Free Press, New York.
Passas, N. & Agnew, R. (1997) *The Future of Anomie Theory*. Northeastern University Press, Boston.

stranger, the

Terri LeMoyne

Simmel defined the field of sociology as the study of social forms, or the assorted patterns that people impose upon social interaction to give it coherent meaning. Social forms are the structured features of interaction, and Simmel argued that the sociologist should ascertain these social forms because actors typically create them unconsciously. In addition, he maintained that "social types," or general character traits, are based upon social forms and are dependent upon social interaction. Therefore, individualisms, or qualities that we oftentimes assume to be uniquely personal, are really rooted in social interaction. "The Stranger"

(1971 [1908]) is but one illustration of a social type.

The notion of distance is important to Simmel in his typology of the stranger, whose social position involves a synthesis of both attachment and detachment. The stranger is someone who can be located within any social environment at any point in time. He is both remote from us while still being close; he is simultaneously a part of the group as well as outside of it.

Simmel utilized "the trader" as an exemplar of the stranger, and more specifically, the European Jew as the classic example of it. By definition, the trader obtains a range of goods for his community from outside groups. Because he is the middleman for trade, he is mobile and is not tied to the group through kinship, locality, or occupation. As a result, he is not completely enmeshed within the group. Because of his unique position, members of his group view him as both far and near.

Because of this unusual social position, others assume that the stranger possesses an objective attitude regarding social matters; he is both involved in and indifferent to the community. Therefore, group members are more inclined to divulge private information to the stranger that they often keep hidden from intimates.

The stranger is also viewed as possessing greater individual autonomy. Simmel writes that the stranger is less apt to distort information because of his differences from the group. This allows him to reach conclusions that more easily deviate from those members who are more entrenched within the collective.

This objective stance provides the stranger with a greater freedom than that experienced by those enmeshed in the group. His attitudes and perceptions are less likely to be distorted because he is not as closely attached to the group. His atypical social position allows him to assess more accurately situations, even close ones, from a distance. This unique freedom allows him to examine a variety of situations with minimal personal bias. As a stranger, he possesses standards that are more general and objective, and his actions are less constrained by customs, religion, or established community practices.

In determining the qualities of the stranger, Simmel writes that group members tend to highlight the general abstract traits that they

share with him. In contrast, when people share a close relationship to someone, they attend to those attributes and qualities that are specific to their relationship. While a focus on general qualities unifies people as a whole, they do not lead particular individuals toward one another. This approach results in a lessening of the bond between people coupled with their awareness of the tenuousness of the relationship. In these cases, the stranger is close to others based upon general similarities like nationality, social position, or occupation, but these same universal attributes make him remote because they also pertain to many others.

Because there is an emphasis on these common general human qualities, they also tend to stress the individual characteristics that they do not share with the stranger. This approach results in a relationship that is characterized by tension. For example, if one is a stranger in terms of nationality or race, these differences are not viewed as individual, but are seen instead as qualities that the stranger shares with other strangers. It is here that strangers are viewed as types rather than people. As types, their nearness is no more specific than their remoteness. Simmel cites the taxation practices of the Middle Ages as an illustration of the Jew as a social type. Where the Christian population was taxed according to their individual assets, all Jews were charged an identical tax no matter what their income. A fixed tax was levied upon the Jews because they were treated as a social position rather than as separate, distinct individuals, with separate, distinct incomes.

In an effort to make this social type more universal, Simmel claims that there is a level of strangeness in all relationships, even the most intimate ones. When entering into romantic relationships people tend to concentrate on what is unique and distinctive about the association, while ignoring any general similarities. This occurs because they believe that no other relationship is comparable to theirs. This love has never existed before. As time passes, each participant will come to question the validity of their relationship when they realize that it is not particularly unique. In fact, relationships just like this one occur with great frequency and each partner could have just as easily met someone else who would have fulfilled this romantic void. All close relationships must endure this assessment because what they all share is never exceptional to them. The outcome of this new-found awareness is an overall level of strangeness within the relationship.

Simmel argues that although varying degrees of remoteness and nearness are present in all relationships, there is a "special proportion and reciprocal tension" between farness and nearness that produce the unique social type of the stranger (Simmel 1971 [1908]: 149). But, Simmel warns, we cannot define or quantify this special proportion with great certainty. All we know is that there are certain amounts of nearness and farness that must be present for this social type to exist.

SEE ALSO: Simmel, Georg; Stranger, The

REFERENCES AND SUGGESTED READINGS

Frisby, D. (2002) *Georg Simmel*, rev. edn. Routledge, New York.

Levine, D. N. (1997) Simmel Reappraised: Old Images, New Scholarship. In: Camic, C. (Ed.), *Reclaiming the Sociological Classics: The State of Scholarship*. Blackwell, Oxford, pp. 173–207.

Levine, D. N., Carter, E. B., & Gorman, E. M. (1976a) Simmel's Influence on Sociology – I. *American Journal of Sociology* 81: 813–45.

Levine, D. N., Carter, E. B., & Gorman, E. M. (1976b) Simmel's Influence on Sociology – II. *American Journal of Sociology* 81: 1112–32.

Simmel, G. (1971 [1908]) The Stranger. In: Levine, D. N. (Ed.), *George Simmel: On Individuality and Social Forms*. University of Chicago Press, Chicago, pp. 143–9.

Spykman, N. J. (2004) *The Social Theory of Georg Simmel*. Transaction, New Brunswick, NJ.

Tabboni, S. (1995) The Stranger and Modernity: From Equality of Rights to Recognition of Difference. *Thesis Eleven* 43: 17–27.

strategic decisions

David C. Wilson

Theoretical and empirical studies of decision-making pervade organization theory. They have done so for over six decades. James March and Herbert Simon suggested in 1958 that managing organizations and decision-making were virtually synonymous. From this broad perspective, decision-making has maintained its centrality to the field of organization theory and is one of the most active areas of current management research, particularly in the field of strategic management. The dynamics of organizing brought with them the need for understanding decision-making. As organizations grew and became more complex, decision-making became a central activity. Managers, in particular, were expected to make choices amongst often uncertain alternatives and to choose wisely – benefiting the organization and its many stakeholders. Scholars were expected to uncover the characteristics of decision processes and to explain ways in which we might, ultimately, improve the ways in which decisions were made in organizations.

The scholarly study of decision-making covers many levels of analysis (from individual cognition to the cultural characteristics of nation-states), and many disciplines inform our knowledge (from mathematics to behavioral theories of social science). The term strategic decision-making is usually used to indicate decisions made in organizations, as opposed to individual choice activity (such as choosing where to go on holiday). Organization includes any collective social, economic, or political activity involving a plurality of human effort. Strategic decisions emphasize the social practice of decision-making as it is carried out amongst and between a group of such individuals. It is the organizing of decision activity as a collective phenomenon which takes center stage, rather than the cognitive processes of individual choice-makers.

Equally, strategic decision-making is not primarily concerned with computation in the field of judgment and choice. Various branches of mathematics can inform us about risk, options, game theory, and choice. All have their utility in understanding choice processes, but are less useful when considering how organizations full of people make decisions. For example, the most well-known variant of game theory (decisions between two players) is the prisoner's dilemma, where two criminals are in separate cells and have to decide whether or not to betray each other (having agreed not to betray in advance of the game). The greatest payoffs come from both prisoners sticking to their agreement, but most betray each other and the payoffs are significantly reduced. The lesson is that computational mathematics could help the players maximize their returns. This is choice theory (rather than strategic decision-making).

Why *strategic* decisions? These decisions are usually large, expensive, and characterized by high levels of uncertainty (no one has done this before). Once implemented, they set the course of many operational (everyday) decisions that follow in their wake. A further characteristic of strategic decisions is that they are difficult to reverse once resources (human and financial) have been committed to their cause. A more robust list of the characteristics of strategic decisions would include the following:

- They are difficult to define precisely (the nature of the problem is elusive).
- Understanding the problem is also part of understanding the solution.
- There is rarely one best solution, but a series of possible solutions.
- Each solution is associated with different tradeoffs and priorities.
- They are difficult to assess in terms of performance, since they tend to continue through the organization without a clear final end point against which performance can be judged.
- They are highly interconnected with other problems in the organization.
- They have high levels of uncertainty associated with them.
- They require strategists to accept fairly high degrees of risk in making decisions.
- Once made, they are difficult to reverse.
- They are likely to be discontinuous and political, with different competing interests trying to influence the outcome in line with their preferences.

At its simplest, strategic decision-making may be considered an instantaneous action, a choice between two or more known alternatives. However, this "point of decision" approach is unable to capture the richness and complexity of:

- the processes that lead up to the point of decision;

- the influences that impact upon putting the decision into action;
- assessing the ultimate performance of that decision.

Decision-making from this choice perspective also assumes that managers have full agency and control over decisions. Sometimes they may have very limited discretion to make decisions or choose amongst alternatives. This could be the case, for example, where strategic decisions in organizations are heavily constrained by interventionist government policies (such as privatization or deregulation), where all strategic decisions are framed and shaped by this wider context. Nevertheless, managers still have some degree of strategic choice even if the wider context (e.g., privatization) is firmly set in place. Managers can still make strategic decisions, for example, concerning such key topics as organizational design, choice of suppliers, choice and sophistication of information systems, and general product or service portfolios.

Theorists such as Drucker (1974) and Weick (1995) showed how decision-making processes in organizations were as much about *defining the question* as they were about *providing an answer*. The important aspects of understanding strategic decisions are deciding whether there is a need for a decision and, if so, what that decision should be about. Weick likens this process to those of boards of inquiry following a disastrous event. Such boards have a number of roles. They are historians – reconstructing the past to allocate responsibility and to prevent future disasters happening through the same processes. Essentially, they take an outcome and interpret it to be the result of a series of decisions (which were often not seen as discrete decisions at the time by those involved). Much of strategic decision-making is about this kind of social reconstruction.

There are many other views of strategic decision-making. You could view strategic decisions as a *plan*: the decision is a consciously intended course of action. In the same way that you might intend to catch an airplane to a specific destination at a particular time, decision-making is a process which is carried out in advance of the action that follows and is developed with a clear purpose. Or you could view strategic decisions as a *ploy*: a decision from this perspective is a set of actions designed to outwit the competition and may not necessarily be the "obvious" content of the decision. For example, a decision to build a new building in order to expand may not be the overt strategy, but is more concerned with increasing barriers to entry for potential competitors. Here, there are connections with strategic decision-making as conceived in its military roots, where the plans of campaigns may have similar characteristics to those of a ploy to outwit the "enemy." You could view strategic decisions as a *pattern*: decisions are not necessarily taken with a planned purpose and decision-makers do not always have access to the range of knowledge required to plan wholly in advance. What happens is that multiple decisions taken over time form a pattern. It is this pattern of resulting (emergent) behavior that we call the strategy of the firm. Strategy is therefore characterized as a pattern that emerges from a stream of decisions.

Strategic decision-making can also be seen as achieving a *position*: decisions are less about the dynamics of planning or gamesmanship and more about trying to achieve a match between the organization and its environment. This position can be one of alignment, so that the organization matches its environment (e.g., highly decentralized structures to match a turbulent and unpredictable environment), or one of trying to secure competitive advantage (where the organization achieves a unique position in the market for some time). Positions, of course, can be planned, emerge, or be a combination of both emergent and planned processes.

Finally, strategic decision-making can be viewed as a *perspective*: decisions are characterized as being a reflection of how strategists in an organization see and perceive the world and their organization. For example, the strategic perspective of Nokia is one of continuous and sometimes radical change (Nokia began as a paper and pulp company); IBM favors a dominant marketing perspective, whilst Hewlett-Packard favors an engineering excellence perspective. This perspective, if pervasive enough, can influence the kinds of decisions taken, in respect of their content and their processes. We can see the effects of this embedded view of decision-making by observing that organizations in similar industries often choose similar strategic decisions. They become institutionalized. Universities tend to follow broadly similar strategies, as do large retailers or service organizations.

Over the last 50 years there have been radical changes in the ways in which strategic decision-making has been researched. For example, the 1950s and 1960s saw an emphasis on the planning approach to decision-making. The focus was on tools and techniques to help managers make informed decisions about future business directions. Such tools included industry structure analyses and portfolio matrices (e.g., the Ansoff matrix or the Boston Consulting Group's Box). Strategic decision-making was mostly about planning. The 1970s onwards saw a different emphasis. Decisions were now supposed to emphasize the payoffs to organizations that may accrue if they pursued different strategic directions. Typical options were diversification decisions, but this was also the era of innovation (R&D), acquisition, joint venture, and internationalization decisions.

The 1980s saw a move away from examining the content of strategic decisions (that is, what they were about) to examining them more as processes. The question now became whether we could map the progress of a strategic decision and make any inferences about why such processes might occur. David Hickson and his colleagues characterized such processes as sporadic (discontinuous), fluid (continuous and smooth), or constricted (restricted to a small group of stakeholders and highly political). This work also underscored the importance of such processes since they underpinned the recognition amongst managers for strategic change. The 1990s onwards have seen a continuing interest in unfolding the characteristics of decision processes, but the emphasis has changed to focus on whether or not there are any links between decision-making activity and performance (did the decision succeed or fail – and do a number of failed strategic decisions lead to failed organizations)? Finally, very recent approaches to strategic decision-making have started to concentrate upon the more micro aspects of how managers think, act, and interpret strategic decisions. This approach has been termed the *strategy and practice* perspective (Whittington 1996).

Strategic decision-making has encountered many attacks on its theoretical and empirical claims to be a discrete field of study. It has not only survived these attacks, but has also prospered in recent years with many established authors returning to some of the original ideas in decision-making (we can see this, for example, in the more recent works of Karl Weick and James March), and there are many newer researchers joining the field. The major criticisms of the field were:

- The decision itself is an inappropriate level of analysis.
- A lack of large-scale empirical studies (too many assumptions based on too few cases).

The first critique argues that studying decisions as the primary unit of analysis "gets in the way" of what is really important. That is, actions occur in organizations where decisions may not have been taken and to isolate and study "the decision" is to miss that process. The counter-argument says that deciding and implementing are matters of degree in quite diffuse processes. Since then, the decision as a unit of analysis has become the firm focus of many theoreticians, with general agreement that in order to understand "strategy" in organizations one has to understand the processes of the handful of decisions which make up that strategy. Key authors in the field (including Henry Mintzberg, James March, Karl Weick, Paul Nutt, David Hickson and colleagues) are today focusing on the decision as the appropriate unit of analysis.

The second critique was more robust until the large data sets of Paul Nutt and Dean and Sharfman in the US and David Hickson and colleagues in the UK began to emerge from the late 1980s onwards. After this empirical work, it was no longer necessary to base the interpretation of decision-making on a few key in-depth cases, but the comparative empirical study of decisions was possible using multivariate tools for analysis. It became recognized in the social science community that strategic decision-making could be argued to be a robust field of study and that it remained theoretically (and empirically) distinct from other related cognate areas such as corporate strategy or individual choice theories such as consumer behavior.

Overall, strategic decision-making research has informed the general field of organization theory in distinct ways. For example, the notion of *incrementalism* (piecemeal attention to small steps in any process) arose from Charles Lindblom's research into how decisions were made. The notion of *problemistic search* (managers only seek information when they have to, or when there is a pressing problem) came out of work by Richard Cyert and James March. The concept of *enacted environments* (managers only see and interpret the bit of the operating environment they focus upon) came out of research by Karl Weick. All of these concepts were developed in the field of strategic decision-making and have become more generically applied to organizational processes in recent years. Strategic decision-making has proved a rich ground for the emergence of such concepts.

The processes of making strategic decisions can appear deceptively simple. Actions are formulated toward the solution of a particular problem. The problem with this approach is that there may be discernible actions and there may be observable outcomes, but they need not necessarily be wholly related to one another. Problems may be solved by factors other than strategic decisions and, sometimes, taking a strategic decision can create a whole new set of problems (without solving the initial problem the decision was supposed to address).

These polar views can be represented as the *planning* versus the *chaotic* processes of strategic decision-making. They are extremes and, although most decisions lie somewhere between the planned and the chaotic, both perspectives are useful for understanding the processes of strategic decision-making. Viewing processes as basically a set of planning tools allows *actions*, *procedures*, and *measurement* to be explicitly addressed. Planning facilitates decision-makers in analyzing and codifying what appear initially as complex problems. Planning simplifies complexity and helps reduce uncertainty. Because of this, planning can also help decision-makers examine current planning practices in their organization and assess their utility in light of current problems. From a behavioral perspective, planning can ensure that others in the organization are involved and are communicated with as fully as possible. Note that although involvement and communication can be explicit parts of the plan, this may not endow those participants with any influence over the process or its eventual outcome. Finally, planning processes help decision-makers identify key performance indicators by which progress of the decision can be monitored and judged.

Chaotic processes mean that organizations can be viewed as an "anarchy" or as a system with chaotic tendencies. Hence decision-makers can neither understand fully nor control decision processes. Means and ends are unlikely to be coupled, which implies that actions do not lead to expected outcomes and are swayed one way or another by other decisions, other actions, and unforeseen circumstances. The main components of a strategic decision-making process (problems, solutions, participants, and choice situations) interact in an apparently haphazard way, a stream of demands for the fluid attention and energies of managers. Participants move in and out of the decision-making process (every entrance is an exit elsewhere), and this can create discontinuity. At other times, participants fight for the right to become involved and then never exercise any influence they may have.

Viewing decision-making processes as chaotic also has some advantages for decision-makers. Unlike the planning approach, the chaos perspective does not seek to simplify and to reduce uncertainty. It avoids any oversimplification of the process and allows decision-makers to appreciate and expect the role of politics and influence to be a natural part of the decision-making process. In theory, the chaos perspective should encourage decision-makers to think creatively around complex problems and help them to avoid thinking solely in linear sequences.

Creativity and innovation may be enhanced by decision-makers being encouraged to take actions that seem unrelated to the decision under consideration. On the other hand, we should bear in mind that the distinction between creativity and madness is a rather fine line. From a decision-making perspective, this means that no one will know whether the tangential explorations were useful or folly until a long way down the track of the decision process.

The work of James G. March characterizes and summarizes many of the basic features and debates in strategic decision-making. The basic decision process can be illustrated as in Figure 1.

The major contribution of this simple flow diagram was that its very simplicity could be misleading. The cycle can be broken or can malfunction at each stage of the process and between stages. James March taught us to beware of assumptions of rationality both in individuals and in organizations. Actions can be taken for a variety of reasons which correspond to the ways in which organizations are structured (each specialized function developing its own view on what should happen). This was added irrevocably to the vocabulary of organizational decision-making in the form of "local rationality" (Cyert & March 1963).

March was later to refine this concept by emphasizing local preferences (rather than rationality). His argument was that in organizational decision-making, the main thing was in forming *interpretations* rather than in making choices. Here, interpretations cover a wide arena

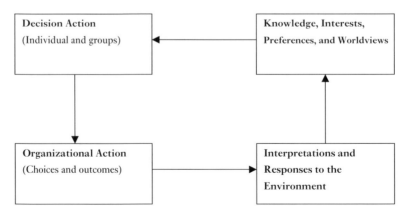

Figure 1   Strategic decision-making processes (James March).

of examining organizational decision-making. In particular, March was keen to show the differences between decisions that were choice based or rule based. The main distinction was whether decision-makers pursue a logic of consequences, making choices amongst alternatives and evaluating their consequences in terms of prior preferences, or do they pursue a logic of appropriateness, fulfilling identities or roles by recognizing situations and following rules which match appropriate behaviors to the situations they encounter? In this respect, organizations provide the context in which such interpretations are formed, sustained, and sometimes changed.

March also alerted our attention to the fact that organizations could engender two very different types of decision behavior. One may be characterized by clarity and consistency and the other by ambiguity, inconsistency, and chaos. In the former case, organization is all about coherence and reducing uncertainty to avoid equivocality. In the latter case, organization is anarchic and acts as a background for decisions which may not be linear in process, may not be logical in a consistent sense, and where solutions may precede outcomes (in the sense that organizations by their very nature are collections of solutions already made – waiting for new decision opportunities to which they can become attached).

Finally, March argued that decision outcomes can be seen as primarily attributable to the actions of autonomous actors in organizations, or can be the result of the systemic properties of organizations as an interacting ecology. Here, the links between organization and decision are made explicit. Is it possible to describe decisions as emanating from the intentions, identities, and interests of independent actors? Or is it necessary to emphasize the ways in which individual actors, organizations, and societies fit together?

There is unlikely to be any resolution of the above theoretical disjunctures. Future work in strategic decision-making may have to try and seek a synthesis – not to force choices amongst epistemologies – so that one can weave together both approaches in ways that allow one to highlight or illuminate the other. Whatever the outcome of this process, it is certain that strategic decision-making will remain at center stage of

the sociology of management and organization for many years to come.

SEE ALSO: Behaviorism; Change Management; Culture, Organizations and; Decision-Making; Existential Sociology; Organization Theory; Strategic Management (Organizations); Structure and Agency; Top Management Teams

REFERENCES AND SUGGESTED READINGS

Cyert, R. & March, J. G. (1963) *A Behavioral Theory of the Firm*. Prentice-Hall, Englewood Cliffs, NJ.

Dean, J. & Sharfman, M. (1996) Does Decision Process Matter? A Study of Strategic Decision Making Effectiveness. *Academy of Management Journal* 39(2): 368–96.

Drucker, P. (1974) *Management: Tasks, Responsibilities, and Practices*. Harper & Row, New York.

Hickson, D., Butler, R., & Wilson, D. (2001) *The Bradford Studies of Decision Making: Classic Research in Management*. Ashgate, London.

Lindblom, C. (1959) The Science of Muddling Through. *Public Administration Review* 19(2): 79–88.

March, J. (1999) *The Pursuit of Organizational Intelligence*. Blackwell, Oxford.

March, J. & Simon, H. (1958) *Organization*. Wiley, New York.

Mintzberg, H. & Waters, J. (1990) Studying Deciding: An Exchange Between Mintzberg and Waters, Pettigrew and Butler. *Organization Studies* 11(1): 1–16.

Nutt, P. (1984) Types of Organizational Decision Processes. *Administrative Science Quarterly* 29(3): 414–50.

Weick, K. (1995) *Sensemaking in Organizations*. Sage, London.

Whittington, R. (1996) Strategy as Practice. *Long Range Planning* 29(5): 731–5.

strategic essentialism

Kristina Wolff

The concept of strategic essentialism is a "strategic use of positivist essentialism in a scrupulously visible political interest" (Fuss 1994: 99).

It utilizes the idea of essence with a recognition of and critique of the essentialist nature of the essence itself. It is a means of using group identity as a basis of struggle while also debating issues related to group identity within the group.

Strategic essentialism emerged out of Gayatri Chakravorty Spivak's critique of the Marxist, historical collective called the Subaltern Studies Group. The collective's main project was to operate as a counter-movement, working to expose elitist representations of South Asian culture, particularly within Indian history. Subaltern studies performed the rewriting of the history of colonial India from the position of subordinated social groups or the *subaltern*. The *subaltern* is often used as a word for the oppressed or "Other" in society. Spivak's usage is based on Antonio Gramsci's definition, which consists of subordinated or non-elite social groups. These groups occupy a space of difference with no or extremely limited access to the culture of the elite. The goal of the Subaltern Studies Group was simply to provide access or space for the subaltern to speak. The subaltern is a product of the network of elites, of differing understandings of what the subaltern *is*, as defined by the elites.

Strategic essentialism recognizes the complexities of occupying a subject-object position, of the subaltern, whether it is a movement, group, or individual. They are working from within a structural position of subordination in society, while also embodying and critiquing that position. For example, a movement for immigrant laborers' rights would be challenging the elites in their definitions of and practices of domination over the workers, while also recognizing the complexities of what it means to be an *immigrant laborer*. The fundamental nature of this concept is that it deliberately suits a particular situation and does not serve as an overarching theory.

Spivak combines the techniques of deconstruction with Foucault's theory of power in the foundational pieces of strategic essentialism. *Deconstruction* as a method of critique provides a means to examine something that is important to how we understand society, perhaps something that is defined as an "essence," while also investigating the complexities of that

essence. Power is examined where it occurs, as a place of domination and of resistance.

Strategic essentialism as applied to feminism serves to utilize essentialist definitions of *woman* while also continually critiquing the concept itself. For example, one of the main goals of liberal feminism is the political struggle to gain equal rights for men and women. This includes providing equal pay for equal work. When arguing for this change in status, the concept of "woman" is used as being as able as men to complete tasks and uphold responsibilities in the working world and therefore they should be judged equally. There is no critique of what being a woman is, but there is a critique as to women's subordinated status in society due to their gender as well as the effects of this on the availability of jobs for women. Strategic essentialism also recognizes that women exist in positions of power within the working world, thus placing them in a position where they may be using female traits that are understood as inherent to all women. This concept moves beyond basic liberal feminist understandings, recognizing that women may be seen as rejecting these "natural" traits in order to fit into a "man's world" of work so that they can be successful. Here women are embodying and rejecting essentialist qualities of being a woman in a calculated manner.

Within the liberal feminist movement, discussions and debates occurred surrounding the ways in which they were utilizing their status as women to fight for their rights. This included the way they fulfilled their expected roles as wives and mothers, as well as using these roles as points of resistance. Additionally, women began to question essentialist definitions of "woman," thus causing great debate within the movement and the development of alternative forms of feminism based on these critiques and definitions of what being a woman means and the effects this has on identity on the individual, group, organization, and societal levels.

Critiques of strategic essentialism often focus on whether it can account for the complexities of race, class, and gender, specifically if it is to focus on a specific situation, within a certain political, geographic, historical context. Others question if those utilizing the technique are always making a strategic choice, as there is an assumption of a certain awareness at play. However, the loudest and most constant critic of strategic essentialism is Spivak. She sees it as morphing into a tool for promoting essentialism rather than serving as a means of critique. Many utilizing it stop short of deconstructing essentialist beliefs serving as the foundation of what is considered essentialist. Strategic essentialism has been adopted and used as a theory rather than remaining a technique, a strategy for understanding the complexity and fluidity of subject/object positions, of identity and power, and of the ways in which subordinated groups operate and work for changing their situations, their status. The indiscriminant use of strategic essentialism broadly to all oppressed groups ignores the importance of tactics and in turn becomes a misapplication of the spirit of the concept. Spivak does find that it can continue to be useful through the consideration of how individuals and others are essentialist in different ways, thus embracing the challenge of the relationship of race, class, gender, and other components of identity.

SEE ALSO: Deconstruction; Essentialism and Constructionism; Foucault, Michel; Liberal Feminism

REFERENCES AND SUGGESTED READINGS

Colesville, C. (2002) Certeau and Foucault: Tactics and Strategic Essentialism. *South Atlantic Quarterly* 100 (2): 18–38.
Danius, S. & Jonsson, S. (2003) An Interview with Gayatri Chakravorty Spivak. *boundary 2* 20(2): 24.
Foucault, M. (1980) *Power/Knowledge: Selected Interviews and Other Writings 1972–1977.* Pantheon Books, New York.
Fuss, D. (1994) Reading Like A Feminist. In: Schor, N. & Weed, E. (Eds.), *The Essential Difference*. Indiana University Press, Bloomington, pp. 98–115.
Rooney, E. (1994) In a Word. Interview. In: Schor, N. & Weed, E. (Eds.), *The Essential Difference*. Indiana University Press, Bloomington, pp. 151–86.
Spivak, G. C. (1996) *The Spivak Reader*. Ed. D. Landry & G. MacLean. Routledge, London.

strategic management (organizations)

David Knights

On being asked to define strategic management, the temptation is to respond by asking what is *not* strategic in management. In other words, as soon as the idea of management is addressed, it is necessary to see it as strategic, although clearly much of management is about managing organizational routines. Such a response begs the question of what is meant not only by strategy, but also by management. Some writers on strategy and management have seen the two as coincident, but others perceive the focus on strategy to be contemporary and linked to the emergence and development of large, often multisite and sometimes multinational corporations. Both terms are in need of definition, even though we know that their meanings are tied to the context of their use. Nowhere is this made more obvious than when consulting the Shorter Oxford English Dictionary, where both terms are treated in terms of usage and would seem to share a similar genesis in activities concerned with battle or the military.

Management has its derivation in managing as controlling the affairs of the household or training horses (to be put through the exercises of the *manège*). Alternatively, it refers to the handling of weapons or instruments to serve one's purposes. It is then about directing both animate and inanimate resources toward a particular objective. But the art of managing can also be seen as the use of contrivances for effecting some purpose, often by way of deceit or trickery. On the other hand, it can refer to indulgence or consideration shown toward a person. As with the term strategy, there is a strong association between management and military activities since it is clear that "handling weapons" and the use of horses cannot be separated from the conduct of battle in medieval warfare. The relationship continues even today, with the police use of horses in managing crowds during mass demonstrations. These activities might be seen as the "hard" practices of management, but the term has links with a "softer" meaning in which it refers to "animal and household husbandry," where it relates to caring for and maintaining what is under its tutelage.

Strategy has its origin in military history and may be defined as the art of projecting and directing the larger military movements and operations of a campaign. Chandler (1962) defined it largely in terms of long-term goals and the means (i.e., courses of action and allocation of resources) for attaining them. In organizations, however, strategy operates at various levels.

- *Corporate strategy* refers to how the corporation defines itself, what business it is in, and its future direction and scope.
- *Business strategy* is concerned with the application of the corporate strategy to a subsidiary, division, or business unit of the corporation.
- *Strategic management* focuses on managers in general acting strategically in order to make the best use of the corporation's competitive advantages, core competences, and market positioning and to advance the corporate mission, while having due regard for external constraints and opportunities.

While these different levels of strategy need to be distinguished, often the term strategic management is used less technically to refer generically to all three levels.

INTELLECTUAL AND SOCIAL CONTEXT

Insofar as the term management was used within the field of productive work, it tended to be associated with engineering and the military; thus, social class was extremely important in the context of recruitment into, and the pay differentials of, managerial positions during the period of the Industrial Revolution. The transparency of this privilege declined after 1790, when payment became attached to the job rather than to the person and seemed to coincide with an erosion of the differential between proprietors and salaried managers, though the latter were more often than not the relatives of the former (Pollard 1965: 139, 145). At this time, however, management was seen as restricted to achieving the goals of the organization as laid down by entrepreneurs, who determined the nature and scope of the business, its goals, finance, and markets (Pollard 1965: 3). In effect, proprietors were rightly seen as entrepreneurs and were responsible for strategic thinking (a term not used at the time), whereas managers were simply functionaries translating their ideas into practice.

Once the joint stock company legislation was passed in 1854, those owning capital could invest their funds without being liable for anything other than the amount invested should the company fail. They therefore took the opportunity to spread risk through owning a portfolio of shares in several companies, thus becoming absentee landlords. Managerial agents were employed to run the business, but they also assumed responsibility for designing strategies against which the owners could evaluate their performance at annual general meetings.

After this institutional separation of ownership from control, the distinction between entrepreneurs and managers began to erode as the latter assumed executive responsibility for both activities, although they were accountable to a board of directors who represented the interests of shareholders. Insofar as managers were clearly beginning to be recognized as of equal, if not greater, importance than the absentee owners, this could be seen as a point of discontinuity between the pre-managerial and the managerial world. This, it could be claimed, provided the conditions that made it possible for strategic management to be practiced and eventually for it to become a topic of academic and popular management discourse.

Although some notion of strategy has been a central feature of armies for centuries, Hoskin and Macve (1986) argued that strategic management only became meaningful when writing, recording, and calculation became common practice within organizations. Strategy and management were identified as virtually synonymous since they were mutually interdependent.

Hoskin (1990) sought to pursue this theme with greater precision, suggesting that modern management had its genesis in mid-nineteenth-century America with the development of the Pennsylvania railroad. By "importing the practices of writing, examination, and grading," Hoskin (1990: 23) argues, Herman Haupt of the Pennsylvania railroad changed the "rules of business discourse" in the direction of being "proactive and future oriented," or what we would now define as strategic. It is this orientation to strategic corporate decision-making that Hoskin identifies as synonymous with a concept of modern management. This is seen as coterminous with the development and transformation of the internal discourses and practices of organizations into a written recorded and calculable form.

Modern management, from this point of view, is grounded in the knowledge and power that make it possible to control labor and the organization of production in pursuit of a set of strategic ends such as profit or corporate expansion. It is accomplished through practices that turn everything and everyone into an "object" to be managed (Miller 1987). Case files on employees and customers are written, recorded, and stored, and their behavior is continuously examined so as to render it calculable in terms of both the present and future prospects of the corporation. Examining, quantifying, and grading people and events brings them readily within the disciplinary gaze and the techniques of surveillance of strategic managers who exercise power and constitute knowledge within organizations.

While so far this analysis has been entirely academic in focus, as with many of the concepts in management, the strategy literature is heavily dominated by managerial approaches that see the academic's role as helping managers to do their jobs more effectively and efficiently in terms of meeting goals presumed to be those of, or defined by, that self-same management. This takes us to an examination of the main approaches and dimensions of strategic management.

MAJOR APPROACHES AND DIMENSIONS

The idea of strategy in management did not become standard in academic discourse until the 1960s, when the Master of Business Administration (MBA) was widely introduced. However, an equivalent notion of planning can be traced as far back as 1916 to the writings of Fayol (1949 [1916]: 43), who, in arguing that

"managing means looking ahead," presumably was reporting on his experience of planning as a practitioner. While business schools were established in the US around the turn of the twentieth century (Wharton, 1881; Harvard, 1908; Stanford, 1925), largely in response to industrialization and the need for "trained managers" (Robinson 1995), it was not until around the middle of the twentieth century that they began to expand dramatically and to begin their development in the rest of the world.

It is possible to identify numerous approaches to strategy (Mintzberg 1994), but these can be contained within two broad perspectives – the rational and the processual. Similarly, there are several levels or dimensions in addition to those of corporate, business, and generic management strategy, but again these can be restricted to issues relating to creation, formation, development, and implementation. It should be noted, however, that these various approaches, levels, and dimensions may differ depending on the area of the business – accounting and finance, customer service, human resource management, information and computer technology, marketing, operations, and so on.

Rational Approach

The rational approach continues to dominate mainstream thinking about strategy, particularly within economics, but also, with some modifications, in organization analysis. One of the most popular rational approaches is Porter's (1980) competitive forces model. Although broadly based on the economic theory of competition, the model also draws on the marketing theory of product differentiation and the organization theory of corporate power. Porter's model is illustrated in Figure 1.

If the magnitude of the five competitive forces is zero, the strategic competitive advantage of the company is infinite for it is, in effect, in a monopoly position, although this is rare. The normal situation is for the five forces of competition to be of variable degrees of magnitude, and all will affect the strategic competitive advantage of the company, the price it can charge for its products or services, and hence its profitability. Product differentiation, especially when supported by expensive advertising,

Figure 1 Porter's model of competitive strategy.

helps to reduce, if not eradicate, product substitution and the threat of new entrants, as do highly capital-intensive operations. However, high levels of profitability will attract new entrants regardless of capital costs and product differentiation, and high prices will encourage both suppliers and buyers to look for substitutions. Powerful suppliers push up costs, as does the effect of competitors, and powerful buyers will force down prices.

Within organizations studies, the rational approach is most vividly represented by the Design School, which sees strategy largely as being designed and developed by senior executives and then distributed through the hierarchy in a top-down, cascade-like fashion. Strategic management is informed by a SWOT analysis, which involves developing the strengths and minimizing the weaknesses of the organization as well as exploiting environmental opportunities and neutralizing any threats. Implementation of the strategy is expected to proceed bureaucratically without divergence or disruption.

Process Approach

The process approach considered the Design School to have a naïve view of organizations, since it presumed rather than demonstrated coherence and consensus. From an examination of the processes whereby decisions are made and implemented, it is clear that there is as much conflict as consensus, as much contest as compliance, and as much competition as cooperation within organizations. Implementation cannot therefore be presumed to be a smooth and uncontested process; it therefore makes sense to adopt a more flexible approach toward strategic management (Mintzberg 1994). In order to secure the commitment of those who have to implement strategies, managers need to "find"

strategies lower down the organization rather than simply trying to impose formal plans from above. This approach seeks to remedy the failings of formal strategic planning, which include its inflexibility, its preoccupation with management control, and the problems that these generate for creative and innovative work. If strategies emerge from below, they will not suffer the same problems of implementation since staff will identify with them. Incremental and emergent conceptions of strategy, where design and implementation go hand in hand on a trial-and-error basis, are more appropriate in contemporary turbulent environments (Mintzberg 1994).

A process approach draws on contingency theories of organization, which reject universal approaches to management in favor of flexibility and responsiveness to the environment, often presumed to be unstable. Scenario planning, in which every aspect of the environment is investigated in order to produce medium- and long-term forecasts of its development, is a necessary prerequisite for this kind of strategic management.

CURRENT EMPHASES IN RESEARCH AND THEORY

Strategic management has tended to assume a different form and content, not only historically, but also in relation to where it is located within the organization. Generally, corporate strategy is a boardroom discourse and practice, although it will usually also be a responsibility of senior managers who advise the board. Business strategy, by contrast, is invariably a cascaded translation of this corporate strategy to the various divisions, departments, or business units of the organization. However, much depends on how power is distributed in the organization since some corporations operate a strict command

and control system, whereas others may simply distribute budgets and leave their divisions, units, or profit centers to manage themselves. A divisionalized structure usually means that strategy is distributed to the divisions or profit centers, but those corporations that retain strategic thinking at the center have clearly not been influenced by the idea of "emergent" strategy.

Corporate strategy may be understood as having passed through at least five phases from the 1950s until the present (Grant 1998). Financial control dominated in the early period, giving way to a concern for planning, then strategic diversification, competitive advantage, and, most recently, a preoccupation with innovation and guru prescriptions. Insofar as these approaches to corporate strategy have been simply recording the fads and fashions of business practice, they remain descriptive in content but often seek to influence practitioners and thereby follow a prescriptive line that suggests a particular approach is more effective than previous ones. Sometimes those academics (e.g., Gary Hamel, Rosabeth Moss Kanter, Tom Peters, Michael Porter) prescribing the "strategic one best way" entered the bestseller lists through entertaining vast armies of business managers with time to kill in airport lounges and on long-haul flights.

Strategy, then, like other aspects of management, is subject to the fads and fashions of managerial thinking. Knights and Mueller (2004) suggested an alternative classification to the rationalist (realist) and processual (social constructionist) approaches, for these are respectively objectivist and subjectivist. A nondualist approach perceives strategy neither as a "thing" nor merely as a "process" to capture but as an ongoing project that reflects and reproduces particular forms of subjectivity. Although closer to the social constructionist than to the objectivist approach, it combines both to theorize a range of rationalities, processes, and politics, but then seeks to delve beneath the surface of discursive practices to explore their dynamic. Whereas the process theory recognizes organizational politics only to seek its eradication on the basis that it is often disruptive to the achievement of strategic objectives, the project theory sees politics as an inescapable but necessary part of securing managerial and staff

commitment to the strategy. Strategy can only be fully accomplished when it coincides with the subjectivity of members of the organization. While strategy clearly is about penetrating existing and new markets, gaining competitive advantage, restructuring, or mergers and acquisitions, an unintended effect is how it transforms individuals into subjects that secure their sense of identity, meaning, and purpose by participating in the activities it invokes (Knights & Morgan 1991). In short, a side-effect of strategy is a stimulation of subjective self-discipline that secures the management control of employees, enrolls the support of fund managers and shareholders, and facilitates the mobilization and incorporation of consumers as loyal customers.

METHODOLOGICAL ISSUES AND FUTURE DIRECTIONS

The major methodological problem in studying strategy is access, because ordinarily corporations are secretive about their strategy on the basis that it contains competitively sensitive data and material. Few academics have managed to secure access to the boardroom to observe rather than speculate on how strategy is formulated. Consequently, most studies of strategy rely on archival or secondary data that are in the public domain. Rarely does research take place in the boardroom where strategy is enacted (see, however, Knights & Willmott 1992; Samra-Fredericks 2000). Only direct observation of boardroom interactions can avoid the selection of material for purposes of impression management, since the ongoing context of seeking to develop or implement a strategy in a boardroom meeting must prevail over any attempt to impress the observer.

The above two studies used the most sensitive of methods – recorded observations – to study boardroom behavior and the data are therefore available for further analysis. They sought to show how strategy was accomplished through, rather than independently of, the boardroom social encounters and that it was both a medium and an outcome of the exercise of power and the concern to secure identity among board members. Samra-Fredericks (2000) not only tape-recorded board meetings but also video-recorded them, thus providing verbal transcripts as well as the various bodily movements and expressions that often reveal more than the words themselves. Both studies used a range of methods, including non-participant observations, work shadowing, interviewing, and documentary investigation.

A fairly limited literature has begun to develop that may be seen as providing some of the missing links on what makes strategy work operationally. Developing a strategy, whether from above or below, does not amount to operationalizing that strategy or translating it into practice. This requires organizational members to be fully conversant with the strategy as well as committed to it. Recent research has used methods that secure access to boardroom meetings where strategy is usually formulated and/or distributed to other members of the organization. Drawing on analytical approaches about subjectivity and self-discipline, this research suggests that strategy is less important for its actual content than for the effect it has on subjects, who may begin to secure a sense of themselves – their meaning, purpose, and identity – through engaging in the discourses and practices that the strategy invokes.

SEE ALSO: Capital: Economic, Cultural, and Social; Change Management; Management; Management Innovation; Management Theory; Methods; Strategic Decisions

REFERENCES AND SUGGESTED READINGS

Ansoff, H. (1965) *Corporate Strategy*. McGraw-Hill, New York.
Chandler, A. (1962) *Strategy and Structure*. MIT Press, Cambridge, MA.
Fayol, H. (1949 [1916]) *General and Industrial Management*. Pitman, London.
Grant, R. M. (1998) *Contemporary Strategy Analysis*. Blackwell, Oxford.
Hoskin, K. W. (1990) Using History to Understand Theory: A Reconsideration of the Historical Genesis of "Strategy." Paper delivered at the EIASM Workshop on Strategy, Accounting, and Control, Venice, October.
Hoskin, K. W. & Macve, R. H. (1986) Accounting and the Examination: A Genealogy of Disciplinary Power. *Accounting, Organizations, and Society*: 105–36.
Knights, D. & Morgan, G. (1991) Corporate Strategy, Organizations, and Subjectivity: A Critique. *Organization Studies* 12(2): 251–73.
Knights, D. & Mueller, F. (2004) Strategy as a "Project": Overcoming Dualisms in the Strategy Debate. *European Management Review* 1(1): 1–7.
Knights, D. & Willmott, H. (1992) Conceptualizing Leadership Processes: A Study of Senior Managers in a Financial Services Company. *Journal of Management Studies* 29(6): 761–82.
Miller, P. (1987) *Domination and Power*. Routledge & Kegan Paul, London.
Mintzberg, H. (1994) *The Rise and Fall of Strategic Planning*. Prentice-Hall Europe, Hemel Hempstead.
Pollard, S. (1965) *The Genesis of Modern Management: A Study of the Industrial Revolution in Great Britain*. Edward Arnold, London.
Porter, M. (1990) *Competitive Strategy*. Free Press, New York.
Robinson, P. (1995) *Snapshots from Hell*. Warner Books, New York.
Samra-Fredericks, D. (2000) Doing "Boards-in-Action" Research: An Ethnographic Approach for the Capture and Analysis of Directors' and Senior Managers' Interactive Routines. *Corporate Governance* 8(3): 244–56.

stratification, distinction and

Wout Ultee

Behind a lot of research on societal stratification lurks the idea that, if persons are given a choice between a large and a small pay packet, they will opt for the larger one. Yet people in general not only want to have more than they already have, they also want to be more than others around them, particularly others who have about as much as they themselves have. This is the subject of distinction within the field of stratification. It became important in sociology through studies by Thorstein Veblen on conspicuous consumption, Norbert Elias on changing standards about what counts as good manners, and Pierre Bourdieu on distinction through leisure activities. Also to be mentioned is work by the art historian E. H. Gombrich on "the logic of vanity fair."

Although the tendency for people to distinguish themselves from others may be assumed to be present in most persons, the tendency supposedly is stronger in societies with open stratification systems, that is, systems where a person's station in life is not fixed at birth, but in which social mobility and marriages between societal strata occur. In societies that to a large extent are closed, visible markers of an elevated position often are restricted by custom and law to the persons with these positions. The game of outdoing the other took place among persons on more or less the same rung of the social ladder in European agrarian societies until the beginning of industrialization and was limited by sumptuary laws and similar devices. Their contemporary form in highly developed societies is the rate of value-added tax on luxury goods, which is higher than that on the necessities of life.

Of the various sociological contributions to the topic of stratification and distinction, perhaps that of Elias is the most important. By way of a comparison of a series of French books on good manners ranging from the fifteenth to the nineteenth centuries, Elias made clear that the tendency for persons to distinguish themselves from others by following the rules of good manners in gatherings and encounters, if imitation of these standards by persons just below them on the social scale is possible, makes the old rules of civility lose their discriminatory power, leading to more strict rules of politeness, which in turn are imitated, and so on. For that reason the process of distinction shows a particular direction unintended by any of the original persons involved. Gombrich has argued that such processes of devaluation of old signs of distinction through imitation stand behind contemporary phenomena such as rapidly changing fashions. One may think here of shorter skirts and louder pop music. The question of where these inflationary processes end is an important topic for research.

SEE ALSO: Bourdieu, Pierre; Conspicuous Consumption; Distinction; Elias, Norbert; Lifestyle; Stratification: Functional and Conflict Theories; Stratification Systems: Openness; Veblen, Thorstein

REFERENCES AND SUGGESTED READINGS

Bourdieu, P. (1984) *Distinction: A Social Critique of the Judgment of Taste*. Routledge, London.
Elias, N. (1978 [1939]) *The Civilizing Process: The History of Manners*. Blackwell, Oxford.
Gombrich, E. H. (1979) The Logic of Vanity Fair: Alternatives to Historicism in the Study of Fashion, Style, and Taste. In: Gombrich, E. H., *Ideals and Idols*. Phaidon, Oxford, pp. 60–92.
Hunt, A. (1996) *Governance of the Consuming Passions: A History of Sumptuary Laws*. Macmillan, Basingstoke.
Veblen, T. (1899) *The Theory of the Leisure Class*. Macmillan, New York.

stratification: functional and conflict theories

Paul M. de Graaf

Every society can be characterized by a set of social positions that are related to the access to the scarce and desired goods in that society. Functional and conflict theories of stratification are formulated to provide an answer to the question how are positions distributed across members of a society.

The functional theory of stratification was formulated by Davis and Moore (1945), who refer to the universal necessity which calls forth stratification in any social system. They explicate the functional theory as follows. Every society has a number of positions (occupational structure), which can be ranked by the importance they have for society and by the skill level required. If position A is more important than position B, and if position A requires more skills than position B, then the rewards of position A must be larger than the rewards of position B, otherwise its attractiveness would not be large enough to be filled by able individuals. Individuals who have either the required native abilities or the required training must have an incentive to fill the most important positions. Functional importance and scarcity of personnel both are relevant for a social position to be highly rewarded. If a position is functionally important but can be filled easily, its rewards do not need to be high to motivate individuals to prepare for it and to acquire the necessary skills. In other words, functional importance is thought to be a necessary but not a sufficient condition for a function to be rewarded highly. Rewards can be diverse, ranging from material rewards like income and wealth, to more symbolic forms of rewards like occupational prestige and admired lifestyles, as long as they motivate individuals to use and develop their talents.

An important element of the functional theory of stratification is that the distribution of social positions varies between societies and between historical periods, mainly because of technological innovation. As a consequence the relevant talents and skills individuals must acquire in order to fill the social position also vary between societies and periods. Examples are the transition from an agricultural to an industrial society, the increasing efficiency in industrial production, and the emerging information technology, which all have changed the occupational structure. Following Blau and Duncan (1967), the modernization process in industrial and post-industrial society could have made educational qualifications more important, a process which was labeled a shift from "ascription" to "achievement" and soon as the leading determinant of status attainment.

The functional theory of stratification has been criticized for at least two reasons. First, functional theory lacks an individual basis. It seems to assume that individuals adjust their careers to support society's need for qualified personnel in a given set of social positions. However, individuals cannot be expected to support the interests of society as a whole; instead, they pursue their individual interests and strive for income, prestige, and power. Second, the functional theory is criticized because it has an eye only for the eufunctions of social stratification: the incentive it provides for all individuals in a society to acquire the skills needs for the given set of social positions. Doing this, it neglects dysfunctions of social stratification, mainly the negative consequences for social cohesion.

The conflict theory of stratification stresses that inequality is not a benefit for all members of society, but mainly for the elites. Power differences mean that some groups take more of the scarce goods than other groups. The privileged groups exploit the subordinate groups. Using their superior resources, elites tend to attempt to increase their share, and to transmit their privileged position to their children. The Marxist interpretation is about economic ownership of the means of production and distinguishes between two *classes*: the bourgeoisie and the proletariat. This Marxian class scheme has been extended in different directions. In international sociology two important class schemes have been developed by Eric Olin Wright and John Goldthorpe. Both are based in the differentiation in the occupational structure, especially on the market situation and employment relations.

The conflict theory of stratification has been developed explicitly by Collins (1971), based on the concept of status groups (Weber). Status groups include persons who share a common culture and lifestyle: behavior and manners, language style, consumption patterns, values, attitudes, and preferences. Status groups are often but not necessarily based on their position in the occupational structure (classes). The struggle for wealth, power, and prestige is assumed to take place primarily between status groups, and education is thought to be the primary battlefield. Schools teach the culture of the dominating status groups, and because education is so important for selection in the labor market, education is the channel of intergenerational transmission of privileged positions. Collins argues that educational requirements for jobs are often not (only) based on technical reasons. Employers select the higher educated because they feel that they are better socialized and more respectable. Bourdieu (1973) adds to this argument that the educational system works in a way that children from the elites feel at home at school. Their parents have provided them with cultural habits and preferences that are parallel to what is expected at schools. The conflict theory of stratification argues that education is serving as a device to transmit social status from one generation to the next. Note that this interpretation of conflict theory can be seen, to some degree, as a conspiracy theory.

Educational expansion is explained by the functional theory of stratification as a logical system answer to technological innovation. The shifts in the occupational structure mean that job requirements have changed and educational growth is a functional consequence of this change. Conflict theory interprets educational expansion as the consequence of individual choices. When education has become a key factor in the selection process of personnel, it becomes worthwhile to invest in it. If people start to invest in education, the logic of the situation means that it becomes necessary for everybody to invest as well. Empirical tests of the functional and conflict theories of stratification are scarce and not very convincing. Whether in modern society education serves as a meritocratic device or as a reproduction channel remains at issue, and both interpretations are probably valuable.

SEE ALSO: Class, Status, and Power; Conflict Theory; Functionalism/Neofunctionalism; Stratification: Gender and; Stratification and Inequality, Theories of; Weber, Max

REFERENCES AND SUGGESTED READINGS

Blau, P. M. & Duncan, O. D. (1967) *The American Occupational Structure*. Wiley, New York.
Bourdieu, P. (1973) Cultural Reproduction and Social Reproduction. In: Brown, R. (Ed.), *Knowledge, Education and Cultural Changes*. Tavistock, London, pp. 71–112.
Collins, R. (1971) Functional and Conflict Theories of Educational Stratification. *American Sociological Review* 36: 1002–19.
Davis, K. & Moore, W. (1945) Some Principles of Stratification. *American Sociological Review* 10: 242–9.

stratification, gender and

Catherine Hakim

The documentation, interpretation, and explanation of structured social inequality has always been a central focus of sociology. Although social stratification lies at the heart of macrosociology, and is the subject of extensive theoretical and empirical analysis, the study of gender and stratification is comparatively recent, and developed in the 1970s onwards as a result of the second wave of the feminist movement in modern western societies (Crompton & Mann 1986). The traditional sociological view was that the subordination and oppression of women could be adequately incorporated into class analysis. Feminist theory insisted that in modern societies the class structure, and the oppression of women within patriarchal systems (i.e., women's oppression by men), were separate but interacting social processes.

In conventional class analysis, women generally, and wives in particular, took the social class position of the males in their family or household: initially their father's social class, then later, after marriage, their husband's social class. This was essentially because occupation, or any other status in the public sphere (such as elected politician), was taken as the most obvious indicator of a family's or household's social class/status in modern capitalist societies. The unit of analysis was the cohabiting and income-sharing social unit, not the individual. The feminist focus on women's oppression within the patriarchal family, and within patriarchal societies, forced sociologists to look at the class/status position of individuals as well. This led to an extended debate among empirical sociologists on whether the family or the individual is the appropriate unit for class analysis and, more specifically, whether wives should be allocated to social classes on the basis of their husband's occupation or on the basis of their own current (or last) occupation (Dex 1990; McRae 1990).

It is now agreed that women's position in society, and in the labor force, should be studied separately from class analysis. Empirical research has shown that the sex segregation of occupations, and the pay gap between men and women, cut across social classes in ways that vary from one society to another, and vary across time (Hakim 1998). Occupational segregation and the pay gap develop and change independently within labor markets as a result of antidiscrimination policies and other social policies (such as family-friendly policies) that often have unintended deleterious effects (Hakim 2004). Similarly, women's position in the family can be studied independently of their position in the class structure, and may depend on their property rights (Crompton & Mann 1986: 69–72, 191–2) or their level of education as much as their position within the labor market (Hakim 2000).

The feminist challenge to conventional class analysis was based in large part on the idea that rising female employment rates in modern western societies were leading to a new situation in which all couples would be dual-career as well as dual-earner, wives would cease to be financially dependent on their spouses, and symmetrical family roles would become the norm, so that it no longer made sense to classify wives by their husband's occupation and social class, especially in the context of serial monogamy and declining marriage rates. Here too, empirical research provided a new perspective and led to the development of preference theory. Hakim (2000, 2004) showed, firstly, that there has in fact been relatively little change in female employment rates in modern societies over the past 150 years and that most of the visible change (in economic activity rates) was due to rising levels of part-time employment, and to some women switching from full-time to part-time employment; in consequence, less than one-quarter of all women of working age achieve the male pattern of continuous full-time, life-long employment by the start of the twenty-first century. In most societies, the female full-time employment rate remains far lower than that for men, and typically wives remain secondary earners in their household rather than equal earners. Rising female employment was exposed as a myth in most European countries, although it is real in the US. Secondly, Hakim showed that, in most modern societies, in Europe as well as North America, women divide into three distinct groups: a minority of work-centered women who follow the male employment profile and are financially self-supporting; a minority of home-centered women who are entirely dependent on their spouses after marriage; and a majority of adaptive women who are generally secondary earners within their households rather than careerists. This heterogeneity of women's lifestyle preferences, and thus their employment profiles, cuts across social classes, education levels, and income levels. This diversity of female lifestyle choices produces a polarization of female employment profiles over the life cycle, and is a major cause of rising income inequality between households in liberal modern societies – as illustrated by the income differences between dual-career childless couples and one-earner couples with several children to

support. Similarly, preference theory predicts that occupational segregation and the pay gap can never be completely eliminated – two goals that are underlined by feminist campaigners and by policymakers in the European Commission.

Female social stratification is thus substantially different from male social stratification in modern societies, because women now have two avenues for achieving higher social status and class position – through the labor market, or through the marriage market. Both are still actively used by women, even in modern societies after the equal opportunities revolution of the 1960s and 1970s (Hakim 2000). In contrast, men are limited to using the labor market almost exclusively. All research shows that the vast majority of women resist the idea of role reversal in marriage, with the female as the sole or main income earner (Hakim 2000). Overall, stratification and inequality among women will tend to be larger than among men. For example, in the US and Britain at the start of the twenty-first century, there were more female than male millionaires, because some women achieved success and wealth through their own activities in the labor market, and some achieved wealth as rich men's widows or ex-wives.

The picture in less developed societies is different, and depends a lot on whether women have independent access to the labor market/market economy, have access primarily through male members of their family (father or spouse), or are expected to refrain from market activities and devote themselves exclusively to homemaking and childrearing activities (reproductive work rather than productive work). In agricultural societies, technology itself has also been an important factor in women's social and economic position, as illustrated by large differences in women's position in economies depending on the hoe or on the plow (Boserup 1970).

The precise importance of patriarchy and male dominance as a cause of women's position in the family and in the social structure continues to be the subject of theoretical debate and empirical research. Feminist theory tends to treat patriarchy as the main cause of women's oppression in all societies, and at all times in history. In modern societies, patriarchy is argued to work through occupational segregation and the pay gap in particular; these are imposed by men on women in order to restrict women's economic independence, force them into financial dependence on men, and thus keep women subject to male control (Hakim 2004: 8–11). However, new research by historians, political scientists, and sociologists suggests that in reality male desire for control of female reproductive work may be far more important as the catalyst for patriarchal systems than male desire to control female productive work. If this analysis is correct, patriarchy will be eliminated by technological advances in reproduction and fertility control. An extensive review of the historical evidence by Lerner (1986) led her to conclude that male desire to control women's sexuality and childbearing, in order to safeguard the inheritance of private property, was the primary cause of the introduction of patriarchal control of women's activities. The control of women's gainful activities outside the home was an accidental side-effect, never the main aim. This conclusion is consistent with the results of analyses of World Values Survey data for 85 countries around the world in all six continents. Inglehart and Norris (2003) and Norris and Inglehart (2004) argue that culture can be viewed as providing a survival strategy for a given society. In subsistence-level traditional societies, life is insecure and short, and the culture encourages maximum fertility. Partly through religious beliefs and institutions, and partly through patriarchal value systems, women's primary role is defined in terms of childbearing and high fertility. In rich secular knowledge societies with long life expectancies, the culture changes to accept low fertility levels but with high-quality children, and women are encouraged to have more diverse social roles – in public life and the labor market as well as in the family. In short, patriarchal values, along with religious values, are maintained by women as much as men, and then jointly abandoned in prosperous modern societies, according to the importance of high fertility as a survival strategy in a given society.

SEE ALSO: Class, Status, and Power; Dual-Earner Couples; Employment Status Changes; Feminism; Feminism, First, Second, and Third Waves; Fertility: Transitions and Measures; Gender Ideology and Gender Role Ideology; Income Inequality and Income Mobility; Inequality/Stratification, Gender; Patriarchy; Sex-Based Wage Gap and Comparable Worth; Stratification and Inequality, Theories of

REFERENCES AND SUGGESTED READINGS

Boserup, E. (1970) *Women's Role in Economic Development*. St. Martin's Press, New York.

Crompton, R. & Mann, M. (Eds.) (1986) *Gender and Stratification*. Polity Press, Cambridge.

Dex, S. (1990) Goldthorpe on Class and Gender: The Case Against. In: Clark, J., Modgil, C., & Modgil, S. (Eds.), *John H. Goldthorpe: Consensus and Controversy*. Falmer Press, London, pp. 135–56.

Hakim, C. (1998) *Social Change and Innovation in the Labour Market*. Oxford University Press, Oxford.

Hakim, C. (2000) *Work-Lifestyle Choices in the 21st Century: Preference Theory*. Oxford University Press, Oxford.

Hakim, C. (2004) *Key Issues in Women's Work: Female Diversity and the Polarization of Women's Employment*. Glasshouse Press, London.

Inglehart, R. & Norris, P. (2003) *Rising Tide: Gender Equality and Cultural Change Around the World*. Cambridge University Press, New York.

Lerner, G. (1986) *The Creation of Patriarchy*. Oxford University Press, New York.

McRae, S. (1990) Women and Class Analysis. In: Clark, J., Modgil, C., & Modgil, S. (Eds.), *John H. Goldthorpe: Consensus and Controversy*. Falmer Press, London, pp. 117–34.

Norris, P. & Inglehart, R. (2004) *Sacred and Secular: Religion and Politics Worldwide*. Cambridge University Press, New York.

stratification and inequality, theories of

David B. Grusky

The term stratification system refers to the complex of institutions that generate inequalities in income, political power, social honor, and other valued goods. The main components of such systems are (1) the social processes that define certain types of goods as valuable and desirable, (2) the rules of allocation that distribute these goods across various roles or occupations in the division of labor (e.g., houseworker, doctor, prime minister), and (3) the mobility mechanisms that link individuals to these roles or occupations and thereby generate unequal control over valued goods. It follows that inequality is produced by two types of matching processes. The social roles in society are first matched to "reward packages" of unequal value, and individual members of society are then allocated to the roles so defined and rewarded. In all societies, there is a constant flux of incumbents as newcomers enter the labor force and replace dying, retiring, or out-migrating workers, yet the positions themselves and the reward packages attached to them typically change only gradually. As Schumpeter (1953: 171) famously put it, the occupational structure can be seen as "a hotel ... which is always occupied, but always by different persons."

There is a growing consensus among academics, policymakers, and even politicians that poverty and inequality should no longer be treated as soft "social issues" that can safely be subordinated to more fundamental interests in maximizing total economic output. This growing concern with poverty and inequality may be attributed to such factors as (1) the dramatic increase in economic inequality in many countries over the last quarter-century; (2) the rise of a "global village" in which spectacular regional disparities in the standard of living have become more widely visible and hence increasingly difficult to ignore; (3) a growing commitment to a conception of human entitlements that includes the right to secure employment and be spared extreme deprivation; (4) an emerging concern that poverty and inequality may have negative macro-level effects on terrorism, ethnic unrest, and total economic output; and (5) a growing awareness of the negative individual-level effects of poverty on health, political participation, and a host of other life conditions. Although the growth of anti-inequality sentiment thus rests in part on an increased awareness of just how unequal and poverty-stricken the world is, it may also be attributed to an ever-evolving and accreting list of human rights (i.e., a "normative" account), as well as a growing appreciation of the negative externalities of inequality and poverty (i.e., a "consequentialist" account).

CONCEPTUALIZING INEQUALITY

The first task in understanding inequality and poverty is to specify the types of assets that are unequally distributed. It is increasingly fashionable to recognize that inequality is "multidimensional," that income inequality is accordingly only one of many forms of inequality, and that income redistribution in and of itself would not eliminate inequality (e.g., Sen 2005). When a multidimensionalist approach is taken, one might usefully distinguish between the eight types of assets listed in the left-most column of Table 1, each understood as valuable in its own right rather than a mere investment item. It must nonetheless be recognized that the assets of Table 1 are also inevitably "resources" that serve some investment functions. For example, most economists regard schooling as an investment that generates future streams of income, while some sociologists likewise regard cultural resources or social networks as forms of capital that can be parlayed into educational credentials, income, and other valued goods. There is much research and theorizing on the social processes by which inequality in one domain is converted into inequality in another domain.

The core task of the contemporary inequality researcher is to develop evidence on how much inequality there is, whether some countries are more unequal than others, and whether inequality is increasing or decreasing within and between countries. Although the vast majority of research within this fact-finding tradition has focused on income distribution, inequality scholars are increasingly examining how distributions of other assets may or may not resemble income distribution. It is now fashionable, for example, to examine the structure of inequality with respect to such outcomes as computer literacy (i.e., the "digital divide"), mortality and health, risks of imprisonment or capital punishment, and lifestyles and consumption practices.

This line of research typically takes the form of an exposé of the extent to which seemingly basic human entitlements, such as living outside of prison, being gainfully employed, freely participating in "digital" culture, or living a reasonably long and healthy life, are unequally distributed in ways that amplify well-known differentials of income. The continuing attraction

Table 1 Types of valued goods and examples of advantaged and disadvantaged groups

Assets		Examples	
Asset Group	Types	Advantaged	Disadvantaged
Economic	Wealth	Billionaire	Bankrupt worker
	Income	Professional	Laborer
	Ownership	Capitalist	Employed worker
Power	Political power	Prime minister	Disenfranchised person
	Workplace authority	Manager	Subordinate worker
	Household authority	"Head of household"	Child
Cultural	Knowledge	Intelligentsia	Uneducated
	Popular culture	Movie star	High-culture "elitist"
	"Good" manners	Aristocracy	Commoner
Social	Social clubs	Country club member	Non-member
	Workplace associations	Union member	Non-member
	Informal networks	Washington "A list"	Social unknown
Honorific	Occupational	Judge	Garbage collector
	Religious	Saint	Excommunicate
	Merit-based	Nobel Prize winner	Non-winner
Civil	Right to work	Citizen	Illegal immigrant
	Due process	Citizen	Suspected terrorist
	Franchise	Citizen	Felon
Human	On-the-job	Experienced worker	Inexperienced worker
	General schooling	College graduate	High school dropout
	Vocational training	Law school graduate	Unskilled worker
Physical (i.e., health)	Mortality	Person with long life	A "premature" death
	Physical disease	Healthy person	Person with AIDS, asthma
	Mental health	Healthy person	Depressed, alienated

of such exposés (at least among academics) may be attributed to our collective discomfort with an economic system that generates rather more inequality than is palatable under contemporary cultural standards. That is, capitalist economic systems are not only highly successful in delivering the goods (i.e., high gross national products), but are also great inequality-producing machines, and we are hard put to reconcile such extreme inequality with our post-Enlightenment cultural commitment to the view that humans are "fundamentally" equal. Although the equalizing reforms of social democracy have historically been a main solution to this tension, the declining legitimacy of such reform (especially in Europe and the US) leaves the tension an increasingly unresolved one.

This tension is only exacerbated by recent trends in income inequality. Arguably, the most dramatic social scientific finding of our time is that income inequality has increased markedly

over the last 35 years, reversing a longstanding decline stretching from the eve of the Great Depression to the early 1970s. According to the classic Kuznets curve (Kuznets 1955), the initial stages of capitalist development will bring about a one-time increase in income inequality as capital is increasingly concentrated among a small number of investors, whereas more advanced forms of capitalism entail a growth in the size of the middle class and a consequent reversal of the upward trend. This story aligns nicely with the facts of inequality up to the early 1970s, but then a dramatic, unprecedented upswing in inequality in the post-1970 period (within many countries) made it clear that history does not end with the much-vaunted middle-class expansion.

We have since witnessed one of the most massive research efforts in the history of social science as scholars sought to identify the "smoking gun" that accounted for this dramatic increase in inequality. Initially, the dominant hypothesis was that deindustrialization (i.e., the relocation of manufacturing jobs to offshore labor markets) brought about a decline in demand for less-educated manufacturing workers, a decline that generated increases in inequality by hollowing out the middle class and sending manufacturing workers into unemployment or into the ranks of poorly paid service work. Although this line of argumentation still has its advocates, it cannot easily be reconciled with evidence suggesting that the computerization of the workplace and related technological change has been a driving force behind a heightened demand for highly educated workers. Because of this result (and other supporting evidence), the deindustrialization story has now been largely supplanted by the converse hypothesis that "skill-biased technological change" has increased the demand for high-skill workers beyond the increase in supply, thus inducing a short-term disequilibrium and a correspondingly increased payoff for high-skill labor. At the same time, most scholars acknowledge that this story is at best an incomplete one and that other accounts, especially more narrowly political ones, must additionally be entertained. Most notably, some of the rise in income inequality in the US is clearly attributable to the declining minimum wage (in real dollars), a decline that in turn has to be understood as the outcome of political contests that increasingly favor pro-inequality forces (e.g., Levy 1999).

The future of income inequality depends on which of these underlying mechanisms is principally at work. The silver lining of the deindustrialization story is that within-country increases in inequality should be offset by between-country declines (as poor countries profit from new manufacturing jobs), whereas the silver lining under skill-biased technological change is that the heightened demand for high-skill workers is presumably a one-time, short-term disequilibrium that will, by virtue of the higher payoff to high-skill jobs, trigger a compensating growth in the supply of high-skill workers. There is, unfortunately, no shortage of competing stories that imply more disturbing futures, even futures consistent with a classical Marxian account in which low-skill workers are emiserated by virtue of a globalization-induced "race to the bottom." Indeed, accounts that focus on

the political sources of rising inequality often take on this more disturbing character, given that social democratic ideologies have fallen largely out of fashion and no longer provide capitalists with a viable high-road of "enlightened self-interest" (e.g., support for labor unions, redistribution). As social democratic agendas come to be viewed with suspicion, political support for the minimum wage and other inequality-reducing institutions may increasingly falter, and market-generated inequality may no longer be much restrained by pre-market or after-market interventions.

CONCEPTUALIZING SOCIAL CLASS

The claim that inequality takes on a "class form" is one of the few distinctively sociological contributions to inequality measurement and stands as the main alternative to approaches that either focus exclusively on income inequality or analyze the many dimensions of inequality independently and separately. The main advantage of class-based measurement, as argued by sociologists, is that conventional class categories (e.g., professional, manager, clerk, craft worker, laborer, farmer) are institutionalized within the labor market and are accordingly more than purely nominal or statistical constructions. The labor market, far from being a seamless and continuous distribution of incomes, is instead a deeply lumpy entity, with such lumpiness mainly taking the form of institutionalized groups (i.e., "classes") that constitute prepackaged combinations of the valued goods listed in Table 1.

Within sociology, the implicit critique, then, of income-based approaches rests not so much on the argument that the income distribution is just one of many distributions of interest (i.e., multidimensionalism), but rather on the argument that measurement strategies based on the income distribution alone impose an excessively abstract, analytic, and statistical lens on a social world that has much institutionalized structure to it. This structure takes the tripartite form of a set of social classes that are privileged under capitalist labor markets (e.g., capitalists, professionals, managers), a set of social classes that are less privileged under advanced capitalism (e.g., routine nonmanuals, craft workers, operatives), and an "underclass" that stands largely outside of the labor market and is accordingly deeply disadvantaged in market systems. The rise of class models should therefore be understood as a distinctively sociological reaction to the individualism of the income paradigm and other unidimensional approaches to measuring inequality.

The foregoing account, which is a largely consensual rendition of the rationale for social class measurement, nonetheless conceals much internal debate within the field on how best to identify and characterize the boundaries dividing the population into classes. These debates can be conveyed by recounting the three phases through which the field has developed.

Structuralist Phase (1945–1985)

The class models of the postwar period rested implicitly or explicitly on the assumption that classes are coherent bundles of endowments (e.g., education levels), working conditions (e.g., amount of autonomy), and reward packages (e.g., income). The middle class of "craft workers," for example, comprises individuals with moderate educational investments (i.e., secondary school credentials), considerable occupation-specific investments in human capital (i.e., on-the-job training), average income coupled with substantial job security (at least until deindustrialization), middling social honor and prestige, quite limited authority and autonomy on the job, and comparatively good health outcomes (by virtue of union-sponsored health benefits and regulation of working conditions). By contrast, the underclass may be understood as comprising a rather different package of conditions, a package that combines minimal educational investments (i.e., secondary school dropouts), limited opportunities for on-the-job training leading to intermittent labor force participation and low income, virtually no opportunities for authority or autonomy on the job (during those brief bouts of employment), relatively poor health (by virtue of lifestyle choices and inadequate health care), and much social denigration and exclusion. The other classes appearing in conventional class schemes (e.g., professional, managerial, routine nonmanual) may likewise be understood as particular combinations of scores on the dimensions of Table 1.

For the purposes of illustration, consider a simplified case in which the multidimensional "inequality space" comprises only three individual-level variables (e.g., education, autonomy, income), thus allowing the class hypothesis to be readily graphed. Additionally, assume that the class structure can be represented by six classes (e.g., professional, managerial, sales & clerical, craft, laborer, farm), signified in Figure 1 by six different symbols (dark squares, light squares, dark circles, etc). As shown in this figure, the two main claims underlying the class hypothesis are that (1) the structural conditions of interest tend to cluster together into characteristic packages, and (2) these packages of conditions correspond to occupational groupings. For a class analyst, the multidimensional inequality space is presumed to have a relatively low dimensionality, indeed a dimensionality no more nor less than the number of postulated classes. The individuals falling within the classes comprising this scheme will accordingly have endowments, working conditions, and reward packages that are close to the averages prevailing for their classes. Moreover, even when individual scores deviate from class averages, the conventional class analytic assumption (albeit wholly untested) is that the contextual effect of the class is dominant and overcomes any individual-level deviations. This type of contextual effect would appear to be ubiquitous; for example, the full professor

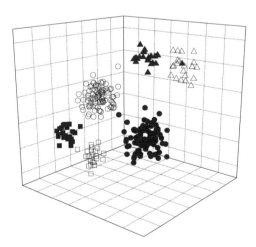

Figure 1 Class regime.

who lacks a PhD is presumably just as market-able as a fully credentialed (but otherwise comparable) full professor, precisely because membership in the professorial class is a "master status" that tends to dominate all other indivi-dual-level ones.

The postwar period also was notable for a flourishing of gradational measurement approaches that again treated occupations as the fundamental units of analysis, but then assumed that such occupations may be ordered into a unidimensional "socioeconomic" scale. In Figure 1 we assumed that the class structure cannot be understood in simple gradational terms, meaning that the underlying individual-level variables did not vary linearly and that at least some classes were formed by combining high values on one dimension with low values on another. It is possible, however, that the structural conditions of interest tend to covary linearly, thus generating a class structure of the very simple type represented in Figure 2. In a regime of this sort, inequality becomes rather stark, as privilege on one dimension implies very reliably privilege on another. There should accordingly be much interest in determining whether inequality indeed takes this form. Unfortunately, inequality scholars of the post-war period did not typically test the linearity assumption, but rather simply assumed that it held and proceeded to develop socioeconomic scales that treated education and income as the main dimensions of interest (and ranked

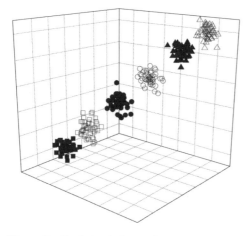

Figure 2 Gradational class regime.

occupations by averaging scores on these two dimensions).

It may be noted that many neo-Marxian scholars during this period also deviated from a strict multidimensional stance by nominating particular dimensions within Table 1 as being theoretically crucial and hence the appropriate basis upon which social classes might be defined. There are nearly as many claims of this sort as there are dimensions in Table 1. To be sure, Marx is most commonly criticized for pla-cing "almost exclusive emphasis on economic factors as determinants of social class" (Lipset 1968: 300), but in fact much of what passed for stratification theorizing during this period amounted to reductionism of some kind, albeit often an expanded version of reductionism in which two or three dimensions were nominated as especially crucial (Wright 1985). When a reductionist position is adopted, the rationale for a class model is not typically that classes are coherent packages of conditions (as repre-sented in Fig. 1), but rather that the nominated dimension or dimensions are crucial in defining interests and will accordingly come to be the main sources of social action. The classic Marx-ian model, for example, has workers ultimately appreciating that their status as workers (i.e., nonowners) defined their interests.

Culturalist Phase (1985–1995)

In the mid-1980s, Bourdieu (1984) and other sociologists (especially Wilson 1996) sought to develop a culturalist rationale for class models, a rationale that rested on the claim that classes are not merely constellations of structural condi-tions (e.g., endowments, outcomes), but are also socially closed groupings in which distinctive cultures emerge and come to influence attitudes, behaviors, or even preferences of class members. Throughout this period many sociologists con-tinued to work with more narrowly structuralist definitions of class (Wright 1997; Goldthorpe and Erikson 1992), but Bourdieu (1984) and Wilson (1996) were instrumental in legitimating the claim that class-specific cultures are a defin-ing feature of inequality systems. The two main forms of closure that serve to generate class-specific cultures are residential segregation (e.g., urban ghettos) and workplace segregation (e.g., occupational associations). As Wilson notes, members of the underclass live in urban ghettos that are spatially isolated from mainstream culture, thus allowing a distinctively oppositional culture to emerge and reproduce itself. The effects of residential segregation operate, by contrast, in more attenuated form for other social classes. After all, residential communities map only imperfectly onto class categories (i.e., the demise of the "company town"), and social interaction within contemporary residential communities is in any event quite superficial and cannot be counted upon to generate much in the way of meaningful culture. If distinctive cultures emerge outside the underclass, they do so principally through the tendency for members of the same occupation to interact disproportionately with one another in the workplace and in leisure activities. In accounting, for example, for the humanist, anti-materialist, and otherwise left-leaning culture and lifestyle of sociologists, class analysts would stress the forces of social closure within the workplace, especially the liberalizing effects of (1) lengthy professional training and socialization into the "sociological worldview," and (2) subsequent interaction in the workplace with predominantly liberal colleagues.

When classes are allowed to have cultures in this fashion, one naturally wishes to better understand the content of those cultures and, in particular, the relationship between such content and the structural conditions (i.e., endowments, outcomes, institutional setting) that a class situation implies. At one extreme, class cultures may be understood as nothing more than "rules of thumb" that encode optimizing behavioral responses to prevailing institutional conditions – rules that allow class members to forego optimizing calculations themselves and rely instead on cultural prescriptions that provide reliable and economical shortcuts to the right decision. For example, Goldthorpe (2000) argues that working-class culture is disparaging of educational investments not because of some maladaptive oppositional culture, but because such investments expose the working class (more so than other classes) to a real risk of downward mobility. In most cases, working-class children lack insurance in the form of substantial family income or wealth, meaning that they cannot easily recover from an educational

investment gone awry (i.e., dropping out), and those who nonetheless undertake such an investment therefore face the real possibility of substantial downward mobility. The emergence, then, of a working-class culture that regards educational investments as frivolous may be understood as encoding that conclusion and thus allowing working-class children to undertake optimizing behaviors without explicitly engaging in decision tree calculations. The behaviors that a "rule of thumb" culture encourages are, then, deeply adaptive because they take into account the endowments and institutional realities that class situations encompass.

The foregoing example may be understood as one in which a class-specific culture instructs recipients about appropriate (i.e., optimizing) means for achieving ends that are widely pursued by *all* classes. Indeed, the prior "rule-of-thumb" account assumes that members of the working class share the conventional interest in maximizing labor market outcomes, with their class-specific culture merely instructing them about the approach that is best pursued in achieving that conventional objective. At the other extreme, one finds class-analytic formulations that represent class cultures as more overarching worldviews, ones that instruct not merely about the proper means to achieve ends but additionally about the proper valuation of the ends themselves. For example, some class cultures (e.g., aristocratic ones) place an especially high valuation on leisure, with market work disparaged as "common" or "polluting." This orientation presumably translates into a high reservation wage within the aristocratic class. Similarly, "oppositional cultures" within the underclass may be understood as worldviews that place an especially high valuation on preserving respect and dignity for class members, with of course the further prescription that these ends are best achieved by (1) withdrawing from and opposing conventional mainstream pursuits, (2) representing conventional mobility mechanisms (e.g., higher education) as tailor-made for the middle class and, by contrast, unworkable for the underclass, and (3) pursuing dignity and respect through other means, most notably total withdrawal from and disparagement of mainstream pursuits. This is a culture, then, that advocates that respect and dignity deserve an especially prominent place in the utility function and that further specifies how those ends might be achieved.

It should by now be clear that sociologists operating within the class-analytic tradition have adopted very strong assumptions about how inequality and poverty are structured. As noted, intrinsic to the class concept are such claims as (1) the space of outcomes and capabilities has a (low) dimensionality equaling the number of social classes, (2) the class locations of individuals become master statuses that dominate (or at least supplement) the effects of individual-level endowments, and (3) such class locations are socially closed and come to be associated with adaptive or maladaptive cultures. The foregoing claims have been unstated articles of faith among class analysts in particular and sociologists more generally. In this sense, class analysts have behaved rather like stereotypical economists, the latter frequently being parodied for their willingness to assume most anything provided that it leads to an elegant model.

Postmodernist Phase (1995–present day)

The third phase of conceptual work within sociology has been marked by an increased willingness to challenge the assumptions underlying the class analytic status quo. In recent years, such criticisms of the class analytic enterprise have escalated, with many postmodernist scholars now feeling sufficiently emboldened to argue that the concept of class should be abandoned altogether. Although the postmodern literature is notoriously fragmented, the variant of postmodernism that is most relevant here proceeds from the assumption that the labor movement is rooted in the old and increasingly irrelevant conflicts of industrial capitalism, that political parties have abandoned class-based platforms in favor of those oriented toward values and lifestyles, and that class-based identities accordingly become ever weaker and more attenuated. The resulting "individualization of inequality" (Beck 1992) implies that lifestyles and consumption practices are becoming decoupled from work identities as well as other status group memberships. The stratification system may be regarded, then, as a "status bazarre" (Pakulski & Waters 1996: 157) in which identities are actively constructed as

individuals select and are shaped by their multiple statuses.

This hypothesis, which is represented in extreme form by Figure 3, has not yet been subjected to convincing empirical test and may well prove to be premature. Moreover, even if lifestyles and life chances are truly "decoupling" from economic class, this ought not to be misunderstood as a more general decline in inequality per se. The brute facts of inequality will still be with us even if social classes of the conventional form are weakening. As was already noted, income inequality is clearly on the rise, and other forms of inequality show no signs of withering away. The postmodernist hypothesis speaks, then, to the way in which inequality is organized, not to the overall amount of such inequality.

CONCEPTUALIZING ALLOCATION

Although inequality scholars have long sought to understand how different "reward packages" are attached to different social positions, an equally important task within the field is that of understanding the rules by which individuals are allocated to the social positions so defined and rewarded. The language of stratification theory makes a sharp distinction between the distribution of social rewards (e.g., the income distribution) and the distribution of opportunities for securing these rewards. As sociologists

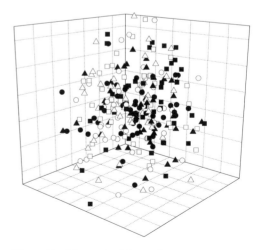

Figure 3   Disorganized inequality.

have frequently noted, it is the latter distribution that governs popular judgments about the legitimacy of stratification. The typical American, for example, is quite willing to tolerate substantial inequalities in power, wealth, or prestige provided that the opportunities for securing these social goods are distributed equally. If the competition has been fairly run, we are quite willing to reward the winners and punish the losers.

The study of opportunities (or "capabilities") is no less fashionable among economists. However, the main motivation among economists for studying opportunities is not some intrinsic interest in mobility processes themselves, but rather a concern that standard outcome-based measures of inequality are tainted by the confounding effect of differential tastes. For example, an employee with a well-developed taste for leisure will presumably opt to work for relatively few hours, leading to low earnings but nonetheless high utility (by virtue of the high valuation placed on leisure). Whenever income inequality is generated through the operation of differential tastes, most economists would argue that it should be regarded as quite unproblematic, given that low-income workers are simply choosing, by virtue of their particular tastes, to tradeoff income for some other valuable good (e.g., leisure). This line of reasoning implies that inequality scholars should measure the distribution of opportunities that prevails before differential tastes can express themselves. The main task of an inequality scholar under this formulation is to determine whether "capabilities" (i.e., opportunities to secure rewards) are equally distributed, not whether rewards themselves, which reflect the operation of tastes, are equally distributed (e.g., Sen 2005).

It follows that sociologists and economists have become quite interested, albeit for different reasons, in the study of opportunity and how it is unequally distributed. In most of the resulting research, the liberal ideal of an open and discrimination-free system is treated as an explicit benchmark, and the usual objective is to expose any inconsistencies between this ideal and the empirical distribution of life chances. This objective leads, then, to analyses of the net effects of gender, race, and class background on income and other labor market rewards. The size of such net effects may be uncovered

statistically by examining between-group differences in income (and other rewards) in the context of models that control all merit-based sources of remuneration. Additionally, experimental approaches to measuring discrimination have recently become popular, most notably "audit studies" that proceed by (1) sending employers resumes that are identical save for the applicant's gender, race, or class, and (2) then examining whether call-back rates (for interviews) are nonetheless different across such groups. Although the available statistical and experimental studies all indicate that opportunities are far from equal, there remains some debate about whether or to what extent such inequalities are declining or will continue to decline.

The main reason that long-run declines in discrimination might be anticipated is that employers who opt to discriminate (in favor of men, whites, or upper-class families) cannot successfully compete against those who select without bias the most qualified and efficient workers (Becker 1957). Furthermore, the spread of egalitarian values renders discriminatory tastes ever more suspect and illegitimate, and indeed some employers now appear to have "tastes for equality" or perhaps even "tastes for reverse discrimination." The ongoing diffusion of egalitarian values additionally underlies the emergence of equality-generating political reform (e.g., affirmative action, anti-discrimination law), as well as the rise of bureaucratic labor markets in which hiring and firing is, at least in principle, rigorously merit-based. This package of equality-generating forces, which is featured in the so-called "liberal theory" of industrialism, suggests that economic rationality will ultimately triumph over discrimination and ascription.

At the same time, each of the main forms of unequal opportunity (i.e., race, gender, class) is actively supported by various countervailing forces that make it difficult to predict how quickly, if at all, discrimination will indeed erode away. There are many countervailing forces of this kind, but perhaps the most important ones are (1) the tendency for African Americans to be segregated into ghettos with few jobs and, some would argue, maladaptive cultures (i.e., "segregation"); (2) the continuing cultural presumption that women are best suited for domestic duties and that men should accordingly invest disproportionately in education, on-the-job training, and other forms of human capital (i.e., "gender essentialism"); and (3) the presumption that parents have a fiduciary responsibility to their children and should therefore assist them in the competition for good jobs by providing them with economic, cultural, and social resources (i.e., "intergenerational transfer"). These countervailing forces of segregation, essentialism, and intergenerational transfer are seemingly organic features of late industrial stratification rather than simple residues that automatically wither away as economies modernize and rationalize. The key question of our time, and one which remains largely unanswered by the evidence of the last half-century, is whether the forces for equality featured in the "liberal theory" are strong enough to overcome such countervailing processes.

SEE ALSO: Educational and Occupational Attainment; Ethnic Groups; Gender, Work, and Family; Income Inequality and Income Mobility; Inequality/Stratification, Gender; Mobility, Intergenerational and Intragenerational; Poverty; Race; Status Attainment; Stratification: Functional and Conflict Theories; Stratification, Gender and; Stratification, Race/Ethnicity and; Work, Sociology of

REFERENCES AND SUGGESTED READINGS

Beck, Ulrich (1992) *Risk Society*. Sage, London.
Becker, G. S. (1957) *The Economics of Discrimination*. University of Chicago Press, Chicago.
Bourdieu, P. (1984) *Distinction: A Social Critique of the Judgement of Taste*. Trans. R. Nice. Harvard University Press, Cambridge.
Goldthorpe, J. H. (2000) *On Sociology: Numbers, Narrative, and the Integration of Research and Theory*. Oxford University Press, New York.
Goldthorpe, J. H. & Erikson, R. (1992) *The Constant Flux: A Study of Class Mobility Industrial Societies*. Clarendon Press, New York.
Kuznets, S. (1955) Economic Growth and Income Inequality (Presidential Address). *American Economic Review* 45: 1–28.
Levy, F. (1999) *Dollars and Dreams*. Russell Sage, New York.
Lipset, S. M. (1968) Social Class. In: Sills, D. L. (Ed.), *International Encyclopedia of the Social Sciences*. Macmillan, New York, pp. 296–316.
Pakulski, J. & Waters, M. (1996) *The Death of Class*. Sage, London.
Schumpeter, J. (1953) *Aufsätze zur Soziologie*. Mohr/Siebeck, Tübingen.
Sen, A. (2005) Conceptualizing and Measuring Poverty. In: Grusky, D. B. & Kanbur, R. (Eds.), *Inequality and Poverty*. Stanford University Press, Stanford.
Wilson, W. J. (1996) *When Work Disappears: The World of the New Urban Poor*. Alfred A. Knopf, New York.
Wright, E. O. (1985) *Classes*. Verso, London.
Wright, E. O. (1997) *Class Counts: Comparative Studies in Class Analysis*. Cambridge University Press, Cambridge.

stratification: partner effects

Paul M. de Graaf

Partner effects refer to the impact that partners (spouses or partners in consensual unions) have on each other's life chances. In stratification research partner effects especially refer to the ways in which partners affect each other's labor market careers with regard to labor market supply and occupational status. Educational homogamy means that partners are similar with regard to their human capital and thus, *ceteris paribus*, an individual approach would predict a similarity with regard to the labor market careers of partners. However, couples face time budget problems when both partners have full-time careers because of the domestic and caring tasks which have to be dealt with, especially when they have children. Couples must decide how to divide the paid and unpaid work, and in this decision process partner effects have proven to be important. The question is: how do partners mutually affect each other's career opportunities?

The notion that stratification research should focus on households and not on individuals has been clear for a long time. However, only recently have the combined status positions of husband and wives, and the interdependencies in their labor market careers, been the object of research (Blossfeld & Drobnič 2001). Earlier, the status position of male family heads was thought to be decisive for the social status of the family. The status of married women was derived from the status of their husbands, even when the wives held positions in the labor force as well. The traditional family model of a male breadwinner and a female caretaker was dominant, in society just as in social studies. This may have been reasonable in times when most women stopped working when they married or when they had their first child. Since the 1960s and 1970s, however, the number of married women who participate in the labor market has increased dramatically, as has the age at which they enter motherhood. The traditional family model is no longer dominant. The increasing labor market supply of women is the result of a modernization and emancipation process. In this process the educational opportunities of girls and boys have become more equal and the labor market has opened for women.

In many households and families in industrial societies both partners add to the family income, although there is still much cross-national variation (Blossfeld & Hakim 1997). In Southern Europe the traditional model is dominant, in Northern Europe many mothers work in part-time jobs and some in full-time jobs, and in the US dual full-time couples are much more common. The possibility of dual careers means that husbands and wives have to decide who is going to work in the labor market and who is going to work in the household, and especially how many hours both partners are going to work inside and outside the household. Economic theory uses an explicit household perspective: it is assumed that decisions are taken by husband and wife together. Exchange theory and bargaining theory argue that individuals pursue their own interests as well, but it is obvious that the household perspective must be taken into account explicitly.

The economic theory of the family (Becker 1981) argues that household and families divide the paid work in the labor market and the unpaid work at home according to the principle of comparative advantage. The partner who has comparative advantage in the labor market will focus on paid work and the partner who has comparative advantage in domestic work will take care of the home and the children. Although this theory can be seen as gender-neutral, it is often believed that wives are more productive in the household and husbands are more productive in the labor market. It is important to note that the human capital investments of young men and women reflect the sex-specific division of work in society in the period they are growing up, and thus some continuation of the prevailing division of work can be expected.

Partners affect each other's labor market careers in positive and negative ways. A positive partner effect means that the labor market career of one's partner is a resource to one's own career, and a negative partner effect means the partner's labor market career is a restriction to one's own career opportunities. It is clear that economic theory predicts negative partner effects. If one's partner is doing well in the labor market, he or she has a comparative advantage and there are fewer incentives for the other spouse to be successful as well. Note that economic theory, quite implicitly, assumes that the comparative advantage in the labor market is more important than the comparative advantage in domestic work. Another way to look at the negative spouse effect comes from the (traditional) additional worker hypothesis, that wives have an incentive to work when their husbands are not able to earn a living. This hypothesis may have special value in periods when one salary is not enough to cope with the costs of living.

Social capital theory argues that partners have positive effects on each other's careers. It is obvious that the partner is an important part of someone's network. If one's partner has a resourceful network and if he or she has access to these resources, this network is an important source of information about labor market opportunities. The idea that resources available through the social capital of one's partner facilitate one's own career goes against the mechanism of specialization. A caveat here is that the close relationship between partners might mean that the social capital of one's partner is not much different to one's own social capital. Partners have a strong tie, and thus it may be that the expected positive effect is not large.

A third mechanism has to do with norms about female labor market participation. Since the more highly educated have less traditional norms about the sex-specific division of labor, it will especially be wives of highly educated husbands who will participate in the labor market. It is clear that this would produce a positive partner effect. On the other hand, if a couple has modern, egalitarian values about the division of labor, it may be that the husbands of highly educated wives are more willing to share in home work and refrain from pursuing only their own career. This would lead to a negative partner effect.

Research has shown that, indeed, a husband's income has a negative effect on his wife's participation in the labor market, but that his level of education has a positive effect on his wife's working hours (Bernasco et al. 1998; Blossfeld & Drobnič 2001), and it has been established that the job levels of partners are associated. Effects of wives on husbands are much less clear, partly because they have not been investigated much, probably because the variation in husbands' participation in the labor market is limited.

Although hypotheses on partner effects have been developed to explain the association between the labor market careers of partners, they can be used in a wide variety of other sociological domains, among them the sociology of religion, social aspects of health (e.g., eating and drinking habits, smoking), leisure-time behavior, and consumption patterns.

SEE ALSO: Connubium (Who Marries Whom?); Dual Labor Markets; Educational and Occupational Attainment; Gender, Work, and Family; Stratification, Gender and

REFERENCES AND SUGGESTED READINGS

Becker, G. (1981) *A Treatise on the Family*. Harvard University Press, Cambridge, MA.

Bernasco, W., de Graaf, P. M., & Ultee, W. C. (1998) Coupled Careers: Effects of Spouse's Resources on Occupational Attainment in the Netherlands. *European Sociological Review* 14: 15–31.

Blossfeld, H. P. & Drobnič, S. (2001) *Careers of Couples in Contemporary Society*. Oxford University Press, Oxford.

Blossfeld, H. P. & Hakin, C. (1997) *Between Equalization and Marginalization: Women Working Part-Time in Europe and the United States of America*. Oxford University Press, Oxford.

stratification, politics and

David Brady

One can divide this area into how stratification shapes politics and how politics affects stratification. Since at least Marx, of course, scholars have highlighted the reciprocal relationship between these two as well. Stratification in this context has meant a system of class inequality, the processes of class attainment, mobility, and disadvantage, and has involved class identities, mobilization, and structuration (how classes become real and manifest in the experiences, actions, and cultures of class members). Stratification and politics increasingly involves racial and gender stratification as well. Politics, in this sense, involves the collective and individual behavior in regards to the state, public authorities, and powerholders. Politics covers the ground from micro-level political ideology to the macro-level welfare state. As Wright explains, stratification and politics integrate the micro-level interactions of locations, practices, and consciousness and the macro-level interactions of structure, struggle, and formation. For our purposes, the focus here is on class voting, class ideology, power resources theory, and the political sources of economic inequality.

Class voting has been one of the most studied areas within political sociology. Early research simply sought to show that the working class was more likely to vote for leftist parties within the advanced capitalist democracies. Indeed, this was the case in the first several decades after World War II, though always less so in countries like the US. Working-class voters were motivated by interest since leftist parties supported welfare state expansion and redistribution. In the last few decades, critical scholars began to document a declining tendency for the working class, albeit crudely defined, to vote leftist. Based on such claims, Clark and Lipset answered affirmatively the question, "Are social classes dying?" Sassoon contends that major reasons for the purported decline include the fragmentation of leftist politics into environmental, gender and racial identity, and social justice movements, and the rising material security and comfort of the working class.

In the past 10–15 years, interest in class voting has revitalized because of methodological and theoretical innovations that led to scrutiny over the decline of class voting. Hout, Brooks, and Manza demonstrated it is essential to use a more sophisticated class schema and measure of class voting than the traditional blue-collar versus white-collar Alford index. With the Erikson-Goldthorpe schema and a measure of the variation in the probability of voting Democrat across the classes (Kappa), they showed that class voting had been stable in the US since 1952. More recently, Manza and Brooks showed that within this stability there have been marked shifts such that the manual working class has become a swing voter, professionals vote predominantly Democrat, while the self-employed and managers vote overwhelmingly Republican. A lively debate has continued over whether class voting is in decline in advanced capitalist democracies and in former state socialist societies. The evidence has been mixed, though it is reasonable to conclude that class remains important to how people vote. Despite this renewed evidence for class voting, one emerging challenge is that regardless of whether class voting is stable or not, race and religion may have far more influence on how people vote, at least in the US.

Research on how stratification shapes ideology has remained vibrant for decades. In the 1970s and 1980s, it was common for scholars to use attitude data to examine the patterning of "stratification beliefs" across classes, occupations, and socioeconomic status. Across advanced capitalist democracies, Wright shows that the working class holds much more anticapitalism views, followed by the middle class, while the bourgeois hold pro-capitalism views. Interestingly, cross-national differences exist in polarization and ideological coalitions. Others show that class, race, and gender shape one's ideology on diverse topics like beliefs about schooling and attainment, job attitudes, poverty and inequality, the welfare state, religiosity, and general moral cosmologies like whether the

world is a just place. These ideologies are a dimension of structuration and a source of class formation, and research in this area has broadened our understanding of why or why not people act politically and mobilize. This research has complicated the assumption that phenomena like class voting are simply a matter of interest (economic or otherwise). Some of the advances in this area have involved the study of how race, gender, and class intersect to shape attitudes. For example, scholars have examined variation in stratification ideologies across ethnic groups and of wives in relation to their husbands and their own class position.

One of the most influential threads in this area is power resources theory. Developed by Korpi, Huber and Stephens, and others, this theory holds that in capitalist societies, the affluent always have greater power than the working class. Since capitalists control the means of production, capitalism distributes greater resources to the elite. Within a democracy, however, the working class can collectively bond together and mobilize politically (e.g., through strikes or voting) to pressure the state to redistribute resources. Thus, the working class's power resources can manifest in labor unions, leftist or social democratic political parties, and even egalitarian ideology. When these power resources mobilize, the welfare state is expanded to ensure that the working class is protected from the insecurity of unemployment, old age, and sickness and the profits of capitalism are redistributed. When an encompassing welfare state is institutionalized, the middle class can become a constituency of beneficiaries that also support the welfare state.

Work influenced by power resources theory has elaborated how politics shape inequality. This work has countered the normal explanation of economic inequality, which focused on the Kuznets curve, economic performance, demographics, and labor markets. Many scholars have shown that advanced capitalist democracies with strong labor unions and powerful social democratic parties have lower poverty and greater social equality. As Brady explained, this is because those power resources channel through the welfare state – causing a more generous welfare state, which then causes reduced poverty. In the labor market, institutions like corporatism (collective labor market organization to ensure management–labor cooperation, long-term planning, and centralized bargaining) and high unionization compress the earnings distribution and raise worker pay. Most recently, scholars have shown that stratification can be driven by the ascent of market fundamentalist, neoliberal ideology and rightist political parties. Rightist parties have ushered in a program of monetarism, privatization, and free markets and have at least sought to dismantle welfare states, labor unions, and social democracy. The rise of rightist parties in Thatcher's Britain and Reagan's US has probably contributed to the Great U-Turn of increased inequality since the 1970s. Certainly, the free market ideology of rightist political parties has become quite powerful in the contemporary era after Keynes and state socialism.

Several questions warrant attention for future research. Can power resources mobilize when traditional working-class organizations appear to be in decline (and if so, how)? After decades of steady decline, unions seem almost irrelevant in much of the US. As a result, it becomes difficult to envision working-class mobilization when class consciousness, structuration and formation, and egalitarianism seem to have been trumped by individualism and political mobilization over cultural, religious, and gender issues. Some recent persuasive research contends that racism and racial divisions are an extremely powerful force undermining public support for the welfare state and working-class formation. Though class voting may or may not have declined, it is hard to argue that the working class votes collectively in its economic interest. Because of developments like these, it is harder to sustain an orthodox power resources theory. Potentially, power resources and research on the politics of inequality can benefit from cross-fertilization with the aforementioned research on stratification beliefs and ideology. Another interesting question could examine how elites, the upper middle class, and corporate power have cultivated an intellectual establishment for market fundamentalist, free market, and neoliberal opinion-makers and public intellectuals. Maybe class politics has not declined per se, but in this era, it might be more about the reassertion of capitalist ideological hegemony in the public sphere. A third question could involve a greater appreciation for the intersection of race/ethnicity/nationality, gender, and class in the politics of stratification. In many of the egalitarian social democracies and even the mid-twentieth-century US higher unionization was facilitated by the exclusion of ethnic minorities and the cohesion of relatively homogeneous groups of male workers. In this era of increased immigration, greater ethnic diversity, and the presence of ethnic minorities and women in the workplace and political arena, stratification politics will have to reconstitute itself in order to remain relevant. How and if that can occur is unclear. Finally, unfortunately, the study of stratification and politics, like so much of sociology, continues to neglect many of the world's regions and peoples. Certainly, this field has disproportionately concentrated on the advanced capitalist democracies, and especially the US. Africa, Latin America, and Asia (outside the former Soviet Union and China) definitely deserve greater scholarly attention. Even applying the traditional debates and theories to these regions would be a rare contribution.

SEE ALSO: Class Consciousness; Class, Status, and Power; Ideology; Political Sociology; Power, Theories of; Stratification, Gender and; Stratification and Inequality, Theories of; Stratification, Race/Ethnicity and; Welfare State

REFERENCES AND SUGGESTED READINGS

Brady, D. (2003) The Politics of Poverty: Left Political Institutions, the Welfare State, and Poverty. *Social Forces* 82: 557–88.

Clark, T. N. & Lipset, S. M. (2001) *The Breakdown of Class Politics: A Debate on Post-Industrial Stratification.* Woodrow Wilson Center Press and Johns Hopkins University Press, Washington, DC and Baltimore.

Hout, M., Brooks, C., & Manza, J. (1995) The Democratic Class Struggle in the United States, 1948–1992. *American Sociological Review* 60: 805–28.

Huber, E. & Stephens, J. D. (2001) *The Development and Crisis of the Welfare State.* University of Chicago Press, Chicago.

Korpi, W. (1983) *The Democratic Class Struggle.* Routledge, New York.

Manza, J. & Brooks, C. (1999) *Social Cleavages and Political Change: Voter Alignments and US Party Coalitions.* Oxford University Press, New York.

Sassoon, D. (1996) *One Hundred Years of Socialism: The West European Left in the Twentieth Century.* Fontana, London.

Wright, E. O. (1997) *Class Counts.* Cambridge University Press, New York.

stratification, race/ethnicity and

Frank van Tubergen

An important research field in the stratification literature is concerned with inequalities along the ascribed characteristics of race and ethnicity. The term race connotes biological differences among people (skin color, facial features) that are transmitted from generation to generation. As such, these biological differences are seen as permanent characteristics of people. However, the notion of race does not make much sense as a biological concept, because the physical characteristics that make people distinctive are trivial. Even though biological differences are superficial, they are important sociologically. For if people believe that others are biologically distinctive, they tend to respond to them as being different. Furthermore, skin color is transmitted from generation to generation by assortative marriage, a prime sociological phenomenon.

Race is considered a social construct and in that sense incorporated in the more general notion of ethnicity. An ethnic group is a subpopulation of individuals who are labeled by the majority and by the members of a group itself as being of a particular ethnicity. The term ethnicity refers to the (perceived) historical experiences of a group as well as its unique organizational, behavioral, and/or cultural characteristics. Thus, ethnic groups can be distinguished by their country of origin, religion, family practices, language, beliefs, and values. The more visible the characteristics marking ethnicity, the more likely it is that those in an ethnic category will be treated differently.

Ethnic inequality is documented in different ways. Important aspects of inequality include education (school dropout, educational attainment), the labor market (unemployment, occupational status, income), wealth, housing quality, and health. These issues are examined at the national level, telling us something about the distribution within a population, and at the individual level, informing us about mobility. Questions on mobility include examinations of the life course of people (i.e., intragenerational) and studies comparing parents and their children (i.e., intergenerational).

The literature on ethnic stratification is divided into three different research lines. The first is concerned with the position of *indigenous populations* that were annexed through military operations and colonization, such as the American Indians in North and South America, Aboriginals in Australia, and Maori in New Zealand. The second focuses on ethnic groups that are the offspring of *slaves* or *involuntary migrants*, such as African Americans in America. The third is concerned with the economic position of *voluntary migrants* and their offspring, such as the Italians who moved to the US at the turn of the twentieth century.

Research on indigenous populations has focused on native Indians in the US. The levels of education attained by Native Americans are below those attained by white Americans. Native Americans are under-represented in white-collar occupations and over-represented in service occupations. For example, in 1990 almost 42 percent of Native Americans were employed in white-collar occupations compared with 61 percent of white Americans. Native Americans tend to have lower-quality housing and lower incomes than whites. Over the last decade the incomes of Native Americans have risen somewhat.

A considerable amount of research on the position of involuntary migrants has focused on the economic position of African Americans in the US. The general assessment is that inequalities between whites and blacks are declining, but still persist long after slavery was abolished. For instance, in 1960, 20 percent of blacks attained a high school degree, compared to 43 percent among whites. In 2000, the figures were 79 percent and 88 percent, respectively. In 1960, 55 percent of blacks were living in poverty; in 2000 this was 23 percent. The black family median income as a percentage of white median income increased from 0.54 in 1950 to 0.68 in 2000.

Research on voluntary migrants has focused on the economic mobility within and between immigrant generations. Chiswick (1978) argued and indeed found that after a certain time, immigrants of the first generation catch up economically with natives in the US. Borjas (1987), however, showed that the assimilation effect was largely due to lowering quality of (un)observed human capital in immigration cohorts. The intragenerational mobility of immigrants still attracts ample research, and the issue of assimilation remains highly debated. Evidence of economic mobility is more convincing with respect to intergenerational comparisons.

Several studies have compared the economic standing of voluntary migrants, involuntary migrants, and indigenous populations simultaneously. One classical study is by Van den Berghe (1967). He found that hierarchies of ethnic stratification are quite similar in Brazil, Mexico, South Africa, and the US. In all countries, those at the top of the ethnic hierarchy are of European ancestry. These are the offspring of voluntary migrants from Portugal (Brazil), Spain (Mexico), Great Britain and the Netherlands (South Africa), and Great Britain (US). At the bottom of the hierarchy are blacks, who either formed the indigenous population (South Africa) or who were imported as slaves (Brazil, Mexico, US). In the countries of North and South America, native Indians fall in between these two groups. A more contemporary study that compares African Americans and white immigrants can be found in Lieberson (1980).

Different explanations of ethnic inequality have been proposed. Some theories have been applied exclusively to one of the three research fields (voluntary migrants, involuntary migrants, indigenous populations), whereas other ideas have been applied to two or all of them.

The idea of assimilation was proposed by Park and Burgess (1969), worked out later by Warner and Srole (1945) and Gordon (1964), and more recently by Alba and Nee (2003). Although the idea has many variants, the core assumption is that over time ethnic groups will gradually integrate into mainstream society. Thus, it was expected that both within and across generations immigrants and ethnic groups will experience upward mobility to the point that their economic position equals that of the native majority.

Chiswick (1978) provided a human capital explanation for the assimilation idea. The human capital theory states that people's life chances depend on their human capital, and that people are aware of this relationship and rationally invest in their own human capital. Chiswick argued that immigrants have a weaker economic position at arrival than natives because immigrants have less human capital: they have less command of the host language, fewer occupational experiences, and less knowledge of the host labor market. Because immigrants invest in post-school training, gradually learn the host language, and acquire knowledge of the host labor market, they improve their position over time. And because the offspring of immigrants obtain their schooling in the host country and have perfect language skills, their position will outperform that of their parents. In this way, the human capital theory explains why ethnic groups will gradually reach economic parity with natives.

One empirical challenge for the assimilation theory and the human capital interpretation is the observation that economic incorporation differs between groups. Why do some immigrant groups rapidly integrate economically, whereas other ethnic groups, such as African Americans, remain economically at a disadvantage? Borjas (1987) and other researchers have tried to explain these issues with an extended human capital framework, incorporating notions of selective migration and the influence of (unobserved) skills, talents, and motivation. Alternatively, researchers have proposed a number of other theories to explain differences between ethnic groups. These are notions of inheritance, cultural values, discrimination, spatial mismatch, and ethnic capital.

One of the oldest explanations of ethnic group differences is the idea that groups have different biological endowments, which are genetically transmitted from generation to generation. Such biological explanations flourished in the US during the late nineteenth and early twentieth centuries, providing "scientific" evidence of the biological inferiority of non-Anglo Saxon groups and justifying their subordinate status. The evidence is typically drawn from studies that compare intelligence test performances of ethnic groups and the native population. One recent example is Herrnstein and Murray's *The Bell Curve* (1994), in which they claim that African Americans and Latinos are less intelligent than whites and for that reason have a lower economic standing. As with other studies that are informed by notions of inheritance, their study was heavily criticized by psychologists and sociologists on theoretical, methodological, and empirical grounds. For instance, contrary to the statement of Herrnstein and Murray that the race–intelligence link is stable over time, researchers showed that intelligence test scores of blacks and numerous ethnic groups improved dramatically over the course of the twentieth century. Overall, most researchers nowadays conclude that inheritance is unable to explain ethnic stratification.

Another, more sociological explanation of group differences in ethnic stratification is concerned with cultural values. Echoing the Weberian notion of the Protestant work ethic, Sowell argues in *Markets and Minorities* (1981) that Asians are model minorities at school and in the labor market because of their cultural traits of effort, thrift, dependability, and foresight. By contrast, the disadvantaged socioeconomic positions of African Americans, Latino Americans, and American Indians today are portrayed as a consequence of their cultural characteristics, which are perceived to be incompatible with a modern industrial society. The cultural approach of Sowell was criticized by several researchers, most notably Steinberg in *The Ethnic Myth* (2001).

Another cultural explanation of ethnic group differences is the hypothesis of "oppositional culture," which argues that black youth develop an oppositional identity relative to whites because they focus on their parents' past experiences of discrimination. As a consequence, blacks distrust the dominant society and develop distinct cultural norms in which they reject schooling as a route to socioeconomic mobility.

Many researchers use notions of discrimination to explain group differences in ethnic stratification. Two different types of ethnic discrimination (i.e., the unequal treatment of minority groups) are outlined: attitudinal and institutional. Attitudinal discrimination refers to discriminatory practices influenced by prejudice. Research shows that prejudice, and, in turn, discrimination, tends to increase when ethnic groups are perceived as threatening to the majority population in terms of cultural, economic, or political resources. Ethnic groups that are numerically large and that are distinct culturally are especially vulnerable to discrimination. This led to theories about ethnic competition and split labor markets. Another important theory is that of statistical discrimination.

Institutional discrimination refers to rules, policies, practices, and laws that discriminate against ethnic groups. This type of discrimination is used to explain the economic difficulties that African slaves and their offspring experienced in the US. For instance, through the first half of the twentieth century, they were formally excluded from acquiring or inheriting property, marrying whites, voting, testifying against whites in court, and attending higher-quality schools. Contemporary evidence on institutional discrimination is provided by Massey and Denton (1993).

Researchers have argued that group differences in ethnic inequality can be explained by the residential concentration of ethnic groups and regional variations in economic opportunities. One influential idea states that the economic opportunities of blacks are hampered because they live in inner-cities. In *The Declining Significance of Race* (1981) and *The Truly Disadvantaged* (1987), Wilson maintained that the economic position of the black inner-city poor has deteriorated because of structural economic changes, including change from goods-producing to service-producing industries, increased industrial technology, and the flight of industries from central cities. The process of deindustrialization has created an economic mismatch between the available jobs and the qualifications of inner-city residents, predominantly blacks. As a result, the economic position of the African American urban poor is diminishing.

Another argument stresses the role of social or "ethnic" capital, that is the resources that are available to a person through their relations with others. A highly debated issue in this respect is whether "ethnic enclaves," in which ethnic capital is shared, promote the economic incorporation of ethnic groups. Authors have argued that more sizable and geographically concentrated ethnic groups develop an independent, mono-ethnic labor market in which their members can obtain positions otherwise held by the native majority. In ethnic economies the returns to human capital are expected to be higher than outside the ethnic economy.

Various research designs have been used to study ethnic stratification. The classical design is the case study, in which a single ethnic group in a single receiving context is examined. Because this design provides little information on contextual effects, comparative macro designs have also been developed. One such popular framework is the "comparative origin" method, which compares multiple ethnic groups in a single location, yielding important insights into ethnic group differences. Similarly, researchers have paid attention to the role of the receiving context by comparing a single ethnic group across multiple destinations, such as cities or nations ("comparative destination" design). More recently, these macro approaches have been combined into a "double comparative" design, which studies multiple-origin groups in multiple destinations simultaneously. This design provides a better understanding of ethnic origin, the receiving context, and the specific interaction between origin and destination ("ethnic community").

Another methodological development in the literature is to rely on dynamic designs. Initially, researchers compared the position of ethnic groups at a single point in time (e.g., by relying on a single cross-sectional survey). By pooling cross-sectional surveys that are apart in time, researchers were able to disentangle assimilation effects from cohort effects ("synthetic cohort design"). Dynamic designs have been improved further by the appearance of panel surveys on immigrants.

In general, three different measures of ethnicity are used: country of origin, nationality, and ethnic self-identification or subjective ancestry. Country of origin and nationality are often used to study *voluntary* migrants. A drawback of using nationality as a measure of ethnicity is that voluntary migrants who are successful in the labor market are more likely to naturalize, leading studies on nonnaturalized migrants to underestimate their economic performance. For that reason, researchers generally prefer the country of origin of the respondent, the parents, and the grandparents.

Research on *involuntary* migrants and *indigenous* populations generally relies on ethnic self-identification and subjective ancestry. These measures are problematic for several reasons. First, like nationality, ethnic self-identification

is partly an outcome of people's economic position, leading the more successful people not to identify with their lower-status ethnic background. Second, ethnic and racial boundaries and self-identified characterizations change over time. For instance, previously "non-white" ethnic groups such as Irish and Italians became "white," often by deliberately distinguishing themselves from blacks. Third, subjective measures of ethnicity assume a single identification, whereas, through intermarriage, a considerable proportion of the population has multiple identifications.

In many countries, general population surveys or specific immigration surveys contain questions on country of origin or nationality, providing a wealth of data for studies on *voluntary* migrants. Large-scale surveys rarely contain subjective measures of ethnicity, leading to fewer data sources available for the study of *involuntary* migrants and *indigenous* populations. An exception is the census of the US. As an alternative, several researchers have conducted small-scale or qualitative studies to examine these populations.

Researchers nowadays agree that ethnicity plays a role in people's life chances, that ethnic groups gradually improve their economic standing across generations, and that the process of assimilation can be interpreted in terms of human capital accumulation. At the same time, it is found that assimilation rates of ethnic groups vary. Initially, researchers have relied on theories of biological traits and cultural dispositions to explain such group differences, but they have been largely replaced by extensions of the human capital theory, ideas on discrimination, the concept of ethnic capital, and spatial differences in economic opportunities. In recent work, researchers have combined the theories explaining group differences with micro-level approaches explaining individual assimilation.

Methodologically, as more large-scale data become available, researchers increasingly prefer to use comparative research methods rather than the case study. Much of the classical and contemporary work on ethnic stratification has been done in the US, but research in other countries is rapidly growing. This opens the possibility of comparing patterns of ethnic stratification cross-nationally, possibly also including ethnic groups in developing countries.

Another important direction of future research is the development and application of dynamic research designs to study ethnic mobility.

SEE ALSO: Assimilation; Ethnic Enclaves; Ethnic and Racial Division of Labor; Ethnicity; Race; Race (Racism); Spatial Mismatch Hypothesis; Stratification, Gender and; Stratification and Inequality, Theories of

REFERENCES AND SUGGESTED READINGS

Aguirre, A. & Turner, J. H. (2004) *American Ethnicity: The Dynamics and Consequences of Discrimination.* McGraw-Hill, New York.

Alba, R. & Nee, V. (2003) *Remaking the American Mainstream: Assimilation and Contemporary Immigration.* Harvard University Press, Cambridge, MA.

Borjas, G. J. (1987) Self-Selection and the Earnings of Immigrants. *American Economic Review* 77: 531–3.

Chiswick, B. R. (1978) The Effect of Americanization on the Earnings of Foreign-Born Men. *Journal of Political Economy* 86: 897–921.

Gordon, M. M. (1964) *Assimilation in American Life.* Oxford University Press, New York.

Lieberson, S. (1980) *A Piece of the Pie: Blacks and White Immigrants Since 1880.* University of California Press, Berkeley.

Massey, D. S. & Denton, N. A. (1993) *American Apartheid: Segregation and the Making of the Underclass.* Harvard University Press, Cambridge, MA.

Park, R. & Burgess, E. (1969 [1921]) *Introduction to the Science of Sociology.* University of Chicago Press, Chicago.

Van den Berghe, P. (1967) *Race and Racism: A Comparative Perspective.* Wiley, New York.

Warner, W. L. & Srole, L. (1945) *The Social Systems of American Ethnic Groups.* Yale University Press, New Haven.

stratification systems: openness

Wout Ultee

All societies are stratified, but some more so than others. Perhaps the most visible variable feature of a society's stratification system is the difference in the standard of living of its inhabitants at a particular point in time. Nowadays, most advanced industrial societies regularly publish statistics on yearly household income, such as the share of all incomes going to the top 20 and bottom 20 percent of all households. Statistics on the causes of income differences are published on a regular basis too, such as figures on inequalities in household wealth, the relation between wealth and income, and the returns to education in terms of income.

For sociologists, these measures fail to capture an important aspect of a society's stratification system: the degree to which it is open or closed. If households are made up of dual-earner couples and the two partners have different incomes, this equalizes the income shares of quintile groups. To the extent that such marriages occur, a stratification system may be said to be open. But what if the individual income shares of quintiles do not change over time? Stability at the societal level does not imply that incomes of individuals remain the same: there may have been an exchange of persons between quintiles. That is why individual or household mobility, along a criterion like income, is also an important aspect of societal openness for sociologists.

Of the classical sociologists, Max Weber most clearly conceived of societal stratification as a process comprising less advanced and more advanced stages of closure. In a society consisting of strata that can be ranked according to some principle from higher to lower, those within a stratum may combine so as to limit the number of newly entering persons, in tacit or explicit cooperation with state authorities and employers. This happened in some countries during the second half of the twentieth century with respect to occupations such as general practice and printing. Medieval guilds also limited the number of new entries and strengthened exclusion by granting sons the right to succeed their fathers. A stratification system is even more closed if the members of two different societal strata do not intermarry. In Europe, the marriage of a member of the nobility with someone from another estate was at least a *mésalliance*. Weber pointed out that the Southern states of the United States forbade marriages between whites and blacks by law around 1900. The sanction against marriages between members of different classes went further in Hindu

India: according to Weber, in the India of his day a child born of a marriage between two castes belonged to a caste lower than either of the castes involved in the marriage. Compared with medieval estates, religion and magic discouraged mixed marriages. It may be added that Nazi Germany went even further: after forbidding marriages between Aryans and Jews, it sought to discourage friendly association between Aryans and Jews by refusing Jews entry to public meeting places like restaurants and cinemas. In the end, Nazi Germany destroyed Jews in specially built gas chambers. Weber referred to the phenomenon of who marries whom as *connubium*, and that of who befriends and shares meals with whom as *convivium* and commensality.

Turning to contemporary sociologists, Lenski (1966) distinguished stratification systems by the number of dimensions along which a society's members may be ranked from more to less advantaged in life chances and endowment in resources (complexity). As the position of a person on the various dimensions need not be the same, inconsistency is another aspect of a society's stratification system. The range of variation along one dimension Lenski called *span*, and movement along one dimension he labeled *mobility*. Lenski hardly focused on connubium and convivium.

Several recent studies attest that in advanced industrial societies with higher income inequalities, mobility is less widespread on average. This was established by Erikson and Goldthorpe (1992) for a dozen advanced industrial societies by way of odds ratios for the relation between father's and son's social class. It has been held that the United States has high income inequality and high mobility, but recent figures seem to indicate that for this country father and son earnings mobility, as computed over a period of several decades, is less widespread than in Sweden and Finland, two countries with limited income inequality. Lipset and Bendix (1959) took father–son mobility and assortative marriage according to broad occupational groupings as interchangeable indices of societal openness. Ultee and Luijkx (1990) established, with figures for 23 advanced industrial societies from around 1970, that greater father–son mobility across the manual/non-manual divide goes hand in hand with more educationally mixed marriages.

SEE ALSO: Connubium (Who Marries Whom?); Convivium (Who is Friends with Whom?); Income Inequality and Income Mobility; Stratification and Inequality, Theories of; Stratification: Technology and Ideology

REFERENCES AND SUGGESTED READINGS

Erikson, R. & Goldthorpe, J. H. (1992) *The Constant Flux*. Oxford University Press, Oxford.

Lenski, G. E. (1966) *Power and Privilege*. McGraw-Hill, New York.

Lipset, S. M. & Bendix, R. (1959) *Social Mobility in Industrial Society*. University of California Press, Berkeley.

Ultee, W. & Luijkx, R. (1990) Educational Heterogamy and Father-to-Son Occupational Mobility in 23 Industrial Countries. *European Sociological Review* 6: 125–49.

Weber, M. (1923) *Wirtschaft und Gesellschaft*. Mohr, Tübingen.

stratification: technology and ideology

Nazneen Kane

Several theories of social stratification have emerged from the discipline of sociology. The ultimate focus of this body of knowledge has quite clearly been the production of a comprehensive understanding of inequality within and across human societies over time and place. Yet, few theories have constructed adequate working models of stratification that satisfy geographical and historical particularities.

Gerhard Lenski's ecological-evolutionary theory of social stratification, however, has quite adequately addressed the research question and has come closest to attaining the goal. His theory was, for the first time ever in the discipline, able to provide a causal explanation of *how* things came to be (Huber 2004). Indeed, Lenski's ecological-evolutionary theory attempts to comprehensively explain the ultimate and proximate causes of societal differences. Although Lenski addressed many realms of societal difference, the focus here is specifically on the relationship between subsistence technology, ideology, and social stratification.

SUBSISTENCE TECHNOLOGY → IDEOLOGY

The theory argues that subsistence technology, "The technology that is used by the members of a society to obtain the basic necessities of life" (Lenski & Nolan 2004: 366), is the key factor in making possible (but not determining) societal differences, including the level of stratification within and across societies. Within societies, ideology, defined as "cultural information used to interpret human experience and order societal life," is then developed in attempts to understand the existing material conditions (p. 363). The main premise of the theory is that societal differences "begin in the realm of technology and extend into almost every other sphere of life" (Lenski 1966: 144). Because the level and form of technology vary across societies, so too does ideology. In short, changes in stratification levels are dependent upon shifts in subsistence technology (Lenski & Nolan 2004). For example, the shift from the wooden digging stick of simple horticultural societies to the metal hoe of advanced horticultural societies also allowed for an increase in economic inequality. Ideologies may then also shift and are often used by elites to legitimate unequal distributions of power and wealth. For example, US slavery was often legitimated by racist ideologies of black inferiority. Thus, the nature and formation of class stratification and other trends in social inequality are all shaped primarily by subsistence technology.

TYPES OF HUMAN SOCIETIES

Hunting and gathering society (average population size: 40; approximate date of first appearance: 100,000 BCE). The subsistence technology of hunting and gathering societies is described as that which can be derived from nature. Wood, bones, and stone are used as tools for survival. Hunting and gathering societies have little or no economic surplus because of their nomadic character and limited subsistence technology. Sharing is the norm and resources are readily available in nature. These societies

consequently experience relative equality in terms of distribution of goods and services.

Inequality in hunting-gathering societies varies but is generally limited to "functional inequality" (Lenski 1966: 105). That is, the elderly, those attributed with possessing supernatural powers, and those with exceptional hunting capabilities are often afforded greater prestige. In general, however, there is very minimal inequality in power, wealth, and privilege and those prestige inequalities that do exist are mainly individually based. The accompanying ideology is often animism, the religious belief that spirits inhabit everything in nature, and is used to explain this prestige inequality. The dominant belief is that those individuals imputed with prestige are more in tune with the rituals of the spirits and are blessed as they please these spirits (Lenski & Nolan 2004: 98). In sum, due to the limited subsistence technology, hunting-gathering societies are relatively equal with little prestige inequality, and ideology has little effect on societal change.

Simple horticultural society (average population size: 1,500; approximate date of first appearance: 8000 BCE). In the gardening economy of simple horticultural societies, the digging stick is the basic subsistence tool. Because land and tools are readily available to any member of society who is willing to put forth the effort, there are no significant inequalities in material possessions. There are, however, both more and varied possessions as compared to hunting-gathering societies. This increase in possessions is due to the fixed character of simple horticultural societies. The digging stick allows for gardening, which in turn decreases reliance upon hunting and stabilizes communities in terms of movement. It is this increased permanence of settlement that is associated with ideology emphasizing the importance of kinship and the increasing incidence of ancestor worship and religious rituals.

Simple horticultural societies demonstrate the population/surplus dialectic. That is, permanency of settlement allows for food surplus, making possible a population increase. In turn, population increase also allows greater productivity. Fixed communities can accumulate more possessions, and a larger population allows for some members of society to specialize in production of goods such as tools, clothes, pottery, and baskets as "leisure" time becomes more prevalent. This leisure is said to allow for ceremonial activities, warfare, and political organization. Social inequalities become more pronounced as society becomes increasingly hierarchical with political subordinates, slavery, wealth inequality (often in the form of wives), and prestige inequality. Forms of prestige are broadened to encompass not only hunting and spiritual recognition, but also political and military prowess.

Advanced horticultural society (average population size: 5,250; approximate date of first appearance: 4000 BCE). In advanced horticultural societies, "inequality is carried to a level far beyond anything ever observed in technologically less developed societies" (Lenski 1966: 154). Indeed, it is in advanced horticultural societies that substantial differences in social inequality emerge. Lenski attributes this to the shift in subsistence technology, from the digging stick to the metal hoe. Metallurgy is the distinguishing technological difference between simple and advanced horticultural societies.

The metal hoe allowed for increased efficiency and permanency of settlements as it could reach nutrients previously unreachable by the digging stick. Consequently, soil was not exhausted as quickly and plots of land could be utilized for longer periods of time. This allowed for greater food production, an increase in population, greater specialization, and a more complex political organization.

The increased complexity and growth of the government led to state building. Those linked most closely to the king tended to make up the small warrior nobility who became increasingly distinguishable from the mass of commoners. The primary determinant of status in advanced horticultural society is the relationship of an individual or group to the king. Metal weapons allowed for successful militaries that not only subjected and controlled the common population, but also allowed for empire building and the subjection of more distant communities. Those privileged in the state hierarchy tended to live in walled urban centers and controlled the redistribution of resources. Redistribution was not equal and often led to severe exploitation of those working the land.

Wealth, privilege, and status are directly tied to this distribution of goods and services.

Extreme exploitation of the king's subjects, a numerous class of slaves with no legal rights, human sacrifice, and the exchange of women are all prevalent in these types of human societies. Lenski and Nolan (2004) argue that it is in these types of societies that ideology begins to play a major role in societal development. Traditional beliefs in the cult of the warrior often led to increased warfare, and hence further shifts in societal development.

Agrarian society (average population size: 100,000; approximate date of first appearance: 3000 BCE). Horticultural societies often evolved into agrarian societies. In this fourth type of human society, the distinguishable subsistence tool was the plow and the harnessing of animate energy. With this major technological shift, cultivated fields replaced gardens, population size greatly expanded, and food production increased (Lenski 1966). "The net effect of all these innovations was the substantial enlargement of the economic surplus. Under agrarian conditions of life, far less of the total product of man's labor was required to keep him alive and productive, and hence more was available for other purposes" (Lenski 1966: 193).

"Other purposes" often meant a greater division of labor and developments in arts, crafts, and particularly in military technology and war, i.e., the strengthening of the state. The simultaneous growth of economic surplus and government meant elites were controlling that surplus. This interdependency of economics and politics allowed significant forms of stratification to emerge (Lenski & Nolan 2004).

A greater division between the governing, landowning, urban literate class and the illiterate rural mass was salient. In many of these societies, peasants were required to give all produced surplus over to elites, exacerbating class inequality to unprecedented levels. Military forces were often used to extract taxes and goods and to control the peasant population. This economic and political control was often justified through appeals to religion. Religion, in fact, becomes a major site of ideological control. Universal faiths such as Buddhism, Christianity, and Islam emerged, and while it was during this era that church and state began to separate, elites remained closely tied to clergy, often giving them land grants, tax exemptions, and generous financial support. Clergy defended elites, justifying their privilege through appeals to divinity and lineage (Lenski & Nolan 2004). Ideology was in this way a tightly controlled outcome that was continually reconstructed to legitimate the status quo. In sum, following the subsistence pattern, as stratification in agrarian societies increased in complexity and inequality, so too did ideology transform.

Industrial society (average population size: 17 million+; approximate date of first appearance: 1800 CE). Industrial society is marked by the technological shift from human and animate energy to machine technology. Industrialization is revolutionary in that the trend toward increasing inequality reverses itself. While the "range of possibilities for inequality" has increased and the stratification system has become more complex, the standard of living for the average person simultaneously increases (Lenski & Nolan 2004: 257). Lenski argues that these changes led to greater specialization, occupational stratification, greater organizational complexity, growth of government, and a rise in market economies. Indeed, specialization meant an increase in societal interdependence, and hence the rise of a moneyed capitalist economy. From these changes come a series of short- and long-term societal changes. For example, within industrial societies, opportunities for participation in political decision-making have broadened, income inequality has been reduced, and "the overall level of inequality in industrial societies is considerably less than that in agrarian societies of the past, or in most nonindustrial societies in the world today" (Lenski & Nolan 2004: 271). However, Lenski also argues that inequality between the rich and poor nations of the world is increasing, as the wealthy consume considerably more of the world's wealth and resources.

Because of the vast increase in economic surplus and consequential socioeconomic transformations, ideologies seemingly shift to make sense of these changes. New secular ideologies such as democracy and capitalism replaced the traditional beliefs of many (Lenski & Nolan 2004). Such ideologies defended free market policies and the interests of wealthy business enterprises. Economic surplus increased, however, unlike the previous trend of increasing economic inequality, and wealth and income were no longer as unequally distributed,

according to Lenski. From this idea came an important line of work concerning the relationship between stratification systems and democracy (Hewitt 1977).

In sum, Lenski's theory of human societies explains not only what society *is*, but *how* and *why* it came to be. Subsistence technology is, for Lenski, the ultimate cause of societal difference. The type of technology used to ensure survival is a necessary precondition for the significant increase in the size and complexity of society. Subsistence technology, then, is not necessarily a determinant of societies, but rather limits what is possible and is the main explanation for great intersocietal (dis)advantage.

Although Lenski does recognize societal variation, his ecological-evolutionary theory provides a general and extensive theory of human societies. From it has emerged a small but significant body of work such as that produced by Joan Huber and Rae Blumberg, both of whom have extended the theory to better understand sex and gender stratification. That an entire issue of *Sociological Theory* (Vol. 22, June 2004) was devoted to Lenski's life, career, and social thought is evidence of this. Lenski's theory of social stratification is not without criticism and much future work remains to be done. Further, Lenski's work sits awkwardly next to sociological theories of *post*-industrial society and postmodernity, a societal type not theorized by Lenski. However, as Patrick Nolan says of Lenski's theory, "a good theory should provoke more questions than it answers" (2004: 336).

SEE ALSO: Class, Status, and Power; Income Inequality, Global; Inequality, Wealth; Stratification, Politics and

REFERENCES AND SUGGESTED READINGS

Barnett, B. (2004) Introduction: The Life, Career, and Social Thought of Gerhard Lenski – Scholar, Teacher, Mentor, Leader. *Sociological Theory* 22: 163–93.

Blumberg, R. (1978) *Stratification: Socioeconomic and Sexual Inequality*. W. C. Brown, Dubuque, IA.

Hewitt, C. (1977) The Effect of Political Democracy and Social Democracy on Equality in Industrial Societies: A Cross-National Comparison. *American Sociological Review* 42: 450–64.

Huber, J. (2004) Lenski Effects on Sex Stratification Theory. *Sociological Theory* 22: 258–68.

Lenski, G. (1966) *Power and Privilege: A Theory of Social Stratification*. McGraw-Hill, New York.

Lenski, G. & Nolan, P. (2004) *Human Societies: An Introduction to Macrosociology*. Paradigm, Boulder, CO.

Nolan, P. (2004) Ecological-Evolutionary Theory: A Reanalysis and Reassessment of Lenski's Theory for the 21st Century. *Sociological Theory* 22: 328–37.

stratification in transition economies

Péter Róbert

Although one could argue that all economies are in transition, permanently, from one state to another, this entry will focus on former socialist societies, which have undergone a post-communist transition both in a political and a socioeconomic sense. Accordingly, economies that experienced a transition to democracy but not to a market economy (e.g., countries in South America) are not considered. Thus, this entry provides information on developments in social stratification in societies as a consequence of political *and* economic changes since the collapse of socialism at the end of the 1980s.

The sociological context is a change in mechanism, which creates social inequalities and generates stratification in socialist planned economies and in capitalist market economies. Former socialist societies represent good test cases for studying these different mechanisms because the same nations with their historical and sociological characteristics can be observed before and after the transformation, in a situation dominated earlier by socialist *redistribution* and later by the capitalist *market*. With respect to these two mechanisms, the basic assumption is that inequalities under socialism are generated by the redistribution and reduced by the market, while inequalities in market economies are produced by the market and decreased by state intervention (Manchin & Szelényi 1987; Szelényi & Kostello 1996).

A more elaborated and detailed set of hypotheses referring to different elements of this transformation process has been developed by Nee (1989) as market transition theory (MTT). One of its assumptions is the *market power thesis* and it expects that the power of the former communist cadres or party members will be replaced by the new power based on marketability. The persistence or feebleness of the advantageous position in the former redistribution system is one of the key issues in stratification of transitional economies. This research question focuses on the elite in these societies and formulates two alternative hypotheses. The first, in accordance with MTT, predicts an elite circulation by assuming that the new elite of transforming societies will replace the former (communist) elite. The second hypothesis expects less circulation but more reproduction and predicts that the former cadres will be able to convert their political capital into economic capital (Hankiss 1990; Staniszkis 1991; Szelényi & Szelényi 1995). A further elaboration of this latter hypothesis adds that only those members of the nomenklatura who have cultural capital and good educational credentials can successfully move from political positions into economic ones.

Another element of MTT is called the *market incentive thesis* and it expects that educational investments will obtain higher financial returns. One of the main features of socialist stratification used to be the low returns to human capital investment (i.e., professionals like engineers, teachers, and doctors were not paid much better than the manual, skilled labor force). Nevertheless, the level and field of education strongly determined occupational chances in these societies, in line with how the planned economy worked under socialism: when leaving the school system, young people could find a job that suited their studies and labor market mobility was restricted even later during further careers.

Another element of MTT focuses on the role of the emerging private sector. The *market opportunity thesis* assumes that individual ambitions, aspirations, and habitus were hindered under socialism when people were employed in big state-owned, inefficient firms, but individual capabilities will lead to higher social status and more salaries when working in the private sector for private companies or as an entrepreneur in one's own business. With respect to the new entrepreneurship under post-communism, Szelényi (1988) formulated the interrupted embourgeoisement theory. This hypothesis predicted that the offspring of previously bourgeois families with appropriate habitus, ambition, and some material capital, who were forced to stay in the "parking lot" under decades of communism, would get into a private market position during the transition process.

MTT expects a kind of *meritocratic* change, which restructures the stratification system of the transition economies. Former merits connected to political trustfulness are replaced by other personal credits like education, ambition, and hard work and these merits will basically determine individuals' status attainment. During this process the stratification of transition economies gets closer to the stratification of advanced market economies. This does not mean, however, that former socialist countries transform simply into capitalist states. Their past and historical roots and experiences influence the transition process in every element of the emerging markets in these countries (Stark 1992).

Two major structural shifts strongly influenced the stratification in transition economies. First, in consequence of privatization, employment in the public sector has shrunk and became restricted to such sectors as health, education, and governance, while employment in the private sector has increased. Privatization techniques varied in the different countries, but a *decrease* in the size of firms and an *increase* in their number is a common feature. The big state-owned companies could not be privatized in one step; they were split into smaller units and smaller private enterprises have been established. At the same time, the old economic structure dominated by heavy and light industry went through a crisis; post-industrialization obtained a push, with new private companies in the service sector, finance, trade, social services, personal services, etc. Second, transition economies, which were characterized by full employment, experienced a huge drop in economic performance and employment in the first half of the 1990s. The new private owners rationalized companies' economic activities and

dismissed part of the labor force. A class system of cadres and workers turned into a dichotomy of *winners and losers*.

With respect to the winners, post-socialism brought new political and economic prospects for a definite group of people. The political elite expanded as the multiparty system replaced the one-party system; the new democratic parties opened up new political positions as well. Privatization increased available managerial positions, since the big state-owned firms turned to several smaller companies, generating special upward mobility paths – a step forward for those who had occupied lower positions. Characterizing this process, some talked about the "revolution of deputies" (Kolosi 2002), others about the rise of managerial capitalism (Eyal et al. 1998). In any case, occupants of the new political and economic elite positions did not come from the "bottom" of society; they had been in good positions either in the redistributive hierarchy or in the quasi-market of the socialist second economy. Thus, empirical evidence does not fully support either the elite circulation or the elite reproduction hypothesis based on former party position, and the interrupted embourgeoisment theory cannot be confirmed either. However, human capital, cultural capital combined with social capital (useful network relationships), helped to maintain advantages in the transition economies, as analysis of privatization reveals (Stark & Bruszt 1998).

As for the losers, their largest group consisted of employees of former big industrial state firms who were not well educated, had restricted skills, and were too old to learn something new and to adapt to the changes. After being dismissed, if they were not able to find a new job, the unemployed went frequently to disabled pension or to old age pension. The hope that the emerging private service sector could provide jobs for everybody who had been dismissed from state industry turned out to be an illusion. Though women could find a job more easily in the service sector, in most transition economies they are over-represented among the unemployed. Early pension programs were an escape for the older representatives of the former political and economic elite without appropriate human and cultural capital. However, unlike manual workers, these former cadres received a specific high allowance when they had to leave their advantageous positions. The level of unemployment is still substantial in several transition economies, but it is not the main reason why the official employment rate is lower in most of these countries. The black economy is also widespread and it employs a sizable fraction of the labor force. Since young school dropouts have difficulty finding a legal job, both unemployment and black employment persist.

Education also takes a leading part in generating stratification in transitional economies. As expected by the market incentive theory, human capital investments have higher returns and tertiary diploma holders especially are better paid. Although transition economies experienced great educational expansion, the tertiary level of schooling pays well, especially if the diploma is obtained in some developing field and if one is employed in the private sector. Nevertheless, the level of schooling of the labor force is still lower in transition economies than in OECD countries. Even with higher income returns in comparison to the socialist era, salaries in transition economies are significantly lower than in developed market economies, while consumer prices are not that much lower. With the lower purchasing power of wages, differences in salaries play a greater role in generating stratification. Income differences used to be low under socialism and increased considerably during the transition. Income differences are still not extremely high, but living on a low income means greater poverty in an absolute sense. Low education is the strongest factor in decreasing the chances of finding a job and increasing the likelihood of becoming unemployed and consequently living in poor conditions.

The occupational distribution of the labor force indicates similar tendencies to those in developed market economies: the proportion of agricultural laborers decreases, employment in the service sector and the percentage of the "service class" (managers and professionals) increases (Domanski 2000). A typical feature of the structural changes was the rapid increase in the numbers of self-employed. Entrepreneurship is a mixed category in transition economies; the distinction between winners and losers is relevant here, too. For some, the market opportunity thesis holds because some people benefited from the transformation: they had the opportunity to follow their ambitions, motives, and habitus for becoming private entrepreneurs and now they earn and live in better conditions. Others, however, were simply forced into self-employment because nobody wanted to employ them, as the employee–unemployed–self-employed sequence indicates in some research on occupational careers.

A further characteristic of the stratification in transition economies is increasing flexibility. Atypical forms of labor-force participation emerged, such as self-employment, part-time work, and employment with fixed-term contracts. This caused growing uncertainty, further increased by the collapse of the safety net and the decline of the state in compensating social inequalities.

SEE ALSO: Communism; Democracy; Educational Attainment; Markets; Meritocracy; Occupations; Schooling and Economic Success; Socialism; Status Attainment; Stratification, Politics and; Transition Economies; Unemployment; Welfare State

REFERENCES AND SUGGESTED READINGS

Domanski, H. (2000) *On the Verge of Convergence: Social Stratification in Eastern Europe*. CEU Press, Budapest.

Eyal, G., Szelényi, I., & Townsley, E. (1998) *Making Capitalism without Capitalists: The New Ruling Elites in Eastern Europe*. Verso, London.

Hankiss, E. (1990) *East European Alternatives*. Clarendon Press, Oxford.

Kolosi, T. (2002) System Change and Elite Change in Hungary. *Central European Political Science Review* 3: 101–25.

Manchin, R. & Szelényi, I. (1987) Social Policy under State Socialism. In: Rein, M., Esping-Anderson, G., & Rainwater, L. (Eds.), *Stagnation and Renewal in Social Policy: The Rise and Fall of Policy Regimes*. M. E. Sharpe, Armonk, NY.

Nee, V. (1989) A Theory of Market Transition: From Redistribution to Markets in State Socialism. *American Sociological Review* 54: 663–81.

Staniszkis, J. (1991) "Political Capitalism" in Poland. *East European Politics and Societies* 5: 127–41.

Stark, D. (1992) Path Dependence and Privatization Strategies in East-Central Europe. *East European Politics and Societies* 6: 17–51.

Stark, D. & Bruszt, L. (1998) *Postsocialist Pathways.* Cambridge University Press, Cambridge.

Szelényi, I. (1988) *Socialist Entrepreneurs: Embourgeoisement in Rural Hungary.* University of Wisconsin Press, Madison.

Szelényi, I. & Kostello, E. (1996) The Market Transition Debate: Toward a Synthesis? *American Journal of Sociology* 101: 1082–96.

Szelényi, I. & Szelényi, S. (1995) Circulation or Reproduction of Elites During the Post-Communist Transformation of Eastern Europe. *Theory and Society* 24: 615–38.

stratified reproduction

Amy Agigian

Stratified reproduction is a term originally coined by Shellee Colen in her classic 1986 study of West Indian nannies and their (female) employers in New York City, which found inequalities of race, class, gender, culture, and legal status played out on a social field that was both domestic and transnational. Colen elaborated the term in her later work to describe situations in which women perform physical and social reproductive labor structured by economic, political, and social forces and differentiated unequally across hierarchies of class, race, ethnicity, gender, and place in a global economy (Colen 1995). Many feminist social scientists since the 1980s have adopted stratified reproduction as a theoretical framework within which to examine a variety of issues relevant to the intersections of reproduction and stratification.

The term stratified reproduction implicitly acknowledges both the sexual politics and the political economy of reproduction. In this way it derives from, and elaborates on, second-wave feminist concerns with removing childbearing (biological reproduction) and domestic labor (social reproduction) from the realm of the "natural" and placing them squarely under critical, social scientific analysis. Researchers of stratified reproduction continue the feminist project, demystifying still relatively unexamined gender relations and gender inequalities, particularly those related to procreation and

carework. Prior to second-wave feminism, social and biological reproduction – pregnancy, childbearing, childcare, housework – was undertheorized within sociology and seen largely as private and "natural," as opposed to political and socially constructed (Laslett & Brenner 1989). Scholars of stratified reproduction examine the ways that reproduction is stratified within and across cultures, with particular attention to the transnational organization of reproduction. For example, Ehrenreich and Hochschild examine global flows of nannies, maids, and sex workers, while Inhorn (2002) analyzes the gendered and cultural impact of "western" reproductive technologies in Egypt. Since reproduction is so inextricably entwined with women's bodies, the political reverberations of the study of stratified reproduction are immediate and often radical. As with other analyses of sexual politics, injustices in people's intimate and private lives become apparent. Similarly, the stains of both colonialism and eugenics on current global hierarchies of embodiment become unavoidable.

As a social scientific framework, stratified reproduction has enabled scholars across fields including sociology, history, political science, and especially anthropology to examine power relations and inequalities in the realm of reproduction. Inherent in this framework is the understanding that certain kinds of reproduction are privileged, encouraged, and supported, while others are stigmatized, discouraged, and oppressed. As Ginsburg and Rapp (1995: 314) note, "Throughout history, state power has depended directly and indirectly on defining normative families and controlling populations." In this understanding, reproduction is shaped by struggles among and within powerful institutional forces such as the state, global capitalism, religion, and gender hierarchies. Reproduction can be, and is, stratified along multiple axes of social status and exclusion. Relevant inequalities include gender, race, class, nation, sexual orientation, age, health and disability status, and legal status. Such social inequalities are played out dramatically in differential access to and use of reproductive technologies such as fetal screening, prenatal care, donor sperm and eggs, and a choice of skilled birth attendant, as well as in reproductive sites such as surrogacy and genetic counseling.

Stratified reproduction can also be seen in the policy realm when some forms of reproduction are encouraged and resourced while others are stigmatized and discouraged. Some children are considered highly worthy of being born, and considerable resources are used to enable their births (e.g., through in vitro fertilization made available to affluent, predominantly white heterosexual couples), while others are strongly discouraged (e.g., through welfare policies that impose "family caps" limiting the subsistence income of poor mothers who have children). Some women are seen as reproductive threats to society and "reproductive sinners" by virtue of their race, class, and/or other characteristics. For instance, Chavez (2004) analyzes popular discourses about the presumably dangerous sexuality and procreation of Latina women in the United States. Roberts (1997) documents the brutal impact of US welfare laws that punish poor, African American women for having children. Conversely, other women are seen as potential "reproductive saviors" of the state, ethnic group, religion, and/or normative family. Kahn's (2000) study of the use and regulation of reproductive technologies in Israel, for example, finds that a strong pronatalist ethic outweighs concerns regarding the potential social disruption occasioned by the new forms of assisted reproduction. Another group that is encouraged to procreate, though in a very different way, is Ivy League-educated, white, blond, tall, "healthy" young women, who are paid tens of thousands of dollars to sell their eggs on the global market. While these incentives and disincentives to procreate may appear to be unrelated phenomena, the theoretical framework of stratified reproduction promotes articulation of the important links among them.

The lens of stratified reproduction overlaps and differs in significant ways from other sociological approaches to the study of reproduction. For example, while it may use demography to understand trends in transnational caregiving, stratified reproduction emphasizes the political and cultural forces shaping migratory caregiving, the care deficits left behind in regions vacated by third world caregivers when they depart for first world households, and the ways that paid caregiving reinscribes patriarchal power in high-earning, heterosexual, two-career households. Similarly, studies of stratified

reproduction in alternative insemination demonstrate how racial, class, homophobic, and phenotypic hierarchies are inscribed in the practices of sperm banking and sperm selection.

Research regarding stratified reproduction tends to favor qualitative methodologies. In-depth, on-the-ground studies of particular sites of stratified reproduction are the bases for the development of theoretical frameworks as well as for claims about the importance of reproduction to all social theory. *Conceiving the New World Order* (1995), edited by feminist anthropologists Faye D. Ginsburg and Rayna Rapp, was a pivotal book in articulating the significance of stratified reproduction as a framework for the burgeoning work of feminist social scientists on reproduction. The second section of the book, "Stratified Reproduction," suggests something of the concept's scope. In addition to Colen's work there are chapters on lesbian motherhood (Lewin); the politics of race, class, and gender in female-headed households (Mullings); and early childbearing (Ward).

The use of the theoretical framework of stratified reproduction appears to be well on its way to becoming mainstreamed in the sociological study of areas including procreation, transnational carework, and reproductive technology.

SEE ALSO: Carework; Family Planning, Abortion, and Reproductive Health; Feminism; Feminism, First, Second, and Third Waves; Feminist Anthropology; Feminization of Labor Migration; Genetic Engineering as a Social Problem; International Gender Division of Labor; Lesbian and Gay Families; New Reproductive Technologies

REFERENCES AND SUGGESTED READINGS

Agigian, A. (2004) *Baby Steps: How Lesbian Alternative Insemination is Changing the World.* Wesleyan University Press, Middletown, CT.

Chavez, L. R. (2004) A Glass Half Empty: Latina Reproduction and Public Discourse. *Human Organization* 63, 2 (Summer).

Colen, S. (1995) "Like a Mother to Them": Stratified Reproduction and West Indian Childcare Workers in New York. In: Ginsburg, F. D. & Rapp, R. (Eds.), *Conceiving the New World Order:*

The Global Politics of Reproduction. University of California Press, Berkeley.

Ginsburg, F. D. & Rapp, R. (Eds.) (1995) *Conceiving the New World Order: The Global Politics of Reproduction*. University of California Press, Berkeley.

Inhorn, M. (2002) The "Local" Confronts the "Global": Infertile Bodies and New Reproductive Technologies in Egypt. In: Inhorn, M. & Van Baal, F. (Eds.), *Infertility Around the Globe*. University of California Press, Berkeley, pp. 263–82.

Kahn, S. M. (2000) *Reproducing Jews: A Cultural Account of Assisted Conception in Israel*. Duke University Press, Durham, NC.

Laslett, B. & Brenner, J. (1989) Gender and Social Reproduction: Historical Perspectives. *Annual Review of Sociology* 15: 381–404.

McCormack, K. (2005) Stratified Reproduction and Poor Women's Resistance. *Gender and Society* 19(5): 660–79.

Rapp, R. (2001) Gender, Body, Biomedicine: How Some Feminist Concerns Dragged Reproduction to the Center of Social Theory. *Medical Anthropology Quarterly* 15, 4 (December).

Roberts, D. (1997) *Killing the Black Body: Race, Reproduction, and the Meaning of Liberty*. Vintage, New York.

stress and health

Jeffrey E. Hall

Stress is an emotional-psychophysiological state that occurs in a situational context when an individual is confronted with cues that elicit fear or anxiety responses. Medical sociologists are interested in stress because the situations that cause it are often social and increase a person's risk of disease by taxing or exceeding his or her adaptive capacities (Wheaton 1994). Admittedly, the word stress has other connotations, but this view captures the essential facets of an extensive body of research that has been expanding for almost a century.

THE STRESS PROCESS

Although various stress process models exist, they generally involve (1) a stimulus problem, (2) a processing state where information regarding the stimulus is organized, and (3) some form of response. The first stage of the stress process involves the presence of stimulus problems or "stressors" consisting of environmental, social, and internal demands that challenge adaptive abilities and call for behavioral adjustments (Holmes & Rahe 1967). The content of stressors varies greatly depending upon individual and group circumstances. For example, adaptive abilities may be significantly challenged by (1) the loss of a job or the death of a loved one; (2) minor but regular annoyances, such as traffic problems and inconsiderate neighbors; (3) enduring exposures to urban problems, such as crowding, environmental pollution, and high rates of crime and unemployment; or (4) disruptive experiences, such as unemployment, war, and acts of terrorism. Such categories of problems are, respectively, labeled life events, daily hassles, chronic strains, and traumas (Pearlin 1989; Thoits 1995). These categories have emerged out of research identifying and measuring stressful stimuli.

Once a stressor is encountered, information regarding the stimuli is evaluated in preparation for the selection or elicitation of a response. Specifically, the threat potential of stressors is assessed and determined based upon the meanings given to these occurrences within specific social contexts (Lazarus & Folkman 1984). This segment of the stress process is termed primary appraisal; the results of activities here vary according to stressor features such as the intensity and controllability of the stimulus and individual traits like personality dispositions.

Logically, appraisal activities also include actions of a secondary nature, hence the use of the term secondary appraisal. Entry into this phase of appraisal is initiated after it is determined that some form of response is needed. Possible responses may include the generation of (1) coping or (2) stress responses. Coping responses are actions that "help individuals maintain psychosocial adaptation during stressful periods; [they] encompass cognitive and behavioral efforts to reduce or eliminate stressful conditions and associated emotional distress" (Holahan et al. 1996). During secondary appraisal, coping repertoires (the possible strategies for dealing with problems) are evaluated first to determine the feasibility of eliminating stressors or reducing their aversive impacts.

If an appropriate coping response is available and perceived as a potentially effective means of dealing with a stressor, then the negative affects of the stressor may be neutralized. If, however, it is determined that a suitable response is not within one's coping repertoire or is available but ineffective, then a stress response is generated.

Stress responses include (1) physiological and biochemical responses, such as the arousal of the sympathetic nervous system and changes in corticosteroid steroid levels (Selye 1936); (2) physical health problems such as cardiovascular disease, hypertension, and ulcers (e.g., Aneshensel & Gore 1991); and (3) reactions involving the onset and course of forms of psychological distress. Initially, stress responses were studied separately with primary attention given to specifying the breadth and depth of stressor impacts upon specific outcomes. Later efforts (e.g., Thoits 1995), however, focused on interconnected and multifaceted stress situations. This effort entails explorations of junctures among physical and psychological health, and attempts to define the implications of stress-induced changes in one domain for functioning in the other. In summary, the stress process links our bodies to the environment by way of our minds and their psychosocial filters. Encountered stimuli become threatening and thus "stressful" if they are appraised as such relative to specific cultural and individual meanings and cannot be adequately responded to using available coping responses.

PERIPHERAL ELEMENTS OF THE STRESS PROCESS: VULNERABILITY FACTORS AND MODERATORS

While the conception presented in the previous section is useful, it is limited in that it only depicts the basic framework of the stress process. The history of stress research also identifies other influential variables. Two classes of these variables are particularly important: vulnerability factors and mediators.

Vulnerability Factors

Early stress research depicted the stress process beginning with the emergence of a potentially stressful stimulus. In contrast, subsequent research has acknowledged the need to model the effects of statuses and dispositions that may increase (1) the probabilities that stressors will be encountered or (2) the likelihood that problems will be experienced in the face of stress. Such statuses and dispositions are considered vulnerability factors (Turner & Avison 1989).

Demographic statuses such as age, race, gender, education level, and marital status have been classified as vulnerability factors because they "determine the stressors to which people are exposed, the mediators they are able to mobilize, and the manner in [and the extent to] which they experience stress" (Pearlin 1989: 241). These statuses are indicators of social location that convey contextual information about the circumstances in which specific stressors are more likely to be generated, contended with, and felt. They also reflect differences in the initial positioning of certain groups relative to society's goals (e.g., sound health and financial success) and in relation to the approved networks and pathways for reaching and retaining them (e.g., quality medical care and stable, lucrative employment). Lastly, they influence the form of the stress response that is called forth when attempts to eliminate stressors are ineffective.

Personality dispositions such as the consistent exhibition of Type A behavioral patterns (TABP) and perfectionist behavior are other factors that may render individuals more susceptible to the adverse effects of stressors. The increased vulnerability associated with the possession of the Type A personality may be attributable to its interference with the "natural" course of secondary appraisal. It inspires the selection of inadequate coping responses that subsequently compromise efforts to diffuse the effects of stressors (Vingerhoets & Flohr 1984). The perfectionist personality type increases stressor vulnerability in quite a different manner. It increases the frequency of encounters with stressors and amplifies their negative psychological effects by changing minor issues into major problems and by increasing the likelihood that failures will be interpreted as signs of personal deficiency (Hewitt & Flett 1993). Social statuses and personality dispositions can affect each stage of the stress process.

Mediators

An extension of the stress process model focuses on the role of constructs that govern the effects of stressors on outcomes and function as barriers to the adverse effects of exigencies. These constructs are called mediators (Pearlin 1989). This entry has already presented one mediator (coping) in its description of options for response that are selected during secondary appraisal. Other constructs that may act as mediators include personal resources and social resources. Coping responses, personal resources, and social resources may improve or protect well-being by reducing the effects of existing stressors and by discouraging the occurrence of secondary stressors.

Coping Responses

Coping responses are elicited or enacted in order to manage specific situational demands (Lazarus & Folkman 1984; Pearlin & Schooler 1978). These responses are intended to regulate or alter stressor effects. The first set of responses is known as "emotion-focused" coping, while the second is "problem-focused" coping. Emotion-focused coping includes behaviors such as venting, positive reframing, religion, acceptance, and the use of emotional support. In contrast, use of instrumental support, active coping, and planning are actions exemplifying problem-focused coping.

A third set of coping responses that may be elicited in response to stressors entail actions that deny the threat posed by potential stressors. Such responses are labeled as either avoidant or disengagement coping styles (Carver & Scheier 1993). Avoidant coping typically involves the initiation of activities or the occupation of mental states that prevent or delay direct confrontations with stressors and their implications for well-being. Such responses include self-distraction, substance use, behavioral disengagement, and the excessive use of humor. Problem-focused, emotion-focused, and avoidant coping responses are elicited based upon the personal and cultural meanings assigned to specific stressors. Coping involves interaction between environmental, personality, and health factors.

Psychological Resources

Psychological resources are personality characteristics that people draw on to help them withstand the threats posed by events and objects in their environment. These resources function as internal "barriers," reducing the impact of stressors on the self and decreasing the levels of distress experienced. Two forms of commonly studied psychological resources are self-esteem and mastery.

Self-esteem refers to the positiveness of one's attitude toward oneself. High self-esteem has been shown to significantly reduce psychological symptoms and to moderate the emotional consequences of stressors (Thoits 1995; Turner & Roszell 1994). Mastery refers to "the extent to which one regards one's life chances as being under one's own control in contrast to being fatalistically ruled" (Pearlin & Schooler 1978: 5). Studies suggest that individuals with higher levels of mastery are less vulnerable to the impacts of stressors, less likely to experience psychological disruptions, and more likely to have better mental and physical health compared to individuals with low mastery levels (Mirowsky & Ross 1990). High levels of mastery and self-esteem may inspire self-appraisals that reduce the level of threat assigned to stressors. In addition, they may elevate confidence in one's ability to control these stimuli. In addition, high levels of mastery may promote greater accuracy in the selection of ways of responding to stressful stimuli, while high self-esteem levels may make it less likely that encountered problems will give rise to self-evaluations that might engender emotional distress.

Self-efficacy, resiliency, and optimism are other psychological resources that may serve as mediators. Although these constructs have received less attention than either self-esteem or mastery, they may have a role in the stress process.

Social Resources

Social resources constitute the final class of mediators considered in the stress literature. These resources consist of various forms of social support: functions performed by others to aid individuals in dealing with stressors (Thoits 1995). Forms of social support used to explain variations in stress responses include: (1) emotional support, which is the expression of positive affect, emphatic understanding, and the encouragement of expressions of feelings; (2) informational support, the offering of advice, information, guidance, or feedback; (3) instrumental support, which is the provision of material aid or behavioral assistance; and (4) expressive support, which involves the expression of love and affection.

Although studies by House and Kahn (1985) indicate that these forms of support are highly correlated, scrutiny of each is warranted since specific forms of support may be more or less effective in counteracting particular stressors (Cohen & McKay 1984). For instance, emotional and expressive support may be required during bereavement, while informational and instrumental support may be vital when confronting the physical limitations accompanying an injury such as an ankle fracture. Furthermore, it is noted that each form may also contribute uniquely and interactively to the acquisition of particular stress outcomes (Rook & Underwood 2000). Emotional and expressive supports directly address basic needs for love and esteem, whereas instrumental and informational supports assist in the performance of problematic activities and provide function promoting regulation. Combinations of emotional, expressive, instrumental, and informational may help to stabilize and strengthen interactions with internal and external environments.

Attention has been given to the perceptual elements of social support and their roles in the stress process. Work in this area illustrates the health-related significance of perceptions concerning resource availability apart from the actual receipt of resources. Specifically, whether or not one receives support has been shown to be less important for health and adjustment than one's beliefs about resource availability. The belief that support is available diffuses stressor impacts by way of the secondary stage of appraisal; it increases the likelihood of concluding that one has "enough" or the "right" coping responses and social resources to deal with specific circumstances. The extent to which stressor effects are mediated by resources depends on ideas about what is supportive, as well as actual resource levels. Stress-related experiences reflect the social dispositions possessed and cognitive postures assumed when stimuli are defined as threatening.

THE STRESS PROCESS AND HEALTH: SYNOPSIS AND SYNTHESIS

Generally, the term stress is used to describe feelings experienced when a person is confronted by disruptions, demands, or challenges. Yet among stress researchers this term is linked to a process that takes shape far before the arousal of any feelings. In this latter context stress has internal and external origins, includes occurrences requiring adjustments acutely, daily, and chronically, and is expressed both emotionally and physiologically. Moreover, the process is seen as affected by factors that increase or decrease exposures to potentially noxious stimuli.

This entry provides an overview of the stress process and health as one of many domains impacted by stressors and mediators. It is limited in that some ideas about the stress process were not covered (e.g., the array of stress model variants depicting relations among vulnerability factors, stressors, mediators, and health; the role of social capital and social networks in the stress process). Information concerning developments in these areas can be obtained by consulting works by Ensel and Lin (1991) among numerous others.

SEE ALSO: Social Support; Stress and Migration; Stress, Stress Theories; Stress and Work; Stressful Life Events

REFERENCES AND SUGGESTED READINGS

Aneshensel, C. & Gore, S. (1991) Development, Stress, and Role Restructuring: Social Transitions of Adolescence. In: Eckenrode, J. (Ed.), *The Social Context of Coping*. Plenum, New York.

Carver, C. & Scheier, M. (1993) Vigilant and Avoidant Coping in Two Patient Samples. In: Krohne, H. (Ed.), *Attention and Avoidance: Strategies in Coping with Aversiveness*. Hogrefe & Huber, Seattle, pp. 295–320.

Cohen, S. & McKay, G. (1984) Social Support, Stress, and the Buffering Hypothesis: A

Theoretical Analysis. In: Baum, A., Singer, J., & Taylor, S. (Eds.), *Handbook of Psychology and Health*, Vol. 4. Erlbaum, New York, pp. 253–67.

Cronkite, R. & Moos, R. (1984) The Role of Predisposing and Moderating Factors in the Stress–Illness Relationship. *Journal of Health and Social Behavior* 25: 372–93.

Ensel, W. & Lin, N. (1991) The Life Stress Paradigm and Psychological Distress. *Journal of Health and Social Behavior* 32: 321–41.

Hewitt, P. & Flett, G. (1993) Dimensions of Perfectionism, Daily Stress, and Depression: A Test of the Specific Vulnerability Hypothesis. *Journal of Abnormal Psychology* 102: 58–65.

Holahan, C., Moos, R., & Schaefer, J. (1996) Coping, Stress Resistance, and Growth: Conceptualizing Adaptive Functioning. In: Zeidner, M. & Endler, N. (Eds.), *Handbook of Coping: Theory, Research, Applications*. Wiley, New York, pp. 24–43.

Holmes, T. & Rahe, R. (1967) The Social Readjustment Rating Scale. *Psychosomatic Research* 11: 213–18.

House, J. & Kahn, R. (1985) Measures and Concepts of Social Support. In: Cohen, S. & Syme, S. (Eds.), *Social Support and Health*. Academic Press, Orlando, pp. 83–108.

Lazarus, R. & Folkman, S. (1984) *Stress, Appraisal, and Coping*. Springer, New York.

Mirowsky, J. & Ross, C. (1990) Control or Defense? Depression and the Sense of Control over Good and Bad Outcomes. *Journal of Health and Social Behavior* 31: 71–86.

Pearlin, L. (1989) The Sociological Study of Stress. *Journal of Health and Social Behavior* 30: 241–56.

Pearlin, L. & Schooler, C. (1978) The Structure of Coping. *Journal of Health and Social Behavior* 19: 2–21.

Rook, K. & Underwood, L. (2000) Social Support Measurement and Interventions: Comments and Future Directions. In: Cohen, S., Underwood, L., & Gotlib, B. (Eds.), *Social Support Measurement and Intervention: A Guide for Health and Social Scientists*. Oxford University Press, New York, pp. 331–4.

Selye, H. (1936) A Syndrome Produced by Diverse Noxious Agents. *Nature* 138: 32.

Thoits, P. (1995) Stress, Coping, and Social Support Processes: Where Are We? What Next? *Journal of Health and Social Behavior*, extra issue: 53–79.

Turner, R. & Avison, W. (1989) Gender and Depression: Assessing Exposure and Vulnerability to Life Events in a Chronically Strained Population. *Journal of Nervous and Mental Disease* 177: 443–55.

Turner, R. & Roszell, P. (1994) Psychosocial Resources and the Stress Process. In: Avison, W. & Gotlib, I. (Eds.), *Stress and Mental Health: Contemporary Issues and Prospects for the Future*. Plenum, New York, pp. 179–210.

Vingerhoets, A. & Flohr, P. (1984) Type A Behavior and Self-Reports of Coping Preferences. *British Journal of Medical Psychology* 57: 15–21.

Wheaton, B. (1994) Sampling the Stress Universe. In: Avision, W. & Gotlib, I. (Eds.), *Stress and Mental Health: Contemporary Issues and Prospects for the Future*. Plenum, New York, pp. 77–114.

stress and migration

Judith T. Shuval

Migration within and between different countries is an ongoing, worldwide phenomenon which is likely to continue well into the twenty-first century and involve over 130 million persons. It is caused by population pressures, environmental deterioration, poverty, wars, persecution, and human rights abuses. Migration is a response to the flow of capital, technology, and cultural innovations in an interactive process across the globe. It links countries by flows and counter-flows of people in sets of networks which are both interdependent and independent of each other. Countries of origin and destination are determined by historical ties based on earlier colonization, political influence, trade, investment, or cultural ties – as well as the present economic, social, and political contexts.

Migrants are extremely diversified. They include a wide variety of people and the various categories of migrants may shift over time from one type to another. The most prominent categories include permanent settlers, temporary and seasonal workers, refugees and asylum seekers, legal and illegal immigrants, diaspora migrants who return to their former homeland, persons who come for purposes of family reunion, skilled and unskilled persons of varying social-class backgrounds, persons of urban and rural origins, wage earners and entrepreneurs, and many varieties of ethnic groups.

Extensive illegal immigration characterizes many of the receiving societies and poses a major threat to the authority and power of the state, since it represents a loss of control in the flow of people and goods over borders. Efforts to control illegals have included penalties on employers who provide them with jobs, as well as limitations on such benefits as welfare payments, tax and housing assistance, family support, student loans, and medical care.

Illegal migrants take the least desired jobs on the market, make their living in the "informal" sector, and satisfy employers' demand for cheap labor. Because of their willingness to accept lower wages, illegals pose a job threat to the local population. Illegals are subject to increased stress in some countries because of their ineligibility for health and welfare benefits, education for their children, and fear of deportation. In many parts of the world there is a concern that immigrants import Islamic fundamentalism and terror as well as increasing crime rates. Humanitarian concerns have been compromised for security considerations by imposing tighter controls on the entry of illegal immigrants.

Stress occurs when an individual confronts a salient situation in which their usual modes of behavior are inadequate and the consequences of not adapting are sufficiently disturbing to result in a disruption in homeostasis. Situations are not objectively stressful, but are constructed as such by individuals in relation to their own social and cultural norms. If one is unable to mobilize personal or social resources to cope with the situation in such a manner as to restore homeostasis, energy will be bound up dealing with the perceived disturbance.

The availability and usability of coping mechanisms constitute the link that determines whether a situation will in fact result in stress for the individual. Indeed, there is considerable evidence for the stress-mediating and stress-buffering roles of coping resources. Such coping resources are of two types: individual (e.g., personal skills, personality traits, intelligence, knowledge) and social (e.g., formal institutions, informal groups, social norms and values). In the context of migration, earlier, familiar coping mechanisms may lose their efficacy in the transition from one cultural setting to another. Furthermore, stress experienced in the country of origin may be "imported" into the destination and even be exacerbated by the newer stresses of the migration process.

Stress may be viewed as both a cause and a consequence of migration. On the causative level, stress in any given location may act as a motivator of migration, when people believe that they can reduce stress and improve their overall situation by migrating to a different setting. In order to serve as an effective motivator, two conditions are required: (1) a level of stress which is perceived as sufficiently powerful and salient to justify uprooting oneself and one's family from a familiar setting; and (2) knowledge about the destination and a belief that conditions there will provide less stress and a more satisfactory setting.

The relationship between migration and stress is best conceptualized in terms of an integrated, macro–micro framework. On the macro level, the changing nature of state responses to the presence of immigrant communities needs to be considered against a background of shifting notions of nationhood and transnational processes. Processes of globalization which induce the circulation of capital, commodities, people, and cultural practices, reconfigure spaces and identities, and change earlier notions of attachment and citizenship. While people from less developed parts of the world try to move to the economically developed regions, there is anxiety in migrant-receiving countries about job loss and changes to national culture which promote state policies to restrict, control, and select international migrants.

On the micro level it is necessary to consider issues of individual and collective identity, life chances, and how immigrants perceive themselves and their social reality. Social networks are micro-structures which play a core role in migration processes by their role in providing assistance at the destination in job location, financial support, practical information, and a base for the migration of additional persons. The ongoing nature of the process is seen in the fact that the larger the number of people who migrate, the thicker the social networks at the destinations and the consequent amount of available help; this tends to decrease the costs and risks of migration for others from the same origin. Widespread policies of "family reunification" reinforce these networks.

The processes of change which are inherent in migration undermine the sense of the self with respect to the individual's place in the social order. One of the major sources of stress for immigrants is the loss of numerous self-identities that were embedded in their former communities, jobs, skills, language, and culture. These represent a serious loss in human capital. Racism, prejudice, and xenophobia exacerbate the difficulties encountered in the reconstruction of identity. Role theorists have suggested that when a person has multiple identities, they are better able to cope with the loss of a specific role because viable alternative identities are available and can be given increased weight in defining one's self.

Migration has stimulated the rise of transnational communities which challenge conventional identities, notions of belonging, rights, and responsibilities. Studies of diaspora migration have highlighted the multiple ethnic identities that are maintained by immigrants – as ties to former homelands are retained through cheap travel and electronic modes of communication. These patterns have challenged older notions of the nation-state and patterns of exclusive loyalty and identity.

On the structural level, migrants are not dispersed at random in a social system, but tend to be located in specific occupational and geographical niches, often in marginal locations. These patterns reflect informal or formal barriers imposed by the host society, as well as immigrants' choices. Since migration is frequently a response to job openings in the host society, the types of jobs available vary widely, from unskilled laborers to skilled technicians or professionals. Limited options for housing and exclusionary mechanisms often force migrants into slum neighborhoods and substandard housing. Thus, the structural location of the migrant in the social system exposes them to different stressors, including health risks.

Occupational and geographic concentration contributes to the visibility of migrants, and this affects both the migrant group itself and other populations in the society. Insofar as the migrants are concerned, a common structural location carries implications for self-identification, solidarity, and feelings of commonality. A sense of cohesion may result, promoting group identification and social support, but may also exacerbate stress by encouraging or reinforcing collective perceptions of exploitation and deprivation.

Ethnic enclaves composed of immigrants and their offspring have attained growing legitimacy as demands for cultural assimilation have been found to be incompatible with democratic values of tolerance and equality. Ethnic pluralism has become normative in many societies. One result has been the long-term persistence and viability of ethnic communities and neighborhoods in which traditional cultural patterns are retained and reinforced over several generations. These have strengthened ethnic cohesion as well as ties with former homelands which encourage the development of cross-national communities. But when such enclaves are perceived as ghettos which serve as a barrier to mobility and achievement, the resulting sense of deprivation is often expressed in hostility or violence focused on other accessible target groups, which include immigrants stemming from different cultural backgrounds or veteran groups in the host society who are perceived as legitimate targets. Indeed, violence as a mode of attaining goals may be part of the normative cultural baggage of some groups of immigrants in a multi-ethnic society.

There is a dynamic quality to structurally determined stressors. During the early period in the host society, migrants often accept low status or deprivation as inevitable; however, there is generally a strong underlying expectation of change for the better. When the host society's culture includes such values as equality, achievement, and social mobility these expectations are reinforced. If improvement is perceived as slow or absent, such lack of change serves as a stressor. Stress is felt by subgroups in such a value context, as they feel they are not succeeding or are not attaining as much as relevant others. Migrants are especially vulnerable to such feelings when they have been in the host society for increasing lengths of time and especially in the second and third generation. Under such conditions, it may be said that the stress induced by migration is multi-generational and its effects can be long term, as they spread to other segments of the population.

Attitudes of groups in the host society toward migrants range from acceptance and tolerance to hostility or overt aggression. In any case, the visibility of the migrants makes possible a clearer focus on them by the host population or by subgroups in it. Expressions of prejudice, intolerance, aggression, or xenophobia may serve as stressors, especially when the more successful migrants are perceived as competing with, or advantaged relative to, veteran members of the society.

Another structural dimension on which migrants are not randomly distributed is the power and influence hierarchy in the host society. At the time of entry, migrants tend to be low on these factors. For migrants who enjoyed and utilized power before their move, its absence may serve as a stressor in the new society. However, when large numbers of immigrants from one country of origin arrive, they may themselves constitute a political power in the host country. Their interests may dictate that they lobby for the admission of groups from specific countries of origin, for limitations in the numbers of immigrants, or for their own special interests.

Absence of power may express itself on the simplest level by lack of citizenship. For a period of time the migrant may be unable to vote, hold office, acquire property, or qualify for certain jobs. Once formal citizenship has been acquired, migrants may still encounter barriers in the economic and political spheres, where positions of power are occupied by veterans who have little interest in relinquishing such influence to newcomers. In open, democratic societies, political organization of migrant groups may provide channels to acquire power and influence within such groups and through them eventually enter into the broader political context.

On the informal level, migration often results in a shift in the balance of power within families and other informal social contexts. Thus, persons who traditionally have wielded power in the family (e.g., grandparents or fathers) may find themselves stripped of their accustomed roles as a result of different patterns of family life in the new society. Unless alternative rewards are found for the demoted traditional leaders, they are likely to experience stress.

The above processes are intensified by globalized media messages which serve to inflate expectations and intensify trends toward increased democratization. Immigrants often expect rapid improvement in their economic and social status in the host society, immediate rewards, and a voice in decision-making. When these are slow in coming, the ensuing frustration may lead to violence.

SEE ALSO: Migration, Ethnic Conflicts, and Racism; Migration: Internal; Migration: International; Migration: Undocumented/Illegal; Stress and Health; Stress and Work

REFERENCES AND SUGGESTED READINGS

Bonneuil, N. & Auriat, N. (2000) Fifty Years of Ethnic Conflict and Cohesion: 1945–94. *Journal of Peace Research* 37: 563–81.

Brown, D. L. (2002) Migration and Community: Social Networks in a Multilevel World. *Rural Sociology* 67: 1–23.

Bruess, J. (2003) Attitudes and Aggressive Actions: Interethnic Tensions Among German, Turkish and Resettler Adolescents. *Migraciones* 13: 209–40.

Center for Immigration Statistics (2003) *Immigration-Related Statistics 2003*. US Government Printing Office, Washington, DC.

Colic-Peisker, V. & Walker, I. (2003) Human Capital, Acculturation and Social Identity: Bosnian Refugees in Australia. *Journal of Community and Applied Psychology* 13: 337–60.

Hoffman-Nowotny, H. J. (2002) Social and Political Tensions in Migration Processes. *Migration* 33–5: 37–49.

Inglis, C. (2000) The "Rediscovery" of Ethnicity: Theory and Analysis. In: Quah, S. & Sales, A. (Eds.), *The International Handbook of Sociology*. Sage, London, pp. 151–70.

Lohrmann, R. (2000) Migrants, Refugees and Insecurity: Current Threats to Peace? *International Migration* 38: 3–22.

Maris, C. & Sahardo, S. (2001) Honour Killing: A Reflection on Gender, Culture and Violence. *Netherlands' Journal of Social Science* 37: 52–73.

Nagel, C. (2002) Constructing Difference and Sameness: The Politics of Assimilation in London's Arab Communities. *Ethnic and Racial Studies* 25: 258–87.

Pecaut, D. (2000) The Loss of Rights, the Meaning of Experience and Social Connection. *International Journal of Politics, Culture and Society* 14: 89–105.

Remennick, L. (2002) Immigrants from Chernobyl-Affected Areas in Israel: The Link between Health and Social Adjustment. *Social Science and Medicine* 54: 309–17.

Shuval, J. T. (1993) Migration and Stress. In: Goldberger, L. & Breznitz, S. (Ed.), *Handbook of Stress: Theoretical and Clinical Aspects*. Academic Press, New York, pp. 677–91.

Shuval, J. T. (2000) Diaspora Migration: Definitional Ambiguities and a Theoretical Paradigm. *International Migration* 38: 41–57.

Shuval, J. T. (2000) The Reconstruction of Professional Identity Among Immigrant Physicians in Three Societies. *Journal of Immigrant Health* 2: 191–201.

Simmons, A. B. (2002) Globalization and International Migration: Trends, Puzzles and Theoretical Models. *Cahiers Quebecois de Demographies* 31: 7–33.

Suarez-Orozco, S. (2001) Immigrant Families and their Children: Adaptation and Identity Formation. In: Blau, J. (Ed.), *The Blackwell Companion to Sociology*. Blackwell, Oxford, pp. 128–39.

Timotijevic, L. & Breakwell, G. M. (2000) Migration and Threat to Identity. *Journal of Community and Applied Social Psychology* 10: 355–72.

Wasti-Walter, D., Varadi, M., & Veider, F. (2003) Coping with Marginality. *Journal of Ethnic and Migration Studies* 29: 797–817.

stress, stress theories

Gerald F. Lackey

What differentiates the study of stress in sociology from similar work in fields like biology or medicine is the attention given by sociologists to the social distribution of mental health and well-being. Sociological inquiry focuses on how the causes of stress, the resources for coping with stress, and the outcomes of stress vary across subgroups in the population. As distinct from a psychological or biological approach, the sociological study of stress focuses on how the social condition can determine a number of different stress outcomes. A significant step forward in this endeavor was made by Pearlin et al. (1981) when they formalized a sociological theory of the stress process.

There are three fundamental concepts that form the core of the stress process: stressors, moderators/mediators, and stress outcomes. Stressors can be external, environmental, or social factors, or internal, biological, or psychological factors that challenge an individual to adapt or change. They can be discrete events such as the destruction of one's home by a tornado or chronic problems such as a degenerative neurological illness like Alzheimer's disease. Related, moderators are the social or personal resources that attenuate the effects of stressors or change the situations that are producing the stressors. In addition to this buffering effect, research also shows that certain resources can have mediating effects on stress outcomes. The three types of moderators/mediators are coping strategies, personal resources, and social support. Lastly, stress outcomes are the psychological, emotional, or physiological conditions resulting from exposure to stressors, after accounting for the the moderators/mediators.

In a simplified model of the stress process, people's position in the social structure exposes them to stressors, which in turn leads to stress outcomes. Moderators and mediators primarily have effects between the stressors and the outcomes, and the social structure and the stressors. This simplified model hides the reciprocal relationships and agentic processes that exist in practice between stressors and moderators, outcomes and stressors, and also individually among stressors, moderators, and outcomes. Nonetheless it accurately represents the underlying connections among the key stress theory concepts (Pearlin 1999).

There are two broad categories of stressors: event stressors and chronic stressors. Event stressors include any sudden and generally unexpected phenomena that result in a stress outcome. Initial work measured the effect of an event stressor by the amount of change it required of an individual (i.e., the larger the magnitude, the more negative the outcome), but subsequent work has shown this to be a poor measure when taken on its own. In defining the effect of an event it is important to take into account whether or not the event was anticipated (e.g., retirement), whether it represents a closure of another stressor (e.g., divorce after a long period of litigation), or even whether the individual deliberately sought the event as a problem-solving strategy to other stressors (e.g., getting fired from a miserable job). Thus, research shows that seemingly negative life events may actually decrease the likelihood of having a negative stress outcome when considered in context of a person's other life course trajectory. In fact, current work embeds an understanding of life events (both positive and negative) within the life course framework of transitions, trajectories, and pathways.

Chronic stressors comprise a wide variety of stressors, including status strains, role strains, ambient strains, and quotidian strains. As their name suggests, status strains are stressors that arise out of a person's position in the social structure (e.g., living in abject poverty). Furthermore, the holding of a status that is stigmatized or devalued by society (e.g., a particular race, gender, sexuality, or religion) can also be a status strain. Role strains focus on the stressors that arise from conflicts or demands within an individual's role-set and they provide stress theory's key link between macro-level influences and individual outcomes. Initial research focused only on the negative effect of having many roles, arguing that they create competing demands on the individual, thus acting as stressors. Yet subsequent research has shown that under certain conditions having many roles can benefit the individual by providing more fungible resources that carry-over from one role to another. Ambient strains focus on the stressors that come from an individual's proximal environment, most often measured as their neighborhood. Here the focus is on threats of crime or violence, or on access to resources like schools, hospitals, fire departments, and other public services. Quotidian or daily strains are perceived to produce the lowest intensity stressors and arise out of the daily hassles of things like waiting in traffic, fighting for a spot on the subway, or cooking. Research suggests that the effect of these strains may stem more from the fact that they are repeated daily than from the individual stressors themselves.

It is important not just to know the types of stressors an individual faces, but also the timing and interrelationship of these stressors. Stressors rarely occur in isolation from one another. Often, some primary stressor leads to several secondary stressors, a process known as stress proliferation. When the sequence of stressors is considered in conjunction with a person's multiple roles, the concept of a carry-over effect is introduced, whereby stressors in one role domain or life stage may have impacts in other domains or stages. For example, facing multiple stressors in childhood may have consequences for adult mental health. Similarly, facing stressors at home may have consequences for anxiety levels at work. The study of sequencing is an increasingly important one in the sociological study of stress, as it can better account for the dynamic link between individuals and society as well as illuminate the long-term consequences of stressors that are often obscured by cross-sectional or short-term studies.

Related to the sequencing of stressors is the sequencing of life events, a concept that is a core component of life course theory. Stress researchers and life course researchers have been combining efforts to investigate how the sequencing of life events and transitions leads to both positive and negative outcomes. Two competing arguments exist as to why the timing of life events produces stressors. One argument is that there are societal norms for when certain transitions should be made relative to others and that when individuals deviate from these paths the society produces stressors. For example, in some societies it is a violation of social norms to have children outside of wedlock, thus if a woman violates this norm it may increase her likelihood of experiencing stressors. The other argument puts less emphasis on the violation of societal norms and more on the belief that certain sequences generate practical, objective obstacles, which in turn create stressors. For example, having a child outside of marriage normally necessitates being both a full-time parent and a full-time mother, something which may or may not generate stressors depending on other factors. In the end, this union of methods, theories, and concepts between life course theorists and stress theorists holds promise for understanding the role of the stress process over a much longer time horizon.

The second major component to the stress model is the role of moderators/mediators like coping strategies, personal resources, and social support. Coping strategies are the changes people make to their behavioral or psychological state in response to the stressors they encounter. Coping strategies may be focused on changing the situation that is causing the stressors (e.g., finding a new job after being fired), on preventing a stressor from occurring (e.g., marriage counseling to prevent divorce), on reinterpreting the stressors in a different light (e.g., looking at increased job responsibility as an opportunity instead of a burden), or on managing the stress outcomes (e.g., including meditation in one's daily routine). In order to make use of these coping strategies individuals need coping resources which can be either personal or social.

Personal resources include a sense of self-mastery or control over one's life and environment, as well as one's self-esteem. More of the research on personal resources has focused on self-mastery and less of it on self-esteem, but both have been shown to directly reduce the severity and prevalence of stress outcomes as both mediators and moderators. More work, however, still needs to be done to understand the interaction effect these personal resources have with social support and coping strategies, as well as their potential to condition the types of social support and coping strategies one receives.

Social support has been the most widely studied resource and continues to show strong, significant direct and buffering effects on stress outcomes. Social support comes chiefly in the forms of instrumental assistance, informational assistance, and emotional assistance from other people. Three major conclusions can be drawn from the literature on social support: (1) being a member of a closely knit group has direct positive mental health benefits, but does not act as a moderator on stress outcomes; (2) perceived emotional support (whether real or not) has both direct and buffering effects on the severity and significance of negative life events for stress outcomes; (3) having an intimate relationship that encourages confiding in one another has the largest effect on attenuating stress outcomes.

The biggest shortcoming with the work on social support is with how the concept is measured. Progress has been made in treating social support as a type of social network with defined measures of range, density, composition, and availability, but this is not standardized. Furthermore, it is largely measured only from the perspective of the individual under observation without acknowledging that these are reciprocal, social relationships. Along similar lines, future work on social support needs to consider the reciprocal relationship between support and stressors, as having too many stressors or too long a duration of stressors may lead to a weakening of one's social support network.

The final step in the stress process model is the stress outcome, which can be any health or mental health illness. Most often sociologists study generalized depression, anxiety, or drug/alcohol abuse, but there is a push to study the co-morbidity of multiple health and mental health outcomes. Aneshensel et al. (1991) were the first to note the importance of studying multiple outcomes in a single study. In their words, "single outcome studies ... are clearly inadequate for identifying the impact of social factors on overall psychological well-being across subgroups of the population." This conclusion is made all the more important given that one of the primary contributions of the sociological study of stress is its focus on the social distributions of mental health and well-being. Much more work is needed on this part of the stress model, but it promises to make an important contribution to researchers in fields outside of sociology.

SEE ALSO: Life Course Perspective; Role Theory; Social Support; Stress and Health; Stress and Migration; Stress and Work; Stressful Life Events

REFERENCES AND SUGGESTED READINGS

Aneshensel, C. S. (1992) Social Stress: Theory and Research. *Annual Review of Sociology* 18: 15–38.

Aneshensel, C. S., Rutter, C. M., & Lachenbruch, P. A. (1991) Social Structure, Stress, and Mental Health: Competing Conceptual and Analytic Models. *American Sociological Review* 56: 166–78.

Lazarus, R. S. & Folkman, S. (1984) *Stress, Appraisal and Coping.* Springer, New York.

Mirowsky, J. & Ross, C. E. (2003) *Social Causes of Psychological Distress*, 2nd edn. Aldine de Gruyter, New York.

Pearlin, L. I. (1989) The Sociological Study of Stress. *Journal of Health and Social Behavior* 30: 241–56.

Pearlin, L. I. (1999) The Stress Process Revisited. In: Aneshensel, C. S. & Phelan, J. C. (Eds.), *Handbook of Sociology of Mental Health.* Kluwer Academic/Plenum Publishers, New York, pp. 395–415.

Pearlin, L. I., Lieberman, M. A., Menaghan, E. G., & Mullan, J. T. (1981) The Stress Process. *Journal of Health and Social Behavior* 22: 337–56.

Thoits, P. A. (1995) Stress, Coping, and Social Support Processes: Where Are We? What Next? *Journal of Health and Social Behavior* 35: 53–79.

Turner, R. J. & Avison, W. R. (2003) Status Variations in Stress Exposure: Implications for the Interpretation of Research on Race, Socioeconomic

Status, and Gender. *Journal of Health and Social Behavior* 44(4): 488–505.

Wellman, B. (1992) Which Types of Ties and Networks Give What Kinds of Social Support? *Advances in Group Processes* 9: 207–35.

stress and work

Johannes Siegrist

While stress is a popular concept in everyday life that describes a feeling of pressure resulting from overload, it is also a scientific term of growing importance. In a scientific perspective, stress differs from the everyday notion in at least two important ways. First, stress defines a reaction to a challenge (stressor) from the external world or from within the organism that interrupts or threatens the usual behavior and normal functioning of a person and that requires specific efforts to meet the challenge. These efforts are termed coping. It is important to note that major stressors that are experienced in everyday life emerge from the social rather than the physical environment. Examples of such social stressors are interpersonal power, role obligations, competition between organizations, groups, or individuals, and social deprivation or inequality. Therefore, stress is an important sociological topic.

A second difference between everyday and scientific notions of stress concerns the distinction of several dimensions of a person's response to a stressor. In scientific terms, four dimensions of the stress response are distinguished: the cognitive, the affective or emotional, the physiological, and the behavioral response. At the cognitive level, a challenge is appraised according to its degree of threat or harm. This appraisal is paralleled by negative or positive affective responses. Most importantly, the experience of threat goes along with intense negative emotions of anger, irritation, or anxiety. At the physiological level, stress reactions elicit arousal of the organism through activation of the autonomic nervous system and the so-called stress hormones. Through this activation the person is prepared to adapt their behavior in terms of fight or flight. If the challenge is met by successful coping efforts, positive emotions of self-esteem and self-efficacy are experienced, and the organism recovers quickly. However, if an overwhelming challenge results in a defeat or in a chronic unresolved struggle, strong negative emotions and sustained autonomic activation are evoked that "get under the skin." In the long run they trigger bodily dysfunction and disease, such as cardiovascular disease, metabolic or gastrointestinal diseases, or affective disorders (Weiner 1992).

Work and employment belong to those core social circumstances that produce recurrent stress responses in exposed people. Therefore, the scientific inquiry into associations of stressful working conditions with health is considered a prominent topic of medical sociology. This subdiscipline of general sociology is in a unique position to bridge the social sciences with the biomedical sciences by combining sociological, psychological, and physiological information in epidemiological study designs. When analyzing associations of work-related stress with health one has to keep in mind that the nature of work has changed considerably over the past several decades in economically advanced societies. Industrial mass production no longer dominates the labor market. This is due in part to technological progress and to a growing number of jobs available in the service sector. Many jobs are confined to information processing, controlling, and coordination. Sedentary rather than physically strenuous work is becoming more and more dominant. New management techniques may be introduced, and economic constraints can produce work pressure, greater rationalization of tasks, and reduction in personnel. These changes go along with changes in the structure of the labor market. More employees are likely to work on temporary or fixed-term contracts, or in flexible job arrangements. Overemployment in some segments of the workforce is paralleled by underemployment, job instability, or structural unemployment in other segments. Overall, a substantial part of the economically active population is confined to insecure jobs, to premature retirement, or job loss.

Why is work so important for human wellbeing, and how does work contribute to the burden of stress and its adverse effects on health? In all advanced societies work and occupation in adult life are accorded primacy for the following reasons. First, having a job is a principal prerequisite for continuous income and thus for independence from traditional support systems (family, community welfare, etc.). Increasingly, level of income determines a wide range of life chances. Second, training for a job and achievement of occupational status are among the most important goals of socialization. It is through education, job training, and status acquisition that personal growth and development are realized, that a core social identity outside the family is acquired, and that goal-directed activity in human life is shaped. Third, occupation defines an important criterion of social stratification. Amount of esteem in interpersonal life largely depends on type of job and level of occupational achievement. Fourth, occupational settings produce the most persuasive continuous demands during one's lifetime, and they absorb the largest amount of active time in adult life, thus providing a source of recurrent negative or positive emotions. It is for these reasons that stress research in organizations where paid work takes place is of particular relevance.

There is now growing awareness among all parties of the labor market that stress at work produces considerable costs, most importantly a high level of absenteeism, reduced productivity, compensation claims, health insurance, and direct medical expenses. Permanent disability and loss of productive life years due to premature death add to this burden. At the same time, scientific evidence on associations between stress at work and health is growing rapidly. This research differs from traditional biomedical occupational health research by the fact that social stressors cannot be identified by direct physical or chemical measurements. Rather, theoretical models are needed that aim at identifying the "toxic" components of stressful work within the complexities and diversities of occupational settings. Ideally, such a sociological model has rather general explanatory power and can be applied to a wide range of different working conditions. With its focus on the social reality of work it may identify specific occupational risk groups and thus explain the burden of work-related illness above and beyond individual susceptibility.

During the past 30 years, several sociological models of work stress have been developed and tested. The "person–environment–fit" approach was probably the first one of these models (Caplan et al. 1980; Cooper 1998; Dunham 2000). More recently, two such concepts received special attention in health-related research: the "demand-control" and the "effort-reward imbalance" models (Karasek & Theorell 1990; Siegrist & Marmot 2004).

The demand-control model is based upon the premise that stress at work occurs when there is high psychological work demand in combination with a low degree of task control. Low control at work is defined in terms of low level of decision latitude (authority over decisions) and a low level of skill utilization. Job task profiles characterized by high demand and low control are assumed to evoke recurrent stress responses among those exposed. Conversely, demanding jobs that offer a high level of decision latitude and skill utilization promote personal growth and thus may be beneficial to health. More recently, the two-dimensional demand-control model was modified to include a third dimension, social support at work. If social support at work is available, it may act as an interpersonal coping resource to buffer the adverse effects of stress on health. On the other hand, high demand/low control conditions at work were shown to produce highest levels of stress reactions among those who work in social isolation or who suffer from inadequate social support.

The effort-reward imbalance model is concerned with contractual fairness at work. It assumes that effort at work is spent as part of a contract based on the norm of social reciprocity where rewards are provided in terms of money, esteem, and career opportunities, including job security. Work contracts often fail to be fully specified and to provide a symmetric exchange between requested efforts and given rewards. In particular, this is the case when there are few or no alternative employment opportunities for the employees. Additional conditions of nonequivalent exchange were identified by the model, including a personal pattern of coping with work demands ("overcommitment"). Non-symmetric work contracts are expected to be frequent in a global economy characterized by job insecurity, forced occupational mobility, short-term contracts, and increased wage competition. The model of effort-reward imbalance claims that lack of reciprocity between the costs and gains (i.e., high cost/low gain condition) elicits recurrent stress reactions due to obvious violation of a basic norm of social exchange, reciprocity. In the long run, the negative emotions that parallel these stress reactions result in increased risks of ill-health and disease. These two models of stress at work complement each other. They offer opportunities for combining information on work stress and health, as conditions of low control and low reward often occur simultaneously in the same work environments.

Evidence of reduced health due to exposure to the social stressors that are defined by the two models is growing rapidly. Overall, prospective epidemiological investigations found a twofold elevated risk of a number of physical and mental disorders among employees working under high demand/low control or high effort/low reward conditions. Elevated risks were documented for coronary heart disease and cardiovascular mortality, for depression, for type II-diabetes, and for alcohol dependence. Although some of the prospective findings seem to be restricted to men, they are not confined to a specific occupational group. Rather, work stress is found to affect the health of employees in industrial as well as in service and administrative occupations and professions. Currently available prospective evidence is supplemented by a large body of data derived from cross-sectional investigations, case-control studies, and experimental findings testing the two work stress models. For instance, higher rates of sickness absence, musculoskeletal disorders, health-adverse behaviors (e.g., smoking), and biomedical cardiovascular risk factors (high blood pressure, elevated blood lipids, and fibrinogen) were observed in association with high demand/low control or effort/reward imbalance (Schnall et al. 2000). Finally, in search of psychobiological mechanisms linking exposure to social stressors with illness susceptibility, elevated levels of stress hormones, reduced competence of the body's immune system, and reduced heart rate variability were documented.

These findings of health-related sociological research have policy implications, given the fact that up to one third of a country's workforce may be exposed to conditions of work-related stress that were identified by the two models.

Moreover, a risk factor that doubles the incidence of frequent disorders, such as cardiovascular disease, depression, or musculo-skeletal disorders, calls for increased preventive efforts. Health promoting improvements of quality of work require specific measures of organizational and personnel development that can be derived from the theoretical models. Concerning the demand-control model they include job redesign in terms of increased autonomy, skill discretion, job enlargement, and enhanced participation. Provision of compensatory wage systems and models of gain sharing, strengthening of non-monetary gratifications (e.g., through leadership training), and ways of improving promotional opportunities and job security are measures derived from the effort-reward imbalance model. Clearly, the power of economic life and the constraints of globalization limit the options and range of worksite health promotion measures. Such measures need to be supplemented by more comprehensive interorganizational and governmental activities that aim at reducing the gap between scientific evidence and policy development. Research on work stress and health illustrates the promising contribution sociology can make to this end.

SEE ALSO: Stress and Health; Stress, Stress Theories; Stressful Life Events

REFERENCES AND SUGGESTED READINGS

Caplan, R. D., Cobb, S., French, J. R. P., Harrison, R. V., & Pinneau, S. R. (1980) *Job Demand and Worker Health: Main Effects and Occupational Differences*. Institute for Social Research, Ann Arbor, MI.

Cooper, C. L. (Ed.) (1998) *Theories of Organizational Stress*. Oxford University Press, Oxford.

Dunham, J. (Ed.) (2000) *Stress in the Workplace: Past, Present and Future*. Worth, London.

Karasek, R. A. & Theorell, T. (1990) *Healthy Work: Stress, Productivity, and the Reconstruction of Working Life*. Basic Books, New York.

Schnall, P. L., Belkic, K., Landsbergis, P., & Baker, D. (Eds.) (2000) The Workplace and Cardiovascular Disease. *Occupational Medicine: State of the Art Reviews* 15: 1–334.

Siegrist, J. & Marmot, M. (2004) Health Inequalities and the Psychosocial Environment: Two

Scientific Challenges. *Social Science & Medicine* 58: 1463–73.

Weiner, H. (1992) *Perturbing the Organism: The Biology of Stressful Experience*. Chicago University Press, Chicago.

stressful life events

William R. Avison

Stressful life events are discrete social experiences or life changes that require individual adjustment or manifest themselves in emotional arousal or physical reactions. The defining characteristic of life events as stressors is that they are observable life changes that have relatively clear onsets and endings. This quality of discreteness distinguishes stressful life events from chronic stressors that typically have more insidious onsets and whose conclusions are less easily demarcated. Chronic stressors tend also to have longer time courses than life events.

Interest in the relationship between stressful life events and health can be traced to Hans Selye's biological research which concluded that events that constitute a threat to the organism produce a series of responses, some of which are adaptive and others of which are maladaptive. Wheaton (1994) argued that an engineering model of stress may be more useful conceptually to social science researchers because it conceives of stress as an external force or pressure that exceeds the capacity to adjust. Both formulations distinguish between relatively discrete or eventful stressors and more continuous, ongoing challenges or threats.

The early work of Thomas Holmes and Robert Rahe in developing a life events checklist (the Social Readjustment Rating Scale) stimulated much of the subsequent research on stressful life events and their consequences for mental health and illness. Their inventory of life events generated a substantial body of subsequent research that took two distinctive directions. Dohrenwend and Dohrenwend (1974) led the way in further developing and refining life events inventories to address contextual effects and the problem of intra-event variability. Their approach retained the life events checklist method but elaborated this approach with additional probes and editing procedures that addressed problems of measurement. Their work focused on the importance of stressful life events as mediators of the relationship between social status and mental health problems. George Brown's approach (Brown & Harris 1989) has been to focus on the psychological meaning of life events by conducting in-depth interviews that focus on the strong emotions that life events produce. Although these two approaches differ substantially in method and emphasis, both have stimulated a wealth of research that documents the association between the experience of stressful life events and a wide range of mental health outcomes.

Despite the early excitement among researchers that the experience of stressful life events might constitute an important determinant of mental health problems, several researchers observed that the magnitude of the association between stressful life events and mental health outcomes was relatively small. This observation generated a vast body of research that attempted to explain how the theoretically compelling association between stressful life events and mental health could be so modest empirically. A number of important conclusions have emerged from this research.

There is substantial evidence of variability in stressful life events both in terms of the events themselves and the social contexts in which they occur. A number of researchers have addressed the issue of intra-event variability by incorporating probe questions in checklists in order to better specify the nature of stressors. From a sociological perspective, a more important development has been the recognition that stressful life events occur in different social contexts. Brown's work has been important in understanding how individuals' life experiences around the occurrence of stressful life events condition their meaning and emotional impact. Other researchers have documented how biographical histories influence the experience of events and how community contexts modify the impact of stressors on mental health. Still others have demonstrated how certain circumstances lead to stress proliferation and how some stressors amplify the effects of other life events on symptoms of mental illness.

In the 1980s there was substantial interest in the possibility that the modest association of stressful life events with symptoms of mental illness might be due to the differential vulnerability, responsiveness, or susceptibility of more disadvantaged social groups to stressors. The sources of this differential vulnerability were hypothesized to be group differences in social resources such as social support, in more personal resources such as mastery or coping capacity, or in other susceptibilities including biophysiological differences. Over time, sociologists have largely concluded that there is little evidence for the hypothesis of differential vulnerability. When exposure to stressors is measured comprehensively and when a wide array of mental health outcomes are considered, social group differences in vulnerability appear to be less important in accounting for variation in mental health outcomes than are differences in exposure to stressors.

These findings have had important implications for a broader conceptualization of the domain of stress. Wheaton (1994) has argued for a much more elaborate stress universe that supplements standard life events checklists with measures of chronic stressors, traumatic experiences in childhood and adolescence, and daily hassles. Subsequent research suggests that consideration of a much broader array of stressors reveals a much more robust association between stressors and mental health than can be observed for stressful life events alone. Moreover, research shows that reliance only on measures of stressful life events may underestimate social group variations in exposure to stress.

Perhaps the most important contribution that sociologists have made to the study of stressful life events and mental health is to document how individuals' positions in the social structure of society profoundly affect their experience of social stressors that ultimately manifest themselves in symptoms of mental illness. Pearlin (1989) clearly articulated this in outlining his vision of the sociological study of stress. Since then, many sociologists have documented how variations in social status and role occupancy are associated with differential exposure to stressful experience.

Another noteworthy development in the sociological study of stress is the incorporation of the life course perspective. Sociologists have increasingly argued for the importance of considering the impact of stressful life experiences on mental health over the life course. The theoretical rationale for this has been specified by Pearlin and Skaff (1996) and George (1999).

The challenge for future sociological research on stressful life events is to integrate concepts and ideas from the broader sociological discipline so that we can better specify the interplay among social structure, stress, and health. In this way, the importance of stress in social life will be better understood.

SEE ALSO: Aging, Mental Health and Well-Being; Mental Disorder; Social Epidemiology; Stress and Health; Stress and Migration; Stress, Stress Theories; Stress and Work

REFERENCES AND SUGGESTED READINGS

Aneshensel, C. S. (1992) Social Stress: Theory and Research. *Annual Review of Sociology* 18: 15–38.

Brown, G. W. & Harris, T. (1989) *Life Events and Illness*. Guilford Press, New York.

Dohrenwend, B. S. & Dohrenwend, B. P. (Eds.) (1974) *Stressful Life Events: Their Nature and Effects*. Wiley, New York.

Elder, G. H., Jr., George, L. K., & Shanahan, M. J. (1995) Psychosocial Stress Over the Life Course. In: Kaplan, H. B. (Ed.), *Psychosocial Stress: Perspectives on Structure, Theory, Life-Course, and Methods*. Academic Press, New York, pp. 247–92.

George, L. K. (1999) Life-Course Perspectives on Mental Health. In: Aneshensel, C. S. & Phelan, J. C. (Eds.), *Handbook of the Sociology of Mental Health*. Kluwer Academic/Plenum, New York, pp. 565–83.

Pearlin, L. I. (1989) The Sociological Study of Stress. *Journal of Health and Social Behavior* 30: 241–56.

Pearlin, L. I. & Skaff, M. M. (1996) Stress and the Life Course: A Paradigmatic Alliance. *Gerontologist* 36: 239–47.

Turner, R. J., Wheaton, B., & Lloyd, D. A. (1995) The Epidemiology of Social Stress. *American Sociological Review* 60: 104–25.

Turner, R. J. & Avison, W. R. (2003) Status Variations in Stress Exposure: Implications for the Interpretation of Research on Race, Socioeconomic

Status, and Gender. *Journal of Health and Social Behavior* 44: 488–505.

Wheaton, B. (1994) The Stress Universe. In: Avison, W. R. & Gotlib, I. H. (Eds.), *Stress and Mental Health: Contemporary Issues and Prospects for the Future.* Plenum, New York, pp. 77–114.

strong objectivity

Nancy A. Naples

The notion of strong objectivity was first articulated by feminist philosopher Sandra Harding. Strong objectivity builds on the insights of feminist standpoint theory, which argues for the importance of starting from the experiences of those who have been traditionally left out of the production of knowledge. By starting inquiry from the lived experiences of women and others who have been traditionally outside of the institutions in which knowledge about social life is generated and classified, more objective and more relevant knowledge can be produced. In fact, Harding (1986) and Hartsock (1983) argue that knowledge produced from the point of view of subordinated groups may offer stronger objectivity due to the increased motivation for them to understand the views or perspectives of those in positions of power.

A scholar who approaches the research process from the point of view of strong objectivity is interested in producing knowledge for use as well as for revealing the relations of power that are hidden in traditional knowledge production processes. Strong objectivity acknowledges that the production of power is a political process and that greater attention paid to the context and social location of knowledge producers will contribute to a more ethical and transparent result. In fact, Harding (1991) argues, an approach to research and knowledge production that does not acknowledge the role that power and social location play in the knowledge production process must be understood as offering only a weak form of objectivity.

Another aspect of traditional approaches to science and knowledge production that contributes to a weak form of objectivity is found in the move to greater and greater generalization.

As a result, material reality is replaced with abstractions that bear little resemblance to the phenomenon originally under examination. Smith (1987), another scholar who has contributed to the development of standpoint theory, explains that the traditional androcentric approach to sociology that privileges a white, middle-class, and heterosexual point of view produces results that are both alienating and colonizing (see Stanley 1990). Harding (1998) has been especially concerned with the role of colonization in marginalizing the situated knowledges of the targets of colonization. Western science has developed through the exploitation and silencing of colonial subjects. In this way, much useful knowledge has been lost or rendered suspect (see Sachs 1996). Strong objectivity involves acknowledging the political, social, and historical aspects of all knowledge (Longino 1993). The strongest approach to knowledge production is one that takes into account the most diverse set of experiences.

Reflexivity is another practice that contributes to strong objectivity. Harding argues for a self-reflexive approach to theorizing in order to foreground how relations of power may be shaping the production of knowledge in different contexts (also see Naples 2003). The point of view of all those involved in the knowledge production process must be acknowledged and taken into account in order to produce strong objectivity. In this way, knowledge production should involve a collective process, rather than the individualistic, top-down, and distanced approach that typifies the traditional scientific method. For Harding (1991), strong objectivity involves analysis of the relationship between both the subject and object of inquiry. This approach contrasts with traditional scientific method that either denies this relationship or seeks to achieve control over it. However, as Harding and other standpoint theorists point out, an approach to research that produces a more objective approach acknowledges the partial and situated nature of all knowledge production (also see Hartsock 1983; Haraway 1988; Collins 1990).

Postmodern critics of this approach point out that the goal of producing a strong objectivity replicates the limitations of traditional scientific methods, namely, privileging one or more accounts as most "accurate" or true (Hekman

1992). Postmodern theorists argue that all social positions are fluid. Such fluidity makes it impossible to identify individual knowers who can represent any particular social group. Furthermore, they insist, the search for truth, even one that is partial, is fraught with marginalizing other accounts. However, those who adopt the stance of strong objectivity argue that it can avoid the "arrogant aspirations of modernist epistemology" (Longino 1993: 212).

SEE ALSO: Black Feminist Thought; Feminist Methodology; Feminist Standpoint Theory; Materialist Feminisms; Matrix of Domination; Objectivity; Outsider-Within; Postmodern Feminism; Reflexivity; Subjectivity

REFERENCES AND SUGGESTED READINGS

Collins, P. H. (1990) *Black Feminist Thought: Knowledge, Consciousness, and the Politics of Empowerment.* Unwin Hyman, Boston.
Haraway, D. (1988) Situated Knowledges: The Science Question in Feminism and the Privilege of Partial Perspective. *Feminist Studies* 14(3): 575–99.
Harding, S. (1986) *The Science Question in Feminism.* Cornell University Press, Ithaca, NY.
Harding, S. (1991) *Whose Science? Whose Knowledge?* Cornell University Press, Ithaca, NY.
Harding, S. (1998) *Is Science Multicultural? Postcolonialisms, Feminisms, and Epistemologies.* Indiana University Press, Bloomington.
Harding, S. (2003) *The Feminist Standpoint Theory Reader: Intellectual and Political Controversies.* Routledge, New York.
Hartsock, N. (1983) *Money, Sex, and Power: Toward a Feminist Historical Materialism.* Longman, New York.
Hekman, S. J. (1992) *Gender and Knowledge: Elements of a Postmodern Feminism.* Northeastern University Press, Boston.
Longino, H. E. (1993) Feminist Standpoint Theory and the Problems of Knowledge. *Signs: Journal of Women in Culture and Society* 19(1): 201–12.
Naples, N. A. (2003) *Feminism and Method: Ethnography, Discourse Analysis, and Activist Research.* Routledge, New York.
Sachs, C. (1996) *Gendered Fields: Rural Women, Agriculture, and Environment.* Westview, Boulder, CO.
Smith, D. E. (1987) *The Everyday World as Problematic: A Feminist Sociology.* University of Toronto Press, Toronto.
Smith, D. E. (1990) *Conceptual Practices of Power.* Northeastern University Press, Boston.
Stanley, L. (Ed.) (1990) *Feminist Praxis: Research, Theory, and Epistemology in Feminist Sociology.* Routledge, New York.

Strong Program

Lena Eriksson

The Strong Program is a programmatic statement that calls upon social scientists to examine the social content and underpinnings of scientific knowledge. It played an important part in the wider development of the field of sociology of scientific knowledge. The Strong Program originated from the so-called Edinburgh school in the mid-1970s and was most famously set out by David Bloor in his 1976 book, *Knowledge and Social Imagery.* Bloor was part of a group of sociologists and historians based in the University of Edinburgh who proposed that social scientists should treat and analyze scientific knowledge claims as they would any other type of knowledge claims: as knowledge constructed and located in a specific societal framework. The Strong Program was inspired by Wittgenstein's argument about rules, which states that to apply a rule, or a taxonomy, or a term, a judgment of similarity or difference is needed. The Edinburgh group introduced the concept of *finitism* to argue for why the content of scientific knowledge could not, and should not, be exempt from sociological analysis. No two cases or events are ever "the same," or "not the same," without a human decision about similarity or difference.

Scientific knowledge claims had hitherto been excluded from sociological analysis – it was considered to be a unique type of knowledge derived by special means. The way in which scientists arrived at their conclusions, via systematic empirical study, granted such knowledge a special status. Scientific knowledge was seen as the simple result of our observations of nature; inextricably linked to that nature by force of the scientific method. Thus, while one could conduct interesting sociological analysis of the circumstances that surround scientific knowledge production, such as Robert Merton's famous studies of scientific institutions, the actual *content* of scientific knowledge was seen as exempt from any social influences. The Strong Program challenged this assumption and instead argued that no distinction should be made between natural knowledge and other types of knowledge. Thus, all knowledge claims should be treated as material for sociological investigation and explanation.

The most well-known part of the Strong Program is the four tenets of causality, impartiality, symmetry, and reflexivity. The tenet of causality is concerned with the conditions that will enable or give rise to a certain belief or state of knowledge. Just as we look for causality in nature, we should systematically examine the causes and conditions that bring about our knowledge about the natural world. One example of such causal conditions could be wider political structures. Many analysts working within the framework of the Strong Program during the 1970s and 1980s invoked external interests of particular groups to explain internal states of knowledge. One pivotal study by historian Steven Shapin correlated the rise of phrenology in Edinburgh during the 1820s with the interests of a burgeoning middle class whose status and legitimacy were boosted by the idea of biological heritage over that of inherited privilege. Such scientific theories were resisted by an upper class, mainly represented by the Royal Society, whose power and legitimacy depended on the idea that ability and fitness to rule were class-dependent.

The tenet of impartiality states that the analyst should examine all beliefs on an equal basis, regardless of whether they are held to be true or false, rational or irrational. This requirement overlaps with the third tenet, that of symmetry. The tenet of symmetry is the most well-known feature of the Strong Program and is perhaps also its lasting legacy in the field of science studies today. Symmetry means that all knowledge claims should be explained in the same way and with the same methods, e.g., in terms of their social causes and by means of detailed empirical investigation. This should be done regardless of their societal status as "true" or "false." Beliefs held to be irrational thus warrant the same level of attention by the sociologist as rational beliefs would. Furthermore, they should be treated and explained by reference to their social causes and conditions, without reference to "nature." Our beliefs about nature are the objects of sociological investigation, and the argument would thus become circular if those beliefs were explained by reference to themselves.

Bloor uses the metaphor of a train crash – it is when things go wrong that we tend to look for "the human factor." Perfectly functioning train services are, of course, as "social" as the ones that go wrong, but we never launch investigations into why trains do not crash. We exempt seemingly unproblematic events from sociological investigation. Social science analysis that explains knowledge or beliefs thought to be false or irrational with reference to its social production, but leaves claims held to be true and rational as in no need of sociological attention, is referred to as a "sociology of error."

Finally, the tenet of reflexivity means that the same types and patterns of explanations should and must be applicable to sociology itself. Sociology does not think of itself as standing apart from other types of knowledge production, and is therefore as viable a material for sociological investigation as any other type of knowledge claim.

The Strong Program has been criticized for containing an inherent asymmetry, as scientific knowledge is explained by reference to social interests, but the social interests themselves are taken as "real" and stable entities. Another weak point is the so-called "problem of imputation" – how do you first identify, for example, a class interest and then show that this is directly linked to a given aspect of scientific belief?

Even though few people today would identify themselves as followers of the Strong Program, its legacy in the wider field of science studies is well recognized and the tenet of symmetry still holds sway, both as a methodological principle and as a theoretical position.

SEE ALSO: Knowledge, Sociology of; Laboratory Studies and the World of the Scientific Lab; Merton, Robert K.; Science, Social Construction of

REFERENCES AND SUGGESTED READINGS

Bloor, D. (1991 [1976]) *Knowledge and Social Imagery*. University of Chicago Press, Chicago.

Merton, R. K. (1973) *The Sociology of Science: Theoretical and Empirical Investigations*. Ed. N. W. Storer. University of Chicago Press, Chicago.

Shapin, S. (1975) Phrenological Knowledge and the Social Structure of Early Nineteenth-Century Edinburgh. *Annals of Science* 32: 219–43.

Wittgenstein, L. (1958) *Philosophical Investigations*. Blackwell, Oxford.

structural equation modeling

Xitao Fan

Structural equation modeling (SEM) has witnessed an exponential growth in its application in social and behavioral science research in the last two decades. Because of its versatility, SEM has been heralded as a unified model that joins methods from econometrics, psychometrics, sociometrics, and multivariate statistics (Bentler 1994). Many statistical techniques can be considered as special cases of SEM, including regression analysis, canonical correlation analysis, confirmatory factor analysis, and path analysis (Bentler 1992; Fan 1996; Jöreskog & Sörbom 2001).

Several aspects of SEM distinguish it from other multivariate procedures (e.g., multivariate analysis of variance, exploratory factor analysis). Unlike other multivariate techniques, SEM takes a *confirmatory* rather than an exploratory approach. The pattern of relations among variables is specified a priori based on theoretical expectations. This characteristic of SEM lends itself especially well to testing theoretical models.

Many researchers in social sciences are familiar with the traditional path analysis for modeling causal relationships. The major weaknesses of path analysis are (1) all variables are assumed to have been measured *without* error;

(2) there is a lack of statistical mechanisms for testing the model–data fit. The assumption that variables are measured without error is obviously unrealistic, because measurement error is the norm in social sciences. Path analysis only describes "causal" relationships among observed variables, and it is not capable of dealing with latent constructs represented by multiple observed indicators. The lack of model–data fit test also imposes a major limitation on the use of path analysis.

Confirmatory factor analysis (CFA) is a submodel (measurement model) of SEM. In measurement practice, a subscale may consist of multiple items (or item composites) as its observed indicators, and an instrument may consist of multiple subscales. Substantively, the subscales often represent different constructs (or latent variables), and these subscales, or latent variables, are often correlated to some degree. Because CFA as a submodel of SEM describes the relationships between measured indicators and latent constructs, and those among the latent constructs themselves, it is particularly useful for construct validation in instrument development.

The distinction among path analysis, CFA, and SEM can be characterized as follows: path analysis examines the "causal links" among observed variables; confirmatory factor analysis examines "causal links" from constructs (factors, latent variables) to their respective observed indicators; and structural equation modeling examines the "causal links" among the latent constructs and those from the latent constructs to their respective indicators. In SEM analysis, a variable is either exogenous or endogenous. An exogenous variable (observed or latent) "gives" effect to other variable(s) in the model, but itself does not "receive" effect from any variable in the model. An endogenous variable "receives" effect from other variable(s) in the model, and it may also "give" effect to other variable(s) in the model. Statistically, the variation in an endogenous variable is assumed to be accounted for by the model (i.e., by other variables in the model), while the variation in an exogenous variable is assumed to be accounted for by something outside of the model. A hypothetical structural equation model is graphically represented in Figure 1.

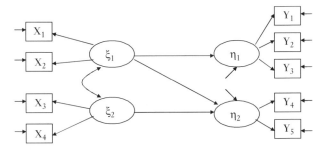

Figure 1   A hypothetical SEM model.

The prerequisite for conducting SEM analysis is to construct a model (e.g., Fig. 1) that represents the theoretical expectations about the data structure (i.e., relationships among the variables). The parameter value of each coefficient in the model will either be specified (i.e., equal to a specific value, including zero) or estimated from sample data. Once the model (including all its path coefficients) is specified, the sample data are used to test the fit of the model–data fit. First, the unspecified parameters are estimated based on an estimation method (e.g., maximum likelihood estimation, generalized least squares). Then the parameter estimates, both those specified by the researcher and those estimated from sample data, are used to reproduce the *model-implied covariance matrix*. The model-implied covariance matrix is compared against the original sample covariance matrix to see how much difference there is between the two matrices. The difference between the two covariance matrices is quantified as the "minimal fit function," and this fit function is translated to a χ^2 (chi-squared) statistic for testing model–data fit. A small difference between the two matrices suggests that the model fits the data well, while a large difference leads to the rejection of the model for its poor fit to the sample data.

Unlike most statistical tests (e.g., *t*-test, regression), in SEM analysis model degrees of freedom (*df*) are based not on sample size but on the difference between the number of unique elements in the sample covariance matrix and the number of parameters to be estimated in the model. For k variables, the number of unique elements in the covariance matrix is $k(k+1)/2$, and we have $df = k(k + 1)/2 -$ (# estimated parameters).

Although testing model–data fit in SEM appears conceptually straightforward, in practice considerable uncertainty and subjectivity often arise. Statistically, the test for model–data fit is the χ^2 test, with the null hypothesis being that the model fits the data. Rejection of the null hypothesis indicates that our theoretical model is not statistically consistent with sample data. Unlike most hypothesis-testing situations, in SEM we usually want to see that the null hypothesis is not rejected. However, statistical significance is heavily influenced by sample size, and SEM is a large-sample technique (Boomsma 1987; Bentler 1998; Jöreskog & Sörbom 2001). Because large sample size results in high statistical power, it is not surprising that, when sample size is large, the χ^2 test may declare a model as having poor fit, even though the model-implied covariance matrix differs minimally from the sample covariance matrix, and the model makes strong substantive sense.

The dissatisfaction with the χ^2 test led to the mushrooming of many goodness-of-fit indices for assessing model–data fit. These fit indices are generally descriptive, in contrast to the inferential nature of the χ^2 test. However, there is a lack of consensus regarding which one(s) to use for decision-making. To get a sense of this variety of indices, one can take a look at the types of fit indices provided by a typical SEM software package (e.g., LISREL, AMOS, SAS/CALIS).

For most social science researchers without sophisticated quantitative training, it is difficult to have a good understanding of all the differences/nuances among the fit indices. However, it is generally advised that information from three sources should be considered in considering model–data fit: (1) χ^2 test; (2) some fit indices (e.g., TLI, RMSEA, SRMR, CFI); (3) the fitted covariance matrix residuals (the difference between the sample and the model-implied covariance matrices). As discussed by many (e.g., Jöreskog & Sörbom 2001), relying solely on one index (especially the χ^2 test) may cloud one's judgment. Although there have been some interesting developments in this area (Hu & Bentler 1998, 1999) in specifying cutoff criteria of fit indices in model–data fit assessment, the issues are still far from being settled (Marsh et al. 2004).

Appropriate application of SEM depends partially on whether some basic assumptions have been met. In SEM application, it is assumed that the variables involved have a multivariate normal distribution. This assumption is relevant because, under typical SEM estimation procedures (maximum likelihood, generalized least squares), the χ^2 test and the standard error estimation in SEM are sensitive to departure from multivariate normality. If this assumption is not met, "the statistical basis of the method is lost and standard errors and chi-square tests have little meaning" (Bentler 1982: 421). When there is evidence that the data depart considerably from multivariate normality, one of several approaches can be taken. First, we may use estimation methods that do not require multivariate normality (e.g., asymptotic distribution-free, or ADF). Alternatively, a test statistic corrected for the effect of data nonnormality can be used (e.g., the Satorra-Bentler scaled χ^2 test), and standard errors corrected for the effect of data non-normality can also be obtained. More recently, the bootstrap method has also been advocated as an empirical approach for dealing with the data non-normality issue in SEM application (e.g., Byrne 2001).

Statistically, the data covariance matrix should be used for SEM analysis. Statistical theories for the estimation methods (e.g., maximum likelihood, generalized least squares) were developed for covariance matrices

(i.e., unstandardized variables), but not for correlation matrices (i.e., standardized variables). As discussed in SEM literature (e.g., Cudeck 1989; Loehlin 1998; Jöreskog & Sörbom 2001), using correlation matrix in SEM analysis may be problematic in several aspects, such as unintentional alteration of the model being tested due to scale changes caused by converting covariance matrix to correlation matrix, possible incorrect χ^2 test and other fit indices, and possible incorrect standard errors for parameter estimates. In practice, the correlation matrix is sometimes substituted for the covariance matrix to circumvent the interpretation problem caused by different measurement scales of the observed variables (Loehlin 1998). This strategy may be deemed acceptable in some practical situations, but it should not be considered as the norm. It would be preferable for the covariance matrix to be analyzed whenever possible. The interpretational difficulty caused by different measurement scales can be compensated by producing a standardized solution, an available option in all SEM software packages.

In SEM application, the model fitted to the data represents a researcher's theoretical expectation about the data structure, and it is typically desirable that the model is not statistically rejected. The power to reject the model, however, increases with the sample size. Statistical theory underlying SEM is such that, for the χ^2 test to be valid, it is assumed that the sample size is sufficiently large. Although there is no rule of thumb about what sample size is sufficiently large, sample size of a couple of hundred (e.g., Boomsma 1987) is usually considered as the minimum, and should be considered in light of the complexity of the model (Floyd & Widaman 1995). The requirement for a sufficiently large sample in SEM application creates a dilemma: large sample size increases the power of the test, and as a result small discrepancies between the model and data tend to lead to the rejection of the model.

In SEM application, the model–data fit may be found to be inadequate, and it may be tempting to modify the model to achieve better model–data fit. SEM computer programs also routinely provide "modification indices" that pinpoint possible model change(s) that lead to better model–data fit. Before revising the theoretical model, it is important to understand the consequences of such post hoc model modification. First, a distinct advantage of SEM is its confirmatory approach. Post hoc model modification may transform the confirmatory approach of SEM into an exploratory analysis. Statistically, it is always possible to obtain better model–data fit by continuously modifying our model, with or without the guidance of substantive theory (Cliff 1983). Second, sample data always contain some idiosyncrasies due to sampling error. In fitting a model to sample data, what we want to obtain is a model that will fit future similar data well, not just to obtain good fit for this particular sample. As Loehlin (1998: 195) discussed, researchers want "genuine improvement in measurement or theory, not just a procedure for decreasing chi-square." If modifications are not based on theoretical considerations, it is very likely that the model revision will capitalize on sample data idiosyncrasies, and the model fit improvement cannot hold for different sample data.

This concern naturally leads to model validation. In research practice, if model modifications are made based on either statistical or substantive considerations, it is imperative that cross-validation be carried out with independent sample data to make sure that the improved model fit is not just the result of sample data idiosyncrasies. Ideally, the cross-validation should be carried out in a new sample. In practice, if the original sample is reasonably large, the model validation issue can be readily accommodated by randomly splitting the original sample into two independent data sets: one used for fitting the initial model and making necessary modifications, and the other used for testing the revised model.

A variety of statistical software packages are available for implementing SEM analysis, such as LISREL, EQS, AMOS, Mplus, SAS/CALIS, SYSTAT, and Mx. These programs typically offer considerable flexibility in conducting SEM analysis, and a researcher's choice of a particular program is usually based on personal preference.

SEE ALSO: Correlation; Factor Analysis; General Linear Model; Latent Growth Curve Models; Methods, Bootstrap; Multivariate Analysis; Path Analysis; Regression and Regression Analysis

REFERENCES AND SUGGESTED READINGS

Bentler, P. M. (1982) Confirmatory Factor Analysis via Noniterative Estimation: A Fast, Inexpensive Method. *Journal of Marketing Research* 19: 417–24.

Bentler, P. M. (1994) Forward. In: Byrne, B. M. (Ed.), *Structural Equation Modeling with EQS and EQS/Windows*. Sage, Thousand Oaks, CA.

Bentler, P. M. (1998) *EQS: Structural Equations Program Manual*. BMDP Statistical Software, Los Angeles.

Bollen, K. A. (1989) *Structural Equations with Latent Variables*. Wiley, New York.

Boomsma, A. (1987) The Robustness of Maximum Likelihood Estimation in Structural Equation Models. In: Cuttance, P. & Ecob, R. (Eds.), *Structural Modeling by Example: Applications in Educational, Sociological, and Behavioral Research*. Cambridge University Press, New York, pp. 160–88.

Byrne, B. M. (2001) *Structural Equation Modeling with AMOS: Basic Concepts, Applications, and Programming*. Lawrence Erlbaum, Mahwah, NJ.

Cliff, N. (1983) Some Cautions Concerning the Application of Causal Modeling Methods. *Multivariate Behavioral Research* 18: 115–26.

Cudeck, R. (1989) Analysis of Correlation Matrices Using Covariance Structure Models. *Psychological Bulletin* 105: 317–27.

Fan, X. (1996) Structural Equation Modeling and Canonical Correlation Analysis: What Do They Have In Common? *Structural Equation Modeling* 4: 64–78.

Floyd, F. J. & Widaman, K. F. (1995) Factor Analysis in the Development and Refinement of Clinical Assessment Instrument. *Psychological Assessment* 7: 286–99.

Hu, L. & Bentler, P. M. (1998) Fit Indices in Covariance Structure Modeling: Sensitivity to Underparameterized Model Misspecification. *Psychological Methods* 3: 424–53.

Hu, L. & Bentler, P. M. (1999) Cutoff Criteria for Fit Indexes in Covariance Structure Analysis: Conventional Criteria versus New Alternatives. *Structural Equation Modeling* 6: 1–55.

Jöreskog, K. G. & Sörbom, D. (2001) *LISREL 8: User's Reference Guide*. SSI Scientific Software International, Lincolnwood, IL.

Loehlin, J. C. (1998) *Latent Variable Models: An Introduction to Factor, Path, and Structural Analysis*, 3rd edn. Lawrence Erlbaum, Mahwah, NJ.

Marsh, H. W., Hau, K. T., & Wen, Z. (2004) In Search of Golden Rules: Comment on Hypothesis-Testing Approaches to Setting Cutoff Values for Fit Indexes and Dangers in Overgeneralizing Hu and Bentler's (1999) Findings. *Structural Equation Modeling* 11: 320–41.

structural functional theory

Jeffrey W. Lucas

Structural functional theory holds that society is best understood as a complex system with various interdependent parts that work together to increase stability. For most of the twentieth century the structural functional perspective (also called functionalism) was the dominant sociological approach in the US and Western Europe. Although the label structural functional theory has subsumed multiple perspectives, there are a few basic elements that generally hold for all functionalist approaches in sociology: social systems are composed of interconnected parts; the parts of a system can be understood in terms of how each contributes to meeting the needs of the whole; and social systems tend to remain in equilibrium, with change in one part of the system leading to (generally adverse) changes in other parts of the system.

HISTORICAL DEVELOPMENT

An irony in the development of structural functional theory as a perspective that essentially came to define the discipline of sociology is that the theory in large part arose out of a nineteenth-century effort to link the emerging field of sociology with other more established disciplines. Comte, the social theorist first to use the term sociology, attempted to gain legitimacy for his emerging field by linking it with the biological sciences. Comte's social theory largely grew out of his vision of a good or correct society. In his view, society had in many ways broken down as a result of influences including the French Revolution, and he sought ways to restore order to society. As an outgrowth of these interests, Comte initiated a focus on how various aspects of society contribute to the functioning of the whole. In this vein, and in an attempt to link sociology with the more established field of biology, Comte likened society to a biological organism. He theorized that society is an ordered system of interdependent parts, but in a sense greater than the sum of those parts, requiring that it be studied as a whole.

With this approach, a reasonable concern becomes how each part of the system contributes to the functioning of the whole. Spencer argued that in order to determine the function of a social institution or arrangement one must determine the need that it meets for society as a whole. Toward this end, he developed the concepts of *structure* and *function* that lie at the core of structural functional theory. To Spencer, understanding society consists of understanding the functions that various structures serve for society as a whole.

Another theorist closely associated with structural functional theory is Durkheim. While rejecting many of the positions of Comte and Spencer, Durkheim retained the primary elements of their functional approaches. Durkheim's sociology focused on the interrelationships among the parts of society and their contributions to the functioning of the whole. For example, Durkheim (1965) discussed the function of religion in society: "Before all, it is a system of ideas with which the individuals represent to themselves the society of which they are members, and the obscure and intimate relations which they have with it. This is its primary function." Durkheim also built on the functionalism of Comte and Spencer in his distinction between causal analysis and functional analysis. Causal analysis, to Durkheim, consists of studying why a structure or social form exists. Functional analysis, in contrast, assesses the functions that a structure performs for society as a whole. Durkheim argued that a sociological analysis of any structure is incomplete without each of these elements.

Talcott Parsons was perhaps most instrumental in promulgating structural functional theory in the twentieth century (Parsons 1937). He constructed a theory of social action which argued that individual action is rooted in the norms of society and constrained by its values. In this way, individuals carry out actions that benefit the whole of society. Drawing on Spencer's work, Parsons also asserted that all societies must meet certain needs in order to survive. His AGIL scheme (Parsons 1951) proposed that all societies must fulfill an *adaptive* function, a *goal-attainment* function, an *integrative* function, and latent pattern maintenance (*latency*).

Following Parsons, Robert K. Merton laid out a working strategy for how to "do" structural functional theory in distinguishing between manifest (or intended) functions and latent (or unintended) functions, noting that the same acts can be both functional and dysfunctional for the social whole. Merton (1968) proposed that sociologists can examine the functional and dysfunctional elements of any structure, determine the "net balance" between the two, and conclude whether or not the structure is functional for society as a whole.

CENTRAL ELEMENTS

Although structural functional theory has taken various forms, there are a few basic elements that are central to the perspective. First, the theory leads to a focus on the functions of various structures. By "functions," theorists in the perspective generally mean consequences that benefit society as a whole, contribute to its operation, or increase its stability. "Structure," in its broadest sense, can mean anything that exists independent of individual actors. Social arrangements such as stratification systems therefore are social structures, as are social institutions such as marriage. Structural functional theorists tend to examine social structures in terms of the functions they serve for society. Davis and Moore (1945), for example, developed a functional theory of stratification in which they argued that a stratification system is a functional necessity, with positions in society that are more functionally important garnering higher rewards.

A second basic element of structural functional theory is rooted in the organic analogies of Comte and Spencer. The theory treats society as an integrated whole with a series of interconnected parts. Further, the theory holds that the various parts contribute to the functioning of the whole. Durkheim, for example, proposed that when all of the parts of the social whole are fulfilling their necessary functions, then society is in a "normal" state. When individual parts are not fulfilling their functions, Durkheim argued, society is in a "pathological" state.

Third, structural functional theorists assume that society rests on the consensus of its members, and that there is widespread agreement on what is good and just for society. Davis and Moore's theory of stratification, for instance, rests on an assumption that members of society generally agree on which social positions are most important for society.

CRITICISMS

In the middle of the twentieth century, structural functional theory became the dominant sociological perspective in the US and Western Europe. In the 1960s, however, criticisms of the theory began to mount. These criticisms took a variety of forms, but two were perhaps most common: the theory deemphasizes social conflict and it does not adequately address social change.

According to critics, structural functional theory overemphasizes social cohesion while ignoring social conflict. By treating society as an interconnected whole, structural functional theory emphasizes integration among the various parts of society. With this approach, critics hold that the theory disregards social conflict. Moreover, because of its focus on social consensus and integration, any attention the theory does pay to conflict tends to treat it as disruptive.

Critics also contend that structural functional theory is ill-equipped to deal with social change. Another consequence of viewing society as a system of interconnected parts is that any changes are seen as having the consequence of disrupting the entire system. To early thinkers in the functionalist perspective, change was a major threat. Herbert Spencer, for example, held that any change made with the objective of benefiting society will have unforeseen negative impacts. While more contemporary theorists in the structural functional paradigm have not been as hostile to social change as was Spencer, the theory still has difficulty in dealing with change. This has led to a criticism of the perspective as being conservative in nature.

A third criticism that can be leveled against structural functional theory stems from its assumption that the parts of society function together to support the whole, while at the same time it seeks to determine the functions of various social structures. In traditional structural functional theory, then, any institution that exists in society must be functional for the whole. For example, Davis and Moore treated stratification as a functional necessity in society. However, because all known societies have contained some level of stratification, it is impossible to find independent evidence for the functional benefits of a stratification system. That is, we cannot know what functions a stratification system serves that would not be served in its absence or that might be served by alternative structures.

Largely as a result of criticisms lodged against it, structural functional theory has seen a decline in sociology since the 1960s. There are, however, contemporary approaches that draw significantly on the roots of the perspective.

CONTEMPORARY FUNCTIONALISM

Perhaps the best-known contemporary variant of structural functionalism is the neofunctionalism of Alexander and colleagues (Alexander 1998; Alexander & Colomy 1990). Neofunctionalism is largely a reconstruction of Parsons's body of work, avoiding many of the pitfalls of earlier structural functional theorists. It accomplishes this in part by not taking social integration as a given, by giving greater weight to social action, and by specifying the role that the perspective should play in the production of knowledge.

Early functionalists, most notably Parsons, took integration of a social system as a given. This thought lay at the root of many of the criticisms brought against structural functional theory. The assumption of social integration led to the perspective's conservative character, its deemphasis of conflict, and its difficulty in dealing with social change. With neofunctionalism, Alexander argues that integration of functional parts should not be considered a fact, but instead should be treated as a social possibility. Although Alexander has distanced himself from the functionalist perspective since his writings in the late 1990s, the neofunctionalist approach he developed with his colleagues remains an important contemporary contribution to structural functional theory.

By treating society as a number of structural elements unified into an integrated whole, structural functional theory has tended to view individuals as constrained by the social system. Further, in his theory of action, Parsons accorded little room to human agency. Neofunctionalism sought to address this shortcoming of structural functionalism. Drawing from symbolic interactionism, ethnomethodology, and exchange theory, Alexander's neofunctionalism offered a theory of action that gives equal weight to social order and to the actions of individuals.

Alexander also argues for a distinction between sociological discourse and sociological explanation. Sociological discourse, in Alexander's distinction, is more speculative and general, while sociological explanation is geared toward empirical evidence and the determination of causal relationships. To Alexander, functionalist approaches should be seen as discourse; that is, not as formal theories but rather as general pictures of social systems and their parts in a descriptive rather than explanatory sense. In this regard, neofunctionalism, and structural functional theory in general, should be seen less as theories with testable propositions and more as orienting strategies comprised of broad assumptions about how society operates.

Another contemporary link to the historical roots of structural functional theory lies in the growing trend in sociology to take human evolution as a framework for social theory. Evolutionary theory, particularly the assumption that organisms retain characteristics that help them to adapt to (or function in) their environments, is an inherently functional perspective. While those carrying out research on the evolution of human characteristics and social structures are not likely to consider themselves structural functional theorists, they share some basic assumptions with the roots of the perspective. In fact, it was an early structural functional theorist, Herbert Spencer, who first popularized the term "survival of the fittest." Although structural functional theory has seen a decline over the past four decades, theoretical perspectives seldom die, but rather become reinvented in new iterations. In this way, structural functional thinking continues to be expressed in contemporary formulations.

SEE ALSO: Comte, Auguste; Durkheim, Émile; Functionalism/Neofunctionalism; Merton, Robert K.; Parsons, Talcott; Spencer, Herbert

REFERENCES AND SUGGESTED READINGS

Alexander, J. C. (1998) *Neofunctionalism and After*. Blackwell, Oxford.
Alexander, J. C. & Colomy, P. (1990) Neofunctionalism: Reconstructing a Theoretical Tradition. In: Ritzer, G. (Ed.), *Frontiers of Social Theory: A New Synthesis*. Columbia University Press, New York, pp. 33–67.
Davis, K. Moore, W. (1945) Some Principles of Stratification. *American Sociological Review* 10: 242–9.
Durkheim, É. (1965 [1912]) *The Elementary Forms of Religious Life*. Free Press, New York.
Merton, R. K. (1968) *Social Theory and Social Structure*. Free Press, New York.
Parsons, T. (1937) *The Structure of Social Action*. McGraw-Hill, New York.
Parsons, T. (1951) *The Social System*. Free Press, Glencoe, IL.

structural strains, successive transition of

Koichi Hasegawa

The successive transition of structural strains refers to the mechanism and social process of the following vicious cycle: a policy or a countermeasure aimed at solving one problem gives birth to another serious problem, and the solution of that problem results in the creation of yet another more serious one and finally reaches a dead end. The first step in the wrong direction leads into deep woods that are impossible to escape. In research into the social impacts of the Tohoku and Joetsu bullet train line construction project, Funabashi (1988) invented this concept and described this vicious cycle. The concept of structural strain, defined as deprivation caused by a structural factor neither personal nor accidental, came from Smelser's

(1963) concept. This perspective reveals how the response to one risk factor can result in the creation of new risks, and that subsequent attempts to address the new risks produce yet further risks, until, finally, no remedy can be found. The concept explains rapid environmental degradation and other social problems.

One example is the mechanism by which huge budget deficits grow rapidly:

slowing down of the economy → increasing public investment → budget deficits → raising tax → recession → revenue deficits → reducing public investment → heavy recession → increasing revenue deficits

Another example is the social process leading to the concentration of nuclear facilities in Rokkasho Village in the northern part of Japan (see Funabashi et al. 1998):

failure of building settlements and cultivating farmland → failure of the proposed Mutsu Steelworks project → failure of cultivating beetroots → setbacks in developing new rice fields → the Mutsu-Ogawara Industrial Park fiasco → the introduction of nuclear fuel processing facilities → the accumulation of radioactive waste → the further concentration of nuclear facilities in the area

We can also observe the workings of this vicious cycle in typical cases of establishing nuclear power stations:

depopulation of the area → electric utility company proposes to establish a nuclear power station → community confrontations over the issue → construction and start of operations at the new nuclear power station → sharp drop in labor demand with completion of construction works → population decrease → local government develops a dependency on revenue from the nuclear power station → local government invites an additional nuclear power plant → construction works and start of operations → increase in the amount of radioactive waste generated → storage of this waste in the area → construction of storage facilities to accommodate spent fuel

The latter two cases clearly illustrate the vicious cycle that compounds environmental degradation: the establishment of a single nuclear facility or plant often results in an ever-expanding number of risky nuclear facilities.

The center or "upstream" area of a society has a lot of alternatives to escape from the vicious cycle. But for peripheral or "downstream" areas where lower-class or minority people are living it is more difficult to escape. For example, the experience of development projects in the global South resulting in steeper economic decline exemplifies this successive transition of structural strains.

SEE ALSO: Daily Life Pollution; Ecological Problems; High-Speed Transportation Pollution; Pollution Zones, Linear and Planar

REFERENCES AND SUGGESTED READINGS

Funabashi, H. (1988) Kozoteki Kincho no Rensateki Ten I (Successive Transition of Structural Strains). In: Funabashi, H., Hasegawa, K., Hatanaka, S., & Kajita, T. (1988) *Kosoku Bunmei no Chiiki Mondai; Tohoku Shinkansen no Kensetsu, Funso to Shakaiteki Eikyo* (Regional Problems of a High Speed Civilization: The Dispute over Construction of the Tohoku Bullet Train Line and Its Social Impacts). Yuhikaku, Tokyo, pp. 155–87.

Funabashi, H., Hasegawa, K., & Iijima, N. (Eds.) (1998) *Kyodai Chiiki Kaihatsu no Koso to Kiketsu: Mutsu Ogawara Kaihatsu to Kakunenryo Saikuru shisetsu* (Vision Versus Results in a Large-Scale Industrial Development Project in the Mutsu-Ogawara District: A Sociological Study of Social Change and Conflict in Rokkasho Village). University of Tokyo Press, Tokyo.

Smelser, N. (1963) *The Theory of Collective Behavior.* Free Press, New York.

structuralism

Mark A. Schneider

Structuralism is a catchall term for a set of explanatory approaches or paradigms in the social sciences that emphasize the causal force of the relations among elements in a system or of emergent properties of their patterning. The character of the elements themselves (beyond what conditions their relations) is viewed as arbitrary and of no explanatory bearing. Various structural approaches have at times been popular in linguistics, psychology, anthropology, and sociology. In the latter two fields, distinct forms developed that can both be traced back to Émile

Durkheim, while sociology has also produced strains of structuralism influenced by Georg Simmel. Arising from Durkheim and Simmel as well has been the programmatic contention that in structuralism alone will be found a basis for distinguishing sociology from other disciplines.

Anthropological structuralism achieved celebrity in the third quarter of the twentieth century through the writings of Claude Lévi-Strauss. He argued that structural factors pattern our cultural expressions so as to make them resonate with us beneath awareness. His explanatory strategy first involved reducing expressive objects (e.g., artwork or mythological stories) to *contrastive structures* in which some elements were opposed to others. These structures were then argued to be similar in form to (or otherwise influenced by) an abstract picture of the social structure in which they were produced. The formal correspondence produced a resonance that explained why particular expressive objects were enjoyed and repetitively consumed. Methodologically, Lévi-Strauss followed Prague School linguists who saw meaning as conveyed structurally by contrasts among sound elements, as well as Ferdinand de Saussure's suggestion that meaning arose from relations among essentially arbitrary linguistic elements. Substantively, Lévi-Strauss followed Durkheim's suggestion in *The Elementary Forms of the Religious Life* and in *Primitive Classification* (written with Marcel Mauss) that certain cognitive constructs have the same form as elements of social life.

For example, in *Tristes Tropiques* Lévi-Strauss reduced the face paintings of the Caduveo of Brazil to a pattern that is diagonally sectioned, defining two dimensions of contrast such as we see in playing cards. The two dimensions played symmetry off against asymmetry to achieve a striking effect unique to the Caduveo among surrounding tribes. To explain this, Lévi-Strauss argued that the Caduveo faced a particular social structural problem that their neighbors had solved. A system of castes which exchanged marriage partners within themselves exerted disintegrative pressures on Caduveo society, pressures reduced in surrounding tribes by marriage rules that forced exchanges across caste lines. This produced a social symmetry that balanced the hierarchic asymmetry of castes and thus held these tribes together. The Caduveo were too snobbish to marry across caste lines, argued Lévi-Strauss, but they produced the same balance of symmetry and asymmetry in their face paintings, which he interpreted as a cultural solution to a social structural problem. In this analysis, both the cultural product and the social structure were reduced to contrastive relations between symmetric and asymmetric features, with social factors influencing cultural phenomena.

In Lévi-Strauss's later work on Amerindian myths (*Mythologiques*), the influence of social structure dropped out and myth was analyzed as an elaborate self-organizing system reflecting fundamental structuring habits of the human mind. The stories that myths told, which often seemed surreal, were viewed as less important to listeners than the harmonies that derived from logical relations among properties of the creatures, artifacts, or incidents that the myths included. It was these harmonies that caused myths to please people, and thus to be told over and over even when they lacked intelligible narrative structure. Lévi-Strauss argued that "savage minds" employed different principles in constructing myths from those we use in stories – ones that were entirely novel and heretofore unimagined. In his decoding of myths, the reduction to contrastive structures was retained, but the explanation of their pattern took a path similar to the generative grammar being formulated in linguistics by Noam Chomsky, looking to features of the human brain rather than social structure.

This revolutionary work soon came under attack. It was seen as too systematic and scientistic by some scholars in the humanities (e.g., Derrida 1978; for an overview, see Culler 1975), whose critiques were instrumental in launching poststructuralism and postmodernism as intellectual currents. At the same time, some anthropologists and sociologists (e.g., Harris 1968; Schneider 1993) criticized it as a form of self-validating idealism that depended upon dubious interpretive methods and unlikely cognitive mechanisms. It never propagated as a method.

In sociology, structuralism has had a longer, more varied, and less meteoric career. One strand of structural analysis follows Durkheim and Mauss in viewing *expressive culture* (which differs from *instrumental culture* – such as our

tools – in being relatively free of practical constraints) as determined by social structure. Another carries forward Simmel's view of social structure as having formal properties that condition behaviors well beyond the domain of expressive culture. They join in viewing social structure as the source of what Durkheim called *social facts*, that is, causal currents that generally operate outside the awareness of social actors.

The attempt to uncover structural determinants of expressive culture has been handicapped by disagreement among sociologists and anthropologists over the precise meaning of social structure. Without consensus over the important dimensions along which social structure varies, not to speak of measures thereof, scholarship has been eclectic and has not given rise to organized research traditions. Two examples must suffice.

In *The Birth of the Gods*, sociologist Guy Swanson argued that the structure of relations among organized groups in society determined how the spiritual world was conceptualized. His approach modified Durkheim's argument in *Elementary Forms* to make it more amenable to testing. Using anthropological sources for a sample of world societies, Swanson showed, for instance, that the concept of a "high god" directing lesser spiritual agents occurred with frequency only in societies with a significant number of hierarchically organized "sovereign groups," each having jurisdiction over an array of human affairs. Societies with lesser numbers of such groups believed either in unorganized spiritual forces or in multiple, competing divinities. Thus the structure of sociopolitical organization was shown to determine relative monotheism within the cultural domain.

Anthropologist Mary Douglas looked to different aspects of social structure in explaining why some cultures or subcultures enjoy rituals while others find them hollow. Drawing on comparative case studies, Douglas hypothesized that impermeably bounded groups divided among many ranked statuses favored ritual, whereas more permeable groups with few ranked statuses viewed ritual as empty, opting for individually crafted or spontaneous ceremonials that were seen as more authentic. Thus important aspects of cultural style were argued to be determined by variation in social structure.

If this Durkheimian strand of structuralism has devoted itself largely to explaining variation in expressive culture, the Simmelian strand has taken a more systematic approach to defining and mapping social structure, and used the result to explain a wider range of social behavior. The main objective is to show how well-defined properties of social structures (or occupancy of particular positions within them) constrain behavior. The structures range from small-scale friendship or work groups, mapped sociometrically, to entire societies, viewed in terms of specific structural properties.

Network theories, for instance, use features of social structure such as the comparative intimacy of social relationships, the proportion of weak to strong ties among individuals, and the relative frequency of bridging ties among groups, to explain an array of social phenomena ranging from the capacity of communities to mobilize politically to the comparative catholicity of cultural tastes. An interesting feature of network theories has been their suggestion that occupants of positions that are connected to other positions in similar ways should behave similarly (Burt 1982). The explanatory power of the principle of structural equivalence is only now being explored.

A somewhat different approach was taken by Blau (1977), who viewed the skeleton of social structure as composed of the different dimensions along which people are differentiated from one another. Among these might be wealth, education, gender, religious confession, political party, and so on. Societies vary in the number of dimensions involved in drawing distinctions (their heterogeneity) and the tendency of dimensions to be ranked (their inequality). They also vary in the degree to which positions allow for interaction with diverse others (the relative intersection of dimensions) and the degree to which ranking on one dimension predicts ranking on others (relative consolidation of dimensions). Blau explores many features of social life that are dependent upon these variables, as well as on the proportions of the population distributed into differentiated groups and rates of mobility among them. For instance, greater intersection of dimensions seems to decrease the likelihood of intergroup conflict.

Bridging this approach and the one derived from Durkheim, DiMaggio (1987) argues that the tendency of societies to view expressive culture as divided among distinct genres is determined by such structural features as social heterogeneity, the prevalence of weak ties, and the relative complexity of role structure in a society. DiMaggio also notes that the relative consolidation of status dimensions within the society determines its tendency to see genres as ranked and their mixing as a species of cultural pollution. Less consolidation leads to less stratification of genres and consequently less concern with their mixing. DiMaggio's theory draws upon symbolic interaction as well as Durkheimian and Simmelian strands of structuralism, and connects with structuralist arguments that were central to Goffman's sociology of culture.

Programmatic structuralism advances the claims of Durkheim and Simmel that the integrity of sociology as a scientific discipline depends upon establishing a realm of causation distinct from those explored by psychology or economics. Among contemporary sociologists, this position has been most forcefully argued and illustrated by Black (1976, 2000). Neither Durkheim nor Simmel, he argues, had the strength of their convictions, since both consistently relied on individual psychologistic explanations despite their evident concern with sociology's disciplinary integrity. All classical and most modern sociology, suggests Black, is psychological, teleological, and individualistic. Its focus is on understanding people rather than understanding social life, with the consequence that it is not really sociological. To finally become sociological, sociologists must replace their interest in people with an interest in social life and how it can be explained structurally.

Black's structural theory attempts to explain the behavior of law as a property of social life. Law, taken to be governmental social control, can be viewed as a quantitative variable. For instance, social life is more regulated by law as the average social distance among individuals increases. Law's "direction" influences its quantity as well. More law flows downward from higher ranking positions in social structures than flows upward, and more flows outward from positions more densely connected to those less densely connected. The greater the vertical and horizontal distance between two positions, the greater the proportion of downward and outward law in comparison with inward and upward. In practice this means that lower ranking and more peripheral litigants succeed in court less frequently against higher ranking and more central litigants, with the imbalance directly proportional to their positional distance. Like DiMaggio, Black shows how these structural effects play out in a wide range of human interaction, connecting his structural analysis to what Goffman called the interaction order.

The above examples illustrate again the lack of agreement among sociologists over how to define social structure. Were consensus reached, problems of measurement would still plague structuralist theorizing, since many of its propositions will be hard to test unless and until metrics are established that allow comparisons across the important dimensions of social structure. Put somewhat differently, a successful structuralism must be able to assign to particular positions an absolute location at the intersection of multiple dimensions of social structure, rather than, as is most often the case today, assigning a relative location along only one dimension. Until this methodological problem can be solved, structuralist theorizing is apt to remain suggestive rather than establishing the core of a purified sociology.

A much more detailed and somewhat broader view of structuralism is available in Turner (1998), who includes an array of sociologists who have made anatomizing social structure and analyzing the processes by which it is reproduced over time the subject of scrutiny.

SEE ALSO: Culture; Deconstruction; Durkheim, Émile; Networks; Paradigms; Poststructuralism; Semiotics

REFERENCES AND SUGGESTED READINGS

Black. D. (1976) *The Behavior of Law*. Academic Press, New York.
Black, D. (2000) Dreams of pure sociology. *Sociological Theory* 18: 343–67.
Blau, P. (1977) *Inequality and Heterogeneity: A Primitive Theory of Social Structure*. Free Press, New York.
Burt, R. (1982) *Toward a Structural Theory of Action*. Academic Press, New York.
Culler, J. (1975) *Structuralist Poetics: Structuralism, Linguistics, and the Study of Literature*. Cornell University Press, Ithaca, NY.
Derrida, J. (1978) Structure, Sign, and Play in the Discourse of the Human Sciences. In *Writing and Difference*. Trans. A. Bass. University of Chicago Press, Chicago.
DiMaggio, P. (1987) Classification in Art. *American Sociological Review* 52: 440–55.
Douglas, M. (1970) *Natural Symbols: Explorations in Cosmology*. Pantheon Books, New York.
Harris, M. (1968) *The Rise of Anthropological Theory: A History of Theories of Culture*. Crowell, New York.
Schneider, M. (1993) *Culture and Enchantment*. University of Chicago Press, Chicago.
Swanson, G. (1960) *The Birth of the Gods: The Origin of Primitive Beliefs*. University of Michigan Press, Ann Arbor.
Turner, J. (1998) *The Structure of Sociological Theory*, 6th edn. Wadsworth, Belmont, CA.

structuration theory

Rob Stones

Structuration theory is a term used by the British sociologist Anthony Giddens in a series of publications in the 1970s and early 1980s as he attempted to define a distinctive approach to the study of social relations. Giddens wanted the term to both embrace and go beyond the more static notion of social "structure." He wanted the praxis and dynamic qualities of agency also to be included within the term. Thus, both structure and agency are captured within the philosophy of structuration. Many commentators soon noted the striking similarity between Giddens's structuration theory and the work of Pierre Bourdieu in France. Bourdieu also wanted to go beyond the reification and objectivism of approaches that emphasized the pressures of the social milieu to the exclusion of individual and collective action. By creating a synthesis of the best from different traditions, Giddens was able to fashion a path between the deterministic tendencies of Marxism and Positivism, on the one hand, and the overly voluntaristic, free-floating approaches of interpretive sociologies such as ethnomethodology and symbolic interactionism, on the other. Bourdieu, working within the French post-war intellectual scene, devised a path between the overly objectivist and dehumanizing tendencies of structuralism and Marxism, and the idealistic and subjectivist tendencies of existentialism, which put far too high a premium on the role of an individual's will power.

Structuration theory includes the weight of structures within its compass, the material, social, and personal inheritances from the past that set the limits to what can be done by people in the present. It also includes the sense that this structural inheritance provides the enabling conditions that are drawn on by individual or collective actors in pursuing their projects. However, it goes beyond these insights in emphasizing the dynamic and recurring processes by which these structures are "worked upon" by actors who draw from them, and who then either reproduce the structures or change them through the very process of acting. The reproduction or the changes can either be intended or unintended outcomes of the agent's practices.

Thus, we have a "duality of structure" whereby agents draw on structures to produce actions that then change or maintain structures. More than this, however, in structuration theory the structures themselves must be conceptualized in terms of praxis. The very existence of social structures themselves relies on their continuing to be "put to work" by the agents within them. A concrete institutional structure such as a library only continues to exist in a meaningful form as long as people continue to run it and use it as a library. This, in turn, requires that these people share a phenomenological understanding of what a library is and of how to "do" things such as cataloging, searching, lending, borrowing, reserving, and so on. The latter emphasis on phenomenology and the sociological traditions it has spawned, including a prominent place for ethnomethodology, is central to Giddens's version of structuration theory. Social actors possess stocks of mutual knowledge that exist within a wider worldview, and it is necessary to hermeneutically interpret and understand these actors' worldviews or "frames of meaning" in order to be truly able to grasp what they do and why they do it. An agent would not be able to act in the world without some "knowledgeability" of her circumstances, and this is always knowledge embedded within a view of the world containing all sorts of formative cultural, social, and religious influences.

The way in which structuration incorporates phenomenology into its approach means that it also conceptualizes a "duality of structure and agency" whereby the social structures "out-there" beyond the agent-in-focus enter "in-here" into her body and mind in terms of knowledgeability and dispositions. For Giddens, the structures out-there that mold or influence the body and perceptions in-here can be analytically divided into three different dimensions. Thus, one can look at any one or all of the structures of power, norms, or meaning and signification in terms of how they provide enabling or constraining conditions for action. Bourdieu gave a particular emphasis to how the cultural discourses and forms of life out-there necessarily mold, influence, and implicate the bodily, perceptual, and appreciative dispositions of agents, capturing this in his celebrated concept of habitus.

The status and significance of this intertwining of structure and agency is one among a series of conceptual issues germane to the structuration project that have been given greater clarity and analytical precision through subsequent debates. Structuration has by now developed beyond its founders as a vibrant, lively tradition in its own right, strengthened and emboldened by critique, counter-critique, diverse empirical applications, and synthesis (Stones 2005). The work of Chris Bryant and David Jary, drawing together and critically dissecting a legion of theoretical contributions and empirical studies, has played a particularly important role in the formation of structuration's status as an internally evolving tradition.

Beyond this there have been a number of key moments in the conceptual elaboration of structuration, all of them much more concerned with empirical application than the early philosophically oriented work of Giddens. Margaret Archer, while supporting the structure–action–structure–action sequencing promoted by structuration theory, famously criticized the way that structuration's emphasis on structures entering into the agent unhelpfully confused the clear boundaries between the agent and her structural context. Archer felt that this undermined our ability to have a clear sense of objective constraints, limits, and possibilities. She argues that we need to maintain a clear "dualism" between structure and agency. Subsequent criticism of Archer accepted that it is important to be able to conceptualize dualism, but argued that this was not incompatible with also needing to conceptualize the duality of structure and agency. Indeed, Nicos Mouzelis works, in effect, with dualism, the duality of structure, and the duality of structure and agency. On this basis he has developed a series of conceptual categories that allow one to distinguish between a subtle variety of structure–agency relationships. These allow one, for example, to distinguish between (1) the degrees of power that different agents possess to affect aspects of the world-out-there; and (2) to investigate whether particular agents have more or less ability to achieve a critical and/or strategic distance from the inherited cultural and normative milieu. Further issues concerning differences between knowledge of the immediate conjuncture and the more general and transposable dispositions captured by habitus; the conceptualization of the relational meso-level of position-practices within which individual practices are enacted (Cohen 1989); the methodology of empirical applications; and the relationship of structuration theory to more traditional macro conceptions of structure, have all been the subject of recent developments in structuration.

SEE ALSO: Bourdieu, Pierre; Ethnomethodology; Existential Sociology; Phenomenology; Structure and Agency

REFERENCES AND SUGGESTED READINGS

Archer, M. (1995) *Realist Social Theory*. Cambridge University Press, Cambridge.
Bourdieu, P. (1977) *Outline of a Theory of Practice*. Cambridge University Press, Cambridge.
Bourdieu, P. & Wacquant, L. (1992) *An Invitation to Reflexive Sociology*. University of Chicago Press, Chicago.
Bryant, C. & Jary, D. (Eds.) (1996) *Anthony Giddens: Critical Assessments*, 4 vols. Routledge, London.
Bryant, C. & Jary, D. (2001) *The Contemporary Giddens: Social Theory in a Globalizing Age*. Palgrave Macmillan, London.
Cohen, I. J. (1989) *Structuration Theory: Anthony Giddens and the Constitution of Social Life*. Macmillan, London.
Giddens, A. (1984) *The Constitution of Society*. Polity Press, Cambridge.
Giddens, A. (1993 [1976]) *New Rules of Sociological Method*. Polity Press, Cambridge.
Mouzelis, N. (1991) *Back to Sociological Theory*. Macmillan, London.
Stones, R. (2005) *Structuration Theory*. Palgrave Macmillan, London.

structure and agency

Rob Stones

The concepts of structure and agency are central to sociological theory. Structures are typically seen as the more fixed and enduring aspects of the social landscape. As used by Durkheim and others working within a similar tradition, *structure* is a metaphor that denotes qualities of society that are akin to the skeleton of a body in the field of anatomy, or to the frame of a building in architecture. Durkheim's work was heavily influenced by his desire to establish a sphere of study for sociology that was distinct from both biology and psychology. To this end he insisted that there are structured ways of acting, thinking, and feeling that are general throughout a society and that act as external constraints over its members. This was to emphasize the role of society in the process of causation, as opposed to individual or group agency. Some writers taking issue with this position went to the other extreme. Weber, for example, emphasized the role of individuals and rejected the idea that terms such as "society" or "group" could refer to any reality other than that of individuals and their actions.

For writers seeking to include both structure and agency in their analytic frameworks, the Durkheimian emphasis on structures is maintained. Now, however, agency is conceived as the more processual, active, dimension of society – analogous to the physiology of an organism or to the activities conducted within the spaces of a building. Agency is the ability of individuals or groups, such as class movements, governments, or economic corporate bodies, to "make things happen" within given structural constraints and opportunities. There is a close parallel between this conception and Marx's dictum that people make history, but not in circumstances of their own choosing. This "middle-way" approach to structure and agency is the dominant conception in contemporary sociological theory. Now debates are less in terms of structure *versus* agency and more about specific emphases and the precise ways in which these two major aspects of social life affect each other or are combined. Key questions within this approach have concerned the extent to which structures constrain or determine the actions of agents, and the extent to which agents act independently of social structures.

Although mutually entwined, structure and agency can still be conceptualized independently. Much of the agency/structure debate revolves around just how independent of each other they are or can be. Lopez and Scott (2000) argued that there are two primary ways of conceptualizing structure, both deriving from Durkheim. The first is the *relational* notion of structure, referring to networks of social relations that tie people together into groups and social systems. These networks of interdependencies, characterized by mutual reliance within divisions of labor, are typically clustered into specialized sectors of social relations such as kinship, religion, the economy, the state, and so on. Durkheim referred to these as *collective relationships*. Georg Simmel similarly emphasized relationships, conceiving of society as a dynamic complex of social forms and interactions. These may involve smaller or larger numbers of people or specific types of association that structure the way that agents behave in one another's presence. Norbert Elias's *figurational sociology* likewise emphasized the webs and networks of relationships within which individual agents must act. Pierre Bourdieu consistently argued against a view of social life that analyzed social entities without placing them in the context of the relations that produced and sustain them, and which provide the fields in which the actions of such entities produce their consequences. Recent work on social and policy networks has also taken a relational viewpoint, looking at such things as the frequency, direction, duration, and quantity of in-house and external relationships between individual and corporate agents.

The second notion of structure, the *institutional*, refers to the beliefs, values, symbols, ideas, and expectations that make up the mutual knowledge of members of a society and that allow them to communicate with each other. Durkheim (1984) referred to this dimension of structure as a society's *collective representations*. The structural-functionalist tradition associated with the work of Talcott Parsons, Robert Merton, and others, captured this aspect of structure under the rubric of "social institutions." Other writers emphasized cultural patterns. Parsons's focus was on the rules and normative expectations into which agents were socialized as children, and on their adaptation to the various roles and positions they occupied as adults. This emphasis on rules and norms held in individual minds within institutions can be seen to continue in various ways in diverse strands of current writing, including the neo-functionalism of Jeffrey Alexander, new institutionalists such as Powell and DiMaggio, and in the work of Pierre Bourdieu and Anthony Giddens.

Both approaches to structure are compatible with another metaphor routinely associated with structure: *pattern*. The notion of a pattern is often included in the very definition of structure. For example, social structure may be seen as "a system of patterned relationships of actors in their capacity as playing roles relative to one another" (Parsons 1945). Such patterns can be produced by agents acting in accordance with normative expectations, as in the institutional version of structure, or in accordance with the requirements of mutual interdependence, as in the relational view of structure.

Both notions exist side by side in many theoretical traditions. Marxism, for example, emphasizes the importance of one's position with respect to the relations and forces of production, and also the significance of ideology or cultural hegemony in the perpetuation of class oppression – themes emerging from the Frankfurt School and from Gramsci and the neo-Gramscians. Nicos Poulantzas's later work also explicitly stressed a relational approach to political strategy. The two notions of structure, relational and institutional, are clearly not mutually exclusive. The precise way in which the two notions should be combined is, however, a much more complex question.

Contemporary theorists increasingly have confronted the uneasy relationship between these accounts of structure and the concept of *agency*. Alan Dawe's account of "Theories of Social Action" noted a theoretical tension between social order – associated with the enduring qualities of structure – and creative, potentially disruptive, social action. To account for the reproduction of relatively stable social circumstances, major theorists such as Parsons ultimately allowed their concern with agency and action to be subsumed by the normative rules, sanctions, and regulations associated with the institutional approach to structure. Structures mold, constrain, and determine the actions of agents. This *substantive* privileging of structure over agency is often associated with structuralist writers such as Claude Lévi-Strauss, Roland Barthes, and Louis Althusser, who tended to treat agents as the mere "bearers" of structures, and with Michel Foucault, whose emphasis on the overwhelming force and imposition of discursive regimes (institutional structure) and multiple power relations (relational structure) led him to pronounce the death of the subject or agent.

Agency theorists have asserted that structural approaches fail to recognize how agents are involved in the production of structured patterns or of social change. From the founding texts of sociology through the 1960s, a variety of ways of establishing and conceptualizing the autonomy of agency have been offered. Two overlapping traditions have dominated. One – the tradition of pragmatism and symbolic interactionism – includes Mead, Blumer, and Goffman (although, intriguingly, Goffman also borrowed heavily from Durkheim). The other includes Weber, Schütz, Berger and Luckmann, and Garfinkel in the neo-Kantian and phenomenological traditions. Their common emphasis is on the internal makeup of agents and action. They assumed from the start that agents and their actions were not subjugated to structures, and thus set out to explore their key characteristics. Weber, for example, distinguished between four different types of social action: *instrumentally rational* action geared towards "the attainment of the actor's own rationally pursued and calculated ends"; *value-rational*

action, which is pursued for reasons of personally held value irrespective of the prospects for success of that action; *affectual action*, determined by the actor's emotional states and orientations; and *traditional action*, "determined by ingrained habituation" (Weber 1968: 24–5). Mead and Blumer emphasized the reflection, reflexivity, and creativity inherent in the very process of interaction itself, and in the making of selves. Schütz, and also Berger and Luckmann, drew attention to the storehouse of preconceptions, typifications, of objects and practices – the latter as "recipe knowledge" – that we draw upon in appropriate circumstances. Garfinkel highlighted the array of competencies, skills, and moral commitments that are intrinsic to agents' routine accomplishments. Goffman, like Garfinkel, emphasized the chronic role played by tacit knowledge in the production of social practices. His insightful cameos prefigured the work of writers such as Bourdieu and Giddens in drawing attention to the ways in which such agential knowledge was permeated by structured social norms. All three writers stress the powerful sense individual agents have that others expect them to behave in manners appropriate to the immediate social context.

Bourdieu, Giddens, and Jürgen Habermas are major contemporary theorists who have each attempted to synthesize the two notions of structure and the two traditions of agency outlined above. The syntheses are facilitated by philosophical insights that help to both reveal and refine previous oversimplifications of core concepts. Each combines structure and agency in a more nuanced and inclusive manner than their predecessors. Each emphasizes not only structures external to agents, and the stocks of knowledge possessed by agents, but also the *social* origins and grounding of agents' knowledgeability. The key mediating concepts are *habitus* for Bourdieu, *practical consciousness* for Giddens, and the phenomenological *lifeworld* for Habermas. Social structures are seen as having entered into agents. These traces of structures within agents are drawn from both the relational and the institutional. Giddens's notion of "virtual" structures within agents, for example, draws on the institutional in stressing normative and significatory structures, whereas the relational seems to be emphasized more with respect to structures of domination or power. Each of these authors also emphasizes the agent's phenomenological frame of meaning and the attendant role played by the agent's situational "horizon of relevance" in affecting how she draws upon stocks of knowledge.

A final way that contemporary theorists acknowledge the separate treatment of structures and agents is *methodological*. Here structures are not thought to subsume agents. Rather, agents are treated as important components of the very makeup of structures (thus complicating and moderating the analogies made with skeletons or the walls of a building), and as having much to contribute to the reproduction or transformation of structures and to the unfolding of events. It is just that the theorist may want to focus temporarily on the conceptualization, mapping, and analysis of specific characteristics of social structures (e.g., on norms, rules, regulations, and on the nature of networked and patterned relations and interdependencies) without attending to the specific characteristics and contribution of agents.

Recent contributions to the development of structure and agency have been made by Nicos Mouzelis, who has elucidated the range and variety of types of interconnection between structure and agency, and Mustafa Emirbayer and Anne Mische, and also Margaret Archer, on different dimensions of relations between temporality, structure, and agency. All have called for more links between the conceptual apparatus of structure and agency and the empirical, *in situ* level. This will necessarily require that greater attention be paid to methodological issues than hitherto. An accompanying call to further refine the concepts themselves has been prompted by a related desire to increase their practical utility.

SEE ALSO: Agency (amd Intention); Bourdieu, Pierre; Durkheim, Émile; Ethnomethodology; Marxism and Sociology; Parsons, Talcott; Phenomenology; Schütz, Alfred; Structuralism; Structuration Theory; Weber, Max

REFERENCES AND SUGGESTED READINGS

Bourdieu, P. (1990) *The Logic of Practice*. Polity Press, Cambridge.

Dawe, A. (1978) Theories of Social Action. In: T. Bottomore & R. Nisvet (Eds.), *A History of Sociological Analysis*. Basic Books, New York.

Durkheim, E. (1984 [1893]) *The Division of Labour in Society*. Macmillan, London.

Emirbayer, M. & Mische, A. (1998) What is Agency? *American Journal of Sociology* 104: 962–1023.

Giddens, A. (1984) *The Constitution of Society*. Polity Press, Cambridge.

Lopez, J. & Scott, J. (2000) *Social Structure*. Open University Press, Philadelphia.

Mouzelis, N. (1991) *Back to Sociological Theory*. Macmillan, London.

Parsons, T. (1945) The Present Position and Prospects of Systematic Theory in Sociology. In: T. Parsons, *Essays in Sociological Theory*, 2nd edn. Free Press, New York.

Stones, R. (2004) *Structuration Theory*. Palgrave Macmillan, London.

Weber, M. (1968) *Economy and Society*. Ed. G. Roth & C. Wittich. Bedminster Press, New York.

student movements

Christopher Rootes

Although students have been prominent among the actors in many revolutions and revolutionary movements, as well as other forms of contentious politics, student movements – social movements comprised wholly or mainly of students, especially university or college students – are a distinctively modern phenomenon. Their emergence is predicated upon the existence in a society of a critical mass of students.

Student movements have emerged in all manner of modern and modernizing societies, often as agents of change, sometimes in reaction against change, but usually as challengers of regimes perceived to lack legitimacy or moral authority. They have appeared in authoritarian states in Europe, Asia, Africa, and Latin America, as well as in the liberal democratic states of the industrialized world.

Student movements have an important place in the development of social movement theory. In the US, it was dissatisfaction with the psychosocial and reductionist explanations of student protest (see, e.g., Feuer 1969) that stimulated explanations that took social movements seriously as forms of political action. In Europe, theories of "post-industrial" society and "new social movements" were developed by Touraine (1971) and others as explanations of the student protest that confounded orthodox Marxist theories.

Sociological interest in student movements was excited principally by the eruption during the 1960s of student protest in the US and in many states in Europe and the Pacific. Protests against the US's prosecution of the war in Vietnam were central to the student movements of the 1960s, but they also had other and deeper causes.

In the US, the student movement emerged in the early 1960s out of the campaign for civil rights for African Americans in the South as well as the socialist Student League for Industrial Democracy, which became Students for a Democratic Society (SDS) in 1960. It came to prominence with the student revolt, in the name of freedom of speech, at the University of California, Berkeley, in 1964, the Berkeley events inspiring new scholarly interest in student movements as well as student mobilizations on other campuses across the US and beyond. The US student movement, fueled by increasing opposition to the Vietnam War, spread nationwide before reaching a crescendo in the spring of 1970. In Western Europe, student movements developed in most countries and, most spectacularly, brought normal life to a halt in much of France in May 1968 when students appeared to put revolution back on the political agenda of liberal democratic states. However, student movements also challenged regimes and/or contested government policies in Australia, Asia, and communist-ruled Eastern Europe.

Student movements emerged in the advanced industrialized societies toward the end of a period of doubling, even trebling, of enrollments in higher education. As a result, students were everywhere unprecedentedly numerous, both relatively and absolutely. The expansion of higher education had various sources. One was demographic pressure – the swelling, consequent upon the post-war "baby boom," of the age cohorts from which most students were drawn. But everywhere the main pressures for expansion were political – from governments influenced by human capital theorists to invest in more highly qualified workforces in the hope of improving economic competitiveness, and from newly affluent parents concerned to ensure the career prospects of their offspring. As socio-technical change sketched in the outlines of the "knowledge economy" and began to transform occupational structures, so demand for and the supply of higher education grew dramatically. At the same time, increasing affluence made it possible for unprecedentedly large numbers of young people to enjoy a moratorium upon adult obligation. Youth as a distinct stage of life was born, and the university was its ideal locus.

The numbers of students expanded just at the time that demographic and socioeconomic changes combined to enhance the status and visibility of youth. The entry of this generation produced strains within universities which, in many countries, were elitist and traditionalist. Inadequate facilities, unreformed curricula, and antiquated rules generated conflicts between students who considered themselves adults and authorities who regarded themselves as acting in loco parentis. These local conflicts with university authorities were, however, symptomatic of wider strains in society.

Yet these were not simply the self-interested complaints of the materially deprived. Everywhere, students were drawn disproportionately from the relatively privileged strata of societies. Actual or anticipated graduate unemployment, sometimes proffered as an explanation of the rise of student radicalism, played little or no part. This was before the peak of the long postwar economic boom and, even in Italy, where the mismatch between output and labor market was legendary, the peak years of the student revolt coincided with historic lows in the frequency of graduate unemployment. If there were grievances about employment prospects, they were less about the lack of jobs than about demands for "jobs worth doing."

Social, demographic, and educational changes provided the actors for student movements, and local difficulties that raised civil libertarian issues often generated the first sparks, but it was events in the wider political arena that accounted for the spread of protest and cross- and intranational variation in its incidence. Students' local grievances generally highlighted political rigidities at state level as university authorities found themselves powerless to respond in ways that might defuse protest, as in France where university rectors had no power even to modify dormitory regulations. However, the general political condition that stimulated the development of student movements was an effective vacuum of political opposition to government policies within the mainstream political arena.

In the US, where only a few legislators voiced opposition to the Vietnam War, the draft compelled students to think seriously about the issues, and student opposition expanded to fill the space available. In Western Europe, the sclerotic politics of states frozen by the communist/anti-communist divide were similarly conducive. In West Germany, the absence of opposition was almost literal, as student socialists had been expelled from the Social Democratic Party and a "grand coalition" government of Social and Christian Democrats overwhelmingly dominated the parliament. The vacuum of opposition was often reproduced at local levels. In Europe, the student movements of the 1960s usually began not at campuses such as the Sorbonne, Heidelberg, Munich, or Rome where the institutionalized left was strong, but at those, such as Nanterre, Berlin, Frankfurt, Trento, and Turin, where the left was weak or absent. The most propitious condition for the development of the utopian student movements that so captured the imagination of observers was their political and social isolation (Statera 1975: 119).

The subsequent development of student movements was the product of interaction between the movements, their environments, and their internal social and political dynamics. Mass media coverage generalized student movements, but raised the stakes and contributed to internal dynamics that were divisive and ultimately destructive (Gitlin 1981). Media attention amplified recruitment but, once the movement had peaked, a "reverse bandwagon" effect exaggerated its decline. By focusing upon the outspoken and the outrageous, media coverage created "leaders" without authority or political acumen, encouraged spectacular and provocative actions, and amplified the incidence of violence. This deepened the movement's political isolation and encouraged political adventurism, with the result that in several countries, including Italy, Germany, and the US, small minorities of student activists drifted into terrorism. More generally, frustrated by the limitations of their student constituencies, they rediscovered Marxism and embarked upon mostly fruitless missions to revolutionize the proletariat. Secular processes may have dictated the inevitable demobilization of student movements, but the turn to sectarian theorizing and Leninist organization everywhere hastened the process, antithetical as they were to the civil libertarian and moral protests that had inspired student mobilization in the first place (Rootes 1980).

Although encounters with apparently unjust authority were crucial to the mobilization of student movements, it was crucial to their survival that official repression should remain moderate and unsystematic. Nowhere in the West did the level of repression of student protest reach the levels usual in Eastern Europe, Asia, or Latin America. Student movements were thus able to develop in the free spaces of liberal democracies aided by the intermittent stimuli of erratic police action. On those few occasions where repression was extreme – as with the 1970 shooting of four students at Kent State University – the immediate reaction was indignant protest, but the longer-term effect was demoralizing and demobilizing. Generally, however, the repression of student movements was mild compared with that of striking workers. State responses were more generally reformist than simply repressive.

In most countries student movements simply declined, but in the US and France they collapsed suddenly. In the US, the invasion of Cambodia demonstrated the impotence of the movement, and the shootings at Kent State raised the stakes. Most students returned to their books, but the most radicalized minority, as the Weather Underground, resorted to clandestine political violence. In France, the student movement was overwhelmed by the political crisis it unleashed, and outmaneuvered by General de Gaulle's appeal to the electorate. Thus disconcerted, the libertarians in the movement were no match for the Marxist sects who, emboldened by the crisis, sought to hegemonize a chimerical worker–student alliance. The student movement's rediscovery of the proletariat occurred almost everywhere and guaranteed the extinction of student movements as activists' mobilizing efforts were directed off-campus.

Only in Germany was the student movement so completely isolated from the working class that, in forming an extra-parliamentary opposition, it looked to broader sections of society, thereby intimating the coalition of forces that eventually coalesced into the Greens.

By 1971, student movements had burned themselves out almost everywhere. The turn to Marxism meant that, in the rare cases where issues stimulated renewed protests by students, they did not generally produce student movements. In 1976, the longest and most widespread student strike in French history paralyzed the universities, but it found little wider resonance, both because the political context had changed and because the prominence of leftist groups determined to portray the protests as anti-capitalist obscured the elements of cultural critique that had made the 1968 revolt so iconic. Because most protesting students rejected leadership of any kind, the presence of the sectarian left was less an aid to more effective mobilization than an obstacle to it, and the collapse of the protests left no significant legacy.

The direct impact of the 1960s student movements upon political structure was extremely limited. Their one nearly universal legacy – the extension of the franchise to 18-year-olds – has made little impact. Nowhere in the West did student movements succeed in overthrowing elected governments. Even in France, the demise of de Gaulle in 1969 was less a delayed result of the student revolt than of his own political miscalculation. Nor did student protests influence elections in the ways they hoped. The election that ended the French student revolt produced a decisive shift to the right. If student protest persuaded Lyndon Johnson not to seek reelection, the outcome was the election not of a liberal anti-war candidate but of Richard Nixon. Student movements' impacts upon policy were probably more positive. Student protest certainly raised the salience of the Vietnam War and probably hastened US withdrawal. But the greatest impacts were in higher education where both curricula and governance underwent reform.

The wider political impacts of student movements were diffuse. Graduates of the "generation of '68" contributed to the radicalization of Labour parties in Britain and Australia, and the secularization of communist parties in Italy and Spain, but their most important legacies were in the other social movements they inspired, the women's and personal liberation movements chief among them. "Movement entrepreneurs" who learned their skills in the student movement moved on to organize workers and the poor as well as to the environmental and anti-nuclear movements that emerged in the 1970s. By these means, student movements contributed to the legitimation of protest and the "participatory revolution" in liberal democracies whose effects continue, especially in Western Europe.

In and since the 1980s, observers, especially in the US, have claimed to detect in various campus-based campaigns – from disinvestment in South Africa under the apartheid regime to that against sweatshop labor in developing countries – the makings of a new student movement comparable to that of the late 1960s. But although students have indeed been among the early activists in such campaigns and in the anti-globalization/global justice movement, none has developed as a fully fledged student movement. The principal reason is that, in all these cases, either students rapidly found allies in other, more powerful social or political actors, or the movements that developed quickly mobilized much broader cross-sections of society.

What is extraordinary about western student movements is not that they so quickly disappeared but that anybody should have expected them to endure. The conditions of student life and the rapid turnover of student generations scarcely favor a politics of the long haul. The student movements of the 1960s arose out of an extraordinary conjunction of demography and social change, sustained rises in living standards, the expansion of higher education in response to technological change and changes in occupational structures, and an effective vacuum of political opposition. It is possible that some of these conditions will recur; it is improbable that they will again occur in such conjunction. The 1960s now appear as a transitional stage in the development of industrialized societies in two respects. First, they marked the point at which youth emerged as a distinct stage of life and was accorded the liberties and rights of adulthood. Second, the 1960s was the crucial decade in the transformation of the university from an elite institution at one remove from society into a site of mass education increasingly integrated with the demands of the market for highly skilled labor.

The transformation of higher education amounts in many places to its dilution. Not only are studies increasingly vocational, but students themselves are less likely to be 18-year-olds straight from school. Students are increasingly obliged to work at least part-time, and policies favoring late entry and recurrent education have encouraged universities to enroll greater numbers of older students. The status of "student" has, in consequence, become less determinate as students are increasingly integrated into the social and economic mainstream. Cultural and moral concerns have not disappeared from student politics, but they have, with the proliferation of the "new" social movements, become more widespread in non-student politics. Distinctively student politics have, as a result, come more closely to resemble the politics of other sectional interest groups.

If student movements have all but disappeared from the liberal democratic states of the advanced industrialized societies, they have continued intermittently to play important roles in authoritarian states. In the 1970s, student movements played critical roles in the democratization of Franco's Spain and of Greece during years of military dictatorship, in Spain because the universities enjoyed a degree of political immunity and so provided space for political discussion and organization not enjoyed by other groups in society, and in Greece because students dared to challenge an increasingly unpopular regime. In Hungary, Poland, and Czecholovakia, student movements repeatedly challenged communist regimes from the 1950s to the 1980s. Sometimes their protests were bloodily repressed – as in Hungary in 1956 – but student movements kept alive democratic aspirations and so contributed to the eventual collapse of those regimes.

The role of student movements in the democratization of Asian societies is even clearer. In Thailand, South Korea, Taiwan, and Indonesia, despite often savage repression, student movements provoked political crises in authoritarian regimes that ultimately issued in the expansion of civil liberties and democratic rights. Student protests against more closed and systematically repressive regimes have, however, had less

fortunate results. The student movement in Burma/Myanmar has been aggressively repressed, but perhaps the best-known example, both for the hopes it raised and the brutal way in which they were dashed, was the Chinese movement that focused upon Beijing's Tiananmen Square in 1989.

What these and the many other instances of student movements in authoritarian states have in common is that it was generally students who first challenged oppressive regimes in the name of universalist principles of liberty, morality, and democracy. The critical conditions for the emergence and development of student movements are a suitably moralistic political grievance, an absence of effective opposition within the polity from other, more powerful political actors, and a lack of powerful allies. Chief among the conditions of their success, however, is their ability to attract allies either from reformists within governing elites or from other sections of society, and upon the vigor of the state's repressive response. Students, who are relatively unconstrained by the obligations of adult life, may be the least inhibited partisans of anti-authoritarianism, but they are seldom able by themselves to achieve their objectives.

The development of student movements in modernizing societies under authoritarian regimes is common, but their development in fully democratic states in economically advanced societies is wholly exceptional.

SEE ALSO: Anti-War and Peace Movements; Global Justice as a Social Movement; Globalization and Global Justice; Modernization; New Left; New Social Movement Theory; Revolutions; Social Movements; Women's Movements

REFERENCES AND SUGGESTED READINGS

Boren, M. E. (2001) *Student Resistance: A History of the Unruly Subject.* Routledge, New York.

Burg, D. E. (1998) *Encyclopedia of Student and Youth Movements.* Facts on File, New York.

Feuer, L. (1969) *The Conflict of Generations: The Character and Significance of Student Movements.* Basic Books, New York.

Gitlin, T. (1981) *The Whole World is Watching: The Mass Media in the Making and Unmaking of the New Left.* University of California Press, Berkeley.

Miller, J. (1987) *Democracy is in the Streets: From Port Huron to the Siege of Chicago.* Simon & Schuster, New York.

Rootes, C. (1980) Student Radicalism: Politics of Moral Protest and Legitimation Problems of the Modern Capitalist State. *Theory and Society* 9(3): 473–502.

Rootes, C. (1990) Student Movements in Advanced Western Societies. *Associations Transnationales* 4: 207–17. Online. www.kent.ac.uk/sspssr/staff/rootes.htm.

Statera, G. (1975) *Death of a Utopia.* Oxford University Press, New York.

Touraine, A. (1971) *The May Movement.* Random House, New York.

subculture

David Muggleton

A subculture in general terms is a group with certain cultural features that enable it to be distinguished from other groups and the wider society from which it has emerged. But before it is possible to attempt a more precise clarification of the concept of subculture, it is necessary to examine the wider and related term "culture." The definition of culture that underpins the analysis of subculture is that which derives from the discipline of anthropology, and is concerned with the study of "a whole way of life" of a group or society. This widely encompassing and democratic definition does, however, raise the issue of what aspects of groups or societies are, or are not, "cultural." Sociologists have always regarded both religious and secular systems of values and beliefs to be cultural, along with those "styles of life" that arise from patterned modes of consumption. More recently, the discipline of cultural studies has reserved the term culture for those "signifying practices" – including cinema, fashion and design, cuisine, popular recreations, advertising, music, and so forth – through which people communicate their tastes and give expressive form to their emergent identities.

This does raise the issue of the level of generality or specificity at which culture is shared. In an age of global communications, certain cultural forms clearly cross national boundaries; yet it is also possible to identify distinctive national cultures. Within nations, cultural patterns are also cross cut by region, religious affiliation, and other social characteristics such as class, gender, age, ethnicity, and sexuality. It might therefore be appreciated why early definitions of subculture proposed the term to refer to a unified subset or division of the wider, national culture, one that had an integrative function for the individual member. Other initial attempts at conceptualization preferred to employ the designations subworld, population segment, or scene. But while precise agreement has never been reached over what constitutes subcultures, they can fundamentally be regarded as social groups whose specific, shared culture, lifestyle, or identity is distinctive enough to mark them off as different in some significant way from their "parent culture" (the immediate cultural milieu from which they arise). They can be organized around many kinds of shared interests and activities, including drug taking, fashion and music, or sport. Any particular social class, age span, gender, or ethnicity could conceivably dominate membership, although sociological studies of subcultures have often focused on those composed of white, male, working-class youths.

In a pluralistic and highly differentiated society, cultural identifications do not all wield the same influence or share equal status; rather, they are unevenly ranked in terms of power, so it is broadly possible to identify cultural clusters that stand in mutual relationships of domination and subordination. While subcultures can emerge from relatively powerful parent cultures, such that they can be considered enclaves within the dominant culture, ultra-radical groups of this kind whose values and activities are too sharply opposed to those of the dominant culture, and/or that are perceived to have developed a potentially revolutionary political self-awareness, tend to be conceptualized as "contra-cultures" or more often "countercultures." On the other hand, the term subculture is rarely used to denote sets of practices that are too conservative, reactionary, or reflective of the dominant culture. The assumption is that subcultures are inherently oppositional in that they are necessarily predicated on some form of disorder, delinquency, or deviance. Furthermore, they are also held to be "subterranean," their underground status and lack of formal barriers to membership contrasting sharply with the bureaucratic entry requirements of "official" organizations and legitimately sanctioned groups. The concept of subculture has therefore more typically been applied to those groups, arising from a subordinated parent class culture, whose position vis-à-vis the dominant culture is less clearly articulated or overtly politicized than those of the countercultures.

Various forms of social inquiry into a range of subcultural groups had taken place long before the concept itself had begun to gain currency in academic circles from the late 1940s onwards; but the pioneering, institutional research in this respect was that conducted by members of the sociology department at the University of Chicago in the period between the two world wars. The Chicago School, as they were collectively known, were concerned with the ecology of the urban environment and specifically the high incidence of crime and delinquency occurring in "zones of transition" – areas of rapidly shifting population and social disorganization in which normative controls had been weakened. By treating the city as a "social laboratory," the resulting case studies of juvenile gangs, hobos, and taxi-dance hall habitués were characterized by the symbolic interactionist principle of examining the world from the point of view of those being studied.

The Chicago School's legacy of commitment to qualitative interviews and ethnographic practice can be discerned in American studies of deviant and delinquent subcultures undertaken throughout the 1950s and 1960s. It also surfaced during this time in a slightly different strain of American sociological research into subcultures, one influenced by anomie theory, which suggests that certain groups, having internalized dominant success goals, find it impossible to realize their aspirations due to their structural position in society. A situation of anomie or "normlessness" results in which legitimate means are abandoned and alternative, "illegitimate" ones proposed. Lower working-class youth, for example, having suffered educational

failure, blocked opportunities, and "status frustration," invert respectable middle-class values, placing emphasis instead upon delinquent activities that are prized from the perspective of their own peer group. In this sense, the delinquent subculture can be said to arise as one collective "problem-solving" device. This paradigm was to dominate US subcultural theory throughout this period, albeit with various attempts at modification (including an analysis of the differential opportunities for illegitimate as well as legitimate means for success). It was also to become influential in Britain during the 1960s and 1970s, but took on slightly different emphases, being allied first with interactionism, then Marxism.

Of the various approaches apparent in British subcultural research during the first two post-war decades, two are particularly worthy of note. The first involved ecological explorations of delinquent, deviant, or impoverished urban communities and of the groups that formed within these neighborhoods. Unlike American studies that emphasized social disorganization or anomie theory as explanations for the formation of subcultures, the British context more usually stressed differential socialization – an adherence to alternative, subterranean working-class values and disassociation from middle-class notions of respectability. The second approach focused more specifically on schools and how streaming and banding (the allocation of pupils to school classes on the basis of perceived academic ability) aided the creation of pro- and anti-school pupil subcultures that respectively revered or rejected the educational ethos of academic achievement. The role of the teacher in ascribing either a positive or negative label to the pupil (such as "hardworking" or "troublemaker") and the response of the pupil in rejecting or, alternatively, accepting and internalizing the label, could also be seen as a factor in the formation of these school-based subcultures; as, indeed, could be the home background of students and their socialization into the parental social-class culture, as well as their involvement in commercialized youth leisure activities.

By the late 1960s and early 1970s, youth subcultures based around highly visible styles of dress became an explicit focus of academic attention in Britain. Initial explorations were concerned with how social reactions to deviance could escalate the problem through the generation of "moral panics" – a form of collective righteous indignation involving calls for greater law enforcement measures and tougher penalties for offenders. This involved an analysis of how the media, along with the agencies of social control such as the police and judiciary, labeled, stereotyped, exaggerated and, in so doing, amplified the very forms of delinquent behavior they sought to contain. Even so, the problem-solving approach was still relied on for structural explanations of the *origins* of the initial deviance and thus of the subcultures themselves. Throughout the 1970s the interactionist dimension of this body of work was displaced by a neo-Marxist mode of theorizing that saw these and other style-based subcultures, such as teddy boys, skinheads, and punks, as attempts by working-class youth to resist "hegemony" – the process by which middle-class (or bourgeois) culture attempts to define and circumscribe on its own terms the experience of subordinate classes. But again, in a manner echoing the American delinquency theory of the 1950s, each successive subculture was seen as an attempt at a solution to a historically specific "problem" faced by its working-class parent culture.

It is important to recognize two very different methodological strands within this general theoretical approach, associated with the Centre for Contemporary Cultural Studies (CCCS) at the University of Birmingham, UK. The first harked back to the classic ethnographic tradition of Chicago School sociology with its use of qualitative interviews and participant observation. The second more innovatively borrowed from French theory the principles of structuralism and semiotic analysis, which enabled all cultural practices to be read like a language. In this way, the styles of the subcultures were "decoded," like texts, for their hidden meanings, without recourse to the subjective motives of the subcultural members themselves. Some of the CCCS work was also notable for its consideration of how British "race relations" and black style subcultures, such as rude boys and Rastafarians, impacted upon the formation of white, indigenous British youth

subcultures. But much of the output by its male academics was silent on issues of gender divisions: the too-close identification with male-dominated groups and the masculine elements of style had rendered "invisible" the presence of girls in subcultures. To date, the few extensive, systematic explorations that have been conducted on females in male-dominated subcultures have confirmed the tentative assumptions made by early feminist critiques of the CCCS – that females use subcultures as a means of negotiating and resisting aspects of conventional femininity.

Although the work of the CCCS has proved highly influential in many other English-speaking countries, its position as the dominant paradigm in subcultural studies has been slowly undermined since the early 1990s by intense criticism from a new generation of academics who, eschewing textual analysis and once more embracing ethnography, have attempted to engage with the rapidly changing cultural conditions of contemporary youth. These developments have been further stimulated by the emergence of the "Acid-house," rave, or techno-party event from the late 1980s onwards. Because this new youth movement could not be easily accounted for by existing youth subcultural theory, academic attempts to come to terms with its prominence have helped advance the field of study. It is perhaps now accurate to say that we are in a situation where no one theoretical perspective dominates, although two of the major contenders for supremacy are those influenced by the work of Pierre Bourdieu and Michael Maffesoli, respectively.

The concept of "*sub*cultural capital" has been developed on the basis of Bourdieu's "cultural capital" to explain the hierarchies of taste operating within both clubbing crowds and subcultures. It refers to that form of "hip" status accrued by having esoteric knowledge regarding what is currently "in or out" on that scene, and is a means by which members of such groups display their "authenticity" – the legitimacy of their underground tastes in comparison to what is perceived to be the mass tastelessness of commercialized, "mainstream" culture. Maffesoli's concept of the "tribus" has, in the guise of "neo-tribe," also been applied to subcultures and dance crowds because of its connotations of transitory membership, eclectic tastes, and multiple allegiances – all markers of the "postmodern," and which are said to characterize contemporary youth movements.

Indeed, the widespread use of such concepts as "clubculture, "neo-tribe" or, in some cases, "lifestyle" has led to a questioning not only of the relevance of existing theory but the very term subculture itself. It would seem, however, that despite the polemical pronouncement that we are now "post-" or "after-" subculture, future work will not necessarily dispense with the concept of subculture, but is likely to emphasize the characteristics of flux, fluidity, and hybridization that these groups do, and perhaps to some extent always have, displayed.

SEE ALSO: Consumption, Fashion and; Consumption, Girls' Culture and; Consumption, Masculinities and; Consumption, Youth Culture and; Lifestyle Consumption; Postmodern Consumption; Sport Culture and Subcultures; Subcultures, Deviant

REFERENCES AND SUGGESTED READINGS

Bennett, A. & Kahn-Harris, K. (Eds.) (2004) *After Subculture: Critical Studies in Contemporary Youth Culture*. Palgrave, London.

Cohen, S. (2003) *Folk Devils and Moral Panics: The Creation of the Mods and Rockers*, 3rd edn. Routledge, London.

Downes, D. (1966) *The Delinquent Solution: A Study in Subcultural Theory*. Routledge & Kegan Paul, London.

Gelder, K. & Thornton, S. (Eds.) (1997) *The Subcultures Reader*. Routledge, London.

Hebdige, D. (1979) *Subculture: The Meaning of Style*. Methuen, London.

Leblanc, L. (2002) *Pretty in Punk: Girls' Gender Resistance in a Boys' Subculture*. Rutgers University Press, New Brunswick, NJ.

Muggleton, D. (2000) *Inside Subculture: The Postmodern Meaning of Style*. Berg, Oxford.

Muggleton, D. & Weinzierl, R. (Eds.) (2003) *The Post-Subcultures Reader*. Berg, Oxford.

Thornton, S. (1995) *Club Cultures: Music, Media and Subcultural Capital*. Polity Press, Cambridge.

White, R (Ed.) (1993) *Youth Subcultures: History, Theory and the Australian Experience*. National Clearinghouse for Youth Studies, Hobart, Tasmania.

subcultures, deviant

T. J. Berard

Subcultures come in an incredible diversity of forms, associated with street gangs, organized crime families, prison inmates, drug addicts, football hooligans, surfers, religious cults, hippie communes, and punk rockers. On a grander societal scale, subcultures include working-class and underclass subcultures, racial/ethnic subcultures, immigrant subcultures, regional subcultures, and youth subcultures. Although not all subcultures are deviant, the term subculture is often used to refer to the values and attitudes of deviant groups, and especially deviant groups of juveniles. Therefore, the study of deviant subcultures has traditionally been associated with the sociology of deviance and crime, criminology, and youth social work. But the study of deviant subcultures has expanded well beyond its traditional disciplinary boundaries.

DEFINING CHARACTERISTICS

The term *sub*culture is similar to culture in that both refer to a shared collection of traits, including beliefs, values, interests, language, behaviors, and a collective identity. The terms subculture and culture can alternately refer to the *group(s)* or *populations* of persons characterized by distinctive traits. The distinction between subculture and culture deals primarily with the relative size of different cultural groups sharing the same territory. Distinctive cultural groups become "sub" cultures by contrast to the conventional or mainstream values of a larger cultural group which serves as the cultural standard, due to its numerical majority and often greater status and power. Because the members of a subculture are characterized by cultural difference in relation to a larger, dominant, or mass culture, these differences are often evaluated as *deviant*, meaning that they violate conventional standards or fall short of conventional expectations. Some subcultures actually oppose or resist dominant culture, and these subcultures can be called *counter-cultures*.

ALBERT COHEN'S DELINQUENT BOYS

The sociology of deviant subcultures was first delineated in Albert Cohen's *Delinquent Boys: The Culture of the Gang* (1955). Cohen combined "cultural transmission" theories of delinquency with a "psychogenic" account at the level of individual psychology. Cohen attempted to explain the prevalence and persistence of urban delinquency in terms of neighborhood subcultures which recruit successive youth groups as subcultural "carriers." Recruitment depends on the provision of subcultural "answers" to problems of adjustment experienced by members of each subsequent cohort of working-class boys, each facing similar risks of status frustration in the face of middle-class norms, especially in school.

Cohen's arguments reference earlier scholarship on delinquency and gangs from the Chicago School of sociology. Clifford Shaw and Henry McKay's *Juvenile Delinquency and Urban Areas* (1942) had revealed higher rates of delinquency in Chicago's working-class immigrant and minority neighborhoods. Cohen attributed the "cultural transmission" theory of delinquency to Shaw and McKay, and to Edwin Sutherland's later theory of differential association. Cohen also drew on Shaw and McKay and subsequent scholarship on the social disorganization or differential social organization of urban working-class communities as causes of delinquency. Frederick Thrasher's study *The Gang* (1927) was related to the structural and ecological theory of social disorganization, although Thrasher was also instrumental in drawing attention to the *group* nature of much delinquency, and for pioneering observational research on gangs. Cohen also attributes to Shaw and McKay the theory of "culture conflict," best known from Thorsten Sellin's *Culture Conflict and Crime* (1938), in which Sellin analyzes crime partly in terms of the existence of different normative groups in society, resulting in a conflict of "conduct norms" or "cultural codes." Cohen acknowledges Shaw and McKay yet again with respect to the "illicit means" theory, which he secondarily attributes to Robert Merton. Merton was responsible for disseminating this theory under the name of anomie or strain theory, which explains economic street crime as an illicit or innovative means of satisfying American cultural norms of materialism and economic success.

One of Cohen's more distinctive contributions was to emphasize that new cultural forms emerge and are perpetuated through social *interaction* in youth peer groups, as youths *collectively* "solve" shared problems of social adjustment through delinquency. Cohen's subcultures thus provide a microsociological bridge between class and neighborhood location and delinquency. Previous usage had often referred to the subcultures of abstract population segments such as classes and races, rather than genuine groups, but in Cohen's hands, the term became more concrete.

SUBSEQUENT STUDIES AND THEORIES OF DEVIANT SUBCULTURES

The institutionalization of deviant subcultures as a topic within the sociology of crime and deviance was cemented when Cohen's *Delinquent Boys* (1955) was followed by Cloward and Ohlin's *Delinquency and Opportunity* (1960). Despite some differences, the two books were similarly theoretical in nature, and both saw deviant subcultures and delinquency as responses to problems of "adjustment" caused by structural issues of class inequality. A third influential author during this period was Miller (1958), who described lower-class culture in terms of a number of "focal concerns," including trouble, toughness, excitement, and autonomy. Cloward and Ohlin, and especially Miller, disagreed with Cohen's thesis that working-class boys experienced status anxiety over failure to live up to middle-class norms, but all agreed that the culture of delinquents should be understood against the background of class structure, with subcultures serving as links between class location and delinquency.

One of the most searching criticisms of the theory of deviant subcultures came with the work of David Matza. Matza's *Delinquency and Drift* (1964) criticized existing positivist theories of deviant subcultures for emphasizing determinism and constraint at the expense of the will or agency of subcultural members. He also argued that the norms of delinquents could not be sharply differentiated from conventional norms. Two related suggestions were that delinquents employ conventional moral techniques for neutralizing norms or excusing violations, and that delinquent culture and conventional culture overlap in a "subterranean" fashion. Jock Young later pursued Matza's subterranean analysis with great effect in his book *The Drugtakers* (1972). Young suggests that values of hedonism and disdain for work, for example, are subterranean values throughout society, and that drug-takers accentuate these values rather than create them as unique features of a deviant subculture.

In the 1970s, subcultural theories of deviance took on new forms in Britain, largely associated with Birmingham University's Centre for Contemporary Cultural Studies. Stuart Hall and Tony Jefferson's collection *Resistance Through Rituals* (1975) signaled the arrival of the British on the scene. The influence of 1960s labeling theory was evident in that British theorists and ethnographers skipped the foundational American concerns with the reform or control of juvenile delinquents. Instead, British scholarship reflected a neo-Marxist project of class analysis sympathetic to the symbolic resistance ostensibly represented by working-class youth subcultures. Paul Willis's *Learning to Labour* (1977), which documents a group of working-class youths leaving school and accommodating themselves to their place in the labor market, became one of the most celebrated ethnographies of deviant subcultures. Another landmark British contribution was Dick Hebdige's *Subculture: The Meaning of Style* (1979), a semiotic analysis of the aesthetics adopted by musical subcultures such as punk rockers. Both Willis and Hebdige suggested, in different manners, that youth subcultures signify ideological resistance to the hegemonic and oppressive nature of post-war capitalist society. The British tradition was distinct in many respects, but generally shared with American studies an underlying tendency to treat culture as secondary to structural and economic conditions, and to treat subcultural responses to structural inequality as ultimately ineffective, if not outright dysfunctional.

POLITICS AND MORALITY

The theoretical contributions of the early Chicago School partly reflected a liberal, reformist position on urban social problems, evident in their arguments that delinquency and crime were to be explained by the social disorganization of communities rather than in terms of individual pathology or racial proclivities. In the 1940s and 1950s, Cohen, and Cloward and Ohlin, raised more critical questions about unequal opportunities in American society, but stopped far short of radical critiques of the American class structure. Such early criminological theory also displayed an underlying correctional morality.

Ethnographic work remains perhaps the least evaluative and least political of traditions in the study of deviant subcultures, although ethnographers often cooperate with social service institutions, and portray their subjects with more sympathy than condemnation. Many British contributors identified unabashedly with the neo-Marxist theoretical tradition, but this in the post-war period when neo-Marxism entailed cultural critique rather than revolutionary politics. British work suggests that the problem is not so much delinquent youth groups as class inequality, unemployment, disruptive urban planning, and the like. In the US the "culture of poverty" argument has been used at times to hold the poor responsible for their poverty. The sociology of deviant subcultures has therefore always been associated with discourse on social problems, whether deviant subcultures serve as targets for reform, as targets for crime control, or as indicators of larger problems rooted in class relations, race relations, and urbanization.

It is important to recognize, however, that the term deviant subculture does not necessarily reflect a sociologist's judgment that particular groups are deviant. While the term can reflect such judgments, it can also be used by sociologists in a purely descriptive, non-judgmental sense, in reference to the common evaluation of a subculture in the wider cultural environment, which the sociologist merely observes to be the conventional evaluation. Howard Becker's *Outsiders* (1963) served as an influential introduction to non-judgmental studies of deviance and deviant subcultures.

METHODOLOGICAL ORIENTATIONS AND ISSUES

Methodologically, the study of deviant subcultures is complicated by the coexistence of two largely distinct traditions of research. Many positivist, quantitative studies starting in the 1960s have tested formal theories of delinquency, but these theories often address subcultures only tangentially, and many are not specifically *cultural* explanations of deviance. In such studies, subcultures might figure as a potential explanation for deviance, rather than as phenomena in their own right. Qualitative studies often describe real subcultural groups, who really deviate from middle-class norms and criminal codes. Qualitative researchers are often not concerned with formal theory testing, formal theory construction, or even causal explanation. Studies of deviant subcultures have often been of the latter, qualitative variety, employing observational and interview methods, which offer accounts of identity, behavior, and commitment as these are related to a way of life and system of meanings.

One of the more reflective methodological discussions is provided by Ned Polsky, a later member of the Chicago School, in his book *Hustlers, Beats, and Others* (1998). Polsky advocates studying criminals in their natural environment, and raises several objections to research trends in the sociology of crime and criminology. Polsky argues that good ethnographic research on criminals requires a disinterested stance on questions of morality and law, and finds fault with those who approach their studies with a social control or social work orientation. He charges that these trends have worsened recently because opportunities for jobs and grants are increasingly weighted towards the practical concerns of criminal justice administration. He objects to the common practices of studying criminals in "anti-crime settings" such as prisons and half-way houses, and criticizes the over-reliance on the recollective testimony of such caught criminals. He criticizes what he

suggests are scientistic prejudices and bureaucratic fetishes leading to the dismissal of unstructured field observations in favor of more structured research methods. The more structured methods, he charges, erect screens between researcher and subjects and prevent the observation of subjects in their ordinary life-situations.

While all of these are serious and important issues, Polsky risks being overly dismissive. Many noteworthy studies have been informed by the labeling/social reaction theory, which studies deviance as a function of social labeling, thus opening up new topics for research. Stan Cohen in his *Folk Devils and Moral Panics* (1972) noted the role of media in constructing a moral panic about youth subcultures, which led ironically to increased affiliations with such subcultures. Similar observations have been made about the gang eradication efforts of social workers and police. Meehan (2000) suggests that gang activities are in an interesting sense constructed by police dispatchers and gang units for bureaucratic and political reasons. Solid work has also been done in correctional settings. John Irwin explored inmate subculture in *The Felon* (1970), and D. L. Wieder's *Language and Social Reality* (1973) analyzes the "convict code" in a half-way house, prefiguring contemporary interest in the relevance of language for displaying subcultural norms.

A more recent discussion is provided by Katz and Jackson-Jacobs (2004) in a survey of gang research. Although the research surveyed includes noteworthy quantitative and positivist studies, Katz and Jackson-Jacobs note several shortcomings of quantitative data. Data from official sources, victim surveys, and self-report surveys are all problematic in different ways. Gang identities can go unremarked and unrecorded, can be recorded erroneously or inconsistently, or can be recorded in insufficient detail. Katz and Jackson-Jacobs argue that the field of gang studies "is structured on a quiet agreement not to press the causal question" (p. 93). They suggest that causal explanations may be tautological, and they ask whether gang membership causes violence, or vice versa. More broadly, these authors note that gangs are often treated as an index of the background social conditions which happen to preoccupy each given theorist, resulting in a failure to document the realities of gang life.

Although many quantitative studies have had minimal impact on subsequent theory and research, the entire project of explaining deviance in terms of subcultures is premised on statistics suggesting different rates of deviance in different segments of the population or in different neighborhoods. Such data cannot demonstrate that deviance is caused by subcultures, but they can be suggestive. The *lack* of statistical differences across groups or neighborhoods can throw subcultural theories into question, also. For this reason, self-report studies indicating that middle-class youth might engage in delinquent behavior at similar rates as poorer youth have added an interesting debate to the study of delinquency, as have studies suggesting that lower-class youth have similar rates of delinquency regardless of membership in delinquent peer groups. The theoretical relevance of quantitative analysis is also limited in part by the theories in question, which have frequently been criticized for being difficult to test or for being tautological. Such issues may ultimately reflect divergent traditions of inquiry. Theories of deviant subcultures have rarely been designed to satisfy the requirements of formal theory, although they have often implied a researchable causal relationship amid largely interpretive accounts of deviant subcultures.

FUTURE DIRECTIONS

By the 1980s the sociology of deviant subcultures had established a core literature, around which much discussion still revolves. This has led to an under-appreciation of historical developments, including the increasingly economic and violent character of street gangs in the US, blamed largely on the drug trade, and the further commercialization of youth subcultures, especially with respect to music and fashion. Academic developments have had greater influence on deviant subcultures scholarship. Sarah Thornton expanded subculture theories by incorporating Pierre Bourdieu's sociology into her *Club Cultures* (1996). The interpretive and linguistic turn in the social sciences has brought new attention to the identities and commitments of subcultural members as understood by the members themselves. Sue Widdicombe and Robin Wooffitt's *Language of Youth Subcultures* (1995) is exemplary in this vein.

Although the first generations of theory and research on deviant subcultures tended to focus on the delinquent behavior of young urban males, the literature has expanded considerably to address a wide range of deviant behavior, in a great variety of settings, and among girls as well as boys, adults as well as juveniles. The expansion of the subject area has occurred hand in hand with the proliferation of relevant theories and perspectives. Within criminology and the sociology of crime and deviance, relevant work is addressed to social learning and differential association theories, social disorganization and social control theories, labeling theory, class conflict and cultural conflict theories, and several others. Many relevant publications appear outside the sociology of crime and deviance, including in youth studies, cultural studies, urban studies, minority studies, and many other fields. Studies of cults, organized crime, hate groups, and other deviant subcultures are often pursued as independent topics, in what are now largely separate literatures. The sociology of youth culture, in particular, has broadened the discussion of subculture towards cultural rather than criminal deviance, for example emphasizing alternative music and dress rather than vandalism and street fights. Michael Brake's *Comparative Youth Culture* (1985) traces as well as represents this trend. Much of the existing momentum in the study of subcultures is now addressed to youth culture, and is associated with the field of cultural studies as well as sociology. Importantly, the early tendency to resort to subcultures primarily as an explanation for the apparently irrational behavior of urban youth, in the context of a structuralist emphasis on class relations, has been counterbalanced to some degree. In recent studies, cultural analysis sometimes appears as an alternative to structural analysis, meaning that subcultural identity, commitment, values, and styles are not always understood as determined and dysfunctional.

The relationship between deviance and cultural groups and cultural differentiation continues to be a rewarding topic of study, and has informed and even generated theoretical and empirical work across a growing variety of disciplines and subdisciplines.

SEE ALSO: Birmingham School; Chicago School; Consumption, Youth Culture and; Cultural Studies; Deviance; Gangs, Delinquent; Subculture

REFERENCES AND SUGGESTED READINGS

Arnold, D. (Ed.) (1970) *A Sociology of Subcultures.* Glendessary, Berkeley.
Bordua, D. (1962) Some Comments on Theories of Group Delinquency. *Sociological Inquiry* 32(2): 245–60.
Downes, D. & Rock, P. (1998) *Understanding Deviance: A Guide to the Sociology of Crime and Rule Breaking*, 3rd edn. Oxford University Press, Oxford.
Gelder, Ken & Thornton, S. (Eds.) (1997) *The Subcultures Reader.* Routledge, New York.
Katz, J. & Jackson-Jacobs, C. (2004) The Criminologists' Gang. In: Sumner, C. (Ed.), *The Blackwell Companion to Criminology.* Blackwell, Oxford, pp 91–124.
Meehan, A. (2000) The Organizational Career of Gang Statistics: The Politics of Policing Gangs. *Sociological Quarterly* 41(3): 337–70.
Miller, W. (1958) Lower Class Culture as a Generating Milieu of Gang Delinquency. *Journal of Social Issues* 14(3): 5–19.

subjectivity

Vivienne Boon

In sociology, subjectivity is often positioned as the opposite of objectivity, with objectivity being the ideal to which all empirical sociology should aspire. When Auguste Comte coined the phrase sociology, he had in mind the objective study of human behavior according to rational principles. A pertinent example of objective sociological analysis is that of Émile Durkheim, who argued that sociologists should analyze the internal (and impersonal) causes of social phenomena through the observation of concrete facts. Another notable example is, of course, the scholarship of Karl Marx, who also believed in a form of social scientism that went beyond

the surface of social life through the analysis of concrete social facts. Durkheim distinguished this analysis from philosophical introspection and generalizations that would be unduly affected by subjective influences such as beliefs and values (Giddens 1993; Crow 2005).

Objective sociology has been criticized by those who believe that the observation of social phenomena cannot and should not be separated from our subjective perspective, since doing so entails a form of distortion and even repression. Here, introspection and philosophical reflection play an important role and social analysis proceeds through the chief methods of "imagination, psychological insight and historical interpretation" (Mayer 1934: 341).

However, subjectivity is more than the mere opposite of objective social research. For it is an intrinsically modern concept that is bound up with ideas of the self as an acting agent. Through secularizing and modernizing processes, it was no longer a universal order that predetermined individual actions but, rather, it was within the thinking subject herself that reason and freedom were to be found. It was as a result of modernization processes that a preoccupation with the flourishing of the authentic individual self emerged (Berman 1970).

In the Enlightenment writings of Immanuel Kant, the transcendental subject stood at the center of all possible knowledge and reason. It was in the unified subject that sensibility and understanding collided, giving rise to the universal (Kant 1968). This idea of the unified subject was already contested by Georg Wilhelm Friedrich Hegel, who argued that the subject was not in and of itself but, rather, became aware of its subjectivity through its relation to surrounding objects and subjects.

Yet, it was with Friedrich Nietzsche that the subject disintegrated and became celebrated as an aesthetic endeavor. For Nietzsche intended to "incalculate a greater degree of personal agency, and the taking of responsibility for one's actions in the process of self-creation" (Hall 2004: 70). Nietzsche is hence often regarded as the forefather of postmodern and poststructuralist thought, which claims that there is no grand knowledge (Lyotard 1984) and no centered (or unified) subject (Lacan 1977; Foucault 1984).

According to Michel Foucault, our subjectivities are formed through our subjection to various discourses that position a subject within a web of knowledge–power relations. Whilst these discourses of power are oppressive, they also provide a site of resistance in that we can continuously reinvent our subjectivities (Foucault 1984: 41–2). It is for this reason that Foucault endeavored to engage in a genealogical critique that consists of a "historical investigation into the events that have led us to constitute ourselves and to recognize ourselves as subjects of what we are doing, thinking, saying" (1984: 46). Thus whilst we are subject to various historical discursive processes, we are also agents acting and interfering in these historical processes.

Appeals to active subjective agents have been made in light of identity and subcultural politics. For example, within identity politics, it is argued that women's voices provide alternative voices (through their female subjectivity) within a political realm that is dominated by a male hegemonic order. Similarly, subcultural styles such as punk have also been heralded as the creation of new subjectivities (Hebdige 1979).

We should be careful, however, not to conflate the notions of identity and subjectivity, even though they are rather difficult to distinguish since they are intrinsically related. It is difficult to think of one's identity without regarding one's subjectivity, just as it is hard to perceive of one's subjectivity without a sense of I, or identity. Yet, as Heidrun Friese notes, identity thinking in the social sciences has often been motivated by the desire for unity of the subject, and has proceeded through the construction of narratives and the process of naming that synthesized the manifold (Friese 2002: 26). Reflection on subjectivity is slightly different from identity thinking in that it is more specifically focused on the consciousness of being, on the medium of one's own mind in the perception of things, and on the awareness of one's subjective feelings. Thus reflection on subjectivity is more related to the idea of consciousness and stands at the intersection of "two lines of philosophical inquiry: epistemology (the study of how we know what we know) and ontology (the study of the nature of being or existence)" (Hall 2004: 4).

SEE ALSO: Belief; Collective Identity; Discourse; Epistemology; Foucault, Michel; Identity Theory; Objectivity; Realism and Relativism: Truth and Objectivity; Strong Objectivity; Values

REFERENCES AND SUGGESTED READINGS

Berman, M. (1970) *The Politics of Authenticity: Radical Individualism and the Emergence of Modern Society*. Atheneum, New York.

Crow, G. (2005) *The Art of Sociological Argument*. Palgrave, Basingstoke.

Foucault, M. (1984) *The Foucault Reader*. Ed. P. Rabinow. Penguin, London.

Friese, H. (2002) Identity: Desire, Name, and Difference. In: Friese, H. (Ed.), *Identities: Time, Difference, and Boundaries*. Berghahn Books, New York.

Giddens, A. (1993) *New Rules of Sociological Method: A Positive Critique of Interpretative Sociologies*. Polity Press, Cambridge.

Hall, D. E. (2004) *Subjectivity*. Routledge, New York.

Hebdige, D. (1979) *Subculture: The Meaning of Style*. Methuen, London.

Hegel, G. W. F. (1977) *The Phenomenology of Spirit*. Oxford University Press, Oxford.

Kant, I. (1968) *Immanuel Kant's Critique of Pure Reason*. Trans. N. K. Smith. Macmillan, London.

Lacan, J. (1977) *Écrits: A Selection*. Norton, New York.

Lyotard, J.-F. (1984) *The Postmodern Condition: A Report on Knowledge*. Manchester University Press, Manchester.

Mayer, J. (1934) Scientific Method and Social Science. *Philosophy of Social Science* 1, 3 (July): 338–50.

Sarup, M. (1993) *An Introductory Guide to Post-Structuralism and Postmodernism*, 2nd edn. Harvester Wheatsheaf, Hemel Hempstead.

suburbs

Judith J. Friedman

Social scientists in the US usually identify a city's suburbs as the municipalities (plus any "urban" unincorporated areas) that are located outside the political boundaries of that city, but are adjacent to the city or to its other suburbs. A city's suburbs form a band around the city that has (1) lower population density overall than the city, yet (2) predominantly urban land uses. Unless the city is located near another city, its suburbs end where farmland or open space predominates. The term suburb refers either to the entire band of suburbs around a city or to particular places within a suburban band. The term suburban also can refer to a way of life identified with suburbs.

The definition of suburb and the characteristics of suburbs differ around the world, in part because of differences in local government structure. In many countries, suburbs are relatively new neighborhoods within a city or within a metropolitan area served by one government. This entry focuses on suburbs in the US, where municipalities, including those considered suburbs, have substantial political and fiscal autonomy. In 2000, half the US population lived in suburbs of metropolitan areas (Hobbs & Stoops 2002).

Early US cities absorbed more people and more activities by (1) using land more intensively, and (2) expanding on the edge, as developers converted farmland to an urban use. Cities routinely annexed the newly urban land. In the nineteenth century, railroads permitted a new kind of small town: a primarily residential town linked by rail to a city. These towns were called suburbs. As the city expanded toward a commuter suburb, well-to-do residents frequently resisted annexation. State laws in Eastern states soon facilitated this method of retaining local political control by making incorporation relatively easy, and annexation difficult.

The US population shifted from small towns and farms to large towns and cities during the nineteenth century, and additional types of suburbs formed. Before 1900, street car lines facilitated lines of urban land use that extended outside city limits. Factory owners built modern factories on the city's outskirts, creating industrial suburbs. Cities annexed some of this newly urban land, but residents of other new places incorporated. New urban land uses eventually surrounded older towns, cities, and commuter suburbs. Despite the resulting diversity among a city's suburbs, the term suburb retained a connotation of new, residential, and middle class.

Factories built during World War II brought more jobs to former farmland around cities, and both residential and commercial construction boomed after the war. Farmland near a city provided ideal locations for large developments, especially when near a highway. Diverse federal and state policies subsidized new schools, hospitals, sewer lines, and other infrastructure, but did little to repair and upgrade existing infrastructure. Federal housing policies combined with banking and real estate practices also tended to put cities at a disadvantage. Some cities, especially cities in the West, continued to annex new development. If a city did not annex growing areas, its suburban band expanded in land area, employment, and population. If the city itself failed to attract new residents and businesses, its property tax revenue declined, putting it at further disadvantage.

As cities stopped routine annexation, social scientists and administrators needed a straightforward definition for this urban land outside city limits, a definition that would facilitate both data collection and comparisons among places and across time. The US Bureau of the Census based such definitions on political boundaries – municipal or county. Standard Metropolitan Statistical Areas (SMSAs) contain a large city and its "ring" – the rest of the county that contains the central city land plus any adjacent counties economically tied to the city. An SMSA can include substantial rural areas. In 1910 the Census identified 25 metropolitan districts – cities plus adjacent "urban" minor civil divisions (Gardner 1999) – but published little information about the "fringe" of each district. In 1950 the Bureau defined 35 urbanized areas, units again based on minor civil divisions. A city's fringe could include incorporated places (residential suburbs, industrial suburbs, older towns and villages) plus unincorporated land that had a population density of 1,000 per square mile or more or was surrounded by other land within the fringe. Since land area and the population size of a city's fringe depended in part on past annexation, large fringe areas were more typical of cities in the Northeast than of cities in the West or South.

In Census reports and in academic research using Census data, a city's fringe (and its ring) became its suburbs. Individual incorporated places within the fringe or ring also are called suburbs. Demographers such as Schnore (1965) emphasized the diversity of these incorporated places, and suggested categories. Schnore reserved "suburb" for primarily residential municipalities; suburban residents still largely commuted to city jobs. Schnore called municipalities that provided substantial employment, and hence had some independence from the city, "satellites."

Even in 1950, distinctions between city and suburb were not always obvious, particularly in highly urban areas. Jersey City, NJ could be a central city or a satellite, but was it a satellite of Newark or of New York City? Similarly, was Newark a city with suburbs, or a part of New York City's suburbs? With each subsequent Census, this situation has become more common and more complex.

Further changes in land use, particularly the growth of jobs in suburbs, have generated a new kind of commute and a new term: exurb. Exurbs are small towns or unincorporated areas with sizable new housing developments. Located outside the suburban fringe, an exurb houses many people who work in suburbs.

The suburbs (and exurbs) of any US city tend to be different from each other, yet internally homogeneous. Employment is no longer a key distinction. Municipal zoning practices, economic development policies, and other local policies mean that a suburb can appear residential, yet have substantial commercial, office, and even industrial activity. Suburbs now concentrate such activities in malls or in "parks" located near highway interchanges, effectively out of sight as corporate landscaping blends into the residential landscape.

The critical difference among US suburbs today involves ability to finance municipal services. US municipalities, counties, and school districts depend heavily upon property tax revenue, and per capita property tax revenue varies substantially. Federal and state funds have not equalized local revenue (and services). A suburb with wealthy residents plus substantial non-residential development can provide services more easily than a primarily residential community with low-income residents. Over time, these differences have produced substantial "stratification of place" among each city's suburbs. As this suggests, there is wide variation in median family income as well. Suburbs are not necessarily middle class.

The processes creating the decline of annexation, suburban stratification of place, and substantial population and housing homogeneity

within each suburban municipality involve more than municipal finance. Long-held beliefs about proper land-use planning, use of local land-use planning (rather than metropolitan area planning), and the importance of home ownership as a financial investment make substantial contributions. The initial characteristics of each suburb also have lasting impact. Older industrial suburbs, for example, tend to follow a different track than older suburbs that began as upper-middle-class residential areas.

Housing stock can be especially important, as it varies with the period in which a suburban municipality experienced rapid growth (Friedman 1994). Suburbs that grew rapidly before World War II include satellites with substantial multi-family housing and other housing built for the working class. Other older residential suburbs can have large homes that have retained, even gained, value. Places that grew rapidly just after World War II are likely to include former defense plants and post-war housing tracts that initially had small houses on small lots. In this period, many municipalities, anticipating future growth, zoned for large-lot single family homes. In part for this reason, average house size increased rather steadily after 1948. Single family homes built in 1955 averaged 1,270 square feet. The mean for new single family homes increased to 1,500 in 1970, 2,080 in 1990, and 2,330 in 2003 (HUD and US Bureau of the Census 2004). Suburbs also vary in the extent they have added condominium and townhouse developments, a possible source of "moderate" cost (but not necessarily "affordable") housing.

The total suburban population of the US is becoming less "white" as others settle in suburbs. By 2000, over half (58 percent) of the Asian population, half (49 percent) of the Hispanic population, but only 39 percent of the black population lived in suburbs (defined as the rings of SMSAs) (Logan 2001). Koreans and Asian Indians are especially suburban, in part because immigrants are settling directly in suburbs. In the entire country, 75 percent of the 2000 suburban population was non-Hispanic white. The remaining 25 percent included 11 percent classified Hispanic, 8 percent black, and 4 percent Asian (US Census).

The suburban history of blacks is complex. US suburbs have always housed and employed

African Americans (Wiess 2004). Before World War II, high-status suburbs typically had neighborhoods that housed African American servants and other local workers. In the South, African Americans typically lived on the outskirts of the city. In the North, freed slaves founded villages and towns that are now within a city's fringe. The vast majority of the housing developments that went up outside (and also inside) city limits before, perhaps, 1970 were, however, entirely white. Homogeneity in residential neighborhoods was "best practice." Realtors and sociologists alike argued that neighborhoods homogeneous in income, race, ethnicity, and other characteristics were more likely to retain property value over time. Further, housing discrimination was legal until the late 1960s. Since then, the percentage of blacks living in suburbs has slowly increased. Informal practices continue, however, to limit housing integration.

SEE ALSO: City Planning/Urban Design; Exurbia; New Urbanism; Residential Segregation; Urban Ecology; Urban Policy; Urbanization

REFERENCES AND SUGGESTED READINGS

Friedman, J. J. (1994) Suburban Variations within Highly Urbanized Regions: The Case of New Jersey. In: Baldassare, M. & Chekki, D. (Eds.), *Suburban Communities, Research in Community Sociology* 4: 97–132.

Gardner, T. (1999) Metropolitan Classification for Census Years before World War II. *Historical Methods* 32: 139–50.

Hobbs, F. & Stoops, N. (2002) *Demographic Trends in the 20th Century.* Census 2000 Special Reports (November), US Census Bureau, US Department of Commerce, Washington, DC.

HUD and US Bureau of the Census (2004) Characteristics of New One Family Homes. Construction Reports, Series C 25. HUD and US Bureau of the Census, Washington, DC.

Logan, J. R. (2001) The New Ethnic Enclaves in America's Suburbs. Lewis Mumford Center for Comparative Urban and Regional Research, State University of New York, Albany.

Rudel, T. (1989) *Situations and Strategies in American Land-Use Planning.* Cambridge University Press, Cambridge.

Salamon, S. (2003) *Newcomers to Old Towns.* University of Chicago Press, Chicago.

Schnore, L. (1965) *The Urban Scene: Human Ecology and Demography.* Free Press, New York.

Wiess, A. (2004) *Places of Their Own: African American Suburbanization in the Twentieth Century.* University of Chicago Press, Chicago.

suicide

Steven Stack

Suicide is among the top ten leading causes of death. Over 30,000 Americans take their own lives each year: about 85 per day. Further, there are an estimated 250,000–600,000 suicide attempts each year. There are at least 5 million living Americans who have attempted suicide in the past. While Americans fear being murdered more than dying by their own hand, the suicide rate is currently double the murder rate.

The dominant mode of analysis of suicide has stressed Durkheim's (1966) concept of social integration – bonds between the individual and society. Subordination of the individual to society is thought to provide meaning and prevent selfishness or "egoism." Groups lacking in ties to society, such as widowers, the divorced, atheists, the unemployed, and non-church members, are at higher than average risk of suicide.

According to Durkheim, the greater the number of religious beliefs and practices shared with co-religionists, the lower the suicide rate of a group. Historically, Catholics were more integrated (e.g., meatless Fridays, confession, weekly church attendance) than Protestants, and had lower suicide rates. In modern times, Islam is a religion with a high level of integration (e.g., prayer is expected multiple times a day). Research finds that the higher the proportion of Muslims in a nation, the lower the nation's suicide rate.

Marriage and parenting are seen as providing a set of responsibilities, such as obligations to a spouse (e.g., giving and receiving emotional support) and children, that act as protections against excessive self-involvement or egoism. A review of 132 studies found strong support for this thesis in 77.9 percent of their findings. For example, in Austria, the suicide rate of divorced persons is 128.6/100,000. This rate is 4.22 times higher than the suicide rate among married persons (30.5/100,000). Divorce rates are the best predictor of suicide rates in the 50 American states for all census years (e.g., 1940, 1950, 1960, 1970).

CHANGES OVER TIME IN THE TOPIC AND ITS TREATMENT

Religion and Suicide

Two new theories have linked religion to suicide. First, Stack's theory of religious commitment and suicide argues that belief in a few life-saving principles (as opposed to the many that Durkheim posited) may be enough to prevent suicide. For example, belief in a blissful afterlife for those who persevere may protect against risk factors such as poverty, divorce, and death of loved ones. Second, Pescosolido's religious networks perspective argues that friends from church (co-religionists) may provide emotional and material support for otherwise suicidal individuals. It may not be religious beliefs per se that save lives, but the social support networks in churches that prevent suicides. Most of the empirical work on these new, perhaps complementary, perspectives has supported the respective theories. For example, in an analysis of 261 Canadian census divisions, a 10 percent increase in the proportion with no religious affiliation (a sign of both low religious commitment and religious networking potential) is associated with a 3.2 percent increase in the suicide rate.

Economic Strain and Suicide

Durkheim argued that poverty was a school of social constraint. The poor were toughened by impoverishment and could handle life's adversities better than the more affluent. However, in the last 50 years, most research on social class and suicide risk has found that lower-status persons have higher, not lower, suicide rates. For example, data for the US indicate that laborers have a suicide rate of 94.4 suicides per 100,000, eight times the national suicide rate. The high suicide rate of lower-class persons is partly a consequence of their high rates of severe mental troubles, alcoholism, and family disruption.

Unemployment can influence suicide by affecting suicide risk factors such as lowering household income, self-esteem, work-centered social networks, and increasing depression levels. For example, in London, the unemployed had a suicide rate of 73.4/100,000, five times that for the general population (14.1/100,000). In Austria the suicide rate for the unemployed was 98.3/100,000, a figure nearly four times that for the general population (25.0/100,000).

Alcohol and Suicide

Durkheim rejected alcohol abuse as a contributing factor to suicide, although his own data, if carefully analyzed, showed a significant association. Nevertheless, alcohol can increase suicide risk through such means as emotional disinhibition, which enhances impulsive behavior including suicide, pharmacological effects, and depression. To the extent that a culture provides positive definitions of alcohol use, it may indirectly promote suicidal behavior. Sociological research over the past three decades has often illustrated an association. For example, at the level of individuals, in a panel study of 40,000 men over four decades, the lifetime prevalence of suicide by age 60 was 4.76 percent for alcohol abusers compared to 0.63 percent for non-abusers.

CURRENT EMPHASES IN RESEARCH AND THEORY

Media and Suicide

Durkheim, on the basis of scant data, viewed media-based stories, such as those in newspapers, on suicide as largely irrelevant to explaining suicide rates. However, since 1967 many of the 106 studies on this issue have found copycat effects. From news and other coverage of suicide, depressed people may learn that there are troubled individuals who commit suicide in response to life's problems. For example, the publication of *Final Exit*, a guide recommending suicide through asphyxiation for the terminally ill, was associated with an increase of 313 percent in suicide by this method in New York City. This was for the year that the book was published. A copy of *Final Exit* was found at the scene of 27 percent of these suicides.

From the standpoint of social learning theory, widely publicized suicides are most likely to trigger copycat suicide if the model is a celebrity, someone that many people identify with, a well-known and admired person. In particular, studies of the widely publicized suicides of entertainment or political celebrities are 14 times more likely to find a copycat effect than studies of ordinary suicides. When famous movie stars commit suicide, there are, on average, 217 additional suicides during the month of news coverage of their suicide.

Gender Suicide Ratio

After a century of converging, the suicide rates of men and women are diverging. For example, while the suicide rate of women was half that of men 50 years ago, it is currently only a quarter that of men in the US. Stack developed a cultural theory of a curvilinear relationship in the gender suicide ratio. First, female rates of suicide would rise along with increases in labor force participation. The cultural definition of women's place as being in the home would promote a certain amount of strain and guilt for many working women, increasing their risk of suicide and closing the gender gap. However, after a critical mass of women was in the labor force, culture defined the working mother in more positive terms. Supportive social institutions such as day-care centers emerged, and women's percentage share of better jobs in the professions increased. Women could take more advantage of the benefits of work, such as adult companionship, careers, and higher household income, and their suicide rate declined. However, the gains for women in such areas as medicine, law, and the professorate represent corresponding losses in occupational mobility for men. Male suicide rates have increased proportionately, thus widening the gender suicide gap. Pampel has successfully applied Stack's curvilinear theory to a sample of other industrial nations.

Sexual Orientation and Suicide

Given significant homophobic tendencies in the cultural systems of western developed societies, one might anticipate that persons with homosexual orientations would have a higher incidence of suicidal behavior. It is often argued that the recognition of one's homosexuality is often associated with anxiety, depression, confusion, and other suicidogenic conditions. The families of many gay youth may multiply the risk of suicidal behavior through the rejection of the gay child. While there are few well-designed research studies on sexual orientation and suicide, two patterns are found in the existing research evidence. First, homosexuals have higher rates of suicide attempts than heterosexuals. For community samples, the prevalence of having attempted suicide among gay males ranges from 20–35 percent and is about twice that of heterosexual males. Among disturbed samples (e.g., runaway youth) the prevalence rate of attempted suicide sometimes exceeds 50 percent. The prevalence of suicide attempts is higher among lesbians, but the gap between lesbian and heterosexual women is smaller than that for men. Second, while completed suicide and sexual orientation is an understudied area, there is no evidence that homosexuals have a higher rate of completed suicide than heterosexuals. Further, the stress and other factors underlying the suicides of gay and heterosexual persons were more similar than different and include relationship difficulties with lovers. However, gay suicides are more apt than heterosexual suicides to use hanging as a method and to have been diagnosed schizophrenic.

QUALITY OF SUICIDE DATA

Data on suicide tend to underreport the phenomenon. Some authorities seek to conceal suicide as a cause of death. The best estimates of underreporting place the suicide undercount as being somewhere between 3 percent and 18 percent. For example, suicide is undercounted by 2.8 percent for males and 5.6 percent for females. These error rates are not large relative to undercounts for crime rates. For example, crime underreporting in federal crime statistics amounts to 67 percent of all index crimes, including 49 percent of the rapes and 50 percent of the burglaries.

Analyses of data for 404 American county groups support the validity of suicide data. Indicators of misreporting in the official statistics have little discernible effect on the relationships between major sociological variables (e.g., divorce rates, religion) and suicide rates. The errors in suicide reporting are not considered large enough to preclude meaningful sociological analyses.

FUTURE DIRECTIONS

The vast majority of sociological studies on suicide deal with suicide as a phenomenon isolated from other forms of deviant behavior. However, recent research finds that suicidal persons, those who are basically depressed and out of touch with the value of life, are involved in a broad range of deviant behaviors. For example, analyses of national data found that suicidal youth are more likely than others to engage in each of the following deviant behaviors: crack cocaine use (9.25 times more likely), marijuana use (3.25 times more likely), binge drinking (2.69 times more likely), heavy smoking (3.17 times more likely), unsafe sex (2.65 times more likely), getting someone pregnant/getting pregnant (4.63 times more likely), carrying a gun (4.73 times more likely), aggravated assaults (6.56 times more likely), and threatened with a weapon (5.23 times more likely). Research on crime and deviant behavior could benefit by viewing deviance, in part, as an expression of suicidality.

Of course, in future research there is the issue of the direction of causality. Does suicidal behavior cause deviance, or does deviance cause suicidality? Perhaps a common factor x may account for many types of deviant behavior, including suicidal behavior. The common factor may be, as Durkheim argued, lack of adequate subordination of the individual to society: low social integration. Factor x may also include a psychological state such as depression, which has been associated with a wide variety of deviant behaviors, especially suicide.

SEE ALSO: Alcoholism and Alcohol Abuse; Divorce; Drug Use; Durkheim, Émile; Homosexuality; Media; Mental Disorder; Religion; Stressful Life Events; Unemployment

REFERENCES AND SUGGESTED READINGS

Durkheim, É. (1966 [1897]) *Suicide*. Free Press, New York.

Pampel, F. (1998) National Context, Social Change, and Sex Differences in Suicide Rates. *American Sociological Review* 63: 744–58.

Pescosolido, B. & Mendelsohn, R. (1986) Social Causation or Construction of Suicide. *American Sociological Review* 51: 80–100.

Pope, W. (1976) *Durkheim's Suicide: A Classic Reanalyzed*. University of Chicago Press, Chicago.

Stack, S. (1982) Suicide: A Decade Review of the Sociological Literature. *Deviant Behavior* 4: 41–66.

Stack, S. (1987) The Effect of Female Participation in the Labor Force on Suicide: A Time Series Analysis. *Sociological Forum* 2: 257–77.

Stack, S. (2000) Suicide: A 15-Year Review of the Sociological Literature Part I: Cultural and Economic Factors; Part II: Modernization and Social Integration Perspectives. *Suicide and Life Threatening Behavior* 30: 145–62.

Stack, S. (2003) Media as a Risk Factor in Suicide. *Journal of Epidemiology and Community Health* 57: 238–40.

Sumner, William Graham (1840–1910)

Bernd Weiler

William G. Sumner, born in Paterson, New Jersey, is commonly regarded as one of the most influential American social scientists in the late nineteenth and early twentieth centuries. In histories of sociology he is often portrayed or – as some would argue – misportrayed as a conservative apologist for "tooth-and-claw" capitalism and as the great Social Darwinist antipode to his progressive and reform-oriented contemporary and fellow-countryman L. F. Ward.

After graduating from Yale in 1863, Sumner, the son of an immigrant mechanic and pious Protestant from Lancashire, attended the universities of Geneva, Goettingen, and Oxford to study languages, history, and theology and to prepare himself for the ministry. In 1866 he returned to Yale as a classics tutor and, shortly afterwards, joined the Protestant Episcopal clergy. In 1872 he was appointed to the newly founded chair of political and social sciences at Yale, a post he held until his retirement in 1909. In the 1870s Sumner also served as a politician for the Republicans. Disillusioned, he left politics after a few years and became a liberal Mugwump. In 1908, two years before his death, Sumner succeeded L. F. Ward as the second president of the American Sociological Society.

Among the main intellectual influences on Sumner's work were classical economic theory, especially Malthus's population theory, the positivistic approach to the study of history (e.g., Buckle), Darwinian evolutionism, Spencerian sociology, and, later in his career, the emerging comparative researches in ethnography and cultural history (e.g., Lippert), as well as the contributions of the "Austrian Struggle School." Like many theorists of his age who converted from religion to social science, Sumner replaced the belief in a divine providential design with a naturalistic conception of the lawfulness of the social world.

Sumner's writings span a broad spectrum of subjects and genres. Apart from extended treatises on American economic history and political biographies, Sumner, in the first part of his career, gained fame as a public intellectual who vigorously supported laissez-faire economics and adhered to a Social Darwinist philosophy. In numerous articles he polemicized against bimetallism, protective tariffs, trade unionism, socialism, governmental paternalism, amateurish "meddling" in social affairs, and utopianism. Far from simply glorifying the status quo and contrary to the prevailing optimism of his time, however, Sumner remained skeptical about societal progress, warned against the danger that plutocrats might undermine the independence of political life, and argued forcefully against the emerging American imperialism.

In the second part of his career, following a breakdown in health in 1890 and accompanying his increasing disillusionment with American society, Sumner turned his attention from current social, political, and economic affairs to the cross-cultural study of the importance of tradition for human conduct. The major works resulting from this research, in the course of which Sumner and his collaborators collected and indexed a massive amount of data from cultural history and ethnography, are the loosely structured treatise *Folkways* (1906) and the voluminous, similarly unsystematic, posthumously published *The Science of Society* (1927). At the core of Sumner's late theoretical work, which was not free from contradictions, lie his identification of four universal needs (hunger, love, vanity, fear), his argument that societies had developed different means or "folkways" to satisfy those needs, his claim of the priority of the group over the individual, his analysis of the antagonistic relationship between "we-groups" vs. "others-groups," his inquiry into the universal nature of "ethnocentrism," and his emphasis on the mighty and unconscious influence that "folkways" exerted over all people, whether "savage" or "civilized." The main thrust of Sumner's late work, however, may be seen in the enormous collection of empirical data. Though Sumner and his disciple Keller neglected the use of statistical methods, were unable to synthesize their data in a satisfactory manner, and were unable to lay the foundations for a comparative science of society, they anticipated and influenced the much more comprehensive and systematic *Human Relations Area Files* that are intimately linked to the name of G. P. Murdock, another Yale scholar.

SEE ALSO: Cultural Relativism; Ethnocentrism; Gumplowicz, Ludwig; Ratzenhofer, Gustav; Social Darwinism; Spencer, Herbert; Ward, Lester Frank

REFERENCES AND SUGGESTED READINGS

Bannister, R. C. (1989) *Social Darwinism: Science and Myth in Anglo-American Social Thought*. Temple University Press, Philadelphia.

Bannister, R. C. (Ed.) (1992) *On Liberty, Society, and Politics: The Essential Essays of William Graham Sumner*. Liberty Fund, Indianapolis.

Bernard, L. L. (1940) The Social Science Theories of William Graham Sumner. *Social Forces* 19(2): 153–75.

Curtis, B. (1981) *William Graham Sumner*. Twayne, Boston.

Hofstadter, R. (1992 [1944]) *Social Darwinism in American Thought*. Beacon Press, Boston.

Starr, H. E. (1925) *William Graham Sumner*. Henry Holt, New York.

Sumner, W. G. (1906) *Folkways: A Study of the Sociological Importance of Usages, Manners, Customs, Mores, and Morals*. Ginn, Boston.

Sumner, W. G. (1919 [1911]) *War and Other Essays*. Yale University Press, New Haven.

Sumner, W. G. & Keller, A. G. (1927) *The Science of Society*, 4 vols. Yale University Press, New Haven.

Sunbelt

Vern Baxter and David Johnson

The Sunbelt is a contested construct adopted by scholars in the late 1970s from journalistic accounts of industrial relocation and shifts in population and political power to the Southern and Western regions of the US after World War II. The Sunbelt is defined by juxtaposing rapid economic growth and the rise of conservative politics in the South and West, with economic collapse and political liberalism in the Northeast and Midwest (Frostbelt). Sunbelt boundaries are ambiguous, depending on whether attention is directed to relocation of old industry, location of new industry, or political realignment. Sale's (1975) early designation of the Sunbelt as that area below the 37th parallel (northern border of North Carolina through lower third of California) was largely confirmed by Rice and Bernard's (1983) survey of business and public perceptions of the region, but other scholars believe the Sunbelt represents a sloppy form of regionalization that combines disparate patterns of growth and prosperity found in the South and West.

While scholars quarrel about geographic boundaries, most agree the Sunbelt represents economic growth and conservative politics in a new urban environment. Spurred by federal investment in military and space programs, the expansion of Sunbelt defense, aerospace, electronics, agribusiness, oil and gas, and tourist industries places the region at the center of the new economy. Industrial restructuring and flexible production methods favor Sunbelt cities as locations of new industry and for relocation of northern manufacturing plants. Sunbelt cities generally offer lower labor costs, non-union workforces, and less stringent environmental and zoning regulations than found in the north. Larger cities like Los Angeles, Houston, and Atlanta now challenge the prominence of New York and Chicago, while medium size Sunbelt cities like Charlotte and Albuquerque are peers to Cincinnati and Providence. Automobile transportation facilitates urban sprawl in Sunbelt cities where annexation and city–county mergers favor private investment and unfettered, if uneven, economic growth. Internal migration to the South and West and extensive immigration from Asia and Latin America increased population and political representation of increasingly Republican Sunbelt states that spearheaded realignment of national politics.

Convergence and uneven development theories provide the broadest explanations of Sunbelt economic growth. Convergence theory emphasizes long-term equilibrium in national market economies. Earlier industrial growth, higher incomes, and lower unemployment in Northern industrial cities was eventually offset by lower wages and factor costs in the Sunbelt. Regional convergence occurred as investors took advantage of lower costs and backlogs of unapplied technologies in industry and agriculture. Rostow (1977) argues that the global economic upswing after 1972 favored the Sunbelt with higher food and energy prices and expansion of electronics and petrochemical investment, while demand stagnated for products like textiles, shoes, steel, and autos produced up north. Ecological theories highlight a filtering process whereby firms move from higher to lower wage regions and take advantage of new infrastructure in the Sunbelt. Both convergence and ecological theories emphasize private rather than public sector impetus for Sunbelt economic growth. The superior business climate that attracts investment to the South and West is enhanced by lower taxes, weak regulation, and local coalitions committed to privately organized growth.

Theorists of uneven development argue that capitalist economies grow in a spatially concentrated and uneven fashion that creates divergent development patterns that engender dependence of one set of cities on another. Watkins and Perry (1977) argue that economic investment is not dispersed throughout the country by some equilibrating mechanism, but that historic conditions change so old centers of growth (Northern steel, autos, rubber) lose momentum and new ones (Sunbelt defense, electronics, oil) emerge. The Sunbelt has not prospered because low-wage manufacturing moved South, but because new high-wage, high-tech industries located in the South and West. Contrary to convergence theory, uneven development theorists emphasize the role of government in the rise of the Sunbelt. They argue that inequities in federal spending broke earlier barriers to Southern industrial development. New Deal era federal spending on highways and infrastructure and Cold War federal spending on defense technology and military bases are critical determinants of Sunbelt growth.

The political importance of the Sunbelt is widely debated. Controversy initially centered on whether the emergent Republican majority in most Sunbelt states would fragment the national polity and undermine the liberal consensus that supported the welfare state. Debate extended to whether regional shifts were occurring in the composition and politics of the ruling class. One view is that political ascendance of the New Right evidences a shift from dominance by moderate Eastern "Yankee" to ultraconservative Southwestern "Cowboy" capitalists. The "Yankee-Cowboy" thesis is that rapid post-World War II economic growth in the Sunbelt created new elites who made money speculating in oil, defense, and real estate. These "Cowboy" elites oppose government intervention in the economy and advocate an expansionist foreign policy, states' rights, weak unions, and individualistic morality. Opponents insist that the 1970s corporate profit squeeze and political reactions to Civil Rights and environmental protection legislation catalyzed a convergence of elite politics on a New Right consensus. Empirical research finds little consistent evidence of a split between "Cowboy" and "Yankee" elites. Salt (1989) finds that Sunbelt capital was more supportive than Northeastern capital of conservative candidates in national elections held between 1978 and 1986, while Midwestern capital was more supportive of the New Right

than either Sunbelt or Northeastern capital. Refutation of the Sunbelt "Cowboy" thesis comes from Cohen (1977), who finds that Sunbelt economic growth remains dependent on Northern and Midwestern banks, accounting, and law firms and that no real shift has occurred in corporate control with the rise of the Sunbelt.

Debates about local politics in Sunbelt cities concern the extent to which governance of Southern cities by white business and civic elites has given way to suburban growth coalitions committed to fiscal conservatism, annexation, and private initiative and urban minority ruling coalitions committed to wealth redistribution. While business-oriented urban and suburban growth coalitions still dominate most Sunbelt cities, black or immigrant minority mayors and minority-based coalitions have risen to power in places like Birmingham, San Antonio, New Orleans, Atlanta, and Miami.

Scholarly interest in the Sunbelt has waned, largely because of difficulties characterizing regional patterns of economic development and political change. Economic growth stagnated in the South and West in the 1980s and whatever growth did occur was uneven and unequally distributed between urban and rural areas and across racial and ethnic groups. It is also difficult to characterize urban politics across the Sunbelt and differentiate them from the politics of Northern cities. For example, traditional ruling coalitions in New Orleans, Nashville, and Memphis look a lot like the party machines that dominated urban politics in the North; and battles over governmental reform in the South resemble similar battles fought in the North.

The Sunbelt remains ambiguous. Perhaps the South and West are too disparate for any regional synthesis to gain explanatory traction. Old distinctions also remain salient between urban and rural and between urban and suburban, and this confounds efforts to highlight regional differences in economic development, culture, and politics. During the 1990s the idea of globalization largely supplanted regional and even national-level analysis of industrial restructuring and decentralization. However, suburban and leisure tourism scholars still find the Sunbelt a useful construct to understand migration and cultural differences in the US, and recent patterns of Hispanic immigration have reinforced the salience of the Sunbelt (Goldfield

2003). To conclude, the Sunbelt construct served as a bridge in the analysis of shifts in the global division of labor and national politics between the eras of post-war industrial prosperity and liberal politics and the current era of globalization and conservative realignment of national politics in the post-industrial economy.

SEE ALSO: Political Economy; Rustbelt; Uneven Development; Urban Political Economy

REFERENCES AND SUGGESTED READINGS

Cohen, R. B. (1977) Multinational Corporations, International Finance, and the Sunbelt. In: Perry, D. C. & Watkins, A. J. (Eds.), *The Rise of the Sunbelt Cities*. Sage, Beverly Hills, CA, pp. 211–26.

Goldfield, D. (2003) Searching for the Sunbelt. *OAH, Magazine of History* (October): 3–9.

Rice, B. R. & Bernard, R. M. (1983) Introduction. In: Bernard, R. M. & Rice, B. R. (Eds.), *Sunbelt Cities: Politics and Growth Since WWII*. University of Texas Press, Austin, pp. 1–30.

Rostow, W. W. (1977) Regional Change in the 5th Kondratieff Upswing. In: Perry, D. C. & Watkins, A. J. (Eds.), *The Rise of the Sunbelt Cities*. Sage, Beverly Hills, CA, pp. 83–103.

Sale, K. (1975) *Power Shift: The Rise of the Southern Rim and Its Challenge to the Eastern Establishment*. Random House, New York.

Salt, J. (1989) Sunbelt Capital and Conservative Political Realignment in the 1970s and 1980s. *Critical Sociology* 16(2, 3): 143–63.

Watkins, S. J. & Perry, D. C. (1977) Regional Change and the Impact of Uneven Development. In: Perry, D. C. & Watkins, A. J. (Eds.), *The Rise of the Sunbelt Cities*. Sage, Beverly Hills, CA, pp. 19–54.

supermarkets

Kim Humphery

Defined in commercial terms a supermarket is a predominantly self-service retail shop selling a range of foodstuffs and household goods. These products are displayed mostly on open shelves, selected by the shopper and placed in a basket or trolley, and purchased by way of moving through a check-out or past a cash register. The supermarket is differentiated from other food stores in terms of the range of foods available within it (which usually includes manufactured and packaged products, fruit and vegetables, and refrigerated produce) and the area of selling space. Supermarkets are generally larger than similar environments such as corner shops or convenience stores, but smaller than other types of large, self-service establishments such as hypermarkets.

Initially, then, the supermarket can be understood as an economic institution, and one which is dominant (or at least highly significant) as a vehicle of everyday retail food distribution within nations as diverse as the United States, Britain, Australia, Germany, France, Japan, and China. This increasing dominance of the supermarket as a retail form is matched in many countries with a high concentration of commercial ownership, such that a small number of retail companies or "chains" own and operate a large number of supermarkets dispersed throughout a region or nation and sporting the same logo, store design, and product profile.

Yet the supermarket is also much more than an economic phenomenon. It is a part of everyday life within many industrialized countries – so much so, that the above definition can seem a little ludicrous, as if to make the very ordinary and already known somehow strange and technical. It is this everydayness, and the position of the supermarket within a much broader field of consumption, that has recently begun to interest those working in the social sciences and humanities. Beyond the economic, the supermarket is a *social space*, in the sense in which it is a terrain of interaction; a *cultural field*, in the sense in which it marks out particular ways of symbolizing and emotionally valuing consumer goods; and a *terrain of politics*, in the sense in which it is embedded within a set of labor practices, global production frameworks, and environmental consequences. Supermarkets, then, may be mundane and ordinary, but they are not simple or unimportant places because of this. On the contrary, supermarkets are central to the nature and levels of consumption within the contemporary highly industrialized world.

Historians and cultural analysts have recently turned their attention to the rise of supermarketing, drawing on and reformulating histories of retailing, shopping, and individual companies. An indisputably "American" phenomenon, the supermarket is seen to have appeared in the 1930s, particularly in New York where there was originally an emphasis on large warehouse-type stores selling a plethora of goods at cheap prices. These stores were integrally dependent on changes in food manufacturing and packaging, on the suburbanization of cities, and on the rise of the automobile as a form of transport. They were also modeled on much earlier retail experimentation in North America, Europe, and elsewhere with the practices of cash-and-carry and self-service. By the 1950s the supermarket was fast becoming the dominant form of retail food distribution in the United States and, as a retail form, it was emerging in Britain, Australasia, Canada, France, Germany, and in other western nations. This pace of development continued, such that by the mid-1960s the supermarket could claim status as a global phenomenon, having spread beyond the West into Southeast Asia, parts of Africa, and elsewhere. In the process, the supermarket had become a preeminent symbol of capitalist modernity, connected with images of choice, convenience, abundance, and everyday luxury. Its internationalization spurned also further retail experimentation, with the development in France of the hypermarket during the early 1960s.

Within a number of countries this consolidation of the supermarket resulted in significant restructuring of the economics of retailing and the social practices of shopping. With the rise of the supermarket the number of retail shops, particularly grocery stores, dramatically decreased within many countries, while the size of retail grocery outlets, in terms of area of selling space, grew significantly. Older forms of retailing, along with the independent shopkeeper, were thus eclipsed by the rise of supermarket chains which, in turn, consolidated the economic dominance of key manufacturers of foods and household goods and fostered highly commercialized forms of agricultural production Socially, the supermarket also quickly transformed everyday consumption, shifting the responsibility for the selection and transport of goods purchased onto the shopper, and thus increasing the domestic workload of many

women who have always constituted the majority of supermarket shoppers. Equally, the goods available within the supermarket gradually contributed to population-wide transformations in dietary intake. Moreover, the supermarket as a social space reframed the experience of shopping, placing people within an environment which blurred class distinctions, partially challenged the highly gendered nature of everyday provisioning, and positioned people as autonomous within an ideological framework of consumer choice.

These and other consumption practices and frameworks mark the contemporary supermarket as well. Yet it is only comparatively recently that scholars have turned their attention to the supermarket and taken it seriously as a subject of social and cultural analysis. This recent work has been productive in terms of exploring the very particular place of the supermarket within the broader historical development of consumption cultures. Analysts have thus explored the supermarket in terms of the rise of mass marketing, transformations in technologies of manufacturing and packaging, the development of post-World War II cultures of capitalist abundance, and shifts in the nature of domestic work. Further, scholars have explored the connections between everyday supermarket shopping and the concepts of self-identity, cultural fragmentation, and rituals of provisioning under conditions of modernity and beyond.

It might also be said, however, that the future direction of such analysis is undergoing timely challenge. The recent study of consumption, and of the supermarket along with it, has arguably been dominated by explorations of the cultural significance and social dynamics of shopping in terms that have been too narrowly focused on questions of identity, meaning, and postmodernity. This has tended to eclipse an analysis of other aspects of supermarket retailing: its placement within global systems of provision, its connection with the logic of global capitalist expansion, and its embeddedness within systems of overconsumption leading to significant individual, social, and environmental costs. It is perhaps to these more avowedly critical explorations of the supermarket, and life within and *beyond* it, that commentators might now turn.

SEE ALSO: Consumption; Consumption, Cathedrals of; Consumption, Food and Cultural; Consumption, Provisioning and; Shopping

REFERENCES AND SUGGESTED READINGS

Bowlby, R. (2000) *Carried Away: The Invention of Modern Shopping*. Faber, London.

Humphery, K. (1998) *Shelf Life: Supermarkets and the Changing Cultures of Consumption*. Cambridge University Press, Melbourne.

Miller, D. (1998) *A Theory of Shopping*. Cornell University Press, Ithaca, NY.

Strasser, S. (1989) *Satisfaction Guaranteed: The Making of the American Mass Market*. Pantheon, New York.

supply chains

Chris Lonsdale

The term supply chain is actually a metaphor for a complex series of interactions between a set of organizations responsible for delivering a product or service to an ultimate customer. Indeed, this series of interactions has more recently been referred to as a network (Hakansson and Snehota 1990; Harland 1996). A supply chain starts with a set of raw materials and ends with the delivery of a finished product or service to the ultimate customer(s). Figure 1 provides a simplified representation of a supply chain.

The term gained prominence within the management field because of the realization that an organization's prospects are dependent not only on its interactions with its immediate customers, competitors, and suppliers, but also on those that take place elsewhere in the chain or network. This can be explained using the hypothetical supply chain in Figure 1. First, organization A can be affected by the actions of organization B, despite having no direct commercial relationship with it. For example, organization B might be ineffective at providing demand information to organizations D and E. If that then affects the ability of those two organizations to interact effectively with

organization A, then this will have an adverse affect on organization A. Given that the problem is poor demand information, the effect could be related to organization A's efforts to plan its capacity.

Alternatively, organization A can be affected by the actions of organization C, again despite having no direct commercial relationship with it. For example, organization C may refuse to adhere to an agreement with organization F, one of organization A's own suppliers. If organization C's actions affect the ability of organization F to supply organization A, then organization A may well suffer adverse effects, perhaps to its production schedule. More dramatically, the same principle means that all of the participants in the supply chain are dependent on the actions of organization G.

While this realization was initially made in the manufacturing context, it is also entirely applicable to both the service and public sector contexts. For example, work has been undertaken on supply chain optimization in the health care sector, the advertising sector and, of course, the defense sector, where considerations of supply chain efficiency have long been a key concern of armed forces. Work in the construction and information systems industries has also shown that the concept of the supply chain can be applied to a project as well as process environment.

The contribution that the concept of the supply chain has made to the study of management and organizations, therefore, has been to broaden the focus of business management from dyadic and direct interactions to the wider terrain of the supply network. It has highlighted the broader range of interdependencies which organizations need to cope with in order to fulfill their objectives (Gadde et al. 2003).

Supply chains and their management have been studied by academics from a vast range of disciplines. For example, contributions have come from the areas of operations management, purchasing and supply, information technology, institutional economics, strategic management, organizational behavior, law, and marketing. However, it is possible to provide some kind of organizing schema. This schema is based upon the view that the supply chain subject area consists of three broad dimensions: structures, relationships, and operations.

Downstream toward
the ultimate customers

Upstream toward the
initial suppliers

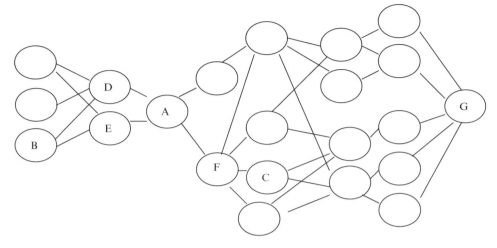

Figure 1 A simplified representation of a supply chain.

The study of supply chain structures has focused on a number of issues, some of which have long been of interest to economists. These include assessments of vertical integration, or its recently fashionable opposite, the virtual organization (Chesbrough & Teece 1996). Related to this has been the study of outsourcing and make-buy decisions. Finally, there has also been interest in the positioning decisions made by organizations within supply chains. Different stages of supply chains offer different levels of profitability and organizations have often shifted their position accordingly (Gadiesh & Gilbert 1998). The literature that has supported this dimension of the study of supply chains has included resource-based theory, institutional economics, and marketing theory.

A second dimension to the study of supply chains has concerned relationships. On the one hand, this has concerned the internal relationships that impact upon organizational buying behavior (Ronchetto et al. 1989). On the other, it has concerned inter-organizational relationships, with contributors again utilizing resource-based theory, institutional economics, and marketing theory, but also accessing information economics, behavioral economics, game theory, and law. Relationships with other customers, suppliers, and competitors have been described in the supply chain literature as a key organizational resource. For example, Gadde et al. (2003) comment: "Firms operate in the context of interconnected relationships, forming networks ... these relationships affect the nature and the outcome of the firm's actions and are their potential sources of efficiency and effectiveness."

If we look at the relationships organizations have with their suppliers, for example, we can begin to understand why Gadde et al. might hold this view. Take IBM. According to recent company statistics, 73 percent of IBM's revenue generated by sales of manufactured goods was accounted for by supply inputs (Urioste 2000). There are two consequences to this. First, the quality of IBM products is heavily dependent upon the performance of suppliers. Second, the ability of IBM to control its costs is heavily dependent on its ability to manage its relationships with suppliers effectively.

Much of the study into relationships within supply chains has investigated the perceived need for organizations to match relationship forms with transactional circumstances. Again using the example of supply-side relationships, it has been shown in the literature that organizations face transactional circumstances that differ in terms of magnitude, complexity, uncertainty, power relations, asset specificity, and likely duration. As a result, most academics studying supply-side relationships have advised managers that they need to adopt a contingent approach to relationship management (Williamson 1985; Cox et al. 2000; Gadde & Hakansson 2001). Similar ways of thinking have been employed in relation to the study of customer relationships.

The third dimension of the supply chain literature concerns operational management. Over the past 20 years, a great deal of attention has been paid to the perceived need for production operations to be integrated or synchronized along the whole of the supply chain. There are sound reasons for this. As has been pointed out, it is literally the case that a supply chain is only as strong as its weakest link. Supply chains that have a mixture of effective and ineffective participants have a tendency to develop "islands of excellence." This can either lead to high levels of inventory in the chain if the offending party is a customer, or production delays if it is a supplier. This logic has led to the operations management discipline broadening its focus from the individual organization to the overall supply chain.

Much work has been undertaken, therefore, on how organizations might integrate their operations. In particular, traditional operational methods such as batch production have been challenged by methods based on just-in-time (JIT) or "pull" systems. Indeed, JIT production, with all of the organizational and information technology integration that it entails, has been put forward by its proponents as a superior approach to supply chain management rather than an alternative (Womack et al. 1990), although as we shall see below this is questioned by many.

There are, therefore, three broad dimensions or domains to the study of supply chains. They each contribute to making the subject area extremely diverse. This is not to say, however, that all academics include all three in their work. For example, the tendency in the US is for supply chain academics to focus on operational issues, whereas in Europe the focus is more (although by no means exclusively) on structure and relationships (Giannakis & Croom 2004).

The debates in the supply chain literature echo those of the management literature in general. Perhaps the most significant debate in the literature concerns the issue of supply chain integration. There is a divide in the supply chain literature between those that are optimistic about the achievement of supply chain integration and those that believe that supply chains or networks will always be messy and the deliverer of highly imperfect outcomes. In considering this debate, it is hard to overstate the impact that the models of integrated supply chain management have had over the past 15 to 20 years. The best known is the lean supply model. The model encompasses two of the three dimensions of the subject area outlined above: operations and relationships. In terms of operations, the lean supply model provides techniques aimed at integrating the supply chain. In terms of relationships, the lean supply model takes a view on the type of relationships required to support the operational techniques.

The lean supply model was originally developed on the basis of comprehensive research into the Japanese automotive industry – particularly Toyota – although over the past 10 years the model has been applied and modified in a range of other industrial contexts. The research highlighted that the Japanese automotive assemblers had a totally different approach to managing the supply chain from their western counterparts. While the supply chains of the western assemblers were conflictual and anarchic, those of the Japanese assemblers were apparently more consensual and orderly, with a network of collaborative relationships referred to as a *keiretsu*.

From these observations of Toyota (and many of its Japanese competitors), a number of academics proceeded to develop the lean supply model. This was then widely disseminated during the 1990s (Womack et al. 1990; Lamming 1993; Hines 1994). There are four key operational principles to the lean supply model. First, there is the insistence that value is specified from a customer perspective. Such a specification requires the abandonment of sectional interests within the supply chain, whether they be at a firm or intrafirm level. Second, it is stated that supply chain participants should then consider how that proposition can be delivered in the most efficient manner possible. The starting point of this task is process mapping.

The aim of process mapping is to (1) identify the total process that currently exists and (2) locate the problems within that process. Once the problems have been located, remedial action can be taken. This remedial action has as its target the reduction of waste. Lean supply identifies seven types of waste: overproduction, unnecessary waiting, excessive transportation, inappropriate processing, unnecessary inventory, unnecessary motions, and defects. In the mapping process, all current supply chain activities are divided into three categories: value-adding, non-value-adding but necessary, and non-value-adding. The aim of lean supply is to minimize the second category and eradicate the third category.

Third, and key to the reduction of waste, is the just-in-time (JIT) principle. JIT is a method of production where a supply chain process only operates when a customer indicates its demand. JIT or "pull" systems are said to benefit the firm by contributing to the reduction of inventory within the chain, reductions in number of defects, a reduction in the requirement for storage space, and an increase in the ability of managers to identify problems early. Finally, the fourth principle of lean supply is that of continuous improvement. Lean supply strongly adheres to the principle of continuous improvement and takes the view that the task of pushing out the productivity frontier is never complete.

These operational principles are then supported within the lean supply model by the development of close, collaborative buyer–supplier relationships. Such relationships include high levels of product/process information exchange (e.g., proprietary or cost information), extensive operational linkages (e.g., aligned information systems), cooperative norms (e.g., a code of conduct), and transaction-specific investments (Cannon & Perrault 1999).

The lean supply model has been very successfully disseminated throughout the world. One of the early texts outlining the model, *The Machine that Changed the World*, by Womack, Jones, and Roos (1990), has sold over half a million copies. This success has not, however, stopped many supply chain academics from criticizing it. In particular, claims that lean supply is a universally applicable model of supply chain "best practice" have been widely contested. In a critique that echoes the realist critiques of many

other management models, Cooney (2002) argues that the "value creation" in the lean supply model is not just dependent on just-in-time flow, but is also contingent on general business conditions (economic cycles), the differing nature of buyer–supplier relationships in a supply chain, and the structure of social and political institutions in different national contexts. These are all factors that, according to Cooney, the lean supply model simply dismisses.

With respect to the nature of buyer–supplier relationships, one of the factors that is said to cast doubt on the universality of the lean model is the existence of buyer–supplier power relations (Ramsay 1996; Ford 1997; Cox et al. 2000; Cooney 2002). The lean supply model requires the development and maintenance of long-term, collaborative relationships throughout the supply chain. However, according to the lean supply model's critics this is not always going to be possible because the nature of buyer–supplier power relations will not permit it.

Ford et al. (1998) seek to make this point by referring back to the original exemplar upon which the lean supply model was based – the Japanese automotive industry. They comment: "It seems that many of the Japanese subcontractors have been more or less forced into relationships involving extensive coordination by a customer because of the considerable power of those customers ... It is likely to be very difficult for a small customer to involve large suppliers in these efforts [collaborative relationships] except on the most favorable terms" (p. 147). Cooney (2002) argues that because of the variable nature of buyer–supplier power relations, other, more traditional methods of managing supply chains (e.g., batch systems of operational production and arm's-length relationships) may well have to be adopted on many occasions.

The general consensus of the critics of the lean supply model is that the management of supply chains cannot be modeled on any set template of "best practice." Rather, their management is about "identifying the scope for action, within existing and potential relationships, and about operating effectively with others within the internal and external constraints that limit that scope" (Gadde et al. 2003: 357). The view is taken that organizations will need to develop many different approaches to operations management, adopt many different customer and supplier relationship types (arm's-length and collaborative, equal and unequal), and understand that the organization will influence and be influenced by such relationships. It will also need to remain flexible in the face of changing supply chain circumstances and understand that change is likely to be incremental rather than the result of strategic planning.

This philosophical divide over the management of supply chains is underpinned by methodological differences. The academics researching the implementation of lean supply and other similar supply chain integration models, such as agile supply (Christopher 2000), are mainly positivists undertaking quantitative research into operational techniques. Those providing the critique are mainly, although not by any means exclusively, critical realists undertaking qualitative research into intra-organizational and inter-organizational relationships and processes. Not surprisingly, many of those that fall into the former camp are those with an operations management background, whereas those in the latter have emerged from the disciplines of marketing, organization theory, political economy, and institutional/behavioral economics.

Consideration of the future direction of research into supply chains and their management brings to mind three comments. First, it is possible that the idea of a contingent approach to the management of supply chains will become more prominent in the coming years. Such an approach is widely accepted among industrial marketing academics (especially those in the influential Industrial Marketing and Purchasing Group) and is slowly gaining more prominence among purchasing and operations management academics.

Second, supply chain academics from all disciplinary backgrounds will have to continue to monitor the impact of the Internet on supply chain management. The Internet-based software that facilitates supply chain relationships and real-time auctions will continue to have an impact on the structural features, relationships, and operational practices within supply chains and has the potential to challenge many closely held assumptions.

Third, it seems that the high-level assumption of the supply chain fraternity – that individuals and organizations need to be seen as operating within a wider network of interdependencies – is likely to become more and more influential within other management disciplines. The network concept can already be seen in the strategy literature (Dyer & Singh 1998) and the human resource management literature (Harris 2002), for example, and this trend only seems likely to continue.

SEE ALSO: Alliances; Management Networks; Operations Management; Outsourcing; Power-Dependence Theory

REFERENCES AND SUGGESTED READINGS

Cannon, J. & Perrault, W. (1999) Buyer–Seller Relationships in Business Markets. *Journal of Marketing Research* 32: 430–60.

Chesbrough, H. & Teece, D. (1996) When is Virtual Virtuous? Organizing for Innovation. *Harvard Business Review* 74: 65–73.

Christopher, M. (2000) The Agile Supply Chain. *Industrial Marketing Management* 29: 37–44.

Cooney, R. (2002) Is "Lean" a Universal Production System? Batch Production in the Automotive Industry. *International Journal of Operations and Production Management* 22(9/10): 1130–47.

Cox, A., Sanderson, J., & Watson, G. (2000) *Power Regimes*. Earlsgate Press, Helpston.

Dyer, J. and Singh, H. (1998) The Relational View: Cooperative Strategy and Sources of Interorganizational Competitive Advantage. *Academy of Management Review* 23(4): 660–79.

Ford, D. (Ed.) (1997) *Understanding Business Markets*. Dryden, London.

Ford, D., Gadde, L.-E., Hakansson, H., Lundgren, A., Snehota, I., Turnbull, P., & Wilson, D. (1998) *Managing Business Relationships*. John Wiley, Chichester.

Gadde, L.-E. & Hakansson, H. (Eds.) (2001) *Supply Network Strategies*. John Wiley, Chichester

Gadde, L.-E., Huemer, L., & Hakansson, H. (2003) Strategizing in Industrial Networks. *Industrial Marketing Management* 32: 357–64.

Gadiesh, O. & Gilbert, J. (1998) Profit Pools: A Fresh Look at Strategy. *Harvard Business Review* 76: 139–47.

Giannakis, M. & Croom, S. (2004) Towards the Development of a Supply Chain Management

Paradigm: A Conceptual Framework. *Journal of Supply Chain Management* 40(2): 27–37.

Hakansson, H. & Snehota, I. (1990) No Business is an Island: The Network Concept of Business Strategy. *Scandinavian Journal of Management* 4(3): 187–200.

Harland, C. (1996) Supply Chain Management: Relationships, Chains and Networks. *British Journal of Management* 7: 63–80.

Harris, L. (2002) Human Resource Management in the Extended Organization. In: Eastham, J., Sharples, L., & Ball, S. (Eds.), *Food Supply Chain Management*. Butterworth Heinneman, London.

Hines, P. (1994) *Creating World Class Suppliers*. Pitman, London.

Lamming, R. (1993) *Beyond Partnership: Strategies for Lean Supply*. Prentice-Hall, London.

Ramsay, J. (1996) The Case Against Purchasing Partnerships. *International Journal of Purchasing and Materials Management* 32: 13–21.

Ronchetto, R., Hutt, M., & Reingen, P. (1989) Embedded Influence Patterns in Organizational Buying Systems. *Journal of Marketing* 53: 51–62.

Urioste, J. (2000) *IBM Global Procurement*. IBM, New York.

Williamson, O. (1985) *The Economic Institutions of Capitalism*. Free Press, New York.

Womack, J., Jones, D., & Roos, D. (1990) *The Machine that Changed the World*. Rawson Associates, New York.

surveillance

David Lyon

Most of us take for granted today that our personal data are required for many purposes and that our images, scans, and traces are used by organizations. When we identify ourselves we usually need evidence to back up our claim: an ID card, a PIN, a drivers' license, or a passport. We are not surprised to see video surveillance cameras in the street or the shopping mall and we are aware that our transactions, phone calls, and emails are logged and processed. Personal data are extremely valuable to many agencies today, from marketers to insurance companies to the police.

Not all ordinary citizens, workers, travelers, or consumers realize, however, the scale or significance of surveillance today. Personal data businesses are worth billions of dollars, and government departments and law enforcement agencies mount massive computer and telecommunications systems to support their processing of such data. Surveillance in these circumstances cannot but involve questions of power and the distribution of rights and responsibilities. While ostensibly personal questions about privacy may well be raised, public issues also demand attention – of how our choices and life-chances are affected by surveillance and how trust and accountability can be enhanced.

Surveillance is as old as human history, but over the past few decades it has risen rapidly to a position of central importance – and controversy – in sociology. The reasons for this are complex, but relatively clear. The use of new technologies in surveillance and their promotion and adoption by a wide range of agencies have created a situation in which surveillance capacities are unprecedented and their effects widespread. Surveillance is also politically disputed. At the same time, sociological tools for understanding and analyzing surveillance have been developed, especially since the groundbreaking work of Foucault. This has also generated debate regarding already existing theory and the possibilities of new theories that question how far Foucault's work really addresses the key issues in surveillance today.

Surveillance may be defined as the focused and systematic attention to personal details for the purposes of influence, management, or control (which is similar to the definition in one of the earliest sociological treatments of surveillance, Rule 1974). Not all "watching" is focused and systematic, but "watching over," as in the French verb *surveiller*, is likely to be so. The watching may be literal, as in daycare assistants "watching over" children, or street intersection cameras "watching out" for speeders who cross the line on a red light, but it may also be metaphorical. Our activities may be "seen" in our telephone records or our credit card purchases. But the watching is always purposeful – in these examples, to care for children or to catch out careless drivers. Marketers may wish to influence consumers, employers to manage their workers, or prison guards to control their inmates.

Before considering some contemporary situations, however, it is worth noting the long history of surveillance. Ancient civilizations such as the Chinese or the Roman used censuses, for example, to keep track of citizens for taxation or conscription purposes. And overseers of work projects have always checked on their labor forces to ensure that the project is done correctly and on time. The use of clocks, from the thirteenth century, aided this endeavor. The making of maps was also a means of locating, in general terms, where people were. So both direct supervision (another English word meaning "watching over") and record keeping are antique practices of coordination and control.

The coming of modernity made many such practices routine and systematic. Indeed, modernity is in part defined by such routinization and systematization. Bureaucratic methods of organizations, within a hierarchy governed by rules, in which communication passes only through certain prescribed channels, and files are kept – on persons as well as transactions and events – were examined classically by Weber (see Dandeker 1990). But Marx also observed astutely that within capitalist organizations there are additional incentives to maintain control, and that, for example, placing workers together under one roof in early factories enabled monitoring and supervision more readily to take place. Such analyses were pursued in the twentieth century, for example in the much-debated work of Braverman on *Labor and Monopoly Capital* (1974).

Another dimension of surveillance, emphasized by Foucault, was modernity's shift away from forceful, coercive, and sometimes brutal methods of social control. In their place, argued Foucault, were "technologies of power" that induced self-discipline through surveillance. For Foucault (1979), the Panopticon, Jeremy Bentham's late eighteenth-century semi-circular prison design with a central watchtower, was the archetype of modern surveillance power. Prisoners would be constantly observed, and, being in back-lit cells, would be continuously visible. At the same time, the inspector in the tower would be obscured from view by slatted blinds, so that prisoners could never be sure that anyone was actually there. But they would develop self-discipline and act appropriately, just in case they were being watched.

The big change on which Foucault made no comment was the use of computers in surveillance. While the earliest surveillance involved direct watching and supervision, plus some basic record keeping, and modern surveillance adopted rational methods of bureaucratic governance, a key development in the later twentieth century was computerization. James Rule researched this in relation to items such as credit card and social security systems, and Gary T. Marx (1985) established some crucial new dimensions of surveillance based on new technologies. He argued that it transcends barriers of darkness and distance and that data storage means it transcends time. New surveillance tends to be capital – not labor – intensive, introduces categorical suspicion, and tries to prevent violations. It is decentralized, hard to discern, is both more intensive and extensive. He warned about the potential for new soft forms of secret manipulation and control.

Of course, social changes relating to computers depend in turn on the perceived needs for and benefits of certain kinds of surveillance. The new technologies do have "effects," but they are also subject to social, economic, and political forces that give them their chance in the first place. Thus some effects are intended – government departments wish to reduce costs, including fraud, and thus install systems to detect violators, for instance – but some are unintended. Notoriously, systems set up to increase production or distribution efficiency in manufacturing may also have surveillance side-effects in allowing workers to be monitored more closely. Similarly, retail surveillance to prevent shoplifting may be expanded to check on staff.

The technologies that facilitate deeper surveillance have appeared at a snowballing pace, each adding another dimension while maintaining previous capabilities. In the later 1980s searchable databases extended surveillance capacities (Lessig 1999) and in the 1990s networked multimedia provided increased opportunities for integration between previously separate databases. Those opportunities were also earnestly sought, for example by policing networks, keen to trace offenders in cross-border activities such as drug smuggling, or corporations desiring to target more precisely their most profitable consumers (Gandy 1993).

A further boost to integrative ambitions came following the "terrorist" attacks of 9/11, when law enforcement bodies ratcheted up their efforts not only to get different departments cooperating more intelligently with each other, but also to obtain personal data from whatever source – including commercial, educational, and medical – that might provide them (Lyon 2003).

It is important to understand, however, that no surveillance system can work fully without the cooperation, witting or unwitting, of its subjects. In many cases ordinary people trigger surveillance practices in the mundane routines of everyday life. When cards are swiped, websites accessed, or when phone numbers or postal codes are given to store clerks, data are extracted. Those data reveal when transactions were made and for how much, and today, cellphones and other locational devices may also indicate where we are geographically. And if ordinary people are involved in enabling surveillance, they may as readily question or block surveillance as simply comply with it. People sometimes withhold information, or alter it slightly, in order to evade the gaze. In particular cases, outcry may be strident, such as when otherwise law-abiding citizens of Athens spray-painted surveillance camera lenses before the 2004 Olympics.

The diagram of the Panopticon provides a useful way of organizing theoretical approaches to surveillance (Wood 2003). It has stimulated an ongoing debate about the best ways to understand and explain what is going on within and under the "gaze." A number of writers (e.g., Poster 1996) proposed that electronic technologies enable the perfection of Bentham's ideas. Software architectures can achieve more completely what the bricks and mortar of the original plan were meant to do – to create control through uncertainty. But others object that the Panopticon's genius cannot be generalized to other situations. It may be present for cases such as welfare recipients, but in other contexts other models must be sought. In this critique, the panoptic paradigm is relevant but limited.

Those who doubt the extent of the Panopticon's usefulness for theory may themselves fall into one or another group. The "pre-panoptics" are those who insist that the works of say, Marx, Weber, or Machiavelli yield plenty of clues about how surveillance works and why

it is expanding and intensifying. Its meanings may be found in the inner workings of capitalism, in bureaucratic management, or in geopolitical control. The "post-panoptics," on the other hand, would now include theorists such as Gilles Deleuze, Michael Hardt and Antonio Negri, or Giorgio Agamben, who work from other guiding models. Deleuze's notion of "societies of control" suggests how surveillance simply closes or opens opportunities for action. Hardt and Negri's "empire" claims that surveillance is vital to new global regimes of imperial power. And Agamben proposes that Foucault never worked out "how sovereign power produces biopolitical bodies" and why exclusion is today a more powerful surveillance effect than inclusion in the Panopticon.

Needless to say, issues of theory provoke questions of methods. How do we know what kinds of surveillance are in place, and what their effects are, given the high degree of secrecy in some corporations and government departments? And how can researchers avoid being seen merely as critics of surveillance with the consequence that access to sites and spokespersons may be blocked by those who argue that the surveillance is necessary or desirable? One could say, of course, that these issues have always produced problems for academic investigation, and that the task of independent researchers is still to find out as much as possible by whatever means are legal and ethical. No doubt critics of surveillance studies would say that the enterprise is hypocritical – have not social scientists always been in the business of surveillance themselves? Such methodological questions do present difficult conundrums, but these can also be placed in context be recalling some key points from the above discussion.

Surveillance is moving steadily closer to the center of social order and governance in technologically advanced societies. New technologies are implicated in this as they facilitate and even "drive" some developments, but those technologies are also themselves shaped by social, economic, and political factors. In the early twenty-first century this is seen clearly in the surveillance responses to security threats in the "war against terror." Much surveillance accompanies current thrusts towards efficiency and safety in the modern world and thus its effects may never be correctly viewed as only negative. Surveillance is always ambiguous. But because questions of trust and responsibility in relation to the handling of personal data are paramount, yoking sociological work to the ethics and politics of information is vital.

SEE ALSO: City Planning/Urban Design; Consumption, Mass Consumption, and Consumer Culture; Credit Cards; Foucault, Michel; Information Technology; Privacy; Social Control; Welfare Regimes

REFERENCES AND SUGGESTED READINGS

Braverman, H. (1974) *Labor and Monopoly Capital.* Monthly Review Press, New York
Dandeker, C. (1990) *Surveillance Power and Modernity.* Polity Press, Cambridge.
Foucault, M. (1979) *Discipline and Punish: The Birth of the Prison.* Vintage, New York.
Gandy, O. (1993) *The Panoptic Sort: A Political Economy of Personal Information,* Westview Press, Boulder.
Lessig, L. (1999) *Code and Other Laws of Cyberspace.* Basic Books, New York.
Lyon, D. (1994) *The Electronic Eye: The Rise of Surveillance Society.* Polity Press, Cambridge.
Lyon, D. (2003) *Surveillance after September 11.* Polity Press, Cambridge.
Marx, G. T. (1985) I'll Be Watching You: Reflections on the New Surveillance. *Dissent* 32 (Winter): 26–34.
Poster, M. (1996) Databases as Discourse. In: Lyon, D. & Zureik, E. (Eds.), *Computers, Surveillance and Privacy.* University of Minnesota Press, Minneapolis.
Rule, J. (1974) *Private Lives and Public Surveillance: Social Control in the Computer Age.* Schocken, New York.
Wood, D. (2003) Editorial for a special issue on the Panopticon. *Surveillance and Society* 2(3) Online. www.surveillance-and-society.org.

survey research

Patricia Snyder

Survey research refers to systematic investigations designed to gather information from populations or samples for the purposes of describing, comparing, or explaining phenomena. Survey research involving samples often is distinguished from census surveys, which involve the study of populations. As Kerlinger noted in *Foundations of Behavioral Research* (1986: 377): "Survey research studies large and small populations (or universes) by selecting and studying samples chosen from the populations to discover the relative incidence, distribution, and interrelations of sociological and psychological variables."

Several types of research approaches are described in the survey methodology literature. *Descriptive or status* survey research focuses on accurately characterizing information about defined units of analysis, such as individuals, social groups, geographic areas, or organizations. In descriptive research applications, surveys are used to quantify phenomena such as unemployment rates in a state, the health status of citizens of the US, or the number of certified teachers in a school district. Public opinion surveys or polls (e.g., Gallup Poll or Harris Survey) are a type of status survey designed to quantify information from defined samples about their subjective preferences, beliefs, or attitudes. *Correlational* survey research is directed toward examining interrelationships among variables. An example of correlational survey research might involve using surveys to examine familial and community factors associated with juvenile delinquency. *Explanatory* survey research typically involves hypotheses testing to explicate relationships between attribute or predictor variables and criterion variables of interest. Although explanatory survey research does not permit causal inferences, because of the lack of experimental manipulation and control, it offers important opportunities to model and test complex relationships among variables of interest using advanced statistical techniques such as multiple regression analysis, structural equation modeling, or hierarchical linear modeling.

Commonly employed survey research designs include cross-sectional and longitudinal designs. In cross-sectional designs, information is collected at a single point in time from a sample of respondents. Three common types of longitudinal designs include panel, trend, and cohort. Panel designs involve data collected at different points in time from the same sample. In trend designs, different samples from the same general population are used at each measurement occasion. Cohort designs involve identifying a specific population who share a common attribute, such as infants born in the US in 2005 or those who graduated from high school in Texas in 2004. The same specific population is involved in the cohort study over time, but a new sample from this population is selected each time survey data are gathered.

Survey research involves processes common to other quantitative research approaches, including identification of the research question, selection of the study design, selection of the sample, development or selection of the survey instrument, pretesting of instruments, data collection, data coding and processing, data analysis, data interpretation, and dissemination of findings. Fowler (1993) characterized the *total survey design* approach as one focused on the complete data collection process and suggested that in survey research particular attention be paid to the quality of the sample, the quality of the measures, the quality of data collection, and the mode of data collection. Decisions made about each of these components impact the accuracy and validity of survey results. In a widely cited text, Groves (1989) details sources of imprecision and bias found in survey research that are associated with four common types of error: sampling, coverage, nonresponse, and measurement.

Sampling decisions are important in survey research, particularly when the intent is to evaluate the precision of sample estimates in relation to population characteristics. Three interrelated processes are associated with sampling decisions: defining the sample frame, determining sample size, and choosing a sampling method. The sample frame is the list of people or objects that comprise the accessible population. Survey samples are selected from the frame by specifying sample size and determining whether probability or nonprobability sampling methods will be used to select units. Probability sampling permits use of statistical tools to estimate the amount of sampling error. Random sampling error occurs due to chance variations in different samples drawn from the same population. Systematic sampling error occurs when inadequate sampling procedures are used. Coverage error is a form of systematic sampling error. An example of coverage error

would be surveying only individuals with access to computers when the variables of interest are related to having or not having computer access. Errors in sampling also can arise from poor definitions of the sampling frame and the use of small sample sizes. Fowler (1993) offers an expanded discussion of factors to consider when making sampling decisions.

Biases associated with low response rates often are problematic in survey research and represent a major source of survey error. Low response rates are particularly problematic when researchers are unable to characterize how responders differ from nonresponders. Dillman (2000) describes tailored design methods and presents strategies designed to enhance response rates.

Survey questions are designed to operationalize variables of interest. Comprehensive instrument development and validation strategies should be used to ensure that questions are well formulated and that reliable and valid data are obtained when surveys are administered across samples of respondents. Pilot testing of survey items and data gathering procedures is uniformly recommended to help reduce measurement error. Reliability and validity should be systematically evaluated each time a survey is used with a sample of respondents because these two characteristics are not static properties of measures.

Modes of survey administration involve face-to-face, telephone, mail, and web-based formats. Use of computers in survey research is becoming commonplace, including laptops and personal data assistant (PDA) devices. Each mode has its strengths and limitations. Decisions related to the mode of administration to be used typically involve considerations of the characteristics of the sample to be surveyed, the types of questions to be asked, the response rate desired, and time and cost considerations. Entire texts are devoted to describing strategies for minimizing systematic error by standardizing interviews and telephone surveys (Fowler & Mangione 1990; Lavrakas 1993).

Survey research is one way to collect quantifiable data in a standardized way from samples or populations. As noted in this review, if not conducted with appropriate rigor, survey research is particularly susceptible to various sources of error related to sampling, measurement, and data collection processes.

SEE ALSO: Convenience Sample; Hierarchical Linear Models; Interviewing, Structured, Unstructured, and Postmodern; Random Sample; Reliability Generalization; Structural Equation Modeling

REFERENCES AND SUGGESTED READINGS

Alreck, P. L. & Settle, R. B. (1994) *The Survey Research Handbook*, 2nd edn. McGraw Hill, New York.

Babbie, E. (1990) *Survey Research Methods*, 2nd edn. Wadsworth, Belmont, CA.

Dillman, D. (2000) *Mail and Internet Surveys: The Tailored Design Method*. Wiley, New York.

Fink, A. (2002) *The Survey Kit*, 2nd edn. Sage, Newbury Park, CA.

Fowler, F. J. (1993) *Survey Research Methods*, 2nd edn. Sage, Newbury Park, CA.

Fowler, F. J. & Mangione, T. W. (1990) *Standardized Survey Interviewing: Minimizing Interview-Related Error*. Sage, Newbury Park, CA.

Groves, R. M. (1989) *Survey Errors and Survey Costs*. Wiley, New York.

Groves, R. M., Fowler, F. J., Couper, M. P., Lepkowski, J. M., Singer, E., & Touangeau, R. (2004) *Survey Methodology*. Wiley, New York.

Lavrakas, P. J. (1993) *Telephone Survey Methods: Sampling, Selection, and Supervision*. Sage, Thousand Oaks, CA.

Scheuren, F. (2004) What is a Survey? American Statistical Association/Section on Survey Research Methods. Online. www.amstat.org/sections/SRMS/index.html.

Sutherland, Edwin H. (1883–1950)

Gilbert Geis

Edwin H. Sutherland is generally regarded as the father of the scientific study of criminology in the United States. In 1924 he published *Criminology*, the first systematic textbook study of crime. Sutherland advanced the principle of differential association, a social learning construct that sought to interpret criminal behavior in theoretical terms. He also coined the term white-collar crime in his 1939 presidential address to the American Sociological Society. In addition, Sutherland wrote a pioneering monograph on confidence scams, as well as highly regarded papers on the death penalty and prisons. He also published journal articles critical of sexual psychopath laws and psychiatric interpretations of illegal behavior.

Sutherland was born in Gibbon, Nebraska, and spent most of his formative years in Grand Island, Nebraska, where his father, a Baptist minister, served as president of Grand Island College. Sutherland did his undergraduate work at the college, and tied with a friend for a Rhodes scholarship that eventually was awarded to the other man. He taught Greek and shorthand at the college for several years, and then enrolled in the divinity program at the University of Chicago, but soon switched to sociology, where he came under the tutelage of Charles Henderson. He later focused on political economy, working with William Hoxie, a labor historian and disciple of Thorsten Veblen, earning a joint PhD, magna cum laude, in sociology and political economy. His dissertation dealt with the work of public employment agencies in Chicago.

Sutherland's first teaching position was at William Jewell College, a Baptist school in Liberty, Missouri, where he remained for six years and published just one article, on the results of rural health surveys. His Chicago connections then served to secure him a teaching job at the University of Illinois (1925–6). The next year, he moved to the University of Minnesota (1926–9). He spent 1930 visiting prisons in England, Western Europe, and Sweden under the auspices of the Bureau of Social Hygiene. Following that, he was appointed to a research position at the University of Chicago, which ended in 1935 under uncomfortable circumstances that are still not clear. In the fall of 1935 Sutherland became the founder and chair of the sociology department at Indiana University, where he assembled a sterling faculty and attracted a cadre of to-be eminent graduate students, including Donald Cressey, Albert Cohen, Lloyd Ohlin, and Karl Schuessler, as well as many others. He remained at Indiana for the next 15 years, until his death.

Sutherland's *Criminology* textbook dominated the study of the subject until the 1960s.

The book (its title altered in later editions to *Principles of Criminology* and then back again) would go through 10 editions over a span of almost 70 years, with Cressey as co-author from the fifth edition until the tenth, when David Luckenbill assumed that role. The text was notable for the strikingly sophisticated analysis of empirical and ethnographic work on lawbreaking. Sutherland would inventory the relevant research findings and then systematically assess their credibility and shortcomings in a list that often would begin "First, …" and then continue through half a dozen or more precise summaries of the state of knowledge on the subject.

The book dropped from its preeminent position primarily because it was too austere and perhaps too erudite for later generations of students and, more importantly, because it analyzed criminal behavior in general in terms of social correlates, such as race and ethnicity, social class, mental competence, and immigration. Successfully competing later textbooks adopted an approach that focused substantively on forms of crime, such as homicide, sex offenses, and robbery. In addition, as criminology became the creche and the graveyard for a plethora of interpretive schemes, the Sutherland text's single-minded focus on differential association left devotees of other approaches out in the cold. Newer textbooks sought to attend to the ever-expanding roster of theoretical postulates in the field of criminology.

Sutherland coined the term white-collar crime, now in common popular and professional use throughout the world, and in 1949 published *White Collar Crime*, a pioneering monograph detailing and interpreting crimes committed by high-status offenders in their occupational roles. He offered varying definitions of what constituted such crime and squabbling about the proper realm of its subject matter has taken up a great deal of the intellectual energy of scholars doing research on such subjects as fraud, anti-trust violations, insider trading, and embezzlement. At the same time, the term white-collar crime has entered into popular usage and, as with pornography, there are many persons who indicate that while they cannot define the term precisely they recognize the behavior perfectly well when they see it.

Hermann Mannheim, an eminent English criminologist, was among many of Sutherland's colleagues who were greatly impressed with *White Collar Crime*. Mannheim wrote that if there were a Nobel Prize for preeminent criminological contributions, then Sutherland assuredly would have earned it for that monograph. On the other hand, critics, especially criminal law scholars, persistently have faulted *White Collar Crime* for what they regard as its muckraking slant and its failure to attend to legal doctrines which differentiate criminal behavior from civil violations and administrative wrongdoing.

White Collar Crime had its roots in the populist, anti-business mood prominent in Nebraska politics during Sutherland's time in the state. It also reflects Sutherland's strong moral values, values that were epitomized in an interview he gave when he taught summer school at the University of Washington in 1942, not long after America's entrance into World War II. He had the courage to tell a reporter for the student newspaper that the evacuation of the Japanese from the west coast and their forced internment in "resettlement camps" had "resulted more from race prejudice than from military necessity."

Sutherland's theory of differential association consists of nine postulates that maintain that crime is a behavior learned from association with others who transmit attitudes, teach tactics, and offer rationalizations that put persons on the path to illegal behavior. The postulates themselves are an uneven conglomerate, some of them core concepts, others rather in the nature of asides. It is arguable that criminal behavior is learned only in primary groups, that is, from family and friends, as Sutherland's theory maintains. A considerable literature now concludes that secondary learning sources, such as television and song lyrics, can lead to violent lawbreaking. Sutherland's formulation also rather gratuitously indicates that crime is *not* the result of imitation, a position enunciated at the time by Gabriel Tarde, a French sociologist, who maintained that what humans did was a product of what they saw being done. Sutherland makes the important point that criminal behavior is not an expression of general needs and values, since noncriminal behavior results from these same conditions. Two people may need money; one will commit a robbery, the other will get a second job pumping gas.

Differential association today is generally regarded as overly simple and absolutely untestable as Sutherland formulated it: how, for instance, can the ratio of experiences favorable to crime and those pushing in the other direction, a key element in the theory, be measured? How can the theory explain why persons who seemingly are exposed to similar experiences respond very differently to these stimuli? The theory also has been faulted for its total neglect of biological and genetic contributions to criminal and to law-abiding behavior. For Sutherland, human behavior is the product solely of those things that we encounter and absorb after birth.

Interestingly, the most pointed critique of the theory was by Sutherland himself in an unpublished essay written in 1944 and circulated among his colleagues. It carried the whimsical title, "The Swan Song of Differential Association." Sutherland noted that he had not given adequate attention to "opportunity" as a necessary correlate of illegal behavior, nor had he sufficiently calibrated the intensity of particular needs in terms of the role they play in triggering criminal acts. He concluded that the sufficiency of differential association as an explanation of criminal acts was "questionable." Nonetheless, the theory continued to dominate the field for several more decades.

Sutherland was not a prolific writer, but what he published tended to be carefully crafted. As three of his close colleagues note: "Sutherland's writing is distinguished by unusual clarity, simplicity, and unpretentiousness. He seldom wasted words, and he seldom repeated himself in different papers." His was a serious, humorless style, though the man himself was an iconic figure to most of the graduate students with whom he worked. Albert Cohen, in a tribute to Sutherland as a mentor, observed: "It was not only that we felt that Sutherland was at the frontier; we felt we were at the frontier." For all the tenacity of Sutherland's own views, Cohen added, he "was never overbearing, never didactic, never arrogant. He invariably treated the students with respect, never humiliated them, always made them feel we were partners in a quest."

In addition to his monograph on white-collar crime, a subject that he came to late in his career, Sutherland used material furnished by Chic Conwell, a skilled con artist, to write *The Professional Thief*, and, with Harvey Locke (one of his very few collaborations) he wrote a monograph about homeless men in Chicago during the Depression. Critics regard the former book as marked by a kind of hero-worship, and insist that Conwell conned Sutherland into accepting a tale that was at best only a partial truth; that Sutherland either was in the dark or chose to ignore Conwell's history of drug addiction. They also argue that while Sutherland was appalled by corporate predators, he romanticized a smooth talker such as Conwell, who boasted that he was an outlaw, and proclaimed that only the greed of his victims allowed him to exploit them.

Sutherland's articles critiquing sexual psychopath laws remain relevant today when community notifications regarding released sex offenders add an extra-judicial penalty to the sentence that the offenders have served. Sutherland's writings on prisons have worn less well. Today, his view that the length of incarceration ought to be left to the professional judgment of social scientists and prison authorities – a common position when he was writing – seems unpromising and likely to be unduly punitive. Objections also are raised that such a program would punish people for what they are rather than only for what they have done. On the other hand, Sutherland's diatribe against corporate criminals, which he sought in vain to camouflage as objective social science, resonates in our time, as major American businesses are charged with crimes involving the theft of extraordinary amounts of money and their culpable executives are handcuffed and led off to prison.

SEE ALSO: Chicago School; Crime, Psychological Theories of; Crime, Social Learning Theory of; Crime, White-Collar; Criminology

REFERENCES AND SUGGESTED READINGS

Cohen, A., Lindesmith, A., & Schuessler, K. (1956) *The Sutherland Papers*. Indiana University Press, Bloomington.

Cressey, D. R. (1955) Changing Criminals: The Application of the Theory of Differential Association. *American Journal of Sociology* 61: 116–20.

Cressey, D. R. (1960) Epidemiology and Individual Conduct: A Case from Criminology. *Pacific Sociological Review* 3: 47–58.

Galliher, J. F. & Tyree, C. (1985) Edwin Sutherland's Research on the Origins of Sexual Psychopath Laws: An Early Case Study of the Medicalization of Deviance. *Social Problems* 3: 100–12.

Gaylord, M. S. & Galliher, J. F. (1988) *The Criminology of Edwin Sutherland*. Transaction Books, New Brunswick, NJ.

Geis, G. (1976) Revisiting Sutherland's *Criminology* (1924). *Criminology* 14: 303–6.

Geis, G. & Goff, C. (1983) Introduction. In: Sutherland, E. H. (Ed.), *White Collar Crime*. Yale University Press, New Haven, pp. ix–xxxiii.

Matsueda, R. L. (1988) The Current State of Differential Association Theory. *Crime & Delinquency* 34: 277–306.

Sutherland, E. H. (1937) *The Professional Thief*. University of Chicago Press, Chicago.

Sutherland, E. H. (1941) The Development of the Concept of Differential Association. *Ohio Valley Sociologist* 15: 3–4.

Sutherland, E. H. (1949) *White Collar Crime*. Dryden, New York.

Sutherland, E. H. (1950) The Diffusion of the Sexual Psychopath Laws. *American Journal of Sociology* 56: 142–8.

Tittle, C. R., Burke, M. J., & Jackson, E. F. (1986) Modeling Sutherland's Theory of Differential Association: Toward an Empirical Clarification. *Social Forces* 65: 405–32.

Suzuki, Eitaro (1894–1966)

Yasushi Suzuki

Eitaro Suzuki is one of the pioneers of Japanese rural and urban sociology. Graduated from Tokyo Imperial University in 1922, he taught at Gifu Agricultural High School and Seoul Imperial University. After World War II, he became a professor at Hokkaido University.

Sociology was introduced to Japan in the 1880s, but empirical research on Japanese society did not develop until the 1920s. By then, Japan had reached an early stage of industrialization and urbanization. Sociology of the family, rural sociology, and urban sociology were launched in this historical context. Suzuki was a pioneer of rural sociology in the 1930s and turned his interest to urban sociology in the post-war era.

Suzuki studied the social structure of Japanese rural villages during the 1930s, under the influence of German cultural science, American rural sociology, and Le Play's (French) School. He published his first major work, *Principles of Japanese Rural Sociology*, in 1940. His main contribution to this field was the introduction of the concept of "natural village" as a unit of sociological analysis. Operationally, he divided "social districts" into three categories, by examining the geographical overlaps of social relations and groups of villagers. The first social district is the small neighborhood, which is a subunit of the natural village. The second is the natural village itself, and the third is the "legal village." The legal village was an artificial construct by the national government after the Meiji Restoration, and typically contained several natural villages within it. The natural village, in contrast, has been a self-sustaining community, typically founded three centuries or more ago, according to Suzuki.

Referring to Sorokin's concept of cumulative community, Suzuki emphasized that the natural village was not only a cumulative community, but also a community with a collective spirit that was the ultimate source of social order in the village. As a cumulative community, it comprised many social relations and groups. It was basically composed of traditional stem families, which were taken over from generation to generation by male successors. It also included other social groups, such as formal residential associations regulated by the local government, traditional mutual aid associations, religious and kinship (Japanese lineage) groups. Moreover, the natural village is a distinctive entity. It owned common forests and properties, and managed water systems collectively (Japanese agriculture typically uses water-laden paddies). It had its own guardian deity and the group of shrine parishioners. They were considered to be the legitimate members of the village. In addition, the natural village held a collective consciousness that Suzuki called "the spirit of the village." It is this spirit that controlled traditional behaviors and attitudes of villagers.

Thus, by describing the social structure of the natural village in the 1930s, Suzuki constructed the ideal type of Japanese rural community. The natural village and its elements have become basic concepts in Japanese rural sociology. Although natural villages have disappeared in the face of rapid urbanization since the 1950s, their remnants today can still be seen, even in highly urbanized areas.

After World War II, Suzuki devoted himself to the study of urban sociology and published his second major work, *Principles of Urban Sociology*, in 1957. This book is not tightly organized, but includes many insightful concepts, a classificatory schema for social relations and groups, and detailed descriptions and analyses of urban traits. Among these, the "nodal organ" thesis, the "normal life of the normal population" thesis, and the concept of "life structure" are widely known among Japanese sociologists.

Based on his observations of various rural and urban communities in Japan, Suzuki developed his own definition of the city: the city is a community that differs from a rural one in the way that it contains nodal organs (social institutions) that connect social interactions to the national society as a whole. This definition is unique in that it has no reference to any demographic or other traits. Rather, he argued that urban traits such as population size, density, heterogeneity, strangeness, and so on are accompanied by the concentration of institutions and that the city should be defined in relation to the nodal function in the national society. The presence of nodal institutions, such as government agencies, retail and wholesale services, and the offices of various kinds of corporations and associations, makes a community a city. He argued that all the communities in the national society are organized in a hierarchical urban–rural system, in which the rural communities are positioned at the lowest level. Thus the characteristics of the nodal institutions in a given community determine its position as a city in the nationwide hierarchy of urban system.

Other Japanese urban sociologists suggested similar definitions. Fukutaro Okui (1996 [1940]), another pioneer of Japanese urban

sociology, argued that although a "city-in-itself" may be defined in terms of its population aggregation and regions, it is important that we study it in relation to the development of the national society as a whole. He claimed that the "essence" of the city is the locus of the central functions in a wider social economic life. Later, Takeo Yazaki (1962) also emphasized the integrative function of urban institutions. These suggestions reflect the fact that Japanese cities have been controlled by the central government and its local agencies since the Tokugawa era. Suzuki made it clear that urban and rural communities are organized within the national hierarchy, and, therefore, cities should be defined and analyzed in relation to the wider society.

In addition to the "nodal organ" thesis, Suzuki suggested a general framework for analyzing the social structure of cities. In order to clarify the urban social structure, he emphasized "the normal life of the normal population," instead of "abnormal life" or "abnormal population." By "abnormal," he meant a state which is unable to reproduce itself if it continues. The "normal life" should therefore constitute the "structure" of complex urban life. The ordinary life of the ordinary urbanite entails commuting between home and the workplace. Suzuki therefore identified households and workplaces (and schools for children) as central axes of the structure. He added neighborhoods and leisure groups to them. Yet he maintained that leisure groups were merely "superficial elements of the structure, or accessories [of urban life], no matter how exaggerated or gorgeous they appear." Although some critics argue that one could find distinctive characteristics (and problems) of urban life within the "abnormal life" and "abnormal population," Suzuki's intent was to emphasize that the urban social structures were not disorganized, as claimed by some of the followers of American urban sociology. While he estimated the number of abnormal populations in cities, he argued that these must be ignored in order to understand the basic urban structures.

Before introducing Suzuki's concept of metropolitan areas, it is worth mentioning his basic concept of the community. By community, he meant "a local social unity that performs the functions of cooperation for living and of collective defense." This conception of community applies to both cities and villages. Both serve the defense function against enemies and disasters (floods, fires, and earthquakes). It is clear that the villagers cooperate for living. As for the city, he claimed that some basic human needs are satisfied within the community by public services and private transactions. This is the critical point, however, for his development of another scheme for analyzing the metropolitan areas: "the pre-social unity existing within and beyond the city." As a site of concentration of nodal institutions, a city interacts with other communities positioned at a lower level. Such interactions produce five types of metropolitan areas: urban living area, urban dependency area, urban users' area, urban dominance area, and urban influential area.

The urban living area is where urbanites lead their everyday life. It constitutes adjoining areas to shop for basic life necessities. The urban dependency area encompasses residents who depend on the city for their livelihood, typified by the commuting sphere. The urban users' area includes all residents who use urban institutions. Since such institutions are typically located in central business districts or subcenters, it constitutes the trading areas of the central city. The urban dominance area is where the institutions of the city deploy their branch offices. In theory, it differs from institution to institution, but in reality they overlap significantly. Finally, the urban influential area extends to all residents who receive information transmitted by the city. Since the mass media in Japan are concentrated in Tokyo, Suzuki suggested that Tokyo's urban dominance area extends across Japanese society as a whole. Other urban centers are, in comparison, "like the light of a candle under the Sun."

Each area is defined in terms of particular types of relationships between persons and institutions. Here, the spatial orders of "the normal life of the normal population" combine with "nodal institutions." This is one dimension of Suzuki's "life structure of the city."

Suzuki defined "life structure" as a set of spatial and temporal orders of the community. It refers to a dynamic aspect of urban life. He argued that the routine activities of persons and institutions must follow a set of spatial and temporal orders, and thus produce cyclic pulses of urban life. These orders are not only the effects of aggregation of individuals' daily activities but also sometimes institutionalized as norms. The norms of workplaces, schools, and households define the time for work, rest, and sleep. Suzuki classified the temporal orders of the city in terms of the temporal units of the cycle (the examples mentioned below are selected from the original text):

- a day – rest, sleep, nutrition, and work for daily workers;
- a week – weekly schedules, leisure, and rest on Sundays;
- a month – salary system, rent payment, etc.;
- a year – new year holidays, gift-giving, annual settlement of accounts;
- lifetime – karmic backlash;
- endlessness – traces of the feudal obligations among traditional families.

Among these, Suzuki focused on the settlement of accounts and the breaks and holidays for workers, illustrating how they occur through various terms of cycles. In addition, he aimed to describe the typical life cycle of the Japanese people. As he had previously developed a model of the life cycle of Japan's traditional stem families, he expected to be able to apply it to urban Japanese. He thought he would be able to identify a distinctive life cycle common to Japanese urbanites but different from their counterparts in other countries.

Suzuki's analytical schemas for urban social structures and the life structures are very clear, and fit the social conditions of Japan at the time. Suburbanization was limited, and there was no need to distinguish the natural city from the legal city. Basically, he established a descriptive framework for Japanese cities in the national context. Yet it is not clear how his definition of the city is related to the schema of the urban social structure. He failed to classify Japanese cities by their distinctive functions, e.g., manufacturing, shipping, political administration, commerce, and tourism, beyond their differential status in the urban hierarchical system. He also failed to explain how the urban social structures differ by size and status. In sum, he delineated the urban social structure common to Japanese cities without delineating their differences.

4906 *symbolic classification*

His theory of rural and urban communities was constrained by time and place, for it was based on Japanese materials in the 1930s to the 1950s. Although the concepts and schemas he developed need to be reviewed and redefined, Eitaro Suzuki's analysis is a distinctive heritage of Japanese sociology. He depicted the typical Japanese villages and cities of his time and their relationships to the national society as a whole. Thus his work continues to provide key concepts and insights for understanding cities and communities in relation to the national and global system.

SEE ALSO: Global/World Cities; *Ie*; Sorokin, Pitirim A.; Traditional Consumption City (Japan); Urban; Urban Community Studies

REFERENCES AND SUGGESTED READINGS

Okui, F. (1996 [1940]) Contemporary Metropolis. In: *Collected Papers of Okui Fukutaro*, Vol. 5. Ozorasya, Tokyo.
Suzuki, E. (1969 [1940]) Principles of Japanese Rural Sociology. In: *Collected Papers of Suzuki Eitaro*, Vols. 1 and 2. Miraisya, Tokyo.
Suzuki, E. (1969 [1957]) Principles of Urban Sociology. In: *Collected Papers of Suzuki Eitaro*, Vol. 6. Miraisya, Tokyo.
Yazaki, T. (1962) *Process of Development in Japanese Cities*. Kobundo, Tokyo.

symbolic classification

Simone Ghezzi

Symbolic classification – literally, complex arrangements of symbols into wholes – refers to the process of classifying and ordering by means of which individuals are able to make sense of the natural and social world. They do so by means of models of categorization that are culturally and socially determined. Such categories are cast in concrete images that we may call symbols, which are, by definition, polysemic and relativistic because they convey different meanings.

Durkheim and Mauss were among the first scholars to pick up the age-old philosophical idea about the ways human beings conceive of time, space, causality, unity, plurality, and so on. Their ideas are elaborated in an article entitled "De quelques formes primitives de classification: contribution à l'étude des représentations collectives," published in *L'Année sociologique* (1903) and translated in English as *Primitive Classification* (1963). The importance of this publication lies in the fact that some of the issues illustrated here were eventually discussed in greater depth in structuralist social theories that emerged several decades later; moreover, it may be regarded as an early contribution to the sociology of knowledge and to sociological epistemology. The central argument of their essay is that there exists a connection between the classification of natural phenomena and the social order. The act of classifying does not occur through the effect of a "spontaneous" attitude of the mind, based for example upon the principles of contiguity, similarity, and opposition among objects or among living beings, but originates within the organization of social life. When they state that the "individual's mind is incapable of classification," it does not mean that the individual's mind lacks "the innate faculty of classification" – indeed, it would be difficult to conceive of a mind incapable of processing information and distinguishing objects of the environment; rather, Durkheim and Mauss insist on the social expression of human knowledge and on the social root of human thought. They oppose the idea both that categories exist before experience (built-in or a priori categories) and that categories are the product of experience (empiricism).

To investigate and elaborate on this assertion, they focus in particular on Aboriginal totemic societies from Central Australia, held at that time to be the most primitive of all, and to a lesser extent on Native American tribes. These societies appeared to classify people, animals, and things according to taxonomic criteria corresponding to the specific organization of their society (moieties, clans, kin). Durkheim and Mauss seek evidence of this by considering the patterns of residence, the arrangements of marriage, and the dominant organizing principles of these societies, and relate these aspects to logical thought processes.

From a functionalist point of view, the classification of categories makes the relationship between phenomena explicable; from an evolutionary perspective, it constitutes the first foundations of scientific thinking. Durkheim and Mauss conclude that among the Australian tribes "the classification of things reproduces the classification of men" (1963 [1903]: 11). The implication is that ideas and worldviews are constructed on a model that reproduces the society from which they have emerged. This argument will be taken up again by Durkheim a few years later in *Les Formes élémentaires de la vie religieuse: le système totémique en Australie* (1912). Some have argued that to prove their point, Durkheim and Mauss omitted cases where social organization and symbolic classification do not correspond; nonetheless, their original ideas have influenced other scholars, such as Lévi-Strauss and Mary Douglas.

Lévi-Strauss analyzes symbolic classification at a much deeper, i.e., unconscious, level. Native categories of thought are the output of universal mental processes (e.g., binary or dual oppositions), which manifest themselves in different ways. Both the cosmologies of "primitive" societies and the scientific thought of industrial societies are founded upon the same bases – the unconscious but structured regularities of human thought. Whereas for Durkheim and Mauss the taxonomy of the classifications reflects the kind of relationships that regulate social institutions, for Lévi-Strauss classifications are viewed and analyzed as cognitive models. Evidence of these two different viewpoints emerges in the theory of totemism. Durkheim explains totemic classifications of animals or plants in terms of a structural homology between the social and the symbolic sphere. A group identifies symbolically with an animal, a plant, or a natural phenomenon, one of which then becomes the symbol of the group itself. By contrast, for Lévi-Strauss totems must be understood metaphorically in terms of the relationship between groups. The identification with a totem is arbitrary; what counts are the differences among animal or plant species because they are used to express differences among groups of people. In such a manner the observed world is used as a sort of template for a symbolic representation of the social world.

The British anthropologist Mary Douglas departs from the epistemology of Durkheim and Mauss's notion of symbolic classification and refines their sociology of knowledge. She avoids their evolutionary typology, i.e., the distinction between primitive and modern symbolic worlds, and insists time and again on the importance of classificatory impurities. To understand the environment, individuals introduce order out of the chaos by means of classification. Yet in this process individuals discover that a few objects, living beings, actions, or ideas appear to be anomalous – matter out of place – which may pollute the entire classificatory system. What does not fit must be dealt with ideologically to keep the anomaly under control, both in the natural and in the social world. Douglas's pollution studies demonstrate how the human body is used to symbolize certain social relations. Bodily substances, processes, and orifices play a significant role in rites and prohibitions by expressing relationships between social groups and categories (Douglas 1966, 1970). The ideas elaborated in the study of symbolic classification have recently been reexamined and employed. This is evident, for example, in studies on ethnicity which deconstruct the ethnic anomalies stressed by a hegemonic system of classification, especially in multi-ethnic societies.

SEE ALSO: Anthropology, Cultural and Social: Early History; Durkheim, Émile; Ethnicity; Knowledge, Sociology of; Semiotics; Sign; Symbolic Exchange; Structuralism; Totemism

REFERENCES AND SUGGESTED READINGS

Douglas, M. (1966) *Purity and Danger: An Analysis of the Concepts of Pollution and Taboo*. Penguin, Harmondsworth.

Douglas, M. (1970) *Natural Symbols: Explorations in Cosmology*. Cresset, London.

Douglas, M. (Ed.) (1982) *Essays in the Sociology of Perception*. Routledge & Kegan Paul, London.

Durkheim, É. (1965 [1912]) *The Elementary Forms of Religious Life*. Free Press, London.

Durkheim, É. & Mauss, M. (1963 [1903]) *Primitive Classification*. University of Chicago Press, Chicago.

Lévi-Strauss, C. (1966 [1962]) *The Savage Mind.* University of Chicago Press, Chicago.

Lévi-Strauss, C. (1967 [1962]) *Totemism.* Beacon Press, Boston.

Needham, R. (1979) *Symbolic Classification.* Goodyear, Santa Monica.

symbolic exchange

Michael T. Ryan

Symbolic exchange is the organizing principle, the cellular structure, of the earliest forms of society, the forms that Anthony Giddens designates as "tribal cultures." The exchanges that take place within and between clans, within and between tribes, and between chiefs and other members of the tribe are more than economic exchanges as we know them in modern societies, and their circulation integrates the members of these societies. Marcel Mauss conceptualizes these exchanges as a form of gift giving, and the gift is a "total social phenomenon." They are multidimensional: economic, moral, religious, mythological, juridical, political, aesthetic, and historical.

Mauss (Durkheim's nephew) created his concept from the work of nineteenth and early twentieth-century anthropologists in Melanesia, Polynesia, and Northwest America. Like Durkheim, he also wanted to demonstrate the social basis for exchanges as a refutation of the utilitarian notion that individual interests were the foundation for the creation of market relations. There was no "natural" economy that had preceded political economy.

Further, while the tribes of the Americas, Africa, and Asia seemed so different, so "other," to Europeans, Mauss wanted to demonstrate through comparative analysis the underlying similarities as well. The complex structure of the gift made it more difficult for Europeans to see these groups as inferior primitives whose annihilation or assimilation would be of no loss to humanity.

Gift giving was obviously an economic phenomenon, although it did not involve the exchange of equivalent values as it does in market economies. In the Kwakiutl tribe the *potlatch*

ritual exchanges were competitive and required a reciprocal exchange at a later moment that was of more value than the original gift. This was how the chief, the clan, or the tribe maintained prestige and power; the chief would distribute the gifts later received to the members of his clan or tribe. The chief was the member of the tribe who shared the most. The goods exchanged were often destroyed in festivals which made the accumulation of wealth impossible.

Gift giving also involved a relation with nature and created a balanced reciprocal relation between society and nature. For example, since tribes deified natural forces in their animistic religions, a wood carver made an offering to the spirits of the forest before cutting down the tree that he would use. The domination of nature is a modern phenomenon; these tribes lived in nature.

Gift giving also included a morality of reciprocity. The members of tribes were obligated to give gifts as well as receive gifts. Failure to do either would mean a loss of status, perhaps enslavement, or possibly war if it occurred between two tribes. The norm of reciprocity bound clan to clan, men to women, and tribe to tribe, and the circulation of gifts reproduced these tribes as tribes.

Thorstein Veblen brought the analysis of symbolic exchange to the consumer practices of wealthy Americans in his *Theory of the Leisure Class.* Veblen developed his concepts of vicarious consumption and conspicuous consumption from the same sources as Mauss, from tribal cultures and agrarian societies. The leisure class originally derived its prestige from avoiding ignoble work and devoting its time to pursuits that had little practical significance: sports, indolence, war, religious activities, and government. They also derived prestige through the idleness and vicarious consumption of their wives, families, and servants. Further, as the members of the middle class took up practical positions as professionals and managers, they derived their prestige from conspicuous consumption, "keeping ahead of the Joneses." Further, the competitive logic of the rat race filtered down throughout the class structure. Although Veblen also recognized that, once his theory had become understood by the leisure class, the members of this elite could reverse course and practice asceticism. Old money has often adopted low profiles in their lifestyles, and the arts and crafts movement with its functional aesthetic was very popular for members of the professional managerial class in the early twentieth century. Veblen also recognized that the pursuits of the leisure class often had functional qualities and were not always a pure waste of time and wealth.

Jean Baudrillard developed his analysis from a critical reading of Mauss, Galbraith, and Veblen. Symbolic exchange for Baudrillard was a way to escape the consumer society and the political economy of the sign. He demonstrated in his early writings how the code of consumption and the system of needs had completed the system of production. The use value of the commodity provided no way out of the capitalist mode of production as it had for traditional Marxists ("to each according to his needs") – it only provided an alibi to exchange value. Consumers were even more alienated in their private lives than they were at work engaging in unequal exchanges with capital and producing surplus value. They were unconscious of the process of semiosis that led through their acts of consumption of commodities with their coded differences to the reproduction of the capitalist mode of production. The only way out of this system was a return to symbolic exchange where the accumulation of wealth and power was impossible and where exchanges were reciprocal and reversible. Symbolic exchange was also likely to restore a balance between society and nature, whereas the logic of the consumer society, predicated on continuous economic growth and the ideology of economic growth, is likely to destroy the environment.

What are the analytical problems with Baudrillard's analysis of symbolic exchange? A number of critics point out that he does not clearly define the concept of code in his writings. But it seems that what he means is that every commodity has a hierarchal structure with the originals at the top that are appropriated by the elite and models of descending quality that are appropriated by the other strata. The consumption of the sign value of each commodity reproduces the code *and* the relations of domination between the programmers of consumption and the consumers. George Ritzer finds "commotion" in Baudrillard's appropriation

of concepts from diverse theorists: Marx, Durkheim, Mauss, structural linguistics, Lévi-Strauss, Lefebvre, etc. But this *is* the procedure for dialectical method. The most serious problem is the criticism that he has given us a romantic possibility without identifying any actual agents or movements of social change.

SEE ALSO: Consumption; Gift; Gift Relations

REFERENCES AND SUGGESTED READINGS

Baudrillard, J. (1975) *The Mirror of Production.* Telos Press, St. Louis.
Baudrillard, J. (1976) *For a Critique of the Political Economy of the Sign.* Telos Press, St. Louis.
Baudrillard, J. (1988) *Symbolic Exchange and Death*, In: Kellner, D. (Ed.), *Jean Baudrillard.* Stanford University Press, Stanford.
Baudrillard, J. (1998) *The Consumer Society.* Sage, London.
Kellner, D. (Ed.) (1988) *Jean Baudrillard.* Stanford University Press, Stanford.
Kellner, D. (1994) *Baudrillard.* Blackwell, Oxford.
Levin, C. (1989) Introduction. In: Baudrillard, J., *For a Critique of the Political Economy of the Sign.* Telos Press, St. Louis.
Mauss, M. (1967) *The Gift.* W. W. Norton, New York.
Poster, M. (1975) Introduction. In: *The Mirror of Production.* Telos Press, St. Louis.
Ritzer, G. (1998) Introduction. In: *The Consumer Society.* Sage, London.
Veblen, T. (1953) *Theory of the Leisure Class.* Mentor, New York.

symbolic interaction

Peter M. Hall

Symbolic interactionism (also known as interactionism) is a uniquely American theoretical perspective that draws its primary inspiration from pragmatism. It refers to humans' distinctive use of language to create symbols, common meanings, for thinking and communication with others. Herbert Blumer (1969) coined the term to express his "reading" of George

Herbert Mead's thought developed in the early 1900s and codified it in the elaboration of three premises: (1) humans act on the basis of the meanings which things have for them; (2) meanings arise in interaction between people; and (3) meanings are handed and modified through an interpretive process used by people in dealing with things encountered.

Another source for the perspective came from early twentieth-century Chicago sociologists W. I. Thomas, Robert Park, and Everett Hughes (a contemporary of Blumer's), who examined urban settings, racial/ethnic hierarchies, work and occupational relations, and social problems. They presented views of social processes, social organization, and social change. While they shared many ideas with Blumer, they gave such ideas as social forces, constraints, and obduracy more emphasis. Students of both Blumer and Hughes (such as Howard Becker, Anselm Strauss, and Helena Lopata) fused the two lines of thought into what is labeled interactionism. Strauss (1993) brings this fusion together in a comprehensive vision for the perspective.

KEY ASSUMPTIONS AND CORE CONCEPTS

G. H. Mead noted two distinctive human qualities: handedness and language. The human hand allows feeling, taking apart, putting together, and modifying the environment. Language (with consciousness and mind) in conjunction with the hand facilitates thinking, imagining, creating, and communication with others to plan, coordinate, and assess social action. Humans are assumed to be at work, active in managing their existence. The hand serves as a metaphor for doing the work of affecting the environment and offering feedback of the results for thought. Society precedes any individual. As humans enter this world and develop they are socialized into it (i.e., learn how to use the hand and language). They are taught or come to know what objects mean and how they are used. They develop a self, make an object of their actions, and use this reflexivity to think and interact with others. From this foundation there are five key assumptions: process, emergence, agency, conditionality, and dialectics.

Process

Rather than static or equilibrium states, interactionists believe things social are always active, in process, ongoing, becoming, and changing. Society and the individual are seen as in process. Even in stability there is process because actions/activity are necessary to maintain that state. Interactionists also deconstruct and dereify totalities and structures into activities and processes.

Emergence

Emergence refers to unique combinations that create qualitatively different manifestations. For example, hydrogen plus oxygen creates water. Similarly, an aggregate of individuals together as a group is more than the sum of the parts. It has different consequences. Thus, the emergent developments of handedness and language lead to human social organization and culture. Emergence also means unpredictability and contingency. Interactionists are relative determinists, who because of vagaries (e.g., ambiguous communication, divergent interests, problematic coordination, and unforeseen obstacles) expect the unexpected, the accidental, novelty, or resistance/deviance. Interactionists remain open to possibilities and potentialities.

Agency

Agency refers to the idea that humans are not robots and have the capacity to exert some control over themselves, others, and the environment. Humans are able to construct, pursue, and achieve their intentions (within limits). Activity and social action are not predetermined but are constructed in the process of doing and therefore capable of being altered to meet whatever circumstances arise. Humans construct social worlds and transform environments.

Constructed Conditionality

Constructed conditionality embeds two processes. The world as we know it is a social construction. Humans have built societies, groups, and relationships. Humans then have to live with the consequences of their constructions. They condition subsequent activity. Humans are born into societies with conditions to which they adapt, respond, and often change. There is an obdurate reality that humans must take into account. The conditions/reality do not necessarily determine social action, prevent agency, or mute social construction, but they cannot be ignored without consequences. The existing conditions shape but do not determine behavior.

Dialectics

There is a rejection of standard dichotomies or dualistic thinking. Western societies have long accepted dualisms such as mind-body, individual-society, and rationality-emotion. Interactionists see these in relational and processual terms. The self is said to be composed of a social aspect (me) and a personal (I) one, which are in conversation, dialogue, and interaction with each other. Thus, self and society are not opposites but implicated in each other and in process. The ideas of relationality, mediation, and dialectics are expressed here as interpenetrative phases and aspects. Interactionists responded to debates about macro-micro, structure-process, and agency-structure by transcending these dualities with alternative conceptualizations.

A set of core concepts draws upon these assumptions. Work as something to be done stands for action. Working things out implies "with others," thus interaction. Interactionists take the dyad or joint action as the basic social unit. From this form and process are built greater complexity. Dyads with relative stability have general agreements about identities, intentions, expectations, and coordination. Joint action occurs because each actor builds upon and completes the actions of the other. But interactionists assume agreements are working consensuses, subject to differences and obstacles, and then renegotiated.

Situations constitute basic contexts for action. Over time actors encounter familiar ones which they recognize and then produce the appropriate and consequent identities, actions, and outcomes. These are routine situations characterized by habitual behavior. When actors encounter obstacles, novelty, or ambiguity the situations are problematic and require social action to define and specify the situation and its interactional requirements.

Much of social life occurs in collectivities of different sizes, forms, and complexities. Collective action, joint action by multiple actors, whether in teams, families, congregations, or social movements, requires significant planning, coordination, timing and spacing, and monitoring. Collectivities may be seen as networks which connect and implicate multiple others, but may vary on how tightly or loosely coordinated the collectivity is. Since such collectivities may not be located in a single space and may have projects that extend for long durations, the ability to maintain, coordinate, and accomplish their goals poses major problems. Interactionists have consequently paid attention to temporality, spatiality, and coordinated action.

Interactionsts have questioned the strengths and stability of conventional organizational forms. They have offered conceptualizations of organizations as negotiated orders stressing the problematic, ambiguous, and contested nature of those contexts and the necessity of actors to reconstitute activity through negotiation. More generally, they have proposed a new concept, "social world," to represent collectivities organized around an activity/idea/purpose but dispersed across space and time with diffuse boundaries and membership. Using this concept, Becker (1982) demonstrated how art worlds involving production, dissemination, and consumption of art were held together in networks by conventions, resources, and context. Others have shown how multiple social worlds come together, interact, and evolve in organizations, institutions, and arenas of public issues and social problems. Social worlds represent a fluid, dynamic, and changing social formation due to problematic circumstances and consequential interaction.

Interactionists prefer the term social organization to social structure because they perceive greater fluidity, looseness, and change. They see dialectical relationships between order-disorder, stability-instability, yet at the same time they see processual ordering through constructed conditionality. There is recognition of structuration, constraints, sedimentation, and inequality. Not all actors have equal access to cultural and material resources and hence agency is restricted. However, there are opportunities, contingencies, alternatives, and imaginations that provide dynamic possibilities. So while one can acknowledge that the inequality orders of class, gender, and race intersect, their ordering can be said to be "tentative, messy and incomplete."

SCHOOLS OF THOUGHT

Interactionism lacks a consensual, integrated, transmitted body of ideas; rather, scholars have taken what they wanted to fit their purposes at hand. Major faultlines in interactionism have been around Herbert Blumer's interpretation of Mead. On the one hand, some scholars believed Blumer minimized social structure and rejected a positivist approach to exploring relations between individuals and society. Others believed Blumer focused too much on the self, symbols, and cognitive aspects and insufficiently on behavior or forms of social interaction.

There are two forms of interactionism that stand in some contrast to conventional symbolic interaction. The first is the Iowa School, which has seen several forms. It was first developed in the 1950s under the leadership of Manford Kuhn, who believed (following his views of Mead and Cooley) that it was possible to pursue the scientific study of the self. His view of the self was more structural than the presumed fluid view of Blumer. Kuhn proposed the Twenty Statements Test as a simple, quantitative way to get data about people's ideas about their selves. Numerous studies were conducted and published using this instrument that led to ultimate understandings of how self-conceptions were altered by social change and new conditions.

Later, in the 1970s, Carl Couch and his colleagues developed the "new" Iowa School with the same interest in systematic, scientific study. They took a position that more attention needed to be given to examining the social act and the problematic coordination of behavior. Their social behaviorism made the core

ontological units, not individuals, meanings or situations, but rather forms of coordinated behavior (e.g., dyad, triad, small group). For them, the basic building blocks of society were two or more people coordinating behavior with experienced, enduring consequences. They did so by studying the emergence of relationships and different forms of relationships in varying contexts. Carl Couch used these studies as the basis for *Constructing Civilization* (1984), which explored the evolution of complex forms of social coordination across expanses of space and time. It remains a foundation piece for interactionist studies of social organization.

The second form, the dramaturgical perspective, most completely developed by Goffman (1959), has been utilized by numerous interactionists, providing an extensive literature (see Brissett & Edgley 1990). It has its formal origins in the writings of Kenneth Burke on dramatism and was utilized by C. Wright Mills in his early work on motives. Gregory Stone and Robert Perinbanayagam were also instrumental in expanding the framework and integrating it with ongoing interactionist analysis. Several factors distinguish it from traditional symbolic interactionism. Like the Iowa School, dramaturgy focuses on actions and situations. It focuses on how people express themselves with others. But that interest involves more than verbal communication. The formulation includes nonverbal elements: appearance, attire, gestures, sounds, and movements. Following Goffman, dramaturgists believe accomplishing expressive actions jointly is problematic, socially emergent, and variable. Dramaturgists believe all social actors have to express themselves to interact, but they may or may not be aware of or be able to control how they do so. Thus, there are numerous possible alternatives in these interactions. The dramaturgical perspective and the language of theater continue to offer insights and methods for interactionists.

METHODOLOGY

Interactionists have used a variety of methods and techniques to develop an extensive empirical base. Use of different methods may arise from varying assumptions about interactionism and social reality. Many practitioners operating from interpretive assumptions have conducted ethnographic fieldwork and depth interviews designed to access actors' perspectives, biographies, and experiences and to reveal detailed observations of group life. Other interactionists whose focus was on social action and social process chose various ways to conduct systematic observations of different behavioral phenomena in laboratory or public settings. Some of these studies utilized multiple observers and/ or videotaping or photographing of social gatherings and interactions (e.g., experimental role-playing or large protest demonstrations). A third approach has utilized questionnaires, hypothesis testing, and statistical analyses to explore connections between self, roles, relationships, and social structures. A final category of empirical study involves content analyses of documents or visual and print media to elicit thematic elements.

Because early ethnographic and qualitative research was criticized as idiosyncratic, Glaser and Strauss (1967) presented grounded theory as a systematic method of relating qualitative data and emerging theory through comprehensive fieldwork strategies, coding, conceptualization, and theory generation. The approach has been extensively elaborated, revised, expanded, and strengthened in later works by Strauss and others. A major recent advance comes from Clarke (2005), which integrates historical, visual, and narrative discourses and structural contexts with grounded theory to produce a more comprehensive basis for conducting qualitative research.

Another significant change in interactionist qualitative research emerges from making explicit the significance of the self in the conduct of the research. Since the researcher's self is the instrument of data gathering, it is imperative to show that their identities, perspectives, actions, and relationships affect and are affected by the field. Reflexivity, the dialogue between self as subject and object, is central to understanding that imperative and requires explication. The subjectivity of the researcher facilitates the research, but also becomes author of the research presentation. That makes the presentation and its form subject to analysis.

One result has been to adopt a narrative approach that is consciously explicit about a rhetorical structure with dramatic appeal.

It is common for interactionists to use multiple methods in their research in order to examine the empirical and theoretical problems with different information. Researchers often combine fieldwork and interviews with document analysis or surveys. Recent work has utilized self-administered questionnaires and interviews with participant diaries and video-taped conversations. Several interactionists have made strong arguments about combining qualitative and quantitative analysis where the latter can provide insightful and appropriate exploration of outcomes, variation, comparisons, and contexts to supplement processual and perspectival analysis. It is in keeping with the pragmatist tradition that the nature of the problem will determine what methods will most appropriately be applicable. Many require multi-method approaches that provide complementary and triangulating assessments of the problem.

RECENT CONTRIBUTIONS

In the last 30 years there have been dramatic changes in interactionist scholarship. The renascence of pragmatism has meant reexamination of early writings and attention to new topics such as temporality, physical objects, science, and society. Scholars have also examined power, organizations, institutions, dynamic social structures, and large-scale social processes (Hall 1997). A particular new and important focus has been inequality, where scholars have examined processes of reproduction, emerging social stratification systems, and the intersection of class, gender, and race inequality (Schwalbe et al. 2000).

Other significant ventures have transformed the field of collective behavior and social movements, eliminating mythical notions of irrational actors and group minds, adding cultural/symbolic elements to instrumental/political social movement analysis, and expanding the scale and scope of studies to encompass expanses of time and space (McPhail & Tucker 2003).

Symbolic interactionists were among the first sociologists to include emotions as a topic of sociological study. Utilizing early work by Cooley, Shibutani, and Goffman, they showed the interplay between cognition and feeling, the definition and categorization of emotions, and the normative shaping of emotional behavior. More recently, interactionists have been attentive to neurocognitive research and its relationship to conceptions of mind, self, emotions, and action (Franks 2003). Recent developments in human genetics and biotechnologies have also renewed interest in biology by interactionists.

SEE ALSO: Blumer, Herbert George; Crowd Behavior; Dramaturgy; Goffman, Erving; Mead, George Herbert; Pragmatism; Public Realm; Role; Self; Social Psychology; Social Worlds

REFERENCES AND SUGGESTED READINGS

Becker, H. (1982) *Art Worlds*. University of California Press, Berkeley.
Blumer, H. (1969) *Symbolic Interactionism: Perspective and Method*. Prentice-Hall, Englewood Cliffs, NJ.
Brissett, D. & Edgley, C. (Eds.) (1990) *Life as Theater: A Dramaturgical Sourcebook*, 2nd edn. Aldine de Gruyter, New York.
Clarke, A. (2005) *Situational Analysis: Grounded Theory After the Postmodern Turn*. Sage, Thousand Oaks, CA.
Franks, D. D. (2003) Mutual Interests, Different Lenses: Neuroscience and Symbolic Interaction. *Symbolic Interaction* 26: 613–30.
Glaser, B. & Strauss, A. L. (1967) *The Discovery of Grounded Theory*. Aldine, Chicago.
Goffman, E. (1959) *The Presentation of Self in Everyday Life*. Doubleday, Garden City, NY.
Hall, P. M. (1997) Meta-Power, Social Organization, and the Shaping of Social Action. *Symbolic Interaction* 20: 397–418.
McPhail, C. & Tucker, C. W. (2003) Collective Behavior. In: Reynolds, L. & Herman-Kinney, N. (Eds.), *Handbook of Symbolic Interaction*. Altamira Press, Lanham, MD, pp. 721–42.
Maines, D. R. (2001) *The Faultline of Consciousness: A View of Interactionism in Sociology*. Aldine de Gruyter, New York.
Reynolds, L. & Herman-Kinney, N. (Eds.) (2003) *Handbook of Symbolic Interaction*. Altamira Press, Lanham, MD.
Schwalbe, M., Goodwin, S., Holden, D. et al. (2000) Generic Processes in the Reproduction of Inequality. *Social Forces* 79: 419–52.
Strauss, A. L. (1993) *Continual Permutations of Action*. Aldine de Gruyter, New York.

system theories

Tom Burns

In the most abstract sense, a system is a set of objects together with relationships among the objects. Such a definition implies that a system has properties, functions, and dynamics distinct from its constituent objects and relationships. A system theoretic approach is not unique to sociology. Many of the major system theorists have belonged to other disciplines, including mathematics, with conceptual and analytic challenges rather different from those confronting sociologists and social scientists. Within sociology there have been several system theories, differing from one another in the extent to which, for example, human agency, creativity, and entrepreneurship are assumed to play a role in system formation and reformation; conflict and struggle are taken into account; power and stratification are part and parcel of the theory; structural change and transformation – and more generally, historically developments – are taken into account and explained. What the various system theories have in common is a systematic concern with complex and varied interconnections and interdependencies of social life. Complexity has been a central concept for many working in the systems perspective. The tradition is characterized to a great extent by a burning ambition and hope to provide a unifying language and conceptual framework for all the social sciences.

MULTIPLE APPROACHES

Below, we consider three general approaches to studying social systems: functionalist and neo-functionalist theories (identified particularly with Parsons); the historical, Marxian approach; and actor-oriented, dynamic system theories (e.g., those of Margaret Archer, Walter Buckley, and the European group including Thomas Baumgartner, Tom R. Burns, and Philippe DeVille). These three approaches are methodologically holistic (Gindoff & Ritzer 1994).

Functionalist Systems Theories

The theorists in this tradition explain the emergence and/or maintenance of parts, structures, institutions, norms, or cultural patterns of a social system in terms of their consequences, that is, the particular functions each realizes or satisfies. This includes, for instance, their contribution to the maintenance and reproduction over time of the larger system. The major functionalist in sociology is arguably Talcott Parsons (1951, 1966). Society in a Parsonian perspective is not just an aggregate of social structures but an actual functioning or operating system, with some varying degrees of coherence, integration, and effectiveness. Societal subsystems such as politics, law, economics, and education are interrelated and may contribute differentially to overall systemic performance, the quality and quantity of which may vary.

Parsons extended earlier functionalist explanations which had left open such questions as: Which are the necessary or requisite functions, if any, of a society or its institutions? Is the number infinite or finite? Is there a prioritizing of functions? Of particular importance is Parsons's theory of universal functions or *requisites*. He identified four universal social functions with which any society must deal in order to be sustainable:

1   Goal attainment (*G*): political and administrative institutions are designed to determine the ends to which a society should orient (both externally and internally): societal goals, priorities, and political and administrative effectiveness.
2   Adaptation or economic efficiency (*A*): institutions deal with the economy and the material environment: transforming material inputs to serve the physical needs of the population and to provide resources to maintain and establish particular institutions of the social system.
3   Latency (*L*): institutions of socialization and social control maintain commitment to, or at least acceptance of, basic cultural patterns, in particular the complex of cultural values, principles, and basic institutional arrangements.
4   Integration (*I*): institutions coordinate and manage individual agents and multiple societal structures to a greater or lesser extent as a coherent, functioning whole.

The performance and effectiveness of AGIL institutions in accomplishing relevant functions may be treated as variables, thus suggesting varying degrees of societal effectiveness and sustainability of any given system. Put otherwise, the reproduction of a system entails the maintenance of "essential variables" within certain limits (Buckley 1998).

In the late 1960s and 1970s criticisms emerged against Parsons's theory and mode of theorizing, his presumed ideology, and even against his person – his religious background, ethnic and cultural heritage, putative support of the power elite, and writing style. The critique of Parsonian systems theory was well placed in many instances, albeit often exaggerated and ad hominem. Fortunately, some sociologists (Jeffrey Alexander, Shmuel N. Eisenstadt, David Lockwood, Peter Munch, David Scuilli, and Bryan S. Turner, among others) continued to work with Parsonian concepts and issues and in a number of instances succeeded in overcoming some of the limitations of his original work. Alexander (1995), in particular, strengthened the theorizing about conflict and power as well as culture in Parsonian systems theory. Another important development related to Parsonian systems theory is Niklas Luhmann's (1995) autopoietic systems theory. While following a functionalist theory line, Luhmann was original in several respects. For instance, he eliminated human agents from his theory, eschewed materiality, developed a purely constructionist approach to systems theorizing, and, above all, stressed self-reflectivity and self-organization. However, the theory still neglected to incorporate or to develop major conceptualizations of central importance to the development of modern sociology and social science, such as institution, human agency, and creativity.

Historical, Political Economic Systems Theory

The Marxian approach to system theorizing clearly points us to sociologically important phenomena: the material conditions of social life, stratification and social class, conflict, the reproduction as well as transformation of capitalist systems, the conditions that affect group mobilization and political power, and the ways ideas function as ideologies. Marx's historical approach conceives of all societies as evolving in a series of stages. Each stage is characterized by a particular structure, a certain mode of production, the "superstructure" of politics, and a culture derived from and dependent on the substructure of production. Human beings generate these structures through their own actions, but not always under the conditions of their own choosing or in the ways they intend. Marx and Marxists focused their theoretical and empirical research on the emergence and transformation of capitalist systems. Because of contradictions between structures – between, for instance, the "forces of production" (such as new knowledge, techniques, and scientific developments that contribute to generating such forces) and the "relations of production" (such as the private ownership of the means of production) – the capitalist system undergoes crises, leading eventually to its transformation.

Marxist theory identifies and explains why certain modes of production or social structures give advantages to one group or class rather than another. The relative power of social classes is determined by the particular mode of production, the ownership of productive property, and the authority system required by a given technology (Collins 1988). Classes have not only different interests (ideology and modes of mental production), but also different capabilities and means of political mobilization and influence. The capitalist system is historically characterized by economic crises, conflicts, and tendencies for continuous transformation, not only of economic relations, but also of other social relationships. Nevertheless, institutions were developed in modern societies to deal with destabilizing developments such as overproduction, as well as other systemic problems of capitalism such as class struggle, multiple social dislocations, volatility, overexploitation of natural resources, environmental degradation, etc.

Marx's historically oriented systems theory and its variants have contributed to the development of a complex of structural concepts and analyses and to a conceptualization of particular forms of reproductive and transformative processes. In contrast to Parsonian and other system theories, however, it has been relatively weak in conceptualizing and taking into account human agency and in developing relevant institutional and cultural theories. Recent developments in neo-Marxist theorizing (which rejects simplistic materialism) have overcome some of these deficiencies. Among other related major developments, world systems theory (Wallerstein 2004) should be mentioned. Inspired by Marxist theories, it addresses dependency among nations and imperialism, placing the evolution of capitalist systems in a global and comparative perspective. Another variant of Marxist system theory is that of Pierre Bourdieu (1977), which unifies the material and the symbolic, as well as agency and structure.

Actor-Oriented, Dynamic Systems Theories

This family of theories – inspired to a great extent by Buckley – is largely non-functionalist. It includes Buckley's (1967, 1998) "modern systems theory," Archer's (1995) "morphogenetic" theory, Burns's "actor-system-dynamics" (also ASD; Burns et al. 1985; Burns & Flam 1987), and the "sociocybernetics" of Geyer and van der Zouwen (1978). Complex, dynamic social systems are analyzed in terms of stabilizing and destabilizing mechanisms, with human agents playing strategic roles in these processes. Institutions and cultural formations of society are carried by, transmitted, and reformed through individual and collective actions and interactions. On the one hand, such structures are temporally prior and relatively autonomous with respect to social action, yet exhibit causal force. They constrain and enable people's social actions and interactions. On the other hand, individual and collective agents through their interactions generate structural reproduction, elaboration, and transformation. The approach concerns not only the identification and development of social structures, but also the specification of the social mechanisms, including *morphostatic* feedback processes that entail stabilizing, equilibrating features, and *morpho-genetic* processes of structural elaboration and transformation. In such terms, social structures help to create and recreate themselves in an ongoing developmental process in which human agents play constructive as well as destructive and transformative roles in the context of complex sociocultural arrangements. The approach entails systematic theorizing of individual as well as collective agents, institutions, and cultural formations and their part in processes of reproduction and transformation. Active agents with their distinctive characteristics, motivations, and powers interact and contribute to the reproduction and transformation of structure. They establish as well as reform such structures as institutions, socio-technical systems, and physical and ecological structures, always within constraints and opportunities, and not always in ways they intend. The selective and structuring mechanisms that reproduce, modify, or transform social structures are themselves based on institutional arrangements and distributions of powers among societal agents and social populations such as classes and ethnic and religious groups.

This approach to systems theory, particularly in the work of Archer and ASD, theorizes institutions and sociocultural formations in their own right, identifying and explaining the real and variegated structures which have emerged historically and are elaborated and developed in ongoing social processes. The approach enables one to identify and analyze the complex mechanisms of stable reproduction as well as of the transformation of societal structures and the genesis of new forms. In other words, human agents constitute and reconstitute institutions and cultural forms through their interactions. Rule interpretation, formation, and development are viewed as a form of normatively guided problem-solving and entrepreneurship.

ASD has drawn to a significant degree upon Marxist theory, redefining key Marxian concepts in modern sociological terms (above all, through institutional and cultural theorizing), including concepts such as class, power, domination, exploitation, conflict and struggle, and unequal exchange and accumulation, reproduction, and transformation.

CONTRIBUTIONS OF SYSTEM THEORIES

System theories have been applied to a wide spectrum of empirical cases and policy issues. Parsons and his followers, in particular, applied their systems theory to diverse empirical phenomena in sociology as well as in other disciplines: modernization, economics, politics, social order, industrialization and development, Fascism and McCarthyism, international relations, social change and evolution, complex organizations, health care, universities, religion, professions, small groups, and family as well as abstract questions such as the place of norms in maintaining social order both historically and cross-nationally. Marxian theory and dynamic system theories have also been applied to a spectrum of diverse empirical and policy subjects.

Among the major contributions of the approaches outlined here is the development of conceptual and methodological tools to investigate *complex* interdependencies of social phenomena, including (1) the multi-dimensionality of social action and interaction, (2) interstructural problems and dynamics, and (3) complex action-structure loops such as those of reproduction and transformation. These are outlined below.

Multi-Dimensionality

Action and interaction has been interpreted and conceptualized as multi-dimensional, entailing the confluence of economic, social, cultural, instrumental, and moral factors. One implication of this perspective is that unidimensional action such as pursuit of profit or gain would tend to be functionally or evolutionarily disadvantageous to a society as a whole. Social integration – the realization in general of other social requisites – is sacrificed to productive efficiency in such a unidimensional perspective on action and interaction. Similarly, purely procedural rationality also proves disadvantageous because it ignores real consequences. More generally, the neofunctional and dynamic system theories as well as neo-Marxist theory have fruitfully addressed multidimensional, multi-level phenomena, taking into account human agency as well as developments in institutionalism and in the sociology of culture.

Interstructural Problems, Forces of Change, and Dynamics

A common thread in system theories has been the analysis of interstructural relations and the instability to which they give rise. Multiple, incompatible structures cause performance failures and disorder. Lockwood (1964) addressed these issues in his distinction between *system integration* and *social integration*. He utilized Parsons's idea of a normative order, incorporating "factual order" or substratum as a determinant of social conflict and social instability. For Lockwood, the key factor in social transformation is system contradiction; for instance, between forces and relations of production. If present at the same time that there is social conflict and struggle between groups of societal agents or classes, then social transformation is likely. Among the major subtypes of interstructural problems are incompatibilities between structures of the social system and structures in the environment. Complex feedback loops between societal orders and their environments may generate uncontrollable instability and non-sustainability (e.g., in connection with soil erosion or other resource depletion).

Reproductive and Transformative Action-Structure Loops

In investigating complex interdependencies in social life, system approaches have typically worked with multiple forms of causality and complex mechanisms of system functioning, stability, and change. A major common interest – although formulated in different ways in the three approaches – relates to processes of system reproduction and non-reproduction (or transformation). The conceptualization of reproduction processes contributes to the explanation of structural stability or morphostasis. Disturbance or blockage of these processes leads typically to restructuring via transformations or morphogenesis.

Social Reproductive Mechanisms

These entail particular types of action-structure loops. Any given social structure consists of constraining and enabling factors for the agents involved. Under certain conditions, these lead to consequences maintaining and reproducing the structure. In a given context, one theorizes factors that may disturb reproductive loops and factors that may handle disturbances so that reproduction can be sustained. Some reproductive loops are consciously designed. That is, particular practices and institutions are constructed so as to contribute to, or set in motion, reproductive loops. Thus, we find in modern societies a spectrum of institutional arrangements designed to prevent or to regulate conflicts between diverse agents and groups. Democratic institutions, court systems, particular government agencies of regulation, and formalized negotiation systems deal with, for instance, labor-capital and commercial conflicts. Along such lines, Sciulli (1992) emphasized procedural norms, collegial forms of organization, and symbolic media of interchange, which facilitate integration and effective collective action in the face of the substantial diversity in agents' beliefs and interests in a modern society. Also, modern societies have developed a number of institutions to deal with destabilizing features of capitalism and to assure its effective reproduction, albeit often in modified form.

Transformative Mechanisms

Endogenous processes such as economic or political competition among agents, and social entrepreneurs responding to incentives, may restructure and transform a system. Under some conditions, these initiatives result in self-sustaining, cumulative transformative processes. As a result of an initial, possibly modest, change in institutional rules and/or rule enforcement activities, different opportunity and constraint structures are shaped, leading to shifts in patterns of action and interaction. These in turn may result in new initiatives, social mobilization, and successful efforts at extensive reform or transformation. In general, a transformative action-structure loop entails a type of circular causality with cumulative transformative effects. In some cases, the initial impetus may have been an external shock.

Power, knowledge, values, and interests are key ingredients in structural innovation and transformation. The power of agents to mobilize resources including wealth, government authority, and coercive powers to maintain or change institutional orders is well recognized in sociology. Emerging groups and movements may also mobilize sufficient power resources to challenge established elites and, under certain conditions, to bring about transformative loops such as revolutions. The interaction between established elites and challenging groups or movements is a common theme in the study of institutional and societal dynamics. Such power mobilization and conflict are fueled by actors' material and ideological interests. They are reflected in paradigms that define appropriate institutional arrangements, strategies, and policies to deal with collective problems, including problems of social order. In general, a political or economic order is historically vulnerable when reproductive loops are eroded or collapse. For instance, one or more of the conditions for rule enforcement, transmission, and self-replication may be unsatisfied (Burns & Dietz 1992). Even initially successful institutionalization of a major reform or revolution can be undermined by complex processes of reproductive failure. There are numerous historical examples of what appeared to be successful institutional innovations, even revolutions with great visions of new, even utopian social orders. Many have collapsed, degenerating into substantially different social orders.

CHALLENGES AND OPPORTUNITIES

The vigorous critique of Parsons in the 1960s and 1970s extended to other system theoretic approaches such as those of Archer, Buckley, and ASD. These other theories generally were treated as "grand theorizing" and regarded as suspect when not rejected out of hand. Sociological textbooks neglected much of the diversity of system theorizing, such as the work of Buckley and his European followers. Including them would have complicated the picture

considerably. For a time, an exception was made for Marxist theory, which was viewed as non-functionalist – although Collins (1988) later disproved this characterization – and more compatible with the ideological tenor of the times.

The general rejection of systems approaches since the 1960s did not stem the incorporation of systems concepts into other theoretical traditions by major American and European sociologists (e.g., James Coleman, Klaus Eder, Anthony Giddens, David Lockwood, Charles Perrow, W. Richard Scott, Arthur Stinchcombe, Piet Styrdom, and Piotr Sztompka). Consequently, much of the language and conceptualization of modern system theories has become part of everyday contemporary sociology (e.g., open and closed systems, loosely and tightly coupled systems, information and communication flows, reflexivity, self-referential systems, positive and negative feedback loops, self-organization and self-regulation, reproduction, emergence, non-linear systems, complexity). Institutionalists and organizational theorists in particular have co-opted a number of system concepts without always pointing out their etiology.

The tendency of neofunctionalist, neo-Marxist, and dynamic system theories to converge through contemporary institutional and cultural analysis is an important part of the ongoing revitalization of systems theorizing. One might ask, why not simply concentrate solely on developing institutional and cultural theories, and forget systems theorizing as such? But the multi-dimensional conceptualization of action and interaction, the interrelatedness of diverse multiple structures, and the action-structure loops of reproduction and transformation call for a more encompassing or holistic approach. The interplay of physical or material structures, sociocultural systems, and interaction orders cannot be properly conceptualized, described, and analyzed through strictly institutional and cultural theories.

Another key factor is the system approach's conceptual and methodological capacity to facilitate cooperation among social, natural, engineering, and medical sciences. Already there is increasing convergence and some cooperation between natural scientists and mathematicians, on the one hand, and social scientists on the other, in constructing models of "multi-agent, dynamic systems." A major force here is the emergence of complexity theory and the theoretical work and simulation of complex "multi-agent systems," of interest to many mathematicians, computer scientists, and natural scientists as well as a growing number of social scientists.

System theories also perform an important intellectual function within sociology, and among the social sciences and humanities: they contribute a common language, conceptualization, and theoretical integration in the face of the extreme fragmentation among the social sciences as well as within sociology. The latter suffers as a result of the institutionalized concentration on mid-level empirical and theoretical research (i.e., "middle range theorizing"). The challenge which Parsons and others including Buckley originally addressed remains to overcome the fragmentation of sociology and the social sciences generally, the lack of synergies, and the failure to develop a cumulative science by providing them a common language and integrative theoretical framework to mediate, accumulate, and transmit knowledge among all branches and sub-branches of the social sciences and allied humanities (Sciulli & Gerstein 1985). On a practical level, there remains the venerable challenge to establish and develop a social science complex that can readily and systematically put pieces of specialized knowledge together to address major contemporary problems – perhaps a type of meta-theoretical framework rather than a single overarching theory.

SEE ALSO: Complexity and Emergence; Function; Functionalism/Neofunctionalism; Marx, Karl; Metatheory; Parsons, Talcott; Political Sociology; Simulation and Virtuality; Social Change; Structure and Agency

REFERENCES AND SUGGESTED READINGS

Alexander, J. C. (1995) *Neofunctionalism*. Sage, London.

Archer, M. S. (1995) *Realist Social Theory: The Morphogenetic Approach*. Cambridge University Press, Cambridge.

Bourdieu, P. (1977) *Outline of a Theory of Practice*. Cambridge University Press, Cambridge.

Buckley, W. (1967) *Sociology and Modern Systems Theory*. Prentice-Hall, Englewood Cliffs, NJ.

Buckley, W. (1998) *Society – A Complex Adaptive System: Essays in Social Theory*. Gordon & Breach, Amsterdam.

Burns, T. R., Baumgartner, T., & DeVille, P. (1985) *Man, Decisions, and Society*. Gordon & Breach, London.

Burns, T. R. & Dietz, T. (1992) Cultural Evolution: Social Rule Systems, Selection, and Human Agency. *International Sociology* 7: 259–83.

Burns, T. R. & Flam, H. (1987) *The Shaping of Social Organization: Social Rule System Theory with Applications*. Sage, London.

Collins, R. (1988) *Theoretical Sociology*. Harcourt Brace Jovanovich, New York.

Geyer, F. & van der Zouwen, J. (1978) *Sociocybernetics: An Actor-Oriented Social Systems Approach*. Martinus Nijhoff, Leiden.

Gindoff, P. & Ritzer, G. (1994) Agency-Structure, Micro-Macro, Individualism-Holism-Relationism: A Metatheoretical Explanation of Theoretical Convergence Between the United States and Europe. In: Sztompka, P. (Ed.), *Agency and Structure: Reorienting Social Theory*. Gordon & Breach, London.

Lockwood, D. (1964) Social Integration and System Integration. In: G. K. Zollschan & H. W. Hirsch (Eds.), *Explorations in Social Change*. Houghton Mifflin, Boston.

Luhmann, N. (1995) *Social Systems*. Trans. J. Bednarz, with D. Baecker. Stanford University Press, Stanford.

Parsons, T. (1951) *The Social System*. Free Press, Glencoe, IL.

Parsons, T. (1966) *Societies: Evolutionary and Comparative Perspectives*. Prentice-Hall, Englewood Cliffs, NJ.

Sciulli, D. (1992) *Theory of Societal Constitutionalism: Foundations of a Non-Marxist Critical Theory*. Cambridge University Press, New York.

Sciulli, D. & Gerstein, D. (1985) Social Theory and Talcott Parsons in the 1980s. *Annual Review of Sociology* 11: 369–87.

Wallerstein, I. (2004) *World-Systems Analysis: An Introduction*. Duke University Press, Durham, NC.

T

Takata, Yasuma (1883–1972)

Kazuo Seiyama

Yasuma Takata was a prominent neoclassical economist in the pre-war era. He was also a tanka poet and published several collections of original poems.

He was born in Kurume, a city in Northern Kyushu, Japan, and graduated in sociology from Kyoto Imperial University. He taught at various universities, including Kyoto, Kyushu, and Osaka, mainly as an economics professor. He wrote more than 100 books, of which about half were on economics and about 30 were sociological.

Although his work was multidimensional he began his career as a sociologist and retained this focus throughout his academic life. His sociological works bridged various sociological fields, such as general theory, class theory, social change, population, social power, and others. He was principally a theoretical sociologist The basics of his theory are principally addressed in his early (and voluminous) *Shakaigaku Genri* (Treatise on Sociology) (1919), in which he endeavored to construct a general sociological theory based on methodological individualism (using the term coined by economist J. A. Schumpeter in 1908, with whom Takata became acquainted sometime later when Schumpeter visited Japan).

A pivotal concept in the *Treatise* was the individual's "desire" as the main factor underlying various social phenomena and social evolution. He assumed that several kinds of desires are naturally given to people and determine their behavior. Important among them were the "desire for power" and "desire for gregarious living." Desire for gregarious living was a ground for basic social formation. On the other hand, desire for power was a basis for dissociation, differentiation, and individuation.

This description might make Takata appear to be an old-fashioned Spencerian sociologist with a hint of Tönnies' conceptual framework thrown in. But the originality of Takata's thinking lies in his way of constructing a large-scale theoretical system beginning from those basic presumptions. Various original concepts were introduced, for example, "homogeneous association and heterogeneous association," "direct association and indirect association," and "fundamental society and derivative society." And several "laws" – such as "the law of fixed quantity of association," "the law of the loss of intermediate societies," and "the law of the decline of fundamental societies" – were formulated. After giving extensive explanations for these concepts and laws, he presented a theory of social evolution which emphasized three major trends: cultural flourishing, the expansion of liberty, and the development of individuality. This main framework of the *Treatise* was followed by *Principles of Sociology*, originally published in 1922 as a more compact version.

In one sense, his sociology may be characterized as a social theory of atomistic liberalism. First, he was entirely opposed to any collectivist or substantivist view of society, although these were so common as to be taken for granted by his contemporary social theorists, especially in Japan. His theory of the relationship between state and society anticipated in many respects the pluralist theory of state formulated by R. M. MacIver and H. J. Laski. Secondly, at the same time, he envisaged a social evolution in the process of individualization, arguing that it would lead to a new type of social integration and solidarity far preferable to the old one. This thesis was later developed in his *Sekai Shakai*

Ron (On World Society) (1947), in which he presented a theoretical future vista of a politically and socially unified global society where nation-states would be extinguished, at least as independent political units. (It is astonishing that this was presented immediately after Japan's devastating defeat in World War II.) Thirdly, his optimistic view of social evolution was grounded in his conviction that fundamentally individual liberties would bring about a desirable and well-ordered society, a view common to neoclassical economics.

Takata's theory of social change is known as "the third view of history" or "the population view of history." Many have interpreted it, mistakenly, as a claim that history is determined by the growth of population. Importantly, it was originally presented as a new interpretation of class theory in an anthology *Kaikyu Oyobi Dai San Shikan* (Class and the Third View of History) (1925), shortly after his *Treatise*. His class theory is well known as a theory of power; that is, what determines class formation and changes in class structure is neither an Idea (*Geist*) nor the relations of production, but social power. In opposition to Marxian class theory in which the power structure is supposedly subordinate to the economic structure, Takata thought that power is the most fundamental determinant of class structure. Hence, his "third view of history" should be understood as basically "a power view of history," meaning that it is neither the first, Hegelian idealist view, nor the second, Marxian materialist view.

He provided three main reasons why Marxian class theory – that class is formed according to people's common location in the relations of production – is wrong: (1) some landowners and capitalists form a class without engaging in any economic activity; (2) in a future classless society, there will still be a division of labor and differences in economic activities; (3) individuals engaged in the same profession may yet belong to different classes. Instead of similarities in economic activities, he insists that similarity in social power is the constitutive factor of class structure.

Although since his earliest work power had been the pivotal concept, his most extensive discussion of power was not produced until relatively late, in *Seiryoku Ron* (On Power) (1940), where his "power view of history" was

systematically presented by articulating and developing both theoretical and historical accounts of power. He considered this to be his major work. And yet, it should be stressed that his basic conceptual framework on power had already been formulated when he presented his extensive class theory (1922). This was well before the sociological power theories, such as those by Weber, von Wiese, or Russell, had appeared or become available to him, let alone the post-war writings of Hunter, Dahl, and other political scientists.

One distinctive feature of his theory is seen in the definition of power, which was initially given as "the ability of governing another's will," but later revised in *On Power* as "the chance of being obeyed." Compared to Weber's "chance of accomplishing one's will," which should have been available to him at that time, the uniqueness of Takata's definition is that it refers simultaneously to both the power-exerciser and the power-obeyer. Hence it is a relational concept, not an action-based concept. At the same time, it is still a broadly individualistic concept, in contrast to the Foucaultian and other current trends in conceptualizing power.

From the contemporary general theoretical perspective, whether power is defined individualistically or collectively is an extremely important issue.

In this regard, what is important for Takata's theory of power is that, while he was from the beginning the foremost individualist sociologist, there are various signs of collectivist ways of thinking about power in his writings. The definition above is the first example. We might note that the power-exerciser does not explicitly appear in this definition. The term "chance," in contrast to "ability," expresses a contextual, relational, or structural property, as per Weber.

To be more precise, Takata's theory of power is double-edged. For example, an important pair of concepts in his theory is "external power" and "internal power" which were borrowed, slightly modified, from Wiese. Basically, external power is that in which a certain individual or group is identified as a power holder, while internal power refers to the power of social norms like customs, laws, or morals, where no particular power holder exists, implying that internal power is collective. Takata considers internal power theoretically very important, and argues that a new power emerges initially as internal power within a small group and then extends its scope as external power to a large part of the population. And yet, he emphasizes that we should not disregard those powers which come from a proper and independent personality. For Takata, power must ultimately be imputed to a person or a group of persons, even if effected by collective elements such as social norms, customs, or laws.

His theory of power fluctuates between methodological individualism and collectivism. In fact, when he describes concrete historical events in terms of power and related concepts, his description betrays his faith in methodological individualism. For example, he argues that the state is an organizational and official power of the first order, and inherently involves the legitimacy of power. And for the latter, Takata rightly emphasizes the importance of "propaganda," "thought," "ideology," and "religion." He even claims that the core of a new wild power which is emerging is a thought, and a new ruling organization is established as a realization of this thought. As for the emergence of modern society in Europe, Takata explains that, as Christianity declines, the status of the pope and religious aristocrats who occupy the special position between God and human beings changed, that the rise of republican thought in Europe had removed several monarchs, and that the spread of egalitarian thought had raised the status of the proletariat class and realized the liberation of slaves. Astonishingly enough, this is a sort of idealist explanation of historical change. Of course, this is another example of the double-edged character of Takata's power theory.

His peculiar position as a central figure in neoclassical economic theory is closely related to this. Being a methodological individualist, he was inherently drawn to neoclassical thinking. But, interestingly, in developing his own economic theory – the power theory of economics – he diverged from the mainstream of economics. He repeatedly emphasized that power, or the relations of power, is the fundamental factor of the economy. He criticized the mainstream for neglecting power or, at best, treating it as a given in theory. He provided several reasons for the significance of power. First, the government and labor unions interfere extensively, as economic powers, in various economic decisions. Secondly, socioeconomic inequalities or differences, such as in wage differences by sex, ethnicity, and educational background, should be conceived as effects of non-economic, social power.

In spite of his laborious insistence and his reputation as a leading economist, Takata's power theory of economics was never fully accepted by Japanese economists such as M. Morishima, who became one of the leading figures in post-war Japanese economics, and nevertheless greatly admired him. In any case, it should be clear that, as an economist, Takata employed a collectivist mode of thinking that was unmistakably revealed in his sociology of power.

Takata's double-edgedness can also be seen in another important aspect: that is, nationalism and globalism. Of course, he was never a narrow-minded nationalist, even during World War II, but was rather a noble and moderate nationalist who was born into a family of Shinto priests. At the same time, though, his sociological theory was entirely cosmopolitan and liberal. In *On World Society* (1947) he envisaged a future global world, politically unified, where individual liberty and equality would prevail. This was overly optimistic from the contemporary perspective.

However, this optimism and the various inner contradictions in his theory are rather charming, and not merely a fault in his sociology. In reading his work we certainly find profound inspirations and stimulations in these days when new social theories are waiting to emerge.

SEE ALSO: Class, Status, and Power; Individualism; Liberalism; Power, Theories of; Schumpeter, Joseph A.

REFERENCES AND SUGGESTED READINGS

Kaneko, I. (Ed.) (2003) *Takata Yasuma Rikabari* (Recovery of Takata Yasuma). Minerva Books, Kyoto.

Kawamura, N. (1992) *Takata Yasuma no Shakaigaku* (Sociology of Takata Yasuma). Inaho Books, Tokyo.

Kitajima, S. (2002) *Takata Yasuma: Riron to Seisaku no Mubaikai-teki Goitsu* (Takata Yasuma: Indiscriminate Combination of Theory and Policy). Toshindo, Tokyo.

Schumpeter, J. A., Takata, Y., & Morishima, M. (1998) *Power or Pure Economics?* Palgrave Macmillan, London.

Seiyama, K. (2000) *Kenryoku* (Power). University of Tokyo Press, Tokyo.

Senda, S. (2003) Takata Yasuma and Morishima Michio on the Collaborative Development in Northeast Asia. *Bulletin of Yokohama City University* 6: 111–32.

Takata, Y. (1956) *An Introduction to Sociological Economics*. Science Council of Japan, Division of Economics and Commerce, Tokyo.

Takata, Y. (1989 [1922]) *Principles of Sociology*. University of Tokyo Press, Tokyo.

Takata, Y. (1995) *Power Theory of Economics*. St. Martin's Press, New York.

Taoism

Chee-Kiong Tong and Cheuk-Yin Lee

Taoism takes its name from the concept of Tao, or Way. In Chinese, the word "Tao" (or *dao* in *hanyu pinyin*) is made up of two components, one depicting a human head, the other a motion verb meaning to pass, go through, or walk. The earliest and most important work on Taoism is a short book of some 5,000 characters known as *Daode Jing* (*Classic of the Way and Virtue*) by the legendary Laozi (literally, Old Master, around sixth century BCE). The oldest manuscripts of the *Daode Jing*, unearthed in 1973 from an ancient tomb in Changsha, Hunan province, China, dated to about 200 BCE. Next to the Bible, it is probably one of the most translated works in the world, with close to 100 translations in English (see Lee et al. 1994).

The "Tao" is conceived as a metaphysical reality, the origin of heaven and earth, and the very beginning and end of all things. In Chapter 42 of the *Daode Jing*, it states: "The Tao gave birth to the One. The One gave birth to the Two. The Two gave birth to the Three. And the Three gave birth to the myriad creatures." This process of creation can also be understood as a process of differentiation from unity to multiplicity.

RELIGIOUS ROOTS AND HISTORICAL DEVELOPMENT

The origin of religious Taoism is extremely complex. As an organized religion, it probably started during the Eastern Han dynasty (25–220 CE). However, religious Taoism did not occur suddenly in a historical and religious vacuum. Rather, it drew upon preexisting ancient Chinese religious ideas and practices, incorporating Chinese ideas of nature worship and ancestor worship. Divination and other religious arts of ancient Chinese religious experts or "shamans" also became part of the repertoire of the Taoist priests. In addition, religious Taoism was influenced by the teachings of ancient Taoist philosophers as well as the cult of immortality promulgated by religious teachers of the Warring States period (475–221 BCE). In this sense, religious Taoism can be seen as a synthesis of several currents of thought going back to the very beginning of Chinese history.

During the reign of Emperor Shun (126–144 CE) of the Han dynasty, Zhang Ling, native of Jiangsu province, established the first Taoist sect in Sichuan, China. He claimed to have received a revelation from the divine Laozi to establish a new Taoist order. Known as the "Celestial Master" sect, it made the Taoist philosophical classic *Daode Jing* the chief scripture of the sect, and followers were taught to venerate the Tao and to repent their sins. By means of sacred incantations, talismans, and purification rites, the Taoist master sought to restore the spiritual and physical health of the followers. The movement attracted a large following and quickly developed into a major religious force. At that time, the Han Empire was already on the brink of disintegration, and the country was plunged deep into civil war. The rise of religious Taoism can be viewed in the context of its ability to provide meaning and meet adherents' spiritual and material needs at a time of sociopolitical and economic strife.

Religious Taoism may have been started as a popular movement, supported mainly by the rural peasants, but by the post-Han period (third century CE) it began to attract the attention of the educated elites. The Taoist master Ge Hong (283–343 CE), an expert in Taoist alchemy and traditional medicine, is one of the key figures responsible for the "upward" swing of the religion. Ge Hong envisioned a synthesis of Confucianism and Taoism, in which spiritual practice and moral cultivation form an inseparable union, combining the Taoist goal of attaining spiritual liberation and becoming an immortal with the Confucian emphasis on moral self-cultivation, filial piety, benevolence, trustworthiness, and other moral virtues. In the fifth and sixth centuries CE, during the Eastern Jin (317–420) dynasty, two new major Taoist sects were formed: the Supreme Purity Sect (*Shangqing*) and the Numinous Treasure Sect (*Lingbao*). Over time, the Supreme Purity Sect became the dominant Taoist group in medieval China. As the hermitage of the sect was on the famous Taoist mountain, Mao Shan, in Jiangsu province, the Supreme Purity Sect came to be known as Mao Shan Taoism. The teachings of the Supreme Purity Sect concentrated on internal spiritual cultivation, supplemented by the study of scriptures and performing good deeds. Unlike the Celestial Master Sect, it does not emphasize the performance of rituals or the use of talismans and other religious devices. The Numinous Treasure Sect had a more outward orientation and emphasized both spiritual cultivation and rituals. It paid close attention to doing good deeds and universal salvation.

During the Southern Song dynasty, around 1167, a new Taoist sect with a strong monastic flavor – the Complete Perfection (*Quanzhen*) Sect – was founded. Its teachings prescribed a heavy dose of monastic discipline. Practitioners had to remain celibate, embrace poverty, abstain from indulgence of all kinds, including food and sleep, and refrain from injuring all forms of life. The Complete Perfection Sect was very successful and attracted a large following. In response, the other Taoist lineages gradually joined forces to form a new orthodoxy known as Right One (*Zhengyi*) Sect (see Qing 1988; Ren 1990).

Both the Complete Perfection and Right One Taoism venerate the "Three Pristine Ones" as the supreme gods of the cosmos. In terms of practice, however, the two are quite different. Complete Perfection Taoism is monastic; all priests must observe celibacy and live in seclusion. Right One Taoism is more lay-oriented; its priests can marry and live among the common people. Doctrinally, Complete Perfection Taoism emphasizes quiet self-cultivation, while Right One Taoism relies mainly on the use of talismans, incantations, prayers, and the performance of rituals.

DIVINE HIERARCHY AND KEY TAOIST IDEAS

In Taoist religion, both Laozi and his follower Zhuangzi are worshipped as gods and founders of the religion. As an incarnation of Tao, Laozi is regarded as the "Supreme Venerable Lord." The "Three Pristine Ones" and the other divinities of Taoism, including the Heavenly Gods, the Earth Gods, and the Human Gods, are all considered to have evolved from Tao. Thus, Religious Taoism is a devotional religion with a polytheistic structure. It has a highly sophisticated and hierarchically structured pantheon with countless gods and goddesses under the command of a sovereign high god and with specific stations in the divine hierarchy. The organizational principle seems to have been modeled on that of the imperial government. However, from the Taoist perspective, the earthly government reflects the structure of the heavenly kingdom.

The highest level of the Taoist pantheon is comprised of the Lordly Spirits of Anterior Heaven. It is headed by the "Three Pristine Ones" (*Sanqing*): the "Celestial Venerable of the Original Beginning" (*Yuanshi Tianzun*), the "Celestial Venerable of the Numinous Treasure" (*Lingbao Tianzun*), and the "Celestial Venerable of the Way and Virtue" (*Daode Tianzun*), also commonly known as the "Supreme Venerable Lord." However, the "Three Pristine Ones" are perceived to be so exalted that they reign, but do not rule. Cosmic governance is delegated to a subordinate chief known as the "Great Sovereign Jade Emperor" (*Yuhuang Dadi*). The Jade Emperor, whose "birthday" is celebrated on the ninth day of the first month in the Chinese lunar calendar, is the supreme high god, the ruler of the Taoist universe. He has direct command over all deities and has absolute control over all human and divine matters. Like the imperial emperor, his counterpart on earth, the Jade Emperor is assisted by a multitude of officials and functionaries. These, in turn, are organized into a divine bureaucracy, and can be classified in terms of their rank, jurisdiction, functions, and responsibilities, such as the God of Wealth, the Earth God, the Kitchen God, and the Door God.

Broadly speaking, Taoism can be divided into three interrelated traditions. A Taoist philosophical tradition associated with Laozi's *Daode Jing*, Zhuangzi's work, and other texts; a religious tradition with an organized doctrine, formalized cult activities, and institutional leadership; and a popular religion tradition, where there is a syncretic mix of Taoist beliefs, folk beliefs and rituals, including ancestor worship, and elements of Confucianism and Buddhism. This tradition is often referred to as a "diffused" religion, with no canonical scriptures and its rituals and religious ideas largely orally transmitted from one generation to the next.

While these are three different traditions, they are interrelated and draw from some of the key ideas of Taoism, such as the conception of *yin* and *yang*, and the five elements. For Taoists, the origin of the universe is known as the Great Beginning. The universe began as a void, from which the great breath (*Taiji*) developed. The Great Breath in turn gathered momentum, and split into two equal breaths; a light pure breath, *yang*, moves upwards and created heaven, while the opaque heavy breath, *yin*, descended and created earth (Robinet 1997: 8). Together, they constitute the cycle of life and death. The positioning of these forces is considered instrumental for social order on earth, and a disjuncture in the correct positioning will result in hazards and natural calamities (Kuah 2003: 23–4). *Yin* and *yang* form the foundation of both philosophical and religious Taoism. From these two forces, the five elements, fire, water, earth, wood, and metal, are produced. These, in turn, govern the four seasons and all aspects of human existence.

RELIGIOUS SPECIALISTS

As noted above, the concepts of *yin* and *yang* form the foundation of both philosophical and religious Taoism. The classical texts of Laozi and Zhuangzi explicate the principles of this philosophy, while the priests, mediums, and so on found in religious Taoism draw on these ideas in the performance of rituals relating to birth, marriage, death, festival cycles, and all

aspects of human life. Taoist priests, *daoshi*, are professionals who earn their living through providing a range of religious services and ritual performance. These ritual specialists, particularly in Taiwan, are called "red-headed" Taoists or barefoot masters as they wear a red turban around their head and are barefoot when dressed in ceremonial ritual costumes.

Curing rituals are the most common of their services. Using divination techniques and traditional Chinese medical knowledge, they diagnose ailments. A simple cure for the illness requires the priest to write a charm, which the patient places in his or her house, or burns to drink the ashes as tea or to wash with. Complex problems may require more elaborate ritual solutions. For example, a *daoshi* may be called upon to exorcise demons that have invaded a person's dwelling or body. He performs dramatic rites, including sword dances and elaborate gestures, to chase the demons away.

In addition to the *daoshi*, there is another class of religious specialists who draw on Taoist ideas. Chinese spirit mediums, or shamans, are called *dang-ki*, literally, "child-diviners." Chinese spirit mediumship is based on the idea that a spiritual being, or *shen*, can temporarily possess a human body. In such a state, the *dang-ki* becomes the personification of the *shen* and mediates between the human and spiritual worlds. Human beings can then consult the spirits seeking advice as well as solutions to human problems. Mediums, when possessed, enter into a state of trance. Rituals performed by spirit mediums include the sacrifice of offerings of food and joss papers, that is, paper printed in gold and silver and sometimes inscribed with prayers that are burnt, to appease the spirits.

There is a clear hierarchical distinction between the *dang-ki* and the *daoshi*. Daoshi are regarded as the religious superiors of the shamans. To be a *daoshi* is to fill an office that is hereditary, and they are considered as the administrators of the spiritual world, a reflection of the bureaucracy that governs the earthly world. In fact, in Taoist traditions, Laozi is regarded as the first Heavenly Master and Zhang Ling (or Zhang Daoling) the universal head of the Taoist liturgical tradition. Succeeding Heavenly Masters have been representatives from this family line. The Heavenly Masters bestow the hereditary office on the *daoshi*, who then become the priests of the regional and lay organizations. Thus, the group of *daoshi* is a confederacy of masters, not a church. The legitimacy of their mastership rests in part on the ownership of the manuscripts for liturgical use: books for reciting, rituals, collection of formularies, secret formulas, talismans and diagrams, passed down from each generation in the family (Schipper 1993: 59).

There is a clear distinction between the vernacular *fashi* and the classical *daoshi*. Besides the contrasting vestments and ceremonial garbs, the rituals performed by the two are significantly different. Vernacular rituals often contain ballads that describe a journey or the myth of the deity invoked. They also tend to give a mythological rendering of the other worlds. The classical rituals, on the other hand, do not contain such mythological aspects or journey narratives, as they are concerned with the expression of moral law and sentiment. They also constantly refer to the abstract cosmology of Taoism. Another distinct difference between the two is the use of trance techniques. Classical Taoism does not practice trance techniques that are quite commonly used by the vernacular Taoist priests. The classical Taoist rejects all forms of individual rites (as opposed to communal rites) such as healing and exorcism. Despite the apparent ritual differences between classical and vernacular Taoist priests, many of the rituals are complementary and may be performed together, as during the *jiao* festival, staged to pacify wandering ghosts, to purify the community's territory, and to reach cosmic renewal (see Liu 2003).

TAOISM AND CHINESE CULTURE

Confucianism, Taoism, and Buddhism form the three pillars of traditional Chinese culture. They provide a window to help understand the Chinese, their values, customs, and way of life. Taoism, unlike other religions that also flourished in China, is an indigenous religious tradition, shaped and formed by native religious beliefs from the start. Taoism can be said to embody a synthesis of traditional Chinese culture. As a popular religion, its teachings influenced the masses. In addition, it penetrated

Confucian traditions and added Taoist features and hues to the Confucian landscape. By blending its doctrine of immortality with Confucian ethics and political philosophy, it had a substantial impact on the educated elite as well.

Taoism also influenced the nature of moral education and self-cultivation in China, with its emphasis on performing good deeds and the accumulation of religious merits. One popular belief is that to become a "celestial immortal" a person is required to perform at least 1,300 good deeds. Later, when the genre of Taoist writings known as "Ledgers of Merit and Demerit" gained currency, the moral teachings of Taoism became even more widespread. Essentially, daily actions are classified into good and bad deeds, each of which is assigned a fixed number of merit or demerit points. In this way, Taoism was able to regulate behavior and promote its vision of the good life.

External alchemy and internal alchemy, natural methods of nourishing and preserving life, represent the two foci of Taoist self-cultivation. External alchemy is above all concerned with the manufacture of an "elixir" of everlasting life and involved an understanding of the nature of chemical processes and the properties of plants and minerals. Internal alchemy is concerned with nourishing and strengthening the internal vital energy that contributed to the concept of *Qi*, which plays a central role in the teachings of religious Taoism. Although external and internal alchemy may no longer be pursued in their classical form, their influence remains today. Rather than through overt missionary effort or deliberate indoctrination, Taoist practices simply merged with the common Chinese conception of physical health and spiritual well-being. Other more conspicuous practices such as hanging a symbol of the "eight trigrams" in the front of a house or pasting talismans on doors to ward off evil spirits, among countless other practices, likewise reflect the pervasive presence of Taoism in Chinese culture.

Taoism was able to sink deep roots in China, not simply because of the worship of many gods and goddesses. The dimension of practice is equally important, especially in terms of various forms of religious arts. Taoism incorporated ancient astronomy, medicine, mathematics, alchemy, and other religious arts into its understanding of Tao, and further developed various forms of divination such as astrology and geomancy. All these activities were and still are intimately related to the everyday life of the Chinese. Many practices that originated from Taoism, from the use of herbs and drugs and the art of *Qigong* (breathing exercise) to certain rituals and customs, have gradually and imperceptibly become part of the daily life of Chinese people.

CONTEMPORARY TAOISM

The classical secularization hypothesis suggests that a consequence of modernity, and for some scholars an inevitable outcome, is the decline in social significance of religion. The process implies that sectors of society are increasingly removed from the domination or religious institutions and symbols. In the main, it is argued that the process of secularization has been dependent on the rise of empiricist thinking and differentiation of roles and functions within society. The religious situation of Taoism in China, Taiwan, and Hong Kong shows that rather than secularization, there has been a revival of Taoist practices and rituals.

Revivalism in China

Despite the tenets of orthodox Marxist theory, and suppression and strict restrictions placed on religions during the communist era, religion in China is thriving, particularly after economic liberalization. Thousands of temples destroyed or damaged during the Cultural Revolution have been restored and increasing numbers of people are taking part in ritual activities. Currently, China has over 1,500 Taoist temples and more than 25,000 Taoist priests and nuns. With the rebuilding and reconsecrating of the temples, many Taoist priests found new job opportunities and returned to work. In addition, many Chinese communities began to celebrate elaborate Taoist *jiao*, communal sacrifices, as well as reviving elaborate funerary and ancestral rituals. There has been a renaissance of popular religion with the growing popularity of temple cults, local deities, and temple festivals. With the boom in economic activity, many Chinese could also afford to rebuild temples to their local god.

The resurgence in religious activities is also linked to the donations from overseas Chinese. They return in large numbers to attend religious rituals and to bury their dead, or at least hold services in their places of origin for those who have died overseas. Many have been persuaded to make large contributions to local schools, hospitals, and roads once they have been allowed to conduct the rituals (see Dean 1993; Fan 2003; Lai 2003a).

Although the state has always wanted the Taoists to conform to the Buddhist ideal of celibacy and monastic life, most of the Taoist priests or *daoshi* live a married life at home, wearing liturgical vestments when performing the rituals. Since they perform services and ceremonies in the context of the cults of various gods in local temples, they are not easily distinguishable from local temple shamans whose religious activities have been criticized as superstitious. In order to legitimize and effectively manage this group of Taoist priests, the National Daoist Association has classified the "correct" or "recognized" *daoshi* of the Zhengyi order. By law, the *daoshi* have to register with their local Taoist association and will receive a "Daoist certificate belonging to the Zhengyi sect," which is issued by the National Daoist Association (Lai 2003a: 424).

Popular religious practices have not lost their importance as China begins its modernization process. Instead, Fan argues that there has been an increase in spirituality among the population as many urban workers who have moved beyond basic struggle for survival are now faced with deeper questions of personal meaning. In his study on religion in the modern city of Shenzhen, Fan shows the trend toward a privatization of popular religion among urban Chinese. To them, religious beliefs are private concerns and the search for spiritual meaning is a personal one. Although many of these urban Chinese do not organize large communal worship events, they still uphold the traditional Chinese popular religion worldview of *mingyun, yuanfen,* and *feng shui* (Fan 2003: 455).

Taiwan's Religious Situation

Since the end of martial law in Taiwan, religion is thriving. Taoism, with over 4.5 million adherents, is one of the most popular religions in Taiwan. The number of Buddhist and Taoist temples in Taiwan nearly doubled in 50 years from 3,661 in 1930 to 5,531 in 1981. According to the statistics provided by the Ministry of the Interior, by 2003 Taiwan was home to 8,604 Taoist temples that had registered with the state. In addition, there are numerous unregistered temples and household shrines (Katz 2003: 396).

Popular religion or folk religion is very widespread. Temple cults in particular have retained their importance as sites for daily worship and community festivals, with popular deities worshipped for their ability to provide health and prosperity. Some of the popular deities include Mazu (patron goddess of the sea and fishermen) and the Royal Lords. Not only are these temple cults and festivals flourishing, they are also moving beyond their local boundaries to play a significant role on the national stage. These temples have also extended their reach into social services, and currently operate a total of 20 hospital and clinics as well as 180 schools ranging from kindergarten to university (Katz 2003).

In Taiwan, another modern, syncretic form of religion similar to those found in the folk or temple cults is currently growing in significance. The *Yi Guan Dao* (Religion of the One Unity) draws upon both traditional teachings and each of the world's major religions. *Yi Guan Dao* adherents try to identify common principles underlying Buddhism, Christianity, Islam, Judaism, and Hinduism. They ascribe to an idea of a god above all other gods called *Mingming Shangdi* (God of Clarity). *Yi Guan Dao* adherents follow many of the Confucian rituals and engage in ancestor worship. They strive to uphold the precepts of not killing, stealing, committing adultery, lying, and drinking alcohol while putting into practice the ideals of benevolence, righteousness, and universal love envisioned by Confucian teaching. As of 2001, the *Yi Guan Dao* had 887,000 believers, making it the third most popular religion in terms of number of adherents.

The Religious Situation in Hong Kong

Buddhism and Taoism, traditional Chinese religions, have a large local following with more than 600 Chinese temples in Hong Kong. Religious practices are still very much observed today. Tablets for ancestors, Master of the Site (*dizhu*), Heaven God (*tiangong*), Kitchen God (*zaojun*), and Door God (*menguan*) are commonly found in homes where there is the practice of local religion. People regularly organize temple festivals to celebrate the birthdays of the local deities and to seek blessings. Leading deities include Buddha, *Kwan Yin*, *Guandi*, and *Luzu*. *Tian Hou*, the Queen of Heaven and Protector of Seafarers, is reputed to be worshipped by 250,000 people. During the *Tian Hou* Festival, which falls on the 23rd day of the third moon, many worshippers visit the most famous *Tian Hou* temple, at Joss House Bay on the Clear Water Bay Peninsula. The *jiao* festival is another popular event for the community. During the major *jiao* event, a large stage is constructed for the Taoist rituals and Cantonese opera. Taoist priests are hired to perform rituals that last several days. After the Taoist ritual, a Cantonese opera is performed for several days to signify the beginning of a new cosmic cycle (Liu 2003). In addition, many participate in deity festivals, birthdays, Hungry Ghost festivals, and communal *jiao* festivals. There are an estimated 500 Taoist masters of the *Zhengyi* tradition (known as Nahm-mouh Taoist masters in Hong Kong) who are in high demand, especially for the performance of funerary rituals (Lai 2003b: 464).

In his research on Hong Kong, Lai (2003b) notes that in contrast to the *Zhengyi* Taoist tradition, which does not usually unite as a community to conduct group worship, many Hong Kong Taoists belong to sects, halls, and temples. Many of these include altars devoted to cult of *Lü Dongbin*. *Lü Dongbin* was a Taoist in the latter half of the Tang dynasty. He is an immortal and was presented as a master of internal alchemy and venerated as the patriarch of the Taoist *Quanzhen* order. He is also worshipped in the popular religious tradition as a deity famed for exorcistic and healing powers. Such *Lü Dongbin* cults were very popular in Guandong and many Taoist altars in Hong Kong are offspring of main altars in Guangdong.

In recent years, the Taoist organizations in Hong Kong have also evolved into socially conscious, charitable organizations. Once offsprings of parent institutions in Guangdong, they have supported the revival of Taoism in mainland China. With greater economic prosperity in Hong Kong, the Taoist organizations have raised millions of dollars to reconstruct temples in China. They have also funded universities, schools, and hospitals, established social services for old people, and set up orphanages, clinics, and study rooms for students (Lai 2003b: 466).

SEE ALSO: Buddhism; Confucianism; Culture; Globalization, Religion and; Plural Society; Popular Religiosity; Religion; Religion, Sociology of; Secularization

REFERENCES AND SUGGESTED READINGS

Dean, K. (1993) *Taoist Ritual and Popular Cults of Southeast China*. Princeton University Press, Princeton.

Fan, L. (2003) Popular Religion in Contemporary China. *Social Compass* 50(4): 449–57.

Katz, P. R. (2003) Religion and the State in Post-War Taiwan. *China Quarterly* 174 (June).

Kohn, L. (1991) *Taoist Mystical Philosophy: The Scripture of Western Ascension*. State University of New York Press, Albany.

Kuah, K. E. (2003) *State, Society, and Religious Engineering: Towards a Reformist Buddhism in Singapore*. Eastern Universities Press, Singapore.

Lai, C.-T. (2003a) Daoism in China Today, 1980–2003. *China Quarterly* 174 (June).

Lai, C.-T. (2003b) Hong Kong Daoism: A Study of Daoist Altars and Lü Dongbin Cults. *Social Compass* 50(4): 459–70.

Lee, C.-Y., Chan, A., & Tsu, T. (1994) *Taoism: Outlines of a Chinese Religious Tradition*. Taoist Federation, Singapore.

Liu, T.-S. (2003) A Nameless but Active Religion: An Anthropologist's View of Local Religion in Hong Kong and Macau. *China Quarterly* 174 (June).

Liu, T.-Y. (1989) *Daojiao shi Shenme (What is Taoism?)*. Institute of East Asian Philosophies, Singapore.

Overmyer, D. L. (2003) Religion in China Today: Introduction. *China Quarterly* 174 (June).

Qing, X. (1988) *Zhongguo Daojiao Shi (History of the Taoist Religion of China)*. Sichuan People's Press, Chengdu.

Ren, J. (Ed.) (1990) *Zhongguo Daojiao Shi (History of the Taoist Religion of China)*. Shanghai People's Press, Shanghai.

Robinet, I. (1997) *Taoism: Growth of a Religion*. Trans. P. Brooks. Stanford University Press, Stanford.

Schipper, K. (1993) *The Taoist Body*. Trans. K. C. Duval. University of California Press, Berkeley.

Welch, H. & Seidel, A. (Eds.) (1979) *Facets of Taoism: Essays in Chinese Religion*. Yale University Press, New Haven.

taste, sociology of

Jukka Gronow

The importance of taste as a sociological concept was emphatically pointed out by Pierre Bourdieu. In his sociology, probably more than anywhere else, taste is a central theoretical concept of analysis. By distinguishing between good and bad, tasteful and tasteless, beautiful and ugly, taste classifies and orders the natural and social world. By taste one classifies oneself and is classified by others. Understood in this way, the sociological concept of taste shares many important features with its predecessor in classical philosophical aesthetics, the power of judgment. In this capacity, taste does not just refer either to individual preferences or dispositions (the term used by Bourdieu), or to some standards used in making choices in consumption. It is an important concept in bridging the gap between an individual's choices and his or her socially shared preferences or habits. In addition, it can refer to more or less automatic responses as well as to highly reflective acts of judgment, and to behavioral responses which share both these aspects at the same time.

TASTE AND POWER OF JUDGMENT IN PHILOSOPHICAL AESTHETICS

The old saying that one should not dispute over matters of taste (*De gustibus disputandum non est*) was not originally understood to refer to the inevitably private nature of judgments of taste. Nowadays, it is often interpreted to mean that since judgments of taste are everyone's private matters, there is no use in arguing about them or presenting any reasons for one's own, presumably superior taste. The lesson to be learnt was rather the opposite. Because taste was something self-evident and shared by all, it was part of "common sense" or *sensus communis*, and it was both futile and unnecessary to argue about it. On the other hand, according to the self-understanding of the representatives of this moral sense theory, taste was based on a sense of feeling about the goodness or badness of objects or forms of conduct. Therefore, it was in principle impossible to formulate any general maxims of good taste. Sole reliance on one's sense or "instinct" of good and bad, tasteful and tasteless, precluded distinction of both beauty and goodness: "sense of beauty" and "sense of right and wrong" were inseparable. Taste was essentially both an aesthetic and a moral category. Thus, decent conduct, dress, and decorum, as well as eating habits, were all indicators of an individual's moral and aesthetic value, or good taste.

In neoclassical economics taste is an exogenous factor. Consumer preferences are taken as given and regarded simply as something which lie behind an individual's choices. Therefore, in economics, individual tastes and the social process of their formation are neither theoretically problematized nor empirically studied.

ANTINOMY OF TASTE

This problem inherent in the common sense of taste (i.e., taste as basically both totally private and subjective, and universally valid and objective) was formulated most poignantly by Immanuel Kant in his third critique, *The Critique of Judgment*. He called it the antinomy of taste. According to Kant, in claiming that something is beautiful we only express our own feeling or subjective taste, but at the same time presume that all others will join us in this judgment. Without this latter presumption, our statements of taste would only express our subjective feelings of sensual pleasure and their general validity would be decided solely empirically by counting how many fellow citizens join us in any particular judgment of taste. In this influential tradition of thought, genuine aesthetic judgments differ from judgments of pleasure exactly because of their claim to universal validity.

Whereas the criterion of good taste gradually disappeared from the aesthetics of fine arts during the eighteenth century, it retained its role in the aesthetics of everyday life and popular culture, in the aesthetics of "lower" arts like gastronomy or popular music, which were often understood to be closer to sensual delights. The philosophical aesthetics in the classical European humanitarian tradition of thought which culminated in Kant's third critique has left deep traces in later sociological thinking and conceptualization of taste. One could claim that his famous antinomy of taste is repeated in two ways in later sociological thinking about taste. First, since it is obvious that people's tastes, in fact, differed, often drastically, from each other, the question of a common or good taste became an empirical question: taste – or good taste – was understood to be either the taste of a certain group of people, representatives of a "high society," or in a more democratic interpretation, of the great majority of people. It became in principle an empirical question to find out to what extent people shared a common taste and to what extent different tastes existed side by side in any society or culture. This tradition of research can, with good reason, be traced back to David Hume's writings on taste. In a sense, the rich and long history of sociological studies of lifestyles and consumer choices or preferences can be understood to originate from this question: to what extent do people, as a matter of fact, share a common taste which unites them in some respects and gives coherence to their choices in various fields of consumption, from housing to clothing, from art and music to food? It is the guiding principle in most market research to search for some standards unifying certain consumer segments and various social groups at the same time as singling them out from others.

Second, taste is an important concept in sociological theories of what constitutes the relation between an individual and his or her social existence and in answering the question of what unifies the members of any social community. In the tradition of classical sociology most prominently represented by Georg Simmel, taste was something which helped to overcome the distance or opposition between an individual and the larger social totality of which she or he was supposedly a part. Through shared taste or style, people would show their affiliation to a common social group as well as preserve their individuality. In social life, as in art, it was possible to share a style, as well as retain one's own individuality and personality, by having a taste of one's own. A painting, for instance, can be characterized as representative of the impressionistic style in art as well as a unique masterpiece painted by the French artist Monet. By the same token, a person can be recognized both as a hip-hopper and an individual called John. Of equal importance was the fact that, ideally, to have a taste in common was thought to restrain an individual's own instincts and preferences less than social norms would, not to mention the legal makeup of a society. In addition, it helped to create social order by coordinating individuals' behavior. Taste united people in taste communities which, supposedly, unlike any kind of political or economic association, allowed people to express their individuality and particularity more.

TASTE AND FASHION

To Georg Simmel, the social formation of fashion was an important phenomenon of modernity. Like Baudelaire's "modern artist" at his best, it can capture the meaning of eternity in one fleeting moment. Fashion is contingent, eternally changing and fleeting. Unlike Hamlet, fashion did not have to decide "whether to be or not to be." In fashion, something could be as well as not be, at the same time. What is now in fashion becomes out of fashion the very next moment. What is even more important, fashion offers in practice, in the everyday life of ordinary people, a sociological solution to Kant's antinomy of taste. As a simultaneous process of social imitation and distinction, it is both individual and social, on the one hand, an expression of an individual's own taste – ideally choosing simply what he or she finds pleasing – on the other, socially shared taste: in fashion, I offer my own choices or judgments of taste for all others to join in and share. The community of fashion is a veritable *sensus communis* – a community of taste – which comes into being only in order to disappear the very same moment. It is just a weak community, notwithstanding effectively creating order in a rapidly changing modern social world.

One of the most pertinent tenets in the social sciences is that taste usually "trickles down"

the social ladder, as do fashionable items. New fashions and styles, just like stylish or fashionable utensils and commodities, always first appear in the higher echelons of society, only to descend, more or less gradually, to its lower groups. The consequence of this presumption is that even though the lifestyles of social classes or status groups always differ, they all have basically the same taste. Since the lower classes or status groups emulate the lifestyles of the higher ones and would prefer to live like their social superiors if only they could, they in fact share the same taste. The process of social imitation is a process motivated by the demand and will of social ascent. The dynamics of consumption in the modern world are characterized by the social aspirations of "status seekers."

Thorstein Veblen's classic study of the conspicuous consumption of what he called the leisure class interestingly emphasized the changes taking place in a modern commercial society. Whereas, earlier, men could distinguish themselves and enjoy their fellow men's esteem because of their superior work performances, in modern societies these generally become increasingly invisible to others. The result of one's labor or one's monetary resources is usually equally invisible. Therefore, "showing off" one's wealth becomes important instead. Taste in a modern society is in the final analysis guided by the aspirations to gain social esteem by explicitly showing off one's pecuniary power. Furthermore, the degree of "uselessness" and instrumental nonfunctionality adherent to an artifact or an occupation, or the amount of idle time required to spend at it competently, seems to equal the high degree of prestige and social esteem afforded its owner/practitioner. This is why, in Veblen's opinion, fine riding horses or pet dogs, just like housewives and domestic servants, among others, serve as ideal and highly visible symbols of one's social standing.

In his classic study of the Paris fashion shows, Herbert Blumer suggested another and competing interpretation of the social mechanism of fashion and of taste formation in general. According to Blumer, taste is a result of collective selection. What Blumer witnessed in the Parisian fashion shows was the process of formation of a collective or common taste. Somehow the fashion designers or representatives of fashion trade could each year select, from among a multitude of dress designs brought to the show, just a few stylistically similar ones. It looked almost as if they had reached a consensus or an agreement by actually negotiating and arguing about the merits of their own favorites whereas, in fact, they chose them largely independently of each other. What was important to Blumer was that this collective taste did not emanate from any powerful or prestigious center, but took place among peers or colleagues. Somehow, almost as if by magic, a taste shared by all crystallized out of a multitude of individual tastes and a new seasonal fashion collectively selected.

Blumer's idea has far-reaching consequences for sociological reasoning because he emphasized that such dynamic social processes like taste formation do not necessarily presume any hierarchical order of superiority. The gravitational center of taste in a modern society is its social center, the middle class, and not its peak. In this respect it reminds one of Gabriel Tarde's classic work on the laws of imitation, where he claimed that in imitating social models people just imitate themselves, or others who are just like them. Consequently, taste is not a class, but a mass phenomenon. The idea of social worlds with their own aesthetics and etiquette of conduct, developed later by symbolic interactionists, makes it possible to take into account social differentiation of taste which is not hierarchic.

Fashion, without a doubt, serves economic interests and ultimately promotes the accumulation of capital by artificially aging otherwise functional products. In clothes fashion strong economic incentives are at play. But it can reasonably be argued that what goes on in the collective selection of taste is similar to a process of aesthetic judgment. The basic criterion of fashion is that it could just as well be otherwise. As far as fashion is concerned, there cannot be any objective criteria of superiority. Therefore, it does not actually matter what, exactly, is the fashion at each point in time, or, say, what will be the fashionable color of the next season or the length of the female dress this autumn. Even if manipulation of taste takes place one can always ask who manipulates the manipulators.

DISTINCTIONS OF TASTE AND SOCIAL DIFFERENCES

One of the most pertinent questions concerning the role of taste in society has been to what extent taste is an expression of an individual's preferences alone. Are the individual's choices in consumption free and conscious choices? To what extent are they socially determined and habitual? In economistic market research such choices are as a rule regarded as individual preferences. Sociologists, contrariwise, emphasize choices' social origin and their socially shared nature. Pierre Bourdieu's work *Distinction: A Social Critique of the Judgment of Taste*, published in English in 1984 (French edition, 1979), has perhaps more than any other single sociological work influenced the sociological discussion of taste during the last decades. Bourdieu's work was explicitly intended as a sociological critique of Immanuel Kant's analysis of aesthetic judgment (and, with him, of the whole tradition of philosophical aesthetics). Bourdieu aimed at revealing the true social nature of good taste, which always presents itself as objectively valid and legitimate.

To Bourdieu, taste is the basic analytical concept of sociology. Distinction is a study of social distinctions of taste and their relationship, on the one hand, to social positions and, on the other hand, to different symbolic activities and lifestyles. An individual's relative social position, and, consequently, lifestyle and taste disposition, is always determined by the specific combination of the three different types of capital: economic, cultural, and social. To an extent, these three forms of capital can be transformed into each other. In Bourdieu's study, the sum total of one's capital, as well as the interplay of these three forms of capital, explain the class differences in taste dispositions and their visible expressions, different lifestyles and, finally, consumer choices.

HIERARCHY OF TASTE

If *Distinction* had only claimed that tastes and lifestyles of various social groups will vary according to the amount and type of capital in their possession, it would not differ much from most ordinary sociological studies, which identify correlations between socioeconomic background factors and various cultural practices and habits. Bourdieu, however, made a further claim. He claimed that in any society tastes are hierarchically ordered. This means that there is a legitimate taste in each society which gains its legitimacy from the very fact that other, lower echelons of society, the middle classes in particular, acknowledge its superiority by aspiring to acquire it and its visible symbols. A process of continuous social emulation reproduces both cultural distinctions and, by doing so, the different forms of capital. This process perpetually forces the upper classes to distinguish themselves from their social competitors by adopting new signs and symbols of excellence. One of the logical consequences of Bourdieu's analysis is that, as a result of the continuous process of making new distinctions, the taste of the upper classes tends to become more and more refined and exclusive. What we have here is, essentially, an aristocrat's taste. The cultural hero of early modernity, the dandy, is its true representative.

CLASS TASTE OR A VARIETY OF TASTES

Bourdieu's strong emphasis on the hierarchical and aristocratic nature of the ruling class taste is what has caused most reservations among sociologists toward his theoretical interpretations. The criticisms address concrete empirical and theoretical questions concerning his model. The dissenting empirical results can be explained both by different and rapidly changing socioeconomic conditions (most notably the democratization of educational opportunities) and by theoretical and methodological differences in the study designs.

An interesting question raised in recent studies is the emergence of a cultural omnivore. According to this idea – proposed by Peterson and Kern (1996) – what distinguishes the present cultural upper class from other classes is not the exclusiveness and refinement of its taste, but rather the very opposite, its inclusiveness. Peterson and Kern's studies of musical tastes

in Northern America revealed that the elite were omnivores – this was true above all of the economic elite graduating from business schools. They appreciated most or several musical genres almost indiscriminately, whereas social groups with less economic and cultural capital were much more restrictive in their tastes, with preferences such as country and western or gospel. Quite unexpectedly, business school graduates are the new cultural heroes.

Another interesting empirical observation to which Bourdieu paid very little attention in his own study are the distinctions according to gender. In virtually all subsequent empirical studies, gender differences seem to lie behind many distinctions in various fields of consumption and culture. They are particularly accentuated in the consumption of goods or in the practices of traditional high culture often associated with established cultural institutions, such as museums, art exhibitions and galleries, theatres, dance performances, etc. All have become leisure time activities for an increasingly female public. What is more important, they are practiced by women of various educational backgrounds, that is, not only by relatively well educated women but even by those in the middling positions. An equally clear distinction between the sexes can often be found, for instance, in eating practices and food tastes.

FUTURE DIRECTIONS

One of the interesting questions facing future research is to what extent does this validate the fact that by increasingly taking over such typically "highbrow" cultural practices women have really become a new cultural elite. Or, conversely, does this signify a general social and cultural degradation of these traditional genres and fields of "highbrow" culture? Or, finally, is it more likely, as suggested by some sociologists, that even though relatively clear cultural distinctions related to different taste preferences exist in present-day societies, they are not in general or in the majority of cases hierarchically ordered? Women and men, or for that matter young people and old people, may just develop different tastes, but this practice does not necessarily have to signify an eternal struggle over the determination of legitimate or good taste. Instead, we may have entered a state of societal development which is characterized by the emergence and coexistence of a number of different and equally good – or, if you like, bad – tastes. Social groups with similar lifestyles may just share a common taste without sharing anything else. Or, finally, as some sociologists claim, taste may have become more individualized and society more fragmented.

SEE ALSO: Blumer, Herbert George; Bourdieu, Pierre; Conspicuous Consumption; Consumption, Fashion and; Consumption, Food and Cultural; Distinction; Highbrow/Lowbrow; Lifestyle Consumption; Simmel, Georg; Veblen, Thorstein

REFERENCES AND SUGGESTED READINGS

Bennett, T., Emmison, M., & Frow, J. (1999) *Accounting for Tastes: Australian Everyday Cultures*. Cambridge University Press, Cambridge.
Blumer, H. (1969) Fashion: From Class Differentiation to Collective Selection. *Sociological Quarterly* 10: 275–91.
Cambell, C. (1987) *The Romantic Ethic and the Spirit of Modern Consumerism*. Blackwell, Oxford.
Gronow, J. (1997) *The Sociology of Taste*. Routledge, New York.
Gronow, J. & Warde, A. (Eds.) (2001) *Ordinary Consumption*. Routledge, New York.
Lahire, B. (2002) *Les Culture de individes: dissonances culturelles et distinction de soi*. La Décovererte, Paris.
Lamont, M. (1992), *Money, Morals and Manners: The Culture of the French and American Upper-Middle Class*. University of Chicago Press, Chicago.
Peterson, R. A. & Kern, R. M. (1996) Changing Highbrow Taste: From Snob to Omnivore. *American Sociological Review* 61: 900–7.
Simmel, G. (1997) *Simmel on Culture: Selected Writings*. Ed. M. Featherstone & D. Frisby. Sage, London.
Tarde, G. (1962 [1890]) *The Laws of Imitation*. Peter Smith, Gloucester.
Veblen, T. (1961 [1899]) *The Theory of the Leisure Class*. Random House, New York.
Warde, A. (1997) *Consumption, Food and Taste*. Sage, London.

tatemae/honne

Jane Bachnik

Tatemae/honne distinguish between the world of social relations (surface reality) and the world of feelings (inner reality). *Tatemae* refers to formal principles or rules to which one is at least outwardly constrained, while *honne* conveys personal feelings or motives, which cannot be openly expressed due to *tatemae*. Rather than a discrepancy between a "false" exterior and "true" interior, *tatemae/honne* are better understood as conveying the existence of more than one kind of truth in social situations. Thus the "truth" of what is appropriate to say directly to others may be different from the "truth" in our hearts. Japanese cocoon their guests in *tatemae* so that a faux pas by a guest, even if it offends the host, will not be communicated directly in *tatemae*. Japanese accept that social communications may not correspond to personal feelings; moreover, they consider the surface reality to be just as "real" as the inner, private reality.

The words *tatemae/honne* came into frequent use only in the post-war period, although the distinctions they characterize are found in literature as far back as the fourteenth century. *Tatemae* refers to the ridgepole (or main beam) in Japanese architecture, which supports the rest of the structure, and psychiatrist Takeo Doi considers the logic of *tatemae/honne* to be manifested in the relationship between the *tatemae* and the finished building. The *tatemae* is not the real aim of the builders, who construct the ridgepole in order to add the roof, walls, and floors that will constitute the completed building. Yet by the same token, it is impossible to complete the rest of the building unless the *tatemae* is raised first (Doi 1986). This logic privileges *tatemae* as the "core structure" of a building, which seems the opposite of its meaning as "surface reality."

But this same logic links *tatemae* to its prime meaning of social conventions, such that *tatemae* supports the "structure" of social life much as the ridgepole supports the house. For example, the *tatemae* of the science fiction novel refers to the conventions for writing this kind of novel, which are created by a consensus that can change over time. In its relationship to social conventions, *tatemae* always implies the existence of people in the background who assent to it, while at the same time keeping their own personal motives and opinions in *honne* (Doi 1986). Rather than being unique to Japan, *tatemae/honne* represent tensions between conforming to social conventions and giving expression to one's heartfelt desires – tensions between individual and society that are a fundamental part of social life everywhere.

In fact these same tensions are represented in a number of paired sets of terms, which include *omote* ("appearance," "in front") and *ura* ("behind the scenes," "in back"). *Tatemae* is part of *omote* as official, public, and social, while *honne* is within *ura* as hidden, secret, and personal, and may also include what is publically unacceptable or even illegal. Another set of terms, *uchi* ("inside," "us," "our-group") and *soto* ("outside," "them"), is also linked to *tatemae/honne*, since *tatemae* constitutes the surface communication of *omote* presented to *soto* outsiders, while *honne* is expressed in the behind-the-scenes *ura* sphere of *uchi* insiders. *Tatemae/omote/soto* are always linked together, as are *honne/ura/uchi*.

The Japanese language also exhibits wide-ranging distinctions manifested in formal/informal grammatical forms which parallel the distinctions contained in the double sets of terms. For example, communication of *soto/omote/tatemae* is characterized by choice of a formal register to express varying degrees of distance and deference through elaborated polite forms of speech. Communication of *uchi/ura/honne* is marked by choice of an informal register to express varying degrees of closeness (and sometimes intimacy) through highly contracted plain forms of speech. These distinctions permeate the entire language, since even single utterances, and certainly anything longer than two-item exchanges, are marked by the use of register.

These language distinctions in tandem with the paired sets of terms indicate two distinct spheres in self and social life, which are nonetheless linked like two sides of a coin. Each sphere mutually defines and constitutes the other, in a way that actually mirrors the constitution of self and society. Thus *honne* exists only in relation to *tatemae*, and *tatemae* is constructed out of *honne*, which manipulates it from behind

the scenes. Consequently, the paired terms have been used as a basis for defining the organization of Japanese self and society. Takeo Doi (1986) developed the organization of a double-sided Japanese self, based explicitly on *omote/ura* and *tatemae/honne*. Chie Nakane (1972) defined *uchi* as a basic and ubiquitous component of Japanese society. Bachnik and Quinn (1994) argued that the paired sets of terms form a theoretical basis for defining self, social life, and language, spelling out pragmatic and practice-oriented perspectives.

Japanese society is distinctive in placing a high value on avoiding direct communication of *honne* problems, disagreements, and other "uncomfortable truths" in *tatemae*. Japanese are taught to sacrifice *honne* for the sake of *tatemae*, and are very skilled at keeping *honne* from "leaking" into *tatemae*. Yet *tatemae* can be seen as one of Japan's "truly excellent features" (Kerr 2001), which infuses daily life in Japanese face-to-face communities with grace and calm. The emphasis placed on preserving *tatemae* over expressing *honne* can be regarded as self-sacrifice for the sake of the greater social good (in this case the smooth functioning of social life).

But by the same token, should the sense of self-service for a greater social good be distorted or lost, the results can be socially corrosive and dangerous. Many authors have noted that *tatemae/honne* distinctions are pervasive in Japanese large-scale institutions, including those at the apex of power in government, big business, and politics. It is also noted that *tatemae/honne* have undergone a shift in meaning, so that *tatemae* now widely conveys falsity and emptiness, while *honne* is considered "true," but tinged with dirtiness and corruption.

At the same time, a shift can be noted in the organization of *uchi/soto* when comparing small-scale family organizations to large institutional organizations. This shift is exemplified by the constitution of *uchi*, which in family organizations consists of family members themselves (as "we," "us," "insiders"), making them privy to the realms of *ura* and *honne*. In contrast, in the government bureaucracy, for example, each government ministry is organized as an *uchi*, whose "inside" realms of *honne* and *ura* are accessible only to its own insider bureaucrats. The public is strictly *soto* to such a ministry and therefore privy only to *tatemae* communication.

Consequently, the inside operations and affairs of each ministry are kept opaque, and the hidden nature of *honne/ura* in these bureaucratic *uchi* gives rise to a circular process, whose aspects have been the focus of considerable research and investigative reporting in English. They include the fostering of dishonest and collusive practices in *uchi*; sabotaging of safety and regulatory procedures; and cosmetic accounting (*funshoku kessan*) to keep information about dishonest practices from reaching the *soto* public.

For example, bid-rigging (*dango*) is pervasive in Japan, particularly in the construction industry, to whom the Construction Ministry channels the considerable funds allocated to public works construction. Ministry officials also participate in *dango* and have publicly defended bid-rigging practices in 2005. *Dango* rests upon a tender system that is both fixed and closed, and such bidding inflates the project costs to the public by 30–50 percent. Crucial to carrying out *dango* is a practice known as *amakudari* (descent from heaven), in which bureaucrats from the ministry shift to high positions in industry or public agencies. *Amakudari*, in effect, creates an *uchi* conduit between the ministry and the firm or agency into which the bureacrat descends. This allows that organization to create *uchi* ties with the ministry to create *dango* (and other *ura* practices) – through a *honne* motivation to maximize profits among themselves.

Such collusion is not limited to the Construction Ministry. In 1996 all of Japan's seven housing loan corporations (known as Jusen) went bankrupt with losses of eight trillion yen. Yet, even though over 90 percent of the loans extended by the Jusen were non-performing by the early 1990s, and the Ministry of Finance knew this, the ministry failed to take any action. This was because six of the seven Jusen were run by *amakudari* directors from the Ministry of Finance, and so the ministry had no desire to "hurt its own," as one critic put it (Bowen 2003). Consequently, in the years before bankruptcy, the *amakudari* executives guided the banks in an elaborate shell game of accounting trickery that is highly developed in Japan. By the time the scandal became public in 1996, the public had to pay hundreds of billions of additional yen to clean up the mess (Kerr 2001).

During the 1990s a series of scandals circulated throughout the ministries, involving almost all of them. The scandals demonstrated the collusive processes outlined above, and one might expect the press to play an investigative role in breaking up such collusions. But since reporters can only get access to the news by being embedded in government-attached press clubs, they also end up in collusion with the institutions in which they are embedded. The result is that the published news is largely *tatemae*.

The collusive relationships outlined above reveal a distinct – and pathological – inversion in the values of *tatemae/honne*, so that personal profiteering in *honne* takes precedence over self-sacrifice for the greater social good in *tatemae*. Here the "good" has been transposed from the public, social good to a selfish, *uchi* good – "taking care of our own" – resulting in a huge variety of corrupt practices. This inversion of the government servant/public service relationship victimizes the public, who ultimately pay for the corruption – through wasted tax money which has created enormous fiscal deficits (and cuts in services), made pension funds insolvent, inflated construction costs, and created numerous safety hazards due to lack of effective regulation.

The kinds of collusive practices described above make it understandable how *tatemae* now connotes falsity and deceit, *honne* conveys dirtiness and dishonesty, and both *tatemae* and *honne* are held in low regard. The crucial question is whether the "excellent features" of *tatemae/honne* can be reclaimed, so that the corrupt and inverted relationship between bureaucrats and the public can be righted and self-sacrifice for the social good take precedence over personal profiteering. These issues of bureaucratic corruption are of interest far beyond Japan, for they pervade today's world. Resolving them would strengthen Japanese democracy, by allowing the people to reclaim power from the bureaucracy and follow the constitution, which places sovereign power in their hands. These steps may also allow the people who produced the "economic miracle" to finally emerge from the quagmire of their 15-year slump.

SEE ALSO: *Seikatsu/Seikatsusha*; *Seken*

REFERENCES AND SUGGESTED
READINGS

Bachnik, J. (2005) *At Home in Japan: What No One
Tells You.* National East Asian Languages
Resource Center in cooperation with the National
Institute of Multimedia Education, Japan. Online.
www.nealrc.osu.edu.
Bachnik, J. M. & Quinn, C. J., Jr. (Eds.) (1994)
*Situated Meaning: Inside and Outside in Japanese
Self, Society, and Language.* Princeton University
Press, Princeton.
Bowen, R. W. (2003) *Japan's Dysfunctional Democ-
racy.* M. E. Sharpe, Armonk, NY.
Doi, T. (1986) *The Anatomy of Self: The Individual
Versus Society.* Kodansha International, Tokyo.
Gibney, F. (Ed.) (1998) Introduction. In: *Unlocking
the Bureaucrat's Kingdom.* Brookings Institution
Press, Washington, DC, pp. 1–15.
Kerr, A. (2001) *Dogs and Demons: The Fall of Modern
Japan.* Penguin, London.
Nakane, C. (1972) *Japanese Society.* University of
California Press, Berkeley.

taxes: progressive, proportional, and regressive

Christine A. Wernet

The generation of government revenue and the
redistribution of income among the population
are two central reasons for taxation (Davies
1986). Governments have used taxation as a
means to generate revenue for centuries, and
some governments have been using taxation as
a means of resource reallocation since at least the
1800s. The three main types of taxation, progressive, proportional and regressive taxes, are
outlined.

Progressive taxes are taxes that require those
who earn more money to pay higher taxes.
Personal income taxes in the US are progressive. For example, those who have a family
income of $100,000 or higher may pay as much
as 29 percent of their total income in annual
taxes, while those in the lowest income bracket,
who may have a family income of $10,000, pay
approximately 4.6 percent of their total income

in annual taxes (Mishel et al. 1999). Proponents
of progressive taxes argue that wealthy individuals have a moral obligation to society to pay
higher taxes. Opponents argue that progressive
income taxation has a negative effect on capital
formation and economic growth.

Proportional taxes refer to taxes that equally
burden all income groups in a society. Proportional taxes are sometimes referred to as a flat
tax. For example, if a society had a proportional
income tax of 15 percent, a family with an
annual income of $100,000 would pay $15,000
a year in income taxes, while a family with an
annual income of $10,000 would pay $1,500 a
year in income taxes.

Regressive taxes burden lower-income groups
more than higher-income groups. Less affluent
individuals spend a higher proportion of their
income on regressive taxes, such as sales taxes
and excise taxes, than do more affluent individuals. For example, $400 of sales tax is a much
larger proportion of $10,000 than it is of
$100,000. Sales tax is tax that is placed on all
items that are sold: food, clothing, furniture,
etc. Some states place a sales tax of, for example,
7 percent on all items sold. In this case, if an
item is purchased for $100 the individual will
owe $7 in sales tax to the government. Another
regressive tax is the excise tax. Excise taxes are
placed on certain items such as alcohol, tobacco,
and gasoline. Excise taxes place a heavier burden on the poor than on the rich because excise
taxes, like sales taxes, account for a larger proportion of their total income.

When all forms of taxation are considered,
some countries, such as the US, actually have
more income inequality after taxation than
before (Devine 1983; Kerbo 2003). Therefore,
while taxation does much to generate revenue
for the government, it may do little to redistribute resources.

SEE ALSO: Class, Status, and Power; Economic Development; Income Inequality and
Income Mobility

REFERENCES AND SUGGESTED
READINGS

Davies, D. (1986) *United States Taxes and Tax Policy.* Cambridge University Press, New York.

Devine, J. A. (1983) Fiscal Policy and Class Income Inequality: The Distributional Consequences of Governmental Revenues and Expenditures in the United States, 1949–1976. *American Sociological Review* 48: 606–22.

Fullerton, D. & Rogers, D. L. (1993) *Who Bears the Lifetime Tax Burden?* Brookings Institution, Washington, DC.

Kerbo, H. R. (2003) *Social Stratification and Inequality: Class Conflict in Historical, Comparative, and Global Perspective*. McGraw Hill, New York.

Mishel, L., Bernstein, J., & Schmitt, J. (1999) *The State of Working America, 1998–99*. Cornell University Press, Ithaca, NY.

Taylorism

Harland Prechel

Taylorism was developed by Frederick Taylor in the 1880s. By the 1920s, together with other forms of scientific management, Taylorism was widely adopted in the US and other industrial societies. Taylor was raised in a prominent Philadelphia family, but rejected his parents' plans for a Harvard education and became an apprentice in a metal-working plant. Later, he obtained a technical degree. Despite his career focus, Taylor retained the ideological bias of his upper-class background that incorporated dimensions of socio-Darwinism and utilitarianism. This doctrine provided the ideological context for Taylor's system of scientific management, which emphasized the idea that economic success is caused by superior abilities and those abilities can be learned.

Changes in the political-legal arrangements in which business enterprises were embedded and the emergence of the modern corporation established the social structural context for implementing Taylorism. In the 1880s and 1890s, New Jersey and other states passed laws that made it easier for industrial firms to use the joint stock holding company. The embeddedness of industrial firms in these institutional arrangements permitted corporate consolidation, which created giant corporations by merging firms and incorporating them as subsidiary corporations (Prechel 2000). Attempts by capitalists to exercise more control over the labor process in these corporations resulted in labor unrest, which was manifested as high rates of absenteeism, labor turnover, and strikes. In response to these historical contingencies, Taylor (1967) claimed there was a need for "greater national efficiency" and efficiency is best achieved through systematic management of people. He argued his system would reduce costs, increase efficiency, and appeal to workers' economic self-interest. Taylor claimed that the increased efficiency from scientific management would result in high profits, which would permit capitalists to increase wages, thereby eliminating labor unrest and workers' desire to join unions.

The technical dimensions of Taylorism focused on the "one best way" to perform work. Taylor (1967) maintained that workers (1) retained knowledge over the production process, and (2) incorporated rest breaks into the production process (i.e., soldiering) that were so sophisticated and complex that capitalists and their foremen could not detect them. To increase control over the labor process, Taylor collected information from workers and located it in a centralized planning department where engineers used this information to establish rules to control the execution of each task by specifying how to complete it and the amount of required time to do it.

Drawing from the Marxian-Hegelian conception of alienation, Braverman (1974) maintained that the separation of conception from execution in Taylorism dehumanizes the worker because it limits the opportunities for individuals to use their creative capacities. This separation occurs when engineers transform craft knowledge into work rules (i.e., bureaucratic controls) and machines (i.e., technical controls) (Edwards 1979). Although the centralization of knowledge also subordinated operating managers to centralized control, these managers retained a substantial degree of control over the managerial process during this historical period. Taylor also developed a reimbursement system that rewarded managers in relationship to their position in the hierarchical division of managerial labor.

There are several long-term effects of Taylorism on class relations. First, the adoption of Taylorist ideology, which assumes that workers are inferior to managers, has been the source of conflict between workers and managers. Second, the emergence of organizational hierarchies and the concomitant ideology of Taylorism encouraged managers and engineers to disregard workers' knowledge of the production process, which created obstacles to improving efficiency. Third, the reimbursement system initiated by Taylor contributed to inequality by establishing a system of pay differentials between managers and workers, which reached a historical high point in the late twentieth and early twenty-first centuries.

SEE ALSO: Alienation; Capitalism; Decision-Making; Fordism/Post-Fordism; Ideology; Labor Process; Marxism and Sociology; Weber, Max; Work, Sociology of

REFERENCES AND SUGGESTED READINGS

Braverman, H. (1974) *Labor and Monopoly Capital.* Monthly Review Press, New York.
Edward, R. (1979) *Contested Terrain.* Basic Books, New York.
Prechel, H. (2000) *Big Business and the State.* State University of New York Press, Albany.
Taylor, F. W. (1967 [1911]) *The Principles of Scientific Management.* W. W. Norton, New York.

teachers

Kristin Gordon

With over 3 million teachers working in the US public school system, teaching attracts considerable attention from sociologists. Many issues have been explored. Dominating the field are questions concerning teachers' roles, quality, professional status, training, gender composition, pay, staffing, and placement. Teachers play multiple roles in the educational process. First, teachers impart academic skills and knowledge (human capital). Second, teachers socialize children in the lifestyles, values, and cultures of society (cultural capital). The importance of the academic, social, and cultural dimensions of this work for children raises one of the foremost questions in research on teachers: Does teacher quality matter? Early research studying the impact of teacher credentials and experience largely indicated that teacher quality did not consistently relate to student achievement. More recent exploration reveals that teacher preparation, particularly subject-matter knowledge, does positively impact student achievement.

In addition to debates over teacher quality, the occupation is plagued by questionable professional status. In an effort to assert teacher professionalism, new models of teacher training have emerged. Historically, normal schools assumed responsibility for instruction in teaching theory and pedagogy. As teachers increasingly turned towards colleges and universities for training, substantive knowledge began dominating the curriculum. Today, reforms aimed at affirming teacher professionalism stress initial and ongoing training in subject-area knowledge.

The gender composition of the occupation also contributes to its questionable professional status. Teaching in the US began as a male occupation. Around 1850, teaching became a predominantly female occupation and this pattern persists today. Despite the fact that teaching is a female-dominated occupation, men are over-represented in administrative positions. This occupational sex segregation reinforces the semi-professional status and low pay of teaching. These factors are held partly responsible for the current staffing problems afflicting the occupation.

Recent research indicates that the US continues to have difficulty staffing classrooms with qualified teachers. Two possible causes of school staffing problems have been investigated: increased enrollments combined with high teacher retirement and teacher turnover. Recent research provides limited support for the notion that staffing problems are the result of increased enrollments and retirements. Rather, the evidence indicates that large numbers of teachers are leaving the occupation in response to problematic working conditions, specifically student discipline problems and insufficient administrative support. One consequence of these school staffing problems is the growing occurrence of out-of-field teaching. This phenomenon, in which a teacher does not possess a major or minor in their teaching field, is particularly important for understanding teachers' careers, satisfaction, turnover, and student achievement.

Cross-national research on teachers and teaching examine similar issues. Questions of teacher quality pervade educational reform in many national contexts. Recent data indicates that in many countries a large proportion of teachers are working without minimum qualifications. While concern over teacher quality appears in many nations' reform agendas, little research supports the contention that variation in teacher quality cross-nationally explains national differences in student achievement.

Like the US, comparative studies reveal that many countries have trouble recruiting and retaining qualified teachers. This can be partially explained by teacher pay. While the salaries of experienced teachers studied by the Organization for Economic Cooperation and Development range from less than US$10,000 in Poland and the Slovak Republic to US $45,000 and more in Germany, Japan, Korea, Luxembourg, and Switzerland, there is agreement among teachers that teaching provides inadequate financial reward. Of those countries that share the US's staffing problems, the most frequent solutions include out-of-field teaching and increasing other teachers' workloads. Interestingly, staffing problems are not universal. Several nations, such as Greece and Korea, actually have an oversupply of teachers, which also introduces policy challenges.

Despite unique contexts, tremendous demands are being placed on teachers in their multiple roles. Debates about teacher quality, professional status, preparation, and placement persist. Continued sociological exploration of teachers and teaching is imperative for understanding these issues.

SEE ALSO: Education; Professions; Professors; Teaching and Gender

REFERENCES AND SUGGESTED READINGS

Darling-Hammond, L., Wise, A., & Klein, S. (1995) *A License to Teach*. Westview Press, Boulder.

Fuller, B. (1986) *Defining School Quality*. In: Hannaway, J. & Lockheed, M. E. (Eds.), *The Contributions of the Social Sciences to Educational Policy and Practice*. McCutchen, Berkeley, CA, pp. 33–70.

Ingersoll, R. (2001) Teacher Turnover and Teacher Shortages: An Organizational Analysis. *American Educational Research Journal* 38: 499–534.

Ingersoll, R. (2005) The Problem of Underqualified Teachers: A Sociological Perspective. *Sociology of Education* 78(2): 175–8.

Lortie, D. (1975) *School Teacher*. University of Chicago Press, Chicago.

National Commission on Teaching and America's Future (1996) *What Matters Most: Teaching for America's Future*. NCTAF, New York.

Organization for Economic Cooperation and Development (2005a) Teachers Matter: Attracting, Developing and Retaining Effective Teachers. OECD Publishing. Online. www.oecd.org/.

Organization for Economic Cooperation and Development (2005b) Education at a Glance: OECD Indicators. OECD Publishing. OECD Publishing. Online. www.oecd.org/.

Strober, M. & Tyack, D. (1980) Why Women Teach and Men Manage. *Signs* 5: 494–503.

Weller-Ferris, L. (1999) Working Conditions. In: Menlo, A. & Poppleton, P. (Eds.), *The Meanings of Teaching: An International Study of Secondary Teachers' Work Lives*. Bergin & Garvey, Westport, pp. 117–48.

teaching and gender

Linda Grant and Linda Renzulli

The study of teachers and teaching has always been an important focus of sociology of education, but the analysis of links between teaching and gender has developed more recently. As Grant and Murray (1999) contend, K-12 teaching and postsecondary teaching are two different occupations and thus relationships between gender and teaching differ at each level. Other researchers have studied gender as it affects pedagogy and curriculum at all levels of schooling. Finally, some scholars, especially those working from a feminist perspective, have explored what students learn about gender in schooling, and how teachers – intentionally or not – affect the gender climates of educational institutions.

GENDER DISTRIBUTIONS IN THE TEACHING PROFESSION

Teaching is a classic example of an occupation that feminized. Today, about 75 percent of teachers in grades K-12 in the US are women. Similarly, in 11 of 20 OECD countries, women make up 70 percent or more of elementary teachers. Preschool teaching is also strongly woman dominated, with precise proportions hard to tabulate because few states license preschool teachers.

Women gained access to teaching in the late 1800s. Not until the 1920s in the US, and not until 1995 in OECD countries, did women represent 70 percent or more of teachers. The feminization of teaching occurred in part because with the growth of the middle class and formalization of schooling, teaching became a full-time job. However, pay did not rise along with increased time demands. Thus, men left teaching in the US and internationally for better higher paying occupations, creating open positions that were relatively attractive for women.

As women entered the profession, the definition, role, and expectation for teachers' work changed. Contracts required that teachers be single women, and teaching was viewed as preparation for motherhood. Teachers' work was nevertheless controlled by male-only school boards and administrators. As in other feminized occupations, women grew in numbers, but not in pay, power, or autonomy. More recently, pay and autonomy have increased, but pay remains low (Ingersoll 2001). In fact, as the rate of feminization increases in OECD countries, teacher salary seems to decrease.

Teaching became an avenue for upward mobility for farm and working-class families and for black and white men and women. By the 1930s, however, most US teachers were middle-class white women. Teaching in segregated schools was an important means of upward class mobility for African Americans. Under segregation, educated blacks' access to positions as teachers and administrators helped to establish a black middle class. When the *Brown* v. *Board of Education* decision ended legally mandated school segregation, many black educators lost their jobs, even when they were more qualified than their white counterparts. Blacks now make up less than 8 percent of public school teachers, although about 17 percent of students are black. Black middle-class women, and other educated minority youth, nowadays seek more lucrative careers.

At the postsecondary level, teaching remains a white-*male* dominated profession. Women and persons of color have made only modest inroads into professor positions in recent decades in the US and in most other countries. Before the mid-1900s, white women in the US comprised only a small fraction of college faculty, concentrated primarily at women's colleges or in feminized disciplines such as home economics, education, or social work in coeducational institutions. Women's enrollments in PhD programs expanded dramatically in the late 1970s, and affirmative action policies adopted by colleges aided their entry into college teaching. By 2004, women were about one-third of postsecondary faculty in the US, up from about 23 percent in 1974. In research-intensive universities, women are only about 14 percent of full professors, but nearly 60 percent of lecturers and instructors (AAUP 2004). Women, however, are better represented across ranks at Historical Black Colleges and Universities (HBCUs) than in colleges generally (NCES 2004).

PAY GAPS

The heavily feminized occupation of preschool teaching is poorly paid, averaging lower hourly wages than bus drivers, secretaries, and practical nurses (Whitebook & Sakai 2004). K-12 teachers also earn relatively low wages, with women averaging only 90 percent of men's wages in 2000. In countries such as Japan and Turkey, where men are more numerous in the teaching ranks, teachers' salaries compare more favorably to the country's cost of living index than is the case in the US.

Several explanations have been offered about the gender gap in teachers' pay. One is the gender-segregated composition of teaching staffs, with women more dominant in elementary grades where pay is low and men more numerous in secondary grades and administrative posts where wages are higher. Men are about three times more numerous among high school as among elementary teachers.

In addition, segregation in types of position within the hierarchy of teaching by gender also occurs (Cognard-Black 2004). Men who enter teaching rise rapidly in status and often are tracked into administrative positions. In the US about 56 percent of principals are men, and male principals average three more years' experience than women counterparts. This contrasts sharply with the disadvantages to advancement that women often face in male-dominated occupations, such as postsecondary teaching.

Gender differences in credentials also account for some of the pay gap. Male teachers are more likely to have advanced degrees, and they average more years of teaching experience than women. In addition, men are more likely to teach in unionized systems, and unions have been successful in raising teacher pay.

Women professors are more poorly paid than their men counterparts in US colleges and universities, with pay gaps even wider than at the K-12 level. In recent years women full professors have lost ground compared with men of similar ranks (AAUP 2004), but at lower ranks they have gained slightly, mostly as a result of wage stagnation for men. Among full professors, women's average salaries are 12 percent lower than men's. HBCUs show a different pattern. Although overall salaries at these institutions average only about 80 percent of college salaries generally, women and men of similar rank are closer to parity (NCES 2004).

Salary gaps reflect in part women's more recent entry into college teaching and consequent lesser seniority and their concentration into lower-paid academic fields. Men have longer records of uninterrupted service and are in types of institutions with higher pay; for example, research universities rather than community colleges. Men also outnumber women in administrative positions. Women faculty are ghettoized into lower-paid fields (e.g., English, foreign languages, or education rather than math, science, business, or law) (NSF 2004). Higher pay for the male-dominated fields usually is justified by arguments that faculty in these disciplines have attractive job opportunities outside of academia. Nevertheless, with controls for rank, degree year, quality of degree, and employer type, margins of difference favor men (AAUP 2004).

Research has been inconsistent about whether men scholars have been more successful than women in publication and grant productivity, a major basis of salary awards in higher education. Earlier studies concentrated largely on natural scientists found productivity gaps favoring men, but more recent works suggest a convergence of publication and tenure rates, of women and men in fields such as sociology where women are not tokens (Hargens & Long 2002).

A comprehensive study of faculty shed light on subtle processes leading to gender inequities (MIT 1999). Women faculty recognized the negative impact of the gender climate on their careers and well-being, but felt that complaints would be fruitless. Women faculty were underpaid relative to comparable men and systematically disadvantaged in areas such as teaching loads, assignment of laboratory and office space, access to mentoring and support, and sponsorship for awards and other special opportunities. Women faculty believed they did more mentoring than their male colleagues. Many had experienced sexual harassment, and women believed they would be seriously penalized for having a child or otherwise investing heavily in family.

GENDER AND PEDAGOGY

Few differences in teachers' pedagogical style by gender appear at either the K-12 or the postsecondary level. Where differences exist, they reflect the differential distributions of women and men across elementary and secondary teaching and their locations in different academic specialties using variable pedagogical approaches. Nevertheless, widespread concern that too few men are entering teaching and that male students in public schools in particular lack male role models has resulted in special programs to recruit men, especially men of color, into teaching. Gender differences in pedagogical style at the postsecondary level are more apparent in patterns of out-of-class mentoring and support than in classroom performance.

CURRICULUM AND GENDER CLIMATES

Studies have explored what is taught in schools about gender, in the formal curriculum and the informal, or hidden, curriculum. Reports by American Association of University Women (AAUW 1992–2004) explore ways in which curriculum and gender climates of educational institutions can marginalize women. The reports critique formal curriculum for excluding or trivializing girls and women and for not addressing issues of particular significance to women's lives; for example, pay equity law, family leave policies, or women's health. Staffing patterns in public schools usually place men in positions of authority over women, modeling patriarchal systems for young learners. Furthermore, teachers do not necessarily create, but often tolerate, gender climates that are hostile to girls and women. The AAUW report has drawn criticism for failing to fully consider educational problems of boys and for blaming teachers for gender inequities that they have little power to influence. In many systems, teachers have proactively addressed gender equity issues via efforts to create gender-equitable curricula and educational climates.

At the postsecondary level, studies of gender and teaching focus on whether women students face chilly climates in college classrooms, especially in male-dominated fields such as math and science, and whether they have adequate opportunities for mentoring and sponsorship. Scholars have also explored harassment and other forms of sexual exploitation as they affect women faculty and students. Finally, a growing body of scholarship has examined whether or not women's scholarship is valued as much as men's in making hiring, tenure, promotion, and salary decisions in colleges and universities.

The impact of gender scholarship and feminist thought has been uneven across disciplines. Nevertheless, substantial change in the influence of women is evidenced by the rapid growth of women's and gender studies curricula, departments, and majors. Academic disciplines now include committees to monitor status of women, organizations of women scholars, and publication outlets for gender research. In sociology, the Sociologists for Women in Society and its affiliated journal, *Gender and Society*, are examples.

CONCLUSION

Gender affects teaching careers and advantages for men persist at all levels of education. Yet we know little about why gender inequities persist in teaching, why men are reluctant to enter teaching (despite salary advantages), and why recruitment and retention of teachers of both genders is increasingly problematic. Possible links between these concerns and the feminization of teaching, its semi-professional status, and the professionalization of the field have not been explored in theoretically sophisticated ways. At the postsecondary level, teaching may be threatened with deprofessionalization, just at a point when women comprise a significant presence.

Although studies in local contexts have established the importance of formal and informal curricula and gender climates for teachers and for students, these issues are rarely researched in national studies. We know more about the content of curricula and the characteristics of gender climates of educational institutions than about the long-range impact on teachers and students. We lack a finely nuanced understanding of the role of teachers and educational institutions in reproducing or challenging gender stratification in society.

At the postsecondary level questions remain about how structural changes in colleges and universities will affect the status of women faculty and gender-inclusive scholarship. Women's proportions of college enrollments at all levels continue to increase, and women are likely to make up larger shares of college teachers in the future. As colleges rely more heavily on part-time, contingent workforces, men are leaving academia, and this trend is partly responsible for increasing proportions of women faculty in many disciplines. The implications of these changes are not yet clear.

SEE ALSO: Education, Adult; Educational Inequality; Gender, Education and; Gendered Organizations/Institutions; Professions; Professors; Teachers

REFERENCES AND SUGGESTED READINGS

American Association of University Professors (AAUP) (2004) Online. www.aaup.org/.
Association of American University Women (AAUW) (1992) *How Schools Shortchange Girls: The AAUW Report*. AAUW Educational Foundation, Washington, DC.

Association of American University Women (AAUW) (2004) Online. www.aauw.org/.

Benjamin, E. (2004) Disparities in the Salaries and Appointments of Academic Women and Men: An Update of a 1988 Report of Committee W on the Status of Women in the Academic Profession. AAUP, Washington, DC.

Cognard-Black, A. J. (2004) Will They Stay, or Will They Go? Sex-Atypical Work Among Token Men Who Teach. *Sociological Quarterly* 45 (1): 113–39.

Grant, G. & Murray, C. E. (1999) *Teaching in America: The Slow Revolution.* Harvard University Press, Cambridge, MA.

Hargens, L. H. & Long, J. S. (2002) Demographic Inertia and Women's Representation among Faculty in Higher Education. *Journal of Higher Education* 73 (4): 494–517.

Ingersoll, R. M. (2001) Teacher Turnover and Teacher Shortages: An Organizational Analysis. *American Educational Research Journal* 38 (3): 499–534.

MIT Report (1999) A Study on the Status of Women Faculty in Science at MIT. *MIT Faculty Newsletter: Special Edition* 11 (4). Online. www.mit.edu/fnl/women/women.html.

National Center for Education Statistics (NCES) (2004) Online. www.nces.ed.gov/.

National Science Foundation (NSF) (2004) Online. www.nsf.gov/.

OECD (2004) Education at a Glance: OECD Indicators 2002. Online. www.oecd.org.

Whitebook, M. & Sakai, L. (2004) *By a Thread: How Child Care Centers Hold On to Teachers, How Teachers Build Lasting Careers.* Upjohn Institute, Kalamazoo, MI.

teamwork

Michael A. West

Teams are a particular form of work group. They are groups of people who share responsibility for producing products or delivering services. They share overall work objectives and ideally have the necessary authority, autonomy, and resources to achieve these objectives. Team members are dependent on each other to achieve the objectives and therefore have to work closely, interdependently, and supportively to achieve the team's goals. Members have distinct and clear roles. Effective teams have as few members as necessary to perform the task and are ideally no larger than six to eight members. And the team is recognized by others in the organization as a team. The team rather than the individual is increasingly considered the basic building block of organizations and team-based working the modus operandi of organizations (West et al. 2003).

There are multiple types of teams in organizations: advice and involvement teams, e.g., management decision-making committees, quality control (QC) circles, staff involvement teams; production and service teams, e.g., assembly teams; maintenance, construction, mining, and commercial airline teams; departmental teams; sales and health care teams; project and development teams, e.g., research teams, new product development teams, software development teams; action and negotiation teams, e.g., military combat units, surgical teams, and trade union negotiating teams.

Why work in teams? In many areas of endeavor, research has shown how team working can lead to greater efficiency or effectiveness. An analysis of the combined results of 131 studies of organizational change found that interventions with the largest effects upon financial performance were team development interventions or the creation of autonomous work teams (Macy & Izumi 1993). Applebaum and Batt (1994) reviewed 12 large-scale surveys and 185 case studies of managerial practices. They concluded that team-based working led to improvements in organizational performance on measures of both efficiency and quality. Similarly, Cotton (1993) reports on studies examining the effects of team working on productivity, satisfaction, and absenteeism. The author reviews 57 studies that report improvements on productivity, seven that found no change, and five that report productivity declines, following the implementation of self-directed teams. Finally, studies in health care have repeatedly shown that better patient care is provided when health professionals work together in multidisciplinary teams.

THE HISTORY OF TEAM THEORY AND RESEARCH

The source of the stream of research on teams can be traced to the Hawthorne studies which established the importance of intergroup relations in organizations, the influences of teams on their members, and the importance of informal groups in influencing work-related behavior.

Two strands of thought about teams emerged in the 1960s and 1970s. The first focused on the whole team and examined unconscious phenomena in work teams (Bion 1961). Bion argued that teams developed "basic assumptions" in discussions of organizational culture, which could impede their effective functioning. These include basic assumptions of *dependence* (one of the team's members will look after the needs of the team and ensure its effectiveness); *pairing* (two team members will join together to produce a leader in some way, leading to a sense of messianic anticipation in the team); and *fight–flight* (the team meets to fight an enemy or run away, and is consequently unable to do any effective work). However, little research has been stimulated by this approach.

The second strand has led to considerably more theorizing and research internationally. The sociotechnical tradition proposed that social and task-related outcomes can be optimized through appropriate task and work design – the well-being of team members can be achieved in conjunction with team performance, through the joint optimization of the application of technology, organization, and the use of human resources.

In the last 20 years, there has been an altogether new emphasis amongst writers concerned with understanding work team effectiveness – the organizational context within which teams perform (Hackman 1990; Guzzo & Shea 1992). Hackman (1990), for example, has drawn attention to the influence of organizational reward, training, and information systems in influencing team effectiveness.

Guzzo and Shea developed a reciprocal model of team effectiveness. They argue that *outcome interdependence* among team members leads to higher team effectiveness. Outcome interdependence refers to the extent to which team members are dependent on each other to achieve organizational rewards such as recognition, career advancement, and financial rewards. *Task interdependence* moderates the relationship between outcome interdependence and effectiveness, because outcome interdependence can only lead to greater effectiveness if team members are required to work interdependently to get the job done. But the most significant element of the model (theoretically) is the concept of *potency*, rather like self-efficacy but at the team level characterized by a team sense of likely success and ability to meet challenges. This is a direct predictor of team effectiveness in the model. They extended this approach by proposing that potency best predicts team effectiveness in conjunction with three other factors – the alignment of team goals with organizational goals, organizational rewards for team accomplishments, and the availability of resources for teams.

Another model of team effectiveness has been developed from a focus on team reflexivity. West (1996) argues that most models of team performance tend to present static rather than dynamic processes, yet teams often change rapidly as a result of experience and member turnover, requiring repeated adaptation of communication and decision-making processes. West proposes that what may best predict team effectiveness is an overarching factor influencing all aspects of team performance – team task reflexivity. He argues that teams are effective to the extent that they reflect upon their task objectives, strategies, processes, and environments and adapt these aspects of their functioning accordingly. In relation to the wider organizational environment, non-reflexive teams will tend to comply unquestioningly with organizational demands and expectancies; accept organizational limitations; fail to discuss or challenge organizational incompetence; communicate indebtedness and dependence on the organization; and rely heavily on organizational direction and reassurance. Reflexive teams, in contrast, are more likely to be agents of innovative change within the organization, developing ideas for new and improved products, services, or ways of working.

This brief account of some of the major theoretical approaches illustrates the move toward less descriptive models, which take into account organizational factors and reveal too that researchers are coming to terms with the inherent complexity and cloudiness of real teams in organizations.

TEAM EFFECTIVENESS

Much effort has been devoted to understanding the factors which promote team effectiveness. The thinking of most researchers has been dominated by an input–process–output model, mainly because of its simplicity and utility. Inputs include the task of the team, team composition (size, functional and demographic diversity, tenure), and organizational context (such as culture, support for team working, structure). Some processes mediate the relationships between inputs and outputs such as participation mediating the effects of diversity upon innovation, while some inputs such as organizational context directly influence outputs. Processes include participation (influence over decision-making, interactions, and information sharing), leadership, conflict, decision-making, interteam processes, and reflexivity. Team outputs include productivity, innovation, team member well-being, and team learning.

Inputs to Teams

The team task. The task a team performs is a fundamental influence on the work team, defining its structural, process, and functional requirements – who is in the team, what their roles are, how they should work together, and the nature and processes of the tasks they individually and collectively perform.

Dimensions for classifying task characteristics include task difficulty; solution multiplicity; intrinsic interest; cooperative requirement tasks which are unitary versus divisible, conjunctive, disjunctive, and additive; conflict versus cooperation elements; and conceptual versus behavioral components. These classification systems, developed by social psychologists, have not been fruitful for researchers exploring team performance and innovation in organizational settings, probably because such goals as producing television programs, battleground training, health care, product development, and providing financial services cannot be neatly categorized into discrete tasks and subtasks.

Sociotechnical systems theory (STST) provides a powerful framework for examining the effects of task design upon work team innovation. Sociotechnical systems theorists argue that autonomous work teams provide a structure through which the demands of the social and technical subsystems of an organization can be jointly optimized. The key to effective performance is then whether the work team can control variation in quality and quantity of task performance at source. The joint optimization of the two subsystems is more likely when work teams have the following characteristics:

- The team is a relatively independent organizational unit that is responsible for a whole task.
- The tasks of members are related in content so that awareness of a common task is evoked and maintained and members are required to work interdependently.
- There is a "unity of product and organization," i.e., the team has a complete task to perform and team members can "identify with their own product."

The *task* characteristics that evoke "task orientation" or intrinsic motivation (and therefore innovation) according to STST are:

- completeness (i.e., whole tasks);
- varied demands;
- opportunities for social interaction;
- autonomy;
- opportunities for learning;
- development possibilities for the task.

Team composition. Team composition – used here to refer to the "mix" of members making up a team – has been examined in various ways. One examines the question of whether heterogeneity is advantageous to groups. The theoretical perspectives that have guided much of the research in this area include the attraction–selection–attrition model, similarity–attraction theory, and self-categorization theory. A basic premise of all three is that we are attracted to those who are similar to us and thus organize, and evaluate, our social worlds accordingly. In the second line of research, it is assumed that heterogeneity is valuable but groups need to have the right mix of members. This approach questions which combination of roles, styles, or skills fits together particularly well and which types of people are needed within groups. Research in this area has tended to focus on heterogeneity in terms of demographic variables, skills, attitudes, cognitive ability, and, more recently, personality traits. Although much of the early research on group heterogeneity examined experimental laboratory-based groups, focus on "real-world" groups has typified more recent research in this area.

Some studies suggest facilitative effects of heterogeneity on team performance. This pattern is most likely when the characteristics in question are skills or educational specialization. Strategic management initiatives appear more likely to be made by groups that were heterogeneous with respect to educational specialization. More recently, studies in health care suggest that the greater the number of professional groups represented in teams, the higher the levels of innovation in patient care. It might be that skill heterogeneity means that each group member is more likely to have non-redundant – and, presumably, relevant – expertise to contribute to the team activities. Groups that include both diverse and overlapping knowledge domains and skills are particularly creative.

Some debate has surrounded the question of whether it is advantageous to have groups that are homogeneous or heterogeneous with respect to cognitive ability. Results of two recent meta-analyses suggest that the relation between ability heterogeneity and performance may be somewhat complex. Based on these analyses, it appears that, in general, ability heterogeneity and performance are unrelated. Thus, there would seem little justification to select team members with a view to dispersing their cognitive ability levels.

Teams which are diverse in task-related attributes are often diverse in relation to attributes inherent in the individual. These relation-oriented characteristics can trigger stereotypes and prejudice which, via intergroup conflict (Hogg & Abrams 1988), can affect group processes and outcomes. For example, turnover rates are higher in groups that are heterogeneous with respect to age. Two studies that have examined ethnicity diversity in groups have suggested that the effects of diversity may change over time. Milliken and Martins (1996) suggested that ethnic diversity in groups can have negative effects on individual and group outcomes, primarily early in a group's life. Similarly, in one of the very few longitudinal studies in this area, Watson et al. (1993) reported that groups that were heterogeneous with respect to culture initially performed, on a series of business case exercises, more poorly than culturally homogeneous groups. As group members gained experience with each other over time, however, performance difference between culturally homogeneous and heterogeneous groups largely disappeared.

Organizational supports. Various organizational contextual factors have been proposed as important in predicting team effectiveness. Reward systems, such as public recognition, preferred work assignments, and money, have long been known to provide motivation and affect performance, particularly when the rewards are contingent upon task achievement. Gladstein found that pay and recognition had an effect, especially upon the leader's behavior and the way the group structured itself. Hackman (1990) identified two contingencies: whether the rewards are administered to the group as a whole or to individuals, and whether the rewards provide incentives for collaboration or delegation of tasks to individuals (the former, in both cases, are associated with positive relationships between rewards and group effectiveness). Feedback is important for setting realistic goals and fostering high group commitment. In addition, high job satisfaction requires accurate feedback from both the task and other group members. However, group feedback can be difficult to provide to teams with either long cycles of work or one-off projects. Limited empirical evidence suggests training is correlated with both self-reported team effectiveness and managers' judgments of effectiveness.

Team Processes

The second major element of the input–process–output model is team processes. Among these, the most consistently important factor in determining team effectiveness is the existence of team goals or objectives (Guzzo & Shea 1992).

Objectives. The clarity or specificity of goals has also been shown to predict team performance outcomes. In order to combine efforts effectively, team members have to understand collectively what it is they are trying to achieve. Much research also indicates that involvement in goal-setting fosters commitment to those goals and consequently better team performance.

Participation. The second factor of central theoretical and empirical concern in the study of team performance is the notion of participation.

Research on participation in decision-making has a long history, revealing that participation tends to foster greater team effectiveness and commitment. When people participate in decision-making through having influence, interacting with those involved in the change process, and sharing information, they tend to invest in the outcomes of those decisions and to offer ideas for new and improved ways of working. In Europe, schemes to increase participation have resulted in higher levels of innovation among industrial workers. At the organizational level, most writers concur that high centralization of decision-making (low participation) inhibits innovation, although there is limited empirical evidence to support these views.

Task conflict. A central theme in the teamwork literatures is that divergent thinking and the management of competing perspectives are important processes in teamwork. Such processes are characteristic of task-related team conflict and controversy. Tjosvold and colleagues have argued similarly that constructive controversy in teams improves the quality of decision-making (Tjosvold 1991). Constructive controversy is characterized by full exploration of opposing opinions and frank analyses of task-related issues. Constructive controversy occurs when decision-makers believe they are in a cooperative team context where mutually beneficial goals are emphasized, rather than in a competitive context, where decision-makers feel their personal competence is confirmed rather than questioned, and where they perceive processes of mutual influence rather than attempted dominance. Another perspective on conflict comes from minority influence theory. A number of researchers have shown that minority consistency of arguments over time is likely to lead to change in majority views in teams (Nemeth & Owens 1996). A homogeneous team in which minority dissent is suppressed will reduce creativity, innovation, individuality, and independence.

Outputs

The final component of the input–process–output model is outputs and this refers to team effectiveness or productivity, team innovation (new and improved products, services, ways of working), team member well-being and satisfaction, and team viability and attachment (the cohesion and commitment to the team shown by team members). This model continues to dominate in research but it is giving way to new concerns.

CURRENT AND FUTURE EMPHASES IN TEAM RESEARCH

The focus of research is increasingly turning toward an understanding of micro and macro processes hitherto neglected by researchers and theorists. The first is a concern with agreement within teams about their perceptions of team processes and outputs manifested in theorizing about team "mental models." These refer to team members' implicit and (to a greater or lesser extent) shared models of their team and its functioning as well as the wider environment with which the team engages (schema congruence and accuracy). High levels of congruence and accuracy are predicted to relate to team effectiveness. The methodological challenges of measuring shared mental models are yet to be overcome.

This concern is matched by a strong focus on trust, identity, and attachment in teams as factors that promote individual cooperation in teams (Korsgaard et al. 2003). Trust is defined as "the individual's intention to accept vulnerability to the group based on the expectation that the group will act in a considerate and benevolent manner toward the individual" (Korsgaard et al. 2003: 116).

However, the most vigorous new developments in this area are likely to relate to research into team-based organizations (Agarwal 2003). The study of work teams has developed rich understanding of social processes and performance in organizations (West et al. 2003) and the future for this area is immensely promising. The challenge now is to understand the functioning of team-based organizations (or multi-team systems) and how they can be structured and developed to maximize the benefits of this basic form of human functioning in modern, large, complex organizational settings. Moreover, as alliances and networks develop within and between organizations, the spotlight of research is also exploring how teams can operate effectively across organizational boundaries (e.g., joint venture teams) and across networks to enable people to cooperate on tasks that no single organization can accomplish.

SEE ALSO: Group Processes; Organizations as Social Structures; Organizations, Voluntary

REFERENCES AND SUGGESTED READINGS

Agarwal, R. (2003) Teamwork in the Netcentric Organization. In: West, M. A., Tjosvold, D., & Smith, K. G. (Eds.), *International Handbook of Organizational Teamwork and Cooperative Working*. Wiley, Chichester, ch. 21.

Applebaum, E. & Batt, R. (1994) *The New American Workplace*. ILR Press, Ithaca, NY.

Bion, W. R. (1961) *Experiences in Groups and Other Papers*. Basic Books, New York.

Cotton, J. L. (1993) *Employee Involvement*. Sage, Newbury Park, CA.

Gladstein, D. (1984) Groups in Context: A Model of Task Group Effectiveness. *Administrative Science Quarterly* 29: 499–517.

Guzzo, R. A. & Shea, G. P. (1992) Group Performance and Intergroup Relations in Organizations. In: Dunnette, M. D. & Hough, L. M. (Eds.), *Handbook of Industrial and Organizational Psychology*, Vol. 3. Consulting Psychologists Press, Palo Alto, CA, pp. 269–313.

Hackman, J. R. (Ed.) (1990) *Groups That Work (and Those That Don't): Creating Conditions for Effective Teamwork*. Jossey Bass, San Francisco.

Hackman, J. R. (1992) Group Influences on Individuals in Organizations. In: Dunnette, M. D. & Hough, L. M. (Eds.), *Handbook of Industrial and Organizational Psychology*, 2nd edn. Consulting Psychologists Press, Palo Alto, CA, pp. 199–26.

Hogg, M. & Abrams, D. (1988) *Social Identifications: A Social Psychology of Intergroup Relations and Group Processes*. Routledge, London.

Korsgaard, M. A., Brodt, S. E., & Sapienza, H. J. (2003) Trust, Identity, and Attachment: Promoting Individuals' Cooperation in Groups. In: West, M. A., Tjosvold, D., & Smith, K. G. (Eds.), *International Handbook of Organizational Teamwork and Cooperative Working*. Wiley, Chichester, ch. 6.

Macy, B. A. & Izumi, H. (1993) Organizational Change, Design, and Work Innovation: A Meta-Analysis of 131 North American Field Studies, 1961–1991. *Research in Organizational Change and Development* 7: 235–313.

Milliken, F. J. & Martins, L. L. (1996) Searching for Common Threads: Understanding the Multiple Effects of Diversity in Organizational Groups. *Academy of Management Review* 21(2): 402–33.

Nemeth, C. & Owens, P. (1996) Making Work Groups More Effective: The Value of Minority Dissent. In: West, M. A. (Ed.), *Handbook of Work Group Psychology*. Wiley, Chichester, pp. 125–42.

Roethlisberger, F. J. & Dickson, W. J. (1939) *Management and the Worker*. Harvard University Press, Cambridge, MA.

Tjosvold, D. (1991) *Team Organization: An Enduring Competitive Advantage*. Wiley, Chichester.

Turner, J. C. (1987) *Rediscovering the Social Group: A Self-Categorization Theory*. Blackwell, Oxford.

Watson, W. E., Kumar, K., & Michaelsen, L. K. (1993) Cultural Diversity's Impact on Interaction Process and Performance: Comparing Homogeneous and Diverse Task Groups. *Academy of Management Journal* 36: 590–602.

West, M. A. (1996) Reflexivity and Work Group Effectiveness: A Conceptual Integration. In: West, M. A. (Ed.), *Handbook of Work Group Psychology*. Wiley, Chichester, pp. 555–79.

West, M. A., Tjosvold, D., & Smith, K. G. (Eds.) (2003) *International Handbook of Organizational Teamwork and Cooperative Working*. Wiley, Chichester.

technological determinism

Alan Bryman

Technological determinism refers to the thesis that the path of social change is directly influenced by technological developments. As such the thesis ascribes agency to an inert object, namely technology, in human affairs and their development.

It is common to distinguish between hard and soft versions of the thesis. The hard version views technology as the sole determinant of social development, whereas the soft version depicts it as one among several other factors and as greatly implicated in the social circumstances out of which it arises. The soft version thus moderates the anti-determinist's dislike of the ascription of agency to a thing and of the marginalizing of human intervention.

Nowadays, technological determinism is considered a discredited thesis about the nature of society. Few social scientists today would describe themselves as technological determinists without qualifying the description considerably. A lingering technological determinism can sometimes be discerned in approaches that seek to depict technology as both cause and effect (e.g., Hughes 1994).

Technological determinism was particularly influential in sociological studies of work and organizations. In the 1950s and 1960s, studies of work contexts like the automobile assembly line frequently construed the largely negative work attitudes of workers as directly produced by the technology with which they worked. The most sophisticated version of this approach can be discerned in Blauner (1964), where four different production technologies in US industry (craft, machine tending, assembly line, and process) were examined. Blauner showed that levels of work alienation varied systematically by the prevailing technology in the industries concerned. Another prominent study was Woodward's (1965) British investigation of technology in relation to organization structure. Woodward showed that structures varied by the prevailing technology of the organization in terms of characteristics like the flatness of the hierarchy. The suggestion that it was necessary to achieve a good fit between technology and organization structure was perceived as a corrective to the view that there could be universal laws of administration that could be applied without regard to an organization's special circumstances.

A number of problems with technological determinism have been identified. First, it is pointed out that a technology is designed with specific purposes and applications in mind, so that the "effects" that technological determinists claim to identify are in fact natural outcomes of how designers envisioned its purpose. Secondly, it is often observed that a technology can be implemented in several different ways, so that the supposed outcomes of its application are in fact the result of the ways in which it is introduced and executed (e.g., Buchanan & Boddy 1983). Third, technologies are interpretively flexible and as such can be construed in

different ways by those responsible for making them operational and by users (Grint & Woolgar 1997). Fourth, in the context of work situations, it is often pointed out that people bring to the workplace a variety of orientations that will also play a significant role in conditioning their work attitudes and behavior (e.g., Goldthorpe et al. 1968).

While technological determinism is frequently seen as outdated, it should not be replaced with the equally extreme view that technologies have no implications for human affairs, since technologies are responsible for constraining responses to them, as several writers have observed (e.g., Law 1992; Orlikowski 1992).

SEE ALSO: Actor-Network Theory; Organization Theory; Organizational Contingencies; Scientific Knowledge, Sociology of; Technology, Science, and Culture; Work, Sociology of

REFERENCES AND SUGGESTED READINGS

Blauner, R. (1964) *Alienation and Freedom*. University of Chicago Press, Chicago.
Buchanan, D. A. & Boddy, D. (1983) *Organizations in the Computer Age: Technological Imperatives and Strategic Choice*. Gower, Aldershot.
Goldthorpe, J. H., Lockwood, D., Bechhofer, F., & Platt, J. (1968) *The Affluent Worker: Industrial Attitudes and Behaviour*. Cambridge University Press, Cambridge.
Grint, K. & Woolgar, S. (1997) *The Machine at Work: Technology, Work and Organization*. Polity Press, Cambridge.
Hodson, R. (1996) Dignity in the Workplace under Participative Management: *Alienation and Freedom*. Revisited. *American Sociological Review* 61(5): 719–38.
Hughes, T. P. (1994) Technological Momentum. In: Smith, M. R. & Marx, L. (Eds.), *Does Technology Drive History? The Dilemma of Technological Determinism*. MIT Press, Cambridge, MA, pp. 101–14.
Law, J. (1992) Notes on the Theory of the Actor-Network: Ordering, Strategy, and Heterogeneity. *Systems Practice* 5(4): 379–93.
Orlikowski, W. J. (1992) The Duality of Technology: Rethinking the Concept of Technology in Organizations. *Organization Science* 3(3): 398–426.
Woodward, J. (1965) *Industrial Organization: Theory and Practice*. Oxford University Press, Oxford.

technological innovation

Polly S. Rizova

The topic of technological innovation has been fascinating generations of scholars, managers, and policymakers ever since Schumpeter's influential *Theory of Economic Development* (1934) appeared in English. In it, he compellingly argued that the survival of firms as well as that of society is dependent upon their ability to perpetually find new uses for the existing resources and to recombine the latter in novel ways. The economic and social changes in the western world, particularly after the Industrial Revolution, are attributed to a considerable degree to technological innovations.

At first addressed by economists, the topic has become of interest to an array of social science disciplines such as sociology, management science, industrial psychology, and the history of technology. Empirical research on the economic and social determinants and consequences of technological innovation surged in the 1980s and 1990s when leading scholarly journals devoted special issues to it: *Administrative Science Quarterly* (1990), *Strategic Management Journal* (1990), and the *Academy of Management Journal* (1996). *Social Studies of Science* was even more specific; in 1992 it published a symposium on "Failed Innovations."

Technological innovation is defined as a process which stretches from the origination to the development, implementation, and diffusion of new products or processes which have market and social value. Innovation is not to be identified with the act of scientific discovery or invention. The latter marks the very first occurrence of an *idea* for a novel product or process; the former encapsulates the deliberate *actions* of people from diverse organizational units – research and development (R&D), manufacturing, and marketing – to develop and to commercialize it. All through, it is ideas and knowledge that are sought, processed, and transmitted by both people and organizations. That is why technological innovation is conceived of as an information and knowledge-processing activity which takes place in an organizational context and goes beyond the generation of a creative idea in the minds of single individuals.

In the years after World War II, a set view regarding what the force is behind technological innovation took prominence; namely, that scientific technical research is the single most important drive for innovation and, consequently, for economic development. Promulgated by Vannevar Bush in *Science: The Endless Frontier* (1945), it became known as the "linear model." This model was the framework used to inform all efforts to organize for successful innovation up to the 1980s. It rests on the assumption that innovation results from the application of science in a process which takes place through well-defined sequential linear stages – scientific research, development, production, and marketing. Not only are the stages neatly defined, but so are their technical objectives and output. According to this understanding, innovation moves from one stage to the next after a successful completion of each stage's goals. Hence, by its nature, the model takes for granted that technological innovation springs from the new scientific knowledge and breakthroughs created in the first stage. Not surprisingly, research from this period addressed the link between science, scientific knowledge, and new technology. This view was also mirrored in the high level of government funding for university research and federal R&D laboratories.

An important shift in the contemporary understanding of technological innovation has been marked by the recognition of what technological innovation is *not* – namely, a linear process. Research in the 1980s demonstrated that although scientific research continues to be a viable source for innovations, the large majority of them began with a recognized market demand. It is often the case that a technological innovation is initiated at the stage located at the very end of the "linear model," from where it moves backward and forward throughout the rest. Hence, it involves nested goal formation and problem-solving activities grounded in an iterative interaction between science, technology, and the market. The relative importance that scientific research and the market play in technological innovation, though, varies over time, with the size of a firm, and between, as well as within, industries. For instance, in *Forces of Production* (1984), David Noble shows that although the preponderance of innovations, as measured in absolute numbers, stemmed from market-driven competition, critical innovations such as supercomputers, integrated circuits, and the digital control of manufacturing were directly linked to government-funded research. A reflection of this new way of looking at *why* and *how* innovation happens is the continuous search for design forms which are to respond to the need for coordination and information exchange between the multiple organizational divisions that take part in the innovation process.

The literature discusses four types of technological innovation. When the classification criterion is the locus of technological change, the differentiation is between *product* and *process* innovations. The former concerns any change to a firm's existing product or service portfolio; the latter refers to a change that the company introduces in the way a product is made or service is provided. More recent research has suggested that it is somewhat misleading to regard the two as completely independent from each other. Rather, as Utterback demonstrates in *Mastering the Dynamics of Innovation* (1994), they ought to be seen in an interrelated relationship in which their relative importance for the firm changes over time. Depending on the degree of technical change that is introduced to a final product or process when compared to the existing state of technology and the knowledge base, a distinction is made between *incremental* and *radical* technological innovations. *Incremental* innovation corresponds to a little departure from the currently existing and relied-upon technical and scientific knowledge and practices; it only adds new features to an already existing product or process. In contrast, *radical* technological innovation involves a drastic departure from the existing technology, knowledge base, and practices; it is normally linked to a breakthrough in knowledge (e.g., the introduction of the airplane) (Damanpour 1998).

An important reason for distinguishing between radical and incremental innovation lies in the complexity of scientific knowledge that they draw upon and the degree of the predictability of the tasks associated with carrying out research and development. As a result, each imposes different requirements on staffing and organizing. For example, testing the conventional mechanical properties of batches of commercial plastics is a highly predictable task. The complexity of a task refers to the requirement that knowledge must be drawn from multiple knowledge domains that are at most only loosely connected to one another. Complex tasks deal with ill-structured, ambiguous technical circumstances that require assessment of the implications of multiple, and perhaps conflicting, knowledge domains to characterize them in terms of the actions needed. Simple tasks, on the other hand, deal with circumstances that are perceived to fall into the range of ordered experience, to conform to a well-established paradigm. Integrating knowledge from medical practice, electronics, chemistry, and mechanical engineering to produce a concept for a medical magnetic resonance imaging device is a highly complex task. So too may be that of deciding which are the important characteristics of a plastic to test, while the selection of procedures to carry out routine tests is generally a simple task.

Technological innovation has been studied qualitatively and quantitatively at the level of the individual, the project, and the organization, as well as at the intra- and interindustry levels. A wide array of topics has received coverage ranging from paradigm shifts, organizational learning, entrepreneurship, knowledge organizations, individual and organizational creativity, and, of course, how to organize for and succeed at innovation.

Much of the empirical research has been focused on structure and the investigation of the effect of the formal organization on the individual and firm behavior and outcomes. After decades of preoccupation with discovering the "one best way to organize," the contingency tradition, which developed in the 1960s, broke the old model. In this tradition, organizational structure is shaped by the nature of the technology and then in turn shapes the relationships between people in the work processes. In *The Management of Innovation* (1961), Burns and Stalker studied the relationship between a firm's innovativeness and organization design in 20 British electronics and rayon firms. They argued that *organic* (decentralized and less formalized) structures are conducive to technological innovation, particularly a radical one, as they are better able to respond rapidly to the ever-changing environment, whereas *mechanistic*

4954 *technological innovation*

(bureaucratic and highly formalized) organization forms tend to be innovation-resistant. The literature on the management of technological innovation has examined various structural aspects and the conditions under which they affect the ability of individuals and organizations to innovate. Examples of those are: centralization, formalization, horizontal and vertical integration, and stage of industry development. The research informed by this tradition mostly relied on large surveys and statistical methodology to infer the effect of different structural arrangements on performance. Ultimately, it produced valuable insights and, much to the dissatisfaction of the managers of technology, one broad design rule: "*it all depends.*"

By the late 1970s, the structural contingency school was heavily criticized for focusing exclusively on the investigation of the formal structural attributes at the expense of neglecting the contribution of informal structures. This void has been filled by another structuralist approach – the social networks perspective. The origin of the social networks perspective can be traced to Simmel's (1950) work on dyads and triads, but it was Granovetter's (1985) seminal article that carved a prominent place in social research for the individuals and the social relations that they establish and maintain. Unlike the traditional structuralist approach which looks at performance as a function of the relationship between positions and people as *prescribed* by an organization chart, the social networks perspective seeks to capture the *actual* patterns of linkages and relations. It is based on the premise that the actors' behaviors and outcomes can be understood through the informal structural configurations (friendship, advice, and collegial networks) that they are a part of, and the positions they occupy within them (high or low respect, status and informal power). At the center of the social network analysis is an examination of the form and content of the stable patterns people develop in their relationships, as well as the effects these create.

The impact of social networks, their structural properties, and the social capital they create on outcomes has been investigated at multiple levels of analysis. This literature is replete with empirical evidence of the advantages that the informal structures offer over the formally prescribed rules and behaviors to technological success (van de Ven 1986; Powell & Brantley 1992; Ibarra 1993). Informal structures have been shown to foster innovation through the creation of opportunities for learning, expanding on one's communication network and easing access to knowledge and information (Allen 1977; Tushman 1977).

Yet another influential stream of research on innovation, a qualitative one, came from the social constructivist perspective. In the 1980s it has been applied to scrutinize the production of scientific knowledge, technology, and technological innovation. The latter, according to this view, is not to be understood as a result of following the natural progression of technological development. Rather, it is seen as emerging from the constant interaction between technology and social processes. It is this interaction that explains how some innovations come to fruition and others do not, and why the same technologically sound projects could be funded under one type of social arrangement and abandoned under a different social cast. This literature gave us the insight that the same technologies could have different meanings to different people; thus, it addressed the question of *how* decisions on technology are reached and what role those who have interest in them play (Bijker et al. 1994).

Despite the impressive amount of empirical studies, the research on technological innovation is marked by inconsistent findings. Years of investigation and valuable contributions have not converged into a dominant theoretical perspective which incorporates the multiple streams of innovation research. This could be, at least, partially explained by the fact that innovation has been studied by researchers who represent a multitude of academic disciplines; their efforts and findings, though, are yet to be integrated. A systematic investigation designed to shed light on the phenomenon from more than a single theoretical perspective simultaneously is also lacking. Furthermore, there is a need for more studies which approach the understanding of innovation from a multilevel standpoint. The future research on technological innovation will need to address these issues.

SEE ALSO: Industrial Revolution; Science, Social Construction of; Scientific Knowledge, Sociology of; Social Network Analysis;

Technological Determinism; Technology, Science, and Culture

REFERENCES AND SUGGESTED READINGS

Allen, T. (1977) *Managing the Flow of Technology*. MIT Press, Cambridge, MA.

Bijker, W., Hughes, T., & Pinch, T. (1994) *The Social Construction of Technological Systems: New Directions in the Sociology and History of Technology*. MIT Press, Cambridge, MA.

Damanpour, F. (1998) Innovation Type, Radicalness, and the Adoption Process. *Communication Research* 15: 545–67.

Fagerberg, J., Mowery, D., & Nelson, R. (Eds.) (2005) *The Oxford Handbook of Innovation*. Oxford University Press, Oxford.

Granovetter, M. (1985) Economic Action and Social Structure: The Problem of Embeddedness. *American Journal of Sociology* 91: 481–510.

Ibarra, H. (1993) Network Centrality, Power, and Innovation Involvement: Determinants of Technical and Administrative Roles. *Academy of Management Journal* 36(3): 471–501.

Powell, W. & Brantley, P. (1992) Competitive Cooperation in Biotechnology: Learning Through Networks? In: Nohria, N. & Eccles, R. (Eds.), *Networks and Organizations: Structure, Form, and Action*. HBS, Boston, MA, pp. 366–94.

Simmel, G. (1950) *The Sociology of Georg Simmel*. Ed. K. H. Wolff. Free Press, New York.

Tushman, M. (1977) Communication Across Organizational Boundaries: Special Boundary Roles in the Innovation Process. *Administrative Science Quarterly* 22: 587–605.

Van de Ven, A. (1986) Central Problems in the Management of Innovation. *Management Science* 32(5): 590–607.

technology, science, and culture

Noah Efron

It is because the sciences, especially the natural sciences, were for so long, and by so many, taken to be divorced from culture that their great interpenetration with culture remains surprising and, in some circles, controversial. In recent decades, historians, sociologists, and anthropologists of science have documented many ways in which cultural influences have affected the development of the sciences, and in which sciences have left an imprint on seemingly far-flung aspects of culture. This scholarship has been vigorously, sometimes viciously, disputed by scientists and others who still see the sciences as largely unswayed by the cultures in which they are practiced. In the 1990s, this dispute became commonly, if rather grandly, known as "the Science Wars."

It is difficult to characterize the relationships between science and culture because neither "science" nor "culture" is easily defined. "Science" typically refers to a set of practices aiming to uncover and formalize regularities in nature, and to the bodies of knowledge these practices produce. Since both the practices and the bodies of knowledge have varied by epoch, place, and discipline, however, any general characterization of science is partial and problematic. "Culture" too is a general term that has no universally accepted referent. Alfred Kroeber and Clyde Kluckhohn famously catalogued over 200 definitions of culture, including "the social legacy the individual acquires from his group," "a way of thinking, feeling, and believing," and "the storehouse of pooled learning." A recent United Nations declaration reckoned culture as the "set of distinctive spiritual, material, intellectual, and emotional features of society or a social group," and that it "encompasses, in addition to art and literature, lifestyles, ways of living together, value systems, traditions, and beliefs." The relationships between "science" and "culture," then, are relationships between hazy and ill-grasped concepts.

Often, these relationships are viewed from one of two opposite directions. One concerns the impacts that culture has on science and technology, while the other concerns the influences of science and technology on culture. This crass division is problematic in the eyes of many because it assumes that "culture" and "science and technology" are fundamentally independent entities. For those who see science as a complex of human activities that are cultural from the ground up, the distinction between culture and science is misleading (making no more sense than similarly distinguishing between, say, culture and music). Still, the notion that science and culture *are* fundamentally independent realms has a long history, and remains influential to this day. For this reason, at least, there is heuristic value in distinguishing between the place of culture in science, and that of science in culture, so long as the limitations of this distinction are acknowledged.

CULTURE IN SCIENCE AND TECHNOLOGY

The view that science is free from cultural influences was most rigorously (and influentially) formulated by a group of scientists and philosophers meeting regularly in 1920s Vienna. This "Vienna Circle," as it became known, included some of the greatest philosophers of the twentieth century – Rudolf Carnap, Karl Hempel, Moritz Schlick, and A. J. Ayer, to name a few – who developed a philosophy that became known as logical positivism, or logical empiricism. These philosophers saw in science the best exemplar of knowledge properly won. Science, as they saw it, ideally had two ways of ascertaining and verifying knowledge: direct observation and logic. No other source of knowledge (like tradition, intuition, or revelation) could be considered credible.

This view implied that good science is by its nature insusceptible to cultural influences, because it is a product solely of the logical manipulation of sense data. If the laws of nature are the same in New York and Nairobi, generating similar sense data, then the logical positivist view of science left no room for local culture to affect science. Indeed, in the view of many philosophers, scientists, and others who embraced this view, the greatest virtue of the scientific method was that it allowed flawed and subjective human beings to produce highly reliable, objective knowledge. As they saw it, science – unlike art, literature, philosophy, politics, couture, cuisine, and practically every other human endeavor – transcends human culture, a view that is sometimes called "scientific exceptionalism."

Though this image of scientific knowledge as uniquely divorced from the culture has retained currency in some circles to the present day, its heyday was brief. In July 1931, a Soviet physicist named Boris Hessen delivered before the Second International Congress of the History of Science and Technology in Kensington, London, an address entitled "The Social and Economic Roots of Newton's *Principia*." In it, Hessen insisted that Newton's physics was influenced by class ideology and by the practical needs of moneyed Englishmen. These claims were embraced by some Marxist philosophers and scientists eager to see a link between early modern science and the culture of emerging capitalism, and they were rejected by many others for whom Hessen's paper was a crass attack on the intellectual purity of science. In 1935, Polish economist Henryk Grossman published in *Zeitschrift für Sozialforschung* a paper further developing Hessen's approach, called "The Social Foundations of Mechanistic Philosophy and Manufacture." In the same year, Ludwig Fleck argued in a book called *Genesis and Development of a Scientific Fact* that "thought styles" in medicine and science greatly influence even seemingly objective observations. One year later, American sociologist of science Robert K. Merton completed a Harvard dissertation entitled "Science, Technology, and Society in 17th-Century England," tracing links between the rise of science and both Puritan ideology and contemporary economic circumstance. These works and other "externalist" accounts (so called because they attributed scientific development to factors outside science itself) challenged the positivist account of the advance of science, suggesting that cultural, social, political, and economic factors greatly affected science, even influencing the very content of scientific theories.

Partly in response to these challenges, in 1938 philosopher Hans Reichenbach distinguished between what he called the "context of discovery" in science, in which accident, human foibles, and social and cultural forces played a part, and the "context of justification," in which objective observation, logic, and reason alone determine which hypotheses are accepted and which are rejected. If cultural factors had any impact upon science at all, Reichenbach and the logical positivists insisted, it was limited to the messy and uninteresting "context of discovery." But over ensuing decades, historians, sociologists, and anthropologists continued to describe cultural and social influences in almost every aspect of science. The most influential of these was Thomas Kuhn, who asserted in *The Structure of Scientific Revolutions* that science does not progress by amassing and correlating observations, but rather through sudden changes in fashion after which prior theories, and even data, acquire new meaning. Echoing Fleck, and drawing some inspiration from gestalt psychology, Kuhn argued that sense data themselves appear different to different researchers working from within different theoretical orientations. A Chinese acupuncturist and a Canadian cardiologist will see different symptoms in the same patient.

Kuhn's book inspired a great deal of research, some challenging his outlook, and some taking it much farther than Kuhn himself could endorse. Philosopher of science Paul Feyerabend concluded that science has no overarching method at all, and that in research "anything goes." Further, he declared in the 1975 introduction to the Chinese translation of his famous book *Against Method* that "First World science is one science among many." Different cultures produce different sciences. One of the most spirited efforts to describe the interpenetration of sciences and sociocultural factors was conceived at about this time in Edinburgh (and advanced by Barry Barnes, David Bloor, Donald MacKenzie, Steven Shapin, Andrew Pickering, and others) and called the "Strong Program." Its aim, according to Bloor, was to show that "it was not possible anymore to hold a vision of science as exempt from social influences." The accuracy or "truth" of a scientific theory can never be taken to explain its acceptance, Bloor and his colleagues insisted, because it is acceptance on the part of a scientific community that determines which theories are considered accurate and "true." Thus, it is not just "logic, rationality, and truth" that explain the progress of science, but also sociocultural negotiations within a scientific community. This view, embraced and expanded by a generation of historians, sociologists, and anthropologists of science, was developed into what became known as the "social constructivist" (or sometimes "social constructionist") view of science, which held that what is taken to be true among scientists reflects social consensus among them, and not bedrock facts about nature. Scholars advocating the "social construction of technology" (SCOT) have similarly described how technologies do not evolve according to an inevitable logic of their own, but are constituted through ongoing negotiations between engineers, consumers, users, marketers, and others, and as a result reflect a mosaic of social and cultural assumptions.

In recent decades, feminist historians and philosophers of science like Evelyn Fox-Keller and Donna Haraway have argued that cultural assumptions about gender greatly influence the production of scientific knowledge. Casual and commonplace sexist presumptions lead scientists to misrepresent women's physiology, psychology, and social roles, as well as to prefer certain sorts of scientific theories (reductive ones, for instance) over other sorts (holistic ones). More radically, Sandra Harding and other feminist scholars of science have argued that scientists' canons of epistemology – what they take to be knowledge and how they seek knowledge – are themselves conditioned in part by gender. In this view, often called "standpoint epistemology," what counts for evidence and argument may differ between female and male scientists. Other philosophers have emphasized that aesthetic considerations have greatly influenced which scientific theories have been accepted and which rejected. ("One can always make a theory, many theories, to account for known facts," wrote Nobel physicist George Thomson, "the test is aesthetic.") Still others have emphasized the impact of literary conventions on science, arguing that canons of literary coherence influence which scientific theories are accepted and which are rejected. Sociologist of science Karin Knorr-Cetina has recently argued that scientific knowledge is mediated through varying "epistemic cultures, shaped by affinity, necessity, and historical coincidence." Taken together, sociologists, anthropologists, historians, and philosophers of science have, in the past 70 years, described how religion, politics, economics, class, gender, race, art, etiquette, and many other ambient aspects of culture and society have affected the process and products of science. Scholars have found traces of these influences in every facet of scientific practice: choice of subject to investigate, experimental design, observation, inference, analysis, publication, and more. These findings have been embraced by many, probably most, scholars who study science, but they have remained a subject of acrimonious debate.

SCIENCE AND TECHNOLOGY IN CULTURE

Little (if anything at all) in modern, western culture remains untouched by science and technology. Science has long found a place in the arts, for instance. Science and scientists have been a recurring theme in modern literature, from John Donne's "The Anatomy of the World: The First Anniversary" and Molière's *The Learned Ladies* to Mary Shelley's *Frankenstein*, Sinclair Lewis's *Arrowsmith*, and on to recent generations' torrent of science fiction. Science has left imprints on centuries of painters and sculptors. Leon Battista Alberti acknowledged as much in his *On Painting* (1435), which applied classical optics and geometry to techniques for producing perspective on canvas. Leonardo da Vinci's painting reflects years of patient empirical study of the human form, as well as of physical and mechanical principles. Andreas Vesalius's *De Fabrica* (1543) was at once an anatomy atlas and a masterpiece of early modern artistic engraving. The tradition of artists consulting natural philosophers and scientists to perfect their craft continued unabated to the modern epoch when, for example, studies of vision carried out by researchers like Hermann von Helmholtz were eagerly devoured by early impressionists like Seurat, who acknowledged the crucial influence of science on his painting. A contemporary observed that a key to Picasso's work was his use of "geometric figures – of a geometry at the same time infinitesimal and cinematic." Around the same time, futurist painters like Giacomo Balla and Umberto Boccioni championed science, and especially technology, as the principal object of their art, calling for a moratorium on nudes, still lives, and other traditional artistic subjects and declaring that instead "we will sing the multicolored and polyphonic surf of revolutions in modern capitals; the nocturnal vibration of arsenals and docks beneath their glaring electric moons . . . factories hanging from the clouds by the threads of their smoke; . . . large-breasted locomotives bridled with long tubes, and the slippery flight of airplanes." More recently, "transgenic artists" and "bio-artists" like Eduardo Kacs have adopted laboratory techniques as an artistic medium, asserting that "new technologies culturally mutate our perception of the human body from a naturally self-regulated system to an artificially controlled and electronically transformed object." Kacs works in the medium of genetic modification, and he is not alone. In fact, for each of these examples, hundreds of similar examples can be adduced.

The influence of science upon music is, if anything, still more longstanding and deeply ingrained. Until modern times, music was itself considered a science (and was one of the mathematical sciences of the classical *quadrivium*, along with astronomy, geometry, and arithmetic). Until after the Renaissance, Boethius's sixth-century *De musica* remained the most influential guide to music, advancing the notion that music expresses the same mathematical principles that govern the relations between all elements in the cosmos. Marin Mersenne investigated pitch in his physical inquiries (describing his findings in his 1636 *Harmonie universelle*), and Galileo Galilei, himself a lutenist of reputation, described his own empirical studies of the sounds produced by vibrating strings in his *Discourses Concerning Two New Sciences*. The relationship between physics and music remained intimate for subsequent centuries, for both scientists like d'Alembert, Bernoulli, Euler, Laplace, and Helmholtz and composers like Bach, Handel, Telemann, and Rameau. In the twentieth century, new technologies allowing sounds to be produced electronically and recorded greatly changed the nature of music. Electric pianos and guitars came into common use by mid-century, finding their place alongside a great number of newly minted instruments, from the Theremin to the Moog synthesizer. By the final decades of the century, synthesized and computer-generated compositions dominated much of both popular and avant-garde music. In some cases, contemporary science was an immediate source of inspiration, as when Iannis Xenakis produced a series of compositions structured according to the kinetic theory of gases.

The impact of science and technology was greater still in newer cultural media like film and television. These media would not exist at all without technological advances produced by modern science. Science and technology have in turn been constant themes in movies and television. From early movies like *Frankenstein* and *Dr. Jekyll and Mr. Hyde* to recent ones like *Contact* and *AI*, the cinema has constantly reflected on science and technology and their effect and meaning. So too has television, in dramas ranging from *Star Trek* to *Dark Angel*, and in hundreds of thousands of hours of science and nature documentaries broadcast over the six decades of the medium's existence. At the same time, advances in computer science have greatly expanded what is possible to depict on screen.

The influence of science on culture reaches well beyond the rarefied reaches of the arts. Historians have shown, for instance, how advances in bacteriology in the first half of the twentieth century changed conventional views of cleanliness, leading in time to a great increase in the time housewives devoted to housework. Advertisers enlisted science, pseudo-science, and fake science to sell soft drinks, clothing, shampoo, baby formula, anti-perspirant, and automobiles. A lab-coated scientist soberly explaining the virtues of a product became one of the most recognizable images in western consumer culture.

Science has also helped fashion modern political culture. Friedrich Engels captured something crucial of Karl Marx's aspirations (if perhaps not his accomplishments) when he said of him in eulogy, "just as Darwin discovered the law of development of organic nature, so Marx discovered the law of development of human history." Throughout its century of growing and waning popularity, Marxism was presented by supporters as a "scientific" politics, its scientific nature warranting its validity and inevitability. In liberal societies, science played a different, though no less important, role as growing armies of economists, sociologists, engineers, and other "scientific experts" have been called upon to help fashion and evaluate every aspect of policy and administration. In a similar way, scientists now exercise great influence in the courts, serving as expert witnesses hired to persuade juries and judges of the veracity of facts, the credibility of litigants and witnesses, and the extent of damages.

SCIENCE, TECHNOLOGY, AND CULTURE

In the end, the complex relations between science and culture are not exhausted by canvassing how culture influences science and science influences culture. It is often the case, and more now than ever, that science and culture are indistinguishable, even in principle. Historian William Everdell has described how in the first years of the twentieth century many came to doubt the possibility of attaining true objectivity, a change that owed at once to the politics, economics, science, and art of the day, and ultimately changed each of these fields. "The belief in objectivity crumbled so that phenomenology and solipsism began to take over not only philosophy, but literature, politics, psychology and at last even physics" (Everdell 1997). More recently, the enormous attention paid to the impact of genetics on human character and behavior reflects a change in the very notion of what it means to be human, which is equally a product of scientific and cultural assumptions and has equally (and enormously) affected both the practice of science and the nature of the societies and cultures that produce science. In such cases, it is impossible to tease apart the mutual influences of science and culture, because the two are so tightly and diversely intertwined as to be inseparable. Many scholars today, expanding on the pioneering work of philosopher and anthropologist of science Bruno Latour, picture social and cultural artifacts, human actors, and natural objects as linked in a single "network." The identity of each element of the network is constituted, in varying degrees, by all other elements in the network. In Latour's system, it makes little sense to hypothesize social and cultural "influences" on science, or even about the "social construction" of scientific knowledge, because these formulations overlook the fact that society and nature (and the sciences that ostensibly study nature) are mutually constituted. This model, though not without problems, captures nicely the inextricability of science and culture.

SEE ALSO: Actor-Network Theory; Feminism and Science, Feminist Epistemology; Kuhn, Thomas and Scientific Paradigms; Laboratory Studies and the World of the

Scientific Lab; Political Economy of Science; Realism and Relativism: Technological Determinism; Technological Innovation; Truth and Objectivity; Science across Cultures; Science, Social Construction of; Scientific Knowledge, Sociology of; Strong Program

REFERENCES AND SUGGESTED READINGS

Barnes, B., Bloor, D., & Henry, J. (1996) *Scientific Knowledge: A Sociological Analysis*. Athlone, London.

Bijker, W. (1995) *Of Bicycles, Bakelites, and Bulbs: Toward a Theory of Sociotechnical Change*. MIT Press, Cambridge, MA.

Bucchi, M. (2004) *Science in Society: An Introduction to the Sociology of Science*. Routledge, New York.

Everdell, W. (1997) *The First Moderns: Profiles in the Origins of Twentieth-Century Thought*. University of Chicago Press, Chicago.

Ezrahi, Y. (1990) *The Descent of Icarus: Science and the Transformation of Contemporary Democracy*. Harvard University Press, Cambridge, MA.

Fuller, S. (1997) *Science*. University of Minnesota Press, Minneapolis.

Golan, T. (2004) *Laws of Men and Laws of Nature: The History of Scientific Expert Testimony in England and America*. Harvard University Press, Cambridge, MA.

Golinski, J. (1998) *Making Natural Knowledge: Constructivism and the History of Science*. Cambridge University Press, Cambridge.

Hess, D. (1997) *Science Studies: An Advanced Introduction*. New York University Press, New York.

Knorr-Cetina, K. (1999) *Epistemic Cultures: How the Sciences Make Knowledge*. Harvard University Press, Cambridge, MA.

Latour, B. (1993) *We Have Never Been Modern*. Harvard University Press, Cambridge, MA.

McAllister, J. (1996) *Beauty and Revolution in Science*. Cornell University Press, Ithaca, NY.

telephone

Nicola Green

The telephone was developed in 1876, and alongside communication technologies such as the telegraph and steam-based transportation systems, it was one of the key technologies that contributed to the transformation of late nineteenth- and early twentieth-century western societies. The ability to transmit sound across long distances in real time was initially treated with either wonder or suspicion, but by the end of the twentieth century the telephone had become a taken-for-granted feature of everyday life in many parts of the western world. It is because of this ubiquity that sociologists have tended to neglect the telephone as a fundamentally social technology. More recently, however, sociologists have come to pay more attention to the extent of its significance in social communication, interpersonal interaction, social organization, and the regulation of social life.

The telephone was a technology that emerged from the era of industrialization, and the first means that sociologists have come to understand its sociological significance is by considering the technology in terms of its social and historical development. As a "new media" of its day, the telephone served to extend the social transformations of the industrial era, not by introducing entirely new social behaviors, but by providing new means to conduct familiar social practices, and prompting the revision of older forms of social organization in new settings. The telegraph and modern transportation systems had already transformed physical space and time by the late nineteenth century by, for example, collapsing distances and altering the perception of natural time and clock time, concentrating the tempo and reach of industrial production and consumption systems. The telephone extended these transformations by allowing communication to take place at a distance between commercial urban centers and businesses conducted from the newly emerging Victorian-era suburbs, contributing to the spatial organization of the cities we see today.

The alteration of time and space in this way also enabled a revision of the boundaries between, for example, public and private life. Whereas one early use of the telephone was as a "broadcast" medium (one-to-many transmissions of, for example, public entertainments such as concerts), the telephone soon became an instrument wired into the homes of wealthy families in the US and Europe to facilitate one-to-one calls, thereby introducing a potential intrusion of the "public" sphere into the "private" life of the home. Whereas it was initially envisaged by telephone companies that telephones in homes would primarily be used by the male head of household to conduct business, or (of secondary and later importance) be used by the female household manager to run the household more effectively, family members soon found the telephone could be used for communications beyond the economic life of the household, to maintain intimate social networks and relationships at a distance. The role of knowledgeable individuals and groups (whether "expert" or not) was therefore to negotiate and manage the revised boundaries of public good and domestic intimacy as framed by the technology.

The uneasy relationship between the public and the private as it was negotiated over the early history of the telephone highlights the central role that gender has played throughout the technology's history. With the disruption of familiar boundaries as telephones were introduced into homes, the roles of men and women with respect to the technology were also called into question. The telephone was originally conceived (along with other "electric" new technologies and media of the time) as a masculine technology, to be used primarily by (technically competent) men as heads of households, communities, and businesses for the public good and in the public sphere. With the development of larger centralized telephone exchanges serving a number of households and small communities, however, "operators" came to be employed to manage the calls to and from individual devices. As it gradually became accepted (through practice, legislation, and the organization of telephone provision) that the telephone could be used to facilitate all kinds of communications between both intimate relations and more distant associates, women operators were specifically enroled to facilitate telephone contact. Social communication and the maintenance of social networks and bonds was held to be a particularly feminine skill, and it was via these means that the association between the telephone and "talk" of all kinds was cemented, and over time in the domestic sphere came to be particularly associated with women and the emotional labor of social contact between family, friends, and social networks.

The management of revised boundaries of time and space, public and private, prompted

by wired, "landline" telephones also presented new dilemmas for the negotiation of interpersonal "presence" and "absence" in human communication. A second way that sociologists have investigated the importance of the telephone in social life is to focus on the technology particularly as a communications medium. Social interactionists in particular have examined the ways that social relationships are mediated, established, and maintained during telephone communications, both with those "co-present" and not directly party to the communication, as well as those "telepresent" others with whom one is communicating at a distance. The ring of a telephone is a "summons" to communicative interaction (prompting some sociologists to ponder why, in contrast to most other communicative media, the telephone has no "off" switch – the summons is designed to be imperative). From this first summons, individuals may choose between a range of responses framed by normative contextual rules and procedures of interaction. In Goffman's terms, the instance of a phone call is a "stage" that needs to be managed via interactional strategies with respect to both co-present and telepresent others. The normative procedures for taking a telephone call in private space where it might be overhead by intimate others conform to one set of rules, those for making a call in public space conform to another. In each case, individuals might develop strategies for deciding to make or take a call by negotiating the relative power of those co-present and telepresent to demand attention and to establish the rules of conversation. The strategies will also include common rituals of negotiating identification, availability, and the purpose of the call. Of particular importance has been the evolution of normative rules and conversational rituals to establish interactional resources through which the relevance and sense of a telephone call can be understood. Goffman's notion of "footing" has been used to explain how mutual understanding and human "presence" are established and maintained when interlocutors are communicating at a distance.

Using conversation analysis, ethnomethodologists in particular have turned their attention to the contextually framed interactional skills used by members of a community in everyday telephone talk. Initially, ethnomethodologists used recorded telephone conversations to investigate the social organization of telephone talk, mutual identification, turn-taking, the achievement of communicative context, and the negotiation of talk content. Of particular interest has been the management of interaction given the absence of physical context. A range of studies have identified common features of telephone interaction, one of the most important of which is verbal exchanges that are paired in turn-taking, one statement or question requiring a matched response. The opening sequences of telephone conversations will conventionally consist of normative telephone greetings, the identification of the caller and recognition, the inquiry as to well being, which all have their ritualized, common paired responses, framed with respect to context and the identity of the caller.

One important outcome of these studies was the recognition that the micro-coordination of telephone talk and interactional norms differed across cultural contexts. A third way of understanding the sociological importance of the telephone has therefore been to examine comparatively the role, uses, and availability of the telephone across cultures, regions, nations, and internationally. Interactional studies have pointed out that conventional norms in telephone talk reflect deeper cultural differences in behavioral norms, the conventional rules of politeness, conversational norms in public spaces, turn-taking, and informational requirements for mutual identification and recognition. Many of these studies have, however, concentrated on cultural differences within and between different nations and cultures in North America and Europe. This in itself points to a wider sociological phenomenon – that of globally unequal availability of a telecommunications infrastructure, and population access to associated technologies. This inequality has historically reflected the unequal division of resources between the developed and developing worlds – a number of sociologists have pointed out that the deployment and use of the landline telephone, especially when positioned in a domestic context, is a particularly western phenomenon. Despite its ubiquity in western settings, it was estimated at the turn of the millennium that around 70 percent of the world's population had no direct access to a landline telephone. By concentrating on comparative research between western nations, sociologists have sometimes neglected alternative configurations of people, cultural practices, and technologies that have evolved around telephony in non-western settings, particularly community based and shared uses of telephones, its role in ritual, religious, and kinship practices, and its uses in the processes of both colonialism and development.

Access to telecommunications infrastructures has itself, however, again been transformed with further innovations in the configuration of telephony itself – in the form of wireless, mobile, or cellphone technology. Throughout the 1980s and 1990s, cellular telephony emerged as a key technological infrastructure in European and North American societies. The transmission of voice over distance no longer relied on fixed-line telephone wires, but rather employed digital signals over radio waves. The devices to send and receive telephony signals were no longer bound to a single place such as the domestic household, and instead became the "handset" or cellphone. This entailed a significant shift in telephone practices, as rather than being attached to a fixed geographical space, telephone devices instead became attached to particular persons and bodies. Via such means, telephony has become further individualized, and in the process, the mobile devices themselves became part of the consumption and commodity systems to an extent not previously seen. Telephone receivers could be highly personalized by, for example, changing the appearance of the handset, and the devices not only carried voice calls, but incorporated address books and answering services more extensive than their fixed-line predecessors, and featured "text messaging" – the ability to send short written rather than oral messages. More recently, mobile phones have also incorporated digital cameras (and the ability to exchange images), as well as hardware and software to support polyphonic "ringtones" and play digital audio files.

This mobilization of telephony has been extensive, most notably in Western Europe, where some countries' mobile phone subscription rates exceed 90 percent of the population. Because mobile telephony does not rely on a wired infrastructure, it has also overtaken subscription to fixed-line telephony in some nations of the developing world. The extent of this change in telephony has led sociologists to reevaluate the social relationships mediated by telephones, where those devices have become mobile.

As was the case with the fixed-line telephone, the presence and use of telephones "on the move" has affected how the public and the private are negotiated in everyday life. Because mobile phones are significantly *personal* devices, they come to symbolize (through voice messaging, address books, and text messages) the social networks of which the individual is a part. At the same time, they are public by virtue of their use in shared spaces, whether those shared spaces are in the home or family relationship, or in collective spaces such as public transport. On the one hand, therefore, mobile phones can establish and maintain the private and personal as in the case, for example, where young people can bypass parental gatekeeping of the fixed-line household phone to engage with their peers. On the other hand, mobile phones can both mediate and disrupt the public – when, for example, peers "gift" one another with text messages and images that can then be displayed to co-present others to demonstrate participation in a telepresent social network, or when phones are used for voice calls in public space disrupting conventional behavioral norms. Similarly, gender is implicated in emerging norms of use, for example in the ways mobiles are used by women to manage their multiple responsibilities with respect to work, household, and extended family.

As was also the case with the fixed-line telephone, the interactional norms governing use and behavior with respect to the mobile phone must be negotiated over time. The conversational norms with both co-present and telepresent others are being rewritten as mobile phones become a more ubiquitous feature of everyday life. The "etiquette" of mobile phone use has been the subject of significant public debate, and continues to be so with the introduction of further features such as cameras that can readily be used across a range of social situations. Sociologists have begun to conduct ethnographies of a range of places and spaces to investigate these emerging norms, and to uncover the ways in which the mobile phone intervenes in social and communicative practices across a number of nations and cultures. They are investigating the historical significance of the mobile

with respect to the technological landscapes and social networks of which they are a part, and considering the organization, hierarchies, and power relations embedded in their production and consumption. As mobile and fixed-line phones continue to converge with technologies such as the Internet, sociology now recognizes that in contemporary societies telephony has a central role in the technology and media landscape, and have adjusted their focus accordingly.

SEE ALSO: Conversation Analysis; Historical and Comparative Methods; Information Technology; Interaction; Technological Determinism; Technological Innovation; Urbanization

REFERENCES AND SUGGESTED READINGS

Brown, B., Green, N., & Harper, R. (Eds.) (2001) *Wireless World: Social and Interactional Aspects of the Mobile Age*. Springer, London.

Fischer, C. (1994) *America Calling: A Social History of the Telephone to 1940*. University of California Press, Berkeley.

Katz, J. & Aakhus, M. (2002) *Perpetual Contact: Mobile Communication, Private Talk, Public Performance*. Cambridge University Press, Cambridge.

Marvin, C. (1988) *When Old Technologies Were New: Thinking About Electric Communication in the Late Nineteenth Century*. Oxford University Press, New York.

Poole, I. de S. (Ed.) (1977) *The Social Impact of the Telephone*. MIT Press, Cambridge, MA.

televangelism

William H. Swatos, Jr.

Initially an American phenomenon, televangelism refers to the use of television for Christian missionary outreach, of an evangelical-fundamentalist type, usually incarnated in a single leadership figure, which became particularly prominent in the 1970s as a result of shifts in broadcasting policies regulated by the United States Federal Communications Commission (FCC) in 1960. Prior to that time, the FCC required the commercial broadcast networks to donate a portion of their airtime to "public interest" use. A convenient way to do this was for the stations to cooperate with large, mainstream religious bodies to produce a variety of non-confrontational, non-sectarian programs that could fit within this category. This ended when the FCC in 1960 ruled that the stations could count commercial programming toward their public interest quotas. The effect was to open a new market, wherein profit interests could redefine the public interest within category limits. Hence, "religious interest" could be met by allowing the religious interests with the most money to have the available slots. This was greatly enhanced as more broadcast frequencies became more easily available. So was born the parallel religious institution of the "electronic church," with its most successful exponents eventually termed "televangelists."

As a part of media coverage of the growth in fundamentalist and evangelical churches in the United States during the 1970s and 1980s, one focus of attention became the concomitant expansion in the activities of religious broadcasters, especially the televangelist stars of Sunday morning. Eventual revelations of scandals involving sexual misconduct and/or financial misrepresentation by some of the best-known television preachers, such as Jim Bakker and Jimmy Swaggart, served to fix popular gaze firmly on the operations of religious broadcasters. Unnuanced and even derisive reporting of these scandals also reinforced persistent stereotypes concerning the rather diverse ministries that jointly inhabit the airwaves. Chief among these is the impression that all religious broadcasters are money-hungry opportunists, accountable to no higher authority, who promise miracles in order to lure huge numbers of the desperate and the gullible – and their financial contributions – away from the putatively sounder fellowship of mainline congregations or secular professional help.

A sociological account of televangelism is better constructed in aspects of the roles that broadcast ministers perform and the economic and organizational constraints within which they work. The electronic church, like other western institutions, is voluntaristic, diverse, market-oriented, entrepreneurial, technologically advanced, and activated by vast amounts of time and money. In the media market, there simply is no ministry without money. In a different sense than is normally intended, within broadcasting time is money – that is, time costs money. Thus, the head of a broadcast ministry, virtuous or not, must always preach with one eye glued to the financial bottom line and one foot planted a step ahead of his creditors. Hence the seeming obsession during religious broadcasts with talk of raising and spending money. Additionally, the very evangelistic nature of religious commitment among conservative Christians reinforces this entrepreneurial style. To their way of thinking, a faith that is not actively being passed on is a faith that is indolent and moribund. Not only is there a Christian imperative to extend the faith, but also a conviction that God has established a (hidden) time limit within which this must be done and that those who do not receive the Christian gospel are eternally lost. The logical conclusion to this line of thought is the incessant appeal for money to retire debts, maintain operations, and advance into the future.

The principal spokesperson for these appeals is the televangelist himself. Because very few current broadcast ministries are the projects of denominations, it is almost always an individual (most frequently the founder) who comes to embody the spirit of a religious program. He becomes the focal point for all that his ministry is and does; for all practical purposes, he *is* his organization. Televangelists are not above turning this condition around, however, and using it to cultivate loyalty among their followers. It is, after all, harder for people to trust an institution than a person, and even harder for them to endorse the worth of an abstract idea. So their gazes settle naturally on the profile of the preacher at center stage; hence, for example, viewers are much more likely to know *who* they watch among the televangelists than they are the actual name of his program.

Audience research shows that despite the sometimes outlandish claims of broadcast preachers themselves, the size of the regular audience for religious television in the United States is rather modest. It is dwarfed by the average ratings for the most popular talk shows and situation comedies on network television and its cable counterparts. The audience for religious television is also heavily concentrated in Southern states, where religious convictions as a whole have greater salience then they do in the rest of the country; hence religious broadcasting may simply intensify already existing convictions rather than change alternative worldviews. Across the entire audience, furthermore, viewers are not ordinary unchurched, but are comparatively religious in the first place. Hence, there is little basis for a concern that religious television is substituting for worshipping with a congregation; the majority of viewers who are not otherwise religiously active are among the elderly, the immobile, and the chronically infirm, who would not swell the participatory ranks of congregants if televangelism were to cease.

SEE ALSO: Fundamentalism; Media; Popular Religiosity; Religion; Television

REFERENCES AND SUGGESTED READINGS

Alexander, B. (1994) *Televangelism Reconsidered: Ritual in the Search for Human Community*. Scholars Press, Atlanta.
Armstrong, B. (1979) *The Electric Church*. Nelson, Nashville.
Hadden, J. & Shupe, A. (1988) *Televangelism: Power and Politics on God's Frontier*. Holt, New York.
Hoover, S. (1988) *Mass Media Religion: The Sources of the Electronic Church*. Sage, Newbury Park, CA.
Schultze, Q. (1991) *Televangelism and American Culture*. Baker, Grand Rapids, MI.

television

Toby Miller

What is television? It is an object that is produced in a factory, then distributed physically (via transportation) and virtually (via advertising). At that point it transmogrifies into a fashion statement, a privileged (or damned) piece of furniture – a status symbol. Finally, it becomes outmoded junk, full of poisons and pollutants in search of a dumping ground. In short, television has a physical existence, a history as an object of material production and consumption in addition to its renown as a site for making meaning. That renown is the focus of most sociological theory and research into the media.

Prior to the emergence of TV appliances and services, people fantasized about the transmission of image and sound across space. Richard Whittaker Hubbell made the point by publishing a book in 1942 entitled *4000 Years of Television*. The device even has its own patron saint, Clare of Assisi, a teen runaway from the thirteenth century who became the first Franciscan nun. She was canonized in 1958 for her bedridden vision of images from a midnight mass cast upon the wall, which Pius XII decided centuries later was the first broadcast. As TV proper came close to realization, it attracted intense critical speculation. Rudolf Arnheim's 1935 "Forecast of Television" predicted it would offer viewers simultaneous global experiences, transmitting railway disasters, professorial addresses, town meetings, boxing title-fights, dance bands, carnivals, and aerial mountain views – a spectacular montage of Broadway and Vesuvius. A common vision would surpass the limitations of linguistic competence and interpretation. TV might even bring global peace with it, by showing spectators that "we are located as one among many." But this was no naïve welcome. Arnheim warned that "television is a new, hard test of our wisdom." The emergent medium's easy access to knowledge would either enrich or impoverish its viewers, manufacturing an informed public, vibrant and active, or an indolent audience, domesticated and passive (Arnheim 1969: 160–3). Two years after Arnheim, Barrett C. Kiesling (1937: 278) said "it is with fear and trembling that the author approaches the controversial subject of television." Such concerns about TV have never receded. They are the very stuff of sociology's inquiries into this bewildering device.

Like most sociological domains, the study of television is characterized by severe contestation over meanings and approaches, not least because its analysts "speak different languages, use different methods," and pursue "different questions" (Hartley 1999: 18). Broadly speaking, TV has given rise to three key topics:

1 Ownership and control: television's political economy.
2 Texts: its content.
3 Audiences: its public.

Within these categories lie several other divisions:

1 Approaches to ownership and control vary between neoliberal endorsements of limited regulation by the state, in the interests of guaranteeing market entry for new competitors, and Marxist critiques of the bourgeois media's agenda for discussing society.
2 Approaches to textuality vary between hermeneutic endeavors, which unearth the meaning of individual programs and link them to broader social formations and problems, and content-analytic endeavors, which establish patterns across significant numbers of similar texts, rather than close readings of individual ones.
3 Approaches to audiences vary between social psychological attempts to validate correlations between watching TV and social conduct, and culturalist critiques of imported television threatening national culture.

There is an additional bifurcation between approaches favored by those working and/or trained in US social sciences versus the rest of the world. These relate to wider intellectual differences, but also to distinctive traditions of public policy. Like so many other areas of social life, TV is principally regarded as a means of profit through entertainment in the US and, historically at least, as a means of governance through information elsewhere. The first tradition focuses on audiences as consumers, the second as citizens. Pierre Bourdieu (1998: 48) refers to these rather graceless antinomies as "populist spontaneism and demagogic capitulation to popular tastes" versus "paternalistic-pedagogic television." Neoliberal deregulation since the 1980s has privatized TV all over the globe under the sign of the US exemplar, but there continue to be theoretical, analytic, and political correlatives to this difference between the US and the rest.

Just as US sociology determinedly clings to a binary opposition between qualitative and quantitative approaches, between impression and science, between commitment and truth, so it has hewed closely to methodological individualism in seeking to explain why people and television interact as they do, looking for links between TV and violence, misogyny, and educational attainment. Conversely, sociologists elsewhere worry less about such issues. They are more exercised by Hollywood's impact on their own countries' cultural expression. Global sociology is inclined to use critical terminology and methods that look at TV as a collective issue, rather than an individual one; a matter of interpretation and politics more than psychological impact. But there is in fact a link between the two anxieties.

In their different ways, each is an effects model, in that they assume television *does* things *to* people, that audience members are at risk of abjuring either interpersonal responsibility (in the US) or national culture (in the rest of the world). In Harold Garfinkel's (1992: 68) words, both models assume that the audience is a "cultural dope … acting in compliance with the common culture." Caricaturing people in this way clouds the actual "common sense rationalities … of here and now situations" they use. Most of the time that the television audience is invoked by sociologists, or by TV's critics and regulators, it is understood as just such a "dope"; for example, the assumption that "children are sitting victims; television bites them" (Schramm et al. 1961: 1).

The dope splits in two, in keeping with dominant audience models. The first appears in a *domestic* effects model, or DEM. Dominant in the US, and increasingly exported around the world, it is typically applied without consideration of place and is psychological. The DEM offers analysis and critique of education and civic order. It views television as a force that can either direct or pervert the audience. Entering young minds hypodermically, TV can both enable and imperil learning. It may also drive viewers to violence through aggressive and misogynistic images and narratives. The DEM is found at a variety of sites, including laboratories, clinics, prisons, schools, newspapers, psychology journals, television stations' research and publicity departments, everyday talk, program-classification regulations, conference papers, parliamentary debates, and state-of-our-youth or state-of-our-civil-society moral panics. The DEM is embodied in the US media theatrics that ensue after mass school shootings, questioning the role of violent images (not hyper-Protestantism, straight white masculinity, a risk society, or easy access to firearms) in creating violent people. The DEM also finds expression in content analysis, which has been put to a variety of sociological purposes. For example, a violence index has been created to compare the frequency and type of depictions of violence on US TV news and drama with actual crime statistics, and content analysis has also been applied to representations of gender and race.

The second means of constituting "dopes" is a *global* effects model, or GEM. The GEM, primarily utilized in non-US discourse, is spatially specific and social. Whereas the DEM focuses on the cognition and emotion of individual human subjects, via observation and experimentation, the GEM looks to the knowledge of custom and patriotic feeling exhibited by populations, the grout of national culture. In place of psychology, it is concerned with politics. Television does not make you a well-educated or an ill-educated person, a wild or a self-controlled one. Rather, it makes you a knowledgeable and loyal national subject, or a *naif* who is ignorant of local tradition and history. Cultural belonging, not psychic wholeness, is the touchstone of the global effects model. Instead of measuring audience responses electronically or behaviorally, as its domestic counterpart does, the GEM interrogates the geopolitical origin of televisual texts and the themes and styles they embody, with particular attention to the putatively nation-building genres of drama, news, sport, and current affairs. GEM adherents hold that local citizens should control TV, because their loyalty can be counted on in the event of war, while in the case of fiction, only locally sensitized producers will make narratives that are true to tradition and custom. The model is found in the discourses of cultural imperialism, everyday talk, broadcast and telecommunications policy, unions, international organizations, newspapers, heritage, cultural diplomacy, and post-industrial service-sector planning. In its manifestation as textual analysis, it interprets programs in ideological terms.

Both models have fundamental flaws. The DEM betrays all the disadvantages of ideal-typical psychological reasoning. It relies on methodological individualism, thereby failing to account for cultural norms and politics, let alone the arcs of history and shifts in space that establish patterns of imagery and response inside TV coverage of politics, war, ideology, and discourse. Each massively costly test of media effects, based on, as the refrain goes, "a large university in the [US] mid-West," is countered by a similar experiment, with conflicting results. As politicians, grant-givers, and jeremiad-wielding pundits call for more and more research to prove that TV makes you stupid, violent, and apathetic (or the opposite), sociologists and others line up to indulge their contempt for popular culture and ordinary life and their rent-seeking urge for grant money. The DEM never interrogates its own conditions of existence; namely, that governments and the media use it to account for social problems, and that TV's capacity for private viewing troubles those authorities who desire surveillance of popular culture. As for the GEM, its concentration on national culture denies the potentially liberatory and pleasurable nature of different forms of television, forgets the internal differentiation of publics, valorizes frequently oppressive and/or unrepresentative local bourgeoisies in the name of maintaining and developing national televisual culture, and ignores the demographic realities of its "own" terrain.

Nevertheless, the DEM and the GEM continue unabated. From one side, Singer and Singer (2001: xv) argue that "psychophysiological and behavioral empirical studies beginning in the 1960s have pointed ... to aggression as a learned response." From the other side, García-Canclíni (2001: 1) notes that Latin Americans became "citizens through our relationship to Europe," while warning that links to the US may "reduce us to consumers."

In contradistinction to the DEM/GEM, a third tendency in sociology picks up on Garfinkel's cultural-dope insight. Endorsing the audience as active rather than passive, it constructs two other model audiences:

1 All-powerful consumers (invented and loved by neoliberal policymakers, desired

and feared by corporations) who use TV like an appliance, choosing what they want from its programming.

2 All-powerful interpreters (invented and loved by utopic sociologists and cultural critics, investigated and led by corporations) who use TV to bring pleasure and sense to their lives.

These models have a common origin. In lieu of citizen-building, their logic is the construction and control of consumers. Instead of issuing the jeremiads of rat-catching psy-doomsayers, they claim that the TV audience is so clever and able that it makes its own meanings from programs, outwitting institutions of the state, academia, and capital that seek to measure and control it. Ownership patterns do not matter, because the industry is "wildly volatile," animated entirely by "the unpredictable choice of the audience" (De Vany 2004: 1, 140). The first approach demonstrates a mechanistic application of neoclassical economics. The second varies between social psychological tests of viewers' gratifications and a critical ethnography that engages cultural and social questions.

A summary of sociological approaches to television up to the present might look like Table 1.

And the future? What are we to make of digitally generated virtual actors (synthespians), desktop computers that produce and distribute expensive-looking images, the New International Division of Cultural Labor's simultaneous production work on TV programs across the world, and broadband home video

access (Miller et al. 2005)? The rhetoric of the new media is inflected with the phenomenological awe of a precocious child who can be returned to Eden, healing the wounds of the modern as it magically reconciles public and private, labor and leisure, commerce and culture, citizenship and consumption. "Television is dead" (de Silva 2000) and the interactive web is the future. That may be. But it is worth remembering that television stations continue to multiply around the world, that TV is adapting to the use of Internet portals, and that the digital divide separating the poor from high technology is not changing. Two billion people in the world have never made a telephone call, let alone bought bookshelves on line.

In any event, the questions asked of television today illustrate its continued relevance. For example, leading bourgeois economist Jagdish Bhagwati (2002) is convinced that TV is partly to "blame" for global grassroots activism against globalization because television makes people identify with those suffering from capitalism, but has not led to rational action (i.e., support for the neoclassical economic policies he supports, which many would say caused the problem). Just a few pages further on in Bhagwati's essay, however, cable is suddenly a savior. There is no need to litigate against companies that pollute the environment, or impose sanctions on states that enslave children to become competitive in the global economy, because the rapid flow of information via the media ensures that "multinationals and their host governments cannot afford to alienate their constituencies"

Table 1 Sociological approaches to television

Origins	Topics	Objects	Methods	Allied disciplines
Global	Regulation, industry development	State, capital, labor	Political economy, neoliberalism	Economics, political science, law, communications
US	Genre	Text	Content analysis	Communications
Global	Genre	Text	Textual analysis	Literary/cultural studies
US	Uses	Audience	Uses and gratifications	Communications, psychology, marketing
Global	Uses	Audience	Ethnography	Anthropology, cultural studies, communications
US	Effects	Audience	Experimentation, questionnaire	Psychology, marketing, communications

(pp. 4, 6). The tie between the medium as a heaven and hell is as powerful as it was in Arnheim's forecast seven decades earlier.

We are perhaps witnessing a *transformation* of TV, rather than its demise. Television started in most countries as a *broadcast*, *national* medium dominated by the state. It is being transformed into a *cable and satellite*, *international* medium dominated by commerce, but still called "television." A TV-like screen, located in domestic and public *spaces*, and transmitting signs from other *places*, will probably be the future.

In many ways, television has become an alembic for understanding society. There is intellectual and political value in utilizing the knowledge gained from sociology to assess this transformation and intervene in it, especially if we borrow from the right traditions. The three basic questions asked by students of the media – "Will this get me a job?" "Is television bad for you?" "How do we get that show back on?" – have direct links to the relationships between text and audience, as understood through ethnography and political economy. The respective answers are: "If you know who owns and regulates the media, you'll know how to apply"; "The answer depends on who is asking the question and why"; and "If you know how audiences are defined and counted and how genre functions, you'll be able to lobby for retention of your favorite programs."

In summary, analyzing television requires interrogating the manufacture and material history of TV sets; creation, commodification, governance, distribution, and interpretation of texts; global exchange of cultural and communications infrastructure and content; and economic rhetoric of communications policies. This can be done by combining political economy, ethnography, and textual analysis into a new critical sociology of TV.

SEE ALSO: Audiences; Culture; Genre; Media; Media and Consumer Culture; Media and Globalization; Media Literacy; Mediated Interaction; Popular Culture

REFERENCES AND SUGGESTED READINGS

Arnheim, R. (1969) *Film as Art*. Faber & Faber, London.

Bhagwati, J. (2002) Coping with Antiglobalization: A Trilogy of Discontents. *Foreign Affairs* 81(1): 2–7.

Bourdieu, P. (1998) *On Television*. Trans. P. P. Ferguson. New Press, New York.

De Silva, J. P. (2000) *La televisión ha muerto: La nueva producción audiovisual en la era de Internet: La tercera revolución industrial*. Editorial Gedisa, Barcelona.

De Vany, A. (2004) *Hollywood Economics: How Extreme Uncertainty Shapes the Film Industry*. Routledge, London.

García-Canclíni, N. (2001) *Consumers and Citizens: Multicultural Conflicts in the Process of Globalization*. Trans. G. Yúdice. University of Minnesota Press, Minneapolis.

Garfinkel, H. (1992) *Studies in Ethnomethodology*. Polity Press, Cambridge.

Hartley, J. (1999) *Uses of Television*. Routledge, London.

Hubbell, R. W. (1942) *4000 Years of Television: The Story of Seeing at a Distance*. G. P. Putnam's Sons, New York.

Kiesling, B. C. (1937) *Talking Pictures: How They are Made, How to Appreciate Them*. Johnson Publishing, Richmond.

Miller, T. (Ed.) (2003) *Television: Critical Concepts in Media and Cultural Studies*. 5 Vols. Routledge, London.

Miller, T., Govil, N., McMurria, J., Maxwell, R., & Wang, T. (2005) *Global Hollywood 2*. British Film Institute, London.

Schramm, W., Lyle, J., & Parker, E. B. (1961) *Television in the Lives of Our Children*. Stanford University Press, Stanford.

Singer, D. G. & Singer, J. L. (2001) Introduction: Why a Handbook on Children and the Media? In Singer, D. G. & Singer, J. L (Eds.), *Handbook of Children and the Media*. Sage, Thousand Oaks, CA, pp. xi–xvii.

terrorism

Douglas Kellner

The term terrorism derives from the Latin verb *terrere*, "to cause to tremble or quiver." It began to be used during the French Revolution, and especially after the fall of Robespierre and the "Reign of Terror," or simply "the Terror," in which enemies of the Revolution were subjected to imprisonment, torture, and beheading, the first of many modern examples of state terrorism.

Over the past two centuries, terrorism has been a highly contested and volatile category. Those accused of terrorism are vilified as enemies of the state and social order, but many labeled "terrorists" insist that they are "freedom fighters," strugglers for national liberation, or *mujaheddin* (holy warrior) or *fedayeen* ("prepared for martyrdom"), ready to die for righteous causes. Many decry terrorists' indiscriminate violence against civilians, while other critics like Chomsky (1988) and Herman (1982) document state use of violence and terror against its perceived enemies.

During the nineteenth century, terrorism was frequently associated with anarchism. Russian anarchists and Narodniks (populists) advocated political terror and were responsible for assassinating Czar Alexander II, a frenzied milieu depicted by Fyodor Dostoevsky in his novel *The Possessed* (1913). Nationalist movements also began to use terrorism in anti-colonial movements, such as the Irish Republican Brotherhood which carried out attacks in England in the name of Irish nationalism, or groups like the Internal Macedonian Revolutionary Organization which was driven by Slavic nationalism (Laquer 1998).

Sociologically, terrorist groups often recruit disaffected and alienated individuals, often motivated by strong ideologies like nationalism or religion to commit terrorist acts. These in turn generate societal fear and exacerbate conflicts and hatred within the social fabric.

During the twentieth century, oppositional political groups ranging from anarchists and nationalists on the left to fascists and the ultra-right used political terror to promote their agendas, engaging in bombing, destroying property, political assassination, and other destructive action to attack the established order. Colonial national liberation movements spread throughout the globe, such as the Mau Mau group in Africa, the Palestinians in the Middle East, the Irish Republican Army in Britain, and the Basque liberation group ETA in Spain.

The term has also been associated in the twentieth century with indiscriminate or excessive use of state violence and has been leveled against actions of Nazi Germany, the Soviet Union, the United States, Israel, and other countries. For instance, Chomsky (1988) and Herman (1982) document a wide range of US state terrorist actions in Southeast Asia, Africa, South America, and elsewhere, with Chomsky pointing out that the US is the only country that has ever been convicted of an international act of terrorism by the World Court, which condemned US acts against Nicaragua during the 1980s.

From the 1980s to the present, terrorists have constructed spectacles of terror to promote their causes, attack their adversaries, and gain worldwide publicity and attention. Terror spectacle has become an increasingly significant part of contemporary terrorism and various groups systematically use spectacles of terror to promote their agenda. Extravagant terrorist acts are thus orchestrated in part as media spectacles to gain worldwide attention, dramatize the issues of the terrorist groups involved, and achieve specific political objectives (Kellner 2003).

The hijacking of airplanes had been a standard terrorist activity, but the ante was significantly upped when, in 1970, the Popular Front for the Liberation of Palestine hijacked three western jetliners. The group forced the planes to land in the Jordanian desert, and then blew up the planes in an incident known as "Black September," which was the topic of a Hollywood film. In 1972, Palestinian gunmen from the same movement stunned the world when they took Israeli athletes hostage at the Munich Olympic Games, producing another media spectacle turned into an academy award-winning documentary film.

In 1975, an OPEC (Organization for Petroleum Exporting Countries) meeting was disrupted in Vienna, Austria when a terrorist group led by the notorious Carlos the Jackal entered, killing three people and wounding several in a chaotic shootout. Americans were targeted in a 1983 bombing in Beirut, Lebanon, in which 243 US servicemen were killed in a truck bombing orchestrated by a Shiite Muslim suicide bomber, which led the US to withdraw its troops from Lebanon. US tourists were victims in 1985 of Palestinians who seized the cruise ship *Achille Lauro*, when Leon Klinghoffer, 69, a disabled Jewish American, was killed and his body and wheelchair were thrown overboard. In June 1985, a double bombing of Air India jets originating from Canada attracted global attention, as did a 1988 bombing of Pan Am Flight 103 over Lockerbie, Scotland.

In 1993, the World Trade Center was bombed in New York by Islamist terrorists linked to Osama bin Laden, providing a preview of the more spectacular September 11 aggression. An American-born terrorist, Timothy McVeigh, bombed the Alfred P. Murrah Federal Building in Oklahoma City, killing 168 and wounding more than 500. Further, the bin Laden group assaulted US embassies in Africa in 1998 and a US destroyer harbored in Yemen in 2000.

Periodic IRA attacks in Britain continued, including a 1998 car bomb attack in Omagh, Northern Ireland that killed 29 and injured hundreds, creating great outrage. On September 11, 2001, terror attacks against the World Trade Center in New York and the Pentagon in Washington, DC became a global media spectacle (Kellner 2003). The September 11 terror spectacle was the most extravagant strike on US targets in its history and the first foreign attack on its territory since the war of 1812. The 9/11 attacks inaugurated a "war on terror" by the Bush administration and was the prelude to highly publicized terrorist bombings in London, Pakistan, Bali, and elsewhere, and Bush administration military interventions in Afghanistan and Iraq as "preemptive" actions in the "war on terror." Many critics accused the Bush administration of state technology in its invasion and occupation of Iraq.

Terrorism and terror war have thus become defining features of the twenty-first century. Governments throughout the world have attempted to more precisely define and criminalize terrorism, while terrorist activities multiply. As weapons of destruction become more deadly and widespread, social divisions between haves and have-nots multiply, and conflict rages throughout the world, terrorism will likely continue to be a major issue and problem of the present era.

SEE ALSO: Violence; War; World Conflict

REFERENCES AND SUGGESTED READINGS

Chomsky, N. (1988) *The Culture of Terrorism*. South End Press, Boston.

Herman, E. (1982) *The Real Terror Network*. South End Press, Boston.

Kellner, D. (2003) *From September 11 to Terror War: The Dangers of the Bush Legacy*. Rowman & Littlefield, Lanham, MD.

Laquer, W. (1998) *Origins of Terrorism: Psychologies, Ideologies, Theologies, States of Mind*. Woodrow Wilson Center Press, Washington.

text/hypertext

Gregory L. Ulmer

Hypertext refers to a network of nodes or lexias (units of content) connected non-sequentially by links, forming a docuverse that includes users in a feedback loop, usually in a computer medium. The first description of hypertext as a concept was by Vannevar Bush, in an article entitled "As We May Think," published in the *Atlantic Monthly* in 1945. Bush imagined a machine-desk called "memex" that could solve the problem of storage and retrieval created by the modern information explosion. Merging the functions of a library and a personal filing system, memex proposed to support and augment an associative indexing corresponding to the actual processes of human thought, memory, and imagination. Individuals researching the branching paths of information related to an inquiry would build trails of connections through the collective archive of recorded information, and these trails would be preserved, shared, and cross-referenced, establishing possibly a new profession of knowledge "trailblazers."

Inspired by memex, Theodor Holm Nelson coined the term hypertext (and also hypermedia, to include multimedia) in 1965. "Such a system as the ELF (Evolutionary List File) actually ties in better than anything previously used with the actual processes by which thought is progressively organized, whether into stories or hypertext or library categories. Thus it may help integrate for human understanding bodies of material so diversely connected that they could not be untangled by the unaided mind" (Nelson 1989: 145). Nelson's vision, called the

Xanadu project (referring to the "magic place of literary memory" in Samuel Taylor Coleridge's poem *Kubla Khan*), extended memex into a global archive in which users could write as well as read. Xanadu's multiple styles of hypertext were at least partially realized in the greatest hypermedia system to date, the World Wide Web. Tim Berners-Lee introduced the document description language HTML (hypertext markup language) in 1989 that made the Internet into a hypertext system. Even with the addition of the graphical browser, created by Marc Andreessen in 1993, however, the available equipment and its applications have not approached the full realization of the hypertext vision. Lev Manovich argued that the most important creators of the twentieth century are the people who invented the hypermedia tools, adding to the names already mentioned those of Douglas Englebart, who invented the mouse and windowed interface, Ivan Sutherland, whose Sketchpad was the first paint program, and J. C. R. Licklider, director of DARPA (Defense Advanced Research Projects Agency). All these figures made their contributions in the 1960s.

To appreciate the full potential of hypertext it is useful to place its development in the context of the concept of apparatus (social machine) commonly used in media studies. To say that hypertext is part of a new apparatus beginning to replace literacy helps avoid the fallacy of technological determinism. A language apparatus includes not only technology, but also institutional practices and human identity formation. It is possible to grasp what is happening in our time by analogy with the shift from orality to literacy in classical Greece, when Plato and Aristotle invented the institution of school, and the practices of alphabetic writing, including logic, method, and the category system of concepts (metaphysics) that eventually produced modern science. To have a term for the digital equivalent of literacy helps identify more easily the full range of inventions in progress across the dimensions of the apparatus. This neologism is "electracy," combining "electricity" with the theory of "trace" used by Jacques Derrida to describe the operations of text (Ulmer 1989).

The beginnings of electracy as technology date from the 1830s, with the invention of photography and Charles Babbage's analytical engine, an information processor (never built) based on the punchcards of the Jacquard loom. The metaphor of "textile" in the root of "text" is worth noting in this context. The separate trajectories of these inventions converged finally in the graphical computer, making possible the mutual mapping between the culture of mass media entertainment operating through television and the culture of disciplinary science supported by the databases of information processors.

Hypertext is not only the result of a history of technology, but also the most recent manifestation of the ancient dream of a perfect or universal language. To deal with the information overload caused by manuscript culture, for example, medieval pedagogy promoted the art of memory. Mnemonic systems, associating real or imaginary settings and striking (violent or sexual) images with bodies of information, facilitated memorization in service of oratory. The practice led to attempts to build actual memory theaters, such as the one designed by Giulio Camillo in the 1530s. Large enough to be occupied by two people, the theater was a hypertextual organization (consisting of cross-referenced drawers filled with slips of writing) of the oeuvre of Cicero.

Mnemonic learning practices served several historical currents, including hermeticism and the trend leading from the search for a universal language to the creation of the encyclopedia in the Enlightenment. Jorge Luis Borges, whose story *The Garden of Forking Paths* (1941) is often mentioned as an allegory of hypertext design, drew upon this tradition of philosophical languages as a source for a number of seemingly bizarre ideas about writing and memory. The most influential fictional representation of what it might be like for an individual to think with complete access to the entire dynamic archive of collective information is William Gibson's cyberpunk novel *Neuromancer*. In the two novels following *Neuromancer*, Gibson, who coined the term cyberspace, drew upon the event of possession in Haitian Vodun as a metaphor for this merger of individual and collective mind.

The key practical issue for those continuing to invent hypertext as an apparatus concerns the nature of the human–computer interface (HCI).

What remains to be invented is the electrate equivalent of logic, rhetoric, and poetics that allows people to be native users of a docuverse. The issue is foregrounded in Michael Joyce's *Afternoon* (1987), the first and still one of the most important examples of hypertext fiction. Composed in StorySpace, a hypertext authoring program developed by Joyce with Jay David Bolter and John B. Smith, *Afternoon* is a detective story in which the reader attempts to figure out the plot by navigating a complex set of nodes and links. The feeling of being lost in a maze reported by many readers of *Afternoon* may be extended to hypertext in general, in which reading is the exploration of an information space, whether in the mode of fiction, game, or encyclopedia. In this regard Espen Aarseth proposed as the two primary rhetorical figures of hypertext the tropes of aporia (impasse) and epiphany (revelation). The pleasure of navigation involves a eureka moment in which the user discovers how to continue the path productively. Aarseth also proposes the term "ergodic" to replace "narrative" to describe cybertexts in which the sequence through the lexias is different at each reading.

The labyrinth effect of hypertext makes explicit what was always implicit in the literate archive. Umberto Eco's study of semiotics clarifies that what hypertext embodies and renders tangible is nothing less than the dynamic, open, and infinite operation of meaning-in-process. Eco describes semiotics as a transition away from the logical categories of literate concepts generated by definition (semantics), to a new kind of category functioning through inference, having more to do with pragmatics. Since the meanings involved are interpretants, including the subjectivity of the individual, they take the form collectively of a labyrinth of the network or rhizomatic type, lacking both center and outside.

What are the practices that enable reading and writing in a labyrinthine docuverse? This is the fundamental active question of hypertext. Within the unifying framework of electracy it is possible to recognize that hypertext is being invented across the apparatus. The fact that hypertextual features are found in certain literary works such as *Tristram Shandy* (digression) or *Wuthering Heights* (nested points of view), not to mention *Finnegans Wake* (trace)

and other experimental works, is explained by the fact that the genealogy of hypermedia is social and cultural as well as technological. *Afternoon* is described as modernist in its aesthetics and postmodernist in its use of technical devices. Lev Manovich has shown that the practices of collage-montage invented by the vanguard arts across the media, especially concentrated in the movements of the 1920s, have been designed into the interface controls of the software used to author in new media. Unfortunately, many artists experimenting with new media complain that the public have yet to internalize the equivalent rhetoric in their worldview, and continue to use as their default model of intelligibility the pop forms of mass entertainment.

The institutional practices appropriate for hypertext have at least been theorized, beginning in the same decade of the 1960s that produced the Xanadu project and the GUI tools, when a group of critics working in France formulated the poststructural theory of "text." When commentators claim that hypertext makes poststructuralism seem obvious, or that the Web is the laboratory for testing poststructural principles, they are referring to the writings of such figures as Roland Barthes, Julia Kristeva, and Jacques Derrida. The new meaning of "text" appearing in the 1960s was the culmination of the "linguistic turn" in the arts and letters disciplines going back to the beginnings of modernism in the nineteenth century. Meaning based on reference to an objective reality was replaced by signification emerging from the relationships among the elements of a system. Structuralism was the science of such systems. Poststructuralism took up the question of pragmatics, concerned with the experience of people within discourse.

Structuralism treated everything in culture as a language, thus doing for theory what the convergence of media in digital technology did for the equipment. The way was prepared for theorizing reading and writing as the traversal of a virtual world designed as a discourse. Roland Barthes (who introduced the term lexia to describe a unit of reading) devoted his entry on "text" for the *Encyclopaedie Universalis* to an exposition of Julia Kristeva's "semanalysis," which he said created an epistemological mutation by integrating linguistics and semiotics with dialectical materialism and psychoanalysis. The old notion of a literary "work" as a unique bounded entity expressing the intentions of an individual author was replaced with the semiotic notion of text as an intertextual transformation of other texts. Kristeva introduced "intertext" to translate Mikhail Bakhtin's "dialogical word" – the idea that every word is a crossroads of other words, opening onto the entire field of language, with meaning as an ideological struggle for possession of the field. Derrida's "trace" expresses a similar idea that every sign carries the traces of all other signs.

The shift of identity experience in electracy is related to the "death of the author," which Barthes reminds us is also the birth of the reader. Or, rather, text deconstructs the opposition between writer and reader, since what it names is not an inherent property of completed works, but a "productivity" of signification produced by the reader reworking the found materials of discourse. Text theatricalizes the encounter of the subject with language. "Subject" is not the person, but the identity position ideologically constructed in culture. The subject does not speak language, but is spoken by it. There is no position of critical distance outside the text, outside history or society, from which to judge events.

This loss of control over intention is compensated for by a new relationship of the subject immersed in discourse, which Barthes characterizes as "bliss." Signification does not concern communication or message, but a new dimension of logic, of inference, which Barthes compares to Freud's dreamwork (condensation and displacement). The technical, vanguard, and theoretical trajectories converge on this insight: the rhetoric of hypertext is precisely poetry (Bush's associative thinking, or what Marcos Novak called liquid architecture). Poetry, or more generally the aesthetic operations observed in all varieties of creative thinking, contains the resources which it is the task of educators and designers today to translate into a "general electracy" that is to digital culture what general literacy is to print culture.

SEE ALSO: Cyberculture; Deconstruction; Digital; Internet; Media Literacy; Postmodernism; Poststructuralism; Semiotics

REFERENCES AND SUGGESTED READINGS

Aarseth, E. J. (1997) *Cybertext: Perspectives on Ergodic Literature.* Johns Hopkins University Press, Baltimore.
Bolter, J. D. (1991) *Writing Space: The Computer, Hypertext, and the History of Writing.* Lawrence Erlbaum, Hillsdale, NJ.
Eco, U. (1995) *The Search for the Perfect Language.* Trans. J. Fentress. Blackwell, Oxford.
Manovich, L. (2001) *The Language of New Media.* MIT Press, Cambridge, MA.
Nelson, T. H. (1989) A File Structure for the Complex, the Changing, and the Indeterminate. In: Wardrip-Fruin, N. & Montfort, N. (Eds.), *The New Media Reader.* MIT Press, Cambridge, MA.
Ulmer, G. L. (1989) *Teletheory: Grammatology in the Age of Video.* Routledge, New York.
Wardrip-Fruin, N. & Montfort, N. (Eds.) (1989) *The New Media Reader.* MIT Press, Cambridge, MA.

theology

Karl Gabriel

The modern conception of theology as both a faithful and rational or scientific way of talking about God dates from the Christian Middle Ages. Theology as a term is rooted in Greek philosophy, which consisted of three parts: the mythology of the gods, theology as a form of philosophy of nature, and political theology as a public cult. Christendom only reluctantly accepted the term. It is only from the twelfth century onwards that the term theology is commonly used for this science of Christian faith in contrast to the term philosophy. The late Middle Ages finds the term entirely accepted and it is even taken over by Martin Luther. In modern times it is especially used to distinguish between religious philosophy and religious studies on the one hand and Christian doctrine on the other.

Christian theology finds its roots in the biblical tradition. In its first phase since the second century, theology was dominated by the apologetical defense of faith from external attack as well as inner gnostic debate. Clement of

Alexandria and Origen developed the first conceptions of systematic knowledge and of an understanding of faith. From the thirteenth century a new prototype of theology as science of faith was established. The West and East developed differently, with western theology concerned with inner processes of systematization and rationalization, while the East was more liturgically and spiritually oriented. Furthermore, philosophy and theology in the West were separated, and challenged faith and science to bring forth their inner connection. Thomas Aquinas thought of God from the rational as well as the revelational points of view. The plurality of theologies was already apparent in the Middle Ages. Thus, scholastic theology with its tendencies to rationalize and intellectualize faith went hand in hand with forms of theology with ties to Augustinian-Neoplatonic thinking or those which were more biblically or affectively oriented, such as the *devotio moderna*. Nominalism in the late Middle Ages came under the pressure of the medieval synthesis of faith and reason until it fell apart during the Reformation.

Modern western theology is marked by schism and conflict with modern society and culture. Reformation, due to the negation of scholastic theology, fell back on the Bible and on patristic theology, as well as trends of mysticism. For Luther, the object of theology was no longer the unity of faith and reason, but "the culpable and forlorn individual and the justificatory or saving God" (WA: 327). Modern trends in Protestant theology are marked either by the search for a connection with modern culture (e.g., the theology of the Enlightenment and liberal theology) or a stress on separation (e.g., Pietism and dialectical theology). At first, modern Catholic theology was anti-Protestant and dominated by controversy. Neo-Scholasticism, which was established in the nineteenth century, combined the critical debate with Protestantism with a separation towards modern culture and society. Approaches in liberal Catholic theology like the "Tübinger Schule" cannot convince or were clerically sentenced during the controversy over modernism. The struggle against modernism did not exclude inner processes of modernization in Catholic theology or in ecclesiastical structures.

Theology conceives of its modern form in processes of inner differentiation which follow the general development of society and science. When it began in the twelfth and thirteenth centuries it was still homogeneous in its interpretation of the Bible, reflection on faith, and introduction to religious practices. The beginnings of the separation of biblical and systematic theology reach back as far as the Middle Ages. In its function of thinking about faith, theology consists of three basic structures: historical, systematic, and practical science. Historical theology gained its modern form through the development of the historical-critical method, which leads to tensions with systematic theology. Pastoral theology reacts to the modern differentiation of religion and society and helps establish practical theological disciplines which specialize in the practical role of the church in society. It is a specific part of modern theology that it reflects and copies the plurality of scientific approaches and disciplines. Today, theology signifies the connection between historical disciplines (contemporary history and exegesis of the Old and New Testament, church history), systematic disciplines (philosophy, fundamental theology, dogmatics, moral theology, social ethics), and practical disciplines (pastoral theology, liturgics, canon law, missionary science, religious education). The unity within the plurality of theologies is nowadays mainly expressed in the challenges it faces: the overcoming of confessional separation, the dialogue between religions, the variety of cultures, and the separation of the world into the poor and the rich. Theology is challenged to demonstrate the unity of the Christian promise of salvation and the culturality of Christian faith. It proves to be most fruitful where it succeeds in interpreting faith as part of a sociopolitical and cultural sphere with a view to its capability for experience and action. This is all the more clear in outlines of contextual theology developed across confessional boundaries, the best known of which are feminist theology, the theology of liberation, the theology of enculturation, and the theology of religions. In the sciences, theology nowadays appears to be an indispensable science of the cultural memory and a challenge to overcome the limitations of the modern understanding of science as a system of hypothetical-deductive propositions within interdisciplinary dialogue.

SEE ALSO: Catholicism; Denomination; Hermeneutics; Orthodoxy; Protestantism; Religion; Science and Religion; Secularization

REFERENCES AND SUGGESTED READINGS

Childs, B. S. (1992) *Biblical Theology of the Old and New Testament: Theological Reflections on the Christian Bible*. SCM Press, London.

Frei, H. W. (1992) *Types of Christian Theology*. Yale University Press, New Haven.

Luther, M. (2002) *Werke. Kritische Gesamtausgabe* [= WA] Bd. 40, II. Böhlau, Weimar.

McGrath, A. E. (1994) *Christian Theology: An Introduction*. Blackwell, Oxford

Murphy, N. (1990) *Theology in the Age of Scientific Reasoning*. Cornell University Press, Ithaca, NY.

Oberman, H. A. (1963) *The Harvest of Medieval Theology: Gabriel Biel and Late Medieval Nominalism*. Harvard University Press, Cambridge, MA.

Osborne, E. (1993) *The Emergence of Christian Theology*. Cambridge University Press, Cambridge.

Schüssler-Fiorenza, E. (1996) *The Power of Naming: A Concilium Reader in Feminist Liberation Theology*. Orbis Books, Maryknoll, NY.

Stenmark, M. (1995) *Rationality in Science, Religion, and Everyday Life*. University of Notre Dame Press, Notre Dame, IN.

Tracy, D. (1975) *Blessed Rage for Order: The New Pluralism in Theology*. Winston Seabury Press, Minneapolis.

theoretical research programs

David G. Wagner

A theoretical research program has three components: a set of interrelated theories, a set of substantive and methodological working strategies used to generate and evaluate these theories, and a set of models for empirical investigation and analysis based on these theories. Theoretical research programs provide accounts of social phenomena as diverse as affect control, status organization, network exchange, resource mobilization, revolution, and coalition formation in political action. Berger and Zelditch (1993, 2002) present detailed discussion and analysis of these and many other programs. Wagner (1984) discusses the source of the concept in the work of philosopher of science Imre Lakatos (1968, 1970) on scientific research programs.

Theoretical research programs are important to our understanding of how sociological knowledge grows. Programs are distinct from the broad, overarching meta-theoretical strategies, such as functionalism and interactionism, which orient the construction of individual theories. Programs are more dynamic than strategies, the latter growing only very slowly and seldom in response to assessment of the theories that they generate. Programs are also distinct from individual theoretical arguments, or *unit theories*, such as Davis and Moore's theory of stratification or Lenski's theory of status crystallization. Although programs generally originate in a unit theory, they become much more complex as a network of interrelated theories emerges over time.

TYPES OF RELATIONS

The interrelation among theories in a program arises from a *core set* of key abstract concepts and assertions that are used in all the theories in the program. For example, the idea of an expectation state is central to the status characteristics program, the notion of a resource flow to the network exchange program. Over time these core ideas come to be used in a variety of different ways that expand our knowledge. Each of these ways represents a distinct pattern of theoretical growth.

First, the ideas may be elaborated to provide a more detailed or specific account of the phenomenon under study. Theory T_2 is an *elaboration* of theory T_1 if it uses the same underlying core ideas to address a similar explanatory domain as T_1, and is more comprehensive or specific or has better empirical grounding than T_1. Usually, T_2 is intended to serve as a replacement for T_1. Elaborations may expand the explanatory scope of a theory, formalize its structure, or enhance the empirical consequences of a theory and its corroboration.

For instance, a distributive justice theory that originally dealt only with situations involving quantity goods later expanded to deal with quality goods.

When combined with a few other new ideas, the core ideas may generate a new theory designed to explain different phenomena. T_2 is a *proliferant* of T_1 if it expands the core ideas (or adds new ones) to address a new explanatory domain or new theoretical problems in the domain of T_1. In this case, both theories are likely to be viable and important explanatory tools, since they address different problems or phenomena. Proliferations significantly expand the range of sociological problems or phenomena to which a program's theories can be applied. For example, the concept of a source evaluator was added to expectation states theory to help explain how significant others affect actors' self-evaluations and subsequent group behavior.

Sometimes two very closely related theories are developed from the same core ideas to develop more precise knowledge about how a process operates. T_1 and T_2 are *variants* of each other if they address the same or very similar explanatory domains, but propose slightly different mechanisms to account for how the process operates within that domain. Variants allow the theorist to consider and resolve small differences in understanding. Often, the result is a specification of different conditions under which each mechanism operates. For example, variant accounts of bargaining processes suggest that the use of threatening tactics either deters others from engaging in punitive behavior or leads to a spiral of conflicting threats that increases the likelihood of punitive behavior. Such variant theories may then be closely compared to determine which account provided the more effective explanation.

A superficially similar kind of relation appears when T_1 and T_2 use different sets of core ideas to address the same or overlapping explanatory domains. In this circumstance the theories are *competitors*. However, because of the significant differences in theoretical structure, it is often much more difficult to resolve explanatory differences between competitors than between variants. For example, one theory for the stabilization of mental illness invokes a labeling process, another focuses on psychophysiological processes, and these have competed with each other without full resolution since they were first articulated in the 1960s.

Finally, ideas in one theory may be combined with ideas from another theory to provide a deeper or more complete account of phenomena or domains that previously were treated separately. Theory T_3 is an *integration* of T_1 and T_2 if it consolidates many of the ideas from the earlier theories, articulating ways in which they may be related. The manner in which integration is accomplished depends on the nature of the relation between T_1 and T_2. If the integrated theories were variants, a common outcome is likely to be conditionalization. That is, T_1 is identified as operating under one set of conditions, T_2 under another set. Thus, when considering deterrence versus conflict spiral accounts of bargaining behavior, research has shown that deterrence occurs as long as the stakes in the bargaining remain relatively low. As the stakes increase, threat tactics prompt like responses, thereby generating the conditions for conflict spiral.

If T_1 and T_2 are proliferants, the integrating theory is likely to describe ways in which the different processes considered by the two earlier theories are interrelated. Accounts of the two processes may remain distinct, but connections between them are specified. For instance, reward expectations theory partially integrates status characteristics theory and the status value theory of distributive justice, the latter two theories previously having been proliferants. Reward expectations theory accomplishes this by specifying how expectations for task performance and expectations for reward allocation may form simultaneously in status situations.

Integrating competitors is most challenging. In this case the integrating theory usually must specify a new set of core ideas with which to describe the phenomena within its domain. Thus, Guillermina Jasso combined ideas from both multiple prior theories of distributive justice in developing her own. Key to her integration was the concept of a justice evaluation function, an idea that did not exist in either earlier theory.

Much more thorough accounts of the types of relation that may occur in theoretical research programs are available in Wagner (1984) and Wagner and Berger (1985). Those sources also include detailed discussion and citation of relevant examples of each type.

WORKING STRATEGIES

Orienting strategies specify the fundamental aims and presuppositions that guide theoretical work. They provide an underlying ontology (what is to be seen as sociologically real) and an epistemology (how we know what is real). They also provide a substantive foundation of presuppositions about such issues as the nature of the actor, action, and the social order. Does the actor have agency? Is action rational? What is the relative importance of conflict and consensus in action? While orienting strategies provide the meta-theoretical framework within which theoretical research programs may grow, they generally do not grow significantly or very rapidly, nor do they generally change in response to developments in the programs they frame.

There are, however, other elements of orienting strategies that do change and grow significantly in association with theoretical research programs. The directives of these *working strategies* are somewhat more specific and concrete than those of an overarching orienting strategy. Methodological working strategies provide concepts and principles dealing with the nature of theory, the logic of inquiry, and the criteria for assessing theories. Herbert Blumer's proposal of a naturalistic method for investigating symbolic interaction is, for example, a methodological working strategy. Substantive working strategies provide concepts and principles specifying what properties of actors, action, and society are considered to be crucial for investigating social phenomena. They identify what kinds of problems are worth solving and what concepts and principles to use in solving them. Merton's proposals for functional analysis represent a substantive working strategy.

Working strategies play an important role in determining what the core ideas in a program should be, what questions should be addressed, and how they should be investigated. The answers generated constitute the different theories in a program. Methodological working strategies specify how these theories are to be constructed and what methodological tools are to be employed in testing them. The foundational directives of orienting strategies provide the premises that justify working strategies; working strategies then specify more concretely how those premises can be realized.

Working strategies do not simply respond to broad foundational directives. They also respond to the success or failure of the elaborations, proliferants, variants, competitors, and integrations they stimulate. In fact, an articulation of at least some of the elements of a working strategy may only emerge gradually as theories in a program develop, broaden, and deepen understanding of the ideas under investigation. (For an illustration of this process, see the conceptualization of social interaction as a state organizing process in expectation states theory, in Berger et al. 1989, 1992). Thus, working strategies grow and change as a part of, and in concert with, the theories in the programs they guide.

MODELS

Another aspect of the development of theoretical research programs is associated with the implementation of theoretically based empirical models for research. Such models may include specifications of concrete instances of phenomena that can be modeled with the concepts and principles of theories in the program; they may specify conditions under which the model is expected to apply; they may identify observational techniques and procedures useful in applying the model; they may provide ways of interrelating elements from different theories in a program to deal with the complexity apparent in a particular application situation.

These are all issues of relevance in evaluating theoretical research programs. Models are central to evaluating the empirical adequacy of a program in representing specific social situations. They are also useful in specifying the range of situations and phenomena to which a program can be applied. Finally, models are essential in assessing how useful a program might be as a basis for intervention and change in specific social situations. (On the role of models in theory growth, see Berger & Zelditch 1998.)

MULTIDIMENSIONALITY OF THEORY GROWTH

Whether and how sociological knowledge is seen to grow thus depends on the unit of analysis chosen for considering the issue. A focus on the broad foundational orienting strategies of the discipline reveals very stable intellectual structures that change only very slowly (if at all) and without being particularly responsive to the fortunes of the theories generated from these strategies. A focus on individual unit theories yields only a consideration of changes in the empirical base for a static theoretical structure. And a focus on organizational and institutional properties like citation analyses and funding patterns reveals only growth in the social structures within which knowledge might occur, not the growth of knowledge itself.

A focus on theoretical research programs reveals *multiple* kinds and sources of growth. Knowledge grows through articulation and refinement of the working strategies that guide the construction of programs. Knowledge grows through the construction of new theories within programs. Elaborations, proliferants, variants, competitors, and integrations increase both the breadth of theoretical issues considered and the depth of understanding of those issues. Knowledge grows through assessments of the empirical adequacy and instrumental utility of the theory-based models programs generate. A consideration of all of these patterns is necessary to fully understand how our sociological knowledge may be improved.

SEE ALSO: Affect Control Theory; Exchange Network Theory; Expectation States Theory; Power-Dependence Theory; Social Justice, Theories of; Stratification and Inequality, Theories of; Theory; Theory Construction; Theory and Methods

REFERENCES AND SUGGESTED READINGS

Berger, J. & Zelditch, M., Jr. (1993) *Theoretical Research Programs: Studies in the Growth of Theory.* Stanford University Press, Stanford.
Berger, J. & Zelditch, M., Jr. (1998) Theoretical Research Programs: A Reformulation. In: Berger, J. & Zelditch, M., Jr. (Eds.), *Status, Power, and Legitimacy.* Transaction Books, New Brunswick, NJ, pp. 71–93.
Berger, J. & Zelditch, M., Jr. (2002) *New Directions in Contemporary Sociological Theory.* Rowman & Littlefield, Lanham, MD.
Berger, J., Wagner, D. G., & Zelditch, M., Jr. (1989) *Theory Growth, Social Processes, and Metatheory.* In: Turner, J. (Ed.), *Theory Building in Sociology.* Sage, Newbury Park, CA, pp. 19–42.
Berger, J., Wagner, D. G., & Zelditch, M., Jr. (1992) A Working Strategy for Constructing Theories: State Organizing Processes. In: Ritzer, G. (Ed.), *Metatheorizing.* Sage, Newbury Park, CA, pp. 107–23.
Lakatos, I. (1968) Criticism and the Methodology of Scientific Research Programmes. *Proceedings of the Aristotelian Society* 69: 149–86.
Lakatos, I. (1970) Falsification and the Methodology of Scientific Research Programmes. In: Lakatos, I. & Musgrave, A. (Eds.), *Criticism and the Growth of Knowledge.* Cambridge University Press, Cambridge, pp. 91–195.
Wagner, D. G. (1984) *The Growth of Sociological Theories.* Sage, Beverly Hills, CA.
Wagner, D. G. & Berger, J. (1985) Do Sociological Theories Grow? *American Journal of Sociology* 90: 697–728.

theory

Barry Markovsky

There are many different views in sociology about what theory is and what it should be. Many of these views are complementary, referring to different aspects of the process of theorizing, or to particular qualities that are more or less emphasized by different theorists. Some views are so disparate, however, as to be mutually incompatible, even while achieving legitimacy within mutually exclusive streams of sociological work. The purpose here is not to critically evaluate sociology's various theories and approaches, but rather to provide a short overview of some of the major strands of theoretical work. The approach will be to present several dimensions along which sociological theories have varied.

First, theories may be distinguished by major "schools," also known as approaches, frameworks, paradigms, metatheories, orientations, traditions, and by other labels as well. These forms of theorizing tend to be relatively unstructured, open to interpretation, and immune to falsification – qualities that contrast markedly with the more parsimonious and rigorous products of formal theorizing. Some argue for reserving the term "theory" just for this more tightly constructed form, as this more clearly distinguishes statements that are considered to *embody* the theory from statements and discussions that are merely *about* the theory. Second, theories may be distinguished along a temporal dimension based upon when they first entered and impacted the discipline's corpus of knowledge. A number of historians of sociology have attempted to rationalize the progression of theories and schools, typically interpreting later developments as reactions against their immediate predecessors. Third, theories may be distinguished according to the extent to which they have been developed and evaluated with explicit reference to scientific standards. This dimension of evaluation should be important to sociology to the extent that its ultimate goal is to develop theories that are general, precise, and systematically evaluated in the empirical world. Finally, several additional properties will be considered that do not fit neatly into the above scheme.

SCHOOLS OF SOCIOLOGICAL THEORIZING

A small number of schools of sociological theorizing appear in virtually all textbooks on the subject. The remainder, a very much larger number (at least 70, judging by the 2005 edition of the *Encyclopedia of Social Theory*), range from near universal coverage to rarely seen in contemporary theory texts. This means that any review covering more than a handful of schools is invoking the personal tastes of the reviewer: there is no agreed-upon metric for evaluating a school's relative success or impact.

Conflict. Conflict theories focus on destabilizing factors such as social inequalities and social change. Karl Marx usually is credited with ushering in this orientation, with his emphasis on struggles between social classes with opposing interests, the emergence of collective consciousness among the oppressed, and the conditions for violent revolutionary change. Early versions

of the perspective were further articulated by Max Weber and Georg Simmel. Beginning in the late 1950s and extending through the 1970s, a succession of theorists extended and refined various strands of thought within the developing tradition. Ralf Dahrendorf, Lewis Coser, Jonathan Turner, and Randall Collins are among the more prominent. Each developed a critique of prior work, and each sought to integrate and streamline some of the disparate insights of his predecessors. The conflict approach since has evolved into other lines of work, e.g., neo-Marxist theories, resource mobilization theory, theories of social revolutions, and breakdown theories of social movements.

Exchange. Social exchange theories reflect a kind of economic approach to social relations. As such, social actors (individuals or collectivities) are regarded as having individual interests that can be satisfied through exchanging goods, information, services – anything that others might accept in return for providing something of value. Many exchange theorists are further concerned with the larger social forces that bind together different interactants even as they pursue their individual interests. Roots of the exchange tradition in sociology can be found in the writings of Marx and Simmel. However, it was the more focused and explicit work of George Homans on behaviorist foundations, John Thibaut and Harold Kelley on rewards and costs in dyadic relationships, and Peter Blau on bridging to macro structures that really established this area's identity by the 1960s. Richard Emerson and his collaborators subsequently developed a formal theory of power–dependence relations based on exchange principles, including an initial foray into social network relations. During this time, James Coleman, David Willer, and others also were developing exchange network theories addressing power, structural change, and other phenomena. Most theories of distributive justice and equity owe a debt to the exchange perspective, and more recent theorizing on group solidarity and commitment, legitimacy, and rational choice are offshoots of, or otherwise connected to, the exchange perspective.

Functionalism. Functionalism (a.k.a. *structural functionalism*) dominated sociology for much of the period between 1930 and 1960. It regards social systems as consisting of differentiated, interdependent substructures having corresponding functions that operate in a coordinated fashion to maintain the integrity of the system as a whole. The basic ideas were first inspired by analogies to living organisms. Many theorists in this area strove to identify a set of universal *requisite* functions that are essential for the survival of any system. Early theorists included Auguste Comte, Herbert Spencer, and Émile Durkheim. In the mid-twentieth century, major figures included Robert K. Merton, who was best known for emphasizing the development of "theories of the middle-range" (between grand and particularistic), and Talcott Parsons, known for his adaptation, goal attainment, integration, and latency (AGIL) model of system functions. Although functionalism lost its dominant status in sociology many years ago, its core ideas have continued to evolve and persist through several other lines of work such as human ecology, organizational ecology, neofunctionalism, evolutionary approaches, and others.

Interactionism. In contrast to the larger field's primary concern with macro-scale social phenomena, the interactionist tradition in sociology gives primacy to what we may call the *social individual.* Charles Horton Cooley's work in the early 1900s on the emergence of self-concepts out of social interaction proved to be seminal. George Herbert Mead became a leading figure in the 1930s and beyond by synthesizing earlier work and making theoretical connections between societal institutions, the social self, and the minds of human actors. Mead's ideas were extended by theorists such as Jacob Moreno and Robert Park, both of whom emphasized the self–society connections inherent in the process of occupying social roles. While the core of this line of work came to be known as *symbolic interactionism,* branches instigated by the likes of Edmund Husserl, Alfred Schütz, Herbert Blumer, Manford Kuhn, and others included phenomenology, ethnomethodology, self theories, role theories, identity theories, emotion theories, sociolinguistics, dramaturgical analysis, conversation analysis, and more. There have been numerous prominent contributors to these theoretical developments including Ralph Turner, Erving Goffman, Aaron Cicourel, Harold Garfinkel, Sheldon Stryker, Theodore Kemper, Randall Collins, and others. Among the more interesting developments are several theories that go against the interactionist preference for discursive theorizing: David Heise's affect control theory, Peter Burke's identity control theory, and Joseph Berger's expectation states theory are all formal theories with roots in interactionism. Each has survived systematic empirical testing and grown increasingly broad and precise over time.

Structuralism. As the label implies, structuralism is concerned with the ways that patterns among social objects determine social behavior. Within this rubric can be found a dizzying array of topics, levels of analysis, and styles of theorizing. Thus, the objects of investigation can range from patterns of individual cognitions to the patterns of political coalitions among nations. The field of structuralist theories was far simpler in the twentieth century when it emerged as a direct extension of certain strands within Marxist, Durkheimian, and Simmelian theorizing. Toward the middle of the century, however, the area experienced an infusion of disparate influences from the French social anthropologist Claude Lévi-Strauss and his cognitive-linguistic approach; from the British anthropologist Alfred Radcliffe-Brown, who emphasized the reality of social structures rather than cognitive representations of them; and from the US by Moreno's sociometry, Alex Bavelas's communication network studies, balance theoretic approaches of Fritz Heider, Theodore Newcomb, Dorwin Cartwright, and Frank Harary, and Blau's macrostructural theory. Today, the more recent approaches emerging from structuralist traditions hardly seem related at all: social network analysis, Pierre Bourdieu's cultural conflict theory, Anthony Giddens's structuration theory, and many others.

Others. The preceding represents only a small sample of schools of sociological theorizing, albeit a sample whose components have had profound impacts on the field. Many others have achieved at least some level of prominence, however. In addition to several schools or perspectives mentioned but not elaborated in the preceding paragraphs, members of another set receive relatively frequent mention in contemporary textbooks and websites. To characterize some of these briefly and in no particular order:

Critical theory is so named based on its critical stance toward modernity, culture, capitalism, or other properties of what at the time is contemporary society. *Ethnomethodology* examines methods by which actors develop a sense of social order and meaning. *Feminist theories* are concerned with examining and elevating the social, political, and economic status of women in society. *Postmodernism* offers non- and anti-scientific commentaries on conditions in post-industrial society. *Systems theories* focus on structures and dynamics constituted by social system components. *Neofunctionalism* offers postpositivist antidotes to some of the limitations of functionalism. *Neo-Marxism* consists of twentieth-century attempts to account for major problems in Marx's earlier theorizing.

In summary, it is evident that sociology has a great accumulation of schools and perspectives. An optimistic view might then be that there is a fantastic "database" of ideas from which to solve intellectual and social problems. A more pessimistic view is that most of the vast proliferation of ideas seem to wax and wane according to factors that have little to do with their precision, generality, parsimony, or communicability. A view that is both realistic and constructive might be that theorists may now focus less on the process of proliferating ideas, and more on the task of weeding out via careful logical and empirical analyses those which cannot demonstrate their merits. This means relegating many ideas strictly to "history of sociology" texts, despite whatever intellectual, political, or emotional appeal they may hold for however many contemporary adherents. Progressive fields improve systematically on their most promising theories and move beyond the rest.

HISTORIES OF SOCIOLOGICAL THEORIZING

There have been many attempts to trace the historical development of sociological theory, usually from a "classical" era in the mid-nineteenth century to the present day. Most efforts interweave temporal and intellectual dimensions. That is, the publication dates of the works that are reviewed in any such reconstruction can be ordered along a timeline. Sometimes the timeline provides the backbone for the entire

review. Otherwise the timeline may be applied within but not across intellectual schools, for instance separately retracing the emergence of functionalism and interactionism via the appearance of publications associated with these respective areas. A third strategy has been to focus on one or more intellectual epochs, interpreting their development as resulting from the influences of contemporaneous intellectual endeavors and other factors. This exemplifies the application of sociology of knowledge to sociology itself: the objects of inquiry are sociological ideas and theories, with historians of the discipline offering speculations as to how empirical factors – prevailing social and political conditions, personal histories of the authors, received theories and perspectives of the day – instigated and shaped emerging schools of thought. Thus, the line between historical description and historical interpretation may blur – a bad thing if one is interested in the bald facts of sociology's history, but a good thing if one is interested in speculating on how sociology came to be the way it is today. Perhaps needless to say, there is high consensus on the temporal dimension of sociological theorizing, but less consensus on the intellectual dimensions that have shaped sociological theory.

The "sociological canon" – the authors whose seminal work is assigned in practically all sociological theory courses – includes Marx, Weber, and Durkheim. Their masterworks comprise sociology's body of *classical theory*, usually along with those of several of their contemporaries and near contemporaries whose selection tends to vary across writers. Classical theory is rife with big ideas and big aspirations. That the theorizing tended to manifest grandiose rhetoric and only selective empirical validation was and is perfectly forgivable: these were trailblazers in new territories.

Sociological theory produced within the current generation of scholars (roughly the last 25 years or so) is deemed *contemporary*. Theorizing that emerged in the years between the classical and contemporary periods also is often called contemporary, or else distinguished from contemporary theory by being called *modern*. In the brief sketches to follow, this period simply will be called *post-classical*, distinct from work residing both in the classical canon and in the most recent decades.

Classical theorizing. The sociological literature cites more or less frequently a number of European scholars that made substantial contributions either during or directly preceding the classical period. In order of their birth years (1770 to 1864) and including those noted above, they were G. W. F. Hegel, Comte, Marx, Spencer, Vilfredo Pareto, Sigmund Freud, Thorstein Veblen, Durkheim, Simmel, Mead, and Weber. Most of these men were multidisciplinary in orientation. "Sociologist" was only beginning to develop its academic identity during these years, and the extent of its assimilation by these theorists correlates positively (though imperfectly) with their chronology. Without a doubt, later theorists were influenced by their contemporaries and predecessors, sometimes building on foundations laid by others, sometimes tearing them down, sometimes launching from them into new territories. Moreover, these theorists cited influences by numerous writers in other disciplines, and almost certainly were further affected by the prevailing states of science, culture, politics, economics, and other bodies of knowledge. Together they initiated, then eventually amassed, a body of scholarship that was sufficiently distinct from others in its substantive topics, value orientations, and level of discourse to warrant its unique name.

Post-classical theorizing. For a half-century after around 1920, sociology experienced an upsurge of activity and visibility. Along with the increasing number of sociologists came an intensification and proliferation of theorizing and debate, much of it operating in the shadow cast by functionalism, the era's dominant school. Some of this activity may be attributed to the rise of the critical theory school, led by Theodor Adorno, Max Horkheimer, and other continental scholars. However, the ascension of American sociology also occurred during this period, most famously (and chronologically) via the so-called Chicago School (including W. I. Thomas, Florian Znaniecki, Park, Cooley, and Blumer), Harvard University (including Pitirim Sorokin, Parsons, and Homans), and Columbia University (including Merton, Paul Lazarsfeld, Daniel Bell, C. Wright Mills, and William J. Goode). Toward the latter part of this period, the aforementioned scholars and their intellectual offspring began to populate new departments of sociology. The resulting decline

in the hegemony of these influential programs did not reflect any decline in the production of sociological ideas, however. Every school of theorizing spawned multiple intellectual offspring, many of which have survived to the present.

Contemporary theorizing. The proliferation and diversification that characterized theorizing in the post-classical era has only accelerated. This most recent phase in the development of sociological theorizing is the most difficult to portray, with many more theorists and would-be theories arriving on the scene, and more complex relationships and influences among them. Textbooks from only five to ten years ago cite what then seemed to be burgeoning new trends that never really panned out. At best, feminist, postmodernist, agency–structure, and modernity approaches, to cite just a few, have achieved a sort of steady state as far as their impact on the "big picture" of sociological theory and research is concerned. Most of these impacts are far from discipline-wide, and some already are shrinking.

Every approach, old and new, is important to some sociologists. Whereas there is near perfect consensus on the classical canon, however, and there is *some* consensus on what we may deem to be important post-classical writings, there is nothing remotely approaching a consensus on important contemporary theorizing. Part of this state of affairs is attributable to the recency of the work. But if the past is any indication, it is more likely due to the sheer number of theoretical offerings being generated combined with the absence of any widely shared disciplinary norms for the evaluation and culling of sociological theorizing.

SCIENTIFIC VS. NON-SCIENTIFIC THEORIZING

Sociology generally is considered to be a social *science*, but a significant proportion of its theorists, researchers, and practitioners operate in ways that are indifferent to scientific norms and practices, and a subset of its members is even overtly anti-science. A central tenet of scientific fields is that research is oriented toward the development and evaluation of explicit, testable theories. In this context, a theory is a set of general, parsimonious, logically related statements containing clearly defined terms, formulated to explain the broadest possible range of phenomena in the natural world. *Formal* theories reside at the most rigorous end of the theoretical spectrum. Authors of such theories pay special attention to the form of their theoretical arguments in the sense that they take care to (1) identify and define all of the theory's key terms, (2) identify all of the theory's key statements (which may be called axioms, assumptions, propositions, or by some other name), (3) ensure that their theoretical conclusions derive logically from the other key statements, and (4) distinguish statements that are *in* the theory from statements made *about* the theory. Many sociologists believe that formal theories are expressed in mathematical languages; however, this is not necessarily the case. The defined terms may be words, and the arguments may consist of linked declarative sentences for which *sentential logic* provides rules and methods used to check for logical correctness.

Scientists regard with skepticism theories that contain ambiguous terms or ambivalent statements, or that do not have a high degree of support gathered through systematic empirical testing. Ideally, scientific theories are public and collectively evaluated in the sense that informed proponents and informed critics all have the opportunity to check them against agreed-upon standards of semantic clarity, logical integrity, and empirical verisimilitude. Science is progressive and self-correcting in the sense that its theories improve over time. This is largely due to the fact that scientists take it as their job to identify problems in theories – e.g., in their clarity, logic, or empirical support. It then becomes the job of a theory's proponents to solve the problems, lest the theory be discarded for a less flawed alternative. In this way, even while the work of individual scientists can be biased by values, politics, wishful thinking, or other factors in the short run, the long-run effect of collective evaluation is theoretical improvement at the level of the scientific discipline.

Some sociologists would prefer to reserve the "theory" label only for the brand of theorizing just described, and use terms such as perspective, metatheory, orientation, framework, or ideology for writings that fail to satisfy the foregoing definition for theory. This view is far from normative, however, and all manner of discursive, non-scientific products are referred to as theories in sociology. Some forms are self-consciously non-scientific, at the end of a spectrum opposite that of formal theories. Here, the explicit goal is not to create or evaluate theories as defined above. It may be, for example, to create rich descriptions of complex empirical phenomena, or to promote ideological or philosophical positions. For example, Marx's concept of *praxis* is often considered to be a component of Marxist theory, but is actually a prescription for revolutionary social action. In a similar way, while some contemporary feminist theories offer explanations for gender inequalities, others are explicit calls to political action. Even more confusing is that a given formulation may blend all three functions – explanatory, descriptive, ideological – and switch among them indiscriminately.

Much theorizing in sociology is non-scientific for yet another reason: the objects of discourse are not phenomena in the empirical world, but instead are other theoretical writings. Most theorists recognize this so that, for example, neofunctionalists who interpret the writings of Talcott Parsons would not claim to be doing science. Whereas the greater good of such activity may be incomprehensible from a scientific standpoint, nevertheless there is a sense in which the intellectual products of such activities grow and evolve, with the potential to discover previously unrealized nuances and insights. From a scientific standpoint, however, these activities fall short of cumulative theoretical development because the internal changes that occur as a result of discussion and debate are not governed by rules of logic and evidence. Factors such as writers' disciplinary status, personal charisma, or rhetorical skill may then produce an unwarranted degree of impact and acceptance of the theorizing they produce.

Arguably, the non-scientific label would also fit a highly *empiricist* form of research that may superficially appear to be scientific. In such work, rather than focusing on the evaluation of abstract and general theory, attention is focused solely on descriptions of observed relationships among indicators in specific data sets. Sometimes the descriptions may be highly quantitative, as would be the case with statistical modeling; or they may be highly qualitative, e.g., "thick descriptions" of observed events in natural settings. Both forms of analysis may be invaluable in the process of theory development, particularly with respect to inducing plausible theoretical conjectures to be assessed later in more diverse empirical settings. Also, such observations may be deemed to be important for some non-theoretical purpose, e.g., inferring practical solutions to problems associated with a particular empirical setting. Nevertheless, most scientists and philosophers of science now agree that observation and data analysis alone cannot sustain a science because they cannot "add up" to a theory without the aid of inductive leaps.

OTHER PROPERTIES OF SOCIOLOGICAL THEORIES

In addition to those discussed above, there are many other properties that a given sociological theory may possess or manifest to varying degrees. A selection of some of the most interesting and significant are mentioned below.

Programmatic structure. Although we may think of great theories as standing the test of time, successful theories tend to not stand still for long. As they are tested and refined, they evolve through stages as a consequence of modifications large and small. They may grow branches that address new classes of phenomena, and they may gain strength by integrating with other theories. The general term for both the ongoing theory-building and theory-testing activities, and for the resulting theoretical product, is *theory program* or *theoretical research program*. Philosopher of science Imre Lakatos was best known for exploring the dynamics of research programs, as well as the implications of conceptualizing theories as developing within programs.

Levels of analysis. To sociologists, "microlevel theorizing" or "micro-theorizing" implies a focus on the level of the individual person or small group, and often considers how they affect or are affected by phenomena at higher levels of analysis – social contexts, organizations, institutions, and so forth. "Macro-theorizing" typically focuses on relationships among larger-scale phenomena at higher levels of analysis, e.g.,

city-level rates of crime as related to levels of urban poverty. Although macro-theorists frequently make implicit assumptions about the capacities and proclivities of individuals, such links to the micro level generally are, at most, peripheral aspects of the macro-theorizing. Traditionally, sociology is a macro-theoretical discipline and so this is understandable. Since around the late 1980s, however, interest has increased in explicitly linking micro and macro levels by constructing *multilevel theories*.

Grounded theorizing. The method of grounded theorizing is used to arrive at a theory that is assured of being consistent with a set of observations. It is an inductive process in the sense that the specific observations in which the theory is "grounded" are used to stimulate the development of more abstract and general definitions and categories. Although this guarantees that the theory will conform to the given observations, it also becomes possible to "over-fit" the theory, i.e., to tailor it too closely to particular nuances of the data at hand and so render it less likely to generalize beyond those data. Until a grounded theory is validated by systematic testing with a variety of methods, data sets, and phenomena not employed in its development, it is more accurate to consider it to be a form of empirical generalization.

Typologies. A typology is a framework for organizing concepts. As the name implies, it is concerned with different types or manifestations of the ideas it organizes. Thus, a simple one-dimensional categorical typology of norms for the allocation of social rewards may include "need," "equity," and "equality." A typological dimension also may be ordered, e.g., ranking degrees of national economic development by the labels "first world," "second world," and "third world." Typologies also may have multiple dimensions. For instance, we could classify nations simultaneously along two dimensions: economic development (as just described) and form of government (monarchy, democracy, etc.). Frequently such typologies are presented in tabular form. Within each cell of the table may be either a general term for that particular cross-classification (e.g., "Type C"), or an illustrative or exhaustive list of empirical referents ("Germany, New Zealand, Costa Rica"). Importantly, only a very broad definition of "theory" would include typology building as a form of theorizing because typologies do not by themselves provide explanations or define theoretical terms. Nevertheless, they can be a powerful theoretical tool by providing systematic refinements of theoretical terms that, in turn, promote finer-grained explanations of the phenomena classified by the typology.

Propositional inventories. Some sociological articles and books offer lists of theoretical propositions highlighted in the body of the text or listed in an appendix. Such lists or inventories are intended to encapsulate the theoretical knowledge contained within the work. However, a list of propositions does not automatically constitute a theoretical knowledge. First, the propositions in a theory should be abstract, general statements linked to one another to form a logical system from which new statements may be derived. There is no such requirement for propositional inventories, and usually they are compiled without concern for the extent or pattern of their propositions' logical interrelatedness. Even so, a subset of propositions within an inventory could provide key components for a theory. Second, propositions in an inventory frequently vary in the extensiveness of the evidence upon which they are based, or in the care taken by the author in defining their terms.

Computer simulations. Although fundamentally they are nothing more than instruction sets, computer simulations (or *computational sociology*) have been adopted as a tool for expressing and logically examining theoretical statements. Just as statements in everyday language may range from particularistic and concrete to general and abstract, so may statements in computer programs depending upon how their terms are defined. When terms in program statements are defined abstractly, and the statements organized so as to model general phenomena and processes, simulations can function exactly like theories. In addition, computer simulation offers tools for automatic logic-checking and dynamic analysis that are unparalleled in traditional methods.

SEE ALSO: Conflict Theory; Exchange Network Theory; Functionalism/Neofunctionalism; Grounded Theory; Knowledge, Sociology of; Mathematical Sociology; Metatheory; Micro–Macro Links; Postmodernism; Postpositivism; Rational Choice Theories; Social Exchange Theory; Social Structure; Stratification and Inequality, Theories of; Structural Functional Theory; Structuralism; Symbolic Interaction; System Theories; Theory Construction; Theory and Methods

REFERENCES AND SUGGESTED READINGS

Alexander, J. (Ed.) (2001) *Mainstream and Critical Social Theory.* Sage, Thousand Oaks, CA.

Berger, J. & Zelditch, M., Jr. (Eds.) (1993) *Theoretical Research Programs: Studies in the Growth of Theory.* Stanford University Press, Stanford, CA.

Berger, J. & Zelditch, M., Jr. (Eds.) (2002) *New Directions in Contemporary Sociological Theory.* Rowman & Littlefield, Lanham, MD.

Calhoun, C., Gerteis, J., Moody, J., Pfaff, S., & Virk, I. (Eds.) (2003) *Contemporary Sociological Theory.* Blackwell, Malden, MA.

Cohen, B. P. (1989) *Developing Sociological Knowledge*, 2nd edn. Nelson-Hall, Chicago.

Fararo, T. J. (1989) *The Meaning of General Theoretical Sociology.* Cambridge University Press, New York.

Kivisto, P. (Ed.) (2003) *Social Theory Roots and Branches: Readings*, 2nd edn. Roxbury, Los Angeles.

Merton, R. K. (1968 [1949]) *Social Theory and Social Structure*, enlarged edn. Free Press, New York.

Münch, R. (1994) Sociological Theory. Vol. 1: *From the 1850s to the 1920s.* Vol. 2: *From the 1920s to the 1960s.* Nelson-Hall, Chicago.

Pampel, F. C. (2000) *Sociological Lives and Ideas: An Introduction to the Classical Theorists.* Worth, New York.

Powers, C. H. (2004) *Making Sense of Social Theory.* Rowman & Littlefield, Lanham, MD.

Ritzer, G. (Ed.) (2005) *Encyclopedia of Social Theory.* Sage, Thousand Oaks, CA.

Stinchcombe, A. L. (1968) *Constructing Social Theories.* University of Chicago Press, Chicago.

Szmatka, J., Lovaglia, M. & Wysienska, K. (Eds.) (2002) *The Growth of Social Knowledge.* Praeger, New York.

Turner, J. H. (Ed.) (1989) *Theory Building in Sociology: Assessing Theoretical Cumulation.* Sage, Thousand Oaks, CA.

Turner, J. H. (2003) *The Structure of Sociological Theory*, 7th edn. Wadsworth/Thomson Learning, Belmont, CA.

theory construction

Murray Webster, Jr. and Barry Markovsky

In sociology, the term theory is used in a variety of ways, not all of which are mutually compatible. For present purposes we adopt a definition that is consistent with how the term is used by many sociologists, and by most scientists outside of our field: a *theory* is a set of explicit, abstract, general, logically related statements formulated to explain phenomena in the natural world. *Theory construction* is then the process of formulating and assembling components of theories into coherent wholes, or the process of revising and expanding theories in light of logical, semantic, and empirical analyses.

HISTORICAL DEVELOPMENT

Sociology's interest in theory construction arose quite suddenly in the 1960s, and tapered off relatively quickly thereafter. As one indicator of this pattern, all of the books that could be found on the subject of building sociological theories were located. None was published before 1960; 13 appeared between 1960 and 1975, seven between 1976 and 1990, and only one since – ironically, a collection of papers from a 1990 conference on the failure of formal theory to thrive in sociology. It is clear that sociology's interest in theory construction is less prominent now, as shown by decreasing numbers of didactic books and journal articles on the topic.

One possible reason for the decline in interest in the topic is that sociologists may be prone to embrace new approaches, only to move on to others as the glow of novelty fades. Also, advocates of the theory construction movement sometimes promoted differing, arcane, and even contradictory methods and rationales. We see two other influences as most significant, however. First, while relatively few sociologists would object to the goals of the theory construction movement (e.g., clear language and sound logic), approaching those goals entails hard work and discursive, informal theories are still the norm in sociology. Second, and

relatedly, the theory construction movement may have seemed to promise more than it delivered. Theories did not leap forward, full-blown paradigms were not replaced, and sociological knowledge appeared to continue growing at a measured pace without the adoption of explicit theory construction methods. Disappointment led some to falsely caricature the movement, creating and then destroying "straw men." Some reached the pessimistic conclusion that, because sociological theory has not advanced as they hoped, it may be impossible to build theory in our field (Cole 2001; for a more hopeful view, see Berger et al. 2005).

There is cause for optimism about sociology's future attention to theory construction issues. Interest in the subject has never disappeared and, over the course of decades, published work increasingly has attended to formal aspects of its underlying theories. It would not be surprising to see a resurgence of interest. This is because theory construction not only is a substantive topic, but also a body of *methods* that can improve theories *and* research, and bind the field more securely to the broader fabric of interdisciplinary knowledge.

ELEMENTS OF THEORIES

All theories are built from just a few basic elements. Different approaches to sociological theory building have emphasized some of these elements more than others, and sometimes elaborated them in ways that mask their simplicity. Nevertheless, theories boil down to just this: *terms* are used to build *statements*; statements are used to build *arguments*; and arguments apply under a set of *scope conditions*.

Terms

Ideally, every word or symbol in a theory is carefully chosen by the theorist to convey an idea or concept. Some terms may not be understood a priori the same way by all readers, however. To promote their clear communication to others, the theorist may assign to a term one or more conditions that must be satisfied in order for something to be considered an instance of it. For example: "*social power*: the capacity to extract resources from another actor against the other's interests." Here, "social power" is a *defined term*. Having "the capacity to extract resources" along with it being "against the other's interests" are conditions of the *definition*. erms, so in any given theory the theorist will need to employ as a foundation some *primitive terms* whose meanings already are clear to the intended audience. A theory should have the minimum number of primitive terms and defined terms that are needed to communicate its claims to an intended audience.

Statements

Theories contain statements, each of which relates the states or values of one or more terms to the states or values of one or more other terms. For example, "The higher the parents' income, the more education is achieved by their children." A more famous example from another discipline: $e = mc^2$.

Arguments

Well-constructed theories combine multiple statements and apply rules of logic to generate new statements. These are called arguments, and their component statements go by various names such as propositions, assumptions, premises, postulates, or axioms. The new statements they generate are called derivations, implications, conclusions, or theorems. Consider the above proposition on income and achievement, to which we add: "The more education a child receives, the higher his/her income upon entry into the workforce." Combining the two statements and applying basic logic, lets us conclude: "The higher the parents' income, the higher the child's income upon entry into the workforce." Note also how the two propositions *explain* the conclusion via the mediating effects of education.

Scope Conditions

Scope conditions are provisional statements that assert the conditions under which a theorist considers the theory to be applicable. Relatively few sociological theories identify scope conditions as such, but nevertheless they are crucial because they provide guidance to researchers who are interested in testing or applying a theory.

PROPERTIES OF THEORIES

Inspiration for a theory can come from anywhere: observation, imagination, modifications to existing theories, and so on. Not all theories are created equal, however, and a variety of criteria exist that allow reasoned selections among alternative theories. In a word, such criteria help us to decide among theories on the basis of their *believability*. Some of these criteria are empirical, as when statistical methods are applied to help decide whether data confirm or refute hypotheses derived from a theory. Here we are most concerned with criteria pertaining to qualities that may be "built-in" at the time the theory is constructed. Their goal is to promote accurate communication, rigorous testing, high accuracy, and broad applicability. They include the following: absence of contradictions, absence of ambivalence, abstractness, generality, precision, parsimony, and conditionality. We will describe each briefly.

- *Absence of contradictions.* If statements in a theory contradict one another (e.g., "If X, then Y" and "If X, then not Y," then the rules of logic dictate that the theory must be false. As such, it cannot fulfill its primary function of explaining phenomena.
- *Absence of ambivalence.* Ambivalent statements such as "If X, then maybe Y" are not themselves contradictory, but they allow other contradictory claims to coexist. In this case, "If X then Y" and "If X, then not Y" are both consistent with the ambivalent statement, but cannot coexist without creating a contradiction. Thus, ambivalence must be eliminated from theories.
- *Abstractness.* If a theory were *concrete* – the opposite of *abstract* – then it could explain only one particular phenomenon at a certain place and time. Abstractness ensures that theories have the potential to explain many phenomena in many times and places, including those that have yet to occur.

- *Generality.* This is a two-pronged criterion. First, a general theory has numerous and varied applications to phenomena in the world. Second, a general theory has survived numerous and varied tests. It is important for a sociological theory to be capable of generating hypotheses about a wide variety of social phenomena, and just as important that the hypotheses survive empirical testing. If a theory has few applications, it will not be useful. If it has not survived tests, it lacks believability.
- *Precision.* A theory could be general, but also imprecise in the sense that it has survived many tests that were not especially stringent. For instance, predicting and verifying that "Group A existed longer than Group B" is not nearly as precise and informative as predicting and verifying that "Group A survived 3 years and 75 days; Group B survived 11 days."
- *Parsimony.* All else being equal, theories with fewer terms and statements are preferable to those having more terms and statements. This facilitates communication, as well as logical and empirical analysis of the theory.
- *Conditionality.* One of the qualities that distinguishes theories from descriptions of phenomena is the conditionality of theories. In particular, the core statements of theories assert how one concept is conditional on another: "If A, then B," or "The greater the X, the greater the Y," or even "e = mc^2." Conditional statements then combine to form theoretical arguments, from which new conditional statements may be derived and tested. In another sense, theories are also conditionalized by their use of scope conditions which express the conditions under which the theory is deemed to apply or not to apply.

Once the components of theories are assembled into a coherent whole, it becomes possible to compare them on each criterion. At present, there is no formula for adding up these qualities into something like an overall "believability index." However, the criteria are useful for thinking about ways to improve individual theories, or to compare multiple theories on particular dimensions when "all else is equal" or nearly so.

BUILDING INDUCTIVELY

In the social sciences, two different motivations account for much of the work that is done with theories. The first is the desire to understand a set of observations by developing a theory to explain them. The second is the wish to explore the untapped consequences of preexisting theory, seeking empirical tests and applications, and thereby evaluating the power of the theory. We refer to these general approaches as *inductive* and *deductive*, respectively. In this section we discuss the former, and then discuss the deductive approach in the next section.

Status characteristics theory (SCT, a.k.a. "the theory of status characteristics and expectation states") will illustrate the inductive aspects of theory construction. SCT's roots can be traced to 1950s research by Robert F. Bales on task-focused, collectively oriented discussion groups. These so-called Bales groups usually included 2–20 individuals, often college students who volunteered to participate. Through open discussions regarding a given problem or issue, groups typically arrived at collective decisions in 30–60 minutes. Members of the research team tallied their observations of such factors as who initiated contributions, the nature of those contributions, and to whom each was directed.

Early Bales group researchers observed four regularities:

1　There were participation inequalities. For instance, in 3-person groups, the highest, middle, and lowest participants initiated about 50 percent, 30 percent, and 20 percent of the group's contributions, respectively.
2　Group members' rates of initiating task-relevant communications tended to correspond with their rates of receiving such communications from others.
3　Once inequalities emerged, typically they remained stable for the rest of the session, then reappeared in any subsequent interactions.
4　Individuals' ranks on participation rates tended to correspond with their ranks on all manner of perceived skills and influence.

Berger (1958) posited that these observed regularities are components of a social structure that arises under certain task-focused interaction conditions. He reasoned that the empirical regularities could be explained by *observable power and prestige orders* that emerge from underlying *performance expectation states* that are built up through the interaction process. The first published version of Berger's new theory came with a set of abstract and general scope conditions, among which were the requirements that group members are task-focused and collectively oriented. Explicit propositions explained the process whereby performance expectations are formed and how expectations are transformed into the group power and prestige order.

While Berger's theory of performance expectations and behavior was subjected to tests in new situations, theorists also began to consider cases in which group members have preexisting status differences – a condition largely absent in Bales groups. For instance, juries are certainly task-focused, collectively oriented groups. Unlike Bales groups, however, jurors typically vary by status characteristics such as age, gender, race, and occupation. What happens in such groups is that power and prestige orders emerge very quickly from initial encounters among members. When jurors choose a foreperson before they deliberate, they have minimal knowledge regarding one another's abilities. Nevertheless, they overwhelmingly favor someone with advantages on their society's status characteristics, such as a member of the racial majority with a high-prestige occupation.

Research from a variety of sources confirms that groups with members differentiated on external status organize their internal power and prestige orders in a manner consistent with advantages the characteristic confers in the larger society. This occurs whether or not members' status characteristics are relevant to the group task. It seems that group members develope expectations for task performance by "importing" cultural beliefs regarding status advantages and disadvantages, and then infer specific skills to group members on that basis. These and many diverse cases became explainable by the SCT as it was extended to include explicit, testable propositions regarding links between status characteristics, performance expectations, and social behavior (Wagner & Berger 2002).

To summarize, the evolution of SCT implies a series of steps through which inductive theory building can transpire:

1 *List empirical generalizations.* In the case of SCT, a body of findings from prior research provided the raw material for theoretical explanation.
2 *Formulate generalizations abstractly.* To build SCT, it was necessary to develop abstract concepts removed from particular studies and historical circumstances.
3 *Explain generalizations theoretically.* That is, additional general propositions are postulated with an eye toward combining them into a theoretical system that permits the focal generalizations to be deduced from others.
4 *Explicate scope conditions.* The purpose here is to demarcate classes of situations within which the general propositions should explain and predict phenomena of interest, and to distinguish these from situations in which the theory does not claim to provide explanations.
5 *Derive and test new consequences.* By deriving general statements and substituting empirical indicators for theoretical terms, it becomes possible to develop and conduct independent tests of the theory.
6 *Identify and conceptualize new applications.* Useful theories never stop developing. In this case, SCT was extended to incorporate predictions for situations of status-heterogeneity as well as for the original equal status cases. SCT also has been extended and refined in a number of other ways, making it far deeper and broader than it was when first developed.

In all this work, there is an interplay of the empirical and the theoretical. The theorist attempts to explain some limited set of phenomena, develops an explanation, and conducts tests independent of the original observations that the theory was designed to explain. The tests may confirm theory, or they may refute it and stimulate modifications. The theorist searches for new applications and attempts to account for them with the theory, leading to new tests and modifications in an endless process of development.

BUILDING DEDUCTIVELY

We illustrate deductive theory building using Blau's (1977) *theory of inequality and heterogeneity*. Blau's original theory was entirely verbal, but later it was formalized by Skvoretz (1983) using an algebraic language. Blau began by considering two groups of different sizes. For convenience, we may think of them as groups of people, but the theory applies as well to any interacting units, whether human, animal, or computer simulated. To say there are two groups suggests there may be a differentiating basis (e.g., skin color or religion). Now suppose there is some interaction across the boundary between the groups, such as friendships or marriages. The theory's first task simply was to analyze how different relative group sizes affect cross-boundary interactions.

If the two groups differ in size, and if interaction across the boundary is essentially random, one can deduce that an individual from the small group is more likely to interact with an individual from the large group than vice-versa. For instance, suppose (1) the differentiating principle is skin color, (2) there are ten times as many in the larger group as in the smaller group, and (3) the interaction basis is friendship. If friendships form at random, then a much larger proportion of the small group (black) will have out-group (white) friends than vice-versa. Blau noted that this explained a lament he had heard among some of his egalitarian white friends who wished they had more black friends. They simply do not encounter enough potential out-group friends in their daily interactions. That could only transpire if there were a high degree of cross-group interaction and black individuals on average were willing to accept ten times as many friends as white individuals. For religion and marriage, the same relations hold. All else being equal, any randomly selected Jew in the US (about 3 percent of the population) has a higher chance of marrying a Christian (about 90 percent of the population) than does a randomly selected Christian of marrying a Jew. It is purely a "numbers effect," independent of other factors such as individual preferences for in-group friends or spouses. After exploring consequences of the basic two-group framework, Blau considered more complex situations by introducing preferences that biased

the random associations, hierarchical factors such as status differences, and intersecting bases of differentiation within and between groups.

In the Christian–Jew example, we know that interaction across groups is not random, and that it is not the case that 90 percent of Jews marry Christians. Interactions between and within groups tend to be biased by the shapes of social networks, and those networks tend to be connected more densely within groups than between them. Skvoretz (1983) took this into account when he formalized Blau's discursive theory using a kind of mathematics called *biased net theory*. He translated Blau's propositions into equations where the dependent or resultant variables were probabilities of in-group associations, and the independent or causal variables were generalized, symbolic versions of factors identified by Blau. Skvoretz's version can claim several accomplishments. First, the formalized theory corrects some errors that are not obvious in the discursive theory. For instance, "salience" in the discursive theory is treated the same as "in-group preference," whereas the formal theory demonstrates the utility of distinguishing the two concepts. Second, the formalized theory is more precise and thus more testable in its implications. Third, the formalized theory is more general, applicable to types of association beyond the friendships and marriages that Blau considered.

To review, this case of deductive theory building proceeded through these stages:

1 *Assert and explore general propositions.* Blau postulated that relative group sizes should affect intergroup associations in predictable ways, independent of all other factors. He explored the consequences of his theoretical propositions for cases of friendship and marriage formation.
2 *Explore new or modified propositions.* Further work explored the effects of additional factors in more complex situations, such as those with in-group preferences, ordered differentiation, and cross-cutting differentiation.
3 *Formalize.* Skvoretz's formalization revealed new and improved predictions, extended the theory's scope, and produced a more rigorous, general theory. Formalizing does not necessarily mean translating words into mathematical expressions, however.

Sentential logic and predicate logic are formalizations that can be applied to well-constructed English sentences, and definitions of terms certainly can be written in carefully formulated prose. Formalization is best thought of as a process for improving discursive theory by sharpening the meanings of terms and the explicitness of arguments.

RECOMMENDATIONS

Once they are built, all good theories are deductive in the sense of having clearly stated propositions from which other statements logically follow. As well, most theories also are inductive in the sense that their propositions, and modifications to their propositions, typically began as conjectures and intuitive leaps. The inductive and deductive approaches we outlined have different emphases, but it is worth noting that any theory-building enterprise can be improved by keeping in mind the following:

1 *Identify all significant terms.* Select primitive terms judiciously, and define the rest at a level of abstraction that will facilitate the construction of general propositions, useful links to empirical phenomena for tests and applications, and comprehension on the part of readers in the intended audience. There is an art to developing a theory's terminological system, along with much trial and error.
2 *Identify general propositions.* Be sure a reader can tell what the theory is arguing (i.e., what it assumes to be true, and what it concludes on the basis of those assumptions). Explicit terms and propositions facilitate logical and empirical analyses of a theory, and also facilitate its formalization.
3 *Identify scope conditions.* It is important for a theorist to place some limitations on the domain in which his or her theory will apply. For tests within its scope, confirmations increase the theory's believability, while disconfirmations diminish it. For tests conducted outside of a theory's scope, neither confirmation nor disconfirmation can impact the theory. If scope conditions are not stated, then its author implicitly claims either that the theory applies everywhere to everything – an impossibility – or that he or she simply has not thought about the theory's limitations, making the theory highly vulnerable to failing tests in settings that the author may not ever have considered to be relevant.
4 *Conduct rigorous tests.* Building theories differs from punditry in the sense that the theorist who seeks out disconfirmations through well-designed tests is more likely to home-in on an accurate explanation than the theorist who only looks for confirmations. Rigorous tests are more likely than weak tests (or no tests) to identify areas where a theory can be improved. *Critical tests* evaluate conflicting hypotheses from competing theories and are thus especially valuable for the advancement of knowledge.
5 *Improve the theory.* Theories improve over time as they are refined and extended. Every element of a theory is subject to modification: terms can be sharpened to incorporate or exclude great swaths of empirical phenomena; scope conditions can be relaxed to permit broader application; propositions may be added to address new kinds of phenomena, and formalized to allow more precise explanations and hypotheses.

We began this entry by noting that theoretical knowledge, far from being mysterious, is actually how we understand the social world. What we *know* about social processes and social structures is exactly that which is embodied in our *theories* of social processes and social structures. Our knowledge is never completely valid and reliable, and it is always provisional, as tomorrow's tests and theoretical modifications alter what we think we know today. At the same time, these changes must be progressive. That is, today's knowledge should be more valid and reliable than it was, say, a few decades ago. And knowledge in a few decades (or sooner) should be better than today's. The more systematic our adoption and application of the tools of theory construction, the more efficiently our knowledge will improve.

SEE ALSO: Blau, Peter; Expectation States Theory; Mathematical Sociology; Micro–Macro Links; Theory; Theory and Methods

REFERENCES AND SUGGESTED READINGS

Berger, J. (1958) Relations between Performance, Rewards, and Action-Opportunities in Small Problem-Solving Groups. Doctoral dissertation, Harvard University, Cambridge, MA.

Berger, J., Willer, D., & Zelditch, M., Jr. (2005). Theory Programs and Theoretical Problems. *Sociological Theory* 23: 127–55.

Blau, P. M. (1977) *Inequality and Heterogeneity: A Primitive Theory of Social Structure.* Free Press, New York.

Cohen, B. P. (1989) *Developing Sociological Knowledge.* Nelson-Hall, Chicago.

Cole, S. (Ed.) (2001) *What's Wrong with Sociology?* Transaction Publishers, New Brunswick, NJ.

Freese, L. (1980) Formal Theorizing. *Annual Review of Sociology* 6: 187–212.

Skvoretz, J. (1983) Salience, Heterogeneity and Consolidation of Parameters: Civilizing Blau's Primitive Theory. *American Sociological Review* 48: 360–75.

Wagner, D. G. & Berger, J. (2002) Expectation States Theory: An Evolving Research Program. In: Berger, J. & Zelditch, M., Jr. (Eds.), *Theoretical Research Programs: Studies in the Growth of Theory.* Rowman & Littlefield, New York.

theory and methods

Barry Markovsky

Theories organize and manipulate elements in a world of ideas. In contrast, *methods* organize and manipulate elements in the natural world, the world of concrete objects and events. Although *theory* has a variety of meanings in sociology, a definition that is both widely shared within the field and also consistent with the term's use in mainstream sciences is the following: a theory is a set of abstract, general, logically related statements formulated to explain phenomena in the natural world. The term method is commonly used two ways in sociology: (1) a procedure enacted in the natural world for the purpose of yielding theoretically relevant observations; (2) an analysis of recorded observations that is intended to summarize or to make inferences about them. The first usage is loosely referred to as *research methods*. The second usage, *methods of data analysis*, encompasses our rather large palette of qualitative and quantitative techniques for working with empirical observations.

Countless books and journal articles have been published on topics in sociological theory and sociological methods over the years. However, there is relatively little information to be found on the details of their interface – the points of contact where correspondences are drawn between theories and the slices of the natural world to which they are intended to apply. This also reflects common practice: published research generally establishes relatively loose and intuitive linkages between theories and their empirical realizations. Sometimes the informality is appropriate, as when new theoretical ideas are being explored and there is uncertainty as to the specifics of their applicability to natural phenomena. Other times the lack of specificity can be highly problematic, such as when researcher A claims to have tested and falsified B's theory, but B contends that the theory was not intended to address the phenomena used in A's test. In general, the burden is on the theorist to clarify terms so that appropriate methods and analyses may be developed by others.

The theory–method interface is a crucial area of concern because, as social scientists, we are motivated to make our theories relevant to the natural world, either for the purpose of understanding it better or to intervene in sociological phenomena in desired ways. It is through our research methods and our methods of data analysis that we attempt to determine the degree of relevance of our theories to the phenomena that we seek to understand. This implies that there is an intimate relationship between theories and methods, but also that they are distinct spheres of operation, each with its own rules and standards. Without a doubt, sociological writings often obscure distinctions between theoretical statements and observation statements, and it may be difficult or even impossible to fully prevent theories from coloring the observations that we make. However, to then presume that theory and method are indistinguishable in some inherent sense only leads to unwarranted confusion.

When developed without the benefit of strong connections to the natural world, theories are no more valid than fantasies, and they deserve no better than highly provisional support. By the same token, when enacted without the benefit of clear theoretical purposes, methods are no more useful to us than undocumented snapshots of unfamiliar objects. Thus, theories rely on methods to make them believable, and methods rely on theories to give meaning to their products.

The interface of theory and methods – where elements in the theoretical realm connect to elements of the natural world – becomes most apparent when theories are written explicitly and succinctly, and their connections to objects in the natural world are rendered unequivocal. This is the ideal situation, and we will conclude by examining it in a bit more detail.

There are three essential components to the theory–methods connection: statements in the theory, statements about particular observations, and statements that link terms in the theory with specific observations. Their relationship is shown schematically in Figure 1.

Theories employ conditional statements, often called propositions or assumptions, to make general claims that can be subjected to scrutiny. An example appears in the upper half of the figure in the "theoretical world." The statement may be read "If A, then B," where A

and B are each simple declarative statements. For example, A may be "A group has a role structure" and B could be "A group has a system of rewards and punishments." The conditional statement $A \rightarrow B$ asserts that if the first statement is true, then the second statement will be true as well.

To link theoretical propositions to the natural world, the terms in the propositions must be connected to actual empirical phenomena. The theoretical terms are abstract constructions (or "constructs"), not at all like descriptions of rich, complex objects in the natural world, but extremely useful from the standpoint of a theory: abstract terms are needed if the theory is to be *general* (i.e., applicable to a wide range of empirical cases). In the figure, each simple statement from the theory is connected to multiple concrete and specific referents in the natural world. For instance, a_1 may be "The Chess Club now active at Fairview High School has three elected positions" and b_1 could be "The Chess Club now active at Fairview High School has trophies for outstanding performance, and rescinds the membership of any member caught cheating." There are also implicit linking statements: " 'The Chess Club now active at Fairview High School' *is an instance of* 'a group' " and " 'A combination of multiple elected and appointed positions' *is an instance of* 'a role structure.' " Now, having translated the theoretical statements into empirical statements, we can derive as many testable *hypotheses* as we have empirical instances (e.g., "If the Chess Club at Fairview High School has multiple elected and appointed positions, then it will have trophies for outstanding performance and rescind the membership of any member caught cheating"). Furthermore, a_2, b_2, a_3, b_3, and so on, can pertain to wildly different kinds of groups, rewards, etc.

Instructions for how to create these linking statements are supplied by the definitions of the theoretical terms; that is, the definitions for terms such "role structure," "reward," and "punishment" in the example above. This is why it is important for a theorist to define terms as clearly as possible. Failing to do so means that researchers will be uncertain as to the theory's proper application, leaving it vulnerable to interpretations that its author never intended for it to cover. At the same time, definitions

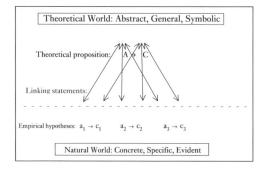

Figure 1 The heart of the theory–methods connection.

must be sufficiently open to interpretation so that the theory will be applicable to the widest possible range of cases. Thus, good theories strike a useful balance between specificity and generality.

Now that the theory can guide the choice of empirical indicators, research methods can be used to gather data, (e.g., through experiments, surveys, participant observation, text analysis, or other means – preferably more than one). The choice of research methods, in conjunction with the specific questions the researcher would like to answer, jointly guide the choice of methods for data analysis.

SEE ALSO: Experimental Methods; Mathematical Sociology; Social Indicators; Theoretical Research Programs; Theory; Theory Construction

REFERENCES AND SUGGESTED READINGS

Bunge, M. (1999) *The Sociology-Philosophy Connection*. Transaction Books, New Brunswick, NJ.
Cohen, B. P. (1989) *Developing Sociological Knowledge: Theory and Method*, 2nd edn. Nelson Hall, Chicago.
Glymour, C. (1980) *Theory and Evidence*. Princeton University Press, Princeton.
Kerlinger, F. N. & Lee, H. B. (2000) *Foundations of Behavioral Research*, 4th edn. Wadsworth, Belmont, CA.
Schutt, R. K. (2004) *Investigating the Social World*, 4th edn. Pine Forge Press, Thousand Oaks, CA.

third world and postcolonial feminisms/ subaltern

Marietta Morrissey

Sociological interest in feminism in the so-called third world nations of Asia, Africa, and Latin America has been conditioned by disciplinary reactions and responses to larger theoretical transformations in the academy. The consequence has been a shift from liberal feminist interpretations to more comprehensive understandings of the range of feminisms that have emerged in conditions of economic dependency, underdevelopment, and globalization. More recently, sociologists have begun to consider the complexity of women's positions and those of other powerless groups – the subaltern – through the lens of postcolonial studies.

THIRD WORLD FEMINISMS

Liberal Feminism: WID and GAD

Sociologists' initial contributions to our understanding of third world feminism coincided with the early stages of the sociological study of women more generally. Emphasizing occupational and educational inequality and gendered wage disparity, sociologists of the late 1970s and early 1980s assumed parallels between feminisms in the first and third worlds. Indeed, many women in poor countries aspired to higher levels of education and occupational achievement. Vibrant liberal feminist movements developed in many nations of the third world. Often led by western-educated women from wealthy families, they encouraged women and girls to seek educational parity with men and success in the occupational and business sectors from which they had been excluded. Progressive women's groups and organizations recognized in traditional cultural norms and male-inspired and dominated development strategies impediments to socioeconomic achievement by women (Boserup 1970).

International development and lending agencies encouraged liberal feminism by promoting Women in Development (WID) policies. Internationally funded economic development projects, particularly those emphasizing entrepreneurship, urged women's participation. Multilateral sponsors often required a WID component in project proposals. Many national governments adopted a similar approach. These practices remain in place today as development agencies recognize more fully women's roles in the production and marketing of crafts and food.

Academic and other critics of WID argued that separating women from families and community ties and the larger context of underdevelopment misunderstands women's positions and thus has had little impact on women's educational or occupational statuses. Meanwhile, men have objected to the exclusive funding of women's business projects in some settings, claiming discrimination (Barriteau 2001). Thus, Gender and Development (GAD) initiatives were launched. They emphasize the relationship between the development process and gender relations and insist that neither men nor women be disadvantaged in nationally and internationally sponsored development projects.

Ultimately, the liberal feminist philosophy embodied in WID and GAD embraces only sectors of populations with access to basic resources. Larger populations of women have economic, health, and political concerns that have gradually come to the attention of scholars both within and outside the third world (Kandiyoti 1988). Researchers and theorists throughout the academy now generally acknowledge that western-defined liberal feminism has little adaptability to women's concerns in third world nations. Indeed, the commonly cited distinctions among liberal, socialist, and radical feminisms deemed appropriate to first world countries do not accurately capture the reality of feminism in the third world.

National Feminisms

The most significant contributors to the redefinition of third world feminism have been activist and academic women working in national contexts. Themselves often from bourgeois backgrounds, they have had access to governmental organizations and NGOs working with the poor. The transmission and interpretation of the voices of low-income and marginalized people broke conceptual barriers and allowed new definitions of third world feminist ideology and political movements to emerge. Representing many different disciplines with a strong affinity to sociology (particularly history, political science, and anthropology), academic work of the late 1980s and the 1990s on feminisms in the third world was often interdisciplinary and privileged the voices of the poor and disenfranchised over methodological issues and debates. No longer strictly or primarily sociological, studies of third world feminisms

from a social science view became part of a core of women's and gender studies literature.

Women's and gender studies caucuses and studies sections within Latin American, Caribbean, Asian, African, Middle Eastern, and other regionally focused organizations have provided important venues for the discussion and dispersal of the work of international feminists that together form interdisciplinary bodies of knowledge about third world women's positions and politics. Within sociology, *Gender and Society* has been an important vehicle for the education of sociologists in the US about work on feminism, women, and gender in third world settings. Of particular note are the literature reviews authored by third world feminist sociologists treating the state of women's and gender studies in their nations and regions (e.g., Ampofo et al. 2004).

POSTCOLONIAL FEMINISMS

Poststructural and Postcolonial Studies

While national scholars within third world nations redefined feminisms in ways pertinent to the social sciences, a parallel process was occurring in humanities disciplines. It began with a theoretical challenge to more traditional interpretive theories from proponents of poststructural approaches to literary and cultural interpretation. With their origins in linguistic theory, poststructural and postmodern critical and interpretive methods have called for the interrogation, deconstruction, and reinterpretation of representation in literature, art, and other cultural forms. Postcolonial theories have considered cultural representations produced in colonial and postcolonial settings. Third world feminist scholars (in particular, Spivak 1988, 1999) have expanded postcolonial theoretical categories in analyzing gender in postcolonial culture.

Postcolonial theories recognize the impact on third world nations of the historic termination of formal political and economic relations in the 1960s and 1970s. Indeed, decolonization was a product, albeit sometimes an indirect one, of third world social movements. However, much postcolonial analysis focuses on consciousness, culture, and ideology, rather than economic, social, or political conditions and responses. Some postcolonial theorists (e.g. Bhabha) follow Foucault in examining the discourses and disciplines of culture and knowledge and the repressing forces internal to them. Bhabha's view, that it is in the interstices of colonial and national experiences that postcolonial culture lies, echoes anthropological work on liminal, syncretic, and other cross-national and cross-group cultural forms. This theoretical tendency complements sociological understandings of colonial and other forms of oppression (including gender) and their impacts on culture in the broadest sense. Others (e.g., Spivak) have been influenced by Said's (1979) efforts to uncover oppressive images and language in the colonizers' literary and cultural representations of the colonized. The latter approach has resonated in humanities disciplines, including postcolonial feminist cultural studies.

Sociological Contributions to Postcolonial Thought

Sociology has only slowly joined the poststructural critique of academic canons (Mirchandani 2005). The strength of hermeneutic and other anti-positivist methodologies in sociology relative to many other disciplines has diminished the attraction of poststructural thought. Nevertheless, sociology has made an impact on indirect contributions to the elaboration of postcolonial theory. Moreover, the debates among sociological theorists about postmodernism as a historical epoch have had important implications for our understanding of globalization and its impacts on international feminisms.

Critical conceptualizations of third world economic development that incorporate understandings of bilateral dependence and global interdependence have been important in sociology since the 1970s. Sociologists James Petras (1973), Immanuel Wallerstein (1974), and others played pivotal roles in the elaboration of worldwide patterns of dependency and sectorally uneven development.

Equally important has been sociologists' reception to research and theory about the consciousness of the oppressed. The work of Franz Fanon (1961, 1967) and Albert Memmi (1965) on the complex intellectual and emotional effects of colonialism – the mixed feelings of cultural inferiority, fear, and anger experienced by the colonized – contributed to sociological understandings of economic and political dependency and echoed issues raised by sociologists regarding other twentieth-century conflicts. W. E. B. Du Bois (1903) wrote about the "dual consciousness" of African Americans, both oppressed by and subjugated by whites and at the same time conscious of oppression and resistant to it. Later, members of the Frankfurt School of European émigrés to the US, in particular Theodor Adorno, Erich Fromm, and Max Horkheimer, used the experiences of those terrorized and violated by the Nazi regime to explore further the duality of consciousnesses and cultures of subjugation and resistance and ideological responses.

Postcolonialism and Feminist Sociology

Feminist sociology has had a significant impact on the development of feminist postcolonialism. Patricia Hill Collins's book *Black Feminist Thought* (1990) has been widely cited in postcolonial feminist studies. Collins draws on the critical theory tradition and later standpoint theories such as that elaborated by Dorothy Smith (1989) to valorize the standpoints and situated group knowledge of African American women and to recognize the layers of oppression and hence knowledge that separate women by ethnicity, income, education, region, etc. Collins's work has thus been valuable in exploring a multiplicity and hierarchy of meanings in representations and in the daily consciousness, culture, and ideology of colonized groups.

Collins's contributions to third world and colonial feminisms go beyond the consideration of these topics within other nations to their discussion within the borders of wealthy nations. Immigrants and internally colonized ethnic minority groups are often termed third world people and their political and cultural ideologies (including gender politics) share dimensions with both the majority population and with other marginalized groups. Third world feminism in the US and other industrial countries shares the liminality and hybridity of feminisms in postcolonial nations. Moreover, the representation of ethnic minority women in cultural works influenced by dominant groups within nations resembles in theme and form those treating women and gender relations in postcolonial nations.

Sociology and the Subaltern

Sociologists have long struggled with the problem of how research methodologies can allow us to hear, present, and interpret the voices of marginalized groups. American sociology's expansion of qualitative techniques beyond the ethnographic to include lengthy interviews and narrative analyses has coincided with the rise of gender studies in the field. Indeed, the concept of feminist methodology, which goes beyond the disciplinary confines of sociology, embodies a commitment to give voice to the powerless (DeVault 1999). At the same time, postcolonial literary and cultural studies have struggled with the challenge of giving means of expression to sectors of third world populations that are estranged from the means of cultural production and representation. The ways in which this problem has been conceptualized once again go back to theoretical work of broad significance to sociology.

From the late 1920s through the mid-1930s, imprisoned Italian political theorist and activist Antonio Gramsci produced a set of "notebooks" treating the difficult political problems of ideological hegemony, critical consciousness, and revolution. Published posthumously, Gramsci's *Prison Notebooks* (1991) are widely cited by neo-Marxist academics eager to understand why objectively oppressed and subjugated classes have been unable to marshal forces to transform the class structure and in the case of fascist regimes seem in fact to embrace ideologies that run dramatically counter to their class interests. Gramsci's references to the subaltern have gained the attention of third world feminists and others trying to give visibility to the interests of marginalized groups.

"Subaltern" refers literally to a military officer rank below the highest levels, but is used more generally to mean subordinate groups. Gramsci wrote about two social categories of the subaltern: incipient challengers to traditional dominant classes and relatively powerless groups subject to constraining ideological

power. The Subaltern Studies Group of South Asian Historians followed Gramsci's lead in considering why Indian workers, peasants, and other "subaltern" groups did not emerge as revolutionary classes. The resulting emphasis on "history from below" has influenced and reinforced social science efforts to reveal and understand the ideology and culture of the powerless and the politically invisible. "Subaltern" has shifted meaning, however, as critical academic writing and postmodern and postcolonial feminists have argued that the conceptual and discursive meanings of Marxist and neo-Marxist thought, including Gramsci's theorization of the subaltern, reproduce the binary and essentialist thinking that has limited third world women's political options. Spivak's (1988) article was particularly influential in moving the "subaltern" away from neo-Marxism to a feminist epistemology that permits women to express unanticipated, untheorized thoughts, emotions and political strategies. Literary and cultural studies have since addressed the meanings of the expressions and representations of subaltern groups, and the implications of their exclusion from political and cultural platforms.

Sociologists have been notably absent in debate about the role of the subaltern per se, although issues of radical and revolutionary consciousness among workers, peasants, and other social groups have long been of interest in the discipline. In adhering to a fundamental disciplinary focus on social stratification and its elaboration in precisely defined social strata, sociologists may find the term subaltern imprecise both with reference to socioeconomic status and assumed group ideology, culture, and consciousness. Sociologists refer more frequently to "marginalized" groups, acknowledging more simply and exclusively an estrangement from economic and political power and privilege.

Globalization and Feminisms

Third world and postcolonial feminisms continue to command scholarly attention and inspire theoretical debate. However, changing economic conditions in rich and poor countries with increased globalization have generated an intense effort in the social sciences to understand women's changing positions.

Sociologists' recent collections on women in the third world (e.g., Blumberg et al. 1995) focus on women's roles in production and community-based efforts to improve women's status.

Academic and policymakers' current discussions of globalization have to some extent supplanted the debates of the 1980s and 1990s about the meaning of late capitalism, postmodernism, and postcolonialism. Methodological and epistemological challenges to structuralist categorizations of cultural and historical change continue to engage feminist and other critical political theorists and activists. However, recent recognition of the breadth and depth of global interdependence has reinvigorated the scholarly quest to explicate the dynamics of global capitalism and the political spaces therein that allow for fundamental change. For third world women, whether in postcolonial or industrial settings, the feminist challenge is ever more complex as the interstices of the colonial and the national multiply and become less distinct.

Third world and postcolonial feminisms/subaltern present vital substantive, methodological, and political challenges and strategies of study that unite humanities and social science disciplines. Sociologists have taken a more prominent role in the interdisciplinary identification of third world women's economic, social, and political positions and interests in both postcolonial nations and in the US. The nearly century-long debate within sociology about biases and inaccuracies produced by positivist-derived methods and techniques and the continuing efforts of important subgroups within the field to reveal and valorize the voices of the marginalized has allowed the discipline to move in tandem with much of the postmodern critique of academic knowledge without joining fully in it. Postcolonial feminism has, in a similar way, engaged elements of sociological theory while accommodating a distinction between humanities disciplines' critical study of gendered cultural representation and social science efforts to understand gendered social relations.

SEE ALSO: Black Feminist Thought; Decolonization; Feminist Activism in Latin America; Gender, Development and; Hybridity; International Gender Division of Labor; Intersectionality; Marginality; Methods, Postcolonial; Orientalism

REFERENCES AND SUGGESTED READINGS

Ampofo, A. A., Beoku-Betts, J., Njambi, W., & Osirim, M. (2004) Women's and Gender Studies in English-Speaking Sub-Saharan Africa: A Review of Research in the Social Sciences. *Gender and Society* 18: 685–714.

Barriteau, E. (2001) *The Political Economy of the Twentieth Century Caribbean.* Palgrave, New York.

Bhabha, H. K. (Ed.) (1990) *Nation and Narration.* Routledge, London.

Bhabha, H. K. (1994) *The Location of Culture.* Routledge, London.

Blumberg, R. L., Rakowski, C. A., Tinker, I., & Montion, M. (Eds.) (1995) *Engendering Wealth and Well-Being: Empowerment for Global Change.* Westview Press, Boulder.

Boserup, E. (1970) *Women's Role in Economic Development.* St. Martin's Press, New York.

Collins, P. H. (1990) *Black Feminist Thought: Knowledge, Consciousness and the Politics of Empowerment.* Unwin Hyman, Boston.

DeVault, M. L. (1999) *Liberating Method: Feminism and Social Research.* Temple University Press, Philadelphia.

Du Bois, W. E. B. (1903) *The Souls of Black Folks: Essays and Sketches.* A. C. McClurg, Chicago.

Fanon, F. (1961) *The Wretched of the Earth.* Grove, New York.

Fanon, F. (1967) *Black Skin, White Masks.* Grove, New York.

Foucault, M. (1972) *The Archaeology of Knowledge.* Pantheon, New York.

Gramsci, A. (1991) *Prison Notebooks.* Columbia University Press, New York.

Kandiyoti, D. (1988) Bargaining with Patriarchy. *Gender and Society* 2: 274–90.

Memmi, A. (1965) *The Colonizer and the Colonized.* Orion Books, New York.

Mirchandani, R. (2005) Postmodernism and Sociology: From the Epistemological to the Empirical. *Sociological Theory* 23 (2): 75–85.

Petras, J. (Ed.) (1973) *Latin America: From Dependency to Revolution.* Wiley, New York.

Said, E. W. (1979) *Orientalism: Western Representation of the Orient.* Vintage Books, New York.

Smith, D. (1989) *The Everyday World as Problematic: A Feminist Sociology.* Northeastern University Press, Boston.

Spivak, G. C. (1988) Can the Subaltern Speak? Speculations on Widow Sacrifice. In: Nelson, G. & Grossberg, L. (Eds.), *Marxism and the Interpretation of Culture.* University of Illinois Press, Urbana, pp. 271–313.

Spivak, G. C. (1999) *A Critique of Postcolonial Reason: Toward a History of the Vanishing Present.* Harvard University Press, Cambridge, MA.

Wallerstein, I. (1974) *The Modern World System: Capitalist Agriculture and the Origins of the European World Economy in the Sixteenth Century.* Academic Press, New York.

Thomas, William I. (1863–1947)

Robert A. Stebbins

W. I. Thomas was born in Virginia and raised in a Protestant, rural, religious milieu. In 1884 he received his bachelor's degree from the University of Tennessee, and after two years of study in Germany followed by teaching English and sociology at Oberlin College, he joined in 1895 the new faculty in sociology at the University of Chicago. He had been among that department's first group of graduate students (he worked under Albion Small), starting in 1893 and receiving his doctorate in 1895. He remained at Chicago until 1918 when, for personal reasons, he retired. In 1923 Thomas returned to active teaching, now at the New School for Social Research, but his teaching was largely part-time, for he preferred to mix teaching with research. Between 1930 and 1936 he went regularly to Sweden to work with the Social Science Institute at the University of Stockholm. He was appointed lecturer at Harvard University in 1936 and 1937, living in New Haven until his move to Berkeley, California, in 1939. He resided there as an independent researcher until his death in 1947.

Thomas is well known for his collaboration with Florian Znaniecki in *The Polish Peasant in Europe and America*, a five-volume study published between 1918 and 1920. Other celebrated works include *The Unadjusted Girl* (1923) and, with Robert Park and Herbert Miller, *Old World Traits Transplanted* (1921). His reputation has lived on in sociology largely in the legacy he left symbolic interactionism in the theoretic sections of the *Polish Peasant*. The analytic framework of this study was based on the transformations in the personality and social structure of the Polish peasant community as it moved to the US.

Thomas had an enduring interest in the pragmatic tradition in sociology, one center of which, at the time, was the University of Chicago. For him, sociology concentrated on human activities, wherein people demonstrated conscious control in developing art, religion, language, forms of government, and the like. More precisely, sociology looks at *attention*, the attitude that takes note of the outside world and then manipulates it. From this stance he wrote a great deal about attitudes and attention, later preferring to conceptualize both as *definition of the situation*. Crises in everyday life, be they large or small (e.g., upsetting a habit), bring people to define the situation in which they occur and then to act accordingly. Development and change in larger, abstract forms of structure and culture occur when many people define similar situations.

Today, Thomas is widely recognized as one of the founders of symbolic interactionism. A dictum from a work co-authored with his wife, "if people define situations as real, they are real in their consequences" (Thomas & Thomas 1928: 571–2), is still frequently quoted.

SEE ALSO: Chicago School; Definition of the Situation; Small, Albion W.; Symbolic Interaction; Znaniecki, Florian

REFERENCES AND SUGGESTED READINGS

Thomas, W. I. (1923) *The Unadjusted Girl: With Cases and Standpoint for Behavior Analysis.* Little Brown, Boston.

Thomas, W. I. (1951) *Social Behavior and Personality: Contributions of W. I. Thomas to Theory and Social Research.* Ed. E. H. Volkart. Russell Sage Foundation, New York.

Thomas, W. I. (1966) *W. I. Thomas on Social Organization and Social Personality: Selected Papers.* Ed. M. Janowitz. University of Chicago Press, Chicago.

Thomas, W. I. & Thomas, D. S. (1928) *The Child in America.* Alfred A. Knopf, New York.

Thomas, W. I. & Znaniecki, F. (1918–20) *The Polish Peasant in Europe and America.* Richard G. Badger, Boston.

Thomas, W. I., Park, R. E., & Miller, H. A. (1921) *Old World Traits Transplanted.* Harper, New York.

time

Peter Clark

Time-reckoning systems contain benchmarks that indicate the passing of time and durational expectancies with respect to sequences, rhythmic features, and periodicities. There is no social ordering without temporal ordering, yet time comprises more than the chronological use of calendar and clock time (CCT) with which most of the world associates it. There are also very significant frames of action calculated through the heterogeneous events located within natural and task-based processes (Gurvitch 1964; Dubinskas 1988; Clark 1985; Bluedorne 2003). Time reckoning is a multilayered, hierarchical, contingent relationship between past, present, and future processes (Gurvitch 1964; Clark 1985; Harvey 1989; Adam 2004). The present is constituted through the differences between the remembered past and images of the future. One aim of an organization or society should be to establish an accessible, robust repertoire of temporal recipes and heuristics which enable the actionable interpretation of those future events that are located in emergent processes and flows.

It is from the processes, flows, cultures, and social structures that time-reckoning frameworks are socially constructed. There are multiple, coexisting frameworks to choose from and choices are consequential. Individual competencies in self-managing the different time-reckoning situations are increasingly demanding. There has been a tendency to understate the times of consumption relative to the work times of the factory and the office (e.g., Thompson 1967; Harvey 1989). The temporality of "consuming for capitalism" is evident in the design of sports like American football, shopping at Wal-Mart, engaging in mass tourism, eating slow food, or watching the media. The emergence of new social and non-social processes associated with globalization depends upon and affords hybrid time-reckoning systems.

Understanding temporal structuring and developing categories of temporality are central problems for practice and theory. Time is a key referential principle and its explication is required to understand the coordination and synchronization within and between different segments of activity. Time and space are closely connected. Currently there is a rich vein of research, theorizing, and critical debate concerning the politics of time.

HOMOGENEOUS INSTRUMENTAL TIME AND EVENT-BASED TEMPORALITY

The distinction between homogeneous instrumental systems of time reckoning and heterogeneous, event-based reckoning is fundamental (Hassard 1996). Homogeneous time-reckoning codes are represented by the calendar (e.g., week, month, year, 1917) and the clock (e.g., day, hour, minute). Calendars provide markers placed at equal standardized intervals derived from astronomical processes. A calendar expresses the rhythms of a society and suggests regularity. The calendar can be cyclical, as in the year when most societies celebrate the event of the "new year" but do so in contrasting ways. The calendar also provides a linear temporal structuring going backward into the past and forward into the future, as in utopian prophecy and scenario writing. Calendrical units are used reflectively to arrange past events, to plan the extended present, and to envisage different scenarios of the future. CCT is non-reversible. So, 1066, 1776, and 1917 are in the past but 2020 is in the future. However, the imagining of different timescapes, including reversing time, is central to the modern and postmodern imagination and the cultural media. Linear event chains formed the basis for the emergence of historical consciousness about nature, especially geology (e.g., Darwin). The regularity of linear calendrical time was supplemented by the major innovation of narrative history and the imposition of determinate patterns (e.g., thesis, antithesis, synthesis). Calendrical time was and is used by powerful elites and their challengers to formulate linear chains of political events and to reveal anachronisms.

In Europe from the fourteenth to eighteenth centuries public clocks came to occupy a different role compared with China (Landes 1983). Christian monasteries, especially the Benedictines, established strict and exacting forms of temporal discipline which structured the day very tightly. Christian bureaucracy initially structured everyday life in the emerging towns. New temporal structures were assembled around the ringing of bells and the display of public clocks. These were variously used to regulate the start and end of activities. Later this was extended to the increasing synchronization of activities within the towns. The escarpment movement clock required immense collective investment and struggle. The use of the clock to conquer space is illustrated by the mid-eighteenth-century development of a chronometer that could be used at sea to calculate the position of a ship relative to its intended trajectory. On land, from the eighteenth century onward the clock came to be used in the workplace by employers seeking to control work discipline. In England clock time was vigorously opposed and subverted by opposition by work groups in certain sectors (Thompson 1967). The Chinese used clocks for status and decoration throughout this period (Landes 1983). Homogeneous world times provided a global network which enabled high-volume consumption.

CCT provides the framing to the world time of capitalism, travel, and trade in the twentieth century (Harvey 1989). CCT is a classificatory system of standardized, formalized units that can be added, subtracted, multiplied, divided, and arranged in linear and recurring patterns. CCT appears to be objective, authoritative, rational, and legitimate, yet CCT inscribes power at multiple levels. The regular units of CCT are tightly intertwined with use of money as medium of stored time. CCT enables planning, synchronizing, and coordinating activities by the state and by corporations.

Heterogeneous time reckoning contains clusters and sequences of events which are anchored in the duration of processes mainly known to local and specific groups of people of varying kinds: engineers and scientists. Events are contextual, directional, and irreversible. The units of event time tend to be pregnant with durational meanings like excitement, fear, and surprise. Scientists and engineers regularly use heterogeneous systems of reckoning (Dubinskas 1988). Marketing departments use event markers and intervals that are irregular and contingent yet have a patterning (Clark 1985).

Heterogeneous time reckoning is characterized by events as markers of intervals and by a heightened awareness of the durational aspects.

The big debate about time has been whether members of industrial and capitalist societies in the twenty-first century use heterogeneous systems. Thompson (1967), in a seminal narrative about capitalism and work discipline, claimed that heterogeneous systems are displaced by homogeneous systems. However, as already indicated, industrialism and capitalism depend upon heterogeneous time reckoning. In practice, time reckoning is always multiple and diverse.

THEORETICAL LINEAGE

The agenda for time is contested. Gurvitch (1964) provides a stimulating history of time from Newton into the mid-twentieth century. Abstract homogeneous time has been a dominating influence. Newton's (seventeenth-century) universal framework, which was anchored in the metaphor of clock time, enabled the dualist separation of static and dynamic analyses. Dualism retained a powerful influence in sociology. Marx moved beyond descriptive chronologies based on calendrical time to construct a teleological, dialectical history of humankind as a journey toward a secular utopia. Marx focused on how capitalists equated homogeneous time units with the costs of production and opportunities for profit. The owners of firms translated units of time into money and commodified time. CCT became the framework in planning and controlling. The owners imposed clock-based discipline, minimized porosity in the turnover time of financial capital, and replaced human time with technology. Weber sought to show a relationship between the measured work time of Taylorism, formal instrumental rationality, and the likelihood of disenchantment. Weber's historicism imposed ideal types on big structures and large processes. Gurvitch claimed that Weber's typological method was overly static and insufficiently processual.

The lineage of Newton and CCT was challenged in the early twentieth century. Bergson contended that the durational qualities of time could not be understood within the temporality derived from Newtonian mechanics because social and biological processes were emergent. Therefore understanding flows, processes, and the future required a new ontology. Gurvitch provides a clear and relevant critique of Bergson's contribution. Durkheim stated that time, space, and causality are representations of collective life and are the solid frame that encloses all thought. Time is a serial order of experiences distinguishing the past, present, and future. The sequences can be cyclical (e.g., seasons), linear (e.g., birth to death), or open-ended. Durkheim's attention to the durational features such as excitement highlighted the elements that distinguished sociology as an emerging discipline.

In the mid-twentieth century Gurvitch sought to restate the sociology of time and history in terms of contingent processes, disjunctures, and a depthful ontology of places (Gurvitch 1964; Clark 1985). His spectrum of social times includes: the extent of continuity, contingency, and surprise; the pace of durations; and the relative influence of the past/present/future. An eightfold typology distinguishes levels in terms of surface or depth for different social formations (Harvey 1989: 224–5). Gurvitch, in contrast to Weber, proposed discontinuous typologies for specific periods and places.

The bold, complex approach of Gurvitch was displaced by Parsons's treatment of time in social systems. Parsons reinstated the dualism of static/dynamic from the Newtonian lineage and theorized time as an abstract objective framework. This complemented the new time-geography, time budgets, and life cycle models. Time-space geography records and maps the trajectories of individuals and cohorts during the day, week, and year as they move through particular spaces. This minimizes contingency and emphasizes chronic recursiveness about human activity (May & Thrift 2001). Time budgets are extensively used to audit activities in the typical day and week. They reveal consistent gender differences and significant differences between some nations. The life cycle model of birth, maturity, and death has become a temporal metaphor used to anticipate, justify, and explain the shifting changes to everyday

life. Commodities can have life cycles – and so can personal relationships.

Contemporary theory is being uneasily shaped by a blending of structuration theory (Giddens), casino capitalism (Harvey 1989), and dissipative structures. Giddens's sociology reconnected time with history whilst also subverting orthodox calendrical narratives. He adapted an objectified time and chronic recursiveness from time-geography. Modernity became the capacity of historical narratives to provide reflexivity about custom and tradition so that existing time-space is bracketed and scrutinized. The emergent future becomes the disrobing of the past of traditions. Innovation became routine. The relevance of time-space distanciation cannot be overstated. Giddens provides a temporal tool kit for examining the stretching of corporations from local entities into massive global firms, of cities into regions, and of the state apparatus in the modern nation-state. Giddens's treatment of temporal agency is much more rampant and controversial than in the alternatives to structuration. He contends that there has been a transformation into "late modernity" or "post-traditional society" rather than a rupture from modernity. Giddens's theory of time provides a protective belt for otherwise unconnected studies in different disciplinary areas: organization theory, historical geography, and information systems (Bluedorne 2003). Harvey (1989), a critical geographer, contends that the temporal mechanisms of finance capitalism have been qualitatively transformed by the instantaneity of information technology to create casino capitalism. This rapid speeding up inserts new time frames on top of older, taken-for-granted time priorities and practices, causing personal disruption, high risk, and uncertainty. Finally, dissipative structures were theorized in modern science to conceptualize and explain the inner temporality of processes as continuous flows of becoming. Adam (2004) draws on this theory to argue that sociological theory needs to address the non-social context and its future consequences for social processes. Dissipative structures confront and challenge "Giddens-time," overturn the dualism of static/dynamic analyses, and promote attention to the multiple event trajectories located within all kinds of processes.

MULTIPLE TIMES

The combination of heterogeneous and homogeneous systems provides temporal orientation and ordering to everyday life and to the specialized activities of the state, religious organizations, science, corporations, and occupations. For example, in the multitude of different disciplines within a typical university, the times of contemporary physics still differ from those found in geology and both differ from those found in sociology or economics. Musical scores and orchestras had been a repository of controlled time, but these orderly conceptions have been complemented and confronted by a blooming of aesthetic temporalities in the humanities and the arts. Times are differently constructed, expended, and experienced in different strata in the same society. Regions may possess repertoires of times that enable or disable economic success. All these processes are pregnant with political conflicts and inequalities.

There are many highly abstract times. Eternal time constructs linear flows from the distant past into a glorious extended present. Italian fascism invoked the Roman Empire. A linear eternal orientation may be utopian or dystopian. Some religions link the past to a future state. The template of eternality underpins the aim of producing universal generalizations in the social sciences. Since the mid-twentieth century there has been the routine and extensive development of temporally open, multistate models that are independent of any context. These start with an undesired state and move through progressive time to further states and arrive at the desired goal. The models provide an abstract, instrumental, multilinear conceptualization of processes such as the diffusion of innovations between nations. The intervals of time are sequential rather than simultaneous, yet irreversibility can be imagined as a game of comparisons and the auditing of performance. The discourse of tasks, events, milestones colonizes the temporal life of everyone. Families in Silicon Valley can coordinate their identities on a daily basis using handheld technologies.

In some theories of modernity it was mistakenly assumed that sacred religious time had been ousted as a major time-setting authority and replaced by the secular temporalities of science, the state, and commerce.

COMMODIFIED WORLD TIME: EXPERTS, CORPORATIONS, AND NATIONS

A market economy depends on and reproduces standardized, decontextualized, and commodified units of time. CCT provides a major discourse in capitalism to the coordination of technologies and labor discipline. The commodification of time and its separation from commodified space is an indicator of the role of the economy in capitalist societies. The market has been the route through which the work rhythms and temporal principles of corporations predominate. Time is experienced in everyday contexts through schedules of all kinds, calendars, deadlines, seasonal events, and project times. Even intimate moments like "quality time" seem scheduled. There are different temporal effects in the metropolitan centers like Los Angeles, Tokyo, and Frankfurt from those experienced in peripheries such as Nigeria producing raw materials or Kenya producing edible products. The metropolitan temporal flows instantiate the supply chains and networks that organize the spatial. The harvesting of flowers in Kenya is temporally orchestrated like a musical score to mesh with both the rate of expected sales in Europe and the fragile, aesthetic perishing of the flowers. A new discourse of flexible temporal principles is being imposed – "serving the consumer" – and contested.

Professional time experts, consultancies, and corporations are the leading edge of compressing and stretching time. They constantly use abstract representations to remove delays and waiting times when the financial return is low and the porosity is high. The evolution of the Gantt method of charting time lines and its inscription in software is very important. Gantt charts became a temporal boundary object in corporate power struggles (Yakura 2002). Time lines are graphical representations of tasks, events, and milestones. Gantt charts make abstract time visible to powerholders. Time experts orchestrate the temporality of urban spaces and search for places that can be more deeply commodified, as in tourism around the Indian Ocean. They are the eyes of capitalist power (May & Thrift 2001) that reflexively search the world to compare practices and to construct sites for simulating novel practices. By enrolling and incentivizing innovation in information technology, they introduce mechanisms and organizational formations which tend to transform sticky processes into flows over vast distances. They develop software for the planning and surveillance of the use of resources in organizations. Time sequencing and synchronizing are embedded in expert systems like enterprise resource planning (ERP). These reduce the porosity of capital accumulation by envisaging the simultaneous actions and flows. A focus upon the cycle time of production can disrupt the total time from design to the consumer's purchase (Clark 1985).

Some corporations (e.g., Toyota) have developed capacities to stretch time through expert systems that embed capacities to design temporal structures which stretch across continents. Large organizations typically calculate an abstract temporal container expressing the aggregate volume of standardized time available to undertake a portfolio of activities over a given calendar period (Clark 1985; Hassard 1996; Bluedorne 2003). Large retailers are streamlining the purchasing function to speed up and control transactions whilst introducing barcode scanners and extending the panoptic gaze of the firm. The temporality is closer to that of supermarket than hospital.

Some nations, their corporations and their professions may be the source of time-reckoning frameworks that are carried across large areas of the world. The key to analyzing the internal dynamics of the capitalist state is that revenue for the state is dependent upon processes of valorization which the state does not directly control. The state frames many of the new forms of temporal ordering through legislative actions (e.g., France). The temporal complexity within America is remarkable and consequential for the world. The spectrum ranges from the ordered times of American football and McDonald's to the event-dominated temporal modularity associated with some West Coast communities and with the emergent segments of information technology. In twentieth-century America, the clock was used most extensively by influential specialist occupations specifically situated with a role in the temporal structuring of workplaces of all kinds, which to some extent occasionally structured home life as well (e.g., funerals). Many of the practices and technologies were commercially developed in and marketed around the world: from Gantt charts to systems of production and inventory control. Currently moreover, time experts and firms specialize in "events" and in historicizing the past in a postmodern history of the future. So, contrary to some views (e.g., Bluedorne 2003), there is a remarkable articulation between homogeneous and heterogeneous time reckoning in America. Celebratory and sacred times are evident in many social occasions.

TIME-SPACE COMPRESSION AND THE POLITICS OF TIME

Critical theorists contend that in capitalism the political control of temporal structures by corporations has unfavorable consequences because we live in an extended present of time-space compression and instantaneity. They contend that we are in an era when established expectations of what comes next are much less clear than in the past: it is a runaway world. If so, established temporal expectations are a poor guide to future navigation. Temporal relations may become so destabilized as a result of constant flux that they can provide little in the way of anchoring for social relations and place-bound nostalgias. Time-space compression means reducing the total cycle time of global financial capital accumulation by quickening the time from design to sale (Harvey 1989; May & Thrift 2001). The time to travel distances is reduced through increases in the speed of sending material goods, information, and people. Most of our electronic devices are dedicated to speeding things up. Commodified times relentlessly colonize and replace the social rhythms with greater speed of transactions. New forms of advertising create an aesthetic audiovisual economy of signs, brands, and logos which can be constantly upgraded. Consequently, the objectified qualities of how we represent the world to ourselves are disrupted and this can lead to a tension between the speed of turnover and the capacity of societies to regenerate. Radically new forms of time disrupt linear homogeneous time with forms of project and event time that can be chaotic and volatile. There is discontinuity and there are new times (Gurvitch 1964). The experience of simultaneity and synchronized processes from the "electronic embrace" is complemented by new possibilities of asynchronicity in situations typified by a consensually grounded grammar. The time of mass production is replaced by mass customization and the opportunities for diversity.

SEE ALSO: Commodities, Commodity Fetishism, and Commodification; Distanciation and Disembedding; Durkheim, Émile; Gurvitch, Georges: Social Change; Management History; Space; Taylorism; Time-Space

REFERENCES AND SUGGESTED READINGS

Adam, B. (2004) *Time*. Blackwell, Oxford.
Bluedorne, A. C. (2003) *The Human Organization of Time: Temporal Realities and Experience*. Stanford University Press, Stanford.
Clark, P. A. (1985) A Review of Theories of Time and Structure for Organizational Sociology. *Research in the Sociology of Organizations* 4: 35–79.
Dubinskas, F. A. (1988) *Making Time: Ethnographies of High Technology Organization*. Temple University Press, Philadelphia.
Gurvitch, G. (1964) *The Spectrum of Social Time*. Reidel, Dordrecht.
Harvey, D. (1989) *The Condition of Postmodernity*. Blackwell, Oxford.
Hassard, J. (1996) Images of Time in Work and Organization. In: Clegg, S. R., Hardy, C., & Nord, W. R. (Eds.), *Handbook of Organization Studies*. Sage, London. pp. 581–98.
Landes, D. A. (1983) *Revolution in Time: Clocks and the Making of the Modern World*. Belknap, Cambridge, MA.
May, J. & Thrift, N. (2001) *Timespace: Geographies of Temporality*. Routledge, London.
Thompson, E. P. (1967) Time, Work-Discipline and Industrial Capital. *Past and Present* 38: 58–97.
Yakura, E. K. (2002) Charting Time: Timelines as Temporal Boundary Objects. *Academy of Management Journal* 45(5): 956–70.

time series

Robert M. Capraro

Time series analysis can be used in two general situations: (1) forecasting and (2) exploring the nature of some event represented by a set of points or observations, with both techniques serving the purpose for establishing theory that can, at some point, represent future events. Time series analyses are often used in business settings by forecasting stock, commodity, and product valuing. Time series is less often used in educational research; therefore, it is this perspective that will be used in all examples to contextualize possible research scenarios where time series analyses would be appropriate.

Among the myriad techniques subsumed by the term time series analyses are autocorrelation, trend, and seasonal variation, which all help in the quest to understand the underlying structure or the fit of a theoretical model. Just as with the general linear model, time series can handle single or multiple dependent variables. Some techniques for fitting a time series include Box-Jenkins univariate and multivariate, and Holt-Winters. The fit techniques, similar to the way classical measurement attempts to differentiate between true and unsystematic error score for each item, attempt to differentiate between data points that are and are not useful in helping to predict future events. Therefore, time series analyses incorporate procedures for dealing with these erroneous data points. Specifically, time series analyses make use of smoothing techniques; the approach to the smoothing differs, as well as the smoothing technique's susceptibility or ability to deal with "noise" or random unsystematic error. The smoothing techniques generally fit into one of two methods, consisting of averaging and exponential smoothing methods.

Generally, univariate time series refers to data that are recorded sequentially, at regular intervals, over some period of time. For example, a case for a univariate time series would be examining the impact of free/reduced lunch programs on school attendance patterns for low socioeconomic status as compared to the other students, for, say, 2 years. These time series data allow the researcher, depending on sampling technique, to examine school attendance trends for these two groups based on their enrolment in the free/reduced lunch program. If trends were detected an additional time series analysis might be undertaken, one in which attendance patterns might help to identify trends in academic success or on high-stakes tests. Currently, as with many statistical analyses, the minimal number of observation points is somewhat debated, but as a general rule of thumb, 50 observation points should suffice.

Two other general types of time series analyses, multivariate and interrupted time series, can be used when additional data points are available and related to the phenomena under investigation or when comparing the effects of an external event on the observations, respectively. From the example above, one might consider that the changes in attendance trends among the groups of interest might be due to other factors. In this case, a multivariate time series analysis might be reasonable and include other measures, such as classroom behavior management referrals, suspensions, or school climate measures such as parent volunteerism, teacher absenteeism, and phone calls to or from parents. When one is considering changes in programs or the impact of new programs, then an interrupted time series is applicable. The kindergarten through twelfth grade public education system provides a rich source of time series appropriate data. Many states hold textbook adoptions every 5 or 7 years. This change in textbooks allows one to consider student academic achievement in an interrupted time series that considers student performance before and after the change in textbooks. On the surface, this study is of marginal interest except if in changing textbooks a downward trend in student academic achievement was detected and this downward trend was predictable with each new adoption – some legislators may attempt to forgo the textbook adoption process for schools and opt for a single textbook. Again, referring to the original example, one might be interested in any of the above additional variables, but also want to consider the impact of new legislation influencing free/reduced lunch in conjunction with the inception of the Head Start legislation on school attendance, which represents an interrupted time series from before and after each of the legislative actions. Interrupted time series allow one to consider the impact of some intervening variable on the phenomenon of interest. Often, interrupted time series make some use of retrospective data collection or the inclusion of extant data along with current data. However, the research question and paradigm should govern when and how to use any of the myriad varieties of time analyses.

RESEARCH PARADIGM

Time series can be useful when the researcher needs to be able to isolate the dependent variable from other exogenous variables. Therefore, it is necessary to find a design that allows for the control of variables that can function as threats to validity. When the researcher needs to interpret a dependent variable from some set of measured variables, why not simply use an experimental design? One option for measuring the outcomes of social interactions or programs is true experiments (Fishman & Weinberg 1992). In a true experiment, individuals are randomly assigned to either an experimental or a control group. The purpose for randomization is that it presumably controls for the effects of unmeasured variables, allowing the researcher to claim that the outcomes are the result of the intervention (i.e., not the result of unmeasured variables or quirky data) (Cook & Campbell 1979; Shadish et al. 2002). In the absence of random assignment or in non-experimental situations, researchers attempt to control the effects of unmeasured variables on the outcome variable. However, in non-experimental designs researchers cannot make causal statements regarding treatment results on the outcome variable. Researchers are limited to statements about linkages between the treatment and the outcome variable situated within the presence of other variables. In social science situations, non-experimental designs can be more attractive than experimental designs because they are less costly, make retrospective longitudinal investigations possible, allow the use of extant secondary databases, and incorporate a reasonable control of extraneous variables. In time series analysis, aggregate data allow for the measuring of global changes, separate from other variables that can impact the outcome variable.

TIME SERIES ANALYTIC METHODS

Several different approaches are available for time series analyses. The time domain approach focuses on the correlation between immediately surrounding points in time by the dependence of the current values on past values. This modeling can be thought of as linear regressions of present values on past values generally considered as a useful forecasting tool. This approach is associated with autoregressive integrated moving average or ARIMA models. Conceptually, ARIMA handles data in the general form of time-correlated events where one presumes that past values are predictive of future events. Just as multivariate analysis of variance better models real-world events (Thompson 1991), multivariate time series can provide a better model by accounting for more than one input series through a multivariate ARIMA or transfer function.

The frequency domain approach focuses on periodicity and the idiosyncratic nature that can be explained by external factors. In social sciences or education one might be interested in monthly attendance patterns across rural, urban, and suburban schools or performance of students on minimal skills testing that occurs during various months across states.

Spectral analysis is often used to examine the various periods of interest in the data. This analytic method examines the variance associated with each interest period separately. This method often works well with long series or when the periods are clearly defined. For instance, the frequency domain approach seems to fit well with analyzing speech. Speech consists of clearly defined periods that can be analyzed by computer software to provide speech-to-text applications. However, in financial applications, one would want to know about summative trends for companies, financial indexes, and sector performance. Just as with education and social sciences, it is important to match what the time series analyst wants to know to the appropriate approach.

Conventionally, whichever approach one chooses the result is presented in graphical form with the *x-axis* being time. There are three general forms for presenting the results. Continuous time series represent data collected longitudinally, and observations could be made at any continuous point in time. Discrete time series use equally spaced points along the time continuum. The discrete nature for the data collection should be purposeful and intentional. Interrupted time series refers to examining related events before or after some intervening variable during the time series. While sampling technique is a non-trivial issue, it is important to note that the sampling rate (frequency) can appreciably change the appearance of the representation of the data. Improper sampling can lead to distorted data, referred to as aliasing.

ANALYTIC DECISIONS AND STUDY FORTITUDE

Finally, in choosing a time series analysis it is important to keep some questions in mind: (1) How much data are required (for an interrupted time series) and how many baseline data points are needed? (2) How many schools/teachers/programs etc. are needed? (3) How large should subject pools be? (4) How many follow-up years should be included in the analyses? These questions address factors influencing estimates of program impact. After the study is complete and these questions are considered in the design, it is important to consider impact. A simple way to represent the precision of a research design is its "minimum detectable effect." Intuitively, this is the smallest impact that has a good chance of being identified if it actually exists. The smaller the minimum detectable effect, the more precise the design. The first step in assessing the minimum detectable effect of a research design is to decide how impacts will be reported. However, the minimum detectable effect does not induct replicability of the observed effects. A popular way to determine effect that does infer replicability, especially for education research, is a measure called effect size. This is simply the impact in its original units (e.g., a scaled test score) divided by the standard deviation of the original measure for the population or sample of interest. Hence, effect sizes are measured in units of standard deviations. Thus, an effect size of 0.25 means a positive impact that is comparable in magnitude to 0.25 standard deviations. An effect size of −0.40 means a negative impact that is comparable in magnitude to 0.40 standard deviations. Although judgments about whether a specific effect size is large or small are ultimately arbitrary, some guidelines do exist. Many researchers use the rule of thumb proposed by Cohen (1988), which suggests that effect sizes of roughly 0.20 be considered small, 0.50 be considered moderate, and 0.80 be considered large. Lipsey (1990) provides empirical support for this approach based on the distribution of 102 mean effect sizes obtained from 186 meta-analyses of treatment effectiveness studies, most of which are from education research. The bottom third of this distribution (small impacts) ranged from 0.00 to 0.32, the middle third (moderate impacts) ranged from 0.33 to 0.55, and the top third (large impacts) ranged from 0.56 to 1.26.

SEE ALSO: Experimental Design; Multivariate Analysis; Variables

REFERENCES AND SUGGESTED READINGS

Box, G. E. P. & Jenkins, G. M. (1976) *Time Series Analysis: Forecasting and Control.* Holden-Day, San Francisco.
Cohen, J. (1988) *Statistical Power Analysis for the Behavioral Sciences.* Lawrence Erlbaum Associates, Hillsdale, NJ.
Cook, T. & Campbell, D. (1979) *Quasi-Experimentation.* Rand McNally, Chicago.
Fishman, M. & Weinberg, D. (1992) The Role of Evaluation in State Welfare Reform Waiver Demonstrations. In: Manski, C. & Garfinkel, I. (Eds.), *Evaluating Welfare and Training Programs.* Harvard University Press, Cambridge, MA, pp. 115–42.
Lipsey, M. W. (1990) *Design Sensitivity: Statistical Power for Experimental Research.* Sage, Newbury Park, CA.
Shadish, W. R., Cook, T. D., & Campbell, D. T. (2002) *Experimental and Quasi-Experimental Designs for Generalized Causal Inference.* Houghton-Mifflin, Boston.
Thompson, B. (1991) Methods, Plainly Speaking: A Primer on the Logic and Use of Canonical Correlation Analysis. *Measurement and Evaluation in Counseling and Development* 24: 80–93.
Vandaele, W. (1983) *Applied Time Series and Box-Jenkins Models.* Academic Press, New York.

time–space

James Slevin

All social life is ordered over time and through space. However, when sociologists attend to the "situated" character of social life, they do not treat time-space as simply the temporal and spatial environment of the phenomena they study. They see social life as not just being "in" time-space, they see time-space as central to all social interaction. The "situatedness" of social life involves time-space as a constitutive feature in the construction and reconstruction of what people do and in the way they do things together. The ordering of social life comes about because social practices are routinely made to come together across time-space as shared experiences. This binding of time-space is expressed in the ways in which societies, institutions, and individuals organize time-space.

Anthony Giddens draws attention to three features that need to be addressed by sociologists when seeking to understand the way in which social life is ordered across time-space. The first involves the construction and reconstruction of regularized social interaction across time-space through informed practices. Take, for example, the actions and interactions relating to the lending and borrowing of a library book. These are knowledgeable activities involving the understanding of a range of time-space relations by both lenders and borrowers. A borrowed book has to be returned before the elapse of a specific time period and returned to a specific place in the library in order for it to be made available for the next person wishing to borrow it. The library staff gather and process information on the whereabouts of the books they have lent out and apply sanctions, where necessary, in order to secure their timely return.

The second feature involves the association of social interaction with purposefully designed spatial and temporal environments. Taking once again the example of a library book, such transactions are embedded in purposefully designed spatial and temporal settings for the storage, distribution, and collection of books. The design of a library building, the spacing of facilities for the storing of books, the catalog access points, the information and administration desks, the reading rooms, etc., are all features integral to the spatial and temporal coordination of library transactions and are integral to what a library is.

The third feature involves the organizational mechanisms which are used to regulate the timing and spacing of social interaction. The lending and borrowing of a library book are organized by means of various time-space organizing devices. A library will have specific opening hours. These may alter depending on which day of the week people wish to visit the library. The annual cycle of opening hours may include calendar dates when there are holiday closures. Other time-space schedules, such as a library's borrowing and cataloging system, regulate the location of books, the total number of books borrowed, and the length of the borrowing period.

The development and use of information, communication, and transportation technology impact on all three of the features set out above. David Harvey's term "time-space compression" describes the reduction of distance experienced through the decrease in the time taken, either to cross space physically by means of transportation, or symbolically by means of communication. People can, for example, use the Internet to access and consult cataloging systems of distant libraries which, due to their far-off location, they would have never considered visiting physically. They can also increasingly download reading material digitally and so cancel out the need for physical transportation altogether. The use of the Internet also impacts on libraries as purposefully designed spatial and temporal settings. For example, library users may browse through books on a computer screen rather than in the open book stacks in a library building. Finally, Internet use impacts on the organizational mechanisms which are used to regulate the timing and spacing of library transactions. People can, for example, consult a library's cataloging system and download reading material even outside a library's opening hours. Moreover, material stored and distributed by a library in a digital form does not need to be returned to the library in order for it to be made available to others.

Time-space compression allows for the stretching of social life across time-space, a phenomenon that lies at the heart of one of the most central transformative processes of our time: globalization. Tomlinson (1999) writes of "the 'proximity' that comes from the networking of social relations across large tracts of time-space, causing distant events and powers to penetrate our local experience." However, as he makes clear, the compression of time-space is not just about physical distance. It is also about social-cultural distance.

SEE ALSO: Culture; Environment and Urbanization; Globalization; Goffman, Erving; Information Society; Media and Globalization; Network Society; Organizations; Space; Surveillance; Urbanization; Time

REFERENCES AND SUGGESTED READINGS

Giddens, A. (1984) *The Constitution of Society*. Polity Press, Cambridge.
Goffman, E. (1959) *The Presentation of Self in Everyday Life*. Doubleday, New York.
Heidegger, M. (1962) *Being and Time*. Blackwell, Oxford.
Innis, H. A. (1950) *Empire and Communications*. Clarendon Press, Oxford.
Thrift, N. (1996) *Spatial Formations*. Sage, London.
Tomlinson, J. (1999) *Globalization and Culture*. Polity Press, Cambridge.
Urry, J. (1995) Tourism, Europe and Identity. In: *Consuming Places*. Routledge, London.

Tocqueville, Alexis de (1805–59)

Sam Binkley

Born into a French aristocratic family in 1805, Alexis de Tocqueville was a French political theorist, sociologist, and cultural and historical commentator whose contributions are equally claimed by the disciplines of sociology, political science, American studies, and American history. In 1831, together with his colleague Gustave de Beaumont, Tocqueville embarked on a tour of the nascent American democracy in an effort to understand the inner workings of the democratic spirit in the everyday lives and social institutions of the American people. On returning to France he wrote his famous two-volume investigation, *Democracy in America* (1835). Tocqueville uncovered within American society a tension between democracy's conflicting imperatives: the egalitarian character of democratic societies, while successfully eliminating forms of despotism identified with feudalism, did not provide sufficient integration of the individual into the social fabric. Hence, democratization, if extended unchecked and in irresponsible ways, could produce excessive individualism (a term Tocqueville coined for this purpose), and ultimately new forms of despotism. In a comparison of the American and French experiences with democracy, Tocqueville pointed to the dangers posed by the French case, in which a sudden leveling of social hierarchies following the French Revolution eliminated the intermediary institutions that maintained the integration of individuals within the larger social fabric, leading to revolutionary despotism, a theme developed more completely in his other major work, *The Old Regime and the Revolution* (1856).

The American case, on the other hand, fostered voluntary democratic institutions which ensured local involvement and instructed in the methods and techniques of self-rule. The American case, however, was possessed of the equally ominous threat of the "tyranny of the majority," or leveling and homogenizing of public opinion by the belief in the ultimate sovereignty of the views held by the greatest number. Tocqueville cited as an example the persecution of the editors of a Baltimore newspaper who, during the war of 1812, after voicing an unpopular view, were besieged by a mob of enraged locals, had their printing presses destroyed, and were jailed and ultimately killed. Tocqueville's assessment of such majoritarian absolutism contributed to later debates around mass society and twentieth-century totalitarianism, conformity, and homogenization, and resonates with David Reisman's *The Lonely Crowd* (Reisman et al. 1950).

Tocqueville's legacy is still very much in dispute, particularly in debates around the welfare state, civic engagement, and democratic citizenship (Goldberg 2001). On the political right,

Tocqueville is cited as a critic of the tyranny of the welfare state and of public assistance as a means of redressing inequality. On the left he is taken up as an advocate of an active role for the state in offsetting the atomization of society through policies that enable associative engagement of individuals in democratic and community participation (Arato & Cohen 1992). Tocqueville's imprint is also visible in contemporary sociological concerns with declining social capital and the erosion of civic engagement in urban, mediated, and postmodern societies (Putnam 2000).

SEE ALSO: Citizenship; Civil Society; Democracy; Individualism; Totalitarianism; Welfare State

REFERENCES AND SUGGESTED READINGS

Arato, A. & Cohen, A. (1992) *Civil Society and Political Theory*. MIT Press, Cambridge, MA.

Goldberg, C. A. (2001) Social Citizenship and a Reconstructed Tocqueville. *American Sociological Review* 66(2): 289–315.

Putnam, R. (2000) *Bowling Alone: The Collapse and Revival of American Community*. Simon & Schuster, New York.

Reisman, D., Glazer, N., & Denney, R. (1950) *The Lonely Crowd: A Study of the Changing American Character*. Yale University Press, New Haven.

Tocqueville, A. de (1987 [1856]) *The Old Regime and the French Revolution*. Ed. K. M. Baker. University of Chicago Press, Chicago.

Tocqueville, A. de (1990 [1835]) *Democracy in America*, Vol. 1. Ed. P. Bradley. Random House, New York.

tolerance

Susanne Karstedt

In 1598, Henri IV King of France decreed the Edict of Nantes that proclaimed the principle of tolerance as guiding principle of the state, its administration, and the life of its citizens. The Edict of Nantes established the principle of tolerance in order to end civil strife and religious conflicts, and to enhance the safety of all citizens, independent of their religious beliefs. Looking back over a period of more than 400 years, the Edict of Nantes is an astonishingly modern document. It granted equal access to the institutions of the state, public office, and educational institutions for all religious denominations, in particular for Protestants. As such, it is a document not only of the toleration of (religious) diversity, but also of the creation of those institutional safeguards and arrangements that underpin tolerance as a lived experience and practice of citizens.

Europe and the United States have been the seedbeds of tolerance, of the philosophical ideas on which it is founded, the legal and institutional framework where it is enshrined, and the education of citizens and their habits, through which tolerance becomes a lived experience. In Europe, tolerance emerged as a mechanism of internal conflict resolution during the period of religious wars and strife, and the Confederation of Warsaw (1573) is one of the earliest documents of (religious) tolerance guaranteed by the state. In the Middle Ages, cities like Toledo or Granada thrived on the established tolerance between Muslim, Christian, and Jewish citizens; Sarajevo is another of these notable examples, all from countries under Islamic occupation (Spain, Bosnia). It took nearly another 250 years after the Edict of Nantes for the principles and institutional foundations of religious tolerance to be firmly established in Europe in the nineteenth century. In this process Europe lagged behind the United States, which had adopted the ideas as well as the legal and institutional framework, had proclaimed religious tolerance in its Declaration of Independence, and guaranteed it in its Constitution. The European and American philosophers of the Enlightenment proclaimed toleration as the notion that all human beings are essentially the same, despite their religious and moral convictions, and that the beliefs of other races and civilizations are equal to those of Christianity. Tolerance emerged as a core concept and value in the formation of modernity and modern societies.

Tolerance is a concept which can only be defined in a negative way, and its essence is defined by the lack of action, social bonds, or emotions. It is not an expression of benevolence, but embodies a sense of disapproval. Tolerance is the deliberate choice not to interfere with conducts and beliefs, lifestyles and behaviors, of which one disapproves. Tolerance is defined by passivity, not activity, and it is non-reaction and non-interference that characterize tolerant attitudes and behaviors. Tolerance means the absence, not presence, of strong emotions, and neither love nor hatred is comprised in the concept of tolerance. As such, tolerant attitudes and behaviors are situated between a positive and negative extreme; at its positive extreme, tolerance expressively includes respect for others, and acceptance and embracement of social diversity and individual difference. At its negative extreme, tolerance can be characterized by total neglect, disregard, ignorance, and avoidance of those individuals and groups who are different. The range covered by tolerance is reflected in thresholds, where behaviors and lifestyles of others are seen as threats to the social and moral order, and as such become "intolerable." How far tolerance can be stretched, and at what tipping points intolerance takes over, varies individually between groups and societies.

Tolerance owes its prominent role in the formation of modernity to its essential character as non-interference. It is decisive for the cultural change from "passions to interests" (Hirschmann 1997 [1977]), which gave birth to modern capitalism. It constitutes the foundation for the development of universalistic and individualistic value patterns, and is essential for the development of the weak ties (Granovetter 1973) that are a defining feature of modern societies. Tolerance is embedded neither within those bonds of solidarity that develop between equals nor within groups, where tolerance of difference is not actually needed. Tolerance is, however, essential in the formation of links between different social groups, and facilitates the everyday interactions of their members. Tolerance is one of the foundations of the transformation from *Gemeinschaft* to *Gesellschaft* (Tönnies). Modern democracy and its "civic culture" (Almond & Verba 1963) are based on the lack of strong bonds and emotions, and tolerance is seen as an indispensable "underpinning of democracy" and cornerstone of civic culture (Sullivan & Transue 1999). The stability of modern democratic regimes is based on acceptance of the majority rule by the minority, succession through elections with winners and losers, and peaceful negotiation of different interests between groups, as well as a specific attitudinal pattern amongst the citizenry that supports these institutions and makes them work.

Tolerance can only flourish where weak ties are strong. Weak ties need a certain level of trust and cohesion amongst the citizenry. Inglehart (1997) shows with data from the World Values Survey that generalized trust in others and tolerance of different and deviant lifestyles are highly correlated in his sample of 43 countries. In particular, generalized trust that links different ethnic groups increases tolerance of and the integration of ethnic minority groups (Jorgensen 2004; Uslaner 2004). Amongst the predictors of intolerance, perceived threat from all who are defined as "others" is an extremely potent, completely exogenous, and by far the most significant predictor of endangered tolerance (Gibson 1992; Sullivan & Transue 1999). This is mirrored by the individual dispositions and personality traits that are linked to intolerance. Adorno et al.'s *Authoritarian Personality* (1950) laid the foundations for an influential stream of research, which linked psychological insecurity and individual dogmatism to intolerance of "others" (Stouffer 1955; Gibson 1992; see Sullivan & Transue 1999). It has, however, proven to be difficult to establish that a "modal" and more authoritarian character is responsible for a higher or lower level of intolerance in a specific society. Rather than individual or collective dispositions, a specific social situation of anomie, felt insecurity, and perceived threats seems to combine into the significant social conditions conducive to intolerance, though these can be based on tradition and history (Gibson & Gouws 2003).

Consequently, transitional societies and emerging democracies seem to be in particular vulnerable to widespread intolerance and ethnic and religious strife, and more affected by resulting violent conflicts with ethnic minorities. The quest for "group rights" in the transition countries of Eastern and Central Europe has been made responsible for a decrease in tolerance and the revival of ethnic conflicts and boundaries, combined with increased violence (Offe 2002; Mann 2005). In divided societies like South Africa, perceived threats still loom large and

endanger tolerance and the building of democracy and civic culture (Gibson & Gouws 2003).

Contemporary societies and democracies put the tolerance and toleration of citizens to the test in new and different ways. They stress individualistic expression, individual autonomy, and identity, and citizens ask for the toleration of their own behavior and identity as much as they are asked to tolerate others. More autonomy and less restraint in behavior exercise the tolerance of citizens. As such, tolerance in modern societies encompasses a much broader spectrum of attitudinal and behavioral patterns than those related to political and/or religious affiliations. Citizens have to cope with new levels of ethnic and cultural diversity in contemporary societies due to the influx of ethnic minorities and immigrant groups, and their different ways of life. They experience increased levels of insecurity through crime and disorder in their neighborhoods and cities, or deep generational gaps between the lifestyles of younger and older generations in society. All this is perceived as threats to the existing "moral order" of groups and communities. Most recent developments indicate that religious affiliation in combination with ethnicity is perceived as a threat again, or that threats from crime become racialized (Frederico & Holmes 2005), thus pointing to highly differentiated patterns of tolerance and intolerance within different social groups. Tolerance has become precarious as citizens increasingly demand higher levels of personal and community security from the state, are increasingly willing to accept restrictions on civil liberties, are increasingly opting for populist solutions to such problems, and are more inclined toward punitiveness and less toward tolerance of deviance than before.

In responding to the challenges to tolerance in contemporary societies, political theory and philosophy have reconfigured the concept of tolerance in terms of liberalism, identity, and difference (Horton 1993; Walzer 1997; Horton & Mendus 1999; Shweder et al. 2002; Castiglione & McKinnon 2003; McKinnon & Castiglione 2003). Traditional notions of political and religious tolerance needed to be broadened in order to account for all aspects of the new forms of diversity in contemporary societies, and to relate them to the institutional framework of democracy, justice, and human rights (Kymlicka & Opalski 2001). Beyond those mechanisms that citizens use to deal with the behavior, actions, and beliefs of "others" that they perceive as a threat to their "moral order," citizens need to link with the institutions of society when they address them for support and help in dealing with such behaviors and the resulting social conflicts. The civic culture that engenders tolerance amongst citizens needs support from the institutions and associations of civil society, as well as strong democratic institutions. It is crucial in this process that freedom from insecurity and perceived threat is distributed equally, and that minorities as well as the majority are equally secure. The provision of security to all citizens by institutions as diverse as criminal justice and welfare is vital in ensuring and developing tolerance in societies. Contemporary societies need to find the balance between closely knit communities and diversity, stability, and disorder that shapes tolerance in all realms of life (Weissberg 1998).

SEE ALSO: Adorno, Theodor W.; Affirmative Action; Citizenship; Civil Society; Democracy; Discrimination; Prejudice

REFERENCES AND SUGGESTED READINGS

Adorno, T. W., Frenkel-Brunswick, E., Levinson, D. J., & Nevitt Sanford, R. (1950) *The Authoritarian Personality*. Harper, New York.
Almond, G. A. & Verba, S. (1963) *The Civic Culture*. Harper, Boston.
Castiglione, D. & McKinnon, K. (Eds.) (2003) *Toleration, Neutrality, and Democracy*. Kluwer, Dordrecht.
Frederico, C. M. & Holmes, J. W. (2005) Education and the Interface Between Racial Perceptions and Criminal Justice Attitudes. *Political Psychology* 26(1): 47–75.
Gibson, J. L. (1992) The Political Consequences of Intolerance: Cultural Conformity and Political Freedom. *British Journal of Political Science* 19: 562–70.
Gibson, J. L. & Gouws, A. (2003) *Overcoming Intolerance in South Africa: Experiments in Democratic Persuasion*. Cambridge University Press, Cambridge.
Granovetter, M. (1973) The Strength of Weak Ties. *American Journal of Sociology* 78: 360–80.
Hirschmann, A. O. (1997 [1977]) *The Passions and the Interests: Political Arguments for Capitalism Before its Triumph*. Princeton University Press, Princeton.
Horton, J. (1993) *Liberalism, Multiculturalism, and Toleration*. Macmillan, London.
Horton, J. & Mendus, S. (Eds.) (1999) *Toleration, Identity, and Difference*. Macmillan, London.
Inglehart, R. (1997) *Modernization and Postmodernization: Cultural, Economic, and Political Change in 43 Societies*. Princeton University Press, Princeton.
Jorgensen, B. (2004) Social Capital in a Tolerant Society? *International Journal of Sociology and Social Policy* 24(1/2): 1–20.
Kymlicka, W. & Opalski, M. (2001) *Can Liberal Pluralism Be Exported? Western Political Theory and Ethnic Relations in Eastern Europe*. Oxford University Press, Oxford.
McKinnon, K. & Castiglione, D. (Eds.) (2003) *The Culture of Toleration in Diverse Societies*. Manchester University Press, Manchester.
Mann, M. (2005) *The Dark Side of Democracy*. Cambridge University Press, Cambridge.
Offe, C. (2002) Political Liberalism, Groups Rights, and the Politics of Fear and Trust. *International Social Science Review* 3(1): 5–17.
Shweder, R., Minow, M., & Markus, H. R. (Eds.) (2002) *Engaging Cultural Differences*. Russell Sage Foundation, New York.
Stouffer, S. A. (1955) *Communism, Conformism, and Civil Liberties*. Doubleday, New York.
Sullivan, J. L. & Transue, J. E. (1999) The Psychological Underpinnings of Democracy: A Selective Review of Research on Political Tolerance, Interpersonal Trust, and Social Capital. *Annual Review of Psychology* 50: 625–50.
Uslaner, E. M. (2004) Trust and Social Bonds: Faith in Others and Policy Outcomes Reconsidered. *Political Research Quarterly* 57(3): 501–7.
Walzer, M. (1997) *On Toleration*. Yale University Press, New Haven.
Weissberg, R. (1998) *Political Tolerance: Balancing Community and Diversity*. Sage, London.

Tönnies, Ferdinand (1855–1936)

Raymond M. Weinstein

Ferdinand Tönnies was born near Oldenswort, Germany, in the northern province of Schleswig-Holstein. He came from a well-to-do farming family and grew up at a time when

Germany was expanding as a colonial empire and undergoing profound changes such as population growth, urbanization, and industrialization. Tönnies's oldest brother was involved in mercantile endeavors and thus he experienced the world of the peasant farmer as well as the town merchant. He received his doctorate in philosophy from the University of Tübingen in 1877, then returned to his native province, and later taught for over a half century as a private lecturer and professor at the University of Kiel.

Tönnies was interested in social philosophy and social science. His best-known work was his first, *Gemeinschaft und Gesellschaft*, published in 1887. Translated into English as *Community and Society* (1957), this book on social change and modernization had a pioneering influence in the new discipline of sociology. Its later editions served to enhance Tönnies's reputation as an important social theorist. *Gemeinschaft* referred not so much to a geographic place as to a "community feeling," intimate and holistic relationships, and a common meeting of minds characteristic of people living in a village or small town. By contrast, Tönnies used *Gesellschaft* to describe the impersonal, limited, and contractual relationships people have in an urban-industrial world, an "associational society." The two terms were meant to call attention to the dramatic shift occurring in the late nineteenth century in social groupings and interpersonal relations.

Tönnies believed all social relationships were governed by human will, the need to belong to groups or associate with others. He spoke of "natural will," the motivation for action derived from the temperament, character, or intellect of the individual. This will is typified by *Gemeinschaft* and is found in kinship groups, neighborhoods, and friendship circles. People are bound together by blood, locality, or common interest and naturally work together or help each other as an end in and for itself. Tönnies believed "rational will" is characteristic of *Gesellschaft*. People associate with one another as a means to an end, for economic or political gain in capitalist society, to rationally choose their associations for practical results rather than personal motives. Tönnies developed his concepts to be ideal-types of historical relationships found in medieval or rural, as opposed to modern or urban, societies.

As a sociologist, Tönnies was ahead of his contemporaries – Durkheim and Weber in Europe and Cooley in the US – who likewise created dichotomies of the changing forces that bind people and different orientations guiding their actions. He was a prolific writer and made contributions to many areas of sociology, publishing over 900 works during his lifetime. In 1910 Tönnies wrote a philosophical treatise on Thomas Hobbes. In 1922 he produced a book about public opinion and research methods. The papers he considered most relevant were collected in three volumes from 1924 to 1929. In 1931 he published an introduction to sociology as a social science. His last book, *The Spirit of Modern Times*, appearing in 1935 shortly before his death, connected theoretically back to *Community and Society* a half century earlier.

Tönnies co-founded the German Sociological Society and served as its president for several years. He came to America in 1904 to lecture at Harvard University. He was removed from his academic post at Kiel by the Nazis in 1933 because of his liberal ideas and public criticism of the regime. After the war, times changed and the father of sociology in Germany was honored by the creation of the Ferdinand-Tönnies-Gesellschaft at Kiel in 1956. The FTG sponsors research, journals, and conferences on sociological topics, and from 1998 published a 24-volume critical edition of Tönnies's complete works. Tönnies's first work, however, composed as a young man, turned out to be the one he would be most remembered for. His ideas continue to move, intellectually and emotionally, younger generations of scholars on both sides of the Atlantic. The German words *Gemeinschaft* and *Gesellschaft* are readily employed without translation by sociologists lecturing and writing in any language.

SEE ALSO: Community and Economy; Cooley, Charles Horton; Durkheim, Émile; Durkheim, Émile and Social Change; Social Change; Urban Community Studies; Weber, Max

REFERENCES AND SUGGESTED READINGS

Adair-Toteff, C. (1995) Ferdinand Tönnies: Utopian Visionary. *Sociological Theory* 13: 58–65.

Christenson, J. A. (1984) Gemeinshaft and Gesellschaft: Testing the Spatial and Communal Hypotheses. *Social Forces* 63: 160–8.

Tönnies, F. (1957) *Community and Society*. Trans. C. P. Loomis. Michigan State University Press, East Lansing.

Tönnies, F. (1971) *On Sociology: Pure, Applied and Empirical*. Ed. W. J. Cahnman & R. Heberle. University of Chicago Press, Chicago.

Tönnies, F. (1998–) *Ferdinand Tönnies Gesamtausgabe*. Ed. L. Clausen, A. Deichsel, C. Bickel, R. Fechner, & C. Schlüter-Knauer. De Gruyter, Berlin.

top management teams

Phyl Johnson and Steven W. Floyd

The top management team (TMT) literature concerns itself with the study of the most senior teams of executive directors in both private and public sector organizations. These teams are studied in terms of their makeup, their activities, and the extent to which either of these variables has a causal relationship with organizational performance. Top management teams are widely acknowledged to play a key role in organizational success and failure and, as such, generate significant research interest.

Although sharing some themes in common, the TMT literature does not normally include work that is interested in boards of directors and issues surrounding corporate governance. These literatures look at the next level up in organizational hierarchy where the decision-making body is made up of directors that are internal (executive) and external (non-executive) to the organization and are answerable to (or representative of) the owners of the business and other key stakeholders.

The TMT literature is tangential to other fields. As the most senior managers within the organization, it is the task of the membership of the TMT to both develop and lead the implementation of the strategy that organization is seeking to follow to achieve success. Therefore, both the leadership and strategic decision-making literatures are relevant to and share common themes with the TMT literature.

Different perspectives have been used to explore the nature, role, and impact of TMTs. One of the more widely known and recognized is the literature on the *demographic* profile (e.g., size, turnover, tenure, occupational background) of TMTs. In general, this research examines relationships between such variables and the organization's strategy or its financial performance. One of the causal mechanisms proposed to account for these relationships is the effect of demographic characteristics on the information processing capacity of the TMT. Thus, for example, Haleblian and Finkelstein (1993) argue that larger TMTs have a greater degree of information processing capacity, that this leads to better strategic decisions, and thus, that the size of the TMT is positively associated with organizational performance. A similar line of causal reasoning connects the demographic characteristics of the TMT to its beliefs or knowledge base. Thus, for example, Michel and Hambrick (1992) argued that the more an organization's diversification posture relied on interdependence among business units, the more likely that operations, marketing, sales, and R&D would be represented in the functional backgrounds of TMT members. The most widely cited work within this genre is Hambrick and Mason's (1984) theoretical paper in which they outline both the rationale and the methodology for using demographic variables in the study of TMTs. This paper is usually recognized as launching this stream of research, which Hambrick and Mason call the "upper echelons perspective."

Another body of work that is focused on the TMT is the *strategic decision-making* literature. One stream of debate and discussion within the strategic decision-making literature breaks the decision-making process into subtasks: scanning for strategic issues, interpreting these issues, and making a strategic choice. Here, the cognitive processes, biases, and routines of the members of the TMT are explored. For instance, one finding is that how strategists categorize a strategic issue influences strategic choice: when issues are categorized as threats, the decision is more likely to affect a significant change in strategy. Other researchers focus much more on the processes associated with strategic choice. One stream of work analyzes the comprehensiveness of strategic decision processes (Fredrickson 1984; Fredrickson & Mitchell 1984). A high degree of comprehensiveness means that the TMT pursues a more rational approach to decision-making, including the articulation of clear goals and the analysis of multiple alternatives, while a low degree of comprehensiveness means that decision-making follows a more incremental pattern, involving a more limited comparison of a potential course of action against the status quo. Another body of work on TMT decision process examines the extent to which TMT members agree or disagree about strategic decisions, i.e., the extent of strategic consensus. Both the antecedents and outcomes of consensus have been explored (e.g., Dess 1987; Dess & Origer 1987; Woolridge & Floyd 1989; Dess & Priem 1995). Others focus on the manner in which the TMT interacts in the process of achieving agreement. Three modes of interaction are usually discussed: devil's advocacy, dialectical inquiry, and consensus building.

A more recent perspective on TMT decision-making has sought to bring a finer-grained understanding to the subject. Here a *cognitive* lens is used to explore how TMT members think about (Huff 1990) or make sense of (Weick 1995) the internal and external organizational environments and their role as strategists. The cognitive strategic groups literature would be an example (e.g., Porac et al. 1989; Reger & Huff 1993; Johnson et al. 1998). Here, researchers seek to account for strategic outcomes in terms of the way strategists think about the structure of their competitive environment.

So far the discussion of TMTs has been focused on the outcomes and nature of TMT activity and has been clearly aligned to the strategic decision-making literature. However, there is a body of work within the TMT literature that is concerned less with the strategic nature of TMT activity per se than with the exploration of the *characteristics* of those who make it to the TMT. This is largely contingency-based theorizing and moreover is more heavily focused on exploring the characteristics of those managers who make it to the CEO role rather than the executive suite generally. Norburn's (1989) study is an example of work that focuses on CEOs; he describes a set of psychological characteristics that predict CEO or director status.

There is a smaller literature that examines characteristics of individual TMT members, not in terms of who makes it to the top, but rather in terms of what happens to executives physically and psychologically when they become members of the TMT. This literature is concerned with the causes and consequences of *executive health*.

Finally, there is a small literature that, encompassing all of the above and more, seeks to create a *typology* of TMTs. Often papers on this topic are designed for a practitioner as opposed to academic audience. Pitcher (1997) is a good example of work that is practically oriented and academically sound.

The primary methodological problem with studying the TMT has been access. That is, the upper echelons of organizations are comprised of powerful people who are not inclined to become objects of research. In the past, the preference has been to theorize using data that are in the public domain. Hence, the demographic methodology discussed at the outset has been used widely. However, the use of such *surrogate measures* (using demographic variables as a surrogate measure of TMT members' attitudes and beliefs) has been criticized (Lawrence 1997; Markoczy 1997) and calls have been issued for researchers to carry out more work that collects primary data from the TMT.

The issue of sensitivity and access remains, however. It is rare for a researcher to gain access to a TMT in order to observe members at work and ask them detailed questions about their activities. Balogun et al. (2003) argue that in order to induce such cooperation there must be a clear quid pro quo for the organization. Also, it is the responsibility of the researcher to have a meaningful contribution to offer the team (over and above feedback from the research itself). This sentiment is also echoed elsewhere in the management literature (Maclean & Macintosh 2002).

SEE ALSO: Leadership; Organization Theory; Organizational Failure; Strategic Decisions; Strategic Management (Organizations); Teamwork

REFERENCES AND SUGGESTED READINGS

Balogun, J., Huff, A. S., & Johnson, P. (2003) Three Responses to the Methodological Challenges of Studying Strategizing. *Journal of Management Studies* 40(1): 197–223.

Campbell Quick, J., Gavin, J., Cooper, C., & Quick, J. (2000) Executive Health: Building Strength and Managing Risks. *Academy of Management Executive* 14(12).

Dess, G. G. (1987) Consensus on Strategy Formulation and Organizational Performance: Competitors in a Fragmented Industry. *Strategic Management Journal* 8: 259–77.

Dess, G. G. & Origer, N. K. (1987) Environment, Structure, and Consensus in Strategy Formulation: A Conceptual Integration. *Academy of Management Review* 12(2): 313–30.

Dess, G. G. & Priem, R. I. (1995) Consensus-Performance Research: Theoretical and Empirical Extensions. *Journal of Management Studies* 32(4): 401–17.

Fredrickson, J. W. (1984) The Comprehensiveness of Strategic Decision Processes: Extensions, Observations, and Future Directions. *Academy of Management Journal* 27: 445–67.

Fredrickson, J. W. & Mitchell, T. R. (1984) Strategic Decision Processes: Comprehensiveness and Performance in an Industry with an Unstable Environment. *Academy of Management Journal* 27: 399–424.

Haleblian, J. & Finkelstein, S. (1993) Top Management Team Size, CEO Dominance, and Firm Performance: The Moderating Roles of Environmental Turbulence and Discretion. *Academy of Management Journal* 36: 844–63.

Hambrick, D. C. & Mason, P. A. (1984) Upper Echelons: The Organization as a Reflection of its Top Managers. *Academy of Management Review* 9(2): 193–206.

Huff, A. S. (Ed.) (1990) *Mapping Strategic Thought*. Wiley, Chichester.

Johnson, P., Daniels, K., & Asch, R. (1998) Mental Models of Competition. In: Eden, C. & Spender, J.-C. (Eds.), *Managerial and Organizational Cognition: Theory, Methods, and Research*. Sage, London.

Lawrence, B. S. (1997) The Black Box of Organizational Demography. *Organization Science* 8(1): 1–22.

Maclean, D. & Macintosh, R. (2002) One Process, Two Audiences: On the Challenges of Management Research. *European Management Journal* 20(4): 383–92.

Markoczy, L. (1997) Measuring Beliefs: Accept No Substitutes. *Academy of Management Journal* 40(5): 1228–42.

Michel, J. & Hambrick, D. C. (1992) Diversification Posture and the Characteristics of the Top Management Team. *Academy of Management Journal* 35: 9–37.

Norburn, D. (1989) The Chief Executive: A Breed Apart. *Strategic Management Journal* 1: 1–15.

Pitcher, P. (1997) *The Drama of Leadership*. Wiley, Chichester.

Porac, J., Thomas, H., & Baden Fuller, C. (1989) Competitive Groups as Cognitive Communities: The Case of the Scottish Knitwear Manufacturers. *Journal of Management Studies* 26, 4 (July).

Reger, R. K. & Huff, A. S. (1993) Strategic Groups: A Cognitive Perspective. *Strategic Management Journal* 14: 103–24.

Weick, K. E. (1995) *Sensemaking in Organizations*. Sage, London.

Woolridge, B. & Floyd, S. (1989) Strategic Process Effects on Consensus. *Strategic Management Journal* 10: 295–302.

totalitarianism

Chamsy El-Ojeili

Totalitarianism refers to a political system in which the people are completely or nearly completely dominated by an all-embracing state. Totalitarianism is often said to involve the lack of independent social sectors, the non-existence of rights and pluralism, and the eradication of politics. The concept is frequently viewed as differing from authoritarianism in a number of ways: being more ideological; involving the domination of a single political party; seeing pervasive state intervention at every level; and being a peculiarly twentieth-century political form.

Totalitarianism is commonly deployed as a concept that encompasses both fascist and socialist social orders. Critics note that the concept thus deals with very different social formations and is of little analytical value. Although there are socialist accounts of totalitarianism (e.g., Franz Neumann, Claude Lefort, Cornelius Castoriadis, Agnes Heller), Marxists tend to be unhappy with the equation of the USSR with Nazi Germany, especially on account of what they see as clear socioeconomic divergences, viewing the concept as largely an expression of Cold War politics and as an inoculation against emancipatory change. Marxists have also criticized the idealism of attempts to trace the genesis of totalitarianism to thinkers such as Hegel and Marx. They have insisted on the complicity of liberal democracies in totalitarianism – even charging that liberal democracies are themselves totalitarian – and some have insisted that the concept falsely implies the absence of conflict within these states. On the other hand, "totalitarianism" has been defended as a useful ideal type, and it has continued to have popular currency.

There have been a number of important contributions to the theory of totalitarianism. Friedrich and Brzezinski (1965) denoted six features of totalitarianism: an elaborate ideology which centers on a final, perfected humanity; a single mass party; a system of terror; near-complete monopoly by the party of the means of mass communication; a near monopoly, too, over the use of weapons of armed combat; and central control of the economy. F. A. Hayek viewed totalitarianism as arising from planning and collectivism; Popper (1945) located the origins of the "closed society" in holism and in the "historicist" notion that history unfolds through knowable general laws towards an endpoint; and Talmon (1961) explored the beginnings of totalitarianism in the thought of Plato, Hegel, and Marx. Arendt (1951) underscored the role of imagined laws of history or nature, a frantic dynamism, terror, and ideology (separating people completely from reality); and she found precedents to, and conditions for, totalitarianism in imperialism, capitalism, and the superfluousness of the mass of people in industrial societies.

Although the term lost some of its intellectual appeal from the 1960s and the 1970s, it has gained something of a renewed currency in postmodernist discourse, which comes to echo the critical theory of the Frankfurt School. Here, an ethical turn has focused variously on the erasure of difference and otherness in totalizing, teleological narratives, on the coercive consequences of the rule of reason and science, and on the normalizing, even totalitarian, tendencies of modernity's desire for order and transparency and its fear of ambivalence.

SEE ALSO: Arendt, Hannah; Communism; Democracy; Fascism; Propaganda; Socialism

REFERENCES AND SUGGESTED READINGS

Arendt, H. (1951) *The Origins of Totalitarianism*. Harcourt, Brace, New York.

Aron, R. (1965) *Democracy and Totalitarianism*. Weidenfeld & Nicolson, London.

Camus, A. (1969) *The Rebel*. Penguin, London.

Castoriadis, C. (1997) *The Castoriadis Reader*. Blackwell, Oxford.

Friedrich, C. J. & Brzezinski, Z. K. (1965) *Totalitarian Dictatorship and Autocracy*, rev. edn. Praeger, New York.

Lefort, C. (1986) *The Political Forms of Modern Society: Bureaucracy, Democracy, Totalitarianism*. Polity Press, Cambridge.

Popper, K. (1945) *The Open Society and Its Enemies*, 2 vols. Routledge, London.

Schapiro, L. (1972) *Totalitarianism*. Pall Mall, London.

Talmon, J. L. (1961) *The Origins of Totalitarian Democracy*. Mercury, London.

totemism

Gaetano Riccardo

The word totemism denotes in a broad sense the complex of beliefs concerning the existence of a sort of kinship between a human group, or a single individual, and an animal or a plant serving as an emblem of this link. This relationship implies a range of rituals and taboos, especially alimentary and sexual ones, which bind those who recognize themselves as members belonging to the same totem. The word itself, in the variant *totam*, was used in 1791 by the English traveler J. Long to designate the link of kinship and the worship of plants and animals by the Algonquin Indians of the Ojibwa, in Eastern North America. Although the term referred to the clan totem, Long used it to describe individual totemism, that is to say, the belief in the existence of a personal link between a person and an animal (more rarely a plant), which is considered as a guardian spirit.

In anthropology, the acceptance of the notion of totemism began in the late nineteenth century and diminished at the beginning of the twentieth century. During this period scholars focused their attention especially on religious aspects of totemism, and they considered it principally as one of the most archaic forms of worship. So conceived, the idea of totemism achieved widespread fame and it was analyzed by various disciplines. Its introduction in the anthropological debate goes back to McLennan, who stressed how totemism was typified by three elements: fetishism, exogamy, and matrilineal descent. To these aspects Rivers would later add another, namely, prohibiting the group from eating the plant or the animal considered as a totem, except during certain ritual events.

While on the one hand the rapid increase of ethnographic data concerning totemism promoted their inclusion in great evolutionistic syntheses suggested by various authors, on the other it already heralded their superseding. The first important comparative exposition of known ethnographic data is due to Frazer's *Totemism and Exogamy* (1910), in which three different hypotheses concerning the origins of totemism are suggested. The first hypothesis states that the first form of totemism is the individual one, involving the idea that there is an external soul dwelling in animals and plants. The second hypothesis stresses the magical aspect of totemism, particularly expressed in its Australian variant. The third hypothesis stresses primitive humans' misunderstanding about the existence of a bond between sexuality and conception, with the consequent idea that the latter could depend on the action of an animal or vegetable spirit.

In Frazer's monumental work the arrangement of the collected ethnographic data concerning totemism aimed particularly to stress western modern rationality, in contrast to primitive thinking. One of the results of this approach was to hide a large variety of differences existing in the ethnographic data. The continuous decrease of this concern enabled scholars to stress how the variety of totemic phenomena was too wide to be ranged in a single typology. Research put forward by other scholars enabled them to identify very different phenomena, and when agreement was rare it was not easy to formulate universal hypotheses. Analogies began to be suggested with greater care, and with consideration of historical and geographical continuities and discontinuities.

Consequently, the age of major diffusion of the notion of totemism coincided with that of its major decline. In the year in which Frazer's monumental work appeared, another author, Goldenweiser (1910), stressed that it was misleading to include such different data as social organizations by clans, their being labeled by names of plants and animals, and, finally, the belief in a real or mystical relationship between clan members and a totemic species in a single institution. All these phenomena were not always equally present. Furthermore, in many cases they were independent of one another.

The evolutionistic approach to the problem of totemism did not necessarily presuppose the comparative method. It was sufficient to assume that totemism could be one of the most archaic forms of religion. Thus Durkheim (1912) was interested only in Australian totemism, which he claimed to be its most archaic form. According to Durkheim the totem is the main symbol of the society itself. In this way his analysis of totemism becomes an illustrative example of the inextricable link between the religious and the social. Durkheim's sociological approach was an alternative to a previous approach in which a psychological explanation concerning the creation of institutions and religious phenomena prevailed. The advance offered by this new approach was evident. Social phenomena were explained by the social itself and not by more or less imaginative conjectures about primitive thinking.

Although Durkheim's arguments were very incisive, the psychological approach to the study of totemism received a new impulse from the father of psychoanalysis, Sigmund Freud. In his work *Totem und Tabu* (*Totem and Taboo*) (1912), Freud tried to establish a parallelism between the two major prohibitions concerning totemism – alimentary and sexual – and the Oedipus complex. Ethnographic data were underestimated by him in favor of the Darwinian hypothesis concerning the prehistoric existence of the so-called primitive horde. Freud supposed a social scenario in which there is not yet a form of exogamy and the whole group is ruled in a despotic way by a single man, the father, who is unable to control his instincts. This despotic father claims to be the only person who has access to the females of the group. Such an intolerable situation would have triggered a violent rebellion of the sons against him. The youngest men killed the despotic father to devour him, and then they were racked with remorse. A sense of guilt for the crime committed led the sons to substitute the father with a symbolic figure, a totemic species. At the same time, the prohibition of sexual relationships with the females of the group, previously ordered by their despotic father, was spontaneously observed by them. This would be the reason for the appearance of totemism and exogamy as well.

Although in opposition to the arguments put forward by Durkheim, this purely psychological explanation of totemism formulated by Freud is to some extent similar because both authors share an evolutionistic and universalistic vision of cultural facts. A loss of interest in the notion of totemism began only when the evolutionistic perspective of analysis was abandoned. Until it was assumed as valid, the interest in totemism was assured by its presumed universalistic aspect, being considered as expressing a particular stage of human evolution. The fact that a particular and empirical form of totemism could not include any traits considered as an integral part of the totemic institution did not seem a problem. In any case, they were necessarily supposed to exist in a different stage of cultural evolution. So ethnographic evidence was considered important not so much for its local relevance as for expressing something considered as universal.

While Elkin was one of the last authors to assume that ethnographic analyses could still be developed in the direction of a more generalized interpretation of totemism, van Gennep (1920) was among the first authors to recognize that it could not be considered as a universal cultural phenomenon. This lack of universality of totemism was reasserted by some American anthropologists. Historical and relativistic methods of analyzing cultural facts gained ground in the United States. Authors such as Boas, Lowie, and Kroeber were very careful to stress the variety of ethnographic data. British functionalists such as Malinowski and above all Radcliffe-Brown moved in an almost identical direction. In the latter's work particularly there are important suggestions concerning the tendency, typical of the most archaic societies, to change animals and plants into objects of worship able to ensure well-being of the group.

A turning point toward the dissolution of the notion of totemism is represented by the publication of Lévi-Strauss's famous book, *Le Totémisme aujourd'hui* (*Totemism Today*) (1962), in which the author speaks of "totemic illusion." He stresses that totemism does not correspond to a primitive form of religion but must be understood within the broader human tendency to classify everything in different species. According to Lévi-Strauss, the core of totemism is represented not so much by a relationship between a group and a species as by the fact that this correspondence with different species is used to conceptualize the differences between the various human groups. Thus the specific nature of totemism would consist in enabling the representation of differences between human groups by resorting to analogies taken from the natural world. Totemism can be understood only on the basis that entire systems of differences, not single elements, are compared. Through totemism, relationships and differences among human groups are conceptualized by analogies with differences among species of animals and plants. According to Lévi-Strauss, this would be the most important aspect of totemism. He supports his opinion through the statement that totemic species are useful for thinking and not for eating.

The analysis of totemism proposed by Lévi-Strauss does not merely represent one opinion among others. It tries also to explain why the notion of totemism had an enduring life among anthropologists, despite its illusory character. According to Lévi-Strauss, the idea of totemism was in a certain sense a sign of the ethnocentrism included in most anthropological works. To talk about totemism meant stressing the discord represented by a kind of thinking that assumed a confusion between natural and cultural spheres, considered quite different in western cultural tradition. Despite the rightness of these observations, the intellectualistic approach adopted by the French anthropologist in his analysis of totemism on the one hand effectively synthesizes the old-fashioned debate concerning the idea of totemism, while on the other it seems to discourage possible alternative ways of research undertaken by other authors. Among these, those which focus their attention on the material and moral implications of totemistic practices assume a certain importance today.

A year before the publication of Lévi-Strauss's book, Raoul and Laura Makarius (1961) resumed the argument concerning the relationship between totemism and exogamy and highlighted a possible "alimentary" origin of the marriage taboo among peoples composing a single group in which meals are shared. Furthermore, the remarks proposed by Valerio Valeri (1999) assume great importance with regard to the moral relevance of totemic taboos. Valeri highlights how the "phonological" approach adopted by Lévi-Strauss does not allow us to appreciate the complexity of relationships between humans and animals, but merely focuses attention on less important aspects of totemism. Totemism constitutes a complex of phenomena reducible neither to an essence nor to a formalism in regard to which the conscious self-representations of groups are considered as a trifling matter.

SEE ALSO: Animism; Durkheim, Émile; Fetishism; Primitive Religion; Religion; Religion, Sociology of

REFERENCES AND SUGGESTED READINGS

Durkheim, É. (1912) *Les Formes élémentaires de la vie religieuse*. Alcan, Paris.

Evans-Pritchard, E. E. (1965) *Theories of Primitive Religion*. Clarendon Press, Oxford.

Frazer, J. G. (1910) *Totemism and Exogamy: A Treatise on Certain Early Forms of Superstition and Society*. Macmillan, London.

Freud, S. (1912) *Totem und Tabu*. Heller, Vienna.

Goldenweiser, A. (1910) Totemism: An Analytical Study. *Journal of American Folklore* 23: 179–293.

Lévi-Strauss, C. (1962) *Le Totémisme aujourd'hui*. Puf, Paris.

McLennan, J. F. (1869–70) The Worship of Animals and Plants. *Fortnightly Review* 6: 407–27; 7: 194–216.

Makarius, R. & Makarius, L. (1961) *L'Origine de l'exogamie et du totémisme*. Gallimard, Paris.

Valeri, V. (1999) *The Forest of Taboos: Morality, Hunting, and Identity Among the Huaulu of the Moluccas*. University of Wisconsin Press, Madison.

Van Gennep, A. (1920) *L'État actuel du problème totémique: Étude critique des théories sur les origines de la religion et de l'organisation sociale*. Leroux, Paris.

tracking

Kathryn S. Schiller

Tracking is the process of differentiating individuals' school experiences through the grouping of students for instructional purposes based on actual or assumed differences in academic development or interests. In theory, such practices can maximize learning by allowing instruction to be tailored to the needs of each classroom of students. In practice, the quality of instruction often varies dramatically based on the group level, such that low track students receive few learning opportunities while high track students are exposed to a rich and rigorous curriculum. When group placements are related to ascribed characteristics such as social class or ethnicity, tracking contributes to social stratification by perpetuating social inequality in not only individuals' current learning opportunities but also future educational and occupational attainment.

The terms *tracking*, *ability grouping*, and *streaming* are frequently used as synonyms. When distinctions are made, ability grouping usually refers to sorting of students in a given grade level into groups that progress through a common curriculum but at different speeds. In contrast, tracking usually refers to differences in students' academic programs, which differ in the topics covered based on the courses taken. Ability grouping is a more frequent practice in primary and elementary schools, while tracking is usually found in secondary schools.

Tracking is a feature of most modern school systems, although the process and extent of stratification and segregation vary dramatically. In the US during the late 1980s, many schools officially eliminated tracking (i.e., *detracked*) in response to political pressures to increase academic standards while reducing gaps in standardized test scores or educational attainment between genders and racial or ethnic groups. However, consistency in group placement across subjects and years indicates that *de facto* petuate social stratification in both the economic and health benefits related to higher levels of educational attainment.

DIMENSIONS OF TRACKING

In sociology, the conceptualization of tracking recognizes that classrooms are the technical core of schools in which students, teachers, and curricular materials combine to create learning environments that vary in quality and quantity of instruction. In addition, students' academic careers consist of series of classroom experiences spanning grade levels that often provide increasingly divergent educational experiences. While the operationalization of tracking varies, the concept in sociological research consistently refers to some aspect of a student's overall academic status at a particular point in time or over a relatively short period of time.

When used synonymously with ability grouping, students' track placement usually refers to their relative status in the academic hierarchy within a classroom or school. Within some elementary school classrooms, tracking occurs when the teacher sorts students into instructional groups based on perceived academic progress or ability. In other elementary schools, students are tracked when they are assigned to classrooms based on similar criteria. These groupings are usually given labels such as *low*, *average*, and *high* or *remedial*, *basic*, *regular*, and *advanced* to reflect relative rankings within the academic hierarchy. In general, most students are expected eventually to cover the same core topics and master a common set of basic skills, although the speed of progress or degree of mastery may differ. Group labels are used to reflect differences in difficulty of the instructional material to which students are exposed, which should build on their prior academic progress.

When referring to secondary schools, tracking is also operationalized as differences in academic programs traditionally described by schools or students as *vocational*, *general*, and *college preparatory*. While now mostly archaic, these terms are used to characterize the types or difficulty of courses students are expected to take based on whether they are expected to enter the workforce or attend college after high school. Students in the college preparatory track, for example, tend to take more academic courses such as advanced placement English, physics, calculus, and foreign languages. In contrast, vocational students tend to take a large number of courses with direct occupational links, such as business English, drafting, bookkeeping, and commercial photography. General track students usually take a combination of less difficult academic courses, such as regular English, and elective courses that might also include one or two vocational courses. To the extent that students are being exposed to distinctly different sets of topics or subjects, self-reported or school-designated track can be a useful summary indicator of a student's general academic experiences during high school.

Since the late 1980s, however, sociologists have recognized that the traditional track labels fail to capture the great diversity of students' academic experiences in American high schools. By 1990, the relationship between sophomores' self-reported track and level of mathematics course did not align consistently, such that knowing one type of classification increased the ability to predict the other by only 14 percent (Stevenson et al. 1994). Several efforts have been made to develop finer-grained measures of academic programs based on detailed analyses of the courses students take at a given time or overall during high school. These *course-based* indicators of track usually use sophisticated statistical techniques to analyze students' high school transcripts. For example, Lucas (1999) developed his track indicators by a detailed mapping of course descriptions onto traditional track designations by taking into account both the level of difficulty and timing of when a student took a course. In this approach, for example, geometry is considered *elite college* track if taken as a freshman but *regular college* track if taken as a sophomore.

Other approaches to characterizing students' academic careers based on course-taking during high school mostly abandon the concept of academic program. In one approach, clustering procedures are used to statistically identify *emergent* tracks based on constellations of course enrolments to which traditional labels may or may not be applied (e.g., Friedkin & Thomas 1997). The goal is to identify students who share similar educational experiences and positions within a particular school or a set of schools without using an a priori classification system. Another approach focuses on indicators of students' progress through a proscribed curriculum by using indicators of whether a student took a given course in a given year and then statistically modeling changes between years to estimate trajectories through a normative sequence of courses (e.g., Schneider et al. 1998). These sequences are likely to be especially clear in high school mathematics due to the hierarchical and standardized nature of the curriculum in which mastery of a basic topic (e.g., functions) is usually required before attempting more advanced topics (e.g., geometry). This approach to characterizing students' academic status allows close examination of learning opportunity sequences, which are primarily a function of the structure and organization of a subject-specific curriculum that link learning opportunities across time, even spanning levels of schooling.

While the comprehensive high school remains an institutionalized feature of American school systems, other countries often track students following a given academic program by placing them in the same school. For example, Germany has a three-tiered system of secondary schools in which *Gymnasium* prepares students for higher education, *Realschule* prepare students for mid-level occupations or careers, and *Hauptschule* provides a basic prevocational education. In Japan, students are admitted based on performance on entrance examinations to selective upper secondary schools, which have tight links to prestigious universities. Only a small portion of those students not intending to go to university attend technical upper secondary schools. Thus, tracking results from the sorting of students into secondary schools.

PROCESS OF SORTING STUDENTS

Tracking is of interest to sociologists as the product of schools' intentional sorting of students into courses or academic programs based on some observed or ascribed characteristic. On the most basic level, the availability of courses is determined by schools' master schedules, which specify which courses will be offered at what times. The master schedule thus constrains the possible combinations of courses students can

take in a given academic year. Within these constraints, assigning students to a selection of courses usually involves processes that consider a mixture of indicators for prior academic performance and individual preferences.

School officials begin the complex process of developing a master schedule for a given academic year in the spring of the prior year. Although they usually use previous years' schedules as templates, school officials must adjust for changes in staffing and student enrolments in light of available instructional resources (e.g., room space) and state regulations (e.g., curriculum and graduation requirements) (Delany 1991). For example, schools need to ensure they offer enough English or literature courses so that all students can meet most states' requirement that students complete 4 years of English to earn a high school diploma. However, a school may offer only one section of honors freshman English in order to free up a teacher for an English as a second language course to serve a growing number of immigrant students. When that honors course will be offered also depends on teacher availability and other courses being offered at the same time. Schools frequently make changes to their course schedules well into the academic year, as they continuously balance resource constraints with student demand.

While assignment policies can vary dramatically, most schools use several indicators of prior academic performance (such as grades or achievement test scores) in making course placement decisions. Turner (1960) described placement procedures that utilized performance on standardized assessments as *contest mobility systems*, in which individuals earn the right of entry into the elite. In contrast, more subjective criteria are used for making placement decisions in *sponsored mobility systems*, in which individuals with unusual qualities are singled out for special assistance. Sociologists have had heated debates over whether the US has more or less of a contest-focused system than either Japan or Great Britain. This debate is the result of most school systems having features of both ideal-type mobility systems, with some students earning placement in higher level courses and others being recruited to the academic elite.

Assignment systems, however, are rarely purely meritocratic due to limitations on the availability of seats in a course and pressures from parents and students to change placements with which they disagree. For example, college-educated parents may be so insistent that their children be given preference in assignment to the single honors English course being offered that other eligible students are prevented from enroling in the class once it reaches capacity. Minority and lower-class students often lack the social and academic resources to object or over-turn undesirable track placements. This may partially account for the historical trend that minority and poor students are less likely to take college preparatory courses than equally talented white students or children of college-educated parents.

ACADEMIC AND SOCIAL CONSEQUENCES

Whether official or *de facto*, tracking not only strongly influences learning and educational attainment, but also shapes the formation of friendships during high school and later occupa-tional attainment and earnings. Organizational, individual, and societal factors influence the process of stratification of learning opportuni-ties and academic outcomes related to course-taking patterns.

Tracking clearly differentiates students' learning opportunities. In secondary schools, some are given academically challenging experi-ences preparing them for college, while others are relegated to classes with curriculum so diluted that they are caricatures of regular courses. Students in honors courses, especially in math and English, are generally exposed to higher-quality learning environments in which they are expected to think critically and creativ-ity is encouraged. In contrast, regular and basic courses often emphasize orderliness and regur-gitation of facts and procedures. Conflict theor-ists such as Bowles and Gintis (1976) argue that these differences in curriculum reflect stu-dents' social origins and are one of the major mechanisms through which social stratification is perpetuated across generations. Lower track courses basically prepare working-class children for menial jobs, while college track courses pre-pare the social elite's children for professional or managerial careers.

The distribution of academic rewards also differs across tracks and courses, with higher grades tending to be awarded in classes attended by students from more advantaged social back-grounds. Theoretically, grades reflect how well students meet their teachers' expectations of learning and behavior in a given course. Thus, differences between courses in the average grade awarded could reflect overall how well students in a given class met their teachers' expectations. However, grade inflation can result from par-ents pressuring teachers and schools to award higher grades in college-preparatory courses to improve their chances of admission to competi-tive colleges and universities. Independent of students' individual achievements, these higher grades awarded in more advanced courses serve as public signals identifying the academic elite in a school.

Track placements also have long-term effects on learning opportunities through what Kerckhoff (1993) described as *institutional iner-tia*, the consistency of placements across grade levels and schools created by organizational dependence on school records and prior place-ment decisions. The positional advantages gained from being placed in more advanced courses earlier in their careers helps academi-cally elite students preserve their status even if they encounter difficulties in that or another course. Positional advantages also accrue from accumulation of prerequisites for later courses that signal to schools that a student was exposed to and gained the knowledge and skills thought necessary to progress. For example, taking alge-bra in middle school is intended to prepare stu-dents to take geometry as high school freshmen, although whether they get much exposure to algebra may be questionable. For these reasons, placement in a more basic course constrains access to advanced courses for even students who may later benefit from a more challenging curriculum. Thus, organizational signals con-cerning students' intellectual abilities and pro-gress sent by prior course placements have lasting effects on their academic careers. When track mobility occurs, students are usually drop-ping down from a higher-level course to a lower level one.

Finally, whether through direct intervention of parents or a more criterion-based system, students' social backgrounds influence their sorting into courses such that they tend to take classes with others similar to themselves. This social class segregation within schools may allow formation of micro-communities with distinct norms and values relating to academic performance. Social capital developed in classes attended by large numbers of children with college-educated parents is likely to create a classroom environment with high levels of academic pressure. Similarly, college-educated parents may lobby for allocation of more qualified teachers and greater resources to the courses taken by their children. Thus, regardless of their own backgrounds, students are likely to benefit academically from attending classes with others from more advantaged social backgrounds.

SEE ALSO: Class, Status, and Power; Conflict Theory; Educational Attainment; Hidden Curriculum; Meritocracy; Mobility, Intergenerational and Intragenerational; Opportunities for Learning; Parental Involvement in Education; Schooling and Economic Success

REFERENCES AND SUGGESTED READINGS

Bowles, S. & Gintis, H. (1976) *Schooling in Capitalist America: Educational Reform and the Contradictions of Economic Life*. Basic Books, New York.

Dauber, S. L., Alexander, K. L., & Entwisle, D. R. (1996) Tracking and Transitions through the Middle Grades: Channeling Educational Trajectories. *Sociology of Education* 69: 290–307.

Delany, B. (1991) Allocation, Choice, and Stratification within High Schools: How the Sorting Machine Copes. *American Journal of Education* 99(2): 181–207.

Friedkin, N. E. & Thomas, S. L. (1997) Social Positions in Schooling. *Sociology of Education* 70(4): 239–55.

Gamoran, A. (1987) The Stratification of High School Learning Opportunities. *Sociology of Education* 60: 61–77.

Gamoran, A. (1992) The Variable Effects of High School Tracking. *American Sociological Review* 57 (December): 812–28.

Hallinan, M. T. (1996) Track Mobility in Secondary School. *Social Forces* 74(3): 983–1002.

Hallinan, M. T. (1994) Tracking: From Theory to Practice. *Sociology of Education* 67: 79–84.

Kerckhoff, A. C. (1993) *Diverging Pathways: Social Structure and Career Deflections*. Cambridge University Press, Cambridge.

Lee, V. E. & Bryk, A. S. (1988) Curriculum Tracking as Mediating the Social Distribution of High School Achievement. *Sociology of Education* 61(2): 78–94.

Lucas, S. R. (1999) *Tracking Inequality: Stratification and Mobility in American High Schools*. Teachers College Press, New York.

Oakes, J. (1985) *Keeping Track: How Schools Structure Inequality*. Yale University Press, New Haven.

Oakes, J. (1994) More than Misapplied Technology: A Normative and Political Response to Hallinan on Tracking. *Sociology of Education* 67: 84–9.

Robitaille, D. F. (Ed.) (1997) *National Contexts for Mathematics and Science Education: An Encyclopedia of the Education Systems Participating in TIMSS*. Pacific Educational Press, Vancouver.

Schneider, B., Swanson, C. B., & Riegle-Crumb, C. (1998) Opportunities for Learning: Course Sequences and Positional Advantages. *Social Psychology of Education* 2: 25–53.

Stevenson, D. L., Schiller, K. S., & Schneider, B. (1994) Sequences of Opportunities for Learning. *Sociology of Education* 67 (July): 184–98.

Turner, R. H. (1960) Sponsored and Contest Mobility and the School System. *American Sociological Review* 25: 855–67.

tradition

Robert Tonkinson

"Tradition" connotes a body of values, beliefs, rules, and behavior patterns that is transmitted generationally by practice and word of mouth and is integral to socialization processes. The content of tradition is shared by a given group and has informational and moral components that concern the nature of things, right and wrong behavior, and unanswerable questions about life and death. Strong connotations of fixity, stability, and continuity are inherent in the notion of "tradition," as a benchmark or beacon guiding a society's body of daily behavior and providing justification for beliefs and practices. In relatively homogeneous small-scale societies, where tradition is the only blueprint for acceptable behavior, it is typically unquestioned and, whatever its truth value, logicality, or consistency, may be regarded as sacred lore (Hunter & Whitten 1976).

Where orally transmitted, however, tradition is always open to variation, contestation, and change; it can also be adjusted, reworked, or reinterpreted to accommodate changing circumstances. Such lability gives the lie to tradition conceived as essentially fixed, immutable, and unchanging over time, and has attracted the attention of historians and anthropologists, particularly in recent decades. In an interesting convergence of focus, two edited volumes on the "construction" and "invention" of tradition appeared in the early 1980s. (Use of the more inflammatory term "invention" by anthropologists ceased after some widely publicized exchanges with indigenous people angered by the implication that they had fabricated their pasts; see Linnekin 1992; Lindstrom & White 1993; see also Turner 1997, on the "authenticity" of invented traditions.)

The first volume (Keesing & Tonkinson 1982) led to a burgeoning interest by anthropologists and others in cognate disciplines in the "politics of tradition." This work reflected the rise of new nationalisms in the Melanesian region that demanded new ways of imagining tradition (Lindstrom & White 1993). Known in Melanesian Tok Pisin lingua franca as *kastom*, semantically opposed to "modern" or "foreign," tradition became a rallying cry of pro-independence movements. In an area famed for its cultural pluralism, the uses of "tradition" highlight the nature of political ideologies and the power of abstract symbols in disguising and mediating contradictions that potentially threaten broader unities (Keesing 1982). In much of Melanesia, the impact of Christianity had caused converts to devalue their traditions and dichotomize their past into a shameful pre-European era of darkness and evil and the Christian era of goodness and light. This prior refiguring of the past was to cause considerable confusion in some areas when leaders of independence movements began invoking the uniqueness and strength of *kastom* (explicitly opposed to non-indigenous European and Christian elements) in their rhetoric aimed at fostering a shared national identity and unity (Tonkinson 1982). Such appeals to tradition encouraged anthropologists to investigate the heuristic possibilities inherent in tradition's seemingly paradoxical malleability.

Most contributors to the 1982 volume adopted a "cultural constructionist" approach, holding that tradition, like culture, is a contested field in which differently located groups struggle to establish and then reproduce their particular symbolic forms and constructions of meaning. Constructions of tradition are always, at some level, about the present, historically contingent, and oppositional (but not always dichotomous) between the western and the indigenous (Lindstrom & White 1993). This perspective inevitably encourages an analytical focus on class and power relations (cf. Keesing 1993), and has become a theoretical imperative for many anthropologists. Linnekin (1992) offers the strongest analytical overview available on the theory and politics of cultural constructionism, and of many anthropologists' unease about the deconstructionist excesses of postmodernism.

The second volume (Hobsbawm & Ranger 1983), by historians, was prompted by two factors: the ubiquity, in Europe and elsewhere, of "traditions" that in form and prominence seem ancient and timeless yet are often relatively recent in origin and are sometimes invented; and the contrast between modernity's unremitting innovation and change and people's attempts to structure elements within their societies as invariant and unchanging (Hobsbawm 1983). Historians are interested principally in the appearance and establishment of such traditions, as well as those that emerge within a brief and datable period yet are less readily traceable. In his Introduction, Hobsbawm defines "invented tradition" as "a set of practices, normally governed by overtly or tacitly accepted rules and of a ritual or symbolic nature, which seek to inculcate certain values and norms of behaviour by repetition, which automatically implies continuity with the past" (p. 1). Besides separating tradition from conventions and routines that are technological rather than ideological, he explicitly contrasts "custom," which is dominant in "traditional societies" and necessarily flexible, with "traditions," including invented ones, which typically stress invariance. Anthropologists have criticized this contrast as denying pre-European-contact dynamism, and as reminiscent of claims that such peoples are "without history" (Jolly & Thomas 1992). Hobsbawm suggests that the seemingly most prevalent post-Industrial Revolution-invented tradition type is "those establishing or symbolizing social cohesion or the membership of groups, real or artificial communities."

Despite ostensible differences in motivation and foci behind these two influential contributions to the literature on tradition, several interesting parallels can be discerned. There is a common interest in symbols and especially the power residing in them when they remain diffuse and undefined. Themes relating to appeals to history and tradition as legitimizing political action, such as resistance to colonial powers, and of reinforcing group cohesion also appear in both treatments. Related to this is another, stronger parallel: the process of nation building, wherein the emergence of new nation-states worldwide and the growth of nationalism necessitate the creation and effective promulgation of symbols of shared identity and belonging, couching the recent, political, and cultural as timeless, "natural," and inevitable. Emergent national identities (informed by tradition) also take on value within the emerging global economic system by supporting tourism (people go to Scotland to see kilts and drink whisky, or to Vanuatu to see land-dives and drink kava) as well as trade in localities and souvenirs.

Discussion and debate about the significance and uses of tradition have continued since the appearance of the two volumes just discussed. The topic has proved remarkably durable, engendering a multilayered body of knowledge about constructions of the past in contemporary societies (Tonkinson 1993). Social actors' received notions of tradition as the solid foundation that underpins customary behavior have been deemphasized in scholarly analyses in favor of conceptions of it as constantly subject to reinterpretation and rereading by each new generation of carriers, who construe their past in terms both of present perceptions and understandings and future hopes and needs (cf. Lindstrom 1982). Tradition becomes a model of past practices rather than a passively and unreflectively inherited legacy (Linnekin 1992). Heuristically, it is perhaps most usefully conceptualized as a resource, employed (or not employed) strategically by individuals and groups (Tonkinson 1993). As Lindstrom (1982) shows, *kastom* is subject to a range of

moral evaluations (or devaluations) by its carriers over time; it is understood by all as a symbol but no one can agree on its meaning, since understandings are embedded within rival groups and become part of competing political ideologies. A notable attribute of tradition is that it can be invoked just as effectively to manifest ethnocentrism and disunity, by emphasizing local differences and reinforcing boundaries, as it can when functioning as a political symbol of unity (in which case it is deliberately left vague and internally undifferentiated, so as to minimize its potentially divisive aspect). The consistent polarity of political uses of tradition between the grassroots, regional, and national levels of society suggests that different analytical strategies may be needed in each case (cf. Tonkinson 1993). In the last decade, the historical turn in anthropological theory has led scholars to attempt to contextualize the emergence of particular constructions of tradition within colonization, missionization, and post-war "development" and in articulation with the global political economy (Lindstrom & White 1993).

SEE ALSO: Constructionism; False Consciousness; Generational Change; Identity Politics/Relational Politics; Social Change; Values

REFERENCES AND SUGGESTED READINGS

Hobsbawm, E. (1983) Introduction: Inventing Traditions. In: Hobsbawm, E. & Ranger, T. (Eds.), *The Invention of Tradition*. Cambridge University Press, Cambridge, pp. 1–14.

Hobsbawm, E. & Ranger, T. (Eds.) (1983) *The Invention of Tradition*. Cambridge University Press, Cambridge.

Hunter, D. E. & Whitten, P. (1976) *Encyclopedia of Anthropology*. Harper & Row, New York.

Jolly, M. & Thomas, N. (1992) Introduction. In: Jolly, M. & Thomas, N. (Eds.), The Politics of Tradition in the Pacific. *Oceania* (special issue) 62(4): 241–8.

Keesing, R. M. (1982) *Kastom* in Melanesia: An Overview. In: Keesing, R. M. & Tonkinson, R. (Eds.), Reinventing Traditional Culture: The Politics of *Kastom* in Island Melanesia. *Mankind* (special issue) 13(4): 297–301.

Keesing, R. M. (1993) *Kastom* Reexamined. In: Lindstrom, L. & White, G. M. (Eds.), Custom Today. *Anthropological Forum* (special issue) 6(4): 587–96.

Keesing, R. M. & Tonkinson, R. (Eds.) (1982) Reinventing Traditional Culture: The Politics of *Kastom* in Island Melanesia. *Mankind* (special issue) 13(4).

Lindstrom, L. (1982) Leftamap *Kastom*: The Political History of Tradition on Tanna. In: Keesing, R. M. & Tonkinson, R. (Eds.), Reinventing Traditional Culture: The Politics of *Kastom* in Island Melanesia. *Mankind* (special issue) 13(4): 316–29.

Lindstrom, L. & White, G. M. (Eds.) (1993) Introduction: Custom Today. In: Lindstrom, L. & White, G. M. (Eds.), Custom Today. *Anthropological Forum* (special issue) 6(4): 467–73.

Linnekin, J. (1992) On the Theory and Politics of Cultural Construction in the Pacific. In: Jolly, M. & Thomas, N. (Eds.), The Politics of Tradition in the Pacific. *Oceania* (special issue) 62(4): 249–63.

Tonkinson, R. (1982) National Identity and the Problem of *Kastom* in Vanuatu. In: Keesing, R. M. & Tonkinson, R. (Eds.), Reinventing Traditional Culture: The Politics of *Kastom* in Island Melanesia. *Mankind* (special issue) 13(4): 306–15.

Tonkinson, R. (1993) Understanding "Tradition" – Ten Years On. In: Lindstrom, L. & White, G. M. (Eds.), Custom Today. *Anthropological Forum* (special issue) 6(4): 597–606.

Turner, J. W. (1997) Continuity and Constraint: Reconstructing the Concept of Tradition from a Pacific Perspective. *Contemporary Pacific* 9(2): 345–81.

Wagner, R. (1975) *The Invention of Culture*. Prentice-Hall, Englewood Cliffs, NJ.

traditional consumption city (Japan)

Yasushi Suzuki

"Traditional consumption city" is one of the categories introduced by Susumu Kurasawa (1968) in his typology of Japanese cities in the early 1960s. His typology emphasizes that the patterns of historical development of cities determine their distinctive social structures. The traditional consumption city refers to cities founded during the feudal era. A contrasting type is the industrial cities that developed largely during the modernization that followed the Meiji Restoration of 1868. (For simplicity, the following description has been updated, although the typology remains essentially the same as Kurasawa's original.)

The traditional consumption cities had, and many still have, castles that served as both the residence and offices for the feudal domain lords designated by the shogunate. In the Tokugawa era (1603–1867), those cities were financially sustained by tributes that were paid by the peasants of the domain and were inhabited by merchants and craftsmen who were largely dependent on the expenditures of the lords.

After the Meiji Restoration, some of these cities became the seats of prefectural governments. Kurasawa categorized the new prefectural seats as type A, other traditional consumption cities as type B. In type A, the prefectural governments provide a financial basis for the city. Other public agencies such as the prosecutor's office, courts, Legal Affairs Bureau, and Land Transportation Offices are concentrated in type A cities, as well as private institutions such as banks, insurance, real estate, transportation, and trading companies. Thus, the type A traditional consumption city is characterized by relatively large numbers of upper-middle-class white-collar workers. The type B cities, in contrast, are populated primarily by self-employed merchants, small factory owners, and their employees. Most of these are locals who grew up in the city and surrounding rural areas.

Of course, even in the type A cities, small entrepreneurs are the majority in numbers, but the managerial, professional, and technical workers provide distinctive characteristics to the urban social structure. These workers are employed by large bureaucratic organizations, public or private, and relocate from city to city as a result of occupational promotion, although clerical and sales workers are usually recruited and promoted locally. Sendai, Kanazawa, and Fukuoka are good examples of the type A city; Hirosaki, Okazaki, and Kurashiki are examples of type B cities. Thus, the traditional consumption types are common among Japanese cities.

Kurasawa classified the industrial cities into three subgroups. First are small, light industrial cities (type C), some of which date back to traditional textile, ceramic, and knifemaking towns. Then there are the heavy industrial cities based on modern industrial technologies for shipping, steel, chemical, electronic, and automobile manufacturing. These are divided into two different subcategories: one-company towns such as Hitachi, Toyota, and Minamata (type D); and those with petrochemical complexes as in Yokkaichi, Kawasaki, and Mizushima (type E). Small industrial towns (type C) had flourished in the late nineteenth and early twentieth centuries, but generally declined by the late 1960s. Now these towns are typically populated by small factory owners, their employees, and small wholesale merchants. One-company towns often developed in rural areas. Kamaishi-city, for example, was a fishing village before the Kamaishi Iron Works was established in the late nineteenth century. Toyota-city was an agricultural village before the Toyota Motors Corporation established its major plants there. The social composition of the one-company town is simple, primarily consisting of the employees of the company, of course, including a handful of executives, managerial, professional, technical, and clerical employees, and a large number of blue-collar workers. Typically, there are also a lot of subcontractors, merchants, and service workers. The social composition of the type E city is quite similar, but it is more complex and less visible, because there are many establishments of different large companies and the sheer size of the city is generally much larger.

Since the type D and E industrial cities have developed in the modern era, they have a purely modern industrial base, although native families may still hold estates and have some influence in the local politics. But most Japanese cities developed as traditional consumption types. Of course, they have modernized in various ways, attracting factories, universities, and tourists and developing airports, expressways, and the superexpress train lines and stations. The three largest metropolitan areas in Japan – Tokyo–Yokohama, Kyoto–Osaka–Kobe, and Nagoya – developed from this type and came to have comprehensive characteristics. In Kurasawa's typology, they are therefore placed in a special category – type M (metropolis). All three initially established their bases in the seventeenth century. As the seat of the Tokugawa shogunate, Edo (now Tokyo) established its primary functions as the center of political control.

Osaka was also formed during the Tokugawa period as the national commercial center, called "the kitchen of the world." Nagoya was simply a great castle town ruled by one of the top three Tokugawa-related families. After the Meiji Restoration, Tokyo inherited its political functions from Edo, and grew to be the capital of the centralized imperial state. Osaka developed as a private commercial center, and Nagoya, a typical traditional consumption city located between the two, gradually developed manufacturing industries. By 1940, Tokyo, Osaka, and Nagoya had grown into great metropolises with populations of 7 million, 3 million, and 1 million people, respectively. During World War II, all three metropolises and many other major cities in Japan suffered heavy bombardment from the US military. However, the three metropolises had all rebuilt their industrial bases by 1955 and began to absorb huge amounts of labor from rural areas. A large number of suburban residential and industrial cities arose in the surrounding areas in the 1960s. Since 1965, deindustrialization and the shift to a service economy have been prominent in the central cities of the metropolitan areas.

Although Susumu Kurasawa's typology was originally published in 1960 and the descriptions presented here have been somewhat updated, globalization and the information technology revolution since the 1980s have dramatically affected the historical paths of cities and transformed urban social structures. Thus this typology might require further revision from the contemporary global perspective. The concept of the traditional consumption city nevertheless remains useful for illuminating the cumulative effect of historical heritage on urban structures.

SEE ALSO: Cities in Europe; Global/World Cities; Metropolis; Suzuki, Eitaro; Urban Community Studies; Urbanism/Urban Culture; Urbanization

REFERENCES AND SUGGESTED READINGS

Kurasawa, S. (1968) *Japanese Urban Society*. Fukumura Shuppan, Tokyo.

traffic in women

Susan Hagood Lee

Traffic in women denotes the practice of transporting women away from their home to a distant location where they are coerced or forced into work or prostitution in slave-like conditions to the profit of their traffickers. Some 2–4 million women are trafficked annually. Women typically are lured into initial cooperation through the deceitful promise of employment at better wages than available in their home area. Traffickers target impoverished regions with few employment opportunities and transfer women to more affluent areas with a market for their labor or sexual services. Some victims are sold into trafficking by relatives or fellow villagers. Most fall prey to criminal organizations with extensive international networks which profit greatly from this lucrative trade. In many regions, legal businesses participate in trafficking under the guise of tourism or entertainment. States profit through taxes on these businesses, and corrupt officials benefit from bribes to protect the industry. In some areas, military installations and peacekeeping operations provide a customer base for trafficking. The international community has responded to trafficking with a Protocol calling on states to enact laws to criminalize all involvement in traffic in women. Heads of state have labeled this growing practice a new slave trade requiring concerted international action.

In a typical trafficking scenario, young women are recruited in their home region by agents who advertise plentiful jobs with high wages and good working conditions in another region. Advertised jobs include waitress, hostess, entertainer, dancer, model, restaurant worker, factory worker, maid, or nanny. The advertisements appeal to impoverished young women with few employment options in their home region due to poor economic development or lack of opportunities for women. The recruiting agents make the departure arrangements and obtain documents such as entertainment visas. The young women leave their home willingly in anticipation of a brighter economic future in which they will be able to contribute to the support of their impoverished families. For many trafficked women, the journey is the first ever out of their home region.

Once at their destination, the recruiters turn the young women over to their new handler in exchange for a fee. The new handler often is a club or brothel owner who has placed an order for female workers with the recruiting agency. Sometimes the young women are presented with an employment contract in a foreign language which they must sign. The handler then takes custody of the women's legal documents and transports the women to a residence in which they are confined. The young women find themselves in an unfamiliar region, often in a foreign country. They lack possession of their legal documents and do not know the language or have any local contacts other than their traffickers. At this vulnerable point, they finally learn the real nature of their new work. They are told that they can leave only if they pay off their debts, including fees for visas, travel, food, shelter, and clothing. The employment contract is used as a seemingly legal document to coerce the young women into compliance. The women may be told that they can be arrested if they break their contract and attempt to leave. Since the police may be paid off by the club or brothel owners, this is not an idle threat.

Many trafficked women resist being prostituted. Sometimes drugs are used to placate the women and create a feeling of complicity in the criminal enterprise. Often, resistant women are severely beaten or gang-raped to break their spirit. Sometimes cooperation is obtained by threatening the safety of the young woman's family. In poor regions, murders can be arranged cheaply, so such threats can be very effective. At other times, the traffickers may persuade the young women that prostitution is the quickest way to pay off their debts and regain their freedom.

There is no transparent accounting of the debts of trafficked women, however, and additional fees are added for ongoing expenses such as rent, clothing, and medical costs such as abortions. In the typical case, trafficked women never succeed in paying off the alleged debt until they become too old or too ill to be useful to the traffickers. Trafficked women are susceptible to HIV infection and AIDS as well as other sexually transmitted diseases. As their economic value diminishes, they suffer increasing abuse, lack of nutrition, and sleep deprivation. Women's self-esteem plummets with this disastrous turn in their lives. They fear the authorities and feel they cannot return home due to the stigma of prostitution. They lose any hope of economic betterment and realize they have lost their marriageability and chances for a normal life. They become depressed and unable to take action to help themselves. Even if they escape from their traffickers, the trauma of trafficking remains with them for a lifetime.

Many parties profit from trafficking. At the village level, women are sometimes sold by relatives or villagers whom they have angered by refusing a suit or divorcing a husband. Recruiting agents profit when they turn a young woman over to the customer who has placed an order. Transnational criminal networks such as the Russian Mafiya, Japanese Yakuza, and the Chinese Triads are involved in recruiting, transporting, and placing impoverished young women in cities where there is a market for sexual services. The CIA found that the Yakuza paid recruiters $6,000 to $10,000 per woman delivered to Japan. Unlike smuggling, where a person pays to be transported illegally, trafficking continues to pay the criminal syndicate long after the young woman is transported into the destination country. The CIA reported that Russian organized crime groups in Israel earn some $1,000 to $4,000 per woman per day. The profits from trafficking can then be used to finance other criminal activity such as corruption or terrorism. Trafficking in women is more profitable than other transnational crimes such as drug or arms trafficking, which do not offer ongoing income after transportation to their destination. Trafficking in women is less risky than drug or arms trafficking since there are fewer laws against trafficking in women. In many countries, trafficked women who come to the attention of the authorities are prosecuted for the crime of prostitution or expelled from the country as criminals themselves.

Legal businesses in the entertainment and tourism sectors sometimes participate in trafficking in women. Individual club owners or entertainment business associations place orders for women as entertainers or waitresses, paying recruitment fees or intermediary brokerage fees. Once hired, the women are pressured or coerced into prostitution roles in addition to their legal waitress or dancer work. Tourism businesses such as hotels, travel agencies, and travel clubs profit from the market for sex tourism. States benefit from the taxes that such tourism and entertainment businesses render to the state treasury. Military bases fuel demand for prostitution and provide a magnet for trafficking activities. For instance, the Korea Special Tourism Association, an association of club owners near US military bases, imports impoverished women on entertainment visas to supply the military market. They charge participating clubs a brokerage fee for new recruits (Seol 2004). United Nations peacekeeping troops have contributed to the demand for prostitution, helping to create a lucrative market for traffickers. In Kosovo, UN and NATO troops constitute 20 percent of the prostitution market despite being only 2 percent of the population, according to an Amnesty International study. With the additional customers, a small-scale prostitution network in Kosovo was transformed into a large-scale industry run by criminal networks.

Trafficking takes place between poor regions with few employment opportunities and more affluent regions with a market for sexual services. The International Organization for Migration (IOM) reports that trafficking is growing most rapidly in Central and Eastern Europe and the former Soviet Union. The economic devastation in these regions following the collapse of the Soviet system has produced many young people desperate for employment and willing to risk migrating for work. Criminal enterprises in Moscow and Kiev transport women to countries such as the US, Germany, Japan, Thailand, and Israel, where markets exist for white prostitutes. Romanian and Moldavian women are trafficked to Asia, where their light-skinned appearance makes them exotic compared to local women. Women from Kazakhstan and Kyrgyzstan are trafficked into Turkey and the Middle East.

In Asia, women from impoverished Bangladesh are trafficked to Pakistan. Rural Nepali women displaced by the Maoist rebellion are trafficked into the urban centers of India. Vietnamese and Cambodian women are trafficked to the more affluent countries of Thailand and Singapore. Korea has become both a sending country and a destination country.

Korean women are trafficked to Japan under the guise of entertainers, while Russian, Chinese, Philippine, and Central Asian women are trafficked to Korea to supply the military base towns.

In Africa, women are trafficked from Sub-Saharan countries such as Ghana, Mali, and Benin to Nigeria and Libya, as well as to the western nations of Italy, Belgium, the Netherlands, and the US. African women are trafficked into the Middle East, lured by employment as domestic servants. President Obasanjo of Nigeria named international trafficking a new slave trade at a Nigeria conference on trafficking in 2000.

In Latin America, less data are available on trafficking. The IOM notes that trafficking takes place out of the war-torn country of Columbia and that women are being trafficked from Latin America to the US and Southeast Asia.

Reliable figures as to the number of persons trafficked annually are hard to obtain, given the illegal nature of this activity. A 1999 CIA report estimated that some 700,000 to 2 million women and children are trafficked globally each year. The report estimated that 45,000 to 50,000 women and children are trafficked into the US annually, mostly from Southeast Asian countries. The United Nations has suggested that perhaps as many as 4 million persons are moved annually within or between countries for trafficking purposes. UN sources estimate that trafficking is a US$5–7 billion operation annually. The ready demand for prostitution services and the ample supply of vulnerable impoverished women account for the profitability of this industry and its appeal to criminal networks.

The phenomenon of sex trafficking takes place at the intersection of poverty and international capitalist enterprises. Female sexuality is commodified and bought and sold on an international market to the highest bidder. The lack of economic development and employment opportunities for women in poor regions fuels the supply side of the equation. The commoditization of women's bodies as instruments of male pleasure contributes to the demand side of the market. Thus the structural context of poverty is coupled with the cultural devaluation of women in patriarchal societies. The AIDS epidemic has impacted the trafficking market due to fears of contracting HIV from a prostitute and cultural beliefs concerning the curative and rejuvenating effect of sex with a virgin. The outcome has been to lower the age of women recruited in trafficking enterprises, with virgin girls fetching a higher price on the international prostitution market.

In 2000 the United Nations adopted a Protocol to Prevent, Suppress and Punish Trafficking in Persons, Especially Women and Children. The Protocol defines trafficking as the "recruitment, transportation, transfer, harboring or receipt of persons, by means of the threat or use of force or other forms of coercion, of abduction, of fraud, of deception, of the abuse of power or of a position of vulnerability or of the giving or receiving of payments or benefits to achieve the consent of a person having control over another person, for the purpose of exploitation." When a person under the age of 18 is recruited into prostitution, the Protocol considers it trafficking even when fraud and coercion are not involved. The Protocol considers consent to trafficking irrelevant, since consent is typically based on the deceitful exploitation of economic vulnerability. Under the terms of the Protocol, crossing an international border is not necessary to qualify as trafficking. Trafficked persons are seen as victims of crime to be protected and assisted, not criminals involved in prostitution. The Protocol requires states to facilitate and accept the return of trafficked persons to their country of origin. Repatriation should be voluntary and take victim safety into consideration.

The Protocol calls on signatories to enact national legislation in order to criminalize trafficking activities and offer assistance to victims. In response, the US enacted the Trafficking Victims Protection Act of 2000. It distinguishes between "severe" forms of trafficking (those involving fraud, force, or coercion) and sex trafficking (other sorts of commercial sexual activity). The Act mandates that severe trafficking be included in the annual State Department country reports on human rights, and it sets minimum standards for countries to meet in order to receive certain forms of assistance from the US. It provides for a new non-immigrant visa category, a "T" visa, for victims of severe trafficking who would suffer extreme hardship upon removal from the US.

SEE ALSO: Crime, Organized; Migration: Undocumented/Illegal; Patriarchy; Prostitution; Sex Tourism; Sexual Markets, Commodification, and Consumption; Slavery

REFERENCES AND SUGGESTED READINGS

American Journal of International Law (2001) International Trafficking in Persons, Especially Women and Children. *American Journal of International Law* 95(2): 407–10.

Amnesty International (2004) "So Does It Mean that We Have the Rights?" Protecting the Human Rights of Women and Girls Trafficked for Forced Prostitution in Kosovo. AI Online documentation archive. AI Index: EUR 70/010/2004.

Bertone, A. M. (2000) Sexual Trafficking in Women: International Political Economy and the Politics of Sex. *Gender Issues* 18(1): 4–22.

Farr, K. A. (2004) *Sex Trafficking: The Global Market in Women and Children.* Worth Publishers, New York.

International Organization for Migration (2001) New IOM Figures on the Global Scale of Trafficking. *Trafficking in Migrants: Quarterly Bulletin*, Special Issue, 23.

Raymond, J. G. (2002) The New UN Trafficking Protocol. *Women's Studies International Forum* 25: 491–502.

Richard, A. O. (2000) *International Trafficking in Women to the United States: A Contemporary Manifestation of Slavery and Organized Crime.* Central Intelligence Agency DCI Exceptional Analyst Program, Washington, DC.

Seol, D.-H. (2004) International Sex Trafficking in Women in Korea: Its Causes, Consequences and Countermeasures. *Asian Journal of Women's Studies* 10(2): 7.

transcarceration

Robert Menzies

Commonly linked with the revisionist social control and new penology literatures of the 1980s and 1990s, transcarceration refers to the widespread profusion of regulatory organizations, practices, authorities, and subjects across and beyond traditional boundaries of institutional governance in contemporary western societies.

The intellectual impetus for the transcarceration concept derived in large part from Michel Foucault's (1977) writings on the rise of the disciplinary society and "carceral archipelago"; from Andrew Scull's (1984) critique of conventional approaches to understanding community criminal justice and mental health initiatives; and from Stanley Cohen's (1985) analysis of late twentieth-century "master patterns" of deviancy classification and punishment. From a range of disciplinary and substantive perspectives, theorists and researchers in the 1980s sought to account for the failings of the diversion, decarceration, rehabilitation, and reintegration schemes of the prior two decades – and of the post-World War II liberal reconstructionist and civil libertarian political philosophies that these movements had embodied.

Transcarceration became both a metaphor and empirical yardstick for the unsettling paradox that state and civil projects aimed at downsizing control structures were in practice having precisely the opposite effect. Instead of disestablishing the old regimes, destructuring movements were generating hybrid systems of institutions, agencies, and programs which were multi-sited, unbounded, virtually impossible to disentangle or evade, and widely dispersed through the contemporary landscape of the "punitive city" (Cohen 1985). In judicial, penal, psychiatric, welfare, and other arenas of human categorization and containment, traditional modernist dualisms between formal and informal, public and private, inside and outside, coercion and provision, were breaking down. Critical observers sought to explain how, having been freed from the oppressive regimes of prisons, asylums, and other exclusionary sites of confinement, untold thousands of citizens were finding themselves subject to new inclusionary modes of control which operated as appendages, not alternatives, to the systems they were supposed to eclipse.

An accumulating body of research showed how, with the proliferation of these "wider, stronger, and different nets" (Austin & Krisberg 1981), people and knowledge were circulating through jails, prisons, probation, parole and welfare offices, hospitals, clinics, halfway and boarding homes, the streets, and assorted other points of enclosure and transmission at ever-accelerating rates. The grim consignment of former patients and prisoners to lives of urban poverty, disease, drugs, and violence was disabusing even its most ardent exponents of the notion that decarceration was truly benefiting this burgeoning population of "conscript clientele" (Friedenberg 1975). Moreover, homelessless – the fate of so many deinstitutionalized people – was ascending into public consciousness as arguably the foremost domestic social problem of the 1980s. Concurrently, while James O'Connor's "fiscal crisis of the state" (1973) might have initially triggered the closure of some public mental institutions (and many beds), the numbers of psychiatrized people continued to escalate as the average length of inpatient committals steadily declined; as mental health networks increasingly extended into general hospital wards, community clinics and the private sector; and as more and more patients faced the experience of being dumped destitute into inner cities only to be later rerouted into criminal contexts (a dynamic that persists into this new century). As for the penal realm, the decarceration era was ironically followed, in short order, by the unprecedented spasm of expansion that became the hallmark of neoconservative law-and-order programs through the 1980s and early 1990s, culminating in a combined jail and prison population of more than 2 million in the US alone.

By the 1980s, progressive scholars and activists were nearly united in acknowledging that the inclusionary agenda of destructuring and decentralization proponents had not only been ruinous in its own right, but had also sparked the punitive backlash and moral panics (Goode & Ben-Yehuda 1994) that came to dominate late twentieth-century penal politics. Socio-legal scholars, radical criminologists, and anti-psychiatrists, among others, came to recognize, in Stanley Cohen's elegantly minimalist phrase, that "we blew it." Accordingly, they set about rethinking some deeply held beliefs about the inherent benevolence and effectiveness of liberal policies and practices in corrections, mental health, and related fields. Moreover, the overarching constructs that had propelled the penal reform era of the 1960s and 1970s – the bifurcation of state and civil society, the public/private divide, the emphasis on individual autonomy and negative rights claims, the very ideas of decarceration and social control (the latter

subsequently described by Cohen (1985) as a Mickey Mouse concept) – were generally agreed to have lost their purchase. What was needed, in the eyes of many, was an utterly new "vision of social control."

The transcarceration construct therefore emerged as a conceptual move toward the rehabilitation of social control theory, and the reworking of critical praxis in relation to this new hypermodern, pluralistic world of penality. Among other aims, revisionist academics and practitioners sought to deinstitutionalize the analysis of control structures and cultures by adopting interdisciplinary, holistic, structurally informed, and materially grounded approaches to the study of social order. Such work is sensitive to the nuances, diversities, and contradictions of all regulatory practices; to the hierarchies of class, gender, race, ethnicity, sexuality, nationality, generation, and (dis)ability within which control and counter-control strategies play out; to the daunting capacity of systems and officials to neutralize, subvert, and coopt even the most well-conceived of reform efforts; and to the cascading (and often unanticipated and unintended) effects of progressive ventures.

The transcarceration construct in many ways prefigured, and continues to resonate through, the legion of writing that has multiplied over recent years within the fields of moral regulation, legal pluralism, and governmentality studies, and on topics as diverse as administrative criminology, actuarial justice, critical penology, the risk and surveillance societies, technologies and cultures of control, and governance of the self. Their variations notwithstanding, these contemporary works are conjoined by what is arguably the key idea yielded from the 1980s revisionist social control literature – namely, that a paradigmatic redrawing of territorial, legal, institutional, and discursive geographies has occurred in the sphere of human regulation, and that any contemporary reformist project must either engage with the actualities of these latterday transcarceral arrangements, or resign itself to failure.

SEE ALSO: Dangerousness; Deinstitutionalization; Deviance, Criminalization of; Deviance, Medicalization of; Deviance Processing Agencies; Homelessness; Mental Disorder; Neoliberalism; Social Control

REFERENCES AND SUGGESTED READINGS

Arrigo, B. A. (1997) Transcarceration: Notes on a Psychoanalytically Informed Theory of Social Practices in the Criminal Justice and Mental Health Systems. *Crime, Law and Social Change* 27: 31–48.

Austin, J. & Krisberg, B. (1981) Wider, Stronger and Different Nets: The Dialectics of Criminal Justice Reform. *Journal of Research in Crime and Delinquency* 18: 165–96.

Chunn, D. E. & Gavigan, S. A. M. (1988) Social Control: Analytic Tool or Analytic Quagmire? *Contemporary Crises* 12: 107–24.

Cohen, S. (1985) *Visions of Social Control: Crime, Punishment and Classification.* Polity Press, Cambridge.

Foucault, M. (1977) *Discipline and Punish: The Birth of the Prison.* Pantheon, New York.

Friedenberg, E. Z. (1975) *The Disposal of Liberty and Other Industrial Wastes.* Doubleday, Garden City, NY.

Goode, E. & Ben-Yehuda, N. (1994) *Moral Panics: The Social Construction of Deviance.* Blackwell, Oxford.

Johnson, W. W. (1996) Transcarceration and Social Control Policy: The 1980s and Beyond. *Crime and Delinquency* 42: 114–26.

Lowman, J., Menzies, R. J., & Palys, T. S. (1987) *Transcarceration: Essays in the Sociology of Social Control.* Gower, Aldershot.

O'Connor, J. R. (1973) *The Fiscal Crisis of the State.* St. Martin's Press, New York.

Scull, A. (1984) *Decarceration: Community Treatment and the Deviant – A Radical View,* 2nd edn. Prentice-Hall, Englewood Cliffs, NJ.

transcription

Linda Skrla

Transcription is the process of converting recordings of social or communicative human interaction into written text. Transcribing audiotaped or videotaped speech acts, conversations, interviews, or other forms of human engagement might be considered to be a relatively simple task, largely a chore or a secretarial matter. After all, to transcribe, one need only write down what was said by the parties involved in the interaction.

The writing down of what was said, however, is viewed by researchers in a variety of fields (including linguistics, communication, psychology, sociology, anthropology, education, and nursing) as only part of the transcription task. In addition to *what* was said, transcription often involves attending to *how* things were said (timing, volume, emphasis, nonverbals), how they were *not* said (silences), and *where* they were said (context and environment).

Furthermore, opinions in various disciplines differ as to what the product of the process of transcription represents. In some instances, a transcript is viewed as a transparent, printed representation of the recorded interaction (a *hard copy*), and it becomes the actual data used for further analysis. Traditions in other fields position transcripts as mediated forms of the original data that are useful aids for analysis, but that never are considered to be identical to the audio or video recordings, which remain the original data and are the primary records for analysis. Other researchers view the transcription process as theory-laden work that fundamentally alters the original data. Kvale (1996), for instance, argues that transcription is a form of translation because of the transcriptionist's key decision-making role.

Numerous decisions must be made when a transcript is prepared, and various fields have developed sets of conventions to guide individual researchers engaged in the process. Opinions differ among fields as to whether the researcher should or must do his or her own transcription work or whether the task can be delegated to others. In either case, transcription conventions cover such considerations as page layout, placement of verbal and nonverbal information, timing (overlaps, pauses, silences), choice of orthographic, phonetic, or combined representation, discourse unit (utterance, proposition, or turn), and symbols. Research fields vary as to the existence of and fidelity to an accepted set of transcription conventions. Conversation analysis is an example of a field that has a widely used set of conventions, the Jeffersonian Transcription System, developed by Gail Jefferson. Examples of symbols from the Jeffersonian System are as follows:

1 Pauses (numbers in parentheses indicate in seconds and tenths of seconds the length of the interval)

J: When I was (0.6) oh five or six we moved
K: To your current house?

2 Sound stretch (a colon indicates that the prior sound is prolonged; multiple colons indicate a more prolonged sound)
A: I re:::ally didn't like it

3 Emphasis (indicated by italics or underscoring; the larger the italics, the greater the stress)
D: That one is *mine*
S: *NO* it is not either yours it's *MINE*

4 Transcriptionist doubt (other than timings of intervals, items enclosed in single parentheses are in doubt)
B: Who were you there to meet?
N: The same guy from the day before (Jeremy)

Standardized transcription conventions such as these have proved useful for handling, comparing, and sharing of language data. However, these conventions have come under criticism for what they do *not* do, such as representing participants' situated meanings, attending to researcher subjectivity, and acknowledging contextual factors. Mishler (1991) and others have argued for a view of transcription that acknowledges the fact that the process is both interpretive and constructive. In other words, exploration is needed of how researchers create representations in their transcripts that follow from their purposes, theories, and worldviews and how this process shapes and constrains subsequent interpretations derived from analysis of transcript data. Suggestions for how this might be accomplished have included calls for researchers to become more reflective about their transcription practices and for them to include discussions of transcription issues along with the presentation of their findings.

SEE ALSO: Conversation Analysis; Interaction; Interviewing, Structured, Unstructured, and Postmodern; Representation

REFERENCES AND SUGGESTED READINGS

Edwards, J. A. (1993) Principles and Contrasting Systems of Discourse Transcription. In: Edwards, J. A. & Lampert, M. D. (Eds.), *Talking Data: Transcription and Coding in Discourse Research.* Lawrence Erlbaum, Hillsdale, NJ, pp. 3–31.
Jefferson, G. (1973) A Case of Precision Timing in Ordinary Conversation. *Semiotica* 9(1): 47–96.
Kvale, S. (1996) *Interviews: An Introduction to Qualitative Research Interviewing.* Sage, Thousand Oaks, CA.
Lapadat, J. C. & Lindsay, A. C. (1999) Transcription in Research and Practice: From Standardization of Technique to Interpretive Positionings. *Qualitative Inquiry* 5(1): 64–86.
Mishler, E. G. (1991) Representing Discourse: The Rhetoric of Transcription. *Journal of Narrative and Life History* 1: 255–80.
Psathas, G. & Anderson, T. (1990) The "Practices" of Transcription in Conversation Analysis. *Semiotica* 78(1/2): 75–99.
ten Have, P. (1999) *Doing Conversational Analysis: A Practical Guide.* Sage, Thousand Oaks, CA.
Tilley, S. A. (2003) Transcription Work: Learning Through Coparticipation in Research Practices. *International Journal of Qualitative Studies in Education* 16(6): 835–51.

transgender, transvestism, and transsexualism

Dave King and Richard Ekins

Twenty years ago a sociological encyclopedia would not have included a separate entry featuring cross-dressing or sex-changing. The medicalization and pathologizing of these phenomena under such categorizations as transvestism, transsexualism, gender dysphoria, and intersex ensured that cross-dressing and sex-changing were considered, in the main, to be the domain of medicine and psychology. The small number of sociological studies relating to "transvestism" and "transsexualism" was considered to be a peripheral concern of historical sociology, the sociology of deviance, and feminism and gender studies. Only Garfinkel (1967) and Kessler and McKenna's *Gender: An Ethnomethodological Approach* (1978) provided a hint of the importance of transsexualism to the discipline of sociology.

This situation began to change in the mid-1980s, a development marked by the more widespread use of the term "transgender" among "transvestites" and "transsexuals" themselves, and the establishment in 1986 of the world's first "transgender archive" housed in a university sociology department. The sociological literature on the topic is still small, but much of sociological interest is to be found in the fields of social anthropology, lesbian and gay studies, women's studies, and (especially in recent years) cultural studies. Most recently, transgender studies is emerging as a specialism in its own right.

The inclusion of an entry on transgender attests both to the greater visibility of transgender phenomena in contemporary society and to the greater interest shown in it by sociologists and other scholars in the arts and social sciences. However, before we trace the evolution of the term transgender, its various meanings and the social phenomena to which it relates, we must go back to the end of the nineteenth century and consider the emergence within medical discourses of what came to be known as transvestism and transsexualism. The immediate origins of contemporary Euro-American conceptualizations of transgender are to be found in the latter half of the nineteenth century, a period which saw the beginning of what Foucault in his *History of Sexuality* (1979) terms the "medicalization of the sexually peculiar." It was during this period that psychiatrists and other medical practitioners began to puzzle over the nature of people who reported that they felt like/dressed as/behaved like a person of the "opposite sex." Such people were initially situated within the category of homosexuality or – in the then common terminology – "inversion," but in the writings of Magnus Hirschfeld and Havelock Ellis a separate category emerged. The term transvestite was coined by Hirschfeld in 1910 to refer to those men who enjoyed behaving and dressing as women, or, indeed, wished to *be* women, and both he and Havelock Ellis (who preferred his own term, eonism) argued that this did not necessarily involve homosexuality. Neither Hirschfeld nor Ellis employed the then fashionable language of degeneracy or perversion, but they nevertheless viewed such people as anomalies to be explained within a medical framework. Edward Carpenter in 1911 translated

Hirschfeld's term as "cross-dressing," a term which along with that of "cross-dresser" has become popular in recent years, being seen to avoid the medical and erotic connotations with which "transvestite" has come to be associated.

Hirschfeld first used the term transsexual in 1923. The first "full" male-to-female (MTF) "sex change" operation (vaginoplasty, following castration and penile amputation) was performed in Berlin at Hirschfeld's Institute for Sexual Science in 1931. However, it was not until the early 1950s following the widespread publicity given to the cases of Christine Jorgensen in America and Roberta Cowell in Britain (both MTF transsexuals) that the terminology of transsexualism was adopted to distinguish those seeking to "change sex" from those who were "content" to cross-dress. During the 1960s "sex reassignment" began to be carried out on an experimental basis in some medical centers, partly due to its legitimation by John Money's influential ideas on the development of gender. From that decade the professional literature on the topic began to grow rapidly. At this time the work of the US-based German endocrinologist Harry Benjamin came to the fore. He argued that carefully selected transsexuals could benefit from "sex reassignment" procedures and for a number of years his *Transsexual Phenomena* (1966) was referred to as the transsexual's Bible.

In the early 1970s the term gender dysphoria entered the literature and quickly became the preferred term used in the titles of medical conferences, associations, books, and articles. However, it was the term gender identity disorder that became enshrined in the official diagnostic nomenclature (American Psychiatric Association, 1973).

Although, within the medical literature, transvestites and transsexuals began to be differentiated from one another from the 1950s onwards, the subcultural groupings that emerged around the same time included both, at least until the early 1980s, when separate transsexual organizations began to consolidate. At the individual-career level there was some slippage between the two categories and a more complex picture than that provided by transvestite/transsexual began to emerge.

The medical centers that began to experiment with sex reassignment during the 1960s provided opportunities for some sociologists to encounter patients seeking such procedures. One such sociologist was Harold Garfinkel, whose *Studies in Ethnomethodology* with its germinal chapter on the transsexual "Agnes" was published in 1967. Garfinkel was interested, though, not in transsexualism (in fact Agnes was initially thought of as intersexed), but in how Agnes's experiences demonstrated the "rules" of doing gender. This approach to transsexuals continued in the work of Kessler and McKenna, among others.

Two other sociologists who were able to study transsexuals via the medical centers were Kando and Sulcov. Kando's *Sex Change* (1973) research began in 1968 and documented the transition of 17 MTF transsexuals who had received surgery at the University of Minnesota. Drawing heavily on the work of Erving Goffman, Kando reported how transsexuals dealt with issues of stigma and information management and how their identities were positioned in relation to the emergence of feminist critiques of traditional femininity. Sulcov, in an unpublished PhD thesis entitled "Transsexualism: Its Social Reality" (1973), focused on the construction of the category "transsexual" by both the medical profession and transsexuals themselves – a theme taken up by a number of later writers.

Other opportunities for research opened up during the 1960s as subcultural groups and organizations began to develop firstly in relation to transvestism and, later, transsexualism. An important figure here was the influential "trans" activist Virginia Prince, whose American organization the Foundation for Personality Expression (for heterosexual transvestites) provided a model for many others around the world. Taylor Buckner carried out a survey of 262 members of Prince's organization for his Masters degree in 1964. Buckner's only publication on the topic contains some useful sociological material. However, the thrust of his article (appropriately published in the journal *Psychiatry*, 1970) was to provide an etiological theory of what he calls a "socially induced 'pathology'": an approach that by that time was out of favor within the discipline of sociology.

Two developments within sociology itself also shaped the approach to transgender phenomena in the mid-1960s. Firstly, there was the rise of the sociology of deviance and a general interest in "alternative" lifestyles reflecting something of what was happening in Anglo-American society at the time. This led in America to a number of empirical accounts of transvestites and transsexuals and their social worlds (e.g., Driscoll 1971; Feinbloom 1976). The second influential development was the (re)emergence of the women's movement and the interest in gender. The distinctions which writers such as John Money and Robert Stoller had drawn between sex and gender were enthusiastically embraced by some sociologists as demonstrations of the lack of a necessary link between gender roles and biological sex. Ann Oakley's influential *Sex, Gender and Society* (1972) drew on this literature and used transsexualism as a demonstration of the independence of sex and gender.

The new sociologists of deviance of the 1960s were generally "on the side" of many of the deviant groupings who were questioning conventional norms at that time. The norms and laws relating to such phenomena as homosexuality, drug use, and abortion were seen as oppressive instruments of power against which the deviant was rebelling. The rebels against gender norms, however, were feminists and, on the face of it, transvestites and transsexuals appeared to be embracing what feminism was questioning. While "radical drag" and "gender blending" were part of the gay liberation scene of the time, changing the content of what were beginning to be called "gender roles" was not what transvestism and transsexualism were about. However, some commentators did consider transvestites and transsexuals as "revolutionaries" who challenged the notion of ascribed gender in the sense that they broke the congruity between sex and gender. These ideas would not seem out of place alongside those of some of the queer theorists that we discuss below.

However, it was the work of Janice Raymond that dominated discussions of the political significance of transsexualism during the 1980s, when her particular style of radical feminism was in the ascendant. Raymond's *The Transsexual Empire* (1980) argues that transsexuals are among the victims of patriarchal society and its definitions of masculinity and femininity. The creation by the male medical profession of transsexualism and its "treatment" by means of sex change surgery obscures the political and social sources of the "transsexual's" suffering. Instead, "transsexuality" is conceptualized as an individual problem for which an individual solution is devised; the "real" problem – patriarchy – remains unaddressed. Moreover, Raymond sees MTF transsexuals and in particular those who identify as lesbian feminists as part of a masculine attempt to undermine feminism. Although Raymond's book probably had little impact on what she called the "transsexual empire," it was influential in some feminist circles. Riddell's early and detailed critique of 1980 was not widely available until it was republished in 1996 (Ekins & King 1996) and, in line with the effect of radical feminism in other areas, most critics of Raymond's position were intimidated into silence. Stone's (1991) landmark riposte heralded a new era of transgender activism and theorization which drew heavily on postmodernism and the newly emerging queer theory. Since then, other critiques of Raymond's work have been published (notably, Califia 1997).

Over the years a number of other empirical studies have appeared, mostly in America and the UK. Woodhouse (1989) reported on her research carried out from a feminist perspective into a small group of English male heterosexual transvestites and is unique for the attention given to their wives. Bolin (1988) followed a small group of North American transsexuals over a period of two years as they transformed their status from that of man to that of woman. In her use of the anthropological concept of liminality she anticipated one of the themes taken up in the theorizing of the 1990s. The first published sociological account from Australia was Perkins's study of a group of transsexual prostitutes in Sydney, somewhat misleadingly entitled *The "Drag Queen" Scene* (1983). Lewins's (1995) study focused on the social process of becoming a woman. This study was based upon interviews carried out in the early 1990s with over 50 MTF transsexuals attending a gender dysphoria clinic in Melbourne.

Rich in empirical data, Ekins's (1997) study also contributed theoretically to exploring the interrelations between sex, sexuality, and gender; self, identity, and social world; and expert, member, and lay knowledge, as they develop over time. Using the methodology of grounded theory, Ekins developed the important conceptualization of "male femaling" which has major ramifications for both the field of transgender and for the analysis of sex and gender more generally.

One theme within the sociology of deviance that was stimulated by the labeling theory of the 1960s was the study of the origins and applications of social labels. In this vein King (1993) sought to understand the nature of transvestism and transsexualism as social categories and documented how and why they have emerged, how they are applied, and their consequences. His work was based on a study of the medical literature, a large number of media reports, fieldwork with transsexuals and transvestites, and, most importantly, interviews with surgeons, psychiatrists, and psychologists and others working in this field. More recently, the historical work of Meyerowitz's *How Sex Changed* (2002) has charted the emergence of transsexualism in America.

As we have seen, the terms transvestite and transsexual had emerged within a medical context and by the 1970s had become enshrined as diagnoses to designate what were seen as essentially pathological phenomena – gender identity *disorders*. Although used by transvestites and transsexuals themselves, the terms remained grounded in professional discourse. By the late 1980s some transvestites and transsexuals were beginning to use the term transgender in an inclusive, "umbrella" sense to encompass both identities. In due time other "gender variant" people (e.g., drag queens and kings and intersexed people) have come to be included within the umbrella term. By the early 1990s it became common to find references to the "transgender community," although the use of the term has not been accepted by all. Although the term transgender has also entered medical and professional discourse (e.g., *International Journal of Transgenderism*), it nevertheless retains its essentially positive and non-pathological meaning. By the mid-1990s Ekins and King (1996) were able to write of the "emerging field of transgender studies." This was seen to encompass the personal experiences of transgendering, the different ways in which those experiences have become socially organized, the ways in which those experiences have been controlled principally by means of medicalization, and the various political issues raised by transgendering.

It is evident that the medical categories of transvestite and transsexual did not encompass the whole range of what we now think of as transgender phenomena. Although some of those who sought sex reassignment had been or were involved in female impersonation for entertainment purposes, the phenomenon of drag itself avoided the medical gaze. With the exception of Esther Newton's important ethnography (*Mother Camp*, 1972), drag also avoided the gaze of social scientists until the 1990s. Since then, Tewkesbury and Gagne and Schact and Underwood have updated the story. Similarly, those people with physically intersexed conditions were absent from the social science literature with one notable exception – Foucault's study of *Herculine Barbin* (1980). Born females who "transgendered" were dealt with mainly in the literature on lesbianism. Little reference was made to the literature on transgenderism in non-contemporary western cultures, except to point to the ubiquity of the phenomenon.

A number of these gaps in the literature have begun to be filled since the early 1990s. There is growth in the literature on "transgender"-related phenomena in non-western cultures. Most of this literature has focused on North American indigenous cultures (e.g., Fulton & Anderson 1992), although there is work on other cultures. Recently, there has been a surge of anthropological interest in transgender, principally in Southeast Asia and in South America (Kulick 1998). Some of this literature has focused on conceptions that have developed without the influence of western medicine, such as the idea of an institutionalized "third" gender or liminal gender space. Nevertheless, it is also evident that western discourses of transgenderism have been exported to many parts of the world and are usurping or are heavily influencing more traditional notions of gender and "transgender" phenomena.

Academic attention has also begun to focus on those people with intersexed conditions. This has been partly stimulated by the development of a more visible and vociferous intersex community. One of the main issues here has been to question the practice of surgically forcing intersexed infants into sexed categories where there is no medical need. Kessler (1998) discusses the ways in which intersex "transgressions" call into question the whole system of binary genders.

One option that was not covered by the medical categories of transvestism and transsexualism was the possibility of living as a member of the other sex without undergoing genital surgery. It was known, of course, that this was a route taken by many transgendered people. Indeed, for most female-to-male (FTM) transsexuals it has remained the only option because of the inability to surgically create a satisfactory penis. However, what was not considered was that this possibility – women with penises and men with vaginas – might be an acceptable status in its own right. Virginia Prince had argued consistently that transvestism was not about sexuality (the erotic) or sex (the body), but was about gender (the social). She argued that it was possible for a man to be a woman socially without altering the body – something which she herself has done since the late 1960s, when she began to refer to herself and others like her who lived as members of the other sex but without surgical interventions as "transgenderal" and, later, as "transgenderist." Prince explicitly distinguishes this group from transvestites and transsexuals.

Until the early 1990s FTMs and cross-dressing females were not very much in evidence in either the literature or in the transgender movement. Since then, FTMs or, more accurately, "female-bodied transpeople" to use Cromwell's (1999) term, have become a more visible feature of the transgender community and in fact have come to play key roles within that community and within transgender politics. They have also been prominent in the emergence of transgender theory. Judith Halberstam's *Female Masculinity* (1998) is a key work in this regard. More specifically, it is female-bodied transpeople who have led the way in linking transgender to revolutionary socialism (Leslie Feinberg's *Transgender Warriors*, 1996); to radical body configurations and pansexualism (Del La Grace Volcano's *Sublime Mutations*, 2000); and to the beginnings of a hitherto neglected transgender approach to class, race, and masculinity (Halberstam 1998).

The rise in popularity of the term transgender has paralleled the rise in academia of queer theory, within which crossing the gender border is seen as subversive and transgressive. Much of this work falls outside the boundaries of sociology and is to be found within what has come to be called cultural studies. This approach has been particularly influential with some trans activists and academics and raises radical questions about the binary and fixed nature of gender categories themselves. Especially influential was Judith Butler's work on gender as performativity. Also influential was Marjorie Garber's *Vested Interests* (1992), which drew on examples ranging across history, literature, film, photography, and popular and mass culture: from Shakespeare to Mark Twain and Oscar Wilde, through transsexual surgery and transvestite support groups, to Elvis Presley and Madonna, indicating the ubiquity of transgender phenomena. In a phrase echoed in a number of other writings she argued "transvestism is a space of possibility structuring and confounding culture: the disruptive element that intervenes, not just a category crisis of male and female, but a crisis of category itself" (p. 17).

It is within this context that the phenomenon of the "drag king" has emerged. The western world has been familiar with drag for a long time, but the term has most commonly been applied to men performing in women's clothes, although it has also been used to apply to women in men's clothes. Only recently though has the use of the suffix "king" emerged. Apparently beginning in the late 1980s with the term becoming more widespread through the 1990s, drag kings entered the academic literature with the publication of Halberstam's *Female Masculinity* (1998). Usually viewed through the lens of queer theory, drag kings are viewed not simply as the female counterparts to drag queens, but as a much more subversive phenomenon because of the mainstream view of masculinity as nonperformative.

Stone's (1991) article can also be seen to provide the starting point for the emergence of a postmodernist approach to transgender, which is now seen by some to be at the very cutting edge of debates about sex, sexuality, and gender. This approach has achieved a position of prominence in a number of recent contributions to cultural studies and queer theory. Stone's image of transsexuals as "outside the boundaries of gender" chimed in well with many of the themes in cultural studies and queer theory, and provided an approach that has been developed extensively in recent years. This idea points to the position of trans people as located

somewhere outside the spaces customarily occupied by men and women, as people who are beyond the laws of gender. The assumption that there are only two (opposite) genders, with their corresponding "masculinities" and "femininities," is opened up to scrutiny. Instead, it is suggested that there is the possibility of a "third" space outside the gender dichotomy to make sense of various gendered identities that transcend dimorphism. Within this approach the idea of permanent core identities and, for some, the idea of gender itself, disappear. The emphasis is on gender transience, fluidity, and performance, as in Kate Bornstein's *Gender Outlaw* (1994).

Despite this late-modern/postmodern approach with its emphasis on diversity, fluidity, and moving beyond the rigidities of the binary gender divide and its celebration of new combinations of masculinity and femininity, for most, in the professional and transgender communities, as in society at large, the binary view of gender prevails.

SEE ALSO: Drag Queens and Drag Kings; Ellis, Havelock; Female Masculinity; Hirschfeld, Magnus; Intersexuality; Queer Theory; Sex and Gender; Sexual Citizenship; Sexual Deviance; Sexual Practices

REFERENCES AND SUGGESTED READINGS

Bolin, A. (1988) *In Search of Eve: Transsexual Rites of Passage*. Bergin & Garvey, New York.

Bornstein, K. (1994) *Gender Outlaw: On Men, Women and the Rest of Us*. Routledge, London.

Califia, P. (1997) *Sex Changes: The Politics of Transgenderism*. Cleis Press, San Francisco.

Cromwell, J. (1999) *Transmen and FTMs: Identities, Bodies, Genders and Sexualities*. University of Illinois Press, Urbana.

Devor, H. (1997) *Female-to-Male Transsexuals in Society*. Indiana University Press, Bloomington.

Driscoll, J. P. (1971) Transsexuals. *Transaction* (March/April): 28–37, 66, 68.

Ekins, R. (1997) *Male Femaling: A Grounded Theory Approach to Cross-Dressing and Sex-Changing*. Routledge, London.

Ekins, R. & King, D. (Eds.) (1996) *Blending Genders: Social Aspects of Cross-Dressing and Sex-Changing*. Routledge, New York.

Feinbloom, D. H. (1976) *Transvestites and Transsexuals: Mixed Views*. Dell, New York.

Fulton, R. & Anderson, S. W. (1992) The Amerindian "Man-Woman": Gender Liminality and Cultural Continuity. *Current Anthropology* 33(5): 603–10.

Garber, M. (1992) *Vested Interests: Cross-Dressing and Cultural Anxiety*. Routledge, New York.

Garfinkel, H. (1967) *Studies in Ethnomethodology*. Prentice-Hall, Englewood Cliffs, NJ.

Halberstam, J. (1998) *Female Masculinity*. Duke University Press, Durham, NC.

Jackson, P. A. & Sullivan, G. (Eds.) (1999) *Lady Boys, Tom Boys, Rent Boys: Male and Female Homosexualities in Contemporary Thailand*. Harrington Park Press, New York.

Kando, T. (1973) *Sex Change: The Achievement of Gender Identity among Feminized Transsexuals*. Charles C. Thomas, Springfield, IL.

Kessler, S. J. (1998) *Lessons from the Intersexed*. Rutgers University Press, New Brunswick.

King, D. (1993) *The Transvestite and the Transsexual: Public Categories and Private Identities*. Avebury, Aldershot.

Kulick, D. (Ed.) (1998) Special Issue: Transgender in Latin America. *Sexualities* 1(3).

Lewins, F. (1995) *Transsexualism in Society: A Sociology of Male-to-Female Transsexuals*. Macmillan, Melbourne.

Stone, S. (1991) The Empire Strikes Back: A Post-transsexual Manifesto. In: Straub, K. & Epstein, J. (Eds.), *Body Guards: The Cultural Politics of Gender Ambiguity*. Routledge, New York.

Woodhouse, A. (1989) *Fantastic Women; Sex, Gender and Transvestism*. Macmillan, Basingstoke.

transgression

Lauren Langman

Transgression, violating a formal rule and/or moral principle, crossing a boundary of acceptable conduct, or exceeding a social limit, is central to understanding social life in general and deviance in particular (Jenks 2003). Although there is no clear-cut distinction between the criminal and moral, few societies ignore theft, while publicly breaking wind or picking one's nose is not usually punished as a criminal offense. At various moments, insanity, masturbation, homosexuality, and adultery have been considered transgressions that have been deemed criminal and/or pathological. At some times, imputed transgressions such as witchcraft were harshly punished. A great deal of social history has concerned the attempts of competing groups to legislate morality – and most of these have been futile.

There are dialectical relations between what is deemed "normal" and what is "pathological" and hence constrained or isolated. Normative standards of right and wrong or good and evil are typically "contested terrains" with "policed boundaries" where powerful actors attempt to define "acceptable" action, thought, and belief. Yet indeed, establishing limits may itself foster the desire to transgress those limits because transgression can be "fun." How does society attempt to thwart transgression, and if that fails, how are transgressions punished? At the same time, how and why are some people impelled to transgress, and yet while transgressions are impelled by individual desire, notwithstanding, some transgressions elicit widespread revulsion, disgust, and outrage, even if they are not against the law?

A long history of thought has attempted to define "good" and "evil." While this has typically been the realm of religion, after the Enlightenment dethronement of faith it has been a concern of sociology. The nature of the "desirable" and "acceptable" ways of being and doing remain vital concerns. Today however, we are informed by the insights of Nietzsche, Durkheim, Freud, and Foucault, as well as Bataille, Bakhtin, Victor Turner, Mary Douglas, and many other scholars who have pondered the ways society constructs limits as well as desires to transgress.

Nietzsche (1989) was among the first to suggest that the "good," as kindness, charity, and humility, was typically an expression of the politics of *ressentiment* in which weak, petty, and banal people, typically majorities, imbued with a "slave mentality" of conformist subjugation, would attempt to stifle the "will to power" of the strong and noble, those who would transcend themselves. While Christian religion sustained servitude and the suppression of will, with modernity and the Death of God, "modern" forms of truth and power fostered the repression of will that in turn enfeebled the person and stunted his/her self-fulfillment as an

Übermensch, the one who authentically trans-cended him/herself in overcoming the restraints of debilitating mediocrity and conformity. If that transcendence might require transgression, indeed cruelty and/or disdain of inferiors, then so be it. Transgression for Nietzsche challenges, overthrows, spoils, and questions the unques-tionable (Jenks 2003: 81).

For Durkheim (1947 [1898]), society as a "moral order," expressed in its *conscience collec-tive* (collective consciousness), depended on shared goals, values, norms, and beliefs, about words, deeds, and actions considered "normal," "right," and those considered "wrong," indeed "pathological," and subject to some kind of repressive sanction. This was evident in the laws that expressed the shared sentiments of tightly bound traditional societies or more dif-fuse modern societies. Such laws might be repressive or restitutive. Yet deviance was socially generated and inevitable in any society. The social structure fostered transgressions to periodically foster the collective outrage that would affirm the sanctity of norms through dramatic, emotion-laden expiatory rituals. Even in a society of saints there must be sinners to affirm the rules among those untouched by the transgression and rekindle the solidarity of the society. Punishment brings the "decent people" together. But so too, at various moments such as festivals, episodic indulgence in the otherwise transgressive could celebrate norms and renew social bonds. At the same time, transgression can be a basis for social change as certain laws and norms are contested. At periods of social change marked by anomie, deviance becomes the basis for innovation and indeed, adaptation to new moral circumstances. What is considered trans-gressive in one era often becomes acceptable in another era and normative even later. Consider the changing notions of sexuality. At one time, masturbation, premarital sexuality (especially of women), and/or homosexuality were seen as psychopathology, criminality, or both.

In a similar vein, Mary Douglas (1966) has examined the relation of "purity" in which pol-lution, as transgression, threatens both elite power and the moral codes of a society. Thus certain kinds of people and/or actions must be kept separated, if not eradicated. Just as notions of ritual pollution safeguarded the tra-ditional caste system of India by affirming social boundaries, so too have various constructions of purity sustained certain class, race, or sex/gen-der boundaries. This can be seen in debates over immigration policies, gays in the military, and even the legality of gay marriage. Those who are "polluted" by virtue of their status or actions, often of a sexual nature, need to be excluded or isolated, lest their pollution "harm" the society as boundaries and norms are challenged.

Foucault, like Durkheim, looked at social structures. His concerns were the smaller insti-tutional structures in which expertise was inter-twined with power. He suggested that the construction of norms and definitions of trans-gression were not simply collective judgments, but indeed a reflection of localized institutional knowledge/power embedded within expert-generated systems of meanings that define who and what is transgressive and prescribe the appropriate actions. Thus, for example, with the growth of rationality in European com-merce, governance, and culture, self-control and a methodical approach to everyday life became valued. The thoughts and behavior of the mad, the "unreasonable," the uncon-trolled became stigmatized as "deviant." Thus as "madness" replaced leprosy as the socially required expression of deviance, psychiatry emerged as a system of knowledge/power whose "scientific" discourses "explained" insanity and prescribed its treatment, the "sequestration of unreason" in asylums (Foucault 1988 [1965]). In much the same way, Foucault argued that wardens and physicians possessed power/knowledge embedded in discursive practices that "explained" criminal or medical deviance, pre-scribed a remedy through their gaze and "expertise," and enhanced the power of expertise.

Similarly, for Jervis (1999), the transgres-sions of the modern are defined by demands of "purposive control and rationality in face of, if not contestation with the repressed other side, the irrational, uncontrolled otherness of the primitive, the insane, the woman and the debauchery of the carnival." The "otherness" of transgression is feared as it questions power. That "otherness" is not only feared but also desired and therefore tabooed, rendered dis-gusting to preserve the "purity" of rational yet repressed modernity.

Such inquiries raise questions about *how* the normative is socially constructed, defined, and sustained and just *why* certain acts, beliefs, and thoughts are proper. In many cases, the transgressive has been punished by death, and often that death was the result of long, slow, painful, public torture. With modernity, transgression was more often punished by sequestration in institutions. Nevertheless, it is the society that creates experts who define and treat the socially generated transgression.

TRANSGRESSION AND DESIRE

As noted, transgression often involves sexuality. In the Victorian era, a "fallen" woman who lost her "virtue" was rendered an immoral outcast, not suitable for marriage. By the end of World War II, the majority of western women had become sexually active before marriage. Today, in the advanced countries, most unmarried youth are sexually active. Sexuality has a long history as a binary in opposition to culture. The construction of unbridled sexuality as transgressive and worthy of retribution was seen in the destruction of Sodom and Gomorrah as punishment for their sexual excesses. This set the tone for the Israelites' opposition to the cultic religions of Baal and Ishtar in which temple prostitution was an essential part of fertility rituals. As an expression of nature, as passion, irrationality, and even death (orgasm as *la petite mort*), sexuality has stood opposed to order and control. This legacy informed Christianity, especially the teachings of Paul and later Augustine, and again in its conquests over paganism. When medieval Christianity became more tolerant of desire, Protestantism would reaffirm asceticism and denial.

The antagonism of civilization and desire, the binary of order versus passion, and the inherent tendency of desire to transgress limits were most clearly articulated by Freud; sexual and aggressive desires were the bases of motivation, while civilized society demanded restraint and control. Transgression presupposed desire, while taboos would prohibit gratifications that would render one dirty, polluted, and dangerous, and perhaps endanger the group. For Freud, the primary taboo was incest; the Oedipal desire of the boy for his mother was repressed or displaced due to the fear of castration as retaliation by the father. Taboo was one of the earliest forms of conscience, internalized social controls of desire.

In much the same way, excreta became tabooed. Freud argued that civilization provided beauty, cleanliness, and order, aka an anal obsession. Civilization required limiting sexuality through rendering most erotic desires and/or their object(s) as tabooed and hence repressed. To ensure that people harmoniously worked together for the sake of collective adaptation, desire needed to be sublimated into work while libidinal aims (gratification) were inhibited so as to enable social ties. Yet such taboos fostered the very desires for transgression that they might thwart. But neither the desire nor the prohibition was likely to abate. However, the repression of desire, sustained by a punitive superego, held most transgressions in check, though the individual would suffer from his/her guilt.

Following Freud, while informed by Sade and Surrealism, Georges Bataille saw taboos on sex and violence rooted in the requirements of economic survival for the tribe. Bataille celebrated eroticism, sexuality purely for the sake of pleasure in the face of finitude – ultimately death. But at the same time, transgressions were ritualized violations of taboos such as in war, sacrifice, or the orgy. From what has been said, transgression is often a reflection of a desire for the tabooed, and indeed, desire is aroused because the act is "prohibited" and gratification rendered artificially scarce. In other words, if the society did not construct prohibitions, then people would not desire what is prohibited.

Finally, it must be noted that Freudo-Marxists such as Wilhelm Reich, and later Herbert Marcuse, argued that sexual repression fostered the conformity required for workers in a capitalist system. But with the rapid expansion of consumer society after World War II, it became necessary to ease the restraints of repression so that people would spend rather than save money. One of the main ways impulse-driven consumerism was encouraged was by linking it to sexuality – sex sells and the erosion of sexual constraints encourages the erosion of thrift and frugality. But society needed to "normalize" sexual transgression, thus it began to encourage fantasies of sexual fulfillment that would be obtained by consuming a particular commodity. Thus societies would tolerate the premarital sexuality of consumers as a form of what Marcuse termed "repressive desublimation," encouraging seeming freedom in the service of domination. Yet as has been seen, the greater toleration of sexuality, straight or gay, has also rekindled a number of fundamentalist movements that would oppose toleration for what had heretofore been transgressive.

THE SEQUESTRATION OF TRANSGRESSION: SPATIAL AND TEMPORAL ISOLATION

As Foucault noted, asylum psychiatry sought to isolate unreason if it could not be transformed. In a similar way, societies provide marginal sites, zones of transition where transgression is tolerated. Victor Turner (1969) has argued that social structures foster "anti-structures," marginal or liminal "in-between" sites where transgressions are tolerated as long as they are isolated from the centers of the society.

In most societies, even those that are quite repressive, the transgressive that is strongly repressed will be desired. Yet perhaps because of that repression it can and will be available. Just as Victorianism fostered bordellos, and Prohibition fostered the "speakeasy," cultures provide encapsulated realms and sites where the otherwise prohibited finds toleration. Thus in certain eras, bordellos, gay bars, or S/M dungeons were sub rosa, hidden to most outsiders. Similarly, every major city in the world has regions where drugs and many kinds of sexual pleasures can be found, even when deemed criminal.

There are certain times that allow, if not encourage, transgression such as vacations and certain festivals. The prototypical time of transgression was carnival, the days before Easter; Bakhtin (1968) argued that the medieval carnival emerged as an episodic popular festival in which the grotesque and transgressive critiqued, through mocking, parody, and inversion, the repressive norms of the elites. In Breughel's *Battle Between Carnival and Lent* we see the joyous, rotund "king" of the carnival doing battle with the haggard, repressed Lent, just as we see the church next to the tavern. The peasants gathered together to drink, dance, and indulge what was otherwise prohibited; most of

these indulgences were bodily, especially erotic licentiousness and all manner of scatological excess. Carnival stood apart from everyday life, transgression was not just tolerated but celebrated. For Bakhtin, transgression embraced far more than sexuality. Carnival valorized the grotesque as a repudiation of elite aesthetic standards. Carnival was a critique of the elites, their lifestyles and seeming "superiority." On the one hand carnival could be seen as a form of resistance, but at the same time that resistance, displaced to the cultural realms, ultimately served to reproduce the political economy.

Bakhtin's work influenced a number of scholars such as Stallybrass and White (1986), and Presdee (2001). For Stallybrass and White, with the ascent of the trading classes and flourishing of coffeehouses, alcohol consumption dropped and fairs and carnivals waned. Presdee, more concerned with criminal transgressions, nevertheless argued that insofar as certain transgressions are labeled criminal, there are joys in such transgressions.

THE COMMODIFICATION OF TRANSGRESSION

In the contemporary era of globalized capitalism, the privatized hedonism of consumption has been universalized as the means of attaining the "goods life." Indeed, consumerism as an ideology, lifestyle, and basis for identity serves to sustain markets and assuage the discontents of the contemporary market-based civilization. More specifically, in the current age, there are three major sources of discontent: (1) economic stagnation and the uncertainty of employment; (2) highly routinized, regulated, and often surveilled work; and (3) the emptiness and shallowness of most forms of "mass culture." Beneath the surface of such discontents lie deeper frustrations and anxieties over social fragmentation and attenuated social ties, problematic agency in an ever more controlled world, finding dignity and recognition, and finally, finding meaning in a world that seems ever more meaningless.

There are at least two reactions to these trends, fundamentalism and transgression, which indeed feed on each other. In the former case, the surrender of the self and subjugation to a higher "moral" authority provides integration into a community of believers, empowerment through prayer and ritual, dignity through piety and purity, and clear-cut meanings, rules, and regulations that disavow the transgressive. At the same time, for a great many people, the transgressive "compensates" for the adversities of modernity. Transgression exalts and rewards the self in its pursuit of hedonistic self-indulgence. But further, transgressive means of assuaging the discontents of capitalism have themselves become commodified. Such commodifications of transgression range from the shocking and grotesque realms of mass culture to transgressive subcultures and lifestyles of goths, punks, or hip-hop. In these commodified transgressions, frustrations are allayed and discontent, anger, rage, and even ennui are contained by, while displaced from, the political economy. Much like the feudal carnival, adverse feelings are dissipated and potential disruption thwarted. Thus not only are discontents allayed, but capitalism finds profit in selling alternatives to its own mainstream and the system is reproduced.

CONCLUSION

Transgression, the crossing of often tabooed moral and frequently criminal boundaries, is not only a universal aspect of human societies but also a fruitful way of understanding how those societies construct and control deviant behaviors, while fostering the very deviance they abhor. In recent years, between the adversities of capitalism on the one hand, and the ever present need to expand the consumer economy on the other, we have seen the transgressive move from the margins to the mainstream. Whether we look at clothing/appearance, lifestyles, or musical styles, the boundaries of morality and the transgressive are quite fluid and variable. And while the embrace of the transgressive may cause many hardships, so too does transgression foster social change and, in the process, reveal much about the society.

SEE ALSO: Crime; Deviance; Deviance, Crime and; Fundamentalism; Norms; Ritual; Subcultures, Deviant; Values

REFERENCES AND SUGGESTED READINGS

Bakhtin, M. (1968) *Rabelais and His World*. Trans. H. Iswolsky. MIT Press, Cambridge, MA.
Douglas, M. (1966) *Purity and Danger: An Analysis of the Concepts of Pollution and Taboo*. Routledge & Kegan Paul, London.
Durkheim, É. (1947 [1898]) *The Division of Labor in Society*. Free Press, Glencoe, IL.
Foucault, M. (1988 [1965]) *Madness and Civilization*. Random House, New York.
Jenks, C. (2003) *Transgression*. Routledge, London.
Jervis, J. (1999) *Transgressing the Modern: Explorations in the Western Experience of Otherness*. Blackwell, Oxford.
Nietzsche, F. (1989) *The Genealogy of Morals*. Vintage, New York.
Presdee, M. (2001) *Cultural Criminology and the Carnival of Crime*. Routledge, London.
Stallybrass, P. & White, A. (1986) *The Politics and Poetics of Transgression*. Cornell University Press, Ithaca, NY.
Turner, V. (1969) *The Ritual Process: Structure and Anti-Structure*. Aldine, Chicago.

transition from communism

Josephine E. Olson and Irene Hanson Frieze

"Transition from communism" refers to the historical process of moving from a centrally planned economy to a market-oriented economy with a dominant private sector. In most cases it has also meant a transition from a totalitarian state to a democracy. Transitions have taken place in European and Central Asian countries formerly under Soviet domination and also in East Asian countries such as China and Vietnam. The transition period is largely associated with the 1990s, but China's transition began in 1978, and transitions are far from complete in many countries. Discussion of the transition generally focuses on economic changes, but many political, legal, social, and psychological changes were also associated with the transition. The focus here is on the transitions in Central and Eastern Europe, the former Yugoslavia, and the former Soviet Union.

Before the fall of the Berlin Wall in 1989 and the collapse of the Soviet Union in 1991, communist countries were centrally planned, with the government and cooperatives owning most means of production. Most communist economies emphasized heavy industry rather than services and consumer goods. Large factories and geographical specialization were common. Energy and transportation industries were often highly subsidized. International trade took place primarily among members of the Council for Mutual Economic Assistance (CMEA). Enterprises were controlled by strict administrative rather than financial constraints; managers had to meet the requirements of the central plan. A single state bank system served to meet the objectives of government economic plans.

All men and women of working age were expected to be employed outside the home, and unemployment was largely unknown. However, there were often provisions for lengthy maternal leaves for women. Services were provided for families, such as housing, government-sponsored childcare centers, and meals at work. Governments provided retirement pensions for all workers, and retirement ages were often in the fifties. Employees received low wages, and wage differentials across jobs were low. By the 1980s, communist governments found they could not offer all the promised services. There were widespread shortages in consumer goods because of price controls, and consumer goods were often of poor quality.

With the breakup of the Soviet Union, Yugoslavia, and Czechoslovakia in the 1990s, there are now 27 transition countries. The German Democratic Republic merged with the Federal Republic of Germany in 1990 and its transition became an internal problem of Germany. The 27 countries are often classified into groups for analysis of the transition. The Baltic countries, Estonia, Latvia, and Lithuania, were part of the former Soviet Union after World War II. The Commonwealth of Independent States (CIS) includes the other countries of the Soviet Union: Armenia, Azerbaijan, Belarus, Georgia, Kazakhstan, the Kyrgyz Republic, Moldova, the Russian Federation, Tajikistan, Turkmenistan, Ukraine, and Uzbekistan. Five Central European countries (the Czech Republic, Hungary,

Poland, Slovakia, and Slovenia) joined the European Union in 2004 along with the Baltic countries. These eight countries are referred to as the Central Europe and Baltic (CEB) countries. The Southeast European (SEE) countries include the countries of the former Yugoslavia except Slovenia (Bosnia and Herzegovina, Croatia, the Former Yugoslav Republic (FYR) of Macedonia, and Serbia and Montenegro) as well as Albania, Bulgaria, and Romania. Bulgaria and Romania expect to join the European Union in 2007 and Croatia and FYR Macedonia are official candidates.

The massive requirements of the transition from communism were unprecedented in history; there were few guidelines to the best process. The following reforms were generally considered necessary to successfully complete the transition to a market economy. Macroeconomic stabilization was required to control inflation and prevent excessive government deficits. This required breaking up the single bank system into a central bank and numerous commercial and investment banks (allowing the entry of new banks). The central bank's responsibilities included limiting the growth of the money supply to control inflation. To avoid large government deficits, controls on government spending, tax reform, and strong tax collection methods needed to be put in place. The tax system had to be reformed so that the government could collect revenue from the private sector that was needed to finance its new responsibilities in a market-oriented economy. Price and trade liberalization were needed so that domestic prices would reflect world prices and encourage efficient allocation of resources. Among other things, this meant the breakup of the CMEA trading bloc.

Hard budget constraints needed to be imposed on companies. This meant eliminating subsidies and non-payment of taxes. Enterprises had to restructure, laying off workers and increasing productivity, to become profitable. Given outdated production methods and previous subsidies, many old enterprises were not viable in a global market and had to liquidate. Methods had to be found to transfer viable government-owned enterprises to a competitive private sector. New businesses needed to be encouraged to increase output and absorb excess workers. Commercial banks needed to make loans based on profit potential and eliminate non-performing loans. A social safety net was required to deal with unemployment and poverty.

Legal and judicial systems and related institutions that would provide a level playing field in a market economy and enforce property rights had to be created. In retrospect, analysts believe that policymakers underestimated the importance of developing legal systems, particularly for the protection of property rights, and related institutions to the proper functioning of a market economy.

The transition in Europe and Central Asia turned out to be far more difficult than expected. The transition initially led to inflation as price controls were removed and as financial crises developed in some countries. There were dramatic drops in output and increased unemployment due to disruptions from the collapse of communist institutions, tight macroeconomic policies, and credit crunches. Although initial drops in output were anticipated, they were much larger than expected: an average fall of about 40 percent. The European Bank for Reconstruction and Development (EBRD) estimated that output fell on average until 1994 and did not begin to rise again until 1998.

Privatization of state-owned enterprises took several forms. Small enterprises were transferred quickly and rather successfully to the private sector, primarily through local auctions. Large and medium-sized state-owned enterprises were handled in a variety of ways. Some countries such as Poland and Slovenia moved slowly to privatize state-owned enterprises, but appointed supervisory boards to run them before privatization. Estonia and Hungary carefully sold off state enterprises to outside buyers, including foreign buyers. Some countries such as the Czech Republic, Lithuania, and Slovakia used voucher plans to quickly transfer ownership shares to most adult citizens. Russia and Ukraine privatized rapidly using primarily subsidized management buyouts. In retrospect, studies suggest that privatization to concentrated outside owners led to better restructuring; privatization to diffuse owners and to enterprise workers and managers often made things worse for restructuring than continued state ownership.

The 1990s were a time of extreme hardship for many people in the transition countries.

The World Bank (2002) estimated that 1 in 20 people in this region had incomes below one dollar per day in 1998 compared to only 1 in 60 in 1988. Aside from drops in output and employment, worsening distributions of income contributed to the growing poverty. Income distribution became more unequal in most countries, but CIS countries like Russia, Armenia, and the Kyrgyz Republic became among the most unequal in the world. War and civil strife in Armenia, Azerbaijan, Georgia, Moldova, and Tajikistan and in most of the states of the former Yugoslavia as well as financial crises, particularly the Russian crises of 1998, undermined the transition in many places. Ethnic and religious strife also hindered transition.

Most countries had shrinking social services and benefits. Fertility and marriage rates dropped, and in some CIS countries average life expectancy fell. There were serious psychological costs for many people due to the greater uncertainty about jobs, social disorientation, and declining standards of living. Value systems based on collectivism began to transform to more individualistic ones. Under communism, people relied on the state to guarantee them a job and to provide social benefits. With the transition, people were confronted with unemployment for the first time. Salaries for government workers were generally quite low, and the private sector, as it developed, provided higher-paying but more demanding jobs. Younger workers, especially men, were most often sought for these new jobs. Women of childbearing age were often not hired, as companies sought to avoid paying maternity benefits. Young, attractive, unmarried women were often the most likely women to be hired and older women experienced the highest levels of unemployment.

The psychological changes resulting from the economic transition often included discontent with the changes. Public opinion surveys conducted in 1999 in the Czech Republic, Hungary, and Poland, three of the more successful transition countries, indicated that more people believed that the losses from the transition exceeded the gains than the reverse. Reactions were even more negative in other countries. But, some young adults have responded positively to the opportunities provided by the private sector and to the increased freedom of political expression in some transition countries. A recent study showed some improvement since the mid-1990s in life satisfaction among residents of transition economies.

Although all the European and Central Asian countries initially suffered significant drops in output and other problems at the beginning of the transitions, there were enormous differences 15 years later. The EBRD (2005) estimated that output in 2004 was 126 percent of its 1989 level in the CEB countries, but only 92 percent in SEE countries and 81 percent in CIS countries. Output, however, has been growing in all countries since 2002 and it has been growing quite rapidly in some of the CIS countries. In 2003, half the countries still reported unemployment of 10 percent or more. The EBRD reported that inflation rates and government deficits were relatively low in 2005. The economic structure of transition countries has changed. Services have grown in relative importance while industry shrank in all countries and agriculture also shrank in the CIS countries. In 2005, the private sector accounted for more than 50 percent of output in all but Uzbekistan (45 percent), Belarus (25 percent), and Turkmenistan (25 percent). In many countries, this change was due to the rapid growth of new private businesses more than privatization of old state enterprises.

The EBRD has a set of transition indicators to track structural and institutional reforms in the transition countries as they move toward mature market economies. Most countries show significant progress in liberalizing prices, in liberalizing international trade and their exchange rate regimes, and in privatizing small-scale enterprises. They are somewhat behind in large-scale privatization and in banking reform and interest rate liberalization. They are still slower in the areas of governance and enterprise restructuring, infrastructure reform, reform in securities markets and non-bank financial institutions, and competition (antitrust) policies. The countries that are the most advanced in reforms are the CEB countries, followed by Croatia, Bulgaria, and Romania. The countries that have made little or no progress in the transition are: Turkmenistan, which has only liberalized some prices and done some small-scale privatization; Belarus; Uzbekistan; and Tajikistan.

It is not surprising that the CEB countries that have joined the European Union and those SEE countries that are in the process of joining the EU have made the most reforms. Many of these reforms are also required for membership in the European Union. In addition, the Central European countries tended to start with some initial advantages, such as relatively high per capita income, high levels of education, shorter times under communism, and proximity to the West. However, the Baltic countries, which were less advantaged initially, are now as advanced as the Central European countries.

SEE ALSO: Capitalism; Communism; Ideology, Economy and; State and Economy; Stratification in Transition Economies; Transition Economies

REFERENCES AND SUGGESTED READINGS

Einhorn, B. (Ed.) (1993) *Cinderella Goes to Market*. Verso, New York.
European Bank for Reconstruction and Development (2005) *Transition Report 2005: Business in Transition*. EBRD, London.
Svejnar, J. (2002) Transition Economies: Performance and Challenges. *Journal of Economic Perspectives* 16(1): 3–28.
World Bank (2002) *Transition: The First Ten Years. Analysis and Lessons for Eastern Europe and the Former Soviet Union*. World Bank, Washington, DC.

transition economies

Rainhart Lang

Societies or economies in transition have been the focus of sociological research since the fall of the Berlin Wall in 1989, which symbolized the demise of the state socialist system. The term *transition economies* therefore applies mainly to post-socialist countries in Central and Eastern Europe, and also in East Asia, despite its wider use in the economic or sociological literature.

The term *transition* is used to describe the process through which a society or economy introduces the institutional facets associated with advanced capitalist economies, such as the legal system, ownership structures, institutions of financial and labor markets, the party system, and the institutions of the independent and democratic state. While the term *transition* is often restricted to a small time span of an economic change, or relates only to an economic view of post-socialist societies, or describes the fixed result of the changes as *the* western type of a market economy or capitalism (Offe 1996), the term *transformation* has been more widely used in the sociological literature, especially in Europe, since the mid-1990s. The latter term covers a wider social process of fundamental political, economic, technological, and cultural change in structures and values, including all areas and levels of the society: organizations, the individual, and collective actors (Nee & Matthew 1996; Clark et al. 2001).

Transformation has been described as both managed and evolutionary, or self-organized, this quality impinging upon the adjoining concept of "follow-up modernization" (Grancelli 1995). In light of this interpretation, economic transition may be regarded as a temporal and spatial element within the wider transformation process in which new economic institutions are formed and established.

Taking into consideration such a broad view of transformational change, transformation might also be seen as an ongoing process also in those post-socialist countries now entering the EU. These nation-states are still confronting processes of adaptation and change at various levels, including the adoption of societal institutions and values. The broader research agenda on radical social change in transformational societies or economies in transition is therefore concerned with various levels and processes in social change, as represented in Figure 1.

The traditional discourse on economic transition has focused mainly on the process of successful transfer and functioning of capitalist institutions such as labor markets, financial institutions, adequate ownership structures, and the privatization and economic restructuring of economic organizations. But as Clarke (1996) contended, "Although the process of privatization has transformed a stratum of office-holders into a potential class of property-owners, private property is not a sufficient condition for the constitution of a capitalist system of social production." A wider perspective on transition economies has therefore demanded consideration of the impact of various other factors and phenomena such as national values, traditional cultures, political interests, and the strategies of individual and collective actors on the development of economic institutions, economic organizations, and economic actors in transforming societies. While American economic sociology has predominantly focused on change or continuity in workers' control over the labor process

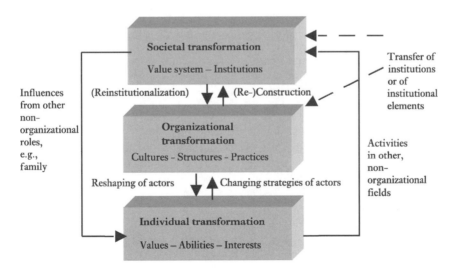

Figure 1 Levels and social aspects of transformation research in transition economies.

(Burawoy & Krotov 1992), on the transformation in income relations as a result of privatization attempts (Nee & Matthew 1996), on privatization and restructuring of enterprises (Stark 1996), and the emergence of new elites (Waldner 2003), the European debate has been much broader, and has manifested an interdisciplinary approach to transformation. The social aspects of economic transition that have been analyzed most frequently since the mid-1990s are delineated below.

At the societal level, *institution transfers vs. institution building*, or reinstitutionalization of social processes, has been at the center of research attempts, this including study of the conflicts between inherent values of the transferred institutions and the local national value systems. (Clarke 1996; Fligstein 1996; Grabher & Stark 1997; Stanojevic 2001; Wang 2001; Lang & Steger 2002; Bakacsi et al. 2002).

The development of new capitalist institutions in the transition economies, introduced with the massive financial and moral support of western institutions such as the World Bank or governmental advisers and consultants, led to difficulties and failure in the respective economies in the mid-1990s. It has transpired that the transferred institutions often did not fit with national cultures in the CEE countries (Bakacsi et al. 2002) or China (Wang 2001), as well as with the special requirements of transformational settings. The traditional national cultures, characterized by strong in-group collectivism and high power distance, consolidated by the past system, differed in their core values from the transferred institutions, which exhibited individualistic "western" cultural norms. Moreover, different transition strategies could be observed, ranging from early shock therapy to an incremental change (Offe 1996).

At the same time, the imposed transfer of western institutions, supported by a tendency towards mimetic processes from inside the transition economies, finally led to inconsistency problems with the historical and cultural background of the local actors, as shown in various studies (e.g., Lang & Steger 2002). Older interests tended to convert the new institutions in ways that stabilized parts of the heritage, as for example shown by Stanojevic (2001) in the case of the transfer of the German system of industrial relations to Slovenia and Hungary. As a result, the transition economies in CEE countries, as well as in post-socialist Asian countries, have developed a new type of capitalism (Stark 1996; Wang 2001) or a special business system, which is characterized by a distinctive mixture between public and private enterprise, and with the strong influence of social networks and groups with particular interests that have underpinned economic activities and institutions (Fligstein 1996; Grabher & Stark 1997). The emergent or newly embedded institutions are the result of a "recombination" of properties (Stark 1996) based on the culture of the past and transformation experiences with the transferred institutions. While classical neoliberal theories were not able to explain these changes, evolutionary theory, network theory, and new institutional theory have been used more often in these studies (see Fligstein's 1996 claim for an integration of institutional theories).

At the level of organizations, the traditional focus of research has been on the privatization and restructuring of the old enterprises as well as the emergence of small private firms as the main forms of organizational transformation. The social aspects analyzed in the wider perspective of organizational transformation include cultural changes in (economic) organizations, and their enabling and limitation effects on economic activities (Burawoy & Krotov 1992), including the emergence and establishment of new practices as a result of "recombination" (Stark 1996; Grabher & Stark 1997) or "bricolage" (Clark et al. 2001). In addition, the interrelated processes of organizational and institutional learning, and their intended or unintended consequences for a co-evolution of the newly established organizations and institutions, have been analyzed, to explain the various steps of adjustment and adaptation (Child & Czegledy 1996; Lieb-Dóczy 2001). The results show that the core values of old organizations and local embeddedness play an important role for a successful organizational transformation, even in the case of a radical restructuring. The learning process in transformational settings could therefore be characterized as an explorative learning process beyond simple adaptive or exploitative learning.

At the level of individual (and collective) actors, the emergence and shape of new social groups of actors, especially entrepreneurs or managers (Puffer et al. 2000; Steger & Lang 2003), and their influence on the development of new organizational forms, values, and the (re-) construction of new institutions have formed an interesting field of transformation research. The results support the expectation of an elite reproduction instead of a radical change within the economic elite. The new owners, managers, or entrepreneurs of small businesses had mainly a management background in the old system, or belonged to distinctive social groupings. Since many of the old cadres, especially from the younger group of technocrats, have managed their individual transformation into the new capitalist system and have created new roles (Clark et al. 2001; Lang & Steger 2002; Waldner 2003), their values and experiences built the background for the new organizations. Not only the new managers but also the new social group of entrepreneurs differ therefore from their western counterparts with respect to values and preferred practices. Moreover, since they belong to informal social networks of different types, they also gain influence in the public sphere. As shown in early publications on transformation in CEE countries (e.g., Dittrich et al. 1995), powerful actors and their respective networks have to be seen as a central explanatory factor in transformation at societal level.

While in the early years of transformation research, surveys and statistics with questionable original data were used, the broader agenda of transformation research is now accompanied by a wider spectrum of research methods, wherein complex case studies and longitudinal type cases play an important role (Puffer et al. 2000; Clark et al. 2001; Clark & Michailova 2004). Even in the early years, statistics and surveys did not reflect the special influence of the informal "gray" market, the problematic state of official statistics, and the ability of the actors to produce a "good looking" surface picture ("social desirability" phenomena). A critical standpoint on the research methodology in transformation research has demonstrated that taking account of the important influence of third party agents such as translators, cultural interpreters, mixed research teams of insiders and outsiders, strangers, and indigenous researchers is helpful in overcoming partial "blindness," mistakes, and misinterpretations (Clark & Michailova 2004).

SEE ALSO: Institutional Theory, New; Networks; Social Problems, Concept and Perspectives; Stratification in Transition Economies; Transition from Communism

REFERENCES AND SUGGESTED READINGS

Bakacsi, G., Takacs, S., & Karacsonyi, A. et al. (2002) East European Cluster: Tradition and Transition. *Journal of World Business* 37: 69–80.

Burawoy, M. & Krotov, P. (1992) The Soviet Transition from Socialism to Capitalism: Worker Control and Economic Bargaining in the Wood Industry. *American Sociological Review* 57: 16–38.

Child, J. & Czegledy, A. P. (1996) Managerial Learning in the Transformation of Eastern Europe: Some Key Issues. *Organization Studies* 17(2): 167–79.

Clark, E. & Michailova, S. (Eds.) (2004) *Fieldwork in Transforming Societies*. Palgrave, New York.

Clark, E., Lang, R., & Balaton, K. (Eds.) (2001) Organizational Change in Transforming Societies. *International Studies of Management and Organization* 31(2).

Clarke, S. (Ed.) (1996) *Labour Relations in Transitions: Wages, Employment and Industrial Conflict in Russia*. Elgar, Cheltenham.

Dittrich, E., Schmidt, G., & Whitley, R. (Eds.) (1995) *Industrial Transformation in Europe*. Sage, London.

Fligstein, N. (1996) The Economic Sociology of the Transition from Socialism. *American Journal of Sociology* 101(4): 1074–81.

Grabher, G. & Stark, D. (Eds.) (1997) *Restructuring Networks in Post-Socialism: Legacies, Linkages and Localities*. Oxford University Press, Oxford.

Grancelli, B. (Ed.) (1995) *Social Change and Modernization: Lessons from Eastern Europe*. De Gruyter, Berlin.

Lang, R. & Steger, T. (2002) The Odyssey of Management Knowledge to Transforming Societies: A Critical Review of a Theoretical Alternative. *Human Resource Development International* 5(3): 279–94.

Lieb-Dóczy, E. (2001) *Transition to Survival: Enterprise Restructuring in Twenty East-German and Hungarian Companies, 1990–1997*. Ashgate, Aldershot.

Nee, V. & Matthew, R. (1996) Market Transition and Societal Transformation in Reforming State Socialism. *Annual Review of Sociology* 22: 401–35.

Offe, C. (1996) *Varieties of Transition: The East European and East German Experience*. Polity Press, Cambridge.

Puffer, S., McCarthy, D. J., & Naumov, A. I. (2000) *The Russian Capitalist Experiment: From State-Owned Organizations to Entrepreneurship*. Elgar, Cheltenham.

Stanojevic, M. (2001) Industrial Relations in "Post-Communism": Work Place Cooperation in Hungary and Slovenia. *Journal of East European Management Studies* 6(4): 400–20.

Stark, D. (1996) Recombinant Property in Eastern European Capitalism. *American Journal of Sociology* 101(4): 993–1027.

Steger, T. & Lang, R. (2003) Career Paths of Elite Former GDR combinates During Post-Socialist Transformation Process. *Journal of World Business* 38: 168–81.

Waldner, A. G. (2003) Elite Opportunity in Transitional Economies. *American Sociological Review* 68: 899–916.

Wang, H. (2001) *Weak State, Strong Networks: The Institutional Dynamics of Foreign Direct Investments in China*. Oxford University Press, Oxford.

transition from school to work

Fabrizio Bernardi

Research on the transition from school to work focuses on the relationship between the level of education and the first job achieved upon entry into the labor market. This has traditionally been a central topic in social stratification and social mobility research. As such, the study of the transition from school to work has reflected the main theoretical positions that have dominated research on social stratification since the end of World War II. Under the influence of functionalist theory, the relationship between education and the first job has been studied in terms of the classical achievement/ascription dichotomy. Thus, scholars were mainly interested in establishing the relative weights of achieved and ascribed factors in the process of status achievement, in particular with regard to the first job. The key research question was whether or not access to better jobs was increasingly dependent on achieved factors, such as education, and less and less dependent on ascribed factors such as the characteristics of the family of origin. In the same period, economists developed the theory of human capital, which assumes that formal education increases individual productivity by providing the skills and knowledge required for the most demanding occupations. According to this theory, individuals can improve their productivity by investing in their own education. Moreover, employers can dispose of perfect information about school leavers' productivity by considering their level of education. Thus, this theory predicts a direct relationship between level of education and quality of the first job achieved.

In opposition to both functionalist sociological theory and human capital theory, credentialist theory, developed in the 1970s, questioned the idea that education increases individual productivity at work. In this interpretation, educational certificates are credentials that certify membership in a given status group, i.e., groups that share a common culture, worldview, and values. While functionalist and human capital theories argued that school leavers are sorted into occupations on the basis of their merits and productivity, credentialist theory suggested that the process of the school-to-work transition is ruled by dominant status groups who define the educational requirements for a given occupation and, in this way, control and limit access to their privileged positions. The critique of the human capital assumption that education increases individual productivity is also the starting point of the signal theory of education that has been developed by both economists and sociologists. According to this theory, employers interpret education as a signal of the future trainability of applicants for a job vacancy. Although the level of education is not directly related to actual productivity, it reflects other individual traits such as commitment and social and communicative skills that are crucial for subsequent success at work. The important implication for the school-to-work transition is that, among other factors, the signaling capacity of educational qualifications is crucially dependent on the number of school leavers with a given level of qualification: as their number increases, the discriminatory information attached to the educational qualification decreases. If this is the case, one might expect the outcome of the school-to-work transition to depend to a greater extent on factors other than the mere level of education.

In more recent years, research on the transition from school to work has reflected and partly fostered a progressive shift from social stratification and social mobility studies toward labor market sociology. This shift has come about with three interrelated epistemological, theoretical, and methodological changes. First of all, more effort has been made to specify the mechanisms underlying the school-to-work transition. Second, the importance of the institutional context in which the school-to-work transition is embedded has been acknowledged. Third, dynamic methods of analysis have been applied to study entry into the labor market, as opposed to the traditional cross-sectional methods.

The first of these changes can be described as an attempt to move from a "variable sociology," mainly interested in establishing the patterns of association between independent and dependent variables, to a "mechanism sociology" that searches for the generative processes of social inequality. In the past, research on the school-to-work transition mainly focused on the net association of individual education and different measures of quality regarding the first job. In recent years, however, it has been recognized that, in order to address the questions "Who gets which job upon entry to work, and why?" one should account for the broader processes underlying the supply and demand side of the labor market and how they match. An explanation of the school-to-work transition should ideally consider the number and characteristics of school leavers (supply side), the availability of jobs with given characteristics (demand side), and, finally, the processes through which the school leavers achieve valuable information about job vacancies and the employers select employees from among the potential candidates for a job (matching processes).

This shift toward broader explanations of the process of entry into the labor market has also led to the acknowledgment of the importance of the institutional context in which the school-to-work transition is embedded. Thus, comparative research has highlighted institutional differences among countries or over time that might affect both the characteristics of the supply and the demand sides and the matching processes in the labor market and, thus, condition patterns of entry into the labor market. With regard to the characteristics of school leavers, a widely applied typology in research on the school-to-work transition distinguishes

between the level of *standardization* of educational provisions, the *stratification* of educational opportunities that characterizes different educational systems, and the level of *credential inflation*. More precisely, standardization refers to the degree to which the quality of education meets the standard in the country under consideration. What is important in this regard is whether curricula are nationally defined, whether teacher training is uniform, whether there is a national standardized examination system, and whether there is any large variation in funding across schools and universities. On the other hand, the concept of stratification points to the degree of separation of students into differentiated educational tracks and to the selection procedures occurring at early ages. Finally, credential inflation refers to the proportion of each cohort that gets to the highest level of the educational system. This last concept is important because it expresses the idea that the value of a certain educational qualification upon entry to the labor market depends on the number of school leavers with the same level of education. In general, it has been argued that, in countries with highly stratified and standardized educational systems and low educational inflation, educational returns upon entry into the labor market are on average higher than in other countries. This is because high levels of stratification and low credential inflation make it possible for employers to select among fewer applicants with clear-cut distinctions in the qualifications. Moreover, higher levels of standardization make the signals provided by education more reliable. The empirical evidence provided by various cross-national studies largely supports this type of argument.

With regard to the matching processes between school leavers and job vacancies, the study of the school-to-work transition has benefited from the insights of *network analysis*. The key research issue in this respect is if and how the process of entry into the labor market is facilitated by the circulation of valuable information on vacancies and job applicants through the network of relatives, friends, or simple acquaintances. Comparative studies have also focused on the nature and strength of the institutional linkages between the educational system and the labor market. In this respect, it has been argued that the school-to-work transition is smoother and the relationship between the level and type of education and quality of the first job stronger in those countries where there are direct linkages or co-linear linkages between the educational system and the occupational structure. *Direct linkages* exist in the dual system types of vocational training, such as the German and Danish ones, where employers and school jointly collaborate in providing training. An additional and rather exceptional case of strong linkage is the situation where the school acts directly as a job placement office, as in the case of Japan. *Co-linear linkages* are found when there is strong congruence between training and certification provided in school and training or legal requirements for specific occupations in the labor market. For instance in the Netherlands, although there is little joint delivery of training by school and employers, there are a large number of occupations which require applicants to have taken training programs in the educational system before entry. Finally, where *no direct linkage*s between school and work exist, as in the US, employers are not involved in any way in schooling and there is no formal congruence between training and certification provided by the educational system and training or legal requirements to access given occupations in the labor market.

Less attention has generally been paid to cross-national differences on the demand side of the labor market that may potentially have severe consequences for the transition from school to work. Obtaining a good job after leaving school depends crucially on the availability of good jobs. In their most general form, demand-side institutional differences that are particularly interesting for the school-to-work transition refer to cross-national variation in the ratio of vacancies of highly skilled/unskilled jobs. All other conditions being equal, more highly educated people will have an advantage in terms of the quality of the job upon entry into the labor market if the demand for skilled jobs is high. Accordingly, the demand for skilled and unskilled labor will depend crucially on the productive system of a country and on the dominant market and organizational strategies of national firms. The political economy literature on the varieties of capitalism and production regimes might offer useful insights on national differences in the demand

for qualified workers for research on the school-to-work transition.

With regard to the most important methodological changes in this area of study, one might mention that in recent years the outcome of the transition from school to work has been conceived not only in terms of the quality of the first job achieved, but also considering the duration of the first job search. Thus, one aspect studied is how different indicators of educational achievement affect the speediness of the transition to work and how the duration of the job search itself influences the quality of its outcome. In this way, the intrinsic dynamic nature of the process under study has been fully acknowledged.

In sum, the study of the school-to-work transition has traditionally been a border area between economics and sociology. One might conclude that in the last decades the progressive broadening of the scope of analysis to include supply, demand, and matching processes, the acknowledgment that the process of entry into the labor market is embedded in different institutional contexts that might vary from one country to another, and, finally, the adoption of a longitudinal perspective have made the sociological contribution in this area most fruitful.

SEE ALSO: Economy, Networks and; Educational and Occupational Attainment; Labor Markets; Stratification and Inequality, Theories of

REFERENCES AND SUGGESTED READINGS

Allmendinger, J. (1989) Educational Systems and Labor Market Outcomes. *European Sociological Review* 5: 231–50.

Bernardi, F., Gangl, M., & van de Werfhorst, H. (2004) The From-School-to-Work Dynamics: Timing of Work and Quality of Work in Italy, the Netherlands, and the United States, 1980–1998. Working Paper No. 201. CEACS, Fundación Juan March, Madrid.

Collins, R. (1979) *The Credential Society: An Historical Sociology of Education and Stratification.* Academic Press, New York.

Rosenbaum, J., Settersten, R., & Maier, T. (1990) Market and Network Theories of the Transition from High School to Work: Their Application to Industrialized Societies. *Annual Review of Sociology* 16: 263–99.

Shavit, Y. & Müller, W. (Eds.) (1998) *From School to Work: A Comparative Study of Educational Qualifications and Occupational Destinations.* Clarendon Press, Oxford.

Sørensen, A. & Kalleberg, A. (1981) An Outline of a Theory of the Matching of Persons to Jobs. In: Berg, I. (Ed.), *Sociological Perspectives on Labour Markets.* Academic Press, New York, pp. 49–74.

transnational and global feminisms

Manisha Desai

Transnational feminism refers both to the practices of women's movements around the world and to a theoretical perspective in which women theorize and strategize for women's rights and gender justice across national boundaries, work in collaboration with women from other countries, and frame their activism in terms that are both local and global. Thus, transnational feminism refers to the flow of ideas, issues, strategies, organizations, and activists across national boundaries. As practice it dates back to the mid- and late nineteenth century when women activists from the US and Europe worked in collaboration around the abolitionist and suffrage movements in those countries, when women from colonizing countries such as England worked together with women in India and other colonies to advance women's rights, particularly suffrage and education, as well as when European women in the communist and socialist parties worked to develop women's organizations around the world on issues of women's economic rights (Rupp 1997). This earlier practice of transnational feminism was limited in several ways: the issues addressed were restricted to suffrage, education, and workers' rights; the nation-state was still the center of activism; the flow of ideas, strategies, and activists was primarily, though not exclusively, from the North to the South; there were few international organizations, all of which were

hierarchical in nature; and the practice was neither widespread nor the dominant mode of feminism. While this practice continued, primarily in its communist and socialist manifestations, it was not until the 1970s when the United Nations declared 1975 as International Women's Year and 1975–85 as International Women's Decade and organized women's world conferences – in Mexico City in 1975, Copenhagen in 1980, Nairobi in 1985, and Beijing in 1995 – that the practice took off and has now become a dominant strategy of women's movements around the world.

As a theoretical perspective, it emerged in the US academy in the 1990s. It was a response to the critique of second-wave, white, middle-class feminism by women of color in the US and the "third world" and by poststructuralism and postcolonialism, as well as to women's solidarities across the world, forged as a result of women's participation in the UN's International Women's Decade and its four world conferences and preparatory national and regional meetings. The term "transnational feminism" was seldom used by the women's movements and international non-government organizations (INGOs) until after the Beijing conference. Today it is widely used but remains contested by some Latin American feminists who are uncomfortable with the term. To them it is too reminiscent of transnational corporations.

Grewal and Kaplan (1994) and Mohanty (2002) were among the early framers of this academic discourse. Their articulation incorporated critiques of western feminisms and postmodernism without jettisoning either. They underscored the need for feminist political practices that addressed the concerns of women around the world in their historic and particular relationships to multiple patriarchies as well as to international economic hegemonies. For a transnational feminist politics, they noted, feminists have to move beyond polarities, without ignoring the histories of unequal power relations that construct them, and build coalitions based on practices that women around the world develop to address the complex realities of their lives. Together, these local feminist practices could lead to transnational solidarities. This formulation of an intersectional analysis and transversal politics came to be defined as transnational feminism in the 1990s.

Such a transnational analytic focus developed not only in feminism but also in other areas of sociology, specifically social movements, gender, race, and sexuality studies, immigration, families, and organizations among others. This focus on the transnational was fueled by the pace of contemporary globalizations and information technology which enabled easy, quick, and reliable communication across national boundaries. Thus, the transnational analytic aim is to understand how the local – in terms of issues, identities, strategies, methods, targets of protest, and worldviews – becomes global and how global is evident in the local. Analysts assume that identities, networks, and communities are as likely to be global as local and that global dynamics and audiences constrain and facilitate local realities.

Transnational feminism became a privileged discourse in the 1990s in the academy at the same time that women's activists began to privilege transnational activism over local activism. In part, this reflects the common realities, of globalization and structural adjustment policies, that began to influence women's lives all around the world as well as the opportunities made possible by the communication technologies and the UN world conferences that enabled women to meet across national borders. Transnational feminist solidarities were being forged among women across national boundaries around several important sites: the UN conferences, specific local struggles, academic and policy research, and the global justice movements. Most analysts agree that the dominant protest repertoire of transnational activism includes education and mobilization, symbolic framing, and strategic use of information. Advocacy, lobbying, support, and direct action are secondary. Furthermore, the major targets of most transnational movements have been policy mechanisms of local, national, regional, and multilateral international institutions. Finally, while a lot of transnational activism is cyber-based, it also involves travel to sites of protests and gatherings. Such a modality privileges educated, middle-class activists over other movement activists and participants.

The four world conferences and accompanying NGO Forums were contentious events with women, not all of whom identified as feminists, from the South challenging Northern women's conceptions of women's issues based solely on gender and sexuality and insisting on bringing in issues of development, nationalism, and neo-colonialism. These differences among women began to be acknowledged and "solidarities of difference" were forged as they continued to meet over the decade and shared experiences of inequalities and struggles for justice. It was the 1985 conference in Nairobi that marked a shift from contention to solidarity and by the fourth conference in Beijing, women despite their differences had found a common language in the human rights framework. "Women's rights are human rights" emerged at the World Conference on Human Rights in Vienna in 1993 but became paradigmatic in Beijing. Thus, the UN conferences and then its specialized agency meetings, such as the Convention on Elimination of all Forms of Discrimination Against Women and the Committee on the Status of Women, became the prime sites of this new phase of transnational activism. Most women who attended the NGO Forums accompanying the UN conferences, which are for government delegations though increasingly many governments include activists and NGO members among their official delegates, were middle-class educated women from INGOS, donors, academics, and activists. Grassroots women are present as well but most participate in their own Forum outside the main workshops in tents, sharing, performing, and selling handicrafts. Only women from the major INGOs and donors are involved in interacting with the official conferences. Thus, when feminists come together across borders around spaces like the UN conferences, they tend to reproduce inequalities among women and privilege women from the North and elite women from the South.

But transnational feminist politics is not limited to activism around the UN. As the burgeoning literature on transnational social movements shows, activists are coming together across national borders at various local levels for specific struggles such as coalitions against sweatshop labor, fair trade cooperatives, slum and shack dwellers' coalitions, anti-privatization of water, and various other social justice movements. When grassroots activists and networks that involve community-based organizations come together across borders for specific struggles, while the tensions and contradictions persist, local women are able to negotiate and influence politics based on their knowledge and resources. Networks such as Women in Informal Economy Globalizing and Organizing (WIEGO) and Slum/Shack Dwellers International (SID) are composed of people affected directly in their homes and communities by the process of globalization, in partnership with NGOs and academic institutions (WIEGO is based at Harvard University) to gather data and to propose people-centered solutions at international, institutional levels and to engage in local organizing. Such networks have been successful in changing perceptions about the poor and marginalized people and their right to participate in decisions that affect their lives as well as their abilities to generate solutions to their situations. Because such networks represent people and are accountable to them, they are more legitimate than other elite and middle-class networks and NGOs that have no connections to the constituency on whose behalf they make claims.

Educated, middle-class, and elite transnational feminist networks – DAWN, WIDE, WEDO, AWMR – however, have also played an important role in research, policy, and advocacy for women's rights (Moghadam 2005). They are an innovative feminist response, participatory and non-hierarchical, and the most effective form of organizing in an era of globalization. They have been effective in generating new knowledge, influencing policies, and advocating on behalf of women's rights in many international institutions such as the UN, World Bank, and the IMF.

Both grassroots and middle-class transnational feminist networks have also come together in the context of the global justice movement. The protests against corporate globalizations that began in Seattle in 1998 and continued through the end of the decade created new networks and led to the consolidation of the global justice movement. It was in the name of the global justice movement and as an alternative to the World Economic Forum in Davos, where leaders of corporate globalization meet, that the first World Social Forum (WSF) was called in January 2001 in Brazil (www. worldsocialforum.org). The WSF was organized as a democratic space for people from around the world to share their struggles and reflect on alternatives. The language of the WSF stresses process and autonomy from state and parties. Feminists were active in the WSF from its inception and gender equality was stressed as one of the important aspects of global justice. Yet the first two WSF did not have as many sessions on gender, nor were women in prominent positions in the International Organizing Committee. To address this, feminists from Latin America, Asia, and Africa formed "Feminist Dialogues" in 2004 to engender the WSF and make it feminist in its focus, method, and participants.

Transnational feminism, both as practice and a theoretical framework, has several implications. As practice, the domination of transnational feminism has led to reproducing inequalities among activists, from the North versus South and also among activists from the South. Organizationally, it has privileged networks over other organizational structures, which has contradictory effects. On one hand, it enables communication and solidarity in a participatory manner across many boundaries. On the other hand, there is very little accountability and responsibility. Transnational feminism has also diverted resources from local to transnational level, and most importantly, because a lot of transnational activism has been around research, policy, and advocacy, the changes have been more discursive than redistributive. Transnational feminist movements have primarily succeeded at the level of discursive power. They have operated on the notion of discursive representation rather than political representation. Discursive representation has sought to be inclusive, open, and self-reflexive. Such an emphasis is in part a reflection of feminists' ability to harness communicative rather than conventional power. Discourses have an empowering function and are an important site of resistance. But feminist discourses have not become hegemonic, they remain an alternative. And when discourses such as gender mainstreaming and women's human rights are taken up by states and international agencies, they tend to become depoliticized and have little impact on actual policy changes.

Theoretically, transnational feminism, and transnationalism in general, have raised issues of methodology. For example, what constitutes a social movement? Some analysts prefer to use networks as the unit of analysis as it has become *the* organizational expression of transnational social movements, while others focus on methods used, i.e., social movements use contentious methods while NGOs and networks tend to use routine means of social change. Yet others use the concept of transnational activism instead of social movements. They define activism as political activities based on a conflict of interest that challenge or support power structures, that are carried out by non-state actors, and that take place outside formal politics (Piper & Uhlin 2004). Such a move blurs distinctions between NGOs and social movements and indicates the difficulties of using categories like social movements that derive from state-centered sociology for transnational politics.

These definitional issues have been central in the current analyses of women's movements as scholars have moved away from "global" or "international" feminist movements to transnational feminist practices and solidarities, debated the use of feminist versus women's movements, and lamented the NGOization of women's movements. These conceptual issues are important because they both construct movements even as they describe them and show a discomfort with the shift in political terrain that has not led to greater equality for women.

Despite these methodological issues, transnational feminism is here to stay both as a theoretical perspective and as practice. To be more effective as practice, transnational feminism will have to devise strategies with other mass movements – such as unions in the informal sector as well as export processing zones that can hold corporations accountable, enforce land redistribution policies, challenge agribusiness to sustainable land use, and promote fair trade economic alternatives and political quotas for women – that can redistribute resources and emancipate women.

SEE ALSO: Colonialism (Neocolonialism); Feminism; Feminism, First, Second, and Third Waves; Feminist Activism in Latin America; Gender Ideology and Gender Role Ideology; Gender Mainstreaming; Gender, Social Movements and; Global Justice as a Social Movement; Mobilization; Social Movements; Third World and Postcolonial Feminisms/Subaltern; Transnational Movements; Women's Movements

REFERENCES AND SUGGESTED READINGS

Alvarez, S. (2000) Translating the Global: Effects of Transnational Organizing on Local Feminist Discourses and Practices in Latin America. *Meridiens* 1(1).

Basu, A. (Ed.) (1995) *The Challenge of Local Feminisms: Women's Movements in Global Perspectives.* Westview Press, Boulder, CO.

Desai, M. (2005) Transnationalism: The Face of Feminist Politics Post Beijing. *International Social Science Journal* 14(51): 493–504.

Grewal, I. & Kaplan, C. (Eds.) (1994) *Scattered Hegemonies: Postmodernism and Transnational Feminist Practices.* University of Minnesota Press, Minneapolis.

Keck, M. & Sikkink, K. (1998) *Activists Beyond Borders: Advocacy Networks in International Politics.* Cornell University Press, Ithaca, NY.

Moghadam, V. (2005) *Globalizing Women: Transnational Feminist Networks.* Johns Hopkins University Press, Baltimore.

Mohanty, C. T. (2002) "Under Western Eyes" Revisited: Feminist Solidarity Through Anti-Capitalist Struggles. *Signs* 28(2): 499–535.

Naples, N. & Desai, M. (2002) *Globalization and Women's Activism: Linking Local Struggles to Transnational Politics.* Routledge, New York.

Piper, N. & Uhlin, A. (2004) New Perspectives on Transnational Activism. In: Piper, N. & Uhlin, A. (Eds.), *Transnational Activism in Asia: Problems of Power and Democracy.* Routledge, New York, pp. 1–25.

Rupp, L. (1997) *Worlds of Women: The Making of an International Women's Movement.* Princeton University Press, Princeton.

transnational movements

Jackie Smith

Social movements emerged in tandem with modern nation-states, as groups of people organized to resist new claims being made by national authorities (such as taxes or military conscription) or to advance their own claims that states provide a variety of public goods and services (such as education, health care, and various forms of financial assistance). Ongoing competition between authorities and citizen challengers generated new structures – including parliaments, bills of rights, and bureaucratic checks and balances – to routinize public participation in national politics and to otherwise enhance the accountability of political leaders to citizenry (see, e.g., Tilly 1984; Markoff 1996). Today, as states increasingly turn to international political arenas to manage their economies and ecologies as well as other aspects of social life, we find that social movements are becoming increasingly transnational in their structure and focus.

Movements are assisted in their transnational organizing efforts by the same rapidly advancing technologies that have assisted in the expansion of a global economy. Relatively cheap airline tickets, more widely available telephone and Internet access, expanding use of English as a global working language, and a globalized mass media help enable people from more diverse classes and geographical origins to share information and cultivate cooperative relationships across huge distances. While transnational social movements were active in the nineteenth and early twentieth centuries promoting international peace, an end to slavery, and women's suffrage, activists in these movements were by and large from privileged backgrounds. Today's transnational activism, which has expanded rapidly since the 1970s and 1980s, involves those of far more modest means. That said, it is still true that many transnational (and other) movements are disproportionately middle class, since people with more and better education as well as time, skills, and resources are the most able to be involved in social movements. But social movement politics by its nature attempts to lower barriers and costs to popular political participation, and many activists seek to confront the inequities they find in their own structures and operations.

Transnational social movements are best seen as networks of actors that are organized at local, national, and international levels. Many include formal organizations that have constitutions, staff members, bank accounts, and boards of directors. Others are neighborhood or friendship groups who meet informally and irregularly and who support each other's work to promote social change. Individuals are also key players in all social movements, and in transnational movements we often find members of government delegations to the United Nations playing key roles in social movements. For instance, governments like that of Mexico have long been supportive of international disarmament efforts, and that government's delegates have helped peace movement activists get access to information and increase their influence on official disarmament negotiations.

United Nations officials, such as those in the United Nations Human Rights Commission, are also frequently involved in supporting the work of the transnational human rights movement. Journalists and academics are also part of many movements, helping to popularize debates or to advance new analyses that can assist social movements. Webs of interpersonal and interorganizational connections help expand the flow of information to different actors within movements. Transnational events like United Nations conferences or transnational meetings of civil society groups have helped increase the strength and density of these network ties, and the increased frequency of these events in recent decades helps account for the rise of transnational movements.

Transnational movements have adopted a number of strategies to promote global change. They can work to advance new international agreements, such as the Convention to Ban Landmines or the International Criminal Court, or to block agreements such as those in the World Trade Organization. They can work to press individual governments to abide by international norms or to ratify treaties. And they can appeal to global institutions or norms in order to strengthen their leverage in national conflicts (see Smith et al. 1997). Margaret Keck and Kathryn Sikkink (1998) refer to the latter of these strategies as the "boomerang effect." They argue that when national political systems are repressive or restrictive, appeals to international norms or alliances can bring international pressure to bear on states, thereby altering the balance of power in national political contests. So when Argentine human rights activists mobilized their transnational networks, they introduced an additional cost (US military aid) to the government if it persisted in flouting international law. In short, transnational movements can and do affect both national and international political processes. Moreover, by shaping international treaties and by working with international institutions, they help define the institutional arrangements of our global political system.

The major distinction of transnational movements is that they mobilize people across national boundaries around a shared aim. They help people define their interests and identities in ways that go beyond the traditional nation-state borders. By facilitating routine communication between people from vastly different regions and cultures, they help enhance understanding and mutual trust while making international friendships more feasible and likely. A member of Amnesty International, for instance, will share more common interests and perspectives with AI members outside her own country than she will with many of her compatriots. Organizations generate their own internal cultures and identities. And because they generally oppose predominant cultural systems, social movement organizations have a particular need for creating supportive identities that can bind members together and support collective action even in the face of repression (see, e.g., Rupp 1997).

As they attempt to define new activist identities, transnational movements must overcome the considerable influence of the national state in defining people's primary allegiances and motivations. However, just as the processes of global economic integration help generate the technologies and other infrastructures that support transnational organizing, here too global processes help break down the monopolies states have on their citizens' loyalties. The globalization of the economy has meant that people's educational backgrounds are more similar, as are their professional lives and working conditions. Moreover, there are increasingly obvious connections between global forces, such as transnational corporations or international trade laws, and one's daily experiences and interests, and these provide important foundations for the creation of shared understandings and meanings outside the framework of traditional state boundaries. Indeed, overcoming differences in national perspectives may be far easier than overcoming other differences within movements (Moody 1997). In other words, we can see important foundations for the globalization of civil society to parallel the globalization of economic and political institutions.

Like all movements, transnational social movements seek to enhance their political influence by cultivating alliances with other groups. A longstanding divide exists between social movements organized around issues such as the environment or civil rights and those organized to promote the interests of labor (Waterman 2005). In many contexts, corporate interests seek to undermine alliance building by framing environmental struggles as contests between jobs or development and environmental conservation. Divisions between richer and poorer activists persist in many movements, as economic class shapes the day-to-day experiences and perspectives of people in important ways. Sometimes, however, transnational movements can help overcome class or caste divisions by providing a broader perspective on the divisions that might exist within a single country. Activists in transnational environmental groups, for instance, are motivated out of a concern for a particular policy, and they will work with any groups they think can help secure their aims. In contrast, within countries we often find that urban–rural divisions or even anti-indigenous prejudices can impede alliance formation within nations. Thus, when the World Social Forum – an annual gathering of social movement and other actors seeking to democratize the global system – was held in Mumbai, Indian activists were forced to confront more directly the claims raised by low-caste Dalit which drew wide and sympathetic attention from international delegates to the Forum.

While social movements address any number of different issues, many work more or less self-consciously to affect the formal means by which citizens can both participate in policy debates and hold their elected leaders accountable for policy decisions. So movements for racial equality have generated laws to protect minority voting rights, and demonstrators protesting against military arms races have helped to advance new legal protections for all forms of public speech. In short, in the course of mobilizing around particular issues, movements help shape the laws and institutions of our democracies. This is exactly what has taken place in the international political arena. As groups mobilized to advocate human rights or to limit the use of military force, they have found themselves involved in the process of helping define the role of citizens in institutions that were established by states.

Global political institutions such as the European Union and United Nations were formally organized by governments with little desire to see much in the way of citizen participation. International diplomacy was seen as "high politics" that needed to be removed from the pressures of what were seen as poorly informed and passionate citizenries. But because a government's participation in any international organization generally required that their national legislature approve of the arrangement, governments were forced to yield some space for citizens' involvement in these bodies. And since the establishment of both these institutions, we have seen efforts by movements to further expand citizen participation in global politics.

Nevertheless, a substantial "democratic deficit" remains, and many national delegates to international institutions are unelected and largely unaccountable to citizens. There are no political parties organizing constituencies beyond the national level. Many international negotiations remain secretive, and even national legislators are denied access to official meetings and documents. Because global institutions have an increasing impact on the policy decisions that affect us, this global democratic deficit has undermined the quality of democracy within nations as well. Some analysts speak of a "hollowing out" of national democracy in recent years as states delegate more of their authority to supranational institutions, privatize more of their services to the corporate sector, and delegate more distributional decisions to local authorities (see Markoff 2004). Thus, after years of growing transnational activism aimed at promoting international agreements for human rights, more equitable development, and environmental protections, more transnational movement groups are demanding global democracy as the twenty-first century unfolds.

Another key emphasis of contemporary transnational movements is a call for a more balanced approach to global integration than policymakers have pursued thus far. Since the late 1970s, key players in global politics have emphasized the development of global markets, and they encouraged all countries to reduce tariffs and other measures that limit the flow of goods and services across national borders. Increased global trade was thought to bring economic growth that would benefit all. Unfortunately, for many reasons this simple economic logic has not proved true, and along with unprecedented increases in global trade we find unprecedented concentrations of wealth amid persistent poverty and environmental degradation.

Beginning in the 1990s, many groups began working transnationally to challenge this predominant neoliberal model of economic globalization. They argued that many decisions should not be left to the "free" market, because markets only respond to those with wealth. And many social goods – such as a clean environment or public health – are not readily reduced to simple cost-benefit calculations. These decisions, activists argue, require informed public debate and consultation. By the last meeting of the World Trade Organization in Seattle in 1999, transnational movements came together with national and local organizers to demand more accountable and less market-oriented international policies. Activists were demanding a greater say in decisions about how our national and local economies (and polities) are organized, as they were finding that global institutions were squeezing out possibilities for citizen input into decisions about what kinds of industries operate in local communities, what protections states can (and more often cannot) enact to preserve their natural environments, and how educational, health, and other services are managed. So we see a sort of "clash of globalizations" pitting a global system driven by markets against a system of global governance where politics determines how public goods are managed and how conflicting interests are reconciled.

In sum, attention to transnational social movements helps us understand the political processes behind globalization. Because movements are working to connect localized citizens with global political processes, they provide the connective tissue that helps integrate our global polity. They are also part of complex processes of contestation that help define the structure of global institutions and the character of local, national, and global polities. By helping shape institutions, policies, and systems of meaning, they are important actors in the global system. By insisting that the global system be made more open and accountable, transnational movements are essential for the preservation of democracy.

Studying transnational movements is difficult. One needs to have expertise in the politics and cultures of different countries, as well as an understanding of the global political system – which constitutes a unique "area study" of its own. Because of these complexities, most studies to date are case studies of how transnational activism affects a particular national context or of particular transnational campaigns or events. The *Global Civil Society Yearbook*, published annually since 2001, has sought to trace the evolution of globally organized social change efforts, and it provides useful information about trends in global organization and activism. Electronic newspaper records have allowed for large-scale, comparative analyses of media coverage of movements. Key questions that emerge from analyses of transnational movements are: How have globalizing trends affected the ways people engage in politics? How do transnational forms of activism compare with national ones? How does participation in transnational activism vary across different countries? And, perhaps most importantly, what impacts do transnational movements have on global political and cultural change?

SEE ALSO: Collective Action; Collective Identity; Democracy; Ecology and Economy; Environmental Movements; Global Economy; Global Justice as a Social Movement; Global Politics; Identity Politics/Relational Politics; Labor Movement; Social Movement Organizations; Social Movements; Social Movements, Networks and; Transnational and Global Feminisms; Transnationalism; Transnationals

REFERENCES AND SUGGESTED READINGS

Anheier, H., Glasius, M., & Kaldor, M. (Annual) *Global Civil Society Yearbook*. London School of Economics, London.
Keck, M. & Sikkink, K. (1998) *Activists Beyond Borders*. Cornell University Press, Ithaca, NY.
Markoff, J. (1996) *Waves of Democracy: Social Movements and Political Change*. Pine Forge Press, Thousand Oaks, CA.
Markoff, J. (2004) Who Will Construct the Global Order? In: Williamson, B. (Ed.), *Transnational Democracy*. Ashgate, London.

Moody, K. (1997) *Workers in a Lean World: Unions in the International Economy*. Verso, New York.
Rupp, L. J. (1997) *Worlds of Women: The Making of an International Women's Movement*. Princeton University Press, Princeton.
Smith, J., Chatfield, C., & Pagnucco, R. (1997) *Transnational Social Movements and Global Politics: Solidarity Beyond the State*. Syracuse University Press, Syracuse.
Tilly, C. (1984) Social Movements and National Politics. In: Bright, C. & Harding, S. (Eds.), *Statemaking and Social Movements: Essays in History and Theory*. University of Michigan Press, Ann Arbor, pp. 297–317.
Waterman, P. (2005) Talking Across Difference in an Interconnected World of Labor. In: Bandy, J. & Smith, J. (Eds.), *Coalitions Across Borders: Transnational Protest in a Neoliberal Era*. Rowman & Littlefield, Boulder, CO, pp. 141–62.

transnationalism

Larissa Remennick

The concept of transnationalism, described as an integral part of the globalization process, is becoming increasingly popular in social and political sciences (Glick Schiller et al. 1995; Guarnizo & Smith 1998; Portes et al. 1999). Originally coined in international economics to describe flows of capital and labor across national borders in the second half of the twentieth century, this concept was later applied to the study of international migration and ethnic diasporas. The transnational perspective became increasingly useful for exploring such issues as immigrant economic integration, identity, citizenship, and cultural retention. Transnationalism embraces a variety of multifaceted social relations that are both embedded in and transcend two or more nation-states, cross-cutting sociopolitical, territorial, and cultural borders. The ever-increasing flows of people, goods, ideas, and images between various parts of the world enhance the blending of cultures and lifestyles and leads to the formation of "hyphenated" social and personal identities (Chinese-American, Greek-Australian, etc.).

Some authors argue that transnationalism may actually be a new name for an old phenomenon, in the sense that most big immigration waves of the past were typified by ethnocultural retention and contacts with the homeland (Van Hear 1998; Guarnizo and Smith 1998). Indeed, historic studies of ethnic diasporas show that immigrants never fully severed their links with the country they left behind. Yet, due to technical and financial limitations of the time, for most migrants these links remained mainly in the sentimental and cultural realm, and were seldom expressed in active shuttle movement or communication across borders. Economic ties with countries of origin were typically limited to monetary remittances to family members. Although up to one-quarter of transatlantic migrants of the late nineteenth and early twentieth centuries eventually returned to their homelands, the decision to repatriate was in fact another critical and irreversible choice to be made. Hence, for the majority of historic migrants, resettlement was an irreversible process always involving a dichotomy: stay or emigrate, or else stay or return (Jacobson 1995; Van Hear 1998).

In the late twentieth century efficient and relatively cheap means of communication and transportation (time- and space-compressing technologies) made this old dichotomy largely irrelevant. As Castells (1996) pointed out, new technologies have virtually created new patterns of social relations, or at least strongly reinforced preexisting tendencies. They allowed numerous diasporic immigrants to live in two or more countries at a time, by maintaining close physical and social links with their places of origin. Transnational activities and lifestyles became widely spread, embracing large numbers of people and playing a significant role in the economy, politics, and social life of both sending and receiving countries. Guarnizo and Smith (1998) introduced a useful distinction between the two types of transnationalism: "from above" and "from below." The former refers to institutionalized economic and political activities of multinational corporations and organizations such as the UN, Amnesty International, or Greenpeace, which set in motion a large-scale global exchange of financial and human capital. On the other hand, the increasing role in these networks belongs to ordinary migrants – grassroots agents of transnationalism who run small businesses in their home countries, organize exchange of material (e.g., ethnic food) and

cultural goods (e.g., tours of folk artists) within the diaspora, pay regular visits to their birthplace, and receive co-ethnic guests. This is called a *transnational lifestyle*.

The migration experience in the context of a global society, where the constant exchange of people, products, and ideas is reinforced by global media networks, has attained a whole new quality. The full-time loyalty to one country and one culture is no longer self-evident: people may actually divide their physical presence, effort, and identity between several societies. Citizenship and political participation are also becoming bifocal or even multifocal, since some sending countries allow their expatriates to remain citizens, vote in national elections, and establish political movements. In this context, international migrants are becoming *transmigrants*, developing economic activities, enjoying cultural life, and keeping dense informal networks not only with their home country, but also with other national branches of their diaspora. The split of economic, social, and political loyalties among migrants, and gradual attenuation of loyalty to the nation-state as such, is seen as problematic by some receiving countries (Glick Schiller et al. 1995; Guarnizo & Smith 1998). Yet some recent studies show that dual citizenship may in fact promote immigrants' legal and sociopolitical attachments to both their home and host countries, rather than reinforce so-called postnationalism (Bloemraad 2004).

Most transnational networks in business, politics, communications, and culture organize along ethnic lines (i.e., include members of the same ethnic community spread between different locales on the map). Common language and cultural heritage are the key cementing factors for the *transnational diasporas* (Jacobson 1995; Van Hear 1998). In most cases, transnationals become bilingual and bicultural, but different communities may exhibit various degrees of cultural separatism versus acculturation in the host society. Over time, many immigrant groups develop cultural hybridism – the mix of the elements of their ethnic language and lifestyles with those adopted from the host culture. The most common expression of this trend is the formation of hybrid immigrant languages – Mexican English, Algerian French, Turkish German, etc. (Glick Schiller et al. 1995;

Guarnizo & Smith 1998; Van Hear 1998). In psychosocial terms, immigrant/transnational identity and personality become increasingly "elastic," if not "fluid," being constantly shaped and reshaped by multiple influences of the different societies migrants actually live in. Transnationals of today experience increasing difficulty in answering the questions, "Who are you? Where do you belong?" In that sense, transmigrant identity emerges as the epitome of postmodern identity (Giddens 1991; Guarnizo & Smith 1998). However exciting, a transnational lifestyle has its underside. While for many immigrants it may be a blessing, enabling them to enjoy the best of two (or more) worlds, for some others it virtually means living in limbo, or in a state of permanent uprooting.

SEE ALSO: Bilingualism; Diaspora; Immigration; Migration: International; Nation-State; Transnationals

REFERENCES AND SUGGESTED READINGS

Bloemraad, I. (2004) Who Claims Dual Citizenship? The Limits of Postnationalism, the Possibilities of Transnationalism, and the Persistence of Traditional Citizenship. *International Migration Review* 38(2): 389–426.

Castells, M. (1996) *The Rise of the Network Society.* Blackwell, Oxford.

Giddens, A. (1991) *Modernity and Self-Identity: Self and Society in the Late Modern Age.* Stanford University Press, Stanford.

Glick Schiller, N., Basch, L., & Szanton Blanc, C. (1995) From Immigrant to Transmigrant: Theorizing Transnational Migration. *Anthropological Quarterly* 68(1): 48–63.

Guarnizo, L. E. & Smith, M.P. (1998) The Locations of Transnationalism. In: M. P. Smith & L. E. Guarnizo (Eds.), *Transnationalism from Below.* Comparative Urban and Community Research Ser., Vol. 6. Transaction Books, New Brunswick, NJ, pp. 3–34.

Jacobson, M. F. (1995) *Special Sorrows: The Diasporic Imagination of Irish, Polish, and Jewish Immigrants in the United States.* Harvard University Press, Cambridge, MA.

Portes, A., Guarnizo, L. E., & Landolt, P. (1999) The Study of Transnationalism: Pitfalls and Promise of an Emergent Research Field. Introduction to Special Issue on Transnational Communities. *Ethnic and Racial Studies* 22(2): 217–37.

Van Hear, N. (1998) *New Diasporas: The Mass Exodus, Dispersal and Regrouping of Migrant Communities.* University College of London Press, London.

transnationals

Ray Loveridge

The term transnational corporation (TNC) is often used interchangeably with that of multinational corporation (MNC) or multinational enterprise (MNE) to mean a firm that owns or controls income-generating assets in more than one country. In the more exacting definition of Bartlett and Ghoshal (1989) the multinational organizational mode is described as one subset of the TNC (see below). Other transnational organizations include intergovernmental bodies such as the United Nations Organization (UNO) and International Monetary Fund (IMF), regulatory or standard-setting agencies such as the Basle Group of Bankers, and a rapidly expanding group of "voluntary" associations known as non-government organizations (NGOs). The focus here, however, will be on TNCs rather than these latter forms of cross-national governance. In popular usage, the TNC is usually seen as being extremely large in terms of its level of employment, financial turnover, and ownership of assets. Indeed, it is usual to compare the turnover and assets of the top TNCs such as General Electric or Wal-Mart with the gross domestic product of nation-states. While not wishing to deny the vividness of this crude comparison, we should be aware of its analytical limitations in assessing both the relative resources of these institutions and the nature of their authority. Also, there is an increasing number of small firms that seek an international presence in order to provide their services across borders. In large part this has to do with the increasing appeal of so-called "world standards" and global presence in purchasing a service or material product. Thus, the United Nations' (UNCTAD 2000) estimate of 45,000 parent-TNCs existent in the mid-1990s is likely to have increased significantly over the ensuing decade and now includes many little-known startup firms that have local joint ventures or affiliates in several countries.

Trading organizations spanning territorial frontiers predate the modern nation-state. Privately owned European corporations such as the East India Company and Hudson Bay Company played a major part in the establishment of overseas colonies of their parent nation from the seventeenth to nineteenth centuries (Hertner & Jones 1986). But the contemporary significance of TNCs can be traced to their varying contributions to the integration of global markets and, more controversially, to the possible convergent effects of "globalization" over the latter half of the twentieth century.

FOREIGN DIRECT INVESTMENT

In the mid-1980s the overall level of foreign direct investment (FDI) taking place between countries overtook that of exports and imports (Hirst & Thompson 1999). There was a major shift from the previously dominant pattern of entrepot trade in which western countries imported raw materials in order to manufacture finished goods for home consumption or for export. As Hirst and Thompson point out, FDI had actually reached a comparatively high level before World War I. However, the nature of foreign investment in the latter part of the twentieth century was fundamentally different from that of the earlier period. Earlier, FDI was largely composed of portfolio investment by European financiers in the material infrastructure of other countries. Today, it is most often carried out within the structure of a single TNC or its affiliates or associated partners in a cross-national supply chain. Dicken (2003: 200–1) sees this temporal change as marking movement between an earlier mode of capitalist investment described by Marx as the circuit of commodity capital to one of finance capital and, most recently, to a global circuit of productive capital.

TNCS AND NATION-STATES

Perhaps of equal analytical significance is the manner in which cross-national transactions now often take place within an "internal market" of bureaucratically structured relations between actors at different stages of the value-adding chain. That is to say that the largest TNCs either exercise direct hierarchical control over operations performed in-house or have a nodal position on global supply networks that enables them to shape outcomes according to managerial priorities rather than to short-term movements in external prices (Dicken 2003: 17).

This shift in the nature of cross-national transactions can be seen as changing the basis upon which national governments manage their economic balance of trade quite significantly. For example, the internal (transfer) value placed on a part-manufactured component or product can be shaped by the desire of TNCs to minimize the amount of tax or tariff paid either to the country in which the exported component was produced or to the recipient importing country where it is to be finally assembled. The true cost of its original production may not be reflected in its "sale" price, and therefore in the national accounts of the supplying country.

In other respects also national governments often negotiate with TNCs from a position of greater or lesser dependency in a manner that has a direct effect on their domestic agenda. Where, as in, say, Nigeria, some 80 percent of capital investment and recorded national income derive from FDI, the local presence of TNCs is critical. Even in older economies such as that of the UK, up to 40 percent of local capital investment can derive from overseas. Indeed, some authors on business strategy see TNCs as becoming one of the most significant agencies of global governance (Ohmae 1995). Nation-states are often seen to be competing with one another to obtain FDI in a "locational tournament." For example, governments can offer advantageous low tax and/or low tariff regimes. Sometimes particular regions are designated as "export processing zones" (EPZ) with zero tariffs on materials imported simply for local processing and immediate reexport. In general, EPZs are designed to provide employment for low-skilled labor. The attraction for the TNC is that of easy access to a cheap, stable, disciplined labor force (Froebel et al. 1980). In other cases the existence of a large potential consumer market that is best serviced "close to market," such as exists in North America, Europe, and East Asia (particularly China and India), attracts investment in the design and assembly of products to suit local tastes (Dicken 2003). For retail chains such as Wal-Mart, Carrefour, and Tesco, as for professional service firms like financial accountants, a local presence is a prerequisite for delivery of their particular direct service.

The country's ability to attract so-called "centers of excellence" (Cantwell & Santangelo 2000) or knowledge-intensive plants such as R&D laboratories, which service the needs of the TNC throughout the world, is the ultimate prize. It has been described by one influential political theorist (Reich 1990) as the future "work of nations." By contrast, where the host country provides only extractive commodities such as mineral oil, metals, or precious stones, the processing of these materials can often be performed elsewhere unless the host state acts to prevent this and/or to reallocate investment income to the development of alternative sectors.

Some state governments consciously pursue a strategy of sponsoring "national champions" or locally based TNCs which occupy a significant place in global markets. The French government has, traditionally, been most overt in its pursuance of what is sometimes described as a "mercantilist" position. In practice, most governments tend to protect their "national interest" in important markets. In developing countries it has become part of conventional wisdom to attempt to create a hub of locally owned large business conglomerates from which to negotiate entry to world markets through joint ventures and learning alliances with more specialized TNCs from the developed world: Japan and South Korea are their models (Amsden 1989). Such government-sponsored conglomerates are often seen as serving the dual function of "creating a local middle class" (Evans 1979).

TNC STRUCTURES AND STRATEGIES

From the viewpoint of the TNC acting as a "rational actor," a number of economic models have been put forward to explain its choice of strategy. These are put most succinctly in Dunning's (1980) "eclectic paradigm." The firm must first possess "ownership-specific" advantages, particularly by comparison with local producers. These may range from greater technological or managerial expertise to its more exotic reputation. Second, the firm must see advantage in keeping its capabilities within its own organization rather than licensing them or subcontracting them to a local supplier. This condition will evidently affect its willingness to share its knowledge with others, or even to allow local employees to appropriate this knowledge. Third, there must be location-specific advantages of the kind described above to make the greater risk of overseas investment worthwhile. These can be expressed in terms of a variety of numerical indices such as geographical differences in labor productivity, wage costs, consumer tastes, sovereign (government) risk, and so on. Other models deployed by economists are modeled on sequential "learning" by the company through exporting or through the overseas assembly of product models that are considered outdated on the home market (see Vernon 1966 on the product cycle model). As markets have become increasingly open to global competition, such sequential models of overseas learning have become less applicable. For example, the Volkswagen Santana, produced in China since it was phased out in Germany in the 1970s, has recently been replaced by a range specifically designed for production in China. Perhaps more importantly, specialized producers of services for global supply chains, as well as so-called dot.com website suppliers such as Amazon, target a cross-national market from the outset, that is, they are global by design.

The analysis of the internal organizational structure of control within the TNC can, therefore, be seen as having an important significance for wider society in both its host and parent countries. Bartlett and Ghoshal (1989) summed prevailing wisdom on organizational form in a four-part categorization of TNC control structure.

- The *global* company based on cost advantages through centralized control of a standardized product and production processes conducted in plants around the world. Examples include early US assembly plants such as automobiles and kitchen equipment. Nowadays, this mode is likely to be found among specialized component suppliers such as microchip producers.

- The *international* company that exploits the knowledge and design capabilities of head office through diffusion and local adaptation in local plants operating under close surveillance. Examples include most final assembly (original equipment) suppliers, but this also can include quasi-professional services offering formulaic solutions such as management consultancy.

- The *multinational* company that seeks to meet the particular needs of local or regional markets and offers a wide mandate to local managers. Examples include retail chains, locally regulated professionals, or any close to market production.

- The *transnational* company in which head office is guided by the knowledge of local needs transmitted upwards by relatively autonomous local managers. It seeks to synthesize these experiences in a manner that allows lessons to be learned across diverse locations. Examples tend to be taken from among currently successful firms such as Unilever, GEC, and ABB, but in general Japanese firms are seen by most prescriptive writers as best in this process of "bottom-up" learning.

A fifth mode, put forward by Hedlund (1986), is that of *heterarchy*. In this structural form, horizontal communication between overseas affiliates becomes a primary method of information passing, which may not involve going through head office. It is most likely that this will occur only where the passing of operational information can enhance immediate efficacy or avoid a crisis. But the widespread use of unmonitored email and chat rooms might well facilitate the emergence of such "communities of practice" in sectors such as oil drilling, logging, construction – or financial trading. In an exploratory study which combined case histories with a sample survey, Nohria and Ghoshal (1997) suggested that the most innovative TNCs were those that adopted a *differentiated network* approach in which affiliates were treated differently according to the "complexity" of their local context and the level of local "resources."

As is suggested in the examples above, some analytic importance can be attached to the sector in which the TNC operates. But, equally, this fivefold structural taxonomy has been treated by some writers as shaped by a temporally staged evolution from the export-driven centralized organization to the dispersed and devolved structures of locally autonomous producers or servicers. On the other hand, the sheer size and internal complexity of its operations may be seen to trigger a devolution of authority. Other contingent factors can include those named by Nohria and Ghoshal (1997) as the contextual complexity and available capabilities to be found in the host country. Under the heading of "complexity" these authors subsume a widespread condition imposed by host governments that local affiliates must be partially owned and/or directed by local citizens. While intended to maintain some direct local control over the management of affiliate organization, these appointments can sometimes contribute to widespread accusations of corruption made against TNCs (Kaufmann 1999).

A different explanation is offered by cultural and institutional theorists adopting a more cognitive approach to strategic formulation. Perlmutter (1969) suggested that the values and interests of corporate elites encouraged one of four predispositions amongst TNC expatriate managers. These were ethnocentrism, polycentrism, regiocentrism, and geocentricism. Again, there is the suggestion that managers move along a learning curve from a home-country dominance in thinking to a recognition of diversity in their local operations, moving toward greater rationalization across regions and, finally, to an integrated view of global strategy matching local capabilities. By contrast, comparative institutionalists such as Whitley (2003) tend to subscribe to the view that formal control structures within the TNC, including those determining job and career structures, are shaped more permanently by the back-home institutions of the parent firm. In what has been the most cited study of managerial values carried out within a single TNC (IBM) in the 1970s, Hofstede (1980) discovered that what he described as "core work values" varied significantly across the 40 countries in which the study was conducted. Empirical evidence produced from a wide sample of TNCs by Harzing and Sorge (2003) suggested that whilst internal control structures appeared to be shaped by those of the parent country, strategic views on the external environment held by TNC executives tend to converge on a pattern shaped by size of company and its sector or industry. Perhaps, then, it is not surprising that the more recent ethnographic work of D'Iribarne (1996) suggests the translation of centrally designed formal control structures can vary in different nationally and locally specific contexts, as can the enactment of "core work values."

HUMAN RESOURCE MANAGEMENT AND CIVIL RIGHTS

The study of human resource management (HRM) or employment practices within TNCs tends to dichotomize between a focus on expatriate management development and another on the workplace conditions of locally recruited operatives. Within these themes there are varying foci. The corporate career and personal needs of expatriate managers provides one set of prescriptive literatures, together with the desirability of a sensitivity toward local cultures (Dowling et al. 1994). Relationships with indigenous managers, particularly in the transfer of technical knowledge, are another more conflictual focus (Bhagat et al. 2002). What seems evident is that TNCs are generally likely to retain expatriates in a number of key functions, such as local financial executive or product development, whilst employing indigenous staff in other functions. Often this appears to be motivated by a desire to reduce salary costs and to satisfy the conditions imposed by the host government. However, over the close of the twentieth century it became evident that an emergent class of highly mobile executives was being appointed to senior positions within TNCs irrespective of nationality. Thus, a Brazilian was appointed to head the Japanese car manufacturer Nissan by its French shareholder, Renault. A US chief executive was externally recruited to the old German family-owned firm of auto and electronic component suppliers, Robert Bosch, and so on.

Knowledge transfer also provides an important theme in the discussion of workplace practices. In the 1980s, research interest focused on the so-called Japanization of work organization, in particular upon the adoption of teamworking and the self-regulation of quality standards within work groups in TNCs' affiliates across different national locations (Boyer et al. 1999). In the following decade, the emphasis tended to shift to the wider effects of rationalization undertaken within global supply chains, in particular to the effects of outsourcing low-skilled work to low-wage countries. In the early years of the present century, this movement spread to many routine office and sales functions of large western firms. This movement might be seen as confirming Reich's (1990) earlier notion of an emergent division of labor across relatively stable national systems in which "mature" economies rely on their capacity to produce knowledge workers ("symbolic analysts"). The response of labor unions in the West has been largely focused on obtaining better working conditions for TNC employees in developing countries with a view to equalizing employment opportunities for their local members in the parent company. However, the effect of cross-national competition for low-skilled jobs will inevitably bring about domestic tensions that may challenge the notion of a stable cross-country division of labor (Storper 1997).

The role of the TNC in eroding boundaries to national markets has evidently been increasingly significant over the latter half of the twentieth century. In general, the literature is dichotomized into the managerially oriented study of organizational structures and strategies and that which describes and critiques the negative effects of the TNC as manifested in "globalization." There is a case for greater ethnographic study of the effect of TNCs on local communities in a manner that might provide a better qualitative understanding of both viewpoints. Most studies are conducted through questionnaires remotely designed and administered by western scholars to a sample of interested executives. Finally, it seems important to recognize that TNC strategies are bureaucratically conceived and can, given sufficient political will and understanding of their effects, be bureaucratically constrained.

SEE ALSO: Capitalism, Social Institutions of; Culture, Organizations and; Organization Theory; Organizations and the Theory of the Firm; Outsourcing; Supply Chains; Transnationalism

REFERENCES AND SUGGESTED READINGS

Amsden, A. (1989) *Asia's Next Giant: South Korea and Late Industrialization*. Oxford University Press, Oxford.

Bartlett, C. A. & Ghoshal, S. (1989) *Managing Across Borders: The Transnational Solution*. Harvard Business School Press, Boston.

Bhagat, R. S., Kedia, B. L., Harveston, P. D., & Triandis, H. C. (2002) Cultural Variations in the Cross-Border Transfer of Organizational Knowledge: An Integrative Framework. *Academy of Management Review* 27(2): 204–21.

Boyer, R., Charron, E., Jurgens, U., & Tolliday, S. (1999) *Between Imitation and Innovation: The Transfer and Hybridization of Productive Models in the Automobile Industry*. Oxford University Press, Oxford.

Cantwell, J. & Santangelo, G. D. (2000) Capitalism, Profits, and Innovation in the New Techno-Economic Paradigm. *Journal of Evolutionary Economics* 10: 131–57.

Dicken, P. (2003) *Global Shift: Reshaping the Global Economic Map in the 21st Century*. Sage, London.

D'Iribarne, P. (1996) The Usefulness of an Ethnographic Approach to the International Study of Organizations. *International Studies of Management and Organization* 26(4): 30–47.

Dowling, P. J., Schuler, R. S., & Welch, D. E. (1994) *International Dimensions of Human Resource Management*. Wadsworth, Belmont, CA.

Dunning, J. H. (1980) Towards an Eclectic Theory of International Production: Some Empirical Tests. *Journal of International Business Studies* 11: 9–31.

Evans, P. (1979) *Dependent Development: The Alliance of Multinational, State, and Local Capital in Brazil*. Princeton University Press, Princeton.

Froebel, F., Heinrichs, J., & Kreye, O. (1980) *The New International Division of Labour*. Cambridge University Press, Cambridge.

Harzing, W.-W. & Sorge, A. (2003) The Relative Impact of Country of Origin and Universal Contingencies on Internationalization Strategies and Corporate Control in Multinational Enterprises: Worldwide and European Perspectives. *Organization Studies* 24(2): 187–214.

Hedlund, G. (1986) The Hypermodern MNC: A Heterarchy? *Human Resource Management* 25(1): 9–35.

Hertner, P. & Jones, G. (Eds.) (1986) *Multinationals: Theory and History*. Gower, Aldershot.

Hirst, P. & Thompson, G. (1999) *Globalization in Question: The International Economy and the Possibilities of Governance*. Polity Press, Cambridge.

Hofstede, G. (1980) *Culture's Consequences*. Sage, Beverly Hills, CA.

Kaufmann, D. (1999) *Governance Matters*. World Bank, Washington, DC.

Nohria, N. & Ghoshal, S. (1997) *The Differentiated Network: Organizing Multinational Corporations for Value Creation*. Jossey Bass, San Francisco.

Ohmae, K. (1995) *The End of the National State: The Rise of Regional Economies*. Free Press, New York.

Perlmutter, H. (1969) The Tortuous Evolution of the Multinational Corporation. *Columbia Journal of World Business* 5(1): 9–18.

Reich, R. B. (1990) *The Work of Nations: Preparing Ourselves for 21st-Century Capitalism*. Alfred Knopf, New York.

Storper, M. (1997) *The Regional World*. Guilford, New York.

UNCTAD (2000) *World Investment Report*. United Nations Organization, New York.

Vernon, R. (1966) International Investment and International Trade in the Product Cycle. *Quarterly Journal of Economics* 80: 190–207.

Whitley, R. (2003) *Divergent Capitalisms: The Social Structuring and Change of Business Systems*. Oxford University Press, Oxford.

transparency and global change

Burkart Holzner

The word "transparent" traditionally means the capacity of light to pass through clear glass so that one can see the things behind it. Transparency also means open, frank, candid, and true, as opposed to opaque or secret. Today, the concept "transparency" in sociology refers to the globally emerging value (and its derivative norms) of information disclosure and access. It asserts that all centers of authority have a "duty to disclose information" and that publics and citizens have a "right to know." The value of transparency does not stand alone; it is part of information value systems that include also its counter-values. Thus, the rules for openness are often circumscribed by norms limiting disclosure, such as secrecy, privacy, confidentiality, and others. There are obviously many different kinds of information linked to these norms, such as personal data, public information, proprietary, and others. However, transparency norms are increasingly expected to be followed by governments, international agencies, professions, corporations, foundations, and civil society organizations.

Transparency as a value is historically recent. It had its origin early in the eighteenth century in Sweden's law of information freedom and later in the US Constitution. However, only in the last decades of the twentieth century were the corresponding norms adopted by states on a nearly global scale. Prior to the recent breakthroughs to create open access of information, most centers of authority relied on secrecy as a matter of course. The history of transparency is linked to the history of global change. The first major political impulses in this direction arose in the Protestant mobilization against corruption in the Catholic Church of the sixteenth century. Much later, in 1766, only Sweden established rules for information freedom. About a decade later, as the US declared independence and wrote its Constitution, free speech and the free flow of open information became novel, liberal institutions pointing in the direction of transparency. In the entire nineteenth century virtually no country adopted such values. The Scandinavian countries followed the example of Sweden only in the early twentieth century.

Starting slowly in the 1970s and more rapidly in the 1980s and the following decades, more and more countries adopted freedom of information laws. According to the Freedominfo.org *Global Survey: Freedom of Information and Access to Government Record Laws Around the World* (May 2004), 50 countries have adopted formal freedom of information acts, and another 30 countries are on their way to adopting such laws. There exists a similar growth in the number of countries that became electoral democracies: according to Freedominfo.org, in 1987 there were 66 democratic countries, but by 2001 there were 121.

Another innovation in the direction of transparency came from Sweden in 1809. It was the creation of the office of the national ombudsman. The ombudsman mediates between government and citizens, and serves to improve communications between them. The other

Scandinavian countries followed Sweden's lead only in the twentieth century. At the close of the 1980s there were 21 countries that had adopted the office. By 2000 there were 111. Indicators for transparency, such as freedom of information laws, electoral democracies, and the establishment of ombudsmen, show a rapidly rising tide of transparency in the last two decades of the twentieth century and beyond.

The number of countries adopting specific laws on transparency norms grew in the late 1990s and in the early twenty-first century. These rules have affected almost all domains of power and influence, such as governments, corporations, accountants, lawyers, health professionals, foundations, and civil society organizations. In addition, many significant organizations find it advantageous to adopt transparency practices on a voluntary basis. Voluntary disclosure practices tend to enhance an organization's legitimacy and freedom from corruption. Further, the norms of transparency are spreading far beyond the countries that initiated them. This circumstance poses the challenge of developing internationally accepted specific transparency measures, for example in the accounting rules for financial disclosures across countries. The International Accounting Standards Board has adopted this challenge for its global profession. Similar "harmonization" of measures is evolving in health care, education, and many other professions.

Corruption is not compatible with transparency. Corruption in any rich or poor country is by now recognized as a grave danger to the public good and a threat to good governance in states and corporations. As late as the early 1990s many governments and international agencies did not consider corruption in other nations a cause for international intervention. It was assumed that the national sovereignty of even blatantly exploitative governments was an insurmountable barrier that provided immunity for the perpetrators. This changed when global anti-corruption movements effectively challenged national sovereignty as a source of immunity for corrupt high officials and persuaded international agencies like the Organization for Economic Cooperation and Development (OECD), the World Bank, and many governments to establish international treaties inhibiting corruption and bribery. The largest and most effective global civil society organization in this field is Transparency International, founded in 1993. It has expanded to become a worldwide network in approximately 80 countries, with a high level of influence in the domestic affairs of these countries, and in international agencies and governments. Transparency has become a major strategy in the effort to improve local as well as international governance.

The spread of transparency as a public value and the upsurge in national and international transparency norms is a very recent and rapidly growing phenomenon. Several increasingly global trends converged to produce the energy for the transparency phenomenon: the increase in global economic interdependence, the spread of demands for civil rights, and the arrival of breathtaking innovations in information technology. Economic interdependence also includes an increase in political interdependence: the demand for transparency soon became a necessity because global economic transactions require the availability of reliable economic and governmental information. Without this, trust at a distance across cultural barriers and boundaries would not be possible. The demands for transparency were a natural outgrowth of the movements for civil rights, women's rights, and consumer rights that started in the West and spread around the world, enhanced by the abolition of colonialism. Anti-colonialism became a movement for autonomy in all former colonies. Initially, developing nations turned to nationalism; gradually, movements of responsible government and transparency are arising in many developing nations. In addition, the information revolution has made rapid communication and the creation of information infrastructures possible, and thereby made transparency technically viable in global change. This has a remarkable effect on the privacy of individuals: technology in the hands of governmental and commercial information systems produces comprehensive profiles of individuals, such as credit records, the value of homes, health data, and more. This development is also part of changing information value systems. It is very much in dispute.

The combination of global transformations, value changes, and the power of information and communication technology has created a historically new constellation of information values. This constellation includes the transparency values of openness – autonomy, accountability, freedom of expression – as well as its counter-values of secrecy and surveillance, with the value of privacy between them. The constellation of information values will have different profiles as perceptions of societal threats or security and general moral frameworks shift. Different interests of stakeholders virtually always lead to different interpretations of accessible information, inevitably provoking public debates.

Global change and intense interactions among regions and nations have given rise to novel border-crossing solidarity formations. The treaties that established the European Union as a major power and supranational political institution are the most obvious example of such emerging transnational solidarities and of the way in which they are being achieved. The diverse transactions that are necessary beyond cultural and political boundaries have become a focus for creating trust-building efforts. Valid transparency of important information is inevitably demanded in such situations. Trust at a distance is based on some form of certification of validity and reliability in the disclosed information. This form of trust at a distance is substantially different from "trust up close" among friends or relatives, or networks of shared commonalities. In fact, trust at a distance requires avoidance of conflicts of interest, cronyism, and insider privileges. Transparency requirements can actually limit or even destroy trust up close. It does need a relatively high degree of public information and formalization as against the friendly whisper.

The sources energizing the public demand for transparency are quite diverse, but they have converging effects. Colossal social upheavals, such as the defeat of Nazi Germany in World War II, have generated massive shifts in societies' moral frameworks. The crimes of the Holocaust and of criminal medical experiments on human subjects brought such outrage that massive reforms were called for by international publics. Certain transparency measures such as the establishment of "informed consent" rules were among the many changes that evolved from the catastrophe of the war. Bringing transparency to national histories became a necessity in order to establish justice for past governmental crimes. Historical transparency has become a major factor in the countries in transition from authoritarianism to democracy, as in Germany, Japan, and in many countries more recently, such as South Africa and Argentina. Major sources of value changes also include lesser events such as scandals as value-rational motives for reforms to adopt transparency. Scandals are very frequently drivers toward transparency – as in recent cases of corporate scandals in the US, or the scandals resulting from malfeasance in other professions such as accounting and medical research, or outright criminal acts on the part of prominent officials. Scandals call for repairs in the social rules and they often call for a shift of the socially accepted moral framework. Not infrequently, acts that were acceptable in the past become unacceptable later. Periods of legal remedial action often increase transparency in a more or less irreversible manner.

Social movements addressing such issues as government accountability, corporate malfeasance, environmental risks, and security problems invariably press for relevant information. They have become powerful sources for transparency demands within countries and globally. No one wants to deal with unknown risks from such sources as faulty products, environmental hazards, and government or corporate corruption. The structures for increasing the flow of information include legal provisions, such as freedom of information acts, ombudsmen, and court actions, market necessities, or the activities of civil society organizations such as the American Civil Liberty Union in the US and State Watch in the European Union.

There are further factors that encourage people to turn to transparency voluntarily. The information technology revolution has made it possible to generate and record information on such things as the value of real estate, the prices of goods, personal data, educational certificates, highway maps, sources of direction, and much more. This means that the historically prevailing condition of opacity – the absence of information about most things – is today shrinking. Many opportunities to use (and misuse) such information have opened up. Under these circumstances, the adoption of transparency can be an important advantage for individuals in visible positions, governments, and corporations. The rapid spread of governmental and corporate

codes of conduct is a function of this phenomenon. Corporate codes of conduct invariably emphasize the need for ethical conduct and transparency.

Very practical and matter-of-course transactions require transparency in markets. In all these various sources of transparency demands there is a need for certifying the validity of truth claims made by the information-disclosing agency. The age of transparency, if we may call it that, is also an era of evaluation and certification, not only on the part of governmental regulators and in professional codes of ethics and their enforcement, but also by professional evaluation researchers in many fields of activity.

The social fact of transparency as a new globally relevant value also includes, of course, currents of resistance. Transparency was a child of the Enlightenment, but it is rapidly becoming a strategy for fighting corruption and authoritarianism in developing countries. These movements transcend civilizational boundaries and local cultural differences. The forms of transparency can vary, but transparency itself is always part of efforts that create open, democratic societies.

SEE ALSO: Authority and Legitimacy; Capitalism; Civil Rights Movement; Civil Society; Collective Trauma; Corruption; Democracy; Development: Political Economy; Social Change; Speaking Truth to Power: Science and Policy; Values: Global

REFERENCES AND SUGGESTED READINGS

Brin, D. (1998) *The Transparent Society: Will Technology Force Us to Choose Between Privacy and Freedom?* Perseus Books, Reading, MA.

Finel, B. I. & Lord, K. M. (2000) *Power and Conflict in the Age of Transparency*. Palgrave, New York.

Florini, A. (2003) *The Coming Democracy: New Rules for Running a New World*. Island Press, Washington, DC.

Held, D., McGrew, A., Goldblatt, D., & Perraton, J. (1999) *Global Transformations*. Stanford University Press, Stanford.

Holzner, B. & Holzner, L. (2002) The Transparency Syndrome in Global Change: A Sociological Concept Paper. *EKISTICS: The Problems and Science of Human Settlements* 152–62.

Robertson, R. (1992) *Globalization: Social Theory and Global Culture.* Sage, Newbury Park, CA.

Stiglitz, J. (2002) *Globalization and Its Discontents.* W. W. Norton, New York.

triangulation

Norman K. Denzin

Triangulation refers to the application and combination of several research methodologies in the study of the same phenomenon. The concept of triangulation, as in the action of making a triangle, may be traced to the Greeks and the origins of modern mathematics. Introduced in the social sciences in the 1950s (Campbell & Fiske 1959), heavily criticized in the 1980s (see Silverman 1985; Lincoln & Guba 1985; Guba & Lincoln 1989) and 1990s (Flick 2004), triangulation is a postpositivist methodological strategy. It has recently returned to favor as a new generation of scholars is drawn to a mixed, or multimethod, approach to social inquiry (Teddlie & Tashakkori 2003).

When introduced in the social sciences the term functioned as a bridge between quantitative and qualitative epistemologies. It was seen as a way of helping qualitative researchers become more rigorous, perhaps allowing them to address a methodological inferiority associated with "a kind of stepchild complex" (Kamberelis & Dimitriadis 2004: 2). Advocates of mixed methods research argue that it allows them to answer questions that other methodologies taken alone cannot. Further, it provides "better inferences based on a greater diversity of divergent views" (Teddlie & Tashakkori 2003: 14–15).

The use of multiple methods in an investigation so as to overcome the weaknesses or biases of a single method is sometimes called multiple operationalism. Indeed, triangulation has become a metaphor for methodological integration, of the postpositivist variety, in the social sciences. The metaphor evokes multiple meanings, including (1) a synonym for mixed method, multimethod, or mixed model designs (Teddlie & Tashakkori 2003: 11, 14); (2) a method of validation; (3) the integration of different mixed-methods approaches; (4) combining quantitative and qualitative methodologies in the same study (Erzberger & Kelle 2003).

However, the history of the term, its uses and meanings, is not without contradictions. For example, some distinguish triangulation from those forms of multiple methods research which are informed by poststructuralism and cultural studies (Richardson 2000). In such projects "there are multiple standards for understanding the social world (epistemological relativism) . . . therefore diversity and contradictions should be incorporated within research accounts" (Spicer 2004: 298; see also Denzin 1989: 246). In contrast, Saukko (2003: 23) observes that the "classical aim of triangulation is to combine different kinds of material or methods to see whether they corroborate one another."

NEED FOR TRIANGULATION

Qualitative research is inherently multimethod in focus. However, the use of multiple methods, or triangulation, reflects an attempt to secure an in-depth understanding of the phenomenon in question. Objective reality can never be captured. We only know a thing through its representations. Viewed thusly, critical or interpretive triangulation is not a tool or a strategy of validation, but an alternative to validation. The combination of multiple methodological practices, empirical materials, perspectives, and observers in a single study is best understood as a strategy which adds authenticity, trustworthiness, credibility, rigor, breadth, complexity, richness, and depth to any inquiry.

The social sciences, in varying degrees, use the following research methods and strategies: social surveys, experiments and quasi-experiments, participant observation, critical performance ethnography, interviewing, case study and life history construction, grounded theory, action inquiry, testimony, unobtrusive methods, including archival materials, visual methods, autoethnography, focus groups, and discourse analysis. Each of these methods and strategies has inherent weaknesses, which range from an inability to enter realistically into the subject's life-world in experiments and surveys, to the problems of reflecting change and process in unobtrusive methods, the attention to rival interpretive factors in participant observation, to an excessive reliance on paper and pencil techniques in surveys and interviewing.

The realities to which sociological methods are fitted are not fixed. The social world is socially constructed and its meanings, to the observers and those observed, are constantly changing. As a consequence no single research method will ever capture all of the changing features of the social world under study. Each research method implies a different interpretation of the world and suggests different lines of action that the observer may take toward the research process. The meanings of methods are constantly changing, and each investigator brings different interpretations to bear upon the very research methods that are utilized. For those reasons, a productive search for sound interpretations of the social world employs triangulation strategies.

HERMENEUTICS OF INTERPRETATION

What is sought in triangulation is an interpretation that illuminates and reveals the subject matter in a thickly contextualized manner. A triangulated interpretation reflects the phenomenon as a process that is relational and interactive. The interpretation engulfs the subject matter, incorporating all of the understandings the researcher's diverse methods reveal about the phenomenon.

A hermeneutic interpretation does not remove the investigators from the study, but rather places them directly in the circle of interpretation. While it is commonplace in the social sciences to place the investigator outside the interpretive process, hence asking research methods to produce the interpretation that is sought, hermeneutic interpretation dictates that the circle of interpretation can never be avoided, but it must be entered the right way. Triangulation is the appropriate way of entering the circle of interpretation. The researcher is part of the interpretation.

TYPES AND STRATEGIES OF TRIANGULATION

While it is commonly assumed that triangulation is the use of multiple methods in the study of the same phenomenon, this is only one form of the strategy. There are four basic types of triangulation: (1) data triangulation involving time, space, and persons; (2) investigator triangulation, which consists of the use of multiple rather than single observers; (3) theory triangulation, which consists of using more than one theoretical scheme in the interpretation of the phenomenon; (4) methodological triangulation, which involves using more than one method and may consist of within-method or between-method strategies. There is also multiple triangulation, where the researcher combines in one investigation multiple observers, theoretical perspectives, sources of data, and methodologies. Additional types of triangulation have been identified, including those labeled reflexive, structural, and multipurpose.

Critical or interpretive triangulation can be viewed as an alternative or incitement to traditional postpositivist forms of validation. Interpretive triangulation opens the space for conversations about how a text authorizes or legitimizes itself through the use of multiple voices and representational forms. These forms may act as catalysts to transgressive validities and to a politics of resistance (Lather 1993).

PROBLEMS IN DESIGNING MULTIPLE-TRIANGULATED INVESTIGATIONS

There are at least four basic problems to be confronted in carrying out multiple triangulated research. These are (1) locating a common subject of analysis to which multiple methods, observers, and theories can be applied; (2) reconciling discrepant findings and interpretations; (3) novelty, or the location of a problem that has not been investigated before; and (4) restrictions of time and money.

The location of a common subject of analysis can only be resolved through a clear understanding of the question the investigator wishes to answer. Divergent and discrepant findings are to be expected. Each inspection of the phenomenon is likely to yield different pictures, images, and findings. Novel or new problems are often, upon inspection, not new, but merely manifestations of familiar topics previously examined from different perspectives and questions. Restrictions of time and money are the least problematic, for if investigators are thoroughly committed to understanding a problem area they will persist in examining it even under difficult circumstances.

CRITICISMS OF TRIANGULATION

It must be noted that the method of triangulation is not without its critics. Several criticisms have been brought to bear upon the traditional treatments of the triangulation strategy.

Data Triangulation

Silverman (1985) has argued that a positivistic bias underlies the triangulation position and that this is most evident in the concept of data triangulation. He argued that a hypothesis-testing orientation is present when authors argue that hypotheses that survive multiple tests contain more validity than those subjected to just one test. He also suggested that to assume that the same empirical unit can be measured more than once is inconsistent with the interactionist view of emergence and novelty in the field situation. If, as Silverman argued, all social action is situated and unique, then the same unit, behavior, or experience can never be observed twice. Each occurrence is unique. Patton (1980: 331) has correctly noted that the comparison of multiple data sources will "seldom lead to a single, totally consistent picture. It is best not to expect everything to turn out the same."

Investigator Triangulation

No two investigators ever observe the same phenomenon in exactly the same way. Guba and Lincoln (1989: 307) suggest that it is a mistake to "expect corroboration of one investigator by another." The argument that greater reliability of observations can be obtained by using more than one observer is thus indefensible. This does not mean, however, that multiple observers or investigators should not be used. Douglas (1976) has suggested that team research (a similar term for the use of multiple observers) allows an investigator to gain multiple perspectives on a social situation. Members of a research team have a multiplier effect on

the research – each adds more than just his or her presence to the knowledge that is gained about the situation being studied.

Theory Triangulation

If facts are theory-determined, then theoretical triangulation consists of using more than one theoretical scheme to interpret the phenomenon at hand. Seen thusly, this form of triangulation helps reveal complexity. However, Lincoln and Guba (1985: 307) argue: "The use of multiple theories as a triangulation technique seems to us to be both epistemologically unsound and empirically empty." They base this conclusion on the argument that facts are theory-determined. Theoretical triangulation simply asks the researcher to be aware of the multiple ways in which the phenomenon may be interpreted. It does not demand, nor does it ask, that facts be consistent with two or more theories.

Methodological Triangulation

This strategy takes the position that single-method studies are no longer defensible in the social sciences. The researcher using different methods should not expect findings generated by different methods to fall into a coherent picture. They will not, for each method yields a different picture and slice of reality. What is critical is that different pictures be allowed to emerge. Methodological triangulation allows this to happen.

Multiple Triangulation

Fielding and Fielding (1986) offered a critical interpretation of this strategy, arguing that multiple triangulation is the equivalent for research methods of correlation in data analysis. They both represent extreme forms of eclecticism. Further, they suggest that theoretic triangulation does not reduce bias, nor does methodological triangulation necessarily increase validity. If there is a case for triangulation, it is because we should combine theories and methods carefully and purposefully with the intention of adding breadth or depth to our analysis, but not for the purpose of pursuing "objective truth."

The goal of multiple triangulation is a fully grounded interpretive research approach. Objective reality will never be captured. In-depth understanding, not validity, is sought in any interpretive study. Multiple triangulation should never be eclectic. It cannot, however, be meaningfully compared to correlation analysis in statistical studies.

ALTERNATIVE VALIDITIES

It is now understood that there are multiple forms of validity, many different ways of authorizing text and its arguments (Lather 1993; Saukko 2003: 18). These ways supplement, if not replace, triangulation as a preferred strategy of validation. Saukko (2003: 19–22) reviews three alternative validities. Dialogic validity asks how well a text captures the point of view of the person being studied. Deconstructive validity addresses a text's historicity, its hidden politics, and its underlying binary oppositions. Contextual validity asks how a text anchors itself in material reality, in concrete historical contexts, in the political economy of daily life. Each of these validities problematizes the positivist concept of a single truth. This opens the door for considering different ways of extending the logic of classic postpositivist triangulation.

ALTERNATIVE PARADIGMS FOR COMBINING METHODOLOGIES

Richardson (2000) disputes the concept of triangulation, asserting that the central image for qualitative inquiry is the crystal, or the prism, and not the triangle. Mixed-genre texts, including performance texts, have more than three sides. Like crystals, montage in film, the jazz solo, or the pieces in a quilt, the mixed-genre text can assume an infinite variety of shapes, substances, and transmutations. Crystals or prisms reflect externalities. They refract within themselves. This creates different colors and patterns, casting off in different directions.

Saukko, building on Richardson (2000), also challenges the classic postpositivist model of triangulation because the model presumes a fixed or semi-fixed view of reality, and a view of methods as magnifying glasses that reflect or reveal this reality. The notion of prism works well with dialogic and deconstructive validity. Like the prism, these validities draw attention to the multiple ways reality is constructed. Classic triangulation disappears under the prism model. Still, with its emphasis on fluid reality, the prism model gives too little attention to history and social context. Thus, Saukko advances a material-semiotic perspective. This model looks at how material reality defracts rather then refracts vision. A defraction model shows how research is a material practice that "alters or creates reality" (Saukko 2003: 27). This visual defraction model is then compared to a participatory, dialogic model where multiple dialogues between multiple realities are created and encouraged. A dialogic framework attunes the researcher to the many different voices at work in a concrete situation. The scholar seeks out and incorporates multiple points of view in the research. This expands the egalitarian base of the project, and enhances its claims to strong objectivity; that is, to the commitment to take into account multiple perspectives (p. 29).

THE INCOMPATIBILITY THESIS

The incompatibility thesis disputes the key claim of triangulation, namely that methods and perspectives can be combined. The incompatibility thesis argues "compatibility between quantitative and qualitative methods is impossible due to incompatibility of the paradigms that underlie the methods" (Teddlie & Tashakkori 2003: 14–15). The incompatibility argument potentially discredits triangulation as a research strategy. Under this scenario researchers who try to combine methods that are incompatible "are doomed to failure due to the inherent differences in the philosophies underlying them" (p. 19). Others disagree with this conclusion, and some contend that the incompatibility thesis has been largely discredited because researchers have demonstrated that it is possible to successfully use a mixed methods approach.

There are several schools of thought on this thesis, including the four identified by Teddlie and Tashakkori: (1) the complementary strengths, mixed methods model; (2) the single paradigm mixed methods model; (3) the dialectical mixed methods model; and (4) the multiple paradigm mixed methods model.

Researchers using the complementary strengths, mixed methods model believe that the use of mixed methods is possible, but that the methods and their findings must be kept separate so that the strengths of each paradigm are maintained. Others argue that methods can be mixed because the paradigms are not pure anyway. In contrast, Morse (2003) warns that ad hoc mixing of methods can be a serious threat to validity. Single paradigm scholars (model 2) seek one paradigm to support their methodological preferences and critiques, for example connecting constructivism and qualitative methods. Pragmatists and transformative emancipatory action researchers posit a link between their model and mixed methods (Teddlie & Tashakkori 2003: 20). Adherents of model (3), the dialectical model, assume that all paradigms (and methodologies) have something to offer and "that the use of multiple paradigms contributes to greater understanding" (Teddlie & Tashakkori 2003: 22). Scholars in this group work back and forth between a variety of tension points, such as etic–emic, value neutrality–value committed.

In model (4), the multiple paradigm mixed methods model, several paradigms and mixed methods models are combined. It is argued that no single paradigm can apply to all designs or methods; that is, particular paradigms may work best with particular epistemologies and methodologies. "Several paradigms may serve as the framework for a triangulation design" (Teddlie & Tashakkori 2003: 23). The multiple paradigm position acknowledges the fact that a complex, interconnected family of terms, concepts, and assumptions surrounds the term qualitative research. These include the traditions associated with postpositivism, postfoundationalism, post-structuralism, and the many qualitative research perspectives and/or methods connected to cultural and interpretive studies.

Clearly, multiple frameworks and understandings circulate in the discourses that define how multimethod approaches are to be taken up at this time in history.

CONCLUSION

Over the past four decades the discourse on triangulation, multiple operationalism, and mixed method models has become quite complex and nuanced. This entry has attempted to present some of this complexity, some of its history. This is not a neat, linear history. Each decade has taken up triangulation and redefined it to meet perceived needs. The very term triangulation is unsettling and unruly. It disrupts and threatens the belief that reality in its complexities can ever be fully captured or faithfully represented.

Drawing again from Saukko (2003), bringing these different views of triangulation and multiperspectival research into play with one another, "holding them in creative tension with one another . . . cultivates multidimensional research and politics" (p. 32). There is no intention of arriving at a final, correct, enlightened view. The goal of multiple or critical triangulation is a fully grounded interpretive research project with an egalitarian base. Objective reality will never be captured. In-depth understanding, the use of multiple validities, not a single validity, and a commitment to dialogue and strong objectivity are sought in any interpretive study.

SEE ALSO: Methods, Mixed; Validity, Qualitative

REFERENCES AND SUGGESTED READINGS

Campbell, D. T. & Fiske, D. W. (1959) Convergent and Discriminant Validation by the Multitrait-Multimethod Matrix. *Psychological Bulletin* 56: 81–105.

Denzin, N. K. (1989) *The Research Act: A Theoretical Introduction to Sociological Methods*, 3rd edn. Prentice-Hall, Englewood Cliffs, NJ.

Douglas, J. D. (1976) *Investigative Social Research: Individual and Team Field Research*. Sage, Beverly Hills.

Erzberger, C. & Kelle, U. (2003) Making Inferences in Mixed Methods: The Rules of Integration. In: Tashakkori, A. & Teddlie, C. (Eds.), *Handbook of Mixed Methods in Social and Behavioral Research*. Sage, Thousand Oaks, CA, pp. 457–88.

Fielding, N. G. & Fielding, J. L. (1986) *Linking Data*. Sage, Beverly Hills.

Flick, U. (2004) Triangulation in Qualitative Research. In: Flick, U., von Kardoff, E., & Steinke, I. (Eds.), *A Companion to Qualitative Research*. Sage, London, pp. 178–83.

Guba, E. G. & Lincoln, Y. S. (1989) *Fourth Generation Evaluation.* Sage, Newbury Park, CA.

Kamberelis, G. & Dimitriadis, G. (2004) *Qualitative Inquiry: Approaches to Language and Literacy Research.* Teachers College Press, New York.

Lather, P. (1993) Fertile Obsessions: Validity after Poststructuralism. *Sociological Quarterly* 34(4): 673–93.

Lincoln, Y. S. & Guba, E. G. (1985) *Naturalistic Inquiry.* Sage, Beverly Hills.

Morse, J. M. (2003) Principles of Mixed Methods and Multimethod Research Design. In: Tashakkori, A. & Teddlie, C. (Eds.), *Handbook of Mixed Methods in Social and Behavioral Research.* Sage, Thousand Oaks, CA, pp. 189–208.

Patton, M. Q. (1980) *Qualitative Evaluation Methods.* Sage, Beverly Hills.

Richardson, L. (2000) Writing: A Method of Inquiry. In: Denzin, N. K. & Lincoln, Y. S. (Eds.), *Handbook of Qualitative Research*, 2nd edn. Sage, Thousand Oaks, CA, pp. 923–48.

Saukko, P. (2003) *Doing Research in Cultural Studies: An Introduction to Classical and New Methodological Approaches.* Sage, London.

Silverman, D. (1985) *Qualitative Methodology and Sociology: Describing the Social World.* Gower, Brookfield, VT.

Spicer, N. (2004) Combining Qualitative and Quantitative Methods. In: Seale, C. (Ed.), *Researching Society and Culture*, 2nd edn. Sage, London, pp. 293–304.

Teddlie, C. & Tashakkori, A. (2003) Major Issues and Controversies in the Use of Mixed Methods in the Social and Behavioral Sciences. In: Tashakkori, A. & Teddlie, C. (Eds.), *Handbook of Mixed Methods in Social and Behavioral Research.* Sage, Thousand Oaks, CA, pp. 3–50.

tribalism

Susan R. Trencher

Tribalism refers to customs and beliefs transmitted and enacted in groups (tribes) sharing a common identity and in which centralized political organization and authority are absent. Academic and public references to tribalism have been expanded to refer to behaviors and beliefs associated with diverse populations, including those that share any one, or all, of the following: race, ethnicity, language, religion, ways of life, kinship, attitudes, worldview, and generation. Sociological interest focuses on aspects of ethnicity and stratification.

In response to "degeneration theory" – a biblically derived idea that non-state societies had degenerated from a previous civilized state – late nineteenth-century anthropologists theorized tribal organization as the second stage of social and political formation in an evolutionary sequence moving from the simple to the complex (band, tribe, chiefdom, state). By the early 1900s, anthropologists discredited these theories and focused on patterns of tribal life to define and differentiate these groups from other social and political entities. Patterns included participation and belief in a way of life where social and political formations are composed of kin-based groups associated with a constellation of societal traits, including non-industrialized modes of subsistence, reciprocal modes of economic exchange, and common group ownership of natural resources. As groups, tribes consist of single populations or small communities living within a limited geographic range that can arrange themselves as a single entity for common purposes. Societal institutions, including economics, religion, and politics, are incorporated into the activities of everyday life. Political processes are significantly egalitarian and include power conferred as authority upon specific individuals on the basis of personal merit. Political positions are not permanent and decisions cannot be imposed by force or other systems of control. Tribes can exist within larger political entities, including states and nation-states.

Changes in the use and meaning of tribalism in part reflect the ways in which members of societies living outside such systems seek to categorize and classify them, as well as the ways in which these populations, often pressed by outside interests, redefine and reassert ethnic, regional, and generational identity. Historically, the term tribe was derived from the Latin *tribus*, traced as a reference to the three original divisions of the Roman people 2,500 years ago. In translations of biblical texts into Latin (and later into English), *tribes* referred to the 12 subdivisions of the peoples of Israel constituted through common kinship and custom. By the late sixteenth century, references to tribalism extended to behaviors and beliefs of races and ethnic groups.

In the nineteenth-century era of Western European expansion, tribalism took on significantly negative connotations as a reference to indigenous populations in non-state societies viewed as inferior, which were to be "civilized" by colonialist regimes. This definition was widely extended to non-western societies even where highly centralized states existed (e.g., the Aztecs). In the US, tribes were given legal status as autonomous political entities with inherent powers of self-government by Chief Justice John Marshall (1831) as "domestic, dependent nations," although they remained subject to the authority of the federal government.

In the early 1950s, tribalism was extended to refer to the behaviors of any group of people characterized by strong group loyalty to an array of characteristics and institutions, including attitudes, language, religion, social causes, political leanings, economic interests, race, and ethnicity. In the 1960s, references to tribalism became increasingly problematic and complex. In anthropology, experts in tribal societies argued that the term had become too ambiguous to be useful (Fried 1967; Helm 1967). Vail (1989) argued that while many academics in the US claimed that tribes did not exist and the term tribalism was a racist label imposed on non-western populations, young Africans in emerging nations were asserting themselves as members of tribes and reasserting historical and existing regional and ethnic identities, as well as enmities between and among such groups. Emerging African governments used accusations of tribalism to denounce groups that objected to the position of the dominant party (Wiley 1981; Vail 1989). Wiley (1981, 1990) argued that group identity along ethnic lines was given positive meaning in western settings, but was referred to as tribal and negative in Africa, Latin America, and indigenous American populations, leading to misdirected foreign and social policies.

Since the 1990s there has been a resurgent use of tribalism in terms similar to those found in the period of colonialism and in the 1950s. In political science and in public rhetoric, Huntington (1993, 1996) has argued that tribalism based on ethnicity, religion, and/or language is the dangerous result of the end of the bipolar enmity of the Cold War. From this standpoint, tribalism is a negative reference to groups seen as inferior and insular that resist and oppose other forms of organization and political authority claimed as legitimate and found in nation-states and global systems.

SEE ALSO: Boundaries (Racial/Ethnic); Colonialism (Neocolonialism); Ethnic Groups; Ethnicity; Indigenous Movements; Indigenous Peoples; Totemism

REFERENCES AND SUGGESTED READINGS

Fried, M. H. (1967) On the Concepts of "Tribe" and "Tribal Society." In: Helm, J. (Ed.), *Essays on the Problem of Tribe*. University of Washington Press, Seattle.
Helm, J. (Ed.) (1967) *Essays on the Problem of Tribe*. University of Washington Press, Seattle.
Huntington, S. P. (1993) The Clash of Civilizations. *Foreign Affairs* 72: 22–8.
Huntington, S. P. (1996) *The Clash of Civilizations and the Remaking of World Order*. Touchstone, New York.
Vail, L. (Ed.) (1989) *The Creation of Tribalism in South Africa*. University of California Press, Berkeley.
Wiley, D. E. (1981) Using "Tribe" and "Tribalism" Categories to Misunderstand Africa. Online. www.africa.wisc.edu.
Wiley, D. E. (1990) Capturing the Continent: US Media Coverage of Africa. *Africa News*. Online. www.allAfrica.com.

trust

Karen S. Cook

A number of social theorists (e.g., Fukuyama 1995) argue that trust is somehow central to the production of social order in society. Trust fosters cooperative relations and lessens the need for monitoring and sanctioning. The strong argument that trust is *required* to produce cooperation, however, cannot be accurate since cooperation occurs in many settings in which there is very little trust. In such settings cooperation is secured by other mechanisms (Cook et al. 2005). In many instances these mechanisms include reliable legal institutions that back property rights and contracts, as well as professional associations that monitor and sanction improper behavior and block the violation of trust relations (e.g., for physicians, lawyers, and others whose clients are often vulnerable).

Trust typically emerges when the parties involved have the opportunity to assess trustworthiness as they interact over time. In this sense trust is most likely to emerge in ongoing social relations in which there is a shadow of the future. It is much less likely (if at all) to emerge in settings in which the parties are strangers who will not encounter each other again. Cultural settings vary in the extent to which parties to an exchange are willing to take a risk on one another in the first instance of an exchange. In the trust literature, the term generalized trust is often used to indicate the extent to which individuals in a culture believe that "most people can be trusted," reflecting a relatively benign environment in which initial contacts are more often positive than negative. Where generalized trust is high, it is argued, exploitation tends to be lower; where it is low, the risks of exploitation are generally higher.

Adopting Hardin's (2002) encapsulated interest view of trust allows us to define trust primarily in relational terms. Actor A trusts actor B with respect to some particular matter(s) x, y, ... z when A believes that her interests are included in B's utility function, so that B values what A desires primarily because B wants to maintain a good relationship with A. Others have adopted a somewhat more general definition of trust as the belief that the trustee will not take advantage of a truster's vulnerability. If there is no risk or vulnerability there is no need for a trust relation to emerge between actors. To the extent that actor A perceives actor B as trustworthy, A is also much less likely to monitor B or to sanction B's negative behavior. It is this fact that leads to the argument that trust reduces transaction costs. Trust may also be essential when there is great risk of exploitation. Exploitation is especially likely when there is a power difference between the actors involved in the interaction.

Understanding trust has become a major enterprise in the social sciences in the past decade, in part because of the changes in the fundamental nature of social relations as individuals in many cultures spend more time outside of the confines of family and small local communities. As Blau (2002) notes, life in large complex societies is very different from life in small isolated communities because in complex societies there has been a decline in the significance of the groups into which one is born, together with the growing significance of reciprocal social relations with relative strangers. Cook and Hardin (2001) refer to this changing circumstance as the move from communal norms of association and social control to networked forms of association and a reliance on other mechanisms of social control, including reliance on trust relations in networks. For social association, strangers in modern societies become "dependent on reciprocated choices," to use Blau's terms, in order to sustain social relations. This social change implies that the types of norms that control behavior in tight-knit communities or small groups are not likely to be effective in the world of networked social relations.

In general a lack of mutual trust in a society makes collective undertakings difficult, if not impossible, since individuals cannot know if they engage in an action to benefit another that the action will be reciprocated. It is not only the problem of not knowing whom to trust, it is also the problem of having others not know they can trust you. The lack of mutual trust, Arrow (1974) points out, represents a distinct loss economically as well as a loss in the smooth running of the political system which requires the success of such collective undertakings. Mutual trust, however, cannot be produced on demand and is difficult to maintain even in close personal relations.

In the global era social contacts extend across regional and national boundaries in social networks defined by business, work, or travel connections and increasingly are maintained by more remote forms of communication, such as computer-mediated interaction. Economic relations also extend far beyond face-to-face contacts. Many economic transactions are secured primarily by social relations or are embedded in social networks, sometimes including trust relations among business partners. As Arrow (1974) notes, trust not only saves on transaction costs, it may also increase efficiency at the system level by reducing other costs, thereby increasing productivity. Arrow points out that many societies in which mutual trust is low are less developed economically, raising the question that Fukuyama (1995) addresses concerning the role of trust in the economic productivity of societies more broadly. The role of trust in Arrow's view is mainly in the production of public goods. When do individuals set aside their own personal interests to respond to the demands of their local community or even the larger society? This general question has also been addressed in a large experimental literature on social dilemmas (Cook & Cooper 2003). Issues of trust will remain central to theories of social order in the new world of broad-ranging networked interactions and a global economy.

SEE ALSO: Collective Action; Economy (Sociological Approach); Social Capital; Social Psychology; Trustworthiness; Uncertainty

REFERENCES AND SUGGESTED READINGS

Arrow, K. (1974) *The Limits of Organization*. Norton, New York.

Blau, P. (2002) Reflections on a Career as a Theorist. In: Berger, J. & Zelditch, M. Jr., (Eds.), *New Directions in Contemporary Sociological Theory*. Rowman & Littlefield, Lanham, MD, pp. 345–57.

Cook, K. S. & Cooper, R. (2003) Experimental Studies of Cooperation, Trust and Social Exchange. In: Ostrom, E. & Walker, J. (Eds.), *Trust and Reciprocity: Interdisciplinary Lessons for Experimental Research*. Russell Sage Foundation, New York, pp. 209–44.

Cook, K. S. & Hardin, R. (2001) Norms of Cooperativeness and Networks of Trust. In: Hechter, M. & Opp, K.-D. (Eds.), *Social Norms*. Russell Sage Foundation, New York, pp. 327–47.

Cook, K. S., Hardin, R., & Levi, M. (2005) *Cooperation Without Trust?* Russell Sage Foundation, New York.

Fukuyama, F. (1995) *Trust: The Social Virtues and the Creation of Prosperity*. Simon & Schuster, New York.

Hardin, R. (2002) *Trust and Trustworthiness*. Russell Sage Foundation, New York.

trustworthiness

J. Amos Hatch

Trustworthiness is a concept that constructivist qualitative researchers have used to establish criteria for judging the adequacy of their scholarly inquiries. Trustworthiness is roughly equivalent to the concept of validity in traditional quantitative research, and the genesis of its development is rooted in attempts by qualitative researchers in the early 1980s to find ways to legitimize their work and persuade others to take it seriously. Constructivist researchers think of trustworthiness as a system of checks and balances that take form in four criteria that reframe traditional, positivist elements of validity. *Credibility* is the constructivist criterion that parallels internal validity in the positivist paradigm; *transferability* parallels external validity; *dependability* stands in for reliability; and *confirmability* takes the place of objectivity. Along with the substitute criteria are corresponding empirical procedures (e.g., prolonged engagement, triangulation, and member checks) designed to affirm the adequacy of qualitative reports.

The term trustworthiness was first used in the context of qualitative research by Guba (1981). Guba contrasted criteria for adequacy between what he called rationalistic and naturalistic paradigms. He then introduced the criteria listed above and described a set of research techniques for enhancing the trustworthiness of naturalistic studies. In the same year, Guba and Lincoln (1981) published an elaboration of the same criteria and procedures. Over time, these authors have changed nomenclature, locating trustworthiness within the constructivist (not naturalistic) paradigm and contrasting their approach to positivist and postpositivist (not rationalistic or conventional) epistemological perspectives, but their descriptions of the trustworthiness concept and its purposes have remained constant (Guba & Lincoln 1994; Lincoln & Guba 2000).

Elements of trustworthiness and research techniques for improving the trustworthiness of naturalistic/constructivist studies are carefully described in Lincoln and Guba (1985). Building on their previous work, an entire chapter is devoted to establishing trustworthiness in naturalistic research. A case is made for the importance of credibility, transferability, dependability, and confirmability as alternative criteria for establishing the merit of naturalistic studies, and research techniques for applying these criteria throughout the research process are detailed. Meeting the credibility criterion means demonstrating the "truth value" of the naturalistic inquiry by showing that multiple constructions of reality have been adequately represented and that the reconstructions of the researcher are credible to the constructors of the original realities. Lincoln and Guba suggest several research techniques designed to increase credibility: *prolonged engagement* (spending sufficient time in the field); *persistent observation* (bringing depth to the examination of salient elements); *triangulation* (using different data sources, methods, investigators, and theories); *peer debriefing* (exposing one's research processes and findings to disinterested peers); *negative case analysis* (looking for alternative or disconfirming interpretations); *referential adequacy* (archiving portions of data for later comparison); and *member checks* (attaining feedback on research processes and results from those being studied).

Addressing the transferability criterion means providing enough information to potential users of research findings so that these individuals can make good decisions about the applicability of the findings to their own situations. Lincoln and Guba offer *thick description* as a technique for addressing transferability concerns. Adequately thick descriptions include sufficient contextual data so that readers can make their own determinations about how well the research settings match with other contexts in which the findings might be applied. Lincoln and Guba operationalize the trustworthiness criteria of dependability and confirmability in the form of an *inquiry audit*, including an *audit trail*. An inquiry audit can bolster a study's dependability and confirmability by providing a careful analysis of the residue of records generated at all stages of the inquiry. The kinds of records that make up an audit trail include raw data, data analysis products, process notes, reflexive notes, and instrument development information. Lincoln and Guba conclude their description of research techniques by presenting *reflexive journal*

writing as a strategy that reaches across all of the criteria for enhancing trustworthiness. A reflexive journal should include a daily record of the logistical implementation of the study, a personal diary recording the researcher's affective experiences, and a methodological log recounting decision processes as the study unfolds. Reflexive journaling and the research techniques associated with each criterion provide tools for increasing the trustworthiness of naturalistic studies.

The major contribution of the trustworthiness construct has been to provide qualitative researchers with an alternative perspective from which to consider issues of warrant that continue to trouble those operating outside the dominant discourse of positivism and quantitative research. In the 1980s, qualitative researchers were dismissed or even attacked for producing work that traditional researchers counted as "slipshod" or "touchy-feely." By identifying the elements of trustworthiness and applying the empirical strategies designed to accomplish them, qualitative scholars are able to make the case that their methods are legitimate. Even when the trustworthiness concept is not explicitly identified, its impact is evident in the frequency with which the strategies for accomplishing it are utilized in all kinds of qualitative reports. As qualitative inquiry has matured, the trustworthiness construct has been adapted to fit emerging research approaches under the qualitative umbrella. For example, Kincheloe and McLaren (1994) describe "critical trustworthiness," Hatch and Wisniewski (1995) include trustworthiness among criteria for assessing narrative research, and Green (2000) points out the utility of trustworthiness for the evaluation of social programs. In the early twenty-first century, qualitative research approaches are facing new threats as conservative political forces seek to return to narrow definitions of what constitutes "scientific" research (Erickson & Gutierrez 2000). Trustworthiness and adaptations of the procedures associated with achieving it continue to be important as qualitative research approaches seek to be acknowledged as legitimate.

Those who have critiqued the usefulness of the trustworthiness concept point out that it is more closely aligned with the assumptions of the positivist paradigm than many find comfortable. In Guba and Lincoln's (1994: 114) own words, "although these criteria have been well received, their parallelism to positivist criteria makes them suspect." Others, who have moved past dividing research paradigms into binaries such as qualitative/quantitative or positivist/constructivist, argue that trustworthiness is not a good fit for evaluating qualitative research undertaken within alternative qualitative paradigms such as those embracing critical/feminist or poststructuralist epistemologies (Lincoln & Denzin 1994; Hatch 2002). Following this logic, seeking to establish trustworthiness remains a worthy goal for naturalistic researchers operating within the assumptions of the constructivist paradigm, but such an attempt would not make sense given the different worldviews that define paradigms other than constructivism.

SEE ALSO: Naturalistic Inquiry; Trust; Validity, Qualitative

REFERENCES AND SUGGESTED READINGS

Erickson, F. & Gutierrez, K. (2000) Culture, Rigor, and Science in Educational Research. *Educational Researcher* 31: 21–4.
Green, J. C. (2000) Understanding Social Programs Through Evaluation. In: Denzin, N. K. & Lincoln, Y. S. (Eds.), *Handbook of Qualitative Research*, 2nd edn. Sage, Thousand Oaks, CA.
Guba, E. G. (1981) Criteria for Assessing the Trustworthiness of Naturalistic Inquiries. *Educational Communication and Technology Journal* 29: 75–91.
Guba, E. G. & Lincoln, Y. S. (1981) *Effective Evaluation*. Jossey-Bass, San Francisco.
Guba, E. G. & Lincoln, Y. S. (1994) Competing Paradigms in Qualitative Research. In: Denzin, N. K. & Lincoln, Y. S. (Eds.), *Handbook of Qualitative Research*. Sage, Thousand Oaks, CA.
Hatch, J. A. (2002) *Doing Qualitative Research in Education Settings*. State University of New York Press, Albany.
Hatch, J. A. & Wisniewski, R. (1995) Life History and Narrative: Questions, Issues, and Exemplary Works. In: Hatch, J. A. & Wisniewski, R. (Eds.), *Life History and Narrative*. Falmer, London.
Kincheloe, J. L. & McLaren, P. L. (1994) Rethinking Critical Theory and Qualitative Research. In: Denzin, N. K. & Lincoln, Y. S. (Eds.), *Handbook of Qualitative Research*. Sage, Thousand Oaks, CA.
Lincoln, Y. S. & Denzin, N. K. (1994) The Fifth Moment. In: Denzin, N. K. & Lincoln, Y. S. (Eds.), *Handbook of Qualitative Research*. Sage, Thousand Oaks, CA.
Lincoln, Y. S. & Guba, E. G. (1985) *Naturalistic Inquiry*. Sage, Beverly Hills, CA.
Lincoln, Y. S. & Guba, E. G. (2000) Paradigmatic Controversies, Contradictions, and Emerging Confluences. In: Denzin, N. K. & Lincoln, Y. S. (Eds.), *Handbook of Qualitative Research*, 2nd edn. Sage, Thousand Oaks, CA.

Truth and Reconciliation Commissions

Kevin Avruch

Truth – or Truth and Reconciliation – Commissions are "bodies set up to investigate a past history of violations of human rights in a particular country – which can include violations by the military or other government forces or armed opposition forces" (Hayner 2002: 14). Such commissions focus on the past (usually on violations committed under a previous regime) and have strictly delimited mandates, both as to duration and what "counts" as violation. In the Chilean commission's mandate, for example, only cases where victims actually died under torture were to be counted as human rights violations and investigated. The majority of commissions were established by executive order (less frequently by legislatures) of the new government. In the case of El Salvador, the United Nations established the commission, and it was (untypically) headed by non-Salvadorans. In a few cases an NGO established the commission, as in Rwanda and earlier in South Africa by the African National Congress to investigate its own abuses. In legal terms, Truth Commissions are to be distinguished from "tribunals" or other more strictly judicial entities, such as War Crimes Commissions, since they do not possess the formal power to prosecute or otherwise render "justice" – an important point to be discussed below. In a few cases, Truth Commissions operate alongside tribunals (East Timor and Sierra Leone), or parallel to other judicial processes (Rwanda).

Since 1974 some 25 Truth Commissions have been established, about 10 each in Latin America (Bolivia, Argentina, Uruguay (twice), Chile, El Salvador, Ecuador, Guatemala, Peru, and Panama), and African countries (Uganda (twice), Zimbabwe, Chad, Rwanda, Burundi, South Africa, Nigeria, Sierra Leone, and Ghana). The remainder occurred in Nepal, Sri Lanka, Haiti, Yugoslavia, and East Timor. They typically complete their work within six months to two years. In a few cases the commissions were disbanded before their work was completed and reports issued (Bolivia and Ecuador), in other cases final reports were completed but never issued publicly (Zimbabwe, Uganda, Philippines), or were issued in severely censored versions (Haiti). By contrast, in South Africa's case the report published in 1998 received extremely wide distribution, and the work of the Commission itself was reported extensively by South African and international media. Argentina's report, issued in 1985, published under the title of *Nunca Mas* ("Never Again"), was widely read in Spanish, translated into English, and republished commercially in Britain and the US.

Such variation in final reporting characterizes other aspects of the commissions, in the scope of their work, the resources or legitimacy they command, and observers' judgments of their ultimate effectiveness or success. With regard to scope for example, a few of these commissions, most notably South Africa's, add the term "Reconciliation" to their title, pointing to wider ambitions in the area of post-conflict peacebuilding, while in some other cases the search for "truth" defines the commission's mandate but the further task of "reconciliation" is intentionally left out (Yugoslavia). Yet even where the search for "truth" is highlighted in the commission's name and mandate, some of the commissions have been able to command wide recognition and respect for their relative impartiality and effectiveness (South Africa and Argentina), while others have been seen as more compromised (Chile's, where members of the old regime remained influential), as reluctant responses to international pressure (Uganda's 1974 commission), or merely as platforms to criticize the old regime and legitimize the new one (Chad).

The majority of commissions were established by newly emerging and often very fragile democracies – "transitional governments" in Kritz's (1995) term – which sought or were pressured to present a formal accounting of the violence and civil and human rights violations of the past. The emphasis here is on the production of an *account*. More difficult questions (political and moral ones) of *accountability* are less adequately addressed by these commissions (Minnow 1998; Rotberg & Thompson 2000). Such questions focus attention on the problem of *justice*, specifically on the ability of the commissions to "deliver" justice to victims by finding perpetrators formally guilty of their crimes and rendering some sort of appropriate punishment – *retributive justice*, in other words. Kritz (1995) and others have argued instead for forms of "transitional justice" appropriate to transitional regimes: less adjudicative, formal, and retributive, but in their lesser stringency and flexibility more able to help a new, fragile regime maneuver around the potential resistance posed by former elites and potential "spoilers," and thus achieve a measure of stability. This is the necessary political compromise some see built into the nature of the Truth Commission, especially if, as in the South African and several other cases, the commission lacks the power to prosecute but not effectively to grant amnesty. The question of amnesty granted perpetrators is among the most controversial aspects of these commissions' work.

Others, however, claim more far-reaching goals and positive achievements for the commissions than retributive justice, delivered in courtrooms or war crimes tribunals, can provide. Bishop Desmond Tutu (1999), for example, has argued that these commissions offer both victims and perpetrators another valid form of justice entirely, *restorative justice*, focused not upon penalty, punishment, and retribution, but upon recognizing harm, encouraging healing, and aiming for reconciliation. Proponents of restorative (or "reparative") justice are more likely to add the notion of "reconciliation" to that of "truth" as among the explicit goals of the commission, and to consider reconciliation, consisting minimally of "contrition" (on the part of the perpetrator) and "forgiveness" (on the victim's part), as crucial elements in the broader project of post-conflict peacebuilding.

Whatever the hoary questions around the intersection of truth and justice, most observers and analysts agree that these commissions often do succeed in providing an authoritative and widely accepted record of what actually took place in the past, and giving to victims (and perhaps also to perpetrators; see Gobodo-Madikizela 2003) a platform and a voice to recount their experience and express their pain and suffering. This is the "truth" part of the commissions' work. In the South African Truth and Reconciliation Commission, such "narrative" or "personal" truths, emerging from testimonies, sought to ensure that individual acts of oppression could never be forgotten, and to create an indelible public memory and record of these events. Yet with respect to "truth" these commissions routinely operate in politically charged worlds that would make the most steadfast of academic postmodernists blush. And facts, even if publicly accepted, do not necessarily conduce to publicly accepted truths. The apartheid security forces and Latin American colonels and generals apparently believed that they were fighting communist subversion under emergency conditions that demanded extraordinary measures to protect national security; and many believe this today, even some among them who appeared before various commissions and admitted their acts and expressed regret for their victims and offered apologies to the survivors (Avruch & Vejarano 2001).

The final question surrounding the work of Truth Commissions has to do with how well change or transformation effected at the individual level of victim and perpetrator "transfers" to the national level and the larger project of national reconciliation. Advocates and critics argue about this, with the South African case often used by both parties in their arguments. But rigorous data are lacking, and claims to assessment are mainly still anecdotal. What can be said is that Truth and Reconciliation Commissions are part and parcel of the larger project in the globalization of human rights and democratization. No one claims they are panaceas for the spread of human rights and democracy, but most of their supporters see them as relevant and appropriate, and not a few, as indispensable.

SEE ALSO: Apartheid and Nelson Mandela; Burundi and Rwanda (Hutu, Tutsi); Ethnic Cleansing; Peace and Reconciliation Processes; Peacemaking; Race and Ethnic Politics

REFERENCES AND SUGGESTED READINGS

Argentine National Commission on the Disappeared (1986) *Nunca Mas: Report of the Argentine National Commission on the Disappeared* (1986) Farrar, Straus, Giroux, New York.

Avruch, K. & Vejarano, B. (2001) Truth and Reconciliation Commissions: A Review Essay and Annotated Bibliography. *Social Justice: Anthropology, Peace, and Human Rights* 2: 47–108. Online. www.trinstitute.org/ojpcr/4_2recon.pdf.

Gobodo-Madikizela, P. (2003) *A Human Being Died that Night: A South African Story of Forgiveness.* Houghton Mifflin, Boston.

Hayner, P. (2002) *Unspeakable Truths: Facing the Challenge of Truth Commissions.* Routledge, New York.

Kritz, N. (Ed.) (1995) *Transitional Justice: How Emerging Democracies Reckon with Former Regimes,* 3 Vols. United States Institute of Peace Press, Washington, DC.

Minnow, M. (1998) *Between Vengeance and Forgiveness: Facing History and Genocide after Mass Violence.* Beacon Press, Boston.

Rotberg, R. I. & Thompson, D. (Eds.) (2000) *Truth v. Justice: The Morality of Truth Commissions.* Princeton University Press, Princeton.

Tutu, D. (1999) *No Future Without Forgiveness.* Doubleday, New York.

United States Institute of Peace. *Truth Commissions Digital Collection.* Online. www.usip.org/library/truth/html.

uncertainty

Jens Zinn

Uncertainty is characterized by cognitive and emotional elements. Uncertainty indicates unclear, ambiguous, or contradictory cognitive constructions, which cause feelings of uncertainty.

In sociology as well as economics, uncertainty is about expectations. It refers to the future and whether our expectations will be met and also to the present and our capacity to produce expectations. Typically, norms and institutions structure our expectations. They support clear and unambiguous notions and expectations even though they are always – to a certain degree – uncertain (Luhmann 1993). Sociological classics (e.g. by Durkheim, Gehlen, Parsons, and Erikson) see the destabilization of institutions and normative expectations caused by social change as something negative. The destabilization of expectations would produce feelings of uncertainty, and can even lead to an increase in suicides (Durkheim 2002 [1952]).

More recently, the term uncertainty became prominent in the discourse on reflexive modernization (Beck 1992; Giddens 1991) and the thesis of the risk society and institutional individualization (Beck 1992). A growing complexity, diversity, and instability would destabilize expectations, and awareness of lack of knowledge, especially regarding new risks (e.g., global warming, ozone-layer depletion, nuclear contamination, genetically modified food) which cannot be calculated and rationally managed, would trigger feelings of uncertainty.

In economics uncertainty is distinguished from risk and ignorance. Whereas ignorance is what we cannot know, risk is understood as calculable and therefore manageable uncertainty.

When the "distribution of the outcomes of a group of instances is known (either through calculation a priori or from statistics of the past experience)" we call it risk. In the case of uncertainty "it is impossible to form a group of instances, because the situation dealt with is in a high degree unique" (Knight 1921). That does not mean that we know nothing about the future, but our knowledge is limited and our expectations therefore more or less certain.

Even though uncertainty is seen as a lack of controllability and therefore as negative, it is widely acknowledged that uncertainty is more the rule than the exception. Especially in entrepreneurial decision-making, there is always a high degree of uncertainty involved because of novelty and unstable markets.

Recent developments in sociology and economics have fundamentally changed the perspective on uncertainty. Since it became evident that we often cannot transform uncertainty into certain expectations, growing interest has developed into how we can manage uncertainties as such. Therefore, new strategies beyond instrumental rationality have appeared (e.g., emotion, trust, fast and frugal heuristics, precaution), while the positive aspects of uncertainty, such as giving space for shaping the future, have been recognized (Zinn & Taylor-Gooby 2006).

SEE ALSO: Risk, Risk Society, Risk Behavior, and Social Problems; Science and the Measurement of Risk

REFERENCES AND SUGGESTED READINGS

Beck, U. (1992) *Risk Society: Towards a New Modernity*. Sage, Newbury Park, CA.

Durkheim, É. (2002 [1952]) *Suicide: A Study in Sociology*. Trans. J. A. Spaulding & G. Simpson. Free Press, New York.

Giddens, A. (1991) *Modernity and Self-Identity*. Polity Press, Cambridge.

Knight, F. H. (1921) *Risk, Uncertainty and Profit*. Houghton Mifflin, Boston.

Luhmann, N. (1993) *Risk: A Sociological Theory*. Aldine de Gruyter, New York.

Zinn, J. & Taylor-Gooby, P. (2006) The Challenge of (Managing) New Risks and Uncertainties. In: Taylor-Gooby, P. & Zinn, J. (Eds.), *Risk in Social Science*. Oxford University Press, Oxford.

unemployment

Mikael Nordenmark

Unemployed persons comprise all those within the economically active population who are able and willing to work, and who are actively seeking jobs, but unable to find one. Unemployment and job loss affects millions of people every year throughout the world and the level of unemployment varies with economic conditions and other circumstances. The unemployment rate is expressed as a percentage of the total civilian labor force, where the latter includes both the unemployed and those with jobs (all those willing and able to work for pay).

Sociological unemployment research contributes to the understanding of the social and economic consequences of unemployment for individuals, family members, and others in the community. A majority of the studies have focused on the relationship between unemployment and mental health. The Great Depression of the 1930s generated some of the first studies of the effects of unemployment on the individual. Above all, it was the negative economic consequences of unemployment that were the focus, but their studies also indicated that unemployment affects individuals' social life, identity, and mental well-being negatively (Jahoda et al. 1971; Bakke 1933).

As a consequence of the development of welfare states and welfare transfers, more recent unemployment research has concentrated on the psychosocial side of unemployment instead of the economic side. As with the investigations from the 1930s, most of these studies show that the unemployed in general have poorer mental health than the employed. However, unemployment does not seem to have the same effect on everyone. The adverse effects of unemployment on mental well-being have been found to be mediated by the individual's economic situation, work involvement, gender, social class, age, marital status, ethnicity, duration of unemployment, and previous unemployment experience.

There has been a debate on how the relationship between unemployment and mental health should be understood in causal terms. Does the level of mental well-being cause unemployment or vice versa – is well-being affected by the labor market situation? Longitudinal studies have shown that it is a question of both selection and effect. People with relatively poor mental health status run an increased risk of becoming unemployed, but also unemployment in itself has a negative impact on mental well-being. However, most studies provide powerful evidence that unemployment causes, rather than merely results from, poor mental health (Gallie & Paugam 2000; Nordenmark & Strandh 1999; Warr 1987).

The most commonly used theoretical perspective for explaining the consequences of unemployment is the functionalistic approach developed by Maria Jahoda (1982). She looks at the consequences of unemployment in the light of the psychosocial meaning of employment. Jahoda maintains that employment, in addition to economic or the manifest functions, also has certain psychosocial functions (time structure, social contacts, participation in collective purpose, regular activity, status, and identity). It is the loss of these functions that is the main cause of poor mental well-being among the unemployed.

One main critique of Jahoda's theory is that it sees all kinds of paid work as equally important for the individual's well-being. Warr (1987) tries to solve this problem with his vitamin theory. According to the theory, there are vitamins that a human being needs for staying healthy and these can be consumed both in an unemployment, as well as in an employment, situation. Because the theory assumes that employment, and the loss of employment, can have different meanings for different individuals, it can be used to explain mental health differences between categories of unemployed.

But perhaps the most serious critique of both Jahoda's theory about the latent functions of employment and of Warr's vitamin theory is the minimal role that the individual, or the actor, is assumed to play. These theories focus on how factors in the social environment affect individuals, rather than on how individuals experience, interpret, and act towards their social structure. This is what could be called a functionalistic perspective on the consequences of unemployment, and it has been criticized for instance by David Fryer (1986). In his agency theory, Fryer assumes that persons are active and motivated individuals who influence their environment and try to do their best to realize themselves. The effects of unemployment on mental health are then dependent on the degree to which the unemployment situation restricts agents from reaching what they see as desirable goals.

While Jahoda and Warr are criticized for overemphasizing the importance of the social structure, Fryer is often blamed for overemphasizing the role of the individual and not paying sufficient attention to the restrictions of the social environment. Therefore, there have been attempts to pay adequate attention to both individual and structural factors within one theory. In his status passage theory, Douglas Ezzy (1993) tries to integrate both structural factors and an acting agent. According to Ezzy, the level of mental well-being among the unemployed is mainly decided by the individual's subjective interpretations of the objective social context.

In the light of previous unemployment research it is possible to distinguish two main dimensions of employment that structure the level of mental well-being among the unemployed: the psychosocial and economic dimensions. In line with Ezzy's thoughts, the PEN model (*psychosocial and economic need* for employment) combines the psychosocial functions and agency perspectives into a conceptual model with which one can understand the interaction of these two needs. The model predicts that unemployed who have both a weak economic need and a weak psychosocial need for employment (for instance, unemployed living with a well-paid partner and strongly involved in activities not directly connected to

employment) should not perceive unemployment as problematic and they may adapt relatively well to their new situation. On the other hand, the combination of both strong psychosocial and economic needs makes the likelihood of poor mental health higher (Nordenmark & Strandh 1999).

An important task for future unemployment research is to further analyze the diverse effects of unemployment in varying social and national settings, and to integrate research from the different social sciences. While unemployment research within the behavioral sciences has focused on mental heath consequences, most economic research has analyzed causes of unemployment and employment. However, the only way to reach a deeper understanding of both the causes and consequences of unemployment is to combine economic research with research from the behavioral sciences.

SEE ALSO: Capitalism; Economic Development; Great Depression; Labor Markets; Occupations; Unemployment as a Social Problem; Welfare State

REFERENCES AND SUGGESTED READINGS

Bakke, E. (1933) *The Unemployed Man*. Nisbet, London.

Ezzy, D. (1993) Unemployment and Mental Health: A Critical Review. *Social Science and Medicine* 37: 41–52.

Fryer, D. (1986) Employment Deprivation and Personal Agency During Unemployment: A Critical Discussion of Jahoda's Explanation of the Psychological Effects of Unemployment. *Social Behaviour* 1: 3–23.

Gallie, D. & Paugam, S. (2000) *Welfare Regimes and the Experience of Unemployment in Europe*. Oxford University Press, Oxford.

Jahoda, M. (1982) *Employment and Unemployment: A Social-Psychological Analysis*. Cambridge University Press, Cambridge.

Jahoda, M., Lazarsfeld, P. F., & Zeisel, H. (1971 [1933]) *Marienthal, the Sociography of an Unemployed Community*. Aldine-Atherton, Chicago.

Nordenmark, M. & Strandh, M. (1999) Towards a Sociological Understanding of Mental Well-being Among the Unemployed: The Role of Economic and Psychosocial Factors. *Sociology* 33(3): 577–97.

Warr, P. (1987) *Work, Unemployment and Mental Health*. Clarendon Press, Oxford.

unemployment as a social problem

Jutta Allmendinger

All industrialized or post-industrial societies consider themselves to be working societies. Work – or more precisely, *gainful* work – defines an individual's worth and status. It is for most people the main means of earning a living and frequently the prerequisite to be eligible for social security coverage. Therefore, unemployment is a principal social and political challenge – in particular since the mid-1970s, when most western countries experienced a marked increase in unemployment as a result of the so-called first oil crisis. This followed an approximately 20-year period during which it was generally assumed that the interwar economic and labor market crisis was a thing of the past. Since then, the western industrial countries have tried, with varying success, to come to terms with the problem of unemployment. The post-socialist economies – to varying degrees as well – are also hit by unemployment.

It is frequently alleged that unemployment results above all from regulatory interventions in the ("free") labor market, including overly generous social benefits. One cites as proof the relatively low unemployment rates in countries such as the US and Great Britain, which, in contrast to most European countries or Japan, have a weakly regulated labor market and residual social security systems, targeted mainly at the poor. Yet countries whose market regulations and/or social benefits are comparable to or even surpass this last-mentioned group of countries (in many respects, this is true of the Scandinavian states) have also been very successful in fighting unemployment.

DEFINITIONS

The definitions and statistical measurement of unemployment differ in international comparison. To be counted as unemployed, an individual must have no or little gainful employment and seek paid work (which can also mean more extensive work than previously). Many countries use the International Labor Organization definition of unemployment, which is based on surveys: an individual is considered unemployed who was not in *any* gainful employment during a specific reference week and who is actively seeking work. In other countries (e.g., Germany) unemployment is defined by a state agency, which counts as unemployed those who register with the Public Employment Service; these individuals, however, are allowed to be employed up to half of the standard working hours of a fully employed person. On the other hand, individuals without any employment at all who are not registered as unemployed (often because they are not entitled to unemployment compensation) are not counted as unemployed, no matter how hard they are seeking paid work. Unemployment *rates* also differ depending on the chosen reference standard. In some countries, this reference group includes all dependent employees; in most other countries, it also includes the self-employed. For the purposes of international comparison, the OECD is trying to standardize national unemployment statistics.

Aside from official unemployment, measured in whatever form, one can assume the existence of so-called discouraged workers (i.e., individuals who would like to pursue gainful employment, but have given up hope of finding employment and thus do not actively seek work). Frequently, individuals who participate in active labor market policy measures are not counted among the unemployed. Therefore, the actual extent of underemployment is generally higher than officially stated.

At the same time, it is important to keep in mind that for many people unemployment is a transitional phase. In fact, one can observe high labor-market dynamics even in times of high unemployment; in most countries more (in some countries, far more) people become unemployed – and for the most part find work again – than corresponds to the average yearly stock of unemployed. The average duration of unemployment and the extent of long-term unemployment (generally defined as unemployment lasting one year or longer), which may serve as an indicator of entrenched unemployment, show large differences in international comparison.

UNEMPLOYMENT AS A SOCIAL PROBLEM

In most countries, the unemployment of individuals with low education is markedly higher – generally by a factor of 2 to 4 – than that of highly qualified workers. Often, the unemployment of younger and older workers is also above average; in the case of the former, this is mainly due to high entry rates to unemployment, while the duration of unemployment is mostly average or even below average. Marked gender differences can be perceived above all in continental European countries, where women's unemployment is often significantly higher than men's, while there are hardly any gender differences in Anglo-Saxon countries with their liberal labor markets or in the Scandinavian countries with their greater emphasis on gender equality. In most cases, ethnic and racial minorities suffer significantly higher unemployment rates than the native-born majority.

Unemployment endangers the livelihood of the unemployed individual and, possibly, also that of his or her family. Regardless of the existence of the so-called working poor, unemployment in many countries is the most important cause of poverty. Only in a few countries (mainly in the Scandinavian states) do social security systems largely compensate for the loss of income due to unemployment. Unemployment is also frequently associated with problems such as crime, right-wing extremism, suicide, and illness.

Generally speaking, these effects increase with the duration of unemployment. Therefore, it is important to ask how long-term unemployment may arise on the individual level, and theories of self-reinforcement of unemployment are perhaps best suited for this task. One explanation refers to employers' behavior. If an individual has been unemployed for some time, employers may assume that this individual has already been "checked out" by other possible employers and been found to be wanting the necessary skills; therefore, the longer a person has been unemployed, the fewer job offers they may receive. Another theory associates unemployment with loss of human capital. The longer a person has been unemployed, the more they are barred from access to the latest

developments in their occupation. Besides, they may also lose more general skills such as perseverance or develop health problems.

Finally, the unemployed often have the least access to (re-)training and further education, although they would need it most, for instance, if they have been working in a declining industry and would fare better if they were to switch to an occupation that offers better prospects for future developments.

Unemployment frequently results in negative consequences, even after having been overcome ("unemployment scarring"). These "scars," for example, can be a lower income, a slower rise in income, or increased occupational instability. It should be added that such consequences need not necessarily arise; for instance, if unemployment has been caused by a bad "match" between the skills offered by the unemployed and those required by the earlier job, this match may be better on the next job.

Another facet of self-reinforcing unemployment is repeated unemployment. Many findings suggest that multiple unemployment in the past increases the risk of renewed unemployment. Frequently, however, the duration of the new unemployment is shorter (i.e., those affected more quickly find new work). Generally speaking, long-term unemployment and repeated unemployment seem to be different phenomena. The former seems to have more to do with (possibly ascribed) individual "deficits" (low education, health problems, age) that make the individual unattractive for employers, the latter with the idiosyncrasies of certain industries or partial labor markets (Andreß 1989).

Persistent unemployment on the societal level is frequently associated with the concepts of underclass and exclusion. The term underclass was coined by Gunnar Myrdal and describes a social group that, because of its lack of access to steady employment, is even below the "working class" and thus cut off from mainstream society; in American inner-city ghettos this tendency is exacerbated by spatial segregation (Wilson 1987). The term underclass, however, was also used by some social scientists to ascribe to people certain traits such as the inability to work due to a lack of skills or the unwillingness to work due to certain values and attitudes; its use in sociology is therefore controversial. The term exclusion (of French origin) plays a bigger role in Europe, yet at the same time is less clearly defined. Partly it is used in the context of a belief, according to which unemployment by definition damages the "social contract" and destroys social cohesion, so that (re)integration into the labor market simultaneously restores social integration. In empirical research, exclusion is operationalized as the extent to which unemployment results in fewer social contacts and lower cultural and political participation (Gallie & Paugam 2000). In critical perspective, the term is used to indicate that contemporary capitalism offers fewer and fewer opportunities to participate socially, especially for the "less productive."

Unemployment is also a political challenge. Those polled in surveys in the European Union most frequently cite unemployment as among the "most important problems facing their country" (with marked variations, depending largely on the level of unemployment in any given country). Enduring unemployment in particular – especially in countries where unemployment benefits are based on the contributions of the employed – poses a challenge to the viability of systems of social security. A labor market crisis in general raises demands for reducing the cost of the work factor by, among other things, lowering the non-wage labor costs; yet high unemployment may necessitate an increase in social security contributions, unless one simply cuts unemployment benefits. More generally speaking, a situation of permanent austerity requires a "new politics of the welfare state" (Pierson 2001), which poses complex challenges for governments. It cannot be assumed, however, that the fight against unemployment has the highest priority everywhere (Korpi 2002); it can conflict with other goals such as price stability, and occasionally the fight against unemployment is undertaken rather as a form of symbolic politics.

It is in this context in particular that the unemployed run the risk of being confronted with "blaming the victim" attitudes on the part of political leaders. Based on a long tradition of distinguishing between the "deserving" and the "undeserving poor," there are repeated attempts to put many unemployed in the latter category, by representing unemployment as voluntary or as an expression of an aversion to work. According to modernized versions of such theses, unemployment is caused above all by overly generous social benefits, which raise the reservation wage of the unemployed above the actual level of productivity or to where the marginal returns of employment would be too small compared to unemployment compensation. If such arguments, which are geared to moral hazard, cannot be wholly dismissed, they fail to recognize the possible positive effects of unemployment benefits. If unemployment benefits are contingent upon continuous contributions, they provide an incentive for gainful employment, and in the case of actual unemployment, unemployment benefits can alleviate the pressure to have to accept the next best job offer and thus improve the match between job and skills (Gangl 2004). In addition, one also has to take into account the non-monetary benefits of employment, such as social contacts or prestige, which make many people accept employment that has little or no marginal return from an economic point of view.

LABOR MARKET POLICIES

It is difficult to provide an exact definition of labor market policies, given that some countries distinguish between a policy of fighting unemployment and a policy of maintaining or raising employment and others do not. In the field of labor market policies in the narrow sense, that is, policies directed at the unemployed, there is usually a distinction between "passive" and "active" labor market policies. Passive labor market policy refers to unemployment compensation; active labor market policy denotes measures that help bring the unemployed back to work. These distinctions are not as clear-cut as they may seem at first sight, since the cutting-down of benefits, which has occurred in most countries during the past decades, often has been justified on account of providing more "incentives" for the unemployed to actively engage in seeking work. Indeed, "activation" of the unemployed has been a central feature of recent labor market policies; in the European Union, this term serves as a central guideline, but the reforms in the US, often referred to as "workfare" (Peck 2001) (i.e., making welfare receipt conditional on being engaged in paid work), likewise can be understood as activation. It may be useful to distinguish between at least two types of activation policies (Torfing 1999; Barbier 2004). "Low end" activation is based on providing low benefits and making them strictly conditional on the unemployed's efforts in seeking work and undergoing "work test" measures. "High end" activation, while not necessarily opposing a tighter grip on the unemployed, emphasizes training the unemployed and possibly also more state-sponsored or subsidized jobs, at least on a temporary basis. Both types of activation seem to bear fruit, as is testified by the success of such divergent countries as Britain on the one hand and Sweden or Denmark on the other. Yet it must not be forgotten that reducing unemployment usually also involves fiscal, monetary, and other types of policies. The Netherlands, for instance, has been rather successful not only in reducing unemployment but also in increasing female labor market participation (even though to a large extent based on part-time work) due to a mix of policies of wage moderation, increased flexibility, tax and welfare reform, and a shift of jobs towards private services (Visser & Hemerijck 1997).

FUTURE OF UNEMPLOYMENT

Unemployment is frequently explained by the transition of capitalist societies to post-industrial and post-Fordist economies. Technological changes lead to a continual rise in productivity, and economic growth in many countries lags behind the ensuing job decline, so that one frequently talks about "jobless growth." Earlier hopes that the jobs lost in the producing sector would be regained in the service sector have not come true in a number of countries. Negative utopias such as Jeremy Rifkin's *The End of Work* (1995) picture a world in which computers, robots, biotechnologies, and the like render human work nearly completely superfluous. Globalization has in recent years become another hotly debated topic; as capital becomes more and more mobile, cheap labor in Eastern Europe or Asia poses a threat to

employment in those countries hitherto considered as the leading nations.

Yet the most likely consequences of globalization are more complex; as some jobs are "exported," new jobs are created that are necessary for firms to survive on international markets. Firms increasingly act as multinational or transnational enterprises and work is distributed over many countries and linked by computer networks. The outcomes of these developments for national labor markets (which still exist for a vast majority of workers, higher transnational mobility on the bottom and the top of the hierarchy of jobs notwithstanding) are less than clear-cut and may vary considerably between countries.

Such variation is even more likely in the light of different production regimes and social models; it is not at all clear that the more "liberal" and uncoordinated economies that can be found in many countries of the Anglo-Saxon world are superior to the coordinated market economies that prevail on the European continent (Freeman 1998; Soskice 1999). While unemployment in Europe is at high levels, it has rightly been pointed out that this is largely due to the problems of four major economies: Germany, France, Italy, and Spain. Most other countries fare substantially better. On the other hand, the drawbacks of (nearly) full employment in countries such as Britain and the US should not be neglected: high wage inequality, large numbers of "working poor," and in the US a huge number of imprisoned adults, mostly black, who otherwise would raise the unemployment rate by about 2 percentage points (Western & Beckett 1999). Yet it is obvious that the European economies, based largely on medium- and high-skilled jobs, have to increase their investments in human capital substantially if they do not want to lose ground and if they want to maintain their higher levels of equality. Also, inclusion of women in the labor market is still lagging considerably behind many Western European countries. At the same time, it may be increasingly necessary to loosen the hitherto tight connection between paid work and entitlements to welfare benefits, as job insecurity most likely will continue to grow and episodes of unemployment will be part of the life course of many individuals for the coming decades.

SEE ALSO: Capitalism; Labor Markets; Poverty; Social Exclusion; Unemployment; Welfare State

REFERENCES AND SUGGESTED READINGS

Andersen, J. G., Clasen, J., van Oorschot, W., & Halvorsen, K. (Eds.) (2002) *Europe's New State of Welfare: Unemployment, Employment Policies and Citizenship*. Policy Press, Bristol.
Andreß, H.-J. (1989). Recurrent Unemployment – the West German Experience: An Exploratory Analysis Using Count Data Models with Panel Data. *European Sociological Review* 5: 275–97.
Barbier, J-C. (2004) Systems of Social Protection in Europe: Two Contrasted Paths to Activation, and Maybe a Third. In: Lind, J., Knudsen, H., & Jørgensen, H. (Eds.), *Labour and Employment Regulation in Europe*. Peter Lang, Brussels, pp. 233–54.
Freeman, R. B. (1998) War of the Models: Which Labour Market Institutions for the 21st Century? *Labour Economics* 5: 1–24.
Gallie, D. & Paugam, S. (Eds.) (2000) *Welfare Regimes and the Experience of Unemployment in Europe*. Oxford University Press, Oxford.
Gangl, M. (2004) Welfare States and the Scar Effects of Unemployment: A Comparative Analysis of the United States and West Germany. *American Journal of Sociology* 109: 1319–64.
Korpi, W. (2002) The Great Trough in Unemployment: A Long-Term View of Unemployment, Inflation, Strikes, and the Profit/Wage Ratio. *Politics and Society* 30: 365–426.
Peck, J. (2001) *Workfare States*. Guilford Press, New York.
Pierson, P. (2001) Coping with Permanent Austerity: Welfare State Restructuring in Affluent Democracies. In: Pierson, P. (Ed.), *The New Politics of the Welfare State*. Oxford University Press, Oxford, pp. 410–56.
Soskice, D. (1999) Divergent Production Regimes: Coordinated and Uncoordinated Market Economies in the 1980s and 1990s. In: Kitschelt, H., Lange, P., Marks, G., & Stephens, J. D. (Eds.), *Continuity and Change in Contemporary Capitalism*. Cambridge University Press, Cambridge, pp. 101–34.
Torfing, J. (1999) Workfare with Welfare: Recent Reforms of the Danish Welfare State. *Journal of European Social Policy* 9: 6–28.
Visser, J. & Hemerijck, A. (1997) *A Dutch Miracle: Job Growth, Welfare Reform and Corporatism in the Netherlands*. Amsterdam University Press, Amsterdam.
Western, B. & Beckett, K. (1999) How Unregulated is the US Labor Market? The Penal System as a Labor Market Institution. *American Journal of Sociology* 104: 1030–60.
Wilson, W. J. (1987) *The Truly Disadvantaged: The Inner City, the Underclass, and Public Policy*. University of Chicago Press, Chicago.

uneven development

A. J. Jacobs

Uneven development refers to the inequitable spatial distribution of wealth and/or economic growth within a city, a metropolitan area, a nation-state, or globally. The term also represents the simultaneous occurrence of economic and wealth expansion in one area accompanied by disinvestment and/or expanding poverty in another area. Urban scholars frequently have measured uneven development statistically, through an examination of the geographic distribution of income and employment within or among metropolitan regions, or by an analysis of changes in these and other variables among municipalities, over time. For example, Hill (1974) utilized zero-order correlations to measure economic class and racial segregation by place within 127 American Metropolitan Statistical Areas. Jacobs (2003) compared the degree of place stratification in the Detroit and Nagoya Auto Regions by calculating the standard deviation divided by mean change in per capita income, population, and private employment in the two regions between 1969 and 2000 (i.e., the coefficient of variation) (see Jacobs 2005).

A prime case of interregional uneven development within a nation-state was the large-scale shift of industrial investment from the American Rustbelt (Northeastern and North Central US) to the American Sunbelt (Southeastern and Western US) that occurred during the 1970s and 1980s. A clear illustration of metropolitan uneven development has been the persistent post-World War II out-migration of population from American central cities to suburbia. In the case of the latter, many push and pull factors have contributed to these outcomes. The pull factors were fairly straightforward. The war, combined with rapid economic growth in the US afterwards, created pent-up demand for new housing in urban areas. However, in the early post-war period, land in central cities was either unavailable or too expensive for the construction of new single-family middle-class residences. Therefore, Americans who dreamed of owning a home rather than renting, or owning a bigger and newer home with a backyard, were attracted to the open spaces and new housing in the suburbs. This phenomenon was supported by national monetary, tax, and infrastructure policies that made it possible for middle-class families to receive secured, long-term, low-interest housing loans, and tax breaks for mortgage interest. It also made suburban locations greatly accessible to urban core employment centers through the construction and subsidizing of highways and water and sewer lines.

Unfortunately, the American dream was not open to everyone. Stated and latent national and local policies, such as those promulgated by the Federal Housing Administration (FHA), which recommended that banks only make loans in homogeneous areas, severely limited the housing opportunities of blacks, other minorities, and the poor. This served to exacerbate existing racial and class segregation in cities and metro areas; Gotham (2002) termed this racialized uneven development. It also allowed for the total abandonment of many inner-city neighborhoods through restrictive covenants and bank redlining (e.g., the total refusal of banks to loan money in certain urban neighborhoods). The totality of these events dramatically heightened interracial animosity in the 1960s, especially in the industrial North. This served to accelerate central-city white flight during the next decade. By the 1980s, hundreds of thousands of middle-class jobs also had left for suburban greenfields. The net result was rapid ex-urban growth accompanied by massive fiscal shortages in the urban core, and place/spatial stratification by race, income, and educational and occupational status within many American metropolitan areas.

The academic literature on uneven development has been vast. Scholars of urban ecology were the first to conduct in-depth studies examining the causes of spatial inequities. One of the most influential early twentieth-century studies was Roderick McKenzie's *American Journal of Sociology* essay, "The Concept of Dominance and World Organization" (1927). In this and other articles, McKenzie utilized biological metaphors to chronicle how human settlement patterns over time had led to a hierarchy of spatial locations. This system included the concentration of command and control activities in urban core areas, and the creation of specialized sub-centers and subordinated periphery areas.

The Chicago School of urban ecology remained significant in the field of urban studies until the 1970s. Nevertheless, many of the most important studies of uneven development between the late 1950s and early 1970s focused on capitalism's impact on international inequities. In *Rich Lands and Poor*, Gunnar Myrdal argued that international place inequities were an inevitable social reality of modern capitalism, and that such unevenness naturally grew wider over time, as developed nations industrialized further, and investment and capital became more concentrated in these areas. In *Capitalism and Underdevelopment in Latin America*, André Gunder Frank argued that development and underdevelopment were like two sides of a coin. Drawing from the work of Paul Baran, he challenged the conventional economic thought of the time by claiming that global capitalism, rather than feudal backwardness, had been the primary cause of stagnation and poverty in certain nations and subnational regions, as well as metropolitan-satellite polarization (developed–underdeveloped). Introducing dependency theory to North American scholarship, he maintained that uneven international and intranational outcomes were expected manifestations of metropolitan capitalist class extraction of surplus value from satellite labor.

While these studies and others were significant, perhaps the most important contributions to the discourse on uneven development during this period were those of Immanuel Wallerstein and Steve Hymer. Mirroring McKenzie, Wallerstein claimed that by the middle of the seventeenth century, capitalist development had already divided the world's territories into three unequal structural positions: core, semiperiphery, and periphery. In his seminal piece, "The Multinational Corporation and the Law of Uneven Development" (1972), Hymer combined McKenzie's human ecology with Alfred Chandler's business organizational analysis to explain the relationship between transnational corporations (TNCs or transnationals) and uneven spatial configurations (Hill & Feagin 1987). He argued that as a corporation evolved from a family firm to a TNC, territorial space was organized and reorganized locally and globally to reflect the internal organization of the firm. He suggested that like the nervous system in the body, political jurisdictions under the influence of TNCs became economically and socially dependent on such firms, rather than autonomous of them. This situation of dominance and subordination then served to both exacerbate social and economic divisions of labor and reproduce them on the spatial landscape.

It was the works of these two scholars that laid the foundation for the development of urban political economy. It has been this theory, whose advocates examine "the relationship between capitalism and urban organization on a global scale," which has been the dominant paradigm in the study of spatial inequities over the past 25 years (Hill & Feagin 1987). For example, the global/world cities hypothesis (to be discussed later) is an urban-centered derivative of Wallerstein's world-systems theory.

One other significant but under-appreciated 1970s contribution to the discourse was Bluestone's (1972) article. Here he wrote that uneven development was inevitable in the American economic system. Over time, those who controlled resources would tend to invest and reinvest in products, geographical areas, and workers that promised them the most profitable return on their investment. Conversely, disinvestment would occur over time in products, places, and people that the dominant class believed offered them a relatively low return on their investment. Moreover, he claimed that uneven development was not restricted to industrial investment alone, but also was clearly evident in employment, education, training, and health care opportunities. This was because American political and business leaders had a vested interest in maintaining an unequal distribution of resources, as it disproportionately concentrated wealth and political influence within a small circle of power elites. Based on this evidence, similar to Myrdal, Bluestone concluded that the American political-economic system inherently produced "continuous growth and relative prosperity" in affluent areas and segments of society, and

relative stagnation and impoverishment in declining areas and sectors, with the gap between the haves and have-nots growing wider over time.

The 1980s represented the peak period for the study of American urban and metropolitan uneven development. For the most part, scholars maintained that American metropolitan unevenness was best understood as a long-term process evolving out of the actions of economic and political elites operating within a complex context of global, national, and local political-economic and social forces. In other words, they believed that America's particular forms of uneven development were deeply embedded within that nation's specific national and subnational contexts. As Smith (1988) claimed, this has been why the widespread and pronounced sprawling development, urban fiscal stress, residential segregation by class, and depopulation of inner-city areas in the US have generally not been found in other advanced capitalist states.

While the urban scholarship of the 1980s focused a great deal on unevenness within and among metropolitan areas, the discourse since the early 1990s has centered on the degree to which globalization has had an impact on spatial unevenness. Extending Wallerstein's approach to the study of cities, global/world cities hypothesis theorists have argued that the continued globalization of the economic functions in modern industrial capitalism has created an international hierarchy/division of labor among cities and metropolitan areas. According to this view, expounded by John Friedmann, Saskia Sassen, and others, this hierarchy has served to expand inequities between core and periphery areas, between transnational elites and low-skilled workers, and between dominant groups and racial minorities. In addition, it has led to an expansion of inner-city ghettos, the development of a dual labor market within world cities, and to excessive rural–urban migration, and periphery–core immigration.

In contrast to global cities theorists, Richard Child Hill, Kuniko Fujita, and others propounding the nested city hypothesis have (re) asserted that national and local political-economic contexts, rather than global capitalism, remain the decisive factors determining spatial configurations. Drawing from this approach, A.J. Jacobs claimed that over the past 30 years, the US Federal Regulatory State's policies promoting fiercely competitive inter-local relations, rather than inter-local cooperation, have, in concert with subnational factors, served to accelerate suburban growth and central city hollowing in the Detroit Auto Region. Conversely, he argued that the reverse had been true in Japan, where national and subnational planning had fostered inter-municipal collaboration, relatively balanced growth, and strong major cities in the that nation's auto region, Nagoya-Tokai.

Over the next decade, cities and metropolitan areas will continue to dominate future research on uneven development. It is also clear that until a more integrated metatheory of spatial development becomes accepted, one which incorporates how the global, national, and local contexts all impact economic and social spatial patterns, the future scholarship on uneven development can be expected to teeter between global theories and embeddedness. Cross-national comparative research should become a prominent method with which to both help settle this debate and shed light on a new metatheory.

SEE ALSO: Dependency and World-Systems Theories; Global/World Cities; Metatheory; Metropolitan Statistical Area; Nation-State; Residential Segregation; Transnationals; Urban Ecology; Urban Political Economy

REFERENCES AND SUGGESTED READINGS

Bluestone, B. (1972) Economic Crisis and the Law of Uneven Development. *Politics and Society* 3: 65–82.

Bluestone, B. & Harrison, B. (1982) *The Deindustrialization of America: Plant Closings, Community Abandonment, and the Dismantling of Basic Industry*. Basic Books, New York.

Darden, J., Hill, R., Thomas, J., & Thomas, R. (1987) *Race and Uneven Development*. Temple University Press, Philadelphia.

Dicken, P. (2003) *Global Shift: Reshaping the Global Economic Map in the 21st Century*, 4th edn. Guilford Press, New York.

Gotham, K. (2002) *Race, Real Estate, and Uneven Development: The Kansas City Experience, 1900–2000*. State University of New York Press, Albany.

Gottdiener, M. (1985) *The Social Production of Urban Space*, 2nd edn. University of Texas Press, Austin.

Hill, R. (1974) Separate and Unequal: Government Inequality in the Metropolis. *American Political Science Review* 68: 1557–68.

Hill, R. & Feagin, J. (1987) Detroit and Houston: Two Cities in Global Perspective. In: Smith, M. & Feagin, J. (Eds.), *The Capitalist City: Global Restructuring and Community Politics*. Blackwell, Oxford, pp. 155–77.

Hymer, S. (1972) The Multinational Corporation and the Law of Uneven Development. In: Bhagwati, J. (Ed.), *Economics and World Order*. Macmillan, New York, pp. 113–40.

Jacobs, A. (2003) Embedded Autonomy and Uneven Metropolitan Development: A Comparison of the Detroit and Nagoya Auto Regions, 1969–2000. *Urban Studies* 40: 335–60.

Jacobs, A. (2005) Has Central Tokyo Experienced Uneven Development? An Examination of Tokyo's 23 Ku Relative to America's Largest Urban Centers. *Journal of Urban Affairs* 27: 521–55.

Sawers, L. & Tabb. W. (Eds.) (1984) *Sunbelt/Snowbelt: Urban Development and Regional Restructuring*. Oxford University Press, New York.

Smith, M. (1988) *City State and Market: The Political Economy of Urban Society*. Blackwell, New York.

unions

Judith Stepan-Norris

Unions are collections of workers who join together for the purpose of defending their common interests as employees. In capitalist societies, union representation provides many workers with their only potential for meaningful input in their workplaces. These workers benefit from unions because employers alone possess legal rights and authority over their property (both land and machinery), and therefore any single worker has limited bargaining power vis-à-vis an employer. In the unionized workplace, the hegemony of capital is manifested in a regime of production based on collective bargaining agreements, which are reinforced by the state. Still, capital's control over the workforce is never complete. Workers struggle and negotiate with employers over the terms of the regime.

When workers organize into unions their representatives normally negotiate collective bargaining agreements with management, which codify the terms and conditions of the labor process. These agreements (or contracts) specify workers' wages, hours, benefits, and seniority and grievance systems, whether or not workers may strike, and whether or not the union cedes managerial prerogatives for a specified period. The managerial prerogatives clause is especially important since it either does or does not give to management the right to hire, fire, discipline, plan production, and change production processes, etc. When this clause is absent, these rights are open for negotiation, usually through the grievance procedure. The contract also specifies the number of union representatives within the workplace. These representatives are called union stewards or committeepersons. Union stewards inform workers of their rights and represent them in grievances against employers.

Contracts may place a total, conditional, or no prohibition against strikes during the term of the agreement. Conditional prohibitions specify situations in which a strike is allowable. Whereas many collective bargaining agreements signed between the 1930s and the early 1950s in the US did not include strike prohibitions, the more recent pattern is for them to be included in these agreements. Still, unions that sign collective bargaining agreements with total strike prohibitions may strike once their contracts expire. Alternatively, workers sometimes take matters into their own hands by conducting "wildcat" strikes, which occur without union authorization.

There are several types of unions. The two main types are craft (or vertical) and industrial (or horizontal) unions. Following the lead of the medieval guilds, the earliest trade unions tended to organize craft workers by their skills. To become a member of a craft union, a worker must be proficient in that craft, and workers are organized across workplaces. As industrialization progressed, a larger proportion of the workforce was employed in non- and semiskilled positions. The industrial unions organized workers by industries (e.g., auto, rubber, steel) and sought to represent all the workers within a particular workplace.

Individual national (and international) unions (e.g., the United Mine Workers of America) normally belong to national umbrella organizations such as the American Federation of Labor (AFL) or the Congress of Industrial Organizations (CIO). The pejorative term "dual unionism" is reserved for instances when two unions (usually belonging to different umbrella organizations) simultaneously organize workers within a single industry or trade. Although the mainstream US labor movement has considered dual unionism to be harmful, it may be associated with innovation and/or subsequent union growth. This was the case with the AFL's challenge to the Knights of Labor in the 1880s and with the CIO's challenge to the AFL in the 1930s.

Unionization rates vary over time, place, and industry. National rates of unionization vary from very low rates in the US and France to very high rates in the Scandinavian countries. The periods of increase in US union membership tend to coincide with the initiation of new and successful labor organizations, and the periods of decline have occurred as employment in highly unionized industries fell (especially when unions have not responded to the changing conditions). US union membership hit its peak during the 1950s, and has declined until the late 1990s, when the newly elected leadership of the American Federation of Labor-Congress of Industrial Organizations (AFL-CIO) began its emphasis on new organizing.

The level of democracy within unions has been an issue of heightened concern, especially during specific periods. The main charge is that unions tend to evolve into oligarchies that are unresponsive to workers' needs. Some researchers have pointed out that during certain periods, union democracy has been prevalent. So union democracy and oligarchy are "alternative possible paths of union development" (Stepan-Norris & Zeitlin 2003).

Often, unions' efforts to organize workers were conducted in alliance with political parties. In Europe, unions tend to organize along industrial lines and to be affiliated with left-of-center political parties (some European countries also have had rival Christian, socialist, and/or communist unions). In the US there has been extensive involvement and interchange between unions and political parties, but seldom any formal ties. Unions have both reacted to and influenced legislative change. In the early period of unionism, unions were prosecuted under existing and newly developed laws that served to control and/or eliminate them. Later, many such laws were repealed or modified. But considerable anti-union legislation continues to exist. In the US the National Labor Relations (Wagner) Act of 1935 provided an important spur to union growth, while the 1947 Taft-Hartley Act represented a severe setback for unions. In Great Britain the Combination Acts restricted and the Trade Union Act of 1871 liberalized labor laws.

Union organizing has been associated with conflict as well as a good deal of violence. Prior to the 1930s, US employers were given considerable leeway in protecting their property and often summoned the aid of state and federal troops to help. Taft and Ross's (1969) "grossly understated" estimate of US labor conflict casualties puts the death count at 700 and serious injuries at several thousand. They estimate that state and federal troops intervened in over 160 disputes. Although labor violence has decreased considerably over time, the US has had the most violent labor history of all industrialized nations.

SEE ALSO: Alienation; Bourgeoisie and Proletariat; Capitalism; Class Consciousness; Deindustrialization; Exploitation; Fordism/Post-Fordism; Industrial Relations; Labor–Management Relations; Labor Movement; Mass Production; Taylorism; Work, Sociology of

REFERENCES AND SUGGESTED READINGS

Freeman, R. & Medoff, J. (1984) *What Do Unions Do?* Basic Books, New York.

Lichtenstein, N. (2002) *State of the Union: A Century of American Labor.* Princeton University Press, Princeton.

Stepan-Norris, J. & Zeitlin, M. (2003) *Left Out: Reds and America's Industrial Unions.* Cambridge University Press, Cambridge.

Taft, P. & Ross, P. (1969) American Labor Violence: Its Causes, Character, and Outcome. In: Graham, H. & Gurr, T. (Eds.), *Violence in America: Historical and Comparative Perspectives.* New American Library, New York, pp. 270–376.

Western, B. (1997) *Between Class and Market: Postwar Unionization in the Capitalist Democracies.* Princeton University Press, Princeton.

urban

Vincent N. Parrillo

Urban is one of those deceptive concepts that seem simple to grasp yet have many layers of complexity that are subject to varying interpretations, depending on one's theoretical and analytical predisposition. Derived from the Latin word *urbanus* (meaning characteristic of, or pertaining to, the city), *urban* essentially holds that same connotation to most people.

Complicating that understanding, however, are varying criteria among the 228 countries with urban populations. These criteria include *administrative function* (a national or regional capital), *economic characteristics* (more than half the residents in non-agricultural occupations), *functional nature* (existence of paved streets, water supply, sewerage, and electrical systems), and *population size* or *population density*. Administrative function is used solely in 89 countries and in combination with other criteria in an additional 20. Economic is one of several criteria in 27 countries, as is functional in 19 countries; functional is also used solely in 5 countries. Population size or density is the sole criterion in 46 countries and in combination in an additional 42. No definition exists in 24 countries, while in Guadeloupe, Hong Kong, Kuwait, Monaco, Nauru, and Singapore the entire population is designated as urban.

Such differences make cross-national comparisons difficult. For example, the lower-range limit for population of an urban area ranges from 200 in Iceland to 10,000 in Greece. A universal standard, say a midpoint from these two extremes of 5,000 inhabitants, would be inappropriate in populous countries such as China or India, where rural settlements with no urban attributes at all could easily contain such large numbers. Using each country's own criteria, the Population Reference Bureau (2003) reported that 47 percent of the world's population was urban. Significant variations existed: Africa, 33 percent urban; Asia, 38 percent; Europe, 73 percent; Latin America and the Caribbean, 75 percent; North America, 79 percent. In Canada and the US the urban population was 79 percent, while in the United Kingdom it was 90 percent. The lowest urban population (5 percent) was in Rwanda, while the highest (100 percent) were in the six countries previously identified.

For centuries the contrast between the city and its surrounding region was simple: urban (the spatially defined city) and rural (everything else). From the eras of ancient and medieval societies with walled cities to the pre-industrial cities of commerce, most people lived outside the city. A symbiotic relationship then existed between the city and its hinterland. The latter provided the necessary agricultural products for survival and the city supplied leadership, protection, advances in science and technology, arts and crafts products, and various other luxury items mostly of value only to city dwellers.

Sociology was born in Europe, a child of the industrial and urban revolutions that transformed human existence. As millions left the countryside and flocked to work in the urban factories, a new breed of social observer analyzed these altered forms of social organization. Although they thought the city could be a liberating force from "barbarism to civilization," Karl Marx and Friedrich Engels (1976) were among the first to describe the excesses of industrialization and appalling lifestyle of exploited urban workers.

In a seminal masterwork, *Gemeinschaft and Gesellschaft* (1887), German sociologist Ferdinand Tönnies – openly acknowledging Marx's influence – described the contrasting elements of urban and rural life from a cultural perspective. His concept of *Gemeinschaft* (community) characterized the small village and surrounding area in which people united by close ties of family and neighborhood shared traditional values and worked together for the common good. In contrast to this "we-ness," *Gesellschaft* denoted the "me-ness" of the city, where a future orientation among a heterogeneous population replaced tradition, leading Tönnies

to a pessimistic view of the city as characterized by disunity, rampant individualism, and selfishness, even hostility. This typology of *Gemeinschaft* and *Gesellschaft* had a lasting influence on other urban sociologists.

Émile Durkheim (1962) also had an enduring effect. His emphasis on contrasting social bonds offered another perspective on urban and rural distinctiveness. He suggested that urban social order rested on an *organic solidarity* in which individual differences, greater freedom, and choice thrive in a complex division of labor where inhabitants are interdependent. Rural life, on the other hand, is organized around *mechanical solidarity*, with social bonds constructed on likeness (common beliefs, customs, rituals, and symbols), where inhabitants are relatively self-sufficient and not dependent on other groups to meet all of life's needs.

For the first half of the twentieth century other social scientists continued in this twofold typology. Their examinations of urban growth and development (urban ecology) – and of behavior, communities, economics, lifestyles, politics, and subcultures within an urban context (urbanism) – mostly rested on a spatial or geographic emphasis on the central city. From this perspective, they examined different variables and compared them to non-urban areas. In the century's second half, however, changing settlement patterns and the evolution of a global economy reduced the analytical value of this simplistic urban–rural dichotomy.

The post-World War II suburban boom in Europe, Japan, and the US initiated an exodus from cities and a growing preference for that lifestyle. At first, this intermediary along the urban–rural continuum was easily understood. Suburbs were mostly bedroom communities on the cities' outskirts, where inhabitants typically lived in one-family houses, but worked, shopped, and enjoyed leisure activities in the city. By ringing the central cities, the suburbs reinforced the original conception of *urban* in a spatial context, and were essentially viewed as residential appendages to the cities.

Much as pre-industrial cities had a mutual interdependence with the hinterland, initially so too did twentieth-century cities and suburbs. That changed with the development of suburban office and industrial parks, shopping malls, megastores, hospitals, and places of worship.

As the suburbs became more self-sufficient, the definition of *suburban* changed into that of a third entity, an alternative to *urban* and *rural*. Even so, larger cities continued to extend their sphere of influence beyond their boundaries, particularly in such areas as culture, fashion, media, professional sports, sightseeing, and tourism. *Metropolitan* is the term describing that extended area of urban influence, which the US Census Bureau calls *metropolitan statistical areas* (MSAs). The official US urban population thus includes not just those living in cities, but also those living elsewhere in *urbanized areas* with populations of 2,500 or more, as well as those living in *urbanized zones* (unincorporated communities of less than 2,500, but on the fringes of metropolitan areas). Metropolitan areas, with varying definitions, exist throughout the world.

Sometimes metropolitan areas overlap each other in their spheres of influence, creating what Jean Gottman (1961) popularized as a *megalopolis*. His example was the region extending from Boston to Washington. The Census Bureau identifies 18 such regions in the US and calls them *consolidated metropolitan statistical areas* (or CMSAs).

Spurred by increasing affluence, transportation improvements, and advances in telecommunications that allowed for working from home, a new form of "urban" living became apparent in the 1980s: the exurb. An *exurb* is an upper-middle-class community in an outlying semi-rural community, where highly educated professionals seek an escape from more congested urban, even suburban, locales. Typically, their residences are large, expensive homes on large, wooded lots. This blend of urban attributes among residents in a semi-rural locale blurred the previous clarity of *urban* based on a spatial conceptualization.

Disparities in urban definitions and the blurring of urban and non-urban elements led social scientists into new considerations. Some scholars prefer a theoretical approach, such as *convergence theory*, which argues that technology will lead cities and communities everywhere to develop similar organizational forms. Its counter-theory is *divergence theory*, which posits that increasingly dissimilar organizational forms will emerge because of differences in the (1) cultural values and histories; (2) timing and pace of urbanization; (3) form of government and planning approaches; and (4) hierarchy of countries in the global economy. Another perspective, *postmodern theory*, rests on the premise that cities develop in ways that are no longer rational or manageable according to the old logic of urban ecology. Instead, global capitalism serves as the underlying rationale for actions by increasingly fragmented urban power structures.

In fact, the still-growing world economic system and ease of worldwide telecommunications serve as the basis for arguments by the "new urban sociologists" that *urban* now displays a global character and is an international process. The economic welfare and changes in cities more often result from causes existing beyond their boundaries. Moreover, both the physical form and social life of cities result less from "natural" processes and more from political and economic institutions at the national and international levels that shape urban life. Conflicts between labor and management or among diverse population segments also impact on the physical and social characteristics of cities. This interplay of global, national, regional, and local forces is an additional complicating factor in explaining what we mean by *urban*.

In the final analysis, *urban* remains subject to varying interpretations, with or without a spatial premise; with a local, regional, national, or global perspective; and with either a positive or negative emphasis. No matter what theoretical and conceptual approach one takes, the term nonetheless remains mostly suggestive of its Latin origins: that of particular qualities associated with people and patterns indeed found in cities.

SEE ALSO: Megalopolis; Metropolis; Metropolitan Statistical Area; New Urbanism; Suburban; Urban Community Studies; Urban Ecology; Urban Policy; Urban Political Economy; Urban-Rural Population Movements; Urban Space; Urbanism/Urban Culture; Urbanization

REFERENCES AND SUGGESTED READINGS

Durkheim, É. (1962 [1893]) *The Division of Labor in Society*. Free Press, New York.
Gottdiener, M. (1994) *The New Urban Sociology*, 2nd edn. McGraw-Hill, New York.

Gottman, J. (1961) *Megalopolis*. Twentieth Century Fund, New York.

Marx, K. & Engels, F. (1976 [1846]) *The German Ideology*. International Publishers, New York.

Parrillo, V. & Macionis, J. (2004) *Cities and Urban Life*, 2nd edn. Prentice-Hall, Upper Saddle River, NJ.

Population Reference Bureau (2003) World Data Base. Online. www.prb.org/datafind/datafinder.htm.

Tönnies, F. (1963 [1887]) *Community and Society*. Harper & Row, New York.

United Nations Population Division (2002) *World Urbanization Prospects: The 2001 Revision*. United Nations, New York.

urban community studies

Farrah Gafford

Urban community studies consist of a range of case studies, comparisons, and local analyses that explore the local cultures, relationships, interactions and identities. As cities in the US experienced rapid growth during the early twentieth century, sociologists speculated about how the interactions and relationships in these urban settings would be influenced by a swelling population, advanced technology, and a mounting flow of immigrants. With the population of urban centers like Chicago approaching a population of 2 million in the early 1900s, urban centers provided sociologists with an opportunity to examine how inhabitants would adjust to the growing populations and the diversity within these spaces. The result of these early inquiries would be the establishment of a premier American school of urban sociology and a long tradition of urban community studies in the field of sociology.

The intellectual roots of urban community studies can be traced to Tönnies's *Community and Society* (1887) and Durkheim's *The Division of Labor in Society (*1893). Tönnies contrasted the types of human interactions present in pre-industrial societies to interactions in industrialized societies. He argued the *Gemeinschaft* world is characterized by close-knit ties among family, kin, and neighbors. In these cohesive societies, individuals are very familiar with one another. However, in the modern *Gesellschaft* world of the city, relationships are based on self-interest, and close-knit relationships are replaced by work-based and interest-based relationships. Continuing this line of thought, Durkheim discussed the type of relationships in societies with a complex division of labor. He argued that in areas characterized by large populations and a highly specialized form of division of labor, solidarity was no longer based on common values, but rather dependence and a reliance on each other's skills. Durkheim described this type of solidarity as *organic solidarity*. In a society with organic solidarity, it becomes harder for individuals to create bonds with each other. As a result, individuals in these societies experienced feelings of alienation.

Tönnies and Durkheim's classic generalizations about the interactions in industrialized societies can be identified in our definitions and perceptions of urban communities today. While community can be viewed as a particular geographic location, the concept of community also assumes that certain types of relationships and social ties exist. With this in mind, scholars typically agree that social ties, interaction, and geographic location are the three essential components for defining community (Hillary 1955).

Over the course of time, Tönnies and Durkheim's ideas on the social relations in urban areas would influence American sociology. Sociologists from the Chicago School were responsible for some of the most prominent studies on urban community life in the US. Comparing the city to an ecological system, studies out of the Chicago School viewed the neighborhood as part of a larger system. Robert Park and Ernest Burgess's *The City* (1929) used concentric circle models to demonstrate the growth of urban areas. The concentric model illustrates the outward expansion of the city from the core or the central business district. Within the zones of urban growth are local districts or communities and these in turn are subdivided into smaller areas called neighborhoods. According to the concentric model, neighborhoods tend to develop according to the growth and development of the city.

Prominent works out of the Chicago School tradition like Harvey Zorbaugh's *The Gold Coast and Slum* (1929) suggested that the term community could only be loosely applied to several of the neighborhoods. He argued that in respect to some of the subdivisions of this area, community only served as a geographical expression. Neighborhoods within the area lacked common traditions and feelings associated with traditional societies. Although the studies out of the Chicago tradition made great contributions to sociology, the school's heavy emphasis on the city and larger ecological forces minimized the role of individuals in creating solidarity or a sense of community within their own neighborhoods.

Years later, Herbert Gans's *The Urban Villagers* (1962) found that a close set of relationships could exist in so-called urban slum neighborhoods. In a slum neighborhood in Boston, Gans observed the interconnectedness of peer groups (or the peer group society), institutions (community), and the out-group or outside world of the residents. The area Gans described had a sense of cohesion or solidarity that was fostered through interactions with peer groups that included not only family or relatives but neighbors as well. Gerald Suttles's *The Social Order of the Slum* (1968) also depicted a form of community solidarity in an urban slum district. Suttles's observations of a Chicago neighborhood found that various ethnic groups were able to share social spaces and connect over the sense of shared space despite intergroup tensions. The sense of belonging to the same place allowed the residents to unite in response to outside threats from other neighborhoods.

Over the past two decades, urban community scholars have focused on the concentration of poverty in metropolitan areas. There is a growing body of literature that seeks to examine the role of neighborhood poverty on individual life chances. The neighborhood poverty literature attempts to understand the connection between neighborhood poverty and unemployment, crime, high school completion, and out-of-wedlock births. While neighborhood effect studies represent a growing concern in the field of urban community work, one of the challenges for those who study neighborhood effects revolves around the conceptualization and measurement of neighborhood.

A neighborhood is more than just a physical location or geographic space. Urban scholars are usually interested in the interactions and

social networks that take place within a particular geographic space, hence the interchangeable use of the terms neighborhood and community. Small and Newman (2001) suggest there are various dimensions to neighborhood, such as a set of institutions, cultures, social spaces, and networks that should all be taken into consideration when designing research on neighborhood effects. Without considering the multiple layers of the concept of neighborhood, it becomes increasingly hard to determine the effects of neighborhoods on individuals.

Researchers who study the effects of neighborhoods also have to consider how neighborhoods are measured in their studies. Census tracts do not always provide an adequate operational definition of neighborhood. One limitation of using census tracts to operationalize neighborhoods is that it does not account for residents' perceptions of neighborhood boundaries. Small and Newman (2001) argue a resident's perception of the neighborhood boundaries can act as a determinant of how a neighborhood affects a resident. One alternative to using census tract data in neighborhood research is to use neighborhood clusters or boundaries drawn by the research for the purpose of studying neighborhood effects.

While contributions of the neighborhood effect literature delineate a range of social problems associated with urban community life, other scholars have attempted to highlight the agency of residents in urban communities. Instead of viewing communities as simply "containers of poverty," this vein of work attempts to demonstrate how residents assign meaning to their communities and how they negotiate the use of public spaces in neighborhoods. In the text *Streetwise* (1990), Anderson argues that the social life in the inner-city community consists of various rules and strategies for various interactions. He examines how residents in an urban community negotiate the use of public spaces. Anderson argues that individuals who are streetwise understand the rules of interaction for specific places within the community. Streetwise individuals know how to interpret gestures and body comportment of those within the community. The mutual respect and understanding of the rules of interaction ultimately contribute to a social order of community life. Anderson emphasizes that although negotiating public space in the community helps to maintain a certain order, it does not totally alleviate the social problems in the urban communities.

Gotham and Brumley (2002) examined how public housing residents "use space" in order both to create and reject identities. While the physical spaces in the neighborhood did influence the actions of the residents, the authors also argue that residents actively create safe spaces, and hot spaces (dangerous spots in the community), through their interactions and actions with one another. Using safe spaces allows residents to create respectable identities and to disavow the negative identities associated with public housing residents.

One of the oldest and most preferred methods used to study urban communities is ethnographic field research. In order to study certain urban communities, sociologists may move into a neighborhood or participate in various neighborhood meetings and organizations. The use of this method can also be traced to the early days of the Chicago School. Park and his colleagues produced a number of ethnographic case studies of neighborhoods. Some of the ethnographic studies out of the Chicago School tradition include William Whyte's *Street Corner Society* (1943) – which focused on life in an Italian American slum district in Boston – and Drake and Clayton's *Black Metropolis* (1945), a study of Chicago's black residential neighborhoods.

Contemporary urban community studies continue to draw on the Chicago School sociological tradition of ethnographic case studies of communities. Recent sociological works from Mary Pattillo-McCoy and Maria Kefalas (2003) provide ethnographic accounts of life in urban communities. Pattillo-McCoy's *Black Picket Fences* (1999) examines the social organization of a black middle-class neighborhood in Chicago. Over a 3-year period, she embedded herself in neighborhood life by coaching cheerleading, participating in church and neighborhood meetings, and working on local campaigns. Kefalas's *Working Class Heroes* (2003) is based on her observations and extensive field notes of meetings and events in a Chicago working-class community. She uses ethnographic accounts to demonstrate how race and class shape residents' attachment to place.

Ethnographic studies have been useful in understanding the organization of certain neighborhoods and the interactions among the residents in urban communities. However, urban ethnographers face a range of challenges while conducting field research. Although a researcher may reside in a neighborhood with the hopes of carrying out research, there is still the issue of gaining access to the community. In many cases, urban ethnographies require the assistance of a gatekeeper. Gatekeepers are individuals who can assist researchers in navigating the community and gaining additional contact within the community (Whyte 1997). In Whyte's *Street Corner Society* (1943) his key informant, Doc, was responsible for introducing him to other contacts in the community and helping him to learn the ropes in the community. Kefalas (2003) also indicates that her gatekeepers introduced her to other members of the community and served as unofficial tour guides. She also acknowledges that information from her informants provided a "foundation" for her work. In addition to gaining access to the field, researchers who study urban communities are also challenged with the task of connecting their work to larger social scientific questions and concerns. Ethnographic studies of urban communities offer audiences vivid depictions of the lives of inhabitants, but thick descriptions and narratives alone will not advance the field of sociology. The data from these ethnographies should advance sociological knowledge by either generating theory or expanding existing theory.

Urban community scholars also rely on survey methods to test models of community participation and residents' attachment to place. For instance, one of the most common models used to explain social interaction in communities is the systemic model put forth by Kasarda and Janowitz (1974). The systemic model suggests that length of residence is more important in predicting attachment to community than variables such as community size and density. Using survey data, the scholars provided support for the systemic model and rejected the linear development model that suggests that size and density are the primary factors that influence attachment to community. Guest (2000) addresses some of the limitations of the systemic model by considering the role of extra-community relations in community attachment.

In addition to testing the models that explain the level of interaction within communities, researchers have used survey studies to test the social disorganization of inner-city neighborhoods. For example, Rankin and Quane (2000) use survey research to test the social isolation thesis by examining the importance of neighborhood characteristics on the networks and community participation of residents. Although survey research has been useful in developing and supporting community models, it can be difficult to find data sets that contain information on a variety of neighborhoods and information on both neighborhood characteristics and individuals (Ainsworth 2002).

Future community research will have to address a range of issues. Sociologists have already recast the community-lost debate, or the argument that the tight-knit associations and interactions among people in a geographic location are gradually eroding. As virtual communities become more prevalent feature of our society, urban community scholars will have to consider how urban communities will be affected by the occurrence of virtual communities. While virtual communities and cyberspace represent a new set of challenges for urban scholarship, some issues linger from previous decades. Urban community scholars are still faced with some of the similar issues that Park and his colleagues addressed over 60 years ago. Issues like immigration, swelling urban areas, and residential segregation are still features of the urban landscape. However, unlike their predecessors, urban scholars now have to tackle these issues in the context of globalization.

SEE ALSO: Chicago School; Ecological Models of Urban Form; Ethnography; Robert E. Park, Ernest W. Burgess, and Urban Social Research; Urban; Urban Ecology; Urban Poverty; Urbanism/Urban Culture; Urbanization

REFERENCES AND SUGGESTED READINGS

Ainsworth, J. (2002) Why Does It Take a Village? The Mediation of Neighborhood Effects on Educational Achievement. *Social Forces* 81(1): 117–52.

Flanagan, W. (1993) *Contemporary Urban Sociology*. Cambridge University Press, Cambridge.

Gotham, K. & Brumley, K. (2002) Using Space: Agency and Identity in a Public Housing Development. *City and Community* 1(3): 267–89.

Guest, A. (2000) The Mediate Community. *Urban Affairs Review* 35: 603–27.

Hillary, G. (1955) Definitions of Community: Areas of Agreement. *Rural Sociology* 20: 111–23.

Kasarda, J. & Janowitz, M. (1974) Community Attachment in Mass Society. *American Sociological Review* 39: 328–39.

Kefalas, M. (2003) *Working-Class Heroes: Protecting Home, Community and Nation in a Chicago Neighborhood*. University of California Press, Berkeley.

Rankin, B. & Quane, J. (2000) Neighborhood Poverty and the Social Isolation of Inner-City African American Families. *Social Forces* 79(1): 139–64.

Small, M. & Newman, K. (2001) Urban Poverty after the Truly Disadvantaged: The Rediscovery of the Family, the Neighborhood and Culture. *Annual Review of Sociology* 27: 23–45.

Whyte, W. (1997) *Creative Problem Solving in the Field*. Alta Mira Press, Walnut Creek, CA.

urban crime and violence

Walter S. DeKeseredy

Defining crime and violence is the subject of much debate. In fact, a review of the extant social scientific literature on these topics reveals a myriad of definitions. However, here, the focus is limited to illegal interpersonal behaviors that threaten people's social, economic, and physical well-being. More specifically, the behaviors examined here are acts such as homicide, assault, robbery, theft, and drug dealing. While these harms affect both rural and urban communities, most of them occur in large metropolitan areas characterized by concentrated poverty and racial segregation (DeKeseredy et al. 2003).

Why are people who live in these neighborhoods at higher risk of committing and/or being victimized by crime? Not surprisingly, there are competing answers to this question. For example, heavily influenced by variants of Marxist thought, one group of scholars contends that lethal and non-lethal crimes plaguing these disenfranchised communities are symptoms of the following factors: the rise of the "contingent" workforce; the outmigration of people who can afford to leave poor urban communities; transnational corporations moving operations to developing countries to pay lower salaries; the "suburbanization" of employment; the implementation of high technology in workplaces; and the shift from a manufacturing to a service-based economy (Massey & Denton 1993; Wilson 1996).

Another group of critical theorists argues that the above structural factors are, indeed, key predictors of urban crime, but asserts that it is a combination of these determinants and relative deprivation that motivate people to commit crimes, most of which are intra-racial and intra-class in nature (Young 1999). There are also sociologists driven by social disorganization theory who state that crime in socially and economically excluded neighborhoods is associated with an absence of collective efficacy. This concept refers to "mutual trust among neighbors combined with a willingness to intervene on the behalf of the common good, specifically to supervise children and maintain public order" (Sampson et al. 1998: 1). Generally, high crime rates are more likely to be located in urban neighborhoods characterized by anonymity, weak social ties with neighbors, and diminished control over people's behavior. However, collective efficacy does not completely mediate the relationship between a community's structural characteristics and crime. For example, Sampson et al. (1997) found that, after controlling for collective efficacy, concentrated disadvantage still exerted independent effects on violent crime.

Another widely read and cited perspective on the relationship between poverty and urban crime is culture of poverty theory. Developed by Oscar Lewis in 1966, this account is popular among and promoted by conservatives. Banfield (1974) is one well-known culture of poverty theorist and he asserts that the values of poor and more affluent people are distinct. For Banfield, unlike more affluent people, the poor commit crime because they lack the discipline and moral fiber to avoid breaking the law if it means achieving short-term gains. There are more recent culture of poverty theories and because they are well documented elsewhere, they are not reviewed here. Nevertheless, an important point to consider is that these perspectives fail to recognize that the poor and

affluent have the same goals and values. Both groups want to be happy, have jobs, decent standards of living, a warm and loving family, a safe neighborhood, and so on. However, only those near or at the top of the socioeconomic ladder have legitimate means of achieving the American Dream and its related status, which is why they are much less likely to engage in criminal forms of anti-social behavior on the streets and elsewhere.

Of course, there are other theories of urban crime and violence and new ones are likely to be developed and tested in the near future. Further, those who study crime in urban communities use a variety of research methods to uncover rich qualitative and quantitative data on a wide variety of illegal activities. Still, there are major shortcomings in the extant empirical and theoretical literature on urban crime that must be overcome or minimized. For example, so far, most of the scholarly attention focuses on western industrialized nations and thus we know very little about urban crime in less developed societies (Crutchfield & Wadsworth 2003). Note, too, that there is a conspicuous absence of empirical and theoretical work on male-to-female intimate violence in poor and racially segregated communities, despite the fact that a few recent studies show that this is the most common form of criminal victimization experienced by women living in them (DeKeseredy & Renzetti 2004).

Another issue worth noting is that crime in public housing communities has received little sociological attention. In fact, to date, most of the information on violent and other offenses occurring in North American urban public housing communities is produced by journalists who portray crimes committed by and against those who live there as little more than "aberrations in an otherwise well-functioning system" (Reiman 2001: 173). Fortunately, however, international scholarship on crime in public housing is starting to grow. Even so, most of this work is quantitative in nature and hence there is a major need for more rich ethnographic work on the contexts in which crimes in these impoverished social settings occur (Lab 2003).

Undoubtedly, these criticisms will be effectively addressed in the near future. Still, for those who directly and indirectly suffer from criminal victimization, the question of what is to be done is much more important than the advancement of scholarship. Obviously, there are many prevention and control strategies currently in place, but most are simply aimed at "fixing poor people" (Crutchfield & Wadsworth 2003). Consider the massive expansion of the US prison population and major cutbacks to the welfare state. These policies, combined with the growing gap between the rich and poor, will only increase the amount of urban crime. Clearly, it is time for a new policy agenda. Rather than punishing the poor and minority populations, progressive scholars argue that we should strive to create stable quality employment, healthy public schools, a higher minimum wage, and other policies that reduce inequality and the anger and frustration it causes.

SEE ALSO: Collective Efficacy and Crime; Crime; Poverty; Social Exclusion; Urban; Urban Poverty; Urban Space; Violence; Violent Crime

REFERENCES AND SUGGESTED READINGS

Banfield, E. C. (1974) *The Unheavenly City Revisited.* Little Brown, Boston.
Crutchfield, R. D. & Wadsworth, T. (2003) Poverty and Violence. In: Heitmeyer, W. & Hagan, J. (Eds.), *International Handbook of Violence Research.* Kluwer, Boston, pp. 67–82.
DeKeseredy, W. S. & Renzetti, C. M. (2004) What about the Women? A Feminist Commentary on Crime Inside Public Housing Units. *Critical Criminologist* 14(2): 1–5.
DeKeseredy, W. S., Alvi, S., Schwartz, M. D., & Tomaszewski, E. A. (2003) *Under Siege: Poverty and Crime in a Public Housing Community.* Lexington, Lanham, MD.
Lab, S. P. (2003) Let's Put It Into Context. *Criminology and Public Policy* 3(1): 39–44.
Massey, D. S. & Denton, N. A. (1993) *American Apartheid: Segregation and the Making of the Underclass.* Harvard University Press, Cambridge, MA.
Reiman, J. (2001) *The Rich Get Richer and the Poor Get Prison: Ideology, Class, and Criminal Justice,* 6th edn. Allyn & Bacon, Boston.
Sampson, R. J., Raudenbush, S. W., & Earls, F. (1997) Neighborhoods and Violent Crime: A Multilevel Study of Collective Efficacy. *Science* 277: 918–24.
Sampson, R. J., Raudenbush, S. W., & Earls, F. (1998) *Neighborhood Collective Efficacy: Does it*

Help Reduce Violence? US Department of Justice, Washington, DC.
Wilson, W. J. (1996) *When Work Disappears: The World of the New Urban Poor.* Knopf, New York.
Young, J. (1999) *The Exclusive Society.* Sage, London.

urban ecology

Michael J. White and Ann H. Kim

Urban ecology is the study of community structure and organization as manifest in cities and other relatively dense human settlements. Among its major topics, urban ecology is concerned with the patterns of urban community sorting and change by socioeconomic status, life cycle, and ethnicity, and with patterns of relations across systems of cities. Of particular concern is the dynamic evolution of cities and contrast in urban structure across time periods, societies, and urban scale. The notion of community is central to urban ecology; a premise of the ecological approach is that the aggregation of persons into communities has important implications for their life chances, for the behavior of groups, and for aggregate outcomes. A further aspect of community organization lies in its geographic manifestation, although a mere geographic reductionism would not accurately capture the theoretical or empirical approach of the ecological perspective.

A sub-area of human ecology – a social science paradigm that seeks to understand the relationship between human organization and its environment, both in terms of physical setting and sustenance – the study of urban ecology has been interdisciplinary. Work in ecology has touched on sociology, demography, geography, economics, and anthropology, usually emphasizing the urban sectors of those disciplines. And at various times, human urban ecology has been more or less connected to biological ecology.

As Franklin Wilson argued, ecology is one of the oldest specializations within sociology and the intellectual roots of urban ecology can be found in the origins of sociology itself. For example, Émile Durkheim's *The Division of*

Labor in Society (1893) argued that modern societies are comprised of functionally interdependent units that are necessary for their survival and progress. As an explicit sociological approach, urban ecology is particularly associated with the Chicago School of sociology in the early twentieth century, even though the connection extends to a wide range of scholars and groups interested in cities and in population processes. The massive growth of cities at this time, fueled by the immigration of diverse-origin populations, helped spur the interest in urban form and function, and hence urban ecology as a subject of interest.

These early thinkers attempted to establish a parallel for human behavior with the topic of ecology in biology to describe local biotic communities. Collections of organisms are seen as communities, and the membership and evolution of communities are seen in a framework of interdependence. Sociological approaches almost universally invoke notions of ecology that are at once aggregate, interdependent, and embedded in a spatial and environmental context. Thus, communities of plants and animals find their parallel in communities of human groups. Both approaches see competition for resources in a spatially delimited setting. A further aspect of the framework is the concept of sustenance, in which one considers the manner in which local organisms, here humans, are sustained by the environment and by organization.

Studies at this time of specific urban communities, such as Louis Wirth's *The Ghetto* (1928) and Harvey Zorbaugh's *The Gold Coast and the Slum* (1929), and of city form and sub-communities more generally, such as Robert Park, Ernest Burgess and Roderick McKenzie's *The City* (1925), offer key illustrations of early treatments by the Chicago School, also known as the classical position. Additional concern in this era was with land rents and gradients, which not only helped explain the distribution of social groups, but also connected to the evolving interest in urban economics.

These early notions of human ecology gave way to more statistically intensive and geographically driven analyses of human organization in urban physical space. Considerable analysis was devoted in the middle to late twentieth century to the dimensions of urban social

structure. These included extensive analyses of patterns of residential segregation, urban growth, and differentiation. The application of factor analysis, or "factorial ecology" in the nomenclature, identified life cycle, socioeconomic status, and ethnicity as key dimensions of urban ecological sorting.

The ecological approach then came under criticism from various quarters, the most notable early critic being Milla Alihan. The biological metaphor was seen as strained, limiting the crucial elements of human volition and cognition. Urban ecology was also at risk of appearing spatially deterministic and attention to the relative spatial position and mapping of social phenomena lent credence to the critique. Furthermore, ecological approaches were criticized methodologically, even generating a phrase, "the ecological fallacy," that has traversed into general social science parlance. The fallacy is the error of making inferences about individual behavior from analysis of phenomena at the aggregate level.

In the middle of the twentieth century, human (and hence urban) ecology received additional formulations, with perhaps the broadest theoretical treatment arising in Amos Hawley's *Human Ecology* (1950). This treatise emphasized the study of the community and the dynamic connections among individuals, human organization, and the environment. Around the same time the widely adopted POET framework came to the fore: Population, Organization, Environment, Technology. This POET paradigm is also part of the neoclassical or neo-orthodox approach and it provides an intellectual rubric for organizing the thinking about urban phenomena and community processes within them.

Much work carried out from the mid-twentieth century for the next several decades was ecological in approach, if not always explicit in name. While one stream of research concentrated on the internal structure of cities, another focused on systems of cities and the relationships among them. Analyses of residential segregation by ethnic and socioeconomic group, the relationship between urban economic base and population growth, and some international comparisons of internal urban structure all took place at this time. Similarly, analysis of metropolitan functional specialization, trade, and the comparative growth of urban settlements were undertaken from an ecological vantage point.

These efforts were again followed by critiques from a variety of points, including Marxist and political economy perspectives. Both explicit and implicit criticisms suggested that the ecological approach missed several crucial elements in the study of urban development, structure, and change: the role of the state, local governments, and capital interests. At the same time, the combination of methodological concerns and the availability of microdata made the classic ecological style of aggregate analysis less attractive.

With the reemergence of concerns for urban issues generally and neighborhood issues specifically, various aspects of urban ecology achieved visibility or were reinvented in the late twentieth century. New data forms and methodological developments helped spur this turn. The wider concern for social exclusion, especially as it had a community or spatial manifestation, incorporated the ecological approach. The framework also continues to be relevant and widely used in the study of ethnic groups. In fact, the increasing ethnic diversification of high-income societies provides increasing impetus for the ecological approach, as Park's adage that spatial distance reflects social distance is put to the test in new settings. Interest in residential integration and sorting still involves the analysis of community patterns of ethnic concentration. Moving beyond classical ecology as applied to ethnic and racial groups, contemporary treatments examine dynamic changes in residential environments, such as in residential attainment, where a minority or disadvantaged group achieves residential parity with members of the advantaged majority. Such work is an extension of classical concerns for the process of residential succession.

An additional research theme is the restructuring of urban areas in light of significant transportation, communication, and industrial transformations. Scholars have noted the trend for the spatial decentralization of urban growth (e.g., suburbanization and urban sprawl, land-use patterns, and corporate activity). Where limitations in transportation and communications necessitated spatial proximity in the past, current technology, to some extent, liberates producers, suppliers, workers, and consumers

from this constraint. Regional factors, including policy variation and climate, may also play a role in shifting urban development. In this context, new urban forms and systems of inter-urban hierarchy emerge.

A more methodological avenue of ecological investigation accompanies the exploitation of multi-level or contextual data, in which individual data (microdata) is merged with characteristics of neighborhoods or a wider geographic area. Individual (person, household) behavior then, is taken to be predicted not only by individual traits, but also by characteristics of the local community. Indeed, the rapid development of the "neighborhood effects" literature, both substantively and methodologically, can be seen as a major intellectual current within sociology (Sampson et al. 2002), and this current taps directly into the central themes of urban ecology. Similarly, the broad interest in the problem of the macro-micro link overlaps significantly with ecologists' interest in community, in multiple levels of aggregation, and in dynamic interchange. Such studies have examined the determinants of escaping distressed neighborhoods, the choice of new neighborhood as a function of its ethnic composition, community effects on child development and crime, and the role of neighborhood traits in determining health outcomes.

The multi-level ecological approach is involved at a larger geographic scale, as well. The existence of social inequalities in health motivates a vein of research in which metropolitan income inequality is seen as playing a role in health outcomes such as infant and child mortality. Such studies have been carried out in some detail for the US. International comparisons also exist, where the "ecological" or aggregate measure is the level of inequality measured at the country level.

The predisposition of urban ecological analysis to spatial phenomena has made urban ecology readily receptive to the use of geographic information systems (GIS). More than merely mapping, GIS technology applied to urban ecology allows the analyst to redefine communities and networks, and to link micro to macro. Whereas social scientists were once bound by the community aggregation defined by others (such as a census agency's tract or ward boundaries), the availability of point coordinates assigned to each person or housing unit, and to natural features and economic activities, would allow a more variegated and refined analysis of the relationship between human organization, sustenance activity, community, and territory. Tests for spatial autocorrelation, which examine the effect of proximity, further add to our toolkit for understanding urban structure and organization.

Such technological developments have stimulated a reconnection with biological ecology. Urban ecological analysis provides a framework for examining integrated human-natural systems. Indeed, in several institutional and academic settings, the use of the phrases "urban ecology" and "human ecology" explicitly link human behavior to the biological environment. Here again human activity is seen as dynamic and community based, both influencing and influenced by its surrounding environment.

While urban ecology may be identified most clearly with American urban sociology and the Chicago School particularly, its adherents and manifestations are much broader. For example, it has been linked to the work of the French historian Fernand Braudel, who studied social system changes in the Mediterranean. It has been applied in analyses of urbanization in socialist countries as well as in the developing world. The paradigm was used to describe the somewhat inverted settlement patterns in Latin American cities. It has further found occasional expression in describing North African and European cities, where ethnic diversity had not yet achieved so clear a place in urban form. Still, the level of knowledge about urban ecology for settings outside of high-income societies is less developed. It is far from certain that the models once applied to North America and Europe (and selected other locations) will apply so readily to other portions of world geography, especially to urban settings in developing countries. Yet themes of internal urban structure, geographical disparities in well-being, and community change are relevant to all of these settings.

SEE ALSO: Ecological Models of Urban Form: Concentric Zone Model, the Sector Model, and the Multiple Nuclei Model; Residential Segregation; Urban; Urbanism/Urban Culture

REFERENCES AND SUGGESTED READINGS

Berry, B. J. L. & Kasarda, J. D. (1977) *Contemporary Urban Ecology*. Macmillan, New York.
Duncan, O. D. (1959) Human Ecology and Population Studies. In: Hauser, P. M. & Duncan, O. D. (Eds.), *The Study of Population: An Inventory and Appraisal*. University of Chicago Press, Chicago.
Frisbie, W. P. & Kasarda, J. D. (1988) Spatial Processes. In: Smelser, N. J. (Ed.), *Handbook of Sociology*. Sage, Newbury Park, CA, pp. 629–67.
Hawley, A. (1950) *Human Ecology: A Theory of Community Structure*. Ronald Press, New York.
Micklin, M. & Poston, D. L. (Eds.) (1998) *Continuities in the Study of Human Ecology*. Plenum Press, New York.
Sampson, R. J., Morenoff, J. D., & Gannon-Rowley, T. (2002) Assessing "Neighborhood Effects": Social Processes and New Directions in Research. *Annual Review of Sociology* 28: 443–78.
Saunders, P. (2001) Urban Ecology. In: Paddison, R. (Ed.), *Handbook of Urban Studies*. Sage, London, pp. 36–51.
Wilson, F. D. (1984) Urban Ecology: Urbanization and Systems of Cities. *Annual Review of Sociology* 10: 283–307.

urban education

Alan R. Sadovnik

Urban education has been the subject of ongoing discussions in the US, with policies aimed at urban school improvement vigorously debated over the last 40 years. Since the 1960s, as cities became increasingly poor and populated by minority groups, urban schools have reflected the problems associated with poverty. Although rural and many suburban schools have similar problems, urban schools represent the most serious challenges. A significant percentage of urban schools have been labeled in need of improvement under federal No Child Left Behind (2002) guidelines, with large city school systems having dropout rates at or above 40 percent and student achievement well below 50 percent proficiency in mathematics and reading. Despite these alarming data, there are significant numbers of high-performing urban schools and a number of reform programs that show promise (Tractenberg et al. 2002).

As urban areas became increasingly poor and segregated, their school systems mirrored the problems of urban poverty, including low student achievement, high student mobility, high dropout rates, and high levels of school failure. Due to the concentration of poor and minority populations in urban areas, urban public schools have significantly higher proportions of low socioeconomic and minority students than their surrounding suburbs. Over the past four decades, affluent white families have either moved to the suburbs or sent their children to private schools. In 2003 the enrollments of some of the 12 largest city school districts in the US were overwhelmingly minority, with the percentage of white students ranging from a low of 5.2 percent in Detroit to a high of 16.4 percent in Philadelphia and the percentage of African American and Hispanic students combined ranging from a low of 73.4 percent in New York to a high of 92.9 percent in Detroit (Ladson-Billings 2004).

Student achievement in urban schools mirrors the relationship between socioeconomic status (SES), race, ethnicity, and educational performance. Students from lower SES backgrounds have lower levels of academic attainment and achievement than students from higher SES backgrounds. African American and Hispanic students also have lower academic achievement than white and Asian American students. Given their high percentage of poor and African American and Hispanic students, urban schools reflect the achievement gaps that NCLB is designed to eliminate.

Since the 1960s the achievement gaps based on social class, race, ethnicity, and gender have been the focus of educational policy, especially in urban areas. These gaps include both group differences in achievement based on standardized tests and grades; attainment based on years of schooling, high school and college attendance and graduation and dropout rates and completion of honors and advanced placement courses; and opportunity based on access to qualified teachers, challenging curriculum placement in special education and investments in education, including state and local funding. The gaps include higher academic achievement by high-income students compared to low-income students, white and Asian American students compared to African American and Hispanic students, even when controlling for socioeconomic level, and male students compared to female students. There have been some improvements since the 1960s, with the gender gap closing dramatically and in some cases with women outperforming men, and social class, race, and ethnic differences lessening until 1988. However, the social class, race, and ethnic achievement gap widened since 1988, despite continued educational policies aimed at reducing them (US Department of Education 2000).

The reasons for the differences in achievement are complex, including factors both outside and inside the schools. Rothstein (2004) argues that much of the achievement gap is due to factors related to poverty, such as inadequate housing, health care, and environmental problems, including lead paint and other toxins in the urban environment. Although this is the case, it is undoubtedly also true that factors within urban schools contribute to low achievement. These include unequal funding, unqualified teachers, low expectations and dumbed-down curricula, and high turnover of teachers and principals.

With respect to investments, in 2001 the nation had an effective funding gap between highest and lowest poverty districts of $1,256 per student, $31,400 for a typical classroom of 25 students, and $502,392 for a typical elementary school of 400 students. These gaps vary by state, with some such as Illinois, New York, and Pennsylvania having large gaps and some such as Delaware, Massachusetts, Minnesota, and New Jersey providing more funding to high-poverty districts (Education Trust 2004). These funding gaps are most pronounced in large differences between urban and suburban districts. While some states, most notably New Jersey, have eliminated these differences through court intervention, children in most US cities receive considerably less funding than their suburban neighbors.

NCLB's requirement that all schools have highly qualified teachers in every classroom highlighted the problem of unqualified teachers in urban schools, many of whom were teaching out of their field of expertise. However, while most teachers meet the highly qualified standards of NCLB, the data indicate significant numbers of classrooms staffed by teachers who are not highly qualified in the particular subject taught. This is the result of the practice called out-of-field teaching – teachers being assigned to teach subjects which do not match their training or education. This is a crucial practice because highly qualified teachers may actually become highly unqualified if they are assigned to teach subjects in which they have little training or education. At the secondary school level, about one fifth of classes in each of the core academic subjects (math, science, English, social studies) are taught by teachers who do not hold a teaching certificate in the subject taught. The data also show that urban schools, especially low-income ones, have more out-of-field teaching than others.

Problems in staffing urban schools have less to do with teacher shortages and more to do with organizational issues inside schools. Principals often find it easier to hire unqualified teachers than qualified ones and the absence of status and professionalism and poor working conditions in teaching lead to high dropout rates in the first five years of teaching. Therefore, urban districts are constantly replacing teachers, which has significant consequences since it takes years to become an expert teacher. Rates of teacher attrition and misassignment are more prevalent in urban and high-poverty schools (Ingersoll 1999, 2003). Ingersoll's research suggests that programs aimed at solving urban school staffing problems at the supply level through alternative teacher education programs such as Teach for America, the New York City Teaching Fellows Program, and New Jersey's Alternative Certification Program (all of which allow college graduates with majors in their teaching field to enter teaching without traditional certification through a college teacher education program) fail to address the organizational problems within schools that are responsible for high turnover rates.

Data from the Education Trust (2004) indicate that many urban schools do not have rigorous academic curricula for all of their students, often track a significant number into non-academic programs, and have low expectations for success for a majority of their students. Bryk et al. (1993) argue that one of the reasons that urban parochial schools have higher academic achievement for low-income

students of color is that these schools require a rigorous academic college preparatory curriculum for all of their students.

Despite these problems, there are also numerous examples of highly successful urban schools (Education Trust 2004). For example, in Newark, New Jersey, taken over by the New Jersey Department of Education in 1995 for, among other things, low student achievement, there are a number of district and public charter schools with high poverty and high minority populations that perform not only above the state averages, but also at the same levels as those in the highest socioeconomic districts (Barr 2004). Over the past 15 years a variety of educational policies have been implemented to replicate these schools and to improve urban schools. These include school finance litigation, comprehensive whole-school reform programs, effective school models, school choice (including charter schools and private school vouchers), and state takeover of failing urban districts (Tractenberg et al. 2002).

These educational reforms have the potential to improve urban schools; however, by themselves they are limited in reducing the achievement gaps (Anyon 2005; Rothstein 2004) unless they also address the factors outside of schools responsible for educational inequalities. In addition to school-based programs such as early childhood programs, summer programs, and after-school programs, Rothstein (2004: 129–50) calls for economic programs to reduce income inequality and to create stable and affordable housing, and the expansion of school-community clinics to provide health care and counseling. He also warns that although school finance suits are necessary to ensure that all children receive an adequate education, without addressing the economic forces outside of schools they will not be sufficient. Rothstein (a liberal) and Anyon (a radical) both conclude that school reform is necessary but insufficient to reduce the achievement gaps without broader social and economic policies aimed at reducing the effects of poverty.

These descriptions of US urban education and urban educational reforms are mirrored internationally. For example, research in the UK (Mortimore & Whitty 1999; Walford 1999; Power et al. 2001) indicates that students living in urban areas and disadvantaged minorities achieve at lower levels than more affluent students. Mortimore and Whitty (1999) and Power et al. (2001) describe similar policies aimed at improving urban education and argue that although school reforms can make a difference, policies aimed at eradicating poverty must complement these. Whitty (1997), Walford (1999), Ladd (2002), and Plank and Sykes (2003) have examined the impact of school choice policies internationally to improve urban schools. Their research suggests that these policies have mixed success at best. Similar problems and policies have been described in Australia (Singh 2005) and numerous other countries (Cookson et al. 1992).

SEE ALSO: Bilingual, Multicultural Education; Educational Inequality; Educational and Occupational Attainment; Parental Involvement in Education; Race and Schools; School Choice; School Segregation, Desegregation; Schools, Charter; Schools, Magnet; Urban Policy

REFERENCES AND SUGGESTED READINGS

Anyon, J. (2005) *Radical Possibilities: Public Policy, Urban Education and a New Social Movement.* Routledge, New York.

Barr, J. (2004) *A Statistical Portrait of Newark's Schools.* Cornwall Center for Metropolitan Studies, Newark, NJ.

Bryk, A., Lee, V., & Holland, P. (1993) *Catholic Schools and the Common Good.* Harvard University Press, Cambridge, MA.

Cookson, Jr., P. W., Sadovnik, A. R., & Semel, S. F. (1992) *International Handbook of Educational Reform.* Greenwood Press, Westport.

Education Trust (2004) *Education Watch: Achievement Gap Summary Tables.* Education Trust, Washington, DC.

Ingersoll, R. (1999) The Problem of Underqualified Teachers in American Secondary Schools. *Educational Researcher* 28: 26–37.

Ingersoll, R. (2003) *Who Controls Teachers' Work? Power and Accountability in America's Schools.* Harvard University Press, Cambridge, MA.

Ladd, H. F. (2002) *Market-Based Reforms in Urban Education.* Economic Policy Institute, Washington, DC.

Ladson-Billings, G. (2004) Landing on the Wrong Note: The Price We Paid for Brown. *Educational Researcher* 33(7): 3–13.

Mortimore, P. & Whitty, G. (1999) School Improvement: A Remedy for Social Exclusion. In: Hayton, A. (Ed.), *Tackling Disaffection and Social Exclusion.* Kogan Page, London, pp. 80–94.

Plank, D. N. & Sykes, G. (2003) *Choosing Choice: School Choice in International Perspective.* Teachers College Press, New York.

Power, S., Warren, S., Gillborn, D., Clark, A., Thomas, S., & Coate, K. (2001) *Education in Deprived Areas.* Institute of Education, University of London, London.

Rothstein, R. (2004) *Class and Schools: Using Social, Economic, and Educational Reform to Close the Black–White Achievement Gap.* Teachers College Press, New York.

Singh, P. (2005). Urban Education, Cultural Diversity and Poverty: A Case Study of Globalization: Brisbane, Australia. In: Kincheloe, J. & Hayes, K. (Eds.), *Metropedagogy: Power, Justice, and the Urban Classroom.* Sense Publishers, Rotterdam.

Tractenberg, P., Holzer, M., Miller, G., Sadovnik, A., & Liss, B. (2002) *Developing a Plan for Reestablishing Local Control in the State-Operated Districts.* Institute on Education Law and Policy, Rutgers University, Newark, NJ. Online. www.ielp/rutgers.edu.

US Department of Education, National Center for Educational Statistics (2000) *The Condition of Education: National Assessment of Educational Progress.* Office of the Under Secretary and Office of Elementary and Secondary Education, Washington, DC.

Walford, G. (1999) Educational Reform and Sociology in England and Wales. In: Levinson, D. L., Cookson, Jr., P. W., & Sadovnik, A. R. (Eds.), *Encyclopedia of Sociology and Education.* Routledge, New York, pp. 211–20.

Whitty, G. (1997) Creating Quasi-Markets in Education: A Review of Recent Research on Parental Choice and School Autonomy in Three Countries. *Review of Research in Education* 22: 3–48.

urban movements

Hans Pruijt

Urban movements are social movements through which citizens attempt to achieve some control over their urban environment. The urban environment comprises the built environment, the social fabric of the city, and the local political process.

An alternative current term is "urban social movements." Pickvance (2003) suggested that the term "urban movements" is to be preferred because it is more straightforward, analogous to "environmental movement" instead of "environmental social movement."

The sociological study of urban movements emerged in the aftermath of May 1968. Previously, urban sociology had tended to focus on community and social integration, at the expense of neglecting the political economy of urban development and conflicts of interest. One of the first to set out to fill this gap was Manuel Castells. In *The Urban Question* (1972) he presented a model of the dynamics of the urban system in which there was one single mechanism for structural change. He called this mechanism "urban social movements." Around the same time, citizens in many cities around the world were mobilizing in response to problems in the urban environment, which helped generate interest in the topic; a number of sociologists drew inspiration from their personal experience as participants in these mobilizations.

The urban movement literature shows a wide range of problems that citizens have responded to with collective action. A large section can be categorized under the heading of "collective consumption": housing shortages, growing discrepancies between rents and wages, landlords' neglect of maintenance – even up to the point of abandonment – and insufficient health care and education. In developing countries, shantytown dwellers face a lack of water supply, sewers, and electricity. A second set of action-provoking problems is related to urban planning: displacement and destruction of beloved cityscapes. Finally, specific groups have mobilized around highly specific issues, such as squatters against anti-squatter policies, property-owners against proposed social housing and against property taxes, racist groups against migrants.

Urban movements tend to draw on a relatively stable set of familiar types of action. The action repertoires found in urban movements very much overlap with the action repertoires of other social movements. Some items, however, are specific for urban movements: the rent strike, squatting, and developing alternative spatial plans.

Organizational patterns can be bottom-up or top-down. Bottom-up mobilization involves building networks of activists and occasional participants, the creation of committees, possibly formal organizations, newsletters, and neighborhood centers. An example in which substantial bottom-up mobilization occurred was the 1970s Citizen Movement in Madrid. Top-down mobilization occurs when political parties build local organizations, such as in the case of the land squatter movement of Santiago de Chile from 1965 to 1973, or when political groups try to take over or make use of a movement that started in a bottom-up fashion. This occurred in the later stages of the Madrid Citizen Movement (examples from Castells 1983). Top-down involvement of political groups or parties is often viewed as detrimental because it can entail a transformation into state-oriented bureaucracy, and because it clashes with the prevalent ideal of self-management (Castells 1983).

Often, urban movements exhibited a capacity for transcending social borders, such as through cross-class mobilization. This has taken the shape of horizontal cooperation of participants from different class backgrounds (as in urban squatters' movements), or instead middle-class activists (such as students) helping poor people (such as immigrant workers). Some urban movements, however, have been restricted in terms of the participants' ethnicity (such as black and Latino mobilizations in US cities in the 1960s and 1970s), class (e.g., rent strikes), or age (the Italian Social Centers Movement).

The relatively prominent role of women in urban movements – as far as social movements go that are not specific women's movements – has often been noted. An example is the 1922 tenants' protest in Veracruz, Mexico (Castells 1983). One explanation for this phenomenon points to the special role of women in collective consumption.

Protest goals are often clear and measurable, such as preventing a particular planned transformation in the built environment, ensuring that particular buildings are repaired instead of being abandoned, getting a street closed to through traffic, preventing the eviction of a building, or achieving a rent reduction. In studies of urban movements we tend to find ample information on whether such goals have been attained. The resulting picture shows a mix of failure and success; it is evident that urban movements can have clear effects. The clearest are the effects of activists' victories in planning conflicts. In several cities (such as Amsterdam), the map shows the traces of urban highway construction projects that were abandoned in mid-execution: a wide street, created as a stretch of urban highway after razing blocks left and right, stopped dead in a maze of ancient streets. Newly built houses or renovated buildings may be seen solidifying the protest movement's victory because the gap that they leave is only wide enough for a narrow street.

Beyond cancelation of individual construction projects we find wholesale transformations of urban planning, in a direction that more or less conforms to demands made by activists. An example is the influence that Castells (1983) ascribed to the Madrid Citizens Movement. Urban movements often are pre-sentient of what later becomes accepted planning wisdom.

Ideally, claims about turns in urban history caused by protest are bolstered by an analysis of the decision-making process and by an attempt to sort out movement influence from other factors, such as financial constraints.

Protesters' victories may be partial, such as a cap put on a rent increase instead of succeeding in preventing it completely, or being unable to prevent an eviction but instead securing rehousing. Also, there may be unintended effects, such as protests against eviction of squats leading to legalization. Some point to the risk that urban action can be self-defeating: improvements in low-income neighborhoods might attract gentrification, which forces the original inhabitants out of their neighborhood.

Some confusion exists as to whether urban movements should be seen as either instrumental movements or identity movements. The clarity in terms of goals that cases of urban protest often possess does not exist at the level of the movement. Movements do not need overarching goals, nor do they need a high level of organizational unification. Therefore, goals ascribed to urban movements tend to be somewhat arbitrary. For example, the same Dutch squatters' movement has been described by some as a "new social movement" or identity movement aiming

to create a new way of life, and by others, equally justifiably, as an instrumental movement fighting for affordable housing.

Urban movement studies tend to move beyond recording and explaining victories and defeats in individual cases of urban action and conflict. A question that has commanded much attention is the contribution that urban movements might make to social change. Castells, especially, has been involved in the search for a general theory. At first (e.g., in his 1972 book *The Urban Question*) he elaborated the idea that urban movements had a latent function in the class struggle. He stated that urban movements could only be significant for social change if they linked up with organizations involved in the class struggle in the sphere of production.

In a later attempt, Castells (1983) stated that the local focus of urban movements precludes transformation of production, communication, and government; the kind of social change that urban movements would be capable of producing is resistance to domination, or, in other words, changing the "urban meaning," resulting in "reactive utopias." Urban movements could achieve their maximum potential for social change (Castells reserved the title of urban *social* movement for this condition) when they were multi-issue, pursuing all of the following three goals: (1) realizing collective consumption demands (such as those related to social housing) within a framework of promoting the city as a use-value against commodification; (2) establishing and strengthening an autonomous cultural identity and promoting communication instead of "programmed one-way information flows"; and (3) territorially based self-management. Other criteria were explicit consciousness that active groups were part of a wider social movement, solidarity with other parts of the movement, expression of movement themes in the media, and – without giving up autonomy – the maintenance of links with professionals and political parties. Castells's model seems most fruitful when treated as an ideal type, i.e., as a conceptual tool for discussing similarities and differences between urban movements. Since the model does not include contextual variables and scarcely any action variables, not too much explanatory value is to be expected.

Rise, fall, and transformation of urban movements have been subject to analysis as well. In his early writings, Castells suggested that mobilization can be explained by the intensity of urban problems or the contradictions behind these. This stimulated other urban sociologists to identify contextual factors that play a role in mobilization, such as the extent to which citizens find themselves in a similar state of deprivation, whether or not it is a zero-sum conflict (one neighborhood's gain is the other neighborhood's loss), and cleavages between tenants and owners or between those who are eligible for rehousing after renewal and those who are not. Insights from the general social movement literature, especially the political opportunity structure approach, apply here too: citizens mobilize in response to widening opportunities as cleavages within elites become manifest and new allies appear on the scene. Another relevant contextual variable is the extent to which urban managers succeed in redefining social issues as either individual or technical problems. Repression is an important factor everywhere, although most dramatically in developing countries where activists risk being murdered when they move against powerful interests (Corr 1999). Besides context, analyses of mobilization need to consider the strategies employed in the mobilization of resources such as influential sympathizers. The skills activists display in framing, i.e., verbalizing urban problems, identifying someone to blame, and proposing a solution, are important too.

Movements tend to have a life cycle; institutionalization (i.e., being channeled into a stable pattern based on formalized rules and laws) and cooptation (activists start performing some task at the request of the government) are often seen as the beginning of the end. It is an open question, however, whether institutionalization is inevitable. The introduction of conventional interaction such as consultation and negotiation does not imply that disruptive tactics necessarily disappear from the movement's action repertoire. Especially when disruptive tactics are part of the movement's identity (e.g., for a squatters' movement, squatting is both means and end) and when repression is moderate, they may remain part of the repertoire. Institutionalization and cooptation may cancel out the impulse toward change, but they may also offer a way to secure the results of a movement's victory.

An emergent area of inquiry concerns the effect of structural regime change on urban movements. Post-Fordist theory suggests that local governments increasingly feel contradictory pressures to decrease welfare bureaucracy and spending and, at the same time, to alleviate poverty. This results in a greater need to coopt urban movement groups, for example as managers of self-help programs. Issues that prompt research and debate are whether activists should expect some influence in return for being coopted, because they perform an essential job, and whether cooptation of some movement groups means that new opportunities for radical groups emerge.

Some recent thinking deemphasizes the *local* focus of urban movements (Hamel et al. 2000). Indeed, we do find clear cases of urban movements that are both local and national or supranational, such as the youth movement that is involved in the creation of social centers, "Critical Mass" and "Reclaim the Streets." But more generally, the fact that urban mobilizations have appeared in at least nationwide wave patterns shows that influences beyond the local are relevant.

SEE ALSO: City Planning/Urban Design; Direct Action; Framing and Social Movements; Gender, Social Movements and; Gentrification; Mobilization; New Social Movement Theory; Political Opportunities; Political Process Theory; Resource Mobilization Theory; Urban Political Economy; Urban Policy; Urban Renewal and Redevelopment

REFERENCES AND SUGGESTED READINGS

Assies, W., Burgwal, G., & Salman, T. (1990) *Structures of Power, Movements of Resistance: An Introduction to the Theories of Urban Movements in Latin America*. Cedla, Amsterdam.

Castells, M. (1983) *The City and the Grassroots: A Cross-Cultural Theory of Urban Social Movement*. Edward Arnold, London.

Corr, A. (1999) *No Trespassing: Squatting, Rent Strikes, and Land Struggles Worldwide*. South End Press, Cambridge, MA.

Fainstein, S. S. & Hirst, C. (1995) Urban Social Movements. In: Judge, D., Stoker, G., & Wolman, H.

(Eds.), *Theories of Urban Politics*. Sage, London, pp. 181–204.

Fisher, R. & Kling, J. (Eds.) (1993) *Mobilizing the Community: Local Politics in the Era of the Global City*. Sage, Newbury Park, CA.

Hamel, P., Lustiger-Thaler, H., & Mayer, M. (Eds.) (2000) *Urban Movements in a Globalizing World*. Routledge, London.

Lawson, R. (Ed.) (1986) *The Tenant Movement in New York City, 1904–1984*. Rutgers University Press, New Brunswick, NJ. www.tenant.net.

Lowe, S. (1986) *Urban Social Movements: The City After Castells*. St. Martin's Press, New York.

Pickvance, C. (Ed.) (2003) Symposium on Urban Movements. *International Journal of Urban and Regional Research* 27: 102–77.

urban policy

Allan Cochrane

Urban policy actively shapes the ways in which people live in cities. As well as reflecting contemporary understandings of the role of cities in economic and social development, it also helps to create those understandings.

Definitions of urban policy are elusive in part because the term appears so self-explanatory. It seems to be no more and no less than the sum of those policies that are intended to help cities or those living in them. Unfortunately, however, this commonsense approach is ultimately not very helpful – since most of us now live in urban areas of one sort or another, almost all public policy might be deemed to be urban policy. Assessing quite why one particular form of policy intervention attracts the soubriquet "urban" while another does not is more difficult than at first appears. Although there is a superficial continuity in the emphasis on "urban areas" rather than particular welfare client groups, the definition of the "urban" on which policy attention is focused has itself varied significantly, even if this has rarely been acknowledged by those making or implementing the policies.

The arrival of urban policy as a form of social policy in its own right (rather than an offshoot of urban planning or housing) can be located in the specific circumstances of the US in the 1960s, in the context of the "War on Poverty" and the political demands of the increasingly urbanized African American population, which also found their expression in the urban riots or rebellions of the late 1960s. In this first incarnation it can be seen as a means of bringing previously excluded groups into the broader post-war welfare settlement, even if still on rather different terms. And it was taken up in analogous ways in many other western countries (most obviously the UK). However, the development of urban policy from this starting point does not reflect a continuing process of learning with a clear and continuing set of aims and ambitions. On the contrary, it is "at least in western society, a chaotic conception" (Atkinson & Moon 1994: 20) because there has been no shared understanding of the "problem" around which policy might be defined.

There have been several quite distinctive attempts to find a means of defining urban policy that is capable of capturing and reflecting its full complexity. Some of its earliest analysts (e.g., Piven & Cloward 1972) saw its arrival in the US of the 1960s as a response to political pressure (whether expressed through the threat or reality of riots or the need to incorporate a rising black middle class) and the importance of such pressure in helping to generate urban policy, particularly in its early years, should not be dismissed. But the way in which it made its transatlantic migration (and has since gone on to become a global phenomenon) suggests that it is not enough to focus on its role as a response to popular pressures.

Another early explanation identified urban policy as an expression of the rise of a new political class: new professionals in government and academia seeking to stake their own position as an alternative policy elite, based around the rise of the social sciences and what has come to be called evidence based policymaking, rather than the traditional culture of the civil service or public bureaucracy (Marris & Rein 1972). This interpretation, too, has its attractions, since it fits well with the shift away from the traditional bureau-professionalism of the Keynesian welfare state that has been widely recognized as a central feature of state restructuring since the 1970s. However, the extent to which urban policy can be closely identified with the rise of a new professional class remains questionable, not least because that class has proved difficult to track or identify.

The emergence of urban policy in practice was accompanied by an explosion of critical theory which set out to place the new agenda in a wider context. At the core of this explosion were approaches that focused on issues of social reproduction, described as "collective consumption" by neo-Marxists such as Manuel Castells. These approaches make it possible to identify a policy area that is not simply reducible to what is (confusingly and inconsistently) labeled "urban" in everyday speech or even the language used by new professionals. They also place the "urban" at the heart of political life and policy debate and the reshaping of contemporary welfare states. Castells (1977: 440) argued: "The essential problems regarding the urban are in fact bound up with the processes of 'collective consumption' or what Marxists call the organization of the collective means of reproduction of labor power." Since in this formulation the "urban" is itself defined by policy – the delivery of services and goods provided by or through the state to support the reproduction of labor power – core aspects of social policy are redefined as urban policy.

Unfortunately, one of the strengths of approaches that focus on collective or social reproduction is also a weakness, since, by identifying a separate sphere for the urban, they effectively exclude from consideration some of the policy initiatives that increasingly define the politics and shape the experience of life in urban areas. Many of the policies that would not be defined as urban in this sense help to define the experience of urban life (including policing and economic development, as well as transfer payments through the social security and benefits systems). Equally important, spending on some programs (such as education and health) might qualify as collective consumption, but they are generally only seen as urban when they are associated with specific area-based initiatives.

If the debates of the 1970s focused on the role of the urban in processes of social reproduction, by the mid-1980s the emphasis had shifted dramatically. Now it was placed increasingly clearly on the role of cities in processes of production, or on the realization of profits from real estate development. So, for example, in a powerful phrase, Logan and Molotch (1987) identify the city as a "growth machine." They argue: "*Local conflicts* over growth are central to the organization of cities … not only the economic imperative of the larger system, but also the striving of *parochial actors* to make money" (p. viii).

In some important respects the insights of these theorists are helpful, particularly because they seem to fit with key aspects of today's actually existing urban policy. They are consistent with some of the policy shifts that have led to the identification of the "entrepreneurial" or the "competitive" city; that is, the policy approach that sees economic success as the necessary precondition for the well-being (or welfare) of citizens rather than the existence of an extensive (social-democratic) welfare state. For some, this understanding has come to form the basis of a critique; for others, it provided the basis of normative policymaking.

However, if Castells and others overemphasized the significance of cities as places of collective consumption, then this approach understates it. Because urban politics is understood through the drive to realize exchange value and generate profits from growth (through rising property values) or from the necessary relations associated with locally dependent business policy, aspects of urban policy that might be focused on other forms of social consumption (e.g., community) tend to be ruled out as irrelevant, or redefined as instrumental infrastructure. So, for example, the significance of urban policy as an attempt to control the disorderly and manage disordered spaces fits uneasily with a structural emphasis on growth as driver of urban policy. Similarly, while it might be possible to claim community-based initiatives (and communitarian thinking) in terms that relate them to issues of production and the competitiveness of cities, the tension between a community-based agenda and a more narrowly defined competitiveness-oriented agenda is hard to ignore.

More recently, attempts have been made to position urban policy rather more explicitly within broader shifts in economy, public policy, and state restructuring. One aspect of this is reflected in the major critique launched by those who see in its contemporary development and definition the working out of a global neoliberal agenda (Brenner & Theodore 2002). This approach invites us to understand urban policy as part of a wider process of change, while also positioning the city as an active agent in shaping that change. In this context, urban policy is seen to take on a key role in the reshaping of post-war welfare states and the settlements associated with them. The rise and development of urban policy helped to shape (as well as reflect) the policy upheavals and state restructuring that characterized the fraying of the Keynesian welfare state and the unsettling of the political, economic, and welfare settlement implied by it. In its contemporary form(s) it begins to suggest the possibility of new political and welfare settlements, even if they remain highly provisional and contested.

The "urban" may often still be used as coded language for "welfare" (and black), but the rise of the "competitive" or "entrepreneurial" city powerfully illustrates the wider direction of change. Historically, the emphasis may have been on "inner cities" and those living in them, but now it is urban economies that are to be revitalized or restructured in order to make cities competitive and improve the economic well-being of residents. Physical and commercial infrastructure is to be regenerated, making urban land economically productive once again, and there has also been a drive towards place marketing and cultural reimagination, so that cities can be made attractive to the "creative class." Local neighborhoods are increasingly targeted either for community renewal (building social capital or community capacity) or for new forms of policing, where they cannot be relied on to police themselves effectively.

The rise of mega-projects, the reimagination of cities as cultural centers, and "global cities" are as marked in Pacific-Asia as in the US and Western Europe. In this context the nature of the urban "problem" is also interpreted differently – instead of a catalog of decline, which urban policy needs to reverse, in the new urban policy cities become potential (and actual) sources of growth and development. Even the "slums" of the new megacities in South America and Africa are now identified by the World Bank as potential hotbeds of entrepreneurialism. There has been a broad shift away from a vision of the state as regulator of the market to one in which the state is defined as agent of the market, with an explicit policy focus on providing the infrastructure for profitable production rather than welfare support to those on the margins. It is within this context that cities are left to bargain and negotiate to achieve different outcomes for their populations.

SEE ALSO: Built Environment; City Planning/Urban Design; Community; Crime, Broken Windows Theory of; Growth Machine; Inequality and the City; Social Policy, Welfare State; Urban Crime and Violence; Urban Political Economy; Urban Poverty; Urban Renewal and Redevelopment; Urbanism/Urban Culture

REFERENCES AND SUGGESTED READINGS

Atkinson, R. & Moon, G. (1994) *Urban Policy in Britain: The City, the State and the Market.* Macmillan, London.

Brenner, N. & Theodore, N. (2002) *Spaces of Neoliberalism: Urban Restructuring in North America and Western Europe.* Blackwell, Oxford.

Castells, M. (1977) *The Urban Question.* Edward Arnold, London.

Cochrane, A. (2006) *Understanding Urban Policy. A Critical Approach.* Blackwell, Oxford.

Euchner, C. & McGovern, S. (2003) *Urban Policy Reconsidered: Dialogues on the Problems and Prospects of American Cities.* Routledge, New York.

Hall, P. & Pfeiffer, U. (2000) *Urban Future 21: A Global Agenda for Twenty-First Century Cities.* Spon, London.

Logan, J. & Molotch, H. (1987) *Urban Fortunes: The Political Economy of Place.* University of California Press, Berkeley.

Marris, P. & Rein, M. (1972) *Dilemmas of Social Reform: Poverty and Community Action in the United States*, 2nd edn. Routledge & Kegan Paul, London.

Piven, F. F. & Cloward, R. (1972) *Regulating the Poor: The Functions of Public Welfare.* Tavistock, London.

Savitch, H. & Kantor, P. (2002) *Cities in the International Marketplace: The Political Economy of Urban Development in North America and Western Europe.* Princeton University Press, Princeton.

urban political economy

Leonard Nevarez

One of sociology's original and most fundamental questions is: how does the city shape social life? The answer provided by urban political economy is: as a mechanism in the accumulation of wealth, with all the power and inequality that results. "Political economy" generally refers to the scholarly paradigm that examines how material processes of production and exchange shape and are shaped by decisions made in economic and political institutions; with "urban," this concern centers around material production *of* and *within* cities. Since the 1970s, urban political economy has influenced the field of urban sociology, bringing insights from other disciplines – particularly social geography (with its conceptualization of social space and place) and political science (the focus on government and law) – while retaining sociology's social constructionist framework. Sociology provides an especially hospitable discipline for urban political economy's investigation of the ways in which the city's economic and political relations cohere and evolve across institutional, legal, and territorial domains.

Urban political economy emerged as a critique of the urban ecology paradigm, particularly the latter's explanation for the growth and structure of cities and regions. By emphasizing the spatial competition for resources by individuals, groups, and institutions, urban ecology has viewed political hierarchies, economic actors and laws, and other social institutions as expressions of more fundamental and pre-conscious forces. Its corollary that city governments, local business elites, urban planners, or racist neighborhood associations, for example, are not the "real" agents of urban structure and relations had long struck a cadre of conflict-oriented urban sociologists as a problematic denial of social power. By the 1950s and 1960s, urban ecology's inability to understand critically the problems of white flight and urban poverty in the US as well as urban and political unrest throughout the world created a breaking point for many urban sociologists. Consequently, a first generation of urban political economists began to emphasize the role of economic structure and social power in explaining urban relations.

THE NEO-MARXIAN TRADITION

Urban political economy updates the theoretical legacy of Karl Marx around the urban condition, a topic he did not address extensively in his nineteenth-century writings. First, neo-Marxians explained the city's evolution as structural expressions of *historical relations of production*. Beginning in the early twentieth century, their argument goes, industrial capitalists promoted the flight of manufacturing to the urban periphery and the growth of residential suburbs to advance their class interests in, respectively, avoiding the costs of aging and inflexible urban infrastructure and dispersing urban hotbeds of labor unrest. Industrialists promoted these interests in the political and cultural realms via federal policies and cultural sentiments promoting homeownership, suburban development, and the encouragement of growth in America's "Sunbelt" region (where the union tradition is much weaker than in the older "Rustbelt"). In urban sociology, these early neo-Marxian claims appeared in the 1970s and 1980s alongside other intellectual agendas that, although not necessarily sharing the same conflict orientation, put urban class relations at the forefront of the field. Research on dual labor markets, immigrant entrepreneurs, ethnic niches, and related issues have all benefited from the neo-Marxian insight that economic forces do not merely express social relations but in fact drive them as well. However, by emphasizing capitalism's causal role, this early urban political economy research in turn raised a question that casts doubt on urban sociology's disciplinary relevance: is the city merely a container for larger social forces?

A powerful rejection of that question began with a largely European cadre of neo-Marxian scholars whose work integrated "urban" with "political economy" in new and compelling ways. First, British geographers starting with David Harvey explained how investment in land provided important functions for capitalism. Borrowing the idea of space as a "secondary circuit of capital" from French sociologist-philosopher Henri Lefebvre (whose urban writings at that time were mostly untranslated in English), Harvey contended that land and the built environment offer capital an important alternate site for investment when industrial investments soured. With this claim, Harvey reframed urban sociology's traditional interest for urban and regional development into a structural Marxist theory of *capital accumulation*. By assigning landed capitalists a distinct role vis-à-vis industrialists and financiers in the structural dynamics of capitalism, Harvey also established a new interest for the social role of landlords, developers, and other capitalists who profit from the built environment. Next, the Spanish-born, French-trained sociologist Manuel Castells theorized that the "urban" corresponds specifically to relations of *collective consumption*, those city-based services, housing, and infrastructure provided by the state with which people reproduce their labor power. His claim particularly resonated in Western Europe and Latin America and launched a neo-Marxian research agenda that examines urban politics, grassroots protest, and urban movements as expressions of class relations distinct from the capitalist–worker conflict usually emphasized by neo-Marxians.

THE NEO-WEBERIAN TRADITION

If Marx gives urban political economy its concern for the structural dynamics of capitalism, Max Weber's legacy provides the conceptual vocabulary with which to understand social power and human agency. This is underscored by the curious fact that for Marx, the notion of a "ruling class" is somewhat a contradiction in terms. Governance involves political processes that, to have theoretical integrity, must not be entirely determined by other social realms; yet Marx famously gave little credence to politics' autonomy from material relations of production. Consequently, structural Marxists like Harvey had no vocabulary with which to understand urban power and political contingency apart from the structural determination and historical conjunctures of the economy.

Reasserting its intellectual relevance, the American school of urban sociology reintroduced the neo-Weberian question, "Who governs the city?" posed previously within political science during the 1950s and 1960s. In this earlier *community power* debate, Floyd Hunter and other proponents of the elitist perspective argued that a core group of private urban elites regularly and successfully promote their interests through city hall. Rejecting this claim, Robert Dahl and other advocates of a pluralist perspective countered that private interest groups may prevail on certain issues, but not consistently enough to dominate urban politics. Eventually, the community power debates reached an impasse over inconclusive findings as well as theoretical and methodological differences. By the 1970s, as urban political economists studied the ways in which cities generate wealth for capitalists, it became clear with hindsight that neither side in the community power debate had theorized the material interests of the city's power-holders in a substantial way.

Consequently, urban political economists adapted neo-Weberian premises to the neo-Marxian problematic and identified the social production of urban space – that is, *city building* – as the institution that organizes the material interests and galvanizes the political dominance of urban elites. This means that urban governance is not confined within urban governments; just as important are the private decisions made by place-based entrepreneurs and businesses to make money. Harvey Molotch crystallized this idea with his theory of the *growth machine*, a territorially defined coalition of urban elites from across public, private, and civic sectors that promotes growth in order to advance its common interests in intensifying land-based exchange values (higher rents for developers and landlords, increasing tax revenues for local governments, new readers for local newspapers, more ratepayers for utilities, more jobs for local trade unions, and so on). With his colleague John Logan, Molotch identified the class relations and political stakes underlying the growth machine, asserting that the exchange-value interests of growth machines invariably portend environmental impacts, infrastructure strain, fiscal constraints on public services, and other material conflicts with the use-value interests of residents. For urban sociologists, the growth machine theory transcended the earlier community power debate by identifying urban growth as the consensus agenda (which elitists emphasized) underlying the overt conflicts and political factions of city hall (which pluralists emphasized).

Contemporary research on urban power has further developed the insights of growth machine theory, which did not theorize in detail on how urban elites engage the political realm, under what conditions they cooperate with one another (in fact, urban elites may be divided by vested interests in different parts of the city or different kinds of growth), or how effective they are in attracting urban growth and achieving political hegemony. These issues have been taken up by urban regime theory, a school of urban political science that has influenced urban political economy since the late 1980s. An *urban regime* is the set of formal and informal arrangements that makes urban governance by a public–private coalition possible. As Clarence Stone has explained, urban regimes vary by the agendas that their participants pursue; some are radically progressive, while others simply maintain the political status quo. However, the most frequently observed type is the development regime enacted by pro-growth elites, although for reasons that go beyond the shared interests of the growth machine. Just as importantly, actors in the development regime most effectively marshal and share the political benefits, business opportunities, and other "selective incentives" that enforce cooperation and prevent dissent within their public–private coalition.

NEW PATTERNS OF URBAN RESTRUCTURING

Since the 1980s, urban political economy has developed in large part as a response to the dramatic shifts in economies, politics, population, and settlement associated with *urban restructuring*. This concept has pushed urban political economists to identify what is qualitatively new and significant about capitalism's transformations of the city. For example, the globalization of traditional American industry, on the one hand, merely demonstrates at a larger scale structural dynamics that spurred the growth of the American Sunbelt decades earlier: industrial capital's vulnerability to site-specific labor costs and labor control, and its benefits from geographically uneven development. On the other hand, the technological and organizational innovations that made globalization possible have generated unanticipated economic, spatial, and social outcomes.

In her *global city* thesis, Saskia Sassen explained how the financial capitals of New York, London, and Tokyo have assumed new centrality in the coordination of transnational corporate (TNC) activity. This is not because these global cities attract TNC headquarters, many of which have in fact left major cities, but instead because they concentrate the social networks of smaller financial and advanced business service firms that oversee, respectively, the capital investments and legal–organizational management needed by TNCs. Sassen's insight that geography, markets, and networks assume a coordinating role formerly contained within corporate bureaucracy parallels a larger theory about the geography of "flexible accumulation." Rejecting the popular wisdom that place no longer matters in globalization, this theory documents the central function of *flexible industrial districts* in industries where skilled labor, entrepreneurial companies, and specialized support systems cluster, such as Silicon Valley (technology), Hollywood (film), Paris (high fashion), and the "Third Italy" (textiles).

Amidst the global context of capital mobility and job flight, these and other economically vibrant cities and regions in fact witness economic polarization and social inequality, due to economic growth as well as stagnation. For instance, well-paid workers in booming technical, cultural, and creative industries create new demand for consumer services that employ low-skill labor. Also, some creative industries remain competitive by relying on local sweatshops (endemic in fashion centers like New York or Los Angeles) or other informal enterprises. Manuel Castells and John Mollenkopf have described the subsequent urban structure with their idea of the *dual city*. In its more glamorous half, new professionals revitalize once-staid urban economies, gentrify abandoned neighborhoods, and stimulate the growth of coffeeshops, bistros, bars, and other high-end consumer services. In its less affluent half, working classes become less secure with the exodus of manufacturing and other activities that once created decent-paying union jobs, while new immigrants leap over older ethnic and racial groups to manage and fill the low-paying service and sweatshop jobs, or to sell goods on the street in informal economies.

Theoretically, globalization underscores how the dynamics of growth and decline extend beyond the scale of any one city, region, or even nation. Not surprisingly, urban restructuring has thus challenged urban political economy's models of human agency. On the one hand, the structural context in which growth coalitions operate has always been "global" to some extent, as companies choose a location from a variety of places, and places' competitive advantages are influenced by non-local factors like state budgets, national federal mandates, and interest rates. On the other hand, capital investment and urban growth increasingly materialize in a decentralized, market form. At least in the new economy's industrial clusters, the decisions that bring growth are made by a number of actors too large for any growth coalition to sway effectively with conventional lobbying. As urban political economy keeps abreast of the structural changes associated with urban restructuring, the paradigm's practitioners continue to reevaluate what constitutes the "political." Does the neo-Weberian focus on political institutions' legitimacy, interest groups' pressure politics, and coalitional power-plays still have explanatory value in this era of urban restructuring? If so, just how much, and at what scale does it explain?

SEE ALSO: Capital, Secondary Circuit of; City; Global/World Cities; Globalization; Growth Machine; Inequality and the City; Social Movements; Uneven Development; Urban Ecology; Urban Policy; Urban Renewal and Redevelopment

REFERENCES AND SUGGESTED READINGS

Castells, M. (1983) *The City and the Grassroots*. University of California Press, Berkeley.

Dahl, R. (1961) *Who Governs?* Yale University Press, New Haven.

Harvey, D. (1982) *The Limits to Capital*. University of Chicago Press, Chicago.

Hunter, F. (1953) *Community Power Structure*. University of North Carolina Press, Chapel Hill.

Logan, J. & Molotch, H. (1987) *Urban Fortunes*. University of California Press, Berkeley.

Mollenkopf, J. & Castells, M. (Eds.) (1991) *Dual City*. Russell Sage Foundation, New York.

Nevarez, L. (2003) *New Money, Nice Town*. Routledge, New York.

Sassen, S. (1991) *The Global City*. Princeton University Press, Princeton.

Stone, C. (1989) *Regime Politics*. University of Kansas Press, Lawrence.

Tabb, W. & Sawers, L. (Eds.) (1978) *Marxism and the Metropolis*. Oxford University Press, Oxford.

urban poverty

David J. Harding

While a technical definition of the urban poor includes those individuals in families with incomes below the federal poverty line who live in metropolitan areas, most research on urban poverty focuses on racial and ethnic minorities living in segregated, high-poverty neighborhoods in central cities. The study of urban poverty lies at the intersection of several sociological fields, including race and ethnicity, immigration, stratification, and urban sociology. As a predominantly problem-oriented field, urban poverty research attempts to understand the roots of urban dilemmas such as crime and delinquency, single motherhood, unemployment, and low levels of education, often drawing theoretical concepts from other areas of sociology such as social capital, networks, and culture. The causes and consequences of spatially concentrated poverty and the intergenerational transmission of poverty are also frequent subjects of inquiry. A recurring debate in this field is whether income inadequacy causes problem behavior or whether problem behavior causes income inadequacy.

The study of urban poverty dates back to the founding of sociology as a discipline in the US with W. E. B. Du Bois's *The Philadelphia Negro*, first published in 1899. Du Bois developed theoretical ideas that remain important to this day, including the connection between spatial isolation and social exclusion. Sociologists of the Chicago School largely viewed urban poverty as a temporary stage in the incorporation of immigrant groups from abroad and of migrants from rural areas. High population turnover, lack of material resources, and ethnic heterogeneity lead to the breakdown of social control in immigrant-receiving neighborhoods, creating higher rates of crime and delinquency. Through processes of neighborhood invasion and succession, they argued, ethnic groups moving upward in economic status also move from crowded, poor, central city neighborhoods through a series of concentric zones to progressively better-off areas further from the central city.

The Great Migration, which brought Southern blacks to Northern and Western cities in great numbers between the two world wars and after World War II, challenged the Chicago School model of invasion and succession, as urban blacks were blocked from the economic and spatial advancement previously experienced by white ethnic groups. Focus shifted to understanding the intergenerational transmission of poverty. Some scholars emphasized structural constraints while others argued for cultural explanations, particularly the development of a culture of poverty, characterized by the intergenerational transmission of norms disparaging education and two-parent families and encouraging crime. In response to the controversial Moynihan report, which argued that matriarchal family structures found in black communities were destructive, researchers began to train attention on the adaptive characteristics of black families and their resilience in the face of racial discrimination, segregation, and economic subjugation. Conservative scholars objected that these accounts ignored the more powerful and perverse incentives of the welfare system that, they suggested, encouraged out-of-wedlock childbearing, single-parent households, and persistent unemployment.

The demographics of poverty shifted dramatically over the course of the twentieth century. Improvements in social security and other government programs for the elderly made urban poverty less of a problem among the elderly, while the spread of single-parent families made urban poverty more of a problem among unmarried mothers and their children, the so-called feminization of poverty.

With the publication of *The Truly Disadvantaged* (1986), William Julius Wilson refocused attention on the spatial or neighborhood context of urban poverty. Wilson argued that the black urban poor were doubly disadvantaged by both their individual poverty and their residence in concentrated poverty neighborhoods. Advances in civil rights in the 1960s had made it possible for middle-class blacks to move out of inner-city ghetto neighborhoods in the 1970s, leaving the poor behind. At the same time, the decline of the manufacturing economy had led to chronic unemployment and underemployment among working-class males, especially blacks. Wilson argued that an underclass emerged, a concentrated population characterized by single motherhood, poverty, joblessness, high school dropouts, and participation in the underground economy. Because of its spatial isolation, this population came to be socially isolated from mainstream society, and in the presence of economic deprivation, came to develop cultural practices that diverged from the mainstream. Though Wilson (1997) would later rename this group the ghetto poor and call special attention to the importance of joblessness, the emphasis on neighborhoods remained.

Wilson's work reinvigorated the study of urban poverty as researchers challenged his claims about the rise of concentrated poverty neighborhoods and tested his hypotheses about the consequences of neighborhood poverty for individuals. Massey and Denton (1993) charged Wilson with ignoring the role of racial segregation in magnifying the consequences of economic segregation, and Quillian (1999) later showed that though middle-class blacks were able to leave ghetto neighborhoods, their new neighborhoods quickly resegregated as whites left. Scholars argued that the decline of manufacturing was important only in the industrial cities of the North, where manufacturing jobs paid well and where blacks were well integrated into the manufacturing workforce (Jargowsky 1997). Others challenged Wilson's emphasis on joblessness and pointed toward the large numbers of working poor in disadvantaged neighborhoods, for whom poverty is the result of low wages rather than unemployment (Newman 1999).

One strand of current research investigates the consequences of neighborhood disadvantage for individual residents. Residents of disadvantaged neighborhoods generally have higher rates of school dropouts, teenage pregnancy, single-parent families, unemployment, crime and delinquency, and other problems, net of differences in observed family and individual characteristics. While there is some question as to whether these differences are the product of unobserved differences between residents of advantaged and disadvantaged neighborhoods, results from mobility experiments and from sophisticated methodological techniques designed to deal with this selection bias have convinced most scholars that neighborhood effects are real. Debate continues, however, on their magnitude relative to other influences.

Attention subsequently turned to understanding the social processes that create neighborhood effects. Jencks and Mayer (1990) suggest four mechanisms by which neighborhood poverty might influence adolescents: relative deprivation, exposure to negative peer influences, collective socialization by neighborhood adults, and formal institutions, which distribute material resources and effect contact with non-neighborhood adults. A social control perspective highlights the ability of neighborhood residents to control behavior in the neighborhood, both through informal sanctions and monitoring and through the acquisition of institutional resources such as police protection. Sampson et al. (1997) show that collective efficacy, or "social cohesion among neighbors combined with their willingness to intervene on behalf of the common good," mediates the relationship between neighborhood structural disadvantages and public disorder and crime.

A second strand of current research seeks to understand the causes of high rates of out-of-wedlock and teenage childbearing among the urban poor. Three explanations have emerged for out-of-wedlock childbearing, though to date there is not enough evidence to adjudicate between them (Small & Newman 2001). The male marriageable pool hypothesis holds that a shortage of economically attractive mates leads poor urban women to eschew marriage. The slavery hypothesis holds that the institution of slavery damaged gender relations among African Americans, leading to fewer permanent marital unions among them. A third hypothesis holds that out-of-wedlock childbearing has become more acceptable in society as a whole, and that the behavior of the urban poor reflects this new normative environment. Edin and Kefalas (2006) argue that poor urban women actually hold marriage and childbearing in such

high regard that they delay or avoid marriage when success is uncertain. Coupled with a belief that motherhood is the most important social role a woman can perform, these cultural understandings of marriage lead to high rates of out-of-wedlock childbearing among the urban poor.

Three explanations have also been offered for the higher rates of teenage childbearing among the urban poor (Small & Newman 2001). The peer culture hypothesis holds that among the urban poor, early sexual activity and early childbearing are a source of status among peers (Anderson 1999). The weathering hypothesis holds that early childbearing is a rational response to the deteriorating health of urban poor women as they age, making the teen years the optimal period for healthy childbearing. Finally, the poverty of relationships hypothesis holds that teenage girls have children to compensate for a lack of other meaningful social relationships and for lack of prospects for finding rewarding work.

As research continues, the study of urban poverty faces a number of methodological and theoretical challenges. First, today's urban poor are quite heterogeneous. For example, while most of the research focus has been on African Americans, Latinos now make up the largest minority group in the US, and Latinos and other immigrants have become an important and understudied segment of the urban poor. Indeed, the Latino paradox – higher rates of poverty but fewer negative outcomes among Latinos – raises fundamental questions about the roles of structure and culture. Second, while social isolation has been used theoretically to understand the consequences of urban poverty, we have only begun to understand how the urban poor are socially isolated or socially connected to others. Third, understanding the dynamics and consequences of high-poverty urban neighborhoods requires new methods and new data for measuring the social and cultural characteristics of these neighborhoods, beyond the structural measures provided by the decennial Census. While methods for measuring the characteristics of urban neighborhoods are being developed, further data are needed to take advantage of these methods.

These three concerns highlight two important weaknesses in the current literature on urban poverty. One is the lack of attention to the mechanisms or social processes by which poverty and poor urban neighborhoods have their effects, including the potential for heterogeneity in mechanisms across neighborhoods. A second weakness is a lack of attention to culture and to individual agency in understanding the causes and consequences of urban poverty. To have an impact, macro-level structural forces such as joblessness or neighborhood disadvantage must affect individual behavior through decision-making processes and cultural or cognitive understandings. While most urban poverty researchers continue to talk in terms of norms and values, the sociology of culture has moved toward a more cognitive view of culture that emphasizes cultural repertoires, strategies of action, frames, cultural capital, and boundary making. Poverty researchers are increasingly questioning current theories of urban space and investigating the strategies the urban poor use to challenge their marginality. Gotham & Brumley (2002) use ethnographic field observations and interviews with public housing residents to argue that the urban poor use space to provide a measure of security and protection, to designate and avoid areas of criminality and drug activity, and to challenge or support the redevelopment of public housing (see also Gotham 2003).

Finally, recent work on urban poverty has expanded into other domains. Health outcomes such as low birth weight, mental health, and disease have been shown to be related to individual and neighborhood disadvantage. Using new statistical techniques that assess the impact of a neighborhood's location within the urban context, researchers have also begun to investigate the importance of neighborhood spatial context.

SEE ALSO: Chicago School; Ethnic Enclaves; Hypersegregation; Social Exclusion; Uneven Development; Urban Crime and Violence; Urban Policy; Urbanization

REFERENCES AND SUGGESTED READINGS

Anderson, E. (1999) *Code of the Street.* Norton, New York.

Brooks-Gunn, J., Duncan, G. J., & Aber, J. L. (Eds.) (1997) *Neighborhood* Poverty, 2 Vols. Russell Sage, New York.

Edin, K. & Kefalas, M. (2006) *Promises I Can Keep.* University of California Press, Berkeley.

Gotham, K. F. (2003) Toward an Understanding of the Spatiality of Urban Poverty: The Urban Poor as Spatial Actors. *International Journal of Urban and Regional Research* 27: 723–37.

Gotham, K. F. & Brumley, K. (2002) Using Space: Agency and Identity in a Public Housing Development. *City and Community* 1: 267–89.

Jargowsky, P. A. (1997) *Poverty and Place: Ghettos, Barrios, and the American City.* Russell Sage, New York.

Jencks, C. & Mayer, S. E. (1990) The Social Consequences of Growing Up in a Poor Neighborhood. In: Lynn, L. E., Jr. & McGreary, M. G. H. (Eds.), *Inner-City Poverty in the United States.* National Academy Press, Washington, DC, pp. 111–86.

Jencks, C. & Peterson, P. (Eds.) (1991) *The Urban Underclass.* Brookings Institution, Washington, DC.

Massey, D. & Denton, N. (1993) *American Apartheid: Segregation and the Making of an Underclass.* Harvard University Press, Cambridge, MA.

Newman, K. S. (1999) *No Shame in My Game: The Working Poor in the Inner City.* Russell Sage/Vintage, New York.

Quillian, L. (1999) Migration Patterns and the Growth of High-Poverty Neighborhoods, 1970–1990. *American Journal of Sociology* 105: 1–37.

Sampson, R., Raudenbush, S., & Earls, F. (1997) Neighborhoods and Violent Crime: A Multilevel Study of Collective Efficacy. *Science* 227: 918–24.

Small, M. L. & Newman, K. S. (2001) Urban Poverty After the Truly Disadvantaged: The Rediscovery of the Family, the Neighborhood, and Culture. *Annual Review of Sociology* 27: 23–45.

Wilson, W. J. (1997) *When Work Disappears: The World of the New Urban Poor.* Knopf, New York.

urban renewal and redevelopment

Gregory J. Crowley

The built environment deteriorates with the passage of time and the stresses of use and neglect. Unemployment, poverty, shortages of affordable housing, health epidemics, and transportation problems often accompany physical decay in modern cities. Attempts to relieve these social problems through the maintenance, rehabilitation, and rebuilding of the physical environment are known as urban redevelopment.

European governments implemented the first large-scale urban redevelopment projects in the nineteenth century. Louis Napoleon Bonaparte of France led the way with his massive renovation of Paris that began in 1853. Thousands of residents were displaced by the creation of a system of wide boulevards that "pierced" diagonally through dense, older neighborhoods of the city. Another wave of urban redevelopment began after World War II. In Europe, government acquisition and demolition of properties played a major role in the rebuilding of cities destroyed by war. Cities in North America meanwhile embarked on their first major effort at demolition and rehabilitation of the built environment. Title II of the 1949 Federal Housing Act, known as "urban renewal," responded to a very different problem: the long-term trend of suburbanization that threatened the stability of the central city.

The sociology of redevelopment in the US grew out of attempts to explain population dispersal and corresponding urban distress. Urban ecology, a leading perspective, explains population shifts in terms of "succession." Competition for scarce resources causes some subspecies to replace, or "succeed," others in a habitat. According to the logic of succession, middle-class whites and blacks moved from central cities in the twentieth century simply because technological changes in transportation allowed them to adopt the higher standard of living promised by suburban areas.

Other scholars have criticized urban ecology for overlooking how social inequalities and power relations are structured in the form of the built environment. Neo-Marxist theory emphasizes that capitalist firms change location not only to accommodate upgraded physical plant, but also to control labor conflict. Gordon (1978) used US Census data to show that manufacturing employment in the "rings" increased at more than twice the rate of centers of industrial cities beginning in the 1890s. The change occurred amid a steady increase in labor strife and well before the technological innovations that would later transform the organization of

work and domestic life. According to Gordon, executives at the turn of the century moved their plants to the suburbs mainly to avoid labor union activity, which was concentrated in central cities.

A third approach is urban political economy, which is critical of both ecology and neo-Marxism for discounting the social and political context in which demographic changes occur. Political economy views territorial shifts in population as a result of urban governing coalitions that shape zoning, transportation, taxation, housing, and other policies affecting patterns of land use and migration within a territory. From the political economy perspective, metropolitan "sprawl" is caused by more than just a demand for high-quality housing on the urban periphery. Urban governing coalitions promoting uncontrolled growth are certainly influential in many cities, but in others "smart growth" advocates attempt to direct new development into existing neighborhoods. Among the policy tools they use are loan programs, tax credits for historic preservation, growth controls, and transportation planning.

Understood as a process, redevelopment involves the mobilization of substantial resources controlled by state as well as non-governmental actors. Community development corporations, tax increment financing (TIF), eminent domain, tax exempt bonds, human capital, and social trust are some of the many resources commonly involved in attempts to improve distressed neighborhoods. Valued resources may be controlled by real estate owners, financial institutions, developers, neighborhood residents, historic preservationists, or environmental groups. Sociological studies of redevelopment tend to revolve around questions relating to how the composition and dynamics of urban governing coalitions influence strategies of redevelopment.

In the 1950s and 1960s community power researchers visited cities across North America in search of data revealing who influences redevelopment and other local policies. In his pioneering study of decision-makers in 1950s Atlanta, Floyd Hunter (1953) answered these questions by documenting who in the community held the greatest reputation for political influence. He identified some 13 leaders, mainly corporate executives, reputed to control important decisions in the city's urban renewal program. Many of Hunter's followers found in other cities the same pattern of corporate business dominance in physical rebuilding projects. Other scholars found "coalitional" power structures such that business elites who initiated urban renewal were less influential in formalizing and implementing specific projects. Still others found multiple competing factions in the community, which caused redevelopment to be neglected for a lack of leadership and common purpose.

Critics of Hunter's "reputational" method charged that it is impossible to determine who actually exercises influence over specific decisions by asking people who they believe has power. Just because business elites have reputations for power does not mean they will be united on all redevelopment issues or even have the time to examine them in sufficient depth to take a position. An alternative is the decision-making approach, developed by Edward Banfield (1961) and Robert Dahl (1961) in their case studies of community power in Chicago and New Haven, Connecticut, respectively. Actual rather than potential control over specific public issues is the topic of decision-making analysis.

When combined with reputational analysis, decision-making has tended to produce more complete explanations of community power by showing the limitations imposed on elites by underlying community divisions. According to Banfield, a small group of corporate executives advocated federal urban renewal in Chicago, but they had to expend considerable political capital persuading other elites, who stood little to gain by the demolition of downtown, to go along with their 100-acre Fort Dearborn clearance and renewal project. The implementation of redevelopment, Banfield concluded, is often compromised by limitations in the stocks of political capital of elites who promote them. Similarly, Dahl attributed the success of urban renewal in New Haven as a result of the quality of New Haven's leadership. Mayor Lee and his urban renewal staff were distinguished in their ability to shape their proposals according to what they believed interest groups and voters in New Haven could be expected to support or reject.

Community power researchers were for the most part unconcerned with the impact of redevelopment on the lives of residents in project areas or on the cultural and economic vitality of the city as a whole. They examined land-use decisions mainly to demonstrate methods for measuring the distribution of community power. Other critically minded scholars attacked national urban renewal after a decade of post-war slum clearance had demolished thousands of affordable housing units without replacement. The most celebrated among these critics was Jane Jacobs. In her *Death and Life of Great American Cities* (1961) Jacobs outlined a theory of urban planning that illustrated how physical features of older, mixed-use neighborhoods – the sidewalks, parks, and corner stores – configure informal social contacts that ensure the safety and vitality of cities. Older, "blighted" neighborhoods in city after city were demolished for the purpose of upgrading them to accommodate high-rise luxury apartments, offices, and large government buildings such as Government Center in the West End of Boston.

In the last section of his classic book *Urban Villagers* (1962), Herbert Gans described how destruction of the built environment caused by urban renewal disrupted relationships among neighbors and extended families in Boston's Italian West End. Gans introduced the important distinction, overlooked by local planners, between a slum and a low-rent district. The West End definitely fell into the latter category, according to Gans, which benefited greatly the working-class families residing there. Gans's work influenced a generation of urban planners to be skeptical towards the view that older neighborhoods must be demolished in order to be saved.

By the 1970s a growing body of research validated earlier criticisms of urban renewal. Most of this work was done by scholars versed in neo-Marxist and political economy literature. They used case methods to develop theories of how class interests – especially those of corporate business and real estate – influence government intervention in the physical redevelopment of cities. Susan S. Fainstein and colleagues (1986) have studied dozens of American and European cities this way. Much government intervention, they argue, is geared toward large-scale real estate projects such as the building of stadia and convention centers, and the redevelopment of older warehousing and retailing districts. Prevailing forms of public support for these projects contribute little to the welfare of existing residents and businesses, even if the new development actually increases commercial activity in the city. Eminent domain authority is used to displace low-income residents and small businesses from project areas, developer subsidies and tax increment financing increase the tax burden of city residents, and rezoning of neighborhoods for large-scale projects can create unwanted traffic and noise, while undermining community identity.

Economic competition between cities also affects the redevelopment process. In his influential book *City Limits* (1981), Paul Peterson presented a theory of why some cities outperform others in the competition for mobile capital and skilled labor. The book became popular in the Reagan era of deep cuts in federal funding to cities and growing competition for private capital. Economic growth and urban redevelopment became the most important local policy arenas in which competition between cities was played out. Local officials must work to raise the value of taxable properties in order to finance public schools, transportation, parks, and other services. For declining municipalities, this means trapping mobile capital in place. As a city attracts investment from the outside, according to the argument, its government performs better and its quality of life rises in comparison to other places. Peterson overlooked the question of who gains and who loses in the struggle for urban growth. In his view, some urban dwellers would necessarily suffer from redevelopment along the lines pointed out by political economists. But the sacrifices of some would repay in the prosperity of the city as a whole.

Current sociological accounts of the distribution of benefits and costs of redevelopment owe much to urban regime theory, a perspective created by scholars familiar with neo-Marxist, political economy, and city limits literature, but unsatisfied with their simplified views on coalition building and conflict management. Fundamental to regime theory is the concept of the city as a "growth machine" (Molotch 1976) made up of property owners, realtors, mortgage bankers, and others who profit from

the intensification of land use. Landed interests are among the most active members in the local polity, and their highest political priority is to create the right conditions for outside investment, which leads to economic growth. This may include low taxes, quality municipal services, a productive and inexpensive labor force, and minimal regulations on business. In the American political economy a division of labor exists between the state, which holds legal authority to act on behalf of all citizens, and the market, where productive assets are owned and controlled. Making and carrying out important policies related to economic growth and redevelopment thus requires the blending of resources from both sectors and the effective management of ensuing conflicts from within and without. Accordingly, the form of local government intervention in land use largely reflects who is incorporated into decision-making and by what formal and informal arrangements decisions are reached.

The regime perspective reflects a more complex and changing reality of urban redevelopment than earlier approaches. It states that one cannot decide in the abstract whether or not large-scale or government-led urban redevelopment is a good or bad thing for the community as a whole or its individual members. Much depends on the nature of governing arrangements and the kinds of "solutions sets" that have evolved for dealing with urban distress. When arts organizations are represented in urban regimes, they shift land-use strategies toward "mixed-use" projects and the rehabilitation of older buildings, along the lines of Jane Jacobs's recommendations. Affordable housing advocates represented in regimes in Boston, San Francisco, and other places have created "linkage" policies, whereby downtown redevelopment projects are assessed a fee to help finance construction or rehabilitation of low and moderate-income housing. Other policies and types of regime exist, to the good or ill of the cities they govern. To be sure, in local redevelopment there remains a strong "systematic bias," as regime theorist Clarence Stone (1989) calls it, towards corporate business interests. As long as productive assets, which create wealth and employment in a commercial republic, remain in private hands, government will seek them as primary partners in urban governance.

Over the past century the physical decline of cities has corresponded more and more with patterns of socioeconomic distress. In the name of relieving distress, officials have facilitated redevelopment of the built environment. At times, government action has contributed to greater decline and distress, such as occurred with federal urban renewal. More often, redevelopment projects have mixed results. Understanding the institutions and coalition forms most conducive to more sustainable growth that meets the needs of all urban residents remains a high-priority agenda for future research.

SEE ALSO: Black Urban Regime; Built Environment; City Planning/Urban Design; Gentrification; Growth Machine; Invasion-Succession; New Urbanism; Redlining; Uneven Development; Urban Crime and Violence; Urban Movements; Urban Political Economy; Urban Poverty; Urbanization

REFERENCES AND SUGGESTED READINGS

Banfield, E. C. (1961) *Political Influence: A New Theory of Urban Politics*. Free Press, New York.
Dahl, R. (1961) *Who Governs? Democracy and Power in an American City*. Yale University Press, New Haven.
Fainstein, S. S., Fainstein, N. I., Hill, R. C., Judd, D. R., & Smith, M. P. (1986) *Restructuring the City: The Political Economy of Urban Redevelopment*. Longman, New York.
Gordon, D. (1978) Capitalist Development and the History of American Cities. In: Tabb, W. K. & Sawers, L. (Eds.), *Marxism and the Metropolis*. Oxford, New York, pp. 25–63.
Gotham, K. F. (Ed.) (2001) *Critical Perspectives on Urban Redevelopment, Research in Urban Sociology*, Vol. 6. Jai Press, New York.
Hunter, F. (1953) *Community Power Structure: A Study of Decision Makers*. University of North Carolina Press, Chapel Hill.
Logan, J. R. & Molotch, H. L. (1987) *Urban Fortunes: The Political Economy of Place*. University of California Press, Berkeley.
Molotch, H. L. (1976) The City as a Growth Machine. *American Journal of Sociology* 82(2): 309–30.
Peterson, P. (1981) *City Limits*. University of Chicago Press, Chicago.
Stone, C. (1989) *Regime Politics: Governing Atlanta, 1946–1988*. University Press of Kansas, Lawrence.

urban revolution

Kevin Fox Gotham

The urban revolution refers to the emergence of urban life and the concomitant transformation of human settlements from simple agrarian-based systems to complex and hierarchical systems of manufacturing and trade. The term also refers to the present era of metropolitan or megalopolis growth, the development of exurbs, and the explosion of primate or mega-cities. Archeologist V. Gordon Childe coined the term *urban revolution* to explain the series of stages in the development of cities that preceded the Industrial Revolution of the nineteenth century. For Childe, the first revolution – the "Agricultural Revolution" – occurred when hunting and gathering societies mastered the skill of food production and began to live in stable and sedentary groups. The second revolution – the "Urban Revolution" – began during the fourth and third millennia BCE in the civilizations of Mesopotamia and the Near East. The urban revolution ushered in a new era of population growth, complex urban development, and the development of such institutions as the bureaucratic state, warfare, architecture, and writing. For Henri Lefebvre (2003), the urban revolution not only signifies a long historical shift from an agricultural to an industrial to an urban world, but also refers to a shift in the internal organization of the city, from the political city of pre-medieval times to the mercantile, then industrial, city to the present phase, where the "urban" becomes a global trend. Today, many scholars use the term urban revolution to connote profound changes in the social organization of societies, but they disagree over the conceptualization, causes, and trajectory of the change.

One major point of debate focuses on issues of conceptualization and addresses questions about when, where, and why the first cities arose. In his oft-cited essay "The Urban Revolution," Childe (1950) described the features of early communities in Mesopotamia that marked the beginning of urban settlements. First, a key feature of the first cities was their immense population size, up to 20,000 residents, and their dense geographic concentration. A second major feature was the production of an agricultural surplus. This important development spearheaded several other changes, including the establishment of specialized groups such as craftsmen, transport workers, merchants, officials, and priests. Third, farmers and peasants gradually came under the control of the city through a system of taxation to support government activity, including standing armies. Fourth, the financing and construction of large public works, and other monuments and temples, came to "symbolize the concentration of the social surplus." Fifth, the production of agricultural surplus created problems over the allocation and control of wealth, leading to the emergence of social stratification. Priests, military leaders, and other elites formed a "ruling class" that exempted themselves from physical labor and pursued "intellectual tasks." Sixth, to control and regulate the growth of surplus, the ruling classes invented systems of recording, numerical calculation, and writing. Seventh, the first cities were the birthplaces of modern science, as the invention of writing "enabled the leisured clerks to proceed to the elaboration of exact and predictive sciences – arithmetic, geometry, and astronomy." Eighth, the specialization of labor gave "a new direction to artistic expression" by providing a cultural foundation for artists and craftspeople to cultivate sophisticated styles and traditions. Ninth, the concentration of surplus helped encourage and expand trade, a development that led to "the importation of raw material, needed for industry or cult and not available locally." Tenth, membership in the community was no longer based on kinship but on residence.

Childe's thesis was highly controversial when it was published and the causes and nature of the urban revolution remain hotly debated. On the one hand, Childe offered a powerful theory of urbanization based on the specialization of work, the differentiation of the division of labor, and the interdependence of skills and tasks. These social relations provide the basis for the development of modern industrial societies. On the other hand, scholars have argued that

Childe's thesis embraces a macro-evolutionary orientation that ignores the diversity of human settlements around the world. Others have maintained that Childe's theory employs an overly deterministic view of urbanization that downplays the important role of culture in development of complex societies. One major criticism is that Childe's thesis is tautological and employs functionalistic assumptions to legitimate its arguments. It is not clear, for example, if the specialized division of labor promoted the early development of cities, or if the social complexity of cities encouraged the growth of a differentiated division of labor. It is also not clear if urbanization was the result or the cause of changes in the social relations of production and technological innovations.

These problems flow into a second point of debate, the periodization and trajectories of the urban revolution. Evidence from archeologists and sociologists suggests that urban development is discontinuous and contingent. While Childe argued that a precondition of cities is an agricultural surplus, others have suggested that human control over rivers and mastery of irrigation led to the development of cities. Other critics such as Jane Jacobs argued that early commercial centers such as those in Catal Hyuk in present-day Turkey developed as centers of trade in the absence of agricultural surplus. Anthropologists have long maintained that ancient civilizations in North America developed complex and sophisticated systems of trade and commerce along the Mississippi River without knowledge of farming. One of the oldest cities, Jericho, had a thriving urban culture based on trade and crafts production over four millennia ago, many centuries before the development of agricultural surplus in the region. In short, Childe's thesis suggests an interpretation of early urbanization in Mesopotamian cities. It's generalizability to other regions and time periods remains in question. Still, Childe's ideas offer an incisive and poignant perspective which generations of scholars have utilized to understand the historical development of human societies.

Third, scholars argue that there is not one urban revolution but several. A "Second Urban Revolution," for example, began about 1750 as the Industrial Revolution generated rapid urban growth in Europe. The economy, physical form, and culture of cities changed dramatically as feudal power broke down and trade and travel increased. Increasing size, density, and diversity of cities combined with the growth of commerce to make urban life more rational, anonymous, and depersonalized. Since about 1950, a "Third Urban Revolution" has been occurring in less developed countries, where most of the world's largest cities are located. The increasing number of primate or mega-cities of more than 8 million inhabitants illustrates profound demographic and population trends of the past century. In 1950, only two cities, London and New York, were that size. In 1975, there were 11 mega-cities, including 6 in the industrialized countries. In 1995, there were 23 total, with 17 in the developing countries. In 2015, the projected number of mega-cities is 36, with 30 of them in the developing world and most in Asia. In short, the urban revolution is a global trend that is taking place at different speeds on different continents. Any convincing attempt to understand and explain these important changes has to offer a coherent conceptualization of urban revolution; an account of causal logic; a clear set of propositions about historical periodization; a specification of impacts; and a sound explanation about the trajectory of the process itself.

SEE ALSO: Cities in Europe; Global/World Cities; Megalopolis; Metropolis; Primate Cities; Uneven Development; Urban/Rural Population Movements; Urbanization

REFERENCES AND SUGGESTED READINGS

Asher, F. (2002) The Third Urban Revolution of Modernity. In: Eckardt, F. & Hassenpflug, D. (Eds.), *Consumption and the Post-Industrial City.* Peter Lang, Frankfurt.
Childe, V. G. (1950) The Urban Revolution. *Town Planning Review* 21 (April): 3–17.
Davis, K. D. (1965) The Urbanization of the Human Population. *Scientific American* (September). Scientific American, New York.
Lefebvre, H. (2003 [1970]) *The Urban Revolution.* Trans. Robert Bononno. University of Minnesota Press, Minneapolis.
Pirenne, H. (1925) *Medieval Cities.* Princeton University, Princeton.

urban–rural population movements

Michael J. White

The movement of the population between rural and urban areas is both a major consequence and a major determinant of social change. From a sociological vantage point, this movement offers potential for significant transformation in sending and receiving communities alike, as various types of individuals (differentiated by age, sex, education, ethnicity, etc.) are added and subtracted from the community. For the individual, the relocation may bring attendant challenges, even as it brings new opportunities. Within the research community, the study of urban–rural population movement would be seen as a subdivision within the broader study of internal migration, urbanization, population redistribution, or migrant adjustment.

From a simple demographic point of view, migration forms one of the basic components of population change, and along with fertility and mortality, determines the growth of populations. Historically, the redistribution of persons between urban and rural regions has been driven mostly by changes in economic opportunity, although policy interventions, shifts in region political fortunes, ethnic relations, environmental stress, and other sweeping societal changes also provoke movement. While for decades, even centuries, the preponderant direction of net population shift was from rural to urban areas, this broad characterization overlooks some important counterflows and other more short-term movement that may not fit the stylized pattern. In more recent decades high-income societies, already highly urbanized, have seen something closer to equilibrium in rural–urban population flows.

DEFINITION OF MOBILITY AND THE CLASSIFICATION OF TERRITORY

Under most conventional definitions, rural–urban population movement occurs when an individual changes "usual place of residence" from a location classified as rural to another classified as urban. This definition, and all the measures that follow from it, rests crucially on aspects of space and time that determine residence, territory, and the interval over which geographical mobility takes place. In general, urban territory is relatively high in population density, often bounded within a separate administrative structure, and linked to non-agricultural production.

This simple urban–rural dichotomy is still used widely in national and international statistical compendia, and also in other social science applications, yet it is problematic. The definition of urban has resisted codification. No consistent definition of urban (and hence, rural) has been adopted by national governments (NRC 2003). A survey of contemporary practice found wide variation in thresholds and the balance between administrative and more functional classifications, with less than a quarter of countries using strict population size and density criteria (NRC 2003: 132). Typically, settlements over 2,000 or 5,000 persons are classified as urban, depending also on administrative considerations. (For the recent country-specific list, see UN 2004: ch. 7.)

An alternative to the simple dichotomy is to identify "urban agglomerations." According to the recent UN compendium, the definition "usually incorporates the population in a city or town plus that in the suburban areas lying outside of but being adjacent to the city boundaries" (UN 2004: 111). The classification of territory as metropolitan helps address the shortcoming of the rural–urban dichotomy, but many classifications do not capture relocations across the wide range of scale of settlements. Many tabulations and presentations of data still abide by a simple dichotomous cutoff. In general, as urban territory is classified and reclassified, the categories of population residence and movement are also determined.

Time matters, too. The notion of a relatively permanent change in usual place of residence eliminates temporary and seasonal movement. In high-income societies seasonal movement for reasons of climate and temporary job relocation are often missed in the study of population movements. In developing societies much short-term movement related to seasonality of agriculture and managing economic risk is absent from official statistics. Rural–urban

population movement may be more likely to be missed in such circumstances.

CONTRIBUTION OF POPULATION MOVEMENT TO URBAN–RURAL BALANCE

Rural–urban migration contributes substantially, but not always overwhelmingly, to urban growth. The scale of the contribution of population movement to overall urban growth depends critically on the relative size (stock) of the urban and rural populations initially, and the relative rates of natural increase in the two sectors. In a typical circumstance that begins as predominantly rural, the contribution of rural–urban migration flow is likely to be quite high initially and then decline over time as the rural stock is depleted and the urban stock incremented. One careful empirical examination of urbanization in developing settings calculated that migration (and reclassification of territory) contributed about 40 percent of urban growth in recent decades in developing countries (Chen et al. 1998). Rural–urban migration generally contributes more to city growth in lower fertility settings (US, Europe, China) than in high fertility settings (Sub-Saharan Africa). Many high-income and industrialized societies already have a large urban population. Thus, modest increases in urban–rural migration rates or declines in rural–urban migration rates could shift the net flow in the direction of rural areas.

OVERVIEW OF RURAL–URBAN POPULATION MOVEMENT TRENDS

For much of the twentieth century, the predominant pattern of population change in industrializing societies was urbanization (i.e., an increasing share of the population classified as urban). The UN projects that the world will become majority urban by 2007 and 61 percent urban by 2030 (UN 2004), up from 29 percent urban in 1950. While much of the shift in the net balance of population is due to rural–urban migration, reclassification of territory usually works to further augment the urban population over time, as settlements pass the definitional threshold to become urban.

Counter-urbanization, by contrast, is a decline in the share of population residing in cities and suburban territory. This reverse trend was noted in the US in the 1970s, and then in Europe and other industrialized societies. While it is correct to characterize the trend as a movement to lower-density settlements, counter-urbanization had several manifestations. Some movement was to exurban areas outside of the formal boundaries of urban agglomerations, some to more remote communities, and some was to smaller places within the urban hierarchy. In fact, from the 1970s through 1990s, several high-income societies experienced competing trends of urbanization, counter-urbanization, suburbanization, and continued selective rural depopulation. The US is illustrative, where the net population flow between non-metropolitan to metropolitan territory fluctuated over these decades. As societies move into spatial equilibrium, and as the social distinctions between urban and rural become blurred, such fluctuations are more likely.

DETERMINANTS OF RURAL–URBAN POPULATION MOVEMENT

Economic opportunity has long been the driver of population movement. During much of the nineteenth and twentieth centuries in contemporary high-income societies, migration was preponderantly from rural to urban areas, as industrialization generated labor demand in cities, and gains in agricultural productivity freed labor from the farms. The movement to the cities is still underway in a variety of middle and low-income nations. China, during its late twentieth-century economic transformation, provided a telling example as the fraction of the population living in urban areas increased steadily, augmented by a steady flow of both authorized and unauthorized migrants from the countryside. In high-income economies as factors of production became less tied to geographic place, the pull of cities and their suburbs lessened, and so did the migratory flow to these central locations. In developed societies urban populations grew modestly in absolute terms and levels of urbanization increased by only a few percentage points during the decades of the late twentieth century (UN 2004).

At the level of the individual migrant, the economic underpinnings of relocation are borne out. Surveys asking individual migrants directly about their reasons for moving repeatedly indicate that the greater the distance, the more likely the move is linked to employment opportunity. These reasons tend to hold in both low-income and high-income societies, but in technologically advanced societies with dispersed employment opportunities, rural–urban and urban–rural population movement may involve a mixture of work and family reasons as life cycle changes drive both. For example, retirees often seek out lower-cost housing and natural amenities, which are factors that generally favor smaller cities or rural areas.

In developing countries, the gender composition of the migration stream may vary with time, as primary migrants of one sex later reunify with family members who follow. Family and kinship related reasons (marriage markets linked to rural-origin social networks, return to a natal village for childbirth) may also generate counter-streams. Finally, sharp swings in economic and political stability may provide further impetus for movement between rural and urban areas.

SOCIAL CONSEQUENCES OF MIGRATION

Adaptation to the new setting of the city has long been of interest in the study of rural–urban migration. For destination cities, there is a parallel concern with the ways in which the influx changes community composition and social processes. Less attention has been paid to the adaptation of individuals and places in the urban–rural counter-stream or those people and places that have been left behind by the migratory flow. A large sociological literature in the early twentieth century grappled with the consequences of the increasing scale of urban living and the social heterogeneity introduced by the influx of migrants from the countryside and, in some cases, from other nations. Ernest Burgess, Georg Simmel, Robert Park, and Louis Wirth, among others, examined these issues.

Migration generally benefits the migrant household economically. Some theories posit the development of a dual-sector urban economy, with migrants relegated to an informal sector of long-term low-wage employment. Nevertheless, one recent assessment concluded that even amid substantial variation in individual outcomes, rural–urban migrants attain improved earnings that compare to urban natives after a period of adjustment (NRC 2003: 353).

Urban living is associated with changes in various sorts of behavior (declining fertility, a shift in health exposure regime) and the access to new sorts of resources (schools, sanitation). The direct effects of urban living certainly exist, but were likely overstated by some early observers. Most intriguing for the sociologist is the manner in which social interactions may shift in urban areas. Various processes of diffusion of new ideas and the development of sub-communities are possible when large numbers of new individuals are introduced into a dense heterogeneous environment.

Rural–urban migration also leaves people behind, and moreover, connects origin and destination communities. Social science has produced far less information about the consequences of migration for origin communities. What is known from examination of the composition of the migration streams is that origin communities tend to lose young adults, the more educated, and those with the most portable skills. Often, such departures are also differential by gender and ethnic group. There is reason to think that selective migration may have some adverse implications for those left behind, but a return flow of remittances and reduced labor market competition for remaining rural jobs may partly compensate for the outflow.

CURRENT DEVELOPMENTS

Several aspects of rural–urban population movement remain poorly understood. In some cases, this is due to the fact that this phenomenon is relatively new. In other cases, it is due to the fact that data collection or scholarly analysis is insufficient to shed light on the issue. Changes in transportation, communication, information technology, and associated economic incentives have made transnational rural–urban migration more extensive and more visible. There is international movement that is also rural–urban:

Southern European guestworkers flowing to major cities of Northern Europe; francophone African migrants to Paris; farmers in Central Mexico leaving for the Southwestern US. Circular, seasonal, and temporary migration has occupied the attention of migration scholars for some time. Such mobility is highly prevalent, and of significant economic and social impact, in some societies. Much of the time in cities is spent in economic activity with wages saved or remitted to the home family and community. At the same time, the absences – which may range from forays of several days to sojourns of several months – may bring the stress that comes with familial discontinuities.

Some new thinking on this topic considers contextual conditions. Migration offers a potential household strategy for managing risk and uncertainty, especially in agricultural regions. By sending some household members to the city, the household can spread its risks across the economic fortunes of agricultural and non-agricultural sectors. Notably, such household behavior can generate seasonal and circular migratory flows. Interest in the migration-development paradox stems from the observation that, contrary to expectation, migration out of impoverished rural communities is often quite low, and actually rises with community socioeconomic level. Some posit that this paradox of lower migration propensity in the face of potentially greater wage gains stems from the absolute lack of resources available to support mobility in the poor communities. This deserves greater examination, and certainly begs the question of how community context helps inaugurate, sustain, and terminate migration flows.

Some of the methodological and theoretical trends in sociology are likely to have particular benefit for the study of rural–urban population movement and other forms of population redistribution. The increasing prevalence of longitudinal data, the technological gains enabling the collection and storage of detailed geographically referenced data, and the growing attention to contextual effects all point to innovations in the future.

SEE ALSO: Global/World Cities; Migration: Internal; Migration and the Labor Force; Urban; Urban Revolution; Urbanism/Urban Culture; Urbanization

REFERENCES AND SUGGESTED READINGS

Champion, A. (1992). *Migration Processes and Patterns.* Belhaven Press, New York.

Chen, N., Valente, P., & Zlotnik, H. (1998) What Do We Know About Recent Trends in Urbanization? In: Bilsborrow, R. E. (Ed.), *Migration, Urbanization, and Development: New Directions and Issues.* United Nations Population Fund & Kluwer Academic Publishers, New York, pp. 59–88.

Hugo, G., Champion, A. G., & Lattes, A. (2003) Toward a New Conceptualization of Settlements for Demography. *Population and Development Review* 29(2): 277–97.

Mather, M. & D'Amico, J. (2004) Slow Going for the Population in Rural America. Population Reference Bureau. Online. www.prb.org.

National Research Council (NRC) (2003) *Cities Transformed: Demographic Change and Its Implications in the Developing World.* Panel on Population on Urban Population Dynamics, M. R. Montgomery, R. Stren, B. Cohen, & H. E. Reed. Committee on Population, Division of Behavioral and Social Sciences and Education. National Academies Press, Washington, DC.

Schachter, J. P., Franklin, R. S., & Perry, M. J. (2003) Migration and Geographic Mobility to Metropolitan and Nonmetropolitan America, 1995–2000. United States Bureau of the Census. Census 2000 Special Reports CENSR-9.

United Nations (UN) (2004) *World Urbanization Prospects: The 2003 Revision.* United Nations, New York.

urban space

Adalberto Agiurre

It is not an easy task to provide a definition of urban space because such a definition must consider the social parameters of its constituent parts: urban and space. The difficulty of defining urban space is enhanced if one considers that urban space is an artifact of urbanization – a social process that describes the manner in which cities grow and societies become more complex. For example, a synergistic perspective of space situates the location of "urban" as an outcome of social and institutional forces associated with urbanization. In contrast, a structural perspective of space identifies "urban" as the product of social structures and relationships that typify urbanization. Combining the synergistic and structural perspectives results in the identification of social features associated with urban space: (1) diversity of social roles and relationships, and (2) institutional arrangements and social networks necessary for efficient social order. No matter which perspective one adopts, one thing is clear: urban space is a dynamic aspect of urbanization. Urban space involves synergistic and structural aspects.

From a synergistic perspective, urbanization is fueled by population growth and institutional expansion. In a simplistic scenario, in order for urbanization to occur, people must come together in large enough numbers that they are situated in a space that makes them noticeably different from less populated human groupings. In addition, the social diversity of the people situated in the same space promotes a form of social interaction characterized by formal role relationships rather than intimate or informal (e.g., familial) role relationships. That is, as a population increases its numbers within the same space it becomes necessary for the maintenance of social order that diversity within the population be characterized by formal role relationships (*Gesellschaft*) rather than informal role relations (*Gemeinschaft*). One might say that a distinction emerges between highly populated space (urban) and less populated space (rural).

The aggregation of people within the same space serves as a social force that brings together persons with diverse lifestyles and work ethics. In most cases people migrated to the same space because of shared interests or shared expectations regarding lifestyles and work ethics. Interestingly, social contact between persons in the population sharing the same space enhances the social diversity of the population by increasing familiarity with different lifestyles and work ethics. In turn, the diversity of lifestyles and work ethics necessitates the development of institutional structures for their expression; for example, churches for religious expression and a labor market for demonstrating a work ethic.

At the institutional level, situating a large number of persons with a diversity of lifestyles and work ethics within the same space required the centralization of social life. The dynamic aspect of increased social contact between persons required the development of formal relationships between persons and institutions. For persons situated within the same space to be able to express their lifestyle and work ethic in an efficient manner required the formation of institutional structures for the performance of diverse lifestyles and work ethics. In particular, centralization was necessary for the efficient operation of institutional structures focused on coordinating the delivery of services vital to the expression of lifestyles and work ethics.

For example, in order to promote the efficient expression of social life, economic organizations such as banks and labor markets developed in order to provide a network of services that utilized labor, raw materials, and capital. The network of services, in turn, centralized the production of services that met the needs of a growing population. As such, a large and growing population, coupled with an institutional structure designed to promote centralization and social efficiency, created a context for defining urban space: the situating of a large number of persons with diverse lifestyles and work ethics in space nested within an institutional structure that promotes centralization and social efficiency. From a commonsense point of view, urban space is often regarded as a rudimentary definition for the city.

Given the preceding definition of urban space one must not assume that it is a twentieth-century or twenty-first century phenomenon. Large urban centers or urban spaces can be identified in the history of societies in the world system. According to some estimates, the city of Babylon had almost a million residents at the height of its social development. Similarly, Rome had almost half a million residents at its peak, while London had about a million residents by the early 1800s. All three cities or urban spaces were characterized by a large population of residents and the operation of institutional structures for promoting social efficiency in a diverse population (e.g., collection of taxes, distribution of raw materials, and the production of work).

The institutional structures that centralized social life in an efficient manner resulted in an outcome that one finds today. As the number of persons sharing the same space intensified, so did the diversification of lifestyles and work ethics. In particular, the centralization of social life resulted in the hierarchical arrangement of persons based on lifestyle and work ethic. That is, class differences became visible and served to partition urban space. The partition of urban space made it possible to observe how persons sharing the same space associated with each other along class lines.

For example, in early nineteenth-century Parisian society the aristocracy and growing bourgeoisie moved to the margins of the city to escape the increasing numbers of the "popular classes" in Paris. The access to capital and valued resources enjoyed by the upper and middle classes allowed them to situate themselves on the margin of urban space. In a sense, access to capital or valued resources served as a social force to extend the boundaries of urban space into rural space. As a result, what is often referred to as a suburb – space adjacent to or on the periphery of urban space – took rudimentary expression as the ability of persons with capital to differentiate themselves by class from persons subject to the homogenizing effects of the "popular class" on persons sharing the same urban space.

One finds in American society a similar phenomenon in the twenty-first century. The increasing perception that urban space is pregnant with social problems such as crime, homelessness, and poverty has resulted in persons and families fleeing to space located on the periphery or within traveling distance of urban space. During the 1970s and early 1980s in the US, moving from urban space to the suburb was often characterized as "white flight" because it was a movement that was mostly driven by white persons and families. These were white persons and families that had accumulated equity in their homes located in urban space that permitted them to sell their homes and buy new larger homes in the suburbs. (Unfortunately, most of those left behind in urban space were racial and ethnic minorities who did not own their homes, thus resulting in the racialization of the suburbs.) Ironically, in some cases the number of persons and families moving from urban space to the suburbs was so drastic that suburbs became mirror images of the urban space persons and families were fleeing. The suburbs have become so much like urban space that persons and families are moving into rural areas, resulting in "suburbs of the suburbs," or what population experts refer to as exurbs.

Interestingly, as persons and families moved from urban to suburban space, the uses of public space have come into question. Who is entitled to occupy public space? In urban centers, the poor and homeless have been identified as targets for city redevelopment projects. For example, redevelopment policies have been used by cities to implement "eminent domain" practices to remove older homes, often occupied by the elderly on fixed incomes, to make room for upscale townhouses or condominiums that appeal to young people and families, especially those with white-collar or professional occupations. Redevelopment policies have been designed by cities that establish vagrancy zones in downtown areas that make loitering on public walkways a misdemeanor – a strategic tool for criminalizing the homeless in downtown areas. As a result, city redevelopment practices seek to remove the poor and homeless from public space not so much to "clean up" the city, but so as to create an attractive locale for bringing back the capital that left the city when persons and families moved to the suburbs.

In the suburbs the fight is over how to allocate public space to parks and recreation areas versus businesses and commercial interests. For example, many of the suburbs' residents commute to work in urban centers. In order to develop a system of services that meet the needs of growing suburbs, city councils in the suburbs have courted businesses, especially manufacturers, to relocate to the suburbs in order to generate sales-tax revenue and jobs, thus keeping residents in the suburbs and improving their quality of life by providing jobs that do not require commuting. The push for attracting businesses, however, comes at a cost to residents. Public space that has been designated for recreational use is used as a carrot by city councils to attract businesses. As a result, public space in the suburb is a contest between resource used by people versus economic benefits for businesses.

In summary, if one considers the social construction of population centers, one might say that urban space is typified by what is called a "city." A city is a collection of people and institutional structures that promote the efficient interaction between persons and place. Urban space has often increased in population to the point that it serves as a synergistic force for the social construction of the suburb. Ironically, suburbs have decided that the only means for their survival is to mirror urban areas – formal social relationships and complex institutional arrangements. In turn, the suburb has served as a synergistic force to create its own alter ego, the exurb. As a result, the rapid growth of suburban populations makes it difficult to exclude the suburb from consideration as urban space because it is a product and catalyst for the social construction of urban space. It is possible to consider the rise of the suburb as an extension of urban space that seeks to accommodate the expression of increasing diversity in lifestyles and work ethics. It is not clear, however, how increasing racial and ethnic diversity in the US population will shape the synergistic link between urban and suburban space. Ironically, what urban and suburban spaces have in common is the transformation of public space into contested terrain.

SEE ALSO: Homelessness; Lefebvre, Henri; New Urbanism; Urban Policy; Urban Tourism

REFERENCES AND SUGGESTED READINGS

Aguirre, Jr., A. & Brooks, J. (2001) City Redevelopment Policies and the Criminalization of Homelessness: A Narrative Case Study. In: Fox, K. (Ed.), *Critical Perspectives on Urban Development*. JAI Press, Gotham, NY, pp. 75–105.

Atkinson, R. (2003) Domestication by Cappuccino or Revenge on Urban Space? Control and Empowerment in the Management of Public Spaces. *Urban Studies* 40: 1829–43.

French, J. (1978) *Urban Space: A Brief History of the City Square*. Kendall/Hunt, Dubuque, IA.

Gotham, K. F. (2000) Restrictive Covenants, and the Origins of the Racial Residential Segregation in a US City, 1901–50. *International Journal of Urban and Regional Research* 24: 616–33.

Graham, S. (2001) Information Technologies and Reconfigurations of Urban Space. *International Journal of Urban and Regional Research* 25: 405–10.

Jimenez, A. (2003) On Space as a Capacity. *Journal of the Royal Anthropological Institute* 9: 137–53.

Mitchell, K. (2000) The Culture of Urban Space. *Urban Geography* 21: 443–9.

Palen, J. J. (2005) *The Urban World*, 7th edn. McGraw-Hill, New York.

Thompson, V. (2003) Telling "Spatial Stories:" Urban Space and Bourgeois Identity in Early Nineteenth-Century Paris. *Journal of Modern History* 75: 523–56.

Weeks, J. (1999) *Population: An Introduction to Concepts and Issues*, 7th edn. Wadsworth, Belmont, CA.

urban tourism

Richard Lloyd

Urban tourism refers to the consumption of city spectacles (such as architecture, monuments, and parks) and cultural amenities (such as museums, restaurants, and performances) by visitors. Studying urban tourism requires taking seriously leisure activities and transient populations, features of the city that much of past urban theory declines to address. However, a number of developments in recent decades have led tourism to assume a larger place in urban scholarship. As industrial manufacturing deserts dense urban areas, entertainment plays an expanded role in many city economies. Leisure and consumption for some means work and profits for others. The attraction and accommodation of visitors has become a central concern for public and private city elites. The sizable but fleeting population of visitors to the city has a surprising influence over local politics, investment choices, and the built environment.

The label "tourist" frequently evokes pejorative connotations, which color not only popular but also scholarly representations. While crude stereotypes of the tourist suggest a plodding brute oblivious to all but the most obvious and pre-packaged attractions of the urban landscape, the leisure activity of tourism in fact contains a wide range of consumption activities and orientations toward the city. Moreover, the "business or pleasure" distinction obscures the fact that many trips are multi-purpose, with business travelers also shopping, visiting museums, and dining out. Susan Fainstein and Dennis Judd advocate the use of the term visitor rather than tourist, and see tourism as a particular mode of activity in which visitors engage. Especially today, even permanent residents may at times use aspects of their own cities "as if tourists," consuming its spectacular, exotic, and heterogeneous amenities (Lloyd & Clark 2001).

Cities have long been privileged destinations for visitors as well as sites of residence. The ancient city was a destination for pilgrims, merchants, political envoys, and adventurers, some of whom produced accounts of the exotic spectacles they encountered. The industrial revolution led to rapid growth in the permanent populations of large European and US cities during the nineteenth and early twentieth centuries. During the industrial epoch large cities remained spaces of spectacle and a multitude of entertainments. In the prototypical industrial city of Chicago, for example, city elites were not satisfied merely being hog butcher to the world, actively seeking to enhance the city's cultural image and attract visitors by launching the Columbian exposition of 1892 (in which the Ferris Wheel was introduced).

Still, the sociological study of the city, grounded in the massive growth of urban areas coinciding with the industrial revolution, has traditionally treated tourism peripherally if at all. The last half century, however, has brought significant change. Industry has increasingly declined in the older cities of the US and other developed nations, enhanced technologies of transportation and communication have made travel far more convenient and widely available, and the aesthetic and experiential dimensions of consumption have come to play an arguably much greater role in the global economy. Fast-growing cities like Las Vegas and Orlando feature economies primarily organized around tourism and consumption. For old and new cities, the active production of spectacle and consumption opportunities is now a crucial feature of the political economy. In this case, tourism can no longer be a tertiary concern for urban theory.

In the 1980s, newly popular theories of postmodernism took the lead in examining the city as a site of spectacle and consumption. Focusing on the signifying qualities of the material landscape, thinkers such as Umberto Eco, Jean Baudrillard, and Mark Gottdeiner direct considerable attention to tourist destinations like the Las Vegas strip and Disneyland. The postmodern tendency to emphasize the transient and the ephemeral in social life likewise results in considerable attention to the spaces and activities of tourists. In this light it is unsurprising that Frederic Jameson identifies Los Angeles's Bonaventure Hotel as the signature space of "postmodernism in the city." While these approaches have been influential, the mostly semiotic method employed in them is dissatisfying for many sociologists.

Disneyland and Las Vegas remain potent models that inform the study of the post-industrial city as an object of consumption. Many theorists advance the notion that the city itself is increasingly constructed as a theme park in order to entice consumers. These approaches, which can be called the "Disneyfication" or "theme park" models of urban tourism (Sorkin 1992; Hannigan 1998; Bryman 2004), emphasize homogenizing tendencies in large cities, as tourist spaces come to look much the same from one city to the next. They focus on the injection of large-scale developments such as sports stadiums, convention halls, and shopping malls into formerly decaying areas. Baltimore's Inner Harbor and Chicago's Navy Pier are signature spaces of this style of redevelopment in the US. These spaces of consumption tend to be highly segregated from the rest of the city and the everyday activity of residents. Hence, Judd (1999) identifies the construction of "tourist bubbles," districts that organize tourist activity in a highly regimented fashion while actively excluding undesirable elements.

The success of Disneyfied tourist entertainment is more uneven than these approaches usually anticipate, and themed entertainment venues like Planet Hollywood and the Rainforest Café routinely failed during the 1990s. Critics like Michael Sorkin (1992) decry the "inauthenticity" of themed spaces; what is increasingly clear is that tourists themselves often wish to consume what they perceive to be authentic attractions within a city. Rather than the homogenization of the urban landscape that Disneyfication anticipates, these attractions derive from specific aspects of local identity. Many cities combine large-scale theme developments with more "indigenous" cultural attractions. Grazian (2003) shows that tourists search for authenticity in entertainments such as the Blues in Memphis and Chicago, or country music in Nashville. Local venues strategize to satisfy these expectations, producing what

MacCannell (1999) identifies as "staged authenticity." Often, tourists practice multiple styles of consumption, in Chicago visiting obligatory attractions like Navy Pier, the Sears Tower Observation Deck, and the splendid shopping of the Miracle Mile, while also attempting to locate the "real" Chicago in smoky Blues clubs "off the beaten path."

Indeed, the attraction of cities for tourists derives from both the breadth and the depth of urban culture. Breadth signals the diversity of attractions that center-city districts are uniquely poised to offer, which can include professional sports, museums of various sorts, high, low, and middlebrow theater, musical performances, and an exceptionally wide range of dining and shopping opportunities. Depth refers to the cumulative nature of a city's identity (Suttles 1984), the resonance that attaches to particular aspects of the built environment and local culture. These include landmarks like the Eiffel Tower, the Golden Gate Bridge, or the Empire State Building. Tourists may experience Yankee Stadium as pleasantly haunted by the ghosts of Ruth and Mantle and the streets of Greenwich Village by past generations of storied bohemians. Thus, while some popular tourist destinations such as Orlando and Las Vegas are constituted almost entirely by prefabricated entertainments, and revel in the absence of depth, many others are valued for a place identity that emerges from distinct and varied histories.

At a more mundane but equally important level, cities contain essential infrastructure, achieved through a balance of public and private investment, which enables them to accommodate large numbers of visitors. Such infrastructure includes airports, convention centers, and significant amounts of lodging. Conventions are major vehicles for attracting visitors, and in these cases corporate expense accounts underwrite consumption in restaurants and other entertainment venues. Just as Chicago competed to win the Columbian Exposition near the end of the nineteenth century, entering the twenty-first century urban boosters are locked in competition for major conventions as well as other high-profile, visitor-attracting events such as the Olympics or the Super Bowl.

Local boosters argue that new tourist attractions generate multiplier effects that will improve the tax base and benefit permanent residents. Actual results have been uneven. While the entertainment economy of large cities implies a substantial workforce, the service jobs created are often far less promising than the manufacturing jobs that they replace, representing a mostly disorganized sector of cleaning personnel, kitchen staff, ticket takers, and the like. Casino gaming, a strategy for attracting tourist dollars recently turned to by the most economically desperate urban districts, including downtown Detroit and Gary, appears to produce particularly dubious effects for the local quality of life of poor residents.

The costs and benefits of tourist enterprises promise to be important objects of both theoretical and policy analyses in coming years. In the wake of the 2001 attack on the World Trade Center, security has emerged as another key factor in the regulation of city visitors that will bear considerable scrutiny. Long ignored, the relationship between cities and their visitors has become a core concern in contemporary urban theory.

SEE ALSO: Uneven Development; Urban; Urban Renewal and Redevelopment; Urban Space; Urbanism/Urban Culture

REFERENCES AND SUGGESTED READINGS

Baudrillard, J. (1989) *America*. Verso, New York.
Bryman, A. (2004) *The Disneyization of Society*. Sage, Thousand Oaks, CA.
Eco, U. (1986) *Travels in Hyperreality*. Harcourt, Brace, Jovanovich, New York.
Gottdiener, M. (1995) *Postmodern Semiotics: Material Culture and the Forms of Postmodern Life*. Blackwell, Oxford.
Grazian, D. (2003) *Blue Chicago: The Search for Authenticity in Urban Blues Clubs*. University of Chicago Press, Chicago.
Hannigan, J. (1998) *Fantasy City: Pleasure and Profit in the Postmodern Metropolis*. Routledge, New York.
Hoffman, L. M., Fainstein, S. S., & Judd, D. R. (Eds.) (2003) *Cities and Visitors: Regulating People, Markets and City Space*. Blackwell, Oxford.
Jameson, F. (1991) *Postmodernism: or, the Cultural Logic of Late Capitalism*. Duke University Press, Durham, NC.
Judd, D. R. (1999) Constructing the Tourist Bubble. In: Judd, D. R. & Fainstein, S. (Eds.), *The Tourist City*. Yale University Press, New Haven.
Lloyd, R. & Clark, T. N. (2001) The City as an Entertainment Machine. *Research in Urban Sociology: Critical Perspectives on Urban Redevelopment* 6: 357–78.
MacCannell, D. (1999) *The Tourist: A New Theory of the Leisure Class*. University of California Press, Berkeley.
Sorkin, M. (Ed.) (1992) *Variations on a Theme Park*. Hill & Wang, New York.
Suttles, G. (1984) The Cumulative Texture of Local Urban Culture. *American Journal of Sociology* 90: 283–304.
Urry, J. (1990) *The Tourist Gaze*. Sage, London.

urban way of life (East Asia)

Yasushi Suzuki

Among the various definitions of the "urban way of life" in Japanese social science, Susumu Kurasawa's (1987) definition is most widely accepted in sociology. "Way of life" here refers to a way of coping with common and collective problems in the community. A "rural way of life" is characterized by a strong capacity of residents' households to deal with common problems and their dependence on the mutual aid systems of laypeople in coping with collective problems. In contrast, the "urban way of life" is characterized by the low ability of households to sustain themselves, and their consequential dependence on the specialized systems of experts and professional institutions.

Kurasawa examined several classic arguments in modern sociology on the issue, such as Sorokin and Zimmerman's (1929) urban–rural dichotomy, Simmel's (1951) analyses of urban life, Wirth's (1938) urbanism as a way of life, as well as Tadashi Fukutake's (1952) and Eitaro Suzuki's (1957) definitions of rural and urban communities. Kurasawa then identified the core of the urban way of life as the specialized systems of professional institutions in urban communities. His argument focuses on occupational diversity, social differentiation, division of labor, and nodal institutions which have been identified as the structural characteristics of urban life, and he excluded from the conception individual and psychological traits such as secondary contacts, superficial and temporary relationships, rationality, impersonality, and alienation. In sum, Kurasawa argued that specialized systems of professional institutions are distinctive traits of urban social organizations. He also proposed his own definition of the city: it is a relatively large, dense settlement of non-agricultural residents in a society at a given time.

While concentrating on defining the city and the urban way of life, Kurasawa's theoretical framework remains unclear. He may have considered the "urban way of life" to be an independent variable that affects both the ecological traits of cities and the social and psychological traits. Or perhaps he considered the "urban way of life" to be an intermediate variable between the two. Either way, his focus was on the concept of the "urban way of life" itself. Treating the concepts of professional and mutual aid systems as a dichotomy, he argued that the professional systems should be complemented by mutual aid systems even in urban settings (Kurasawa 1988). In effect, this can be used as an analytical framework for describing urban problems.

In the late 1960s and 1970s, suburbanization produced many new problems in urban Japan, such as a deficiency in infrastructures. Kennichi Miyamoto, one of the leading urban economists in Japan, argued that since the "urban way of life" includes concentration of population, commodity consumption, and collective consumption (i.e., public facilities such as water supply and sewerage systems, streets, parks, and schools), contemporary urban problems were distinctively characterized by the deficiencies in the means of collective consumption (Miyamoto 1980).

Another issue associated with them is the creation of local urban communities. Citizen's movements and public policymakers addressing urban problems advocated the creation of communities in cities. Kurasawa, as we have seen, recommended that local communities should play a significant role in providing mutual aid systems within the urban way of life.

Defining the urban way of life in terms of the reliance on specialized systems of professional institutions thus implies that most urban problems result from expert systems. They may be caused by the deficiency of collective goods provided by governments or by excessive dependency on goods and services provided by markets. Local communities may complement the specialized systems and help alleviate the associated problems. This view remains limited, however, to the consumption sphere, as does Miyamoto's "urban way of life" (and Manuel Castells's similar arguments on "collective consumption"). More recently, specialized systems have been reconsidered in relation to the problems of trust and the risks of the "abstract systems" of modern societies (Giddens 1990). The conception of the "urban way of life" in terms of specialized systems may obtain further significance if it is connected to an analysis of the broader consequences of specialization on modern mental life, as with Simmel's argument in the early twentieth century.

SEE ALSO: Risk, Risk Society, Risk Behavior, and Social Problems; Simmel, Georg; Suzuki, Eitaro; Traditional Consumption City (Japan); Urban; Urban Community Studies; Urbanism/ Urban Culture

REFERENCES AND SUGGESTED READINGS

Castells, M. (1976) Theoretical Propositions for an Experimental Study of Urban Social Movements. In: Pickvance, C. G. (Ed.), *Urban Sociology: Critical Essays*. Tavistock, London.

Fukutake, T. (1952) Structures of Society. In: Fukutake, T. & Hidaka, R., *Sociology: Elementary Theory on Society and Culture*. Kobunsya, Tokyo, ch. 2.

Giddens, A. (1990) *The Consequences of Modernity*. Polity Press, Cambridge.

Kurasawa, S. (1968) *Japanese Urban Society*. Fukumura Shuppan, Tokyo.

Kurasawa, S. (1987) An Introduction to Urban Way of Life. In: Suzuki, H., Kurasawa, S., & Akimoto, R. (Eds.), *Sociological Theory of Urbanization*. Minerva, Kyoto.

Kurasawa, S. (1988) Socialization of Consumption. In: Takahashi, Y. (Ed.), *Textbook Sociology V: Local Community*. Yuhikaku, Tokyo.

Miyamoto, K. (1980) *Urban Economics: Political Economy on the Conditions of Collective Life*. Chikuma Shobo, Tokyo.

Simmel, G. (1951) Metropolis and Mental Life. In: Hatt, P. K. & Reiss, A. J. (Eds.), *Cities and Society*. Free Press, Glencoe, IL, pp. 635–46.

Sorokin, P. A. & Zimmerman, C. C. (1929) *Principles of Rural–Urban Sociology*. Holt, New York.

Suzuki, E. (1969 [1957]) *Principles of Urban Sociology*. In: *Collected Papers of Suzuki Eitaro*, Vol. 6. Miraisya, Tokyo.

Wirth, L. (1938) Urbanism as a Way of Life. *American Journal of Sociology* 44: 3–24.

urbanism, subcultural theory of

Charles R. Tittle

Claude Fischer's (1975, 1995) urban theory is designed to explain how and why social relationships vary by size of population in settlements. According to the theory, urban life is bifurcated into public and private domains. In the public domain social relationships are typically superficial because people are usually interacting with others whom they do not know personally and may not see again. Such interactions are based mainly on the obvious roles people are playing at the time, such as bus rider, store clerk or customer, and pedestrian. Thus, the public domain, which varies directly with the size of the population, is characterized by anonymity, impersonality, tolerance, and lack of social bonding with others.

However, urbanites, even those in settlements with very large populations, have private lives characterized by interpersonal networks of friends, associates, and family, just as do people in smaller settlements. In addition, urbanites are more likely to be involved in other private networks with people who share interests that are somewhat uncommon and often unconventional. Through interaction concerning those peculiar interests, people within such networks develop distinct norms, a particular set of meanings and legitimations, status systems, and other social characteristics that distinguish them as *subcultures*. Thus, in their private worlds, urbanites are no less socially bonded interpersonally than people in other places and, in addition, they are more likely to be involved in subcultural networks.

Cities promote subcultural formation because their large populations make it more likely that a number of people will share a given interest even though it may be statistically rare or unconventional. Moreover, the freedom implied by an anonymous, impersonal, tolerant public domain permits urbanites with peculiar interests to locate each other and interact sufficiently to produce subcultures. Fischer uses the term *critical mass* to refer to a situation where there are enough people with similar but unusual interests to form a subculture. The larger the city, the greater the number of critical masses and the larger the likelihood of subcultures of many types.

Because so many and so many different kinds of subcultures blossom and grow in cities, urban dwellers become more tolerant of the peculiar behaviors or interests that various subcultural affiliates embrace. In addition, subcultural affiliation provides supportive networks, distinct normative expectations, and social controls to encourage those who participate in them to embrace the behaviors around which the subcultures are oriented. Since many of those subcultures are concerned with unconventional or unacceptable things from the point of view of the wider normative context, their participants are likely to exhibit enhanced rates of deviant behavior. As a result, the larger the settlement, the higher the rates of misbehavior, including criminal behavior.

Hence, in a rather straightforward way, subcultural theory also implies a connection between changes in population and crime rates. As the size of a population increases, the critical mass for any given specialized interest also goes up, as do the critical masses for larger numbers and varieties of interests. Growing populations will therefore have enhanced chances of developing criminal subcultures as well as elevated chances of greater diversity in kinds of subcultures, especially unusual ones. Urban subcultures may facilitate innovation and diffusion of new ideas as well as promote unconventionality or unacceptable behavior, so they also help distinguish cities as inspirational places for cultural change.

Fischer's theory has been especially important because it helped resolve contradictions between earlier urban theories. For example,

Wirth (1969) portrayed the city as a place of social isolation with consequent ineffective social control and high likelihood of social pathologies. Additionally, Gans (1962) had contended that urban social relationships and behavioral patterns were entirely the result of the socio-demographic characteristics of their residents without urban contexts themselves having any causal effects. Fischer's account borrows from each, but it also adds a unique subcultural element.

However, because part of the theory concerns supra-individual, ecological-level phenomena that are hard to measure with city-wide data, the complete theory has not been thoroughly tested. The evidence does seem consistent with the notion that urban dwellers maintain interpersonal and familial ties while simultaneously occupying a public world of relative (though not as extreme as earlier accounts suggest) indifference, that many kinds of subcultures do thrive in cities, and that those who are affiliated with such subcultures are more likely to engage in the peculiar behaviors they promote. However, it has not yet been established that cities are the birthplaces or the most nurturing contexts for all subcultures and it is not yet clear whether modern communication systems, particularly the Internet, render cities less relevant to subcultural formation or the behaviors presumably generated by them.

SEE ALSO: Compositional Theory of Urbanism; Deviance; Subcultures, Deviant; Urban Crime and Violence; Urbanism/Urban Culture

REFERENCES AND SUGGESTED READINGS

Fischer, C. S. (1975) Toward a Subcultural Theory of Urbanism. *American Journal of Sociology* 80: 1319–41.
Fischer, C. S. (1995) The Subcultural Theory of Urbanism: A Twentieth-Year Assessment. *American Journal of Sociology* 101: 543–77.
Gans, H. (1962) Urbanism and Suburbanism as Ways of Life: A Reevaluation of Definitions. In: Rose, A. M. (Ed.), *Human Behavior and Social Process*. Houghton Mifflin, Boston, pp. 625–48.
Wirth, L. (1938 [1969]) Urbanism as a Way of Life. In: Sennett, R. (Ed.), *Classic Essays on the Culture of Cities*. Appleton-Century-Crofts, New York.

urbanism/urban culture

Joanna Hadjicostandi

"With a year-old son and a husband who traveled several days a week, she knew she wanted something more than a neighborhood. She wanted a community" (Richards 2005: 64).

"Urbanism" refers to the distinctive social and cultural patterns that develop in cities. "City," "urban site," "urban society," and "urbanization" are often used to refer to the physical structures as well as the social activities in an urban society. Cities have always been key sites for transcultural connections such as local and long-distance trade and the transmission of innovations. They further have been the centers where political and economic power relations are instituted and maintained. Within urban centers multiple cultures develop, interact, and create social change.

Urbanism is not a monolithic term, but one that is complex, multifaceted, and centrally placed in history.

When discussing urbanism, Deitrick and Ellis (2004: 427–8) present a long list of key patterns that dominate urban areas. The first pattern they refer to is the creation of metropolitan regions that are composed of a structured hierarchy of cities, towns, villages, and neighborhoods. They recognize patterns revitalizing city centers with interconnected streets that are friendly to pedestrians and cyclists. They further argue that there is a very careful placement of unaesthetic structures such as garages and parking spaces with a transit-oriented development. Well-designed buildings and gathering places along with high-quality parks and conservation lands are used to define and connect neighborhoods and districts. Finally, there is respect for local history and regional character in new architectural development. This can be particularly observed in neighborhoods that retain the character of their traditional inhabitants. Thus, we have Little Italy in the North End in Boston, or Chinatown in the middle of New York City and San Francisco, Astoria in New York, Soho in London, and so on. Interestingly, the nature of those neighborhoods and how they are viewed by the population have tremendous historical and ethnic/racial significance. For instance, visiting

Chinatown or Little Italy is a night out on the town as opposed to visiting Roxbury, a low-income, economically depressed, black-dominated neighborhood in Boston.

Others claim that urbanism is a cluster of variables. Cowgill (2004) defines a city as a permanent settlement within the larger territory occupied by a society considered home by a significant number of residents whose activities, roles, practices, experiences, identities, and attitudes differ significantly from those of other members of the society who identify most closely with "rural" lands outside such settlements. Beyond the structure of the city, he theorized about individuals and their practices, interests, and emotions; the extent to which the first cities were deliberately created rather than merely emerging as byproducts of increasing sociopolitical complexity; the internal structure of cities and the interplay of top-down planning and bottom-up self-organization; social, economic, and political relations between cities and their hinterlands; interactions of cities with their physical environments; and the difficult "city-state" concept.

GLOBALIZATION AND URBANISM

The city is a place where people typically lead in economic and technological developments as well as artistic and intellectual experiments. Foreigners and endogenous extramodal cultural elements contribute to the creative potential of these innovations.

Migration patterns have changed dramatically in the past two to three decades due to many socioeconomic and political changes that have occurred globally. The new waves of migrants stem from many Asian and African countries, as well as from Central and Eastern Europe and South and Central America. The great numbers of migrants from such diverse backgrounds and differences in lifestyle, with heterogeneous habits, food, clothing, music, film, dance, and literature, have instigated a shift of research focus in race, class, ethnicity, age, and gender. They have also become involved in the construction of new political spaces that cross conventional boundaries between nations and ethnic groups.

RACIAL SEGREGATION AND URBANISM

Although urbanism involves different patterns of cohabitation between groups, some kind of segregation exists almost in every city.

For example, most North American cities remain deeply segregated by race, economic status, or ethnic affinity. Although overt racism has decreased over the last 30 years, racial segregation continues to be a persistent feature of North American cities. Economic segregation continues, sometimes acting as a proxy for racial segregation, strengthened by ideologies justifying "neighborhood protection." Ethnic enclaves persist as protective way stations for recent immigrants as well as distinctive and valued urban neighborhoods.

A host of other problems, such as the lack of both public services and private enterprise in inner-city black, Hispanic/Latino, or Chinese neighborhoods, have persisted in part because of this segregation. The challenge today is to address the legacy of nearly a century of institutional practices that supported racial and ethnic ghettos deep in our urban demography. Specifically, the practices of mortgage lenders and property insurers may have done more to shape housing patterns than bald racism ever did (Squires 1999).

In 1989, Urban Institute researchers found that the dual housing markets are perpetuated by racial steering, insurance decisions, and other forms of disparate treatment of minorities such as concentrating public housing in central city locations and financing highways to facilitate suburban development. Dismantling cities' dual housing markets will require appropriate political strategies that address the structural causes.

GENTRIFICATION

N. Smith (2002) uses several events in New York in the late 1990s to launch two central arguments about the changing relationship between neoliberal urbanism and so-called globalization. First, much as the neoliberal state becomes a consummate agent of – rather than a regulator of – the market, the new revanchist urbanism that replaces liberal urban policy in cities of the advanced capitalist world increasingly expresses the impulses of capitalist production rather than social reproduction. As globalization bespeaks a rescaling of the global, the scale of the urban is recast. The true global cities may be the rapidly growing metropolitan economies of Asia, Latin America, and (to a lesser extent) Africa, as much as the command centers of Europe, North America, and Japan. Second, the process of gentrification, which initially emerged as a sporadic, quaint, and local anomaly in the housing markets of some command-center cities, is now thoroughly generalized as an urban strategy that takes over from liberal urban policy. No longer isolated or restricted to Europe, North America, or Oceania, the impulse behind gentrification is now generalized; its incidence is global, and it is densely connected into the circuits of global capital and cultural circulation. What connects these two arguments is the shift from an urban scale defined according to the conditions of social reproduction to one in which the investment of productive capital holds definitive precedence.

URBAN CULTURES/NEW URBAN PLANNING MOVEMENT

The new urbanism, a movement in urban town planning that developed in the late 1980s and early 1990s, is built on the belief that physical environments really matter and shape people's lives in ways they might not recognize. The principle of new urbanism is to erect fabricated "small towns" with an increased density of friendly residential neighborhoods, and all the facilities within walking (or skipping) radius of their home.

The objective is to facilitate everyday social interaction through the strategic design of public and private spaces, creating the sense of real neighborhoods. Traditional neighborhoods wove people together in economic interdependence, allowing for residents as well as most professionals to be deeply involved in the local society.

The most notorious new urbanism development is the Disney-owned Celebration in Florida. Unveiled in 1994, this $2.5 billion project nestled on 4,900 acres a mere 5 miles south of

Walt Disney World is the new urbanism embodiment of Walt Disney's utopian vision of an ideal planned community.

Ladera Ranch, an Orange County, California, development, is designed to mix homes, neighborhood shops, and jobs to get away from the developing individualism (Richards 2005). Houses are set close to the street and to each other, and are equipped with front porches to encourage social interaction, while banishing garages to the back. The community also employs six salaried event planners who organize at least a dozen functions a year, from harvest festivals to holiday lighting celebrations to garage sales to movies in the park. Residents are also linked around the clock on their own intranet system, Ladera Life, where message boards, chat rooms, and activity schedules are always accessible. Such innovations attempt to make people the moving force in the life of a neighborhood. Ladera embraces its mission with such intensity that residents joke that they are living on a stationary cruise ship. There are some who think that the intensive communitarian social engineering that distinguishes Ladera or other communities like it may ultimately work against it. Nicolaides insists that too much planning can thwart natural community involvement, which has to grow organically over time to be real.

Another distinctive urban engineering project is Ave Maria, Florida. This intentional community, founded by pizza entrepreneur Tom Monaghan, is the expression of a community comprehensively embracing and enforcing the religious values of Roman Catholicism.

Another example of new urbanism is the creation of urban cultural parks, which was inspired by a Lowell park development (www. braypapers.com/new.html). There, planners found that the powerful architectural and urban artifacts of the industrial era could be used to transform a city where everything was perceived to be dull into a city where everything is interesting. New life was given to century-old mill buildings and canals through adaptive uses. Urban cultural parks represent a major leap from the nineteenth-century concept of the park as a retreat or escape from the city. In an urban cultural park, the entire urban landscape, with its amalgam of cultural and natural resources, becomes the "park," which serves as a unifying force, helping the city develop an integrated, resource-based planning effort that addresses the goals of preservation, education, recreation, and economic development.

ARCHITECTURE, ART, AND SOCIAL CONDITION

KATARXIS is a website (luciensteil.tripod.com/katarxis/) dedicated exclusively to a new traditional architecture and urbanism that incorporates a reevaluation of the many world cultures in cities and includes the heritages of the West and the East. Another artistic development is the creation of murals in cities, honoring cultural backgrounds, political beliefs, anger, love, despair, or hope.

J. S. Smith (2002) analyzes the Hispanic urban experience as a window through which an intense attachment to rural places of origin can be examined. Hispanics, like Greeks, Italians, Polish, or Irish immigrants, have a deep attachment to the village of their family's roots. This is quite visible in the way they structure their lives and cultures in the new urban setting. It is not unusual to witness people sipping their coffee under a grapevine, just as they did in their Greek village, in a small street in Allston, Massachusetts. Similarly, Hispanics show their attachment to the rural village ideal in beautiful murals painted on neighborhood walls or the desire to be buried in the town of origin. Rural-based, intensely local music and other kinds of public art frequently mark the territory of an urban ethnic enclave. The murals remind urban-dwelling Hispanics of their cultural roots, reinforcing cultural identity and giving them feelings of comfort, security, belonging, and continuity with a long-cherished historical tradition. These are physical and cultural features that are documented, but each also connotes a whole range of broader psychological and spiritual life, much as rural landscape always has.

COMMUNITY ORGANIZING

Community organizing has always been crucial in developing social movements, whether these are in response to lack of government funding and support (Stoecker & Vakil 2000) or in objection to immigration policy proposals.

Organizing has been particularly powerful among the youth in most countries. Throughout the 1960s, most countries globally witnessed youth movements. The student uprising in Athens, Greece, is a good example of change in the country's political power. On November 14, 1973, students at the National Technical University of Athens (also known as "Athens Polytechnic" or *Polytechnion*) went on strike and started protesting against the regime of the colonels. There was no response to their demands, so the students barricaded themselves in and built a radio station that broadcast across Athens. Soon thousands of workers, citizens, and youngsters joined them, which marked the beginning of the end of the regime.

Generally in the 1960s, youth desired to crack the many codes that maintained sexual, social, racial, and political oppressions. Student revolts were connected with movements of rebellion in a number of sexual, social, racial, and political spheres. The intellectual resources came from writers and theorists such as Mao in the Cultural Revolution, Marcuse on sexuality, one-dimensional man, art and socialism, and feminism. Alternative collective lifestyles were proposed, encompassing popular music forms, drug use, and living in environmentally friendly ways.

Today, two youth movements and cultures can be mentioned as examples. The first is hip-hop, evolving in the US in the late 1970s and 1980s, exerting an ever-stronger global influence. The code it cracked was that of complacency and passivity, which had socialized successive urban youth cultures into accepting unemployment and racial and ethnic oppression. The code it proposed in its place was a mixture of rap, music, dance, and graffiti. Oppressed ethnic/racial identities are celebrated by marginalized communities by challenging majoritarian aesthetic authority. This self-assertion includes redefinition of language, and radical challenges to liberal and conservative social norms. The intellectual roots are in an indigenous people's aesthetic rebellion against Eurocentric Caribbean colonial authorities. It began with Caribbean artists such as King Stitt and Kool Herc, and developed its alternative code through American pop artists such as Snoop Dogg and Ice-Cube.

The second example is that of the development of new communities through the Internet. These communities overcome the limits of space and time upon communication. Resources develop organically on the basis of its users' interests, practices, and intentions. Users do not necessarily intend a reproduction of the norms that dominate in face-to-face communication. There are, however, a number of parallels, as in the email practice where messages are designed to *flame* and *insult* their recipients. This is paralleled by the face-to-face version of the open, raised-voice argument where the intention is to provoke and bully the other party (Dobson 2002).

Cowan (2005) also presents popular music associated with urban culture, with entries on The Clash, Dancing in the Streets, and hip-hop among others. The promiscuous mingling in the book of higher and lower culture, of professional jargon and street slang, is rather like real life that documents social change in the making.

SEE ALSO: Counterculture; Gentrification; Migration: Internal; New Urbanism; Popular Culture Forms (Hip-Hop); Social Movements; Urban Renewal and Redevelopment; Urbanism, Subcultural Theory of; Urbanization

REFERENCES AND SUGGESTED READINGS

Atkinson, R. (1996) From Urbanization to Cities. *Capital and Class* 60: 149–51.

Bar-Yosef, R. W. (2001) Children of Two Cultures: Immigrant Children from Ethiopia in Israel. *Journal of Comparative Family Studies* 32(2): 231–46.

Cochrane, R. (2005) Women and Globalization in Ireland: Interview with Siobhan O'Donoghue of Dublin's MRCI. *Women and Environments International Magazine* 64/65, 32–3 (Fall).

Cowan, R. (2005) *The Dictionary of Urbanism*. Streetwise Press, New York.

Cowgill, G. L. (2004) Origins and Development of Urbanism: Archaeological Perspectives. *Annual Review of Anthropology* 33: 525–49.

Deitrick, S. & Ellis, C. (2004) New Urbanism in the Inner City. *Journal of the American Planning Association* 70(4): 426–42.

Dobson, S. (2002) *The Urban Pedagogy of Walter Benjamin: Lessons for the 21st Century*. Goldsmith Press, New Cross.

Garrett, S. & Beneria, L. (2005) Gender, Development, and Globalization. *Women and Environments International Magazine* 64/65, 43 (Fall/Winter).

Geronimus, A. T. (2000) To Mitigate, Resist, or Undo: Addressing Structural Influences on the Health of Urban Populations. *American Journal of Public Health* 90(6): 867–72.

Gordon, D. & Vipond, S. (2005) Gross Density and New Urbanism. *Journal of the American Planning Association* 71(1): 41–54.

Hartigan, J., Jr. (1997). Green Ghettos and the White Underclass. *Social Research* 64: 339–65.

Henderson, A. & Singh, S. (2005) The Global Significance of Local Resistance: A Feminist, Postmodern Look at Anti-Globalization Politics: Interview with Janet Conway. *Women and Environments International Magazine* 64/65, 26–8 (Fall/Winter).

Holizki, A. (2005) Vancouver's Grassroots Women Link the Local and the Global. *Women and Environments International Magazine* 64/65, 34–5 (Fall/Winter).

McLaughlin, J. P. (2005) City Urbanism and Its End. *Publius* 35(4): 641–3.

Moch, L. P. (2004) Cultures in Contact. *Journal of Social History* 38(1): 215–17.

Modtich, R. (2005) Greek Women Experience Corporate Globalization: Interview with Andriana Vlachou and Sissy Vovou. *Women and Environments International Magazine* 64/65, 12–15 (Fall/Winter).

Oneil, G. (2005) Just Work: The SCM Explores the Impact of Corporate Globalization in North America. *Women and Environments International Magazine* 64/65, 38–9 (Fall/Winter).

Richards, S. E. (2005) Backlash in the Burbs. *Psychology Today* 38(5): 64–8, 70, 72.

Sieber, R. E. (2003) Public Participation Geographic Information Systems Across Borders. *Canadian Geographer* 47(1): 50–61.

Smart, A. & Smart, J. (2003) Urbanization and the Global Perspective. *Annual Review of Anthropology* 32: 263–85.

Smith, J. S. (2002) Rural Place Attachment in Hispano Urban Centers. *Geographical Review* 92(3): 432–51.

Smith, N. (2002) The Urbanization of Neoliberalism: Theoretical Debates. New Globalism, New Urbanism: Gentrification as Global Urban Strategy. *Antipode* 34(3): 427.

Squires, G. D. (1999) The Indelible Color Line: The Persistence of Housing Discrimination. *American Prospect* 42: 67–70.

Stoecker, R. & Vakil, A. (2000) States, Cultures, and Community Organizing: Two Tales of Two Neighborhoods. *Journal of Urban Affairs* 22(4): 439–58.

Tucker, P. (2005) Urbanization Models Examined. *Futurist* 39(6): 11.

Uribe, V. M. (2005) Resistencia: Hip Hop in Colombia. *Journal of Latin American Anthropology* 10(1): 269–70.

Vickers, A. (2004) The Country and the Cities (FN1). *Journal of Contemporary Asia* 34(3): 304–17.

urbanization

Anthony M. Orum

Urbanization refers to the process whereby ever larger numbers of people migrate to and establish residence in relatively dense areas of population. It is a phenomenon that has existed throughout the ages, from ancient times to the present. Large numbers of people have gathered and created urban sites in places like ancient Rome and Cairo as well as in ancient Peking in China. Yet, in recent times, the process of urbanization has gained increasing momentum and with it greater attention as well. Today, more than half of the world's population live in what are considered urban places, and demographers project that by the year 2050 much of the world's population will reside in them.

If urbanization were simply about large numbers of people living in dense residential settlements, it would hold little interest for sociologists. In fact, it is about considerably more. One of the questions posed about urbanization has to do with the reasons why people move into urban areas. What, in particular, draws people into urban areas and, once there, why do they remain? Even more importantly, what happens to people and to their lives as human beings once they move into the compact spaces of urban areas? These are questions that have prompted some of the most interesting and perceptive of sociological writings.

For many sociologists, life in the metropolis constitutes the essence of what societies are all about. If one can understand, for example, the nature of communities as they form in cities,

some would argue, then one can develop a good grasp of those elements that help people to bond with one another, in general. Others would point out, too, that a study of the lives of people in these dense and compact settlements provides great insight into such central sociological issues as the nature of social inequality and the roots of social conflict.

Urbanization thus is something that holds great interest for sociologists and the theories they develop about the way the world works. The first of the major sociological theorists to write about urbanization and its connections to social life was the German social theorist, Georg Simmel. He saw in the nature of urbanization and the growth of the modern metropolis elements that were characteristic not merely of cities, but of the broader development and change unfolding in the modern world. Simmel insisted that the modern city compelled people to treat one another in an indifferent and cool manner. People did not relate to one another as intimates, for example, but rather in an instrumental and calculating fashion: what can you do for me, in effect, rather than let us get to know one another better. This sense of rational calculation and its effects on the lives of people in large urban areas were pervasive throughout city life, Simmel argued, as the result of the emergence of these major centers of population: it shaped the character of society in the metropolis and it demanded that people adapt to its dictates and constraints. Life was swift in the city, relations transitory, and people were compelled to adapt to it by taking a new mental attitude.

Simmel, in effect, set the tone for much of the sociological writing about cities and urbanization over the course of the next several decades. His ideas, coupled with somewhat parallel ideas in the writings of thinkers such as Ferdinand Tönnies, became the building blocks for how others would come to think of urbanization and the metropolis. The next major perspective on urbanization and urban areas, in fact, came from a scholar who helped to create the Chicago School of sociology, Louis Wirth. Wirth, in effect, synthesized many of the key insights of Simmel in a work that would become perhaps the most famous essay about the urban condition in the twentieth century, "Urbanism as a Way of Life." Wirth insisted that the pace of life in the city forced people to deal with one another in an impersonal fashion. People tended to become anonymous in the city; as a result, this influenced their own sense of comfort and security. The city, because of its size and the pace of its life, could become a place that helped to produce various forms of social disorganization, including divorce and crime. Urbanization also placed people into new relationships with one another, the effect being to undermine or to deemphasize the intimacy they had found in smaller places. Moreover, the city also gave birth to new and singular social developments, among them a range of new organizations, such as voluntary associations, not to say also new business groups. In effect, Wirth formalized and extended the basic insights of Simmel, creating both a sociological and a social psychological portrait of the city – a portrait that would remain in place for many decades and provide both an inspiration and a foil for subsequent sociological research.

Other writers and researchers from the Chicago School, among them Park and Burgess, helped to embellish and to flesh out this vision of what urbanization and cities were all about. The Chicago School, in effect, became that branch of sociology that would be devoted to understanding, interpreting, and even seeking remedies for the urban condition created in the modern world. The Chicago School sociologists turned to questions of immigration, for example, because of the great numbers of immigrants that began to enter cities like Chicago at the turn of the twentieth century. Park also turned to other issues, including race and race relations. Drawing on the work of plant ecologists, he developed notions about how immigrants and natives adapt to one another as they come into contact. The foremost theory of race relations during the twentieth century – the theory of assimilation – originated in the work of Park, from his own insights and views gleaned from his and his students' studies of urbanization and the city.

Eventually, the ideas and research of Park and Burgess and their students would become known as the school of human ecology. Taking their inspiration from plant ecologists, they used concepts of population, conflict, and change to talk broadly about what happens when urban areas are created, and as different social groups come into contact with one another. They believed that urbanization necessarily implied tension and conflict, and that such conflict came about because social groups, possessed of different national origins and often different cultures, competed for scarce resources (in particular, land and space) in the city. The city itself seemed to be animated by some basic underlying forces. They argued, for example, that land values at the center of the city were the highest across the metropolis because the land there was the most prized, especially by business. These initial insights were later turned into a sophisticated and complicated theory of people and space by Hawley (1950).

For a long while, these ideas about the city – its impersonality, its conflict between different population groups, and its underlying population dynamics – remained at the forefront of sociological research into cities and urbanization. Then, in the 1970s, these ideas were challenged sharply by a new school of social theory about urban areas and urbanization, that of the neo-Marxists. Central writers like Castells and Harvey argued that the conflict and change within cities – the various social changes that accompanied the process of urbanization – were the result not of some underlying features of urbanization per se, but rather of the growth and development of modern capitalism. It was capitalism – its inequalities and its tensions between the rich and the poor – that should be held to account for the underside of urbanization, they insisted. With such general assertions as these, then, Castells and Harvey, along with French social theorist Henri Lefebvre, introduced a fresh set of ideas into the thinking and writing about urban areas.

Today, it is the writings of this latter group of social thinkers, and others who share their basic orientation, that tend to dominate research and thinking about urbanization. Issues of poverty and inequality, in particular, seem to have emerged across the world as the world itself has become increasingly urbanized. New and compelling questions arise: How will the newcomers be treated within urban areas? Are conflict and poverty forever inevitable features of urban growth? And why is poverty persistent, especially among some groups of new immigrants to the city, but not among others?

In recent years scholars have begun to rethink the way they conceive both of cities and of the broader process of urbanization. Lefebvre urged students of urbanization to turn their attention to urban areas as spaces, and to investigate the way such spaces were created. In particular, he insisted that the broader social forces of modern capitalism have much to do with the configuration and arrangement of spaces in the city. Thus, for example, the nature of work and the way that people must travel to work helps to account not only for the development of transportation routes and modes of transportation, but also for the nature of social life and the sites of residential settlements in urban areas.

Other scholars have taken up such themes and pushed them in new directions. David Harvey, for example, is particularly intent on uncovering the ways in which inequalities emerge in the spaces of cities. His ambition, among other things, has been to show how cities are constantly made and destroyed, a process that is a result, he argues, of the broader processes of capitalism that are devoted, in essence, to the creation of profit. The spaces and sites of cities thus become the pawns for capitalist enterprises: new buildings arise and others disappear because of the constant search for profit and its rise and fall over time. Sharon Zukin has explored these themes even further, noting the ways in which certain spaces of the city have been remade once the older industrial enterprises created during the early part of the twentieth century declined. Zukin also borrows from the work of Joseph Schumpeter, noting how the "creative destruction" of urban areas – the dismantling of old houses, for example, and the creation of new mansions in their place – is emblematic of the growth of market forces in cities, but also of the decline of cities as special places for the lives of human beings.

We tend to think of urbanization and the sites it creates as "places." In recent years, more and more attention has been devoted to how people develop an attachment to the places of cities, and why such an attachment emerges as a key element in their lives. Anthropologists, historians, and philosophers have begun to create a new, broader perspective on the city that emphasizes it as a "place" – a specific site in social space where people regularly gather. The growth of this new view of urbanization and urban areas is somewhat ironic at this time, given that new global forces are playing such a large and impressive part in driving urbanization and in reshaping urban areas.

One of the prominent themes in recent research deals with the forces that promote the growth and development of cities. When scholars such as those of the Chicago School wrote about the growth of urban areas in the past, they most often were concerned about the specific local factors that brought migrants into the city. Naturally, the most important of such factors, both to sociologists and to other scholars, were economic ones: the history of American and European cities in the nineteenth century, for example, provided ample evidence of the ways in which booming industries and new jobs, not to mention the right kind of civic leadership, provided just the right incentives for people to move into cities.

Today, however, the local has become global. Individual cities, and the attraction they hold for new migrants, must compete not only with other cities in their own immediate regions and surroundings, but also with cities worldwide. Moreover, there is a new stratification system that has emerged among cities. Sassen (2001) has argued that some cities have become global forces, their economic structures and enterprises so powerful that their decisions can actually override those of national governments. When taken to its broadest conclusion, this sense of the significance of global forces suggests that broad economic movements can have an impact on urbanization across the world: people will tend to migrate from the poorer places to the richer ones, and those movements no longer are dictated simply by local forces, or even national governments, but rather are the work of major economic firms and the movement of capital across the world.

The original sociologists of urbanization and urban areas, Simmel and Park, for example, observed the migration of people into cities and the emergence of new forms of life and activity there. Among the things they found were forms of class stratification within the city: in central areas they were the places where the dominant financial enterprises were found; nearby were warehouses where the goods of manufacturing were located; within this area and adjacent to it were the new ethnic villages that emerged, along with the growth of a substantial working class; in the outer areas of cities would be found the wealthier residents – those people who could afford to commute into the city on a regular basis. This was essentially the pattern uncovered in America of space and the distribution of wealth. In other nations, such as France, spatial inequalities took somewhat different forms: the poorer immigrants would settle in the outskirts of cities, with the central parts of such cities still reserved for the wealthier residents. And in Latin American and African countries there was a similar pattern of class segregation that would emerge: in such instances, the relatively well-off people in the cities themselves were surrounded by thousands of poor people who lived their lives in shacks and poverty.

Today, a century after many modern cities were formed, social and economic inequalities remain intact. Poor people continue to live apart from rich ones, whether they reside in the inner cities or on their outskirts. Major sociological attention has been devoted to this phenomenon – of poverty and spatial inequalities – over the course of the past two decades, driven initially by the powerful writings of William Julius Wilson on the American underclass. Cities continue to be spatially segregated, and sociologists seek to understand the nature of such segregation better. Poverty has been understood not to be a transitory state for many people, but rather it persists, especially for African Americans. As cities become the destination of ever growing numbers of immigrants, the poor among them (e.g., Mexicans in the US, Turks in Germany, Africans in the Netherlands), the story of race and inequality seems to be repeating the same tales of hardship and dislocation that happened to black Americans. Two major arguments now compete to explain this recurrent phenomenon of race and poverty: (1) that the roots of poverty are primarily economic, born of an inability of people in urban areas either to find high-paying jobs or, given limited education, to qualify for them; (2) that the problem of race and poverty is even more pernicious, and that racism is a phenomenon that does not easily disappear, but rather influences the ways in which poor people are treated in many urban areas of the world.

The early sociologists of urbanization, it could be argued, seemed to think that the city itself created a space in which new forms of social life and a new kind environment would emerge, and that these elements would reshape the character of life. What the research and findings of recent work on urbanization, poverty, and despair now show us is that there are indeed broader and more intractable forces at work in shaping urban areas – and that unless human beings work collectively to eliminate such elements as racism or the class segregation of cities, the lives of the poor and the rich will continue to exist as worlds apart. Urbanization, we now realize, is not simply a broad impersonal fact of modern life, but it is something that people and social forces create – and thus it is something that can be changed as well.

SEE ALSO: Chicago School; City; Ecological Models of Urban Form: Concentric Zone Model, the Sector Model, and the Multiple Nuclei Model; Global/World Cities; Park, Robert E. and Burgess, Ernest W.; Robert E. Park, Ernest W. Burgess, and Urban Social Research; Simmel, Georg; Urban Revolution; Urbanism/Urban Culture

REFERENCES AND SUGGESTED READINGS

Castells, M. (1977) *The Urban Question*. Trans. A. Sheridan. MIT Press, Cambridge, MA.

Harvey, D. (1988) *Social Justice and the City*. Blackwell, Oxford.

Hawley, A. (1950) *Human Ecology: A Theory of Community Structure*. Ronald Press, New York.

Lefebvre, H. (1991) *The Production of Space*. Trans. D. Nicholson-Smith. Blackwell, Oxford.

Orum, A. M. & Chen, X. (2003) *The World of Cities: Places in Comparative and Historical Perspective*. Blackwell, Oxford.

Park, R. E., Burgess, E. W., & McKenzie, R. D. (1925–6) *The City*. University of Chicago Press, Chicago.

Sassen, S. (2001) *The Global City: New York, London, Tokyo*, 2nd edn. Princeton University Press, Princeton.

Simmel, G. (1903) Die Grossstadte und das Geisteleben. In: Petermann, T. (Ed.), *Die Grossstadte*. Dresden, pp. 187–206.

Zukin, S. (1991) *Landscapes of Power*. University of California Press, Berkeley.

use-value

Rob Beamish

Marx begins *Capital* with an analysis of the use-value of the commodity, suggesting, perhaps, that all useful concrete things have use-values – but that is incorrect and the distinction, fine as it might seem, between the utility of a thing and the use-value of a commodity is important. First, not every useful thing is a commodity, although every commodity, except one, is a useful thing. There are many things in the world around us – some may have no apparent use and others have known utility. As a thing – of utility or non-utility – it is a concrete object with qualitatively distinct, physical properties; it is part of the natural order; it may have uses but it does not have use-value. Use-value inheres only in a commodity and the difference between utility and use-value indicates the significant social dimension of a commodity.

The use-value of a commodity appears to be the same as the utility of a non-commodity thing. As use-value, a commodity is also a qualitatively distinct, concrete object that can satisfy human want directly in consumption or indirectly as material in further production. Like all useful things, commodity uses are discovered in history and many have standard measures appropriate to their use – yards of linen, kilograms of steel.

Use-value differentiates a commodity from things found in nature or procured or produced by private labor for personal use because the commodity is secured or produced to enter into a social relation of exchange. It enters exchange as a qualitatively distinct, concrete object – giving it physical utility or use – which simultaneously contains a quantity of socially necessary, abstract labor – giving it value (hence, use-value). A use-value's qualitatively concrete form determines its use and also constitutes the material embodiment of wealth that is congealed within it as a quantitatively comparable social substance – units of abstract, socially necessary labor time. A use-value's form is concrete; its substance is social and abstract. The use-values of commodities constitute a special branch of commercial knowledge that focuses on their concrete utility and their abstract value.

One use-value is unique – it is not a thing but the capacity to do work within a social relation of exchange. The capacity to do work in general has no use-value even though it has ontological significance and is important in one's private activities. However, as a qualitatively unique, concrete capacity, engaged in social labor – labor that will be congealed in a product that will enter the social relations of exchange – the capacity to labor has a concretely human form and a quantitatively comparable, abstract, social substance (the value required to restore the capacity to labor after a period of expenditure). Labor power is a unique use-value because it can, under given conditions of social production, produce more abstract value than necessary to replace it. This unique use-value is the source of surplus-value.

SEE ALSO: Commodities, Commodity Fetishism, and Commodification; Exchange-Value; Labor/Labor Power; Marx, Karl; Values

REFERENCES AND SUGGESTED READINGS

Krader, L. (1979) *Treatise on Social Labor*. Assen, Van Gorcum.
Marx, K. (1976) *Capital*, Vol. 1. Trans. B. Fowkes. Penguin, Harmondsworth.

utopia

David W. Lovell

Utopia is a type of imaginary ideal society. It generally takes a literary form, but it plays a role in social and political thought. From being playful, "utopian" has become a term of opprobrium, warning that a proposed scheme for improvement is not just impossible, it is perfidious. For there is a wide range of (different and often incompatible) notions of what is "ideal," and attempting to realize one person's dream may become another's nightmare.

As with many concepts that have a long history, "utopia" has no agreed definition. Invented by Sir Thomas More for his book

Utopia, published in 1516, More's neologism was a play on the Greek words for "good place" and "no place." Thus began a tradition of writing about ideal societies, though ideal societies themselves were not new.

The diversity among what are commonly called "utopias" is vast. They include: Plato's *Republic*, a hierarchical society exemplifying justice; More's *Utopia*, an island on which communal ownership, material security, and the obligation to work were key features; Tommaso Campanella's *City of the Sun* (1602), a city built in seven concentric circles, with citizens dedicated to knowledge; Francis Bacon's *New Atlantis* (1627), a society run by scientists; utopias by Enlightenment thinkers such as the Abbé de Mably, Morelly, and Denis Diderot; socialist utopias of the early nineteenth century sketched by Charles Fourier, Étienne Cabet, and others; and (at the time) very popular utopias, based loosely on Marxism, in Edward Bellamy's *Looking Backward* (1888) and William Morris's contrasting *News from Nowhere* (1891).

Most utopias take the form of literary representations of ideal societies. Indeed, Kumar (1991b: 25) argues that what makes "utopia" distinctive is that it is a novel. In literature utopia should be distinguished from futuristic genres such as science fiction, where the technology may be extraordinary but the social relations are conventional (or even medieval). Nevertheless, as literature, utopia is unsatisfying because it abolishes the friction and opposition needed for character and plot development.

Utopia, however, is not just a type of literature, for it normally includes some plans that have been associated with social and political projects. Nor should it simply be equated with the notion of an ideal society, though it often is (Manuel & Manuel 1979). "Ideal society" is too broad, encompassing other-worldly places such as "Heaven," or legends of a "Golden Age," or "Arcadia," or "Paradise." It also includes the "Land of Cockaigne" and similar dreams of extravagance and excess, and the Millennium, a vision of apocalyptic deliverance popular with some religions.

What sets "utopia" apart from other ideal societies is that in utopia human nature is not drastically altered: it is an imperfect society where social controls and discipline eliminate disharmony (Davis 1981). Utopias accept a basic problem of social life: the scarcity that arises from our wants constantly outstripping our attempts to satisfy them. Thus, utopian institutions are designed to deal with the results of potential social conflicts that arise from this problem. "The utopian idealizes not man nor nature but organization" (Davis 1984: 9). While utopia relies on a malleable, and even perfectible, humanity (Kumar 1991a: 29), it is not a final, perfect state – an important distinction (Passmore 1970).

"Utopia" has meant different things to different people, and different things at different times. This is not so surprising, since our imagination – on which utopias must draw, at least in part – is historically conditioned. At its simplest, we might thus say that earlier utopias are technologically simple, while more recent utopias are high-tech. Levitas (1990: 7) emphasizes this historical point in her argument that utopia is best considered as a "desire for a better way of living and being." Particular utopias tell us something about the conditions under which people live, because they show us what desires their historical circumstances generate but do not fulfill. Recent developments in utopian thinking, for example, have reflected changing social concerns: Callenbach's *Ecotopia* (1990) is an ecological utopia, while Piercy's *Woman on the Edge of Time* (1977) is a feminist utopia.

It is nevertheless difficult to link too closely the appearance and characteristics of particular utopias with their historical contexts, and utopias exhibit a number of recurring themes. From the time of Plato, many utopias have proposed common ownership, or stressed the evils of private property. Many rely upon benevolent despots or kings (in More's Utopia, the ruler Utopus laid down ideal laws 900 years previously). Some invoke rule by enlightened elites (the "guardians" in Plato's Republic; scientists and industrialists in Saint-Simon's New Industrial World), and have a class system based on social function. But the most important common feature of utopias is their stress on social harmony, order, and a strong sense of community. Many of them therefore have the characteristics (both good and bad) of what Ferdinand Tönnies called *Gemeinschaft*, an organic community with face-to-face social relations.

What, then, have utopias looked like? Most have an elaborate system of rules, along with punishments for disobedience (Campanella's strict punishments, including community executions, are extreme, but even More was generous in this department). Most, however, devote very little attention to the community's processes of rule-making in response to changing circumstances because of an implicit assumption that the social organization is static and thus that rules, once established, will not need to be changed. Politics as a dynamic process of peacefully reconciling different interests does not exist. Relations between utopia's inhabitants have not until recent times been envisaged as equal, but as conforming to a natural or functional hierarchy of roles, for the root of social disorder is never inequality as such, but rather the rejection of inequality. Some utopians have pushed their preference for order to the point of insisting on a particular architecture, as with Campanella's geometric patterns and Fourier's functional *phalanstères*. Children are sometimes reared in individual families, or more often by the community. How the citizens of utopia spend their daily lives depends largely on when the utopia was written, for many conventional matters (including gender relations and workplace issues) are unseen and unquestioned. This becomes particularly important in the wake of industrialization, when utopias can either be industrial or bucolic.

Even if utopias implicitly embody a critique of their host society by addressing unfulfilled desires, very few are written to generate movements for social change, or to inspire the creation of experimental settlements. More's *Utopia* was published in Latin, and was thus inaccessible to the vast majority of his countrymen. Linking utopias to revolutionary movements is actually a post-Enlightenment phenomenon (Rose 1987: 36). Furthermore, the socialist and religious traditions – Cabet, Victor Considérant, the Fourierists and Saint-Simonians, on the one hand, and the Quakers on the other – began to establish experimental communities to implement their visions. The stress on community as mutual dependence even extended, in the Saint-Simonian experimental community at Ménilmontant in the 1830s, to being compelled by virtue of the design of clothes to assist one another to dress. Many of these communities were created in the United States, perhaps because of its relative openness (Holloway 1966). One of the longest-lived was the Oneida Community (1848–81) in New York State, founded on religious doctrines developed by John Noyes. But Australia too – somewhat surprisingly, given its reputation as a "social laboratory" in the late nineteenth century – spawned a well-known utopian, William Lane. Lane established "New Australia" in Paraguay in 1893, a short-lived attempt at a socialist colony.

Experimental utopias have consistently dashed the expectations they raised. Begun with enthusiasm and sometimes in the face of great hardship, they display that mix of virtue and vice, communal spirit and individualism, and sacrifice and selfishness that is characteristic of societies in general. Physically isolating themselves from the corrupting influence of society also meant that such communities tended to turn inwards and ultimately devour themselves. However far people travel, they cannot escape their social relations. As for social cement, experimental utopias have been united (at least for a time) by allegiance to a charismatic leader, or by a sense of mission, whether social or religious. In literary utopias, there is a sense that fellow-feeling will be the mainspring of community, and that the inhabitants will recognize the justice of its arrangements, however they are described.

Is Marx's vision a utopia? Given his emphatic critique of the "utopian socialists" in the *Communist Manifesto*, and Engels's determined contrast between socialism, utopian and scientific, it is often (understandably) assumed that Marxism is not utopian. Marx was, first of all, an analyst and critic of capitalism. But the contrast that he and Engels sought to draw between themselves and their socialist competitors was chiefly a difference over means, not ends. The Saint-Simonians, Fourier, Cabet, and others of their ilk were indeed naïve about class struggle and industrial development, about the power of the state, about the chances for successful utopian settlements, and about the power of moral example for social change. Yet their goals were very similar to those of Marx: social harmony and material security.

Marx's critique of alienation and his expectation of its transcendence is central to understanding his utopia, even if the concept "alienation" was overshadowed in his later work by the language and methods of political economy. Like other utopias, the triumph over alienation means the end of politics: the rule over men, according to Marx, will be replaced by the administration of things. But Marx understood the limitations of literary representations of ideal societies, so he refused to write "recipes for cookshops of the future" and left his vision open-ended. Beilharz (1992) has argued that socialists, in response to Marx's diverse assumptions about the future (whether human fulfillment will be found in labor, or in leisure, in harmony with nature or in subduing nature), have constructed a range of competing visions with quite different political consequences.

It is not surprising that some have questioned the possibility of a utopian reign of harmony, community, and security. With the attempt to implement a communist utopia in Russia after 1917, which imposed murderous uniformity on the masses and privileged the new rulers, "utopia" became sullied by association. It was dogged by "dystopias," literary attempts to describe the malign effects on human beings (particularly individuals) of the imposition of the ideal rules of some utopias, drawing strongly on the contrast between rulers and ruled. This tradition began with Yevgeny Zamyatin's *We* (1920), and went on with Aldous Huxley's *Brave New World* (1932), but achieved its greatest influence with George Orwell's *Nineteen Eighty-Four* (1949).

One of utopia's functions is social criticism. But the line between utopia and other kinds of social theory is not clear-cut. It has been described as a "mobilizing myth" to change society by Karl Mannheim (1936), though Mannheim distinguishes it from "wishful thinking," by which he meant most of what are usually called utopias. Bauman (1976) champions socialism as an "active utopia" because it challenges people to bring about a better world. Geras (1999: 43) has promoted the virtues of a "maximum utopia," insofar as it encourages people to reflect on social life. Utopias mix critique, projections, hopes, and desires in a variety of ways, not all of them considered positive. Indeed, opinion is split over whether utopia

is valuable or dangerous. Oscar Wilde said that "a map of the world which does not include Utopia is not worth even glancing at, for it leaves out the one country at which Humanity is always landing," yet respected thinkers have condemned "utopia" as the source of totalitarianism in the modern world (Kateb 1963).

Utopias nowadays are not written with much confidence, yet they remain an important way of reflecting on society. We should not disparage utopian thinking as mere escapism, nor lightly dismiss utopias. They help us to think beyond the everyday, the mundane, and the routine, and encourage us to question what is possible in human affairs. For we are inclined to confuse the possible with the familiar. For all its value, however, there seems to be a limit to how much utopian thinking is able to contribute to illuminating the complexity of social existence. The fundamental issues – whether they concern how to reconcile the individual and the community, who is to rule, how to prevent bad rulers from doing harm, or how to distribute scarce goods justly – are caricatured by those who envisage simple formulae, fixed rules, or an ultimate value. As a novel, utopia can have thought-provoking effects; as a program for social renovation, it is insufficient.

SEE ALSO: Communism; Individualism; Marx, Karl; Politics; Property, Private; Social Order; Socialism

REFERENCES AND SUGGESTED READINGS

Bauman, Z. (1976) *Socialism: The Active Utopia.* George Allen & Unwin, London.
Beilharz, P. (1992) *Labour's Utopias: Bolshevism, Fabianism, Social Democracy.* Routledge, London and New York.
Callenbach, E. (1990) *Ecotopia: The Notebooks and Reports of William Weston.* Bantam, New York.
Davis, J. C. (1981) *Utopia and the Ideal Society: A Study of English Utopian Writing, 1516–1700.* Cambridge University Press, Cambridge.
Davis, J. C. (1984) The Chronology of Nowhere. In: Alexander, P. & Gill, R. (Eds.), *Utopias.* Duckworth, London.
Geras, N. (1999) Minimum Utopia: Ten Theses. In: *Socialist Register 2000: Necessary and Unnecessary Utopias.* Merlin Press, Suffolk.

Holloway, M. (1966) *Heavens on Earth: Utopian Communities in America, 1680–1880*, 2nd edn. Dover, New York.

Jouvenel, B. de (1966) Utopia for Practical Purposes. In: Manuel, F. E. (Ed.), *Utopias and Utopian Thought*. Houghton Mifflin, Boston.

Kateb, G. (1963) *Utopia and its Enemies*. Free Press, New York.

Kumar, K. (1991a) *Utopianism*. University of Minnesota Press, Minneapolis.

Kumar, K. (1991b) *Utopia and Anti-Utopia in Modern Times*. Blackwell, Oxford.

Levitas, R. (1990) *The Concept of Utopia*. Philip Allan, New York.

Mannheim, K. (1936) *Ideology and Utopia: An Introduction to the Sociology of Knowledge*. Routledge & Kegan Paul, London.

Manuel, F. E. & Manuel, F. P. (1979) *Utopian Thought in the Western World*. Blackwell, Oxford.

Passmore, J. (1970) *The Perfectibility of Man*. Duckworth, London.

Piercy, M. (1977) *Woman on the Edge of Time*. Fawcett Crest, New York.

Rose, R. B. (1987) Utopias and the Enlightenment. In: Kamenka, E. (Ed.), *Utopias*. Oxford University Press, Melbourne, pp. 35–47.

validity, qualitative

Patti Lather

Validity is not just one of many issues in science but the crux of the issue: the claims of science to a certain privilege in terms of author- itative knowledge. How scientific knowledge is made credible is, hence, a longstanding issue. If one looks at validity as a social construction, one sees how the very calculus of credibility of what is deemed "good science," the very deter- mination of warrants of validity, has shifted across time, place, and various fields.

In the contemporary moment, the crisis of legitimation occurring across knowledge sys- tems is registered in a cacophony of postpositi- vism, non-foundationalism, kinds of realism and post-realism, warranted assertability, logics of inquiry, construct validity, carefully con- trolled inference, objectivism, situational valid- ity, and Cronbachian insights regarding the decay of generalizations. As a result, discourse practices of validity in qualitative research exemplify a proliferation of available framings in terms of the legitimation of knowledge, par- ticularly the power and political dimensions of the issue of demarcation.

Various turns have characterized research in the human sciences over the last few decades, shifts that are not so much linear as multiple, simultaneous, and interruptive. It is as if the critiques of truth in Nietzsche, self-presence in Freud, referential language in Saussure, and metaphysics in Heidegger were finally coming home to roost in the social sciences. Across this dizzying array of in-movement shifts, these turns challenge the "view from nowhere" and the tra- ditional foundations of knowledge that continue to undergird so much of contemporary research. The following outlines twentieth-century turns

toward epistemological indeterminacy in order to underscore contemporary interest in situated- ness, perspective, relationality, narrative, poesis, and blurred genres. It then surveys across the field of social inquiry in terms of the variety of available discourses of validity in order to delineate the weakening of any "one best way approach" to validity.

EPISTEMIC INDETERMINACY AND THE WEAKENING OF HOMOGENEOUS STANDARDS

In exploring the work of science in an era of blurred genres, validity is a "limit question" of research, one that repeatedly resurfaces, one that can be neither avoided nor resolved. Within a context of epistemic anti-foundation- alism, validity is about much more than the limits of objectivity: "It bores into the essence of science itself" (Kerlinger 1986: 432). What follows argues in a Foucauldian manner that validity be situated as practices toward spaces of constructed visibility and incitements to see which constitute power/knowledge. This post-epistemic focus decenters validity as about epistemological guarantees and shifts it into practices that are situated, multiple, partial, endlessly deferred, a reflexive validity inter- ested in how discourse does its work.

From a post-epistemic focus, validity is a boundary line for what is acceptable and not acceptable in research. Validity is, in short, power, the power to determine the demarcation between science and not-science. Such a post- epistemic focus shifts the validity question in some interesting directions. Some argue for dis- missing validity altogether as too much about the continuation of positivist ideals. Others worry that qualitative work that fails to provide systematic depth analysis and analytic rigor threatens the fragile legitimacy that qualitative research has established and holds it to a scientistic accounting. This is made most obvious in recent moves by the federal government to warrant experimental design as the "gold standard" for good science.

In contrast, Pam Moss, writing out of psychometrics and assessment, argues that all social science research is under theoretic pressure in terms of foundational assumptions. Moss (1996) argues for a reflexive complementarity between varied approaches to the social sciences in order to think reflexivity about our taken-for-granted practices and perspectives. Moss sees a reciprocity of accountability in this purposeful engagement across paradigmatic assumptions and her expansion of validity echoes Mishler's (1990) argument that the "problem" of validity is about deep theoretical issues that technical solutions cannot begin to address. Ever since Cronbach and Meehl's (1955) essay on the problems with construct validity in psychological testing, validity has been the problem, not the solution. Various post-positivist efforts have been made to resolve the problem, from the naturalistic and constructivist paradigms of Lincoln and Guba that dominated the early discourse of qualitative research to discourse theory, ethnographic authority, critical, feminist, and race-based paradigms and more recent poststructuralisms. Some efforts toward validity in qualitative research remain deeply inscribed in a correspondence model of truth and assumptions of transparent narration, while others attempt validity practices that take into account the crisis of representation. And some call for new imaginaries altogether, where validity is as much about the play of difference as the repetition of sameness. Rather than exhausting the problem, all exemplify how the effort to answer the problem of validity is always partial, situated, temporary.

The following traces these provisional "solutions" as an effort to displace normative criteria of quality. Normative criteria posit themselves as universal and attempt to regulate "best way" procedures, whereas socially grounded criteria are situated, relational, temporal/historical. Unlike standardized regulatory criteria, such criteria move away from compelling conviction to some essence and toward contextually relevant practices that both disrupt referential logic and shift orientation from the object to the relations of its perception, to its situation of address and reception.

COUNTERPRACTICES OF AUTHORITY: FROM QUALITY CRITERIA TO SOCIAL PRACTICES

Just a decade ago, Lincoln and Guba's delineation of validity served as a sort of mantra across qualitative work in the social sciences. This evidences the importance of a validity discourse appropriate to qualitative research, but most interesting is how Guba and Lincoln's early delineation worked in unanticipated ways to undercut representational logic and spawn increasingly post-epistemic practices of validity. This section traces the movement of their thinking across a decade of validity formulations. To set the stage for this, the first layer in the story of validity in qualitative research is the standard story from the side of positivism.

Whereas the criteria for the credibility of quantitative research are based on the validity and reliability of instruments and internal validity, in qualitative research the primary criterion is the credibility of the study. Credibility is defined as the extent to which the data, data analysis, and conclusions are believable and trustworthy as based on a set of standard practices. Markers of credibility include triangulation, the use of different methods, samples of people and/or times and places. Reliability is the fit between what occurs and what is recorded, and is established by: detailed fieldnotes, a team approach, participant confirmation of accuracy of observations, mechanized recording of data (tape recorders, videotapes, photographs), use of participant quotations, and an active search for discrepant data. Internal validity refers to the match between researchers' categories and interpretations and what is actually true. It is claimed via prolonged engagement, thick description, thorough delineation of research process, and unobtrusive entry and participation in the setting. Finally, external validity shifts from generalizability based on sampling to reader assessment of transferability.

While this treatment of generalization evidences some attention to post-positivist assumptions, the preceding is grounded in the sort of scientificity that is at issue here. Guba and

Lincoln (1989), for example, argue that internal validity, as an assessment of the degree of isomorphism between a study's findings and the real world, cannot have meaning as a criterion in a paradigm that rejects a realist ontology. Additionally, external validity or generalizability has little meaning if realities are multiple and constructed. Erickson's (1986) idea of "particularizability" seems more useful: documenting particular cases with "thick" description, so that the reader can determine the degree of "transferability." Most interesting in this standard treatment of validity in qualitative research is the rather unremarked work of the concept of "transferability." Displacing a validity of correspondence with a focus on the terms of address, of reception, shifts orientation to the reader who determines the degree to which a study is "transferable" to his or her own context of interest.

The next layer in the story of validity is a standard treatment of validity from the side of post-positivism.

Michael Patton's *Qualitative Evaluation and Research Methods* (1990 [1980]) was one of the most widely used texts prior to the bestselling *Handbook of Qualitative Research* (Denzin & Lincoln 2000 [1994]). Patton elaborates on methodical reporting of systematic procedures of data collection and analysis. Particularly concerned about researcher effects, he cautions against the sort of self-importance that often leads to overrating this problem. The key is that reducing distortions is based on "empathic neutrality," a kind of impartiality that works to minimize researcher effect while recognizing that "the data inevitably represent perspective rather than absolute truth" (p. 475). In delineating legitimating practices, Patton surveys across the most frequently noted figures: Lincoln and Guba and Miles and Huberman on specific validity practices; LeCompte and Goetz and Kirk and Miller on reliability and validity; Michael Scriven on rethinking objectivity; Denzin on triangulation; Peshkin on subjectivity as a resource; and Cronbach on generalizability. The basic assumptions of this canonical discourse on validity in qualitative research can be traced by unpacking the work of, arguably, the central figures in the validity debates in qualitative research, Guba and Lincoln.

In the summary chart in *Naturalistic Inquiry* (1985), Lincoln and Guba summarize the techniques for establishing trustworthiness as (1) credibility (prolonged engagement and persistent observation; triangulation of sources, methods, and investigators; peer debriefing; negative case analysis; referential adequacy; and member checks); (2) transferability via thick description; (3) dependability and confirmability via an audit trail; and (4) the reflexive journal (p. 328). Each practice is more or less developed, with the member check positioned as the most crucial technique. This involves taking back to the participants what you have learned from them and can range from a minimalist "transcript check" to a more involved reaction to a preliminary analysis to a maximal feedback loop in regards to the final write-up. All are offered in the hopes of working against prescription and orthodoxy.

By 1989, Guba and Lincoln had moved to a delineation of three different approaches: parallel or quasi-foundational criteria, now called trustworthy criteria; the nature of the hermeneutic process itself; and a new set of nonfoundational criteria, termed the authenticity criteria. The parallel criteria map onto the 1985 formulation, but they are more clearly located in a post-realist ontology, for example, triangulation is deemphasized as "too positivist" in its assumptions of "unchanging phenomena" (p. 240). "The hermeneutic process as its own quality control" argues the difficulty of falsity because of the interactive, dialogic nature of the research process. The most noteworthy feature of the authenticity criteria is the break with more traditional methodological criteria into criteria that blur the line between ethics and validity. Termed *fairness* and *ontological, educative, catalytic,* and *tactical authenticity,* the criteria are about balancing viewpoints, encouraging the learning of both researcher and researched, sharing knowledge democratically, and fostering social action. The emphasis here is the move of validity from a set of epistemic concepts to a space of relational practices in situated contexts of inquiry.

By 1995, Lincoln shifted fully into an antifoundational discourse interested in research as relational and fostering of action and social justice. Quality criteria are posited as fluid and emergent, with a focus on criteria that collapse the distinction between rigor and ethics.

Tracing both the history and the rationale for the continued importance of rigor criteria, Lincoln notes her continued use of the parallel foundationalist criteria with her doctoral students as a place to begin. She then delineates emerging criteria that, while all relational, are differently aware of the exclusionary function of quality criteria and the inevitability of partial and incomplete standpoints. Regarding the latter, "detachment and author objectivity" become "barriers to quality, not insurance of having achieved it," as she urges researchers to "come clean" about their own stances (p. 280). Epistemology is situated as an ethical issue, and objectivism is displaced by linking research as a community project to social action. Key practices are delineated: the use of multiple voices, reflexivity regarding the relationships and contradictions of research processes, reciprocity, sacredness, and sharing royalties as a way to address the cultural and economic capital that academics make out of the lives of others. This includes movement toward action inquiry. The interest here is the move beyond the search for uniform criteria toward criteria that emerge as a natural consequence of the inquiry effort. This is a call for a profusion of situated validities, immanent validities, within the context of a particular inquiry.

Seeing validity as an apparatus of betterment, as a cure for what ails us, Lincoln's panegyric contrasts starkly with Scheurich (1996) who, rather than pay tribute, deconstructs "the masks of validity." Across both positivism and post-positivism, Scheurich organizes discourses of validity into three categories. The first, *originary validity*, translates conventional science concerns into post-positivism, for example Lincoln and Guba's parallel criteria. *Successor validity* recasts the concepts that arose in opposition to conventional notions of science, for example the concept of catalytic validity that grows out of advocacy research or "research as praxis" (Lather 1986a, b). Finally, *interrogated validity* deconstructs the policing function of validity, for example Cherryholmes's argument that construct validity is "of and about power" (1988: 450). Scheurich argues that to the extent discourse practices of validity are about policing the borders between "the accepted from the not true or the unaccepted or the not yet accepted" (1996: 5), they are "imperial" in allowing the same and disallowing the different. At the heart of the western knowledge project, Scheurich writes, is this "Same/Other power binary" (p. 6) that is more about "Eating the Other" (quoting bell hooks) than it is about increasing knowledge. "Validity practices are unconscious instantiations of a western philosophical ... dualism" (p. 8) that is not about individual conscious intentions but about the western "civilizational project, an imperial project" (p. 7). To undermine this dualism, he urges new imaginaries of validity that both unmask dualisms and celebrate polyphony and difference, the shifting complexities of truth as multiply perspectival.

As a possibility, Scheurich unpacks Lather's (1993) delineation of transgressive validities – ironic, paralogical, rhizomatic, and situated/embodied/voluptuous. All unsettle truth regimes, implode controlling codes, and work against the constraints of authority. All foreground the insufficiencies of language and the production of meaning effects, foster differences and heterogeneity, put conventional discursive procedures under erasure, and embody a situated, partial, positioned, explicit tentativeness. All anticipate a politics that desires both justice and the unknown, generate new locally determined norms of understanding, and proliferate open-ended and context-sensitive criteria that enact practices of engagement and self-reflexivity. All bring ethics and epistemology together. Intended to "incite" the proliferation of validity discourse practices, this effort leaves Scheurich unsatisfied, however, still worried about the capacity of "our restless civilizational immodesty" to reappear with new masks in its continuing absorption of the other into the same (1996: 10). Turning to the accelerating proliferation of marginalized voices, he calls for "a Bakhtinian dialogic carnival, a loud clamor of a polyphonic, open, tumultuous, subversive conversation on validity" (p. 10). Here validity has moved from a discourse about *quality* as normative to a discourse of *relational practices* that evokes an epistemic disruption, a transgression of set forms.

This exemplifies how validity is being used to further change the terms of the legitimation of knowledge beyond discrete methods and toward the social uses of the knowledge we construct. Across shifts in episteme and the consequent weakening of homogeneous standards and the proliferation of counterpractices of authority in qualitative research, the intelligibility and availability of alternative discourse practices of validity work to loosen positivism and suggest the critical potential of validity to put under theoretic pressure the claims of scientificity.

SEE ALSO: Culture; Legitimacy; Methods; Reliability; Representation; Science, Social Construction of; Scientific Knowledge, Sociology of; Theory; Theory and Methods; Trustworthiness

REFERENCES AND SUGGESTED READINGS

Cherryholmes, C. (1988) *Power and Criticism: Poststructural Investigations in Education*. Teachers College Press, New York.
Cronbach, L. & Meehl, P. (1955) Construct Validity in Psychological Tests. *Psychological Bulletin* 52: 281–302.
Denzin, N. & Lincoln, Y. (Eds.) (2000 [1994]) *Handbook of Qualitative Research*, 2nd edn. Sage, Thousand Oaks, CA.
Erickson, F. (1986) Qualitative Methods in Research on Teaching. In: Wittrock, M. C. (Ed.), *Handbook of Research on Teaching*. Macmillan, New York, pp. 119–61.
Guba, E. & Lincoln, Y. (1989) *Fourth-Generation Evaluation*. Sage, Newbury Park, CA.
Kerlinger, F. (1986) *Foundations of Behavioral Research*, 3rd edn. Holt, Rinehart, & Winston, New York.
Kvale, S. (1995) The Social Construction of Validity. *Qualitative Inquiry* 1(1): 19–40.
Lather, P. (1986a) Research as Praxis. *Harvard Educational Review* 56(3): 257–77.
Lather, P. (1986b) Issues of Validity in Openly Ideological Research: Between a Rock and a Soft Place. *Interchange* 17(4): 63–84.
Lather, P. (1993) Fertile Obsession: Validity After Poststructuralism. *Sociological Quarterly* 34(4): 673–93.
Lincoln, Y. (1995) Emerging Criteria for Quality in Qualitative and Interpretive Research. *Qualitative Inquiry* 1(3): 275–89.
Lincoln, Y. & Guba, E. (1985) *Naturalistic Inquiry*. Sage, Newbury Park, CA.
Mishler, E. (1990) Validation in Inquiry-Guided Research: The Role of Exemplars in Narrative Studies. *Harvard Educational Review* 60(4): 415–42.
Moss, P. (1996) Enlarging the Dialogue in Educational Measurement: Voices from Interpretive Research Traditions. *Educational Researcher* (January/February): 20–8, 43.
Patton, M. (1990 [1980]) *Qualitative Evaluation and Research Methods*. Sage, Newbury Park, CA.
Scheurich, J. (1996) The Masks of Validity: A Deconstructive Investigation. *Qualitative Studies in Education* 9(1): 49–60.

validity, quantitative

Karen Lahm

The term validity can be defined and explained in a plethora of ways. In quantitative research, validity is most commonly discussed when a researcher is developing measures of variables or concepts to put on a survey or use in an experiment, etc. Specifically, validity is synonymous with accuracy in that a valid measure is one that is actually or in reality measuring the concept or variable that it is supposed to be measuring. For example, say a researcher needed to develop a measure for the variable IQ (Intelligence Quotient). So the researcher decides that he is going to ask his sample to get on a scale and weigh themselves in pounds. Such a measure of IQ (body weight in pounds) would be an invalid measure of one's intelligence because in reality body weight tells us nothing about one's IQ. A more valid measure of one's intelligence would be to give an IQ test and compute IQs from the answers gathered on the test.

In order to ensure validity, researchers strive to meet several criteria when they create their measures of concepts and/or variables. First, they try to ensure that their measure has face validity. Face validity provides a check to see if "on its face" or literally it is a measure appropriate for a concept. The example above lacks face validity because in reality body weight does not tell us anything about how intelligent one is. A second criterion for assessing measures is content validity. This suggests that a measure must cover a range of meanings for a given concept or variable. For example, if a researcher wanted to measure someone's criminality, he would not just ask them about how many times they shoplifted. He would have to ask them about all types of criminal behavior (i.e., from shoplifting to violent crime) in order to cover the entire range of the variable. Third is criterion-related or predictive validity. Predictive validity assesses whether or not a measure can adequately predict the future behavior or outcome that it is supposed to. For example, many researchers believe that SAT/ACT scores are good measures of college success because they have a high degree of predictive validity. SAT/ACT tests are standardized college entrance exams taken by high school students in America. The purpose of these exams is to test whether or not a high school student has learned what they needed to be successful in college. Thus, the higher one's score on these exams the more likely it is one will be successful in college (at least, that is what the testing services say). Predictive validity can be established through regression analysis. One can use the value and sign of a correlation coefficient (Pearson's r) as an indicator of predictive validity of the independent variable upon the dependent variable.

The fourth criterion for creating valid measures is construct validity. Construct validity ensures that one's measure "fits" within the theoretical system examined in the research. For example, in the field of criminology, social disorganization theory suggests that neighborhoods or cities with high levels of disorganization (i.e., poverty, ethnic heterogeneity, high population turnover) have less social control and thus more crime. Let us say a researcher came up with some measures of these concepts and went out and gathered some data on them. This researcher, through his data analysis, found that in his sample of cities higher levels of social disorganization led to more social control and less crime. These findings are opposite to what research in this area typically indicates, so he should go back and check the validity of his measures of variables because his finding does not jibe with what the theory suggests. It is important to note that some measures meet all of these criteria for validity, while some measures do not. Also, one measure is not universally valid in all times and places.

Once valid measures are created it is also important for a researcher to ensure both internal and external validity. Both internal and external validity most often come into question within the field of experimental research; however, their importance encompasses all scientific endeavors. In most scientific research the goal is to establish causal connections between concepts or variables. One step in establishing cause is to ensure internal validity. Internal validity refers to the degree to which the researcher eliminates or controls for confounding variables in the study. For example, let us say a researcher wanted to establish that attending a study session will increase test score. In this example, there are many confounding variables that could be influencing test scores besides attendance at a review session. For instance, maybe the students studied more outside of the review session, maybe they got lots of sleep the night before the exam, maybe they ate healthier in the weeks leading up to the exam and were more alert.

To ensure more internal validity, the researcher could do several things, like add a control group or a group of students who did not have the exam and see how their scores compared to the experimental group who received the study session. The researcher could also have given a pre-test to examine scores both before and after the study session. The researcher would also want to make sure students were randomly assigned to both the experimental and control groups, so that it was not only the smart students that attended the review session. Moreover, the researcher would also want to make sure that the control group and experimental group do not have contact with one another. He would want to make sure no one drops out of the study. He would also want to make sure the pre-test and post-test are the same instruments and that there are no other review sessions or outside study groups being offered to either set of participants.

Also important is external validity. It refers to the degree to which the results of an experiment can be generalized to the rest of the population. Think of this as the universality of your findings. Can your findings apply to other people at other places at other times? Some ways to ensure external validity is to randomly select experimental and control groups from the general population. Also, one should replicate their study in a variety of settings, times, etc. These techniques may help to ensure the generalizability of one's findings to the larger population.

SEE ALSO: Reliability; Reliability Generalization

REFERENCES AND SUGGESTED READINGS

Babbie, E. (2003) *The Practice of Social Research*, 10th edn. Wadsworth, Belmont, CA.

Carmines, E. & Zeller, R. (1979) *Reliability and Validity Assessment*. Sage, Thousand Oaks, CA.

Creswell, J. (2002) *Research Design: Qualitative, Quantitative, and Mixed Methods Approaches*, 2nd edn. Sage, Thousand Oaks, CA.

Schutt, R. (2003) *Investigating the Social World: The Process and Practice of Research*, 4th edn. Pine Forge Press, Thousand Oaks, CA.

value

Rob Beamish

Value and theories of value might begin in economics but they have significant sociological importance. As with economics, two divergent conceptions of value dominate sociological thought: an objective, intrinsic, production-centered theory versus a subjective, consumption-focused conception of value – best represented in Marx and Simmel's works, respectively. Marx's systematic presentation of value's form and substance in *Capital* critically extended Adam Smith, David Ricardo, and other political economists' labor theory of value, while Simmel developed the sociological importance of subjective conceptions of value that began with political economist Jacques Turgot and William Jevons and the Austrian School developed with theories of marginal utility, value, and price.

Theories of value extend back at least to Aristotle and the social production of value and its social significance reach back to points in history when humankind lived in primitive-communal groupings and the unit of production and consumption coincided. Group members worked collectively to meet their material needs and wants. Labor was communal and the communal product was shared. Products of labor were considered only for their concrete utility, with no conception of value (abstract or concrete; subjective or objective).

Production above the material wants of the group and periodic interchange created the conditions for intermittent and then ongoing exchange between groups or communities and later within them. Surplus production allowed the social relations of primitive commodity exchange to emerge and a social division of labor between and within groups developed. As production was directed to both communal wants and social exchange, production changed from concrete, primitive-communal to communal-social and a separation of abstract and concrete labor within the commodity arose.

The form of communal life remained a kin, tribal, or communal group or village, but the substance of the social relations among members within production became increasingly mediated as exchange was introduced and expanded. Exchange created a social relation between the qualitatively unique concrete labors of commodities requiring their comparison as abstract, quantitatively comparable labors. Exchange also introduced mediate social relations between production and consumption. Exchange created the value form and labor created its substance. The form and substance of value permitted class division to develop and the accumulation of abstract wealth – value.

In his critique of classical political economy, Marx used Hegel's dialectic of quantity and quality, general and specific, form and content, and form and substance to analytically-synthetically, rather than historically, present an objectively based labor theory of value that would expose the underlying dynamic of exploitation within capitalist production and serve as the departure point for a synthetically based comprehension of capitalism's totality. Marx argued that beneath a commodity's qualitative, concrete appearance there are abstract, quantitatively comparable units of socially useful, socially necessary, simple, abstract labor. This objective substance of value pertains to all commodities, including the "capacity for work" or the labor power workers sell to capital in the labor market. In return for the full and fair exchange of the value of their labor power, workers contract themselves to work a specific period of time at certain levels of productivity, under particular conditions. Due to labor power's unique nature, in the course of a workday it can produce commodities with a total value that is greater than the value substance of labor power itself – creating a surplus of value (or surplus-value). The key contradiction in capitalist production is that workers, receiving full value for their ability to do work, can still generate a surplus which maintains and builds the social relations of production that confront them, appropriate the social surplus, and exploit them. As Hegel began the *Phenomenology* with the single, simple category of sense certainty, and its immediate contradictions, to build an increasingly complex conception of human reason's totality, Marx established the objective substance of value as his departure point for an increasingly synthetic analysis of the contradictions of capitalist production, circulation, and then the system as a whole.

While value was not as central to Simmel's sociology as it was to Marx's critique of political economy, Simmel's discussions of value stem directly from his sociological perspective, illustrate his approach to understanding social phenomena, and represent a key "culturist" critique of historical materialism. Simmel's conception of value stemmed from his interest in money as one of many potential, heuristic concepts that sociologists could use to formulate understandings of social relationships. Simmel explored the ways in which money – one of the more important and highly complex cultural forms of social interaction – was a form in and through which particular types of social interaction occurred and how that interaction held broader social and historical implications.

Individual subjects, Simmel argued, assess and attach value or values to objects to overcome the physical distance and separation between them and the objects of their interest. In exchange processes, people assess their own relationship to an object as well as others' expectations to arrive at a particular, subjectively established value of the object – expressed or made concrete in the money form. Value, through the money form, is objectified; value becomes a "cultural objectivation." Unlike Marx, any labor substance to value is inconsequential. Value is a cultural product; it is produced through subjective understanding and assessment and, most significantly, stems from and further develops a particular worldview.

The calculation of value creates and reinforces a cultural form that seeks uniformity within diversity, rationality from within affective attachment, and individuation through interaction. Value, and its expression in money, establishes an economic rationality that progressively expands into a broader, more encompassing instrumental rationality. Like Weber, Simmel saw, through value and money, the increasing domination of a rational, instrumental approach to social relationships.

Despite their differences over value, Marx and Simmel's analyses led to similar concern with alienation in commodity-based societies. Similarly, value served as a key departure point for more complex, comprehensive social analyses.

SEE ALSO: Exchange-Value; Labor/Labor Power; Money; Use-Value

REFERENCES AND SUGGESTED READINGS

Dobb, M. (1973) *Theories of Value and Distribution Since Adam Smith*. Cambridge University Press, Cambridge, MA.
Krader, L. (2003) *Labor and Value*. Peter Lang, New York.
Marx, K. (1976) *Capital*, Vol. 1. Trans. B. Fowkes. Penguin, London.
Simmel, G. (1978) *The Philosophy of Money*. Trans. T. Bottomore & D. Frisby. Routledge & Kegan Paul, London.

values

Giuseppe Giordan

Values represent beliefs and ideals which form the basis for choices and preferences, both at an individual and collective level. Generally speaking, a value is defined as that which is "good" and which is desired and is able to make one happy. Such long-lasting and immaterial ideas regard both current conduct and one's ultimate objective in life: they are different from simple interests, which are not particularly characterized by duration, and also from moral laws, which indicate what is the "right thing to do." Values propose a certain lifestyle and "how to be" rather than purely concrete rules of behavior.

The utilization of the concept in sociology has been the object of lively debate owing to the difficulty of clearly defining what is meant by values. Sociologists often stress how difficult it is to provide a definition that is usable in empirical research and they underline the relativity and subjectivity of the definition itself. However, all researchers highlight the connection between values, social structure, and actual behaviour of social subjects. Hechter et al. (1993) identify some difficulties in the study of values: (1) they are not visible; (2) there are no theories capable of satisfactorily explaining the connection between values and behaviors both at individual and collective levels (and besides we lack theories explaining how values are formed); (3) they are not easily measurable.

Values are not to be confused with attitudes, norms, and needs or with the peculiarities of personal traits (Hitlin Piliavin 2004). Values are centered on ideals; hence, they have an abstract role in building self-identity, while attitudes directly refer to the actual behavior of individuals. Compared to norms, then, values are perceived by individuals not as imposed from outside, but rather as outcomes of free personal choice. In addition, while needs refer to the biological sphere, values highlight the various cultural responses that can be given to such needs. The need for food or sex meets different responses according to the values of the different cultures where such needs are felt. Values also differ from traits because traits refer to the actual fixed aspects of personality, while values are abstract judgment criteria constantly inclined towards self-transcendentalism.

Empirical research on values emphasizes how their origin can be traced to a heterogeneous multiplicity of factors such as biology (genus, race, ethnicity) and the various characteristics of the social structure to which the individual belongs (e.g., literacy level, occupation, professed religion, social class, family). The concept of values is found in various cognitive spheres and there is a multiplicity of definitions which vary according to the point of reference, be it economics, philosophy, psychology, or sociology, all of which offer significant contributions to a more complete understanding of the concept.

ECONOMICS AND PHILOSOPHY

In the field of economics a value may be defined as that which defines two interconnected but different prospects: on the one hand, the characteristic of a good is that it may be exchanged for other goods ("exchange-value"); on the other hand, all the characteristics which enable any given good to satisfy the multiple needs of humankind are defined as "use-value." The definition of the concept of value from an economic perspective is extremely important, as it has significant consequences in the sociocultural and psychological spheres: values also are conditioned by subjective, not objective evaluation and are identifiable and comprehensible in relation to a specific historical period and particular circumstances and therefore do not have an absolute or eternal character.

This dialectical relationship between the absoluteness of values and the relativism of historical perspective constitutes the heart of the philosophical debate that directly connects concepts of value to that which is good: this provides the reference for the objectives of life and the moral dimension of life. In classical philosophy (particularly Stoicism) the concept of values is explained in a subjective sense and defines the object of ethically good choices. Nietzsche, however, dramatically changed such philosophical reflection in both social and cultural terms at the end of the nineteenth century. His explicit proposal was to radically overthrow the order of traditional values which were based on metaphysics, logic, morals, and religion: all these values were identified principally by the Christian tradition, based on renouncement and asceticism. Nietzsche opposed to them the "vital values" centered on the free expression of the will of man.

From a phenomenological perspective, Max Scheler underlined the "objective" character of values and highlighted absoluteness and eternity: these may be grasped not only via the intellect but also intuitively via the emotional experience of the conscience. Scheler suggested a hierarchy of values, among which are values of the senses (pleasure is contrasted with displeasure), vital values, spiritual values (legal, aesthetic, cognitive) and finally the supreme value of holiness. For Scheler, the ultimate foundation of values is the discovery of the unitary principle of love. Nicolai Hartmann also underlined the original emotional characteristic of values and interpreted this concept in a rigorously realistic manner: the perception of values may vary and may be completely absent, but values exist independently of subjective conscience.

It is easy to see how the foregoing influences the perception and the role that values play in the construction of identity: this process develops as a result of the need for certainty provided by secure and reliable points of reference and also as a result of the relativity of different situations and different historical periods.

VALUES AND IDENTITY

Values are found at the crossroads between different fields of cognizance, particularly evident when one takes into consideration their roles in the construction of identity, both at a personal and at a collective level. The theme of values is significant for in-depth study of the complex relationship between the individual and the society and culture to which they belong, thus highlighting a nexus of interrelationships (the contribution of psychology, anthropology, and sociology are of particular importance). In addition to needs and attitudes, values constitute fundamental psychic contents: while needs "push" us into action, values "attract" our project-making capacity. Thus, we are not made only to satisfy physical needs, but also to face risks and uncertainty in the search for and attainment of new goals and ideals.

Values have a specific function at the heart of one's mentality: they provide identity and they are traction elements of the entire mental apparatus. In other words not only do values unify the diverse components of "I," but they also push the individual to greater realization in the search for a positive identity. One's aim of surpassing the limits of the simple and everyday gives meaning to life. This search for the meaning of life provides one with free choice in spite of continual clashes with the conditions of one's own situation. Although the search is highly personal, the values of the individual are part of their social and cultural context. From a sociocultural point of view, values constitute a specific element of every culture: they are closely linked to the symbols, laws, and rituals which regulate the various dimensions of collective life. Thus, it is clear that values have the function of uniting individual and social praxis; it is this unity which coherently guarantees the link between the individual and society. From a sociological point of view, it is the complex mechanism of the transfer of values from one generation to another which constitutes the socialization process, within which the interaction between society and the individual and thus various aspects of culture become important for the individual.

Seen from the perspective of the social sciences, values do not concern the dimension of absoluteness and transcendence of the philosophical context, but are linked to precise historical, geographical, and social contexts related to various economic, political, and religious structures. The anthropologist Clyde Kluckhohn (1951) defined three fundamental dimensions of values. The entire emotional dimension underlines the profound link between values and the emotions of the subject. The intensity of this link depends on the degree of interiorization of the system of values within any given society. The cognitive dimension is where values implicate the consciousness and the capacity of rational justification on the part of the individual. Kluckhohn then underlines the selective function played by values: these are the criteria by which the subject judges, selects, and orders different behavior and the various ways of thinking which make up their social context: thus, values are fundamental in orienting social behavior.

VALUES AND SOCIAL CHANGE

The sociocultural approach to the topic of values relates to the phenomenon of social change. Knowing all the values which guarantee cohesion and guide the development of a social system is decisive for the comprehension of factors which have moved traditional society to modern and postmodern society. It suffices to reflect on the value of progress, which is comprehended as a permanent innovation that ought to guarantee the development of humanity to ever-improving conditions, and has been the tool used to back the change from traditional to modern society. In addition to progress, modernity is characterized by the affirmation of the individual's freedom of choice, which democracy must guarantee.

The contemporary situation can be characterized by what Inglehart (1977) defined as the "silent revolution": he referred to American and western society in general and underlined the fact that since 1945 society has been moving away from general values. Although the process is slow and gradual, there has been a move away from "materialistic values" to "post-materialistic values" in the last few decades. In the past importance was given to physical and economic security; now, however, growing importance is given to the sense of belonging, self-realization, and intellectual and aesthetic satisfaction. Although post-materialists do not deny the importance of material issues in life, they emphasize quality of life, safeguarding the environment, and freedom of expression. Subjective quality of life and subjective well-being are no longer expressed purely in economic terms.

Bellah et al. (1985) connect the search for happiness with the obtainment of increasingly elevated levels of freedom. Individualism seems to be the characteristic trait of American and western society in general: the need to establish personal freedom and the search for success in economic terms as spurred on by the spirit of personal initiative and creativity, however, tend to isolate members of a community and thus often create discrimination.

"CRISIS OF VALUES" AND THE CHALLENGE OF CULTURAL PLURALISM

The rapid and profound changes which have touched society and culture in recent years have resulted in widespread discomfort, both for individuals and for collective life. Technological innovation encroaches upon the origins of life; interpersonal relations are based increasingly on emotions and temporariness; widespread emigration results in the cohabitation of different customs and traditions in the same territory – all often create difficulties between peers and between different generations. An increasingly accentuated diversity in lifestyles results in the questioning of consolidated traditions, which were, until recently, accepted as unquestionable and eternal.

This has been defined as the crisis of values, an expression which is not easy to define precisely unless one refers to the disorientation caused by the speed of change and the construction of identity and daily life in modern to postmodern society. The crisis of values principally signifies the need to underline the profound change in the process of legitimization of values. This legitimization is no longer to be found in the certainty of institutions and within the law, but is instead based upon individual freedom of choice and a desire for self-realization. No longer is there obedience to a unique authority of tradition, but rather there is social recognition of the multiplicity of values. In addition, the crisis of values refers to a new "range of values" which may be adopted both by various societies and by individuals: these options are not always easy to match and reconcile with a common point of reference. Thus, the crisis of values is not a disappearance of values, but is rather the result of their excessive, incoherent, and often-contradictory proliferation.

A result of social complexity is the creation of diverse possibilities in the composition of values and social change. These positions may be schematically recapitulated in fundamentalist and relativist models, as well as by the possibilities offered by cultural pluralism. The fundamentalist model (often, but not always, inspired by religious legitimization) aims to safeguard eternity and the immutability of values, negating the possibility of interaction with the concrete social and cultural context of the values themselves. The relativist conception stresses the radical freedom of the individual in the construction of personal values, as far as (in its extreme form) the affirmation of the impossibility of humankind's recognition of the foundation of good and evil.

The outlook of cultural pluralism aims at safeguarding the diversity of different cultural concepts through the legitimization of their very diversity. Surpassing an ethnocentric vision (which encompasses the belief that one's own cultural values are superior to those of other cultures) opens up one's system of values to comparison and relations with other cultural systems and values. Cultural diversity is now the biggest challenge for the construction of social systems which are able to guarantee the free expression of the values of individuals and the community to which they belong.

SEE ALSO: Culture; Fundamentalism; Identity: Social Psychological Aspects; Identity Theory; Plural Society; Religion; Social Change; Values: Global

REFERENCES AND SUGGESTED READINGS

Bellah, R., Madsen, R., Sullivan, W. M., & Swidler, A. (1985) *Habits of the Heart: Individualism and Commitment in American Life*. University of California Press, Berkeley.
Bem, D. (1970) *Beliefs, Attitudes, and Human Affairs*. Brooks-Cole, Monterey, CA.
Hechter, M., Nadel, L., & Michod, R. E. (Eds.) (1993) *The Origin of Values*. De Gruyter, New York.
Hitlin, S. & Piliavin, J. A. (2004) Values: Reviving a Dormant Concept. *Annual Review of Sociology* 30: 359–93.
Inglehart, R. (1977) *The Silent Revolution: Changing Values and Political Styles Among Western Publics*. Princeton University Press, Princeton.
Inglehart, R. (1997) *Modernization and Postmodernization: Cultural, Economic, and Political Change in 43 Societies*. Princeton University Press, Princeton.
Joas, H. (2000) *The Genesis of Values*. Polity Press, Cambridge.
Kluckhohn, C. (1951) Values and Value-Orientations in the Theory of Action: An Exploration in Definition and Classification. In: Parsons, T. & Shils, E. (Eds.), *Toward a General Theory of Action*. Harvard University Press, Cambridge, MA, pp. 388–433.
Sciolla, L. (1998) Valori. In: *Enciclopedia delle Scienze Sociali*, Vol. 8. Istituto della Enciclopedia Italiana, Rome, pp. 750–9.
Weber, M. (1958) *The Protestant Ethic and the Spirit of Capitalism*. Charles Scribner's Sons, New York.
Weber, M. (1963) *The Sociology of Religion*. Beacon Press, Boston.

values: global

Dusko Sekulic

Social values are relatively abstract and generalized standards or principles of what the individuals in a society consider good and desirable. Equality, justice, and freedom are examples of such values. They are the basis for creating evaluative criteria for judging concrete social behavior as good or bad, desirable or despicable, acceptable or unacceptable. Values are the source of concrete prescription for behavior in practical situations of everyday life. Where the general value is equality, the norms of teacher impartiality or the presumption of innocence in courts are concrete norms derived from the abstract value.

There are two important points to be made regarding values and their role in understanding social life. First, society is partially constituted through values and the study of sociology is the study of values. Society can usually tolerate highly diverse attitudes, but it requires some degree of homogeneity and consistency in the values held by people. This provides a commonality of shared values, which shape social and political consensus. To what extent shared values are a necessary precondition for society to survive is a hotly debated issue in sociology. In Parsonian sociology, social order depends on the existence of such general and shared values. They are regarded as legitimate and binding, and act as standards by which particular actions are selected. The linkage of social and personality systems is achieved by the internalization of values through socialization processes. The critique states that functionalism overemphasizes the importance of shared values in maintaining social order. Conflict theorists would argue that socialization, and the maintenance of common values, hides the underlying interests of those in power to preserve the existing order. The emphasis on the value of homogeneity underestimates the human capability to handle contradictions or simply to compartmentalize them.

Second, as much as society is partially constituted through values, it is also observed that the contents of values vary tremendously. All ethical and religious systems claim universal validity of the values they profess. The empirical reality is that none of these values is universally accepted, and values prevailing in different societies do not reflect some universal value system characterizing humanity.

The practical reaction to this empirical fact can vary between ethnocentrism, the practice of judging another culture and its values by the standards of one's own culture and values, to cultural relativism, the practice of evaluating value systems by their own standards. Both positions have tremendous ethical and moral consequences. What are the standards that allow the ethnocentrist to claim superiority of his/her values? For cultural relativists, the moral dilemma stems from the fact that if almost any kind of behavior is normative and accepted somewhere in the world, does that mean everything is equally right? Sociology, not being a normative science, does not provide answers to these normative questions. But there are several approaches within sociology that are preoccupied with the question of global or universal values.

We divide these approaches into three broad groups. The first tries to detect some common values derived from human nature in general. The widely used approach of this type is that of sociobiology. The second approach is based on comparative social psychology, which claims that some universal value structures can be discovered. Here we must emphasize that universal structure does not mean universal value *content*, but the universal *structure* of value systems. The third approach tries to detect shifts toward acceptance of some global values as a result of social change and globalization processes.

Sociobiology starts from the assumptions that values are at least partly rooted in our biological nature. If that is the case, our common "biological" human nature gives basis to some common universal tendencies. If altruistic behavior can be derived from inclusive fitness, then the positive values connected to such behavior, including universal positive evaluation and the great significance that is attached to kinship bonds, can be derived from our biological nature (van den Berghe 1979). The maintenance of values in populations could therefore be explained by a combination of biological and cultural mechanisms (Cavalli-Sforza & Feldman 1981).

The second approach claims that there is a universal structure of human values, and that comparative research can discover such universal structures. Although the emphasis and frequency of particular values differ among societies, the underlying structure is the same and can be applied in every society. One such approach can be found in the work of Schwartz (1992, 1994). He developed empirically a schematic representation of what he finds to be an almost universal structure of human values. It is comprised of two higher-order dimensions of values, and motivational types of values derived from the higher-order values. The two higher-order dimensions are openness to change versus conservation, and self-enhancement versus self-transcendence.

The first dimension indicates the degree to which individuals are motivated to engage in independent action and are willing to challenge themselves for both intellectual and emotional realization. The second dimension reflects the distinction between values oriented toward the pursuit of self-interest and values related to a concern for the welfare of others. Within these two general dimensions, ten motivational value types could be distinguished. These ten values are hedonism, power, achievement, stimulation, self-direction, universalism, benevolence, conformity, tradition, and security. Schwartz also adds spirituality, which can be differentiated in some, but not all, of his comparative samples. Adjacent values share motivational emphases. Achievement and hedonism both focus on self-centered satisfaction, and power and achievement focus on social superiority and esteem.

Schwartz has found that the system of values is essentially the same worldwide. Initially his samples were limited to Western Europe, but recently his modified method replicated the structure in the Far East and South America (Schwartz 2004). Schwartz goes a step further and reports that there is a "surprisingly widespread consensus regarding the hierarchical order of values" across probed societies. Benevolence is most often ranked first, followed by self-direction, universalism, security, conformity, achievement, hedonism, stimulation, tradition, and power. Values on the top and bottom of the scale are ranked most consistently, with the middle of the scale much less so.

Hofstede (2001) made a comparative study of values based on analysis of 117,000 IBM employees worldwide. He grouped societies together based on five value dimensions obtained using factor analysis. The dimensions are power distance (acceptance of inequality), uncertainty avoidance, individualism/collectivism, masculinity/femininity, and long versus short time orientations. The individualism/collectivism dichotomy is a widely researched topic within the comparative perspective. In this tradition, the individualistic cultures of the West are contrasted with the collectivistic cultures of the East and Latin America (Triandis 1995; Kagitcibasi 1997).

The third approach starts from analyzing the impact of broadly defined modernization processes, especially those of globalization, on value changes. It is a universally accepted truism that changes in social conditions of life produce changes in values, as values influence acceptance of certain material practices. Diffusion as a more benign form of variable producing change, and subjugation of one society by another as a more malignant form, all produce changes in values.

In the social sciences, a new concept, globalization, is used to describe supposedly historically unique phenomena of ever-increasing flows of goods, information, and people. Will a homogeneous global culture and a universal value system be the consequence of such a trend? Is it true that the areas of the world, and the social groups more enmeshed in globalizing processes, are developing more universalistic values? The most comprehensive theory originating from this framework is Inglehart's theory of value change. His analysis is based on the World Value Surveys that have been collected in regular five-year waves starting in 1981, and on the Euro-Barometer surveys that started in the 1970s. The main conclusion from his research is that a phenomenon, which he calls the "postmodern shift," is occurring.

This shift should be put into the framework of broad historical and economic changes that influence value changes. Inglehart is very careful to emphasize reciprocal causal linkages between economy, culture, and politics. Economic change, cultural change, and political change are linked in a coherent pattern and the postmodern shift is part of that broad pattern.

The modernization process resulted in increasing emphasis on individual economic achievement, and this emphasis on individual success made modernization possible, as described by Max Weber.

This shift toward materialistic priorities entailed the acceptance of social mobility and a deemphasis on communal obligations. The main ingredient of the postmodern shift is that the value of economic achievement as the top priority is giving way to an increasing emphasis on the quality of life. In a major part of the world, the disciplined, self-denying, and achievement-oriented values and norms of industrial society are yielding to increasingly broad latitude for individual choice of lifestyles and individual self-expression. The shift from "materialist" values, emphasizing economic and physical security, to "post-materialist" values, emphasizing individual self-expression and quality-of-life concerns, are the key elements of occurring change.

This shift in the dominant values of modern society springs from the fact that there is a fundamental difference between growing up with an awareness that survival is precarious and growing up with the feeling that one's survival can be taken for granted. The origin of the shift is rooted in the economic miracles that occurred first in Western Europe and North America, and later in East Asia and then in Southeast Asia. Coupled with the safety net of the modern welfare state, this has produced unprecedented high levels of economic security.

This new security shifted the authority away from both religion and the state to the individual, with an increasing focus on individual concerns such as friends and leisure. The root cause of the postmodern shift has been the gradual withering away of value systems that emerged under conditions of scarcity, and the spread of security values among a growing segment of the public of these societies.

This change in the direction of a domination of post-materialist values does appear as a gradual process. It takes place as the younger generation replaces the older in the adult population of society. This is the consequence of the socialization hypothesis introduced into sociology by Mannheim's famous essay on generations. The main idea is that one's basic values reflect the conditions that prevailed during one's pre-adult years. Those raised under conditions of unprecedented security can tolerate more ambiguity and are less in need of rigid rules. In accordance with the principles of diminishing marginal utility in economic theory and Maslow's concept of a need hierarchy in psychology, subjective well-being and quality of life become higher priorities than economic growth.

Materialist/post-materialist value priorities are, according to Inglehart, only one component of the much broader configuration of values constituting the postmodern dimension. This dimension has proven to be remarkably robust over time and it is comprised of two clear clusters of statements ranked by respondents. The post-materialist statements clustering together deal with less impersonal society, more say in job, more say in government, ideas counting more than money, and freedom of speech. Opposites of these are materialist statements clustered in the opposite direction. They deal with a strong defense force, fighting rising prices, fighting against crime, maintaining order, economic growth, and maintaining stable economy. This clustering shows stability in a large number of surveys around the world with the gradual emergence of the domination of post-materialist values in the youngest generations of the highly developed societies. Inglehart's interpretation is not in the sense of the life cycle, but as a cohort effect. That means that a global hierarchy of values in the developed societies is changing with important consequences for politics, culture, and society in general (Inglehart 1977, 1990, 1997; Inglehart & Baker 2000).

Two great shifts documented on the basis of the World Value Surveys are the rise of more egalitarian values and attitudes toward the roles of women and men. Generation comparisons suggest that post-industrial societies have experienced a parallel liberalization of moral values toward sexuality among younger generations, and as this generation is replacing the older, the global shift will occur (Inglehart & Norris 2003). The second area is the most empirically founded support for the secularization thesis (Norris & Inglehart 2004).

Finally, we are faced with the dilemma of the presumed universal nature of the values of modernity. Here, the empirical and normative dimensions are intertwined, and it is very difficult to separate one from the other. To what extent are the values of democracy, human rights, individual rights, and children's rights empirical expressions of the changes that are happening in the social structures of modern and postmodern globalizing societies? Or to what extent are they simply a reflection of the ideological goals of dominant sectors of the most modernized parts of highly developed societies? Are individual human rights the expression of the "natural" rights of all individuals reflecting some basic values deeply rooted in human nature? Do human rights reflect human nature in the same way as Adam Smith claimed that the existence of the market reflects "man's propensity to barter, truck and exchange one thing for another"?

If that is true, then as the market is the institution best suited to human nature, so the same can be said for political democracy of the western type. Is human nature an empirical fact or a construction of the ideological mind? Is the fact that these rights are trampled in so many societies just the result of bad institutions? Would their removal and replacement with the "normal" democratic institutions establish the "natural, order of things," with the sanctity of the individual as the dominant societal value? Or to use another perspective, is the insistence on Asian values just the ideologized defense of Asian authoritarian regimes or a genuine defense of the endangered principal values of traditional culture confronted with the imperial domination of the West?

SEE ALSO: Ethnocentrism; Functionalism/ Neofunctionalism; Globalization; Ideology; Individualism; Norms; Values

REFERENCES AND SUGGESTED READINGS

Cavalli-Sforza, L. & Feldman, M. (1981) *Cultural Transmission and Evolution.* Princeton University Press, Princeton.

Hofstede, G. (2001) *Culture's Consequences: Comparing Values, Behaviors, Institutions, and Organizations Across Nations.* Sage, Beverly Hills, CA.

Inglehart, R. (1977) *The Silent Revolution: Changing Values and Political Styles Among Western Publics.* Princeton University Press, Princeton.

Inglehart, R. (1990) *Culture Shift in Advanced Industrial Societies.* Princeton University Press, Princeton.

Inglehart, R. (1997) *Modernization and Posmodernization: Cultural, Economic, and Political Change in 43 Societies*. Princeton University Press, Princeton.

Inglehart, R. & Baker, W. E. (2000) Modernization, Cultural Change, and the Persistence of Traditional Values. *American Sociological Review* 65: 19–51.

Inglehart, R. & Norris, P. (2003) *Rising Tide: Gender Equality and Cultural Change Around the World*. Cambridge University Press, Cambridge.

Kagitcibasi, C. (1997) Individualism and Collectivism. In: Berry, J. W., Segall, M. H., & Kagitcibasi, C. (Eds.), *Handbook of Cross-Cultural Psychology*, Vol. 3. Allyn & Bacon, Boston.

Norris, P. & Inglehart, R. (2004) *Sacred and Secular: Religion and Politics Worldwide*. Cambridge University Press, Cambridge.

Schwartz, S. H. (1992) Universals in the Content and Structure of Values: Theoretical Advances and Empirical Tests in 20 Countries. In: Zanna, M. P. (Ed.), *Advances in Experimental Social Psychology*. Academic Press, San Diego.

Schwartz, S. H. (1994) Are There Universal Aspects in the Structure and Content of Human Values? *Journal of Social Issues* 50: 19–45.

Schwartz, S. H. (2004) Mapping and Interpreting Cultural Differences Around the World. In: Vinken, H., Soeters, J., & Ester, P. (Eds.), *Comparing Cultures: Dimensions of Culture in a Comparative Perspective*. Brill, Leiden.

Triandis, H. C. (1995) *Individualism and Collectivism*. Westview, Boulder, CO.

van den Berghe, P. L. (1979) *Human Family Systems: An Evolutionary View*. Elsevier, New York.

variables

Nina Baur

VARIABLES AND CASES

Variables (indicators, items) are an important concept in methods of social research and epistemology. A variable is a superordinated attribute, characteristic, or finding that exists in at least two distinct subordinated categories (classes, groups, units of measurement, values). Cases (individuals) can differ – vary – on the variable concerning the category they belong to. Variables thus are used to classify cases. Very often, cases are persons as members of an organization, a region, a nation, etc. Note that in statistical terminology "individuals" and "persons" are not the same. Instead, many different types of cases can be conceptualized. Some examples are given in Table 1.

These cases can be assigned to categories of variables. For example, if John Smith was an American man voting for the Republicans and favoring tax cuts, he could be ascribed the attribute "male" on the variable "gender," "American" on the variable "nationality," "Republican" on the variable "preferred political party," and "in favor of tax cuts" on the variable "attitude towards tax cuts." Following the same logic, the film *Titanic* could be referred to the category "1997" on the variable "production year," "PG-13" on the variable "rating," and "11" on the variable "number of Oscars won." Similarly, any type of case can be assigned to categories of variables.

Applying this principle, all cases of a sample or population can be allocated to variables. Categories should be mutually exclusive, meaning that any individual can only be allocated to one category. They should also be exhaustive (i.e., each individual should be assignable to one category). If for some reason one does not know what category a case belongs to, this is called missing data or missing value.

All cases assigned to the same category count as "the same" (concerning this variable). If two cases are allotted to different categories, they are regarded as being dissimilar. For example, the films *Titanic* and *10 Things I Hate About You* are of the same rating (PG-13), but differ concerning the number of Oscars they won and the year they were released.

VARIABLES AND MEASUREMENT

Although both qualitative and quantitative research use the principle of variables in the sense that cases are classified, the concept is more important in standardized research, especially in survey research, as it links questionnaires and statistics: each question in a questionnaire (usually) can be considered as one variable, each possible answer to a question as a category (value). Some researchers reserve the term "item" for lists of similar questions

Table 1 Types of cases and groups

Case (= individual)	Examples for specific cases	Possible population
Person	John Smith, Mary Jones	All employees of a company
Country	US, Japan, France	All countries in the world
Software program	SPSS, Stata, SAS	Statistical packages
Newspaper article	Leading article of the *New York Times* on 11/17/2005 Third article in page 15 of the *Washington Post* on 12/23/2005	All newspaper articles in American newspapers
Conflict situation	Jim and Jane are fighting at 11.15 a.m. on 01/06/2006 Mary and Sue are spatting at 09.47 a.m. on 01/09/2008	Interaction behavior in American kindergartens
Film	*Titanic, 10 Things I Hate About You*	Romantic films
Organization	Amnesty International, Greenpeace	NGOs

with the same response spectrum. Using a coding system, the answers given have to be coded (i.e., they have to be transformed into figures in order to make them processible by statistics). Here, the problem of measurement arises (i.e., the verbal responses have to be correctly transferred into numbers without distorting their meaning). Defining a concept in a way that it can be measured is called operationalization.

Measurement is especially difficult in international comparative research as respondents might mean completely different things using the same concepts. For example, the German word *fremd* could mean "foreign," "alien," "strange," or "external" in English.

Correct measurement is important, as any statistical procedure assumes that data are free from distortion. One can only achieve valid results if this assumption is true. On the other hand, these methods are very efficient because they can investigate the relation between variables independent of context. Univariate statistics describe the distribution of one variable, bivariate statistics analyze the relation between two variables, and multivariate statistics model the relation between three or more variables. Typically, one distinguishes dependent, independent, and intervening variables for statistical analysis. However, Abbott (2001) has criticized variable-centered analysis methods because researchers using them tend to forget that not variables but human beings are acting. The latter are formalized in survey research as cases.

TYPES OF VARIABLES

One of the factors influencing which statistical analysis procedures are allowed and how results may be interpreted is variable type. There are multiple ways of classifying types of variables. First, variables can be classified by the number and discernibility of their categories (see Table 2).

Secondly, variables can differ concerning the level of analysis (level of aggregation) of the cases concerned. Researchers can study individuals (e.g., persons or single newspaper articles): (1) variables can describe these individuals' genuine characteristics; (2) relational variables describe a case's interrelationship to other cases (e.g., "Jim (case 1) is married to Jill (case 2)"; (3) contextual variables capture a case's embeddedness in a collective (e.g., "Jim (case) lives in the US (aggregate)").

Researchers can also examine collectives (aggregates, higher levels of analysis) (e.g., countries). These collectives can be regarded as individual cases themselves, but they also consist of individuals of lower analysis levels. Global (integral) variables are variables describing characteristics genuine to the aggregate (e.g., western countries could be allocated to the variable "Welfare Regime" as "Liberal," "Conservative," "Social Democratic," "Familistic," or "Post-Socialist"). Analytical (aggregative) variables have to be calculated from variables measuring characteristics of lower-level cases

Table 2   Classification of variables by characteristics of categories

Type of variable	Characteristics of categories	Example	
		Variable	Categories/Values
Binary variable (= Dummy variable)	Two categories with clear boundaries that should be coded with "1" and "0"	Gender	Male Female
Discrete and polytomous	More than two (but finite number of) categories with clear boundaries	Continent	Africa, America, Asia, Europe, Australia
Continuous	Large (often infinite) number of categories that make the boundaries between categories hard to distinguish	Income in US $	Any value from 0 to an infinite number

Table 3   Classification of variables by level of measurement

Measurement level	Variable type	Characteristics of categories	Example	
			Variable	Categories/Values
Low ↑	Categorial variable (= Index, Nominal variable, Qualitative variable)	Categories are just different, but there is no rank between categories	Gender	Male Female
	Ordinal variable (= Dimension, scale in the narrow sense)	Additionally, categories can be ranked	Attitude toward tax cuts	Completely agree Partly agree Partly disagree Completely disagree
	Metric variable (variable of interval scale)	Additionally, the distance between any two adjacent categories is the same	IQ	Any value from about 80 to about 180
↓ High	Variable of ratio scale	Additionally, a true point of zero exists	Number of children	Any value from 0 to about 20

(e.g., a country's "unemployment rate" has to be calculated from dividing the number of unemployed by the number of persons fit for work in the country). Structural variables are calculated from information on the relation between lower-level cases (e.g., "strength of local networks" could be measured by dividing the number of existing contacts between local actors by the number of all theoretically possible contacts).

Thirdly, variables differ in level of measurement (scale in the broader sense); that is, on the question how categories can be arranged (see Table 3). The higher the scale type, the more severe are the measurement rules, but the more statistical methods are allowed as well.

Fourthly, variables differ on how they can be operationalized. Manifest variables can be observed and measured directly. For example, a person's size can be assessed by using a tapeline and ascribing the number reading on the scale to the person (e.g., 1.67m). In contrast, latent variables cannot be directly observed (e.g., conservatism could be measured by a person's attitude toward many political issues. Special methods, such as factor analysis, can be used to reconstruct latent variables, which are sometimes also called dimensions or scales.

Fifthly, for some variables, individual values can be interpreted directly, without knowing other cases' values (e.g., if "size" is measured in meters and a person is "1.67m," one can imagine how tall this person is). In contrast, for other variables, one needs to know the whole range of values to assess the meaning of a single case's value. For example, if "size" is measured by the categories "short" – "medium" – "tall," and a person is classified as "tall," it makes a big difference if this person lives in the US or China. In the US a "tall" person is probably at least 1.80m, while in China a person might be called "tall" if she were 1.60m, which would probably be categorized as "short" in the US.

SEE ALSO: Computer-Aided/Mediated Analysis; Quantitative Methods; Survey Research; Variables, Control; Variables, Dependent; Variables, Independent

REFERENCES AND SUGGESTED READINGS

Abbott, A. (2001) *Time Matters: On Theory and Method.* Chicago University Press, Chicago.
Bartholomew, D. J. (Ed.) (2006) *Measurement*, 4 vols. Sage, Thousand Oaks, CA.
Harkness, J. A., Mohler, P. P., & Van de Vijer, F. J R. (Eds.) (2003) *Cross-Cultural Survey Methods.* John Wiley & Sons, Hoboken.
Little, R. A. & Schenker, N. (1994) Missing Data. In: Arminger, G., Clogg, C. C., & Sobel, M. E. (Eds.), *Handbook of Statistical Modeling for the Behavioral Sciences.* Plenum Press, New York, pp. 39–75.
Netemeyer, R. G., Bearden, W. O., & Sharma, S. (2003) *Scaling Procedures: Issues and Applications.* Sage, Thousand Oaks, CA.
Stolzenberg, R. (Ed.) (2003) *Sociological Methodology*, Vol. 33. Blackwell, Oxford.
Viswanathan, M. (2005) *Measurement Error and Research Design.* Sage, Thousand Oaks, CA.

variables, control

Hung-En Sung

Control variables are variables included in multivariate analyses to identify spurious associations. In assessing whether X is associated with Y, it is important to examine whether the covariation between them persists after the effects of other variables on this association are removed (McClendon 2002). Here, "control" means to hold constant. A variable is controlled when its influence on the other variables in the model is held constant.

In laboratory experiments a variable Z can be controlled by setting a fixed value for it and observing the relationships between X and Y for that fixed value. The experiment can then be repeated at other fixed values of Z to see whether the same results occur. However, in most social science research, values of variables such as race, education, age, and income cannot usually be manipulated before obtaining the data. In correlational studies the portion of the association between X and Y that is caused by variation in Z can be removed by comparing only cases with equal or similar values of Z at a time. A spurious relationship exists between X and Y if both variables are dependent on Z, so that the association between X and Y disappears when Z is controlled (see Fig. 1).

Informed and methodological application of control variables is crucial to the advancement of scientific knowledge. Social research establishes causal claims by demonstrating temporally ordered covariation of variables and by discrediting alternative explanations as implausible (Sobel 1995). For example, earlier studies reported an inverse relationship between levels of female government officials and levels of corruption and urged countries to raise the number of women in public offices to fight corruption (see Fig. 2). But replications that included measures of liberal democracy (e.g., independent judiciary, freedom of the press, and universal suffrage) as control variables found that when forced into the same model, the effects of gender on corruption became statistically insignificant, whereas liberal democracy remained a very

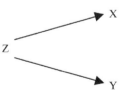

Figure 1 Graphical representation of a spurious relationship between X and Y.

Figure 2   Graphical representation of a causal relationship between gender and corruption.

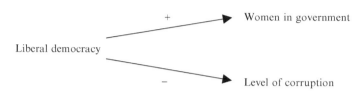

Figure 3   Graphic representation of a spurious relationship between gender and corruption.

powerful predictor (Sung 2003). The inclusion of the right control variables prompted the discovery that the observed association between gender and corruption was largely spurious and mainly caused by a political system that promoted both gender equality and better governance (see Fig. 3).

It is not always theoretically evident which variables should be controlled in multivariate analysis. Researchers should thus develop a thorough knowledge of the theory and previous work relating to their field of research so that one will be more likely to recognize possible spurious relationships and to control relevant variables, thus not giving too much importance to an observed bivariate statistical association.

SEE ALSO: Multivariate Analysis; Theory and Methods; Variables; Variables, Dependent; Variables, Independent

REFERENCES AND SUGGESTED READINGS

McClendon, M. J. (2002) *Multiple Regression and Causal Analysis*. Waveland Press, Long Grove, IL.
Sobel, M. E. (1995) Causal Inference in the Social and Behavioral Sciences. In: Arminger, G., Clogg, C. C., & Sobel, M. E. (Eds.), *Handbook of Statistical Modeling for the Social and Behavioral Sciences*. Plenum Press, New York, pp. 1–38.
Sung, H.-E. (2003) Fairer Sex or Fairer System? Gender or Corruption Revisited. *Social Forces* 82: 705–25.

variables, dependent

Ernest T. Goetz

Research involves identification and description of characteristics of organisms, objects, events, and locations. When these characteristics can take on different values (e.g., when they differ between people or from one time to another for the same person), they are referred to as *variables*. The variables involved in any particular research study are determined by the interests and intentions of the researcher. Much research focuses on the relationships between variables, particularly *causal relationships*. In such research, *dependent variables* are the presumed outcomes or effects of *independent variables*. In research about causal relationships, measurement (i.e., systematic assignment of numerical values to variables) of the dependent variable (or multiple dependent variables) is used to determine if the independent variable had the hypothesized effect or predicted relationship. For example, people's income might be measured to see if it is dependent on or predicted by their occupation. Their occupation, in turn, might be measured to see if it is dependent on or predicted by their education level. Thus, depending on the focus of a study or model, the same variable may function as a dependent variable or independent variable (Pedhazur & Schmelkin 1991).

Note also that income, occupation, and education level differ in the type of *measurement* (i.e., "assignment of numbers to aspects of objects or events according to one or another rule or convention") (Stevens 1968: 850) they represent and the information they convey. A commonly used system for classifying variables in this regard was developed by Stevens (1951, 1958). It should be noted at the outset that this analysis can be applied to variables serving different roles in a research design, statistical analysis, or theoretical model. Stevens identified four *scales of measurement*, which can be ordered from least to most informative or mathematically sophisticated. At the lowest level are *nominal scales*, in which different categories (e.g., male, female; Democrat, Republican; dentist, electrician) are arbitrarily assigned different numerical values. Note that the numbers so assigned (e.g., male $= 1$, female $= 2$) convey no information other than category membership (e.g., the values shown above do not indicate that females have more or less of anything than males). *Ordinal scales* convey information about relative degrees or amounts. They are constructed by assigning numbers to indicate rank ordering based on an attribute of interest (e.g., education levels might be ordered as follows: high school diploma, associate's degree, bachelor's degree, master's degree, doctoral degree; also Stevens's scales of measurement). The numbers assigned in an ordinal scale communicate relationships of less than/ greater than, but tell you nothing about the magnitude of the differences. Thus, the number of years required or the amount of knowledge gained between a high school diploma and an associate's degree may not be the same as that involved in progressing from a master's degree to a doctoral degree. In *interval scales* (e.g., Fahrenheit and Celsius temperatures, calendar dates in years), differences between the numbers assigned to observations indicate the distance or interval between them on the dimension of interest and are invariant across the measurement scale. Thus, the difference in temperature between 37° and 42° Fahrenheit is the same as the difference between 79° and 84° Fahrenheit. However, it is not the case that 84° Fahrenheit is twice as hot as 42° Fahrenheit. Such statements can only be made for *ratio scales*, which have a true or absolute zero (e.g., Calvin temperatures, number of children, income in dollars).

The nature of the measurement constrains the statistical procedures that can be used to summarize data. According to Stevens (1958), the only permissible statistical operations for nominal scales are tabulation of the number of cases of each category and identification of the most frequent category (mode). Interval scales permit the identification of the median and percentiles and the calculation of rank order correlations. It is only with interval and ratio level scales that one can appropriately calculate a mean, standard deviation, and product moment correlation. Thus, there is a strong pull to interpret data in the social sciences as representing interval scale measurement when a more conservative ordinal interpretation might be more appropriate (e.g., rating scale data, standardized test scores).

In interpreting the information provided by measurement of dependent variables, it is also essential to consider their *reliability* and *validity*. Reliability refers to the accuracy or precision of the scores, that is, the extent to which they are free from error. Validity, on the other hand, refers to the appropriateness and utility of the interpretation of data derived via measurement procedures (Cronbach 1971). Although data must be reliable in order to permit valid interpretations, misguided or erroneous interpretations of reliable data also are possible. Thus, reliability is necessary but not sufficient for validity. Depending on the intended purpose of the interpretation, different approaches to gauging validity are possible. *Content validation* entails an examination of the appropriateness of the types of items included in an assessment to the domain being measured. Thus, a test of high school algebra should include items appropriate for that content area and level of instruction, and a survey of views on a president's performance should include questions covering the major issues of the day. *Criterion-related* validation is accomplished by examining the relationship between the measure whose validity is being assessed and some criterial outcome or measure. For example, the criterion-related validity of a measure of an incumbent president's popularity as a predictor of his or her reelection might be assessed by examining the ability of a poll of the president's approval rating before an election to predict the outcome of the election. More generally, criterion-related validity is measured via correlation between the measure in question and the criterial measure. For example, the criterion-related validity of exit polls in a presidential election might be tested by correlating exit polls with final vote counts in a sample of precincts. *Construct validation* is less straightforward. The term *construct* refers to human attributes such as knowledge, beliefs, attitudes, and opinions that are of theoretical importance to social scientists. Pedhazur and Schmelkin (1991) described construct validation as a never-ending process that involves careful attention to the definition of the concept, item content, measurement procedures and scoring procedures, and internal structure analysis. Although concept validation is complex, it is essential to ensuring the validity of many measures such as surveys and tests as indices of the attributes they are intended to measure.

Finally, it is important to note that the operalization of the dependent variable can play an important role in determining the size of the effect observed for the dependent variable. Wilson and Lipsey (2001) synthesized the results of 319 meta-analyses encompassing 16,525 studies of psychological treatments (primarily in mental health and education) and found that study methods, which included type of design, method quality, and operalization of dependent variables, accounted for nearly as much of the variance in outcomes of these studies as the nature of the treatments, with operalization of the dependent variables being one of the most important aspects of study methods.

SEE ALSO: Experimental Design; Hypotheses; Intervention Studies; Multivariate Analysis; Regression and Regression Analysis; Reliability; Structural Equation Modeling; Variables; Variables, Control; Variables, Independent

REFERENCES AND SUGGESTED READINGS

Cronbach, L. J. (1971) Test Validation. In: Thorndike, R. L. (Ed.), *Educational Measurement*, 2nd edn. American Council on Education, Washington, DC, pp. 443–507.
Pedhazur, E. J. & Schmelkin, L. P. (1991) *Measurement, Design, and Analysis: An Integrated Approach*. Lawrence Erlbaum Associates, Mahwah, NJ.
Stevens, S. S. (1951) Mathematics, Measurement, and Psychophysics. In: Stevens, S. S. (Ed.), *Handbook of Experimental Psychology*. Wiley, New York, pp. 1–49.
Stevens, S. S. (1958) Measurement and Man. *Science* 127: 383–9.
Stevens, S. S. (1968) Measurement, Man, and the Schemapiric View. *Science* 161: 849–56.
Wilson, D. B. & Lipsey, M. W. (2001) The Role of Method in Treatment Effectiveness Research: Evidence from Meta-Analysis. *Psychological Methods* 6: 413–29.

variables, independent

Ernest T. Goetz

Research involves identification and description of characteristics of organisms, objects, events, and locations. When these characteristics can take on different values (e.g., when they differ between people or from one time to another for the same person), they are referred to as *variables*. The variables involved in any particular research study are determined by the interests and intentions of the researcher. Much research focuses on the relationships between variables, particularly *causal relationships*. In such research, *independent variables* are the presumed causes whose effects are measured via changes in the value of *dependent variables*. Independent variables are temporally or theoretically prior to (and therefore independent of) dependent variables. For example, the manner in which the prosecutor and defense attorney present their closing arguments to a jury precedes the jury's deliberations and verdict, and so may influence them. Thus, various aspects of the closing arguments might be viewed as independent variables. According to Cohen et al. (2003), there are four requirements for the treatment of a variable X as a cause (or independent variable) of variable Y (the effect or dependent variable):

1   X precedes Y in time (temporal precedence).
2   Some mechanism whereby this causal effect operates can be posited (causal mechanism).

3 A change in the value of X is accompanied by a change in the value of Y on the average (association).
4 The effects of X on Y can be isolated from the effects of other potential variables on Y (non-spuriousness or lack of confounders).

It is important to note that (3) above entails a probabilistic view of causality, which is at the core of causal research in the social sciences (Pearl 2000). Thus, a change in the independent variable is likely to be associated with a change in the dependent variable, but the occurrence, direction, and size of the change may differ from one individual or occasion to the next. In social science research, the probabilistic nature of causal relationships is compensated by the use of multiple observations.

Evidence of the causal relationship between independent variables and dependent variables is strongest in experimental research, which has long been held as the "gold standard" in the study of causality and sometimes anointed as "the scientific method." The causal interpretation of relationships between variables in non-experimental research is gaining increased acceptance and legitimacy (e.g., Cohen et al. 2003), although some authors still caution against causal interpretations of non-experimental research and advocate the use of the term *predictor variable* in place of *independent variable* in such research (e.g., Brewer 2000).

In a prototypical experiment, causal relationships are tested by manipulating the independent variable (or variables) while keeping other factors constant (i.e., controlled). For example, the effect of hydrochloric acid on iron could be studied under laboratory conditions designed to eliminate the potential effects of other chemical agents or physical conditions (e.g., temperature, air pressure). Although this level of control is seldom if ever possible in social science research, researchers attempt to control or account for other potentially confounding variables. Thus, one might study the effect of mode of presentation of an argument in a study in which other potentially confounding variables (e.g., sex and age of the audience) are controlled by matching or by statistical procedures (e.g., removal of associated variance through *regression*).

In non-experimental research, support for causal relationships is provided through tests of association, preferably by testing a priori causal models. Naturally occurring variation in the independent variable (or variables) is measured (that is, the independent variable is not manipulated), and its predictive value is tested after controlling or accounting for potential confounds. Although it is not possible to eliminate all potential confounds, judicious selection of control variables can help to minimize the problem. Thus, the effect of the sex of an audience member on response to a given form of argument might be studied by having men and women of the same age and education level listen to the same presentation. Research, both experimental and non-experimental, can also explore the effects of more than one independent variable, and measure outcomes in terms of more than one dependent variable. Further, a fuller understanding of the relationship between independent and dependent variables may require consideration of *moderator variables*, which influence the relationship between independent and dependent variables, and *mediator variables*, which elaborate the relationship between independent and dependent variables through the specification of intervening processes or states in the causal process.

As Pedhazur and Schmelkin (1991) point out, the same independent variable can be manipulated in one study and non-manipulated in another study. For example, sex is a non-manipulated variable in the examples presented above, but it would be a manipulated variable in an experiment where male and female "attorneys" presented the same argument to different audiences. Further, the same variable can be an independent variable in one study and a dependent variable in another study. Thus, sex would be a dependent variable in a test of a drug whose intended effect was to increase the likelihood of giving birth to a female or male child.

Like dependent variables, variation in independent variables takes several forms. If one were to study the effect of a drug, one might compare various levels of dosage of the drug, or one might compare its effects to those of other drugs. In the first instance, variation is said to be *continuous* or quantitative; in the latter, variation is said to be *categorical* or qualitative. Statistical procedures have been developed that are particularly appropriate to each type of independent variable: effects of categorical independent variables typically are assessed through *analysis of variance* and its variants (e.g., multivariate analysis of variance), while effects of continuous independent variables typically are assessed via regression and its variants (e.g., *multivariate* and *multiple regression*). There are also statistical techniques that are compatible with both categorical and continuous regression (e.g., *analysis of covariance, semantic equation modeling*). Sometimes researchers take continuous independent variables (e.g., age) and reduce them to categorical data by dichotomization. One common form of dichotomization is the median split, in which values above the median are lumped together in one group, while those below are lumped into another. By ignoring variation within these artificially constructed groups, dichotomization results in a loss of information, which makes the outcomes of statistical analyses less informative and reliable (Cohen 1983; MacCallum et al. 2002).

SEE ALSO: Experimental Design; Hypotheses; Intervention Studies; Multivariate Analysis; Regression and Regression Analysis; Reliability; Structural Equation Modeling; Variables; Variables, Control; Variables, Dependent

REFERENCES AND SUGGESTED READINGS

Brewer, M. B. (2000) Research Design and Issues of Validity. In: Reis, H. T. & Judd, C. M. (Eds.), *Handbook of Research Methods in Social and Personality Psychology*. Cambridge University Press, Cambridge, pp. 3–16.

Cohen, J. (1983) The Cost of Dichotomization. *Applied Psychological Measurement* 7: 249–53.

Cohen, J., Cohen, P., West, S., & Aiken, G. (2003) *Applied Regression/Correlation Behavior Analysis for the Behavioral Sciences*, 3rd edn. Lawrence Erlbaum Associates, Mahwah, NJ.

MacCallum, R. C., Zhang, S., Preacher, K. J., & Rucker, D. D. (2002) On the Practice of Dichotomization of Quantitative Variables. *Psychological Methods* 7: 19–40.

Pearl, J. (2000) *Causality: Models, Reasoning, and Inference*. Cambridge University Press, Cambridge.

Pedhazur, E. J. & Schmelkin, L. P. (1991) *Measurement, Design, and Analysis: An Integrated Approach*. Lawrence Erlbaum Associates, Mahwah, NJ.

variance

Ernest T. Goetz

Variability is one of the key characteristics of a set of scores. Measures of variability are used to provide an indication of the extent to which characteristics of people (e.g., income, education), events (e.g., attendance at concerts), or things (e.g., capacity of concert venues) differ from one another. Of the statistical indices of variability (e.g., range, semi-interquartile range), the variance and standard deviation are the only ones that reflect the exact value of each score. In this respect, they are analogous to the mean, the measure of centrality from which they are derived. For this reason, the variance and standard deviation are the measures of variability used in parametric statistics (e.g., analysis of variance (ANOVA), correlation, general linear modeling, hierarchical linear modeling, regression and regression analysis, structural equation modeling).

The variance and standard deviation depict variability of a set of scores in terms of their distances from the mean, or deviation scores. A deviation score is computed by subtracting the mean of the set of scores from the score. Therefore, like the mean, deviation scores can only be computed for interval scales (e.g., Fahrenheit or Celsius temperatures) or ratio scales (e.g., height, weight, Kelvin temperatures), in which differences between scores are meaningful and consistent. Because of the way that deviation scores are defined and computed, the sum of the deviation scores is zero for all sets of scores. Therefore, the average deviation score (which also is zero by definition) is of no value as a measure of variability. This difficulty is overcome by squaring the deviation scores.

To illustrate, suppose we were to count the number of books high school students were carrying in their backpacks. A list of five students and the number of books in their backpacks is presented in the first two columns of Table 1. The mean number of books being carried by these students is six (i.e., $30/5 = 6$). The deviation scores for each student (i.e., number of books they are carrying minus the mean number of books, six in this case) are shown in column three. As previously noted, these add up to zero

Table 1

Student	Score	Score – Mean	(Score – Mean)^2
Júan	12	6	36
Laurie	1	–5	25
Ronghua	9	3	9
Tufan	5	–1	1
Yolanda	3	–3	9
Total	30	0	80

with an average of zero, as they would for any set of scores.

In descriptive statistics, in which you are interested in characterizing the set of scores that you have, the variance is found dividing the sum of the squared deviation scores (shown in the final column) by the number of scores in the set, or $80/5 = 16$ for our example. However, in inferential statistics, in which you want to *estimate* the variability of a large set of scores of interest (i.e., population) from some smaller set of scores that are available (i.e., sample), this approach systematically underestimates the variance of the population. To correct for this bias, the sum of the squared deviation scores is divided by the number of scores minus one, or $80/4 = 20$ in the present case. It should be noted that inferences about a population based on a sample of scores are most valid when they are based on a random sample of scores in which each member of the population (e.g., all US high school students) has an equal chance of being selected. Further, as sample size increases, so does the accuracy of the inferences that can be drawn regarding the population.

Since calculation of the variance yields a metric in which the unit of measurement is squared and sometimes interpretable (e.g., books squared), variability is most often reported in terms of the standard deviation. The standard deviation is found by taking the square root of the variance, which brings the number back to the original unit of measurement. In our example, if the set of scores were the population of interest, the standard deviation would be $\sqrt{16} = 4$. If the set of scores were a sample that was being used to make inferences about a larger population of scores, the standard deviation

would be $\sqrt{20} = 4.47$ (note that the disparity between the results of the two computational formulas decreases as sample size increases).

Thus, the standard deviation can be viewed as a modified average deviation score, adjusted to accommodate for the fact that the sum of the deviation scores is always zero. In our example, the variability of the number of books as measured by the standard deviation (4.47) is quite large compared to the mean number of books (6), assuming that the five students are a random sample of all the students in the high school. However, given the fact that our sample of students is small, the accuracy of our estimates would be limited, resulting in wide confidence intervals, or range of values in which the population parameters (i.e., statistics descriptive of the full set of scores of interest, here the average number of books carried in the backpacks of all US high school students) might be expected to fall.

It is important to note, however, that variance is more than just an intermediate step on the road to the calculation of the standard deviation. Directly or with modifications, it is used in the description and estimation of the relationships between two or more variables. For example, the strength of the relationship between two interval or ratio scales (e.g., height and weight) is measured using the *Pearson product moment correlation*, or Pearson r. The Pearson r is calculated using the variance of the two sets of scores and their covariance, which is an analogue of variance in which the deviation score of one variable is multiplied by the deviation score of the second variable for each observation in the data set (e.g., Margot's height and weight). The proportion of variance accounted for by one or more variables is a metric of effect size that is commonly used in inferential statistics.

SEE ALSO: ANOVA (Analysis of Variance); Confidence Intervals; Descriptive Statistics; General Linear Model; Hierarchical Linear Models; Measures of Centrality; Random Sample; Regression and Regression Analysis; Statistical Significance Testing; Statistics; Structural Equation Modeling; Validity, Quantitative; Variables, Dependent; Variables, Independent

REFERENCES AND SUGGESTED
READINGS

Bolen, K. A. (1989) *Structural Equation Modeling with Latent Variables*. Wiley, New York.
Glass, G. V. & Hopkins, K. D. (1996) *Statistical Methods in Education and Psychology*, 3rd edn. Allyn & Bacon, Boston.
Keith, T. Z. (2006) *Multiple Regression and Beyond*. Pearson, Boston.
Shavelson, R. J. (1996) *Statistical Reasoning for the Behavioral Sciences*, 3rd edn. Allyn & Bacon, Boston.

Veblen, Thorstein (1857–1929)

Matthias Zick Varul

Thorstein Veblen, US economist and social theorist, argued for an evolutionary-institutionalist approach to social development. History is a non-teleological process in which, by quasi-Darwinian selection, institutions survive according to their fit with the current "state of the industrial arts." Inert institutions inhibit further technological progress beyond the state they are adapted to facilitate. In this context, Veblen developed the theory of latecomer advantages and technological borrowing.

Veblen sees two driving motivational forces in the development of technology and institutions. The first, more primordial, is the *instinct of workmanship*, which motivates cooperative productive work for the good of the community. Having been dominant in a peaceful, egalitarian, and matriarchal *age of savagery*, it has been subdued by the second motive, the *predatory instinct*, seeking competitive advantage for the individual at the cost of others in a warlike and patriarchal *barbaric age*. In this setting, a non-productive leisure class dominates the productive industrial classes of farmers, workers, craftsmen, and technicians.

This dominance is perpetuated in modern capitalism, although in a pacified form. Cultural dominance lies with a leisure class of rentiers and absentee owners and industry is dominated by a managerially active business class. While industrial workers and particularly engineers adhere to the logic of production and efficiency, the business class follows the logic of profit, often fueling industrial innovation, but frequently also sabotaging efficiency and technological progress where doing so enhances monetary outcomes.

Widely seen as Veblen's sociologically most significant achievement is the analysis of consumerism in his *Theory of the Leisure Class*. With the ability to waste being the principal determinant in class structure, the leisure class engages in conspicuous leisure and consumption to assert their social position. The sole utility of the goods thus consumed lies not in their capacity to satisfy any substantive need but in their capacity to demonstrate spending power and habitual abstention from productive work. Ascending groups try to *emulate* upper-class habits of consumption and leisure. This sets off a dynamics of consumer good innovation as the emulated upper classes, in order to keep ahead of the runners-up, constantly have to refine their *pecuniary canons of taste*. Those innovations then will trickle down to lower classes in a cascade of competitive emulation inspired by *invidious comparison*.

SEE ALSO: Conspicuous Consumption; Consumption, Mass Consumption, and Consumer Culture; Institutionalism; Leisure Class

REFERENCES AND SUGGESTED
READINGS

Brown, D. (Ed.) (1998) *Thorstein Veblen in the Twenty-First Century*. Edward Elgar, Cheltenham.
Edgell, S. (2001) *Veblen in Perspective*. E. Sharpe, Armonk, NY.
Tilman, R. (1992) *Thorstein Veblen and His Critics*. Princeton University Press, Princeton.
Veblen, T. (1899) *The Theory of the Leisure Class*. Macmillan, New York.
Veblen, T. (1904) *The Theory of Business Enterprise*. Schreibner's Sons, New York.
Veblen, T. (1914) *The Instinct of Workmanship and the State of the Industrial Arts*. Macmillan, New York.
Veblen, T. (1915) *Imperial Germany and the Industrial Revolution*. Macmillan, New York.
Veblen, T. (1919) *The Place of Science in Modern Civilization*. Huebsch, New York.
Veblen, T. (1921) *The Engineers and the Price System*. Huebsch, New York.

verstehen

Larry Ray

Usually translated as "understanding," the concept of *verstehen* has become part of a critique of positivist approaches to the social sciences. Associated with the sociology of Max Weber, *verstehen* derives from the hermeneutic critique of positivism that emerged in German universities in the 1880s and 1890s that gave rise to a dispute over method in the social sciences (*Methodenstreit*). *Verstehen* refers to understanding the meaning of action from the actor's point of view. It is entering into the shoes of the other, and adopting this research stance requires treating the actor as a subject, rather than an object of one's observations. It also implies that unlike objects in the natural world, human actors are not simply the product of causal forces. Individuals are seen to create the world by organizing their own understanding of it and giving it meaning. To do research on actors without taking into account the meanings they attribute to their actions or environment is to treat them like objects.

Wilhelm Dilthey's sociology provided a more elaborated method of understanding than Weber's. Based on the view that since sociologists participate in the cultural worlds of those they study it is possible to gain a kind of inner understanding of social life that is impossible in the natural sciences, Dilthey distinguished several levels of understanding. The most formal level of understanding is based on signs and symbols, which make mental content intelligible but reveal nothing about the inner mental life of the subject. Then there is direct understanding – recognizing a symbol *as* something, which involves decoding the communication of expressions, gestures, and actions, or, say, the meaning of a sentence or mathematical expression. This infers intention from observation of action – so if we see someone hitting a nail with a hammer we might infer what their intention might be; similarly, we recognize certain facial expressions as indicating grief or happiness. Further, there are "higher" levels of understanding involving empathy and reexperiencing, which involve projecting oneself into a text or form of life and appropriating it on the basis of shared

experience. For example, to share the experience of poetic love one must have loved, to imagine suffering one must have suffered, and so on. Then on the basis of empathy arises the "highest" form of understanding, where one recreates or relives the process of cultural production. This occurs in *reverse order* to the sequence of events, and moves from the completed product or event back to the context and intentions that inspired it.

The procedure of placing oneself within the worldview of frames of meaning of contemporary or historical actors is crucial to making sense and thereby explaining social actions and outcomes. We are surrounded by Roman ruins, cathedrals, and summer castles, as Dilthey put it, fragments of the history of mind that can be understood only by interpretive techniques grounded in the life process of individuals.

This empathetic approach to social inquiry, it is argued, finds no analogy in the methods of the natural sciences, but aims to reconstruct the relationship between expressions and meanings and intentions of actors (Dilthey 1986). Its objective is less to explain the world and more to understand and reconstruct meaning to regain the lost unity of the act of creation of texts, cultures, artworks, institutions, and historical events. In this sense, as Delanty (1997) argues, hermeneutics had a more conservative orientation than positivism. Whereas the latter arose in the context of revolt against the authority of tradition and political absolutism, hermeneutics has tended to value community, be uncritical of social institutions, and ignore power relations. However, understanding is resolutely universalistic in its assumption that a common (and therefore comprehendible) humanity underlies all processes of cultural and historical creation.

Weber's use of the method of *verstehen* attempts to reconcile interpretation of action with causal explanation in a way that establishes an interaction between the two. So causal explanations must have adequacy on the level of meaning, while meanings themselves may constitute causes. One of the most systematic uses of this method by Weber is in *The Protestant Ethic and the Spirit of Capitalism* where he supplements structural and economic accounts of the origin of capitalism in Europe with empathetic reconstruction of the worldview of seventeenth-century Calvinist and other Protestant groups. He argues that Calvinist belief in predestination, which precluded achieving salvation through good works, provoked "an unprecedented inner loneliness" and search for signs of salvation. Through attempting to resolve this paradox the theological quest for evidence of divine grace was transposed into the worldly but ascetic pursuit of capital accumulation, success in which was interpreted by Calvinists as signaling divine selection. What this example illustrates is that only through empathetic reconstruction of actors' meanings is it possible to explain critical events like the growth of capitalism.

However, the use of *verstehen* is open to criticism. First, critics have argued that this is not a distinct method, but an elaboration of what all social actors do routinely in everyday life. Secondly, there is no way of validating *verstehende* interpretations since they cannot be tested against replicable evidence. Thirdly, it is claimed that interpretation of meanings adds no new knowledge and by definition recycles what is already known about society. Fourthly, *verstehen* is at best a source of hypotheses that then require testing against evidence. Fifthly, it is accused of over-emphasizing meaning at the expense of material structures and unintended consequences of actions. To some extent these criticisms focus on *verstehen* as a form of introspection or imaginative reconstruction of meanings rather than as a systematic dialogue with a range of social materials – texts, archives, conversations, worldviews, and cultural artifacts – in which suggested interpretations can be "tested" with reference to the extent that they open up new layers of understanding.

SEE ALSO: Hermeneutics; Positivism; Weber, Max

REFERENCES AND SUGGESTED READINGS

Delanty, G. (1997) *Social Science: Beyond Constructivism and Realism*. Open University Press, Buckingham.

Dilthey, W. (1986) Awareness, Reality: Time. In: Mueller-Vollmer, K. (Ed.), *The Hermeneutics Reader*. Blackwell, Oxford, pp. 149–64.

O'Hear, A. (Ed.) (1996) *Verstehen and Human Understanding*. Cambridge University Press, Cambridge.

Outhwaite, W. (1975) *Understanding Everyday Life*. Allen & Unwin, London.

Ray, L. J. (1999) *Theorizing Classical Sociology*. Open University Press, Buckingham.

Weber, M. (1984) *The Protestant Ethic and the Spirit of Capitalism*. Allen & Unwin, London.

Viagra

Meika Loe

Viagra is a blood-circulation drug (the first in its drug class as a PDE5 inhibitor) prescribed to treat erectile dysfunction. This drug, marketed by Pfizer Pharmaceuticals and approved by the FDA in 1998, has been widely cited for its record-breaking sales and its "blockbuster" status. Specifically, Viagra set records as the fastest-selling drug in America, and netted over a billion dollars in its first year. Viagra was the first FDA-approved oral therapy for sexual dysfunction. After five years of consistent sales, competitors Levitra and Cialis (also PDE5 inhibitors) have entered the market, claiming to work faster and for longer periods of time. The financial success of Viagra has helped to construct and finance research and product development in sexual medicine.

Sociologists have treated the Viagra phenomenon as an opportunity to analyze the social construction of medicine, masculinity, sexuality, marketing, and aging. Viagra, when read as a social artifact of our times, is emblematic of changing social realities in the twenty-first century. In sum, Viagra exemplifies the medicalization of social problems at a time when biomedicine is hegemonic, with increasing jurisdiction over areas of life not previously medicalized.

Viagra reflects the emergence of the pharmaceutical era, in which the increasingly consolidated pharmaceutical industry is the most profitable industry in America, with "unprecedented levels of control" over medical education, drug regulation, research, marketing, and advocacy. Viagra reveals the merging of science and capitalism in the pharmaceutical era, as medical researchers and experts are increasingly affiliated with this industry. Viagra was also one of the first drugs to be marketed directly to consumers, after the ban on DTC advertisements was lifted in 1997. In the pharmaceutical era, drugs such as Viagra can be used as tools for the construction of personhood and idealized identities. In this way, the Viagra phenomenon heralds the commodification of sexuality and masculinity. The male body becomes an important new site for medicalization and marketing. Sexuality is increasingly a site for biomedical intervention, and Viagra represents the McDonaldization of sex in a culture that emphasizes efficiency and a quick-fix mentality. Finally, as more products emerge to "treat" symptoms of aging, Viagra will be remembered as one of the first blockbuster drugs marketed to an aging populace, with senator and war veteran Bob Dole as its spokesperson. More recently, sexual medicine is marketed to a wider demographic in terms of age, ethnicity, and gender.

Viagra's debut is a perfect opportunity to examine the construction of social norms, ideals, and expectations, particularly because it renders visible and influences many taken-for-granted social assumptions about sex, aging, gender, and medicine. For example, since Viagra's debut, "normal sex" in America is more and more narrowly defined and difficult to achieve. Then again, normal sex is a seeming requirement for normal personhood. More recently, we have heard that "normal" for women means sexually desirous, easily aroused, fully lubricated, and orgasmic. With such elevated standards, normal sex in the Viagra era likely requires medical or pharmaceutical intervention.

SEE ALSO: Body and Sexuality; Consumption; Gerontology; McDonaldization; Popular Culture; Sexuality, Masculinity and

REFERENCES AND SUGGESTED READINGS

Loe, M. (2004) *The Rise of Viagra: How the Little Blue Pill Changed Sex in America.* New York University Press, New York.
Mamo, L. & Fishman, J. (2001) Potency in all the Right Places: Viagra as a Technology of the Gendered Body. *Body and Society* 7(4): 13–35.
Marshall, B. (2002) Hard Science: Gendered Constructions of Sexual Dysfunction in the "Viagra Age." *Sexualities* 5(2): 131–58.
Potts, A. (2000) The Essence of the Hard-On. *Men and Masculinities* 3(1): 85–103.
Tiefer, L. (2004) *Sex is Not a Natural Act and Other Essays.* Westview Press, Boulder.
Tiefer, L. & Kaschak, E. (2001) *A New View of Women's Sexual Problems.* Haworth Press, New York.

victimization

Tancy J. Vandecar-Burdin

Victimization is the action of victimizing, or fact of being victimized (Viano 1976). Until a variety of factors converged during the 1960s, individual victims were not always given much attention by the criminal justice system. During this time, the women's movement began to address the victim-blaming often seen with sexually violent crimes. Child abuse as a societal problem was also coming to the attention of local and state leaders. Finally, rapidly growing crime rates between 1960 and 1980 brought greater scrutiny to the criminal justice system, in part through President Johnson's 1967 Commission report. Victimization was one focus of this report. The culmination of these factors began the discussion about the victim's role in the criminal justice process, what services should be provided to victims, and data gathering about victimization in the US (Doerner & Lab 1995).

The 1980s were an active time in the history of victims' rights. In 1981 President Reagan established the Annual National Victims of Crime Week in April and in the following year he created the President's Task Force on Victims of Crime, which developed a series of recommendations regarding several victims' issues (Davis & Henley 1990). The 1983 Omnibus Victim/Witness Protection Act addressed the rights of victims and witnesses of federal crimes. The Act stated that victims should not be subjected to intimidation by the offender, have the right to be consulted about possible plea bargains, and can provide victim impact statements for sentencing consideration. Many states have followed the federal example by allowing the same protections for victims (Doerner & Lab 1995).

The 1984 Victims of Crime Act (VOCA) established the Crime Victims Fund of $100 million to help provide grants to victim assistance and compensation programs (Doerner & Lab 1995). In fiscal year 2002, VOCA provided over $93 million in victim compensation funds to the states (OVC 2003). The Office for Victims of Crime (OVC), established in 1988, now provides management for the fund, which is maintained by fines and other monies collected from federal offenders (Doerner & Lab 1995; OVC 2004). The OVC also provides training and education about victims, supports projects to improve victims' rights and services, and maintains and distributes a variety of publications about victim issues.

Information about victimization in the US can be found in a variety of sources. The Uniform Crime Report (UCR) collects crime information from law enforcement agencies throughout the country and is managed by the Federal Bureau of Investigation. The UCR collects data on crimes known to the police in two categories: personal and property offenses. Personal offenses include the violent crimes of murder, forcible rape, robbery, and aggravated assault. Property offenses include burglary, larceny, motor vehicle theft, and arson. While the UCR provides a way for law enforcement to consistently report crime data from year to year and locality to locality, there is very little information about the victim or offender (if the offender is never arrested). Also, the UCR can only report crimes made known to the police (Doerner & Lab 1995). Property crimes are more numerous than violent crimes and crime rates have generally been declining since the early 1990s. The number of violent crimes decreased 25.6 percent from 1994 to 2003. Property crimes decreased 14 percent during the same period. In 2003, about 1.38 million violent crimes were known to the police, compared to 10.44 million property crimes. This translates to 475 violent crimes per 100,000 people and 3,588 property crimes per 100,000 (FBI 2004).

The National Crime Survey (NCS) began in 1972 with a sample of 72,000 households. Each member within the household over the age of 12 was interviewed. The household remained in the sample for three years and was contacted every six months during that time. Each member was interviewed to obtain individual victimization data and one member was selected to give information about crimes committed against the household. However, this one person may not have knowledge of all crimes committed against the household (Doerner & Lab 1995). Several revisions to the NCS beginning in 1979 led to changing the name of the instrument to the National Crime Victimization Survey (NCVS). Changes included changes to the screening questions, the addition of supplemental special topic questions, and allowing for the use of the telephone to conduct interviews after the initial data gathering session were implemented. In 1992, the NCVS was further revised to capture more extensive data on rape, sexual assault, intimate partner violence, and vandalism. The NCVS now collects victimization data on rape, sexual assault, robbery, aggravated and simple assault, purse snatching/pocket picking, household burglary, motor vehicle theft, theft, intimate partner violence, and vandalism (Bureau of Justice Statistics 2002).

The percentage of households experiencing a property or violent crime as defined by the NCVS has been declining since 1994. In 2002, about 15 percent of 110.3 million US households experienced one of the NCVS-measured crimes. This compares to 25 percent of households in 1994. Three percent of households in 2002 experienced a violent crime and 13 percent experienced a property crime. Theft and simple assault were the two most common offenses within each category (Bureau of Justice Statistics 2004). In terms of individual victimizations, there were about 5.5 million personal crime victimizations (this includes the violent crimes and purse snatching) in 2002. Property crime victimizations numbered about 17.5 million (Bureau of Justice Statistics 2003).

Certain demographic factors are associated with greater risks of victimization. The risk of victimization decreases with age after peaking in the 16–24 age group. The elderly (ages 65 and older) have much lower victimization rates than younger individuals (Laub 1990). Men in general are more likely to experience a violent crime than are women. Men experienced crimes of violence at a rate of 25.5 per 1,000 persons aged 12 or older compared to 20.8 per 1,000 for women in 2002. Women are more likely to experience rape or sexual assault than are men (1.8 victimizations per 1,000 compared to 0.3 per 1,000, respectively, in 2002), as well as simple assault with minor injury (4.2 victimizations per 1,000 compared to 3.6 per 1,000, respectively). Blacks are also more likely to experience crimes of violence than other minorities and whites. Blacks had a violent crime victimization rate of 27.9 per 1,000 persons aged 12 or older in 2002, compared to 22.8 per 1,000 for whites and 14.7 for other minorities. Blacks are slightly less likely than whites to experience simple assault (14.6 victimizations per 1,000 in 2002, compared to 15.9 for whites) (Bureau of Justice Statistics 2003).

However, demographics alone cannot fully explain victimization and criminal behavior. Theories of victimization began in the 1940s with Hans von Hentig and his theory of victim–perpetrator interaction. Von Hentig observed that victims often contributed to their victimization by somehow provoking the offender or by putting themselves in situations that would make them prone to criminal acts. Ezzat Fattah stressed the link between victimization and offending and argued that the criminal act as a whole needs to be examined because of the interaction of the victim and offender. Victims can be offenders and vice versa (Adler et al. 2004).

Hindelang, Gottfredson, and Garofalo developed the lifestyle theory of crime in 1978. Changing gender roles (women working outside the home) and work schedules means that people live different lifestyles, spend varying amounts of time in public, and interact with different kinds of people. This theory is based on several propositions, including that increased time spent with non-family members and in public places increases the chances for victimization. "Variations in lifestyle affect the number of victimization risks that a person experiences" (Adler et al. 2004: 223).

The lifestyle theory of crime is very similar to the routine activities approach to explaining criminal behavior and victimization. Cohen and Felson argue that a crime can only occur when there is a likely offender, a suitable target, no other person present to somehow prevent the crime ("capable guardian"), and no "personal handler" to control the likely offender. If all of these factors come together spatially then the potential for criminal perpetration is high. Through the routine activities of everyday life – such as going to work or school, participating in recreational activities, and so on – potential victims can come into contact with potential offenders. And if no capable guardians or personal handlers are present, the chances increase that a criminal act with occur.

SEE ALSO: Crime; Crime, Hot Spots; Measuring Crime; Routine Activity Theory

REFERENCES AND SUGGESTED READINGS

Adler, F., Mueller, G. O. W., & Luafer, W. S. (2004) *Criminology*. McGraw Hill, New York.

Bureau of Justice Statistics (2002) *Crime and the Nation's Households, 2000*. US Department of Justice, Office of Justice Programs, Washington, DC.

Bureau of Justice Statistics (2003) *Criminal Victimization in the United States, 2002 Statistical Tables*. US Department of Justice, Office of Justice Programs, Washington, DC.

Bureau of Justice Statistics (2004) *Crime and Nation's Households, 2002*. US Department of Justice, Office of Justice Programs, Washington, DC.

Davis, R. C. & Henley, M. (1990) Victim Service Programs. In: Lurigio, A. J., Skogan, W. G., & Davis, R. C. (Eds.), *Victims of Crime: Problems, Policies, and Programs*. Sage, Newbury Park, CA, pp. 157–71.

Doerner, W. G. & Lab, S. P. (1995) *Victimology*. Anderson Publishing, Cincinnati, OH.

Federal Bureau of Investigation (2004) *Crime in the United States 2003*. US Department of Justice, Washington, DC.

Laub, J. H. (1990). Patterns of Victimization in the United States. In: Lurigio, A. J., Skogan, W. G., & Davis, R. C. (Eds.), *Victims of Crime: Problems, Policies, and Programs*. Sage, Newbury Park, CA, pp. 23–49.

Office for Victims of Crime (2003) *Report to the Nation 2003: Fiscal Years 2001 and 2002*. US Department of Justice, Office of Justice Programs, Washington, DC.

Office for Victims of Crime (2004) *OVC Fact Sheet: What is the Office for Victims of Crime?* US Department of Justice, Office of Justice Programs, Washington, DC.

Viano, E. C. (1976) From the Editor: Victimology: The Study of the Victim. *Victimology* 1: 1–7.

video games

Greig de Peuter

Video games are played via a dedicated console connected to a television (e.g., Sony's Play Station) and computer games are played on a personal computer, or PC. These two forms of digital play comprise a lucrative sector of the global entertainment complex, an immersive, simulation-based interactive medium, a high-profile domain of youth-oriented popular culture, and a preferred leisure activity for millions of media consumers. Emerging early in the new millennium, game studies is the field of multi-disciplinary scholarship devoted to the analysis of video and computer games.

The origins of digital play lie in the US military–university complex. Cold War-era technologies that were intended to combat the "socialist threat" and to boost industrial productivity were turned upside down – from work to play – when, in 1962, student hackers at Massachusetts Institute of Technology created *Spacewar!*, one of the first computer games. This breakthrough was harnessed in the 1970s by Atari, the US corporation that led the transformation of digital play into a cultural industry. A harbinger of the "information society," the spread of video arcades and the launch of the first home-based consoles in the 1980s saw interactive entertainment suffuse cultural space, commodify "free time," and prepare many young people for the digital age.

Combining audacious marketing campaigns and innovative game design, two video game companies with roots in Japan – Nintendo and Sega – significantly expanded the gaming audience in the late 1980s and early 1990s. Giants of information capitalism Sony and Microsoft entered the business in the mid-1990s, perceiving Internet-ready game consoles as a vessel for the delivery of diverse digitalized media content into homes. Gaming meanwhile became a predominant use of PCs, driven especially by hardcore players of modem-linked games. In the first decade of the 2000s, digital play further saturated virtual space and everyday life, with the rise of "massively multiplayer" online games and mobile phone games.

Generating higher revenues than the movie box office, video and computer games are a burgeoning cultural industry. The video game side of the industry has typically featured only three console manufacturers (i.e., Microsoft, Nintendo, Sony), an oligopolistic industrial structure that makes brand marketing aggressive. Every four years or so an upgraded generation of consoles is released, galvanizing a new cycle of game production and consumption. Increasingly hit-driven, the software side of the industry has two arms: *development* involves the technical and creative labor of making games, a process that can require 50 people, nearly three years, and up to $200 million; *publishing* involves the financing and marketing of games, a sector in which ownership is highly concentrated. The computer game side of the industry is more disparately organized, because proprietary licensing agreements do not restrict what software can be made for a PC.

Kline et al. (2003) argue that the interactive entertainment industry exemplifies the technological, cultural, and marketing dynamics of production and consumption in post-Fordism: perpetual innovation, intellectual property, immaterial labor, cybernetic marketing, synergistic promotion, and "experiential" commodities whose value is rapidly exhausted. Transnationally organized, the largest games companies are headquartered in the US, Europe, or Japan, but manufacturing is frequently outsourced to countries such as China and Mexico – also the emerging consumer markets for games. Games corporations deepen the global digital divide by hyper-exploiting manufacturing labor, while they also contribute (driven by the compulsion of market expansion) to the formation of a world-spanning game audience.

The nascent field of game studies is evolving a vocabulary and an approach through which to examine games and gaming. Scholars variously emphasize that video and computer games are storytelling media (Murray 2004), narrative spaces (Jenkins 2004), and a new art form (Poole 2000). Others deconstruct the semiotics of games, looking at how the representation in game worlds of, for example, gender and violence, reproduce hegemonic ideologies and power relations. Still others emphasize the non-representational dimension of games, specifically "game mechanics," or the pro-grammed set of rules and freedoms that establish the parameters of "gameplay." The precise qualities of this medium vary widely across the diversity of game genres (e.g., first-person shooter, puzzle, role-playing, sports).

Surrounding digital play is a multifaceted gamer culture. The militaristic roots of interactive entertainment and consumer-research-led game design have etched into the culture of digital play a symbolic-subjective nexus of "militarized masculinity" (Kline et al. 2003: 246–68). Game culture is, moreover, thoroughly promotionalized. Games companies have constructed a dense web of promotional media, from magazines to online forums, that not only advertises games but also monitors players' criticisms and creative proposals; that information is fed back into the game design process, closing the loop between game production and consumption. Games are further integrated into the cross-promotional weave of popular culture via synergistic marketing (Kinder 1991). There is, however, also a bottom-up, participatory gamer culture, with hackers, culture jammers, artists, and activists altering the content of existing games and creating new ones through various "modification" techniques, from laying female "skins" over male avatars to "patching" anti-war messages into military-themed online games.

Future research on video and computer games will need to develop in three directions: (1) media theory, to grasp the particularity of this new medium, the grammar of game design, and the nature of gamers' experience of interactivity, simulation, and virtuality; (2) political economy, to examine the cultural consequences of the game sector's concentrated ownership structure and high-intensity marketing, the intellectual property battle between game companies and game piracy, and the relation between the games sector and the military; and (3) cultural studies, to inquire into the creative labor of game development, the ideological content of game narratives, and the active agency of gamers in both the commercial and the bottom-up culture of digital play.

SEE ALSO: Consumer Culture, Children's; Consumption, Youth Culture and; Culture Industries; Cyberculture; Media and Consumer Culture; Postmodern Consumption

REFERENCES AND SUGGESTED READINGS

Cassell, J. & Jenkins, H. (Eds.) (1998) *From Barbie to Mortal Kombat: Gender and Computer Games.* MIT Press, Cambridge, MA.

Jenkins, H. (2004) Game Design as Narrative Architecture. In: Wardrip-Fruin, N. & Harrigan, P. (Eds.), *First Person: New Media as Story, Performance, and Game.* MIT Press, Cambridge, MA, pp. 118–30.

Kinder, M. (1991) *Playing with Power in Movies, Television, and Video Games.* University of California Press, Berkeley.

Kline, S., Dyer-Witheford, N., & de Peuter, G. (2003) *Digital Play: The Interaction of Technology, Culture, and Marketing.* McGill-Queen's University Press, Montreal.

Murray, J. (2004) From Game-Story to Cyberdrama. Wardrip-Fruin, N. & Harrigan, P. (Eds.), *First Person: New Media as Story, Performance, and Game.* MIT Press, Cambridge, MA, pp. 2–11.

Newman, J. (2004) *Videogames.* Routledge, London.

Poole, S. (2000) *Trigger Happy: The Inner Life of Videogames.* Fourth Estate, London.

Raessens, J. & Goldstein, J. (Eds.) (2005) *Handbook of Computer Game Studies.* MIT Press, Cambridge, MA.

violence

Trutz von Trotha

Violence is a form of power, of the "ability of human beings to prevail over forces which are directed against them" (Popitz 1999: 22). It is really power in action, "action-power," as Popitz says, a way of action, above all of harm, based on the power physically and materially to hurt other creatures or to be harmed. It is determined by the boundless relation of human beings with violence: the motivations for violence are so varied and numerous that they cannot be exhausted by any list. No genetic program limits the violent behavior of humans to certain situations. Anyone can become a perpetrator and no one and almost nothing, neither human nor anything else, whatever category, is safe from victimization. Violence means to kill, to harm, to destroy, to rob, and to expel. These are the five basic forms of violence. All varieties of violence are variants and hybrids of these forms.

Among the basic forms of violence, killing stands out especially. It represents the extreme limit of violence. There is no unlimited progressive grading of violence. With killing there is *absolute* violence, an extreme limit of all social conflict, the end of dominance, power, and even sociation. As power over life and death, absolute violence is the experiential area for the idea of complete power, the source of absolute impotence, and the starting point for unlimited violent fantasies of immeasurable destruction and safe omnipotence – just as in the case of suicide, absolute violence is the source of absolute freedom. Deadly action-power constitutes the antinomy of absolute power and the fact that all power of human beings over one another is imperfect. Both can become the trigger for fundamental legitimations: for the god-like superiority of the killer and for unconditional opposition. The all-powerful ruler is surrounded by those who attempt an assassination or a coup, become martyrs, or free themselves from the ruler's absolute power by committing suicide. They all definitively limit the power of death of the ruler. Absolute violence is present in all other forms of violence, whether openly or latently. Violence is action-power within the experiential realm of the unsurpassable act of killing. These special characteristics differentiate killing from all other forms of violence.

Non-lethal, physical violence is action-power which leads to the deliberate physical harm of others or directly threatens this – ranging from the slap to sexual rape, from "police arrest" to torture. Unlike killing it can be graded. It is a form of sociation by way of the subordination and concretization of the other and the space of unlimited victim fantasies, in which all that is possible in powerless torment, despair, and humiliation is anticipated. In this sense physical violence belongs to the realm of lack of freedom, even when it is companion to the overthrow of more or less unfree political and social orders. As concerns the victim, the act of killing is pure action-power. Consequently, "binding action-power" (Popitz 1999: 47), which creates lasting instances of power and relations of domination, is in the case of killing only for the survivors. By contrast, physical violence can become binding action-power both for others and for those who are struck by physical violence.

Absolute violence and physical violence are both aimed immediately at the body, at the natural vulnerability and mortality of human beings. Therefore, notions and ideas of natural superiority and inferiority are typically associated with these forms of power – in the direct assault on the essential nature of human beings, absolute and physical violence seem to be a part of nature itself. Together with the threat of death and violence, they both as a rule stand at the beginning and end of centralized rule and of the state in particular. At the same time they are included among the most reliable guarantees for domination and its institutions of political and administrative rule.

Destructive violence and robbery are aimed at materially damaging others. It is a question of the property of others. If destructive violence – ranging from vandalism, the numerous strategies of anti-guerrilla struggle, and the "fight against terrorism" to a scorched earth policy and carpet bombing – is the deliberate physical destruction of the property of others, then the armed robber or mugger, plunderer or raider uses or threatens to resort to physical violence when stealing others (e.g., slave raids) or when depriving them of their material goods. Unlike the case of destruction, which may indirectly lead to the acquisition of the property of others or of a territory, robbery is an immediate source of enrichment.

Expulsion, especially as a collective act, is typically accompanied by all the forms of violence mentioned hereto, and may be considerably determined by the aim of enrichment. Unlike robbery, it is a case of membership – the violent or threatened violent exclusion of people beyond the physical boundaries of a social unit. In expulsion, the protagonist forces others to abandon their "house and home," their physical living space, whether it is a building, a neighborhood, or even a state territory. As in the case of killing, expulsion is notice to quit a society; however, unlike killing, this notice to quit is not absolute and is therefore in principle reversible.

Death and physical suffering, destruction of house and home, abduction, kidnapping and material loss, flight and loss of country and home town are, together with all the psychic, mental, emotional, social, and symbolic harms which always accompany them, the physical and material wounds which violence imposes. The five basic forms of violent action-power are the essential and non-extendable core of the concept of violence. The core consists of the fact that violence is not a structure but an act of power, typically and particularly in the case of collective violence combined with other forms of violence. Death, complete power, complete impotence, and physical harm throw a shadow on all forms of violence.

In the lengthy discussion which is still going on today about the concept of violence, on the one hand the long tradition of political philosophy is continued in which power and violence are seen as opposites (Arendt 1970). On the other hand, the signification of the concept of violence has either been covered over by other more general concepts or extended to become unrecognizable. Together with the concept of aggression developed in ethology and above all in psychology, the concepts of structural, cultural, and symbolic violence have proved themselves to be the longest lasting and most successful, and have been joined also by the concept of psychic violence (Nunner-Winkler 2004). Analytically, the problematic nature of these concepts lies in the fact that the connection to the above named forms of violence is lost. As a result, the sharp distinction between the numerous forms of inequalities, stigmatizations, and processes of exclusion and psychic mistreatment are lost. This emphasizes all the more the fact that the concept of violence is in particular evaluatively and normatively loaded, that it lies at the heart of the constitutive need for legitimation by power and violence, that it is an important part of legitimation discourse in political and social struggles and moral crusades, and that the idea of what violence *is* is historically interculturally and intraculturally highly variable.

In general, in sociological theory until very recently violence and especially war were neglected. Violence is one of the preferred topics of the sociology of deviance, criminality, and social problems. The latter and the sociological mainstream research into violence are first and foremost *aetiological* research into violence and have a close link to cycles and fashions of the discourses of violence and social and criminal policy. They investigate the conditions under which violence is more likely to occur, whereby the explanation for violent criminality as individual behavior and its aggregation in the form of rates of crime are foregrounded. In the sociological aetiology of violence the main emphasis is on sociostructural and institutional relations and macrosociological processes of change. Anomie, poverty, social segregation, and marginalization belong here; social groups and subcultures, social opportunity structures, family relations, socialization, and education processes no less so than general social processes of economization, individualization, and social disintegration. Among the most influential theories in which violent crimes are topicalized as one of the many forms of criminality are the unchanged continuations of classical sociology, such as anomie theory, the theory of legitimate and illegitimate opportunity structures, and the theory of subcultures. In the 1980s and 1990s control theories – where not so much criminal behavior as conformity is seen to require explanation – and the macrosociological theory of individualization and social disintegration attracted a lot of attention. With the rise of neoliberal economic policy and its driving force in the field of criminal policy, aetiological theories and research were challenged by utilitarian theory on the basis of the general theory of rational choice, which understands criminal behavior to be the result of a cost-benefit calculation. However, its reliability is treated with some skepticism. This is particularly true in the case of violent crime (Albrecht 2003).

An impressive number of analytical dimensions have shown themselves to be fertile, ranging from learning processes within the family and peer group to the transformation of whole political systems, societies, and cultures. They reflect the change in prominent incidences of violence, such as the change in public discourse about violence. Included here is the rise in civil wars, violent ethnic conflicts, terrorism, and (especially in Europe) right-wing extremist violence, as well as the "rise of the victim," where the traditional focus on the perpetrator has been abandoned in favor of the victim of violence. An enormous amount of literature has been published about violence towards children, in heterosexual partnerships, against gays, lesbians, bisexual, and transsexual victims, in the family, at school, at work, and in road incidents. The gender theory of violence is one of the most politically influential and one of the most interesting discourses for the theory of violence and attempts to provide an answer for the fact that three quarters to 99 percent of those suspected of having committed violent crimes are men: violence is primarily a male phenomenon. With the theory of patriarchy, men's studies, and gender-focused socialization theories, gender theory has taken a prominent place in the theory of violence and research into it. However, insofar as the one neglects the homosocial dimension of male violence, the others are primarily deficit theories of male violence, and attention is increasingly focused on the double distinction and dominance logic of doing masculinity: masculinity and violent masculinity in particular are established by men who set themselves apart from women, as well as from other men (Meuser 2002).

All in all, there arises from this diverse research the picture of a present in which violence is not only omnipresent but in western societies (not least as a result of scholarship and social movements) is also perceived to be all-pervasive. As political violence, violence seems to have given up its utopian-revolutionary character and can hardly be linked with a demanding western concept of politics. On the contrary, it asserts the claims of identity, belonging, and exclusion and is used as a strategy for escalation in the pursuit of power and recognition. It is a seismograph for growing social inequalities, especially as far as the segregation of the job market and housing are concerned. It is "individualized" insofar as, on the one hand, it displays the loss of social bonding forces, and on the other, the extremely varied extent of individual ways of coping with social problems. It is, however, mainly a violence which is anchored in extremely multifaceted social conditions and processes and consequently contradicts all the more the "thematization traps" (Heitmeyer & Hagan 2003) into which science and public discourse regularly

fall: the pitfalls of "reinterpretation" (i.e., of framing violence as an individual or social pathology or as a biological, genetic deficiency), the pitfalls of reductionism, "inflation," "moralization," and "scandalization," and the latter's uneven sister, the "normality trap."

In addition to the many levels of analysis, a pluralism of methods and a lively pleasure in experimentation and methodical imagination (which happened with the Chicago School at the beginning of sociology and of the sociology of deviance and crime in particular) are now enjoying a new heyday (Heitmeyer & Hagan 2003). In quantitative research the analysis of criminal statistics and research by means of questionnaires remains dominant. In the context of the former, the historical comparative research of criminal statistics is particularly relevant (Thome 2004). In Europe they show a U-shaped curve for homicide: a clear decline in the homicide rate from the fifteenth century to the middle of the twentieth century, followed by another rise since the 1960s, which would appear to be long term. The theories of Elias (2000) compete with those of Durkheim (1951, 1957) as the most appropriate explanation for this development. Elias traced the process of civilization to the relationship between the state monopoly of violence, growing interdependence, corresponding control by others, and self-control. While Durkheim saw the civilizing force in the complex differentiation and individualism of modern society, he also had a clear vision of the anomic side of the latter, which is taken up by the current prominent theories of individualization and disorganization. The use of questionnaires has continued, especially in the field of research into hidden crime, in spite of numerous methodological hurdles, including the over- or underestimation of violent criminality as a result of too small chance random samplings.

Qualitative methods of all kinds are predominantly used where little is known of the environments and cultural connections of the violent actors, either as individuals or as a collective, and for the reconstruction and analysis of subjective and collective meanings of violence, the way of life of violent protagonists, and the processes of violent interaction. An ethnography of violence has developed here for which ethnographic journalism (Buford 1991) and especially war reporting play an important role – it is still one of the most difficult and yet most banal methodological problems of research into violence that the immediate, academic observation of violence rarely occurs and is limited to a few forms and contexts. The Milgram experiment is a striking example of this: it still offers rich insights today (Blass 2000) and at the same time raises far-reaching ethical research questions.

As for the future development of violence and its discourses, six circumstances deserve particular attention: the decline of the state, the rise of terrorism and asymmetrical war, the multiplication of basic conflicts of belonging, the increasing connection between religion and violence, the pleasure in violence, and the triumphant advance of the victim. Nowadays it seems that the triumph – anchored in colonialism – of the modern western state, characterized by the monopoly of violence, in many parts of the world is rather more formal than substantial. The modern state as welfare state is under pressure even in western societies. Violence, which arises from the many precarious forms of statehood, and which is connected with the decline of the state, its transformations, and accompanying inequalities underlines the fact that the sociological problem of violence is again to be conceptualized as it was analyzed by Thomas Hobbes, Arendt, and Popitz: as a problem of order which violence both endangers and creates and guarantees, and is therefore not exclusively the domain of specialized sociologists, as is the case with the sociology of crime or of social problems. The problem of violence lies at the heart of general sociology and in particular of the sociology of power. The sociology of violence is an intercultural, comparative, historical, and political sociology of the "forms of order of violence" (Hanser & von Trotha 2002). It is a sociology of institutions, rules, meanings, perceptions, and emotional patterns, which determine how societies and cultures deal with human violence; the most important and significant among them are the political systems of rule which, as Hobbes and other political philosophers have argued, are answers to the question how people can protect themselves from violence.

They are at the same time cause as well as product of the decline of the state and

increasingly determine the appearance of and the discourses about violence (Schwab-Trapp 2002): basic conflicts of belonging where – in the shape of ethnic, religious, and racist conflicts – membership is denied and groups of people, determined by category, are violently excluded, raped, and destroyed (Wimmer et al. 2004), terrorism, and asymmetric war (Münkler 2002). With the war in the Balkans and the 9/11 attacks on the World Trade Center and the Pentagon, war has returned to Europe and the territory of the US. This has given rise to a rapid increase in research into and publications about these phenomena. It has led the sociology of war to gain a certain and hitherto unknown momentum, and contrary to the aetiological mainstream analysis of violence sociologists and anthropologists have begun to highlight that violence is not a structure but a process of interaction and escalation (Elwert et al. 1999). This is particularly true of the sociology of the asymmetric war, which in the shadow of atomic and conventional war (which itself has developed a historically incomparable potential for destruction) has become the main form of war with the greatest losses, chiefly among the civilian population. The rise of the asymmetric war has hardly foreseeable consequences for international order, foreign and domestic policy, law, and the constitution of the societies concerned. The latter include developments toward the disappearance of the traditional modern division between war and crime, and the commercialization of war.

The growing link between religion and war can be seen in many violent and war-like conflicts–the conflict between Israel and Palestine, the global small war of al-Qaeda, and the legitimization of preemptive war by means of Christian-fundamentalist missions and eschatologies by evangelical movements in the US (Armstrong 2000). It will probably pose the greatest challenge for international order, policy, culture, and society, as well as for sociology. In Europe and in sociology rooted in the modern European world, where modernization equals secularization, it is particularly difficult to face up to this challenge theoretically and empirically.

What is almost as inaccessible for this western self-image is the return of pleasure in violence. Violence is action and like sexuality it is the epitome of sensual experience – the pleasure of emotion, excitement, and physical experience, the immediacy of the moment, an escape out of the mundane into the freedom of power and the now, the appetite of youthful masculinity and of action. The pleasure in violence is a powerful element of any social order. Elias's theory of civilization is one of the most influential, contemporary social scientific theories about such pleasure. It is a sociology of power arguing that by means of the monopoly of violence and the extended chain of actions made possible by it, the pleasure in violence is removed from the members of the modern state in their daily lives; it is "civilized." However, opposing developments are too evident to enable the analysis of Elias to be continued. In asymmetrical wars and violent, ethnic, and religious conflicts, the pleasure in violence has become a cult of unchained cruelty. Even in western states the pleasure in violence is still present in various forms: in the subcultures of misery and everyday violent criminality in the French "quartiers d'exil" (Dubet & Lapeyronnie 1992), in the inner-city areas of the American equivalent, in networks of organized crime, the subcultures of prostitution and child pornography, the youth subcultures of the German "Skins," "Hools," or "Autonomous" and their soulmates in other European and non-European countries. These phenomena are only the most obvious. They require a phenomenology and ethnography of violence. In the German-speaking sociology of violence, such a debate is being held between "mainstreamers" and "innovators" (Imbusch 2004).

The rise of the culture of the victim goes together with a rise in the discourse of the victim, in which empathy and identification with the victim are self-evident. The fact remains that the culture of the victim nowadays is becoming increasingly a source for the legitimization of violence, revenge, and extensive claims to security. The world of armed conflict is determined by a discourse pattern of accusation and self-pity; the more irreconcilable, the more demanding and righteous it is, the more violent the action-power becomes. The everyday, political side of this discourse is a discourse of criminalization, punishment, and revenge by the actual or potential victims of violence (Waldmann 2003). It is directed at "security" – above all at the *sense* of security – and against all actual or potential "perpetrators of violence" that can be

imagined by the fertile imaginations of the victims. Its protagonists are a mixed bunch whose social space extends from workers to academics, from police associations and political parties to the society for the protection of minors, workers in women's safe houses, and feminist movements. Its "successes" have radically changed the reality of North American criminal law in particular: the merciless execution of the death penalty, a policy of incarceration which has meant an all-time high rate of imprisonment in the US, the return of public humiliation, and the ritual exclusion of sex offenders (Wacquant 1999). While Europe has until now largely opted out of this development, the discourse of the victim in connection with the problems of dramatically increasing social inequalities and social exclusions, of terrorism and organized crime, has however provided influential justification for the dissolution of classic legal principles. Once again it makes the Janus face of violence only too clear: it looks upon order and disorder; and in the face of order it can become a threatening grimace.

SEE ALSO: Aggression; Anomie; Bourdieu, Pierre; Capital Punishment; Civilizing Process; Conflict Theory; Crime; Criminology; Dangerousness; Domestic Violence; Ethnic Cleansing; Football Hooliganism; Fundamentalism; Gendered Aspects of War and International Violence; Genocide; Hate Crimes; Holocaust; Homicide; Marginalization; Poverty; Power, Theories of; Rape Culture; Religion; Sexual Violence and Rape; Social Disorganization Theory; Terrorism; Urban Crime and Violence; Violent Crime; War

REFERENCES AND SUGGESTED READINGS

Albrecht, G. (2003) Sociological Approaches to Individual Violence and Their Empirical Evaluation. In: Heitmeyer, W. & Hagan, J. (Eds.), *The International Handbook on Violence Research*. Kluwer, Dordrecht, pp. 611–56.
Arendt, H. (1970) *On Violence*. Harcourt, Brace & World, New York.
Armstrong, K. (2000) *The Battle for God: Fundamentalism in Judaism, Christianity and Islam*. HarperCollins, London.

Blass, T. (Ed.) (2000) *Obedience to Authority: Current Perspectives on the Milgram Paradigm.* Lawrence Erlbaum, Mahwah, NJ.

Buch, H. C. (2001) *Blut im Schuh. Schlächter und Voyeure an den Fronten des Weltbürgerkrieges.* Eichborn, Frankfurt am Main.

Buford, B. (1991) *Among the Thugs.* Secker-Warburg, London.

Dubet, F. & Lapeyronnie, D. (1992) *Les Quartiers d'exil.* Seuil, Paris.

Durkheim, É. (1951 [1897]) *Suicide: A Study in Sociology.* Free Press, Glencoe, IL.

Durkheim, É. (1957 [1950]) *Professional Ethics and Civic Morals.* Routledge & Kegan Paul, London.

Elias, N. (2000 [1936]) *The Civilizing Process: Sociogenetic and Psychogenetic Investigations.* Blackwell, Oxford.

Elwert, G., Feuchtwang, S., & Neubert, D. (Eds.) (1999) The Dynamics of Violence: Processes of Escalation and De-Escalation in Violent Group Conflict. *Sociologus,* Supplement No. 1. Duncker-Humblodt, Berlin.

Hanser, P. & von Trotha, T. (2002) *Ordnungsformen der Gewalt. Reflexionen über die Grenzen von Recht und Staat an einem einsamen Ort in Papua-Neuguinea.* Rüdiger Köppe, Köln.

Heitmeyer, W. & Hagan, J. (Eds.) (2003) *The International Handbook on Violence Research.* Kluwer, Dordrecht.

Imbusch, P. (2004) "Mainstreamer" versus "Innovateure" der Gewaltforschung. Eine kuriose Debatte. In: Heitmeyer, W. & Soeffner, H.-G. (Eds.), *Gewalt.* Suhrkamp, Frankfurt am Main, pp. 125–48.

Meuser, M. (2002) Doing Masculinity. Zur Geschlechtslogik männlichen Gewalthandelns. In: Dackweiler, R.-M. & Schäfer, R. (Eds.), *Gewalt-Verhältnisse. Feministische Perspektiven auf Geschlecht und Gewalt.* Campus, New York, pp. 53–78.

Münkler, H. (2002) *Über den Krieg. Stationen der Kriegsgeschichte im Spiegel ihrer theoretischen Reflexion.* Velbrück Wissenschaft, Weilerswist.

Nunner-Winkler, G. (2004) Überlegungen zum Gewaltbegriff. In: Heitmeyer, W. & Soeffner, H.-G. (Eds.), *Gewalt.* Suhrkamp, Frankfurt am Main.

Popitz, H. (1999) *Phänomene der Macht.* Mohr, Tübingen.

Schwab-Trapp, M. (2002) *Kriegsdiskurse. Die politische Kultur des Krieges im Wandel 1991–1999.* Leske-Budrich, Opladen.

Thome, H. (2004) Theoretische Ansätze zur Erklärung langfristiger Gewaltkriminalität seit Beginn der Neuzeit. In: Heitmeyer, W. & Soeffner, H.-G. (Eds.), *Gewalt.* Suhrkamp, Frankfurt am Main, pp. 315–345.

Wacquant, L. J. D. (1999) *Les Prisons de la misère.* Raisons d'agir, Paris.

Waldmann, P. (2003) *Terrorismus und Bürgerkrieg. Der Staat in Bedrängnis.* Gerling Akademie, Munich.

Wimmer, A. et al. (2004) *Facing Ethnic Conflicts: Toward a New Realism.* Rowman & Littlefield, Lanham, MD.

violence among athletes

Kevin Young

Aspects of violence among athletes, including behaviors encompassed within the rules as well as outside the rules of sport, have traditionally been condoned in many settings as "part of the game." This is witnessed in the way that aggressive, high-risk, or injurious practices that would be socially and/or legally intolerable apart from sports are encouraged and expected to occur in connection with sports. Further, in many countries, sport is immersed in fervent *cultures* of aggression that may serve to compromise participant safety and limit the possibility of change. Such cultures may also have influenced sport scholarship, since sociologists have paid far less attention to violence among athletes than to violence among fans.

Most sociologists agree that while there is no single cause of violence among athletes, understanding the phenomenon requires examining socialization processes associated with many sports and, indeed, with the institution of sport in general, where athletes learn from an early age that behaviors such as hitting and being hit, and conceiving of violence as a vehicle to resolve conflicts (Coakley 1989), are acceptable and easily rationalized. Combined with an emphasis in many commercialized sports on heroic values, physical dominance, and winning at all costs, thinking and behaving aggressively is simply part of the learning that individuals and groups undertake in sport. Violence among athletes is one outgrowth of this learning.

Several typologies of player violence exist, but one of the most popular and useful comes from Canadian Michael Smith (1983), who classified violence among athletes into four categories, the first two being relatively legitimate and the last two relatively illegitimate in the eyes of sports organizations and the authorities. *Brutal body contact* includes ordinary occurrences such as tackles, blocks, and body checks – acts that can be found within the official rules of many sports, and to which most would agree that consent is given or implied. *Borderline violence* involves acts prohibited by the official rules of a given sport but occur routinely and are more or less accepted by persons connected with the game (e.g., the fist-fight in ice hockey). These actions carry potential for causing injury as well as prompting further violence between players – such as, in ice hockey, the bench-clearing brawl. Historically speaking, sanctions imposed by sports leagues and administrators for borderline violence have been light and often tokenistic. *Quasi-criminal violence* violates the formal rules of a given sport, the law of the land, and, to a significant degree, the informal norms of players. This type of violence usually results in serious injury that precipitates considerable official and public attention. Quasi-criminal violence in ice hockey may include practices such as dangerous stick work, which can cause severe injury, and which often elicit in-house suspensions and fines. Finally, *criminal violence* includes behaviors so seriously and obviously outside the boundaries of acceptability for sport and the wider community that they are handled as exceptional, and possibly unlawful, from the outset. Consequently, it becomes possible to conceive of violence among athletes as sports "crime" (Young 2002). In-depth assessments of how sports violence and sports injury cases are adjudicated by the courts, and the sorts of legal defenses available to prosecuted athletes, have been advanced in a number of countries (Horrow 1980; Gardiner et al. 1998; Young 2004).

Smith's sociolegal approach is useful, but it has two limitations. First, prompted by shifting scales of public and legal tolerance since approximately the 1970s, there has been some "collapsing" of his categories. For example, incidents considered ten years ago as "quasi-criminal" or even "borderline" violence may today be brought before the courts and scrutinized seriously under law as "criminal" sports violence. In this connection, while Smith's typology addresses the important sociological

question of the "legitimacy of violence" – that is, the legitimation/delegitimation process with regard to what is perceived as acceptable violence and what is not (Ball-Rokeach 1971) – it requires updating to fit a dynamic sociolegal climate (Young 2004).

Second, Smith's typology overlooks the way in which aspects of violence among athletes may result from gender processes. Feminist work on sport and gender (Bryson 1987; Theberge 1997) allows us to understand male tolerance of risk and injury linked to aggression and violence in sport as a constituting process enhancing masculine or subcultural identity. In this respect, playing sport in a hyperaggressive way and causing or incurring injury are means of establishing positive status and career success in the form of reputational and/or material benefits. How strongly hegemonic codes of masculinity insert themselves into different sports and sports cultures varies, but it is clear that numerous sports contain "patriarchal dividends" (Connell 1995: 79) for males who are willing to "sacrifice their body" in violent ways in order to win. However, research on the masculinization of player violence is complicated by the fact that studies demonstrate that many female athletes also revere risk and the use of aggression (Rail 1992; Young & White 1995; Theberge 1997). Female involvement in high-risk, aggressive, and violent sport values thus suggests that sport socialization may be more important than gender socialization but, on this important question, far more research is needed.

A trend toward the assessment of "sports-related violence" in its broader context is evident in the way that sociologists have recently expanded their conception of "violence among athletes" to encompass actions away from the field of play. Included here are "rape cultures" that pervade locker rooms, abusive initiation ("hazing") practices, and athletes (professional and amateur) involved in domestic violence, partner abuse, as well as crimes of violence in the wider community. Such cases have not traditionally been viewed as "violence among athletes," but clearly, they are potentially abusive, injurious, or otherwise unlawful practices, performed with some consistency by athletes, that cannot easily be separated from the sports process and that only begin to make sense when the socially embedded character of sport is closely examined. Strong gender effects are visible here too, for while female athletes certainly participate in disturbing hazing rituals (Bryshun & Young 1999), it is clear that athletes involved in misogynist locker-room cultures (Curry 1991) and acts of domestic violence and "street crimes" are predominantly male (Crosset et al. 1995; Benedict & Klein 1997). Fascinating questions of the interface between hegemonic sports codes (competition, winning, dominance, etc.), hypermasculinity, poverty, and race are thus raised but remain, to this point, largely unanswered.

The literature on violence among athletes is not new, but it remains limited. First and most importantly, sociologists have not exercised care in definitional and conceptual matters. *Aggression*, which most people would accept is a normative (though not necessarily agreeable) feature of many sports, is not the same thing as *violence* itself, which is often vaguely conceived of as the "unwanted" version of the sorts of aggressive behaviors and attitudes many sports simply require. Unraveling such definitional quandaries is important, though this is admittedly complicated by varied sport-specific traditions where the definition of "wanted" and "unwanted" behavior is concerned.

After a hiatus in the late 1980s and early 1990s, sociolegal work on the relationship between sports violence and the law is being revitalized. Cross-cultural comparisons of official responses to violence among athletes have not been made available to date. From a burgeoning literature, we know something about the relationship between violence, injury, and pain, but more information is needed. Because the bulk of this research has focused on the experiences of men, studies of risk-taking, physicality, and injury among girls and women are again required, especially in light of evidence from some countries that, as opportunities open up, females are increasingly turning to aggressive, traditionally male-defined sports such as rugby, ice hockey, boxing, and martial arts.

After years of research on the sports violence/media nexus, an impressive body of material has been amassed on coverage styles, but the question of "media effects" remains prickly, and the ways that audiences deconstruct and are impacted by mediated sports violence remain uncertain.

Finally, very little is known about forms of *sports-related violence* that occur away from the field of play – the involvement of athletes, as victims or offenders, in practices such as hazing, abuse, and street crime. A recent shift by sociologists of sport in this direction, coupled with increasing media attention to and public awareness of athletes behaving badly, will expand knowledge of these additional dimensions of violence among athletes.

SEE ALSO: Deviance, Sport and; Sport as Catharsis; Sport Culture and Subcultures; Violence; Violence Among Fans

REFERENCES AND SUGGESTED READINGS

Ball-Rokeach, S. (1971) The Legitimation of Violence. In: Short, J. F. & Wolfgang, M. E. (Eds.), *Collective Violence*. Aldine, Chicago, pp. 100–11.
Benedict, J. & Klein, A. (1997) Arrest and Conviction Rates for Athletes Accused of Sexual Assault. *Sociology of Sport Journal* 14: 86–95.
Bryshun, J. & Young, K. (1999) Sport-Related Hazing: An Inquiry into Male and Female Involvement. In: White, P. & Young, K. (Eds.), *Sport and Gender in Canada*. Don Mills, ON; Oxford University Press, Oxford, pp. 269–93.
Bryson, L. (1987) Sport and the Maintenance of Masculine Hegemony. *Women's Studies International Forum* 10: 349–60.
Coakley, J. J. (1989) Media Coverage of Sports and Violent Behavior: An Elusive Connection. *Current Psychology: Research and Reviews* 7(4): 322–30.
Connell, R. (1995) *Masculinities*. University of California Press, Berkeley.
Crosset, T., Benedict, J., & Mac Donald, M. (1995) Male Student-Athletes Reported for Sexual Assault: Survey of Campus Police Departments and Judicial Affairs. *Journal of Sport and Social Issues* 19: 126–40.
Curry, T. (1991) Fraternal Bonding in the Locker Room: A Feminist Analysis of Talk about Competition and Women. *Sociology of Sport Journal* 8: 119–35.
Gardiner, S., Felix, A., James, M., Welch, R., & O' Leary, J. (1998) *Sports Law*. Cavendish, London.
Horrow, R. (1980) *Sports Violence: The Interaction between Private Lawmaking and the Criminal Law*. Carrollton Press, Arlington, VA.
Rail, G. (1992) Physical Contact in Women's Basketball: A Phenomenological Construction and

Contextualization. _International Review for the Sociology of Sport_ 27(1): 1–27.

Smith, M. (1983) _Violence and Sport._ Butterworths, Toronto.

Theberge, N. (1997) "It's Part of the Game": Physicality and the Production of Gender in Women's Hockey. _Gender and Society_ 11: 69–87.

Young, K. (2002) From "Sports Violence" to "Sports Crime": Aspects of Violence, Law, and Gender in the Sports Process. In: Gatz, M., Messner, M., & Ball-Rokeach, S. (Eds.), _Paradoxes of Youth and Sport._ State University of New York Press, New York, pp. 207–24.

Young, K. (2004) The Role of the Courts in Sport Injury. In: Young, K. (Ed.), _Sporting Bodies, Damaged Selves: Sociological Studies of Sports-Related Injury._ Elsevier, Oxford, pp. 333–53.

Young, K. & White, P. (1995) Sport, Physical Danger, and Injury: The Experiences of Elite Women Athletes. _Journal of Sport and Social Issues_ 19(1): 45–61.

violence among fans

Kevin Young

Multiple definitions of fan violence exist in the sociology of sport. Some are limited to specific behaviors, such as hand-to-hand fighting or acts of vandalism, or to violence committed in the context of a particular sport, whereas others are more expansive. Because research shows that the phenomenon is diverse, the latter definitional approach is more useful. Therefore, _violence among fans_ is best understood as involving direct or indirect acts of physical violence by sports spectators, at or away from the sports arena, that result in injury to persons or damage to property.

Unlike acts of violence among athletes, violence among fans elicits anxious responses from the authorities and often is closely policed. The occurrence of numerous injurious, and several deadly, crowd episodes has sensitized the public and social controllers to the need for careful regulation of sports crowds. In many countries fan violence is seen as a serious social problem, and strict measures, including new laws, have been introduced (Young 2000, 2002). Fans of British and European soccer have certainly

gained notoriety for their violent rituals and practices, but, in fact, violent crowd disturbances occur regularly worldwide. Many sports have been affected, some more consistently than others, and some perhaps more surprising than others. These include, but are not restricted to, baseball, cricket, ice hockey, boxing, horse racing, basketball, American and Canadian football, rugby, and, of course, soccer. It is equally apparent that violence among sports fans has a long history (Guttmann 1986).

Most sociological research has focused on forms and causes of British soccer hooliganism. In step with a popular, but not necessarily accurate (Dunning et al. 1988), perception that hooliganism began in the 1960s and 1970s, and with several tragic episodes resulting in multiple injuries and deaths at soccer games, especially in the 1980s, the literature expanded rapidly during this period, though it has diminished of late. The debates between scholars on this issue have been complex and occasionally fractious, but certain strands within this research may be identified.

One of the initial explanations of hooliganism was social psychological. Building on Tiger's (1969) controversial study of aggression among _Men in Groups_, and on presumptions of the "need" for male bonding, Peter Marsh et al. (1978) developed the "Ritual of Soccer Violence Thesis" following observations at Oxford United Football Club. Employing a so-called "ethogenic method" to explore the organization and motives of hooligan fans from an insider's point of view, Marsh et al. conceptualized aggression as a means of controlling the social world in the process of achieving certain outcomes. Therefore, fan violence at soccer matches was viewed as a cultural adaptation to the working-class environment for male British adolescents – a "ritual of teenage aggro." The contention that hooliganism is largely a ritualistic "fantasy" of violence has been severely criticized, especially for failing to explain the regularity of serious injuries at soccer games, and offering superficial explanations of the social class background of participants. There _are_ ritualistic elements to soccer "aggro" in Britain and elsewhere (for instance, many of the crowd chants and gestures, and even aspects of intergroup provocation, are certainly ritualistic), but to argue that the essence of hooliganism is ritualistic, and that actual violence seldom occurs, raises doubts about the potential of this approach, particularly when hooligan encounters have been widely reported, routinely injurious, and occasionally fatal.

In the 1970s and 1980s, Marxist criminologist Ian Taylor (1971, 1987) offered a macrosociological and class-sensitive account of soccer hooliganism. For him, hooliganism was associated with two different phases in the development of the British game and of British society more generally. First, Taylor looked historically to the emergence of soccer in working-class communities, and to the disruptive effects of commercialization on the game. Commercialization, he argued, fractured a formerly rich "soccer subculture" that weaved its way through such communities. Practices such as the invasion of playing fields and vandalism were interpreted as attempts by the remnants of this subculture to reclaim a game that had become increasingly removed from its control. In the 1980s, and clearly moved by the tragic events of the 1985 Bradford fire and Heysel Stadium riot, as well as the 1989 Hillsborough Stadium crush which resulted in the deaths of dozens of innocent lives (Young 2000), Taylor revised portions of his earlier thesis to argue that contemporary manifestations of soccer hooliganism could better be understood if placed against crises of the British state. Specifically, he argued that increasing dislocation within working-class communities and the development of an "upper" working-class jingoism (or "Little Englanderism") during the tenure of Prime Minister Margaret Thatcher's Conservative rule exacerbated Britain's hooliganism problem, and helped fuel a long sequence of xenophobically violent exchanges between fans of English club teams and of the English national team abroad and those of teams from other countries.

While sensitive to questions of history and social class, Taylor's work has been criticized for "romanticizing" any real "control" working-class fans may ever have exerted over the game during its early phases, for ignoring very early "hooligan" encounters (during, for instance, the early twentieth century and alleged "soccer consciousness" phase), and for misidentifying the majority of hooligan fans as "upper" (and thus more affluent and resourceful) working class. The fact that Taylor's ideas, while provocative, were never based on any acknowledged empirical protocol has not helped their durability, though his attempts to offer a form of "social deprivation thesis" have certainly influenced subsequent North American accounts of fan violence (Young 2002).

Taylor's Marxist views on dynamic class culture and on the development of the British game were echoed at approximately the same time by several writers at the Center for Contemporary Cultural Studies at Birmingham University, England where, once again, soccer hooliganism was viewed as a reaction by working-class males to commercializing processes, such as the increasing presentation of soccer as a market commodity, emerging in what had traditionally been construed as "the people's game." Examining deep structural changes in working-class communities, Clarke (1978) and others added a strong subcultural/ethnographic component to their class analysis, allowing them to explain the presence in the 1960s and 1970s hooligan "phases" of flamboyant skinhead groups combining traditional working-class values (such as the fierce defense of local and national identities, and love of football) with interests in commercial youth style. Relating soccer hooliganism to the context of a culture in flux is a helpful framework of analysis, and the sociohistorical approaches of Taylor, Clarke, and others certainly offer considerably more explanatory insight into a complex social problem than the microsociological ventures of Marsh et al. However, as with Taylor's early work, Clarke and colleagues actually produced little concrete evidence to support the argument that hooliganism was a response to changing working-class traditions and values. Stability of working-class social relations in an allegedly "hooligan-free" past (i.e., in the pre-1960 era) is a view that both parties tended to assume too uncritically – this, again, has not gone unnoticed by critics.

A group of sociologists at the University of Leicester (Dunning et al. 1988) have been interested to examine the "social roots" of British soccer hooliganism. Unlike Marsh and Taylor, however, the Eliasian/figurational work of the Leicester group is grounded in extensive comparisons of the phenomenon in its past and present contexts. Principally, Dunning and his colleagues argue that aggressive standards of behavior displayed by soccer hooligans are directly influenced by the social conditions and values inherent in the class-cultural background of those involved.

A predominant theme of their work, and one which represents a direct counterpoint to Taylor's "Little England" thesis, is that hooligan groups are largely comprised of individuals from the roughest and lowest (rather than "upper") sectors of the working classes. They argue that the hooligan's relatively deprived social condition is instrumental in the production and reproduction of normative modes of behavior, including strong emphases on notions of territory, male dominance, and physicality. It is precisely the reproduction of this social condition that is seen to lead to the development of a specific violent masculine style manifested regularly in the context of soccer. Notions of dynamic territoriality are also offered which allow the Leicester researchers to account for the shifting allegiances of fan support (and thus shifting expressions of fan violence) at local, regional, and international levels. While there are several unique features to the ideas of the Leicester "School," perhaps the most important is the adoption of a long-term Eliasian view regarding the development of soccer hooliganism, which allows them to demonstrate that forms of spectator disorder have existed for over a century. The Leicester research has been heavily influential in Britain and internationally, both within the academy and with policymakers.

As comprehensive as these four approaches are, they do not represent the full spectrum of work available on fan violence in the UK. Other studies which have contributed to the "hooligan debate" include, but are not limited to, Murray's (1984) social history of religious sectarianism in Scottish football, Robins's (1984) accounts of the intersections between soccer violence and the popular cultural interests of young British men, and studies of soccer, violence, and gender in Ireland (Bairner 1995).

This impressive volume of research on soccer hooliganism has not been matched elsewhere, despite the known existence of problems with violence among sports fans. In North America, for instance, where there is clear evidence of fan disorders (Young 2002), remarkably little sociological work has been tendered. The work that does exist is neither as thorough nor as theorized as the British work. Notwithstanding several

notable attempts (Smith 1983) to explain North American fan violence in terms of its social causes, there seems to be a general reluctance on the part of researchers to take the phenomenon seriously, and far more work is needed. Indeed, despite the fact that the bulk of the research on violence among fans relates to transatlantic contexts and experiences, many countries where organized sport is played and valued have recorded problems with fan violence at one time or another. Regrettably, however, the research, and especially that portion of it written in or translated into English, remains slim, and there are no clear ways of classifying or categorizing this work into thematic "schools" or coherent bodies of theory.

Janet Lever's (1983) work on fan violence associated with Brazilian soccer set an early marker for the international research. Using a structural functionalist approach, Lever sought to show how sport in South America can represent both unifying and divisive properties – unifying in the sense that it may enhance community awareness and loyalty, but divisive because it underlines social class distinctions. Fan violence, she argues, is but one side-effect of failed attempts by the Brazilian authorities to deal with poverty and such class distinctions – soccer stadiums have often been used as a venue for the expression of class conflict such as missile throwing from the "poorer" stadium sections into the "richer" sections. Arguably, Lever's functionalist approach cannot easily account for these tensions and her study is now outdated, but it nevertheless represents groundbreaking sociological work on fan violence in South America. A more contemporary account of fan violence in this context may be found in Archetti and Romero (1994).

By now, most serious students of sports violence understand that the argument that soccer hooliganism is a "British Disease" is a myth. In their early figurational studies, Williams et al. (1984) unearthed over 70 reports of fan violence at soccer games in 30 different countries in which English fans were not involved between 1904 and 1983. Slightly later, Williams and Goldberg (1989: 7) identified numerous cases of hooliganism where English fans were, in fact, the "victims of foreign hooliganism" rather than the assailants. Today, cases of fan violence in diverse international contexts are routinely reported in the popular media and over the Internet.

Notwithstanding cultural variance in the nature and extent of fan violence, evidence indicates that soccer hooliganism expanded throughout the 1980s in a number of European countries. A considerable European research literature also emerged at this time. Greece, France, Spain, Belgium, Austria, Sweden, the Netherlands, Germany, and Italy are among countries known to have experienced significant problems with soccer hooliganism (Young 2000: 389). In many of these locations, fan violence has been shown to intersect with far right-wing politics and racist ideologies, demonstrating a clear sociological link between problems in sport and those in the wider society.

While care must always be taken to differentiate between injuries caused by intentional fan violence and those caused by "accidental" crowd surges or stampedes prompted by such things as over-ticketing, negligent policing, or stadium collapses, in terms of total numbers of injuries and fatalities, some of the most serious cases of injurious and fatal fan episodes have occurred in South and Central American locations. For example, a by now well-known riot broke out at the National Stadium in Lima, Peru in May 1964, resulting in over 300 deaths, and in another notorious case of soccer-related violence, a so-called "Soccer War" lasting several days was waged between Honduras and El Salvador in the summer of 1969 following a game played between the two countries. More recently, 83 people were killed and over 150 others injured in a stampede linked to the distribution of forged tickets at a 1996 World Cup qualifying game held in Guatemala City (Young 2000: 389).

Violence among sports fans is a multidimensional and complex topic that has generated a huge volume of research on matters such as causes, manifestations and responses, and media coverage, but this research shows serious imbalances. For example, while there seems little doubt that the most substantial and rigorously theorized body of work in this area has examined forms and causes of British soccer hooliganism, relatively little is known about fan violence in other parts of the world. Again, this is true of North America, for instance, where the phenomenon is acknowledged by sports organizations and authorities alike, but where, with only a few exceptions, much of what we know comes from descriptive and often less than reliable media accounts (Young 2002).

The portion of the research on fan violence summarized here underlines the importance of approaching the topic in ways that respect a historically informed sociology of cultural practices like sport. Culture is important because the often heterogeneous manifestations and meanings of fan violence develop in distinct ways in distinct places, as we can see from the varied manner in which fans from European countries differentially aggress at soccer games (Williams & Goldberg 1989). History is important because these manifestations and meanings always emerge from prior social arrangements, as the work of the Leicester School ably demonstrates. And, a sociology of fan violence is critical because, far from existing in a vacuum, the actions and practices of unruly sports fans coexist relationally with wider social institutions and processes, as can be witnessed by the deeply gendered character of fan violence, which remains a predominantly male activity. Again, cultural differences exist in this regard.

Finally, part of the complexity of explaining fan violence concerns the methodological fact that it is not easy to study. As with other aspects of crime and social "deviance," while outlining the main behavioral components of the phenomenon is relatively uncomplicated (we know how fan violence is *done*), detailing its causes, extent, and nature is not. This is particularly the case where fan violence is not restricted to one sport or one level of sport (Young 2002). Understanding the causes, extent/nature, and motives and meanings of fan violence requires careful and committed research that must overcome familiar problems of access, "entry," and reliability. To this point, the British research stands out as that body of work that has most consistently tackled these dilemmas, but the continued existence of violence among fans in other countries surely means that others must follow suit in due course.

SEE ALSO: Figurational Sociology and the Sociology of Sport; Football Hooliganism; Soccer; Sport as Catharsis; Sport Culture and Subcultures; Subcultures, Deviant; Violence; Violence Among Athletes

REFERENCES AND SUGGESTED
READINGS

Archetti, E. P. & Romero, A. C. (1994) Death and
Violence in Argentinian Football. In: Giulianotti,
R., Bonney, N., & Hepworth, M. (Eds.), *Football
Violence and Social Identity*. Routledge, London,
pp. 37–73.
Bairner, A. (1995) Soccer, Masculinity, and Violence
in Northern Ireland. Paper presented at the North
American Society for the Sociology of Sport,
Sacramento, CA, November 1–4.
Clarke, J. (1978) Football and Working-Class Fans:
Tradition and Change. In: Ingham, R. (Ed.), *Foot-
ball Hooliganism: The Wider Context*. Inter-Action
Inprint, London.
Dunning, E., Murphy, P., & Williams, J. (1988)
*The Roots of Football Hooliganism: An Historical
and Sociological Study*. Routledge & Kegan Paul,
London.
Guttmann, A. (1986) *Sports Spectators*. Columbia
University Press, New York.
Lever, J. (1983) *Soccer Madness*. University of Chi-
cago Press, Chicago.
Marsh, P., Rosser, E., & Harré, R. (1978) *The Rules
of Disorder*. Routledge & Kegan Paul, London.
Murray, B. (1984) *The Old Firm: Sectarianism, Sport,
and Society in Scotland*. John Donald, Edinburgh.
Robins, D. (1984) *We Hate Humans*. Penguin,
Markham, ON.
Smith, M. D. (1983) *Violence and Sport*. Butter-
worths, Toronto.
Taylor, I. (1971) Soccer Consciousness and Soccer
Hooliganism. In: Cohen, S. (Ed.), *Images of
Deviance*. Penguin, New York, pp. 134–65.
Taylor, I. (1987) Putting the Boot into a Working-
Class Sport: British Soccer after Bradford and
Brussels. *Sociology of Sport Journal* 4: 171–91.
Tiger, L. (1969) *Men in Groups*. Thomas Nelson,
London.
Williams, J. & Goldberg, A. (1989) Spectator Beha-
viour, Media Coverage, and Crowd Control at the
1988 European Football Championships: A
Review of Data from Belgium, Denmark, the Fed-
eral Republic of Germany, Netherlands, and the
United Kingdom. Council of Europe, Strasbourg.
Williams, J., Dunning. E., & Murphy, P. (1984)
*Hooligans Abroad: The Behaviour and Control of
English Fans in Continental Europe*. Routledge &
Kegan Paul, London.
Young, K. (2000) Sport and Violence. In: Coakley, J.
& Dunning, E. (Eds.), *Handbook of Sports Studies*.
Sage, London, pp. 382–408.
Young, K. (2002) Standard Deviations: An Update
on North American Sports Crowd Disorder.
Sociology of Sport Journal 19: 237–75.

violent crime

Rosemary Gartner

In popular discourse, violent crime is the intentional, malicious physical injury of one person
by another, with assault, rape, and murder being
obvious and apparently uncontroversial examples. In legal discourse, violent crime is behavior
that leads to particular legal procedures and is
thereby legally sanctionable. Here violent crime
is constituted by legal reactions, not by characteristics inherent in behaviors or people. Legal
definitions may appear precise and objective,
but because they are created and applied
through social and political processes, legally
defined violent crime is historically and socially
constructed. Social scientists acknowledge this
but typically rely on legal definitions to delimit
the violent acts they study (Jackman 2002).

Documenting and explaining the distribution
of violent crime across time, place, and persons
are the major tasks of those who study it. Most
nations and sub-national jurisdictions compile
reports on crimes known to police, which
include information on accused, victim, and
incident characteristics. There are two principal
limitations to these official statistics. First,
because legal definitions of even serious crimes
vary across time and place, official statistics may
not accurately measure differences in the prevalence of violent behaviors across societies or
over time. Second, because characteristics of the
legal agencies that collect information on crime
influence how acts are interpreted and reported,
official statistics do not accurately measure
levels of violent crime even within a single
society. Some violent acts that fit legal definitions are subject to criminal enforcement less
often than others. For example, in most nations,
well under half of physical and sexual assaults
are reported to police (Nieuwbeerta 2002). Since
authorities learn about violent crime primarily
from the public, popular views on the serious-
ness of particular violent acts, as well as perceptions of the legitimacy of legal officials, also
influence which acts are reported. Official statistics on violent crime therefore underrepresent
its true prevalence.

Unofficial data sources, such as general population surveys, avoid some of these problems by

providing information on violent crimes not known to officials. Victimization and self-report surveys, which ask people about their violent victimization and/or offending over a specified period, yield higher estimates of the prevalence of violent crime than do official statistics. Victimization surveys also show that the likelihood that violent crimes will become known to officials depends partly on their severity, as well as on characteristics of victims, offenders, and the relationships between them. However, because victimization and self-report surveys rely on the honesty, memory, and perceptions of respondents, they have their own limitations and biases.

Is there more violent crime today than in the past? The most reliable historical evidence comes from Western Europe and North America, where trends over the last six or seven centuries have been downward, albeit punctuated by short-term crime waves (Eisner 2003). This decline reversed somewhat in North America and Western Europe in the 1970s and in Eastern Europe in the 1980s, when violent crime rates rose dramatically. Nevertheless, interpersonal violence has become a much less customary part of daily life over the long term.

Are some societies more prone to violent crimes? Data from victimization surveys and public health records suggest that rates of lethal violence vary greatly, even among similar societies (Nieuwbeerta 2002). For example, homicide rates are about three times higher in the US than in Canada and four times higher in Venezuela than Chile. Countries in Northern Africa and the Middle East appear to have lower rates of serious interpersonal violence, as do many Asian countries. Interestingly, rates of sub-lethal and lethal violence do not correlate highly: countries with high homicide rates do not consistently have high rates of assault and robbery (Zimring & Hawkins 1997).

What social processes, conditions, or policies affect rates of violent crime? The centuries-long decline in violence in the West was likely due to the expansion of state powers, the Protestant Reformation, and the rise of modern individualism (Eisner 2003). In contemporary societies, homicide rates are higher where inequalities in income and wealth are greater and where there are few restrictions on the ownership and use of firearms. Some of the factors commonly thought to affect violent crime (e.g., urbanization, unemployment, or the death penalty) do not, in fact, appear to do so.

Are some people more likely to be involved in violence? Serious violent crimes tend to be the domain of young, economically disadvantaged males virtually everywhere (Reiss & Roth 1993). Most violent offenders have criminal records, but few specialize in violence. Victims of violent crime, with the exception of rape victims, generally share many characteristics with their victimizers (i.e., they also tend to be young, economically disadvantaged males). Females are more likely to be victims than offenders; most female victims are attacked by males they are related to or are intimately involved with. A substantial proportion of violent crimes occurs among relatives or persons well known to each other, though this proportion is smaller in the US than other countries, and has been declining.

Most sociological explanations of violent crime focus on one of three levels of analysis: the individual, the situational, or the structural-cultural (Sampson & Lauritsen 1994). Individual-level analyses look for characteristics that predispose or fail to discourage people from violence. Situational approaches attend to the context and processes immediately surrounding violent events, such as the nature of the interaction among participants and the presence of weapons or bystanders. Structural-cultural approaches look at broader social forces, processes, and value systems shaping violent motivations and opportunities.

Most sociological research on violent crime has focused on interpersonal violence among individuals. But with recent changes in global politics and governance, sociologists are now confronted with violent behaviors, such as terrorist acts and war crimes, that present both challenges to traditional methods and theories, as well as opportunities for evaluating accepted knowledge about violent crime.

SEE ALSO: Crime; Domestic Violence; Hate Crimes; Homicide; Measuring Crime; Rape/Sexual Assault as Crime; Sexual Violence and Rape; Urban Crime and Violence; Violence

REFERENCES AND SUGGESTED READINGS

Eisner, M. (2003) Long-Term Historical Trends in Violent Crime. In: Tonry, M. (Ed.), *Crime and Justice: A Review of Research*, Vol. 30. University of Chicago Press, Chicago, pp. 83–142.

Jackman, M. (2002) Violence in Social Life. *Annual Review of Sociology* 28: 387–415.

Nieuwbeerta, P. (Ed.) (2002) *Crime Victimization in Comparative Perspective*. Boom Juridische uitgevers, Den Haag.

Reiss, A. J. & Roth, J. A. (Eds.) (1993) *Understanding and Preventing Violence*. National Academy Press, Washington, DC.

Sampson, R. J. & Lauritsen, J. (1994) Violent Victimization and Offending: Individual, Situational, and Community-Level Risk Factors. In: Reiss, A. J. & Roth, J. (Eds.), *Understanding and Preventing Violence*, Vol. 3. National Academy Press, Washington, DC, pp. 1–114.

Zimring, F. E. & Hawkins, G. (1997) *Crime is Not the Problem: Lethal Violence in America*. Oxford University Press, New York.

virtual sports

Michael Atkinson

Virtual sports are symbolic representations of embodied, expressive, and "real world" athletic experiences. These sports can involve complete "out of body" practices wherein participants "play" a sport without exerting their bodies in a traditionally athletic way (i.e., a sports video game), or more embodied performances involving physical activity in a simulated sports environment (i.e., athletic movement in a modified sports setting like a cyclists' wind tunnel). Centrally, virtual sports involve human beings as either real or represented athletes in a technologically enhanced setting. Although certain ludic activities might be considered representations of sport (e.g., "touch" football, "pick up" ice hockey, or go-kart racing), virtual sports are those that place either embodied or computer generated athletes in simulated sports spaces.

Virtual sport has, by and large, escaped sociological scrutiny. Nevertheless, three types of virtual sport are ripe for investigation. First, and perhaps most commonly, virtual sports abound in home and arcade video games. Through the advent of home entertainment systems in the 1970s and 1980s such as Atari, Intellivison, Collecovision, and Vectrex, sports video games became a staple of both popular and youth cultures in North America. From the 1980s onward, game players have competed in virtual sports ranging from hockey to basketball to hunting to skateboarding. Indeed, one of the very first video games commercially marketed in the US, Pong, resembled a crude form of table tennis. Since then, digitally refined and interactively dynamic computer systems such as Sega, Nintendo, Odyssey, Play Station, and X-Box have enabled consumers to play practically every mainstream western sport. Sports games presently account for approximately 20 percent of video game sales in North America, the world's largest gaming market, grossing US$8 billion yearly (Liberman 2003).

Second, virtual sports enthusiasts now have access to physically interactive video games. For example, players may literally "step into" virtual golf courses. A person stands on an Astroturfed tee box holding an electronically sensored golf club, and swings at a virtual ball. A simulated ball instantaneously appears on a large video screen situated several feet in front of the tee box, and flies down the virtual course according to the celerity and spin at which it had been virtually struck. Individuals may play an entire round of golf on the machine, selecting from any number of professional courses. People may also use similar machines (for a cost of US$10–100) to drive virtual race cars, bat against virtual Major League Baseball pitchers, shoot virtual basketballs, ride virtual race horses, or even paddle virtual kayaks.

Third, simulated sports environments may be utilized as training tools for elite athletes. Virtual training machines carefully monitor and strictly control the effort levels of athletes in order to study and help improve their physical abilities. For example, swimmers are often placed in "current tanks" to scientifically evaluate the efficiency of their strokes and pinpoint $VO_2(max)$ rates. Elite-level ice hockey players' skating strides are technically studied in laboratories by using treadmills with simulated ice surfaces. Professional cyclists straddle stationary racing bikes in wind rooms and "peddle through" virtual rides that appear on video screens in front of them; twisting and turning when they go through turns, and exerting effort when tackling hills.

The ascendance of virtual sport over the past 30 years points to how a host of "sociogenic" (Elias 1994) shifts within western cultures have altered our understandings of embodied athleticism. First, virtual sports are of increasing importance at a time in which both amateur and professional sports are intensely commercialized. Sociologists of sport suggest that, particularly in western nations with state-sponsored, rigidly institutionalized and professional sports cultures, the entire sporting experience is fragmented into market commodities, including sport simulations that allow users to become more actively involved fans. As sport is consumed as a popular culture commodity, sports organizations profit by aggressively tapping home entertainment/gaming markets. Many global and national sports organizations license and/or package virtual game experiences for consumers, allowing them to create fantasy leagues and manipulate player performance at the push of a button or thrust of a joystick.

Second, athletic contests are globally promoted as contexts of social "mimesis" (Elias & Dunning 1986) by sports marketers. Audiences are sold virtual sport as symbols of emotionally charged and risky, yet rule-bound, scenarios of physically intense competition. Because of the openness of the aggression, struggle, and toughness in sports, they provide a type of "exciting significance" for audiences. Virtual sports games highlight and exaggerate the taken-for-granted physicality and mimesis inherent in both mainstream and alternative sports. Extreme hitting, bloodletting, brutal tackling, and flamboyant injuries, for example, are common in virtual sports games. Rules are broken without penalty, virtual players do not experience the catastrophic effects of rough play, and users receive reward incentives within games for the number of on-field hits levied or styles of aggressive play mastered.

Third, the booming popularity of virtual sports games should be contextualized against what postmodern sociologists like Baudrillard (1983) refer to as the "simulation" of social reality. Virtual sports games, for instance, create hyper-representations of embodied athleticism

and transform social constructions of "real" sport for users. The games not only mimic what actually occurs in sport, they now partially define what audiences expect from embodied sports. Virtual games may also be more accessible forms of sport for many users, as one can play dozens of sports regardless of physical fitness level. Furthermore, one is granted an unprecedented agency to mold the contours and parameters of an athletic contest at whim (i.e., players involved, physical settings, length of competitions, speed of games, and rule structures). Comparatively, for athletes who are "plugged into" virtual sports machines, simulated sports fields allow for incredible physical exertion without many of the physical dangers inherent in competition. Therefore, performance evaluating or rehabilitating sports machines generate simulated contexts of performance so that athletes may become "swifter, higher, and stronger" during competition.

Fourth, virtual sports underscore how machines and bodies cybernetically intersect in western cultures. Donna Haraway (1991) noted, some time ago, that the postmodern era is one in which corporeality is increasingly breeched by technology. For Haraway and others, it is difficult to conceive of any social activity, including a full gamut of sports performances, that has evaded technological improvement, innovation, control, and monitoring. When individuals are able to kick a soccer ball, catch a baseball, throw a javelin, or perform a ski jump by tapping a computer button or moving the body expressively in a "sports-like motion" in front of video sensors, one cannot overlook how athleticism is deeply tied to computer technology.

Fifth, the prominence of virtual sports reflects emergent cultural preferences for stationary, home-based digital entertainment. Virtual sports participation through video game play jibes with athletically inactive North American lifestyles. Virtual sports fit nicely into the social "sit down" lifestyles widely attributed to long school or work days, poor dietary practices, and exposure to computers as everyday tools. Troublingly, at a time when physical passivity in the leisure sphere and overall obesity rates are on the rise in North America, and as physical education programs are disappearing from educational curricula at all institutional levels, virtual games are a primary form of sports participation for "growing" populations of North Americans (Clocksin et al. 2002).

Extant theoretical deconstructions of virtual sports are narrow in both scope and content. The bulk of the limited empirical research on virtual sports addresses how exposure to aggressive sports games is correlated with aggressive interpersonal behaviors (Bensley & Van Eenwyk 2001). Virtual sports are especially targeted in the contemporary moral panic about youth deviance and the consumption of violent video games. Using a blend of social psychological, behavioral, and sociobiological theories, researchers argue that virtual sports games desensitize users to extreme violence and confound users' understanding of real-world aggression. Yet despite nearly three decades of concentrated empirical research on youth violence and video game play, there is no consensus among social scientists that virtual sports play a causal role in any category of criminal or otherwise assaultive behavior.

Second, political economists study virtual sports as vacuous cultural commodities. Authors including Postigo (2003) weave a pastiche of Marxist, cultural studies, and post-industrial theories to evidence how virtual sports have little use-value but great exchange-value among youth groups. Virtual sports alienate users from embodied athletic experiences and diminish the socially interactive aspects of competitive sport. As critics of virtual sport, political economists contend that athletes, teams, and leagues utilize video games as vehicles for crassly soliciting fan investment into athletics. Furthermore, they argue, virtual sports like video games discourage the first-hand experience of athleticism in sport, and motivate individuals to participate passively via video interface.

Third, sociologists of sport employ post-modernist theories to examine the impacts of computer technology on athlete training, performance, and rehabilitation. Sociologists including Debra Shogan (1999) study athletes' bodies as fragmented, technologically invaded, and subject to penetration/improvement at the hands of therapists, doctors, and trainers. Athletes, as the subjects and targets of medical knowledge bases, are strategically crafted into cybernetic entities that resemble carefully engineered machines rather than embodied agents. Virtual sport machines used in athletic training or in recreational leisure pursuits blur the boundaries between "natural" human performance and artificially engineered, hyperreal athletics. The postmodern athlete is one whose performance is carefully mapped, dissected, analyzed, predicted, and monitored by a full spectrum of computer systems.

Existing research on virtual sports explores only a small range of data collection techniques and strategies. Social experiments, self-report surveys, content analysis, and to a lesser extent interviewing, are the main methods structuring empirical investigations of virtual sports and their cultural significance. Dominant research questions tend to focus on popular sports video games played, the impact of virtual sports on fan communities, and the significance of virtual sports for improving real-world athletic performance.

Future research on virtual sports should encourage methodological diversity. At present, the population of virtual sports enthusiasts is not well defined, nor is the social significance of virtual sports across cultural lifestyles sufficiently probed. This is largely due to the methodological targeting of certain populations of "home system" game players (typically, young males from the middle class), online players (a similar population as home system players), or elite-level athletes. We must determine, in the broadest sense, what groups participate in virtual sport, which have access to virtual sport, and how they are intersubjectively defined as socially meaningful. In particular, questions pertaining to users' interpretive constructions of virtual sports should be pursued via qualitative methods. More exploratory and in-depth ethnographic methods (i.e., participant observation, visual ethnography, or auto-ethnography) might be tapped with greater fervor in this process.

Substantively, future research should venture beyond "game play-aggression" hypotheses and cyborg case studies. Dominant approaches to the study of virtual sports highlight the solitary, anti-social, and disembodied natures of game play for participants. Resultantly, we know very little about the socially integrative function of virtual sports or their creative insertion into everyday group practices. Particular attention might be given to online, multi-user, "real-time" sports gaming. Through the advent of online MUDs (Multi-User Domains), MOOs (MUD

Object Oriented systems), and other forms of computer-mediated-communication (CMC), virtual sports enthusiasts cooperatively interact within digital game worlds. Online virtual sport spaces are relationship building and socially organizing contexts wherein individuals socially interface through shared games. Sport-specific online leagues form through the efforts of hundreds or even thousands of participants scattered across the world. As part of studying ongoing globalization processes in sports worlds, sociologists might inspect how the innovation of online, virtual sports cultures erodes traditional time/space social barriers.

Future research on virtual sport should also examine potential ethical problems accompanying the increased reliance on computer technologies in athletics. For example, sociologists should question: Are virtual sport technologies available to all elite athletes, and if not, is this a source of stratification among them? Are unfair advantages created for athletes who access the premier virtual training and rehabilitation technologies? Does the adoption of virtual sport in training stress the science of athletic performance over its humanistic elements? Does video game play discourage rigorous physical activity and athleticism? Are youth cultures persuaded to consume sport in commodity form, and not as athletes? What role does virtual sport hold in the thickening of westerners' waistlines? Do online virtual sports actually facilitate community building and social interchange in ways embodied sports involvements do not?

SEE ALSO: Cyberculture; Figurational Sociology and the Sociology of Sport; Simulation and Virtuality; Sport; Sport and the Body; Video Games

REFERENCES AND SUGGESTED READINGS

Baudrillard, J. (1983) *Simulations*. Semiotext(e), New York.

Bensley, L. & Van Eenwyk, J. (2001) Video Games and Real Life Aggression: Review of the Literature. *Journal of Adolescent Health* 29(4): 244–57.

Clocksin, B., Watson, D., & Ransdell, L. (2002) Understanding Youth Obesity and Media Use: Implications for Future Intervention Programs. *Quest* 54(4): 259–74.

Elias, N. (1994) *The Civilizing Process*. Blackwell, Oxford.

Elias, N. & Dunning, E. (1986) *The Quest for Excitement: Sport and Leisure in the Civilizing Process*. Blackwell, Oxford.

Haraway, D. (1991) *Simians, Cyborgs, and Women: The Reinvention of Nature*. Free Association Press, New York.

Liberman, N. (2003) Sports Video Games Still Scoring Big. *Street and Smith's Sports Business Journal* 6(11): 7–13.

Postigo, H. (2003) From Pong to Planet Quake: Post-Industrial Transitions from Leisure to Work. *Information, Communication and Society* 6(4): 593–607.

Shogan, D. (1999) *The Making of High Performance Athletes: Discipline, Diversity and Ethics*. University of Toronto Press, Toronto.

W

war

Wolfgang Knöbl

To find an uncontested definition of war is an almost impossible task. Although definitions characterizing wars as major and oftentimes longlasting conflicts between political groups (especially states or nation-states) and carried out by armed forces seem to be useful and convincing at first sight, they are not without problems. The difficulty lies not so much in the vagueness of terms like "major conflict" (how many injured or dead people make a war?) or "longlasting conflict" (there were certainly wars in history that lasted decades; however, can there be wars that last only hours?). The real problem with such definitions is the close link between war and the state. This link is a nuisance for those social scientists who – as social anthropologists or historians – have to deal with conflicts in areas or periods without states. And it is an obstacle for sociologists and political scientists who deal with contemporary conflicts in regions where once existing states have vanished as sovereign political units and where a variety of groups use their potential of violence in an often gruesome way. Is this form of mass violence to be called "war"? Or is it another type of conflict? Thus, the problem of definition is on the agenda again.

Although analyses of war (and peace) are probably as old as historiography, *systematic* research into this topic did not start before the European Enlightenment. This research, however, focused much more on the conditions of peace than on the realities of war: with clearly normative intentions, philosophers from Thomas Hobbes to Jean-Jacques Rousseau and Immanuel Kant reflected on the possibilities of *preventing* war. It was only after that period that

a first analysis of war *as dynamic process* was published, Carl von Clausewitz's famous and posthumously published treatise *On War* (1832). Clausewitz interpreted war as a continuation of politics by other means, but he never regarded war as a process planned and carried out exclusively by rational actors. On the contrary, Clausewitz framed war with his "trinitarian formula," arguing that war has to be seen as an intersection of actions of governments, populations, and military commanders, actions that are motivated by rationality, but also by hatred and hostility and by daring calculations of chances.

The publication date of Clausewitz's treatise ironically coincided with the beginning of sociology since it was exactly around that time that Auguste Comte wrote his *Cours de la philosophie positive*—"ironically," because Comte already seemed to belong to a completely different world; whereas Clausewitz's thinking was deeply shaped by the experience of the Revolutionary and Napoleonic Wars, Comte's writings were impregnated by the liberal belief in continuous progress toward a peaceful and rational society. It was Comte who argued that history can be divided into three periods, a theological, a metaphysical, and a scientific era, the last one Comte's own period dominated by a scientific spirit that in the end will eradicate all militaristic ambitions and adventures. Thus, Comte formulated a thesis that became a kind of premise for the majority of sociologists in the second half of the nineteenth and twentieth centuries, the liberal thesis of a strict incompatibility between war and industrial society. According to this thesis, war is some kind of archaic and disappearing relic that therefore does not need to be analyzed in much detail, a point – though somewhat transformed – ironically shared by socialists and Marxists alike, since they also expected the end of war, at least within the historical stage of socialism. It is revealing that both liberal and socialist theorists of imperialism (Hobson and Schumpeter; Lenin and Luxemburg) were much more interested in the political or economic causes of imperialist wars, not in war itself and its consequences.

Thus, within the early phase of the history of the discipline, it is difficult to find sociologists seriously and systematically analyzing war – precisely because of this liberal (and socialist) premise. True, in Max Weber's huge oeuvre one will always find scattered though certainly interesting hints at the consequences of warfare for societal development. But it is also true that most of the other founding fathers of sociology were rather quiet on that subject. It was only during World War I that Émile Durkheim, Georg Simmel, or George Herbert Mead were more or less forced to write something about war, but the pieces they published were definitely not at the heart of the ideas for which they became famous. Werner Sombart's well-known book *Krieg und Kapitalismus* (*War and Capitalism*, 1913), in which he sketched war's positive economic effects on the economy of early modern Europe, remained an exception.

Interestingly, the sociological neglect of matters of war did not really change that much with the coming of the two world wars: World War II and its aftermath saw the establishment of military sociology in the United States and the publication of Samuel Stouffer's marvelous *The American Soldier*, but – strangely enough – this alone did not put war on the sociological agenda: although one of the four volumes of Stouffer's multivolume work described and theorized "combat experience" and thus one of the central topics of war, the other volumes focused much more on the military as an institution and thus laid the groundwork for military sociology as a subdiscipline which above all analyzes organizational structures and problems of armed forces. War was only a side aspect of this research program. Thus, only some isolated figures shouldered the task of analyzing war and its societal consequences, notably Emil Lederer during World War I, Hans Speier just before and during World War II, and Stanislaw Andreski, Raymond Aron, and Morris Janowitz in the three decades after 1945.

It was not until the rise of historical sociology in the late 1970s and the coming of a new world order after the collapse of the Soviet Empire that war, and especially *the consequences of war*, really began to be theorized in a systematic way by closely connected groups of researchers. Starting with Theda Skocpol's *States and Social Revolutions* (1979), the debate focused very much on how European modernity was shaped by the impact of wars. Whereas Skocpol had argued that especially the French and the Russian Revolutions and their outcomes can only be understood by focusing on international contexts, and particularly on the crises of state administrations weakened by longlasting or lost wars, others emphasized how the modern state and its monopoly of violence were the result of violent interstate conflicts: it was only by constant warfare that large state bureaucracies were built in Europe, bureaucracies for the purpose of extracting resources out of civil society in order to finance large standing armies. Even the rise of democracy and welfare states historically seemed to be closely connected with war since suffering populations could organize and successfully demand suffrage and social rights (see Porter 1994). And, last but not least, war was also linked to internal repression since the militarization of societies as a consequence of war sometimes led to ethnic cleansing or even genocide (Shaw 2003).

However, this kind of historical-sociological research also made clear that war is not a homogeneous variable since different kinds of war have very different effects. Even within the context of the nineteenth and twentieth centuries at least four types of war are to be distinguished: (1) interstate wars between neighboring or competing nations; (2) colonial wars in which mostly European expeditionary forces usually defeated indigenous groups and populations in various parts of the world; (3) civil wars between established state apparatuses and rebels; and (4) wars of national liberation against mostly European colonial powers, a type of war that only came into being after 1945.

The common feature of all these types of war is that a more or less powerful state is at least on one side of the conflict. But what about major conflicts in which states are missing? As indicated above, this increasingly becomes a problem for researchers specialized in some regions of the contemporary world where states have ceased to exist – but not mass violence. The debate on state failure and state breakdown that had started at the beginning of the 1980s and focused very much on some African and Latin American regions had a huge impact on war research as well. Some analysts have begun to talk about so-called "new wars" (Kaldor 1999) that usually take place in spaces where the state monopoly of violence has vanished and where various types of combatants – armed bandits, ethnic groups, parts of former state elites, etc. – are violently fighting for resources. These conflicts – so the argument goes – are not shaped by clearly defined ideological or political goals any longer as, for example, the wars of liberation in the period of decolonization. On the contrary, this type of war is almost exclusively dependent on its own peculiar economy (Jean & Rufin 1996) since in the era of globalization combatants are able to use resources brought in by humanitarian organizations and ethnic and other groups living abroad. Since aid and transfer payments usually continue for a long time, these "new wars" can last a long time as well, wars in which clear-cut demarcations between combatants and civilians can no longer be detected and in which so-called child soldiers as well as private military firms play a significant role.

As these troubled spots and spaces and their "new wars" are often seen as major threats to either particular western states or to the world community as a whole, the number of military interventions by mostly western states (or UN forces) has dramatically increased since the end of the 1990s. Thus, one of the latest trends within social science research is the focus on these interventions. In contrast to former periods, the high-tech warfare of western states often does not seem to affect western civilian populations very much and does not even risk the lives of western soldiers – but does often lead to many casualties among the population of those regions where western armed forces strike (see Shaw's term "risk-transfer war"). It remains to be seen, however, whether warfare really does not have much effect on the homefront of (western) democratic societies, since wars – even those fought in faraway places and without many body bags coming home – do always restructure the domestic political scene. That research, however, has only recently started (see Merom 2003).

SEE ALSO: Anti-War and Peace Movements; Democracy; Ethnic Groups; Gendered Aspects of War and International Violence; Genocide; Liberalism; Military Research and Science and War; Military Sociology; Modernity; Nation-State; Peace and Reconciliation Processes; Peacemaking; Sovereignty; World Conflict

REFERENCES AND SUGGESTED READINGS

Andreski, S. (1954) *Military Organization and Society*. Routledge & Kegan Paul, London.
Aron, R. (1962) *Paix et guerre entre les nations*. Calmann-Lévy, Paris.
Centeno, M. (1997) Blood and Debt: War and Taxation in Nineteenth-Century Latin America. *American Journal of Sociology* 102(6): 1565–605.
Clausewitz, C. von (1976 [1832]) *On War*. Ed. and Trans. M. Howard & P. Paret. Princeton University Press, Princeton.
Goldstein, J. S. (2001) *War and Gender: How Gender Shapes the War System and Vice Versa*. Cambridge University Press, Cambridge.
Janowitz, M. (1976) Military Institutions and Citizenship in Western Societies. *Armed Forces and Society* 2(2): 183–203.
Jean, F. & Rufin, J.-C. (Eds.) (1996) *Économie des guerres civiles*. Hachette, Paris.
Joas, H. (2003) *War and Modernity*. Blackwell, Cambridge, MA.
Kaldor, M. (1999) *New and Old Wars: Organized Violence in a Global Era*. Stanford University Press, Stanford.
Kalyvas, S. N. (2001) "New" and "Old" Civil Wars: A Valid Distinction? *World Politics* 54(1): 99–118.
>Lederer, E. (1915) Zur Soziologie des Weltkrieges. *Archiv für Sozialwissenschaft und Sozialpolitik* 39: 347–84.
Merom, G. (2003) *How Democracies Lose Small Wars: State, Society, and the Failures of France in Algeria, Israel in Lebanon, and the United States in Vietnam*. Cambridge University Press, Cambridge.
Porter, B. D. (1994) *War and the Rise of the State: The Military Foundations of Modern Politics*. Free Press, New York.
Shaw, M. (2003) *War and Genocide: Organized Killing in Modern Society*. Polity Press, Cambridge.

Skocpol, T. (1979) *States and Social Revolutions: A Comparative Analysis of France, Russia, and China*. Cambridge University Press, Cambridge.
Sombart, W. (1913) *Krieg und Kapitalismus*. Duncker & Humblot, Munich.
Speier, H. (1989) *The Truth in Hell and Other Essays on Politics and Culture, 1935–1987*. Oxford University Press, New York.
Stouffer, S. et al. (1949) *The American Soldier*, 4 vols. Princeton University Press, Princeton.

Ward, Lester Frank (1841–1913)

Michael R. Hill

Lester Frank Ward, a man of modest origins born in Joliet, Illinois, was a major architect of American sociology. Prior to Ward's election to the first presidency (1906–7) of the American Sociological Society (ASS, now the American Sociological Association), academic sociology in the US had no independent national disciplinary organization save the unifying voice of the *American Journal of Sociology*, then edited by Albion W. Small at the University of Chicago. The ASS, under Lester Ward's pioneering and able leadership, catapulted sociology into the American intellectual and academic mainstream.

Following horrific service in the Union army during the US Civil War (Ward was seriously wounded, the details of which are found in *Young Ward's Diary*), he earned his undergraduate degree from Columbian University (now George Washington University) in 1869 and won a master's degree, in botany, in 1871. Like the interdisciplinarian Roscoe Pound, who later excelled in botany, law, and sociology, Ward was a formally trained botanist and a self-taught, pioneering sociologist. Working as a paleobotanist in various government offices, including the US Geological Survey, Ward privately developed his systematic analyses of human society and, like several early sociologists, personally underwrote the publication of his books. Ward's major works include: *Dynamic Sociology* (1883), *The Psychic Factors of Civilization* (1893), *Outlines of Sociology* (1898), *Pure Sociology* (1903),

and *Applied Sociology* (1906). His six-volume *Glimpses of the Cosmos* (1913) is replete with autobiographical commentary on the origins of his voluminous writings.

Ward's early books and his 1895 contribution of a seminal article on "The Place of Sociology among Sciences" to the inaugural issue of the *American Journal of Sociology* (*AJS*) demonstrate his leadership at the forefront of sociological thinking. From 1900 to 1903, Ward presided over the international Institut de Sociologie, foreshadowing his subsequent role as president of the ASS. In 1906, Ward achieved a formal academic post, as Professor of Sociology in Brown University.

Ward's interest in Darwinism, notions of systemic "synergy," his concept of "gynecocentrism," and his advocacy of civilization's progressive "telic" forces allied him in promoting many of the same intellectual trajectories advocated by sociologists Edward A. Ross and Charlotte Perkins Gilman.

Ward died on April 18, 1913. His papers, manuscripts, and professional files repose in multiple locations, including the following major depositories: Smithsonian Institution Archives; Brown University Archives; George Washington University Archives and Special Collections; and the Manuscripts Division of the Library of Congress.

SEE ALSO: American Sociological Association; Gilman, Charlotte Perkins; Pound, Roscoe; Small, Albion W.

REFERENCES AND SUGGESTED READINGS

Chugerman, S. (1939) *Lester F. Ward: The American Aristotle – A Summary and Interpretation of His Sociology*. Duke University Press, Durham, NC.
Findlay, B. (1999) Lester Frank Ward as a Sociologist of Gender: A New Look at His Sociological Work. *Gender and Society* 13 (April): 251–65.
Gerver, I. (1963) *Lester Frank Ward*. Crowell, New York.
Ward, L. F. (1913) *Glimpses of the Cosmos*. G. P. Putnam's Sons, New York.
Ward, L. F. (1935) *Young Ward's Diary*. Ed. B. J. Stern. G. P. Putnam's Sons, New York.
Ward, L. F. (1967) *Lester Ward and the Welfare State*. Ed. H. S. Commager. Bobbs-Merrill, Indianapolis.

waste, excess, and second-hand consumption

Nicky Gregson

Waste is a quotidian facet of all societies. All societies discard things; all societies have to deal with what remains of things, from human and animal bodies to vegetable peelings; and all societies are shaped through value regimes which acknowledge waste and/or rubbish as a category, albeit that they vary considerably in their determination of what exactly might befit this category, in how much matter is placed in this category, and what they do with it. While disciplines such as archeology and anthropology and interdisciplinary fields such as material culture have long recognized the disclosing capacities of waste, and while others (notably cultural studies) have begun to explore its metaphorical purchase, sociology largely has left waste alone (O'Brien 1999). This silence is unlikely to remain, for theoretical and empirical reasons. Together with its close theoretical referent excess, waste poses questions which go to the heart of current sociological debates about materiality and mobility, about reflexivity and subjectivities, and about commodity exchange. Waste has begun to be good to think through and not just about. But waste itself matters, increasingly. What happens to the remains of things, and what should happen to them, is now at the forefront of political debate, globally, nationally, and locally. Rubbish defines us: it places us in the world and our relation to it discloses key social divisions, inequalities, and distinctions.

Waste's absence from the sociological frame has in no small measure been bound up with the frequent identification of waste matter with acts of disposal. Seen thus, waste is located as the end point in the commodity chain; as matter whose utility to networks of producers and consumers has been lost and which is therefore open to disposal. As a consequence, waste is cast in trajectories that position it within socio-technical waste management systems that are more commonly the academic preserve of engineers and environmentalists rather than social scientists. This is critical. Waste management systems separate waste matter from sites of production and consumption. They carry matter away from households, for example through the medium of containers such as bins and skips, and they remove them from processing plants, for instance in sealed drums and road tankers. As such, waste management systems render waste as matter out of sight, beyond everyday fields of vision and beyond the sociological frame. Waste management is constituted as a practice not for public display; as known of yet not widely known about, and as a process that discloses considerable ambivalence. In leaving waste alone, sociology has been both acknowledging these ambivalences and acknowledging disciplinary boundaries.

Recent work in sociology and more broadly within the social sciences, however, has begun to turn the mirror to waste. This is discernable in both empirical work on consumption and everyday life and in theoretical writings on consumption.

WASTE, CONSUMPTION, AND EVERYDAY LIFE

Susan Strasser's (1999) study of the history of trash in the US positions waste and disposal as an effect of mass production and mass consumption. For Strasser, manufactured obsolescence, shaped through the imperatives of fashion and technological change, is a post-1950s phenomenon; one in which the ready availability of replacements combines with discourses of disposal to render throwing away the no-longer wanted or needed, and not just the worn out, a routine, easy act of convenience. Strasser shows this development to be predicated upon the rise of public health discourses in the US in the late nineteenth century, to relate to changes in municipal trash collection services, and to changes in the design of house interiors, notably the reduction in available space for storage in both apartment and suburban dwelling structures. However, she also argues that these changes constitute a transformation in people's relationships to objects. For much of human history, she argues, this has been a relationship of stewardship, in which practices of caring for things, repair, handing-down, and making-do run parallel with the art of bricolage. Citing quilt-making, "turning" articles of clothing, and rug-making as emblematic of this sense of stewardship, she goes on to argue that mass production and mass consumption have brought about a far more ephemeral relation to things. Indeed, Strasser argues that the second half of the twentieth century ushered in a period in which the mantra of convenience, cleanliness, and disposability was regarded as the positive to stewardship's negative.

There are clear parallels between Strasser's work in the US and that of Shove and Chappells and Shove in the UK. Liz Shove (2003) highlights the importance of comfort, cleanliness, and convenience to understandings of key practices of contemporary consumption in the UK, but it is in her work with Chappells (Chappells & Shove 1999) that she addresses the importance of waste management systems directly, arguing that the changing technologies of household waste management disclose the changing meanings of household waste. Beginning with eighteenth-century asphalt privies and moving through to early twentieth-century metal bins, and thence to a late twentieth-century combination of "wheelie bins" (garbage bins with wheels) and recycling bins, Chappells and Shove argue that these technologies are indicative of changing boundaries between the public and private management of waste. Although the advent of wheelie-bin technology is considered to have increased the amount of household waste being disposed of, sorting and separating waste matter for disposal through kerbside recycling schemes is argued to have instigated a growing sense of collective responsibility around waste matter and its management. At the same time, recycling activities highlight the importance of a rather different sense of stewardship to that discussed by Strasser, one that goes beyond caring for things to connect practices of reuse and recycling to a stewardship of the planet and to arguments regarding sustainable futures.

Contemporaneous with the above work is the plethora of recent work on second-hand exchange and consumption. Addressing a number of sites of second-hand exchange and consumption (including car boot sales and charity shops), Gregson and Crewe (2003) have highlighted the poverty of commodity chain analyses which identify first-cycle retail as the end point of concern, emphasizing instead how value is recursively created in acts of second-hand exchange and not just produced through value regimes (Thompson 1979). At the same time, Clarke (2000) through her work on nearly new sales has shown the importance of moral economies of mothers. In both sets of work many of Strasser's arguments about stewardship reappear: practices of handing down and handing around, of care and of bricolage are shown not to have disappeared but to have been recast. Moreover, as Gregson and Crewe suggest, the proliferation of sites of second-hand exchange, both face to face and virtual, not only works to reinstate the possibility of reuse, but also establishes hierarchies in sites of second-hand exchange and works to defer the declarations of rubbish value that waste depends upon. Placing lots on eBay, doing a car boot or garage sale, taking worn and/or unwanted items of clothing or books to the local charity shop are all acts which, at least in part, seek to extend the economic and social life of things by placing them in conditions that allow for their revaluation. Furthermore, such sites of exchange connect with international economies in second-hand goods. So that which remains unsold in several of these arenas may be sold on to intermediaries and displaced geographically to places which provide the conditions for their potential revaluation, usually in the third world. Clothing provides one of the best examples of this process, with unwanted garments from the UK and US traveling to Zambia to be reworked as a hybrid fashion (Tranberg-Hansen 2000), but there are others too, notably mobile phones, spectacles, and computers.

Research on second-hand exchange and consumption has not only extended understandings of the commodity chain and the complexities of value, but also highlights how acts of disposal are not necessarily acts of waste-making. Developments within the waste management industry itself also warn against the easy, yet erroneous, identification of disposal with waste. Waste economies per se constitute a huge tertiary sector, spanning everything from the handling of the most hazardous by-products of the nuclear and chemical industries, to clinical (body-related) waste and household discards. Within this, waste minimization through the expansion in markets for recyclables is a particular growth area, and likely to expand considerably within the European Union in the next decade. Fleeces from plastic, pencils from drinks vending machine cups, pens from computer printers, and mouse mats from recycled car tires are just a few examples of the expanding market in recyclables alongside more ubiquitous generic products such as recycled paper. Indeed, selling provenance is now not just a geographical matter but a material one too, as manufacturers proclaim a previous material configuration to their products either alongside or in place of a supply chain that appeals to both transparency and fair trade. "I used to be a car tyre" and "We used to be plastic cups" are just two of the logos that feature in the advertising of a UK-based design company specializing in recyclables. Note that this is not just working with previous histories as consumer objects: these things also have an identity, they are "I's" and "We's." As such, these examples point to the way in which an ethics of care can be mobilized within discourses of recycling. Going beyond stewardship-of-the-planet notions of sustainability, this is a custodial relation that mobilizes anthropomorphism, and one that simultaneously points to a flatter ontology of humans and things akin to that encountered within actant-network theory (ANT).

Most recent empirical work in this field positions discussions of waste within debates about value and the commodity form, while paying attention also to the arguments of Appadurai (1986) and Kopytoff (1986) regarding the social life of things. Theoretical work on waste, however, regards waste as a category, integral to the ordering of both self and society and to the ordering of society through consumption.

WASTE, ORDER, AND EXCESS

It was Mary Douglas's key text *Purity and Danger* (1966) which first drew attention to the social significance of societies' ridding of certain sorts of waste matter. She highlighted the centrality of expulsion and disposal to social classification, specifically to both the constitution of boundaries and the making of social order. Of particular significance here is the placing-out, either on or beyond the margins, of matter deemed to be troublesome, particularly the symbolically polluting or contaminating by-products of human bodies. Similarly, Gail Hawkins (2001) regards the passage of waste matter, and specifically its spatial separation from the body, as central to the ordering of self, maintaining the boundary between what is deemed to be self and what is not. In so doing, this process is regarded as providing the conditions for the renewal of the self through acts of loss. In this and in later work, Hawkins connects this more phenomenological sense of being with waste to theories of subjectivity and to garbage, in what is an explicit attempt to constitute an ethics of waste. Taking as one of her starting points the various "Don't litter" invocations evidenced in many environmental campaigns in the US, Europe, Australia, and New Zealand during the 1990s, Hawkins argues that such imploring works with a Foucauldian sense of an (un)disciplined self. Campaigns such as these are argued to highlight a self who is unable to regulate its actions in the interests of social and environmental order. Moving on, Hawkins outlines how the complexities of dealing with and putting out the garbage are an endless cycle of ritual and repetition dominated by time-consuming acts of classification and sorting in which self-surveillance and self-scrutiny are at a premium. The self here is reflexively made in and through relations with waste. But this is also a self made in and through relations to others, as forged through technologies of waste management. This is a maneuver which takes Hawkins initially in the direction of Foucault's later writings on subjectivity and technologies of the self, through the governmentality literature, and thence to Deleuze and Connolly. Keen to move away from an ethics of waste which highlights normative moralities such as the Reduce–Reuse–Recycle mantra, and which promote recycling as virtue-added disposal, Hawkins attempts to explore Connolly's politics of disturbance to create different, more uncertain and provisional ways of living and being with waste (Hawkins 2003). In a move which both echoes and reverses the discourses identified in Dominic Laporte's groundbreaking *History of Shit* (2002), this takes Hawkins to what many would surely regard as an alternative, utopian world of living with shit and without drains; to a world which turns upside down modernist notions of civilization, in which shit remains within the domestic sphere, rather than being transported away, unsmelt and hidden via extensive networks of underground drains and sewers.

Although far from prominent in theoretical writing on the sociology of consumption, in which desire and distinction have figured centrally, waste has had a presence, even in the earliest writings. Frow (2003) for example, highlights how in one of the formative early texts on consumption, Thorstein Veblen pinpointed the capacity to be wasteful as critical to the sumptuary systems of nineteenth-century capitalism, alongside the more commonly emphasized ownership of desired consumer objects. Frow emphasizes that Veblen saw the conspicuous wasting of time, and not just the wasting of desired things, as central to aristocratic notions of leisure, and therefore to the development of a theory of the leisure class. Waste's metaphoric power has been harnessed more recently, notably in relation to debates about organizations within the late twentieth and early twenty-first centuries. Richard Sennett, for example, in *The Corrosion of Character* (1998), has emphasized how waste and specifically waste reduction and minimization are held-up as metaphorical markers of creativity within the contemporary workplace. Although written nearly a century apart, both Veblen and Sennett's readings begin to touch on waste's relation to excess. For Veblen, this is construed in relation to an absolute need for humans to consume, which profligate acts of consumption exceed. Sennett, however, points to how excess in the workplace is identified with excess labor capacity and operational inefficiencies, and how the elimination of excess is regarded as imperative to the emergence of leaner, more flexible, and more competitive organizations. It is, however, in the work of the French philosopher Georges Bataille that the connections between waste, excess, and consumption are most fully explored.

In *The Accursed Share* (2002), Georges Bataille begins to develop a work of general economy which centers on the importance of consumption rather than production and which locates the expenditure of wealth, or the surplus, as at the heart of consumption in all societies. Although these arguments are connected to some rather opaque comments about energy and resources, it is the surplus which is "the accursed share" of Bataille's title, and it is this which he argues must be expended, given away, lost, or destroyed by all societies. According to Bataille, then, the surplus – the excess – must of necessity be wasted. This theoretical position is one which is grounded in sacrifice and the gift economy of the potlatch, and not in the utility of commodity exchange. Although several commentators have highlighted the almost wilful disregard of historical evidence in Bataille's writings on both sacrifice and potlatch, the theoretical significance of both to an understanding of waste as excess is considerable. Both practices are concerned with managing the surplus and both appropriate objects (often including sentient beings) from the utility of productive consumption to arenas of conspicuous wasting. However, as others have remarked, as important to both sacrifice and potlatch is the cultural work performed by both practices and the social transformations wrought through these rituals. Sacrifice, then, is not just about wasting. Neither is it simply a devotional ritual to a divine being, but it is about a reaffirmation of a transcendent force.

A further recent theoretical development considers the connections between waste, disposal, and consumption, but without reference to excess. Kevin Hetherington (2004) disrupts the associations drawn frequently between waste and disposal. He argues that waste's lack of dynamism makes it a problematic category, and that disposal is best regarded not as an end point in consumption, but as constitutive of consumption as a social and ethical act. Hetherington begins his paper by critiquing Douglas's work, maintaining that in establishing the placement-out of troublesome matter as a binary (there: not here), she misses how social order is always uncertain, provisional, and constantly open to being remade. In contrast, and drawing on the work of both Munro and Hertz, Hetherington argues that disposal is a constant act of placing absences through conduits of disposal. Attics, wardrobes, drawers, and even fridges are all argued to provide gaps between presence and absence, and to allow for questions of value to be considered. Making a case for the importance of absence within sociological thinking, and hinging this to non-linear ways of thinking about time and space characteristic of non-representational work, Hetherington argues that the presence of the trace works to ensure that disposal is never a finished business. Instead, our lives are haunted by ghostly presences and absent presences. Disposal is the means through which we manage our social relations, through absence.

FUTURE DIRECTIONS

Recent theoretical and empirical work on waste has been proceeding in parallel universes, and there are some notable points of difference between authors. At the same time as there are clear differences between theorists, so too are there differences between theorists and those whose concerns are more empirical. Few of those conducting empirical research on waste, for example, would concur with Hetherington's argument that waste is an end point, or with his assertion that waste is unhelpful to think through given its lack of dynamism, a position supported by Bataille's emphasis on the exuberant qualities of waste as excess. Furthermore, waste matter is the stuff of value creation and its handling, even the location and manner of its handling, is a "frontline" governance activity. Increasingly, empirical research in this field is moving to address practices of divestment, ridding, and loss as these relate to things, and the transformations of waste. Its theoretical points of reference center on ideas of transience, durability, and materiality, and emphasize the traces in things and the depths to things. In such work it is the matter of matter which starts to matter. To paraphrase Laporte, shit is . . . shit, and its qualities as such really do matter. Future sociological work on waste is likely to confront the materiality of waste, and not just content itself with thinking through it.

SEE ALSO: Bataille Georges; Commodities, Commodity Fetishism, and Commodification; Conspicuous Consumption; Consumption, Green/Sustainable; Consumption, Mass Consumption, and Consumer Culture; Veblen Thorstein

REFERENCES AND SUGGESTED READINGS

Appadurai, A. (Ed.) (1986) *The Social Life of Things: Commodities in Cultural Perspective*. Cambridge University Press, Cambridge.
Bataille, G. (2002) *The Accursed Share*, Vol. 1. Zone Books, New York.
Chappells, H. & Shove, E. (1999) The Dustbin: A Study of Domestic Waste, Household Practices and Utility Services. *International Planning Studies* 4: 267–80.
Clarke, A. (2000) Mother Swapping: The Trafficking of Nearly New Children's Wear. In: Jackson, P. et al. (Eds.), *Commercial Cultures: Economies, Practices, Spaces*. Berg, Oxford, pp. 85–100.
Frow, J. (2003) Invidious Distinction: Waste, Difference and Classy Stuff. In: Hawkins, G. & Muecke, S. (Eds.), *Culture and Waste: The Creation and Destruction of Value*. Rowman & Littlefield, Lanham, MD, pp. 25–38.
Gregson, N. & Crewe, L. (2003) *Second-Hand Cultures*. Berg, Oxford.
Hawkins, G. (2001) Plastic Bags: Living with Rubbish. *International Journal of Cultural Studies* 4: 5–23.
Hawkins, G. (2003) Down the Drain: Shit and the Politics of Disturbance. In: Hawkins, G. & Muecke, S. (Eds.), *Culture and Waste: The Creation and Destruction of Value*. Rowman & Littlefield, Lanham, MD, pp. 39–52.
Hetherington, K. (2004) Second-Handedness: Consumption, Disposal and Absent Presence. *Environment and Planning D: Society and Space* 22: 157–73.
Kopytoff, I. (1986) The Cultural Biography of Things: Commodification as a Process. In: Appadurai, A. (Ed.), *The Social Life of Things: Commodities in Cultural Perspective*. Cambridge University Press, Cambridge, pp. 64–94.
Laporte, D. (2002) *History of Shit*. MIT Press, Cambridge, MA.
O'Brien, M. (1999) Rubbish Power: Towards a Sociology of the Rubbish Society. In: Hearn, J. & Roseneil, S. (Eds.), *Consuming Cultures: Power and Resistance*. Macmillan, London, pp. 262–77.
Shove, E. (2003) *Comfort, Cleanliness and Convenience*. Berg, Oxford.
Strasser, S. (1999) *Waste and Want*. Metropolitan Books, New York.
Thompson, M. (1979) *Rubbish Theory: The Creation and Destruction of Value*. Oxford University Press, Oxford.
Tranberg-Hansen, K. (2000) *Salaula: The World of Second-Hand Clothing and Zambia*. University of Chicago Press, Chicago.

weak ties (strength of)

D. B. Tindall and Todd E. Malinick

Weak ties are relationships between individuals marked by relatively low intensity and emotional closeness. By contrast, strong ties are relationships that involve high levels of intensity and emotional closeness. The importance of weak ties to a variety of sociological phenomena has been most influentially articulated by Mark Granovetter (1973) in one of the best-cited articles in sociology, "The Strength of Weak Ties" (SWT).

Granovetter argues that most people intuitively expect strong ties to generally be more important than weak ties, because those to whom we are closely tied are more motivated to help us, and are also more likely to be stronger sources of social influence and social support. However, basing his argument on principles of social psychology, Granovetter argues that weak ties are – paradoxically – more important for a variety of phenomena, from helping people obtain a job, to the diffusion of ideas and innovations, to facilitating collective action. Granovetter also argues that insights provided by the "strength of weak ties" principle have implications for understanding the linkages between the micro and macro levels of social reality. His insights about the importance of weak ties have, in part, motivated a variety of methodological endeavors such as operationalizing tie strength, developing techniques to accurately estimate

network size, assessing the accuracy of respondents' recall of ties, and the development of network sampling methods.

Granovetter utilizes network graphs to illustrate his theoretical insights. In one graph there are two egos of interest, A and B. Their set of friends is represented as S = C, D, E, F, G, H. All of the individuals in the set S have ties to either A or B. Granovetter argues that the stronger the tie between A and B, the larger the proportion of individuals in S to whom they will both be tied (connected by either a strong or weak tie). Granovetter predicts that the overlap will be least when the tie between A and B is absent, it will be greatest when the tie between A and B is strong, and it will be intermediate when the tie between A and B is weak.

Next, Granovetter introduces the notion of the forbidden triad. This is a set of three individuals in which A and B are strongly linked, A has a strong tie to a friend C, but the tie between C and B is absent. Granovetter argues that due to pressures on the actors to maintain balanced relationships with their alters (as articulated by Heider's balance theory), this type of triad is very unlikely to occur. In elaborating the application of this idea to larger social networks, Granovetter introduces the concept of a bridge. A bridge is a line in a network which provides the only path between two points (see Fig. 1). He also distinguishes between more narrowly defined "bridges" (as described previously) and "local bridges," the latter being a line in a graph that provides the only local path between two points. Granovetter notes that

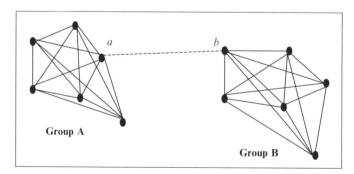

Figure 1   Simplified diagram of Granovetter's concept of a bridging tie. Points depict nodes, or individuals, and lines depict relations. The solid lines represent strong ties and the dashed line represents a weak bridging tie.

bridges are theoretically important to diffusion processes.

Granovetter argues that if, as theory suggests, the "forbidden triad" is absent, then it is unlikely that a strong tie will ever serve as a bridge. A strong tie can be a bridge only if neither ego has any other strong ties. This is unlikely in a social network. However, this constraint does not apply to weak ties. Weak ties are not automatically bridges, but according to Granovetter *all bridges are weak ties*. Granovetter asserts that in large networks it is unlikely that a specific tie provides the only path between two points, but local bridges may be functionally important. The significance of weak ties is that those which are local bridges create more and shorter paths. Consequently, whatever is to be disseminated can reach a larger number of people and cross greater social distance when it is diffused through weak ties rather than through strong ones.

Based on the notion of the "forbidden triad," Granovetter reasons that strong ties should tend to be people who not only know one another, but also have few contacts not tied to ego as well. An ego's weak ties in general, by contrast, will not be tied to one another but will tend to be tied to individuals not tied to ego. Granovetter posits that indirect contacts are typically reached through ties in this weak tie sector; and such ties are of importance not only in ego's manipulation of networks, but also in that they are the conduits through which ideas, influences, or information socially distant from alters may reach ego. The fewer indirect contacts ego has, the more restricted she will be in terms of knowledge of the world beyond her own friendship circle. In a later article, Granovetter (1983: 208) clarified his argument by asserting that "only *bridging* weak ties are of special value to individuals; the significance of weak ties is that they are far more likely to be bridges than are strong ties."

In his SWT article, and a related book, Granovetter goes on to describe the results of a study he undertook examining the role contacts play in helping an individual to get a job amongst recent professional, technical, and managerial job changers in a suburb of Boston. In his study, the majority of jobs were obtained through weak ties.

Granovetter's SWT insights have spawned substantial work on the relationship between the tie strength between egos and contacts and job search outcomes, though there has been some variation in findings regarding the role and importance of weak ties. Some reasons for these varied results are: that measures of tie strength have varied; there may be differential effects for different types of outcomes (any job offer versus level of position of job offered versus salary offered); and there may be differential effects for different types of occupations/sectors of the economy. Other relevant factors may include whether or not the job is a "first job," and there may be different patterns in nation-states with different socioeconomic and political conditions (see Lin et al. 1981; Montgomery 1992).

Granovetter's SWT insights also have implications for collective action at both the whole network and egocentric network levels. Granovetter has argued that at the level of whole networks, weak ties are important because they are more likely (than strong ties) to serve as bridges between otherwise isolated cliques in a community.

It is also worth considering the weak/strong tie distinction and its implications for collective action from the ego-network perspective. Granovetter argues that at the level of egocentric networks, weak ties are important because they are more likely (than strong ties) to provide novel information (e.g., about social movement activities). McAdam (1986) distinguishes between high-risk cost (hrc) activism (e.g., activities that entail potential physical risks to the individual, or that are costly in terms of time and money) and low-risk cost (lrc) activism. He then relates the risks and costs involved in activism to tie strength and ideological commitment, and cites empirical evidence which suggests that prior ties to a recruiting agent are the most powerful predictor of recruitment to low-risk activism. McAdam points out, however, that ideological commitment to low-risk activism does not have to be high in order for individuals to participate. For instance, if an ego is asked to participate in a low-risk cost demonstration for a seemingly worthwhile cause, low amounts of social pressure from weak ties (e.g., from acquaintances at work or school) might be enough to tip the cost/benefit ratio in the direction of participating. In contrast to lrc activism, McAdam suggests that under conditions of hrc activism, strong ties are more important (than weak ties). One reason for this is that strong ties are much more likely to provide social support, and under conditions of hrc this may be crucial for participation (Tindall 2002).

Various definitions of tie strength between individuals have been developed, many of which overlap; these include: (1) felt closeness (e.g., emotional closeness); (2) frequency of contact (how frequently ego communicates with alter); (3) duration (the length of time the relationship has persisted); (4) role definition (e.g., using ties to "acquaintances" to indicate weak ties and ties to "close friends" and/or "immediate family members" to indicate strong ties); (5) reciprocation (reciprocal identification as a strong tie, or reciprocation of a particular type of exchange); (6) volume and type of exchanges; (7) multiplexity (being related through multiple ties of different content); (8) social homogeneity (social similarity); (9) ordinal rank of intimate ties; and (10) network overlap (ego and alter share members of their personal networks).

According to Granovetter (1973: 1361), the strength of an interpersonal tie is a combination of the amount of time, emotional intensity, intimacy, and reciprocal services that characterize the tie. Marsden and Campbell (1984) have provided a thorough conceptual and empirical review of the notion of tie strength. They argue that a distinction should be made between *indicators* and *predictors* of tie strength. Indicators are components of tie strength (e.g., closeness as a measure of the intensity of a relationship). Predictors, by contrast, are aspects of relationships that are associated with tie strength but are not components of it (e.g., role relationships such as neighbor or co-worker statuses that arise out of interactions based on particular foci). Based on an analysis of empirical data, Marsden and Campbell (1984) concluded that closeness (the measure of the emotional intensity of a tie) is the best indicator of tie strength (among those available to them in their study).

These definitions primarily apply to ties between individuals. Additional definitions have been developed regarding ties amongst

groups. For instance, when an officer of company A sits on the boards of companies B and C, there is a strong link between A and B, and a strong link between A and C, but also a weak tie between B and C. In the former two cases the interlock is direct and thus strong, and in the latter it is incidental and thus weak (Granovetter 1983). Powell (1990) has looked at ties relative to interorganizational structure and views tie strength as a function of several factors in addition to those already mentioned, including trust, complementarity, accommodation, indebtedness, collaboration, and history. However, while the concept of tie strength has been incorporated into analyses examining relationships amongst larger social units (e.g., companies), it is unclear whether the logic of Granovetter's SWT argument applies to such relationships, as his arguments are rooted in balance theory and relationships amongst individuals.

Somewhat surprisingly given the importance of tie strength in the sociological literature, there has been relatively little methodological work done on refining the conceptualization and measurement of tie strength. Further, most of the effort on conceptualizing tie strength has focused on ties between individuals. Less attention has been given to conceptualizing the strength of ties linking larger social units (e.g., organizations, corporations, nation-states).

The SWT argument is implicitly connected to a number of substantive and theoretical problems in sociology; some of these include "small world studies," network sampling, estimating personal network size, techniques for assessing and improving the accuracy of responses, and understanding the creation of weak ties.

Small world studies have examined social cohesion, the extent to which individuals are integrated into society, and the social distance that exists between pairs of individuals and/or different social groups. Understanding the prevalence of weak ties and the roles that bridging weak ties play in society is crucial to understanding cohesion/social distance.

In order to describe the structure of weak and strong ties in large bounded populations, one needs to be able to sample such populations because, amongst other reasons, it is impractical to collect network information on large populations. Granovetter has also contributed to research in this area, as have others.

Being able to describe the potential effects of weak ties on outcomes for individuals is predicated on having a good estimate for how many weak ties an individual has in the first place. A variety of techniques have been developed for eliciting responses about ties, including *name rosters*, *name generators*, and *position generators*. Researchers have also worked at trying to assess the accuracy of respondents' reports of the number of ties they have and have developed techniques for the accuracy of recall and for improving recall of forgotten alters.

Finally, understanding the differential creation of weak ties is crucial for understanding their effects. Research has shown that social structures produce foci where individuals with similar social characteristics tend to meet and form ties. Researchers have examined tie strength in the context of patterned tie formation in communities and in voluntary organizations.

SEE ALSO: Cognitive Balance Theory (Heider); Networks; Social Capital; Social Movements, Networks and; Social Network Analysis; Social Network Theory

REFERENCES AND SUGGESTED READINGS

Granovetter, M. (1973) The Strength of Weak Ties. *American Journal of Sociology* 78: 1360–80.

Granovetter, M. (1983) The Strength of Weak Ties: A Network Theory Revisited. *Sociological Theory* 1: 201–33.

Lin, N., Ensel, W., & Vaughn, J. (1981) Social Resources, Strength of Ties, and Occupational Status Attainment. *American Sociological Review* 46(4): 393–405.

McAdam, D. (1986) Recruitment to High-Risk Activism: The Case of Freedom Summer. *American Journal of Sociology* 92: 64–90.

Marsden, P. V. & Campbell, K. E. (1984) Measuring Tie Strength. *Social Forces* 63: 482–501.

Montgomery, J. D. (1992) Job Search and Network Composition: Implications of the Strength-of-Weak-Ties Hypothesis. *American Sociological Review* 57: 586–96.

Powell, W. (1990) Neither Market nor Hierarchy: Network Forms of Organization. *Research in Organizational Behavior* 12: 295–336.

Tindall, D. B. (2002) Social Networks, Identification, and Participation in an Environmental Movement: Low–Medium-Cost Activism Within the British Columbia Wilderness Preservation Movement. *Canadian Review of Sociology and Anthropology* 39: 413–52.

wealth

Claudia W. Scholz and Juanita M. Firestone

Wealth is defined as assets held by an individual or household. These assets may include financial wealth such as savings accounts, stocks, or bonds as well as property such as the family home, farm, or business. Some estimates of household wealth also include consumer durables such as vehicles and refrigerators.

Wealth is an important dimension of stratification because property can be passed down from generation to generation. Families use accumulated assets or savings to bridge interruptions in income, preventing downward social mobility. In spite of its importance, sociologists tend to leave wealth out of their measures of socioeconomic status, because of the difficulties in obtaining valid and reliable data on household assets. Using the data that are available, sociologists and economists have determined that in American society, the distribution of wealth is far more unequal than the distribution of income. The US exhibits the highest levels of wealth inequality in the developed world.

For economists, wealth represents forgone consumption – income that is saved rather than being spent on daily necessities or consumer desires. It is important to note that not all individuals are equally able to save. The accumulation of assets is extremely difficult for the working poor because nearly all of their income goes to fulfill daily needs and because their needs are not subsidized by their employer through medical or childcare benefits.

Recent economic indicators suggest that more and more American families are having trouble saving a portion of their incomes. Net household liabilities have exceeded net asset accumulation in the United States since 1999, which means that Americans are not only failing to accumulate wealth, they are also accumulating personal debt at unprecedented rates. Households that have seen an increase in net worth over the past few years have benefited from rising home values and stock prices rather than increasing personal savings rates. Some research indicates that US households in the bottom quintile have no wealth at all, and a large portion of these have negative wealth (i.e., debt).

Throughout the history of the United States, government initiatives have sought to encourage the acquisition of wealth by American households. These programs have enabled many families to secure homeownership and save for retirement. Unfortunately, many of these government subsidies have benefited native-born white families far more than other groups, resulting in a large wealth gap patterned by race and ethnicity. For example, on average, African American households possess only 8 cents in wealth for every dollar possessed by white families. This disparity persists, even though the income gap between African American and white households has shrunk. African American households are also more likely to possess wealth in the form of residential property than in a more liquid form such as stocks or bonds. Recently, providers of social services have begun to address these disparities in wealth by implementing asset-based poverty reduction programs that help low-income families secure homes and save for education and retirement.

SEE ALSO: Income Inequality and Income Mobility; Inequality, Wealth; Stratification and Inequality, Theories of; Stratification, Race/Ethnicity and

REFERENCES AND SUGGESTED READINGS

Collins, C. & Yeskel, F. (2000) *Economic Apartheid in America: A Primer on Economic Inequality and Insecurity*. New Press, New York.

Conley, D. (1999) *Being Black, Living in the Red: Race, Wealth, and Social Policy in America*. University of California Press, Berkeley.

Keister, L. (2000) *Wealth in America: Trends in Wealth Inequality*. Cambridge University Press, New York.

Weber, Max (1864–1920)

John Drysdale

German sociologist Max Weber, the first child of Max Weber, Sr., and Helene Fallenstein Weber, was born in Erfurt, Thuringia, April 21, 1864. When Max was 5 years old the family moved to Berlin, where Max, Sr., an attorney, became active in both municipal and national politics, and following German unification served as a member of the *Reichstag*, 1872–84. During these heady years the Weber household was often visited by leading politicians and professors. While the conversations of frequent guests provided much stimulation for the young Weber, there is no doubt that the most important and formative influence on him was provided by his mother, a devout Protestant, spiritually sensitive, ethically concerned and active, and intellectually curious.

Weber studied history, economics, philosophy, and law at the universities of Heidelberg, Göttingen, and Berlin. Along the way he completed his military training for an officer's commission. By 1889 he was awarded a doctorate *magna cum laude* with a dissertation on medieval commercial partnerships, and completed his legal training, entitling him to serve briefly as a junior barrister (*Referendar*) in Berlin. In his choice of Heidelberg for undergraduate study as well as in his study of law, the young Weber was following in the footsteps of his father. However, he eventually decided to pursue an academic career. In 1893 he married a distant cousin, Marianne Schnitger, who was to become perhaps his most important intellectual companion. The following year he accepted an appointment as professor of economics at Freiburg. Weber began to attract wide attention with his inaugural public lecture, "The National State and Economic Policy," given in May 1895. This address was a testament to Weber's economic nationalism and, when it was published, sparked a controversy over Weber's claim that economic policy was the servant of the national state. In 1896 he was lured to Heidelberg to take the professorial chair in political economy previously held by Karl Knies, one of his former teachers.

Just as he appeared to be settling into a promising academic career, Weber suffered a psychological breakdown in 1897, unable to resume scholarly work until 1902. His attempts to return to classroom lectures were unsuccessful, however, leading him to forsake his professorial salary and appointment. His breakdown is thought to have been occasioned by a serious altercation with his father during a parental visit in Heidelberg in the summer of 1897. His father died several weeks later without their becoming reconciled.

Having resumed scholarly writing in 1903, Max ventured to extend his activities and responsibilities to editing a journal and to professional travel. In 1904 Max and Marianne traveled as part of a delegation of German academics to represent their country at the World Exposition in St. Louis, Missouri, where he lectured on rural society and economy in Germany. The couple spent several weeks traveling around several regions of the US, visiting relatives, sightseeing, and pursuing contacts with various academics and social leaders (e.g., Booker T. Washington and W. E. B. Du Bois).

In the same year, Weber assumed the lead editorial responsibilities for the major social science journal of the time, *Archiv für Sozialwissenschaft und Sozialpolitik* (Archives for Social Science and Social Policy). He also completed work begun the previous year on a pair of extended essays under the title "The Protestant Ethic and the 'Spirit' of Capitalism." From this point on to the end of his life he maintained an intense pace of scholarly work. Over the next few years he wrote several essays on methodological problems, replied to critics of his work on Protestantism, wrote further on religious sects in North America, conducted research and wrote about the psychophysics of industrial work and about agrarian conditions in ancient society. Beyond these topics he found time to contribute to public exchanges on various topics, including conditions of academic freedom in German universities and the status of women in employment. With the incipient revolution against the tsar in Russia, Weber learned Russian well enough to keep up with events in Russian newspapers and journals. He also published his political-sociological analyses of current conditions in Russia in the wake of the 1905 revolution.

In 1910 he joined with his brother, Alfred, and a few other colleagues, including Robert Michels, Georg Simmel, Ferdinand Tönnies, and Ernst Troeltsch, to establish the German Sociological Society. Having begun his career in the study and practice of law and the academic appointments at both Freiburg and Heidelberg as a political economist, he began to identify himself also as a sociologist in the last decade of his life. The common thread in all three of these identities was his interest in the historical dimensions of social and cultural phenomena, including legal, political, economic, and religious spheres.

With the outbreak of war, Weber served for a brief time as an administrator for a military hospital in Heidelberg. Even during the war he continued to work on multiple research and writing projects. One of these, published after his death, became known as *Economy and Society*, part of a large-scale handbook series in the social sciences. A second project became his largest body of work, his comparative studies of what he called "world religions," again published posthumously under the rubric of the "economic ethic of world religions," better known in the English-speaking world as his sociology of religion.

Toward the end of his life, Weber again tried to resume university teaching. He taught a summer course in Vienna in 1918 before accepting an appointment to the chair of political economy at Munich for the academic year 1919–20. Here he lectured on economic history and sociology, among other subjects. He completed revisions to "The Protestant Ethic and the 'Spirit' of Capitalism," but was still working on other revisions for the first volume of his multi-volume series on the economic ethic of the world religions when he became ill with influenza in early June 1920. He succumbed to pneumonia at his home in Munich on June 14.

EARLY WORK AND VISION OF THE SOCIAL SCIENCES

Weber's earliest projects were historical and empirical. On the historical side were his doctoral and habilitation dissertations, the first on the history of commercial partnerships in medieval Europe (1889), the second on agrarian

Roman economic history (1891). Each won accolades from his professors and attention from scholars. Weber's foray into empirical and quantitative research began as early as 1892 with his participation in a large-scale survey of East Prussian agricultural conditions sponsored by the *Verein für Sozialpolitik* (Association for Social Policy) with a focus on conditions of rural labor. Weber joined the study in midstream but contributed significantly to the interpretation of the empirical findings. This work was related to the emerging fields of agricultural economics and rural sociology. Among other things Weber concentrated on the policy implications of the transition from patriarchal agrarian social and economic structures and traditional attitudes to more modern and rational entrepreneurial forms and practices associated with emergent capitalism. Also, the study of agricultural labor represented for Weber a shift away from legal toward economic perspectives.

Between 1903 and 1908 Weber published several so-called "methodological" essays in which he addressed a wide range of questions concerning the goals, subject matter, and methods of the social sciences. The most famous of these essays was "'Objectivity' in Social Science and Social Policy," published in 1904 as Weber was assuming the co-editorship of the influential journal *Archiv für Sozialwissenschaft und Sozialpolitik*. He sketched his vision of the social sciences as grounded in cognitive interests that are in part historical and in part theoretical, and as seeking relevance to questions of value and contemporary social policy.

Weber's extended discussion of concept-formation focused on his notion of "ideal-type" concepts. Ideal types are conceptual instruments that seek to represent the most relevant aspects of a given object (e.g., "city," "patriarchy," "capitalism") for purposes of social scientific inquiry. They are formed as deliberate constructs through a process of selection, abstraction, and idealization. Ideal-type concepts aim to be useful rather than descriptive, for they are not intended to represent actual phenomena. Weber maintained that they were in fact indispensable for purposes of inquiry and clear exposition. Moreover, ideal types are well-suited to a vision of social science concerned with representing the cultural significance and value-oriented aspects of social phenomena

within the context of historically oriented causal inquiries. When it is forgotten that social scientific concepts of phenomena and processes are mere constructs, the result is the fallacy of *reification* with respect to objects (e.g., the view that "rationality" is real) or to processes (e.g., the view that "rationalization" is a real force). On similar grounds Weber was distrustful of both organicism (e.g., the view that collectivities as such are real) and evolutionism (e.g., the view that processes of change are lawlike, real forces moving in any single direction) as found in the nineteenth-century sociological positivism of Comte and Spencer. Weber's position with respect to these issues has been variously characterized as methodological individualism, atomism, and nominalism.

WEBER'S RESEARCH PROGRAM: TWO MACROSOCIOLOGICAL STUDIES

Weber came to identify his work with the field of sociology relatively late in his career and only through a circuitous route that began with his training in law and proceeded through his early academic work in economic history and political economy. Initially skeptical of Comte and Spencer's sociology, in the last decade of his life Weber participated in the German Sociological Society and began to identify his work with sociology. His sociology was largely historical and comparative, a valuable complement to the historical study of economics, politics, and religion. His greatest substantive contributions to sociology were associated with two great macrosociological projects that occupied most of the last decade of his life.

Economy and Society in World-Historical Perspective

Weber's first major project became known as "Economy and Society." This title actually was assigned to Weber's incomplete contribution to a multi-volume series that was to include works from many social scientists under Weber's general editorship. The large-scale project *Outline of Social Economics* was planned around 1910 and occupied a great deal of Weber's time and labor for the rest of his life. At the time of his death, his own contribution consisted of two unfinished sets of manuscripts. The longer one, published as Part Two of *Economy and Society*, was written mostly between 1910 and 1914. A more compressed manuscript, published as Part One, was written in his last years. Following his death in 1920, his editors, chiefly Marianne Weber, had to decipher Weber's intentions regarding the inclusion and arrangement of these fragmentary manuscripts.

The book *Economy and Society*, although lacking in rigorous internal order and coherence, nevertheless represents an enormous achievement of encyclopedic scholarship with a global reach. Guenther Roth has called it a kind of "sociologist's world history." Its conceptual and theoretical foundations were first outlined in published form in Weber's 1913 essay "Some Categories of Interpretive Sociology." There he sketched a vision of an "interpretive" sociology that included both the interpretive understanding and the causal explanation of intelligible human conduct. "Social action" was treated as the core of human social life. This type of conduct has two chief characteristics. First, it is undertaken by an individual actor on the basis of a subjectively intended meaning. Second, it is oriented toward the behavior of other people. Such conduct is amenable to intelligible explanation despite varying degrees of rationality and familiarity in terms of an observer's experience. As Weber put it: one "need not be Caesar to understand Caesar." Any social action has both subjective meaning and objective conditions, both of which are important in sociological explanation. Weber's dualistic conception of social action can be understood as a synthesis of two scholarly traditions or paradigms: hermeneutics, which emphasized the understanding of meaning, and positivism, which focused on the causal explanation of empirically observable conditions.

Part of the opening chapter, "Basic Sociological Terms," in Part One of *Economy and Society*, includes Weber's extended treatment of social action as the basic conceptual building block for the interpretation of human conduct. There he develops a typology of social action in the form of a series of "ideal types." The types of action are delineated, first, in terms of a distinction between rational and non-rational action, where "rational" refers to more or less conscious consideration of one's action as a way of achieving a given end. Rational social action can be of two types: *instrumentally rational*, in which there is calculation of the choice of means to achieve a chosen purpose, and *value-rational*, in which the calculation is limited to the possible means to be undertaken to pursue a value treated as an end in itself. Non-rational action also displays two main types: *emotional-affectual*, in which action is determined by immediate emotions toward someone or something without pausing to calculate choices in terms of relations of means to ends or likely consequences, and *traditional* action, in which action is guided by ingrained habituation, and may involve little consciousness, much less calculation. Weber intended the typology to provide value-free concepts by which observers could interpret actions of people in virtually any kind of social context. In real life most, if not all, social action represents some mixture of these types. Traditional, or habitual, action is very common in all societies, as is emotional-affectual action. Though perhaps less common, the rational types of action exhibit more individual mastery or self-control over one's conduct, and imply also the possibility of taking responsibility for the values and consequences associated with individual conduct.

Consistent with the aims of a comprehensive reference work, much of Part One of *Economy and Society* presents a broad array of relatively abstract typologies, ranging from types of social action and social relationships to organizations, institutional structures, and social stratification. Also in line with the multidisciplinary reach of the work are typologies of economic and political action and structures. In general, Weber's procedure is, first, to stipulate a definition of a given concept as an "ideal" or "pure type," and then to provide illustrations and commentary based on historical and comparative research. The best-known and most widely used of the dozens of typologies in Part One is Weber's threefold typology of political authority or legitimate domination (*Herrschaft*). *Rational-legal authority* rests on a belief in the legality of a framework of enacted rules by which rulers are selected and by which they govern. Constitutional republican forms of government and parliamentary democracies exemplify rational-legal authority. *Traditional authority* rests on a belief in the time-honored sanctity of traditions.

Traditional leaders are chosen in accordance with inherited, unwritten rules and are obeyed on account of their traditional status. They often rule by personal loyalty based on either kinship or common upbringing. Among the types of traditional rulership Weber mentions gerontocracy, patriarchalism, and patrimonialism. Finally, *charismatic authority* rests on a belief in the special, even divine or superhuman, qualities (sanctity, heroism, exemplary character) of a person to rule, apart from inherited traditions or laws. Obedience is owed to the person and commands of the individual leader on the basis of personal *charisma* (literally, "gift of grace"), which may include magical powers or a record of heroic achievements in the hunt or in war. Charismatic rule may be involved to a greater or lesser degree in religious, military, and political contexts. Weber seems to have adopted the concept of charisma, modeled on the case of Jesus Christ, and extended it to apply to non-religious contexts, for example, Alexander the Great and Napoleon.

In the second part of *Economy and Society* Weber elaborates his well-known and highly influential concept of *bureaucracy*. Although bureaucracies existed in one form or another in ancient and non-western contexts, such as Confucian China and Hindu India, Weber was interested primarily in the role of bureaucracy in modern western societies. In its purest form bureaucracy exhibits the following characteristics: a hierarchical organization of offices (official functions) is governed by laws or administrative regulations; each office has a specific and limited jurisdiction within which it has the authority to carry out its specialized activities; appointment to official positions requires technical qualifications and training; staff members are typically employees who regard their jobs as careers, but they do not own the resources or "means of production" associated with their offices; and official rules, decisions, and actions are recorded in writing and maintained on file as part of the organization.

In Weber's view the development of bureaucratic forms of organization in the modern West was part of a marked trend toward *bureaucratization* across a broad range of institutions. Bureaucracy came to epitomize the modern national state in its legal system, and in its military and civilian administrative (e.g., civil service)

structures and procedures. The state was not alone, however, as a site of bureaucratic organization and control. Bureaucracy, which had arisen early on in the context of church organization, was adopted as the most efficient means of organizing work and decision-making in economic units such as corporations and banks, educational institutions such as academies and universities, and other public services such as hospitals, transportation, and communications.

While bureaucracy was not a modern invention, nor exclusive to the western world, it became greatly elaborated within modern western institutions, especially in the government of modern national states. Weber regarded bureaucracy as particularly consonant with the rational-legal type of political domination, also increasingly typical of western modernity. All the designated properties of bureaucracy, especially its governance of action by impersonal standards and systematic procedures, its organization of work activities in the name of efficiency, and its codification of rules and records, were harmonious with rational-legal domination as opposed to governance based on personal loyalties to either traditional or charismatic rule.

Bureaucratization – the development and spread of bureaucracy – in turn, is conceived by Weber as part of a historical process of *rationalization*, which is the extension of various types of rationality. Bureaucracy represents *formal*, as opposed to *substantive*, *rationality*, given the character of bureaucracy as merely an instrument or tool which can serve virtually any set of (substantive) ends or purposes. That is, the rationality of bureaucracy is limited to its form rather than the aims or purposes of any particular organization. Weber envisioned the extension of rationalization in part through the growth of bureaucracy in ever widening sectors of society.

Bureaucracy cannot be judged to be completely good or bad in its consequences either for individuals or for the society as a whole. On the one hand, bureaucracy represents the most efficient form of organization for the achievement of a broad range of human purposes and values. For instance, the development of capitalism, which Weber termed "that most fateful power in our modern life," has been greatly facilitated by bureaucracy with respect to the internal organization of economic enterprises and in the environment in which these enterprises function (e.g., financial and governmental organizations) by providing for calculability. Indeed, in all the arenas of modern life, bureaucratic apparatuses enable the most efficient possible means for the achievement of complex tasks. On the other hand, bureaucracy has its costs and even irrational consequences. For one, the actions of bureaucratic staff are highly constrained by the framework of impersonal, abstract rules, and the personalities and attitudes of the staff tend to become habituated to the impersonal, emotionally indifferent patterns of behavior in the bureaucracy. The individual bureaucrat is reduced to the status of a small cog in a large and complex machine, prescriptively devoid of any exhibition of love, hate, or any other emotion or value-commitment. At the societal level, the existence and intensity of value diversity and conflict are exacerbated by the very efficiency of organizations devoted to fundamentally different and perhaps incompatible goals such as capital versus labor, and public versus private interests.

Bureaucracy is only one of 16 chapters in more than a thousand pages of Part Two of *Economy and Society*. Three other chapters have been published separately as books and have achieved classic status in their own right: *The Sociology of Religion*, *The Sociology of Law*, and *The City*. Of these topics, religion most concerned Weber during his last years, although he never treated it in isolation from other institutions and spheres of life. It is also the topic that most obviously connects *Economy and Society* with his other major substantive project, discussed next.

The Comparative Studies of Civilizations: The "Economic Ethic of World Religions"

Weber's second major project was conceived under the rubric of "the economic ethic of the world religions." Massive in scope, this study focused on each of several "world religions," including Confucianism, Taoism, Buddhism, Hinduism, ancient Judaism, Islam, and Christianity. (The treatment of the latter two religions was left incomplete upon his death.) The focus on religion as indicated in the titles of component parts (e.g., *The Religion of China*,

The Religion of India) was misleadingly narrow. In actuality these were comparative civilizational studies, showing how religion is implicated in all the major spheres of society and culture in each case.

The design as well as the execution of Weber's research program, culminating in this comparative-historical project on major civilizations *cum* world religions, developed in stages over the last two decades of his life. The starting point can be traced to his renowned study of the relation of the Protestant ethic to the "spirit" of modern capitalism, dating from 1904–5.

The Protestant Ethic and the Spirit of Capitalism

In this earliest stage of his research Weber was interested in ascertaining the contribution made by a set of religious beliefs and practices to the development of the specific form of modern ("rational") capitalism as found in Western Europe and the US. What marked this modern form of capitalism as new was especially the emphasis on the systematic organization of work done by laborers hired on a formally free market, and enterprises devoted to the pursuit of increasing profit without the constraints of traditionalism. Here as elsewhere in his work Weber recognized that there had been other prior forms of capitalism in Europe as well as non-western capitalistic forms and practices. Likewise, he acknowledged that the rise of capitalism as a specific economic system in modern Europe had many causes, both material and cultural. His central problem here was, first and primarily, to explain the rise, not of capitalism as a system, but of the peculiar "spirit" (ethos, mentality) of this new economic system, and second, to show how this new ethos made specific contributions to the intensive growth of modern capitalism in its most crucial stages, especially in the eighteenth and nineteenth centuries. Hence, the problems he addressed were complex, yet circumscribed, as were his hypotheses, lines of argument, interpretations of evidence, and conclusions. This is not to say that his arguments were free of ambiguities, nor that the evidence he marshaled was completely convincing.

What was the new "spirit" of capitalism that Weber took as the object of his inquiry? He described it as an ethic, albeit a secular one, lacking immediate religious foundation or reference, yet prescribing as a moral duty the pursuit of earning more and more money as an end in itself. Whether as an entrepreneur, independent craftsman, or laborer, an individual is obliged to make the acquisition of money from their occupation the center of their life. At the same time, the individual is also duty-bound not to pursue wealth in order to spend money for the enjoyment of luxury or leisure. The acquisition of wealth is its own reward. Waste of time or money is admonished; frugality, reinvestment, and credit-worthiness are virtues. Although the historical origins of this distinctly modern frame of mind are unclear, Weber believed that this new positive moral outlook on the acquisition of money had emerged in America and Western Europe by the eighteenth century. One of the surprising claims is that Weber's spirit of capitalism grew and flourished largely independently of the system of capitalism itself. Weber acknowledges that Benjamin Franklin, though a great exemplar of the new spirit, did not fit the model of the modern capitalist, nor was capitalism very advanced in its development in Franklin's America. This fact of the independent origin of the capitalist spirit, however, served Weber's view that it was not an ideology springing from the economic system that was its rationale, as Marxism might have posited. However, if the modern spirit of capitalism was not a product of the form or system of capitalism, the question becomes all the more urgent: What were the sources of this new attitude toward the acquisition of wealth, an attitude that became, as Weber put it, a leading principle of capitalism?

In his search for the historical origins of capitalism's modern spirit, Weber took as his point of departure the contemporary controversies over the respective orientations of Roman Catholics and Protestants toward capitalistic economic activities. In this context it had been noted as a matter of empirical fact that Protestants were more likely than Catholics to be involved in the more innovative and technically skilled types of capitalistic activity and at the same time were more likely to pursue the patterns of training and education appropriate for such work. Likewise, they tended to be more prosperous than their more tradition-bound

Catholic counterparts. The attempts to explain these differences were the stuff of wide-ranging if unproductive controversies at the time Weber himself began to take up the questions.

As Weber probed the possible sources of the differences he found them to lie in the early history of Protestantism. First, Luther and Lutheranism made key contributions, particularly in advancing the idea that worldly economic activities in pursuit of a livelihood were worthy "vocations," thereby providing enterprise and work with moral sanction. This, Weber reasoned, provided the impetus for individuals to devote themselves to worldly economic activity to a greater extent than in circumstances where tradition had dictated that work was either morally neutral or even evil, albeit necessary for economic sustenance. Second, Calvin and Calvinism provided additional, crucial incentives to work unstintingly in one's economic vocation. Here, Weber's line of argument about the connections between religious beliefs and economic activities becomes intricate and turns on the paradox of unintended consequences.

The central doctrine of original Calvinism was the belief in the predestination of one's soul to ultimate salvation or damnation, a fate that the individual believer could neither know nor change. This harsh doctrine was later moderated by pastoral interpretation (e.g., by the seventeenth-century English minister, Richard Baxter) to alleviate the anxieties of believers tormented by their lack of knowledge concerning their personal salvation. Individuals were admonished to avoid self-doubt regarding their status as members of the elect on the grounds that such doubts could be the work of the devil. Moreover, the best way to gain and sustain self-assurance of one's salvation was to work tirelessly in one's earthly vocation. Thus, the only possible relief from the psychological isolation of salvation anxiety was to work assiduously and single-mindedly in one's chosen economic vocation.

In Weber's interpretation the significant result of following this kind of religious counsel was the production of a new *this-worldly rational asceticism* – "this-worldly" in that the consequences were visible purely in the mundane world of work; *rational* in that the individual assumed self-conscious control over their actions and life course; *ascetic* in that self-discipline and avoidance of temptations (idleness, pleasure, materialism) through complete devotion to labor came to dominate everyday life. With some variations this Calvinist asceticism permeated several other Protestant sects by the eighteenth century: Pietism, Methodism, and the Baptist sects, including Baptists, Mennonites, and Quakers, as well as Congregationalists and various independent sects.

According to Weber, this Protestant asceticism connected with the secular spirit of capitalism exemplified by Benjamin Franklin in the late eighteenth century. The exact nature of the linkage has been the subject of much dispute among Weber's interpreters and critics. Was Protestant asceticism the cause and capitalism's spirit the effect? Or was it mere parallelism, consonance, consistency, or "elective affinity" between the two? Or was it a case of historical metamorphosis, transformation, or secularization from the Protestant ethic to the later spirit of capitalism? Regardless of the exact nature of the connection between the religious ethic and the secular spirit, the potential economic consequences are easy to discern: employers and workers thoroughly dedicated to the program of capitalistic enterprise unfettered by the distractions of the world outside the factory, the workshop, or the firm. To the extent that Calvinism actually had these effects, they were clearly and paradoxically the unintended consequences of the religious doctrines and interpretations. Moreover, the contribution of Protestant asceticism in providing moral legitimacy and meaning to participation in modern capitalistic enterprises, however important in the crucial early stages of modern capitalism, began to fade into irrelevance during the nineteenth century. Capitalism had freed itself from religious and ethical moorings. By the early twentieth century the motivation to work had devolved into a mere compulsion in order to support an ever more prosperous and materialistic lifestyle, a compulsion likened by Weber to a "steel-hard casing."

Economic Ethic of World Religions

If modern capitalism and its spirit were spurred initially by Protestant asceticism, and given that capitalism flourished in Western Europe, Britain, and North America as never before and as nowhere else, the question became how to explain the relative lack of such capitalistic development in other times and places. In order to address this question Weber devised and partially executed a large-scale study of civilizations, especially those of China, India, and the ancient Near East, a study that occupied much of his time during the last several years of his life. Of the multi-volume work *Collected Essays on the Sociology of Religion*, he managed to complete only the first volume, which began with a revised version of the essay on the Protestant ethic, and included his essay on Protestant sects in America, his substantial study of Confucianism and Taoism, and finally an important essay on how various life spheres become differentiated from religion and from one another – "Intermediate Reflections: Religious Rejections of the World and their Directions." Further volumes were to include his studies of Hinduism, Buddhism, ancient Judaism, Islam, and early Christianity.

In each of these studies Weber examined a wide range of material and structural factors that in other times and places tended to retard a "rational" form of capitalism as it developed in the modern West. He reserved his central focus, however, for the role of the various religions, especially through the kinds of "economic ethic" they promulgated. In spite of significant differences among them they all lacked the kind of "this-worldly rational asceticism" found in the modern West. Lacking this frame of mind and pattern of life inspired by the ideal of being God's instrument in, though not of, the world, none of the other world religions was in a position to support an ascetic, but energetic, spirit of rational capitalism.

RECEPTION AND LEGACY

In late 1917 Weber delivered a public lecture on "Science as a Vocation" at the University of Munich. This was followed in early 1919 by his lecture on "Politics as a Vocation" delivered at the same venue. The common theme of the two lectures was the importance of self-renunciation involved in devoting one's life to either scholarship or politics. In both cases, however, the ascetic element was accompanied by a humanistic commitment to the values underlying the pursuit of knowledge and public responsibility. In the lecture on science Weber was returning to a theme about which he had frequently spoken and written: the complex relation of values to science. On the one hand, scientist-scholars are obliged to restrain their own value judgments from biasing inquiry. On the other hand, the problems of inquiry should be selected and constructed so as to make relevant contributions not only to knowledge but to social policy formation as well. In the lecture on politics, Weber distinguished between two "ethics" as alternative models of political leadership: the "ethic of conviction" by which leadership is based on the pursuit of an ultimate value as a "cause," and the "ethic of responsibility" in which the emphasis is on taking responsibility for the consequences of decisions and actions. Weber clearly advocated the latter.

By the last stage of his career Weber had achieved a national reputation both for his scholarship and his politics. World War I had ended in Germany's defeat, and Weber had assumed an advisory role to the defeated military and civilian authorities. As Germans looked forward to what became known as the Weimar Republic as the successor to the fallen *Kaiserreich* there was even some talk of Weber becoming a political leader. That possibility was cut short by his death in the early days of the new republic.

While Weber was widely recognized in Germany as a scholar and public figure, his work was not yet well known outside the country. None of his works had been translated into English prior to his death. Not until 1930 was *The Protestant Ethic* translated by Talcott Parsons. A complete English edition of *Economy and Society* had to wait until 1968. Even today it is still difficult to evaluate Weber's reception and legacy. This is partly due to the fact that his work and perspective consistently transcended the boundaries of any single social science discipline of his time or ours. Thus, in addition to being claimed as a leading founder of twentieth-century sociology and a major contributor to modern political science, public administration, and political theory, he has been recognized for significant contributions to the fields of economic history, historical jurisprudence, the study of ancient civilizations (most especially Rome and the Near East), and the comparative study of religions. He was a historian who

became a sociologist, a sociologist who remained an economist, a serious student of ancient society who contributed significantly to the understanding of modern western culture, its distinctiveness, and its development. He was equally captivated by the study of economics and religion, of material and ideal factors, of social structure and individual action. In sociology his contributions are recognized especially in the areas of law, religion, and the economy; in the study of social stratification, political, urban, and rural sociology, and the sociology of culture. In terms of the method and general conception of sociology, Weber insisted that social action is the conceptual foundation of our understanding of societal structures. Insofar as action carries meaning it is intelligible through the use of *Verstehen* (understanding) in the context of interaction and of sociological observation. As important as action is, Weber gave even more attention to what he called order and to what sociologists later came to view as social structure. Action and structure, for Weber, interact in complex loops, with structure emanating either directly or indirectly as a result of action, yet with subsequent action both enabled and constrained by existing structure. Weber is rightly regarded as the founder of structural sociology (stratification, institutions) as well as the sociology of action.

Weber's influence, already enormous, is likely to increase. Not all of Weber's writings have yet been translated into English or Japanese, the two major languages for the reception and study of his writings. Nor is the end yet in sight to the monumental project of collecting, editing, and publishing all Weber's surviving writings and correspondence, the *Max-Weber-Gesamtausgabe*.

In preparation for the 14th World Congress of Sociology in Montreal in 1998, the International Sociological Association surveyed its members around the world to determine the most influential books written by sociologists in the twentieth century. Weber's *Economy and Society* was selected as the most influential book of the past century, followed not far behind by his *Protestant Ethic and the Spirit of Capitalism* (ranked fourth). Weber was also chosen as the most influential author of the twentieth century by both male and female sociologists among the 455 respondents to the survey. Given the broad sweep of Weber's historical-comparative sociology and the recent and planned publications of Weber's works in German, English, Japanese, Chinese, and other languages, his legacy is likely to increase in global influence.

SEE ALSO: Asceticism; Authority and Legitimacy; Bureaucracy and Public Sector Governmentality; Capitalism; Class, Status, and Power; Historical and Comparative Methods; Ideal Type; Law, Economy and; Marianne Weber on Social Change; Objectivity; Protestantism; Rational Choice Theories; Rational Legal Authority; Religion; Theory; *Verstehen*

REFERENCES AND SUGGESTED READINGS

Chalcraft, D. J. & Harrington, A. (Eds.) (2001) *The Protestant Ethic Debate: Max Weber's Replies to his Critics, 1907–1910*. Trans. A. Harrington & M. Shields Liverpool University Press, Liverpool.

Kalberg, S. (1994) *Max Weber's Historical-Comparative Sociology*. University of Chicago Press, Chicago.

Kalberg, S. (Ed.) (2005) *Max Weber: The Confrontation with Modernity*. Blackwell, Oxford.

Lehmann, H. & Roth, G. (Eds.) (1993) *Weber's Protestant Ethic: Origins, Evidence, Contexts*. German Historical Institute, Washington, DC, and Cambridge University Press, Cambridge.

Marshall, G. (1982) *In Search of the Spirit of Capitalism: An Essay on Max Weber's Protestant Ethic Thesis*. Columbia University Press, New York.

Mommsen, W. J. (1989) *The Political and Social Theory of Max Weber: Collected Essays*. University of Chicago Press, Chicago.

Mommsen, W. J. & Osterhammel, J. (Eds.) (1987) *Max Weber and his Contemporaries*. Allen & Unwin, London.

Schluchter, W. (1989) *Rationalism, Religion, and Domination: A Weberian Perspective*. Trans. N. Solomon. University of California Press, Berkeley.

Turner, B. S. (1992) *Max Weber: From History to Modernity*. Routledge, London.

Turner, S. (2000) *The Cambridge Companion to Weber*. Cambridge University Press, Cambridge.

Weber, Marianne (1988 [1926]) *Max Weber: A Biography*. Trans. & ed. H. Zohn. Transaction Books, New Brunswick, NJ.

Weber, Max (1946) *From Max Weber: Essays in Sociology*. Trans. & ed. H. H. Gerth & C. W. Mills. Oxford University Press, New York.

Weber, M. (1949) *The Methodology of the Social Sciences*. Trans. & ed. E. A. Shils & H. A. Finch. Free Press, New York.

Weber, M. (1951) *The Religion of China: Confucianism and Taoism*. Trans. ed. H. H. Gerth. Free Press, New York.

Weber, M. (1952) *Ancient Judaism*. Trans. & ed. H. H. Gerth & D. Martindale. Free Press, New York.

Weber, M. (1954) *Max Weber on Law in Economy and Society*. Ed. M. Rheinstein. Trans. E. Shils & M. Rheinstein. Harvard University Press, Cambridge, MA.

Weber, M. (1958a) *The City*. Trans. & ed. D. Martindale & G. Neuwirth. Free Press, New York.

Weber, M. (1958b) *The Religion of India: The Sociology of Hinduism and Buddhism*. Trans. ed. H. H. Gerth & D. Martindale. Free Press, New York.

Weber, M. (1963) *The Sociology of Religion*. Trans. E. Fischoff. Beacon Press, Boston.

Weber, M. (1968) *Economy and Society: An Outline of Interpretive Sociology*, 3 vols. Ed. G. Roth & C. Wittich. Trans. E. Fischoff, H. H. Gerth, et al. Bedminster Press, New York.

Weber, M. (1976) *The Agrarian Sociology of Ancient Civilizations*. Trans. R. I. Frank. New Left Books, London.

Weber, M. (1981 [1927]) *General Economic History*. Trans. F. H. Knight. Transaction Books, New Brunswick.

Weber, M. (1982–present) *Max-Weber-Gesamtausgabe (Collected Works)*. Ed. H. Baier, M. R. Lepsius, W. J. Mommsen, W. Schluchter, & J. Winckelmann. J. C. B. Mohr, Tübingen.

Weber, M. (2002) *The Protestant Ethic and the Spirit of Capitalism*. Trans. S. Kalberg. Roxbury, Los Angeles.

Weber, M. (2003) *The History of Commercial Partnerships in the Middle Ages*. Trans. L. Kaelber. Rowman & Littlefield, Lanham, MD.

welfare dependency and welfare underuse

Hartley Dean

Welfare dependency is a term that refers to the use that people make of publicly provided cash benefits (sometimes called cash transfers) or human services. Welfare underuse is the term applied when people who are entitled to publicly provided benefits and services fail to take them up.

WELFARE DEPENDENCY

Welfare dependency, therefore, is a feature of advanced industrial societies with developed welfare states, whose citizens enjoy specific "social" rights (e.g., to social security, health care, social support, and education). The premise on which the advocates of state welfare provision promoted its development was that, as the social division of labor in society becomes more complex, the "states of dependency" that arise at various points in the human life course can be defined and recognized as collective responsibilities (Titmuss 2001: 64). However, the social policymakers who fashioned the modern welfare states of the post-World War II era were often "reluctant collectivists" (George & Wilding 1985). They may have favored guaranteed basic minimum provision by the state, but they also wanted people to depend on income from paid employment on the one hand and on support from their families on the other. Welfare states have developed in different ways in different parts of the capitalist world, and while social-democratic welfare states (e.g., Sweden) have sustained relatively high levels of state welfare dependency, liberal (e.g., the US) and conservative (e.g., Germany) welfare states have tended to discourage it in favor of labor market or family dependency, respectively (Esping-Andersen 1990).

Since the 1970s, the idea of welfare dependency has become increasingly contested as support for state welfare provision has declined. Economic globalization, it was claimed, put welfare state spending under pressure (because it was alleged to make national economies uncompetitive); social and demographic changes in western societies placed what some regarded as unsustainable demands on welfare states (for example, because of population aging, and because of rising numbers of lone-parent households); and the political rise of the New Right presented a wholesale challenge to the legitimacy of state welfare dependency. Despite this, where people depend on state education, contributory state pension schemes, or health care provision, these have by and large retained popular and political support, but cash benefits for people of working age and public housing provision by and large have not. In some countries – particularly the US – the term welfare has been associated specifically with means-tested

or income-related social assistance for the poorest and has acquired a distinctly pejorative connotation (Fraser 1997). Just as the Poor Law regimes that had preceded the development of modern welfare states had deliberately stigmatized the undeserving poor, dependency on the state for income and/or housing and for certain kinds of social support entailed an inherently and increasingly stigmatized status.

Theorists of the New Right (e.g., Murray 1984) claimed that the perpetuation of welfare dependency undermines society by eroding individual responsibility and that it discourages people from sustaining themselves through employment and/or within their families. Earlier anthropological studies had suggested that urban slums in various parts of the world exhibited a culture of poverty that was transmitted from generation to generation. Now, it was claimed, the welfare state was breeding a culture of idleness, irresponsibility, and dependency and was contributing to the creation in many developed western societies of an "underclass." Unemployment and lone-parenthood were blamed on the ready availability of cash benefits and public housing which acted as disincentives to self-sufficiency and economic independence on the one hand and to marriage and family life on the other.

Critics of this thesis have drawn upon evidence that people who depend on cash benefits from the state exhibit no signs of a culture of dependency: on the contrary, they tend to subscribe to the same values, aspirations, and prejudices as does mainstream society (Dean & Taylor-Gooby 1992). It has been argued that we are witnessing a form of "dependency fetishism" that obscures our understanding of the interdependency that characterizes human society. Popular and political discourse tends perversely to regard our dependency on employment and within families as "independence," but uniquely to problematize state welfare dependency.

When one considers the total value of all the benefits and services citizens in developed countries typically receive from the welfare state, most of this is likely to have been self-financed through the various taxes and social security contributions that they will have paid in the course of their lifetimes (Falkingham & Hills 1995). The availability of new forms of longitudinal social data enables us to consider the dynamics of poverty, and to see that for many unemployed people and lone parents who claim cash benefits provided by the state, their dependency is likely to be a relatively short-lived and not necessarily an enduring experience (Leisering & Walker 1998).

WELFARE UNDERUSE

Welfare underuse is in substantial part, but by no means solely, attributable to the stigma often associated with welfare dependency. It is important to distinguish between the underuse of cash benefits, transfers, or their equivalent in kind (e.g., food stamps or food cards) and the underuse of public or social services.

The underuse of cash benefits provision is often referred to as a failure of benefits "take up." A considerable body of research on benefits take up was conducted in the 1970s and 1980s (for an overview, see Craig 1991). It is widely recognized that conditional means-tested benefits or social assistance schemes have much lower rates of take up than universal or contributory benefit schemes (under which citizens may have an automatic entitlement or an entitlement based in social insurance contributions). This was attributed by researchers to the sense of stigma that may attach to claiming such benefits, to ignorance on the part of potential claimants, and/or to the administrative complexity of the schemes. The research drew either upon psychological models, which assume a set of behavioral thresholds that potential claimants must overcome, or econometric models, which assume that potential claimants weigh up the utilities and disutilities associated with claiming their entitlements. Subsequent comparative research, however, has informed an "interactive model" of take up that looks at multi-level influences at the scheme or systemic level, at the administrative level, and at the level of the claimant or client (Oorschott 1995). This sociological approach emphasizes both the structural features of welfare systems and the consequences that may flow, for example, from the behavior of administrators, bureaucrats, and caseworkers, who may develop informal methods to ration access to welfare provision.

The underuse of public services may similarly result from structural and administrative features of those services. Of particular concern is the differential use of services by different social classes or minority groups. Certain kinds of public services, such as health care and education, may be more extensively used and provide greater benefits to middle-class families than to the poorest families who need them the most (Le Grand 1982). One of the most spectacular failures of many modern welfare states is reflected in the fact that benefits of advances in medical science and health technologies have been so unequally distributed (Wilkinson 1996). Even in countries with a universal national health service (e.g., the UK) people from lower socioeconomic classes and/or from minority ethnic groups experience significantly higher mortality and morbidity rates and make less use of health services than people from higher socioeconomic classes and from the white population. The reasons for this are complex. They reflect the extent to which inequalities in income may be translated more generally into inequalities in life chances and inequalities of power. But they also reflect some of the subtle ways in which public service providers may discriminate against, or be culturally insensitive to, particular groups in society.

The majority of the population in developed capitalist welfare states will during particular stages of their life course depend upon or make use of publicly provided or state financed health, education, and welfare services. That is a measure of the level of a country's "social development." Social policymakers and sociologists may, however, be concerned about whether, by whom, and why dependency upon such provision becomes excessive; or conversely about whether, by whom, and why such provision may be underused.

SEE ALSO: Citizenship; Lone-Parent Families; Social Policy, Welfare State; Social Services; Stigma; Unemployment; Welfare Fraud; Welfare Regimes; Welfare State

REFERENCES AND SUGGESTED READINGS

Craig, P. (1991) Costs and Benefits: A Review of Research on Take-Up of Income-Related Benefits. *Journal of Social Policy* 20(4): 537–66.

Dean, H. & Taylor-Gooby, P. (1992) *Dependency Culture: The Explosion of a Myth.* Harvester Wheatsheaf, Hemel Hempstead.

Esping-Andersen, G. (1990) *The Three Worlds of Welfare Capitalism.* Polity Press, Cambridge.

Falkingham, J. & Hills, J. (Eds.) (1995) *The Dynamic of Welfare: The Welfare State and the Life-Cycle.* Prentice-Hall/Harvester Wheatsheaf, Hemel Hempstead.

Fraser, N. (1997) *Justice Interruptus: Critical Reflections on the "Postsocialist" Condition.* Routledge, New York.

George, V. & Wilding, P. (1985) *Ideology and Social Welfare.* Routledge & Kegan Paul, London.

Le Grand, J. (1982) *The Strategy of Equality.* Allen & Unwin, London.

Leisering, L. & Walker, A. (1998) *The Dynamics of Modern Society: Poverty, Policy and Welfare.* Policy Press, Bristol.

Murray, C. (1984) *Losing Ground: American Social Policy 1950–1980.* Basic Books, New York.

Oorschott, W. van (1995) *Realizing Rights.* Avebury Press, Aldershot.

Titmuss, R. (2001 [1955]) Lecture at the University of Birmingham in Honour of Eleanor Rathbone. Republished in: Alcock, P., Glennerster, H., Oakley, A., & Sinfield, A. (Eds.), *Welfare and Well-being: Richard Titmuss's Contribution to Social Policy.* Policy Press, Bristol.

Wilkinson, R. (1996) *Unhealthy Societies: The Afflictions of Inequality.* Routledge, New York.

welfare fraud

Siegfried Lamnek and Ralf Ottermann

Sociologists define *fraud* as any deception the intended outcomes of which are knowingly in breach of norms (of honesty, reciprocity, solidarity, etc.), and define *deception* as any intentional non-disclosure and/or misrepresentation of relevant information, which is to make others behave in a way they would not if they were well informed (Ottermann 2000). Many frauds do not violate laws and/or are considered relatively harmless. But some frauds are regarded not just as unfair or illegitimate, but also as illegal acts of deception. Such is *welfare fraud*, committed in order to obtain unauthorized benefits, which is seen as a violation of statute, as an offense against the rules that regulate the welfare system. In legal terms,

welfare fraud (benefit fraud, public assistance fraud) is defined as making a false or misleading statement or committing an act intended to mislead, misrepresent, conceal, or withhold facts concerning the eligibility for public assistance, which is determined, for instance, by (dis)informations of the current marital status, household composition, employment status, income, receipt of monetary and in-kind gifts, bank accounts, and other resources of the claimants or clients. Welfare fraud is committed when persons make false statements, and/or misrepresent facts, or when (changed) situations are not reported to the departments of social services, in order to obtain public funds for which the beneficiaries would not otherwise be eligible. Labeled a crime, welfare fraud can result in imprisonment, probation, repayment, recoupment, or becoming ineligible for assistance for a certain length of time.

Welfare fraud is socially perceived as an illegal as well as an immoral act of deception and treated as a *social problem* in public discourse. In contrast to similar offenses against the state and its welfare system, such as minor tax evasion or illicit work ("moonlighting," "doing something on the side"), welfare fraud is easily scandalized and stigmatized by opinion leaders and moral entrepreneurs, since it is often seen as an "underclass fraud" and as such as a behavior of already otherwise stigmatized minorities predominantly problematized and combatted by the "moralizing upper-under and middle classes" and the "legislating political elites" (social scientists included). Welfare cheats have few defenses since nearly all the circumstances of their lives are under public scrutiny and they carry a "moral taint" as persons unable – if not unwilling – to earn a living (Barker et al. 1990). Thus, people who intend and commit welfare fraud have to face and to deal with the fact of extraordinary *social control*. But even if they try, they will be less successful in doing stigma management than illicit workers and tax evaders, and this in spite of the fact that the latter are often perceived as doing the greater harm to the public purse (Schäfer 2002). Despite the relatively low costs caused by welfare fraud to the public purse, an outraged public opinion – fueled by mass media campaigns and pronouncements by politicians – led to the establishment of relatively expensive anti-fraud squads specialized in the detection and prosecution of welfare cheats (Pemberton 1990). This raises doubts whether the latter makes sense fiscally in regard to the former (Matt & Cook 1993). Moreover, the public (mis)perception of welfare fraud is often (mis)used as a justification of tax evasion and welfare cuts, and vice versa. However, there has to be a welfare system for people to commit welfare fraud, and people have to appear needy: they have to meet certain criteria, such as poverty and helplessness and/or a basic willingness to work, in order to at least seem eligible for public assistance (Lamnek et al. 2000).

The welfare state was originally not designed just for the poor; instead, it should prevent all people from becoming too poor and deprived, and hence becoming a risk for social order and cohesion. It was supposed to offer social protection for everyone, even though people depending on welfare should not be better off than self-sufficient laborers, therefore relying on deterrence and the stigmatization of (potential) welfare recipients as a way of policing the boundaries. However, social welfare has shifted back towards minimum provision of the poor and the stigmatization of welfare recipients (Spicker 2002). The policy of holding down support for the poor and unemployed is supposed to minimize the incentives to claim benefits and remain on welfare unnecessarily and to maximize the willingness to work for the purpose of self-sufficiency, thereby protecting laborers' dividends of conformity with the central rules of the *occupational society*. Welfare policy can then be seen as a form of social control which creates social values (e.g., the value of work) and shapes social identities (e.g., as deserving or not) and relationships (e.g., between taxpayers and the poor) (Raftopoulou 2004). But the policy of minimal provision plus financial cuts in the name of work has the unanticipated consequence of making illicit work while claiming benefit ("doing the double") more attractive – even for the employers of welfare cheats and contrasting with the stereotype that people on welfare usually are unwilling to work. The real issue is that legal employment opportunities ("proper jobs") to make a living are especially rare and declining for the less qualified, trained, and educated "reserve army of cheap labor" (Evason & Woods 1995).

In public discourses welfare cheats are often (mis)used as scapegoats for structural problems of social change and for unemployment in modern developed societies. Challenges (e.g., resulting from the mobility of global players or demographic aging) have limited the resources available to the welfare state, while at the same time increasing the extent and magnitude of welfare needs. Especially during economic recession, when financial resources are short and governments intend to redress budgetary deficits, the connection between socioeconomic positions and prospects on the one hand and people's attitudes towards welfare on the other hand is becoming obvious. The perceived (in)efficiency, (un)fairness and/or (il)legitimacy of the welfare system induces (non-)compliance with the system and, as a result, (in)tolerance of welfare fraud, tax evasion, and moonlighting. The extent of compliance with the system, the degree of tolerance of fraudulent practices, and the tendency to minimize versus dramatize fraudulent behavior in public discourses correspond to differing conceptions of *distributive justice*. According to the principles of distributive justice, people believe that goods and burdens in a society should be fairly distributed. The principle of achievement or contribution contrasts with the principles of equality and neediness. Ideas of individual responsibility, minimal taxes and entitlements, private provision, and self-help partly collide with notions of welfare. In public opinion, a social policy of minimal support and welfare cuts seem the more legitimate the more welfare is associated with fraud, abuse, social irresponsibility, laziness, waste of public funds, tax burdens, and welfare costs. Politicians claim lean welfarism as an appropriate method to divide the deserving from the non-deserving. However, minimum welfare and maximum control of the welfare recipients also reduce the chances of the really needy escaping from welfare dependency. This in sum may lead to resentments against the system and the willingness to cheat it for socioeconomic reasons. These varying conceptions of distributive justice on attitudes towards the welfare state correlate with socioeconomic positions and prospects, risks, strains, aims, and claims. People use conceptions of distributive justice to legitimate welfare fraud. They can "blame the system," for instance, as "being rigged" and/or "fostering social injustices." In contrast, it is easier to scandalize welfare fraud when it is seen as "part of the system" (e.g., as a symptom of so-called "welfarization"). When people are convinced that fraudulent behavior (welfare fraud, tax evasion, and illicit work) is widespread, they prepare themselves for such a behavior, which is, in the first place, to increase or keep their own socioeconomic resources (Lamnek & Luedtke 1999).

Public discourses of welfare fraud (e.g., its rise and fall as a social problem) are a subject of *discourse analyses* and historical and comparative sociology. In contrast to official statistics which mainly deliver the results of the (selective processes brought about by the) social control of welfare fraud, *social surveys* provide more valid data concerning intra- and intercultural differences in the public opinion of welfare fraud, as well as its incidences. *Self-reports*, focused *group discussions*, and *interviews* display the perspectives and motives of the cheats and their patterns of interpretation of the situation(s) and corresponding neutralizations of social norms (which lower the anticipated moral costs of deviant/delinquent behavior). *Life-history approaches* give insight into so-called de-shaming processes (which reduce the costs of self- and peer-imposed punishment and stigmatization, and therefore, for example, explain, opportunity structures notwithstanding, why welfare cheats tend to engage or to be involved in further "criminality"), while *case studies*, *field observations*, and *ethnographic research* expose the impact of social milieus, such as differential associations and processes of (the offenders') social learning and informal patterns of the agencies of (formal) social control. The combination of qualitative and quantitative methods seems to be the best practice for exploring the macro-social and micro-social dimensions of welfare fraud, as well as for generating and testing theories along the macro–micro–macro link.

As far as welfare fraud as a *deviant/delinquent behavior* is concerned – as a social action which makes sense to (potential) offenders – sociologists have found that anticipated threats and rewards through informal sanctions have greater effects on people's behavior than anticipated threats and rewards through formal sanctions. Internal self-control, the clear versus bad conscience which is anticipated, is – as far as social

norms have been internalized and cannot be neutralized – more important than the anticipated external social control. The anticipation of other people's perceptions of one's own actions is the more crucial the less is the social distance. Thus, besides the threat of legal sanctions and the feelings of guilt that individuals might impose upon themselves when they offend their own conscience by engaging in behaviors they consider morally wrong, there is also the threat of shame, embarrassment, and social disapproval that individuals might experience when they violate norms which people they value support (Yaniv 1998). Sociologists investigated the comparative deterrence effect of formal and informal sanctions (i.e., the perceived certainty and severity of legal punishment on the one hand and the anticipated peer-imposed punishments on the other hand) and found that, apart from past criminal involvement, which plays a significant social-biographical role in so-called de-shaming processes, informal sanctions have a greater effect on welfare fraud than formal sanctions. Only such persons who have nothing to lose (e.g., being chronically short of money and de-shamed since already marginalized and stigmatized as "on welfare") are out of control. Thus, people have to be socially included, not excluded, if society is really interested in diminishing "underclass fraud." If full employment turns out to be a social fiction, we will be in need of a change in social policy and therefore in need of sociological thought.

SEE ALSO: Deviance, Crime and; Distributive Justice; Poverty and Disrepute; Social Control; Social Exclusion; Social Integration and Inclusion; Social Policy, Welfare State; Unemployment as a Social Problem; Welfare Dependency and Welfare Underuse; Welfare Regimes; Welfare State; Welfare State, Retrenchment of

REFERENCES AND SUGGESTED READINGS

Barker, C., Watchman, P., & Rowan-Robertson, J. (1990) Social Security Abuse. *Social Policy and Administration* 24: 104–19.

Evason, E. & Woods, R. (1995) Poverty, Deregulation of the Labour Market and Benefit Fraud. *Social Policy and Administration* 29: 40–54.

Lamnek, S. & Luedtke, J. (Eds.) (1999) *Der Sozial-staat zwischen "Markt" und "Hedonismus"?* (Economic Pressure, Free Riders, and the Welfare State). Leske & Budrich, Opladen.

Lamnek, S., Olbrich, G., & Schäfer, W. J. (2000) *Tatort Sozialstaat* (Abusing the Welfare State: On Moonlighters, Tax Dodgers, and Illegitimate Recipients of Benefits). Leske & Budrich, Opladen.

Matt, G. E. & Cook, T. D. (1993) The War on Fraud and Error in the Food Stamp Program. *Evaluation Review* 17: 4–26.

Ottermann, R. (2000) *Soziologie des Betrugs* (Sociology of Fraud). Kovac, Hamburg.

Pemberton, A. (1990) Discipline and Pacification in the Modern Administrative State: The Case of Social Welfare Fraud. *Journal of Sociology and Social Welfare* 17: 125–42.

Raftopoulou, C.-E. (2004) *Targeting Benefit Fraud.* Political Studies Association, Stoke-on-Trent.

Schäfer, W. J. (2002) *Opfer Sozialstaat* (Victim Welfare State). Leske & Budrich, Opladen.

Spicker, P. (2002) *Poverty and the Welfare State.* Catalyst, London.

Yaniv, G. (1998) *Welfare Fraud and Welfare Stigma.* Paper presented at the 2nd International Research Conference on Social Security, Jerusalem.

welfare regimes

Stephan Lessenich

Thinking in terms of "regimes" and "regime types" has become popular in comparative welfare research since the late 1980s. Originally stemming from international relations studies (Krasner 1983), the "regime" concept has been discovered for and adapted to welfare state research mainly by Danish sociologist Gøsta Esping-Andersen, who used it in his seminal work on *The Three Worlds of Welfare Capitalism* e institutional nexus of work and welfare in advanced capitalist societies. Building on a welfare regime's capacity to reduce the market dependency of individuals ("decommodification"), its implications for the structure of social inequality ("stratification"), and the relative importance of state, market, and the family (or households) in the production of social welfare, Esping-Andersen claimed that the modern welfare state comes in three ideal typical variants: the "liberal," the "conservative," and the "social democratic" model. The great advance for welfare research brought about by this regime typology is twofold. On the one hand, the "three worlds" constitute a suitable tool for bringing order into the complex "real world" of welfare capitalism. On the other hand, and when it comes to specify the differences between advanced welfare states, the concept of welfare regimes focuses not simply on social expenditure data but on the qualitative aspects of welfare state policies, i.e., on the welfare state's relevance as a means of ordering social relations according to specific ideological convictions and normative principles. According to Esping-Andersen, the relative weight of "liberal," "conservative," and/or "social democratic" convictions and principles in different national welfare regimes today depends on the power resources with which the respective social movements were able to engage in the "democratic class struggle" (Korpi 1983) around the welfare state, its emergence and its design, in the late nineteenth and early twentieth centuries.

Esping-Andersen's "regime approach" has been the object of broad conceptual, methodological, and empirical criticism and, at the same time, guiding principle of much of the comparative research on social policy and the welfare state over the last 15 years. While the first wave of critique concentrated on the question of whether and how individual cases (i.e., national welfare states) could be subsumed to one (or another) of the three regime types, subsequent work focused on amending, extending, and transposing Esping-Andersen's "holy trinity." Whereas some authors discovered alternative institutional models of linking work and welfare in Southern Europe, the Antipodes, or the emerging welfare states of Central and Eastern Europe, others contrasted Esping-Andersen's male-biased "decommodification regimes" with more gender-sensitive "care regimes." In *Social Foundations of Postindustrial Economies* (1999), the author of *The Three Worlds of Welfare Capitalism* assumed part of that criticism, emphasizing the different welfare regimes' capacity of "defamiliarization" (i.e., of exonerating individuals from family burdens) and reformulating his regime types as different ("residual," "corporatist," or "universalistic") "models of solidarity." In any case, the ultimately academic and futile struggle about whether there are three, four, or *n* "worlds of welfare" out there eventually has been settled. The future of the concept of welfare regimes lies in further analyses of the interplay (and possible "elective affinities") between Esping-Andersen's "worlds of welfare" and different "varieties of capitalism" and, above all, in in-depth case studies of the changing nature of national welfare regimes in times of accelerating social change, permanent economic austerity, and, not least, growing political transnationalization as it is most prominently reflected in the European integration process. In fact, this is where today the comparative study of welfare regimes may again, as back in the 1980s, profit from research on international regimes and their effects on policymaking and social agency.

SEE ALSO: Capitalism; Conservatism; Democracy; Institutionalism; Liberalism; Markets; Social Policy, Welfare State; Socialism

REFERENCES AND SUGGESTED READINGS

Castles, F. G. (Ed.) (1993) *Families of Nations: Patterns of Public Policies in Western Democracies.* Dartmouth, Aldershot.
Ebbinghaus, B. & Manow, P. (Eds.) (2001) *Comparing Welfare Capitalism: Social Policy and Political Economy in Europe, Japan, and the USA.* Routledge, London.
Esping-Andersen, G. (1990) *The Three Worlds of Welfare Capitalism.* Polity Press, Cambridge.
Esping-Andersen, G. (Ed.) (1996) *Welfare States in Transition: National Adaptations in Global Economies.* Sage, London.
Esping-Andersen, G. (1999) *Social Foundations of Postindustrial Economies.* Oxford University Press, Oxford.
Goodin, R. E., Headey, B., Muffels, R., & Dirven, H.-J. (1999) *The Real Worlds of Welfare Capitalism.* Cambridge University Press, Cambridge.
Korpi, W. (1983) *The Democratic Class Struggle.* Routledge & Kegan Paul, London.
Krasner, S. (Ed.) (1983) *International Regimes.* Cornell University Press, Ithaca, NY.
Lessenich, S. & Ostner, I. (Eds.) (1998) *Welten des Wohlfahrtskapitalismus. Der Sozialstaat in vergleichender Perspektive* (*Worlds of Welfare Capitalism: The Welfare State in Comparative Perspective*). Campus Verlag, Frankfurt.
Rein, M., Esping-Andersen, G., & Rainwater, L. (Eds.) (1987) *Stagnation and Renewal in Social Policy: The Rise and Fall of Policy Regimes.* M. E. Sharpe, Armonk, NY.
Sainsbury, D. (Ed.) (1999) *Gender and Welfare State Regimes.* Oxford University Press, Oxford.

welfare state

Markus Gangl

The essence of the modern welfare state lies in its institutional commitment to reconcile equity issues with the efficient operation of economic markets in industrial and post-industrial capitalist societies. As capitalism institutionally relies on the free competition of autonomous individual agents in exchange markets to achieve economic efficiency, but meets with real-world economies exhibiting an unequal distribution of wealth holdings, economies of scale in production, significant transaction costs, and imperfect information regarding prices and preferences, the unfettered operation of economic forces is likely to result in anything but an egalitarian distribution of economic well-being in a society. As an institutional antidote, modern welfare states have developed various policy instruments to realign the distributional outcomes of the market with broader social objectives of governments and their constituencies – and hence, the welfare state has rightly come to be seen as institutionally expressing and preserving social solidarity in highly complex societies made up of socially as well as economically highly heterogeneous populations.

WELFARE STATE INSTITUTIONS

Historically, the foundations of the modern welfare state emerged in late nineteenth-century Europe when governments responded to social upheaval generated by the transition to full-fledged industrial economies. From the introduction of public health and pension insurance in Bismarckian Germany in the 1880s onwards, governments began – partly in response to dramatic social change itself, partly to check the threat of a growing labor movement – to recognize the need to establish institutional mechanisms to guarantee that the broad majority of the population, especially the working class, would actually participate in economic growth generated by technological progress and an intensified transition to the capitalist mode of production. However, whereas the origins of welfare states have been in the social integration of the working class, welfare states have considerably expanded their scope and objectives, and have much refined their policy instruments over much of the twentieth century.

Nowadays, modern welfare states in fact consist of a broad array of institutions, policies, and programs aiming to secure adequate standards of living, broadly defined, for an encompassing majority of the population in industrialized societies. In consequence, welfare state institutions today comprise poverty relief through social assistance programs, social insurance against old age, ill health, job-related accidents or unemployment, family policies through child benefits, childcare subsidies, and parental leave schemes, service provision in the form of job counseling, public employment offices, public childcare facilities or public systems of care for the elderly, public housing, and often extensive social worker services. Moreover, these welfare state programs, narrowly defined, have become embedded in systems of public education at the primary, secondary, and tertiary level of education, extensive public regulation of markets, extensive judiciary systems, systems of public policies to conserve the environmental bases of affluent industrial societies, and, last but not least, a tax system raising the financial means necessary to fund these various instruments of government intervention.

Clearly, existing real-world welfare states differ significantly in both the level and range of welfare state commitments across the industrialized world. Encompassing welfare states and a respectively significant role of the state in social stratification as well as economic markets has been a hallmark of European societies. Due to strong labor movements and a long history of social democratic governance, Scandinavian countries, notably Sweden, feature particularly extensive welfare states that provide encompassing transfer systems compensating for social hardships, extensive public services to families and the elderly, as well as a significant public sector providing these. As demonstrated by the historical experience of continental European countries like France or Germany, welfare state development was also spurred by Catholic social thought and dominantly Christian democratic politics, although resulting welfare states are typically more bent toward regulation, prefer social insurance to universal transfer systems, and are weaker on public service provision than their Scandinavian counterparts. In comparison, welfare programs are much less generous, and hence the role of the state in social stratification much more limited, in the United States, Britain, Australia, and New Zealand after the reforms of the 1980s, but also in most post-communist countries of Eastern Europe.

ECONOMIC EFFECTS

Whatever the precise institutional arrangements, i.e., the specific national welfare mix institutionally balancing responsibilities and rights of families, markets, and government in any given society, there can be little doubt about the fact that the above policy instruments may constitute a veritable government intervention into private households' decisions on economic and social affairs. By providing transfers to compensate for social risk, governments deliberately alter the nexus between market incomes and household standard of livings, governments deliberately alter price structures by providing services and by subsidizing childrearing or education, governments deliberately alter households' market power by providing information, legal services, and regulation, and, last but not least, governments typically set up progressive tax systems to fund their services disproportionately through revenue generated from the well-off as well as from prospering firms and sectors. As these and other effects are likely to significantly affect the structure of economic incentives and constraints, welfare states are equally likely to engender significant economic consequences in terms of both economic behavior of individuals and households at the micro level and with respect to societies' larger macroeconomic prospects – in fact, soliciting respective economic effects may well be considered, after all, the whole point of establishing welfare state institutions. Given that welfare state institutions often fundamentally affect societies' economic structure, it is hardly surprising to find the empirical magnitude as well as the normative desirability of respective effects a matter of much social science discourse as well as public debate. To survey some of the key arguments and results, we address welfare state effects with respect to distributional outcomes, allocation, economic capabilities, and macroeconomic efficiency below, although this hardly provides an exhaustive list of total welfare state impact on the structure of advanced industrial societies.

Redistribution

To most, the welfare state simply is redistribution. Evidently, by providing income support to the needy and by funding these transfers through progressive taxes, welfare states succeed in redistributing income from the wealthy to the poor and hence contribute to alleviating relative poverty and to provide for minimally acceptable standards of living for practically the full population in the industrial world. To obtain empirical estimates of welfare states' redistributive impact, social scientists typically rely on data on household equivalent income, thus measuring standards of living by household income adjusted for household size. Defining (relative) poverty as standards of living falling below a threshold of 50 percent the national median household equivalent income, data from the cross-nationally comparable Luxembourg

Income Study compiled in Table 1 indicate both generally low poverty levels in advanced industrial societies and a significant role played by the welfare state in bringing this about. In a country like Sweden, poverty rates measured for market incomes alone amount to about 15 percent, yet taking into account welfare state taxes and transfers, less than 5 percent of all households remain below the 50 percent poverty line. Apparently, much the same holds true for other European countries as well, whereas the United States clearly stands out for its weakly developed welfare state showing but little redistributive impact.

Furthermore, Table 1 also shows that welfare state redistribution extends well beyond the low-income strata. Using the Gini coefficient – a measure ranging from 0 (perfect equality, i.e., everyone enjoying the same standard of living) to 100 (perfect inequality, i.e., all income earned by a single household) – to indicate the extent of overall income inequality in a given society, Table 1 again points to a significant reduction in income inequality due to welfare state efforts. Clearly, anti-poverty transfers have their share in this as well, yet more detailed analyses make it plain that transfers to the non-poor population like child benefits and particularly social insurance payments to the unemployed, the ill, and (although not included in the data of Table 1) the elderly are integral to welfare states' redistributive efforts in the population at large. As this points out, reducing the welfare state to mere anti-poverty transfers would be to severely misrepresent its redistributive role: in

Table 1　Poverty and income in equality in western countries (working-age households only), 1980s–1990s

Country	Poverty rate (50% median income)			Income inequality (Gini coefficient)		
	Market income (%)	Disposable income (%)	Poverty reduction (%)	Market income (%)	Disposable income (%)	Inequality reduction (%)
Sweden	14.8	4.8	64.5	32.7	20.2	37.9
France	21.8	6.1	57.9	39.4	29.4	25.4
Germany	9.7	5.1	46.9	32.2	26.2	18.7
United Kingdom	16.4	8.2	48.7	38.2	29.3	22.7
United States	17.2	15.1	12.1	39.8	32.8	17.6

Source: Moller et al. (2003) (poverty rates); Bradley et al. (2003) (Gini coefficients).

particular, as social insurance seeks to protect households against income losses from adverse events, welfare states deliberately redistribute incomes to non-poor households temporarily hit by income shocks in order to promote economic security and consumption smoothing over the life cycle. Accordingly, both pro-poor redistribution through targeted transfers and redistribution over the life cycle through social insurance are decisive for the redistributive impact of the welfare state.

Allocation

Against the significant role of the welfare state in reducing economic inequality, social scientists have wondered whether these redistributive efforts might not generate negative side-effects on the economic behavior of individuals and households. Most prominently, neoclassical economics asserts that high tax loads required to fund extensive welfare programs generate work disincentives or, at least, incentives to evade taxes by the high-income households expected to fund the welfare state. Similarly, mainstream economic theory expects transfer programs like social assistance or unemployment benefits to create significant work disincentives among those actually receiving transfers since many low-income households may hardly hope to command much higher market wages than what they might expect to receive from transfer programs.

Empirically, however, respective effects on work disincentives are typically found to be rather weak in general – labor force participation rates in the universalist Swedish welfare model, for example, are on a par with those in the United States, where a weak welfare state might be considered to induce the least significant distortions of economic incentives. In part this negative evidence might be related to the fact that work has intrinsic value to most people, that industrial economies successfully continue to maintain appropriate work norms, that workers are willing to pay payroll taxes that are seen as insurance premiums, or it might be the case that institutional provisions like job search requirements, minimum entitlement periods, and other qualifying conditions actually prevent transfer recipients from exploiting benefit systems.

On the other hand, many European welfare states clearly have been facing issues of high influx of older workers into unemployment or disability benefit systems as a form of early retirement, so that potential problems with work disincentives induced by welfare state programs are not easily to be dismissed at least for specific subgroups of workers.

What is also missing from the standard economic account of the relationship between welfare states and the allocation of economic effort, however, is the fact that welfare states might actually generate positive allocative impact that might act to counterbalance any presumed disincentive effects. In fact, tying transfer benefits to contribution records may induce workers to seek employment in the legal sector of the economy in order to qualify for benefits later on, thus implicitly also broadening the welfare state's tax base. Moreover, welfare states will alter the structure of the economy itself where, as perhaps most clearly to be seen in the case of women's labor force participation, welfare state provision of care and other social services increases demand for, and at least helps to build, a formal market for services and thus women's labor. Obviously, this in the very least implies a redistribution of employment and earnings opportunities in favor of women.

Capabilities

Efforts to systematically enhance the economic potential of individuals and households may in fact be seen as a constituent element of modern welfare states that is strangely absent from most discussions of the economic role of the welfare state in economics. Quite obviously, however, systems of public education are more than likely to improve access to training and skills, especially among lower-class youth. Similarly, job counseling and retraining programs offered to displaced workers or disadvantaged youth represent veritable welfare state investment in worker human capital unlikely to be undertaken by either employers or workers themselves. Finally, anti-discrimination laws and similar labor market regulation requiring equal treatment of different worker groups may have promoted economic opportunities for women and minority workers. Again, these efforts to strengthen individual and household earnings power will counter potential disincentive effects of the welfare state and will generally contribute to a redistribution of labor market, i.e., income chances in the population.

Macroeconomic Efficiency

The strain between various and potentially counteracting economic effects of the welfare state is equally evident in work on welfare state effects on overall macroeconomic efficiency and growth. Clearly, macroeconomic efficiency is all important to welfare states committed to provide high standards of living to a broad majority of the national population. Against this background, neoclassical economics has once again nurtured doubts about the macroeconomic viability of extensive welfare states that would reduce incentives to save and invest and hence undermine societies' long-term economic prospects. In fact, economists have compiled consistent empirical evidence from cross-national research on post-war economic growth that indicates a potential Achilles' heel of the welfare state: in general, countries that spent most on transfers and government consumption already back in the 1960s indeed incurred lower average growth rates up to the late 1990s.

However, economic research is also crystal clear that successful welfare states do have the means to prevent their own demise and that the key recipe to sustain extensive welfare systems is to maintain a balance between redistribution and investment in education and training. The same economic research indicating growth-inhibiting effects of transfers and government size consistently points out that societies exhibiting more highly educated workforces are those that have been seeing significantly above-average growth prospects over the post-war period due to the intensified technological change thus induced. Facing intensified economic progress and globalization partly spurred by its own success, the welfare state of the twenty-first century may thus, ironically enough, be very much in the same position as during its inception: on the one hand, the welfare state entails a significant redistribution of resources that threatens to create negative economic externalities, and, on the other hand, it is the very same redistribution

of economic capacities that legitimizes and thus indeed makes it possible to fully exploit the economic potential of a capitalist economy.

SEE ALSO: Affirmative Action; Capitalism, Social Institutions of; Education and Economy; Family Poverty; Income Inequality and Income Mobility; Life Chances and Resources; Poverty; Risk, Risk Society, Risk Behavior, and Social Problems; Social Policy, Welfare State; Stratification, Politics and; Taxes: Progressive, Proportional, and Regressive; Welfare Fraud; Welfare Regimes; Welfare State, Retrenchment of

REFERENCES AND SUGGESTED READINGS

Atkinson, A. B. (1999) *The Economic Consequences of Rolling Back the Welfare State*. MIT Press, Cambridge, MA.

Barr, N. (1998) *The Economics of the Welfare State*, 3rd edn. Oxford University Press, Oxford.

Barro, R. J. & Sala-i-Martin, X. (2004) *Economic Growth*, 2nd edn. MIT Press, Cambridge, MA.

Bradley, D., Huber, E., Moller, S., Nielsen, F., & Stephens, J. (2003) Distribution and Redistribution in Postindustrial Democracies. *World Politics* 55: 193–228.

Esping-Andersen, G. (1990) *The Three Worlds of Welfare Capitalism*. Polity Press, Cambridge.

Esping-Andersen, G. (1999) *Social Foundations of Postindustrial Economies*. Oxford University Press, Oxford.

Estevez-Abe, M., Iversen, T., & Soskice, D. (2001) Social Protection and the Formation of Skills: A Reinterpretation of the Welfare State. In: Hall, P. A. & Soskice, D. (Eds.), *Varieties of Capitalism: The Institutional Foundations of Comparative Advantage*. Oxford University Press, Oxford, pp. 145–83.

Goodin, R. E., Headey, B., Muffels, R., & Dirven, H.-J. (1999) *The Real Worlds of Welfare Capitalism*. Cambridge University Press, Cambridge.

Korpi, W. & Palme, J. (1998) The Paradox of Redistribution and Strategies of Equality: Welfare State Institutions, Inequality, and Poverty in Western Countries. *American Sociological Review* 63: 661–87.

Moller, S., Bradley, D., Huber, E., Nielsen, F., & Stephens, J. (2003) Determinants of Relative Poverty in Advanced Capitalist Democracies. *American Sociological Review* 68: 22–51.

Okun, A. M. (1975) *Equality and Efficiency: The Big Tradeoff*. Brookings Institution, Washington, DC.

welfare state, retrenchment of

Olli E. Kangas

Retrenchment of the welfare state pertains to various cost containment efforts that governments have tried to introduce. Retrenchment has taken different forms in different countries and different policy areas. It can include cuts in generosity and increasing qualification conditions to make benefits less universal and restrict the number of recipients. Also, changes in the form of financing can be used. In many countries financial responsibilities have been transferred to individuals themselves. The state has limited its role and citizens have more responsibility for their own welfare. The naming of the policies varies. Sometimes retrenchment is used synonymously with cutting, rolling-back, restructuring, reforming, recasting, recalibrating, and dismantling the welfare state.

The "crisis" of the welfare state is as long as the history of the welfare state. When the very first social policy programs were introduced 100 years ago there were worries about the overly excessive public spending that would hamper economic growth and erode individual morality and the competitiveness of the country. Thus, the theme is nothing new, but there have been fluctuations in policy priorities.

The oil crises of the 1970s changed the prevailing socioeconomic doctrine and more vociferous voices were raised against public spending, and public social spending in particular. The welfare state was seen as too costly and impossible to sustain. "A vicious spiral" metaphor obtained the upper-hand. Influential international organizations warned against cost expansion caused by deteriorating economic growth rates, generous welfare provisions, and aging populations. It was anticipated that these factors would increase public expenditure, especially spending on pensions, to economically unsustainable levels. As a consequence, many countries introduced a series of austerity measures to reverse the development and adapt social policies to the immediate crisis and in the longer run to disarm the "pension bomb" triggered by demographic changes.

The changing economic and political climate also changed the sociological research agenda. Up to the early 1980s, analyses of the causes of the growth of the welfare state gave way to studies revolving around retrenchment. In that sense, Flora's huge comparative research project *Growth to Limits* (1987) was an omen. The welfare state had (seemingly) grown to its limits.

Just as Esping-Andersen's *Three Worlds of Welfare Capitalism* (1990) launched an avalanche of studies on welfare state typologies and explanations of them, Pierson's *Dismantling the Welfare State?* (1994) inaugurated a new era of retrenchment studies in which welfare cuts (not improvements) were in focus. Consequently, a shift in explanatory factors took place. Previously, a power-resource approach emphasizing the role of politics had been successfully used to explain country-specific variations in welfare benefits, but gradually neo-institutionalism and various forms of structural-functionalist explanations (referring to globalization and demographic pressures) gained ground.

The political discourses that emphasize the decisive role of economic and demographic variables and constraints caused by globalization are not that novel. The old structural functionalism was revitalized after a period of stagnation in the 1980s and early 1990s. The new argument in the new politics of welfare was that policy goals had changed. Instead of seeking credit for improvement of the citizens' well-being, governments in their retrenchment policies must try to avoid blame and to minimize political costs (Pierson 1994). In its blame avoidance politics a government has two devices at its disposal. It can obfuscate and make things too difficult for the general public to understand (e.g., mathematical formulas to calculate pensions are such a device). And there is the so-called grandfather/mother clause that leaves current recipients intact but introduces cuts in future benefits. Again, the pension area is the best example.

Sociological retrenchment studies lean toward institutionalism and path-dependent explanations. Here the argument goes that once established, social policy institutions have their own impact on possibilities to cut these institutions. The welfare state was changed from explanandum to explanans. On the one hand, clients of social policy constitute influential pressure groups that politicians must take into consideration when deliberating about cuts in benefits. The central political question is blame avoidance (i.e., how to avoid punishment from the electorate). On the other hand, the welfare state itself has become an institution that has strong feedback loops to politics. Due to the impact of these loops, some schemes are easier to change, whereas other have stronger institutional inertia. One important stream in the retrenchment discourse has dealt with the degree of inertia. The idea that underpins this is that previous decisions constrain future options. Institutions are put on a specific track which creates path dependency.

The degree of path dependency varies between welfare state programs and regimes. Pension programs are the best example of a scheme that is difficult to change. In the pension area the state has given individuals certain promises that extend to 30 or 50 years in the future. Therefore, most pension reforms must be incremental to give individuals possibilities to adapt themselves to the new situation.

Historical analyses show that state corporatist programs – programs administered on a bi- or tripartite basis either between social partners or between partners and the state and financed through social security contributions – are harder to change than, for example, schemes that are based on pure political administration and tax financing. In the former case social partners usually have a number of institutional veto points at which to reject any cuts proposed by the government. Moreover, insurance contributions paid by employees create a feeling that they have paid for the benefits, whereas the link between general taxes and benefits is more obscure and taxes do not create a basis for strong claim rights.

Institutional approaches are often divided into two or three variants. In rational choice institutionalism emphasis is on political actors who in their self-interested rent-seeking react/ act in the institutional surroundings that the welfare state creates, whereas historical institutionalists are more interested in how, for example, the welfare state as such constructs interests and formulates actors' images of their interests. The most constructivist variant, sociological institutionalism, employs discourses and

consequently the politics of retrenchment is much more about discursive or ideological struggles over the right to give interpretation to "reality." From time to time the hegemonic interpretations are changed, which leads to changes in welfare policies. The shift from Keynesianism to monetarism is an example of a paradigmatic shift in the mode of thinking that in turn changes politics.

An important theme in the retrenchment debate concerns the possibilities for changing the existing welfare state. For structuralists, power-resource sociologists, and sociological institutionalists, the answer is rather easy. Changes take place when structural preconditions, political constellations, and policy paradigms are changed. Path dependency and institutional stickiness may cause some problems in explaining change. A handy solution that adopts elements of all the above-mentioned approaches is to say that welfare institutions (notably pensions) enjoy long periods of stability, but occasionally the stability is punctuated by crises – be they changes in structural, political, or discursive contexts or combinations of such factors – that may bring pathbreaking changes. The new path is then followed up to the next punctuation point. The problem in this kind of retrenchment discussion is that a pathbreaking change is supposed to be abrupt. However, many fundamental changes may go unnoticed and be based on non-decisions: small-scale adjustments can ultimately alter the whole system, including the underlying ideology of the responsibilities of the state vis-à-vis the market and the individual. To make the picture a bit more complicated, the severity of retrenchment depends on the indicator we look at. A change in the basic ideology (e.g., from means-testing to universalism) may not yield better benefits to the clients. Social spending figures may give a totally different picture of the impacts of retrenchment policies than indicators of social rights. Moreover, consequences of cuts in terms of poverty and social exclusion/ inclusion will be visible after a time lag of decades, which means that sociologists will also wrestle with these questions in the future. Perhaps, then, the strong western bias in welfare state retrenchment discourse will be changed and social policy debates will deal much more with the distribution of resources in a global perspective.

SEE ALSO: Functionalism/Neofunctionalism; Globalization; Institutionalism; Political Sociology; Politics; Social Policy, Welfare State; Social Problems, Politics of; Welfare Fraud; Welfare Regimes; Welfare State

REFERENCES AND SUGGESTED READINGS

Castels, F. & Pierson, C. (Eds.) (2000) *The Welfare State: A Reader*. Polity Press, Cambridge.

Esping-Andersen, G. (1990) *Three Worlds of Welfare Capitalism*. Polity Press, Cambridge.

Flora, P. (Ed.) (1987) *Growth to Limits: The Western European Welfare States Since World War II*, Vols. 1–4. De Gruyter, New York.

Korpi, W. & Palme, J. (2003) New Politics and Class Politics in the Context of Austerity and Globalization: Welfare State Regress in 18 Countries, 1975–95. *American Political Science Review* 90(3): 425–46.

Pierson, P. (1994) *Dismantling the Welfare State? Reagan, Thatcher, and the Politics of Retrenchment*. Cambridge University Press, Cambridge.

Pierson, P. (Ed.) (2001) *The New Politics of the Welfare State*. Oxford University Press, Oxford.

Steinmo, S., Thelen, K., & Longstreth, F. (Eds.) (1992) *Structuring Politics: Historical Institutionalism in Comparative Analysis*. Agathon Press, New York.

whiteness

Howard Winant

Like water to the proverbial fish, whiteness has been largely invisible in the "modern world-system" of European creation. This invisibility is somewhat unique among the racial categories. The uniqueness does not consist of the "normalization" of whiteness: the idea that whiteness is the "default" racial status, that whites are "just people" who "don't have a race." Nor does its uniqueness consist in the "transparency" of whiteness: the way in which whiteness is taken for granted in the world's powerful countries and thus not seen, like water by the fish. In many places, especially where one racially defined group predominates, that group's raciality is relatively invisible. Think of much of Africa, Han China, or Yamato Japan.

No, the uniqueness of whiteness's invisibility lies in the contradictions therein: while whiteness partakes of normality and transparency, it is also dominant, insistently so. And it is also beleaguered, nervous, defensive. These qualities in turn belie claims for the "normality" of whiteness, the default status of the concept.

Whiteness can hardly be hidden in a social system based on racial domination, one in which races are necessarily relational matters. White supremacy has never gone unresisted, for one thing, so whites (colonists, settlers, planters, etc.) have always had to "circle the wagons": they had to theorize whiteness, defend its "purity," and justify their rule. They had to take up their "White Man's Burden," carry out their "*Mission Civilisatrice*," fulfill their "Manifest Destiny."

From the early days of conquest and slavery, from the early phases of European empire building right down to the present, there has been white unease about the very white supremacy employed to organize and justify European rule. "What if. . ., what if. . ."

Resistance. What if the blacks, the natives, the kaffirs, the wogs, rose up against us? (Indeed, they often have done so.) What if they treated us as we have treated them? In white horror at the Haitian revolution, at Sepoy, at the Mau Mau, at Nat Turner, at the revolt of the Muslim Malês of Bahia in 1835, at the putative barbarity of the Algerian revolution (and in endless other instances), we see the inner fears and guilt that accompany white rule.

Migration. How can we keep ourselves from being "swamped" by the "rising tide of color"? Lothrop Stoddard (1920) and Madison Grant's (1916) bestsellers contemplated with dread the declining fortunes of European rule, conceiving whiteness as a fortress, a laager, besieged by the lesser breeds who sought to immigrate, to overrun the "advanced" outposts of civilization, to drag down all the higher accomplishments of Europe and its avatars. North American nativism of course preceded their panicky alarums by more than a century (Higham 1955). Mrs. Thatcher revived the "swamping" metaphor in her campaigns, and it continues to thrive under the careful tending of Le Pen, Haider, Fini, Tom Tancredo, and many other politicians in every white-dominated metropole in the world.

Sexual purity. Miscegenation is a threat to whiteness authored by whites, notably white men, themselves. "Carnal knowledge and imperial power" (and slavocratic power too) have always gone together, as Stoler (2002) has most effectively demonstrated. Danger, race-mixing ahead! Rape and concubinage, the problematic and ambiguous identities of mixed-race offspring, the thrill of desire for the racialized "other," and the constant risk that whites will "go native" (Torgovnick 1991) have always represented a risk to white purity, and thus white identity itself.

So despite numerous claims of universality, racelessness, and "colorblindness" (Bonilla-Silva 2003), whiteness is not only still present but also racially particular in its own right. "White" is a racial category, and "whites" something of a racial group, of course partaking of huge variation across space and time. But what is "whiteness," anyway?

In much radical literature, largely recent but not without precedent, whiteness is portrayed entirely in the negative: as the explicit absence of "color," of raciality. Whiteness substitutes for class consciousness, subverting it by racially linking rulers and ruled. The social fact of *not* being black, *not* being "of color," is seen as its essential quality. Ignatiev (1995), Lott (1993), Roediger (1991), and others have advanced this analysis, drawing to various degrees on Du Bois's account in *Black Reconstruction* (1935) of the "psychological wage" derived by the North American white worker from the choice of racial rather than class identity. Whiteness arises as if to say, "I may be poor and exploited, but at least I'm white." Morgan's (1975) history of Virginia colonialism takes a similar view.

Other currents dispute this view at least in part, noting the problematic and partial character of the "achievement" of whiteness by many European immigrants (Jacobson 1998) and the weird reversals of white supremacist obsessions

with purity and beleagueredness that echo in such arguments. Some have argued that "white trash" is itself a distinct racial category, pointing to the persecution of the supposedly "feeble-minded" during the heyday of eugenics, and the continuing contempt expressed for the white poor today (Wray & Newitz 1997). But the most telling objection to the idea that whiteness is a purely negative racial category, and hence something that could be "abolished," is the recognition that racial identity is relational in character. However socially constructed the creation and perpetuation of racial identities may have been, these identities can no more be discontinued than can such other similarly situated human attributes that we now see as fundamental: gender, class, and nation, for example.

Beyond this, racialization is notoriously synthetic and absorptive. In forging its whiteness, Europe incorporated a great many of the characteristics of those over whom it ruled, imparting to them in turn many of its own qualities: not only resources, not only migrants, not only diseases, not only gametes, flowed in both directions across various racial divides, but so too did language, technology, and knowledge, both sacred and profane.

Thus the chief distinction between the racial category of whiteness and other racial designations is not some supposedly all-encompassing negativity of white identity; indeed, the claim that whiteness is merely the "absence of color" is quite questionable. Rather, the concept's problematic nature stems from its continuing (if often flexible and today often disavowed) involvement with domination. To adapt Lincoln's formulation: whiteness cannot forever endure half-asserting itself, and half-denying itself. A whiteness that abandoned its ambivalent claims to "colorblindness" (another way of reclaiming invisibility) and that recognized that its gestation and development, right down to the present, have been tainted by "unfair gains, unjust enrichments, and unearned advantages" (Lipsitz 1998), could perhaps redeem itself by breaking decisively with that history. Could whiteness not be reinvented by such means as practical measures of redistribution and thoroughgoing racial democratization? After all, there have been many anti-racist whites; from where did their motivations arise? Might not white people yet achieve admission to a pluralist global community that acknowledged racial difference but refused racially based stratification or hierarchy? Since history has not ended, the final judgment on such questions has yet to be made.

SEE ALSO: Color Line; Double Consciousness; Race; Race and Ethnic Consciousness; Race (Racism); Racism, Structural and Institutional; Scientific Racism; Stratification, Race/Ethnicity and

REFERENCES AND SUGGESTED READINGS

Bonilla-Silva, E. (2003) *Racism Without Racists: Color-Blind Racism and the Persistence of Racial Inequality in the United States.* Rowman & Littlefield, Lanham, MD.

Du Bois, W. E. B. (1977 [1935]) *Black Reconstruction: An Essay Toward a History of the Part which Black Folk Played in the Attempt to Reconstruct Democracy in America, 1860–1880.* Atheneum, New York.

Grant, M. (1936 [1916]) *The Passing of the Great Race; Or, The Racial Basis of European History.* Scribner, New York.

Higham, J. (1955) *Strangers in the Land: Patterns of American Nativism, 1860–1925.* Rutgers University Press, New Brunswick, NJ.

Ignatiev, N. (1995) *How the Irish Became White.* Routledge, New York.

Jacobson, M. F. (1998) *Whiteness of a Different Color: European Immigrants and the Alchemy of Race.* Harvard University Press, Cambridge, MA.

Lipsitz, G. (1998) *The Possessive Investment in Whiteness: How White People Profit from Identity Politics.* Temple University Press, Philadelphia.

Lott, E. (1993) *Love and Theft: Blackface Minstrelsy and the American Working Class.* Oxford University Press, New York.

Morgan, E. S. (1975) *American Slavery, American Freedom: The Ordeal of Colonial Virginia.* Norton, New York.

Roediger, D. R. (1991) *The Wages of Whiteness: Race and the Making of the American Working Class.* Verso, New York.

Stoddard, L. (1920) *The Rising Tide of Color Against White World-Supremacy.* Scribner, New York.

Stoler, A. L. (2002) *Carnal Knowledge and Imperial Power: Race and the Intimate in Colonial Rule.* University of California Press, Berkeley.

Torgovnick, M. (1991) *Gone Primitive: Savage Intellects, Modern Lives.* University of Chicago Press, Chicago.

Wray, M. & Newitz, A. (Eds.) (1997) *White Trash: Race and Class in America.* Routledge, New York.

widowhood

Kate Davidson

There has been a slow but discernible increase in sociological interest in the experience of widowhood in later life in the last three decades of the twentieth century, which has come about as a result of two major western world trends: demography and feminism. People are living longer, and as a result of a decrease in birth rates, the proportion of older people in the population is steadily increasing. For example, in the UK, the 2001 census data revealed that 48 percent of women compared to 17 percent of men over the age of 65 were widowed. Second wave feminism's imperative has been to examine women's experiences and circumstances, and to reflect on what societal norms and values inform meaning and self-conceptualization in relation to being female. Gradually now, feminism is addressing the issue of aging. The conjunction of these two trends has seen the steady emergence, particularly in North America, of sociological study of widowhood as experienced by women (Lopata 1996).

However, minimal sociological attention has been paid to the lives of widowed men, primarily because of their relative invisibility, both numerically and in welfare distribution statistics. The research there has been on widowers has principally focused on the health outcomes and psychological disorientation caused by an unanticipated disjunction: a husband does not expect to predecease his wife. Nevertheless, the issue of "who suffers more," widowers or widows, is shown to be contentious. Parkes and Weiss in their *Recovery from Bereavement* (1983), which looked at widows and widowers across all ages, revealed that both widowed men and women were found to have lower psychological well-being than their married counterparts. Health status and social networks were major predictors of psychological well-being. Among women, close female friends contributed more to psychological well-being than family contact, while among men, family contact was more important.

In the Netherlands, Stevens (1995) examined the well-being and living conditions of older widows and widowers in order to establish gender differences in adaptation to conjugal loss. Her results indicated that there were remarkable similarities in the reported well-being of the respondents. Availability of resources such as income, education, and freedom from limiting disability advantaged the widowers, but widows benefited from the support of close female friends and neighbors as well as adult children. Few significant differences were found in the reported personal relationship needs, although the relational patterns were different: the women tended to have more "emotionally intimate" female friends. The men were content with male friends for "sociability," but also wished for a cross-gender romantic relationship. The men, Stevens discovered, derived satisfaction from the presence of new partners or partner-like relationships and tended to depend more on adult children than did the widows. She found that while widowed women were disadvantaged regarding income, education, and health resources, they reported similar life satisfaction to the widowed men. She concluded that this was because women had been socialized into greater flexibility and adaptability over the life course. This helped them with the major change brought about by widowhood and mediated the instrumental disadvantages.

Early research on spousal bereavement (almost exclusively for women) conceptualized widowhood as "role loss" and "role exit." Bereavement was analyzed in terms of role change from wife to widow, which in turn considered a widow to be a "roleless wife," who lacked any duties towards others in the social system. Widowhood was viewed as *involuntary disengagement* and as such the individual was thought to be rendered powerless. These disengagement theories have contributed to the literature which views widowhood as a totally negative state. The literature does not highlight whether this process is the same or different for widowers since the male identity is differently socially structured. The primary social role of a man is not husband and father, his sense of self-identity is derived from his occupational status rather than his marital status.

The death of a spouse is a devastating experience for the vast majority of people, but the consequential adaptation from "we" to "I" is substantially different for men and women. Later sociological theory such as that explored by Anthony Giddens in *Modernity and Self-Identity* (1994) permits us to reconceptualize loss in terms of ontological security, which takes into consideration adaptation as a *process* mediated by age, gender, culture, and social capital. In doing so, we can contextualize these older people's experience within a life-course perspective, the outcome of which is not always unrelentingly depressing. Indeed, some widows express a sense of liberation and personal development after the loss of their husband. The few studies carried out on widowers indicate that it is the loss of the person whose care allowed them independence, and the need to take on the role as self-carer, that requires psychological and social adjustment (Bennett et al. 2003). Men therefore rarely view widowhood as a time of freedom. Depending upon age, health, and financial status – that is, the younger, fitter, and richer they are – the more likely they are to seek cross-gender companionship, with (preferably) or without sexual relations. Contrary to received wisdom, older widowers' main motive for seeking a new partnership is not to have instrumental help from a housekeeper, but to assuage the loneliness they feel at the death of the most central person in their life. It is ironic that the men, socialized into independence and autonomy, seem to be less psychologically prepared to cope with aloneness.

SEE ALSO: Aging, Demography of; Aging and Social Support; Later-Life Marriage; Retirement

REFERENCES AND SUGGESTED READINGS

Bennett, K., Hughes, G., & Smith, P. (2003) "I think a woman can take it": Widowed Men's Views and Experiences of Gender Differences in Bereavement. *Ageing International* 28: 408–24.

Lopata, H. Z. (1996) *Current Widowhood: Myths and Realities*. Sage, Thousand Oaks, CA.

Stevens, N. (1995) Gender and Adaptation to Widowhood in Later Life. *Ageing and Society* 15: 37–58.

Williams, Raymond (1921–88)

Tony Bennett

Born in 1921 in Wales, Raymond Williams was educated at Cambridge and, after wartime military service and an initial academic position in Oxford's Extra-Mural Delegacy, returned there on a permanent basis as Lecturer in English in 1961, subsequently becoming Professor of Drama in 1974.

A lifelong socialist, Williams was an active member of the Labour Party and a key figure in the British new left. These and his other political involvements – in the Campaign for Nuclear Disarmament (CND), for example – provided the horizon for his intellectual work. This took varied forms. A moderately successful novelist, Williams was much in demand as a political and cultural commentator and he wrote a number of specialist studies on specific literary and dramatic genres.

His most enduring impact, however, was a theoretical one focused on new ways of thinking about the relationships between culture and society that have had considerable influence on debates in sociology and, for cultural studies, remain of foundational significance.

Developed initially in *Culture and Society* (1958) and *The Long Revolution* (1961), Williams's central accomplishment was to dispute, and provide an alternative to, the terms in which the relations between culture and society had been debated in British social thought in the nineteenth and early twentieth centuries. Reviewing the writings of Samuel Taylor Coleridge, John Ruskin, Matthew Arnold, T. S. Eliot, and others, Williams took issue with their sense of culture as an elite standard of perfection that had to be defended against the deadening influence of the masses, a view that informed the literary criticism of Williams's contemporary, F. R. Leavis.

Objecting that there are no masses, only different ways of seeing people as masses, Williams challenged this tradition of thought on two main grounds. First, drawing on the anthropological concept of culture proposed by Edward Burnett Tylor in his *Primitive Culture* (1871), Williams argued that any socially viable contemporary understanding of culture had to concern itself not only with the selective tradition of high artistic and intellectual culture but also with the beliefs, customs, and traditions – the everyday ways of life – of different social classes and groups.

His second contention was that such ways of life should not be studied in isolation from each other. Analysis should rather encompass the whole set of relations that organized the interactions between ways of life. Williams attributed to these a patterned complexity which – in a term whose exact meaning has proved elusive – he called the "structure of feeling" characterizing a particular period or society. The early work of the Birmingham School in cultural studies was profoundly shaped by its engagements with these aspects of Williams's work and the more empirically developed traditions of subcultural analysis coming out of American sociology (Hall & Jefferson 1976).

Williams's work took a different direction in the 1970s, mainly as a consequence of his exposure to the continental tradition of "western Marxism" that *New Left Review* made widely available in English translation. His intellectual engagement with European Marxism bore its most distinctive fruit in *Marxism and Literature* (1977) in which, while committing to a Marxist position, he also sought to reform it.

In earlier work, Williams had distanced himself from the Marxist formulations of the relations between culture and society that were then available to him. In *Marxism and Literature*, the influence of Antonio Gramsci, Lucien Goldman, and others led to a more favorable reading of Marxist thought on the condition that its understanding of the relations between culture and society be detached from the determinist implications of the base/superstructure metaphor. The result was a distinctive formulation of the relative autonomy of culture which Williams fashioned into a probing account of the role of materialism in Marxist thought – issues he returned to in *Problems in Materialism and Culture* (1980).

Other key texts include *The Country and the City* (1973), a commanding overview of the representation of the relations between rural and urban social life in British literature and social thought, and *Television: Technology and Cultural Form* (1974) which, in rebutting determinist accounts of the relations between media technologies and society and discussing the significance of flow in the organization of the television text, had a long-term influence on the development of television studies. *Keywords* (1976) made an original contribution to public scholarship in its historical survey of the key terms in the English vocabulary of the relations between culture and society.

Williams died in 1988, shortly after retiring. While he remained intellectually active to the end – *The Politics of Modernism* (1989) was published posthumously – his later work spoke less centrally to changing political concerns. For Williams, the key point of social reference for discussing culture was always class. His work therefore yielded little purchase on the increasingly important questions regarding gender, sexuality, and culture that feminist thought had placed on the agenda. The exclusively national and white British framework of this thought was also incapable of addressing questions of race and ethnicity – an aspect of his legacy that Paul Gilroy (1987) drew attention to.

There are several critical commentaries on Williams's life and work and one biography (Inglis 1995). Williams, however, had always made commentary on his life a part of his work in a manner that was and remains distinctive. His interviews with the editors of *New Left Review*, published as *Politics and Letters* (1979), are still the most absorbing manifestation and portrayal of this interweaving of life and work.

SEE ALSO: Base and Superstructure; Birmingham School; Class Consciousness; Cultural Studies, British; Culture; Materialism; Media; New Left; Subculture

REFERENCES AND SUGGESTED READINGS

Dworkin, D. L. & Roman, L. G. (Eds.) (1993) *Views Beyond the Border Country: Raymond Williams and Cultural Politics*. Routledge, London and New York.

Eagleton, T. (Ed.) (1989) *Raymond Williams: Critical Perspectives*. Polity Press, Cambridge.

Gilroy, P. (1987) *There Ain't No Black in the Union Jack*. Hutchinson, London.

Hall, S. & Jefferson, T. (Eds.) (1976) *Resistance Through Rituals: Youth Sub-Cultures in Post-War Britain*. Hutchinson, London.

Inglis, F. (1995) *Raymond Williams*. Routledge, London and New York.

O'Connor, A. (1989) *Raymond Williams: Writing, Culture, Politics*. Blackwell, Oxford.

Wollstonecraft, Mary (1759–97)

Cynthia Siemsen

Mary Wollstonecraft has been widely regarded at least since the 1970s as the first feminist thinker of consequence on women's sociopolitical condition. The label "feminist" is perhaps a misnomer considering the historical context of her life and the relative youth of the term. However, if the litmus test for feminist thought is opposition to gender hierarchy, acceptance that gender is socially constructed, and belief that women as a social group need collective action to bring about equality, Mary Wollstonecraft is a proto-feminist thinker. Her writings appear on the shelves of literature, political philosophy, and women's studies. Wollstonecraft's life is also the subject in its own right of psychology, anthropology, and literature. However, the consideration of her contribution to classical sociological thought is more recent. Wollstonecraft's theoretical absence is not a reflection on her sociological contributions; rather, it symbolizes the patriarchal nature of society when sociology as a discipline emerged, and the everyday reality of most societies throughout history, including our own.

The statement that social theory cannot be disentangled from the life and historical moment of the thinker takes on great meaning when applied to Mary Wollstonecraft. Her biography reads like the plot of a great tragedy: berated daughter, servant, vilified political writer, at-times suicidal lover, briefly happy wife, and early death from the complications of child-birth which delivered a great gothic novelist. The tendency to emphasize "Wollstonecraft, the subject" over "Wollstonecraft, the social thinker" is difficult to resist. However, Wollstonecraft's biography informed her thought and her theory influenced her life. But Wollstonecraft's theory goes beyond the particulars of her life to expose the gendered power relations of larger social institutions.

Wollstonecraft was born in the crowded East End of London. She was the second child of seven, and oldest daughter to a ne'er-do-well farmer who was a violent alcoholic and who beat his wife. Wollstonecraft recollected that she slept on the landing outside her parents' bed-room in the event she should have to protect her mother from her father's abuse. Wollstonecraft (1798) remembered her father as a tyrant and her mother as his willing victim. She was continually reminded of the status difference between herself and her parents' firstborn son. Although she remained bitter toward her brother, and the institution of inheritance, later in life Wollstonecraft grew to appreciate poverty's odd benefits. Wollstonecraft reasoned that, had she led the sheltered social existence of her middle-class female counterparts, she may have developed physical and mental inadequacies fostered by patriarchal environments.

Wollstonecraft fled her parents' house at 19 years to pursue a life of economic independence from men. Through service to moneyed women, Wollstonecraft became convinced that middle-class women's inadequacies grew from their dependencies upon husbands, which were supported by the spirit and letter of English law. A married woman legally could not own property in her own name; furthermore, as subservient to her husband, she had no legal control over her own children. Divorce was nearly impossible.

Wollstonecraft was for the most part self-taught. During her early years of independence, she combined her talents with those of her friend Fanny Blood, and opened a school for girls. Although the school folded following Blood's death due to complications of child-birth, the endeavor led Wollstonecraft to write her first work for money. *Thoughts on the Education of Daughters* (1787) stressed the power of women to cultivate their minds through education and reason, in order to realize independence

and virtue. While her first piece was less than original – a frequent criticism of Wollstonecraft (Sapiro 1992) – *Thoughts* reflected Wollstonecraft's later preoccupation with outcomes of blind obedience, whether within the family or within the state.

Wollstonecraft wrote *Mary: A Fiction* (1788) the following year. The now 27-year-old governess depicted a young woman who was belittled by her parents and forced to educate herself as a means of survival. The novel closes by reflecting on a "world where there is neither marrying, nor giving in marriage." Obviously, *Mary* is not pure fiction, but it demonstrates Wollstonecraft's potential for radical thought.

By the end of 1787, Wollstonecraft adopted the identity of a professional writer with the aid of the Dissenting publisher Joseph Johnson. Wollstonecraft joined Johnson's political circle that included British poet and painter William Blake, American Revolutionary Thomas Paine, British political theorist William Godwin, and moral philosopher Richard Price. Wollstonecraft's first great work would not be published until 1790; in the interim she became a frequent book reviewer for Johnson's *Analytical Review*. Of note is her critique of Rousseau's *Confessions*.

The Vindication of the Rights of Men (1790) was the first of many responses to Edmund Burke's *Reflections on the Revolution in France* (1790), the most famous being Thomas Paine's *The Rights of Man*. With the falling of the Bastille in 1789, England was thrust into a controversy over human rights. Burke declared that the principles of the French Revolution might prove the ruin of France (and perhaps England) if liberty and equality prevailed. Burke conceived those institutions threatened by the revolution – the monarchy, class distinctions, inheritance, and property – as the basis of social order. Without them society might revert to its previous brutish state where innate human passions ran rampant.

Less than a month after *Reflections* was published, Wollstonecraft dashed off her heated response that synthesized her ideas with those of Locke, Rousseau, and Richard Price. Wollstonecraft's *The Vindication of the Rights of Men* was considered rude (especially after she revealed her identity), rushed, and emotionally personal. Despite its anger, *Rights of Men* has

been described as "one of the most sophisticated essays on political argument and political
psychology of her day" (Sapiro 1992: 24–5).
Wollstonecraft (1790) followed Locke in defining rights as God-given to "such a degree of
liberty, civil and religious, as is compatible with
the liberty of every other individual with whom
he is united in a social compact" (pp. 7–8).
Following Rousseau, liberty in civil society
was only an ideal that obscures the reality of
private property. For Wollstonecraft, human
rights were rational rights; they were inherited
at birth by humans, as rational creatures;
rational rights cannot be undermined by tradition or other social institutions. She criticized
Burke's view of human malice present at birth.
For Wollstonecraft (1790), "children are born
ignorant, [consequently] innocent" (p. 72). Following Price, morality was not an instinct; it
existed in the sphere of human reason. Wollstonecraft ridiculed Burke for supporting the
aristocracy and class distinctions; she instead
stressed the bad effects of privilege on the person, for "the respect paid to rank and fortune
damps every generous purpose of the soul"
(p. 52). Wollstonecraft argued that upper-class
women were only half human, their biggest
concern being to please men.

However, *The Vindication of the Rights of
Woman* (1792) was the first place she identified –
in today's words – women as an oppressed
group, crossing class lines. In it she set forth
two theoretical propositions. First, she argued
that the absolute monarchism of her day was
tied to four institutions: the aristocracy, military, church, and most of all, the patriarchal
family. Second, true freedom for all human
beings (i.e., economic, political, and intellectual) would never exist as long as women and
men were not equals. Wollstonecraft repeatedly
asserted the right of women to prove their
equality through enlarged opportunities (e.g.,
education) and independence from men. However, its more sociological reading is that just as
the tyranny of men injures the character of
women, so the tyranny of government harms
its people.

By the end of 1792 Wollstonecraft had traveled to France to witness the revolution first
hand. In a departure from liberal thought,
Wollstonecraft grappled with power and domination in *An Historical and Moral View of the
Origin and Progress of the French Revolution*
(1794), addressing both the political violence
of the *ancien régime* and the violence of the
Terror she witnessed. Wollstonecraft's years
in France are most often linked to her romantic
liaison with American writer and entrepreneur
Gilbert Imlay. By the end of 1793 France and
England were at war and British expatriates
were being arrested in France. Wollstonecraft
sought protection at the American Embassy by
registering as the "wife" of Imlay. Although
they never married, Imlay fathered Wollstonecraft's first daughter, Fanny, and was the
impetus behind *Letters Written during a Short
Residence in Sweden, Norway, and Denmark*
(1796).

Imlay lost interest in Wollstonecraft after
Fanny's birth, plunging her into a deep depression. Todd (2000: 279–80) writes: "She took no
comfort from the stern words in *The Rights of
Woman* about the stupidity of women who put
their trust in romantic hopes." The knowledge
of Imlay's interest in other women led to Wollstonecraft's first suicide attempt. To help her
recover, Imlay sent Wollstonecraft (and Fanny)
to Scandinavia as his business agent – a lost
cargo ship needed recovery.

Wollstonecraft's last great work began as part
of a new genre, the travelogue; it also lapses into
a memoir of a troubled woman struggling to
find peace of mind. (Wollstonecraft did not
achieve peace of mind on her travels to Scandinavia. Her affair with Imlay ended only after
another suicide attempt.) However, it was also a
treatise on society and human nature. Wollstonecraft's consciousness of power's oppressive nature was keener than ever. She witnessed the
tyranny of Denmark against its weaker neighbors, men over women, and found power's root
in private property. Observing convicts on a
road one day she reflected that the gold keys
of the nearby noblemen were a greater disgrace
than the prisoners' chains. Whether a person
was the aristocrat or the prisoner, they would
feel the ill-effects of the same unjust society at
the level of their characters.

One of *A Short Residence*'s readers was
William Godwin, who wrote: "if ever there was
a book calculated to make a man in love with
its author, this appears to me to be the book"
(Ferguson & Todd 1984: 89). Wollstonecraft
and Godwin's intellectual and love relationship

was short-lived. After learning of Wollstone-craft's pregnancy they chose to marry despite their public statements on the evils of the marriage contract as an artificial bond. While pregnant, Wollstonecraft was in the process of writing a novel she would never finish. At 38 years of age, Wollstonecraft died from complications after childbirth. Her infant, Mary Godwin Shelley, survived and went on to write *Frankenstein*. Although she never completed *The Wrongs of Woman, or Maria* (1798), in that work Wollstonecraft gave her most radical statement of the relationship between patriarchy, the state, and the family. She argued that the family represents a small commonwealth of the state, and that a husband is not only its patriarch, but also its police.

What earns Mary Wollstonecraft a place of prominence in pre-sociological philosophy is her early articulation of micro and macro levels of analysis. On the one hand, she describes social environmental influences on the formation of the gendered self. Wollstonecraft's analysis also extends beyond her personal experience and close observation of gender roles of her day; she also demonstrates the tie between gender and power in the relations of dominance and subordination within social institutions such as the aristocracy, military, church, and family.

SEE ALSO: Feminism; Patriarchy; Women's Empowerment

REFERENCES AND SUGGESTED READINGS

Ferguson, M. & Todd, J. (1984) *Mary Wollstonecraft*. Twayne, Boston.

Harper, L. M. (2001) *Solitary Travelers: Nineteenth-Century Women's Travel Narratives and the Scientific Vocation*. Associated University Presses, Cranbury, NJ.

Sapiro, V. (1992) *A Vindication of Political Virtue: The Political Theory of Mary Wollstonecraft*. Chicago University Press, Chicago.

Todd, J. (2000) *Mary Wollstonecraft: A Revolutionary Life*. Columbia University Press, New York.

Wollstonecraft, M. (1989a [1787]) *Thoughts on the Education of Daughters*. In: Todd, J. & Butler, M. (Eds.), *The Works of Mary Wollstonecraft*. New York University Press, New York, Vol. 4, pp. 1–49.

Wollstonecraft, M. (1989b [1788]) *Mary: A Fiction*. In: Todd, J. & Butler, M. (Eds.), *The Works of*
Mary Wollstonecraft. New York University Press, New York, Vol. 1, pp. 1–73.

Wollstonecraft, M. (1989c [1790]) *A Vindication of the Rights of Men*. In: Todd, J. & Butler, M. (Eds.), *The Works of Mary Wollstonecraft*. New York University Press, New York, Vol. 5, pp. 1–266.

Wollstonecraft, M. (1989d [1792]) *A Vindication of the Rights of Woman*. In: Todd, J. & Butler, M. (Eds.), *The Works of Mary Wollstonecraft*. New York University Press, New York, Vol. 5, pp. 63–266.

Wollstonecraft, M. (1989e [1794]) *An Historical and Moral View of the Origin and Progress of the French Revolution*. In: Todd, J. & Butler, M. (Eds.), *The Works of Mary Wollstonecraft*. New York University Press, New York, Vol. 6, pp. 1–235.

Wollstonecraft, M. (1989f [1796]) *Letters Written during a Short Residence in Sweden, Norway, and Denmark*. In: Todd, J. & Butler, M. (Eds.), *The Works of Mary Wollstonecraft*. New York University Press, New York, Vol. 6, pp. 237–66.

Wollstonecraft, M. (1989g [1798]) *The Wrongs of Woman, or Maria*. In: Todd, J. & Butler, M. (Eds.), *The Works of Mary Wollstonecraft*. New York University Press, New York, Vol. 1, pp. 75–184.

Wollstonecraft, M. (2003) *The Collected Letters of Mary Wollstonecraft*. Ed. J. Todd. Columbia University Press, New York.

womanism

April L. Few

In 1983, Alice Walker contrasted Afrocentrism, black feminism, and white feminism using the term *womanist* to render a critique of possibilities for women and men who felt ostracized by the mainstream women's movement in the United States. Walker's much cited phrase, "Womanist is to feminist as purple is to lavender," reflects this comparison. Walker derived the term womanist from the Southern black folk expression of mothers to female children, "You acting womanish." Womanish girls and women "act out in outrageous, courageous, and willful ways." They are free from traditional conventions that limit white women's experience and relating. Walker stated that womanish girls and women want to know more and in greater depth than what was considered good for them. They are "responsible, in charge, and serious" when relating to themselves and the world.

In her classic essay "In Search of Our Mothers' Gardens," Walker describes womanism as being rooted in black women's particular history of racial and gender oppression in the United States. Yet, womanists are "traditionally universalists." Womanism is a gender-progressive worldview that emerges from black women's unique history, is accessible primarily to black women yet also extends beyond women of African descent, as evidenced in the works of other multi-ethnic feminists. Therefore, womanism is a pluralist vision of black empowerment and consciousness. Because it is a pluralist vision, womanism requires both women and men to be aware of the nature of gendered inequalities and to share a commitment to work toward social change.

Walker (1983) describes a womanist as many things. A womanist "loves herself . . . regardless." She is a black feminist or feminist of color who is "committed to the survival and wholeness of an entire people, both male and female." A womanist prefers women's culture and has an appreciation for women's flexibility and the strengths to negotiate adversity. Yet, a critique of womanism is that it does not address interracial cooperation among women. She loves the spirit of black women and the struggle to confront and to overcome. Walker (1983: xi) also describes a womanist as "a woman who loves women, sexually and/or nonsexually." The writings of many womanists are rather silent about this aspect of Walker's womanism. As black feminist Barbara Smith suspects, this omission may speak to either ambivalence or homophobia in black communities.

Other scholars have described womanism similarly. Geneva Smitherman defined a womanist as an African American woman who is rooted in the black community and committed to the development of herself and the entire community. Jannette Taylor stated that the word "womanist" incorporates the complexity of experience for black women and that the framework allows the experiences to be shared through the language and principles of black communities. Delores Williams believed that womanism reflects Afrocentric cultural codes. These codes are female-centered and relate to the conditions, meanings, and values that have

emerged from black women's activities in their communities. In "Some Implications of Womanist Theory," Sherley Anne Williams (1986) argued that womanist theory is especially accessible to black men because, while it calls for feminist discussions of black women's texts and for critiques of black androcentrism, womanism places black psychic health as a primary objective. In 1994, Layli Phillips and Barbara McCaskill created the scholarly journal *The Womanist: Womanist Theory and Research* to demonstrate the interdisciplinary, intercultural, and international nature of womanist perspectives in the academy and to feature womanist-grounded pedagogical and theoretical articles, creative writing, and art of black women.

In the late 1980s, black female theologians began to incorporate race and gender critiques into theology. Walker's definition of womanism has played a significant role in raising consciousness among female seminarians regarding the moral agency of black women scholars, particularly and initially active members in the Academy of Religion and the Society of Biblical Literature who sought to create analytical frameworks to advance theoretically black women's religious discourse. Womanism has been used by black women theologians to challenge and critique religious traditions and ecclesiastical-political processes. Womanist theologians also have sought to clarify women-centered aspects of biblical studies, church history, systematic theology, and social ethics. Katie Cannon's *Black Womanist Ethics* (1988), Jacquelyn Grant's *White Women's Christ and Black Women's Jesus* (1989), Delores S. Williams's *Sisters in the Wilderness: The Challenge of Womanist God-Talk* (1993), Emilie Townes's *A Troubling in My Soul: Womanist Perspectives on Evil and Suffering* (1993), and Cheryl Kirk-Duggan's *Exorcizing Evil: A Womanist Perspective on the Spirituals* (1997) are significant Christian womanist texts that center the essence of black feminism in Protestant theology. Even Christian womanist self-help books such as Renita Weems's *Just a Sister Away: A Womanist Vision of Women's Relationship in the Bible* and *I Asked for Intimacy: Stories of Blessings, Betrayals, and Birthings* (1993) have been published to extend womanism's reach beyond the academy and seminary.

Some womanists like Clenora Hudson-Weems (1993) argue that the feminist–womanist tie should be separated by locating womanism in the words of Sojourner Truth (i.e., *Ain't I A Woman*) and Afrocentric cultural values. Africana womanism is this theoretical framework. Hudson-Weems identified the characteristics of Africana womanism as self-naming, self-defining, role flexibility, family-centeredness, struggling alongside men against multiple oppressions, adaptability, black sisterhood, wholeness, authenticity, strength, male compatibility, respect for self, others, and elders, recognition, ambition, mothering, nurturing, and spirituality. Hudson-Weems believes that mainstream white feminism was too self-centered or female-centered with its focus on self-realization and personal gratification. Africana womanists, on the other hand, are family-centered and community-centered, interested in collective outcomes and group achievement. It should be noted that although Africana womanists see sexism as an important problem, some do not see sexism as an objective more important than fighting racism. This perspective on sexism reflects the nationalist roots of womanism and is another critique of womanism.

SEE ALSO: Black Feminist Thought; Feminism, First, Second, and Third Waves; Women, Religion and; Women's Empowerment

REFERENCES AND SUGGESTED READINGS

Cannon, K. (1995) *Katie's Canon: Womanism and the Soul of the Black Community*. Continuum, New York.
Hudson-Weems, C. (1993) *Africana Womanism: Reclaiming Ourselves*. Bedford, Troy, MI.
Walker, A. (1983) *In Search of Our Mothers' Gardens: Womanist Prose*. Harcourt Brace Jovanovich, New York.

women, economy and

Elizabeth Esterchild

Women's position in the economy and their general well-being in all other spheres of life depend heavily on the type of society in which they reside. All societies have a complex division of labor by sex. In some, men's and women's tasks are not differentially evaluated and rewarded; in others differential evaluation is so strong that men receive the lion's share of property, material goods, and rights and privileges while women become the property of men and their work and work products are controlled by men. Societies differ because of alternative modes of organization of the productive forces and the subsequent differences in the parts played by the two sexes in these economic arrangements. Gerhard Lenski (1966) described six different types of societies based on the level of technology of the primary means of production, while gender scholars (Dunn et al. 1999) filled in the distinct implications for women.

In the earliest foraging and simple horticultural societies, women's contributions to food, clothing, and shelter ensured respect for them, as families depended on women's work for survival. Meanwhile, men garnered a bit more prestige because they hunted for the highly prized meat and distributed it outside the family. Material inequality was almost unknown because redistribution norms prevailed and each member of society had access to the means of production (Lenski 1966).

When the steel-tipped hoe was introduced, societies were able to produce a surplus. People in these new, advanced horticultural societies demanded more land; both warfare and trading with other societies became widespread. Only men and eventually only certain men could participate in the military and the emerging governing class. The expectation that men would accumulate possessions replaced redistribution norms, and material inequality increased greatly (Lenski 1966). Women's lives and work became more and more subordinated to men's desires, and although a few were able to set themselves apart by being excellent traders or wives of high-ranking men, the huge majority were completely occupied with producing more warriors, feeding their families, and working to produce surplus that was placed in the hands of men (Chafetz 1986). These changes in the economic structure and the division of labor had profound negative effects on women's status. A double standard of sexuality emerged, divorce was virtually impossible to obtain, and women were eventually viewed as property. Daughters could be traded as brides for military alliances;

wives, including sometimes multiple wives, were used to promote the husbands' interests. Women became interchangeable; women who were stolen or captured from other societies could be incorporated to produce more heirs and perform the same work for which wives were responsible. It is likely that the first patriarchal bargains were struck in this type of society. In the bargain, women, albeit reluctantly, traded their work to their husbands in return for the protection husbands provided.

The introduction of another mode of production – plow agriculture with several associated increases in level of technology – simply accelerated all these trends. A larger military and political apparatus appeared, and distinctions among ranks increased. The emergence of propertied classes coincided with a huge increase in the amount of material inequality. The elite class was made up of the highest-status people from the military, the state, and the propertied classes; all were in a position to benefit from the labor of a large peasant class, a smaller artisan class, and sometimes a large number of slaves (Lenski 1966). As hereditary inequality solidified, women's status increasingly depended on the status of their fathers and husbands. More important, women of the elite classes were not allowed to participate in the military, the state with its expanding bureaucracy, or to own significant property. Elite women were unable, then, to directly reap the rewards associated with high status. Middle-class women had plenty of duties to perform. They and peasant women – the bulk of the population – saw their work devalued in part because it did not produce anything for the market. Women were still responsible for feeding their families, so they labored in large gardens and with small animals, but they were denied access to the major means of production: the oxen and the plow. As a result, women's status deteriorated and an ideology of inferiority developed which carried over into industrial society (Chafetz 1986).

In the United States, ideological changes that accompanied the move to industrialization fueled the fires of classism, racism, and sexism. Capitalist employers were happy to fan the flames to keep the fires burning. They propagated the ideas that "real men" did not have a wife employed for pay, that woman's place was in the home, and that a good wife is one who can make her husband look good by spending his money very wisely. In this way, employers had a large number of men who worked very hard, who were well cared for by their wives, and whose wives were seduced to become a market for consumer goods. As well, employers kept the labor market segmented into many distinct occupational niches and hired different categories of people in each. They did their best to forestall the formation of unions, while unions were not always willing to incorporate women into their organization. Many workers at different levels opposed hiring of minority women and men as well as white women in "their" jobs, thus helping perpetuate job segregation.

In the United States, at the beginning of the 1900s, male workers demanded a family wage, and employers were happy to push the twin myths that men were being paid a wage large enough to support a family and that women were only working until marriage or to supplement their husbands' income so they did not need a living wage (Charles & Grusky 2004). Over the course of the twentieth century, these ideas eroded somewhat as more and more women acquired an education and moved into the labor force. At mid-century, unmarried women had been employed for quite some time, as had divorced and poor married women. Married women with high school-age children joined the labor market after World War II, and beginning in the 1970s, more and more middle-class women with preschool or school-age children entered the labor market. Their fortunes were limited, however, as unequal pay scales continued, and women were crowded into relatively low-paying clerical, service, and factory jobs. Most employed women were now doing a double shift, both working to feed their families and taking care of the emotional and physical needs of their husbands and children (Charles & Grusky 2004).

Moreover, as health care improved and people lived much longer, women were often faced with being the primary caretaker for their elderly parents or for their husbands' elderly relatives. Indeed, it was not uncommon to see women caught among the triple roles of raising their own children, caring for elderly parents, and keeping their own careers up and running. As employers recognized the need to keep women committed to working for them, some began offering support for childcare, flexible working hours, and more generous family leave policies. Other women adapted by working part-time or part-year, but such strategies left them ineligible for even pro-rated benefits (Reskin 1998; Gregory et al. 1999). Truly meaningful part-time jobs that allow both husbands and wives to meet family needs as well as have some time to enjoy their lives are still very few in number.

Today, the United States, Japan, and some European nations have moved into a post-industrial phase in which few workers actually produce goods but provide services instead (Lenski 1966; Charles & Grusky 2004). Auto-mation and other technological advances free many workers – both women and men – from the factory but leave their future uncertain because of the loss of steady, relatively well-paying blue-collar jobs (Sernau 2006). Many production jobs moved overseas where employ-ers are free from government taxes and restric-tions and can employ an ever ready supply of laborers who work for low pay and few bene-fits. These shifts have left some men employed at high-end jobs that pay well, but pushed more downward on the pay scale. In these early years of the new century, it appears that the market for women workers is becoming bifur-cated as well.

Currently, around the world there is enor-mous variability in women's economic partici-pation. The many so-called developing societies result from the imposition and then the throw-ing off of colonial rule. Historically, colonizers exploited native people for natural resources and for labor. Today as well, third world socie-ties supply a market for some goods and cheap, throwaway laborers for production. The desta-bilizing effects of colonization disrupted tradi-tional family and cultural practices, frequently drew men away from their households to work, and left women to fend for themselves. Women in these traditional societies often lose rights to the land and hence face great difficulty in grow-ing food for their children and elders (Sernau 2006). Today, a few women in these societies are gaining an education and moving into white-collar positions in urban labor markets. Many more are forced by circumstances to work in the informal sector as housemaids, selling food or handmade objects on street corners, or as day

laborers. In most instances, their work is unac-knowledged in computations of the gross national product and largely unregulated.

In post-industrial societies, government poli-cies designed to remedy employment discrimi-nation often meet extreme resistance fueled by misunderstandings among the public and ser-ious obstacles from employers who do not want to yield control over their business practices. The combined forces of anti-discrimination laws and remedies, affirmative action regula-tions, and comparable worth campaigns are far from eliminating the deleterious effects of employment discrimination on white women or minority people of either sex (Reskin 1998).

Employees are reluctant to bring charges under anti-discrimination laws and thereby risk their jobs. Class action suits have won major concessions from a handful of large companies in the United States; in the European Union, however, only individuals can contest instances of discrimination (Gregory et al. 1999). Affir-mative action policies require employers to exert concerted efforts to ensure equal opportu-nities before choosing workers. They require employers to actively seek out women and min-ority applicants and make sure that they are not lumped into a limited array of job categories. Affirmative action requires quotas and time-tables *only in those extremely rare cases* when employers have systematically and obviously discriminated against potential employees and have repeatedly failed to adjust their practices to more equitable arrangements (Reskin 1998).

Comparable worth policies offer a solution to the enduring problem that occupations in which women frequently work are often undervalued and underpaid. Because sex segregation of work is likely to endure for generations to come, advo-cates recommend a complete reevaluation of the demands and contributions of all job categories and gradually raising the pay of each underva-lued occupation until pay equity is achieved. Despite the federal Equal Pay Act, comparable worth has most often been implemented – at least partially – in state and municipal employ-ment rather than in private employment (Reskin 1998; Kahn & Figart 1999).

Contemporary women are rarely found in the ranks of the elite wealthholders but are more than numerous among the poor, especially those who are single and the mothers of small children. Older women, especially those who are widowed, are most likely to have to depend on social security payments to subsist. Meanwhile, middle- and working-class couples typically find it necessary to have both wife and husband employed regardless of the ages and stages of the children and despite the fact that one or both draw relatively high wages. Improvements in the economic position of women await major changes in ideological patterns and in the institutional structure of work.

SEE ALSO: Affirmative Action; Divisions of Household Labor; Gender, Development and; Gender, Work, and Family; Occupational Segregation; Sex-Based Wage Gap and Comparable Worth; Stratification, Gender and

REFERENCES AND SUGGESTED READINGS

Chafetz, J. (1986) *Sex and Advantage: A Comparative, Macrostructural Theory of Sex Stratification.* Rowman & Allanheld, Totowa, NJ.

Charles, M. & Grusky, D. (2004) *Occupational Ghettos: The Worldwide Segregation of Women and Men.* Stanford University Press, Stanford.

Dunn, D., Almquist, E., & Chafetz, J. (1999) Macrostructural Theories of Gender Inequality. In: England, P. (Ed.), *Theory on Gender/Feminism on Theory.* Aldine, New York, pp. 69–90.

Figart, D. & Martin, E. (1999) Global Feminization and Flexible Labour Markets. In: Gregory, J., Sales, R., & Hegewisch, A. (Eds.), *Women, Work, and Inequality: The Challenge of Equal Pay in a Deregulated Labour Market.* St. Martin's Press, New York, pp. 44–57.

Gregory, J., Sales, R., & Hegewisch, A. (Eds.) (1999) *Women, Work, and Inequality: The Challenge of Equal Pay in a Deregulated Labour Market.* St. Martin's Press, New York.

Hoskins, C. (1999) Then and Now: Equal Pay in European Union Politics. In: Gregory, J., Sales, R., & Hegewisch, A. (Eds.), *Women, Work, and Inequality: The Challenge of Equal Pay in a Deregulated Labour Market.* St. Martin's Press, New York, pp. 27–43.

Kahn, P. & Figart, D. (1999) Public Sector Reforms in a Changing Economic and Political Climate: Lessons from Michigan. In: Gregory, J., Sales, R., & Hegewisch, A. (Eds.), *Women, Work, and Inequality: The Challenge of Equal Pay in a Deregulated Labour Market.* St. Martin's Press, New York, pp. 183–95.

Lenski, G. (1966) *Power and Privilege.* McGraw-Hill, New York.

Lorber, J. (2005) *Gender Inequality: Feminist Theories and Politics.* Roxbury, Los Angeles.

Reskin, B. F. (1998) *The Realities of Affirmative Action in Employment.* American Sociological Association, Washington, DC.

Sales, R. & Gregory, J. (1999) Immigration, Ethnicity, and Exclusion: Implications of European Integration. In: Gregory, J., Sales, R., & Hegewisch, A. (Eds.), *Women, Work, and Inequality: The Challenge of Equal Pay in a Deregulated Labour Market.* St. Martin's Press, New York, pp. 97–114.

Sernau, S. (2006) *Worlds Apart: Social Inequalities in a Global Economy,* 2nd edn. Pine Forge Press, Thousand Oaks, CA.

women, information technology and (Asia)

Helen Johnson

New information and communication technologies (ICT) challenge and have the potential to promote change in women's social status and socioeconomic opportunities in various ways. Some sociologists argue that innovative ICT embody the key characteristics required to provide women with effective opportunities to participate in mainstream economic activities in Asian societies, others that ICT are yet another tool of masculinized social, economic, and political power that is merely perpetuating gender differentiation.

"Asia" cannot be fully defined but the term is a useful shorthand to describe the array of countries whose economies now engage with ICT. "Asia" can encompass Japan, Singapore, and South Korea as three of the world's most technologically developed nations. Asian countries in general hold leading positions in the ICT arena, and nations such as India are sites for technology industries and practices that add significantly to the region's economies, societies, and cultures. While "women" cannot be considered a homogeneous group, "gender" is one of the major ways that humans organize their lives. Many Asian sociologists link ICT to the analytical prism of "gender" to add detail to the social practices that imbricate ICT usage, examine the ways these may be shaped by gendered and cross-cultural difference, assess the potential for marginalization of some social groups via ICT innovation, and add to current debates in the Asia-Pacific region surrounding the development of social policies that address issues of social marginalization caused by ICT.

Female Internet use in Asia continues to increase, with women, in 2001, in South Korea comprising 45 percent of the online population, in Hong Kong 44 percent, and in Singapore and Taiwan 42 percent and 41 percent, respectively. Furthermore, women themselves are appraising the benefits of ICT. Previous international research on gender and ICT has focused on the participation of women in computer science as a profession; issues of access analyzed through the prisms of race, class, and gender; the diversity of social interactions on the Internet and their potential for the constitution of multiple identities; the gendering of information systems; and issues of sexual harassment and online pornography. Further studies argue that feminist historical analyses illuminate a range of concepts and actions missing from mainstream social studies of technology and highlight women's active use of the Internet for social change, support networks, and self-expression. Others consider how gender is a factor online via experimentation with identity, and how the Internet can be a transformative space where gender categories are reconfigured. Haraway (1985, 1997) has theorized how traditional and innovative media have reconfigured social possibilities for bodies, technologies, and gender. Consalvo and Paasonen have critiqued the ways that technologically neutral or determinist positions do not question the social structures and cultures enveloping new media nor the social differences such as age, caste, class, and nationality that exist between women. Joshi's (1997) edited collection questions the potential for new ICT to expand the gender gap and/or to create more democratic environments in "Asian" nation-states.

Analyses of the gendered access to and use of the Internet in the United States have stirred debate about whether the Internet perpetuates regressive social structures or enables progressive female agency in Asian nation-states (see,

for Japan, Aoshima 1993; Kanai 1993; Kurano 1993; Hirose 1997; and for other nation-states in Asia, Joshi 1997). They also detail the time and financial constraints that hinder women's access and argue that providing access to cyber-empowerment is fundamental. Gan (1997) asserts that the gender marking of technology as a male domain has been transferred to the Internet via gender-coded societal conditions in Singapore and, despite the government's vigorous program to place technology in the hands of all citizens, social attitudes about women's roles and capabilities must also change. Lumby (1997) notes that technological literacy has been defined against women's skills, and questions about whether the Internet is yet another tool of masculinized social, economic, and political power are deemed vital. Ang (2001) and Tan (1991) explore how researchers ignore, to their loss, how local peoples invoke different gendered perceptions to further their interests. And researchers such as Gupta and Singh (1994) and Hobart (1993) detail how geographical information systems (GIS), as computer programs for mapping definitive geographical identifications which can be linked to information databases about local peoples, have been critiqued for privileging spatial coordinates at the expense of incorporating and understanding poetry and performance as important components of local and indigenous communities' knowledge.

The ways in which ICT may change modes of thinking as well as practices have also been examined. Wong (2000) shows how new technology changes not only material reality but also the ways people think about reality, explores social relations and attitudes to cyberspace and the Internet, styles of interaction with new ICTs and perceived possibilities of identity formation, and argues that cyberspace not only connotes the possibility of transcending one's body but also provides a utopian space for transcendence to a higher state of being. Deconstructing the images and language used to describe cyberspace, Wong notes that most users are ambivalent, with attitudes spinning between idealism, cynicism, and indifference. Wong also explores how language is styled by the influences of the Internet as it becomes interwoven throughout society, and the appeal of the Net for adolescents in terms of relative empowerment, word games, and flaming for entertainment. Of significance is her presentation of the Japanese Industrial Standard (JIS) character, its use to subvert ASCII text's globalism, and its development of a different range of emotions to express Japanese sentiments. Razak (1997) explores changes to modes of thinking via an index to Malay women's social consciousness, ascertaining how media technologies act to reinforce women's concepts of identity. She notes that improvements in women's consciousness of their rights and responsibilities are occurring and that women are receiving greater media coverage of their familial contributions and their broader social achievements.

Information literacy is examined via Amin's (1997) proposal that ICT may have a different meaning within the context of a "developing" nation such as Bangladesh, in that it must include older technologies such as fax and telephones. She suggests that ICT has a liberating potential in giving women the ability to choose from a wider range of occupations. While Amin's analysis does not take into consideration how class issues may impact on education and access, Joshi (2004) does discuss the difficulties of ensuring that a range of people participate in digitally empowered development in India and focuses particularly on the ways in which women's issues such as health, health education, and access to means of communication evolve. Rajesh (2002) also examines the potential for social disadvantage that is exacerbated by technological development, concentrating on issues of access, whereas Bhatnagare and Schware (1999) examine how ICTs are forming a significant component of rural development. Cheuk (2000) explores information literacy in the workplace via a user-centered approach, considers common strategies that are exhibited by people in a group, and the diverse strategies of each individual adopted at different times, in order to gain a holistic understanding of information literacy and thence to improve education in this area.

Current research focuses on how women specifically engage with ICTs across cultures in Asia, the problems of access that face socially disadvantaged sectors of the region's many constituent communities, and the potential impact of technology on local peoples, particularly in relation to the loss or ignorance of local knowledge.

SEE ALSO: Culture, Gender and; Gender Bias; Gender Ideology and Gender Role Ideology; Information Technology; Internet; Social Change, Southeast Asia

REFERENCES AND SUGGESTED READINGS

Amin, A. (1997) NCTs: Helping Hands for Women. In: Joshi, I. (Ed.), *Asian Women in the Information Age: New Communication Technology, Democracy, and Women.* Asian Media Information and Communication Center, Singapore.

Ang, I. (2001) Desperately Guarding Borders: Media Globalization, "Cultural Imperialism," and the Rise of "Asia." In: Souchou, Y. (Ed.), *House of Glass: Culture, Modernity, and the State in Southeast Asia.* Institute of Southeast Asian Studies, Singapore.

Aoshima, N. (1993) WINET: Its Structure and Characteristics. *Fujin Kyouiku Joha (Women's Education Information)* 28.

Bhatnagare, S. & Schware, R. (Eds.) (1999) *Information and Communication Technology in Rural Development. Case Studies from India.* Washington, DC.

Cheuk, B. W. (2000) Exploring Information Literacy in the Workplace: A Process Approach. In: Bruce, C. & Candy, P. (Eds.), *Information Literacy Around the World: Advances in Programs and Research.* Center for Information Studies, Wagga Wagga, NSW.

Gan, S.-L. (1997) Singapore: Empowerment or Impediment? In: Joshi, I. (Ed.), *Asian Women in the Information Age: New Communication Technology, Democracy, and Women.* Asian Media Information and Communication Center, Singapore.

Gupta, V. S. & Singh, R. (Eds.) (1994) *Communication Planning for Socioeconomic Development.* Har-Anand, New Delhi.

Haraway, D. (1985) *Simians, Cyborgs, and Women.* Routledge, New York.

Haraway, D. (1997) *Modest_Witness@Second_Millennium, FemaleMan©_Meets_OncoMouse: Feminism and Technoscience.* Routledge, New York.

Hirose, Y. (1997) Japan: Equalizing Opportunities. In: Joshi, I. (Ed.), *Asian Women in the Information Age: New Communication Technology, Democracy, and Women.* Asian Media Information and Communication Center, Singapore.

Hobart, M. (Ed.) (1993) *An Anthropological Critique of Development: The Growth of Ignorance.* Routledge, London.

Joshi, I. (Ed.) (1997) *Asian Women in the Information Age: New Communication Technology, Democracy, and Women*. Asian Media Information and Communication Center, Singapore.

Joshi, J. (2004) People's Participation in Digitally Empowered Development: Challenges and Initiatives. The Second Biennial Conference of the Indian Assoication for Asian and Pacific Studies, January.

Kanai, T. (1993) Women's Movements and Information. *Fujin Kyouiku Joha (Women's Education Information)* 28.

Karim, W. J. (Ed.) (1995) *"Male" and "Female" in Developing Southeast Asia*. Berg, Oxford.

Kurano, Y. (1993) Reference Services and the Use of WINET in National Women's Education Centre. *Fujin Kyouiku Joha (Women's Education Information)* 28.

Lumby, C. (1997) *Bad Girls: The Media, Sex, and Feminism in the '90s*. Allen & Unwin, Sydney.

Rajesh, R. (2002) *Bridging the Digital Divide: Gyandoot the Model for Community Networks*. Tata McGraw-Hill, New Delhi.

Razak, R. (1997) Malaysia: Reinforcing Women's Social Consciousness and Identity. In: Joshi, I. (Ed.), *Asian Women in the Information Age: New Communication Technology, Democracy, and Women*. Asian Media Information and Communication Center, Singapore.

Tan, A. J. (1991) A Study of Women Managers Among Private Enterprises in Peninsular Malaysia. *Malaysian Management Review* 26(3): 23–32.

Wong, A. (2000) Cyberself: Identity, Language, and Stylization on the Internet. In: Gibbs, D. & Krause, K.-L. (Eds.), *Cyberlines: Languages and Cultures of the Internet*. James Nicholas, Albert Park, Victoria.

women, religion and

Sally K. Gallagher

Women's religious commitments, ideals, and involvement are increasingly of interest to sociologists within both the sociology of religion and other fields. While early research on religion focused on the origins, functions, meaning, and measurement of religion, the past few decades have witnessed a burgeoning interest in women's spirituality, the involvement of women within religious institutions, and religiously based women's social movements. Part of this shift is the result of the growth of gender studies within sociology, as well as increased religious pluralism and expression across the religious landscape.

Women's involvement in religion varies depending on whether we are considering personal beliefs and practices or institutional affiliation and leadership. Some scholars have been critical of women's marginalization within religious institutions. Some critics, such as theologian Mary Daly, argue that women's historic exclusion from positions of leadership and authority within western religious traditions is evidence that the Judeo-Christian tradition itself is inherently patriarchal and oppressive and should be abandoned in favor of non-patriarchal feminist spiritualities. The recent growth of neo-pagan (Neitz 2000), goddess worship, and other forms of feminist spirituality suggest that some women are moving away from traditional western religious institutions because they do not adequately meet their needs or provide the kind of overarching moral narrative that gives meaning to women's lives.

Others, however, argue that religion itself (especially western Christianity) is not inherently oppressive to women, but that the gender egalitarian teachings of these traditions and the historical involvement of women as leaders, teachers, and writers have been minimized for political and economic reasons. Thus, within both the Roman Catholic Church and evangelical Protestantism, for example, feminist organizations have emerged in an effort to restore more gender equitable practices and beliefs. Christians for Biblical Equality, the Evangelical and Ecumenical Women's Caucus, and the Women's Ordination Conference are examples of organizations that seek to advance feminist goals within conservative Protestant and Roman Catholic churches. Countering these are a number of conservative organizations and institutions that promote "traditional gender roles" in which women's nurturing is seen as a natural complement to men's responsibilities as leaders, protectors, and providers within both family and the church (Concerned Women for America and the Council on Biblical Manhood and Womanhood are two such examples). Although less and less willing to describe these relationships as one of women's submission and men's leadership, the model these groups promote is nevertheless one in which men have final

decision-making authority and spiritual responsibility for family life. The abuses of this power
have led to an increase of scholarship on links
between religious teaching on women's submission and domestic abuse (Kroeger & Nason-
Clark 2001).

Sociology of religion has also explored the
dimensions of women's leadership as clergy and
lay leaders within the church. Adair Lummis,
Nancy Ammerman, and Paula Nesbitt are
examples of scholars who have written on the
struggles of women in positions of leadership
within conservative denominations and traditions and the organizational barriers women
face as effective clergy.

What the above research highlights is how
women's connections to religious institutions
vary based on underlying ideas about the nature
of masculinity and femininity themselves. The
teachings of some religious institutions and
traditions are that women and men are essentially different, and because of those differences should be differently involved in religious
worship, teaching, and leadership. Orthodox
Judaism, Roman Catholicism, Eastern Orthodoxy, Islam, and many conservative Protestant
denominations are examples of religious traditions in which specific leadership positions and
responsibilities are reserved for men. Within
some of these traditions, religious ritual and
family responsibilities are also gendered – with
women and men being seen as having separate
practices and obligations inside and outside the
household.

Not all theologically conservative religions,
however, are necessarily or uniformly conservative when it comes to the place of women in
religious life. The past decade has seen a movement away from debates over androgyny and
hierarchy toward a growing emphasis on complementarity and ideological egalitarianism.
Both those who argue that there are essential
gender differences and those who argue for gender equality have moved toward a pragmatically
egalitarian approach in which symbolic offices
and authority may remain limited to women, but
women's increasing opportunities to teach, lead,
and participate in institutional religious life are
paralleled by greater emphasis on men's responsibility to become more involved in everyday
family life as husbands and fathers (Gallagher
2003; Bartkowski 2004; Wilcox 2004).

In terms of personal religious life, sociologists
of religion have been particularly interested in
the appeal of conservative religious traditions to
women and the articulation of religion and
family life. Rather than focusing on women's
institutional involvement, this body of research
explores the personal benefits women find in
religious observance. Recent studies of conservative Protestants (Manning 1999; Bartkowski
2001; Gallagher 2003), Pentecostals (Griffith
1997; Brasher 1998), Latter Day Saints (Beaman
2001), and newly Orthodox Jewish women
(Davidman 1991; Manning 1999) have all made
the case that women find personal satisfaction,
growth, community, and family support
through religious life. Small group participation, prayer services, and family rituals are particularly important in creating a sense of
community and care for women within these
traditions.

SEE ALSO: Church; Feminism, First, Second,
and Third Waves; Fundamentalism; Gender
Ideology and Gender Role Ideology; Religion,
Sociology of; Sexuality, Religion and; Spirituality, Religion, and Aging

REFERENCES AND SUGGESTED READINGS

Bartkowski, J. P. (2001) *Remaking the Godly Marriage: Gender Negotiation in Evangelical Families.*
Rutgers University Press, New Brunswick, NJ.

Bartkowski, J. P. (2004) *Promise Keepers: Servants,
Soldiers, and Godly Men.* Rutgers University Press,
New Brunswick, NJ.

Beaman, L. G. (2001) Molly Mormons, Mormon
Feminists, and Moderates: Religious Diversity
and the Latter Day Saints Church. *Sociology of
Religion* 62(1): 65–87.

Brasher, B. E. (1998) *Godly Women: Fundamentalism
and Female Power.* Rutgers University Press, New
Brunswick, NJ.

Davidman, L. (1991) *Tradition in a Rootless World:
Women Turn to Orthodox Judaism.* University of
California Press, Berkeley.

Gallagher, S. K. (2003) *Evangelical Identity and Gendered Family Life.* Rutgers University Press, New
Brunswick, NJ.

Griffith, R. M. (1997) *God's Daughters.* University of
California Press, Berkeley.

Kroeger, C. C. & Nason-Clark, N. (2001) *No Place
for Abuse.* Intervarsity Press, Downers Grove, IL.

Manning, C. (1999) *God Gave Us the Right: Conservative Catholic, Evangelical Protestant, and Orthodox Jewish Women Grapple with Feminism*. Rutgers University Press, New Brunswick, NJ.

Neitz, M. J. (2000) Queering the Dragonfest: Changing Sexualities in a Post-Patriarchal Religion. *Sociology of Religion* 61(4): 399–408.

Wilcox, W. B. (2004) *Soft Patriarchs, New Men*. University of Chicago Press, Chicago.

women in science

Anne Kerr

The history and present status of women in science are of interest to sociologists because of the longstanding disparities in women's and men's relative rank and levels of productivity in science, but also because of the male domination of the sciences as a whole. A range of psychological, structural, and cultural explanations have been developed to explain these circumstances and a whole plethora of initiatives and schemes have been implemented to redress the gender imbalance within science. Disparities nevertheless remain and their entrenchment is the subject of continued theoretical and empirical debate.

Women have not always been a minority within science. As Carolyn Merchant has demonstrated, the scientific revolution was premised upon the formal exclusion of women from the new institutions of science. Wise women and midwives were persecuted and "well-born" women intellectuals were confined to the home as the division between public and private life intensified. At the same time, dichotomies between mind and nature, reason and feeling, and male and female hardened. Great women scientists like Christine de Pizan (1365–ca. 1430) and Laura Bassi (1711–78) were nevertheless rediscovered in the 1970s as second-wave feminists took up their predecessors' quest to show that women can do science just as well as men. They also concentrated their attention on the barriers to women's achievement in science, spawning a rich and diverse literature on the history and culture of science at a time when women were entering science

at a rapid pace. As Schiebinger notes, by 1995, 23 percent of US scientists and engineers were women. Yet it also became apparent that women's fortunes in science wax and wane according to the political and economic climate as well as the development of scientific institutions. Progression is far from linear.

There are copious amounts of empirical evidence to demonstrate that girls excel in science in the right context but that women drop out of science at each and every significant transition throughout the typical scientific career. Women are more likely to be found in low-status, insecure jobs, and to devote themselves to the least valued aspects of academic life, particularly teaching. This means that their record of research fund-raising is not as good as men's and, relatedly, their publication rates and their promotional prospects are worse. The glass ceiling has become something of a cliché but there is no doubt that it is very real. The proportion of female professors in the sciences is minuscule, and the rate of increase is far lower than the increases in women gaining PhDs in the sciences.

As Mary Frank Fox has convincingly argued, the organizational context of science is fundamental to these gender inequalities. Women are least likely to succeed in organizational contexts where the criteria of evaluation and assessment are informal and subjective. In environments where their contribution is not actively encouraged, they participate less in policy discussions and collaborative enterprises. The individualistic culture of some science departments means that graduate education in particular is essentially "privatized" and it is in this type of environment that implicit norms of masculinity flourish, and those who "look like" those currently in positions of authority are privileged. What Knorr-Cetina has called the "epistemic culture" of science, sustained in part through the secrecy and informality of many peer review mechanisms, privileges already established scholars and those like them, and marginalizes female and other minority groups as "the other."

Women's domestic situation is also crucial to their success in science. The long hours culture of science does not suit women's double burden of paid work and unpaid domestic labor.

The widespread and entrenched cultural belief that women have prime responsibility for child-care and the tendency for a woman's career to take second place to that of her husband are other obvious contributory factors. On a more positive note, women's marriages also give them access to different networks of influence, and it seems that women who are married to other scientists are more successful than their counterparts.

Of course there is a burgeoning industry of psychological research and pseudo-scientific speculation in the wider culture which offers reductionist and essentialist explanations of women's lack of success in science. Differences in women's and men's patterns of speech, sociability, cognitive processing, visual–spatial ability, and levels of aggression have all been deployed to explain women's underrepresentation in science. These have been convincingly debunked by proponents of the "gender similarity hypothesis," whose meta-analyses have shown that women and men are more alike than they are different, except in a few largely inconsequential characteristics like the ability to throw objects long distances. As authors such as Janet Shibley Hyde have pointed out, there is a high cost to the prevailing cultural emphasis on gender difference, as it undermines women's sense of their ability to succeed in the workplace (and men's sense of their ability to nurture). Low expectations of girls' and women's mathematical ability and scientific prowess undermine their confidence and perpetuate inequalities. In short, stereotypes matter.

SEE ALSO: Feminism; Feminism, First, Second, and Third Waves; Feminism and Science, Feminist Epistemology; Feminist Standpoint Theory; Scientific Revolution

REFERENCES AND SUGGESTED READINGS

Etzkowitz, H., Kemelgor, C., Uzzi, B., & Neuschatz, M. E. (2000) *Athena Unbound: The Advancement of Women in Science and Technology.* Cambridge University Press, Cambridge.
Fox, M. F. (2001) Women, Science, and Academia: Graduate Education and Careers. *Gender and Society* 15, 5 (October): 654–66.
Hyde, J. S. (2005) The Gender Similarities Hypothesis. *American Psychologist* (September): 581–92.
Knorr-Cetina, K. (1981) *The Manufacture of Knowledge: An Essay on the Constructivist and Contextual Nature of Science.* Pergamon, Oxford and New York.
Merchant, C. (1982) *The Death of Nature: Women, Ecology, and the Scientific Revolution.* Harper & Row: San Francisco.
Schiebinger, L. (1999) *Has Feminism Changed Science?* Harvard University Press, Cambridge, MA.

women, sexuality and

Tiina Vares and Annie Potts

Western thought is underpinned by hierarchical binaries or dualisms, for example, mind/body, culture/nature, masculine/feminine, active/passive, to name but a few. Within this framework, "woman" is associated with terms such as passive, responsive, and inferior. These are constructed in opposition to "man," described as active, aggressive/predatory, and superior. The cultural investment in binarization, particularly between the two sexes, also produces heterosexuality as the only normative form of desire and privileges so-called masculine values and experiences over so-called feminine. With respect to sexuality, Luce Irigaray, in *This Sex Which is Not One* (1985), argues that western culture has persistently negated or repressed those modes of sexual experience that may be specific to women and which do not fit with masculinist assumptions about women's sexuality.

Western knowledge about human sexuality prior to the nineteenth century has been largely attributed to the Greeks. The framing of women's sexuality as inferior to men's sexuality can be found in the works of early philosophers such as Plato and Aristotle, as well as Galen, the influential second-century physician and theorist. Plato, for example, popularized the idea that a "wandering (inactive) uterus" causes female hysteria in women who do not bear children. While Galen accepted the Aristotelian thesis that a woman is like a man, but lower in the hierarchy of being, he disputed Plato's idea of the wandering uterus (Tuana 1993). Women's genitals, Galen argued, were like those of men but found inside the body. This was explained by "arrested development" and supported Aristotle's idea that woman is "less perfect" than or a "misbegotten" man. Galen's thesis that women's sexuality was similar, although inferior, to men's sexuality remained popular well into the eighteenth century. With respect to hysteria, it is worth noting that this became increasingly medicalized from the seventeenth century onwards. By the nineteenth century, it had become the source of attribution for myriad ailments and symptoms supposedly associated with "woman" and firmly connected with women's sexuality (Ussher 1997).

In *Making Sex: Body and Gender from the Greeks to Freud* (1990), Thomas Laqueur argues that it was only from the late eighteenth century that "sex as we know it" was invented. Until this period, he argues, a "one-sex" model of sexual difference dominated western medico-biological thought. The shift to a "two-sex" model was the result of social, political, and economic changes in the late eighteenth century rather than scientific developments. These created the context in which sexual differences needed to be articulated to support shifting gender arrangements. Although women were no longer seen as inverted replicas of men, the association of women's bodies and sexuality as reproductive and nurturing, as opposed to sexual and passionate, was reinforced. The anatomical and physiological differences between males and females were thus used to reproduce assumptions about the nature of "heterosexuality," positioning men as more active, stronger, superior, women as weaker, passive, and inferior, and positioning penile-vaginal penetration as "natural" and central to all conceptions of human sexuality (Potts 2002).

Sexology, the "scientific study" of sexuality, was first constituted as an object of medical and scientific knowledge in the nineteenth century. Two of its pioneers, Richard von Krafft-Ebing (*Psychopathia Sexualis*, 1886) and Havelock Ellis (*Studies in the Psychology of Sex*, 1913), drew on biological and evolutionary understandings of sexuality which continued to endorse the inevitability of male domination and female submission. They equated sex and gender and saw male and female sexuality as fundamentally opposed. Although Ellis supported the possibility and importance of female genital pleasure,

he nonetheless saw women as creatures weakened by their reproductive biology, since the "worm" or menstruation "gnaws periodically at the roots of life" (Segal 1994). Furthermore, women's sexual activity was seen as being primarily for reproductive purposes. Although it was given a more autonomous existence in the writings of Ellis, it still required a man to initiate and release it. Thus, while some saw Ellis as promoting a liberal shift away from the sexual repression of Victorian times, Margaret Jackson (1987), for example, argues that his theories eroticized the oppression of women.

In the mid-twentieth century, sexologist Alfred Kinsey argued that a liberal, as opposed to repressive, attitude to sexuality was necessary for men and women to be more effective sexual partners. His aim was to promote better understanding between men and women and increase women's orgasmic satisfaction (Segal 1994). As a zoologist, Kinsey framed sex as a straightforward biological function and a purely physical phenomenon. His reports on male and female sexuality detailed what people actually did sexually and hence challenged popular sexual norms. For example, Kinsey and his colleagues, in *Sexual Behavior in the Human Female* (1953), found that almost a quarter of women had extramarital sexual relations, 3 percent of the female population were homosexual, and there were high rates of premarital sex among women and men. Kinsey also challenged the notion of female frigidity by indicating high rates of sexual responsiveness among women. In opposition to Freud, he reported that the clitoris was the main site of sexual responsiveness. In fact, he claimed the vaginal orgasm was a physiological impossibility and criticized Freud and others for projecting male constructs of sexuality onto women (Irvine 2002). Furthermore, Kinsey challenged the idea that masturbation was a dangerous sexual practice and argued that it was the best way for women to reach orgasm. While Kinsey's work was seen by some as opening up more "positive" attitudes to sex by countering gendered sexual norms of the period, others argued his emphasis on the power of the male drive perpetuated the positioning of males as agents and females as passive recipients of the sexual act (Potts 2002). Furthermore, Kinsey's refusal to acknowledge the significance of ethical, social, or emotional factors in the study of sexuality, and his use of a biologically deterministic theory of sexuality, supported the common assumptions about women's sexuality he was attempting to disrupt.

The popularization of sexological research, in particular the notions that women "enjoy" sexual intercourse and that orgasms are the sign of that enjoyment, reinforce what Paula Nicolson (1993) calls the coital and orgasmic imperatives. The coital imperative asserts that penile-vaginal intercourse is a "natural" and "normal" activity, while the orgasmic imperative posits that all sexual activity culminates in orgasm. Nicolson (1994) argues that these imperatives provide clear definitions of pleasure for women to adhere to, in spite of Kinsey's claim that orgasm through intercourse is not necessarily common for women, or Shere Hite's assertion, in *The Hite Report: A Nationwide Study of Female Sexuality* (1977), that this is not what most women themselves see as constituting pleasure. This also set the scene for the medicalization of "female sexual dysfunction" by prescribing what constitutes "normal" and hence "abnormal" female sexual function/experience (see below).

The medico-biological, psychological, and sexological approaches which dominated eighteenth- to mid-twentieth-century theorizing and research on women's sexuality drew on "sexual essentialism," that is, the notion that sex "is a natural force ... eternally unchanging, asocial and transhistorical" (Rubin 1984). Feminist anthropologist Gayle Rubin argued that sexual essentialism is a fixed phenomenon in the West, but that the domination of sexual knowledge by disciplines such as medicine and sexology reinforced this essentialism. Within such a framework, sex was "a property of individuals [residing] in their hormones or their psyches" and having "no history and no significant social determinants."

Over the past few decades, essentialist understandings of women's sexuality have been increasingly challenged. For example, while many feminist approaches have pointed to the social construction of sexuality, these have produced tensions with feminist approaches informed by essentialist understandings. Nonetheless, since the first wave of feminism in the nineteenth century, the issue of women's sexuality has been central to feminist theorizing and research. For example, prior to the emergence of the "human

sexuality" of the medical experts, nineteenth-century feminists began to discuss questions that would later be categorized under "sexual politics." The attempt to politicize sex and gender relations was carried out indirectly through discussions of prostitution and the double standard (Valverde 1985). With the rise of second-wave feminism in the late 1960s and early 1970s, feminists challenged what were defined as "male-dominated" or "patriarchal" understandings of women's sexuality and assumptions about heterosexuality. For many feminists, heterosexual relations were seen as detrimental to women and implicit in women's subordination. The feminist slogan, "the personal is political," is often thought to refer primarily to bringing women's sexuality out into the open and exposing it as a major domain for the deployment and exercise of domination (Tiefer 1995).

Over the past decades, much feminist theorizing and debate about women's sexuality can be considered in terms of the title of Carol Vance's edited volume, *Pleasure and Danger: Exploring Female Sexuality* (1984), a collection of papers presented at the Feminist Conference at Barnard College in 1982. Vance explains that the conference attempted to explore the ambiguous and complex relationship between sexual pleasure and danger in women's lives and feminist theory. In part, this was a response to a focus on "sexual pessimism" or the "dangers" of sexuality for women.

Some of the "dangers" of heterosexual sex for women, for example, were highlighted in what was referred to as the lesbian–heterosexual split. This occurred in the women's movement in the 1970s. Lesbianism was first defined as central for women in the struggle against male dominance. Then, with the framing of heterosexuality as an eroticized institution through which male supremacy is maintained, came the assertion that heterosexual women were "sleeping with the enemy." Thus lesbianism became almost a "categorical imperative" for feminists (Faderman, cited in Segal 1994). What was referred to as "political lesbianism" entailed a significant theoretical revision in feminist thinking about women's sexuality, as well as behavioral changes (Segal 1994). However, this focus on the dangers of heterosexuality for women drew on, as well as reinforced, more essentialized understandings of *differences* between men's and women's sexuality. Women's sexuality was framed as gentle, nurturing, and loving, in opposition to an aggressive and dominating male sexuality.

This situation was intensified in the 1970s and 1980s when feminist theorizing about women's sexuality became inseparable from theorizing men's violence against women. For example, Susan Brownmiller, in *Against Our Will* (1975), focuses on rape as the primary means by which men have kept women subordinate throughout history. Here, sexuality is seen as the fundamental source of men's oppression of women. The work of Catharine MacKinnon (e.g., *Feminism Unmodified: Discourses of Life and Law*, 1987) and Andrea Dworkin (*Pornography: Men Possessing Women*, 1979, and *Intercourse*, 1987) on pornography has been hugely influential in perpetuating the idea that heterosexual sex is coercive, violating, and disempowering for women. MacKinnon and Dworkin targeted the pioneers of sexology and their descendants for entrenching women's oppression by encouraging them to speak about pleasure in heterosexual relations, an encounter in which, they argue, women are inevitably positioned as subordinate (Segal 1994). Once again, this radical feminist theorizing drew on essentialist understandings of men's and women's sexuality as fundamentally different and neglected historical and sociological analyses in favor of naturalistic assumptions about what sexuality "really is" (Valverde 1985). This also worked to silence the voices of heterosexual women/feminists about their sexual lives and pleasures.

Much feminist theorizing in the 1980s and 1990s draws on the work of Michel Foucault, and poststructuralism more broadly, to explore the ways in which sexuality is constructed in discourse. Lynne Segal (1994) and Stevi Jackson (2003), for example, critique phallocentric and essentialist models of women's sexual pleasure as "eroticized submission," in particular the way in which these denied agency to heterosexual women (seen as either misguided victims or dupes). While acknowledging the "dangers" in heterosexual relationships, such as sexual coercion and sexual violence, much feminist theorizing has focused on the discursive construction of heterosex and the diversity of heterosexual experiences and bodily

contacts. This includes a focus on women's sexual agency. Queer theory has also influenced contemporary understandings of sexuality and facilitated a shift to exploring the diversity and fluidity of sexual identities, preferences, practices, and meanings.

However, attention to the dangers of sexuality for women also remains a central component of theorizing and research. In the new millennium, sexual violence against women, from domestic violence to rape and the more recent "date rape," is prevalent. Recent work attempts to explore the complex ways in which normative understandings of heterosexuality and women's sexuality provide the "cultural scaffolding" (Gavey 2005) for rape and sexual violence against women. Attention to the location of discourses about sexuality within specific sociohistorical contexts and the ways in which individuals are positioned within, and negotiate with, normative discourses underpins much contemporary research. Gavey (2005), for example, works to unsettle rigid gender binaries around both active desiring sexuality and physical aggression, as well as those around the possibilities of victimization. She advocates a transformation of the cultural conditions of possibility for gendered ways of being sexual and "aggressive."

Other contemporary feminist ways to "recorporeograph" women's sexuality (Potts 2002) include decentralizing the penis, disrupting the masculine (active)/feminine (passive) dichotomy, and promoting the autonomous female sexual subject. Examples of such reframings include: rethinking heterosexual intercourse in terms of engulfment or embracement of the man's penis by the woman's active vagina, thinking in terms of the "phallic woman" or destabilizing impressions of female bodies as vulnerable interiorized spaces and eroticizing the "receptive" male, and promoting active female sexuality through attention to the "female ejaculation" (Bell 1991).

Challenging understandings of what constitutes normative heterosex, for example the coital and orgasmic imperatives, is therefore a central endeavor in much critical theorizing and research on women's sexuality. This extends to the recent critiques of the medicalization of women's sexuality. Since the 1990s there has been an increasing focus on women's sexual problems, located primarily within medical and sexological frameworks. Female sexual dysfunction, as a sexual disorder, was "made" in the late 1990s and is routinely reported to affect around 40 percent of women (despite serious concerns about this figure by sex researchers). "Female sexual dysfunction" refers to women's sexual difficulties with arousal, penile-vaginal penetration, and orgasm and promotes a specific norm of sexually correct genital performance. The necessary ingredients for "successful" sexual experience are desire (vaguely indicated as being "for sex"), genital arousal, a timely orgasm, and the ability to enjoy vaginal penetration (Tiefer 2001). On the one hand, there is acknowledgment of women's new sexual agency and rights, yet on the other hand, the medical model ignores the non-medical nature of sexual problems and difficulties, in spite of women repeatedly telling researchers that these are their primary areas of sexual distress. Tiefer argues that the medical model promotes the idea that all women want the same thing out of sex, with routine orgasmic genital function as the centerpiece and physical manifestations as the main source of difficulty. It tells women there is something wrong with them whenever they experience a pattern of sexual desire, arousal, or orgasm defined by experts as "abnormal."

The escalating medicalization of women's sexuality provoked Leonore Tiefer (2001) to think about a "new view" of women's sexual problems. Tiefer, together with a grassroots group of feminist social scientists, sex educators, therapists, sex researchers, physicians, and activists, developed the Campaign for a New View of Women's Sexual Problems. In contrast to the medical model, the "new view" emphasizes sexual diversity, social context, education, empowerment, and attention to the ways in which sexual norms are constructed. It is hoped this "new view" will influence sexuality theory, research, and education.

SEE ALSO: Ellis, Havelock; Essentialism and Constructionism; Femininities/Masculinities; Feminism; Feminism, First, Second, and Third Waves; Freud, Sigmund; Heterosexuality; Kinsey, Alfred; Krafft-Ebing, Richard von; Lesbian Feminism; Lesbianism; Patriarchy; Personal is Political; Queer Theory; Sex and Gender; Sexual Identities; Sexual Politics; Sexual Practices; Sexual Violence and Rape; Sexuality Research: History

REFERENCES AND SUGGESTED READINGS

Bell, S. (1991) Feminist Ejaculations. In: Kroker, A. & Kroker, M. (Eds.), *The Hysterical Male: New Feminist Theory*. St. Martin's Press, New York, pp. 155–69.

Gavey, N. (2005) *Just Sex? The Cultural Scaffolding of Rape*. Routledge, London.

Irvine, J. (2002) Towards a "Value-Free" Science of Sex: The Kinsey Reports. In: Phillips, K. & Reay, B. (Eds.), *Sexualities in History: A Reader*. Routledge, New York and London, pp. 327–56.

Jackson, M. (1987) Facts of Life or the Eroticization of Women's Oppression? Sexology and the Social Construction of Heterosexuality. In: Caplan, P. (Ed.), *The Cultural Construction of Sexuality*. Tavistock, London, pp. 52–81.

Jackson, S. (2003) Heterosexuality, Heteronormativity and Gender Hierarchy: Some Reflections on Recent Debates. In: Weeks, J., Holland, J., & Waites, M. (Eds.), *Sexualities and Society: A Reader*. Polity Press, Cambridge, pp. 69–83.

Nicolson, P. (1993) Public Values and Private Beliefs: Why Do Women Refer Themselves for Sex Therapy? In: Ussher, J. & Baker, C. (Eds.), *Psychological Perspectives on Sexual Problems: New Directions in Theory and Practice*. Routledge, London, pp. 56–78.

Nicolson, P. (1994) Anatomy and Destiny: Sexuality and the Female Body. In: Choi, P. & Nicolson, P. (Eds.), *Female Sexuality: Psychology, Biology, and Social Context*. Harvester Press, New York and London, pp. 7–26.

Potts, A. (2002) *The Science/Fiction of Sex: Feminist Deconstruction and the Vocabularies of Sex*. Routledge, London and New York.

Rubin, G. (1984) Thinking Sex: Notes for a Radical Theory of the Politics of Sexuality. In: Vance, C. S. (Ed.), *Pleasure and Danger: Exploring Female Sexuality*. Routledge & Kegan Paul, Boston, pp. 267–319.

Segal, L. (1994) *Straight Sex: Rethinking the Politics of Pleasure*. University of California Press, Berkeley and Los Angeles.

Tiefer, L. (1995) *Sex is Not a Natural Act, and Other Essays*. Westview Press, Boulder, CO.

Tiefer, L. (2001) A New View of Women's Sexual Problems: Why New? Why Now? *Journal of Sex Research* 38(2): 89–96.

Tuana, N. (1993) *The Less Noble Sex: Scientific, Religious, and Philosophical Conceptions of Women's*

Nature. Indiana University Press, Bloomington and Indianapolis.

Ussher, J. (1997) *Fantasies of Femininity: Reframing the Boundaries of Sex*. Penguin, London.

Valverde, M. (1985) *Sex, Power, and Pleasure*. Women's Press, Toronto.

Vance, C. (Ed.) (1984) *Pleasure and Danger: Exploring Female Sexuality*. Routledge & Kegan Paul, Boston.

women's empowerment

Denise A. Copelton

Women's empowerment is a central concern of the women's movement. It refers to the general process through which women gain knowledge about the structures that oppress them, and seek to alter the power imbalances in society. Bookman and Morgen (1988: 4) define empowerment broadly as the "process aimed at consolidating, maintaining, or changing the nature and distribution of power in a particular cultural context" that can range from "acts of individual resistance to mass political mobilizations." Given women's diverse experiences of inequality, women's empowerment has been partially achieved through a variety of strategies and within a number of different historical, institutional, and cultural contexts. For example, in the first wave of the women's movement in the US, women's empowerment was linked explicitly to political power in the form of voting rights. In the second wave, women's empowerment was linked to such issues as reproductive rights, workplace rights, freedom from men's violence, and furthering women's political rights and legal protections through the Equal Rights Amendment (ERA). Not all of these issues were successful, however, as the ERA never passed into law, violence against women continues, and reproductive rights are not shared equally by all women. Nevertheless, that large numbers of women demanded changes to the unequal institutional arrangements in politics, law, medicine, and intimate relationships illustrates the process of women's empowerment. Though the concept and process of women's empowerment is far reaching and factors into all areas of women's lives, the discussion below focuses on those

areas of women's lives in which the concept of empowerment has taken center stage. These include second-wave US feminist organizing; women, sports, and self-defense; women's health care; and women and development.

In the US, women's empowerment figured especially prominently in the second-wave women's liberation movement of the late 1960s and 1970s and took the form of consciousness-raising groups. As practiced by second-wave feminist groups, consciousness raising is quite similar to the development of a sociological imagination, which allows its possessor to reframe her problems as collective rather than individual, as emanating from political or institutional structures rather than personal failings. The multistep process of consciousness raising began with sharing personal experiences with other women, connecting those experiences with larger institutional forces, and linking all of the above to larger theories of oppression and privilege (Ferree & Hess 1995). The process often facilitated a "click" experience or epiphany and politicized a large number of women as they collectively reframed their personal experiences as the result of institutionalized sexism and gender discrimination. The feminist slogan "The personal is political" resonated strongly with this overall process of consciousness raising. However, not all women wanted to press for political and institutional change. Some second-wave feminist organizations' use of consciousness raising as a tool of empowerment functioned more like a self-help "rap" session or feminist support group than as a collective strategy to press for societal change. In some groups, the process of consciousness raising never progressed to its final phase – that of facilitating political activism. Instead, some consciousness-raising groups functioned merely as psychological support groups or self-help groups, places where women could receive support from other women as they attempted to make changes in their personal lives.

In the 1970s, the women's health movement emerged out of second-wave feminist organizing in the US. Feminist critics charged that medicine in general and physicians in particular mystified women's bodies and argued that if physicians shared information about women's bodies at all, they did so in complicated scientific terms which rendered such information inaccessible to most women without a medical background. The medicalization of childbirth came in for special scrutiny as feminists argued that the medical treatment of childbirth placed control over this natural process entirely in the hands of medical experts, leaving childbearing women powerless to determine the course of their own care. Activists in both the feminist and childbirth reform movements believed that women must be empowered to wrest control away from physicians and reconceptualize health care to minimize power differentials between providers and patients, or as they were increasingly called, clients. Thus, women's empowerment in health care would come, they argued, through sharing medical information with women and leveling the power differentials embedded in the traditional doctor–patient relationship. A host of second-wave publications such as *Our Bodies, Ourselves* and *How to Stay Out of the Gynecologist's Office* intended to make medical information accessible to women and empower women to take charge of their own health.

Feminist women's health centers, in particular, took seriously the goal of women's empowerment. Jan Thomas (2000) notes that feminist health centers empower women patients through three principal mechanisms. First, instead of merely providing care to women, these centers aim to educate and inform clients about their own health and health care options so women clients can become active participants in their own care. Second, feminist centers seek to break down institutional barriers to care by reducing the physical and social distance between clients and providers, increasing the average length of provider–client interaction, and by becoming visible in the local community. Finally, centers seek to treat all clients with dignity and respect. Thomas (2000: 144) writes that empowerment "takes place over time through the mutual sharing of information, knowledge, and skills" and "culminates in a woman's active control of her health care."

The concept of women's empowerment has also factored heavily in arguments for women's sports and self-defense courses. Title IX of the Educational Amendments Act of 1972 banned sex discrimination in US schools, including school sports programs. Passage of Title IX was seen as a victory for girls not only because

it banned school-based sex discrimination of all sorts, but also because it required schools to offer girls opportunities for sports participation that were equal to those of boys. Advocates for girls' and women's sports argued that sports empower girls and women by improving self-esteem, developing positive body images, offering a sense of accomplishment, and promoting self-confidence, which then may translate into higher grades and standardized test scores, lower high school dropout rates, and higher college attendance rates. In other words, participation in sports empowers girls to develop greater confidence in their own abilities and thereby challenge gender stereotypes and power imbalances in societal institutions.

Advocates of self-defense training for women and girls argue that self-defense can prevent women's victimization by strengthening their physical and psychological capacity to resist male violence. By teaching women basic martial arts techniques, feminist self-defense courses empower women to resist traditional gender role socialization that encourages passivity, and to develop instead both the self-confidence and physical skills necessary to resist and flee an assailant. About the impact of women's physical development through sports, Roth and Basow (2004: 262) write, "as our bodies are transformed, so are our minds." Women's participation in sport and feminist self-defense, these scholars argue, therefore empowers women to contest traditional assumptions concerning the frailty of women and women's bodies and thereby challenge the power dynamics embedded in traditional gender roles that leave women susceptible to potential male violence.

Recently, the concept of women's empowerment has factored heavily in development discourse and practice, particularly among nongovernment organizations (NGOs). One of the ways that women's empowerment is currently being pursued in developing countries is through micro-credit lending. Historically, development programs focused on women only as a means of controlling fertility. Programs promoting women's education were thus often justified with reference to the lower fertility rates these programs would facilitate. Focusing almost exclusively on familial roles, such development programs typically ignored women's economic roles and rarely promoted women's well-being for its own sake. Development policies and programs also typically construed women as in need of aid or welfare, rather than as in need of sustainable income-generating projects, despite the fact that many studies showed that women were often the main income earners within their households. However, since the mid-1970s development discourse and policy have increasingly recognized that women's equity in developing nations is tied to their income-generating activities. Recognition that rural women earned a livelihood from a variety of economic activities besides waged labor led the Grameen Bank of Bangladesh to organize micro-credit lending schemes aimed at poor women. NGOs and other private funders have adopted the model of micro-lending in part, because of the higher loan repayment rates associated with micro-lending compared to other credit schemes aimed at the poor.

Research examining the impact of micro-lending on women's empowerment has found mixed results. Because micro-lending is primarily concerned with women's economic position, providing credit to enterprising women who might not otherwise qualify for credit, its results have largely expanded women's economic resources while leaving untouched other sources of gender inequality. Offering micro-credit to women in developing nations does not always result in women's control of economic resources. Thus, if women's empowerment means control over resources, increased self-reliance, greater independent decision-making, and shared decision-making with men, then micro-lending has been only partially successful.

SEE ALSO: Black Feminist Thought; Consciousness Raising; Feminism; Feminism, First, Second, and Third Waves; Gender Ideology and Gender Role Ideology; Gender, Sport and; Personal is Political; Sex and Gender; Sociological Imagination; Women's Movements

REFERENCES AND SUGGESTED
READINGS

Afsar, R. (2003) Micro Finance and Women's Empowerment: Insights from a Micro-Level Sociological Study. *Pakistan Journal of Women's Studies: Alam-e-Niswan* 10: 129–59.

Bookman, A. & Morgen, S. (1988) *Women and the Politics of Empowerment*. Temple University Press, Philadelphia.

Buechler, S. M. (1990) *Women's Movements in the United States*. Rutgers University Press, New Brunswick, NJ.

Ferree, M. M. & Hess, B. B. (1995) *Controversy and Coalition: The New Feminist Movement Across Four Decades of Change*. Routledge, New York.

Izugbara, C. O. (2004) Gender Micro-Lending Schemes and Sustainable Women's Empowerment in Nigeria. *Community Development Journal* 39: 72–84.

McCaughey, M. (1998) The Fighting Spirit: Women's Self-Defense Training and the Discourse of Sexed Embodiment. *Gender and Society* 12: 277–300.

Mehra, R. (1997) Women, Empowerment, and Economic Development. *Annals of the American Academy of Political and Social Science* 554: 136–49.

Morgen, S. (2002) *Into Our Hands: The Women's Health Movement in the United States, 1969–1990*. Rutgers University Press, New Brunswick, NJ.

Roth, A. & Basow, S. A. (2004) Femininity, Sports, and Feminism. *Journal of Sport and Social Issues* 28: 245–65.

Searles, P. & Berger, R. J. (1987) The Feminist Self-Defense Movement: A Case Study. *Gender and Society* 1: 61–84.

Thomas, J. E. (2000) Incorporating Empowerment into Models of Care: Strategies from Feminist Women's Health Centers. *Research in the Sociology of Health Care* 17: 139–52.

women's health

Diane S. Shinberg

Women's health encompasses physical, emotional, and social health and well-being associated with female reproductive and sexual development over the life cycle, or any medical condition more common among women. The sociology of women's health includes the study of gendered politics within medicine, medical training, doctor–patient interactions, self-care, illness behavior, and health care utilization. Women's health can be more broadly construed to include the relationships between gender inequality (gender as a social institution) and health, even among men.

The pervasiveness of biological essentialism, the ideological emphasis on biology as *the* explanation for apparent differences between men and women, is one reason women's health is such a broad and dynamic area of sociological study. Gender inequality – the social constraint, devaluation, and oppression of women – historically has been justified on the basis that the female sex status is frail with respect to anatomy, physiology, hormones, development, sex, procreation, and, most recently, genes. The use of biomedical authority in theories regarding the fundamental differences between the sexes supports the pervasive belief in women's biologic vulnerability as "the weaker sex." Such ideology has had social consequences, for example, as manifest in barring women from pursuing higher education because intellectual activities supposedly would divert the flow of blood to the brain from the uterus, leading to uterine atrophy, decreased fertility, and even barrenness. More recently, hormonal fluctuations associated with menstruation, premenstrual syndrome, post-partum depression, and menopause are cited as causes of mental imbalance and unpredictability which prevent women from holding the reigns of power in political and corporate offices.

DEMOGRAPHY AND EPIDEMIOLOGY OF WOMEN'S HEALTH

In post-demographic transition societies women on average live longer than men. Mortality declines and gains in life expectancy were most substantial, especially among women, in the early to mid-twentieth century, a trend related to declines in maternal and infant mortality. According to the National Center for Health Statistics for 2002 in the US, total female life expectancies at birth, at age 60, and at age 85 were 79.9, 83.5, and 92 years versus 74.7, 80.3, and 90.9 for males, respectively.

Despite a so-called female physiological advantage in terms of survival, women apparently experience more sickness and ill-health than men, contributing to a so-called gender paradox in health where "women are sicker, but men die quicker." However, this generalization is overly simplistic; indeed, careful

assessments reveal a more complex story about excess female sickness when specific aspects and definitions of health are considered. While women tend toward higher levels of overall physical illness, disability days, and health care utilization, men experience more life-threatening ailments such as heart disease, respiratory disease, and cancer. Despite Americans' mistaken belief that female-specific illnesses such as breast cancer are the leading cause of death among women, men and women die from largely the same set of causes, such as heart disease.

Biomedical approaches to sex differences in health and illness emphasize the portion of gender differences in morbidity attributable to female reproductive problems or to physiological differences between males and females that contribute to different rates of disease processes and aging among men and women. Although biophysiology may contribute to static sex differences in morbidity and mortality, it may be unlikely that such differences, per se, account for change in gender differences in health and death over time.

By contrast, sociomedical approaches to gender disparities in health consider social constructionism and gender role theories. Gender differences in material circumstances, social roles, social support, and lifestyle explain historical change in and gender patterning of health and mortality. People's social roles and characteristics are related to their health, and those roles that women tend to hold more than men may be important in explaining gender disparities in health. These acquired risks (e.g., low socioeconomic status, non-employment, parenting, care-giving, and certain health habits) decrease health status. Compositional gender differences in these acquired risks contribute to gender differences in health that favor men. Secondly, the social construction of gender roles is related to health in that traditional feminine role obligations are more compatible with illness behavior and sick-role incumbency than traditionally masculine roles. Reproductive role obligations, such as nurturing and care-giving, requires cognizance of the nutritional and behavioral requirements of others, and an awareness of what constitutes normal (versus deviant, sick, or out of the ordinary) behaviors and needs of other family members. Such responsibilities may foster sensitivity to sickness and may foster adoption of health-promoting behavior on one's own behalf and on behalf of others, and women tend to be the primary agent for health within the family. Finally, sociomedical approaches suggest gendered artifacts of health-reporting behavior, help-seeking behavior, and recall and response rates may contribute to measured gendered differences in subjective health.

ILLNESS BEHAVIOR, HEALTH CARE UTILIZATION, AND MEDICALIZATION

In general, women go to the doctor more than men, with rates of physician visits overall 40 percent higher among women compared to men. According to the National Center for Health Statistics, among 25–44 year olds, women go to the doctor twice as often as men. Men seek preventive health care half as frequently as women do.

There is an apparent congruity between emphasized femininity and the sick role, with these associations influencing illness behaviors, such as help-seeking. By contrast, an incongruity between hegemonic masculinity and sick-role behavior is manifest among health lifestyles in which masculinity supports risk-taking and negative health behaviors such as drinking, smoking, low seatbelt use, and health care avoidance. Men are twice as likely as women to have had no health care visits in the past 12 months and are three times as likely as women to have had no health care contacts whatsoever during a three-year period.

Perhaps the predominant sociological focus on women's health has been the medicalization of the female life cycle. Medicalization refers to the process through which aspects of life fall under the purview of medicine and come to be defined as medical problems or illnesses. As women are more often patients than men, women's lives may be more easily subject to medicalization; for example, menstruation, premenstrual syndrome (PMS), pregnancy, birth, breast-feeding, infertility, and menopause have all become medicalized to some degree with respect to medical language and to medical practice.

While the medicalization of birth in the US was strongly associated with the rise of medicine as a profession and medical control over the use of forceps in the early twentieth century, the medicalization of pregnancy is a more recent and ongoing process. Through technological advancements (e.g., sonograms, amniocentesis) and legal and insurance constraints (e.g., managed care and malpractice insurance), the definition of what is considered as a "high-risk" pregnancy has expanded so that more technological interventions are brought to bear upon the pregnant and laboring woman (Rothman 2000). Infertility, once considered a social problem for unfortunate couples, is highly medicalized since 1978 and the birth of Louise Brown, the first "test tube baby" or child conceived as a result of *in vitro* fertilization. Although healthy birth rates resulting from hi-tech assisted reproductive technologies remain modest, many private health insurance plans now cover some assisted reproduction trials. Other examples of medicalization research in women's health include Anne Figert's study of the politics of defining PMS as a medical and psychological disorder and Margaret Lock's research on the divergent medicalization of menopause in the US and Japan. With respect to medicalized language, Emily Martin has detailed how biomedical textbooks employ gendered language to describe gamete production, conception, menstruation, and menopause.

GENDER AND THE INSTITUTION OF MEDICINE

As feminism enhanced women's entry into medical fields, more women have access to medical schools today (nearly half of medical students are women). However, while about a quarter of doctors in the US are women, nursing remains a female-dominated occupation; about 95 percent of nurses are women. Gender stratification operates at all levels within these fields: women who become doctors tend to specialize in pediatrics, family practice, and obstetrics/gynecology at higher rates than male doctors. Within more exclusive branches of medicine, such as advanced surgical specialties, women's representation remains scant. Overall, male doctors earn more than female doctors, while female doctors are more likely to be salaried and less likely to be self-employed than their male counterparts. Among full-time physicians, women tend to work somewhat shorter hours than men, although total office hours spent with patients are similar. However, female physicians tend to spend slightly more time (about 2 minutes longer) with patients and thus tend to see fewer patients than male doctors. Given the gender distribution among doctors, nurses, and patients, the predominant dyads within medicine (doctor–patient and doctor–nurse) are gendered as well as hierarchical. Thus, medical settings have contributed to studies of dominance, authority, and gender (Fisher 1988).

The heightened inclusion of women in the profession of medicine has contributed attention to the differential treatment of women as second-class patients relative to men and to the exceptional treatment of women as patients who receive excessive intervention. It is important to remember that differential and/or exceptional treatment of women as patients is not necessarily the result of overt discrimination. The gender system is strongly related to ideas about illness, etiology, and treatment. In the example of heart disease, McKinlay (1996) identified patient, provider, health system, and technologic influences on the gendered detection of illness.

WOMEN'S HEALTH MOVEMENT, POLICY, AND SCHOLARSHIP

The last decades of the twentieth century were a dynamic period for women's health scholarship and activism. The modern women's health movement not only changed the US health care system but also applied the important sociological concepts of authority, deviance, labeling, and medicalization to resist stigma associated with being female.

The successes of the women's health movement in the 1970s buoyed larger movements in self-help and consumerist health care. For example, activists concerned about coercive female sterilization practices against poor women, women of color, and Medicaid recipients fought for informed consent protocols for such procedures. The National Women's Health Network lobbied the US Food and Drug Administration (FDA) to provide more information to women who opted to take contraceptive birth control pills; thus, the Pill became the first prescription drug in the US to include a mandatory patient package insert which disclosed potential side effects.

Pressure from groups outside medicine and from growing cohorts of women scientists, including doctors, forced a change in the way biomedicine was conducted and organized in the US. For decades, women were routinely excluded from clinical trials due to concerns over chemical exposures and reproductive vulnerabilities. Many medications had not been tested on women and thus physicians were on their own in prescribing dosages and assessing drug interactions. However, in 1990 the National Institutes of Health founded an Office of Research on Women to oversee the systematic inclusion of women in clinical studies. This development may be seen as an example of medicine's growing reliance on evidence-based approaches to the clinical treatment of patients.

Just as sociology has shifted from a consideration of the sociology of women to the sociology of gender, the meaning of women's health is expanding to include gender and health. This provides opportunities to configure women's health to include many aspects of interlocking systems of domination, (e.g., race, class, sexuality, age, etc.) and to address ways in which gender as a social institution influences health. Other important influences within sociology include research on the sociology of the body and on aging and the life course.

The sociology of women's health will need to better understand the renewed interest of biomedicine in sex-specific biology (Wizemann & Pardue 2001). Future developments in gender and health will address the continuation of medicalization, with new opportunities for gender-based case comparisons (e.g., sexual dysfunction); the intersections of gender, disability, and the body; and gendered life course trajectories in health practices and outcomes.

SEE ALSO: Health Behavior; Health and Medicine; Illness Behavior; New Reproductive Technologies; Sick Role

REFERENCES AND SUGGESTED READINGS

Boston Women's Health Book Collective (1998) *Our Bodies, Ourselves for the New Century: A Book by and for Women*. Simon & Schuster, New York.

Fisher, S. (1988) *In the Patient's Best Interest: Women and the Politics of Medical Decisions*. Rutgers University Press, New Brunswick, NJ.

Kuh, D. & Hardy, R. (Eds.) (2003) *A Life Course Approach to Women's Health*. Oxford University Press, Oxford.

Lorber, J. & Moore, L. J. (2002) *Gender and the Social Construction of Illness*, 2nd edn. Alta Mira Press, Walnut Creek, CA.

McKinlay, J. B. (1996) Some Contributions from the Social System to Gender Inequalities in Heart Disease. *Journal of Health and Social Behavior* 37: 1–26.

Morgen, S. (2002) *Into Our Own Hands: The Women's Health Movement in the United States, 1969–1990*. Rutgers University Press, New Brunswick, NJ.

Rothman, B. K. (2000) *Recreating Motherhood*, 2nd edn. Rutgers University Press, New Brunswick, NJ.

Wizemann, T. M. & Pardue, M. (Eds.) (2001) *Exploring the Biological Contributions to Human Health: Does Sex Matter?* National Academy Press, Washington, DC.

women's movements

Carol Mueller

Women's movements arise from the gendered social constructions that have accompanied the biological differences between male and female. Because social distinctions based on gender are the most basic forms of human differentiation, they pervade social life. Throughout history, across classes, ethnicity, nationality, sexuality, and religious groupings, the gendered division of labor has been associated with differential roles, rewards, and with an associated politics. That is, the political processes by which rules are made and valued objects and services are distributed have institutionalized gender differences since the beginning of human history. In only rare circumstances have these differences not been associated with the subordination of women. Traditional systems of political thought, supported by most religions, have relegated women to a secondary status. Thus, the potential beneficiaries of "women's movements" conceivably encompass more than half of humanity throughout history.

Yet women are also divided by all of the other social distinctions and sources of subordination to which the human experience gives rise. These distinctions are characterized variously in terms of "multiculturalism," "intersectionality," and, for the last few years, the all-embracing language of "human rights." Women's differences present both obstacles to mobilization and a multiplicity of competing claims characterized in terms of identity struggles (Hobson 2003). Others, however, argue that the resolution of differences occurs in an ongoing process of negotiation in specific sociopolitical contexts within which no long-term historic actor is forged (Stephen 1997: 275–9). This perspective could help account for the periodic societal amnesia regarding the collective struggles associated with women's movements. Negotiating and defining who "women" are in terms of their competing identities, nature of subordination, and associated claims constitute some of the major processes of women's movements (see, for instance, Hobson 2003; Reger 2006).

We should also recognize that not all of women's mobilizations are full-blown social movements. In fact, many are local campaigns restricted to neighborhood or community. Most of these remain local, such as the neighborhood groups that Naples describes in the New York area during the 1960s War on Poverty. Historically, the most famous of the shortlived women's protests was the October 1789 march on Versailles to protest increases in the price of bread, one of the defining *journées* of the French Revolution. Other local mobilizations by women have become national and then internationally modeled by other women. Such was the case with the Mothers (and Grandmothers) of the Plaza de Mayo in Buenos Aires in the late 1970s and the 1980s. The mothers' protests on behalf of their disappeared children were taken up by mothers throughout Latin America (Stephen 1997). In these cases, women were bound together by their identities as "mothers of the disappeared." Women in Black offer another example where gender alone is a binding identity. Their signature protests against violence and warfare originated among Palestinian and Israeli women and then spread to Serbia and Ireland, and are now found all over Europe and North America.

FEMINISM AND WOMEN'S MOVEMENTS

To speak of "women's" movements, however, requires attention to the distinction between movements made up of women as a constituency or organizational strategy and those movements in which the empowerment of women is both a goal and source of theoretical and ideological negotiation and contestation, that is, "feminist" movements (Ferree & Mueller 2004). The distinction is that between an organizational or identity choice of female membership that may or may not be feminist and a mobilization that is based in ideology, framing, cultural discourse, and practices concerned with women's subordination, potentially made up of men as well as women. Women's movements take action on behalf of home and family as well as supporting principles like peace and justice as the responsibility of women in their roles as wives and mothers. Most of the short-term mobilizations of women described above are of this nature.

Women's mobilizations can become feminist and vice versa, as when women in the anti-slavery movement of the early nineteenth century became the founders of the US suffrage movement (Flexner 1959). The recent origins of feminism in the US began with women who felt they had received second-class treatment in the Civil Rights Movement and the new left of the 1960s. Similarly, Lynn Stephen notes that "Latin American women's activism ... often combines a commitment to basic material survival for women and their families with direct or indirect challenges to women's subordination to men" (1997: 267). For the sake of consistency, in the following discussion, the term "feminist" will be used to designate those movements concerned with rectifying women's subordination despite the fact that their goals are frequently much broader.

Although feminist mobilizations are always concerned with the subordination or self-actualization of women, the elasticity of that definition has led to enormous variety in feminist movements. The term itself is a product of intellectual discourse in late nineteenth-century France, but the "woman question" had been a matter of public concern in Europe since the sixteenth century among literate men and women. To emphasize ideas as the defining characteristic of a feminist movement is only to recognize a historic fact. As Karen Offen notes in her history of European feminism, "an expanding body of feminist criticism in print precedes by centuries the development of the women's groups which do begin to form, from 1789 on" (2000: 25). Like most of the social movements associated with modernity, feminist movements were also empowered by the spread of literacy and a print culture (Tarrow 1998). As Offen points out, the Enlightenment was as much about the "woman question" as it was about citizenship, democracy, science, and the authority of reason.

Among women and men who might be considered feminists, there have been many schools of thought on the subordination of women that have continuously served as major sources of ideological and political conflict. Despite this diversity, the most consistent division globally and historically has been between liberal and socialist feminisms. Prior to 1848, it seemed that socialists and feminists were pursuing the same goals, but after mid-century, an intense rivalry developed in Europe that was echoed in most parts of the world where both systems of thought fought for dominance. Pre-Marxist socialist visionaries on both sides of the Atlantic supported egalitarian utopias with communalized family systems like the Owenites in England and the Oneida Community in upper New York state. By the last half of the century, however, August Bebel, Friedrich Engels, Karl Marx's daughter, and Clara Zetkin made it clear that class had political primacy over sex in socialist thinking (Offen 2000). These differences have influenced positions on protective labor legislation, prostitution, state support for mothers, and, most importantly, the question of whether women's subordination is a result of capitalism or some more universal relationship between men and women.

The pervasive socialist/liberal difference between feminists is still found, for instance, in Raka Ray's (1999) comparison of feminist organizing in Bombay and Calcutta; in European and North American feminists' responses to neoliberal political and social restructuring (Banaszak et al. 2003); and in Latin American women's responses to authoritarian governments, where the Zapatista rebellion in Chiapas shows the closest approximation to revolutionary socialist practice (Stephen 1997). In the US and Canada, with weak traditions of socialism, feminist union women such as the Women of Steel described by Fonow (2003) have, nevertheless, begun to make significant progress in building international coalitions.

MODES OF MOBILIZATION AND MOVEMENT LONGEVITY

As one of the major social movements developing in the modern period, feminist movements have, to some extent, shared the same repertoire of collective action (Tarrow 1998) as labor, environment, male suffrage, and other "rights" movements. While feminists' mobilizing structures may have been located in beauty shops, garden clubs, churches, and neighborhood groups rather than taverns, sporting events, and men's clubs, to some extent the resulting repertoires were similar despite the relative absence of violence, or of strikes and revolutionary attempts to take over the state. If we look back at the women's suffrage movements of the nineteenth and early twentieth centuries, we see a very similar repertoire of mass meetings, petitions, demonstrations, and electoral campaigns that were associated with the birth of other social movements attempting to influence the state. The ultimate success of these movements is also credited to the formal organizations that coordinated national campaigns over decades and across large distances.

At the same time, nineteenth-century feminists challenged cultural norms and values through a more symbolic and discursive repertoire associated today with "new social movements" (Melucci 1989). "Bloomer girls" defied the strictures of women's clothing as well as Victorian sensibilities (Flexner 1959). Among other radical challenges to nineteenth-century culture was the call for free love and the end of marriage by leaders of the National Suffrage Association, echoing the programs of communal utopians early in the century. While these claims sprang from the center of equal rights/ liberal feminism in the United States, Engels and other socialists were making similar attacks on the institution of marriage as "legalized prostitution" in Europe.

A similar combination of cultural and political repertoires has characterized the more recent phase of feminist mobilization. The US feminist movement has, in fact, been primarily identified in terms of an equal rights branch engaged with the state (Costain 1992) and a women's liberation branch which has challenged basic cultural assumptions. The former has had its program institutionalized through legislation, court decisions, lobbying, formal organizations, electoral campaigns, and the increasing support of women in electoral and administrative offices. The latter branch of the movement achieves long-term influence through the creation of women's studies programs in colleges and universities, performance art, books, journals, and music, book stores, coffee shops, and entire communities of feminists. The impressive success of Eve Ensler's *Vagina Monologues* has demonstrated how performance art can serve as a venue for consciousness-raising. As Katzenstein (1998) points out, this distinction in repertoires exists even in the "unobtrusive" mobilizations of feminists within highly structured, patriarchal institutions like the US military and the Catholic Church.

Like most long-running international movements, feminists have gone through periods of highly public mobilization followed by "abeyance" periods (Rupp & Taylor 1987). When the public visibility of the movement is lost, low-profile organizations, networks, and communities can sustain the ideologies, framing, and collective memory of the movement. In Europe and North America, this periodicity or cycle of protest (Tarrow 1998) has been characterized in several ways. The most common is the "wave" analogy in terms of first and second waves, with younger scholars pointing to a third wave since the mid-1990s. The first wave, from the mid-nineteenth century until after World War I, is associated with the campaign for women's suffrage, although the movement actually had a much broader agenda. The second wave is associated with the 1960s and, in terms of equal rights, the creation of the State

Commissions on the Status of Women leading to the formation of the National Organization for Women and a host of legislation for women, including the Equal Rights Amendment (Costain 1992). On the cultural side, women's liberation groups engaged in street theater against the Miss America Contest in Atlantic City, released mice at the New York Marriage Fair, and hexed Wall Street. While these "waves" span decades, Whittier (1995) points out that "generations" of feminists can change identities, claims, and repertoires as often as every few years in highly mobile grassroots organizations. Beginning in the 1990s, a "third" wave has been widely debated in terms of how much current feminist issues and practices are discontinuous from earlier mobilizations (see Reger 2006). These discussions are so pervasive that there are increasing arguments for other metaphors.

Regardless of the analogy, what seems very clear is that these transformative moments redefining the relationship of women to men and to society have historically been quickly suppressed by countermovements that reestablished women's traditional subordination. This was true until women gained a firm foothold in the polity through suffrage movements of the late nineteenth and twentieth centuries. Offen (2000) describes such a process of French movement and countermovement occurring repeatedly in 1789, 1830, 1848, and 1871. Institutionalized access to the polity has been a necessary, but not sufficient, condition for achieving cumulative gains toward eliminating women's subordination.

At the local level, periodicity and protest cycles are strongly influenced by sociopolitical conditions and the rise of countermovements. Globally, however, war and depression have played the primary role in suppressing transnational communication, travel, conferences, and organizational development (Ferree & Mueller 2004). Although the major effect of both world wars of the twentieth century was the suppression of women's international mobilization, as was the Cold War, all three conflagrations led to the creation of institutions that furthered global feminist movements. The League of Nations, the Organization of American States, the United Nations, and the decade of international conferences that followed the collapse of the Soviet Union all served as targets of feminists' mobilizations, as forums for debates on differences in women's subordination North and South, and, eventually, as sources of both resources and legitimation.

A GLOBAL MOVEMENT?

By the time European powers encircled the globe with their empires in the nineteenth century, some of the ideas associated with feminism had become embedded in the larger cultural package of "modernity" (Kandiyoti 1991). Indigenous leaders in the European colonies sometimes entertained these ideas along with other modern systems of thought as a way of coming to terms with the imperial powers. Thus, attacks on footbinding in China, *sati* in India, and female circumcision in East Africa were largely campaigns sponsored by coalitions of western missionaries and modernizing local leaders with support from information campaigns aimed at European audiences of men as well as women (Keck & Sikkink 1998). As nationalist movements led to the overthrow of colonial powers in the twentieth century, feminist ideas were in danger of being attacked for their association with western imperialism and discredited "modern" ideas (Kandiyoti 1991). Similarly, when the Soviet system collapsed late in the twentieth century, ideas about women's equal participation in politics and the paid labor force were discredited in many countries of Eastern Europe because of their association with an imposed Soviet-style socialism (Jacquette & Wolchik 1998). Despite these setbacks, both liberal equal rights and socialist interpretations of feminism have circled the globe.

In the late nineteenth century, railways and steamships increased the opportunities for travel, and international postal networks enhanced the opportunities for building transnational networks. The World Expositions held in Paris, London, and Chicago provided opportunities for feminists to hold their own parallel congresses, much as women have done in the late twentieth century during international UN conferences. With the Second International of 1889, socialists identified a common platform with class oppression given preference over the subordination of women as an accepted political priority. The first wave of feminist mobilization in the late nineteenth century led to the creation of international organizations that merged women's concerns for peace and the end of poverty with feminist concerns about women's subordination. In a series of meetings before and after World War I, conferences were held to bring international attention to all of these issues and to create mechanisms for pursuing these aims between conferences.

In a surprising historic parallel, the late twentieth century saw comparable international expansions in opportunities for communication, travel, and networking. Air flights became increasingly affordable. By the end of the century, the Internet provided instant access to the far corners of the globe. Organizationally, the creation of the Commission on the Status of Women (CSW) within the United Nations gave feminists their initial entrée into the major governmental body with international legitimacy (see Meyer & Prügl 1999). From their beachhead in CSW, feminists were successful in lobbying for an International Women's Year (IWY) conference in Mexico City for 1975 which became a starting point for a series of global conferences that brought together an increasing number of governmental representatives and movement organizers. In preparation and in response to these conferences, women's organizations flourished. Feminists also took their agenda(s) to UN conferences on the environment (Rio, 1983), human rights (Vienna, 1993), and population (Cairo, 1994). By the time of the UN conference for women in Beijing (1995), estimates placed the number of official and unofficial participants at 30,000 to 40,000 – the largest gathering of women in world history. Despite this impressive showing of global feminism as historic actor, the global face of the movement has received scant notice from the mainstream media.

Early in the twenty-first century, the Internet was alive with debates over whether, when, and where further UN conferences for women should be held. Organizers feared the countermovement taking shape in the alliance between the Vatican and representatives from Muslim countries that appeared in Cairo and again at the Beijing Conference that would be reinforced by delegations appointed by conservative administrations in Australia, the United States, and other western countries. Countermovements, however, have occurred as frequently as the feminist movements they oppose. There seems little likelihood that either feminists or their opposition will disappear in the coming century.

SEE ALSO: Collective Action; Colonialism (Neocolonialism); Feminism; Feminism, First, Second, and Third Waves; Feminist Activism in Latin America; Gender Ideology and Gender Role Ideology; Gender, Social Movements and; Modernization; Nationalism; New Social Movement Theory; Social Change; Social Movements; Socialism; Transnational and Global Feminisms; Transnational Movements

REFERENCES AND SUGGESTED READINGS

Banaszak, L. A., Beckwith, K., & Rucht, D. (Eds.) (2003) *Women's Movements Facing the Reconfigured State*. Cambridge University Press, New York.

Costain, A. (1992) *Inviting Women's Rebellion*. Johns Hopkins University Press, Baltimore.

Ferree, M. M. & Mueller, C. (2004) Feminism and Women's Movements. In: Snow, D. A., Soule, S.A., & Kriesi, H. (Eds.), *The Blackwell Companion to Social Movements*. Blackwell, Oxford, pp. 576–607.

Flexner, E. (1959) *Century of Struggle*. Harvard University Press, Cambridge, MA.

Fonow, M. M. (2003) *Union Women*. University of Minnesota Press, Minneapolis.

Hobson, B. (Ed.) (2003) *Recognition Struggles and Social Movements*. Cambridge University Press, New York.

Jaquette, J. S. & Wolchik, S. L. (Eds.) (1998) *Women and Democracy*. Johns Hopkins University Press, Baltimore.

Kandiyoti, D. (Ed.) (1991) *Women, Islam, and the State*. Macmillan, London.

Katzenstein, M. (1998) *Faithful and Fearless*. Princeton University Press, Princeton.

Keck, M. E. & Sikkink, K. (1998) *Activist Beyond Borders*. Cornell University Press, Ithaca, NY.

Melucci, A. (1989) *Nomads of the Present*. Hutchinson Radius, London.

Meyer, M. K. & Prügl, E. (Eds.) (1999) *Gender Politics in Global Governance*. Rowman & Littlefield, Boulder, CO.

Offen, K. (2000) *European Feminism: 1700–1950*. Stanford University Press, Stanford.

Ray, R. (1999) *Fields of Protest*. University of Minnesota Press, Minneapolis.

Reger, J. (2006) *Different Wavelengths*. Routledge, New York.

Rupp, L. & Taylor, V. (1987) *Survival in the Doldrums*. Ohio State University Press, Columbus.

Stephen, L. (1997) *Women and Social Movements in Latin America*. University of Texas Press, Austin.

Tarrow, S. (1998) *Power in Movement*, 2nd edn. Cambridge University Press, New York.

Whittier, N. (1995) *Feminist Generations*. Temple University Press, Philadelphia.

work, sociology of

Melissa Bonstead-Bruns

Work is typically described as the activities involved in the production of goods and services. The sociology of work, then, involves the systematic study of the interrelationship between the people and institutions associated with the production of goods and services. The general heading of the sociology of work subsumes many topics, which can be separated roughly into individual-level approaches and structural-level approaches. Individual-level approaches treat the individual as the unit of analysis and typically focus on ascribed characteristics such as gender, race, and age. They also commonly address achieved characteristics such as education, promotion, compensation, and other labor force outcomes. Individual-level approaches may also examine the impact of work over time by looking at the life course or career trajectory of individuals.

The units of analysis of structural-level approaches range from jobs, to occupations, to industries, and may even focus on the individual *within* the larger structure. Common topics addressed under a structural rubric include occupational structures, internal labor markets (ILMs), bureaucracies, unionization, skills, professions, and globalization. Overlapping these two approaches is work on particular occupations or areas of employment, and work on public policy issues related to the labor market, such as affirmative action, comparable worth, welfare-to-work programs, and the welfare state in general.

Over the course of its evolution, the sociology of work has diverged into three separate subfields. One still goes by the name sociology of work, and the other two are industrial sociology and formal organizations. The sociology of work encompasses three main theoretical movements. The first spanned the years roughly between 1920 and 1950. It was rooted in the Chicago School of sociology and was strongly influenced by symbolic interaction and the pioneering work of Everett Hughes. His and other early approaches had a primarily micro focus and addressed the issues of worker culture and interpersonal relations, especially with regard to workplace problems.

The next two decades saw the field turning its focus from a symbolic interactionist concern for individual issues to a more structural focus where the individual worker was viewed as an actor constrained by various organizational impediments. Critics of this structural approach argued that it lost sight of the worker as a purposeful agent, with structure supplanting self-determination. At the same time, research shifted from primarily qualitative to heavily quantitative, in part to increase generalizability of research findings. As such, multivariate analysis became the norm. On the theoretical side, sociological theories such as structural functionalism, social conflict theory, neo-Marxist theory, and systems theory heavily influenced the research during this time. Arguably, the most significant work of this period is Blau and Duncan's *The American Occupational Structure* (1967), which mapped the factors that contribute to an individual's success, such as personal achievement and family background. By situating individuals within a status-ranked occupational structure, Blau and Duncan systematically measured social placement while laying the groundwork for studying social *mobility*.

The third and most current movement emphasizes a synthesis of work done at the individual and structural levels. Two dominant subspecialties and countless other minor subspecialties are situated in this most recent movement. The first of the dominant subspecialties has its roots in Marx's *Capital* and was ignited by Harry Braverman (1974). Braverman introduced the idea of *labor process* to describe how capitalists have degraded the organization of work, leading to the homogenization of workers. Though other theorists have criticized Braverman's work, it reinvigorated the Marxist influence on the sociology of work and led to future studies on worker organization and resistance, worker satisfaction, the role of the state, deskilling, and the role of class in the workplace.

The second dominant subspecialty examines various work structures, such as occupational structures, industries, and firms, and incorporates them into individual-level models of inequality focusing on such issues as income and segregation. This *new structuralist* approach owes much to Averitt (1968). The new structuralists viewed work structures as segmented; thus, analysis focused on how work structures divide the economy, labor market, and labor force and on the inequalities inherent in these divisions. For example, dual labor market theorists such as Doeringer and Piore (1971) highlighted the existence of two distinct labor markets. The *primary labor market* is where the "good" jobs are: those with high wages, unions, good benefits, international markets, and, most importantly, internal labor markets. *Secondary labor markets* are marked by jobs that offer lower wages, are not unionized, have few if any benefits, and little opportunity for advancement. Current structuralist approaches have moved beyond the simplistic dualist approach in favor of more sophisticated models of segmentation.

Much of the current research in the area of sociology of work involves inequality. Researchers apply various theories to phenomena such as segregation (by job, occupation, firm, and industry), the wage gap, advancement and mobility, and problems stemming from disparate treatment and disparate impact. Ascribed characteristics such as race, ethnicity, age, and others are the keys to understanding inequality in the labor process, though inequality based on sex and gender is the most heavily researched.

Researchers interested in gender inequality largely concentrate on segregation and the wage gap. Occupational segregation has been the subject of a great deal of research as women tend to be crowded into a small number of traditionally female occupations such as nursing, teaching, clerical work, and other fields commonly associated with caregiving, service, or relating with others. Men, on the other hand, tend to be concentrated in engineering, architecture, protective services (e.g., police and fire fighters), skilled craftwork, construction, mechanical repair, and other fields seen as requiring instrumental action, supervisory skills, physical strength, and analytical abilities. Explanations for occupational segregation vary. Individual explanations point to prevailing gender roles and gender role socialization to explain occupational choices made by men and women. However, a valid counterargument to this claim is that strong social pressures to bear the primary burden of child and household duties, the fear of disparate treatment in the workplace, and actual disparate treatment and disparate impact in the workplace constrain women's choices. Structural explanations examine how various work structures function to keep men and women in different fields. Segmented labor market theorists argue, for example, that statistical discrimination on the part of employers leads to a tendency to view women as less productive and subsequently leads to a funneling of women into "bad" jobs and men into "good" jobs. Even when women enter the firms where the good jobs are located, structural theorists argue that structures such as internal labor markets are often segregated as well.

The bulk of the research done on gender differences at work involves the wage gap. Though the size of the gap varies according to hours worked, career stage, age of worker, and human capital investments, a gap persists nonetheless. Again, the individual-level explanations focus on worker choice and the tendency of women to choose lower-wage options, often as a result of perceived family and household obligations. Structural explanations look to the gender structuring of occupations, the crowding of women into certain occupations, and the devaluation of skills commonly associated with women. This type of structural explanation has spurred interest in comparable worth (pay equity) policies. Comparable worth policies seek to assign equal rewards to men and women in positions that are comparable on the basis of skills, responsibilities, working conditions, and effort (England 1992). Researchers attribute the recent trends in the reduction of the wage gap between men and women more to the decline in wages for men as a result of changes to the occupational structure and the loss of high paying manufacturing positions than to significant gains made by women.

Occupational segregation and inequalities in labor force outcomes such as wages and promotion also affect individuals who are members of racial or ethnic subpopulations. Minorities are disproportionately concentrated in peripheral firms, in low-wage, low prestige positions, with little opportunity for advancement. Discrimination in the hiring process, educational inequalities, concentration effects, and class differences also factor heavily into the inequalities faced by racial and ethnic subpopulations.

The relationship between work and family is closely related to, and often overlaps, issues of gender and work. A reciprocal relationship exists between family life and work life; as for most families, changes in one lead to changes in the other. The impact of family life on the work experience differs for men and women, especially with regard to labor force outcomes such as income. This became especially apparent as the number of dual-earner households surpassed the number of households following a more traditional division of labor. Some researchers have argued that men receive a wage premium for getting married and having children, while women receive a wage penalty, and that women retain the primary responsibility for the bulk of domestic work even when they work full-time outside the home. However, factors such as social class, level of acceptance for egalitarian ideals, level of education, timing of marriage and family within one's career, and differences in earnings and occupational status between partners may temper these differences. Researchers also see the family–work connection as relevant to level of productivity, career advancement and aspirations, and individual well-being and mental health.

Workers are increasingly feeling the effects of a global economy. Patterns of global communication, global migration, and global trade have led to numerous cross-cultural studies of work along with research on the implications of a global economy. Extreme concentrations of power in the hands of a few multinational corporations and the rise of free trade zones where environmental and human rights concerns have been on the rise have led to a resurgence in worker organization and solidarity. Hence, much work in the field has concentrated on worker rights and collectivization.

Sociologists of work regard many of the problems associated with increased globalization as a result of unevenness in the process of industrialization, which has led to vast wealth and power differences cross-nationally. Three theories seek to explain this phenomenon. First, modernization theory purports that societies evolve through predictable stages of development and industrialization according to their own internal dynamics, which include technological advances and patterns of consumption. Second, dependency theory challenges modernization theory, claiming instead that, within the global economy, more developed countries place less developed countries in a position of dependency. Third and most recently, world systems theory also challenges modernization theory by rejecting the notion that nations evolve in a singular predictable pattern. Instead, it views the global economy as a system of interdependent parts where trade relations function to reproduce existing power differences.

The growth of the service economy and the impact of technology on the world of work and the economy have also taken center stage in recent years. One theoretical approach to these shifts in the organization of work is optimistic in that it sees a move toward a service economy as part of a natural economic process. Thus, theorists predict that changes in technology will improve the quality of work and work life for workers. A second and more pessimistic approach sees changes in the economy as heightening the inequality between skilled and unskilled workers, with technology leading to deskilling or even supplanting the worker.

Researchers expect much of the future growth in the field of the sociology of work to be in continued globalization, increased technological advances, and a continuing evolution of the structure of work and the growth in the service economy. As long as inequality in labor market outcomes exists, however, research will continue on gender, race, and the family, as well as other research programs addressing inequality. Future research will also likely continue the current trend of increasing methodological sophistication, as the quantitative methods currently employed in the field have become increasingly complex. Additionally, researchers recently have called for more integration and cooperation with other disciplines and subspecialties such as economics, economic sociology, industrial psychology, and others.

SEE ALSO: Braverman, Harry; Bureacratic
Personality; Gender, Work, and Family; Global
Economy; Occupational Mobility; Occupational
Segregation; Occupations; Organizations and
the Theory of the Firm; Professions; Unions;
Workplace Diversity

REFERENCES AND SUGGESTED
READINGS

Abbott, A. (1988) *The System of Professions: An Essay
on the Division of Expert Labor*. University of Chi-
cago Press, Chicago.
Averitt, R. T. (1968) *The Dual Economy: The
Dynamics of American Industry Structure*. Norton,
New York.
Blau, P. M. & Duncan, D. (1967) *The American
Occupational Structure*. Wiley, New York.
Braverman, H. (1974) *Labor and Monopoly Capital:
The Degradation of Work in the Twentieth Century*.
Monthly Review Press, New York.
Burawoy, M. (Ed.) (1979) *Manufacturing Consent*.
University of Chicago Press, Chicago.
Doeringer, P. B. & Piore, M. (1971) *Internal Labor
Markets and Manpower Analysis*. Heath, Lexing-
ton, MA.
England, P. (1992) *Comparable Worth: Theories and
Evidence*. Aldine, New York.
Kalleberg, A. L. (1989) Linking Macro and Micro
Levels: Bringing the Workers Back Into the
Sociology of Work. *Social Forces* 67: 582–92.
Marx, K. (1962) *Capital: A Critique of Political Econ-
omy*, Vol. 1. International Publishers, New York.
Simpson, I. H. (1989) The Sociology of Work:
Where Have the Workers Gone? *Sociology of Work*
(March): 563–81.

workplace diversity

Stella Nkomo

Workplace diversity appears to have a rather
short history as a field in organization studies
if one locates its emergence only within contemporary scholarship (Nkomo & Cox 1996). Issues
that commonly fall within the study of workplace diversity have always existed. Yet, early
conceptualizations of organizations were rooted
in universalistic approaches that largely ignored
race, ethnicity, gender, culture, sexuality, and
other social identities (e.g., Clegg 1990). Race

and gender in organizations gained some attention after the passage of equal employment legislation in the United States during the 1970s as
well as in the UK. This work appeared under
the rubric of women in management and in
studies of the effects of affirmative action and
workplace discrimination (for a review see Cox
& Nkomo 1990).

Substantive attention to workplace diversity in
organizations is attributed primarily to the publication of *Workforce 2000* (Johnson & Packer
1987). This report forecasted a radical increase
in the number of women and racial/ethnic minorities entering the United States workforce. It
seems this forecast was largely on target although
some changes in the profile of the workforce
were unforeseen, including an increase in the
number of workers with disabilities and growing
religious diversity. Women constitute 48 percent
of the United States workforce. By 2020, 32 percent of the US labor force is projected to be ethnic
minorities, and four of every ten people entering
the workforce from 1998 to 2008 will be members of minority groups. Hispanics are now the
largest minority group in the United States, surpassing African Americans.

The authors of *Workforce 2000* urged organizations and decision-makers to identify ways to
"manage" this growing diversity (Nkomo & Cox
1996). Consequently, the field was initially prac-
titioner-driven with scholarly attention lagging.
Some would argue this accounts for the frequently lodged criticism that much of the literature on workforce diversity is atheoretical
(Nkomo & Cox 1996; Cassell & Biswas 2000).
However, in the last ten years, the research on
workplace diversity has escalated (Ragins &
Gonzalez 2003).

The conceptualization of and research on
workforce diversity has largely emanated from
North America, primarily the United States.
Consequently, much of the extant literature
represents a perspective rooted in the social
and political history of the United States. More
recently, the topic of workplace diversity has
gained currency in Europe (e.g., Dick & Cassell
2002; Maxwell et al. 2003; Point & Singh 2003),
with its growing immigrant population from
Asia, Africa, and the Caribbean, as well as in
other regions of the world, including Africa,
Australia, and New Zealand (e.g., Jones et al.
2000; Nyambegera 2002; Hartel 2004).

Defining the concept of diversity remains problematic. Some scholars take a narrow approach, focusing on what has been referred to as surface-level diversity or visible immutable identities (e.g., race, gender, age, ethnicity). Still others argue for a more expansive definition that encompasses surface- as well as deep-level diversity (Harrison et al. 1998). The latter refers to personality, attitudes, values, and beliefs. Another classification scheme uses demographic diversity, which is similar to surface-level diversity, and job-related diversity, which is defined as experiences, skills, and functional work responsibilities. Although the categorizations may differ, there appears to be a trend toward broader definitions of workplace diversity rather than narrow ones. Broader definitions suggest workplace diversity should focus on all the ways individuals differ from one another. Nkomo and Cox (1996: 339) argued that despite the level of disagreement over what constitutes diversity, the concept of identity is at the core of understanding workplace diversity in organizations. They suggest diversity refers to identities based on membership in social and demographic groups, and how differences in identities affect social relations in organizations.

A number of theoretical perspectives have been utilized to study workplace diversity. Most often, scholars have turned to the rich body of theory on intergroup relations. Social identity theory, embedded intergroup theory, and organization demography have been the dominant theoretical perspectives for examining workplace diversity. Generally, these perspectives focus on the effects and consequences of diversity in organizations. Research utilizing social identity theory typically examines the categorization processes that create in-group and out-group memberships, resulting in one's own group being more highly valued. This body of work suggests that social identification and related processes produce both negative and positive effects in organizations. Some studies have shown that diverse work groups make better decisions than homogeneous groups, while other results suggest diverse work groups evoke greater conflict and less cohesiveness (Ragins & Gonzalez 2003). The solution to managing diversity in the workplace within a social identity framework is a reduction in the salience of group boundaries.

While social identity theory is largely a cognitive theory, scholars examining workplace diversity have also sought to identify specific contextual influences on categorization processes. For example, contextual factors such as intergroup competition, faultlines, and ongoing within-group interaction are seen as important predictors of the saliency of group boundaries (Lau & Murnighan 1998). Scholars have also acknowledged the influence of two-way or reciprocal identification processes between organizational/work group members as well as the realization that members of any given social group or category vary in the extent to which identity group membership is a central and salient aspect of their overall self-concept (Hogg & Terry 2000).

Alderfer and Smith (1982) developed embedded intergroup theory specifically for understanding identity group memberships within an organizational setting. Their theory posits that two types of groups exist within organizations: identity groups and organization groups. Their theory can also be seen as another way of classifying the content of workplace identities in organizations. An identity group is defined as a group whose members share similar biological or demographic characteristics such as sex or race. An organization group is viewed as one in which members share common organization positions or equivalent work experiences. A person's identity in an organization is composed of their group memberships as well as organization group membership. Alderfer and Smith (1982) propose complex interactions among these identities. For example, they argue that conflicts and tensions arise when the two identities are mirror societal positions. For example, often there may be a correlation between identity group membership and organization membership that reflects broader societal patterns. In the United States and in many countries, leadership and management positions tend to be dominated by heterosexual white males. The theory suggests workplace diversity in organizations requires an understanding of identity group membership, organization membership, as well as the broader societal context in which those relations are embedded. Much of the research on race and ethnicity in organizations has relied heavily on embedded intergroup relations theory to demonstrate how attitudes toward minorities and their structural position in the broader society affect the workplace experiences (e.g., Bell & Nkomo 2001).

Organizational demography focuses on the causes, consequences, or distribution of employees in an organization (Tsui & Gutek 1999). Scholars studying workplace diversity have utilized organizational demography theory to focus primarily on the group identities of age, tenure, education, and functional background. However, Tsui and Gutek (1999: 15) emphasize that diversity and demography are not the same. They argue that demography experts focus on understanding the meaning of demographic diversity and analyzing the effects of such diversity on individuals, groups, and organizations. Their interest is not in prescribing action or change but in explanation. Demographic analysis employs three approaches to uncover the effects of demographic differences: categorical demography, composition demography, and relational demography. Categorical research focuses on the effects of an individual's demographic characteristics on work-related behavior and attitudes. Composition demography is concerned with the effects of demographic compositions of work units and organizations on individuals or groups. Relational demography focuses on social relationships between an individual and the group with respect. The interest is in effects of the difference in the individual's demographic attributes and those of the other members in the group. For example, the situation of a lone female manager in a top management team is argued to be different from being a female in a top management team comprised mainly of females (Tsui & Gutek 1999). An important assumption of demography theory is equivalence among all types of diversity. The interest is in the effects of relative heterogeneity and homogeneity rather than the subjective meaning of the demographic identity (Ragins & Gonzalez 2003).

Recently, a more critical analysis of workplace diversity has emerged from critical management and postmodern theories. This work problematizes the very concept of diversity and its assumptions, particularly the discourse of diversity (Dick & Cassell 2002; Zanoni & Janssens 2003). Scholars have analyzed diversity as a rewriting project that overlooks the issue of inequality of power among groups in the workforce (Linnehan & Konrad 1999) as well as viewing it as an effort to obscure the need for attention to issues of discrimination and oppression. Zanoni and Janssens (2003) analyzed the texts on diversity produced in 25 interviews with Flemish human resource (HR) managers from a critical discourse analysis and rhetorical perspective. They found that HR managers' diversity discourses reflect existing managerial practices. Similarly, Kelly and Dobbin (1998) argue equal employment opportunity/affirmative action specialists, primarily in the United States, retheorized anti-discrimination and affirmative action practices as diversity management to make them more digestible and to ensure their institutional positions. Other scholars argue that the extant literature promotes an essentialist understanding of people and their identities (De los Reyes 2000). There is also work demonstrating the ways in which workplaces are fundamentally gendered and racialized (Fletcher 2001).

A review of the trajectory of the extant scholarship on workplace diversity reveals a great deal about its nature. Initial research was dominated by the question of how to manage workplace diversity and its effects. Scholars focused on research to uncover the effects of diversity and how organizations should manage diverse work groups. An implicit assumption was that diversity is a problem to be managed. Diversity was also assumed to reside in "others," not within dominant group members. Valuing diversity became the next dominant theme. Efforts were made to change the view of diversity from being a problem to a positive feature in workplaces and to make a business case for workplace diversity. Some scholars have attempted to empirically measure the effects of workplace diversity on the bottom line. Richard (2000) tested the effects of racial diversity on firm performance but did not find direct effects. Instead, racial diversity combined with business strategy to have a positive effect on performance. However, most of the literature advocating the valuing of diversity has been prescriptive. Thomas and Ely (1996) argued for the adoption of an "integration and learning" paradigm for workplace diversity. This approach seeks to incorporate diversity throughout the organization, vertically and horizontally, inclusive of the nature of the organization's approach to processes, strategy, and work. According to Thomas and Ely under this paradigm, cultural differences among organization members are recognized as sources of skill and insight that can have a direct impact on the organization's core tasks.

The current trajectory suggests a questioning mode. On one hand critical management and postmodern approaches question the very ontology, essence, and aims of workplace diversity (Zanoni & Janssens 2003). At the same time, there is an evident broadening in the level of complexity in the study of workplace diversity within scholarship from a positivist and functional orientation. More attention is being given to the context in which diversity effects may occur as well as recognizing that individuals have multiple identities, not a singular identity. Others question whether enough attention has been paid to the effects of religious diversity, sexual orientation, disability, and class (Ragins & Gonzalez 2003). Despite the volume of research generated over the past ten years, clearly there remain a number of pertinent complex issues and unanswered questions. Not least among them is the persistence of discrimination, racism, sexism, and homophobia as well as continued inequality in the workplace. Ragins and Gonzalez (2003) noted that doing research on workplace diversity requires traversing a slippery slope. Yet, it is clear that there is still much research needed to understand the meaning, effects, and consequences of workplace diversity as well as how best to address the stubborn issues of inequality.

SEE ALSO: Affirmative Action; Age Prejudice and Discrimination; Discrimination; Diversity; Doing Gender; Ethnic Groups; Ethnicity; Gendered Organizations/Institutions; Postmodernism; Race; Race (Racism); Racialized Gender; Social Identity Theory; Work, Sociology of

REFERENCES AND SUGGESTED READINGS

Alderfer, K. & Smith, K. K. (1982) Studying Intergroup Relations Embedded in Organizations. *Administrative Science Quarterly* 27(1): 35–65.

Bell, E. & Nkomo, S. M. (2001) *Our Separate Ways: Black and White Women and the Struggle for Professional Identity*. Harvard University Press, Boston.

Cassell, C. M. & Biswas, R. (2000) Managing Diversity in the New Millennium. *Personnel Review* 29(3): 268–73.

Clegg, S. (1990) *Modern Organization: Organization Studies in the Postmodern World*. Sage, London.

Cox, T. H., Jr. & Nkomo, S. M. (1990) Invisible Men and Women: A Status Report on Race as a Variable in Organization Behavior Research. *Journal of Organizational Behavior* 11(6): 459–77.

De los Reyes, P. (2000) Diversity at Work: Paradoxes, Possibilities, and Problems in the Swedish Discourse on Diversity. *Economic and Industrial Democracy* 21(2): 253–66.

Dick, P. & Cassell, C. (2002) Barriers to Managing Diversity in a UK Constabulary: The Role of Discourse. *Journal of Management Studies* 39(7): 953–76.

Fletcher, J. K. (2001) *Disappearing Acts: Gender, Power, and Relational Practice at Work*. MIT Press, Cambridge, MA.

Harrison, D. A., Price, K. H., & Bell, M. P. (1998) Beyond Relational Demography: Time and the Effects of Surface- and Deep-Level Diversity on Work Group Cohesion. *Academy of Management Journal* 41(1): 96–107.

Hartel, C. E. J. (2004) Towards a Multicultural World: Identifying Work Systems, Practices, and Employee Attitudes That Embrace Diversity. *Australian Journal of Management* 29(2): 189–200.

Hogg, M. A. & Terry, D. J. (2000) Social Identity and Self-Categorization Processes in Organizational Contexts. *Academy of Management Review* 25(1): 121–40.

Johnson, W. & Packer, A. (1987) *Workforce 2000: Work and Workers for the 21st Century*. Hudson Institute, Indianapolis.

Jones, D., Pringle, J., & Shepherd, D. (2000) "Managing Diversity" Meets Aotearoa/New Zealand. *Personnel Review* 29(3): 364–80.

Kelly, E. & Dobbin, F. (1998) How Affirmative Action Became Diversity Management. *American Behavioral Scientist* 41: 960–85.

Lau, D. C. & Murnighan, J. K. (1998) Demographic Diversity and Fault Lines: The Compositional Dynamics of Organizational Groups. *Academy of Management Review* 23: 325–40.

Linnehan, F. & Konrad, A. (1999) Diluting Diversity: Implications for Intergroup Inequality in Organizations. *Journal of Management Inquiry* 8(4): 399–414.

Maxwell, G., McDougall, M., Blair, S., & Masson, M. (2003) Equality at Work in UK Public Service and Hotel Organizations: Inclining Towards Managing

Diversity? *Human Resources Development International* 6(2): 243–58.

Nkomo, S. M. & Cox, T., Jr. (1996) Diverse Identities in Organizations. In: Clegg, S. R., Hardy, C., & Nord, W. R. (Eds.), *Handbook of Organization Studies*. Sage, London.

Nyambegera, S. M. (2002) Ethnicity and Human Resource Management Practice in Sub-Saharan Africa: The Relevance of the Managing Diversity Discourse. *International Journal of Human Resource Management* 13: 7.

Point, S. & Singh, V. (2003) Defining and Dimensionalizing Diversity: Evidence from Corporate Websites Across Europe. *European Management Journal* 2(6): 750–61.

Prasad, A. (1997) The Colonizing Consciousness and Representations of the Other: A Postcolonial Critique of the Discourse of Oil. In: Parsad, P., Mills, A., Elmes, M., & Prasad, A. (Eds.), *Managing the Organizational Melting Pot: Dilemmas of Workplace Diversity*. Sage, Newbury Park, CA, pp. 285–311.

Ragins, B. R. & Gonzalez, J. A. (2003) Understanding Diversity in Organizations: Getting a Grip on a Slippery Construct. In: Greenberg, J. (Ed.), *Organizational Behaviour: The State of the Science*, 2nd edn. Lawrence Erlbaum, Mahwah, NJ, pp. 125–63.

Richard, O. C. (2000) Racial Diversity, Business Strategy, and Firm Performance. *Academy of Management Journal* 43(2): 164–77.

Thomas, D. A. & Ely, R. (1996) Making Differences Matter: A New Paradigm for Managing Diversity. *Harvard Business Review* (September/October): 79–90.

Tsui, A. S. & Gutek, B. (1999) *Demographic Differences in Organizations: Current Research and Future Directions*. Lexington Books, Lanham, MD.

Zanoni, P. & Janssens, M. (2003) Deconstructing Difference: The Rhetoric of Human Resources Managers' Diversity Discourses. *Organization Studies* 25(1): 55–74.

world conflict

Gordon Fellman

Fights of one kind or another show up in archaeological and anthropological studies of early societies as well as later ones. Usually limited to ritualized encounters, these conflicts seem more like sport than anything else; two groups of men fight, the action ending when someone is hurt.

If war means using weapons deliberately to kill, in order to gain food, booty, land, honor, or other prizes, then war appears to start 12,000–15,000 years ago, probably around the time of the onset of agriculture and the settled communities that accompanied it. Surely the idea of taking food and other things from people who have them would occur to people more than once. Fighting strategies and weapons developed early on, as did the killing of civilians as well as warriors.

Historians can tell us about wars among and within tribes, city-states, empires, and nations. What qualifies, though, as a world conflict? Here it is suggested that a world conflict must involve at least three continents and have an outcome with serious effects in much of the world. World War I mainly involved Western Europe and the United States. By contrast, World War II included the Pacific, Asia, Africa, Europe, and North America. It concluded with the end of most of colonialism that had flourished for up to two centuries; the Cold War, which lasted almost half a century; escalation in the deadliness of weapons systems; and the spread of "free market" economics, liberal democracy, and totalitarianism to places that had known little of these ideologies and practices before.

World conflicts can be examined in terms of at least four dimensions: economic, political, religious, and social psychological. It will not do to seek the "cause" of a given war. Nazism, for example, is a consequence of the humiliation of Germany in the Versailles Treaty marking the end of World War I, but it also reflects on the dire straits the Great Depression brought to much of the West, the romance of German nationalism, and the social psychology of the relationship between a charismatic demagogue and almost an entire people.

"World conflicts" do not mean only war in the traditional sense. In the twenty-first century, "terrorism" has emerged as a variant on traditional war and a central form of world conflict. "Terrorism" has been applied recently to non-state violence directed at civilians and combatants in contests of will, power, and systems. "Terrorism" can also include organized violence against civilians no matter where it comes from. Hence, nations bombing civilians under any circumstances can qualify as "state terrorists," as distinct from "extra-state terrorists" all the way from organized movements to ad hoc suicide bombers.

In the twenty-first century, terrorism is the most dramatic and overtly war-like form of world conflict. Globalization is another. Whatever its multiple meanings, globalization brings about major conflicts between employers and workers, whether those fired in a developed country to save a company money or those working for low wages in less developed countries.

Another aspect of globalization-based world conflict is between forces wishing to preserve the planet in healthy ways and those wishing to disrupt and even destroy delicate resource systems for profit. This includes damage in the ways resources are extracted and the use of fossil fuels in manufacturing and in transporting resources and goods over much of the world. These are all aspects of economy-based world conflicts.

Politically based world conflicts are between political systems vying for dominance. The Cold War was partly about western capitalism and the so-called communist alternative wanting to eliminate each other, but also between societies with at least a partially democratic underlay and those with totalitarian cores. The Cold War organized and stabilized world conflict from 1945 to 1989, when the Soviet Union disintegrated. The end of the Cold War represents a crisis in the nation-state and the secularism that most often has accompanied it in the West. Before the great nation-state period began in the eighteenth century, ethnic/national and religious identifications were paramount in much of the world. Part of the accomplishment of the secular nation-state as defined, for example, by France and the United States in the eighteenth century was that national identity and politics edged aside ethnic and religious identities.

Major western nations developed somewhat democratic institutions along with capitalist economic systems. These two factors combined with industrialization to produce unprecedented goods, trade, and wealth. And also great disparities between the rich and the poor.

With the end of colonialism and imperialism, which were fundamental to the development of liberal democracy and capitalism, world conflict came to be defined as conflict between nations' policies that favored manufacturers, traders, and bankers and the peoples whose resources, economies, and lives were disrupted, controlled, and even ruined by them. As industrialization grew, so did the exploitation of child and female labor, urban crowding, slums, poverty, disease, violence, prostitution, and family breakdown. Thus world conflict was defined heavily by the differences in interests between elites who ran economic and political systems and the majority of people who did not benefit very much from the elites' policies and actions.

Objections to this state of affairs were articulated most forcefully by Karl Marx, who foresaw the brutalities of capitalism as a necessary precondition for liberation from them in the form of a successor society that would allow comfort and fulfillment for all people rather than primarily elites. Marx warned that Russia would ruin his ideas if it tried to implement them, as it had barely entered capitalist industrialization, the full development of which, according to Marx, was necessary before the true human liberation of socialism and communism could proceed.

It was Lenin who decided that communism could skip the full development of capitalism. Whatever the outrages and failures of the effort he set in motion, it at least maintained itself for hundreds of millions of people as an image of an eventually more humane alternative to capitalism. But between its own internal problems and pressures against it from outside, the Soviet alternative collapsed near the end of the twentieth century. This supposedly left the US as the surviving, triumphant system, but that was not exactly the way much of the world experienced the outcome of the Cold War. Even as the Soviet system ended, the seemingly triumphant American system hit some great snags. Its elites assumed that the US was now free to act as it wished in the world. It could take what it wanted on its own terms and could make wars with impunity.

This condition did not, though, sit well with vast numbers of people in the world and even in the US. The collapse of the Soviet alternative and the mistrust and loathing of US efforts in much of the world provoked massive repudiation of both systems and widespread reversion to ethnic and religious identifications.

In the new century, world conflicts take forms other than traditional wars. One finds ethnicities (e.g., Hutus and Tutsis in East Africa) and religions (e.g., Catholics and Protestants in Northern Ireland), and combinations of religions and ethnicities (e.g., Sinhalese and Tamils in Sri Lanka, Israelis and Palestinians in the Middle East) pitted against each other. These conflicts blend anger over differences in wealth and control with belief in one's own group's legitimacy and the illegitimacy of its opponent.

The second current form of violent world conflict is terrorist movements against nation-states. Some see this form of conflict as based on totalitarian commitments of one party versus democratic political commitments of the other.

The liberal hope of endless economic growth, increasingly fair distribution of goods and services, democratic political institutions, and the privacy of religious commitments and behavior seems to have run up against vast objections and rejections. The totalitarian alternative appeared in major force in Leninism/Stalinism, Nazism, and Maoism in the twentieth century, and appears to be gaining force in Islamism and some forms of Judaism and Christianity in the twenty-first century. These movements and their ethnic-nationalist counterparts appear to represent, individually and collectively, a rejection of relativism, "progress," electoral democracy, and the separation of religion and state.

The advertised freedoms of the market and democratic systems seem less and less attractive to more and more people. How can we explain this? At least two approaches come to mind. One harks back to a post-World War II social science classic, *The Authoritarian Personality* (1950), by Theodor Adorno and three other European refugees. The authors set themselves the task of understanding not so much the rise of Hitler as the willingness of most Germans to support him. Adorno et al. found that the "authoritarian personality" harbors an "intolerance of ambiguity." They saw the contrasting term, "tolerance of ambiguity," as characterizing the "democratic personality," which they obviously preferred.

Certain kinds of leaders can provide a community feeling, a sense of bonding with similar others that appears to be lacking in the modern world of free market economics and pseudo-democratic politics ("pseudo" because few if any "democracies" realize very fully the potential of the democratic ideal; money interests, media that seem more intent on keeping the lid on things than informing the electorate, cynical manipulations of emotions and information, and other forces operate to undermine the true potential of democracy). The yearning for strong leadership and absolute, unambiguous declarations about the world suggests a yearning for community which modernism seems to undermine. It also suggests that in some peoples at some times, emotional needs are not congruent with rational needs. For example, the needs for adequate shelter, food, employment, education, and health care do not necessarily define people's approaches to political choices.

The part of the brain that deals with emotions is older and more primitive than the part dealing with reason. Feelings are, of course, far stronger and more dominating for the first several years of life than is reason, and it is completely likely that the salience of feelings is never really abandoned. Rather, it becomes disguised and channeled into institutional behavior.

Young children rely on the authority and approval of parents they often experience as perfectly strong, caring, loving, and wise. Around age 6 or 7, the awareness dawns that parents are not perfect at all. This is a crucial moment, for societies intuitively understand that disillusionment with the imperfect parent does not lead the child to discard the wish for the parent previously idealized. Society offers metaphors, usually religious and national, for those ideal parents lost. The "perfect parent" is a cult figure or God or Nazism or Communism or Islamism, or fundamentalist Christian, Jewish, Hindu, or other clergy or secular national leaders.

At the heart of this are two compelling questions that absolute authority answers for the willing follower. One is, what am I to do with my love, which is so insistent and strong that it impels me way beyond the family in which I first learned its pleasures and centrality? The second question is, what am I to do with my anger, which is so insistent and strong that it impels me way beyond the family in which I first learned it in its numerous manifestations?

Absolute leaders instruct their followers to love certain people and hate the rest. Such leaders take upon themselves the judgmental capacity and conscience of the followers. They say in effect, you do not need to bother yourself making judgments about good and bad, right and wrong, life and death. I will relieve you of those complex, painful decisions and reduce it all to easy contrasts and slogans. This will simplify your life while giving me the absolute power that every child dreams of but gives up fairly early on. I will speak to that child in you that wished to be omnipotent and also that child in you that wished for the perfect and all-knowing parent. You will love the people I tell you to love and hate and even kill those I tell you to oppose.

And here we get to the least studied crucial issue in human behavior in our time: anger (which includes such manifestations as rage, wrath, hatred, loathing, fury, vilification, and much more). Like all emotions, anger originates in the self's predisposition to feel that emotion and in real experiences that draw it out. Children commonly are so consumed with anger that it frightens them as well as the adults who witness and feel it.

With loving, accepting care on the part of adults, children's anger can be accepted, understood, and contained. More commonly, though, the anger is not fully accepted, not completely understood, and not adequately contained. The child who has this experience, and most people have had it, is left with a field of metal rods representing numerous experiences of unfulfilled anger. Culture offers what amount to magnets that fly over those fields of anger rods and pull them swiftly to the magnet. In a racist society, culture says, take that free-floating anger and use it against people whose skin color is different from yours. Or gender. Or nationality. Or religion. Or sexual orientation. Or anything else that offers an opportunity to attach anger to something and let it out there, even though it does not actually originate or belong there.

What conflict does on the world scale is to galvanize endless and countless rods of anger to the magnets of racism, nationalism, religious

superiority, and so forth, "opposition structures" that capture that free-floating hatred and use it to accomplish domination, vilification, exploitation, and war. Certain leaders with excessive tendencies in this direction engage their own anger to organize and perpetuate opposition structures and encourage followers, who have their own reservoirs of anger, to join them in the enterprise.

When this anger is organized into structures that exploit economically and humiliate politically, we find the major alternative, in explaining terrorism, to the anti-modernist one. This interpretation identifies terrorism as a form of war made by the weak against the strong, in retaliation for economic exploitations and political humiliations, Note that the anti-modernist interpretation assumes war to the finish as the only solution. This other interpretation offers an entirely different view and hope.

Conflict at its base draws on anger in two forms: proactive and reactive. Those who ruin other cultures, tear out their resources, force their populations into cities and degradation, and put profit above the well-being of humans, communities, and the environment are people who, in addition to making money, proactively find outlets for their anger. They do not act from malice or sadistic design so much as unacknowledged inner pressures they cannot identify and which they fear to face. "Acting out" those inner pressures is far easier and more familiar than facing them and working to overcome them.

The "structural violence" of domination, exploitation, and humiliation – all operating normatively through economic and political institutions, among others – often draws on physical violence in order to coerce the victims of political and economic strategies of domination to submit to the more powerful party. Familiar with violence as the objects of it, the victims turn to violence in reaction to it. Reactive anger – likely that of the bulk of terrorists in the world at this time – is a response to the proactive anger of someone else.

But there is an option, slowly working its way into the public consciousness of our species, which is non-violent conflict resolution. This is ethically the most recent and most humane alternative to violence in world conflicts. In the recent period, its exponents and practitioners trace a line from Thoreau through Gandhi, Martin Luther King, Jr., the Dalai Lama, Thich Nhat Hanh, and Aung Sang Suu Kii, among others.

If those who lead peoples into violent conflict draw on their followers' reservoirs of hatred – call them "war leaders" – the major and recent alternative leaders – "peace leaders" – draw on their followers' unfulfilled yearnings for peace, community, kindness, and love. These are as natural and fundamental human needs and desires as those for vengeance, hatred, and killing. But they speak to less raw, unsocialized parts of our selves, which it appears are harder to provoke and manipulate than the others. It is more difficult to bond with people than to separate from and oppose them. Those who would end violent conflict in the world need to recognize and take into account this deep, painful, but potentially liberating reality.

The ending of violent conflicts depends also on extending awareness of the true history of peace. In 1905, popular movements in Norway and Sweden forced two governments to withdraw troops massed at their shared border and ready for war. After the breakup of the Soviet Union, almost all its components moved to other forms of government and economy without violence. At the turn of the twenty-first century, long-time conflicts in Northern Ireland and Sri Lanka were on the verge, at last, of non-violent resolution. Numerous projects bring Israelis and Palestinians together in non-violent encounters that point toward peace.

There appears to be a dialectical process between old war customs and new peace visions and practices. Peace visions in this era must include the needs of all people on the planet for environmental health and safety, vibrant and viable communities and societies, and productive, fulfilling lives in relationship with others and the planet.

Organizations and movements that promote peace number in the thousands or tens of thousands throughout the world. They are less developed, disseminated, and experienced than organizations and movements promoting and practicing war, but they are clearly in motion. If they gain the momentum they need to banish war to the history books, we will still face a slew of grave conflicts that will require inventiveness, patience, and determination to solve satisfactorily. There is no greater challenge to those concerned about the nature and fate of world conflict.

SEE ALSO: Aggression; Anti-War and Peace Movements; Capitalism; Conflict Theory; Environmental Movements; Gendered Aspects of War and International Violence; Global Justice as a Social Movement; Globalization, Culture and; Globalization and Global Justice; Military Research and Science and War; Political Economy; Social Movements, Non-Violent; Social Psychology; War

REFERENCES AND SUGGESTED READINGS

Adorno, T., Frenkel-Brunswick, E., Levinson, D. J., & Sanford, R. N. (1950) *The Authoritarian Personality*. Harper, New York.

Anon (2004) *Imperial Hubris: Why the West is Losing the War Against Terrorism*. Brassey's, Washington, DC.

Berman, P. (2003) *Terror and Liberalism*. Norton, New York.

Boulding, E. (2000) *Building a Global Civic Culture*. Syracuse University Press, Syracuse.

Fellman, G. (1998) *Rambo and the Dalai Lama: The Compulsion to Win and Its Threat to Human Survival*. SUNY Press, Albany.

Freud, S. (1959) *Group Psychology and the Analysis of the Ego*. Norton, New York.

Goldstein, J. (2001) *War and Gender*. Cambridge University Press, Cambridge.

Kohn, A. (1986) *No Contest*. Houghton Mifflin, Boston.

Reich, W. (1970) *The Mass Psychology of Fascism*. Farrar, Straus, & Giroux, New York.

world-systems theory

See *dependency and world-systems theories*

writing as method

Elizabeth Adams St.Pierre

Writing as a method of inquiry refers to a research practice of foregrounding and investigating how researchers construct knowledge about people, themselves, and the world by writing. This concept, introduced by Laurel Richardson (2000 [1994]) and developed by Elizabeth St. Pierre (Richardson & St. Pierre 2005) and others, brings the idea that writing is thinking from the humanities to the social sciences.

Writers have always used writing to help them think about their lives and their work, but that function of writing has seldom been taken advantage of in that area of social science research that mimics research in the natural sciences by assuming that language can describe reality. However, after the linguistic turn, the crisis of legitimation, and the crisis of representation, many social science researchers no longer assume that language is transparent and can simply mirror or represent reality; rather, they understand that language helps to create reality. Writing is therefore not an objectifying practice or a mopping-up activity at the end of a research project but a creative practice used throughout to make sense of lives and culture, to theorize, and to produce knowledge.

Since the Enlightenment, writing has been divided into two kinds: literary and scientific. Literature has traditionally been associated with personal expression, rhetoric, physicality, emotions, and subjectivity. Science writing is associated with facts, the truth, reality, rationality, and objectivity. Literature is soft and suspect; science writing is hard and true. Enlightenment thinkers such as René Descartes and Francis Bacon set up binary oppositions – mind/body, objective/subjective, fact/fiction – in which the first term is privileged and scientific. The scientific method assumes that the rational mind can divorce itself from its irrational body and produce true knowledge employing criteria of exactitude, rigor, and systematicity. In this scenario, mathematics is the perfect language, supposedly pure and uncontaminated by the inexactitude, imprecision, and precariousness of everyday life. Science is thus above life, and science writing should reflect the same detachment, rationality, and control.

Of course, such a neat division of writing, and the world (scientific and non-scientific), was never entirely successful, and events of the twentieth century, in particular, brought into question the idea that the knowledge produced by science could cure the problems of humankind. Indeed, the sometimes disastrous effects of an objective, rational science brought the entire enterprise into question after the atrocities of World Wars I and II, Algeria, and Vietnam. The social movements of the 1960s and 1970s demanded that science – both social and natural science – be taken to task for its complicity in perpetuating poverty, racism, sexism, homophobia, ageism, and so forth. Texts encouraging a mind–body connection resisted Descartes's 300-year-old theory and doubted that the mind and body had ever been separate. Scholars began to move out of their own fields, blurring disciplinary boundaries, as they sought different methods to use to produce different knowledge that might allow different possibilities for living. The "soft" social sciences began to claim the status of the natural sciences, no longer content to be called underdeveloped natural sciences or pre-scientific. Physicists began writing for popular audiences, and social science writers began using the genres of the humanities.

Social scientists have always represented their work in words and written texts; however, after the blurring of the genres, forms of representation such as drama and film were increasingly used to report scientific knowledge. Form constrains content, and different genres of writing encourage different thinking and produce different knowledge. No particular genre of writing is superior to another; each has possibilities and limits. Though a conventional scientific research report modeled after that of the natural sciences has been privileged for some time in the social sciences, science does not require a particular genre. A poem can convey as much meaning (and a different meaning) as an academic essay. In fact, to learn as much as they can about their topic, researchers might write up data from a single project using a variety of forms – personal narrative, expository essay, autobiography, fiction, and poetry – in order to engage those data in more and more complex ways, thereby complicating the making of meaning and illustrating the very partial and fragile nature of the work we call science.

Researchers who have special talents have indeed experimented with alternative forms of representation, including poetry, drama, auto-ethnography, fiction, performance texts, poly-vocal texts, hypertext, readers' theater, comedy and satire, visual presentations, mixed genres, and even painting and dance. Social scientists concerned with disseminating their work widely often write very different texts about the same project for different audiences.

The tenuous relation between language and meaning that emerges from postmodern theories of the last half of the twentieth century is central to the idea that writing is a method of inquiry. In *Of Grammatology* (1967), Jacques Derrida explained that language cannot contain and fix meaning. He theorized the concepts *différence* and *writing under erasure* to explain that meaning escapes language and so is always deferred. "Word and thing or thought never in fact become one" (Spivak 1974: lvii). When we write under erasure, we let go of meaning at the moment we introduce it. As a result, meaning cannot be a portable property that words can carry from one person to another, and language cannot "represent" the world.

Postmodern discourses differ from the interpretive discourses used in conventional social science inquiry that assume there is a deep, hidden, prelinguistic meaning that can be found and brought to discourse. If there is no mimetic link between a deep (or transcendental) Truth and a particular instantiation, then the copy theory of truth upon which some theories of representation are structured cannot hold. Postmodernism, after the linguistic turn, suggests that interpretation is not the discovery of meaning but the introduction of meaning. Because of this, writers can never control readers' interpretations since there is always an excess of meaning as people bring their own lived experiences to the texts they read. Writing, then, is not a neutral activity of expression that simply matches word to world. It becomes a task of responsibility as researchers create people, practices, and cultures in the texts they write.

Researchers also collect data in the texts they write, so writing can be a *method of data collection*. Researchers write throughout the research process as they document their day-to-day activities, their impressions of events, their formal interviews and informal conversations with participants, and their formal and informal observations. Some of these data are conventional – data from formal interviews and observations, for example, that are textualized in interview transcripts and fieldnotes. These are official data that are described in social science textbooks.

Other data are transgressive (St.Pierre 1997) and may include memories of the past and the future, dreams, sensualities, emotions, the words of other scholars, the novel just read, a neighbor's comment. These data are found in every study, though their presence and importance are seldom acknowledged. Writers cannot simply erase these transgressive data from their minds and bodies as they think and write about the more conventional data in their interview transcripts and fieldnotes. They bring the richness of their lives to their research. Thus, different researchers studying the same topic think with different conventional and transgressive data and necessarily produce different knowledge. There is no separation between the knower and the known in the work, and the unique positioning of the researcher is valued. *Bias* is not thinkable in this structure, but that does not mean that one does not discriminate among representations, that "anything goes." It means that readers develop more complex ideas of what good research is. Validity is not dismissed but constantly reworked as appropriate.

Since writing is thinking it can also be a *method of data analysis*. Writing allows us to think things we might not have thought by thinking alone. Writing takes us places we might not have gone if we had not written. We must think in order to write the next word, the next sentence, the next theory. An idea simply thought may seem brilliant until it is written. A brilliant unthought idea may appear as we write. Writing forces us to textualize the rigorous confusion of our thinking, and that work is analysis. This analysis is much more complicated than what is usually called data analysis – positivist practices of coding data, sorting it into categories that are grouped into themes that become section headings in an outline that organizes writing in advance of writing. Those practices ignore the work of writing as thinking, as analysis. They assume that writing only documents what is already known. Using writing as a method of inquiry, however – as a method of data collection and data analysis – acknowledges and builds into the research process the generative work of writing.

The linguistic turn that recognized that meaning (the Truth) about people and culture could not be captured and closed off in language led to the crises of representation and legitimation that recognized that meaning (truth) is always partial, situated, contingent, inaccurate, and, thus, dangerous to some extent. The resulting burden of authorship led to the ethical turn that recognized that researchers' texts do not capture truth but produce it. Leery of writing texts that might misrepresent or even harm participants, social science researchers began to ask different questions about their work. Instead of asking "What does [marriage, race, subjectivity] mean?" they posed questions such as those Paul Bové (1990: 54) asked about discourse: "How does discourse function? Where is it to be found? How does it get produced and regulated? What are its social effects? How does it exist?"

From these questions comes a different question about writing: "What else might writing do except mean?" Some researchers, particularly postmodern researchers, have begun to question whether the goal of social science research should even be representation (the goal of interpretivism), and they are increasingly hesitant to get to the bottom of meaning, to gratify the interpretive entitlement of readers to *know* their participants. They are no longer willing to write comfort texts with rich, thick descriptions that provide easy access to and lay bare people's lives, whether exotic or ordinary. Their writing does not encourage an uncomplicated and sentimental identification that erases the difference of the Other. Rather, they shift the focus from their participants to the topic of their research – marriage, race, subjectivity – using conventional and transgressive data to theorize without delivering anyone or any place in authentic, more adequate, persuasive representations. People and lives are no longer the epistemological end of the study – objects that can be known – but provocateurs – lines of flight that lead elsewhere. This elsewhere is the promise of writing as a method of inquiry, of discovery, of coming and going, of movement past what is known.

This kind of post-representational work can be accomplished in any genre, but it requires that we understand writing differently. Writing becomes a field of play in which we are always unprepared to make meaning, and whatever meaning we make will always come too late to rescue us. Nevertheless, we write because we know that, in writing, anything can happen – and will. Like other writers, we may produce knowledge that will change the world.

SEE ALSO: Author/Auteur; Deconstruction; Discourse; Methods; Methods, Mixed; Poststructuralism; Representation

REFERENCES AND SUGGESTED READINGS

Bové, P. A. (1990) Discourse. In: Lentricchia, F. & McLaughlin, T. (Eds.), *Critical Terms for Literary Study*. University of Chicago Press, Chicago, pp. 50–65.

Richardson, L. (2000 [1994]) Writing: A Method of Inquiry. In: Denzin, N. K. & Lincoln, Y. S. (Eds.), *Handbook of Qualitative Research*, 2nd edn. Sage, Thousand Oaks, CA, pp. 923–48.

Richardson, L. (1997) *Fields of Play: Constructing an Academic Life*. Rutgers University Press, New Brunswick, NJ.

Richardson, L. & St.Pierre, E. A. (2005) Writing: A Method of Inquiry. Denzin, N. K. & Lincoln, Y. S. (Eds.), *Handbook of Qualitative Research*, 3rd edn. Sage, Thousand Oaks, CA, pp. 959–78.

Spivak, G. C. (1974) Translator's Preface. In: Derrida, J., *Of Grammatology*. Trans. G. C. Spivak. Johns Hopkins University Press, Baltimore, pp. ix–xc.

St.Pierre, E. A. (1997) Methodology in the Fold and the Irruption of Transgressive Data. *International Journal of Qualitative Studies in Education* 10(2): 175–89.

X

xenophobia

Paul R. Jones

Derived from the Greek words *xeno*, meaning "foreigner," "stranger," or "guest," and *phobia*, meaning fear, xenophobia literally refers to a phobic attitude toward foreigners. However, "phobia" in this context is not meant in the clinical sense but rather refers to a part of the network of racist ideologies predicated on discriminatory discourse and practice. Xenophobia is thus a term that describes fear or prejudice with respect to something or someone perceived as "foreign" or "other." As such, xenophobia is an exclusionary logic whose focus is primarily cultural, being directed toward those artifacts or cultural expressions considered somehow "different." As with all discriminatory ideologies, xenophobia constructs a hierarchical order of people and cultures.

As xenophobia both maintains and constructs such social and cultural boundaries, it can entail a deliberate or unconscious misrecognition of other cultures. Indeed, the designation of certain attributes to other cultures expresses power in itself, as meanings can be imposed on one group by a more dominant group. Given this broad definition, xenophobia could be generalized to a wide range of social situations, but primarily it operates as an ideological basis for nationalism (when such discourses devalue and stigmatize the cultures of other nations) and for related anti-immigrant discourses. Accordingly, xenophobia underpins much of the ideology of right-wing political parties that emphasize cultural difference and perpetrate the myth of cultural incompatibility. By framing their arguments in terms of real or imagined cultural differences, radical right populist parties have increasingly used xenophobic discourse to "legitimate" their racist policies.

Some commentators have suggested the existence of "xeno-racism," a confluence between xenophobia and racism, which is not only directed at black and minority ethnic groups and individuals but also is a "xenophobia that bears all the marks of the old racism, except that it is not colour-coded" (Sivanandan 2001: 2). The displacement of poor white populations forced to seek asylum has shifted the focus of right-wing political parties toward these dispossessed communities; the concept of "xeno-racism" is useful for analyzing the growing racism in popular media and political discourses directed toward white people seeking asylum. Xenophobia is an important concept for sociologists and political theorists researching how such categorizations of the "other" are constructed and subsequently stigmatized or devalued.

SEE ALSO: Ethnocentricism; Hate Crimes; Ideology; Imagined Communities; Nationalism; Race; Race (Racism); Racist Movements; Social Exclusion

REFERENCES AND SUGGESTED READINGS

Baumgartl, B. & Favell, A. (Eds.) (1995) *New Xenophobia in Europe*. Kluwer, London.

Betz, H.-G. (1994) *Radical Right-Wing Populism in Western Europe*. Macmillan, London.

Eatwell, R. (2003) Ten Theories of the Extreme Right. In: Merkl, P. H. & Weinberg, L. (Eds.), *The Extreme Right in the Twenty-First Century*. Frank Cass, London.

Fekete, L. (2001) The Emergence of Xeno-Racism. *Race and Class* 43(2): 23–40.

Mudde, C. (2000) *The Ideology of the Extreme Right*. Manchester University Press, Manchester.

Rydgren, J. (2004) The Logic of Xenophobia. *Rationality and Society* 16(2): 123–48.

Sivanandan, A. (2001) Poverty is the New Black. *Race and Class* 43(2): 1–5.

Triandafyllidou, A. (2001) *Immigrants and National Identity in Europe*. Routledge, London.

Van Dijk, T. (2001) *Ideology: A Multidisciplinary Approach*. Sage, London.

Yanagita, Kunio (1875–1962)

Takami Kuwayama

Kunio Yanagita is widely regarded as the founder of Japanese folklore studies or folkloristics. His influence transcended disciplinary boundaries and was felt in many other fields, including sociology and anthropology. Even today, he continues to be discussed, both inside and outside academic circles. Although little known outside East Asia, Yanagita is indisputably one of the intellectual giants of the modern world.

PERSONAL HISTORY

Yanagita was the sixth son of a poor family in the village of Tsujikawa, Shintō Province, known today as Kanzaki, Hyōgo Prefecture. His father made a living by teaching Chinese classics as a private tutor. Until he was adopted by the Yanagita family at the age of 27, he carried his father's surname, Matsuoka. In 1887, when Kunio was 13 years old, he moved to Ibaraki Prefecture, located northeast of Tokyo, where his brother practiced medicine. Three years later, in 1890, Kunio moved to central Tokyo to receive higher education, but his major interest at that time was literature. He thus joined a literary circle to study poems and became acquainted with some young talented men of letters. Yanagita maintained throughout his young adulthood a keen interest in literature, but eventually studied agricultural policy at the School of Law, Tokyo Imperial University. In 1900, soon after graduation, he found his first job as a bureaucrat in the Department of Agriculture and Commerce.

Having been adopted by a prestigious family in the next year, Kunio Yanagita assumed some important governmental posts, which culminated in 1914 in the appointment as chief secretary in the House of Peers. During office, Yanagita wrote articles about Japanese agriculture, in which he emphasized the need to implement structural reform, but his proposals were turned down. Discouraged, he gradually developed an interest in Japan's folk customs, and visited remote places in the countryside. His field trips resulted in the production of some pioneering books on Japanese folklore. It was about this time that he read James Frazer's *Golden Bough*.

In 1919, at the age of 45, Yanagita put an end to his career as a bureaucrat and started writing for *Asahi Shinbun*, Japan's leading newspaper. Soon afterwards, he was dispatched to Europe as Japan's delegate to the League of Nations. He took advantage of this opportunity to attend lectures at Geneva University. Yanagita was an avid reader of books published in Europe, being well versed in the latest scholarship there. In the early 1930s he resigned from all his public posts to devote himself to the study of folklore. Despite his reputation, he only occasionally taught at universities because he was convinced that folkloristics would only flourish when researchers lived side by side with *jōmin* (ordinary people). He thus kept his distance from professional scholars, organizing instead nationwide networks of independent researchers. Many of his lectures on folklore were given for these researchers at his house in Tokyo. Besides his specialty, Yanagita distinguished himself as a public intellectual who addressed a variety of social issues. In 1951 he was awarded the Order of Cultural Merit, the highest honor to be bestowed on Japanese academics. After his death in 1962, his numerous books and articles were compiled in the form of *zenshū* (complete works), the latest version of which began to be published in 1997. This version, when completed, will comprise a total of 38 volumes, each containing no fewer than 600 printed pages.

JAPANESE FOLKLORISTICS

To appreciate Yanagita's scholarship, some major characteristics of Japanese folkloristics should be mentioned first. In Japan, folkloristics and ethnology, now better known as social or cultural anthropology, have developed as twin disciplines since the late nineteenth century. This contrasts with Great Britain and the US, where the two fields have separate histories, except at the beginning. The Japanese situation is related to the relatively late modernization of the country. In Japan's countryside, researchers from the cities discovered many old manners and customs comparable to those found by western ethnologists in "primitive" society. Japanese intellectuals found a foreign culture within their own country. This discovery led Japanese folklorists to study a wider range of topics than their counterparts in the English-speaking countries. Generally, in Great Britain and the US, the scope of research tends to focus on folktales, ballads, legends, and so forth, whereas in Japan topics like social structure and ideology are also explored. Thus, Japanese folkloristics may best be understood as the anthropological study of Japan by the Japanese. It is a typical example of what Takami Kuwayama (2004) called native anthropology.

THEORY AND METHODOLOGY

Folkloristics as a Historical Science

Yanagita regarded his discipline as a historical science. He criticized orthodox historiography of his time for two major reasons. First, it was concerned almost exclusively with the lives of great individuals and dramatic events. It revealed very little of commoners' history. Second, orthodox historiography reconstructed the past by using only written documents as data. As long as this methodology was followed, Yanagita thought, it was impossible to explore the folk traditions that had been passed on for generations without being recorded. He thus proposed to gather data by doing fieldwork. More specifically, he devised ethnographic methods in which researchers interviewed people about their customs, both past and present. The rationale was that, because Japan modernized relatively late, old customs were still practiced in everyday life, so that thinking about the past was tantamount to thinking about the present. For Yanagita, history referred to the past within the present. Yanagita maintained that language contained the history of ideas and things, and he thus paid particular attention to the analysis of the words and phrases actually used during the interviews. There is, therefore, much etymological discussion in his writings. In today's terminology, Yanagita tried to write the social history of the Japanese people at large. One major difference, though, between Yanagita and today's social historians is that Yanagita aimed at discovering the general *pattern* of history. Put another way, he was interested in discovering the possible "laws" governing the changes that had occurred in ordinary people's lives. The history he wrote is often called *ikkaisei no nai rekishi* (history without unique events).

Folklore Research by Natives for Natives

Yanagita explained the fundamentals of his methodology in *Minkan Denshōron* (On Popular Tradition) and *Kyōdo Seikatsu no Kenkyūhō* (Methods in the Study of Local Community Life), published in 1934 and 1935, respectively. He classified the objects of folklore research into three categories: (1) material culture; (2) verbal art; and (3) mentalities. The first is a translation of *yūkei bunka* (literally, culture that has a form), which includes the following: habitat; clothing; food; transportation; labor; villages; family and kinship; funerals; annual events; religious festivals; and children's games and toys. According to Yanagita, these merely scratch the surface of a folk culture, and even travelers can study them. The second category, *gengo geijutsu* (literally, language and art), comprises the following: new words; new expressions; proverbs; riddles; prayers; children's language; songs and ballads; and narratives, folktales, and legends. This category is concerned with audible phenomena, which are more complex than the first because understanding them requires language competence, but they are still not particularly deep. The third category is a translation of *shin'i genshō* (literally, psychosemantic phenomena), which roughly corresponds to mentalities in the sense of the term used by the Annales School of French history. It consists of knowledge, life skills, and purposes of life. Yanagita was convinced that only compatriots or natives could fully understand the mentalities of their people. Thus, he excluded foreigners from the study of mentalities. For Yanagita, folkloristics was *jisei no gaku* (science for self-reflection).

Yanagita's model of research is similar to that of Bronislaw Malinowski's. In *Argonauts of the Western Pacific* (1922), Malinowski classified ethnographic research into three parts in ascending order of complexity: (1) the organization of the tribe and the anatomy of its culture; (2) daily life and ordinary behavior; and (3) the native mind. There is, however, a definitive difference between the two scholars. As noted above, Yanagita considered it practically impossible for non-natives to understand the native mind, whereas Malinowski had no doubt concerning their ability to grasp it. If anything, Malinowski argued that natives were so absorbed in the details of everyday life that they could not observe themselves objectively. He further contended that the natives lacked the intellectual capacity to study their own culture, so that it must be studied and represented by professionally trained outsiders – western anthropologists.

There are both merits and demerits in these contrasting views. Yanagita's position, on the one hand, regards natives in the non-western world as active agents of research into their culture. They are considered knowledge producers in their own right, rather than passive objects of research. In the age of colonialism, when the natives were denigrated as "primitive" and "uncivilized," Yanagita's view was innovative. On the other hand, it underestimates the ability of trained outsiders to investigate foreign cultures. It even generates a blinkered nationalism that excludes foreigners from the study of one's own country. By contrast, Malinowski's position encourages cultural research by qualified outsiders, but, in the name of science, it tends to elevate their status to the final judges on the cultures they are studying – a point criticized by many native intellectuals engaged in indigenous rights movements today.

Concentric Area Theory

One of the best-known theories presented by Yanagita is called *shūkenron*, which, for lack of suitable translations, is rendered here as concentric area theory. Proposed in his 1930 book *Kagyūkō* (On Snails), this theory first divides Japan into many blocks, which are then arranged to form concentric circles, with Kyoto, Japan's ancient capital, at the center. Based on the premise that new ideas and things develop at the center/urban, concentric area theory holds that new forms of culture will gradually spread toward the periphery/rural, replacing the old with the new in the process of diffusion. Thus, according to Yanagita, customs more commonly practiced on the periphery at the time of investigation are older than those practiced at the center.

This theory grew out of Yanagita's research on dialects. The example he used was that of the snail, for which many different terms exist in Japan. Having collected hundreds of local terms, Yanagita drew a lexical map and demonstrated that, as they moved away from the capital city, snails were called, in descending order of proximity to the center, *dedemushi*, *maimai*, *katatsumuri*, *tsuburi*, and *namekuji*. (These terms were prototypes from which similar local terms had been derived.) Particularly interesting was the case of *namekuji*, which Yanagita considered the oldest term for the snail. In standard Japanese, *namekuji* means slug, but Yanagita discovered that, in many remote areas, slugs were lexically indistinguishable from snails. Significantly, these areas were usually located both at the southwestern and the northeastern frontiers of the country. This discovery was later named the correspondence of outlying areas, which Yanagita interpreted as indicating that the center's influence had not yet penetrated through the peripheral areas. The implication was that the periphery was not yet "civilized," and that it would eventually be assimilated into the center as civilization spread. In this way, Yanagita turned spatial differences (i.e., different terminologies used in different parts of Japan) into temporal differences (i.e., different stages of civilization or "progress" in which these areas were supposedly placed). Yanagita also maintained that his language analysis could also be applied to cultural analysis in general.

In western scholarship, this conversion of space into time, technically known as comparative method, is a distinctive feature of the nineteenth-century social evolutionism represented by, among the most notable, Edward Tylor and Lewis Morgan.

A major problem of concentric area theory is the assumption that Japan constitutes a single national community. Without this assumption, it would have been impossible for Yanagita to contend that new customs had first developed at the center/urban and then spread gradually toward the periphery/rural. Concentric area theory would only apply on the assumption that Japan is a homogeneous nation, with a powerful centralized government situated at the geographical core. At least, it does not fully consider the possibility of external influences, such as prolonged contact with other people, which could have prevented the unchecked flow of culture. In today's critical theory, which emphasizes the multiplicity of cultural experience, Yanagita's theses have been much criticized for having overlooked Japan's internal diversity. It should be noted, however, that, in the early stage of his career, Yanagita enthusiastically studied minority groups, such as hunters and wood-turners in the mountains. He in fact hypothesized that these people were genealogically separate from Japan's majority group, rice-cultivating peasants on flat land. This hypothesis, however, was later discarded by Yanagita himself and fell into oblivion as his interest shifted to the study of Japan's national culture.

Another problem of concentric area theory is the neglect of Hokkaido, located at the northern end of the Japanese archipelago. Indeed, Yanagita left out Hokkaido from the lexical map of the snail mentioned above without giving any reason. Throughout his career, Yanagita paid only scant attention to Hokkaido, probably because it was (and still is) strongly associated with Ainu people. By contrast, Yanagita had been fascinated with Okinawa, Japan's southernmost island, since he was young. He even regarded it as the archetype of Japan. In his last book, *Kaijō no Michi* (Ocean Routes) (1961), he asserted that the ancestors of the Japanese people had first migrated from southern China to Okinawa, sailing on the Japan Current, in order to seek out porcelain shells, and then moved further north to mainland Japan, where they had eventually settled as rice cultivators. This theory has only partially been supported by later archeological research, but illuminates how Yanagita assumed contrasting attitudes toward Okinawa and Hokkaido.

PROSPECTS FOR FUTURE RESEARCH

Despite such problems, there is no doubt that Yanagita was an intellectual giant whose influence continues to be felt today. Among his legacies that have yet to be fully explored, the idea of *sekai minzokugaku* or global folkloristics deserves special attention. Presented in *Minkan Denshōron* (1935), this idea has long been neglected for complex reasons. Recently, however, a new interpretation has been proposed (Kuwayama 2004), which holds that Yanagita originally conceived of global folkloristics as an international forum for dialogue, in which researchers from around the world could exchange ideas without privileging one or a few leading countries. In this new interpretation, global folkloristics is understood as an assemblage of different "national folkloristics" practiced in different parts of the world: it reflects Yanagita's strong desire to make folkloristics a global discipline without sacrificing each country's scholarly tradition. If the ideal of global folkloristics is realized, it will promote the study of one's own culture by natives, who have long been treated as no more than "research assistants" for the "real" researchers from the West.

SEE ALSO: Annales School; Culture; Eurocentrism; *Jōmin*; Malinowski, Bronislaw K.; *Minzoku*; *Nihonjinron*

REFERENCES AND RECOMMENDED READINGS

Fukuta, A. (1984) *Nihon Minzokugaku Höhö Josetsu* (An Introduction to the Methods in Japanese Folkloristics). Köbundö, Tokyo.

Fukuta, A. et al. (Eds.) (1999–2000) *Nihon Minzoku Daijiten* (Comprehensive Dictionary of Japanese Folklore), 2 Vols. Yoshikawa Köbunkan, Tokyo.

Kawada, M. (1993) *The Origin of Ethnography in Japan*. Trans. T. Kishida-Ellis. Kegan Paul International, London.

Koschmann, J. V., Oiwa, K., & Yamashita, S. (Eds.) (1985) *International Perspectives on Yanagita Kunio and Japanese Folklore Studies*. East Asia Program, Cornell University, Ithaca, NY.

Kuwayama, T. (2004) *Native Anthropology*. Trans Pacific Press, Melbourne.

Morse, R. A. (1990) *Yanagita Kunio and the Folklore Movement*. Garland, New York.

Yanagita, K. (1998) *Yanagita Kunio Zenshü* (The Complete Works of Kunio Yanagita), 38 Vols. Ed. M. Ito et al. Chikuma Shobō, Tokyo.

youth/adolescence

Sue Heath

Youth and adolescence are terms which are often used interchangeably to refer to a phase of the life course between childhood and adulthood, yet are often positioned as contrasting approaches within academic discourse. Sociologists use the term youth to refer to a socially constructed life phase which is not only culturally specific, but which is also the product of particular historical conjunctures. Within this approach, youth is broadly construed as a collective experience which is shaped by social structures, age-specific institutions, and societal expectations. In contrast, the term adolescence emphasizes processes of individual social and/or physiological and psychological development and as such is much more closely associated with the disciplines of developmental psychology and clinical medicine. Within this approach the phase between childhood and adulthood is often equated with puberty, and is represented as a time marked by experimentation and emotional storm and stress. Classic theorists of adolescence include G. Stanley Hall (1844–1924) and Erik H. Erikson (1902–94).

CONCEPTUALIZING YOUTH

There are a number of different approaches to the sociological conceptualization of youth. An approach which has been particularly influential in recent years defines youth as a period of *transition*, emphasizing young people's movement through key transitional stages towards the attainment of adulthood. Writing from a Northern European perspective in his book *Youth and Social Policy* (1995), Coles, for example, focuses on three key transitions: the transition from school to work, from the family of origin to a family of destination, and from the parental house to a house of one's own. The assumption of linear progression that underpins this model has attracted criticism in recent years. It is further argued that the model is rendered obsolete by the increasingly widespread deferral of some of the traditional markers of adulthood and the increased visibility of alternative lifestyles which challenge the assumed desirability of attainment in these areas.

An alternative approach focuses on youth as a *relational* concept, which derives its existence and its meaning from its relationship to the concept of adulthood. This approach foregrounds and critiques the relative powerlessness of young people in relation to the world of adults, regardless of how adulthood may be defined over time and across different cultures. Wyn and White (1997), for example, argue that "if youth is the state of 'becoming,' adulthood is the 'arrival.' At the same time, youth is also 'not adult,' a deficit of the adult state" (p. 11). The concepts of both youth and adolescence thus can be employed to legitimate the differential treatment of younger people, and to justify adult intervention in their lives. As Griffin (1993) argues, this tends to result in the portrayal of young people in one of two ways: as either *victims* of social problems or as *perpetrators* of those same problems. Both portrayals serve to marginalize them in relation to adults.

A third approach focuses more on the political economy of youth, regarding youth as a period defined by the various *age-related legal strictures* – including social policies – that regulate young people's lives. Phil Mizen (2004) has argued, for example, that "the simple fact of possessing a certain biological age brings with it differential access to social power, while age also provides the means through which young people are brought into a more or less common relationship with many of the central institutions of modern life" (p. 9). This approach, then, is closely related to the notion of youth as a relational concept. However, it places particular emphasis on the political underpinnings of the concept, and foregrounds the significance of age as a means by which full citizenship is denied.

Youth is a culturally specific concept. Access to age-related citizenship rights, for example, or social norms regarding key transitional stages, varies hugely across different societies and across different cultures and regions within specific societies (Brown et al. 2002). The prevalence of young people among the global population of street people, sweated laborers, sex workers, and militia powerfully underlines this point. Conceptualizations of youth are also historically specific. For example, it is often argued that the emergence of youth as a category which is separate and distinct from adulthood *and* childhood has tended to occur in parallel with processes of industrialization, in order to serve the needs of emergent capitalism.

DISTINCT TRADITIONS WITHIN THE SOCIOLOGY OF YOUTH

Earlier conceptualizations of youth within Europe and North America were strongly influenced by the *functionalist* theories of writers such as Talcott Parsons and, slightly later, Shmuel N. Eisenstadt. Within functionalist accounts, the period of youth serves as a means of facilitating the smooth transition from the particularistic values of the family of origin to the normative values of broader society. Youth culture plays a key role in facilitating this movement, although the exact nature of a young person's cultural affiliation is rendered theoretically irrelevant by the primary role of youth culture in ensuring the maintenance of social order. In contrast, the writings of Karl Mannheim on *youth and generation* point to the historically significant role of younger generations. Mannheim defined generation in terms of groups of individuals who, by belonging to the same birth cohort, share a common "generation location" in relation to key social and historical circumstances, and it is this common location that shapes their attitudes and actions as a distinct generation. While nonetheless arguing that some generations are noted more for their contribution to the status quo, Mannheim recognized the agency of young people by arguing that certain generations are very much in the vanguard of social change, whether for good or ill.

The *cultural studies tradition* within youth research originated in the work of the Chicago School in the first half of the twentieth century. Classic ethnographies such as Thrasher's *The Gang* (1927) and Foote Whyte's *Street Corner Society* (1943) highlighted the impact of urbanization in producing the stigmatized category of deviant youth. In the period following World War II, a more overtly political perspective on youth culture emerged. The Centre for Contemporary Cultural Studies (CCCS) at the University of Birmingham defined the field in terms of a class-based critique of young people's roles as consumers and producers of mass and ghetto cultures. The classic CCCS collection *Resistance Through Rituals* (1976) contended that youth subcultures represented an attempt by working-class young people both to give meaning to, and to solve, the "working-class problematic," namely, their marginalization from hegemonic middle-class society. Through studying a variety of colorful youth subcultures, it was concluded that such allegiances nonetheless represented "imaginary solutions" to this problematic and served to reinforce the alienation of working-class youth.

Over time, the original CCCS position has attracted considerable criticism, including accusations of over-interpreting the significance of "style" and of over-emphasizing the place of leisure in young people's lives. The relative invisibility of young women in their accounts also generated a strong feminist critique. More recent work within the cultural studies tradition has attempted to address these criticisms, and has also moved beyond the earlier focus on social class. In the UK, key writers in the field use the language of "post-subculture," "scenes," and "tribes" to argue that class is no longer of relevance to an understanding of contemporary manifestations of youth culture (Bennett & Kahn-Harris 2004), although this is a contested position. Similarly, in the US there is greater focus on the diversity of youth cultures and a concern to explore the formation of cultural identity, particularly in relation to ethnic identity and hybrid youth cultures (Lee & Zhou 2004).

The *youth transitions tradition* has emerged as another influential strand within the sociology of youth over the last two decades, particularly in Northern Europe and Australasia. Transitions researchers have pointed to the disruption of relatively safe and predictable transitional routes and their replacement by *fractured* and *extended transitions* to adulthood, especially in the economic sphere. The transitions tradition is also distinctive for its focus on the impact of social class, gender, and ethnicity on young people's life chances and, more recently, its engagement with debates concerning social exclusion, social capital, and the putative youth underclass. The approach has, however, been criticized for over-emphasizing the impact of social structure and for adopting an over-deterministic approach to understanding young people's lives.

More recently, Ulrich Beck's *individualization thesis* has been utilized by transitions researchers and others seeking to understand the experiences of young adults in "late modernity." In *Risk Society* (1992), Beck argues that there is an increasing tendency for young people to "write their own biographies" in a world characterized by rising levels of risk and bewildering choice. However, while the proliferation of individualized biographies might suggest that class, ethnicity, and gender are no longer determinants of young people's life chances, and have encouraged younger generations to feel that they are no longer constrained by these factors, critics argue that the old indicators nonetheless remain firmly in place. In *Young People and Social Change* (1997), Furlong and Cartmel refer to this paradox as "the epistemological fallacy of late modernity." This has led some youth researchers to distinguish between "normal" and "choice" biographies, the former marked by continuity with gender-divergent "traditional" working-class transitional routes and the latter marked by the emergence of gender-convergent destandardized pathways among well-educated and/or affluent young adults (du Bois-Reymond 1998).

CURRENT THEMES AND METHODOLOGICAL CONCERNS

The subject matter of sociological youth research is wide-ranging, with few aspects of young people's lives left unexplored by contemporary researchers. Certain themes, such as youth culture and leisure, education and work, and health-related behaviors, are perennial concerns. More recent topics of interest have included social space, globalization, new technologies, consumption and lifestyle, intimacy and sexuality and, as more overarching concerns, identity and subjectivity. A broader conceptual debate relates to the (re)definition of youth in late modernity and the blurring of the boundaries of childhood, youth, and adulthood among younger generations (see for example Cote's *Arrested Adulthood*, 2000, and Dwyer and Wyn's *Youth, Education and Risk*, 2001). The theme of youth (in) crisis is also common in youth research in many parts of the world. This is often a racialized debate, highlighting the pathologization of racial identity (see, for example, Giroux's *Fugitive Cultures*, 1996). There is also a strong gender dimension to the youth crisis debate, focusing on the global trend towards rising levels of academic achievement among young women and associated claims of a contemporary "crisis of masculinity."

In exploring these themes, youth sociologists have traditionally drawn upon a wide variety of methods for researching young people's lives, ranging from detailed ethnographic studies through to large-scale national and subnational cohort studies. Recent developments include the adoption of narrative and auto/biographical interviewing techniques by many youth researchers, and the increasing use of visual methods, including photo elicitation, video diaries, and spatial mapping techniques. This in part reflects a desire to use research methods which are deemed to have an intrinsic appeal to young people. There is also a growing emphasis on qualitative longitudinal research, and some moves towards greater inclusiveness in terms of sampling, incorporating groups who are often sidelined in mainstream youth research, such as young lesbians and gay men, disabled young people, students, young people from socially privileged backgrounds, and young people from rural areas. Finally, participatory youth research – youth research *for* and *by* young people – is becoming more common, and has been a particularly useful vehicle for giving voice to some of these excluded groups.

SEE ALSO: Age Identity; Birmingham School; Childhood; Consumption, Youth Culture and; Leaving Home in the Transition to Adulthood; Life Course Perspective; Mannheim, Karl; Transition from School to Work; Youth Sport

REFERENCES AND SUGGESTED READINGS

Bennett, A. & Kahn-Harris, K. (2004) *After Subculture: Critical Studies in Contemporary Youth Culture*. Palgrave, Basingstoke.

Brown, B. B., Larson, R., & Saraswathi, T. S. (Eds.) (2002) *The World's Youth: Adolescence in Eight Regions of the Globe*. Cambridge University Press, New York.

Du Bois-Reymond, M. (1998) "I don't want to commit myself yet": Young People's Life Concepts. *Journal of Youth Studies* 1: 63–79.

Griffin, C. (1993) *Representations of Youth*. Polity Press, Cambridge.

Lee, J. & Zhou, M. (2004) *Asian American Youth*. Routledge, New York.

Lesko, N. (2001) *Act Your Age! A Cultural Construction of Adolescence*. New York, Routledge.

Mitterauer, M. (1992) *A History of Youth*. Oxford, Blackwell.

Mizen, P. (2004) *The Changing State of Youth*. Palgrave, Basingstoke.

Mortimer, J. T. & Larson, R. W. (Eds.) (2002) *The Changing Adolescent Experience: Societal Trends and the Transition to Adulthood*. Cambridge University Press, Cambridge.

Wyn, J. & White, R. (1997) *Rethinking Youth*. Allen & Unwin, St. Leonards.

youth sport

Paul De Knop and Marc Theeboom

Youth is defined for the purposes of this discussion as youngsters between 6 and 18 years. Sport means all sport activities practiced outside the physical education curriculum. Consequently, school sport as extra-curricular activity is also included.

With the start of the Sport for All movement in the 1960s and 1970s, this period can be characterized as the years of growth for sport. Youth sport at that time was mainly an activity for adolescents and pre-adolescents that took place in sports clubs or during extra-curricular training at school. Now the age to begin participating in youth sport has decreased to 7 years or even younger. This policy of attracting younger children to become involved in organized sport is based not on pedagogical objectives but on those related to "survival." Sports clubs want to remain in the market because their economic existence is threatened.

Sport has become a very popular leisuretime activity among youth. In most countries, at least 50 percent of all children in their early teens are active in various sports. Most of these activities take place in a sports club or during extra-curricular training at school. More boys than girls are active in sports. Sports segregate the sexes as few other phenomena do. Boys and girls seldom take part in sports together.

Some of the most common youth sports globally are soccer among boys and swimming among both boys and girls. Among activities outside a sports club, jogging, cycling, and walking are the most popular. The most common sports are almost always universal. There are hardly any popular sports in a country that are played in that specific country alone. Sport has thus become international, not least with the help of television, with rules for performance that are understood by almost all individuals regardless of nationality and language.

The most common motives for taking part in sports are characterized by intrinsic values such as enjoyment and social aspects. These motives are more common than success in competition and better performance. Middle-class children are overrepresented in organized youth sport. Membership of sports clubs is strongly related to gender, social class, and family situation.

Since the 1970s there have been important changes in sport and ideas about childhood and psychosocial development. The general value systems and norms in many societies have undergone significant transformations, and traditions and traditional social networks in local districts have been weakened. The way families have been individualized has led to less rigid authority structures, and a number of commercial and educational "adjustments" have taken place. Because of these changes, young people are more directed toward creating their own identities. Also, greater emphasis is placed on the role of institutions involved in leisuretime activities, to offer coherent experiences and guidance for the formation of identity among young people. Schultz Jørgensen and colleagues (1986) suggested that the time of youth has become a waiting period for the formation of a psychosocial identity. Sport plays a major role in this formation of identity.

The following trends in youth sport are noticeable.

1 The number of opportunities for youth sport participation have increased substantially since the early 1990s, and youth sports have become more specialized and differentiated at the same time as performance demands have increased.
2 Sport has become institutionalized. Traditional sports, such as team sports, are not played spontaneously to the same extent as before. In some countries spontaneous, informally organized sports have almost disappeared. Children's knowledge about and performance in sport have been more differentiated, and the extent and intensity of physical activity have become more varied. Two extreme groups of children can be identified today. In one group, children train intensively several times a week, some every day. In the other group, children are not physically active at all during their leisure time. As a result, physical capacity and sports skills vary considerably between children.
3 During recent decades more children have entered organized sport. Differences between boys and girls as regards both extent and trends have decreased, mainly because girls' sports habits have come to resemble those of boys. This trend is most common in Nordic countries, although it also exists in countries where there are increased opportunities for girls to participate in organized sports programs.
4 While the flow to organized sport seemed to have stopped and even diminished in many countries, activities in commercial training centers where there is an emphasis on systematic training and skill development have increased. What is significant about these centers is that, although possibilities for making social contacts exist, there are no far-reaching obligations. Youngsters can come and go as they please and are not dependent on parents' engagement.
5 There has been a professionalization of sports delivery, including a need for quality assessment and control in organized sports programs.
6 There is an increased adaptation of rules, equipment, and competitive forms to children's developmental stages and physical abilities.
7 Sports organizations have started to develop schemes to specifically attract young people to their sports.
8 There are an increasing number of initiatives in which organized sports are provided for youth at risk.

Problems in youth sports have received a great deal of attention in research. A dropout problem among teenagers, especially among girls, is reported in many countries. During adolescence there is a decrease in the number of participants. Interest in organized sports seems to have reached a breakpoint in many countries and is now even declining.

Youth sports have been shaped to a large extent by adult sports, and adult norms and values predominate. For example, rules for team sports are similar for adults and young children. In addition, youth sport often contains only specialized activities with sport-specific training.

Youth sport has become more serious and less playful. Children are not allowed to play to the same extent as before. This problem increases with the decreasing age of participants. Youth sports have become heavily organized. Different sports compete for children's interest, resulting in a focus on increasingly younger children becoming members of sports clubs.

Youth sport participation is far from democratized as involvement is related to children's age and gender as well as their parents' socioeconomic status. Many children are dependent on their parents for financial and logistical support, for example transportation. Often, a certain economic standard is a prerequisite for participation.

Ethical questions in youth sport have been raised in many countries. In order for sport to serve educational purposes for youth, the following principles have been formulated: (1) rules and regulations should be followed; (2) respect should be shown to other players and officials; (3) particants should demand the same from themselves as from others; and (4) participants should display a sense of justice and be loyal and generous.

Western competitive sports have developed in the direction of a greater emphasis on the importance of winning. This development can also be noticed in youth sport and can be regarded as a threat for the child orientation of sport. It is also reported from several countries that qualified youth sports leaders are hard to find. There is a heavy dependency on volunteers, which creates a high turnover and inconsistent quality of leadership and coaching.

Other problems also exist. For example, there is a need for effective cooperation between sports clubs, schools, and municipalities. The most successful programs have been those in which different actors have worked in partnership to make better provision of sporting opportunities for young people. Furthermore, the number of sports injuries among children and adolescents has been increasing in all nations where medical data are available.

In light of these problems, several policy recommendations have been made for youth sports programs. Some of these are listed below.

- One of the main objectives of a future policy for youth sport should be to increase quality from a pedagogical point of view. Such a policy needs to focus on the following topics: developing a cooperative approach to the provision of youth sport instead of "competition" between the different organizations; ensuring youth sports coaches have appropriate pedagogical qualifications; setting up specific youth sports coaching programs; persuading parents that informal play during childhood is more important than formal sports participation; promoting sport for youth with an emphasis on enjoyment and its social aspects; and scientifically evaluating the effectiveness of sports promotional campaigns.
- Sports among children must be made more accessible and should be offered close to residential areas. There should be greater possibilities for all children to try different sports, and better conditions should be created for varied physical activities.
- The intrinsic values of youth sports (play and learning) must have priority at all times.
- Training must be individualized and rich in variations. Firmly controlled and formalized training can be counterproductive. Sports clubs should aim to develop talent in the

best way possible instead of trying to find new talent. Selection and specialization of individuals should not be made before they have reached their teens. Distinct variations in the maturing process among youth make any early prognoses of success in later years very uncertain.

- A child's relation to sports and to her own body as well as the experience of her own physical ability are the result of learning motor skills. But sport is also a question of learning norms and values related to behavior and lifestyle. Children are socialized into sports and thus also into the value system of sports. Youth sport is one of the most important environments for socialization. Sports must therefore also be valued as such and given due significance in children's lives and development. Sport is perhaps the most important norm setter, second only to family and school. On the strength of its range and importance, sport must mediate and recreate essential values for the continued existence of a particular culture. In other words, it has a reproducing function. Therefore, it is vital that sport follow a sound ethical code. Also, in youth sport, leaders' personal characteristics and behavior are highly important.
- One of the greatest challenges facing youth sport is the development of a cooperative and coordinated approach by schools and clubs with the aim of offering sports as an educational environment for all children that enables them to develop at their own speed and according to their own interests.
- Quality improvement or quality control will need to become essential elements of sports policy with a focus on encouraging quality awareness, developing quality standards, measuring instruments and remedial techniques, and monitoring through research and transfer of knowledge.

In conclusion, youth sport can serve many purposes. It can be a meaningful activity for many children and give them a lifelong interest in physical activity as an important part of a healthy way of life and as a source of pleasure and relaxation. It can also form future elite sportsmen and women and become a means for self-realization and success for young people who have a talent for sports. For many children, sports are also an important environment for socialization and they play a vital role in the reproduction of culture. However, given the recent developments outlined above, many steps still need to be taken in order for youth sports to fulfill any of these aims in an optimal way.

SEE ALSO: Health and Sport; High School Sports; Leisure; Socialization and Sport; Youth Adolescence

This article is updated from De Knop, P., Engström, L. M., Skirstad, B., & Weiss, M. R. (Eds.) (1996) *Worldwide Trends in Youth Sport*. Human Kinetics, Champaign, IL. Copyright 1996 by Human Kinetics Publishers, Inc. Adapted with permission. Part of this article was published as "European Trends in Youth Sport: A Report from 11 Countries," *European Journal of Physical Education* 1 (1996): 36–45. Adapted with permission.

REFERENCES AND SUGGESTED READINGS

Gatz, M., Messner, M. A., & Ball-Rokeach, S. J. (Eds.) (2002) *Paradoxes of Youth and Sport*. State University of New York Press, Albany.

Hantrais, L. & Kamphorst, T. J. (1987) *Trends in the Arts: A Multinational Perspective*. Giordano Bruno, Amersfoort, The Netherlands.

Heinemann, K. (1986) The Future of Sports: Challenge for the Science of Sport. *International Review for Sociology of Sport* 21: 271–85.

Kamphorst, T. & Roberts, K. (1989) *Trends in Sports: A Multinational Perspective*. Giordano Bruno, Culemborg, The Netherlands.

Kremer, J., Trew, K., & Ogle, S. (Eds.) (1997) *Young People's Involvement in Sport*. Routledge, London.

Schultz Jørgensen, P., Gamst, B., & Andersen, B. (1986) *Efter skoletid (After Schooltime)*. Socialforskningsinstituttet, Copenhagen.

Zimbardo Prison Experiment

Markus Kemmelmeier

Social psychologist Phillip Zimbardo (b. 1933) conducted a well-known prison study known as the Stanford Prison Experiment. Funded by the US Navy to investigate conflict in military prisons, Zimbardo and his graduate students, Craig Haney and W. Curtis Banks, rejected the idea that the personality characteristics of prisoners and guards in the prison system were primarily responsible for conflicts as they occurred in the prison system. Broadly consistent with Goffman's (1961) concept of a total institution, Zimbardo and his team identified individual anonymity and loss of identity as the most prominent characteristics of prisons, which Zimbardo's (1970) deindividuation theory linked to antisocial behavior. Without room for individual identities, Zimbardo and colleagues reasoned that the social roles of prisoner and guard would be the dominant influence on behavior and allow participants to behave in ways that would otherwise be unimaginable to them.

Zimbardo and his team of researchers used newspaper ads to recruit volunteers to participate in a two-week-long "prison simulation" in exchange for payment of $15 per day. From 75 applicants, researchers selected 24 young men, predominantly white and middle class (21 active participants and 3 alternates), whom pretests showed to be healthy, normal, and well adjusted. Through the toss of a coin, participants were randomly assigned to the role of prisoner or guard. Zimbardo assumed the role of "superintendent," an undergraduate research assistant played the role of "warden," and Zimbardo's graduate students

were "psychological counselors." The involvement of an ex-convict consultant in planning and running the prison simulation ensured its realism. The prison was physically located in the remodeled basement of the psychology department at Stanford University. It included a small closet used as solitary confinement facility, quarters for the prison staff, as well as an interview-testing room, which was also used for "parole" meetings. The mock prison was equipped with hidden video and audio recording equipment, allowing subsequent analysis of much of the activity that occurred.

The prison study began on August 14, 1971 with a guard orientation establishing the prison hierarchy and its procedures. The 11 guards were dressed in khaki military-style uniforms and dark sunglasses to provide a sense of anonymity. They were also given whistles and nightsticks as symbols of power. Guards were to work in eight-hour shifts, but would otherwise pursue their normal lives outside of the study. Over the course of the study, many volunteered extra hours without additional pay. Guards received no formal training, but were allowed to run the prison in whatever way they wished, with the only stipulation being that physical violence would not be tolerated.

Having secured the cooperation of the Palo Alto Police Department, on August 15 Zimbardo had real police officers arrest the 10 prisoner participants at their residences. The alleged charges were burglary or armed robbery. After having been advised of their legal rights, prisoners were ferried off to the police station, where they were booked, fingerprinted, and had their mugshots taken. After a brief period in a police holding cell, prisoners were blindfolded and brought to the "Stanford County Prison," where they were stripped naked, deloused by the guards (using a deodorant spray), and then had their blindfolds removed. (Prisoners were never aware that they were in a university building.) As their only piece of clothing, they were given a pair of rubber sandals and a "Muslim smock," onto which their prisoner number was sewn. No underwear was issued. Prisoners also received a nylon stocking cap to further conceal any distinctive features. Three prisoners were housed to a cell, with no personal belongings allowed, and prisoners were only referred to by their number. All procedures were aimed at fostering a sense of anonymity and humiliation, a sentiment reinforced by a lock and chain that prisoners wore around their ankles as a constant reminder of their oppressed state.

The study quickly devolved into a situation of great hostility and open tension, in which prisoners and guards quickly absorbed their respective roles. After a relatively uneventful first day of the study, on the second day many prisoners revolted against the degrading conditions by ripping off their prisoner numbers and barricading themselves in their cells. Without intervention from the research staff, the guards successfully crushed the riot by imposing harsh punishment that included stripping prisoners naked, solitary confinement, withholding of meals, and withholding of blankets and pillows, physical exercise, and various arbitrary activities. The guards further divided the prisoners by pitting "good," privileged cells against "bad" cells, and leading the latter to suspect that there were informers among them. In doing so, the guards affirmed the power and authority associated with their roles as well as a sense of unity against the prisoners. The subsequent harassment on the part of the guards and staff caused serious emotional disturbance in one of the ringleaders of the rebellion, Prisoner #8612. Because they had not anticipated the intensity of the interactions and reactions, initially Zimbardo and his colleagues did not give in to #8612's request to be released, but instead tried to recruit him as a "snitch." Although the prisoner was released later on the same day, the rumor persisted that prisoners would not be released under any circumstances.

Over the course of the following days, the guards' behavior became increasingly sadistic and abusive. Regular prisoner lineups, originally instituted as administrative procedures to familiarize prisoners with their number, devolved into hour-long ordeals. Food and even going to the bathroom turned into privileges that could be granted and withheld. Mattresses and bedding were removed from the "bad" cells, forcing prisoners to sleep on the concrete floor. Prisoners were forced to clean the toilet with their bare hands or were forced to stand naked in front of the guards. Occasional admonishments on the part of the psychological counselors to refrain from certain actions had limited effects, partly because the guards rejected any interference with the exercise of their "duty." Because surveillance was limited, some abusive behavior and even mild physical violence occurred outside of the supervision of the research staff.

Prisoners showed varied reactions to the abuse including "extreme emotional depression, crying, rage and acute anxiety" (Haney et al. 1973: 81). Disorganized thinking and uncontrollable emotional outbursts were common. Some sought to avoid punishment by becoming model prisoners and "zombie-like" following guards' orders. A total of five prisoners had to be released, including one prisoner who experienced a sudden rash upon hearing that his request for early parole had been denied by a parole board consisting of secretaries and graduate students and chaired by Zimbardo's ex-convict consultant. Zimbardo initially denied the sick prisoner's request to be released, on suspicions that he was faking illness to "con" his way out of the prison.

Following the failed revolt, the only resistance against the oppressive regime of the guards came from Prisoner #416, who joined the experiment as a replacement. In light of the terrible conditions, Prisoner #416 went on a hunger strike, which resulted in his being put in solitary confinement for several hours. The guards offered prisoners the choice to either give up their blankets and have #416 released, or keep their blankets and have #416 stay overnight in solitary confinement. Viewing #416 as a troublemaker, all prisoners decided to keep their blankets. (Upon the researchers' intervention, #416 was returned to his cell.)

The oppressive reality of the prison simulation was underscored by the fact that a visitor familiar with penal environments, who came to see the prisoners during Visitors' Night, described prisoners' reactions as those typical of first-time offenders. A public defender who visited the prison in its final phase testified to the similarity of the mindset and behavior of the prisoners to real inmates. Additional evidence showed that prisoners had internalized their roles. On the fifth day of the study, Zimbardo offered the remaining five prisoners a deal to lose all their pay in exchange for "parole," and most prisoners accepted. When all parole requests were turned down, none of the prisoners requested to be released, suggesting that they believed that the only way out was to receive parole or go "crazy," as all other previously released prisoners. In retrospect #416 commented: "It was a prison to me. I don't regard it as an experiment or a simulation. It was a prison run by psychologists instead of run by the state."

Zimbardo admits that he, as well as others on his staff, was increasingly absorbed by his role in the experiment, and failed to recognize its inhumanity. For instance, on the fourth day, rumors of an impending prison break had him enter a Stanford undergraduate student into the experiment in order to spy on the other prisoners. Zimbardo's request to the Palo Alto Police Department to avert the outbreak by transferring his prisoners to a more secure detention facility was turned down. Zimbardo recalls being angry and disgusted at this lack of professional cooperation.

Originally scheduled for a period of two weeks, the experiment was ended after 6 days with the arrival of Christine Maslach, who had been asked to conduct interviews. As a social psychologist unrelated to the study, she objected to the horrifying conditions of the mock prison and convinced Zimbardo to terminate the study. Prisoners expressed great relief, whereas many guards were disappointed. Zimbardo notes that roughly 100 individuals had visited or participated, yet not one had challenged its legitimacy.

Results of this experiment illustrate the potential power of social contexts in shaping human behavior. The fulfillment of social roles within a closed social system overwhelmed individual moral intentions and standards. With preexisting personality difference providing no value in predicting the behavior of prisoners and guards, Zimbardo and colleagues concluded that the roles assigned to individuals within evil social systems are able to turn good people to evil. This idea was consistent with Stanley Milgram's (1974) famous obedience research. Milgram found that most participants

in the role of a subordinate followed the orders of a legitimate authority, even when aware that doing so would likely cause the death of an innocent person. As a result of their research, Zimbardo and Haney have become vocal advocates of prison reform and frequent commentators on prisoner abuse, like that suffered at the Abu Ghraib prison at the hands of American military.

Even though the Stanford Prison Experiment had been approved by Stanford's Human Subjects Review Board, it represented an ethical fiasco. All participants signed consent forms agreeing to have some of their civil rights temporarily suspended, but they were unable to anticipate the harm to which they would be subjected. Further, Zimbardo and his team were unable to anticipate the prison dynamics and, by aligning themselves with the guards in running the prison, failed to protect the human rights of the prisoners. Consequentially, this study has led to a tightening of regulations and practices in protecting human research participants.

Various criticisms have been leveled against this experiment. Some critics argued that prisoners and guards were only acting out familiar stereotypes of prisoners and guards. Zimbardo contends that it was role-playing initially, but that participants internalized their roles over the course of the study – a notion which is supported by most participants and documented in the movie *Quiet Rage*. Other criticism concerns the nature of the data and the fact that documentation of the study was incomplete and often anecdotal, with conclusions often being drawn subjectively. Audio and video recording was focused on more spectacular events that confirmed the expected effects of anonymity and social roles, but did not document existing differences in the behavior of guards. Much of the documentation focused on the cruelest guard nicknamed "John Wayne," with little attention devoted to much kinder guards. Further, it is unclear to what extent the simulation reflected actual conditions at prisons where this level of anonymity and humiliation is uncommon. Lastly, because the study was never replicated, the generality of its findings is unclear.

In 2002, social psychologists Steven Reicher and Alex Haslam, in conjunction with the BBC, set up a prison simulation study, which differed in many important aspects from the Stanford

Prison Experiment. Among other things, this research used an on average older and more diverse set of participants while allowing a much greater degree of experimental control and documentation. Results of this study differed dramatically, for instance, in that no prisoner abuse occurred.

The Stanford Prison Experiment inspired the novel *Black Box* by Mario Giordano, which was made into the German feature film *Das Experiment* directed by Oliver Hirschbiegl.

SEE ALSO: Aggression; Authority and Conformity; Experimental Methods; Goffman, Erving; Milgram, Stanley (Experiments); Organizations as Total Institutions; Role; Role Theory; Social Psychology

REFERENCES AND SUGGESTED READINGS

Goffman, E. (1961) *Asylums: Essays on the Social Situation of Mental Patients and Other Inmates.* Doubleday Anchor, New York.
Haney, C., Banks, W. C., & Zimbardo, P. (1973) Interpersonal Dynamics in a Simulated Prison. *International Journal of Criminology and Penology* 1: 69–97.
Milgram, S. (1974) *Obedience to Authority: An Experimental View.* Harper & Row, New York.
Musen, K. & Zimbardo, P. G. (1991) *Quiet Rage: The Stanford Prison Study.* Film. Psychology Department, Stanford University, Stanford.
Reicher, S. D. & Haslam, A. (2004) *The Experiment.* Video recording. BBC Education and Training. Films for the Humanities, Princeton.
Reicher, S. D. & Haslam, S. A. (2006) Rethinking the Psychology of Tyranny: The BBC Prison Study. *British Journal of Social Psychology.*
Zimbardo, P. G. (1970) The Human Choice: Individuation, Reason, and Order Versus Deindividuation, Impulse and Chaos. In: Arnold, W. J. & Levine, D. (Eds.), *1969 Nebraska Symposium on Motivation* 27. University of Nebraska Press, Lincoln, pp. 237–307.
Zimbardo, P. G. (2005) Stanford Prison Experiment. Online. www.prisonexp.org.
Zimbardo, P. G., Maslach, C., & Haney, C. (2000) Reflections on the Stanford Prison Experiment: Genesis, Transformations, Consequences. In: Blass, T. (Ed.), *Obedience to Authority: Current Perspectives on the Milgram Paradigm.* Lawrence Erlbaum, Mahwah, NJ, pp. 193–237.

Znaniecki, Florian (1882–1958)

Robert A. Stebbins

Florian Znaniecki was born to a well-to-do Polish family living in Russian-occupied territory. His active support of Polish nationalism resulted in his dismissal from the University of Warsaw and an extended stay abroad. He studied at the University of Geneva and the Sorbonne. He later returned, this time to the University of Cracow, receiving his doctorate there in 1910. While helping Poles to migrate he met W. I. Thomas, who in 1914 invited Znaniecki to join him at the University of Chicago. Shortly thereafter the two began work on the famous five-volume study *The Polish Peasant in Europe and America*, published between 1918 and 1920. Znaniecki taught at Columbia University (1916–17), at the University of Chicago (1917–19), and in 1920, following Polish independence, became professor of philosophy at the new University of Pozna. Here he helped to establish sociology, founded the Polish Institute of Sociology, in 1929 and launched a Polish sociological journal. Following the conquest of Poland in World War II, he was invited to Columbia University (1939). In 1941 he went as professor of sociology to the University of Illinois, retiring from there in 1951. Before his death in 1958, he was elected president of the American Sociological Society (1955).

Znaniecki, with W. I. Thomas and others, is often singled out as one of the founders of symbolic interactionism, primarily for his work in the theoretic sections of the *Polish Peasant*. Still, one of the best discussions of definition of the situation is found in his *Cultural Sciences: Their Origin and Development* (1952). Znaniecki's other books tackle different subjects, as in *The Method of Sociology* (1934) where he argues that we must avoid regarding the static and dynamic sides of society as mutually exclusive perspectives. In *The Social Role of the Man of Knowledge* (1940) he examines the scholar from the perspective of the sociology of knowledge.

In *The Method of Sociology* Znaniecki moves away from symbolic interactionism toward sociological functionalism. By abstracting, generalizing, and then expanding on Pareto's concept of system, Znaniecki makes a unique contribution to sociology: social life is a *plurality* ther, that sociology must determine whether a particular system is included in a larger system and whether the particular system encompasses one or more smaller systems (Martindale 1981: 460–1). Sociology's task is to analyze causal relations within systems and then move from there to a more inclusive picture of comprehensive changes. In *The Social Role of the Man of Knowledge*, though in many ways influenced by symbolic interactionism, Znaniecki also treats culture as a system of knowledge. Participation in this system is determined by people's activities enacted through roles linked in social systems.

Znaniecki died at work, in the sense that he left upon his death an unfinished manuscript entitled "Systematic Sociology." It was published posthumously in 1965 as *Social Relations and Social Roles*. It includes a complete list of his works, compiled by his daughter, Helena Z. Lopata.

SEE ALSO: Definition of the Situation; Functionalism/Neofunctionalism; Pareto, Vilfredo; Role; Symbolic Interaction; Theory; Thomas, William I.

REFERENCES AND SUGGESTED READINGS

Martindale, D. (1981) *The Nature and Types of Sociological Theory*, 2nd edn. Houghton Mifflin, Boston.

Thomas, W. I. & Znaniecki, F. (1918–20) *The Polish Peasant in Europe and America*. Richard G. Badger, Boston.

Znaniecki, F. (1934) *The Method of Sociology*. Farrar Rinehart, New York.

Znaniecki, F. (1940) *The Social Role of the Man of Knowledge*. Columbia University Press, New York.

Znaniecki, F. (1952) *Cultural Sciences: Their Origin and Development*. University of Illinois Press, Urbana.

Znaniecki, F. (1965) *Social Relations and Social Roles*. Chandler, San Francisco.

Znaniecki, F. (1969) *Florian Znaniecki on Humanistic Sociology*. Ed. R. Bierstedt. University of Chicago Press, Chicago.

Select Bibliography

The select bibliography is meant to be a partial listing of the most cited works from the entries in this encyclopedia. It is *not* intended to be a comprehensive list of the most widely cited or influential books in the field. While ideally these two lists would overlap, this is not necessarily the case. Every attempt has been made to include cited works from the full spectrum of areas and topics represented in these volumes.

Addams, J. (1998 [1910]) *Twenty Years at Hull House*. Penguin, New York.

Adler, P. A. & Adler, P. (1987) *Membership Roles in Field Research*. Sage, Newbury Park, CA.

Adorno, T. W. & Horkheimer, M. (1977) The Culture Industry: Enlightenment as Mass Deception. In: James Curran, M. G. & Woollacott, J. (Eds.), *Mass Communication and Society*. Edward Arnold, London.

Adorno, T. W. & Horkheimer, M. (2002 [1947]) *Dialectic of Enlightenment*. Stanford University Press, Stanford.

Adorno, T. W., Frenkel-Brunswik, E., Levinson, D. J., & Sanford, R. N. (1950) *The Authoritarian Personality*. Harper & Row, New York.

Alatas, S. F. (1993) A Khaldunian Perspective on the Dynamics of Asiatic Societies. *Comparative Civilizations Review* 29: 29–51.

Alexander, J. C. (1982–3) *Theoretical Logic in Sociology*. University of California Press, Berkeley.

Alexander, J. C. (1987) *Twenty Lectures: Sociological Theory Since World War Two*. Columbia University Press, New York.

Alexander, J. C. & Colomy, P. (1985) Toward Neo-Functionalism. *Sociological Theory* 3: 11–23.

Allan, G. & Crow, G. (2001) *Families, Households, and Society*. Palgrave, Basingstoke.

Althusser, L. (1970) *For Marx*. Vintage, New York.

Anderson, B. (1991) *Imagined Communities*, rev. edn. Verso, London.

Andrews, D. L. & Jackson, S. J. (Eds.) (2001) *Sport Stars: The Culture Politics of Sporting Celebrity*. Routledge, New York.

Anzaldúa, G. (1987) *[Borderlands] La Frontera: The New Mestiza*. Aunt Lute, San Francisco.

Appadurai, A. (1996) *Modernity at Large: Cultural Dimensions of Globalization*. University of Minnesota Press, Minneapolis.

Arber, S. & Ginn, J. (Eds.) (1995) *Connecting Gender and Ageing: A Sociological Approach*. Open University Press, Milton Keynes.

Archer, M. (1982) Morphogenesis versus Structuration: On Combining Structure and Action. *British Journal of Sociology* 33: 455–83.

Arendt, H. (1951) *The Origins of Totalitarianism*. Harcourt, Brace, New York.

Arendt, H. (1965) *On Revolution*. Viking, New York.

Ariès, P. (1965) *Centuries of Childhood: A Social History of Family Life*. Vintage, New York.

Aron, R. (1960) *The Industrial Society: Three Essays on Ideology and Development*. Weidenfeld & Nicolson, London.

Asch, S. E. (1955) Opinions and Social Pressure. *Scientific American* 193: 31–5.

Auge, M. (1995) *Non-Places: Introduction to an Anthropology of Supermodernity*. Verso, London.

Axford, B. & Huggins, R. (Eds.) (2001) *New Media and Politics*. Sage, London.

Baca Zinn, M. (1979) Field Research in Minority Communities: Ethical, Methodological, and Political Observations by an Insider. *Social Problems* 27: 209–19.

Bandura, A. (1977) *Social Learning Theory*. Prentice-Hall, Englewood Cliffs, NJ.

Barker, C. (1999) *Television, Globalization, and Cultural Identities*. Open University Press, Buckingham.

Barthes, R. (1972) *Mythologies*. Cape, London.

Bataille, G. (1992) *Theory of Religion*. Zone, New York.

Baudrillard, J. (1975) *The Mirror of Production*. Telos Press, Saint Louis, MI.

Baudrillard, J. (1983) *Simulations*. Semiotext(e), New York.

Baudrillard, J. (1990 [1983]) *Fatal Strategies*. Semiotext(e), New York.

Baudrillard, J. (1998 [1970]) *The Consumer Society*. Sage, London.

Bauman, Z. (1989) *Modernity and the Holocaust*. Polity Press, Cambridge.

Bauman, Z. (1993) *Postmodern Ethics*. Blackwell, Oxford.

Bauman, Z. (2000) *Liquid Modernity*. Polity Press, Cambridge.

Beauvoir, S. de (1980 [1949]) *The Second Sex*. Random House, New York.

Beck, U. (1992) *Risk Society: Towards a New Modernity*. Sage, London.

Beck, U. (1997) *The Reinvention of Politics: Rethinking Modernity in the Global Social Order*. Polity Press, Cambridge.

Beck, U. (1999) *What is Globalization?* Polity Press, Cambridge.

Beck, U., Giddens, A., & Lash, S. (1994) *Reflexive Modernization*. Stanford University Press, Stanford.

Becker, H. S. (1963) *Outsiders: Studies in the Sociology of Deviance*. Free Press, New York.

Becker, H. S. (1982) *Art Worlds*. University of California Press, Berkeley.

Becker, H. S., Greer, B., Hughes, E., & Strauss, A. (1961) *Boys in White: Student Culture in Medical School*. University of Chicago Press, Chicago.

Beilharz, P. (1994) *Postmodern Socialism*. Melbourne University Press, Melbourne.

Bell, D. (1973) *The Coming of Post-Industrial Society: A Venture in Social Forecasting*. Basic Books, New York.

Bell, D. (1976) *The Cultural Contradictions of Capitalism*. Basic Books, New York.

Bellah, R. N. (1991) *Beyond Belief: Essays on Religion in a Post-Traditional World*, 2nd edn. University of Chicago Press, Chicago.

Benedict, R. (1943) *Race, Science, and Politics*. Viking, New York.

Benjamin, W. (1969) The Work of Art in the Age of Mechanical Reproduction. In: Arendt, H. (Ed.), *Illuminations*. Schocken, New York.

Benjamin, W. (1985 [1928]) *One-Way Street and Other Writings*. Verso, London.

Benjamin, W. (2000) *The Arcades Project*. Harvard University Press, Cambridge, MA.

Ben-Yehuda, N. (1985) *Deviance and Moral Boundaries*. University of Chicago Press, Chicago.

Berger, J. (1992) Expectations, Theory, and Group Processes. *Social Psychology Quarterly* 55: 3–11.

Berger, J., Conner, T. L., & Fisek, M. H. (Eds.) (1974) *Expectation States Theory: A Theoretical Research Program*. Winthrop, Cambridge, MA.

Berger, J., Fisek, M. H., Norman, R. Z., & Zelditch, M., Jr. (1977) *Status Characteristics and Social Interaction*. Elsevier, New York.

Berger, P. L. (1967) *The Sacred Canopy*. Anchor Books, Garden City, NY.

Berger, P. L. & Luckmann, T. (1966) *The Social Construction of Reality: A Treatise in the Sociology of Knowledge*. Doubleday, Garden City, NY.

Bernal, J. D. (1964 [1939]) *The Social Function of Science*. MIT Press, Cambridge, MA.

Bernard, J. (1976) *The Future of Marriage*. Pelican, Harmondsworth.

Bhabha, H. (1994) *The Location of Culture*. Routledge, London.

Black, D. (1998) *The Social Structure of Right and Wrong*. Academic Press, San Diego.

Black, T. R. (1999) *Doing Quantitative Research in the Social Sciences: An Integrated Approach to Research Design, Measurement, and Statistics*. Sage, London.

Blalock, H. J. (1969) *Theory Construction: From Verbal to Mathematical Formulations*. Prentice-Hall, Englewood Cliffs, NJ.

Blau, P. M. (1964) *Exchange and Power in Social Life*. Wiley, New York.

Blau, P. M. (1970) A Formal Theory of Differentiation in Organizations. *American Sociological Review* 35: 201–18.

Blau, P. M. & Duncan, O. D. (1967) *The American Occupational Structure*. Wiley, New York.

Bloor, D. (1991 [1976]) *Knowledge and Social Imagery*. University of Chicago Press, Chicago.

Blumer, H. (1937) Social Psychology. In: Schmidt, E. (Ed.), *Man and Society*. Prentice-Hall, New York.

Blumer, H. (1969) *Symbolic Interaction: Perspective and Method*. Prentice-Hall, Englewood Cliffs, NJ.

Bonilla-Silva, E. (2003) *Racism Without Racists: Color-Blind Racism and the Persistence of Racial Inequality in the United States*. Rowman & Littlefield, Lanham, MD.

Booth, C. (1902–3) *Life and Labour of the People of London*, 17 vols. Macmillan, London.

Bottomore, T. (1965) *Classes in Modern Society*. Allen & Unwin, London.

Bottomore, T. (1993) *Elites and Society*. London. Routledge.

Bourdieu, P. (1977) *Outline of a Theory of Practice*. Cambridge, UK, Cambridge University Press.

Bourdieu, P. (1984) *Distinction*. Cambridge, MA, Harvard University Press.

Bourdieu, P. ([1984] 1988) *Homo Academicus*. Cambridge, UK, Polity.

Bourdieu, P. & Wacquant, L. J. D. (1992) *An Invitation to Reflexive Sociology*. University of Chicago Press, Chicago.

Braverman, H. (1998 [1974]) *Labor and Monopoly Capital: The Degradation of Work in the Twentieth Century*. Monthly Review Press, New York.

Brown, R. H. (1987) *Society as Text: Essays on Rhetoric, Reason, and Reality*. University of Chicago Press, Chicago.

Bryman, A. (1984) The Debate about Quantitative and Qualitative Research: A Question of Method or Epistemology. *British Journal of Sociology* 35: 75–92.

Bryman, A. (2004) *The Disneyization of Society*. Sage, London.

Buchanan, J. (1975) *The Limits of Liberty*. University of Chicago Press, Chicago.

Burawoy, M. (2005) For Public Sociology. *American Sociological Review* 70: 4–28.

Burgess, E. W. (1926) The Family as Unity of Interacting Personalities. *Family* 7: 3–9.

Burke, P. (1991) Identity Processes and Social Stress. *American Sociological Review* 56: 836–49.

Burr, V. (1995) *An Introduction to Social Constructionism*. Routledge, London.

Butler, J. (1990) *Gender Trouble: Feminism and the Subversion of Identity*. Routledge, New York.

Butler, J. (1993) *Bodies That Matter: On the Discursive Limits of "Sex."* Routledge, New York.

Cahill, S. E. (1998) Toward a Sociology of the Person. *Sociological Theory* 16: 131–48.

Calhoun, C. (1995) *Critical Social Theory: Culture, History, and the Challenge of Difference.* Blackwell, Cambridge, MA.

Campbell, C. (1989) *The Romantic Ethic and the Spirit of Modern Consumerism.* Blackwell, Oxford.

Campbell, J. L. (2004) *Institutional Change and Globalization.* Princeton University Press, Princeton.

Cardoso, F. H. & Faletto, E. (1969) *Dependencia y desarrollo en America Latina [Dependency and Development in Latin America].* Siglo XXI Editores, Mexico City, Mexico.

Casper, L. M. & Bianchi, S. M. (2001) *Continuity and Change in the American Family.* Sage, Thousand Oaks, CA.

Castells, M. (1977) *The Urban Question.* MIT Press, Cambridge, MA.

Castells, M. (1996) *The Rise of the Network Society.* Blackwell, Oxford.

Castoriadis, C. (1987) *The Imaginary Institution of Society.* MIT Press, Cambridge, MA.

Certeau, M. de (1984) *The Practice of Everyday Life.* University of California Press, Berkeley.

Chafetz, J. S. (1990) *Gender Equity: An Integrated Theory of Stability and Change.* Sage, Newbury Park, CA.

Chandler, A. (1977) *The Visible Hand.* Harvard University Press, Cambridge, MA.

Chaney, D. (1994) *The Cultural Turn: Scene-Setting Essays on Contemporary Social History.* Routledge, London.

Cheal, D. (1992) *Family and the State of Theory.* Harvester Wheatsheaf, Hemel Hempstead.

Cherlin, A. (Ed.) (2005) *Public and Private Families,* 4th edn. McGraw-Hill, Boston.

Chodorow, N. (1999 [1978]) *The Reproduction of Mothering: Psychoanalysis and the Sociology of Gender.* University of California Press, Berkeley.

Chomsky, N. (1957) *Syntactic Structures.* Mouton, The Hague.

Chomsky, N. (2002) *Media Control: The Spectacular Achievements of Propaganda,* 2nd edn. Seven Stories Press, New York.

Chomsky, N. & Herman, E. (2002 [1988]) *Manufacturing Consent: The Political Economy of the Mass Media.* Pantheon, New York.

Cicourel, A. (1964) *Method and Measurement in Sociology.* Free Press, New York.

Cicourel, A. (1974) *Cognitive Sociology: Language and Meaning in Social Interaction.* Free Press, New York.

Cipriani, R. (2000) *Sociology of Religion: An Historical Introduction.* Aldine, New York.

Clarke, A. (2005) *Situational Analysis: Grounded Theory After the Postmodern Turn.* Sage, Thousand Oaks, CA.

Clough, P. (1994) *Feminist Thought.* Blackwell, Cambridge, MA.

Coakley, J. & Dunning, E. (Eds.) (2000) *Handbook of Sport Studies.* Sage, London.

Coakley, J. & Dunning, E. (2004) *Sports in Society: Issues and Controversies.* McGraw-Hill, New York.

Coale, A. (1973) The Demographic Transition. In IUSSP (Ed.), *International Population Conference,* Vol. 1. IUSSP Liège, Belgium.

Cockerham, W. (2004) *Medical Sociology,* 9th edn. Prentice-Hall, Upper Saddle River, NJ.

Coleman, J. S. (1964) *Introduction to Mathematical Sociology.* Free Press, Glencoe, IL.

Coleman, J. S. (1988) Social Capital in the Creation of Human Capital. *American Journal of Sociology* 94: 95–120.

Coleman, J. S. (1990) *Foundation of Social Theory.* Harvard University Press, Cambridge, MA.

Coleman, J. S., Campbell, E. Q., Hobson, C. J., McPartland, J., Mood, A. M., Weinfall, F. D., & York, R. L. (1966) *Equality of Educational Opportunity.* Department of Health, Education, and Welfare, Washington, DC.

Collins, P. H. (1990) *Black Feminist Thought: Knowledge, Consciousness, and the Politics of Empowerment.* Unwin Hyman, London.

Collins, P. H. (1998) *Fighting Words: Black Women and the Search for Justice.* University of Minnesota Press, Minneapolis.

Collins, R. (1972) *Conflict Sociology: Toward an Explanatory Science.* Academic Press, New York.

Collins, R. (1979) *The Credential Society.* Academic Press, New York.

Collins, R. (1981) On the Microfoundations of Macrosociology. *American Journal of Sociology* 86: 984–1014.

Collins, R. (2000) *The Sociology of Philosophies: A Global Theory of Intellectual Change.* Harvard University Press, Cambridge, MA.

Combahee River, Collective (1997) A Black Feminist Statement. In: Nicholson, L. (Ed.), *The Second Wave: A Reader in Feminist Theory.* Routledge, New York.

Comte, A. (1830–42) *The Positive Philosophy of Auguste Comte.* Calvin Blanchard, New York.

Connell, R. W. (1977) *Ruling Class, Ruling Culture.* Cambridge University Press, Melbourne.

Connell, R. W. (1995) *Masculinities.* Polity Press, Cambridge.

Conrad, P. & Schneider, J. W. (1992) *Deviance and Medicalization: From Badness to Sickness.* Temple University Press, Philadelphia.

Cook, K. S. & Emerson, R. M. (1978) Power, Equity, and Commitment in Exchange Networks. *American Sociological Review* 43: 712–39.

Cook, K. S., Emerson, R. M., Gillmore, M. R., & Yamagishi, T. (1983) The Distribution of Power in Exchange Networks: Theory and Experimental Results. *American Journal of Sociology* 89: 275–305.

Cooley, C. H. (1963 [1909]) *Social Organization: A Study of the Larger Mind*. Schocken, New York.

Cooley, C. H. (1964 [1902]) *Human Nature and the Social Order*. Schocken, New York.

Coser, L. (1956) *The Functions of Social Conflict*. Free Press, New York.

Crane, D. (Ed.) (1994) *The Sociology of Culture*. Blackwell, Oxford.

Crenshaw, K. (1991) Mapping the Margins: Intersectionality, Identity Politics, and Violence Against Women of Color. *Stanford Law Review* 43: 1241–99.

Crouch, C., Le Galès, P., & Voelzkow, H. (2001) *Local Production Systems in Europe: Rise or Demise?* Oxford University Press, Oxford.

Cumming, E. & Henry, W. (1961) *Growing Old: The Process of Disengagement*. Basic Books, New York.

Cyert, R. M. & March, J. G. (1963) *A Behavioral Theory of the Firm*. Prentice-Hall, Englewood Cliffs, NJ.

Dahl, R. A. (1961) *Who Governs?* Yale University Press, New Haven.

Dahrendorf, R. (1959) *Class and Class Conflict in Industrial Society*. Stanford University Press, Stanford.

Darwin, C. (1964 [1859]) *On the Origin of Species: A Facsimile of the First Edition*. Harvard University Press, Cambridge, MA.

Davidoff, L. & Hall, C. (1987) *Family Fortunes: Men and Women of the English Middle Class, 1780–1850*. Unwin Hyman, Chicago.

Davie, G. (2000) *Religion in Modern Europe*. Oxford University Press, Oxford.

Davies, J. C. (1962) Toward a Theory of Revolution. *American Sociological Review* 27: 5–19.

Davis, A. (1981) *Women, Race, and Class*. Random House, New York.

Davis, K. & Moore, W. (1945) Some Principles of Stratification. *American Sociological Review* 10: 242–9.

Debord, G. (1977) *The Society of the Spectacle*. Black & Red, Detroit.

Deleuze, G. & Guattari, F. (1983) *Anti-Oedipus: Capitalism and Schizophrenia*. University of Minnesota Press, Minneapolis.

Deleuze, G. & Guattari, F. (1987) *A Thousand Plateaus: Capitalism and Schizophrenia*. University of Minnesota Press, Minneapolis.

Dennis, N., Henriques, F., & Slaughter, C. (1956) *Coal is Our Life: An Analysis of a Yorkshire Mining Community*. Eyre & Spottiswoode, London.

Denzin, N. (1999) Interpretive Ethnography for the Next Century. *Journal of Contemporary Ethnography* 28: 510–19.

Denzin, N. & Lincoln, Y. (2001) *The Landscape of Qualitative Research*. Sage, Thousand Oaks, CA.

Derrida, J. (1974) *Of Grammatology*. Johns Hopkins University Press, Baltimore.

Derrida, J. (1978) *Writing and Difference*. University of Chicago Press, Chicago.

DeVault, M. (1999) *Liberating Method: Feminism and Social Research*. Temple University Press, Philadelphia.

Dewey, J. (1954 [1923]) *The Public and its Problems*. Swallow Press, Chicago.

Di Maggio, P. J. & Powell, W. W. (1983) The Iron Cage Revisited: Institutional Isomorphism and Collective Rationality in Organizational Fields. *American Sociological Review* 48: 147–60.

Downes, D. (1966) *The Delinquent Solution: A Study in Subcultural Theory*. Routledge & Kegan Paul, London.

Du Bois, W. E. B. (1899) *The Philadelphia Negro: A Social Study*. Ginn & Company, Boston.

Du Bois, W. E. B. (1903) *The Souls of Black Folk*. A. C. McClurg, Chicago.

Duncan, O. D. (1966) Path Analysis: Sociological Examples. *American Journal of Sociology* 72: 1–16.

Dunning, E. (1999) *Sport Matters: Sociological Studies of Sport, Violence, and Civilization*. Routledge, London.

Durkheim, É. (1933 [1893]) *The Division of Labor in Society*. Macmillan, New York.

Durkheim, É. (1951 [1897]) *Suicide: A Sociological Study*. Free Press, New York.

Durkheim, É. (1964 [1895]) *The Rules of the Sociological Method*. Free Press, New York.

Durkheim, É. (1965 [1912]) *The Elementary Forms of the Religious Life*. Dutton, New York.

Easterlin, R. (1978) The Economics and Sociology of Fertility: A Synthesis. In: Tilly, C. (Ed.), *Historical Studies of Changing Fertility*. Princeton University Press, Princeton.

Ehrlich, P. R. (1968) *The Population Bomb*. Ballantine Books, New York.

Eisenstadt, S. N. (1978) *Revolution and the Transformation of Societies: A Comparative Study of Civilizations*. Free Press, New York.

Eisenstadt, S. N. (2003) *Comparative Civilizations and Multiple Modernities*, 2 vols. Brill, Leiden.

Elder, G. H., Jr. (1999 [1974]) *Children of the Great Depression*, 2nd edn. University of Chicago Press, Chicago.

Elias, N. (1978) *What is Sociology?* Columbia University Press, New York.

Elias, N. (1982) *The Civilizing Process*, 2 vols. Pantheon, New York.

Emerson, R. M. (1962) Power-Dependence Relations. *American Sociological Review* 27: 31–41.

Emirbayer, M. & Goodwin, J. (1994) Network Analysis, Culture, and the Problem of Agency. *American Journal of Sociology* 99.

Emirbayer, M. & Mische, A. (1998) What is Agency? *American Journal of Sociology* 10: 962–1023.

Engels, F. (1972 [1884]) *The Origins of the Family, Private Property, and the State*. Pathfinder Press, New York.

England, P. (1992) *Comparable Worth: Theories and Evidence*. Aldine, New York.

Evans, S. (1979) *Personal Politics: The Roots of Women's Liberation in the Civil Rights Movement and The New Left*. Vintage, New York.

Evans-Pritchard, E. (1937) *Witchcraft, Oracles, and Magic Among the Azande*. Oxford University Press, Oxford.

Fajnzylber, F. (1970) *Sistema Industrial y Exportacios de Manufacturas: Analisis de la experiencia Brasilena*. CEPAL, Rio de Janeiro.

Fanon, F. (1967) *Black Skins, White Masks*. Grove, New York.

Fausto-Sterling, A. (2000) *Sexing the Body: Gender Politics and the Construction of Sexuality*. Basic Books, New York.

Fayol, H. & Coubrough, J. (1930 [1916]) *Industrial and General Administration*. Sir I. Pitman, London.

Feagin, J. R. (2001) Social Justice and Sociology: Agenda for the Twenty-First Century. *American Journal of Sociology* 66: 1–20.

Featherstone, M. (1991) *Consumer Culture and Postmodernism*. Sage, London.

Featherstone, M. & Wernick, A. (1995) *Images of Ageing*. Routledge, London.

Festinger, L. (1957) *A Theory of Cognitive Dissonance*. Stanford University Press, Stanford.

Feuerbach, L. (1989 [1841]) *The Essence of Christianity*. Prometheus, Buffalo, NY.

Fine, G. A. (1993) The Sad Demise, Mysterious Disappearance, and Glorious Triumph of Symbolic Interactionism. *Annual Review of Sociology* 19: 61–87.

Folbre, N. (2001) *The Invisible Heart: Economics and Family Values*. New Press, New York.

Foucault, M. (1965) *Madness and Civilization: A History of Insanity in the Age of Reason*. Pantheon, New York.

Foucault, M. (1970) *The Order of Things: An Archeology of the Human Sciences*. Random House, New York.

Foucault, M. (1973) *The Birth of the Clinic: An Archeology of Medical Perception*. Pantheon, New York.

Foucault, M. (1977) *Discipline and Punish: The Birth of the Prison*. Pantheon, New York.

Foucault, M. (1978) *The History of Sexuality*. Vol. 1: *An Introduction*. Pantheon, New York.

Frankenberg, R. (1966) *Communities in Britain*. Harmondsworth, Penguin.

Freud, S. (1953 [1900]) *The Interpretation of Dreams*. Hogarth, London.

Freud, S. (1975 [1930]) *Civilization and Its Discontents*. Hogarth, London.

Friedan, B. (1963) *The Feminine Mystique*. Dell, New York.

Friedson, E. (1970) *Professional Dominance*. Aldine, Chicago.

Fuller, S. (1988) *Social Epistemology*. Indiana University Press, Bloomington.

Fuss, D. (1991) *Inside/Outside: Lesbian Theories, Gay Theories*. Routledge, New York.

Gagnon, J. H. & Simon, W. S. (1973) *Sexual Conduct: The Social Sources of Human Sexuality*. Aldine, Chicago.

Galbraith, J. K. (1969) *The Affluent Society*. Mentor, New York.

Gamson, J. (1994) *Claims to Fame: Celebrity in Contemporary America*. University of California Press, Berkeley.

Gans, H. (1962) *The Urban Villagers*. Free Press, New York.

Garfinkel, H. (1967) *Studies in Ethnomethodology*. Prentice-Hall, Englewood Cliffs, NJ.

Geertz, C. (1973) *The Interpretation of Cultures*. Basic Books, New York.

Gergen, K. (1991) *The Saturated Self: Dilemmas of Identity in Contemporary Life*. Basic Books, New York.

Gergen, K. (1994) *Realities and Relationships: Soundings in Social Construction*. Harvard University Press, Cambridge, MA.

Germani, G. (1955) *Estructura Social de la Argentina* [*The Social Structure of Argentina*]. Editorial Raigal, Buenos Aires.

Giddens, A. (1984) *The Constitution of Society: Outline of the Theory of Structuration*. University of California Press, Berkeley.

Giddens, A. (1990) *The Consequences of Modernity*. Polity Press, Cambridge.

Giddens, A. (1991) *Modernity and Self-Identity: Self and Society in the Late Modern Age*. Stanford University Press, Stanford.

Giddens, A. (1994) *Beyond Left and Right: The Future of Radical Politics*. Polity Press, Cambridge.

Gilligan, C. (1982) *In a Different Voice: Psychological Theory and Women's Development*. Harvard University Press, Cambridge, MA.

Gilman, C. P. (1903) *The Home: Its Work and Influence*. McClure Phillips, New York.

Gitlin, T. (1980) *The Whole World is Watching: Mass Media in the Making and Unmaking of the New Left*. University of California Press, Berkeley.

Glaser, B. G. & Strauss, A. L. (1965) *Awareness of Dying*. Aldine, Chicago.

Glaser, B. G. & Strauss, A. L. (1967) *The Discovery of Grounded Theory: Strategies for Qualitative Research*. Aldine, Chicago.

Glass, D. (1954) *Social Mobility in Britain*. Routledge & Kegan Paul, London.

Glassner, B. (1999) *The Culture of Fear: Why Americans are Afraid of the Wrong Things*. Basic Books, New York.

Goffman, E. (1959) *The Presentation of Self in Everyday Life*. Doubleday Anchor, Garden City, NY.

Goffman, E. (1961) *Asylums: Essays in the Social Situation of Mental Patients and Other Inmates*. Anchor, Garden City, NY.

Goffman, E. (1963) *Stigma: Notes on the Management of Spoiled Identity*. Prentice-Hall, Englewood Cliffs, NJ.

Goffman, E. (1974) *Frame Analysis: An Essay on the Organization of Experience*. Harvard University Press, Cambridge, MA.

Goldthorpe, J. H. (1980) *Social Mobility and Class Structure in Modern Britain*. Clarendon Press, Oxford.

Goldthorpe, J. H., Lockwood, D., Bechhofer, F., & Platt, J. (1968) *The Affluent Worker: Industrial Attitudes and Behaviors*. Cambridge University Press, Cambridge.

Goode, W. J. (1963) *World Revolution and Family Patterns*. Free Press, Glencoe, IL.

Goodwin, J. (2000) *No Other Way Out: States and Revolutionary Movements, 1945–1991*. Cambridge University Press, Cambridge.

Gould, R. V. (1995) *Insurgent Identities: Class, Community, and the Protest in Paris from 1848 to the Commune*. University of Chicago Press, Chicago.

Gould, S. J. (1996) *The Mismeasure of Man*, 2nd edn. W. W. Norton, New York.

Gouldner, A. W. (1970) *The Coming Crisis of Western Sociology*. Avon, New York.

Gramsci, A. (1971) *Selections from the Prison Notebooks of Antonio Gramsci*. International, New York.

Granovetter, M. S. (1973) The Strength of Weak Ties. *American Journal of Sociology* 78: 1360–80.

Greeley, A. (1972) *Unsecular Man*. Schocken Books, London.

Guigni, M., McAdam, D., & Tilly, C. (Eds.) (1999) *How Movements Matter: Theoretical and Comparative Studies on the Consequences of Social Movements*. University of Minnesota Press, Minneapolis.

Habermas, J. (1984) *The Theory of Communicative Action*, 2 vols. Beacon, Boston.

Habermas, J. (1989 [1962]) *The Structural Transformation of the Public Sphere: An Inquiry into a Category of Bourgeois Society*. MIT Press, Cambridge, MA.

Hage, J. & Powers, C. H. (1992) *Post-Industrial Lives: Roles and Relationships in the 21st Century*. Sage, Newbury Park, CA.

Halberstam, J. (1998) *Female Masculinity*. Duke University Press, Durham, NC.

Halbwachs, M. (1992 [1925]) *Social Frameworks of Memory*. University of Chicago Press, Chicago.

Hall, S. (1980) Encoding/Decoding. In: *Culture, Media, Language*. Hutchinson, London.

Hammersley, M. & Atkinson, P. (1995) *Ethnography: Principles in Practice*. Routledge, London.

Haraway, D. (1990) A Manifesto for Cyborgs: Science, Technology, and Socialist Feminism in the 1980s. In: Nicholson, L. J. (Ed.), *Feminism/Postmodernism*. Routledge, New York.

Haraway, D. (1991) *Simians, Cyborgs, and Women: The Reinvention of Nature*. Routledge, New York.

Harding, S. (Ed.) (1987) *Feminism and Methodology*. Indiana University Press, Bloomington.

Hardt, M. & Negri, A. (2000) *Empire*. Harvard University Press, Cambridge, MA.

Hardt, M. & Negri, A. (2004) *Multitude: War and Democracy in the Age of Empire*. Penguin, London.

Hargreaves, J. (1986) *Sport, Power, and Culture*. Polity Press, Cambridge.

Harris, C. C. (1983) *The Family in Industrial Society*. Allen & Unwin, London.

Hartsock, N. (1981) The Unhappy Marriage of Marxism and Feminism: Towards a More Progressive Union. In: Sargent, L. (Ed.), *Women and Revolution*. South End, Boston.

Hartsock, N. (1998) *The Feminist Standpoint Revisited and Other Essays*. Westview, Boulder, CO.

Harvey, D. (1988 [1973]) *Social Justice and the City*. Blackwell, Oxford.

Harvey, D. (1990) *The Condition of Postmodernity*. Blackwell, Oxford.

Hegel, G. W. F. (1988 [1807]) *Phenomenology of Mind*. Oxford University Press, New York.

Hegel, G. W. F. (1995 [1840]) *Lectures on the History of Philosophy*. Vol. 3: *Medieval and Modern Philosophy*. University of Nebraska Press, Lincoln.

Heidegger, M. (1963) *Being and Time*. Harper & Row, New York.

Heise, D. R. (1979) *Understanding Events: Affect and the Construction of Social Action*. Cambridge University Press, New York.

Hekman, S. (1997) Truth and Method: Feminist Standpoint Theory Revisited. *Signs: Journal of Women in Culture and Society* 22: 341–65.

Helanko, R. (1957) Sports and Socialization. *Acta Sociologica* 2: 229–40.

Hicks, A. (1999) *Social Democracy and Welfare Capitalism*. Oxford University Press, New York.

Hillery, G. (1955) Definitions of Community: Areas of Agreement. *Rural Sociology* 20: 72–84.

Hochschild, A. (1979) Emotion Work, Feeling Rules, and Social Structure. *American Sociological Review* 85: 551–75.

Hochschild, A. (1983) *The Managed Heart*. University of California Press, Berkeley.

Hochschild, A. (1997) *The Time Bind: When Work Becomes Home and Home Becomes Work*. Metropolitan Books, New York.

Hoggart, R. (1957) *The Uses of Literacy*. Chatto & Windus, London.

Homans, G. C. (1958) Social Behavior as Exchange. *American Journal of Sociology* 63: 597–606.

Homans, G. C. (1961) *Social Behavior: Its Elementary Forms*. Harcourt Brace & Javonovich, New York.

hooks, b. (1989) *Talking Back: Thinking Feminist, Thinking Black*. South End, Boston.

hooks, b. (2004) *We Real Cool: Black Men and Masculinity*. Routledge, New York.

Horkheimer, M. & Adorno, T. (1972 [1944]) *The Dialectic of Enlightenment*. Herder & Herder, New York.

Horwitz, A. (2002) *Creating Mental Illness*. University of Chicago Press, Chicago.

House, J. S. (1977) The Three Faces of Social Psychology. *Sociometry* 40: 161–77.

Hume, D. (1964 [1739–40]) *A Treatise of Human Nature*, Vols. 1–2. Dent, London.

Husserl, E. (1970 [1900–1]) *Logical Investigations*. Routledge & Kegan Paul, London.

Imanishi, K. (1941) *Seibutsu no Sekai* [*The World of Living Things*]. Kobundo shobo, Tokyo.

Irigaray, L. (1985) *Speculum of the Other Woman*. Cornell University Press, Ithaca, NY.

Jackson, B. & Marsden, D. (1962) *Education and the Working Class*. Routledge & Kegan Paul, London.

Jacobs, J. (1961) *The Death and Life of Great American Cities*. Random House, New York.

James, W. (1890) *Principles of Psychology*. Henry Holt, New York.

Jameson, F. (1991) *Postmodernism, or the Cultural Logic of Late Capitalism*. Duke University Press, Durham, NC.

Janowitz, M. (1960) *The Professional Soldier: A Social and Political Portrait*. Free Press, Glencoe, IL.

Jasper, J. M. (1997) *The Art of Moral Protest*. University of Chicago Press, Chicago.

Jasso, G. (1980) A New Theory of Distributive Justice. *American Sociological Review* 45: 3–32.

Kant, I. (1999 [1781]) *Critique of Pure Reason*. Cambridge University Press, New York.

Kant, I. (2002 [1788]) *Critique of Practical Reason*. Hackett, Indianapolis.

Katzenstein, P. J. (1978) *Between Power and Plenty*. University of Wisconsin Press, Madison.

Kellner, D. (2003) *Media Spectacle*. Routledge, New York.

Kimmel, M. S., Hearn, J., & Connell, R. W. (Eds.) (2005) *Handbook of Studies on Men and Masculinities*. Sage, Thousand Oaks, CA.

Kirk, D. (1996) Demographic Transition Theory. *Population Studies* 50: 361–87.

Klein, N. (2000) *No Logo*. Flamingo, London.

Knorr Cetina, K. (1981) *The Manufacture of Knowledge: An Essay on the Constructivist and Contextual Nature of Science*. Pergamon, Oxford.

Kohn, M. L. & Schooler, C. (1983) *Work and Personality: An Inquiry Into the Impact of Social Stratification*. Ablex, Norwood, NJ.

Kroeber, A. L. & Kluckhohn, C. (1963 [1952]) *Culture: A Critical Review of Concepts and Definitions*. Vintage, New York.

Kuhn, M. & McPartland, T. S. (1954) An Empirical Investigation of Self-Attitudes. *American Sociological Review* 40: 68–76.

Kuhn, T. (1962) *The Structure of Scientific Revolutions*, 2nd edn. University of Chicago Press, Chicago.

Kutchins, H. & Kirk, S. (1997) *Making Us Crazy*. Free Press, New York.

Lacan, J. (1966) *Écrits*. Norton, New York.

Lareau, A. (2003) *Unequal Childhoods: Class, Race, and Family Life*. University of California Press, Berkeley.

Lasch, C. (1977) *Haven in a Heartless World*. Basic Books, New York.

Latour, B. (1993) *We Have Never Been Modern*. Harvard University Press, Cambridge, MA.

Latour, B. & Woolgar, S. (1979) *The Social Construction of Scientific Facts*. Sage, Thousand Oaks, CA.

Lawler, E. (2001) An Affect Theory of Social Exchange. *American Journal of Sociology* 107: 321–52.

Lawrence, P. & Lorsch, J. (1967) *Organization and the Environment*. Harvard University Press, Cambridge, MA.

Lazarsfeld, P. F. (1958) Evidence and Inference in Social Research. *Daedalus Journal of the American Academy of Arts and Sciences* 87: 99–130.

Lechner, N. (1977) *La Crisis del Estado en America Latina* [*The Crisis of the State in Latin America*]. Siglo XXI, Madrid.

Lefebvre, H. (1991) *The Production of Space*. Blackwell, Oxford.

Lefebvre, H. (2002) *Critique of Everyday Life*, 3 vols. Verso, London.

Lengermann, P. M. & Niebrugge-Brantley, J. (1998) *The Women Founders: Sociology and Social Theory, 1830–1930. A Text with Readings*. McGraw-Hill, New York.

Lenski, G. (1964) *Power and Privilege*. McGraw-Hill, New York.

Lesthaeghe, R. & Surkyn, J. (1988) Cultural Dynamics and Economic Theories of Fertility Change. *Population and Development Review* 14: 1–45.

Lévi-Strauss, C. (1995 [1978]) *Myth and Meaning: Cracking the Code of Culture*. Knopf, New York.

Lippman, W. (1922) *Public Opinion*. Macmillan, New York.

Lockwood, D. (1958) *The Blackcoated Worker: A Case Study in Class Consciousness*. George Allen & Unwin, London.

Lofland, J. (1984) *Analyzing Social Settings*. Wadsworth, Belmont, CA.

Lorber, J. (1994) *Paradoxes of Gender*. Yale University Press, New Haven, CT.

Luckmann, T. (1967) *The Invisible Religion*. Macmillan, New York.

Luhmann, N. (1982) *The Differentiation of Society*. Columbia University Press, New York.

Luhmann, N. (1995) *Social Systems*. Stanford University Press, Stanford.

Lukács, G. (1971 [1923]) *History and Class Consciousness: Studies in Marxist Dialectics*. MIT Press, Cambridge, MA.

Lukes, S. (1974) *Power: A Radical View*. Macmillan, London.

Lynd, R. & Lynd, H. (1929) *Middletown*. Harcourt Brace, New York.

Lyotard, J.-F. (1984) *The Postmodern Condition: A Report on Knowledge*. University of Minnesota Press, Minneapolis.

McAdam, D. (1999 [1982]) *Political Process and the Development of Black Insurgency, 1930–1970*, 2nd edn. Chicago, University of Chicago Press.

McChesney, R. W. (1999) *Rich Media, Poor Democracy: Communication Politics in Dubious Times*. New Press, New York.

McIntosh, P. C. (1971) *Sport in Society*. C. A. Watts, London.

McLuhan, M. (1964) *Understanding Media: The Extensions of Man*. McGraw-Hill, New York.

Maines, D. (2001) *The Faultline of Consciousness: A View of Interactionism in Sociology*. Aldine, New York.

Malinowski, B. (1922) *Argonauts of the Western Pacific*. Routledge & Kegan Paul, London.

Malthus, T. (1965 [1798]) *An Essay on Population*. Augustus Kelley, New York.

Mann, M. (1986) *The Sources of Social Power*, Vol. 1. Cambridge University Press, Cambridge.

Mann, M. (1993) *The Sources of Social Power*. Vol. 2: *The Rise of Classes and Nation States, 1760–1914*. Cambridge University Press, Cambridge.

Mannheim, K. (1936) *Ideology and Utopia*. Harcourt, Brace, & World, New York.

Marcuse, H. (1964) *One-Dimensional Man*. Abacus, London.

Markovsky, B., Willer, D., & Patton, T. (1988) Power Relations in Exchange Networks. *American Sociological Review* 53: 220–36.

Martineau, H. (1962 [1837]) *Society in America*. Transaction, London.

Marx, K. (1988 [1844]) *Economic and Philosophic Manuscripts of 1844*. Prometheus Books, Amherst, NY.

Marx, K. (1992 [1867]) *Capital: A Critique of Political Economy*, Vol. 1. International Publishers, New York.

Marx, K. (1993 [1858]) *Grundrisse: Foundations of the Critique of Political Economy*. Penguin, New York.

Marx, K. & Engels, F. (1992 [1848]) *The Communist Manifesto*. Bantam Books, New York.

Marx, K. & Engels, F. (1998 [1845]) *The German Ideology*. Prometheus Books, Amherst, NY.

Masao, M. (1961 [1957]) *Denken in Japan [Japanese Thought]*. Suhrkamp, Frankfurt a. M.

Mauss, M. (1966) *The Gift: Forms and Functions of Exchange in Archaic Societies*. Routledge & Kegan Paul, London.

Mayhew, H. (1967 [1851]) *London Labour and London Poor*. Frank Cass, London.

Mayo, E. (1933) *The Human Problems of an Industrialized Civilization*. Macmillan, New York.

Mead, G. H. (1934) *Mind, Self, and Society*. University of Chicago Press, Chicago.

Merton, R. K. (1938) Social Structure and Anomie. *American Sociological Review* 3: 672–82.

Merton, R. K. (1949) *Social Theory and Social Structure*. Free Press, New York.

Merton, R. K. (1973) *The Sociology of Science: Theoretical and Empirical Investigations*. University of Chicago Press, Chicago.

Messner, M. (1997) *Politics in Masculinities: Men in Movements*. Sage, Thousand Oaks, CA.

Milgram, S. (1963) Behavioral Study of Obedience. *Journal of Abnormal and Social Psychology* 67: 371–8.

Miller, D. (1998) *A Theory of Shopping*. Polity Press, Cambridge.

Mills, C. W. (1951) *White Collar: The American Middle Classes*. Oxford University Press, New York.

Mills, C. W. (1956) *The Power Elite*. Oxford University Press, New York.

Mills, C. W. (1959) *The Sociological Imagination*. Oxford University Press, New York.

Mirowsky, J. & Ross, C. (2002) Measurement for a Human Science. *Journal of Health and Social Behavior* 43: 152–70.

Mohanty, C. T., Russo, A., & Torres, L. (Eds.) (1991) *Third World Women and the Politics of Feminism*. Indiana University Press, Bloomington.

Molm, L. D. (2003) Theoretical Comparisons of Forms of Exchange. *Sociological Theory* 21: 1–17.

Moore, B. (1966) *Social Origins of Dictatorship and Democracy*. Beacon Press, Boston.

Moraga, C. & Anzaldúa, G. (Eds.) (1983) *This Bridge Called My Back: Writings by Radical Women of Color*. Kitchen Table: Women of Color Press, New York.

Mosca, G. (1939 [1884]) *The Ruling Class*. McGraw-Hill, New York.

Myrdal, G. (1944) *An American Dilemma: The Negro Problem and Modern Democracy*. Harper & Brothers, New York.

Naples, N. A. (2003) *Feminism and Method: Ethnography, Discourse Analysis, and Activist Research*. Routledge, New York.

Newcomb, T. M. (1961) *The Acquaintance Process*. Holt, Reinhart, & Winston. New York.

Nicholson, L. (Ed.) (1997) *The Second Wave: A Reader in Feminist Theory*. Routledge, New York.

Nietzsche, F. (1927 [1887]) *Genealogy of Morals*. Modern Library, New York.

Oakley, A. (1974) *The Sociology of Housework*. Martin Robertson, Oxford.

O'Kelly, C. & Carney, L. (1986) *Women and Men in Society: Cross-Cultural Perspectives on Gender Stratification*. Wadsworth, Belmont, CA.

Olson, M., Jr. (1965) *The Logic of Collective Action*. Harvard University Press, Cambridge, MA.

Pareto, V. (1980 [1916]) *The Mind and Society*. University of Minnesota Press, Minneapolis.

Park, R. E. & Burgess, E. W. (1921) *An Introduction to the Science of Sociology*. University of Chicago Press, Chicago.

Park, R. E., Burgess, E. W., & McKenzie, R. D. (1926 [1925]) *The City*. University of Chicago Press, Chicago.

Parkerson, D. H. & Parkerson, J. A. (2001) *Transitions in American Education: A Social History of Teaching*. Routledge, New York.

Parsons, T. (1937) *The Structure of Social Action*. Free Press, New York.

Parsons, T. (1951) *The Social System*. Free Press, Glencoe, IL.

Parsons, T. (1964) *Social Structure and Personality*. Free Press, New York.

Parsons, T. & Shils, E. A. (1951) *Towards a General Theory of Action*. Harvard University Press, Cambridge, MA.

Pearlin, L. I. (1981) The Stress Process. *Journal of Health and Social Behavior* 22: 337–56.

Peirce, C. S. (1923) *Chance, Love, and Logic: Philosophical Essays*. Harcourt Brace, New York.

Pfeffer, J. (1997) *New Directions in Organization Theory: Problems and Prospects*. Oxford University Press, New York.

Platt, J. (2000) *The British Sociological Association: A Sociological History*. Sociology Press, Durham.

Plummer, K. (1981) *The Making of the Modern Homosexual*. Hutchinson, London.

Polanyi, K. (1944) *The Great Transformation: The Political and Economic Origin of Our Time*. Beacon, Boston.

Popper, K. R. (1969) *The Logic of Scientific Discovery*. Hutchinson, London.

Poulantzas, N. (1980) *State, Power, and Socialism*. New Left Books, New York.

Price, J. & Shildrick, M. (Eds.) (1999) *Feminist Theory and the Body: A Reader*. Routledge, New York.

Pugh, D. S., Hickson, D. J., Hinings, C. R., & Turner, C. (1968) The Context of Organizational Structures. *Administrative Science Quarterly* 14: 91–114.

Putnam, R. D. (2000) *Bowling Alone: The Collapse and Revival of American Community*. Simon & Schuster, New York.

Radcliffe-Brown, A. ([1922] 1964) *The Andaman Islanders*. Free Press, New York.

Ragin, C. C. (1987) *The Comparative Method: Moving Beyond Qualitative and Quantitative Strategies*. University of California Press, Berkeley.

Ravetz, J. R. (1971) *Scientific Knowledge and its Social Problems*. Clarendon Press, Oxford.

Rex, J. & Mason, D. (1986) *Theories of Race and Ethnic Relations*. Cambridge University Press, Cambridge.

Rex, J. A. (1962) *Key Problems of Sociological Theory*. Routledge & Kegan Paul, London.

Rich, A. (1980) Compulsory Heterosexual and Lesbian Experience. In: Stimson, C. R. & Person, E. S. (Eds.), *Women, Sex, and Sexuality*. University of Chicago Press, Chicago.

Richardson, D. (Ed.) (1996) *Theorizing Heterosexuality*. Open University Press, Buckingham.

Riesman, D. (1950) *The Lonely Crowd*. Doubleday, New York.

Risher, R. A. (1935) *The Design of Experiments*. Oliver & Boyd, London.

Ritzer, G. (1975) *Sociology: Toward a Multiple Paradigm Science*. Allyn & Bacon, Boston.

Ritzer, G. (2004a) *The McDonaldization of Society: Revised New Century Edition*. Pine Forge Press, Thousand Oaks, CA.

Ritzer, G. (2004b) *The Globalization of Nothing*. Pine Forge Press, Thousand Oaks, CA.

Rizal, J. ([1887] 1990) *Noli Me Tangere [Touch Me Not]*. Nalandangan Press, Manila.

Robertson, R. (1992) *Globalization: Social Theory and Global Culture*. Sage, London.

Robinson, W. I. (2004) *A Theory of Global Capitalism: Production, Class, and State in a Transnational World*. Johns Hopkins University Press, Baltimore.

Rojek, C. (2000) *Leisure and Culture*. Palgrave, Basingstoke.

Rorty, R. (1979) *Philosophy and the Mirror of Nature*. Princeton University Press, Princeton.

Rorty, R. (1991) *Objectivity, Relativism, and Truth: Philosophical Papers*, Vol. 1. Cambridge University Press, Cambridge.

Rose, H. (1984) *Love, Power, and Knowledge: Towards a Feminist Transformation of the Sciences*. Polity Press, Cambridge.

Rosenberg, M. ([1979] 1986) *Conceiving the Self*. Krieger, Melbourne, FL.

Rosenhan, D. L. (1973) On Being Sane in Insane Places. *Science* 179: 250–8.

Rosich, K. J. (2005) *A History of the American Sociological Association, 1981–2004*. American Sociological Association, Washington, DC.

Rostow, W. W. (1969) *The Stages of Economic Growth*. Cambridge University Press, Cambridge.

Rowe, D. (1995) *Popular Cultures: Rock Music, Sport, and the Politics of Pleasure*. Sage, London.

Rowntree, B. S. (1901) *Poverty: A Study of Town Life*. Macmillan, London.

Said, E. (1978) *Orientalism*. Routledge, London.

Sanderson, S. K. (1990) *Social Evolutionism: A Critical History*. Blackwell, Oxford.

Sandoval, C. (2000) *Methodology of the Oppressed*. University of Minnesota Press, Minneapolis.

Sapir, E. (1921) *Language*. Harper, New York.

Sartre, J.-P. (1993) *Being and Nothingness*. Washington Square Press, New York.

Sassen, S. (1991) *The Global City: New York, London, Tokyo*. Princeton University Press, Princeton.

Saussure, F. de (1966) *Course in General Linguistics*. McGraw-Hill, New York.

Savage, M., Barlow, J., Dickens, P., & Fielding, A. (1992) *Property, Bureaucracy, and Culture: The Middle Classes in Contemporary Britain*. Routledge, London.

Scheff, T. J. (1966) *Being Mentally Ill: A Sociological Theory*. Aldine, Chicago.

Schor, J. (1998) *The Overspent American: Why We Want What We Don't Need*. Harper Perennial, New York.

Schultz, T. W. (1961) Investment in Human Capital. *American Economic Review* 51: 1–17.

Schumpeter, J. A. (1934 [1911]) *The Theory of Economic Development*. Harvard University Press, Cambridge, MA.

Schumpeter, J. A. (1976 [1942]) *Capitalism, Socialism, and Democracy*. Allen & Unwin, London.

Schütz, A. (1932) *The Phenomenology of the Social World*. Heinemann, London.

Schütz, A. & Luckmann, T. (1974) *The Structures of the Life-World*, Vol. 1. Heinemann, London.

Scott, J. (1991) *Who Rules Britain?* Polity Press, Cambridge.

Sedgwick, E. K. (1990) *Epistemology of the Closet*. University of California Press, Berkeley.

Seidman, S. (1996) *Queer Theory/Sociology*. Blackwell, Cambridge, MA.

Senna, J. J. & Siegel, L. J. (2002) *Introduction to Criminal Justice*, 9th edn. Wadsworth, Belmont, CA.

Sennett, R. (1977) *The Fall of Public Man: On the Social Psychology of Capitalism*. A. Knopf, New York.

Shannon, C. L. (1989) *The Politics of the Family: From Homo Sapiens to Homo Economicus*. Peter Lang, New York.

Shariati, A. (1980) *On the Sociology of Islam*. Mizan Press, Berkeley, CA.

Siegel, J. (1980) On the Demography of Aging. *Demography* 17: 345–64.

Sigerist, H. E. (1946) *The University at the Crossroads*. Henry Shuman, New York.

Simmel, G. (1950) The Metropolis and Mental Life. In: Wolff, K. (Ed.), *The Sociology of Georg Simmel*. Collier-Macmillan, London.

Simmel, G. (1970 [1900]) *The Philosophy of Money*. Routledge, New York.

Simmel, G. (1971) *On Individuality and Social Forms*. University of Chicago Press, Chicago.

Skinner, B. F. (1953) *Science and Human Behavior*. Free Press, New York.

Skinner, B. F. (1974) *About Behaviorism*. Knopf, New York.

Sklair, L. (2002) *Globalization: Capitalism and its Alternatives*, 3rd edn. Oxford University Press, Oxford.

Skocpol, T. (1979) *States and Social Revolutions: A Comparative Analysis of France, Russia, and China*. Cambridge University Press, New York.

Slater, D. (1997) *Consumer Culture and Modernity*. Polity Press, Cambridge.

Smelser, N. (1962) *Theory of Collective Behavior*. Free Press, New York.

Smelser, N. & Swedberg, R. (Eds.) (2003) *Handbook of Economic Sociology*, 2nd edn. Princeton University Press, Princeton.

Smith, A. (1976 [1776]) An Inquiry into the Nature and Causes of the Wealth of Nations. Clarendon Press, Oxford.

Smith, D. (1987) *The Everyday World as Problematic: A Feminist Sociology*. Northeastern University Press, Boston.

Smith, D. (1990) *Texts, Facts, and Femininity: Exploring the Relations of Ruling*. Routledge, New York.

Smith-Lovin, L. & Heise, D. R. (1988) *Affect Control Theory: Research Advances*. Gordon & Breach, New York.

Snow, D. & Benford, R. (1988) Ideology, Frame Resonance, and Participant Mobilization. In: *International Social Movement Research: From Structure to Action*. JAI Press, Greenwich, CT.

Soja, E. W. (1989) *Postmodern Geographies: The Reassertion of Space in Critical Social Theory*. Verso, London.

Sombart, W. (1976 [1906]) *Why Is There No Socialism in the United States?* Macmillan, London.

Sorokin, P. (1927) *Social Mobility*. Harper, New York.

Sorokin, P. (1947) *Culture, Society, and Personality*. Harper & Brothers, New York.

Spencer, H. (1954 [1850]) *Social Statics*. Robert Schalkenbach Foundation, New York.

Spencer, H. (2002 [1874–96]) *The Principles of Sociology*. Transaction Books, New Brunswick, NJ.

Spillman, L. (1995) Culture, Social Structure, and Discursive Fields. *Current Perspectives in Social Theory* 15: 129–54.

Stacey, J. (1997) *In the Name of the Family: Rethinking Family Values in the Postmodern Age*. Beacon Press, Boston.

Starr, P. (1982) *The Social Transformation of American Medicine*. Basic Books, New York.

Stehr, N. (1994) *Knowledge Societies*. Sage, London.

Stein, A. & Plummer, K. (1996) "I Can't Even Think Straight": "Queer" Theory and the Missing Sexual Revolution in Sociology. In: Seidman, S. (Ed.), *Queer Theory/Sociology*. Blackwell, Cambridge, MA.

Stinchcombe, A. (1959) Bureaucratic and Craft Administration of Production. *Administrative Science Quarterly* 4: 168–87.

Stone, J. & Dennis, R. M. (2003) *Race and Ethnicity: Comparative and Theoretical Approaches*. Blackwell, Malden, MA.

Stouffer, S. A., Suchman, E. A., Devinney, L. C., Star, S. A., & Williams, R. M. (1949) *The American Soldier: Adjustment During Army Life*, Vol. 1. Princeton University Press, Princeton.

Straus, R. (1957) The Nature and Status of Medical Sociology. *American Sociological Review* 22: 200–4.

Stryker, S. (1980) *Symbolic Interactionism: A Social Structural Version*. Benjamin-Cummings, Menlo Park, CA.

Sutherland, E. H., Cressey, D. R., & Luckenbill, D. F. (1992) *Principles of Criminology*, 11th edn. General Hall, Dix Hills, NY.

Swidler, A. (1986) Culture in Action: Symbols and Strategies. *American Sociological Review* 51: 273–86.

Swingewood, A. (1977) *The Myth of Mass Culture*. Macmillan, London.

Sztompka, P. (1993) *The Sociology of Social Change*. Blackwell, Oxford.

Taylor, F. (1998 [1911]) *The Principles of Scientific Management*. Dover, New York.

Thibaut, J. W. & Kelley, H. H. (1959) *The Social Psychology of Groups*. Wiley, New York.

Thomas, W. I. & Thomas, D. S. (1928) *The Child in America: Behavior Problems and Programs*. Knopf, New York.

Thompson, W. (1929) Population. *American Journal of Sociology* 34: 959–75.

Thye, S. (2000) A Status Value Theory of Power in Exchange Relations. *American Sociological Review* 65: 407–32.

Tilly, C. (1978) *From Mobilization to Revolution*. Addison-Wesley, Reading, MA.

Tilly, C. (1990) *Coercion, Capital, and European States, AD 990–1990*. Blackwell, Oxford.

Tocqueville, A. de ([1835] 2000) *Democracy in America*. Bantam Books, New York.

Tong, R. P. (1998) *Feminist Thought: A More Comprehensive Introduction*, 2nd edn. Westview, Boulder, CO.

Tönnies, F. (1957 [1887]) *Gemeinschaft and Gesellschaft* [*Community and Society*]. Michigan State University Press, East Lansing.

Touraine, A. (1971) *The Post-Industrial Society*. Random House, New York.

Touraine, A. (1981) *The Voice and the Eye*. Cambridge, New York.

Toynbee, A. J. (1934–61) *A Study of History*, 12 vols. Oxford University Press, Oxford.

Troeltsch, E. (1960) *The Social Teaching of the Christian Churches*. Harper & Row, New York.

Truman, D. (1971) *The Governmental Process: Political Interests and Public Opinion*. Knopf, New York.

Turner, B. S. (1974) *Weber and Islam*. Routledge, London.

Turner, B. S. (1984) *The Body and Society*. Blackwell, Oxford.

Turner, B. S. (1987) *Medical Power and Social Knowledge*. Sage, London.

Turner, B. S. (1993) *Citizenship and Social Theory*. Sage, London.

Turner, J. H. (2002) *The Structure of Sociological Theory*, 7th edn. Wadsworth, Belmont, CA.

Turner, R. (1976) Real Self: From Institution to Impulse. *American Journal of Sociology* 81: 989–1016.

United Nations (since 1948) *Demographic Yearbook*. Department of Economic and Social Affairs, New York.

United Nations Development Program (1990 to date) *Human Development Report*. Oxford University Press, New York.

Urry, J. (2003) *Global Complexity*. Polity Press, Cambridge.

Van den Berghe, P. (1967) *Race and Racism*. Wiley, New York.

Vanneman, R. D. & Cannon, L. W. (1987) *The American Perception of Class*. Temple University Press, Philadelphia.

Veblen, T. (1953 [1899]) *The Theory of the Leisure Class: An Economic Study of Institutions*. Viking, New York.

Virilio, P. (1986) *Speed and Politics: An Essay on Dromology*. Semiotext(e), New York.

Virilio, P. (2000) *The Information Bomb*. Verso, London.

Wade, R. (1990) *Governing the Market: Economic Theory and the Role of Government in East Asian Industrialization*. Princeton University Press, Princeton.

Wallerstein, I. (1974) *The Modern World System*, 3 vols. Academic Press, New York.

Warbasse, J. (1909) *Medical Sociology: A Series of Observations Touching Upon the Sociology of Health and the Relations of Medicine to Society*. Appleton, New York.

Warner, W. L. (1949) *Social Class in America*. Harper & Row, New York.

Weber, M. (1968 [1914]) *Economy and Society*. Bedminster Press, New York.

Weber, M. (1995 [1923]) *General Economic History*. Transaction, New Brunswick, NJ.

Weber, M. (1998 [1905]) *The Protestant Ethic and the Spirit of Capitalism*. Roxbury, Los Angeles.

Weeks, J., Heaphy, B., & Donovan, C. (2001) *Same-Sex Intimacies*. Routledge, London.

Weick, K. E. (1995) *Sensemaking in Organizations*. Sage, Thousand Oaks, CA.

West, C. & Zimmerman, D. H. (1987) Doing Gender. *Gender and Society* 1: 125–51.

Whyte, W. F. (1943) *Street Corner Society*. University of Chicago Press, Chicago.

Wilcox, W. F. (1891) *The Divorce Problem: A Study in Statistics*. Columbia University Press, New York.

Williams, R. (1958) *Culture and Society 1780–1950*. Penguin, London.

Williams, R. (1975) *Television: Technology and Cultural Form*. Schocken Books, New York.

Williams, R. (1976) *Keywords: A Vocabulary of Culture and Society*. Oxford University Press, New York.

Williamson, O. E. (1981) The Economics of Organizations: The Transaction Cost Approach. *American Journal of Sociology* 87: 548–77.

Wilson, W. J. (1987) *The Truly Disadvantaged: The Inner City, the Underclass, and Public Policy*. University of Chicago Press, Chicago.

Wittgenstein, L. (1958) *Philosophical Investigations*. Blackwell, Oxford.

Wollstonecraft, M. (1988 [1792]) *A Vindication of the Rights of Woman*. Norton, New York.

Wright, E. O. (1978) *Class, Crisis, and the State*. Verso, London.

Wright, E. O. (Ed.) (2005) *Approaches to Class Analysis*. Cambridge University Press, Cambridge.

Yoshida, T. (1990) *Jyoho to Jiko Soshiki-sei no Riron* [*Theory of Information and Self-Organizing Systems*]. University of Tokyo Press, Tokyo.

Young, M. & Willmott, P. (1957) *Family and Kinship in East London*. Routledge, London.

Zeitlin, I. (1994) *Ideology and the Development of Sociological Theory*, 5th edn. Prentice-Hall, Englewood Cliffs, NJ.

Zelizer, V. (1985) *Pricing the Priceless Child*. Princeton University Press, Princeton.

Zelizer, V. (1994) *The Social Meaning of Money*. Princeton University Press, Princeton.

Žižek, S. (1989) *The Sublime Object of Ideology*. Verso, London.

Znaniecki, F. (1934) *Method of Sociology*. Farrar & Rinehart, New York.

Zukin, S. (1991) *Landscapes of Power: From Detroit to Disney World*. University of California Press, Berkeley.

Zurcher, L. A., Jr. (1977) *The Mutable Self: A Self Concept for Social Change*. Sage, Beverly Hills, CA.

Selected Websites

American Sociological Association
www.asanet.org

Asia Pacific Sociological Association
www.asiapacificsociology.org

Association of Black Sociologists
www.blacksociologists.org

Association for Humanist Sociology
www.humanistsoc.org

Association of Population Centers
www.popcenters.org

Association for Qualitative Research
www.aqrp.co.uk

Association for the Sociology of Religion
www.sociologyofreligion.com

Australian Sociological Association
www.tasa.org.au

Blackwell Sociology Resources
www.blackwellpublishing.com/sociology

British Sociological Association
www.britsoc.co.uk

Canadian Census Bureau
www12.statcan.ca/english/census01/home/
index.cfm

Canadian Sociology and Anthropology
Association
www.csaa.ca

Chinese Sociological Association
www.cass.net.cn/chinese/s09_shx/english

Consortium of Social Science Organizations
www.cossa.org

Dead Sociologists' Society
www2.pfeiffer.edu/~lridener/DSS/
DEADSOC.HTML

European Association for Population Studies
www.eaps.nl

European Association for the Study of Science
and Technology
www.easst.net

European Social Survey
www.europeansocialsurvey.org

European Society for Rural Sociology
www.esrs.hu

European Sociological Association
www.valt.helsinki.fi/esa

Euro Studies
www.sosig.ac.uk/eurostudies

French Census Bureau
www.insee.fr/fr/recensement/
page_accueil_rp.htm

French Sociological Association
www.afs-socio.fr

German Sociological Association
www.soziologie.de

Global Social Work Network
www.gswn.com

Indian Sociological Society
www.insoso.org

International Network for Social Network
Analysis
www.insna.org

International Social Science Council
www.unesco.org/ngo/issc/

International Society for the Sociology of
Religion
soc.kuleuven.be/ceso/sisr

International Sociological Association
www.ucm.es/info/isa

International Sociology of Sport Association
www.uq.edu.au/~asjmckay/info.htm

International Union for the Scientific Study of
Population
www.iussp.org

Italian Sociological Association
www.sociologi.it

Japanese Census
web-japan.org/stat/category_01.html

Japan Sociological Society
wwwsoc.nii.ac.jp/jss/index-e.shtml

Kinsey Institute for Research in Sex, Gender, and Reproduction
www.indiana.edu/~kinsey

Korean Sociological Association
www.ksa.re.kr/index.php

Latin American Sociological Association
www2.udec.cl/~alas

Marxists Internet Archive
www.marxists.org/

Norbert Elias and Process Sociology
www.usyd.edu.au/su/social/elias/
eliasframe.html

Population Association of America
www.popassoc.org

Population Association of Japan
wwwsoc.nii.ac.jp/paj/home-e.htm

Rural Sociological Society
ruralsociology.org

Select Great Social Theorists Page
www.faculty.rsu.edu/%7Efelwell/Theorists/
Four/index.html

Social Science History Association
www.ssha.org

Social Science Information System
www.sociosite.net

Society for the Advancement of Socio-Economics
www.sase.org/homepage.html

Society for Applied Sociology
www.appliedsoc.org

Society for the Scientific Study of Sexuality
www.sexscience.org

Society for Social Studies of Science
www.4sonline.org

Society for the Study of Social Problems
www.sssp1.org

Society for the Study of Symbolic Interaction
sun.soci.niu.edu/~sssi

Sociological Association of Aotearoa New Zealand
saanz.rsnz.org

Sociologists' Lesbian, Gay, Bisexual, and Transgendered Caucus
www.qrd.org/qrd/www/orgs/slgc/SLGC.
html

Sociologists Without Borders
www.sociologistswithoutborders.org/

Sociologists for Women in Society
newmedia.colorado.edu/~socwomen

Sociology of Education Association
www2.asanet.org/soe

South African Sociological Association
general.rau.ac.za/sasa

Spanish Sociological Society
www.fes-web.org

Statistical Resources on the Web
www.lib.umich.edu/govdocs/stats.html

United Kingdom Census Bureau
www.statistics.gov.uk/census

United Nations
www.un.org

United States Census Bureau
www.census.gov